For Chrissie

Convergence in Broadcast and Communications Media

The fundamentals of audio, video, data processing and communications technologies

John Watkinson

Focal Press

OXFORD AUCKLAND BOSTON JOHANNESBURG MELBOURNE NEW DELHI

Focal Press
An imprint of Butterworth-Heinemann
Linacre House, Jordan Hill, Oxford OX2 8DP
225 Wildwood Avenue, Woburn, MA 01801-2041
A division of Reed Educational and Professional Publishing Ltd

A member of the Reed Elsevier plc group

First published 2001

British Library Cataloguing in Publication Data
A catalogue record for this book is available from the British Library

Library of Congress Cataloguing in Publication Data
A catalogue record for this book is available from the Library of Congress

ISBN 0 240 51509 9

Composition by Genesis Typesetting, Rochester, Kent
Printed and bound in Great Britain

Contents

Preface

There are two key inventions which have brought about this book, and neither of them are new. The digital computer is one of these, and turned from a curiosity into a powerful tool as early as the Second World War. The idea of pulse code modulation (PCM) which allows continuous signals to be handled by digital hardware is even older.

Digital video and audio are another form of data and so the convergence with computers and communications networks has always been inevitable, although it has taken 50 years to become an economic reality.

Now that convergence is a reality, products and systems combining audio, video, data processing and communications are emerging. Without adequate fundamental knowledge of the four core technologies, products could be flawed or even fail.

Traditional experience does not serve well in convergence. Computer engineers suddenly find they need to understand audio, imaging and data systems delivering with an accurate timebase. Audio and video engineers find they need to understand file servers and computer networks. This book is designed to meet those needs. Without assuming a background in any of them, the four core technologies of image reproduction, sound reproduction, data processing and communications are all treated here.

Specialist industries evolve their own buzzwords and acronyms in order to save time, but these terms have the side effect of making the technology incomprehensible to the outsider. Communications and networking are possibly the worst offenders in the acronym department, with MPEG and DVB close behind. In order to cross disciplines with any hope of success, the only approach which will work is to use plain

English first and to introduce the inevitable buzzwords and acronyms later.

Another important aspect of this book is that the reader is asked to take very little on trust. Instead of presenting facts which are as likely to be challenged as they are to be forgotten, this book gives reasons which can be followed, supported by references. For example, all the criteria involved in image and sound quality should be based on studies of the human senses and so it is here.

These studies have advanced our knowledge considerably, but this has not always resulted in parallel improvements in television and hi-fi equipment because these have become commoditized and riddled with tradition. The reader from a computer background should not make the mistake of thinking that current audio and television practice represents the best that can be done. This book does not simply describe current television and audio practice. Instead it goes far beyond that to the limits of what can be done and how to do it.

John Watkinson
Burghfield Common, England

1

Introduction to convergent systems

1.1 What this book is about

The range of products and services which can be based on various combinations of audio, video and computer technology is limited only by the imagination. From the musical greetings card through videophones, digital photography, MP3 players, Internet video and video-on-demand to flight simulators, electronic cinema and virtual reality, the same fundamentals apply. The wide scope of this book has made it essential to establish some kind of order.

The purpose of this chapter is to show why binary coding and digital processing are so powerful, to introduce a number of key concepts and to give some examples of convergent systems and their far-reaching consequences. The explanations of this chapter are deliberately brief to avoid obscuring the overall picture with too much detail. Instead it will be indicated where in the book the in-depth treatment can be found. Figure 1.1 shows the key areas of convergent systems and how they interact. Figure 1.2 shows some of the systems which depend on the subjects treated here.

In the digital domain it is possible economically to perform any conceivable process on data. These processes can only be applied to audio and video if the sounds and images can be converted from their original form into the digital domain and back again. Realistic digital sound reproduction requires an understanding of the human hearing system, transducers such as microphones and loudspeakers as well as precision conversion techniques. Chapter 5 considers all these aspects of audio interfacing.

Image reproduction in Chapter 7 is based on a detailed study of the human visual system in Chapter 6 which shows how the eyeball's

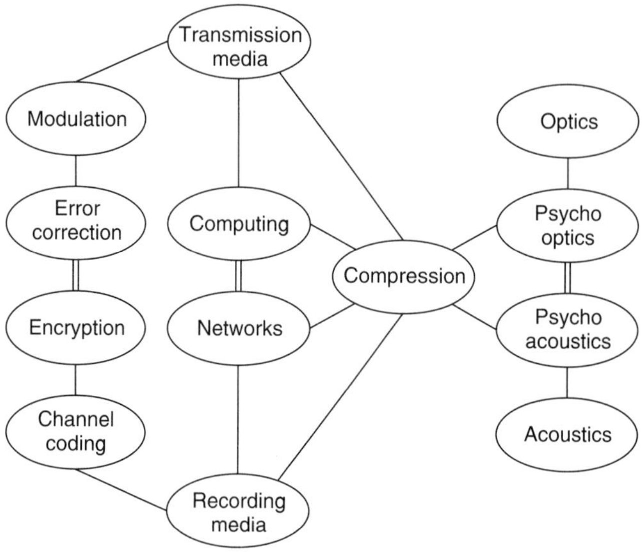

Figure 1.1 The enabling technologies of convergent systems are shown here. Combining these in various ways produces an infinity of information-related services and products.

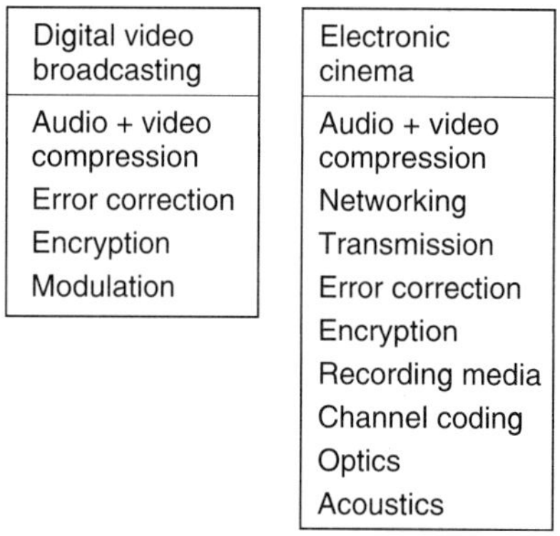

Figure 1.2 Some examples of convergent systems and the technologies in them.

tracking ability has significant consequences. All good imaging systems should look the same, but today's film, television and computer images look different even to the casual bystander. The reasons for these differences will be seen to reside in a number of key areas. Colour accuracy is particularly difficult to achieve in convergent systems and familiarity with colorimetry is essential. Motion portrayal, the way that moving images are handled, is not well done in traditional systems, leading to a loss of realism. Chapter 7 also makes a detailed comparison of various scanning methods to see where progress can be made.

Imaging systems can only be as good as the transducers. Chapter 8 considers displays from the well-established CRT through LCDs up to modern display technologies such as micromirrors, plasma and lasers.

For a given quality, real-time audio and video require a corresponding data rate. Often this rate is not available for economic or practical reasons. This has led to the development of compression techniques such as MPEG which allow the data rate to be reduced. Chapter 9 looks at compression techniques and points out where quality can be lost by the unwary.

Once in the digital domain, audio and images can be manipulated using computer techniques. This can include production and post-production steps such as editing, keying and effects, or practical requirements such as resizing to fit a particular display. Although in principle any digital computer could operate on image data, the data rates needed by some imaging applications are beyond the processing power of a conventional computer and the data rates of its storage systems.

Moving-image processing needs hardware which is optimized for working on large data arrays. The general term for this kind of thing is digital signal processing (DSP). Chapter 2 explains how computers and digital signal processors work.

Data storage is a vital enabling technology and must be treated in some detail. Data can be stored on various media for archiving, rapid retrieval or distribution. The principles and characteristics of magnetic and optical recordings on tape and disks will be found in Chapter 11.

Data can be sent from one place to another in local or wide area networks, on private radio links or public radio broadcasts. Chapter 12 considers all principles of data transmission on copper, optical or radio links.

Whether for storage or transmission, the reliability or *integrity* of the data is paramount. Data errors cause computer crashes, pops and clicks in the audio and flashes on the screen. The solution is error checking and correction and this is the subject of Chapter 10. Encryption is related strongly to error correction and is important to prevent unauthorized access to sensitive or copyright material. Encryption is also treated in Chapter 10.

1.2 Why binary?

Arithmetically, the binary system is the simplest numbering scheme possible. Figure 1.3(a) shows that there are only two symbols: 1 and 0. Each symbol is a binary digit, abbreviated to *bit*. One bit is a datum and many bits are data. Logically, binary allows a system of thought in which statements can only be true or false.

What is binary?

(a) Mathematically:
The simplest numbering scheme possible, there are only two symbols:

1 and **0**

Logically:
A system of thought in which there are only two states:

True and **False**

(b) Binary information is **not** subject to misinterpretation

Black	**White**
In	**Out**
Guilty	**Innocent**

(c) Variables or non-binary terms:

Somewhat	**Undecided**
Probably	**Not proven**
Grey	**Under par**

Figure 1.3 Binary digits (a) can only have two values. At (b) are shown some everyday binary terms, whereas (c) shows some terms which cannot be expressed by a binary digit.

The great advantage of binary systems is that they are the most resistant to misinterpretation. In information terms they are *robust*. Figure 1.3(b) shows some binary terms and (c) some non-binary terms for comparison. In all real processes, the wanted information is disturbed by noise and distortion, but with only two possibilities to distinguish, binary systems have the greatest resistance to such effects.

Figure 1.4(a) shows an ideal binary electrical signal is simply two different voltages: a high voltage representing a true logic state or a binary 1 and a low voltage representing a false logic state or a binary 0. The ideal waveform is also shown at (b) after it has passed through a real system. The waveform has been considerably altered, but the binary information can be recovered by comparing the voltage with a threshold which is set half-way between the ideal levels. In this way any received voltage which is above the threshold is considered a 1 and any voltage below is considered a 0. This process is called slicing, and can reject significant amounts of unwanted noise added to the signal.

The signal will be carried in a channel with finite bandwidth, and this limits the slew rate of the signal; an ideally upright edge is made to slope. Noise added to a sloping signal (c) can change the time at which the slicer judges that the level passed through the threshold. This effect is also eliminated when the output of the slicer is reclocked. Figure 1.4(d) shows

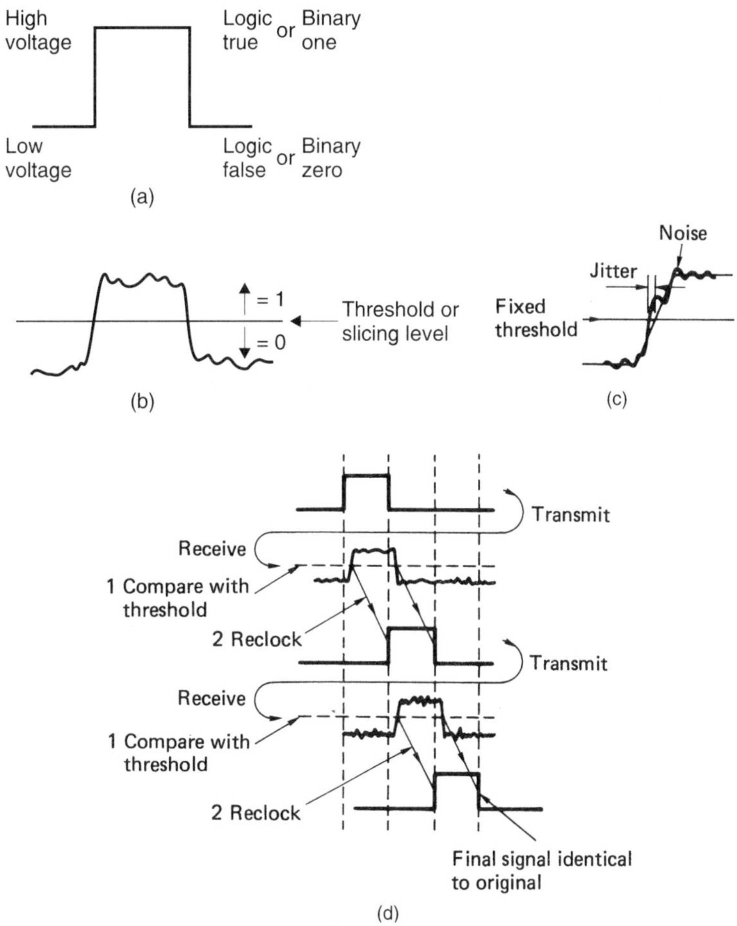

Figure 1.4 An ideal binary signal (a) has two levels. After transmission it may look like (b), but after slicing the two levels can be recovered. Noise on a sliced signal can result in jitter (c), but reclocking combined with slicing makes the final signal identical to the original as shown in (d).

that however many stages the binary signal passes through, the information is unchanged except for a delay.

Of course, an excessive noise could cause a problem. If it had sufficient level and the correct sense or polarity, noise could cause the signal to cross the threshold and the output of the slicer would then be incorrect. However, as binary has only two symbols, if it is known that the symbol is incorrect, it need only be set to the other state and a perfect correction has been achieved. Error correction really is as trivial as that, although determining which bit needs to be changed is somewhat more difficult.

Figure 1.5 shows that binary information can be represented by a wide range of real phenomena. All that is needed is the ability to exist in two

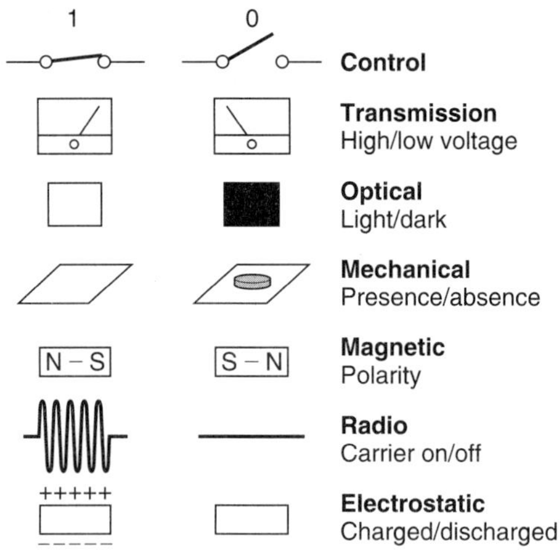

Figure 1.5 A large number of real phenomena can be used to represent binary data.

states. A switch can be open or closed and so represent a single bit. This switch may control the voltage in a wire which allows the bit to be transmitted. In an optical system, light may be transmitted or obstructed. In a mechanical system, the presence or absence of some feature can denote the state of a bit. The presence or absence of a radio carrier can signal a bit. In a random access memory (RAM), the state of an electric charge stores a bit.

Figure 1.5 also shows that magnetism is naturally binary as two stable directions of magnetization are easily arranged and rearranged as required. This is why digital magnetic recording has been so sucessful: it is a natural way of storing binary signals.

The robustness of binary signals means that bits can be packed more densely onto storage media, increasing the performance or reducing the cost. In radio signalling, lower power can be used.

In decimal systems, the digits in a number (counting from the right, or least significant end) represent ones, tens, hundreds, thousands etc. Figure 1.6(a) shows that in binary, the bits represent one, two, four, eight, sixteen, etc. A multi-digit binary number is commonly called a word, and the number of bits in the word is called the wordlength. The right-hand bit is called the least significant bit (LSB) whereas the bit on the left-hand end of the word is called the most significant bit (MSB). Clearly more digits are required in binary than in decimal, but they are more easily handled. A word of eight bits is called a byte, which is a contraction of 'by eight'.

Figure 1.6(a) shows some binary numbers and their equivalent in decimal. The radix point has the same significance in binary: symbols to the right of it represent one half, one quarter and so on. Binary is

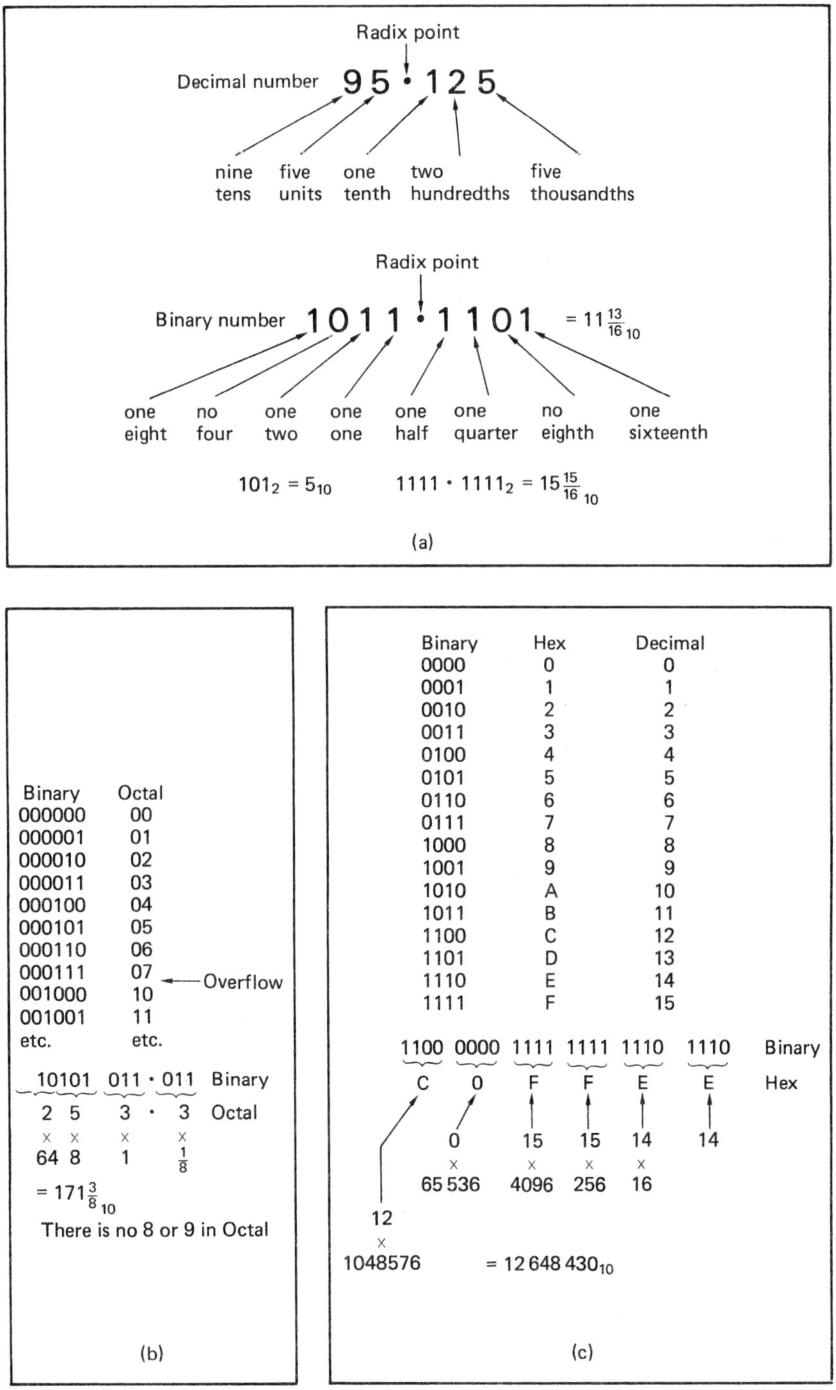

Figure 1.6 Binary digits represent powers of two as shown in (a). Some examples of binary conversion are shown in (b). (c) In hex, groups of four bits make one symbol O–F. Note how much shorter the number is in hex.

convenient for electronic circuits, which do not get tired, but numbers expressed in binary become very long, and writing them is tedious and error-prone. The octal (b) and hexadecimal (c) notations are both used for writing binary since conversion is so simple. A binary number is split into groups of three or four digits starting at the least significant end, and the groups are individually converted to octal or hexadecimal digits. Since sixteen different symbols are required in hex. the letters A–F are used for the numbers above nine.

The number range is found by raising two to the power of the wordlength. Thus a four-bit word has sixteen combinations, and could address a memory having sixteen locations. A sixteen-bit word has 65 536 combinations. Figure 1.7(a) shows some examples of wordlength and resolution.

Binary words can have a remarkable range of meanings; they may describe the magnitude of a number such as an audio sample, an image

Wordlength and resolution

The wordlength determines the possible range of values:

Wordlength	**Range**
1	2 (2^1)
2	4 (2^2)
3	8 (2^3)
•	
•	
•	
•	
8	256 (2^8
•	
10	1024 (2^{10})
•	
•	
•	
•	
•	
16	65 536 (2^{16})

(a)

Round numbers in binary

10000000000_2	=	1024	= 1 k (kilo in computers)
1 k × 1 k	=	1 M	(Mega)
1 M × 1 k	=	1 G	(Giga)
1 M × 1 M	=	1 T	(Tera)

(b)

Figure 1.7 The wordlength of a sample controls the resolution as shown in (a). In the same way the ability to address memory locations is also determined as in (b).

pixel or a transform coefficient. Binary words may specify the address of a single location in a memory, or the instruction to be performed by a processor. The capacity of memories and storage media is measured in bytes, but to avoid large numbers, kilobytes, megabytes and gigabytes are often used. A ten-bit word has 1024 combinations, which is close to one thousand. In physics 1k (where the k is lower case) means 1000, whereas in digital terminology, 1K (where the K is upper case) is defined as 1024. However, the wrong case is frequently used. A kilobyte (KB) of memory contains 1024 bytes. A megabyte (1 MB) contains 1024 kilobytes and would need a twenty-bit address. A gigabyte contains 1024 megabytes and would need a thirty-bit address. Figure 1.7(b) shows some examples.

1.3 Conversion

Figure 1.8 shows that many different types of information can be expressed as data, or more precisely as binary words. As will be seen, standards have to be agreed for the way in which the range of values the information can take will be mapped onto the available binary number range. Clearly both source and destination must comply with the same standard, otherwise the information will be incorrectly interpreted.

One of the simplest standardized mappings is the American standard code for information interchange (ASCII). Figure 1.9 shows that this is simply a table specifying which binary number is to be used to represent *alphanumeric* information (letters of the alphabet, numbers and punctuation). As ASCII has limited capability to handle the full richness of the world's tongues, word processors and typesetters have to define more sophisticated mappings to handle the greater range of characters such as *italics*, *subscripts* and *superscripts* and so on.

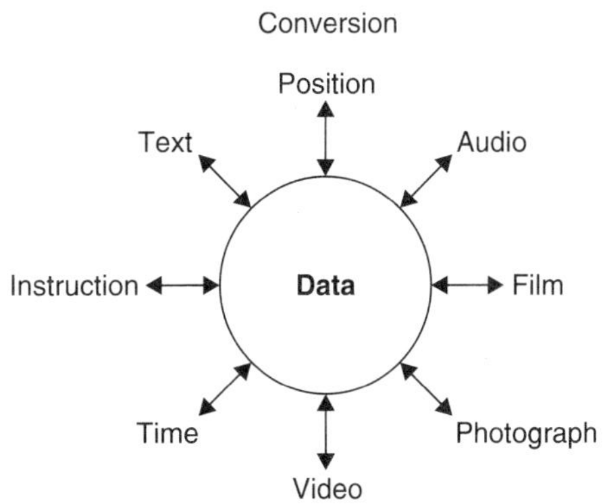

Figure 1.8 A wide variety of information types which can be expressed as binary numbers.

Text as data

ASCII = American standard code for information interchange

A	=	41 hex	
•		•	
•		•	U.C.
•		•	
Z	=	5A	
a	=	61	
•		•	
•		•	L.C.
•		•	
z	=	7A	

7 bits needed for 128 symbols

In practice 1 byte = 1 symbol

1000 words of typical text ≏ 5–6 K bytes of data

Figure 1.9 The ASCII code maps alphanumeric characters onto a binary number scale.

Alphanumeric characters are discrete and it is obvious to allocate one binary word to each character. Where the information is continuous a different approach is necessary. An audio waveform is continuous in one dimension, namely time, whereas a still picture is continuous in two axes, conventionally vertical and horizontal. The shape of a solid object will need to expressed as three-dimensional data for use in CAD (computer aided design) systems and in virtual reality and simulation systems.

The solution here is to use a combination of sampling and interpolation. Sampling is a process of periodic measurement and this can take place in time or space. Interpolation is a filtering process which returns information from discrete points to a continuum. Filtering is inseparable from digital techniques and Chapter 3 treats the subject in some detail.

Sampling can convert the shape of an analog waveform or the surface of a solid into a set of numerically defined points. In image portrayal a grid of defined points is created in the plane of the image and at each one the brightness and colour of the image is measured.

It is vital to appreciate that although the samples carry information *about* the waveform, they are not themselves the waveform. The waveform can only be observed after the interpolator. Samples should be considered as information-efficient instructions which control an interpolator to re-create a continuum. The failure to interpolate causes distortions and artifacts which may be justified by the need for economy but which are not fundamental to sampling. This topic is important for quality and will be considered in Chapter 4.

Those who are not familiar with digital principles often worry that sampling takes away something from a signal because it is not taking notice of what happened between the samples. This would be true in a system having infinite bandwidth, but no continuous signal can have infinite bandwidth. All signals from transducers have a resolution or frequency response limit, as do human vision and hearing. When a signal has finite bandwidth, the rate at which it can change is limited, and the way in which it changes becomes predictable. If the sampling rate is adequate, a waveform can only change between samples in one way, it is then only necessary to convey the samples and the original waveform can unambiguously be reconstructed from them.

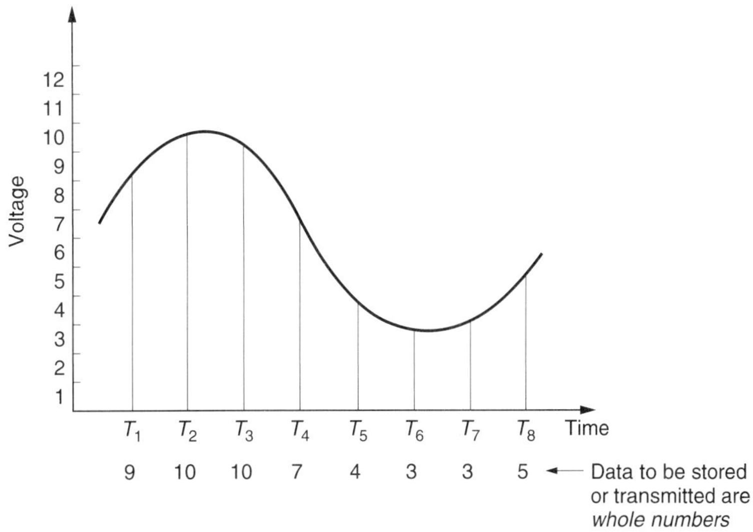

Figure 1.10 In pulse code modulation (PCM), the analog waveform is measured periodically at the sampling rate. The voltage (represented here by the height) of each sample is then described by a whole number. The whole numbers are stored or transmitted rather than the waveform itself.

An audio waveform is sampled in the time domain at a constant sampling frequency F_s as shown in Figure 1.10. In contrast, images are sampled in space. Figure 1.11 shows that a monochrome digital image is a rectangular array of points at which the brightness is stored as a number. The points are known as picture cells, generally abbreviated to pixels, although sometimes the abbreviation is more savage and they are known as pels. As shown in Figure 1.11(a), the array will generally be arranged with an even spacing between pixels, which are in rows and columns. By placing the pixels close together, it is hoped that a combination of the filtering action of the display and the finite resolution

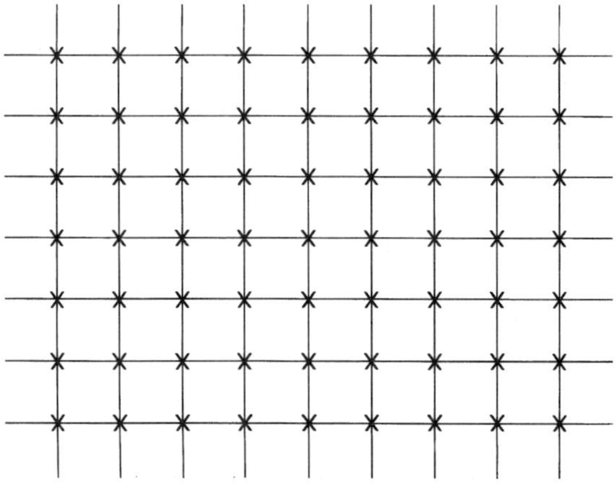

Figure 1.11(a) A picture can be stored digitally by representing the brightness at each of the above points by a binary number. For a colour picture each point becomes a vector and has to describe the brightness, hue and saturation of that part of the picture. Samples are usually but not always formed into regular arrays of rows and columns, and it is most efficient if the horizontal and vertical spacing are the same.

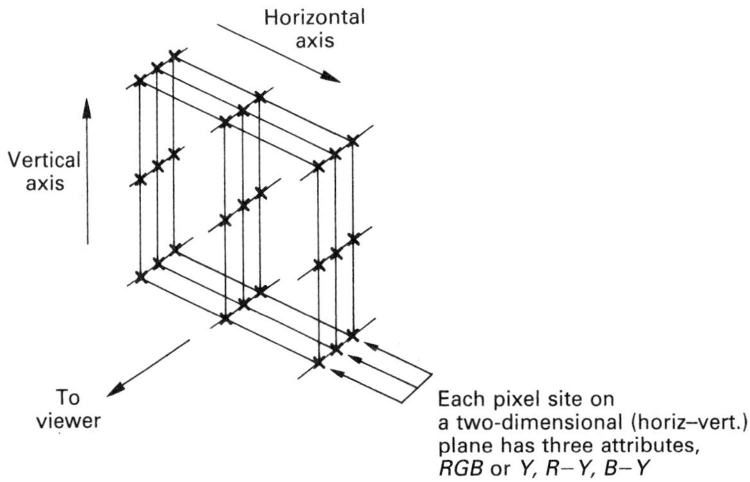

Figure 1.11(b) In the case of component video, each pixel site is described by three values and so the pixel becomes a vector quantity.

of the eye will cause the observer to perceive a continuous image. Obviously the finer the pixel spacing, the greater the resolution of the picture will be, but the amount of data needed to store one picture will increase as the square of the resolution, and with it the costs.

The most efficient system is one in which the horizontal and vertical spacing between pixels is the same. This is because as the viewer approaches the screen, the eye is able to resolve the individual pixels at the same time in both axes. Given a choice, the viewer would then back off until the pixel structure just vanished. Samples taken in this way are called *square pixels* although this is a misnomer: it is the sampling grid which is square. Computer graphics have always used square pixels, whereas digital television frequently does not.

In displays, colour is created by the additive mixing in the display of three primary colours, typically Red, Green and Blue. Effectively the display needs to be supplied with three video signals, each representing a primary colour. Since practical colour cameras generally also have three seperate sensors, one for each primary colour, a camera and a display can be directly connected. *RGB* consists of three parallel signals having the same bit rate, and is used where the highest accuracy is needed. *RGB* is seldom used for broadcast applications because of the high cost.

If *RGB* is used in the digital domain, it will be seen from Figure 1.11(b) that each image consists of three superimposed layers of samples, one for each primary colour. The pixel is no longer a single number representing a scalar brightness value, but a vector which describes in some way the brightness, hue and saturation of that point in the picture. In *RGB*, the pixels contain three unipolar numbers representing the proportion of each of the three primary colours at that point in the picture.

In colour printing, subtractive mixing is used, which is quite different from the additive mixing of television. In subtractive mixing, the primaries are cyan, magenta and yellow. If all these are used together, the result is black, but it is easier to use black pigments for this purpose and so colour printing uses four channels, cyan, magenta, yellow and black or *CMYK*. It is possible to convert from *RGB* to *CYMK* so that images captured by video cameras or digital still cameras can be reproduced as prints. Chapter 6 deals with colour conversion.

Samples are taken at instants in time or space and the value of each one is then mapped onto a range of binary numbers by a process called *quantizing*. The range is determined by the wordlength. As the wordlength is an integer, the binary number ranges available always differ by a factor of two.

In video signals, which are non-linear, eight-bit words allowing 256 combinations are adequate. Linear light coding requires as much as fourteen-bit resolution. In a Compact Disc, the numbers have sixteen bits and 65 536 different codes are available. For audio production purposes longer wordlengths are needed. Audio information is *bipolar* and is handled by the two's complement coding scheme discussed in section 2.4.

Perfect quantizing causes artifacts in both audio and video and a technique known as *dither* is essential to overcome the problem. Quantizing and dither techniques are discussed in Chapter 4.

There are two ways in which binary signals can be used to carry sample data and these are shown in Figure 1.12. When each digit of the

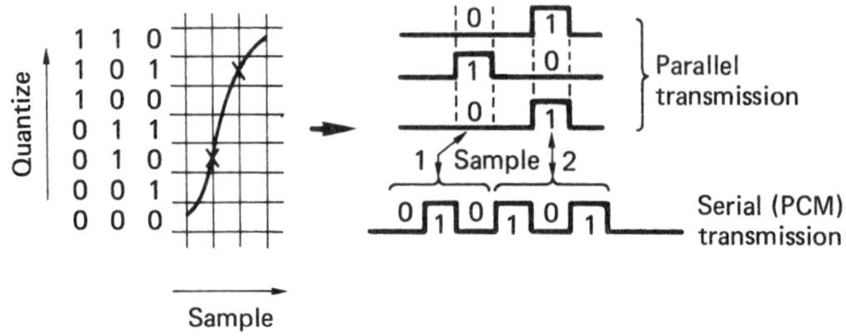

Figure 1.12 When a signal is carried in numerical form, either parallel or serial, the mechanisms of Figure 1.4 ensure that the only degradation is in the conversion process.

binary number is carried on a separate wire this is called parallel transmission. The state of the wires changes at the sampling rate. Using multiple wires is cumbersome, and a single conductor or fibre can be used where successive digits from each sample are sent serially. This is the definition of pulse code modulation which was patented by Reeves.[1] Clearly the clock frequency must now be higher than the sampling rate.

A single high-quality PCM audio channel requires around one million bits per second. Digital audio came into wide use as soon as such a data rate could be handled economically. A PCM standard definition moving colour picture requires around 200 million bits per second. Clearly digital video production could only become common some time after digital audio. Consumer digital video applications could only become possible when technology became available to reduce or *compress* the data rate.

Whichever type of information in Figure 1.8 is used, the result is always the same: binary numbers. As all binary numbers look the same, it is impossible to tell whether a set of such numbers contains images, audio or text without some additional information. File name extensions are one approach to this. In general, binary data only become meaningful information when they arrive at a destination which adheres to the same mapping as the encoder, or at a DSP device which is programmed to understand that mapping so that it can manipulate the data. Storage and transmission systems in general couldn't care less what the data mean. All they have to do is deliver it accurately and it becomes the problem of the destination to figure out what it means. This is a tremendous advantage because it means that storage and transmission systems are generic and largely independent of the type of data.

In practice the only significant differences between types of data that concern transmission and storage devices are the tolerance of the data to error and the degree to which real time needs to be approached at the destination.

1.4 Integrated circuits

Integrated circuits are electronic systems where all the components have been shrunk to fit in a single part. They are also commonly called chips although strictly this refers to the actual circuit element inside the protective housing. The advantage of integrated circuits is that the unit cost can be very low. The development and tooling cost, however, is considerable, so integrated circuits are only economically viable if they are made in volume. Consumer products are an ideal market.

The smaller each component can be, and the closer they can be packed, the more functionality can be obtained from the part, without any increase in cost. Inside such circuits, the small spacing between the wires results in *crosstalk* where signals in one wire are picked up by others. Binary systems resist crosstalk and allow denser packing than would be possible with linear or analog circuits. As a result, binary logic and integrated circuits form a natural alliance. The integrated circuit has been the subject of phenomenal progress in packing density which continues to drive costs down.

When it became possible to put all the functionality of a central processing unit (CPU) on a single integrated circuit, the result was the microprocessor. Computing power came within the reach of the consumer and led to the explosion in personal computers.

The functionality of integrated circuits goes up with time with the following results:

(a) Existing processes become cheaper: e.g the price of pocket calculators.
(b) Processes which were previously too complex become affordable; e.g. error correction and compression.
(c) The cost of RAM falls.

As a result, devices based on complex processes become available not when they are invented but when the economics of integrated circuits make them feasible. A good example is the Compact Disc. The optical storage technology of CD is much older, but it became possible to use it as a consumer digital audio product when real-time error-correction processors became available at consumer prices. Similarly, digital television was not viable until compression processors, which are more complex still, became economic.

1.5 Storage technology

Advances in integrated circuits do not just improve the performance of RAM and computers. Integrated circuits are used in storage devices such as disk drives to encode and correct the data as well as to control the mechanism and make the heads follow the data tracks. If more complex coding and control can be used, the storage density can rise. In parallel with this, the performance of heads and media continues to improve and when compounded with the coding and control improvements, each generation of storage device displays a significant reduction in the cost of storing a given quantity of data. This makes new applications possible which were previously too expensive. For example, the falling cost of the hard disk drive led first to the word processor in the 1970s, which needs a relatively small amount of data, next to the digital audio editor in the 1980s and then to the video editor in the 1990s.

Storage devices are generally classified by their access time and the cost per bit. Unfortunately these two parameters are mutually exclusive and improving one usually worsens the other. Figure 1.13 shows the relative merits of RAM, disks and tape. RAM has the fastest access, but is extremely expensive because every bit has to be individually fabricated inside the integrated circuit. Magnetic recording is cheaper because the medium is uniform and the bits are created by the passage of the head. Disks are optimized for speed whereas tapes are optimized for capacity. As a result, various different storage technologies co-exist because no single one has all the ideal features. The performance of all storage technologies increases with time, but the relative performance tends to stay the same.

Winchester disk	Tape	Optical disk
Fast access speed High cost per bit Non-exchangeable	Slow access speed Low cost per bit Exchangeable	Medium access speed Low cost per bit Exchangeable

Figure 1.13 Different storage media have different combinations of attributes and no one technology is superior in all aspects.

Optical disks such as CD/CDROM and DVD are optimized for mass replication by pressing and cannot be recorded. Recordable optical disks such as CD-R and DVD-R are also available and these have the advantage of high capacity and exchangeability but usually fall behind magnetic disks in access time and transfer rate.

1.6 Noise and probability

Probability is a useful concept when dealing with processes which are not completely predictable. Thermal noise in electronic components is random, and although under given conditions the noise power in a system may be constant, this value only determines the heat that would be developed in a resistive load. In digital systems, it is the instantaneous voltage of noise which is of interest, since it is a form of interference which could alter the state of a bit if it were large enough. Unfortunately the instantaneous voltage cannot be predicted; indeed if it could the interference could not be called noise. Noise can only be quantified statistically, by measuring or predicting the likelihood of a given noise amplitude.

Figure 1.14 shows a graph relating the probability of occurrence to the amplitude of noise. The noise amplitude increases away from the origin along the horizontal axis, and for any amplitude of interest, the probability of that noise amplitude occurring can be read from the curve. The shape of the curve is known as a Gaussian distribution, which crops up whenever the overall effect of a large number of independent phenomena is considered. Thermal noise is due to the contributions from countless molecules in the component concerned. Magnetic recording depends on superimposing some average magnetism on vast numbers of magnetic particles.

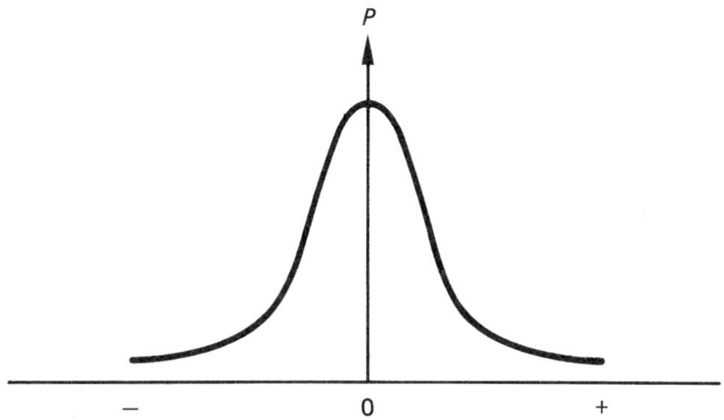

Figure 1.14 The endless nature of the Gaussian curve means that errors will always happen and a correction scheme is usually necessary.

If it were possible to isolate an individual noise-generating microcosm of a tape or a head on the molecular scale, the noise it could generate would have physical limits because of the finite energy present. The noise distribution might then be rectangular as shown in Figure 1.15(a), where all amplitudes below the physical limit are equally likely. The output of a random number generator can have a uniform probability if each possible value occurs once per sequence.

If the combined effect of two of these uniform probability processes is considered, clearly the maximum amplitude is now doubled, because the two effects can add, but provided the two effects are uncorrelated, they

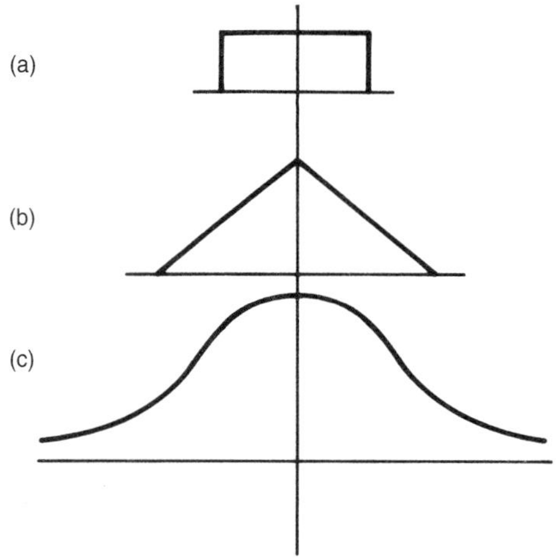

Figure 1.15 At (a) is a rectangular probability; all values are equally likely but between physical limits. At (b) is the sum of two rectangular probabilities, which is triangular, and at (c) is the Gaussian curve which is the sum of an infinite number of rectangular probabilities.

can also subtract, so the probability is no longer rectangular, but becomes triangular as in Figure 1.15(b). The probability falls to zero at peak amplitude because the chances of two independent mechanisms reaching their peak value with the same polarity at the same time are understandably small.

If the number of mechanisms summed together is now allowed to increase without limit, the result is the Gaussian curve shown in Figure 1.15(c), where it will be seen that the curve has no amplitude limit, because it is just possible that all mechanisms will simultaneously reach their peak value together, although the chances of this happening are incredibly remote. Thus the Gaussian curve is the overall probability of a large number of uncorrelated uniform processes.

Many people have difficulty dealing with probability or statistical information. A motorcyclist once told me he would not fly in a helicopter because they are unsafe. When told that smoking increases the probability of lung cancer, many people will cite some 80-year-old relative who has smoked every day for 60 years and is still fit. This is not at odds with statistics at all. The Gaussian curve is infinite and permits, indeed requires, a *small* number of surviving heavy smokers.

There two wonderful examples of extremes of probability. At the high probability end are the chances of a celluloid cat being chased through hell by an asbestos dog, for which gem I am indebted to Robert Pease. At the low probability end is a quote from a competition held by *New Scientist* for newspaper headlines which would amuse scientists: National Lottery winner struck by lightning!

1.7 Time compression and expansion

Data files such as computer programs are simply lists of instructions and have no natural time axis. In contrast, audio and video data are sampled at a fixed rate and need to be presented to the viewer at the same rate. In audiovisual systems the audio also needs to be synchronized to the video. Continuous bitstreams at a fixed bit rate are difficult for generic data recording and transmission systems to handle. Most digital storage and network systems work on blocks of data which be individually addressed and/or routed. The bit rate may be fixed at the design stage at a value which may be too low or too high for the audio or video data to be handled.

The solution is to use time compression or expansion. Figure 1.16 shows a RAM which is addressed by binary counters which periodically overflow to zero and start counting again, giving the RAM a ring structure. If write and read addresses increment at the same speed, the RAM becomes a fixed data delay as the addresses retain a fixed relationship. However, if the read address clock runs at a higher frequency, but in bursts, the output data are assembled into blocks with spaces in between. The data are now time compressed. Instead of being an unbroken stream which is difficult to handle, the data are in blocks with convenient pauses in between them. In these pauses numerous processes can take place. A hard disk might move its heads to another track. In all types of recording and transmission, the time compression of the samples allows time for synchronizing patterns, subcode and error-correction words to be inserted.

Subsequently, any time compression can be reversed by time expansion. This requires a second RAM identical to the one shown. Data are written into the RAM in bursts, but read out at the standard sampling rate to restore a continuous bitstream. In a recorder, the time expansion stage

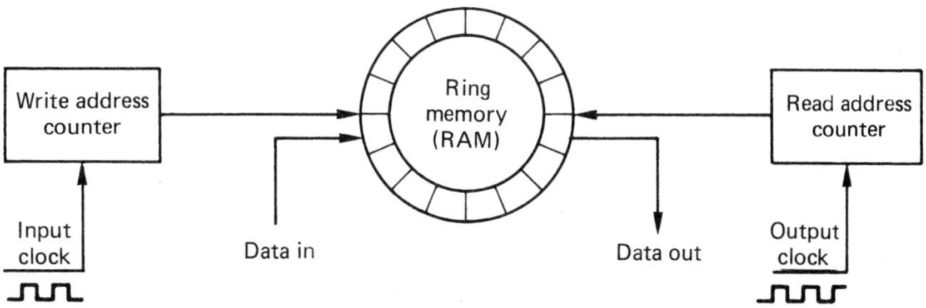

Figure 1.16 If the memory address is arranged to come from a counter which overflows, the memory can be made to appear circular. The write address then rotates endlessly, overwriting previous data once per revolution. The read address can follow the write address by a variable distance (not exceeding one revolution) and so a variable delay takes place between reading and writing.

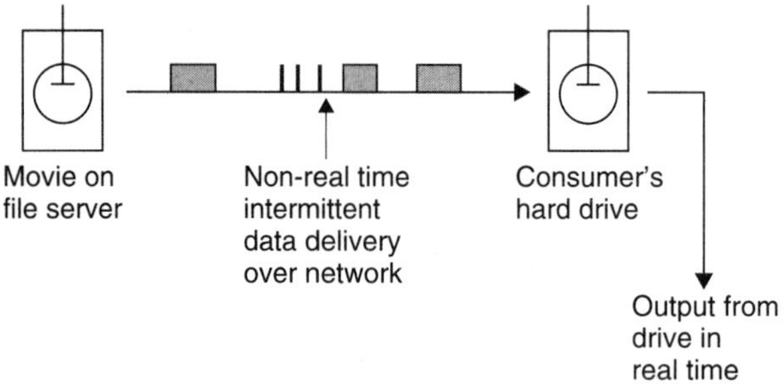

Figure 1.17 In non-real-time transmission, the data are transferred slowly to a storage medium which then outputs real-time data. Movies can be downloaded to the home in this way.

can be combined with the timebase correction stage so that speed variations in the medium can be eliminated at the same time. The use of time compression is universal in digital recording and widely used in transmission. In general, the *instantaneous* data rate in the channel is not the same as the original rate although in real-time systems the *average* rate must be the same.

Where the bit rate of the communication path is inadequate, transmission is still possible, but not in real time. Figure 1.17 shows that the data to be transmitted will have to be written in real time on a storage device such as a disk drive, and the drive will then transfer the data at whatever rate is possible to another drive at the receiver. When the transmission is complete, the second drive can then provide the data at the correct bit rate.

In the case where the available bit rate is higher than the correct data rate, the same configuration can be used to copy an audio or video data file faster than real time. Another application of time compression is to allow several streams of data to be carried along the same channel in a technique known as *multiplexing*. Figure 1.18 shows some examples. At (a) multiplexing allows audio and video data to be recorded on the same heads in a digital video recorder such as DVC. At (b), several TV channels are multiplexed into one MPEG transport stream.

1.8 Error correction and concealment

All practical recording and transmission media are imperfect. Magnetic media, for example, suffer from noise and dropouts. In a digital recording of binary data, a bit is either correct or wrong, with no intermediate stage. Small amounts of noise are rejected, but inevitably, infrequent noise impulses cause some individual bits to be in error. Dropouts cause a larger number of bits in one place to be in error. An error of this kind is

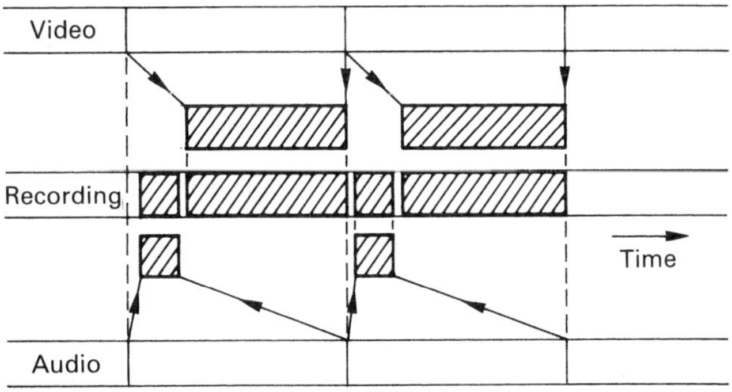

Figure 1.18(a) Time compression is used to shorten the length of track needed by the video. Heavily time-compressed audio samples can then be recorded on the same track using common circuitry.

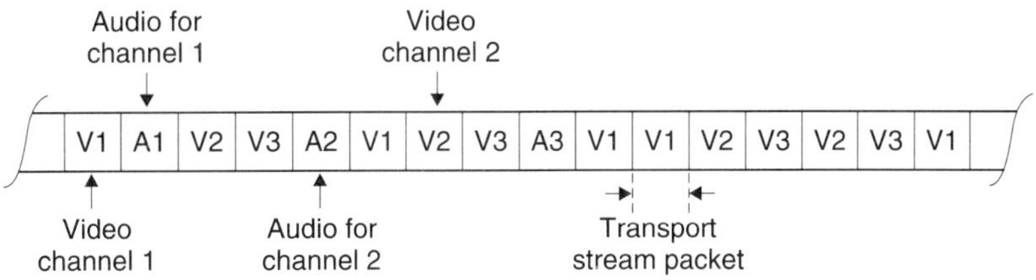

Figure 1.18(b) In MPEG, multiplexing allows data from several TV channels to share one bitstream.

called a burst error. Whatever the medium and whatever the nature of the mechanism responsible, data are either recovered correctly or suffer some combination of bit errors and burst errors. In optical disks, random errors can be caused by imperfections in the moulding process, whereas burst errors are due to contamination or scratching of the disk surface.

Before attempting to specify an error-correction system, the causes of errors must be studied to quantify the problem, and the sensitivity of the destination to errors must be assessed. In video and audio the sensitivity to errors must be subjective. Figure 1.19 shows the relative sensitivity of different types of data to error.

Whilst the exact BER (bit error rate) which can be tolerated will depend on the application, digital audio is less tolerant of errors than digital video and more tolerant than computer data. The use of compression changes the picture if redundancy has been removed from a signal, it becomes less tolerant of errors.

In PCM audio and video, the effect of a single bit in error depends upon the significance of the bit. If the least significant bit of a sample is wrong, the chances are that the effect will be lost in the noise. Conversely, if a high-order bit is in error, a massive transient will be added to the waveform.

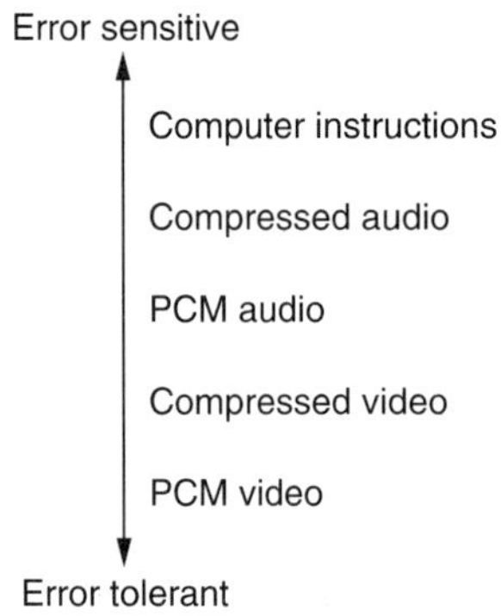

Figure 1.19 Data vary in their tolerance to error. Compressed data are more sensitive to error.

MPEG video compression uses variable-length coding. If a bit error occurs it may cause the length of a symbol to be incorrectly assessed and the decoder will lose synchronism with the bitstream. This may cause an error affecting a significant area of the picture which might propagate from one picture to the next.

If the maximum error rate which the destination can tolerate is likely to be exceeded by the unaided channel, some form of error handling will be necessary.

There are a number of terms which have idiomatic meanings in error correction. The raw BER is the error rate of the medium, whereas the residual or uncorrected BER is the rate at which the error-correction system fails to detect or miscorrects errors. In practical digital systems, the residual BER is negligibly small. If the error correction is turned off, the two figures become the same.

It is paramount in all error-correction systems that the protection used should be appropriate for the probability of errors to be encountered. An inadequate error-correction system is actually worse than not having any correction. Error correction works by trading probabilities. Error-free performance with a certain error rate is achieved at the expense of performance at higher error rates. Figure 1.20 shows the effect of an error-correction system on the residual BER for a given raw BER. It will be seen that there is a characteristic knee in the graph. If the expected raw BER has been misjudged, the consequences can be disastrous. Another result demonstrated by the example is that we can only guarantee to detect the same number of bits in error as there are redundant bits.

There are many different types of recording and transmission channel and consequently there will be many different mechanisms which may result in errors. Although there are many different applications, the basic principles remain the same.

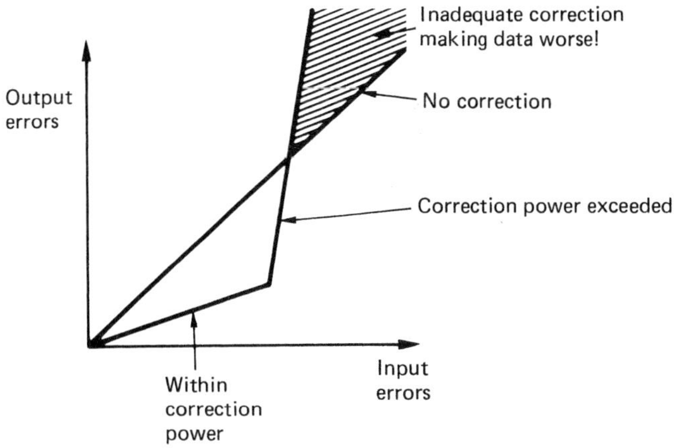

Figure 1.20 An error-correction system can only reduce errors at normal error rates at the expense of increasing errors at higher rates. It is most important to keep a system working to the left of the knee in the graph.

In magnetic recording, data can be corrupted by mechanical problems such as media dropout and poor tracking or head contact, or Gaussian thermal noise in replay circuits and heads. In optical recording, contamination of the medium interrupts the light beam. Warped disks and birefringent pressings cause defocusing. Inside equipment, data are conveyed on short wires and the noise environment is under the designer's control. With suitable design techniques, errors can be made effectively negligible. In communication systems, there is considerably less control of the electromagnetic environment.

In cables, crosstalk and electromagnetic interference occur and can corrupt data, although optical fibres are resistant to interference of this kind. In long-distance cable transmission the effects of lightning and exchange switching noise must be considered. In digital television broadcasting, multipath reception causes notches in the received spectrum where signal cancellation takes place. In MOS memories the datum is stored in a tiny charge well which acts as a capacitor (see Chapter 2) and natural radioactive decay can cause alpha particles which have enough energy to discharge a well, resulting in a single bit error. This only happens once every few decades in a single chip, but when large numbers of chips are assembled in computer memories the probability of error rises to one every few minutes.

Irrespective of the cause, error mechanisms cause one of two effects. There are large isolated corruptions, called error bursts, where numerous bits are corrupted all together in an area which is otherwise error free, and there are random errors affecting single bits or symbols. Whatever the mechanism, the result will be that the received data will not be exactly the same as those sent. It is a tremendous advantage of digital systems that the discrete data bits will be each either right or wrong. A bit cannot be off-colour as it can only be interpreted as 0 or 1. Thus the subtle degradations of analog systems are absent from digital recording and transmission channels and will only be found in convertors. Equally if a binary digit is known to be wrong, it is only necessary to invert its state and then it must be right and indistinguishable from its original value!

Some conclusions can be drawn from the Gaussian distribution of noise.[2] First, it is not possible to make error-free digital recordings, because however high the signal-to-noise ratio of the recording, there is still a small but finite chance that the noise can exceed the signal. Measuring the signal-to-noise ratio of a channel establishes the noise power, which determines the width of the noise distribution curve relative to the signal amplitude.

When in a binary system the noise amplitude exceeds the signal amplitude, but with the opposite polarity, a bit error will occur. Knowledge of the shape of the Gaussian curve allows the conversion of signal-to-noise ratio into bit error rate (BER). It can be predicted how many bits will fail due to noise in a given recording, but it is not possible to say *which* bits will be affected. Increasing the SNR of the channel will not eliminate errors, it just reduces their probability. The logical solution is to incorporate an error-correction system.

Figure 1.21 shows that error correction works by adding some bits to the data which are calculated from the data. This creates an entity called a codeword which spans a greater length of time than one bit alone. The statistics of noise mean that whilst one bit may be lost in a codeword, the loss of the rest of the codeword because of noise is highly improbable. As will be described later in this chapter, codewords are designed to be able totally to correct a finite number of corrupted bits. The greater the

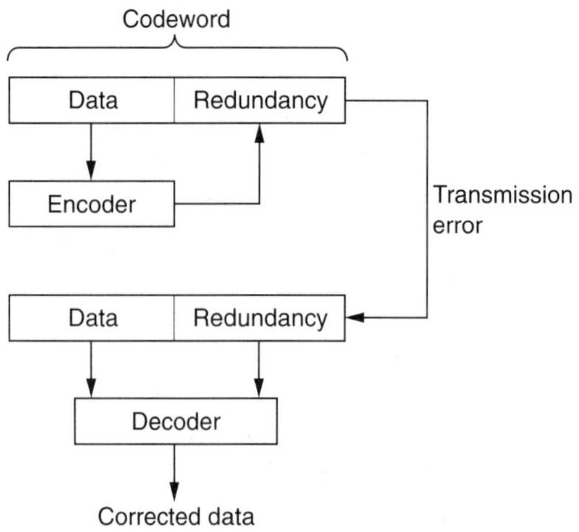

Figure 1.21 Error correction works by adding redundancy.

timespan over which the coding is performed, or, on a recording medium, the greater area over which the coding is performed, the greater will be the reliability achieved, although this does mean a greater encoding and decoding delay.

Shannon[3] disclosed that a message can be sent to any desired degree of accuracy provided that it is spread over a sufficient timespan. Engineers have to compromise, because an infinite coding delay in the recovery of an error-free signal is not acceptable. Most short digital interfaces do not employ error correction because the build-up of coding delays in production systems is unacceptable.

If error correction is necessary as a practical matter, it is then only a small step to put it to maximum use. All error correction depends on adding bits to the original message, and this, of course, increases the number of bits to be recorded, although it does not increase the information recorded. It might be imagined that error correction is going to reduce storage capacity, because space has to be found for all the extra bits. Nothing could be further from the truth. Once an error-correction system is used, the signal-to-noise ratio of the channel can be reduced, because the raised BER of the channel will be overcome by the error-correction system.

In a digital television broadcast system the use of error correction allows a lower-powered transmitter to be used. In a magnetic track, reduction of the SNR by 3 dB can be achieved by halving the track width, provided that the system is not dominated by head or preamplifier noise. This doubles the recording density, making the storage of the additional bits needed for error correction a trivial matter. In short, error correction is not a nuisance to be tolerated; it is a vital tool needed to maximize the efficiency of systems. Convergent technologies would not be economically viable without it.

Figure 1.22 shows the broad approaches to data integrity. The first stage might be called error avoidance and includes such measures as creating bad block files on hard disks or using verified media. The data pass

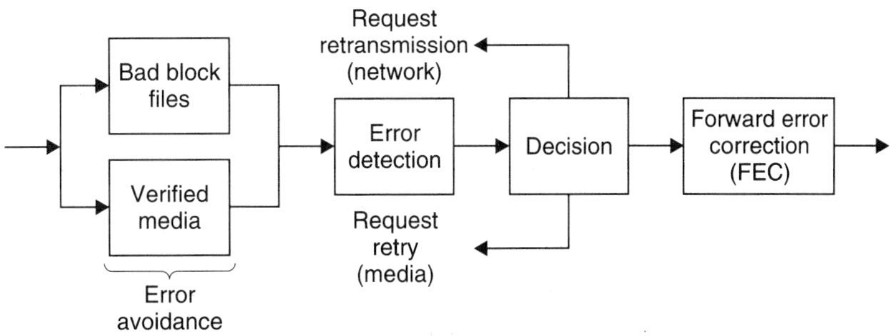

Figure 1.22 Approaches to errors. See text for details.

through the channel, where corruption may occur. On receipt of the data the occurrence of errors is first detected, and this process must be extremely reliable, as it does not matter how effective the correction or how good the concealment algorithm, if it is not known that they are necessary! The detection of an error then results in a course of action being decided.

In many cases of digital video or audio replay a retry is not possible because the data are required in real time. However, if a disk-based system is transferring to tape for the purpose of backup, real-time operation is not required. If the disk drive detects an error a retry is easy as the disk is turning at several thousand rpm and will quickly re-present the data. An error due to a dust particle may not occur on the next revolution. Many magnetic tape systems have *read after write*. During recording, offtape data are immediately checked for errors. If an error is detected, the tape will abort the recording, reverse to the beginning of the current block and erase it. The data from that block are then recorded further down the tape. This is the recording equivalent of a retransmission in a communications system.

In binary, a bit has only two states. If it is wrong, it is only necessary to reverse the state and it must be right. Thus the correction process is trivial and perfect. The main difficulty is in identifying the bits which are in error. This is done by coding the data by adding redundant bits. Adding redundancy is not confined to digital technology, airliners have several engines and cars have twin braking systems. Clearly the more failures which have to be handled, the more redundancy is needed. If a four-engined airliner is designed to fly normally with one engine failed, three of the engines have enough power to reach cruise speed, and the fourth one is redundant. The amount of redundancy is equal to the amount of failure which can be handled. In the case of the failure of two engines, the plane can still fly, but it must slow down; this is graceful degradation. Clearly the chances of a two-engine failure on the same flight are remote.

The amount of error which can be corrected is proportional to the amount of redundancy, and it will be shown in Chapter 10 that within this limit, the data are returned to exactly their original value. Consequently *corrected* samples are undetectable. If the amount of error exceeds the amount of redundancy, correction is not possible, and, in order to allow graceful degradation, concealment will be used. Concealment is a process where the value of a missing sample is estimated from those nearby. The estimated sample value is not necessarily exactly the same as the original, and so under some circumstances concealment can be audible, especially if it is frequent. However, in a well-designed system, concealments occur with negligible frequency unless there is an actual fault or problem.

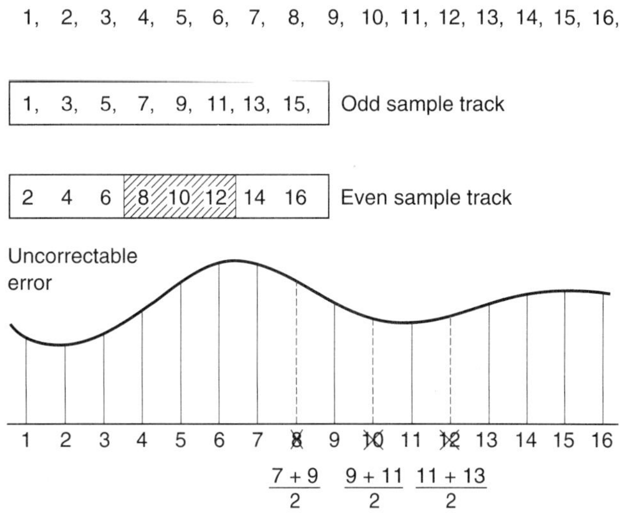

Figure 1.23 In cases where the error correction is inadequate, concealment can be used provided that the samples have been ordered appropriately in the recording. Odd and even samples are recorded in different places as shown here. As a result an uncorrectable error causes incorrect samples to occur singly, between correct samples. In the example shown, sample 8 is incorrect, but samples 7 and 9 are unaffected and an approximation to the value of sample 8 can be had by taking the average value of the two. This interpolated value is substituted for the incorrect value.

Concealment is made possible by rearranging the sample sequence prior to recording. This is shown in Figure 1.23 where odd-numbered samples are separated from even-numbered samples prior to recording. The odd and even sets of samples may be recorded in different places on the medium, so that an uncorrectable burst error affects only one set. On replay, the samples are recombined into their natural sequence, and the error is now split up so that it results in every other sample being lost in a two-dimensional structure. The picture is now described half as often, but can still be reproduced with some loss of accuracy. This is better than not being reproduced at all even if it is not perfect. Many digital video recorders use such an odd/even distribution for concealment. Clearly if any errors are fully correctable, the distribution is a waste of time; it is only needed if correction is not possible.

The presence of an error-correction system means that the video (and audio) quality is independent of the medium/head quality within limits. There is no point in trying to assess the health of a machine by watching a monitor or listening to the audio, as this will not reveal whether the error rate is normal or within a whisker of failure. The only useful procedure is to monitor the frequency with which errors are being corrected, and to compare it with normal figures.

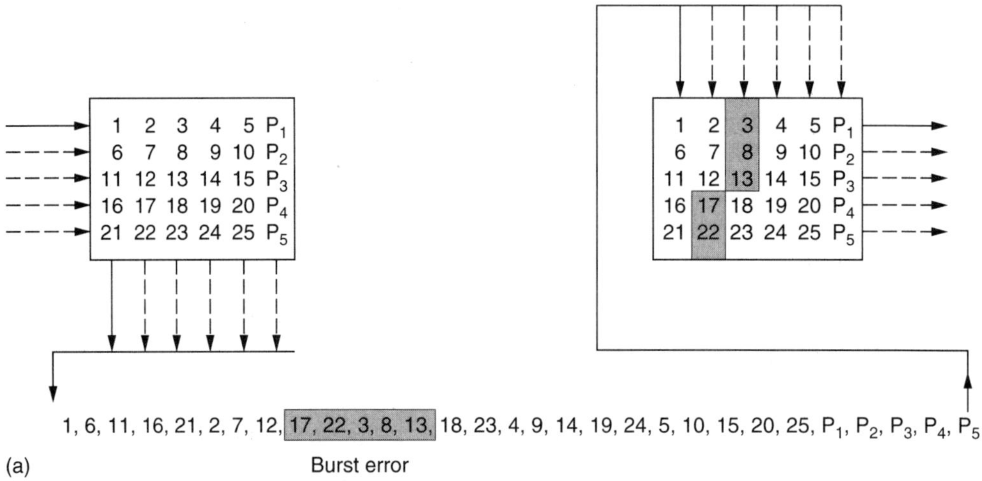

Figure 1.24(a) Interleaving is essential to make error-correction schemes more efficient. Samples written sequentially in rows into a memory have redundancy P added to each row. The memory is then read in columns and the data sent to the recording medium. On replay the non-sequential samples from the medium are de-interleaved to return them to their normal sequence. This breaks up the burst error (shaded) into one error symbol per row in the memory, which can be corrected by the redundancy P.

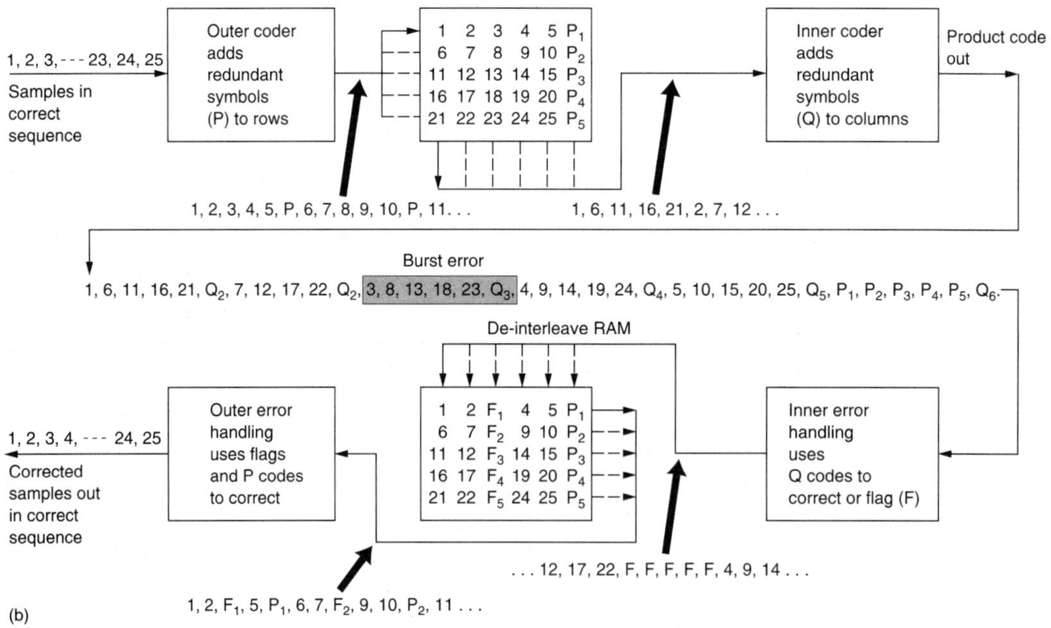

Figure 1.24(b) In addition to the redundancy P on rows, inner redundancy Q is also generated on columns. On replay, the Q code checker will pass on flag F if it finds an error too large to handle itself. The flags pass through the de-interleave process and are used by the outer error correction to identify which symbol in the row needs correcting with P redundancy. The concept of crossing two codes in this way is called a product code.

Digital systems such as broadcasting, optical disks and magnetic recorders are prone to burst errors. Adding redundancy equal to the size of expected bursts to every code is inefficient. Figure 1.24(a) shows that the efficiency of the system can be raised using interleaving. Sequential samples from the ADC are assembled into codes, but these are not recorded/transmitted in their natural sequence. A number of sequential codes are assembled along rows in a memory. When the memory is full, it is copied to the medium by reading down columns. Subsequently, the samples need to be de-interleaved to return them to their natural sequence. This is done by writing samples from tape into a memory in columns, and when it is full, the memory is read in rows. Samples read from the memory are now in their original sequence so there is no effect on the information. However, if a burst error occurs as is shown shaded in the figure it will damage sequential samples in a vertical direction in the de-interleave memory. When the memory is read, a single large error is broken down into a number of small errors whose size is exactly equal to the correcting power of the codes and the correction is performed with maximum efficiency.

An extension of the process of interleave is where the memory array has not only rows made into codewords, but also columns made into codewords by the addition of vertical redundancy. This is known as a product code. Figure 1.24(b) shows that in a product code the redundancy calculated first and checked last is called the outer code, and the

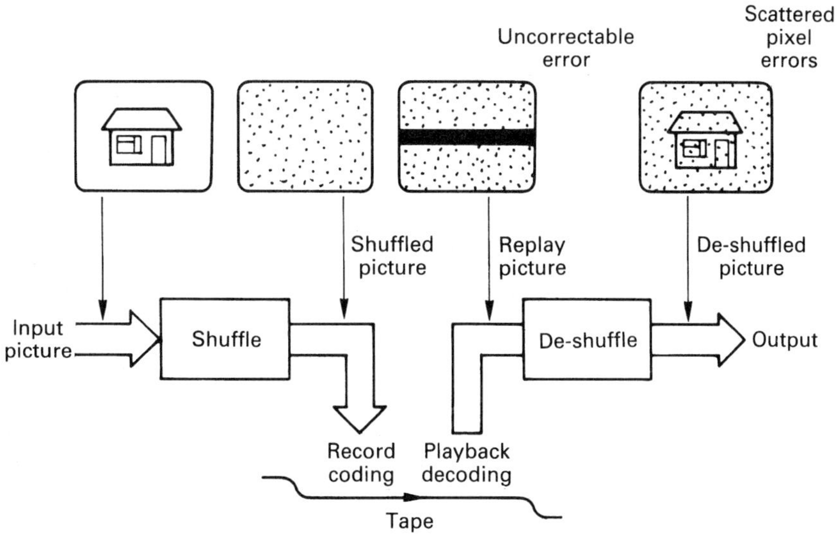

Figure 1.25 The shuffle before recording and the corresponding de-shuffle after playback cancel out as far as the picture is concerned. However, a block of errors due to dropout only experiences the de-shuffle, which spreads the error randomly over the screen. The pixel errors are then easier to correct.

redundancy calculated second and checked first is called the inner code. The inner code is formed along tracks on the medium. Random errors due to noise are corrected by the inner code and do not impair the burst-correcting power of the outer code. Burst errors are declared uncorrectable by the inner code which flags the bad samples on the way into the de-interleave memory. The outer code reads the error flags in order to locate the erroneous data. As it does not have to compute the error locations, the outer code can correct more errors.

The interleave, de-interleave, time-compression and timebase-correction processes inevitably cause delay.

When a product code-based recording suffers an uncorrectable error in an image such as a TV picture or a computer graphic, the result is a rectangular block of failed sample values which require concealment. Such a regular structure would be visible even after concealment, and an additional process is necessary to reduce the visibility. Figure 1.25 shows that a shuffle process is performed prior to product coding in which the pixels are moved around the picture in a pseudo-random fashion. The reverse process is used on replay, and the overall effect is nullified. However, if an uncorrectable error occurs, this will only pass through the de-shuffle and so the regular structure of the failed data blocks will be randomized. The errors are spread across the picture as individual failed pixels in an irregular structure.

1.9 Channel coding

In most recorders used for storing data, the medium carries a track which reproduces a single waveform. Clearly data words contain many bits and so they have to be recorded serially, a bit at a time. Some media, such as optical or magnetic disks, have only one active track, so they must be totally self-contained. DVTRs may have one, two or four tracks read or written simultaneously. At high recording densities, physical tolerances cause phase shifts, or timing errors, between tracks and so it is not possible to read them in parallel. Each track must still be self-contained until the replayed signal has been timebase corrected.

Recording data serially is not as simple as connecting the serial output of a shift register to the head. Data words may contain strings of identical bits. If a shift register is loaded with such a sample and shifted out serially, the output stays at a constant level for the period of the identical bits, and no event is recorded on the track. On replay there is nothing to indicate how many bits were present, or even how fast to move the medium. Clearly, serialized raw data cannot be recorded directly, it has to be modulated into a waveform which contains an embedded clock irrespective of the values of the bits in the samples. On replay a circuit called a data separator can lock to the embedded clock and use it to separate strings of identical bits.

The process of modulating serial data to make it self-clocking is called channel coding. Channel coding also shapes the spectrum of the serialized waveform to make it more efficient. With a good channel code, more data can be stored on a given medium. Spectrum shaping is used in optical disks to prevent the data from interfering with the focus and tracking servos, and in hard disks and in certain tape formats to allow rerecording without erase heads.

Channel coding is also needed to broadcast digital television signals where shaping of the spectrum is an obvious requirement to avoid interference with other services. The techniques of channel coding for recording and transmission are described in Chapter 10.

1.10 Compression, JPEG and MPEG

In its native form, PCM audio and images may have a data rate which is too high for the available channel. One approach to the problem is to use compression which reduces that rate significantly with a moderate loss of subjective quality. The human eye is not equally sensitive to all spatial frequencies and in the same way the ear is not equally sensitive to all temporal frquencies. Some coding gain can be obtained by using fewer bits to describe the frequencies which are less well perceived. Images typically contain a great deal of redundancy where flat areas contain the same pixel value repeated many times. In moving images there is little difference between one picture and the next, and compression can be achieved by sending only the differences.

The ISO has established compression standards for audio, still and moving images. The still image coding was standardized by the Joint Photographic Experts Group (JPEG), whereas the moving image and audio coding was standardized by the Moving Picture Experts Group (MPEG).

Whilst these techniques may achieve considerable reduction in bit rate, it must be appreciated that lossy compression systems reintroduce the generation loss of the analog domain to digital systems. As a result high compression factors are only suitable for final delivery of fully produced material to the viewer.

For production purposes, compression may be restricted to exploiting the redundancy within each picture individually and then with a mild compression factor. This allows simple algorithms to be used and also permits multiple-generation work without artifacts being visible. Such an approach is used in disk-based workstations.

A consumer product may need only single-generation operation and has simple editing requirements. A much greater degree of compression can then be used, which takes advantage of redundancy between pictures. The same is true for broadcasting, where bandwidth is at a premium. A similar approach may be used in disk-based camcorders which are intended for ENG purposes.

The future of television broadcasting (and of any high-definition television) lies completely in compression technology. Compression requires an encoder prior to the medium and a compatible decoder after it. Extensive consumer use of compression could not occur without suitable standards. The ISO–MPEG coding standards were specifically designed to allow wide interchange of compressed video and audio data. Digital television broadcasting and DVD both use MPEG standard bitstreams and these are detailed in Chapter 9.

Figure 1.26 shows that the output of a single compressor is called an *elementary stream*. In practice audio and video streams of this type can be combined using multiplexing. The *program stream* is optimized for recording and the multiplexing is based on blocks of arbitrary size. The *transport stream* is optimized for transmission and is based on blocks of constant size.

In production equipment such as workstations and VTRs which are designed for editing, the MPEG standard is less useful and many successful products use non-MPEG compression.

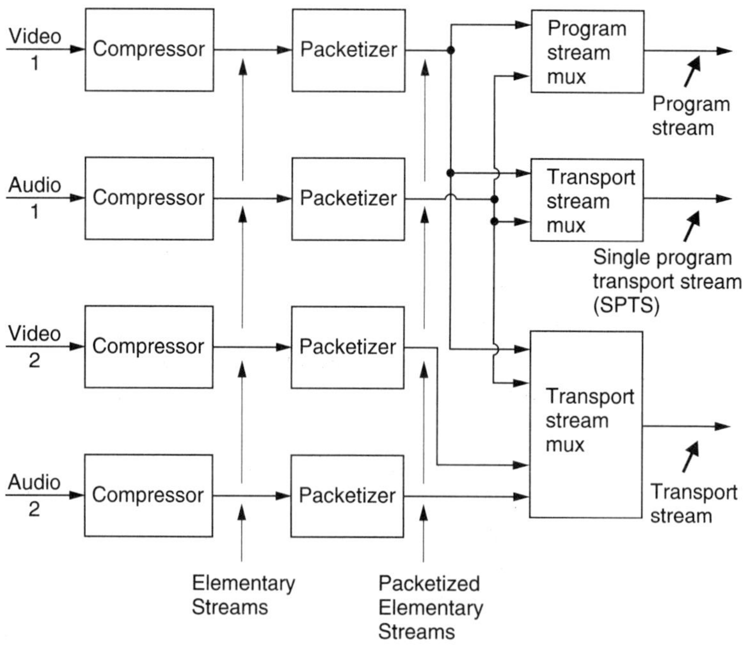

Figure 1.26 The bitstream types of MPEG-2. See text for details.

Compression and the corresponding decoding are complex processes and take time, adding to existing delays in signal paths. Concealment of uncorrectable errors is also more difficult on compressed data. Many compression techniques are based on transforms which are treated in Chapter 3.

1.11 Convergence and commercial television

When television had little or no competition, it could pretty much do what it liked, but now there are alternatives. As a carrier of information, commercial television doesn't work very well because its business model is based on the assumption that commercials and programs are inseparable. Aesthetically speaking, advertising and entertainment do not sit well together and the business model is a crude one which evolved when technology was equally crude.

Today convergent technology allows advertising and entertainment to be separated calling into question the business model of commercial television.

The prospective purchaser looking for product or service is alert and has in the author's mind the constraints and desired qualities needed to solve a real-world problem with some time pressure. In contrast when the same person wants to relax and be entertained the real world and its pressures are not wanted. As commercial television tries to serve both requirements at once it must fail. If it sets out to entertain, the artistic thread of any worthwhile drama is irrepairably damaged by commercial breaks. On the other hand, if it sets out to advertise, it does so very inefficiently. Conventional television advertising is like carpet bombing. The commercial is shown to everybody, whether they are interested or not.

The biggest vulnerability of commercial television is that it is linear. Everything comes out in a predetermined sequence which was at one time out of the viewer's control. It is useful to compare television with magazines. These contain articles, which correspond to programs, and advertising. However, there is no compulsion to read all the advertisements in a magazine at a particular time or at all. This makes a magazine a non-linear or random-access medium.

The development of the consumer VCR was a small step to end the linearity of commercial television. Increasing numbers of viewers use VCRs not just as time shifters but also as a means of fast-forwarding through the commercial breaks.

The non-linear storage of video was until recently restricted by economics to professional applications. However, with the falling cost of hard drives, non-linear video storage is now a consumer product.

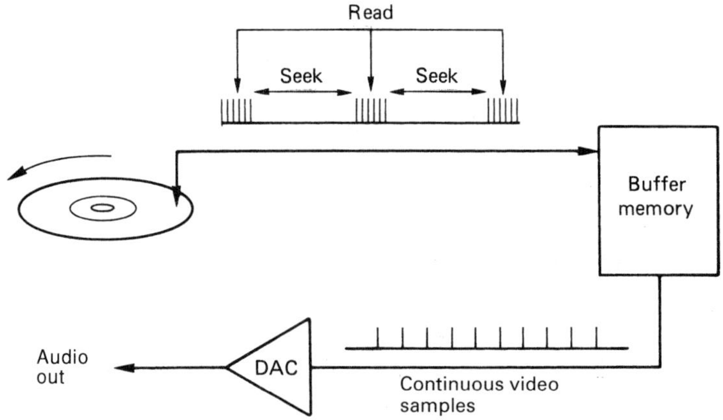

Figure 1.27 In a hard disk recorder, a large-capacity memory is used as a buffer or timebase corrector between the convertors and the disk. The memory allows the convertors to run constantly despite the interruptions in disk transfer caused by the head moving between tracks.

The operation of a hard drive is explained in Chapter 11. What matters here is what it can do. Unlike tape, which can only record or play back but not both at the same time, a PVR can do both simultaneously at arbitrary points on a time line. Figure 1.27 shows how it is done. The disk drive can transfer data much faster than the required bit rate, and so it transfers data in bursts which are smoothed out by RAM buffers. The disk simply interleaves read and write functions so that it gives the impression of reading and writing simultaneously. The read and write processes can take place from anywhere on the disk.

Clearly the PVR can be used as an ordinary video recorder, but it can do some other tricks. Figure 1.28 shows the most far-reaching trick. The disk drive starts recording an off-air commercial TV station. A few minutes later the viewer starts playing back the recording. When the commercial break is transmitted, the disk drive may record it, but the viewer can skip over it using the random access of the hard drive. With suitable software the hard drive could skip over the commercial break automatically by simply not recording it.

When used with digital television systems, the PVR can simply record the transmitted transport stream data and replay it into an MPEG decoder. In this way the PVR has no quality loss whatsoever. The picture quality will be the same as off-air.

Whilst the PVR threatens commercial TV as it is being watched, other technologies threaten to reduce the amount of off-air viewing. The growth of personal computers and the Internet means that there is now an alternative way for the individual to locate products. The would-be purchaser can find a web site which offers the kind of product he or she

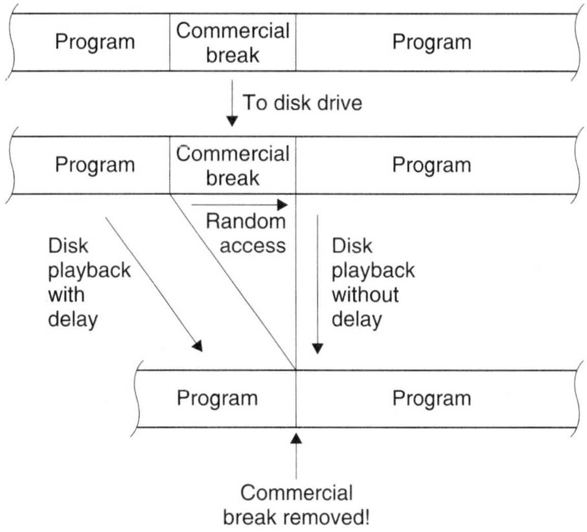

Figure 1.28 The ability of the consumer to use random access to skip over commercial breaks may destroy commercial television as it exists today.

is looking for, and browse through a virtual catalogue. By clicking on an item of interest, it can, for example, be portrayed in action in a moving video sequence. If it suits, it can be bought there and then.

The Internet allows moving pictures to be delivered to the home without using radio technology. Surely radio technology is only necessary when equipment needs to be genuinely mobile. When a television set is permanently chained to the wall by the power cord, why are we using radio to communicate with it? Most PCs are now capable of playing DVDs, which further erodes off-air viewing.

1.12 Electronic cinema

The traditional film-based cinema has hardly changed in principle for about a century. One of the greatest difficulties is the release of a popular new movie. In order to open simultaneously in a large number of cinemas, an equally large number of prints are needed. As film is based on silver, these prints are expensive. The traditional solution was to divide the world up into regions and rely on poor communications so that new films could be released in each region at a time.

When the digital video disk (DVD) was developed, although it is not expensive to duplicate, Hollywood attempted to impose area codes on the disks so they would not play in another region's players. The idea was that DVDs would not be available until after the cinema release.

The region code of DVDs is exactly the wrong solution. Instead of preventing the reasonable use of a successful modern technology because it reveals the shortcomings of an older technology, the correct solution must be to improve the older technology.

Digital technology allows an arbitrary number of copies of moving image data to be delivered anywhere on earth, and so in principle every electronic cinema on the planet could screen the same movie, ending forever the problem of release prints. Digital technology also eliminates film scratches and dirt, and encryption prevents piracy.

References

1. Reeves, A.H., US Patent 2,272,070
2. Michaels, S.R., Is it Gaussian? *Electronics World and Wireless World*, 72–73 (Jan. 1993)
3. Shannon, C.E., A mathematical theory of communication. *Bell System Tech. J.*, **27**, 379 (1948)

2

Digital processing principles

In this chapter the basics of digital processing will be considered. Starting from elements such as logic gates, the chapter builds steadily to an explanation of how computers and digital signal processors work.

2.1 Introduction

However complex a digital process, it can be broken down into smaller stages until finally one finds that there are really only two basic types of element in use, and these can be combined in some way and supplied with a clock to implement virtually any process. Figure 2.1 shows that the first type is a *logic* element. This produces an output which is a logical function of the input with minimal delay. The second type is a *storage* element which samples the state of the input(s) when clocked and holds or delays that state. The strength of binary logic is that the signal has only two states, and considerable noise and distortion of the binary waveform can be tolerated before the state becomes uncertain. At every logic element, the signal is compared with a threshold, and can thus can pass through any number of stages without being degraded. In addition, the use of a storage element at regular locations throughout logic circuits eliminates time variations or jitter. Figure 2.1 shows that if the inputs to a logic element change, the output will not change until the *propagation delay* of the element has elapsed. However, if the output of the logic element forms the input to a storage element, the output of that element will not change until the input is sampled *at the next clock edge*. In this way the signal edge is aligned to the system clock and the propagation delay of the logic becomes irrelevant. The process is known as reclocking.

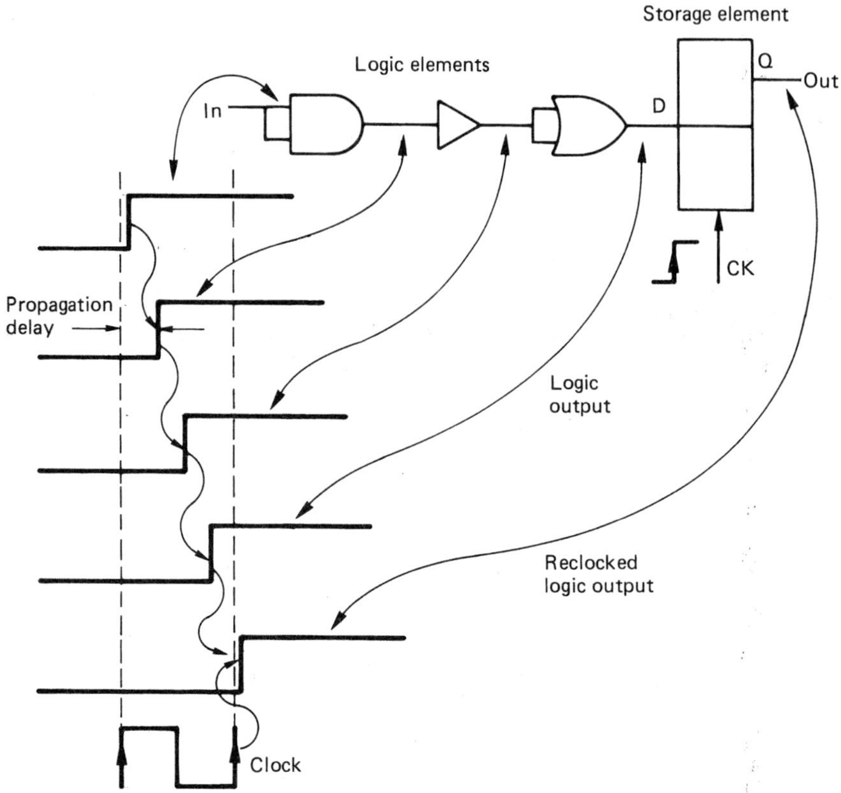

Figure 2.1 Logic elements have a finite propagation delay between input and output and cascading them delays the signal an arbitrary amount. Storage elements sample the input on a clock edge and can return a signal to near coincidence with the system clock. This is known as reclocking. Reclocking eliminates variations in propagation delay in logic elements.

2.2 Logic elements

The two states of the signal when measured with an oscilloscope are simply two voltages, usually referred to as high and low. The actual voltage levels will depend on the type of logic family in use, and on the supply voltage used. Supply voltages have tended to fall as designers seek to reduce power consumption. Within logic, the exact levels are not of much consequence, and it is only necessary to know them when interfacing between different logic families or when driving external devices. The pure logic designer is not interested at all in these voltages, only in their meaning.

Just as the electrical waveform from a microphone represents sound velocity, so the waveform in a logic circuit represents the truth of some statement. As there are only two states, there can only be *true* or *false* meanings. The true state of the signal can be assigned by the designer to either voltage state. When a high voltage represents a true logic condition and a low voltage represents a false condition, the system is known as *positive logic*, or *high true* logic. This is the usual system, but sometimes the low voltage represents the true condition and the high voltage represents the false condition. This is known as *negative logic* or *low true* logic. Provided that everyone is aware of the logic convention in use, both work equally well.

Positive logic name	*Boolean expression*	*Positive logic symbol*	*Positive logic truth table*	*Plain English*
Inverter or NOT gate	$Q = \overline{A}$	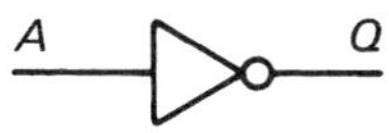	A | Q 0 | 1 1 | 0	Output is opposite of input
AND gate	$Q = A \cdot B$	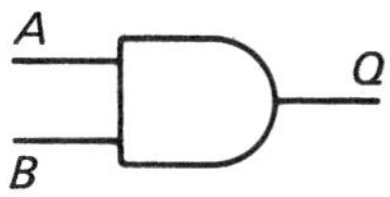	A B | Q 0 0 | 0 0 1 | 0 1 0 | 0 1 1 | 1	Output true when both inputs are true only
NAND (Not AND) gate	$Q = \overline{A \cdot B}$ $= \overline{A} + \overline{B}$	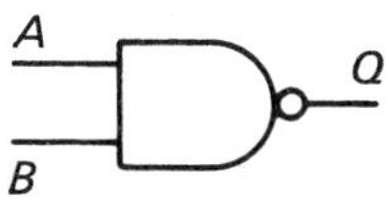	A B | Q 0 0 | 1 0 1 | 1 1 0 | 1 1 1 | 0	Output false when both inputs are true only
OR gate	$Q = A + B$	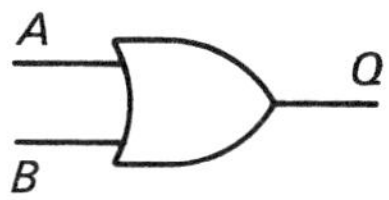	A B | Q 0 0 | 0 0 1 | 1 1 0 | 1 1 1 | 1	Output true if either or both inputs true
NOR (Not OR) gate	$Q = \overline{A + B}$ $= \overline{A} \cdot \overline{B}$	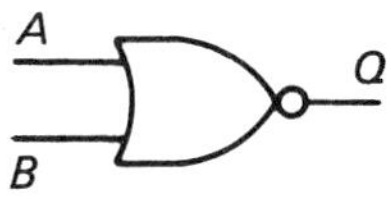	A B | Q 0 0 | 1 0 1 | 0 1 0 | 0 1 1 | 0	Output false if either or both inputs true
Exclusive OR (XOR) gate	$Q = A \oplus B$	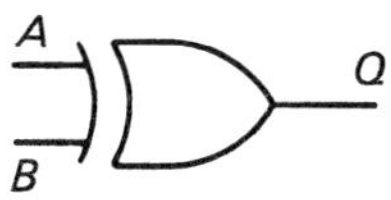	A B | Q 0 0 | 0 0 1 | 1 1 0 | 1 1 1 | 0	Output true if inputs are different

Figure 2.2 The basic logic gates compared.

In logic systems, all logical functions, however complex, can be configured from combinations of a few fundamental logic elements or *gates*. It is not profitable to spend too much time debating which are the truly fundamental ones, since most can be made from combinations of others. Figure 2.2 shows the important simple gates and their derivatives, and introduces the logical expressions to describe them, which can be compared with the truth-table notation. The figure also shows the important fact that when negative logic is used, the OR gate function interchanges with that of the AND gate.

If numerical quantities need to be conveyed down the two-state signal paths described here, then the only appropriate numbering system is binary, which has only two symbols, 0 and 1. Just as positive or negative logic could be used for the truth of a logical binary signal, it can also be used for a numerical binary signal. Normally, a high voltage level will represent a binary 1 and a low voltage will represent a binary 0, described as a 'high for a one' system. Clearly a 'low for a one' system is just as feasible. Decimal numbers have several columns, each of which represents a different power of ten; in binary the column position specifies the power of two.

Several binary digits or bits are needed to express the value of a binary sample. These bits can be conveyed at the same time by several signals to form a parallel system, which is most convenient inside equipment or for short distances because it is inexpensive, or one at a time down a single signal path, which is more complex, but convenient for cables between pieces of equipment because the connectors require fewer pins. When a binary system is used to convey numbers in this way, it can be called a digital system.

2.3 Storage elements

The basic memory element in logic circuits is the latch, which is constructed from two gates as shown in Figure 2.3(a), and which can be set or reset. A more useful variant is the D-type latch shown at (b) which remembers the state of the input at the time a separate clock either changes state, for an edge-triggered device, or after it goes false, for a level-triggered device. A shift register can be made from a series of latches by connecting the Q output of one latch to the D input of the next and connecting all the clock inputs in parallel. Data are delayed by the number of stages in the register. Shift registers are also useful for converting between serial and parallel data formats.

Where large numbers of bits are to be stored, cross-coupled latches are less suitable because they are more complicated to fabricate inside integrated circuits than dynamic memory, and consume more current.

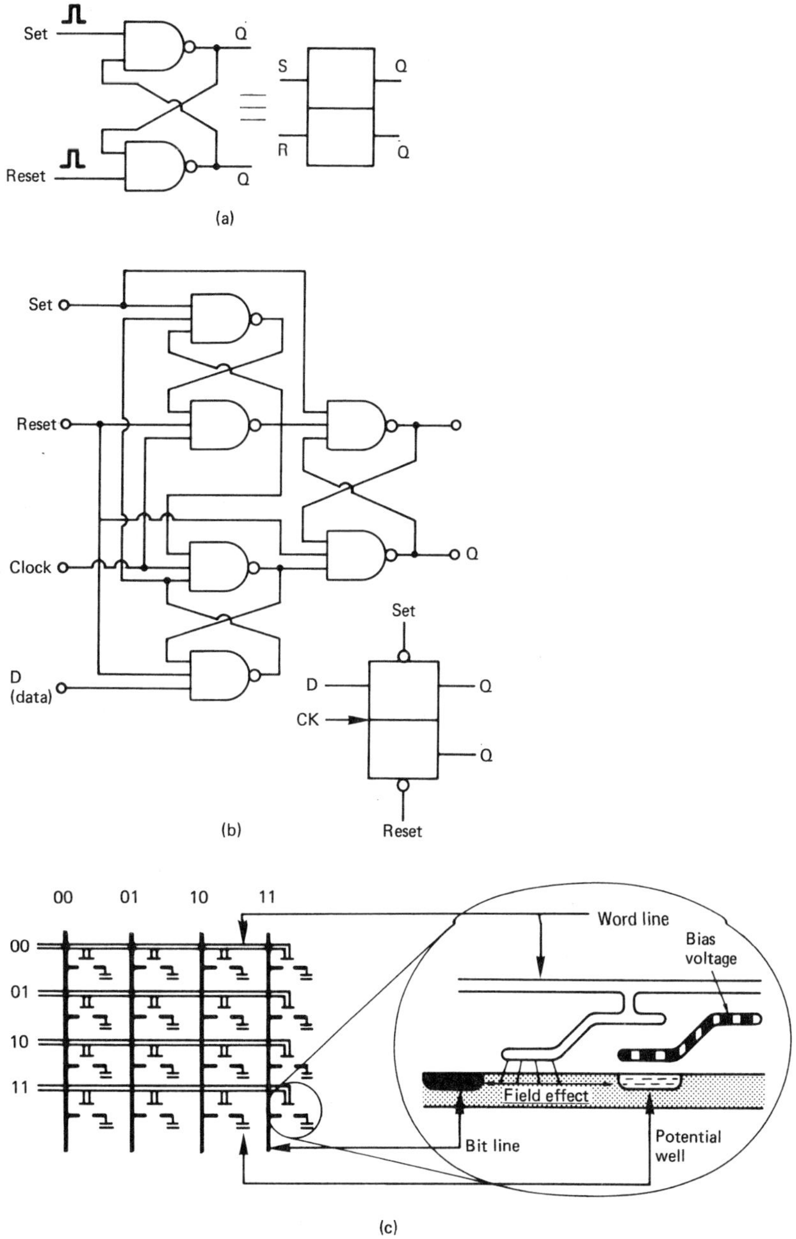

Figure 2.3 Digital semiconductor memory types. In (a), one data bit can be stored in a simple set-reset latch, which has little application because the D-type latch in (b) can store the state of the single data input when the clock occurs. These devices can be implemented with bipolar transistors or FETs, and are called static memories because they can store indefinitely. They consume a lot of power.

In (c), a bit is stored as the charge in a potential well in the substrate of a chip. It is accessed by connecting the bit line with the field effect from the word line. The single well where the two lines cross can then be written or read. These devices are called dynamic RAMs because the charge decays, and they must be read and rewritten (refreshed) periodically.

In large random access memories (RAMs), the data bits are stored as the presence or absence of charge in a tiny capacitor as shown in Figure 2.3(c). The capacitor is formed by a metal electrode, insulated by a layer of silicon dioxide from a semiconductor substrate, hence the term MOS (metal oxide semiconductor). The charge will suffer leakage, and the value would become indeterminate after a few milliseconds. Where the delay needed is less than this, decay is of no consequence, as data will be read out before they have had a chance to decay. Where longer delays are necessary, such memories must be refreshed periodically by reading the bit value and writing it back to the same place. Most modern MOS RAM chips have suitable circuitry built in. Large RAMs store many megabits, and it is clearly impractical to have a connection to each one. Instead, the desired bit has to be addressed before it can be read or written. The size of the chip package restricts the number of pins available, so that large memories use the same address pins more than once. The bits are arranged internally as rows and columns, and the row address and the column address are specified sequentially on the same pins.

Just like recording devices, electronic data storage devices come in many varieties. The basic volatile RAM will lose data if power is interrupted. However, there are also non-volatile RAMS or NVRAMs which retain the data in the absence of power. A type of memory which is written once is called a *read-only-memory* or ROM. Some of these are programmed by using a high current which permanently vaporizes conductors in each location so that the data are fixed. Other types can be written electrically, but cannot be erased electrically. These need to be erased by exposure to ultraviolet light and are called UVROMS. Once erased they can be reprogrammed with new data. Another type of ROM can be rewritten electrically a limited number of times. These are known as *electric alterable* ROMs or EAROMS.

2.4 Binary coding

In many cases a binary code is used to represent a sample of an audio or video waveform. Practical digital hardware places a limit on the wordlength which in turn limits the range of values available. In the eight-bit samples used in much digital video equipment, there are 256 different numbers, whereas in the sixteen-bit codes common in digital audio, there are 65 536 different numbers.

Figure 2.4(a) shows the result of counting upwards in binary with a fixed wordlength. When the largest possible value of all ones is reached, adding a further one to the LSB causes it to become zero with a carry-out. This carry is added to the next bit which becomes zero with a carry-out and so on. The carry will ripple up the word until the MSB becomes zero

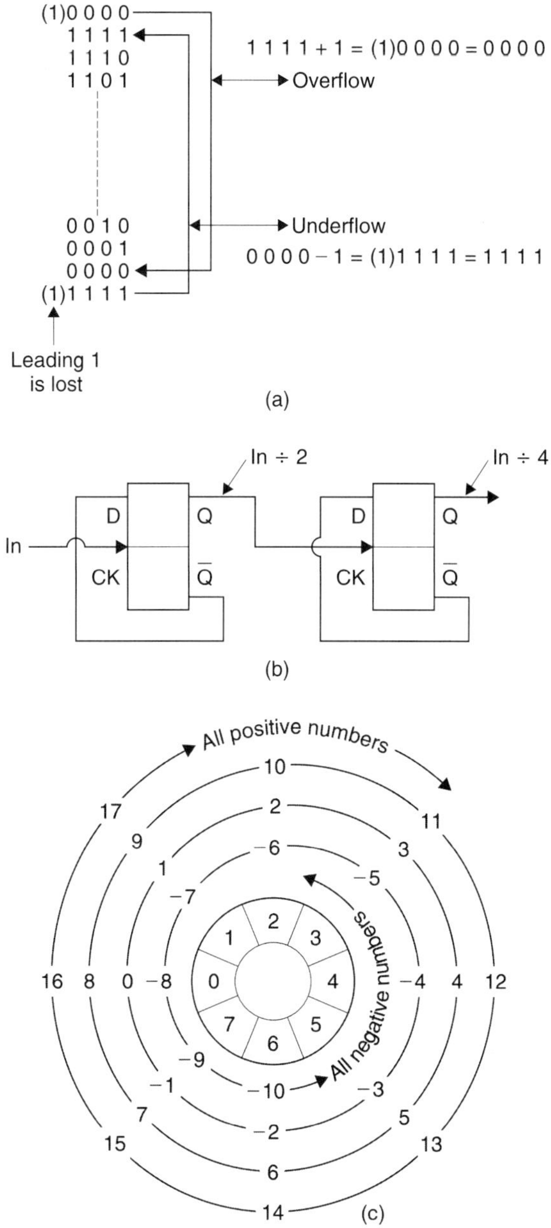

Figure 2.4 Counting up in a fixed wordlength system leads to overflow (a) where the high-order bit is lost. A binary counter can be made by cascading divide-by-two stages. Overflow results in wraparound as shown in (c).

and produces a carry-out. This carry-out represents the setting of a bit to the left of the MSB, which is not present in the hardware and is thus lost. Consequently when the highest value is reached, further counting causes the value to reset to zero and begin again. This is known as an *overflow*. Counting downwards will achieve the reverse. When zero is reached, subtracting one will cause an *underflow* where a borrow should be taken from a bit to the left of the MSB, which does not exist, the result being that the bits which do exist take the value of all ones, being the highest possible code value.

Storage devices such as latches can be configured so that they count pulses. Figure 2.4(b) shows such an arrangement. The pulses to be counted are fed to the clock input of a D-type latch, whose input is connected to its complemented output. This configuration will change state at every input pulse, so that it will be in a true state after every other pulse. This is a divide-by-two counter. If the output is connected to the clock input of another stage, this will divide by four. A series of divide-by-two stages can be cascaded indefinitely in this way to count up to arbitrarily high numbers. Note that when the largest possible number is reached, when all latches are in the high state, the next pulse will result in all latches going to a low state, corresponding to the count of zero. This is the overflow condition described above.

Counters often include reset inputs which can be used to force the count to zero. Some are presettable so that a specific value can be loaded into each latch before counting begins.

As a result of the fixed wordlength, underflow and overflow, the infinite range of real numbers is mapped onto the limited range of a binary code of finite wordlength. Figure 2.4(c) shows that the overflow makes the number scale circular and it is as if the real number scale were rolled around it so that a binary code could represent any of a large possible number of real values, positive or negative. This is why the term *wraparound* is sometimes used to describe the result of an overflow condition.

Mathematically the pure binary mapping of Figure 2.4(c) from an infinite scale to a finite scale is known as *modulo* arithmetic. The four-bit example shown expresses real numbers as Modulo-16 codes. Modulo arithmetic will be considered further in section 2.7.

In a practical ADC, each number represents a different analog signal voltage, and the hardware is arranged such that voltages outside the finite range do not overflow but instead result in one or other limit codes being output. This is the equivalent of clipping in analog systems. In Figure 2.5(a) it will be seen that in an eight-bit pure binary system, the number range goes from 00 hex, which represents the smallest voltage and all those voltages below it, through to FF hex, which represents the largest positive voltage and all voltages above it.

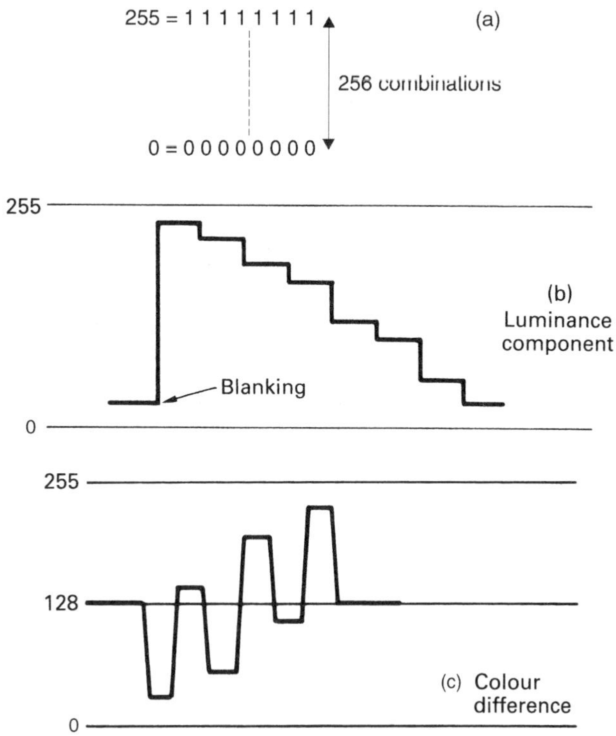

Figure 2.5 The unipolar quantizing range of an eight-bit pure binary system is shown at (a). The analog input must be shifted to fit into the quantizing range. In component, sync pulses are not digitized, so the quantizing intervals can be smaller as at (b). An offset of half scale is used for colour difference signals (c).

In some computer graphics systems these extremes represent black and peak white respectively. In television systems the traditional analog video waveform must be accommodated within this number range. Figure 2.5(b) shows how this is done for a broadcast standard luminance signal. As digital systems only handle the active line, the quantizing range is optimized to suit the gamut of the unblanked luminance and the sync pulses go off the bottom of the scale. There is a small offset in order to handle slightly misadjusted inputs. Additionally the codes at the extremes of the range are reserved for synchronizing and are not available to video values.

Colour difference video signals (see Chapter 7) are bipolar and so blanking is in the centre of the signal range. In order to accommodate colour difference signals in the quantizing range, the blanking voltage level of the analog waveform has been shifted as in Figure 2.5(c) so that the positive and negative voltages in a real signal can be expressed by binary numbers which are only positive. This approach is called offset binary and has the advantage that the codes of all ones and all zeros are

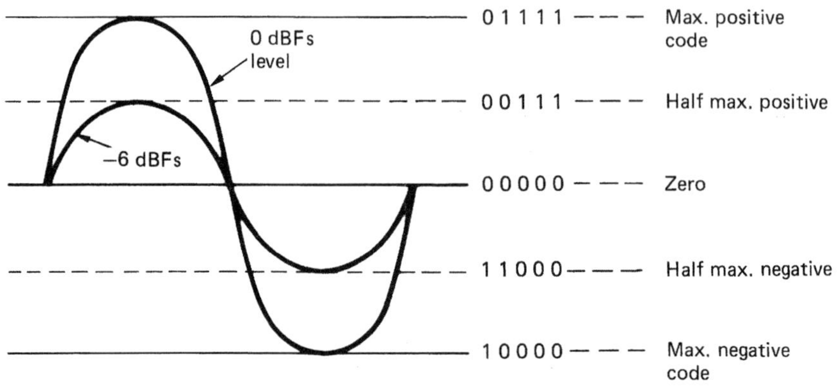

Figure 2.6 0 dBFs is defined as the level of the largest sinusoid which will fit into the quantizing range without clipping.

still at the ends of the scale and can continue to be used for synchronizing.

Figure 2.6 shows that analog audio signal voltages are referred to midrange. The level of the signal is measured by how far the waveform deviates from midrange, and attenuation, gain and mixing all take place around that level. Digital audio mixing is achieved by adding sample values from two or more different sources, but unless all the quantizing intervals are of the same size and there is no offset, the sum of two sample values will not represent the sum of the two original analog voltages. Thus sample values which have been obtained by non-uniform or offset quantizing cannot readily be processed because the binary numbers are not proportional to the signal voltage.

If two offset binary sample streams are added together in an attempt to perform digital mixing, the result will be that the offsets are also added and this may lead to an overflow. Similarly, if an attempt is made to attenuate by, say, 6.02 dB by dividing all the sample values by two, Figure 2.7 shows that the offset is also divided and the waveform suffers a shifted baseline. This problem can be overcome with digital luminance signals simply by subtracting the offset from each sample before processing as this results in positive-only numbers truly proportional to the luminance voltage. This approach is not suitable for audio or colour difference signals because negative numbers would result when the analog voltage goes below blanking and pure binary coding cannot handle them.

The problem with offset binary is that it works with reference to one end of the range. What is needed is a numbering system which operates symmetrically with reference to the centre of the range.

In the two's complement system, the mapping of real numbers onto the finite range of a binary word is modified. Instead of the mapping of

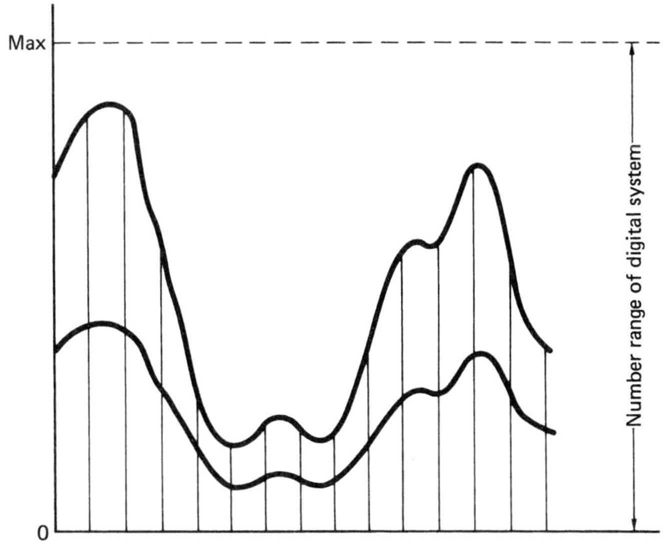

Figure 2.7 The result of an attempted attenuation in pure binary code is an offset. Pure binary cannot be used for digital video processing.

Figure 2.8(a) in which only positive numbers are mapped, in Figure 2.8(b) the upper half of the pure binary number range has been redefined to represent negative quantities. In two's complement, the range represented by the circle of numbers does not start at zero, but starts on the diametrically opposite side of the circle such that zero is now in the centre of the number range. All numbers clockwise from zero are positive and have the MSB reset. All numbers anticlockwise from zero are negative and have the MSB set. The MSB is thus the equivalent of a sign bit where 1 = minus. Two's complement notation differs from pure binary in that the most significant bit is inverted in order to achieve the half-circle rotation.

Figure 2.9 shows how a real ADC is configured to produce two's complement output. At (a) an analog offset voltage equal to one half the quantizing range is added to the bipolar analog signal in order to make it unipolar as at (b). The ADC produces positive-only numbers at (c) which are proportional to the input voltage. This is actually an offset binary code. The MSB is then inverted at (d) so that the all-zeros code moves to the centre of the quantizing range. The analog offset is often incorporated into the ADC as is the MSB inversion. Some convertors are designed to be used in either pure binary or two's complement mode. In this case the designer must arrange the appropriate DC conditions at the input. The MSB inversion may be selectable by an external logic level. In the broadcast digital video interface standards the colour difference signals use offset binary because the codes of all zeros and all ones are at

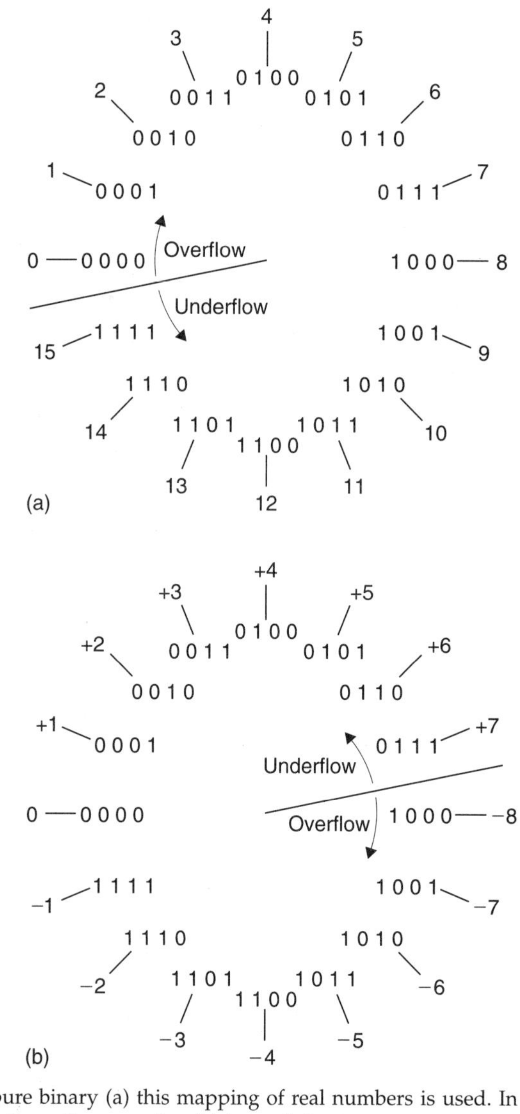

Figure 2.8 In pure binary (a) this mapping of real numbers is used. In two's complement an alternative mapping (b) is used. See text.

the end of the range and can be reserved for synchronizing. A digital vision mixer simply inverts the MSB of each colour difference sample to convert it to two's complement.

The two's complement system allows two sample values to be added, or mixed in audio and video parlance, and the result will be referred to the system midrange; this is analogous to adding analog signals in an operational amplifier.

Figure 2.10 illustrates how adding two's complement samples simulates a bipolar mixing process. The waveform of input A is depicted by

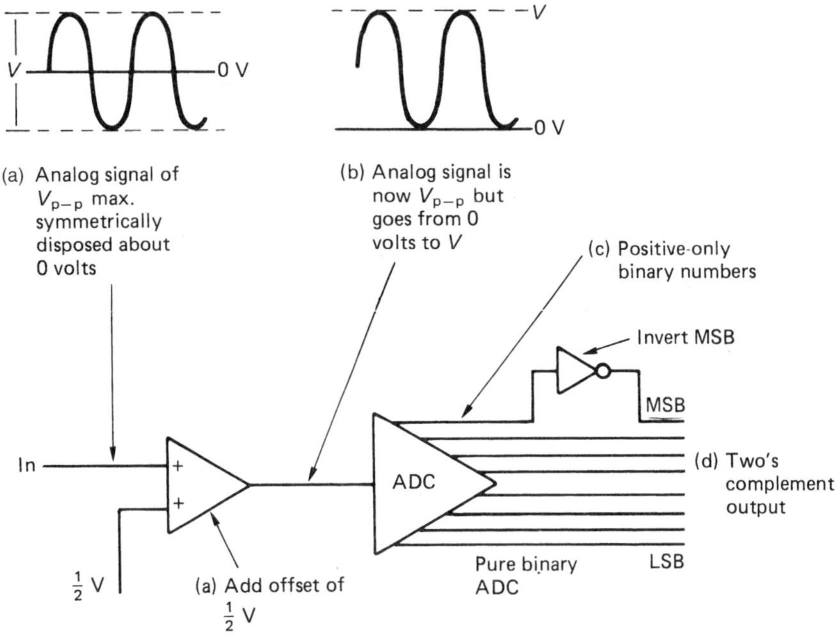

Figure 2.9 A two's complement ADC. At (a) an analog offset voltage equal to one-half the quantizing range is added to the bipolar analog signal in order to make it unipolar as at (b). The ADC produces positive only numbers at (c), but the MSB is then inverted at (d) to give a two's complement output.

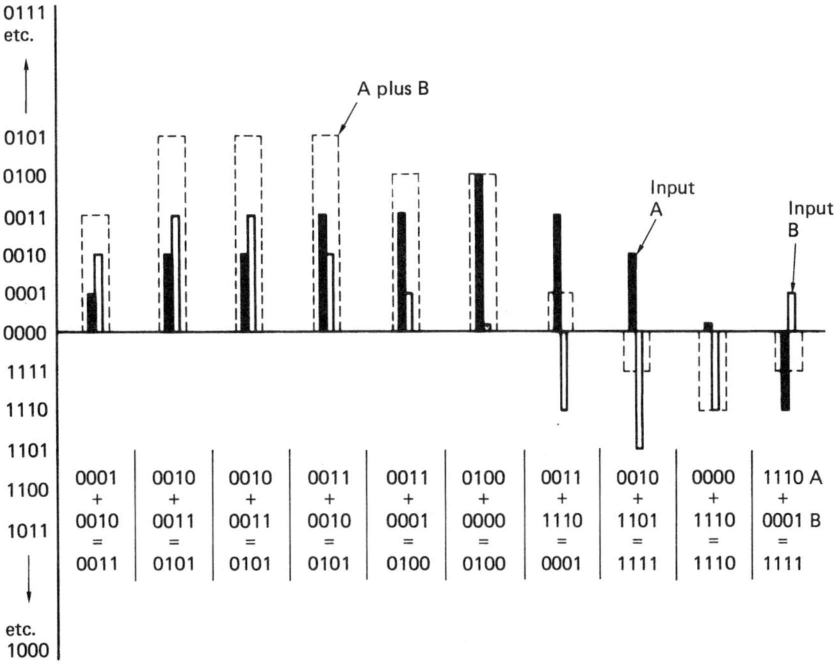

Figure 2.10 Using two's complement arithmetic, single values from two waveforms are added together with respect to midrange to give a correct mixing function.

solid black samples, and that of B by samples with a solid outline. The result of mixing is the linear sum of the two waveforms obtained by adding pairs of sample values. The dashed lines depict the output values. Beneath each set of samples is the calculation which will be seen to give the correct result. Note that the calculations are pure binary. No special arithmetic is needed to handle two's complement numbers.

It is interesting to see why the two's complement adding process works. Effectively both two's complement numbers to be added contain an offset of half full scale. When they are added, the two offsets add to produce a sum offset which has a value of full scale. As adding full scale to a code consists of moving one full rotation round the circle of numbers, the offset has no effect and is effectively eliminated.

It is sometimes necessary to phase reverse or invert a digital signal. The process of inversion in two's complement is simple. All bits of the sample value are inverted to form the one's complement, and one is added. This can be checked by mentally inverting some of the values in Figure 2.8(b). The inversion is transparent and performing a second inversion gives the original sample values. Using inversion, signal subtraction can be performed using only adding logic.

Two's complement numbers can have a radix point and bits below it just as pure binary numbers can. It should, however, be noted that in two's complement, if a radix point exists, numbers to the right of it are added. For example, 1100.1 is not –4.5, it is –4 + 0.5 = –3.5.

The circuitry necessary for adding pure binary or two's complement binary numbers is shown in Figure 2.11. Addition in binary requires two bits to be taken at a time from the same position in each word, starting at the least significant bit. Should both be ones, the output is zero, and there is a *carry-out* generated. Such a circuit is called a half adder, shown in Figure 2.11(a) and is suitable for the least-significant bit of the calculation. All higher stages will require a circuit which can accept a carry input as well as two data inputs. This is known as a full adder (Figure 2.11(b)). Such a device is also convenient for inverting a two's complement number, in conjunction with a set of inverters. The adder has one set of inputs taken to a false state, and the carry-in permanently held true, such that it adds one to the one's complement number from the invertor.

When mixing by adding sample values, care has to be taken to ensure that if the sum of the two sample values exceeds the number range the result will be clipping rather than overflow. In two's complement, the action necessary depends on the polarities of the two signals. Clearly if one positive and one negative number are added, the result cannot exceed the number range. If two positive numbers are added, the symptom of positive overflow is that the most significant bit sets, causing an erroneous negative result, whereas a negative overflow results in the most significant bit clearing. The overflow control circuit will be designed

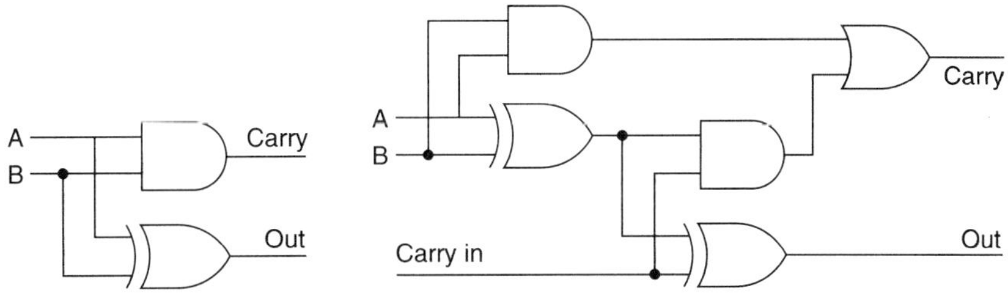

(a)

Data A	Bits B	Carry in	Out	Carry out
0	0	0	0	0
0	0	1	1	0
0	1	0	1	0
0	1	1	0	1
1	0	0	1	0
1	0	1	0	1
1	1	0	0	1
1	1	1	1	1

(b)

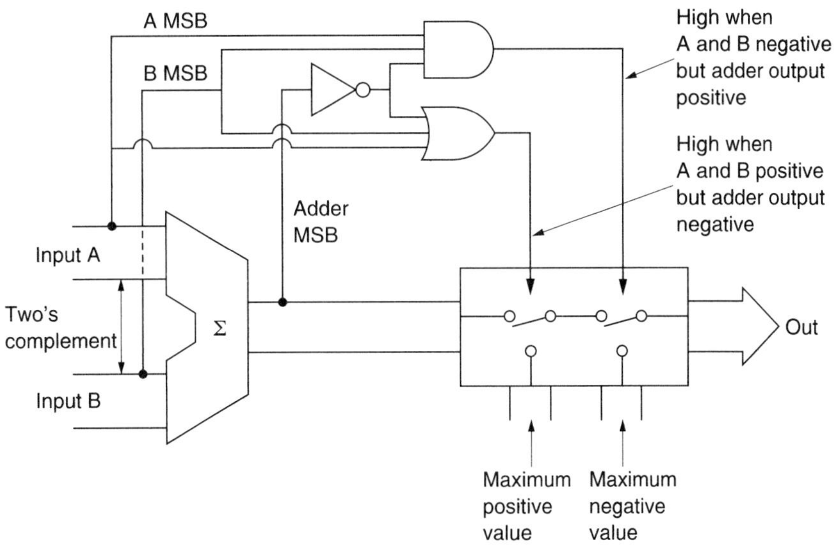

(c)

Figure 2.11 (a) Half adder; (b) full-adder circuit and truth table; (c) comparison of sign bits prevents wraparound on adder overflow by substituting clipping level.

to detect these two conditions, and override the adder output. If the MSB of both inputs is zero, the numbers are both positive, thus if the sum has the MSB set, the output is replaced with the maximum positive code (0111 . . .). If the MSB of both inputs is set, the numbers are both negative, and if the sum has no MSB set, the output is replaced with the maximum

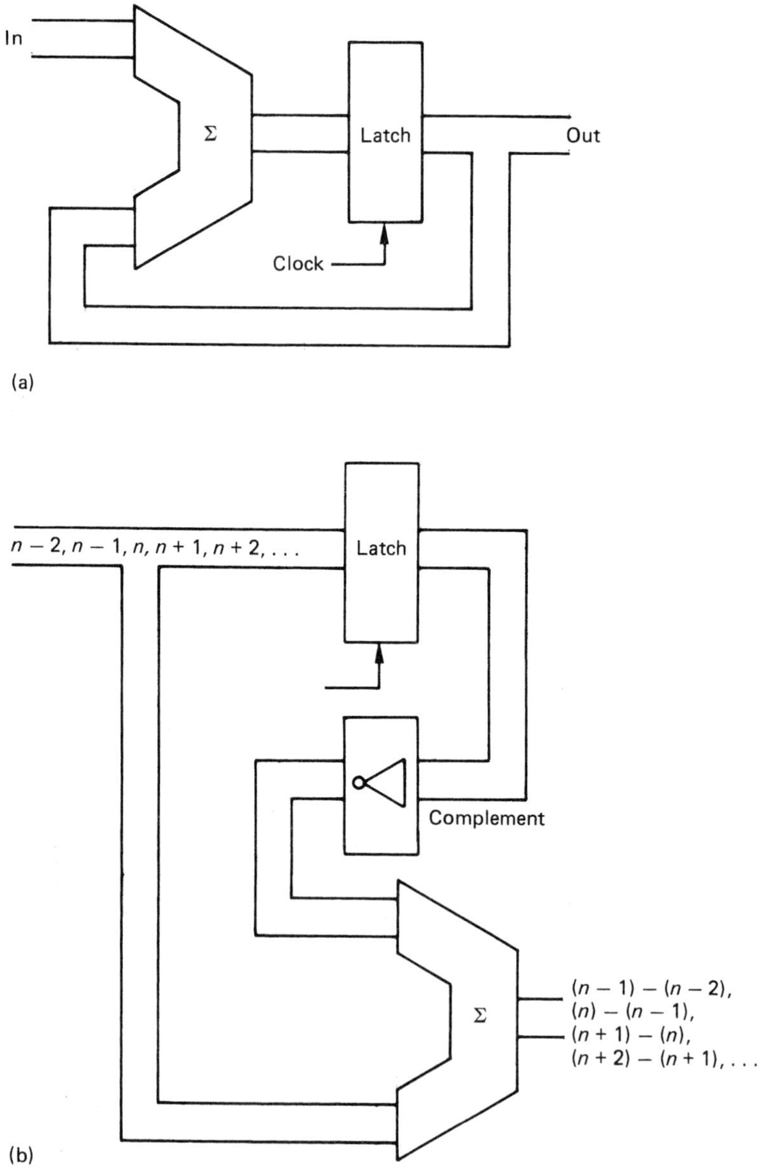

Figure 2.12 Two configurations which are common in processing. In (a) the feedback around the adder adds the previous sum to each input to perform accumulation or digital integration. In (b) an invertor allows the difference between successive inputs to be computed. This is differentiation.

negative code (1000 . . .). These conditions can also be connected to warning indicators. Figure 2.11(c) shows this system in hardware. The resultant clipping on overload is sudden, and sometimes a PROM is included which translates values around and beyond maximum to soft-clipped values below or equal to maximum.

A storage element can be combined with an adder to obtain a number of useful functional blocks which will crop up frequently in digital signal processing. Figure 2.12(a) shows that a latch is connected in a feedback loop around an adder. The latch contents are added to the input each time it is clocked. The configuration is known as an accumulator in computation because it adds up or accumulates values fed into it. In filtering, it is known as an discrete time integrator. If the input is held at some constant value, the output increases by that amount on each clock. The output is thus a sampled ramp.

Figure 2.12(b) shows that the addition of an invertor allows the difference between successive inputs to be obtained. This is digital differentiation. The output is proportional to the slope of the input.

2.5 Gain control

When processing digital audio or image data the gain of the system will need to be variable so that mixes and fades can be performed. Gain is controlled in the digital domain by multiplying each sample value by a coefficient. If that coefficient is less than one attenuation will result; if it is greater than one, amplification can be obtained.

Multiplication in binary circuits is difficult. It can be performed by repeated adding, but this is too slow to be of any use. In fast multiplication, one of the inputs will be simultaneously multiplied by one, two, four, etc., by hard-wired bit shifting. Figure 2.13 shows that the other input bits will determine which of these powers will be added to produce the final sum, and which will be neglected. If multiplying by five, the process is the same as multiplying by four, multiplying by one, and adding the two products. This is achieved by adding the input to itself shifted two places. As the wordlength of such a device increases, the complexity increases exponentially.

In a given application, all that matters is that the output has the correct numerical value. It does not matter if this is achieved using dedicated hardware or using software in a general-purpose processor. It should be clear that if it is wished to simulate analog gain control in the digital domain by multiplication, the samples to be multiplied must have been uniformly quantized. If the quantizing is non-uniform the binary numbers are no longer proportional to the original parameter and multiplication will not give the correct result.

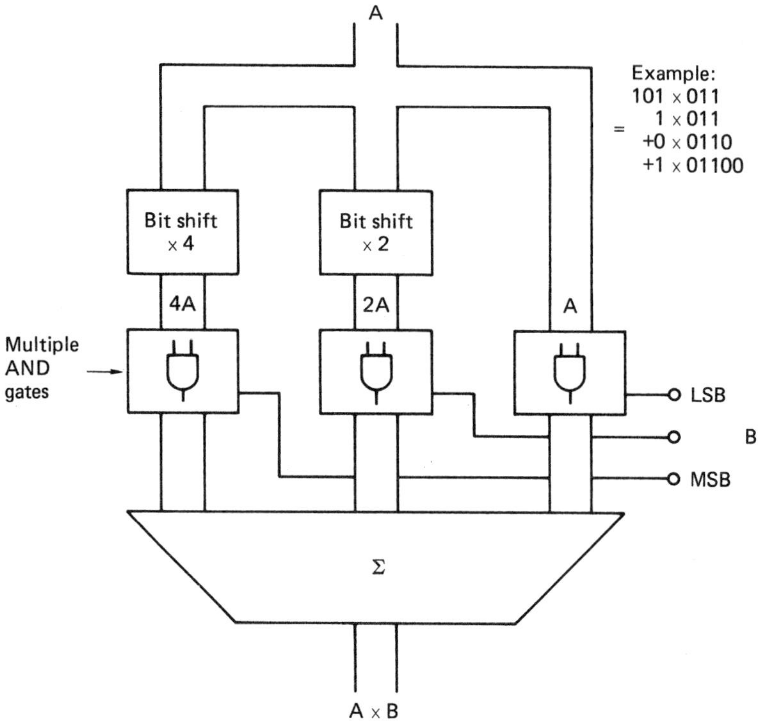

Figure 2.13 Structure of fast multiplier: the input A is multiplied by 1, 2, 4, 8, etc., by bit shifting. The digits of the B input then determine which multiples of A should be added together by enabling AND gates between the shifters and the adder. For long wordlengths, the number of gates required becomes enormous, and the device is best implemented in a chip.

In audio, uniform quantizing is universal in production systems. However, in video it is not, owing to the widespread use of gamma which will be discussed in Chapter 6. Strictly speaking, video signals with gamma should be returned to the uniformly quantized domain before processing but this is seldom done in practice.

2.6 Floating-point coding

Computers operate on data words of fixed length and if binary or two's complement coding is used, this limits the range of the numbers. For this reason many computers use *floating-point coding* which allows a much greater range of numbers with a penalty of reduced accuracy.

Figure 2.14 shows that in pure binary, numbers which are significantly below the full scale value have a number of high-order bits which are all zero. Instead of handling these bits individually, as they are all zero it is good enough simply to count them. Figure 2.14(b) shows that every time

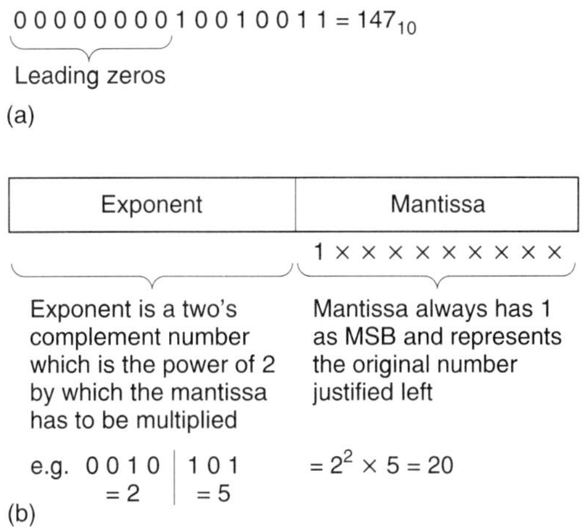

Figure 2.14 Small numbers in a long wordlength system have inefficient leading zeros (a). Floating-point coding (b) is more efficient, but can lead to inaccuracy.

a leading zero is removed, the remaining bits are shifted left one place and this has the effect in binary of multiplying by two. Two shifts multiply by four, three shifts by eight and so on. In order to re-create the number with the right magnitude, the power of two by which the number was multiplied must also be sent. This value is known as the *exponent*.

In order to convert a binary number of arbitrary value with an arbitrarily located radix point into floating-point notation, the position of the most significant or leading one and the position of the radix point are noted. The number is then multiplied or divided by powers of two until the radix point is immediately to the right of the leading one. This results in a value known as the *mantissa* (plural: mantissae) which always has the form 1.XXX.... where X is 1 or 0 (known in logic as 'don't care').

The exponent is a two's complement code which determines whether the mantissa has to be multiplied by positive powers of two which will shift it left and make it bigger, or whether it has to be multiplied by negative powers of two which will shift it right and make it smaller.

In floating-point notation, the range of the numbers and the precision are independent. The range is determined by the wordlength of the exponent. For example, a six-bit exponent having 64 values allows a range from $1.XX \times 2^{31}$ to $1.XX \times 2^{-32}$. The precision is determined by the length of the mantissa. As the mantissa is always in the format 1.XXX it is not necessary to store the leading one so the actual stored value is in the form .XXX. Thus a ten-bit mantissa has eleven-bit precision. It is possible to pack a ten-bit mantissa and a six-bit exponent in one sixteen-bit word.

Although floating-point operation extends the number range of a computer, the user must constantly be aware that floating point has limited precision. Floating point is the computer's equivalent of lossy compression. In trying to get more for less, there is always a penalty.

In some signal-processing applications, floating-point coding is simply not accurate enough. For example, in an audio filter, if the stopband needs to be, say, 100 dB down, this can only be achieved if the entire filtering arithmetic has adequate precision. 100 dB is one part in 100 000 and needs more than sixteen bits of resolution. The poor quality of a good deal of digital audio equipment is due to the unwise adoption of floating-point processing of inadequate precision.

Computers of finite wordlength can operate on larger numbers without the inaccuracy of floating-point coding by using techniques such a *double precision*. For example, thirty-two-bit precision data words can be stored in two adjacent memory locations in a sixteen-bit machine, and the processor can manipulate them by operating on the two halves at different times. This takes longer, or needs a faster processor.

2.7 Modulo-*n* arithmetic

Conventional arithmetic which is in everyday use relates to the real world of counting actual objects, and to obtain correct answers the concepts of borrow and carry are necessary in the calculations.

There is an alternative type of arithmetic which has no borrow or carry which is known as modulo arithmetic. In modulo-n no number can exceed n. If it does, n or whole multiples of n are subtracted until it does not. Thus 25 modulo-16 is 9 and 12 modulo-5 is 2. The count shown in Figure 2.4 is from a four-bit device which overflows when it reaches 1111 because the carry-out is ignored. If a number of clock pulses m are applied from the zero state, the state of the counter will be given by m mod.16. Thus modulo arithmetic is appropriate to digital systems in which there is a fixed wordlength and this means that the range of values the system can have is restricted by that wordlength. A number range which is restricted in this way is called a finite field.

Modulo-2 is a numbering scheme which is used frequently in digital processes such as error correction, encryption and spectrum spreading in recording and transmission. Figure 2.15 shows that in modulo-2 the conventional addition and subtraction are replaced by the XOR function such that:

$$(\text{A} + \text{B}) \text{ Mod.2} = \text{A XOR B}$$

When multi-bit values are added Mod.2, each column is computed quite independently of any other. This makes Mod.2 circuitry very fast in operation as it is not necessary to wait for the carries from lower-order bits to ripple up to the high-order bits.

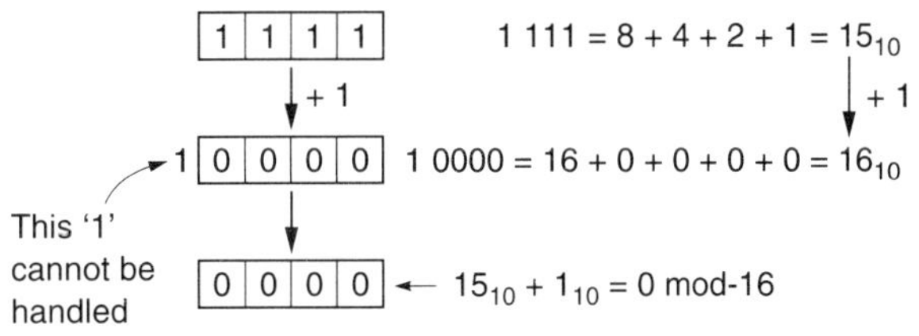

Figure 2.15(a) As a fixed wordlength counter cannot hold the carry-out bit, it will resume at zero. Thus a four-bit counter expresses every count as a modulo-16 number.

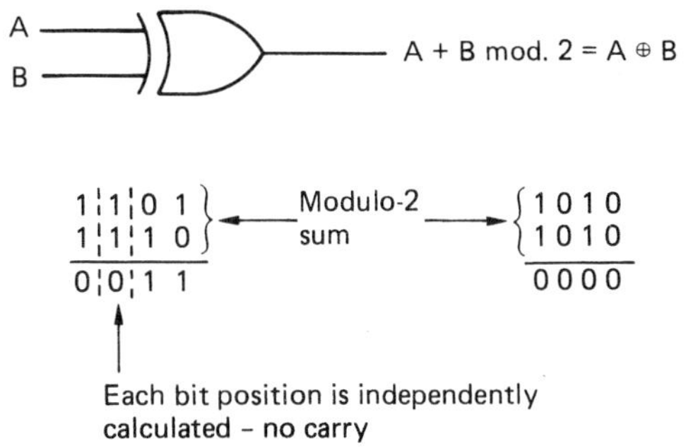

Figure 2.15(b) In modulo-2 calculations, there can be no carry or borrow operations and conventional addition and subtraction become identical. The XOR gate is a modulo-2 adder.

Modulo-2 arithmetic is not the same as conventional arithmetic and takes some getting used to. For example, adding something to itself in Mod.2 always gives the answer zero.

2.8 The Galois field

Figure 2.16 shows a simple circuit consisting of three D-type latches which are clocked simultaneously. They are connected in series to form a shift register. At (a) a feedback connection has been taken from the output to the input and the result is a ring counter where the bits contained will recirculate endlessly. At (b) one XOR gate is added so that the output is fed back to more than one stage. The result is known as a twisted-ring counter and it has some interesting properties. Whenever the circuit is clocked, the left-hand bit moves to the right-hand latch, the centre bit moves to the left-hand latch and the centre latch becomes the XOR of the two outer latches. The figure shows that whatever the starting condition of the three bits in the latches, the same state will always be reached again after seven clocks, except if zero is used.

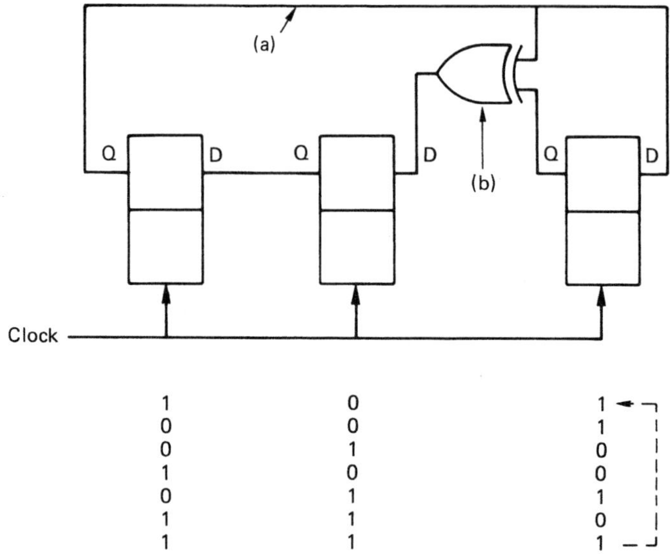

Figure 2.16 The circuit shown is a twisted-ring counter which has an unusual feedback arrangement. Clocking the counter causes it to pass through a series of non-sequential values. See text for details.

The states of the latches form an endless ring of non-sequential numbers called a Galois field after the French mathematical prodigy Evariste Galois who discovered them. The states of the circuit form a maximum length sequence because there are as many states as are permitted by the wordlength. As the states of the sequence have many of the characteristics of random numbers, yet are repeatable, the result can also be called a pseudo-random sequence (prs). As the all-zeros case is disallowed, the length of a maximum length sequence generated by a register of m bits cannot exceed $(2^m - 1)$ states. The Galois field, however, includes the zero term. It is useful to explore the bizarre mathematics of Galois fields which use modulo-2 arithmetic. Familiarity with such manipulations is helpful when studying error correction, particularly the Reed – Solomon codes which will be treated in Chapter 10. They will also be found in processes which require pseudo-random numbers such as digital dither, treated in Chapter 4, and randomized channel codes used in, for example, DVB.

The circuit of Figure 2.16 can be considered as a counter and the four points shown will then be representing different powers of 2 from the MSB on the left to the LSB on the right. The feedback connection from the MSB to the other stages means that whenever the MSB becomes 1, two other powers are also forced to one so that the code of 1011 is generated.

Each state of the circuit can be described by combinations of powers of x, such as

$$x^2 = 100$$

$$x = 010$$

$$x^2 + x = 110, \text{ etc.}$$

The fact that three bits have the same state because they are connected together is represented by the Mod.2 equation:

$$x^3 + x + 1 = 0$$

Let $x = a$, which is a primitive element.
Now

$$a^3 + a + 1 = 0 \tag{2.1}$$

In modulo-2

$$a + a = a^2 + a^2 = 0$$

$$a = x = 010$$

$$a^2 = x^2 = 100$$

$$a^3 = a + 1 = 011 \text{ from (2.1)}$$

$$a^4 = a^3 \times a = a(a + 1) = a^2 + a = 110$$

$$a^5 = a^2 + a + 1 = 111$$

$$a^6 = a \times a^5 = a(a^2 + a + 1)$$

$$= a^3 + a^2 + a = a + 1 + a^2 + a$$

$$= a^2 + 1 = 101$$

$$a^7 = a(a^2 + 1) = a^3 + a$$

$$= a + 1 + a = 1 = 001$$

In this way it can be seen that the complete set of elements of the Galois field can be expressed by successive powers of the primitive element. Note that the twisted-ring circuit of Figure 2.16 simply raises a to higher and higher powers as it is clocked; thus the seemingly complex multibit changes caused by a single clock of the register become simple to calculate using the correct primitive and the appropriate power.

The numbers produced by the twisted-ring counter are not random; they are completely predictable if the equation is known. However, the sequences produced are sufficiently similar to random numbers that in many cases they will be useful. They are thus referred to as pseudo-random sequences. The feedback connection is chosen such that the expression it implements will not factorize. Otherwise a maximum-length sequence could not be generated because the circuit might sequence around one or other of the factors depending on the initial condition. A useful analogy is to compare the operation of a pair of meshed gears. If the gears have a number of teeth which is relatively prime, many revolutions are necessary to make the same pair of teeth touch again. If the number of teeth have a common multiple, far fewer turns are needed.

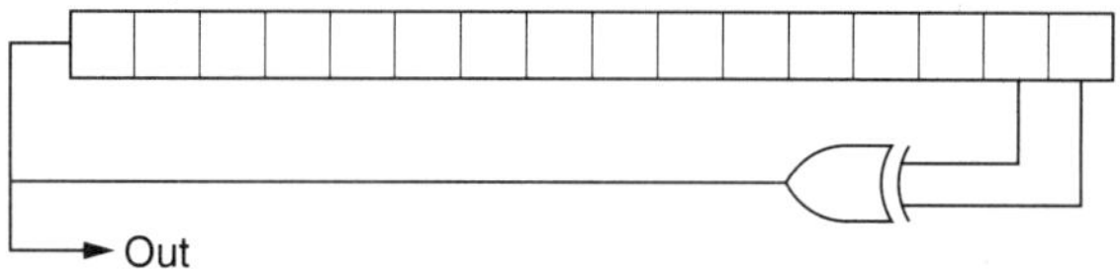

Figure 2.17 The PRS generator of DVB.

Figure 2.17 shows the pseudo-random sequence generator used in DVB. Its purpose is to modify the transmitted spectrum so that the amount of energy transmitted is as uniform as possible across the channel.

2.9 The phase-locked loop

All sampling systems need to be clocked at the appropriate rate in order to function properly. Whilst a clock may be obtained from a fixed frequency oscillator such as a crystal, many operations in video require *genlocking* or synchronizing the clock to an external source. The phase-locked loop excels at this job, and many others, particularly in connection with recording and transmission.

In phase-locked loops, the oscillator can run at a range of frequencies according to the voltage applied to a control terminal. This is called a voltage-controlled oscillator or VCO. Figure 2.18 shows that the VCO is driven by a phase error measured between the output and some reference. The error changes the control voltage in such a way that the error is reduced, such that the output eventually has the same frequency as the reference. A low-pass filter is fitted in the control voltage path to prevent the loop becoming unstable. If a divider is placed between the VCO and the phase comparator, as in the figure, the VCO frequency can be made to be a multiple of the reference. This also has the effect of

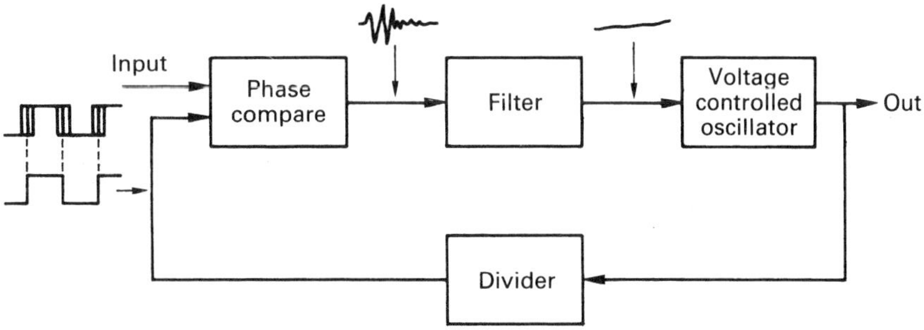

Figure 2.18 A phase-locked loop requires these components as a minimum. The filter in the control voltage serves to reduce clock jitter.

making the loop more heavily damped, so that it is less likely to change frequency if the input is irregular.

In digital video, the frequency multiplication of a phase-locked loop is extremely useful. Figure 2.19 shows how the 13.5 MHz clock of component digital video is obtained from the sync pulses of an analog reference by such a multiplication process.

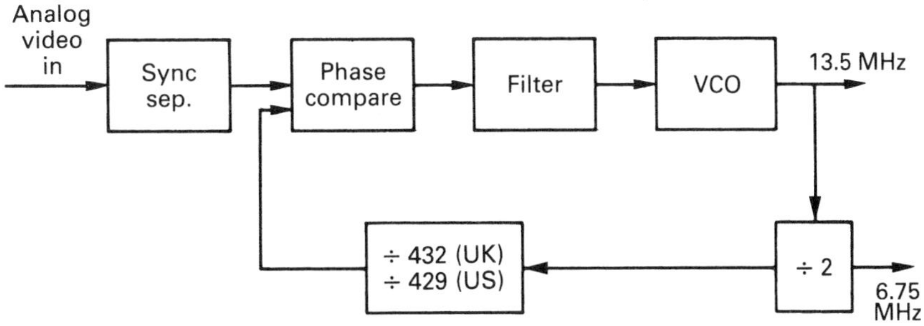

Figure 2.19 In order to obtain 13.5 MHz from input syncs, a PLL with an appropriate division ratio is required.

Figure 2.20 shows the NLL or numerically locked loop. This is similar to a phase-locked loop, except that the two phases concerned are represented by the state of a binary number. The NLL is useful to generate a remote clock from a master. The state of a clock count in the master is periodically transmitted to the NLL which will recreate the same clock frequency. The technique is used in MPEG transport streams.

2.10 Timebase correction

In Chapter 1 it was stated that a strength of digital technology is the ease with which delay can be provided. Accurate control of delay is the

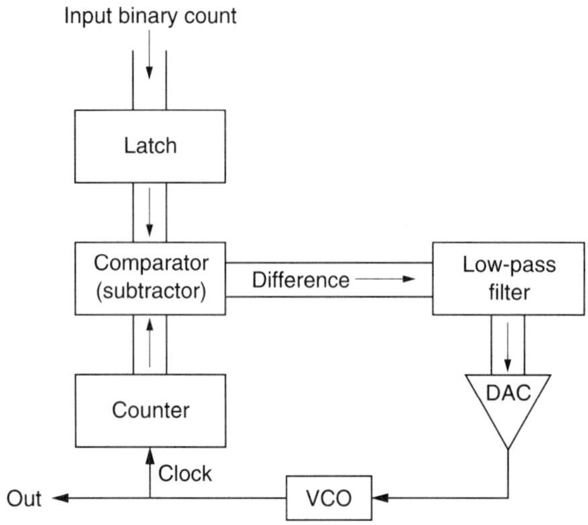

Figure 2.20 The numerically locked loop (NLL) is a digital version of the phase-locked loop.

essence of timebase correction, necessary whenever the instantaneous time of arrival or rate from a data source does not match the destination. In digital video, the destination will almost always have perfectly regular timing, namely the sampling rate clock of the final DAC. Timebase correction consists of aligning jittery signals from storage media or transmission channels with that stable reference.

A further function of timebase correction is to reverse the time compression applied prior to recording or transmission. As was shown in section 1.8, digital recorders compress data into blocks to facilitate editing and error correction as well as to permit head switching between blocks in rotary-head machines. Owing to the spaces between blocks, data arrive in bursts on replay, but must be fed to the output convertors in an unbroken stream at the sampling rate.

In computer hard-disk drives, which are used in digital video workstations and file servers, time compression is also used, but a converse problem also arises. Data from the disk blocks arrive at a reasonably constant rate, but cannot necessarily be accepted at a steady rate by the logic because of contention for the use of networks by the different parts of the system. In this case the data must be buffered by a relative of the timebase corrector which is usually referred to as a silo.

Although delay is easily implemented, it is not possible to advance a data stream. Most real machines cause instabilities balanced about the correct timing: the output jitters between too early and too late. Since the information cannot be advanced in the corrector, only delayed, the solution is to run the machine in advance of real time. In this case,

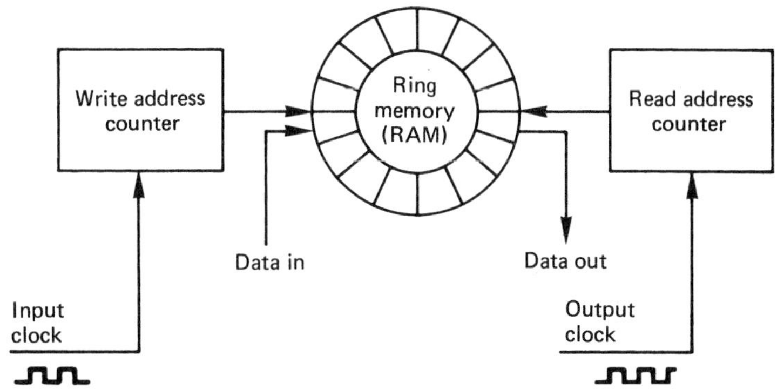

Figure 2.21 Most TBCs are implemented as a memory addressed by a counter which periodically overflows to give a ring structure. The memory allows the read and write sides to be asynchronous.

correctly timed output signals will need a nominal delay to align them with reference timing. Early output signals will receive more delay, and late output signals will receive less delay.

Section 2.3 showed the principles of digital storage elements which can be used for delay purposes. The shift-register approach and the RAM approach to delay are very similar, as a shift register can be thought of as a memory whose address increases automatically when clocked. The data rate and the maximum delay determine the capacity of the RAM required. Figure 2.21 shows that the addressing of the RAM is by a counter that overflows endlessly from the end of the memory back to the beginning, giving the memory a ring-like structure. The write address is determined by the incoming data, and the read address is determined by the outgoing data. This means that the RAM has to be able to read and write at the same time.

The switching between read and write involves not only a data multiplexer but also an address multiplexer. In general the arbitration between read and write will be done by signals from the stable side of the TBC as Figure 2.22 shows. In the replay case the stable clock will be on the read side. The stable side of the RAM will read a sample when it demands, and the writing will be locked out for that period. The input data cannot be interrupted in many applications, however, so a small buffer silo is installed before the memory, which fills up as the writing is locked out, and empties again as writing is permitted. Alternatively, the memory will be split into blocks, such that when one block is reading a different block will be writing and the problem does not arise.

In many digital video applications, the sampling rate exceeds the rate at which economically available RAM chips can operate. The solution is to arrange several video samples into one longer word, known as a

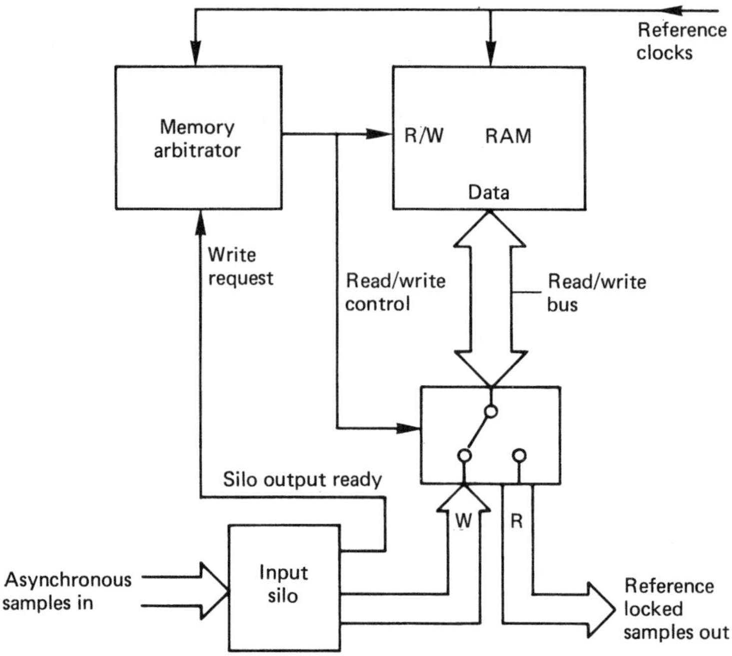

Figure 2.22 In a RAM-based TBC, the RAM is reference synchronous, and an arbitrator decides when it will read and when it will write. During reading, asynchronous input data back up in the input silo, asserting a write request to the arbitrator. Arbitrator will then cause a write cycle between read cycles.

superword, and to construct the memory so that it stores superwords in parallel.

Figure 2.23 shows the operation of a FIFO chip, colloquially known as a silo because the data are tipped in at the top on delivery and drawn off at the bottom when needed. Each stage of the chip has a data register and a small amount of logic, including a data-valid or V bit. If the input register does not contain data, the first V bit will be reset, and this will cause the chip to assert 'input ready'. If data are presented at the input, and clocked into the first stage, the V bit will set, and the 'input ready' signal will become false. However, the logic associated with the next stage sees the V bit set in the top stage, and if its own V bit is clear, it will clock the data into its own register, set its own V bit, and clear the input V bit, causing 'input ready' to reassert, when another word can be fed in. This process then continues as the word moves down the silo, until it arrives at the last register in the chip. The V bit of the last stage becomes the 'output ready' signal, telling subsequent circuitry that there are data to be read. If this word is not read, the next word entered will ripple down to the stage above. Words thus stack up at the bottom of the silo. When a word is read out, an external signal must be provided which resets the bottom V bit. The 'output ready' signal now goes false, and the

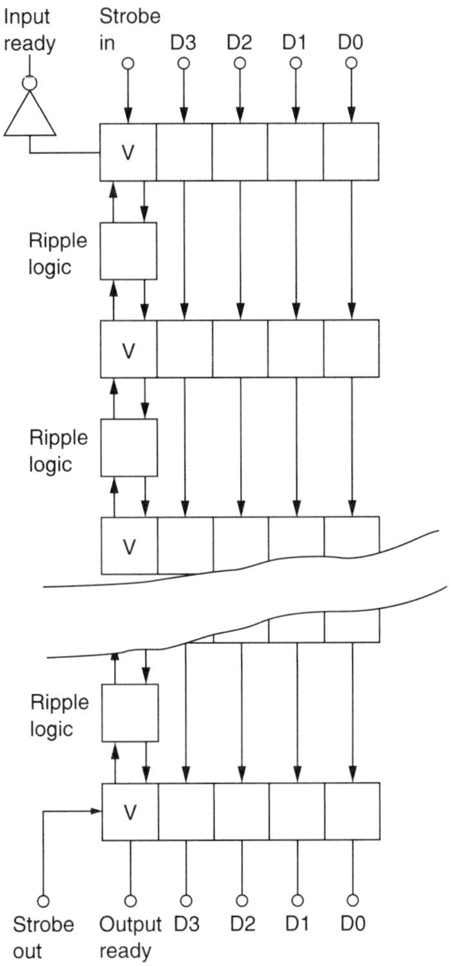

Figure 2.23 Structure of FIFO or silo chip. Ripple logic controls propagation of data down silo.

logic associated with the last stage now sees valid data above, and loads down the word when it will become ready again. The last register but one will now have no V bit set, and will see data above itself and brIng that down. In this way a reset V bit propagates up the chip while the data ripple down, rather like a hole in a semiconductor going the opposite way to the electrons.

When used in a hard-disk system, a silo will allow data to and from the disk, which is turning at constant speed. When reading the disk, Figure 2.24(a) shows that the silo starts empty, and if there is bus contention, the silo will start to fill. Where the bus is free, the disk controller will attempt to empty the silo into the memory. The system can take advantage of the interblock gaps on the disk, containing

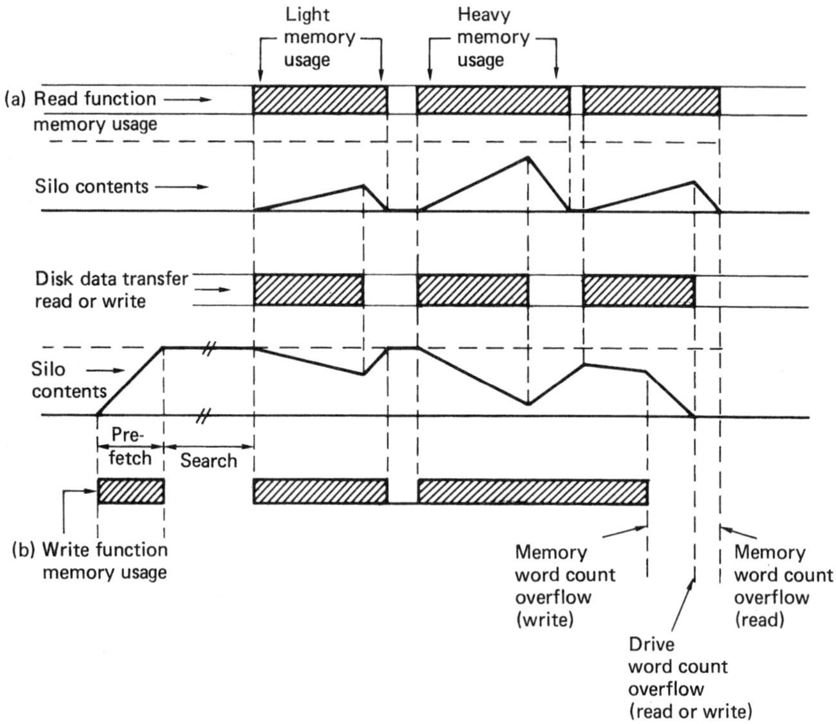

Figure 2.24 The silo contents during read functions (a) appear different from those during write functions (b). In (a), the control logic attempts to keep the silo as empty as possible; in (b) the logic prefills the silo and attempts to keep it full until the memory word count overflows.

headers, preambles and redundancy, for in these areas there are no data to transfer, and there is some breathing space to empty the silo before the next block. In practice the silo need not be empty at the start of every block, provided it never becomes full before the end of the transfer. If this happens some data are lost and the function must be aborted. The block containing the silo overflow will generally be reread on the next revolution. In sophisticated systems, the silo has a kind of dipstick, and can interrupt the CPU if the data get too deep. The CPU can then suspend some bus activity to allow the disk controller more time to empty the silo.

When the disk is to be written, as in Figure 2.24(b), a continuous data stream must be provided during each block, as the disk cannot stop. The silo will be pre-filled before the disk attempts to write, and the disk controller attempts to keep it full. In this case all will be well if the silo does not become empty before the end of the transfer. Figure 2.25 shows the silo of a typical disk controller with the multiplexers necessary to put it in the read data stream or the write data stream.

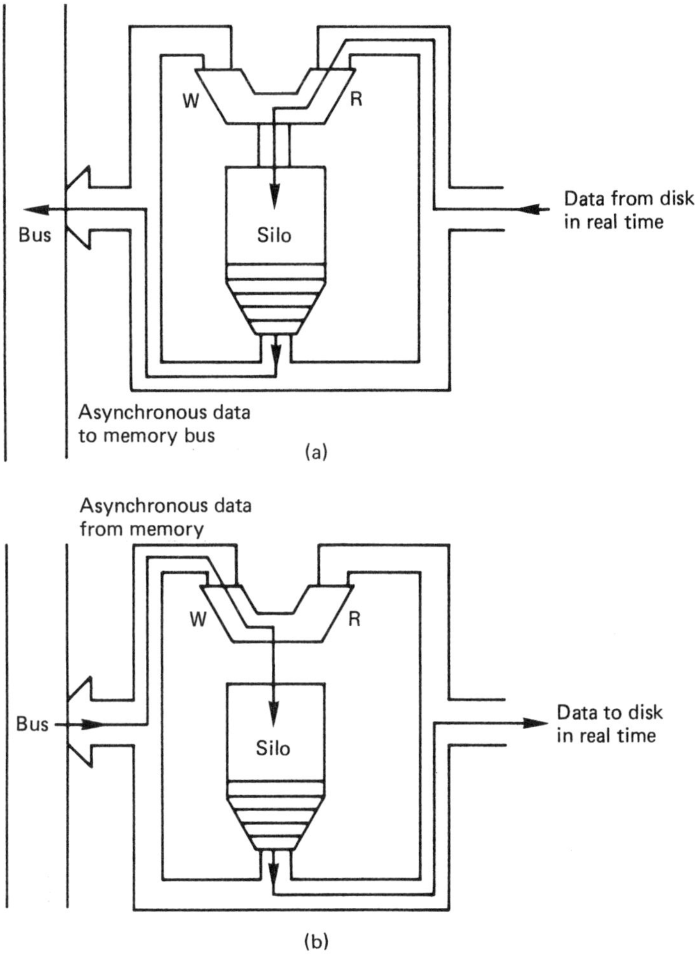

Figure 2.25 In order to guarantee that the drive can transfer data in real time at regular intervals (determined by disk speed and density) the silo provides buffering to the asynchronous operation of the memory access process. At (a) the silo is configured for a disk read. The same silo is used at (b) for a disk write.

2.11 Programmers

Figure 2.26 shows a simple system in which a counter is driven by a clock and counts steadily. At each state of the count, a different address is generated by the counter which is fed to a ROM. At each count state, the ROM is programmed with codes which determine what should happen. These are a simple form of instruction. This simple system assumes that each instruction takes the same amount of time and that the same sequence of events is needed come what may. This is not suitable for any but the simplest applications. Even a device like a washing machine takes a variable time to fill up and to heat its water.

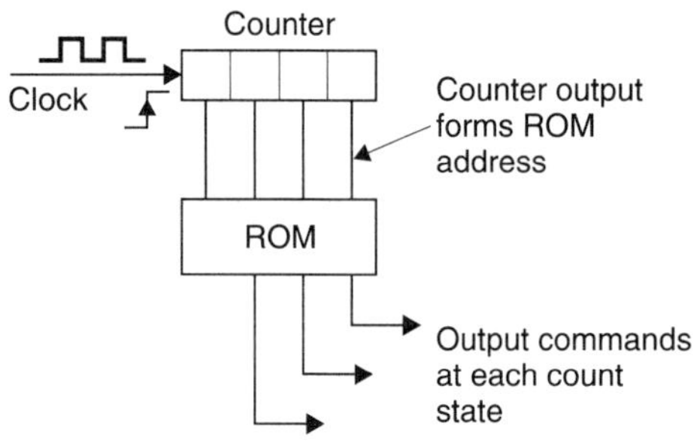

Figure 2.26 A simple sequencer which consists of a counter driving a ROM.

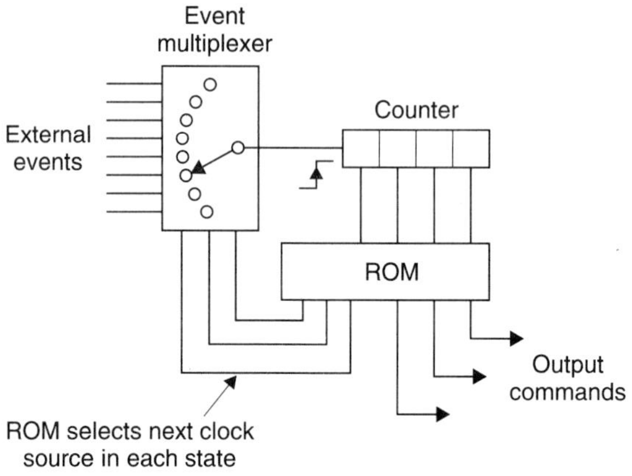

Figure 2.27 Part of the ROM output in each state selects the source of the next clock pulse.

Figure 2.27 shows that variable instruction time is easily arranged by increasing the wordlength of the ROM. Now, part of the instruction drives a source selector or multiplexer which chooses the source of the next clock pulse. To continue with the example of the washing machine, if the instruction were to fill up with water, the clock selector would choose the water level switch. Upon reaching the required level, the counter would be clocked and move on to the next instruction. This might be to heat the water, and the clock selector might then choose the thermostat.

Such a system is still only capable of performing the same sequence, and it cannot select a new sequence in response to changing conditions.

Figure 2.28 shows a slightly more complex arrangement. Here the instruction word has been further extended. At each state, in addition to an instruction and a clock source selector, there is an additional field which forms the address of the next state. Instead of a counter, the ROM

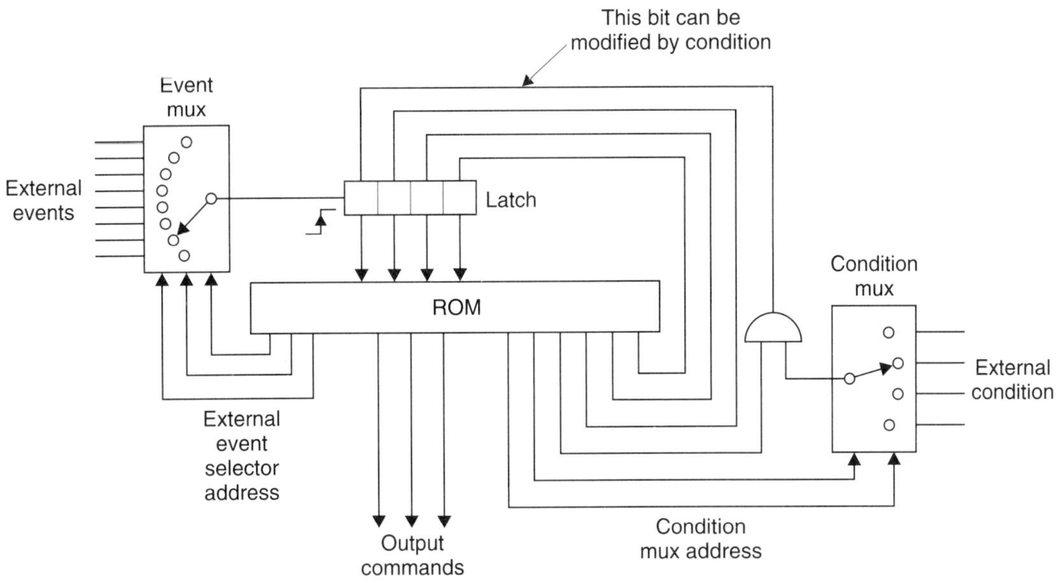

Figure 2.28 An external input can modify the sequence of states by changing the next address.

is addressed by a latch which holds the address from the ROM when clocked. Now, the program does not need to be written in sequential ROM locations, because each location contains the address of the next instruction. However, more importantly, it is possible to modify the sequence by interfering with the next address. Figure 2.28 shows that in the connection from the ROM to the address latch, there is a gate which allows an external signal to modify one bit of the address. The next address will have two possible values depending on the external signal.

This allows the system to react to external circumstances. The term *conditional branching* is used when the normal sequence of instructions is altered by an external event.

A device of the type found in Figure 2.28 is known as a microsequencer and the codes in the ROM are called microinstructions. Inside a processor, many steps are needed to carry out one instruction. Each of these steps is controlled by a microinstruction.

2.12 The computer

The computer is now a vital part of convergent systems, being used both for control purposes and to process audio and video signals as data. In control, the computer finds applications in database management, automation, editing, and in electromechanical systems such as tape drives and robotic cassette handling. Now that processing speeds have advanced sufficiently, computers are able to manipulate certain types of digital video in real time. Where very complex calculations are needed, real-time operation may not be possible and instead the computation proceeds as fast as it can in a process called *rendering*. The rendered data are stored so that they can be viewed in real time from a storage medium when the rendering is complete.

The computer is a programmable device in that operation is not determined by its construction alone, but instead by a series of *instructions* forming a *program*. The program is supplied to the computer one instruction at a time so that the desired sequence of events takes place.

Programming of this kind has been used for over a century in electromechanical devices, including automated knitting machines and street organs which are programmed by punched cards. However, the computer differs from these devices in that the program is not fixed, but can be modified by the computer itself. This possibility led to the creation of the term *software* to suggest a contrast to the constancy of hardware.

Computer instructions are binary numbers each of which is interpreted in a specific way. As these instructions don't differ from any other kind of data, they can be stored in RAM. The computer can change its own instructions by accessing the RAM. Most types of RAM are volatile, in that they lose data when power is removed. Clearly if a program is entirely stored in this way, the computer will not be able to recover fom a power failure. The solution is that a very simple starting or *bootstrap* program is stored in non-volatile ROM which will contain instructions which will bring in the main program from a storage system such as a disk drive after power is applied. As programs in ROM cannot be altered, they are sometimes referred to as *firmware* to indicate that they are classified between hardware and software.

Making a computer do useful work requires more than simply a program which performs the required computation. There is also a lot of mundane activity which does not differ significantly from one program to the next. This includes deciding which part of the RAM will be occupied by the program and which by the data, producing commands to the storage disk drive to read the input data from a file and to write back the results. It would be very inefficient if all programs had to handle these processes themselves. Consequently the concept of an *operating system* was developed. This manages all the mundane decisions and creates an environment in which useful programs or *applications* can execute.

The ability of the computer to change its own instructions makes it very powerful, but it also makes it vulnerable to abuse. Programs exist which are deliberately written to do damage. These *viruses* are generally attached to plausible messages or data files and enter computers through storage media or communications paths.

There is also the possibility that programs contain logical errors such that in certain combinations of circumstances the wrong result is obtained. If this results in the unwitting modification of an instruction, the next time that instruction is accessed the computer will crash. In consumer grade software, written for the vast personal computer market, this kind of thing is unfortunately accepted.

For critical applications, software must be *verified*. This is a process which can prove that a program can recover from absolutely every combination of circumstances and keep running properly. This is a non-trivial process, because the number of combinations of states a computer can get into is staggering. As a result most software is unverified.

It is of the utmost importance that networked computers which can suffer virus infection or computers running unverified software are never used in a life-support or critical application.

Figure 2.29 shows a simple computer system. The various parts are linked by a bus which allows binary numbers to be transferred from one place to another. This will generally use tri-state logic so that when one device is sending to another, all other devices present a high impedance to the bus.

A typical bus is shown in Figure 2.30. There are three kinds of signal in a bus. These are addresses, data and control/status signals. The control signals are sent by a controlling device to cause some action such as writing data. Status signals are sent by a controlled device to indicate that it has complied, or in the case of a fault, cannot comply. The address is asserted by the controlling device to determine where the data transfer is

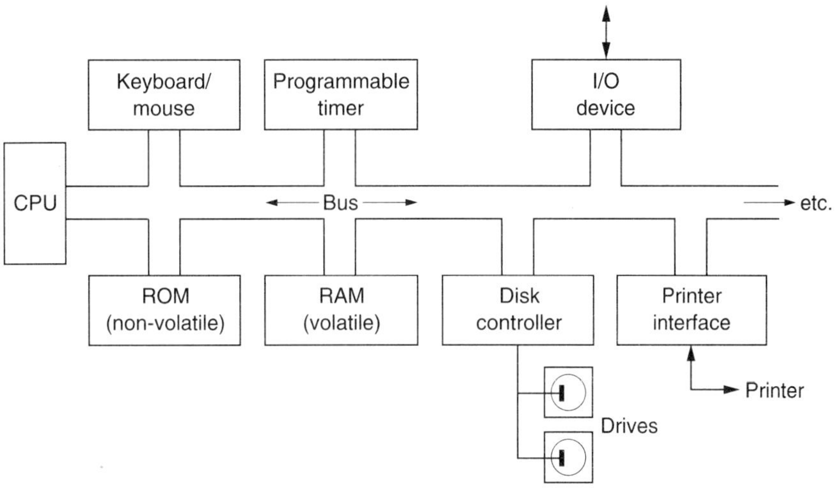

Figure 2.29 A simple computer system. All components are linked by a single data/address/control bus. Although cheap and flexible, such a bus can only make one connection at a time, so it is slow.

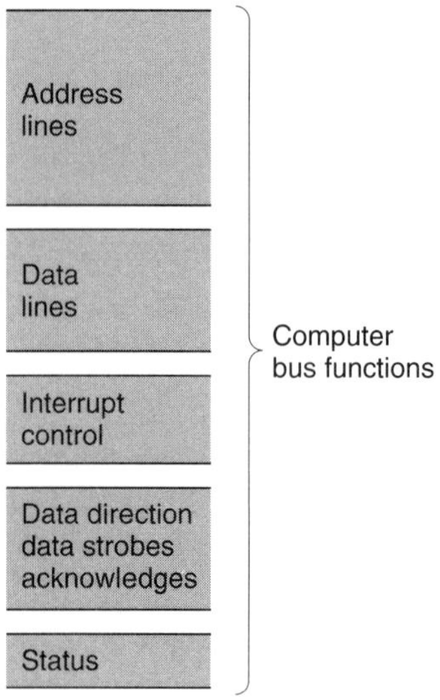

Figure 2.30 Structure of a typical computer bus.

to take place. Most of the addresses relate to individual locations in memory, but a further unique address range relates to peripheral devices.

The ROM stores the startup program, the RAM stores the operating system, applications programs and the data to be processed. The disk drive stores large quantities of data in a non-volatile form. The RAM only needs to be able to hold part of one program as other parts can be brought from the disk as required. A program executes by *fetching* one instruction at a time from the RAM to the processor along the bus.

The bus also allows keyboard/mouse inputs and outputs to the display and printer. Inputs and outputs are generally abbreviated to I/O. Finally a programmable timer will be present which acts as a kind of alarm clock for the processor.

2.13 The processor

The processor or CPU (central processing unit) is the heart of the system. Figure 2.31 shows a simple example of a CPU. The CPU has a bus interface which allows it to generate bus addresses and input or output data. Sequential instructions are stored in RAM at contiguously increasing locations so that a program can be executed by fetching instructions from a RAM address specified by the program counter (PC) to the instruction register in the CPU. As each instruction is completed, the PC is incremented so that it points to the next instruction. In this way the time taken to execute the instruction can vary.

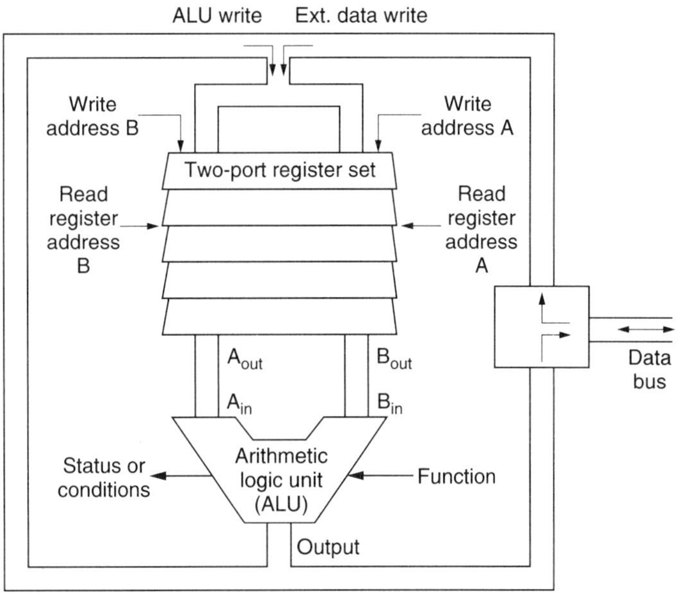

Figure 2.31 The data path of a simple CPU. Under control of an instruction, the ALU will perform some function on a pair of input values from the registers and store or output the result.

The processor is notionally divided into data paths and control paths. Figure 2.31 shows the data path. The CPU contains a number of general-purpose registers or scratchpads which can be used to store partial results in complex calculations. Pairs of these registers can be addressed so that their contents go to the ALU (arithmetic logic unit).

The ALU is a programmable device which performs various functions as a result of a control word supplied to it from a microsequencer. These functions include arithmetic (add, subtract, increment, etc.) or logical (and, or, etc.) functions on the input data, and conditional functions which allow branching of the program due to earlier results such as a calculation being zero, or negative or whatever. The output of the ALU may be routed back to a register or output. By reversing this process it is possible to get data into the registers from the RAM.

Which function the ALU performs and which registers are involved are determined by the instruction currently in the instruction register that is decoded in the control path. One pass through the ALU can be completed in one cycle of the processor's clock. Instructions vary in complexity as do the number of clock cycles needed to complete them. Incoming instructions are decoded and used to access a look-up table which converts them into *microinstructions*, one of which controls the CPU at each clock cycle.

2.14 Interrupts

Ordinarily instructions are executed in the order that they are stored in RAM. However, some instructions direct the processor to jump to a new memory location. If this is a jump to an earlier instruction, the program will enter a loop. The loop must increment a count in a register each time, and contain a conditional instruction called a branch, which allows the processor to jump out of the loop when a predetermined count is reached.

However, it is often required that the sequence of execution should be changeable by some external event. This might be the changing of some value due to a keyboard input. Events of this kind are handled by *interrupts*, which are created by devices needing attention. Figure 2.32 shows that in addition to the PC, the CPU contains another dedicated register called the *stack pointer*. Figure 2.33 shows how this is used. At the end of every instruction the CPU checks to see if an interrupt is asserted on the bus.

If it is, a different set of microinstructions are executed. The PC is incremented as usual, but the next instruction is not executed. Instead, the contents of the PC are stored so that the CPU can resume execution when it has handled the current event. The PC state is stored in a reserved area of RAM known as the *stack*, at an address determined by the stack pointer.

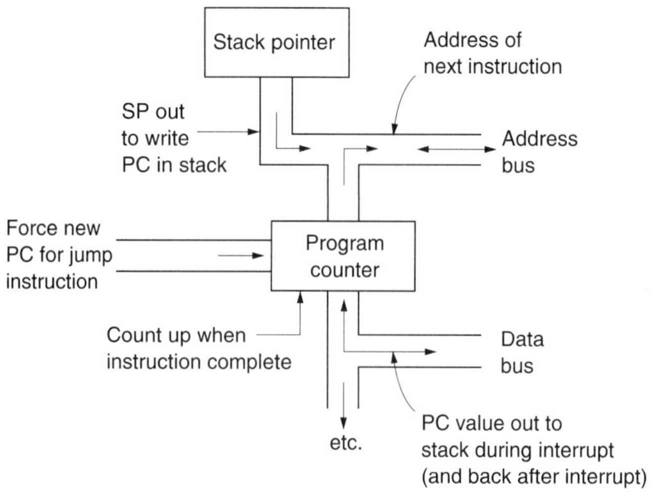

Figure 2.32 Normally the program counter (PC) increments each time an instruction is completed in order to select the next instruction. However, an interrupt may cause the PC state to be stored in the stack area of RAM prior to the PC being forced to the start address of the interrupt subroutine. Afterwards the PC can get its original value back by reading the stack.

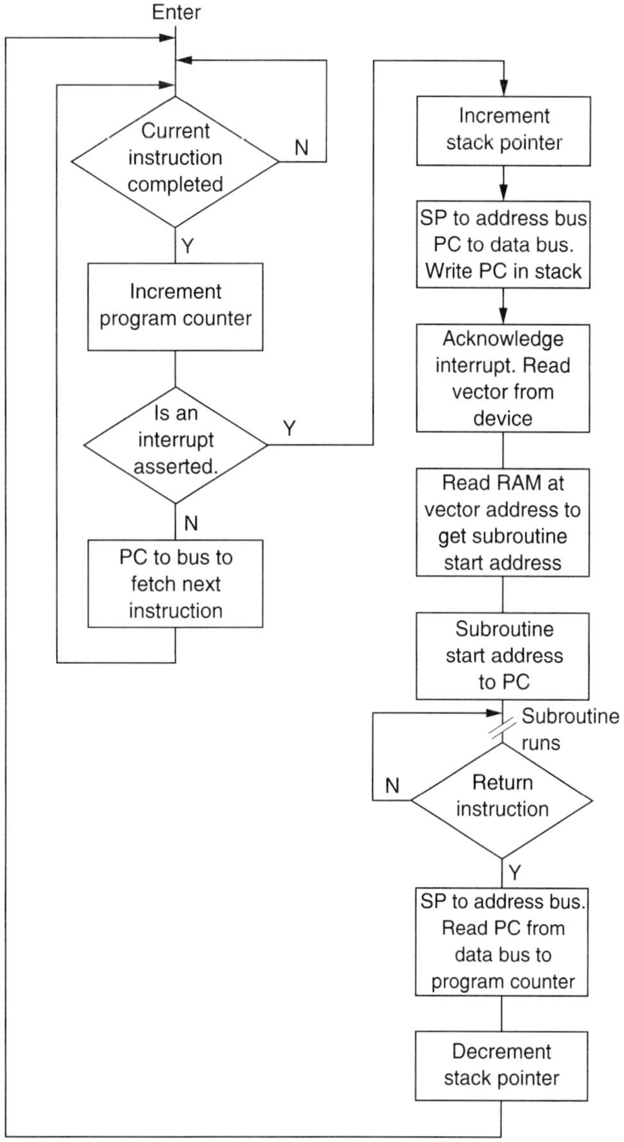

Figure 2.33 How an interrupt is handled. See text for details.

Once the PC is stacked, the processor can handle the interrupt. It issues a bus interrupt acknowledge, and the interrupting device replies with an unique code identifying itself. This is known as a *vector* which steers the processor to a RAM address containing a new program counter. This is the RAM address of the first instruction of the *subroutine* which is the program that will handle the interrupt. The CPU loads this address into the PC and begins execution of the subroutine.

At the end of the subroutine there will be a return instruction. This causes the CPU to use the stack pointer as a memory address in order to read the return PC state from the stack. With this value loaded into the PC, the CPU resumes execution where it left off.

The stack exists so that subroutines can themselves be interrupted. If a subroutine is executing when a higher-priority interrupt occurs, the subroutine can be suspended by incrementing the stack pointer and storing the current PC in the next location in the stack.

When the second interrupt has been serviced, the stack pointer allows the PC of the first subroutine to be retrieved. Whenever a stack PC is retrieved, the stack pointer decrements so that it always points to the PC of the next item of unfinished business.

2.15 Programmable timers

Ordinarily processors have no concept of time and simply execute instructions as fast as their clock allows. This is fine for general-purpose processing, but not for time-critical processes such as video. One way in which the processor can be made time conscious is to use programmable timers. These are devices which reside on the computer bus and which run from a clock. The CPU can set up a timer by loading it with a count. When the count is reached, the timer will interrupt. To give an example, if the count were to be equal to one frame period, there would be one interrupt per frame, and this would result in the execution of a subroutine once per frame, provided, of course, that all the instructions could be executed in one frame period.

2.16 Memory management

The amount of memory a computer can have is determined by the wordlength of the memory address bus. A typical processor has a wordlength of sixteen bits and this can only address 64 K different addresses. Most computers have more memory than this, which leads to the question, how can the processor address large memories?

The solution is the use of memory management or mapping. Figure 2.34 shows that the program counter (PC) of the processor does not address the memory directly. Instead it passes through the memory management unit which is capable of adding constants to the address from the PC. As a result the actual memory location addressed (the physical address) is not what the processor thinks. This leads to the state of the processor PC being called the *virtual address*.

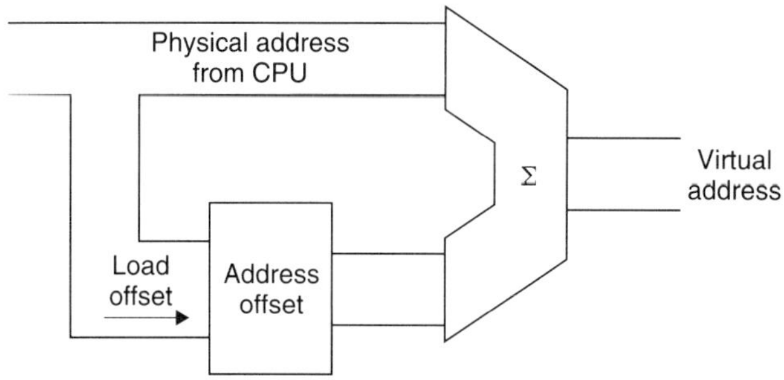

Figure 2.34 Using memory mapping, the processor produces only a virtual address which is converted to a physical address by the addition of an offset.

The constants are loaded into the memory management unit by the operating system. When a program is loaded from, for example, the disk drive, the operating system determines where in the memory the program will reside. This will obviously be a different area from the program currently executing. When the new program is to be executed, the existing program is halted and the memory mapping offsets are changed so that the same virtual address range now addresses the new program.

Correct use of memory management means that user programs cannot access peripheral devices so that faulty user code cannot corrupt the peripheral devices. When a user program needs to obtain data from a peripheral, it must do so via a request to the operating system. As a result the most frequent mode change in the processor will be between running the user program and running the operating system. In addition to requiring a change of memory mapping constants, a mode change also requires that all of the processor's register contents are stored in memory so that they can be restored when the mode reverts. This takes time.

In some processor designs the CPU has more than one register set connected to the ALU and the buses. One of these is called the user set and the other is called the *kernel* set which is used by the operating system. This approach allows faster mode changes because the processor registers do not have to be saved and reloaded. Instead the processor simply switches register set.

Having kernel hardware makes computers much more secure and reliable. For example, if something goes wrong with a user program, it may crash and the user registers can be left in total chaos, but the error will alert the operating system which will simply switch to the kernel register set and carry on working normally. If the memory management registers can only be changed from kernel mode, then there is no possible way in which a user program can change any of the computer's key settings or affect the peripherals because user virtual addresses will never be mapped to peripheral or control register addresses. This makes computers virus resistant.

It should be clear from the virus-prone crash-riddled reputation of the PC that it lacks such features. PCs are consumer devices and their sole advantage is low cost. They are not suitable for critical applications.

2.17 The human interface

In many processes, direct interaction with the human operator is required. The system will present data to the human operator and the operator will present data to the system in the form of movements of the controls. The relative importance of the two data flows depends somewhat on the application. The skilled operator of a digital image production workstation will produce significantly more data than the viewer of a digital television set or a web browser and this will reflect in the type of controls made available. The digital television can be controlled by a simple remote handset with a few buttons. The PC can be controlled with a keyboard and a mouse.

However, in applications which require speed and convenience, a greater number and variety of controls are needed. Professional operators must be able to adjust parameters immediately without having to descend through nested menus. The large number of controls on professional audio and video mixers is a direct consequence of that.

Figure 2.35 shows how a mouse works. The ball is turned in two dimensions as the mouse is moved over a flat surface and a pair of rollers mounted orthogonally (at 90°) operate pulse generators which are

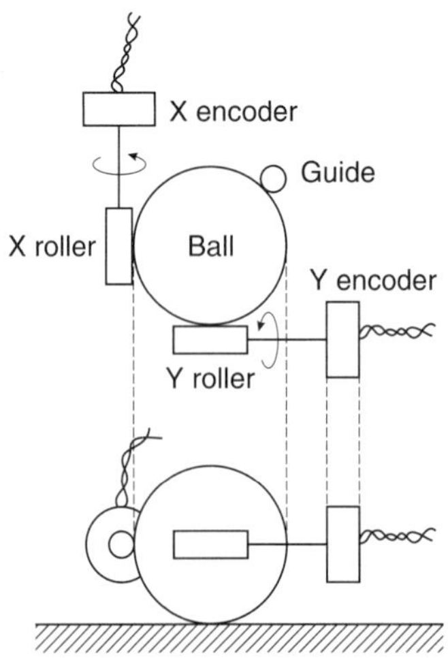

Figure 2.35 A mouse converts motion of the ball in two axes into a series of pulses.

sensitive to direction. These may be optical and consist of slotted vanes. Two suitably positioned light beams falling on photocells will produce outputs in quadrature. The relative phase determines the direction and the frequency is proportional to speed. The pulses from the mouse move the cursor across the display screen until it is over one of the available functions. This function can then be selected by pressing a key on the mouse. A trackball is basically an inverted mouse where the operator rotates the ball in two dimensions with the fingertips.

An alternative is the touch-screen. This is a display which can sense when and where it has been touched by a fingertip. The mechanism may be ultrasonic, optical or capacitive, but it allows a large number of selections to be made quickly. The disadvantage of the touchscreen is that it is tiring to use for long periods as the operator has to extend an arm for each touch.

In a digital audio or video mixer, the gain of each signal is controlled by hand-operated faders, just as in earlier analog machines. Analog faders may be retained and used to produce a varying voltage which is converted to a digital code or gain coefficient in an ADC, but it is also possible to obtain position codes directly in digital faders. Digital faders are a form of displacement transducer in which the mechanical position of the control is converted directly to a digital code. The position of other controls, such as jog wheels on VTRs or editors, will also need to be digitized. Controls can be linear or rotary, and absolute or relative. In an absolute control, the position of the knob determines the output directly. In a relative control, the knob can be moved to increase or decrease the output, but its absolute position is meaningless.

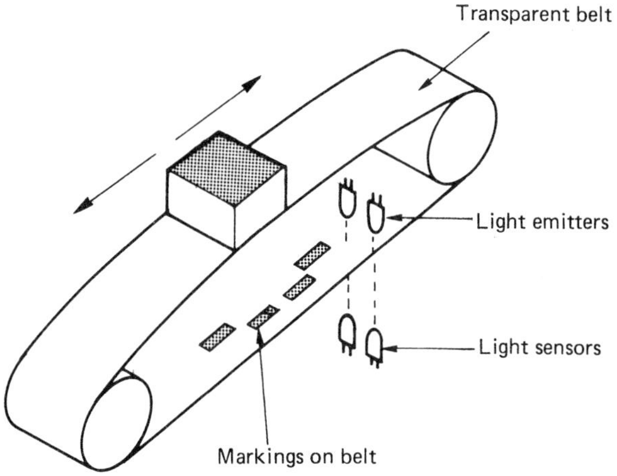

Figure 2.36 An absolute linear fader uses a number of light beams which are interrupted in various combinations according to the position of a grating. A Gray code shown in Figure 2.37 must be used to prevent false codes.

Figure 2.36 shows an absolute linear fader. A grating is moved with respect to several light beams, one for each bit of the coefficient required. The interruption of the beams by the grating determines which photocells are illuminated. It is not possible to use a pure binary pattern on the grating because this results in transient false codes due to mechanical tolerances. Figure 2.37 shows some examples of these false codes. For example, on moving the fader from 3 to 4, the MSB goes true slightly before the middle

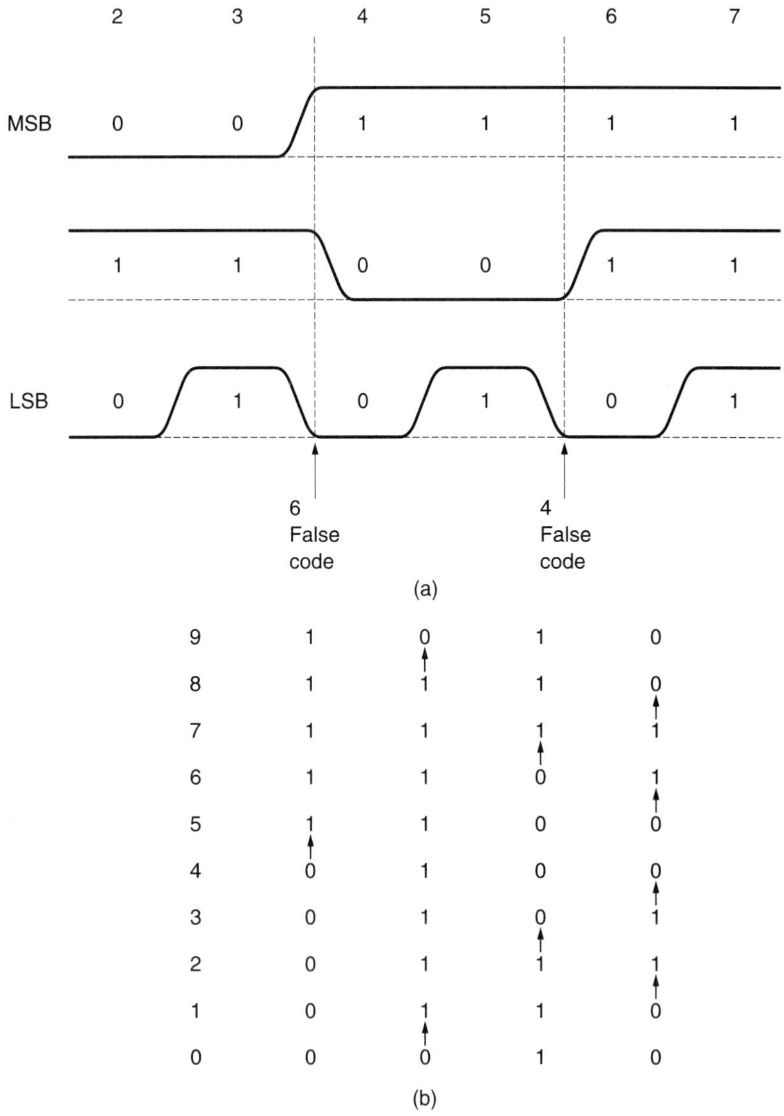

Figure 2.37 (a) Binary cannot be used for position encoders because mechanical tolerances cause false codes to be produced. (b) In Gray code, only one bit (arrowed) changes in between positions, so no false codes can be generated.

bit goes false. This results in a momentary value of 4 + 2 = 6 between 3 and 4. The solution is to use a code in which only one bit ever changes in going from one value to the next. One such code is the Gray code which was devised to overcome timing hazards in relay logic but is now used extensively in position encoders. Gray code can be converted to binary in a suitable PROM, gate array or as a look-up table in software.

Note that in audio faders, the relationship between the gain and the fader position is logarithmic because this is how the ear senses loudness. The analog volume control in a transistor radio has a tapering resistance track to give this characteristic. In digital faders the logarithmic response can be obtained as an additional function of the Gray code look-up process.

Figure 2.38 shows a rotary incremental encoder. This produces a sequence of pulses whose number is proportional to the angle through which it has been turned. The rotor carries a radial grating over its entire perimeter. This turns over a second fixed radial grating whose bars are not parallel to those of the first grating. The resultant moiré fringes travel inward or outward depending on the direction of rotation. These fringes can be detected by a pair of light beams and sensors, whose relative phase will indicate direction. The encoder outputs can be connected to a counter whose contents will increase or decrease according to the direction the rotor is turned. The counter provides the position output.

2.18 DSP

Although general-purpose computers can be programmed to process digital audio or image data, they are not ideal for the following reasons:

1 The number of arithmetic operations, particularly multiplications, is far higher than in data processing.
2 Processing is required in real time; data processors do not generally work in real time.
3 The program needed generally remains constant for the duration of a session, or changes slowly, whereas a data processor rapidly jumps between many programs.
4 Data processors can suspend a program on receipt of an interrupt; audio and image processors must work continuously for long periods.
5 Data processors tend to be I/O (input–output) limited, in that their operating speed is constrained by the problems of moving large quantities of data and instructions into the CPU.

Audio processors in contrast have a relatively small input and output rate, but compute intensively, whereas image processors also compute intensively but tend to outstrip the I/O capabilities of conventional computer architectures.

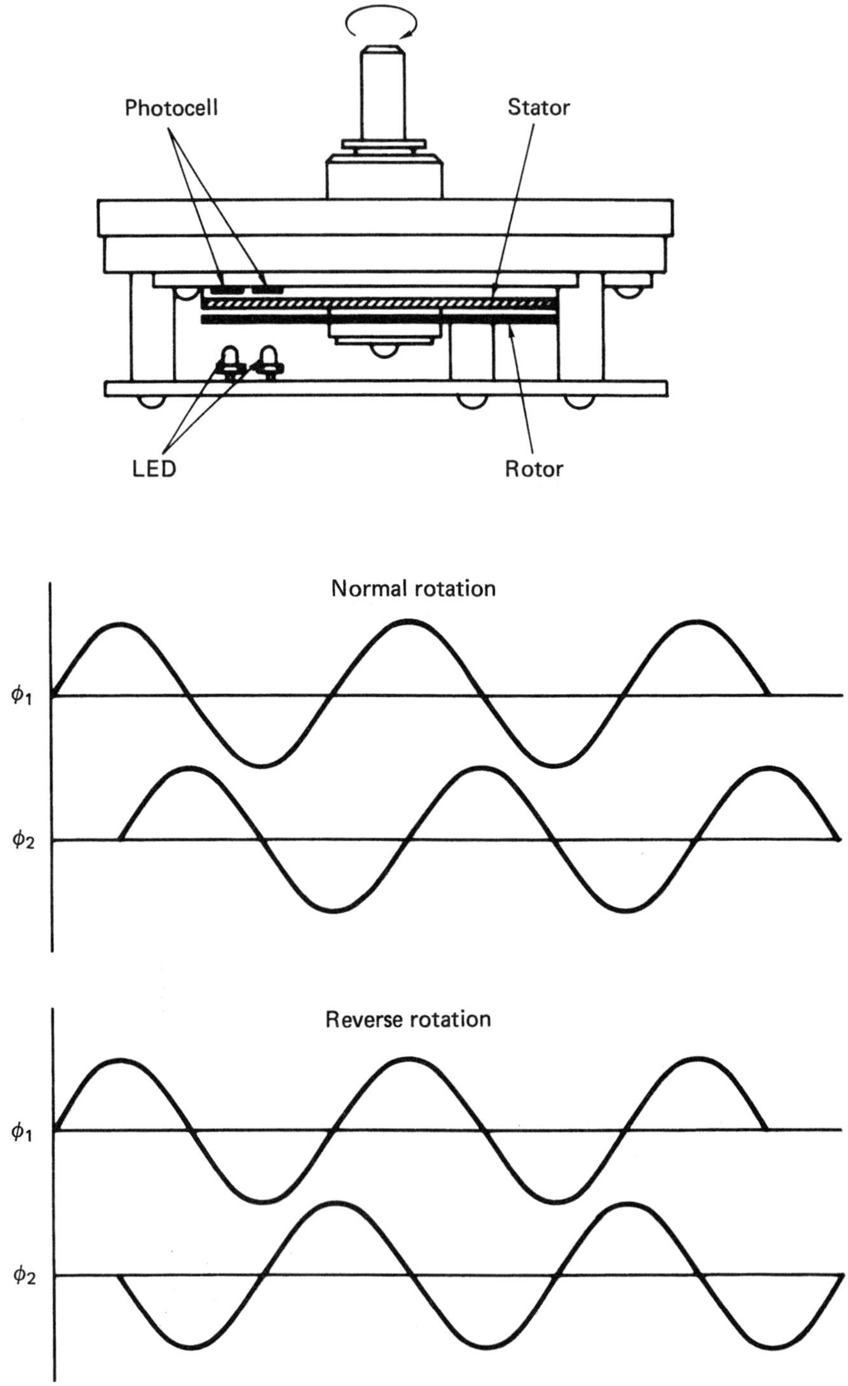

Figure 2.38 The fixed and rotating gratings produce moiré fringes which are detected by two light paths as quadrature sinusoids. The relative phase determines the direction, and the frequency is proportional to speed of rotation.

A common video process is spatial interpolation used for resizing or oversampling. Spatial filters compute each output pixel value as a function of all input pixel values over a finite-sized window. The windows for the output pixels have extensive overlap. In a conventional CPU, shortage of internal registers means that a filter algorithm would have to fetch the input pixel values within the window from memory for every output pixel to be calculated. With an 8×8 window size, one input pixel falls within 64 different windows with the result that the conventional processor would have to fetch the same value from the same location 64 times, whereas in principle it only needs to be fetched once.

This is sufficient justification for the development of specialized digital signal processors (DSPs). These units are equipped with more internal registers than data processors to facilitate implementation of, for example, multi-point filter algorithms. The arithmetic unit will be designed to offer high-speed multiply/accumulate using techniques such as pipelining, which allows operations to overlap. The functions of the register set and the arithmetic unit are controlled by a microsequencer which interprets the instructions in the program. Figure 2.39 shows the interior structure of a DSP chip.

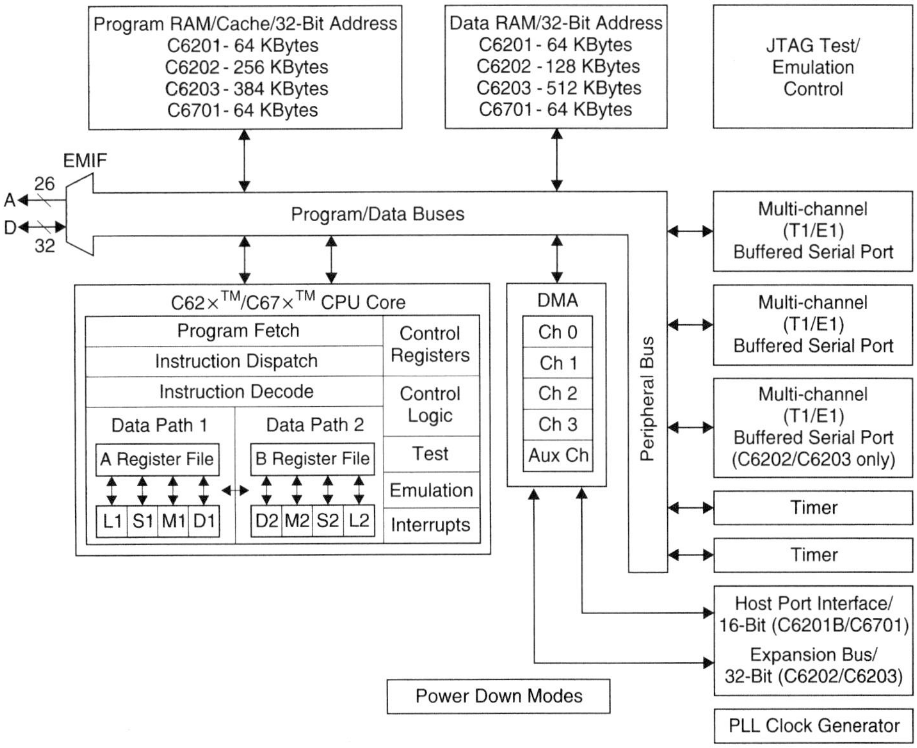

Figure 2.39 A DSP (digital signal processor) is a specialized form of computer. (Courtesy of Texas Instruments.)

Where a DSP is designed specifically for image processing, it is possible to incorporate one CPU per pixel. With a massively parallel approach such as this, the speed of each CPU can be very slow and it can be implemented serially, making it trivially easy to optimize the wordlength of the calculation to the accuracy requirement.

DSPs are used in many other industries where waveforms which were originally analog need to be manipulated in the digital domain. In fact this is probably the best definition of DSP which distinguishes it from

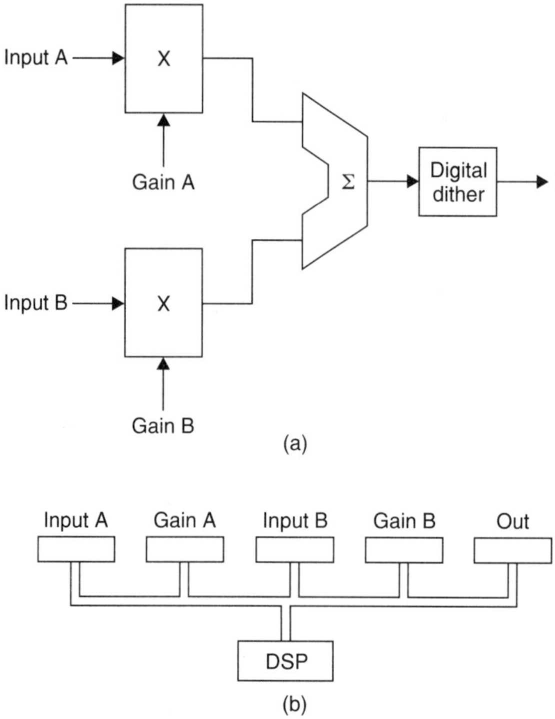

Clear accumulator
Fetch input A
Fetch gain A
Multiply input A and gain A
Accumulate product
Fetch input B
Fetch gain B
Multiply input B and gain B
Accumulate product
Increment pseudo-random sequence
Add pseudo-random value to accumulator
Round off accumulator
Output accumulator value
Wait for sampling rate clock edge
Loop

(c)

Figure 2.40 (a) A simple mixer built conventionally. (b) The same mixer implemented with DSP. The instructions at (c) operate the DSP.

computation in general. Equipment intended for convergent audio/video systems can take advantage of DSP devices designed for applications such as synthetic aperture radar and pattern recognition.

Figure 2.40(a) shows a simple digital mixer which accepts two PCM inputs, sets the gain of each and then mixes (adds) the two together. The sum will have increased in wordlength and must be digitally dithered prior to rounding to the required output wordlength.

Figure 2.40(b) shows a simple DSP system which is designed to do the same job. The hardware is trivial; a few ports and a DSP chip (known colloquially as an 'engine'). The program which is needed to operate the DSP is shown in (c). This has been written in English rather than in DSP language which is incomprehensible to most humans. If all the steps in the program are executed in turn, the output value ought to be the same as if the hardware of (a) had been used.

One problem is that the DSP engine is designed to run as fast as its technology allows whereas in PCM results are required at the signal sampling rate. This is solved by using interrupts. The interrupt signal can occur at any time with respect to the processor clock without causing difficulty as it will only be examined when an instruction has been completed, prior to executing another one. The normal program is suspended, and a different program, known as a subroutine, is executed instead. When the subroutine is completed, the normal program resumes. In a PCM DSP application, the normal program may be an idling program; i.e. it doesn't do anything useful or it may rotate the lights on the front panel. The sample calculation is contained in the subroutine. The master sampling rate clock from a phase-locked loop is then used to generate interrupts to the DSP just after input samples have been made available.

Figure 2.41 shows that if this is done the subroutine is executed at the sampling rate with idling periods between. In practice this is only true if the subroutine is short enough to be executed within the sample period.

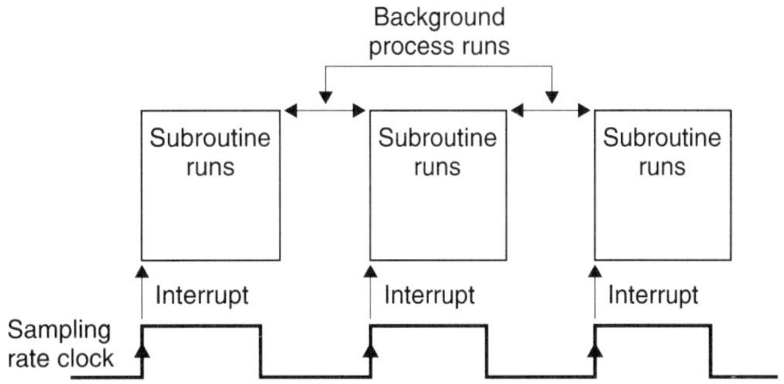

Figure 2.41 Synchronizing a signal processor with real time using interrupts. The processing is carried out by a subroutine.

If it can't, a more elegant program or a more powerful 'engine' must be sought.

2.19 Multiplexing principles

Multiplexing is used where several signals are to be transmitted down the same channel. The channel bit rate must be the same as or greater than the sum of the source bit rates. Figure 2.42 shows that when multiplexing is used, the data from each source has to be time compressed. This is done by buffering source data in a memory at the multiplexer. It is written into the memory in real time as it arrives, but will be read from the memory with a clock which has a much higher rate. This means that the readout occurs in a smaller timespan. If, for example, the clock frequency is raised by a factor of ten, the data for a given signal will be transmitted in a tenth of the normal time, leaving time in the multiplex for nine more such signals.

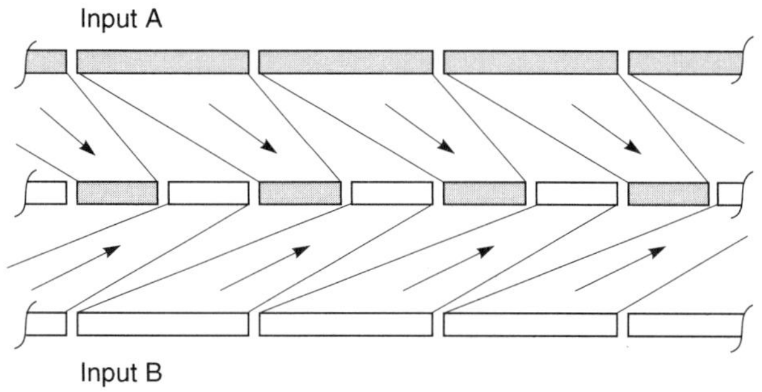

Figure 2.42 Multiplexing requires time compression on each input.

In the demultiplexer another buffer memory will be required. Only the data for the selected signal will be written into this memory at the bit rate of the multiplex. When the memory is read at the correct speed, the data will emerge with its original timebase.

In practice it is essential to have mechanisms to identify the separate signals to prevent them being mixed up and to convey the original signal clock frequency to the demultiplexer. In time-division multiplexing the timebase of the transmission is broken into equal slots, one for each signal. This makes it easy for the demultiplexer, but forces a rigid structure on all the signals such that they must all be locked to one another and have an unchanging bit rate. Packet multiplexing overcomes these limitations.

2.20 Packets

The multiplexer must switch between different time-compressed signals to create the bitstream and this is much easier to organize if each signal is in the form of data packets of constant size. This approach is used in commonly in networks such as Ethernet and ATM (see Chapter 12) as well as in MPEG transport streams. Figure 2.43 shows a packet multiplexing system.

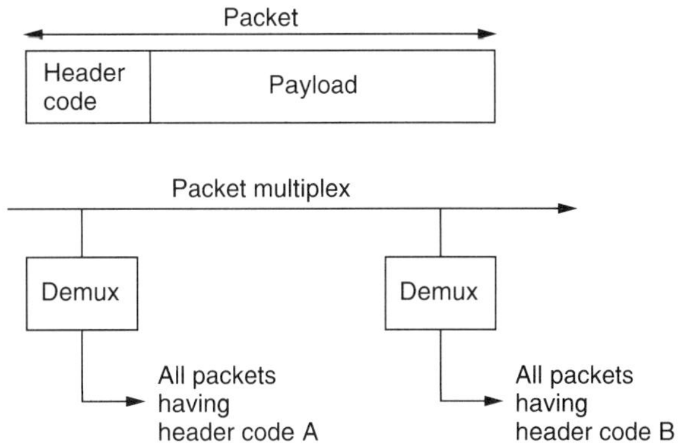

Figure 2.43 Packet multiplexing relies on headers to identify the packets.

Each packet consists of two components: the header, which identifies the packet, and the payload, which is the data to be transmitted. The header will contain at least an identification code (ID) which is unique for each signal in the multiplex. The demultiplexer checks the ID codes of all incoming packets and discards those which do not have the wanted ID.

In complex systems it is common to have a mechanism to check that packets are not lost or repeated. This is the purpose of the packet continuity count which is carried in the header. For packets carrying the same ID, the count should increase by one from one packet to the next. Upon reaching the maximum binary value, the count overflows and recommences.

2.21 Statistical multiplexing

Packet multiplexing has advantages over time-division multiplexing because it does not set the bit rate of each signal. A demultiplexer simply checks packet IDs and selects all packets with the wanted code. It will do this however frequently such packets arrive. Consequently it is practicable to have variable bit rate signals in a packet multiplex. The multiplexer has to ensure that the total bit rate does not exceed the rate of the channel, but that rate can be allocated arbitrarily between the various signals.

As a practical matter is is usually necessary to keep the bit rate of the multiplex constant. With variable rate inputs this is done by creating null packets which are generally called *stuffing* or *packing*. The headers of these packets contain an unique ID which the demultiplexer does not recognize and so these packets are discarded on arrival.

In an MPEG environment, statistical multiplexing can be extremely useful because it allows for the varying difficulty of real program material. In a multiplex of several television programs, it is unlikely that all the programs will encounter difficult material simultaneously. When one program encounters a detailed scene or frequent cuts which are hard to compress, more data rate can be allocated at the allowable expense of the remaining programs which are handling easy material.

In a network using statistical multiplexing, such as ATM, efficient use of transmission capacity can be made by combining mixed data types with different priorities. If real-time MPEG video is being carried, clearly this must be given priority over non-real-time data to provide the required quality of service. However, when the instantaneous bit rate of the video falls, an ATM system can increase the amount of non-real-time data sent.

2.22 Networks

In the most general sense a network is a means of communication between a large number of places. Some networks deliver physical objects. If, however, we restrict the delivery to information only the result is a telecommunications network. The telephone system is a good example of a telecommunications network because it displays most of the characteristics of later networks.

It is fundamental in a network that any port can communicate with any other port. Figure 2.44 shows a primitive three-port network. Clearly each port that must select one or other of the remaining ports is a trivial switching system. However, if it were attempted to redraw Figure 2.44 with one hundred ports, each one would need a 99-way switch and the number of wires needed would be phenomenal. Another approach is needed.

Figure 2.45 shows that the common solution is to have an exchange, also known as a router, hub or switch, which is connected to every port by a single cable. In this case when a port wishes to communicate with another, it instructs the switch to make the connection. The complexity of the switch varies with its performance. The minimal case may be to install

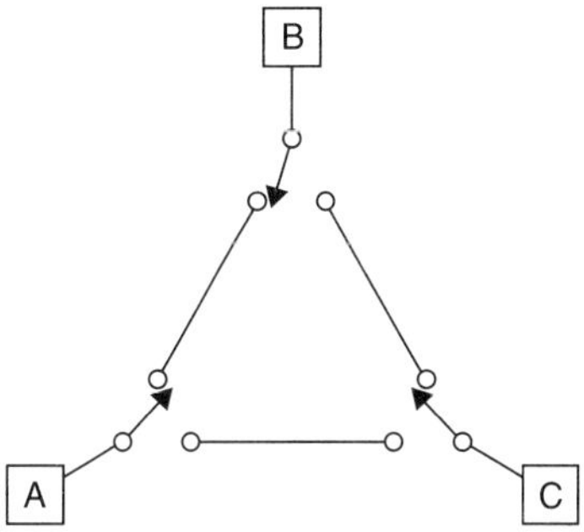

Figure 2.44 A simple three-port network has trivial switching requirements.

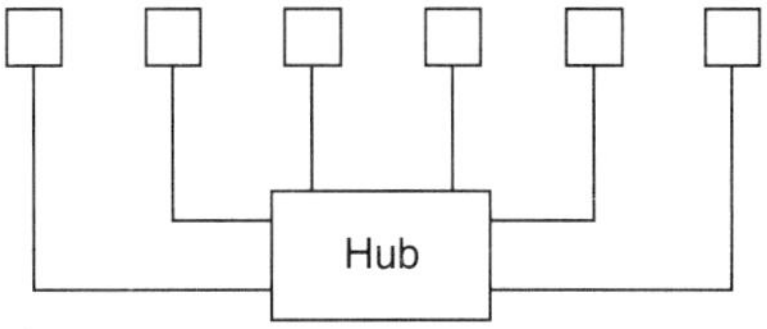

Figure 2.45 A network implemented with a router or hub.

a single input selector and a single output selector. This allows any port to communicate with any other, but only one at a time. If more simultaneous communications are needed, further switching is needed. The extreme case is where every possible pair of ports can communicate simultaneously.

The amount of switching logic needed to implement the extreme case is phenomenal and in practice it is unlikely to be needed. One fundamental property of networks is that they are seldom implemented with the extreme case supported. There will be an economic decision made balancing the number of simultaneous communications with the equipment cost. Most of the time the user will be unaware that this limit exists, until there is a statistically abnormal condition which causes more than the usual number of nodes to attempt communication. This is known as *congestion* in communications parlance.

The phrase 'the switchboard was jammed' has passed into the language and stayed there despite the fact that manual switchboards are only seen in museums. This is a characteristic of networks. They generally only work up to a certain throughput and then there are problems. This doesn't mean that networks aren't useful, far from it. What it means is that with care, networks can be very useful, but without care they can be a nightmare.

There are two key factors to address in a network. The first is that it must have enough throughput, bandwidth or connectivity to handle the anticipated usage and the second is that a priority system or algorithm is

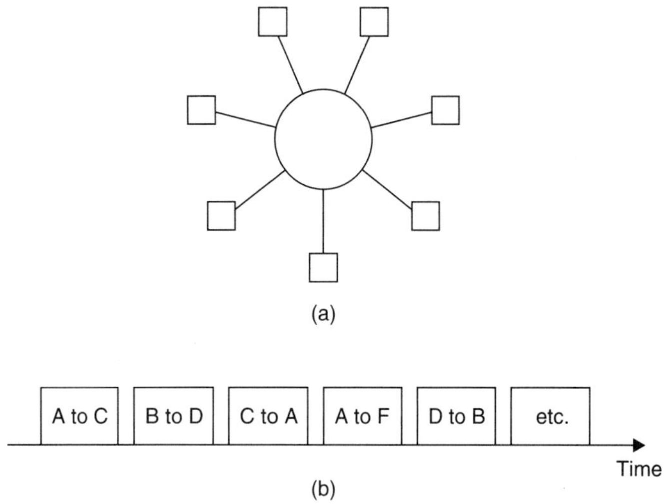

Figure 2.46 Radial network at (a) has one cable per node. TDM network (b) shares time slots on a single cable.

chosen which has appropriate behaviour during congestion. These two characteristics are quite different, but often come as a pair in a network corresponding to a particular standard.

Where each device is individually cabled, the result is a radial network shown in Figure 2.46(a). It is not necessary to have one cable per device and several devices can co-exist on a single cable if some form of multiplexing is used. This might be time-division multiplexing (TDM) or frequency division multiplexing (FDM). In TDM, shown in (b), the time axis is divided into steps which may or may not be equal in length. In Ethernet, for example, these are called frames, whereas ATM calls them cells. During each time step or frame a pair of nodes have exclusive use of the cable. At the end of the time step another pair of nodes can communicate. Rapidly switching between steps gives the illusion of simultaneous transfer between several pairs of nodes. In FDM, simultaneous transfer is possible because each message occupies a different band of frequencies in the cable. This approach can also be used in optical fibres where light of several different wavelengths can be used. Each node has to 'tune' to the correct signal. In practice it is possible to combine FDM and TDM. Each frequency band can be time multiplexed in some applications.

Data networks originated to serve the requirements of computers and it is a simple fact that most computer processes don't need to be performed in real time or indeed at a particular time at all. Networks tend to reflect that background as many of them, particularly the older ones, are asynchronous.

Asynchronous means that the time taken to deliver a given quantity of data is unknown. A TDM system may chop the data into several different transfers and each transfer may experience delay according to what other transfers the system is engaged in. Ethernet and most storage system buses are asynchronous. For broadcasting purposes an asynchronous delivery system is no use at all, but for copying a video data file between two storage devices an asynchronous system is perfectly adequate.

The opposite extreme is the synchronous system in which the network can guarantee a constant delivery rate and a fixed and minor delay. An AES/EBU digital audio router or an SDI digital video router is a synchronous network.

In between asynchronous and synchronous networks reside the isochronous approaches which cause a fixed moderate delay. These can be thought of as sloppy synchronous networks or more rigidly controlled asynchronous networks.

These three different approaches are needed for economic reasons. Asynchronous systems are very efficient because as soon as one transfer completes another one can begin. This can only be achieved by making every device wait with its data in a buffer so that transfer can start immediately. Asynchronous systems also make it possible for low bit rate devices to share a network with high bit rate ones. The low bit rate device will only need a small buffer and will send few cells, whereas the high bit rate device will send more cells.

Isochronous systems try to give the best of both worlds, generally by sacrificing some flexibility in block size. Modern networks are tending to be part isochronous and part asynchronous so that the advantages of both are available. Details of this approach will be found in Chapter 12.

3

Filters and transforms

The various chapters of this book concentrate on some specific subjects, but in all of these some common principles or processes arise. The most important of these is filtering, and its parallel topic of transforms. Filters and transforms are inseparable from this technology. They are relevant to sampling, displays, recording, transmission and compression systems.

3.1 Introduction

In convergent systems it is very important to remember that the valuable commodity is information. For practical reasons the way information is represented may have to be changed a number of times during its journey. If accuracy or realism is a goal these changes must be well engineered. In the course of this book we shall explore changes between the continuous domain of real sounds and images and the discrete domain of sampled data. A proper understanding of these processes requires familiarity with the principles of filters and transforms, which is why this chapter precedes the treatment of conversion in Chapter 4.

Figure 3.1 shows an optical system of finite resolution. If an object containing an infinitely sharp line is presented to this system, the image will be an intensity function known in optics as a *point spread function*. Such functions are almost invariably symmetrical in optics. There is no movement or change here, the phenomenon is purely spatial. A point spread function is a spatial impulse response. All images passing through the optical system are convolved with it.

Figure 3.1(b) shows that the object may be scanned by an analog system to produce a waveform. The image may also be scanned in this way.

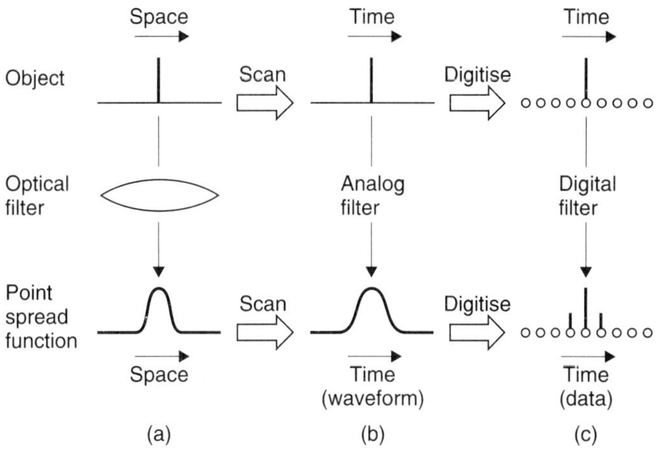

Figure 3.1 In optical systems an infinitely sharp line is reproduced as a point spread function (a) which is the impulse response of the optical path. Scanning either object or image produces an analog time-variant waveform (b). The scanned object waveform can be converted to the scanned image waveform with an electrical filter having an impulse response which is an analog of the point spread function. (c) The object and image may also be sampled or the object samples can be converted to the image samples by a filter with an analogous discrete impulse response.

These waveforms are now temporal. However, the second waveform may be obtained in another way, using an analog filter in series with the first scanned waveform which has an equivalent impulse response. This filter must have linear phase, i.e. its impulse response must be symmetrical.

Figure 3.1(c) shows that the object may also be sampled in which case all samples but one will have a value of zero. The image may also be sampled, and owing to the point spread function, there will now be a number of non-zero sample values. However, the image samples may also be obtained by passing the input sample into a digital filter having the appropriate impulse response. Note that it is possible to obtain the same result as (c) by passing the scanned waveform of (b) into an ADC and storing the samples in a memory.

Clearly there are a number of equivalent routes leading to the same result. One result of this is that optical systems and sampled systems can simulate one another. This gives us considerable freedom to perform processing in the most advantageous domain which gives the required result. There are many parallels between analog, digital and optical filters, which this chapter treats as a common subject.

It should be clear from Figure 3.1 why video signal paths need to have linear phase. In general, analog circuitry and filters tend not to have linear phase because they must be *causal*, which means that the output can only occur after the input. Figure 3.2(a) shows a simple RC network and its impulse response. This is the familiar exponential decay due to the

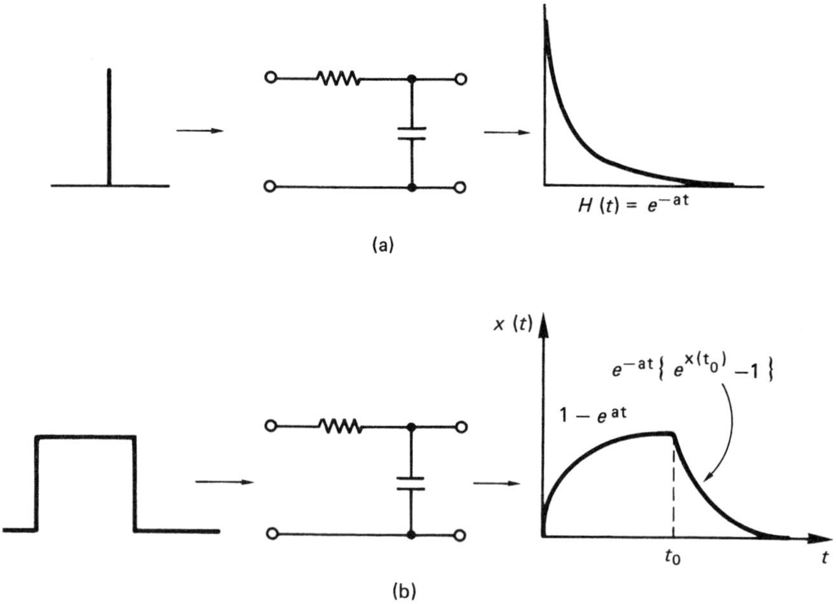

Figure 3.2 (a) The impulse response of a simple RC network is an exponential decay. This can used to calculate the response to a square wave, as in (b).

capacitor discharging through the resistor (in series with the source impedance which is assumed here to be negligible). The figure also shows the response to a squarewave at (b). With other waveforms the process is inevitably more complex.

Filtering is unavoidable. Sometimes a process has a filtering effect which is undesirable, for example the limited frequency response of an audio amplifier or loss of resolution in a lens, and we try to minimize it. On other occasions a filtering effect is specifically required. Analog or digital filters, and sometimes both, are required in ADCs, DACs, in the data channels of digital recorders and transmission systems and in DSP. Optical filters may also be necessary in imaging systems to convert between sampled and continuous images. Optical systems used in displays and in laser recorders also act as spatial filters.[1]

Figure 3.3 shows that impulse response testing tells a great deal about a filter. In a perfect filter, all frequencies should experience the same time delay. If some groups of frequencies experience a different delay than others, there is a group-delay error. As an impulse contains an infinite spectrum, a filter suffering from group-delay error will separate the different frequencies of an impulse along the time axis.

A pure delay will cause a phase shift proportional to frequency, and a filter with this characteristic is said to be phase-linear. The impulse response of a phase-linear filter is symmetrical. If a filter suffers from

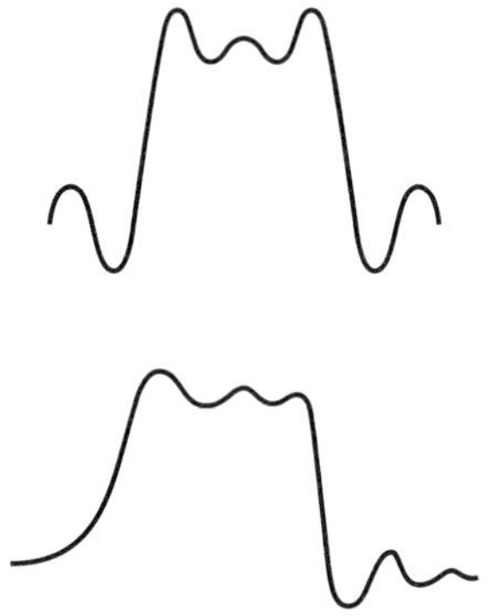

Figure 3.3 If a filter is not phase-linear, different frequencies will emerge at different times if an impulse is input. This is undesirable in video circuitry.

group-delay error it cannot be phase-linear. It is almost impossible to make a perfectly phase-linear analog filter, and many filters have a group-delay equalization stage following them which is often as complex as the filter itself. In the digital domain it is straightforward to make a phase-linear filter, and phase equalization becomes unnecessary.

Because of the sampled nature of the signal, whatever the response at low frequencies may be, all PCM channels (and sampled analog channels) act as low-pass filters because they cannot contain frequencies above the Nyquist limit of half the sampling frequency.

3.2 Transforms

Transforms are a useful subject because they can help to understand processes which cause undesirable filtering or to design filters. The information itself may be subject to a transform. Transforming converts the information into another analog. The information is still there, but expressed with respect to temporal or spatial frequency rather than time or space. Instead of binary numbers representing the magnitude of samples, there are binary numbers representing the magnitude of frequency coefficients. The close relationship of transforms to convergent technologies makes any description somewhat circular as Figure 3.4 shows. The solution adopted in this chapter is to introduce a number of filtering-related topics, and to return to the subject of transforms whenever a point can be illustrated.

Transforms are only a different representation of the same information. As a result what happens in the frequency domain must always be consistent with what happens in the time or space domains. A filter may modify the frequency response of a system, and/or the phase response,

DVB			
Image sampling	DCT-based compression	Randomizing	OFDM modulation
Transforms help explain Nyquist rate and resolution	Transform makes video data easier to compress	Transforms explain why randomizing optimizes transmitter spectrum	Modulator performs an inverse transform

Figure 3.4 Transforms are extensively found in convergent systems. They may be used to explain the operation of a process, or a process may actually create a transform. Here the relationship between transforms and DVB is shown.

but every combination of frequency and phase response has a corresponding impulse response in the time domain.

Figure 3.5 shows the relationship between the domains. On the left is the frequency domain. Here an input signal having a given spectrum is input to a filter having a given frequency response. The output spectrum will be the product of the two functions. If the functions are expressed logarithmically in deciBels, the product can be obtained by simple addition.

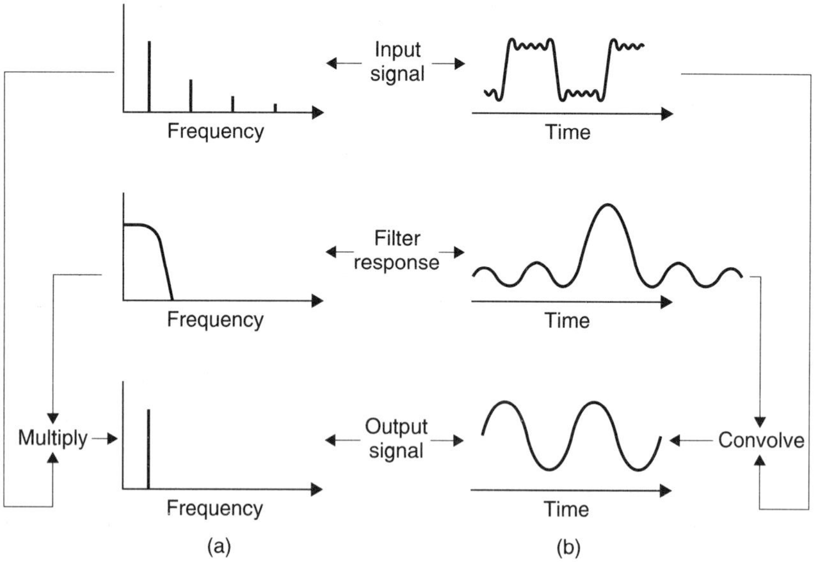

Figure 3.5 If a signal having a given spectrum is passed into a filter, multiplying the two spectra will give the output spectrum at (a). Equally transforming the filter frequency response will yield the impulse response of the filter. If this is convolved with the time domain waveform, the result will be the output waveform, whose transform is the output spectrum (b).

On the right, the time-domain output waveform represents the convolution of the impulse response with the input waveform. However, if the frequency transform of the output waveform is taken, it must be the same as the result obtained from the frequency response and the input spectrum. This is a useful result because it means that when image or audio sampling is considered, it will be possible to explain the process in both domains.

3.3 Convolution

When a waveform is input to a system, the output waveform will be the convolution of the input waveform and the impulse response of the system. Convolution can be followed by reference to a graphic example in Figure 3.6. Where the impulse response is asymmetrical, the decaying tail occurs *after* the input. As a result it is necessary to reverse the impulse response in time so that it is mirrored prior to sweeping it through the input waveform. The output voltage is proportional to the shaded area shown where the two impulses overlap. If the impulse response is symmetrical, as would be the case with a linear phase filter, or in an optical system, the mirroring process is superfluous.

The same process can be performed in the sampled, or discrete time domain as shown in Figure 3.7. The impulse and the input are now a set of discrete samples which clearly must have the same sample spacing. The impulse response only has value where impulses coincide. Elsewhere it is zero. The impulse response is therefore stepped through the input one sample period at a time. At each step, the area is still proportional to the output, but as the time steps are of uniform width, the area is proportional to the impulse height and so the output is obtained by adding up the lengths of overlap. In mathematical terms, the output samples represent the convolution of the input and the impulse response by summing the coincident cross-products.

3.4 FIR and IIR filters

Filters can be described in two main classes, as shown in Figure 3.8, according to the nature of the impulse response. Finite-impulse response (FIR) filters are always stable and, as their name suggests, respond to an impulse once, as they have only a forward path. In the temporal domain, the time for which the filter responds to an input is finite, fixed and readily established. The same is therefore true about the distance over which a FIR filter responds in the spatial domain. FIR filters can be made perfectly phase-linear if a significant processing delay is accepted. Most

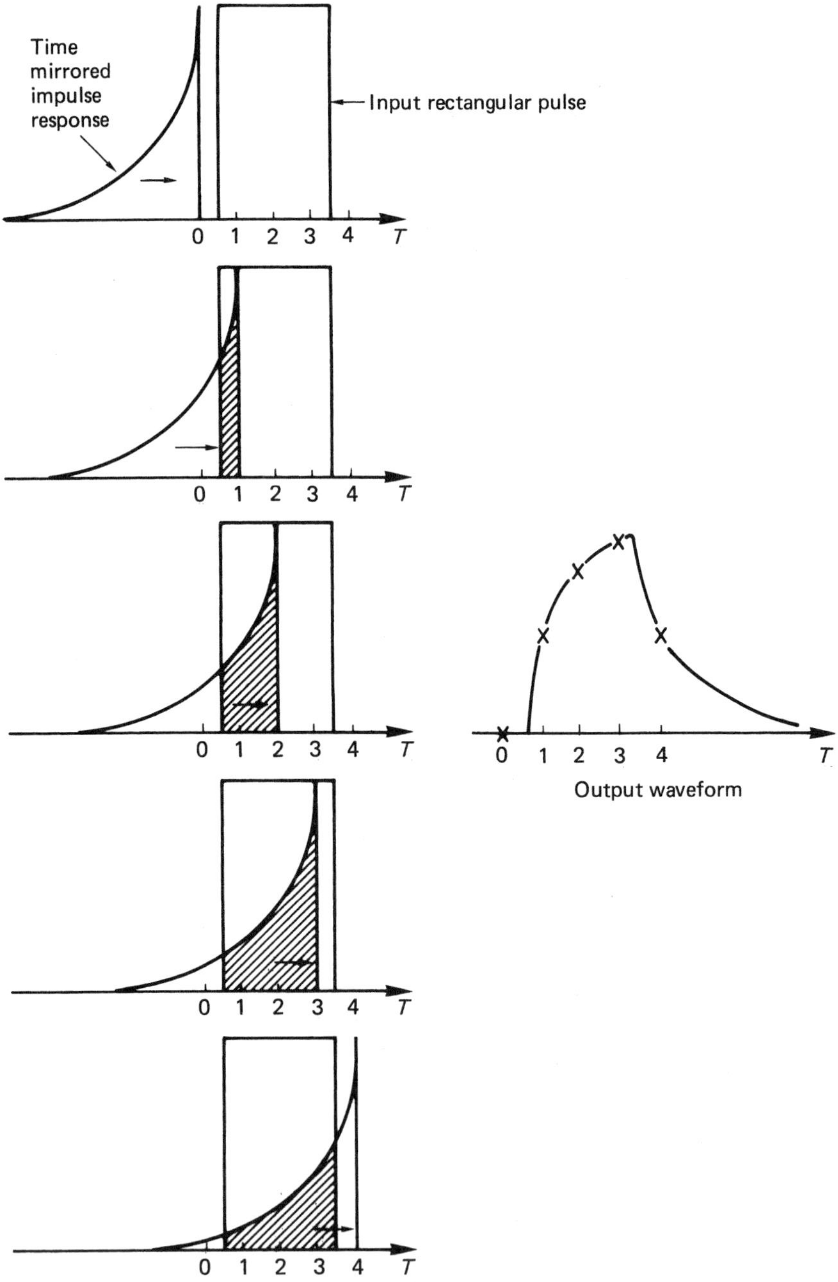

Figure 3.6 In the convolution of two continuous signals (the impulse response with the input), the impulse must be time reversed or mirrored. This is necessary because the impulse will be moved from left to right, and mirroring gives the impulse the correct time-domain response when it is moved past a fixed point. As the impulse response slides continuously through the input waveform, the area where the two overlap determines the instantaneous output amplitude. This is shown for five different times by the crosses on the output waveform.

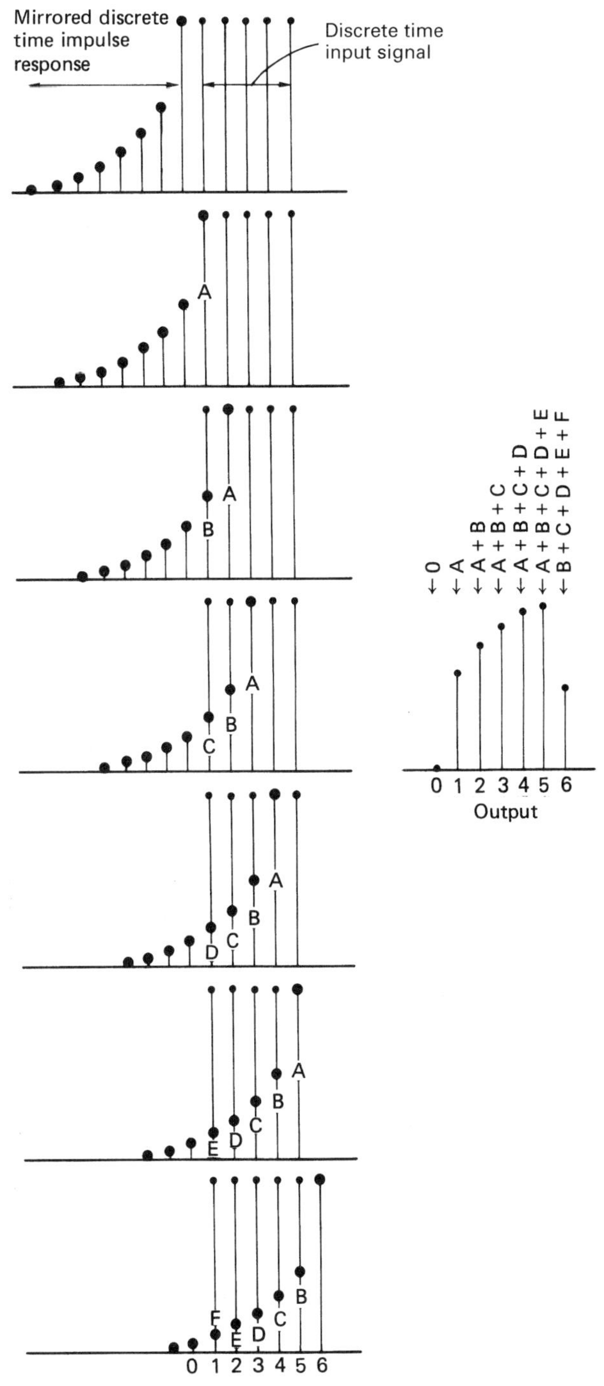

Figure 3.7 In discrete time convolution, the mirrored impulse response is stepped through the input one sample period at a time. At each step, the sum of the cross-products is used to form an output value. As the input in this example is a constant height pulse, the output is simply proportional to the sum of the coincident impulse response samples. This figure should be compared with Figure 3.6.

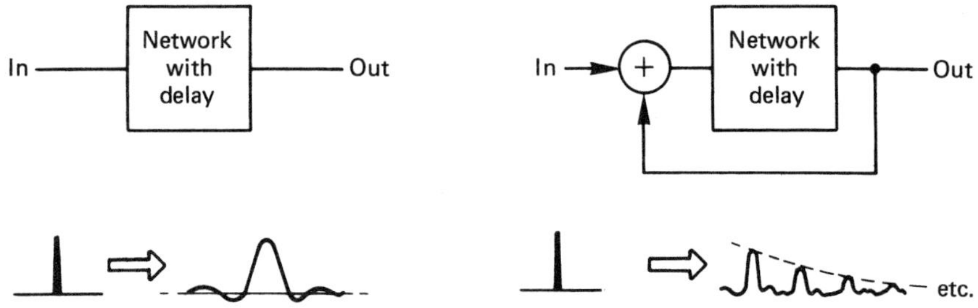

(a) Finite impulse response (FIR)

(b) Infinite impulse response (IIR)

Figure 3.8 An FIR filter (a) responds only once to an input, whereas the output of an IIR filter (b) continues indefinitely rather like a decaying echo.

filters used for image processing, sampling rate conversion and oversampling fall into this category.

Infinite-impulse response (IIR) filters respond to an impulse indefinitely and are not necessarily stable, as they have a return path from the output to the input. For this reason they are also called recursive filters. As the impulse response is not symmetrical, IIR filters are not phase-linear. Audio equalizers often employ recursive filters.

3.5 FIR filters

A FIR filter performs convolution of the input waveform with its own impulse response. It does this by graphically constructing the impulse response for every input sample and superimposing all these responses. It is first necessary to establish the correct impulse response. Figure 3.9(a) shows an example of a low-pass filter which cuts off at $\frac{1}{4}$ of the sampling rate. The impulse response of an ideal low-pass filter is a $\sin x/x$ curve, where the time between the two central zero crossings is the reciprocal of the cut-off frequency. According to the mathematics, the waveform has always existed, and carries on for ever.

The peak value of the output coincides with the input impulse. This means that the filter cannot be causal, because the output has changed before the input is known. Thus in all practical applications it is necessary to truncate the extreme ends of the impulse response, which causes an aperture effect, and to introduce a time delay in the filter equal to half the duration of the truncated impulse in order to make the filter causal. As an input impulse is shifted through the series of registers in Figure 3.9(b), the impulse response is created, because at each point it is multiplied by a coefficient as in (c).

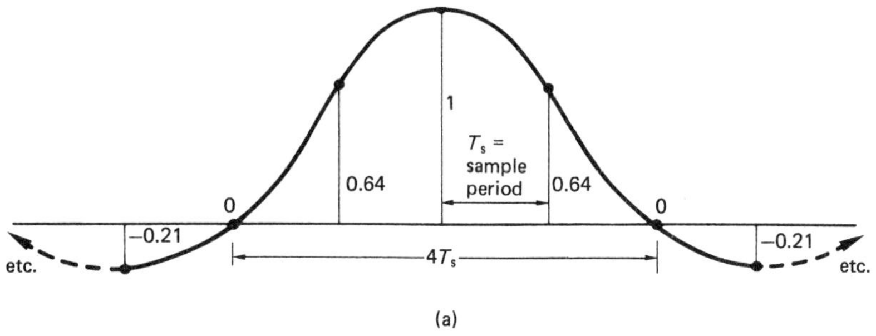

Figure 3.9(a) The impulse response of an LPF is a $\sin x/x$ curve which stretches from $-\infty$ to $+\infty$ in time. The ends of the response must be neglected, and a delay introduced to make the filter causal.

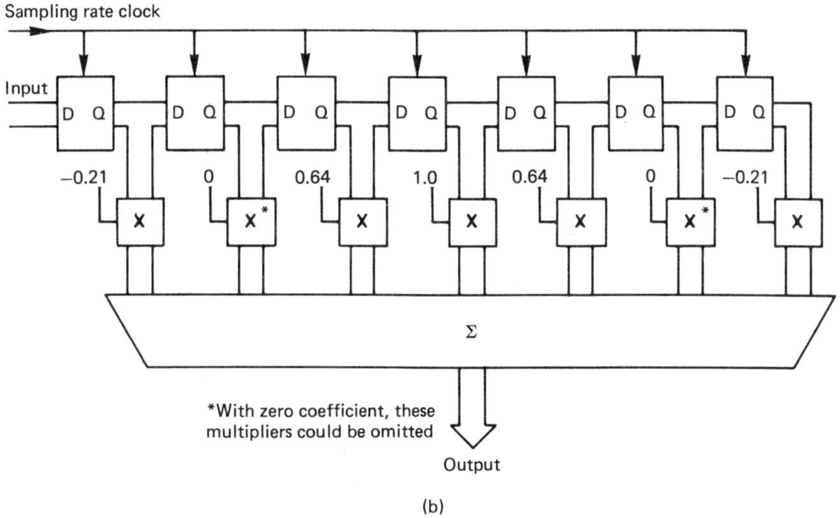

Figure 3.9(b) The structure of an FIR LPF. Input samples shift across the register and at each point are multiplied by different coefficients.

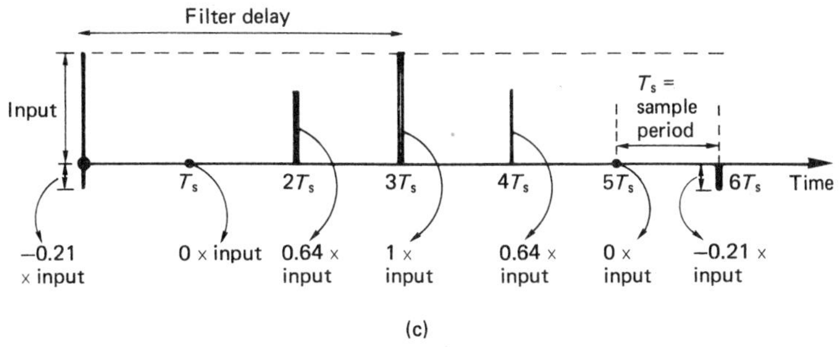

Figure 3.9(c) When a single unit sample shifts across the circuit of Figure 3.9(b), the impulse response is created at the output as the impulse is multiplied by each coefficient in turn.

These coefficients are simply the result of sampling and quantizing the desired impulse response. Clearly the sampling rate used to sample the impulse must be the same as the sampling rate for which the filter is being designed. In practice the coefficients are calculated, rather than attempting to sample an actual impulse response. The coefficient wordlength will be a compromise between cost and performance. Because the input sample shifts across the system registers to create the shape of the impulse response, the configuration is also known as a transversal filter. In operation with real sample streams, there will be several consecutive sample values in the filter registers at any time in order to convolve the input with the impulse response.

Simply truncating the impulse response causes an abrupt transition from input samples which matter and those which do not. Truncating the filter superimposes a rectangular shape on the time-domain impulse response. In the frequency domain the rectangular shape transforms to a $\sin x/x$ characteristic which is superimposed on the desired frequency response as a ripple. One consequence of this is known as Gibb's phenomenon; a tendency for the response to peak just before the cut-off frequency.[2,3] As a result, the length of the impulse which must be considered will depend not only on the frequency response, but also on the amount of ripple which can be tolerated. If the relevant period of the impulse is measured in sample periods, the result will be the number of points or multiplications needed in the filter. Figure 3.10 compares the performance of filters with different numbers of points. A high-quality digital audio FIR filter may need in excess of 100 points.

Rather than simply truncate the impulse response in time, it is better to make a smooth transition from samples which do not count to those that do. This can be done by multiplying the coefficients in the filter by a window function which peaks in the centre of the impulse. Figure 3.11 shows some different window functions and their responses. The rectangular window is the case of truncation, and the response is shown

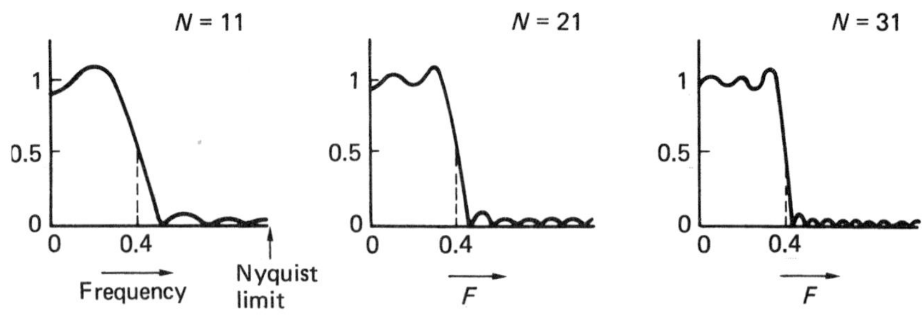

Figure 3.10 The truncation of the impulse in an FIR filter caused by the use of a finite number of points (N) results in ripple in the response. Shown here are three different numbers of points for the same impulse response. The filter is an LPF which rolls off at 0.4 of the fundamental interval. (Courtesy *Philips Technical Review*.)

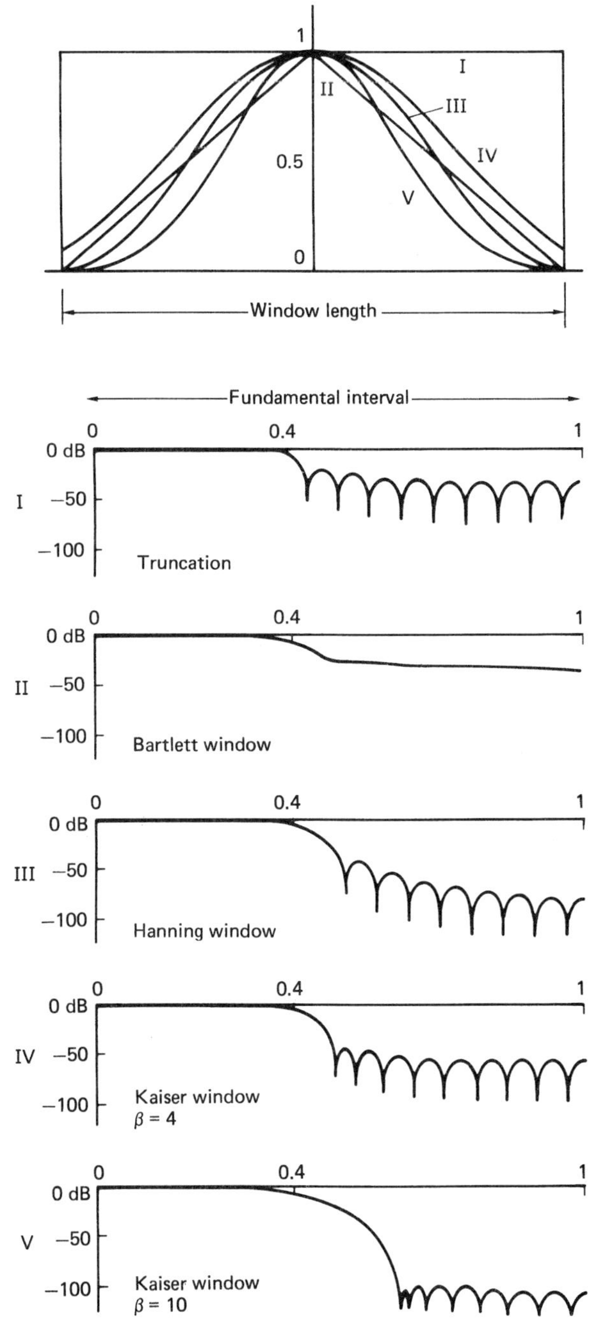

Figure 3.11 The effect of window functions. At top, various window functions are shown in continuous form. Once the number of samples in the window is established, the continuous functions shown here are sampled at the appropriate spacing to obtain window coefficients. These are multiplied by the truncated impulse response coefficients to obtain the actual coefficients used by the filter. The amplitude responses I–V correspond to the window functions illustrated. (Responses courtesy *Philips Technical Review*.)

at I. A linear reduction in weight from the centre of the window to the edges characterizes the Bartlett window II, which trades ripple for an increase in transition-region width. At III is shown the Hann window, which is essentially a raised cosine shape. Not shown is the similar Hamming window, which offers a slightly different trade-off between ripple and the width of the main lobe. The Blackman window introduces an extra cosine term into the Hamming window at half the period of the main cosine period, reducing Gibb's phenomenon and ripple level, but increasing the width of the transition region. The Kaiser window is a family of windows based on the Bessel function, allowing various trade-offs between ripple ratio and main lobe width. Two of these are shown in IV and V.

The Dolph window[4] shown in Figure 3.12 results in an *equiripple filter* which has the advantage that the attenuation in the stopband never falls below a certain level.

Filter coefficients can be optimized by computer simulation. One of the best-known techniques used is the Remez exchange algorithm, which converges on the optimum coefficients after a number of iterations.

In the example of Figure 3.13, a low-pass FIR filter is shown which is intended to allow downsampling by a factor of two. The key feature is that the stopband must have begun before one half of the output sampling rate. This is most readily achieved using a Hamming window

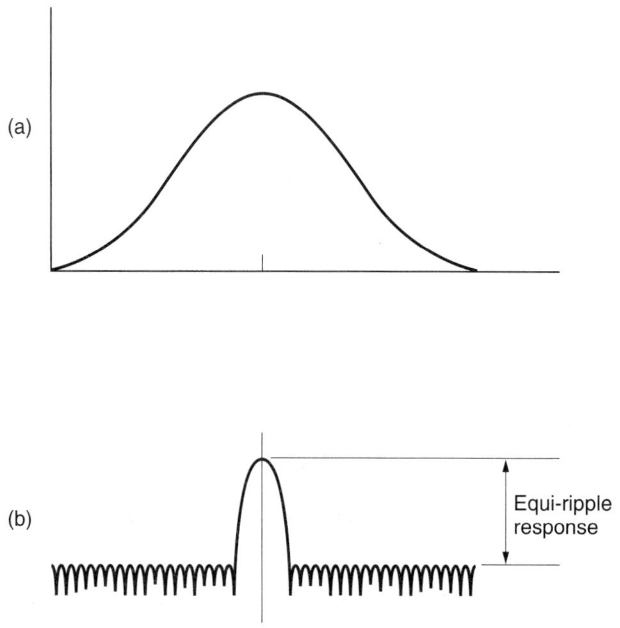

Figure 3.12 The Dolph window shape is shown at (a). The frequency response is at (b). Note the constant height of the response ripples.

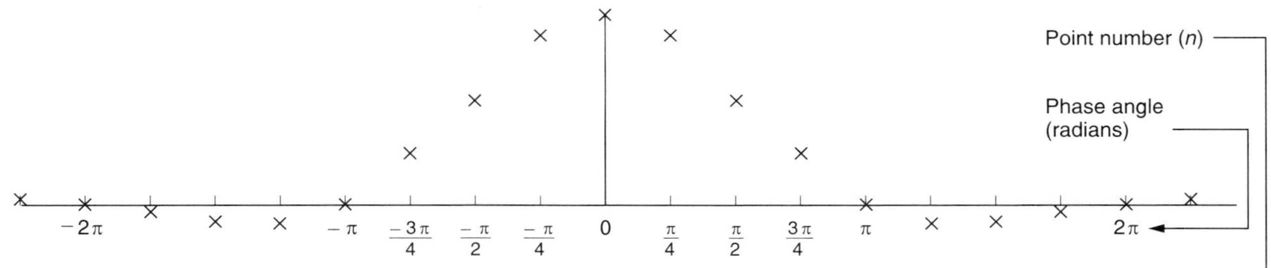

Point number (n)	0	1	2	3	4	5	6	7	8	9	10	11	12	13	14	15	16	17	18 (N)
sin x/x	0.1	0	−0.09	−0.21	−0.18	0	0.3	0.64	0.9	1	0.9	0.64	0.3	0	−0.18	−0.21	−0.09	0	0.1
Hamming window	0.08	0.11	0.19	0.31	0.46	0.62	0.77	0.89	0.97	1	0.97	0.89	0.77	0.62	0.46	0.31	0.19	0.11	0.08
Windowed response	0.01	0	−0.02	−0.07	−0.08	0	0.23	0.57	0.87	1	0.87	0.57	0.23	0	−0.08	−0.07	−0.02	0	0.01

Hamming window function $W = 0.54 - 0.46\cos\left(\frac{2\pi n}{N-1}\right)$

where n = point number, N (in this example) = 18

Figure 3.13 A downsampling filter using the Hamming window.

because it was designed empirically to have a flat stopband so that good aliasing attenuation is possible. The width of the transition band determines the number of significant sample periods embraced by the impulse. The Hamming window doubles the width of the transition band. This determines in turn both the number of points in the filter, and the filter delay. For the purposes of illustration, the number of points is much smaller than would normally be the case in an audio application.

As the impulse is symmetrical, the delay will be half the impulse period. The impulse response is a $\sin x/x$ function, and this has been calculated in the figure. The equation for the Hamming window function is shown with the window values which result. The $\sin x/x$ response is next multiplied by the Hamming window function to give the windowed impulse response shown.

If the coefficients are not quantized finely enough, it will be as if they had been calculated inaccurately, and the performance of the filter will be less than expected. Figure 3.14 shows an example of quantizing coefficients. Conversely, raising the wordlength of the coefficients increases cost.

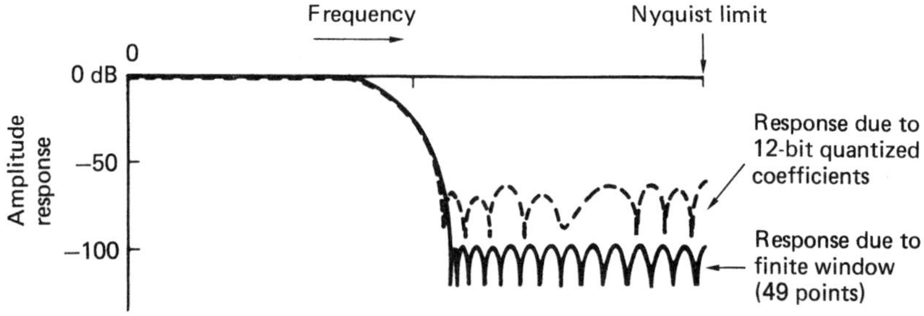

Figure 3.14 Frequency response of a 49-point transversal filter with infinite precision (solid line) shows ripple due to finite window size. Quantizing coefficients to twelve bits reduces attenuation in the stopband. (Responses courtesy *Philips Technical Review.*)

The FIR structure is inherently phase-linear because it is easy to make the impulse response absolutely symmetrical. The individual samples in a digital system do not know in isolation what frequency they represent, and they can only pass through the filter at a rate determined by the clock. Because of this inherent phase-linearity, a FIR filter can be designed for a specific impulse response, and the frequency response will follow.

The frequency response of the filter can be changed at will by changing the coefficients. A programmable filter only requires a series of PROMs to supply the coefficients; the address supplied to the PROMs will select the response. The frequency response of a digital filter will also change if the clock rate is changed, so it is often less ambiguous to specify a frequency of interest in a digital filter in terms of a fraction of the fundamental interval rather than in absolute terms. The configuration shown in Figure 3.9 serves to illustrate the principle. The units used on the diagrams are sample periods and the response is proportional to these periods or spacings, and so it is not necessary to use actual figures.

Where the impulse response is symmetrical, it is often possible to reduce the number of multiplications, because the same product can be used twice, at equal distances before and after the centre of the window. This is known as folding the filter. A folded filter is shown in Figure 3.15.

3.6 Sampling-rate conversion

Sampling-rate conversion or interpolation is an important enabling technology on which a large number of practical digital video devices are based. In digital video, the sampling rate takes on many guises. When analog video is sampled in real time, the sampling rate is temporal, but where pixels form a static array, the sampling rate is a spatial frequency.

Some of the applications of interpolation are set out below:

1 Video standards convertors need to change two of the sampling rates of the signal they handle, namely the temporal frame rate and the vertical line spacing, which is in fact a spatial sampling frequency. In some low-bit rate video applications such as Internet video, the frame rate may deliberately be reduced. The display will have to increase it again to avoid flicker.
2 In digital audio, different sampling rates exist today for different purposes. Rate conversion allows material to be exchanged freely between such formats.
3 To take advantage of oversampling convertors, an increase in sampling rate is necessary for DACs and a reduction in sampling rate is necessary for ADCs. In oversampling the factors by which the rates are changed are simpler than in other applications.
4 In image processing, a large number of different standard pixel array sizes exists. Changing between these formats may be necessary in order to view an incoming image on an available display. This technique is generally known as *resizing* and is essentially a two-dimensional sampling rate conversion. The rate in this case is the spatial frequency of the pixels.
5 Rate conversion allows interchange of real-time PCM data between systems whose sampling clocks are not synchronized.

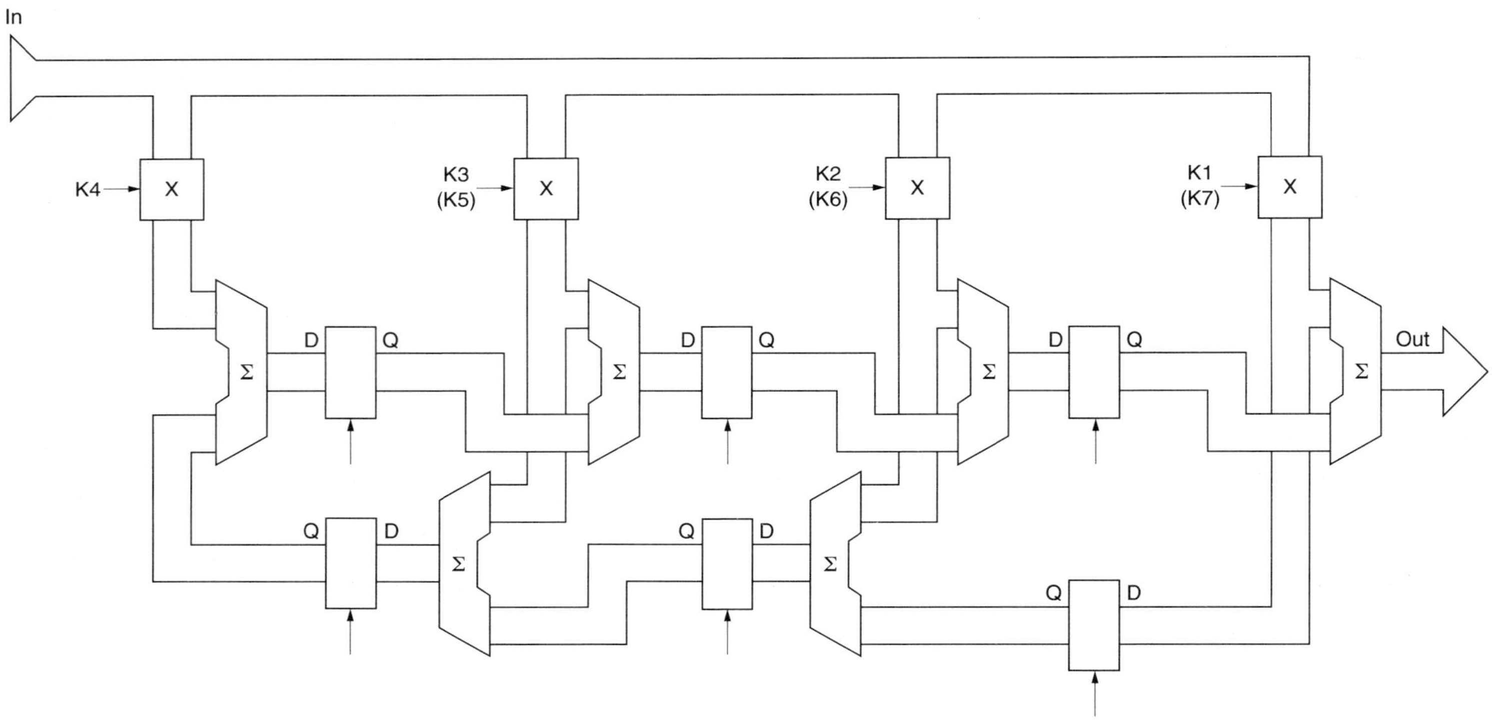

Figure 3.15 A seven-point folded filter for a symmetrical impulse response. In this case K1 and K7 will be identical, and so the input sample can be multiplied once, and the product fed into the output shift system in two different places. The centre coefficient K4 appears once. In an even-numbered filter the centre coefficient would also be used twice.

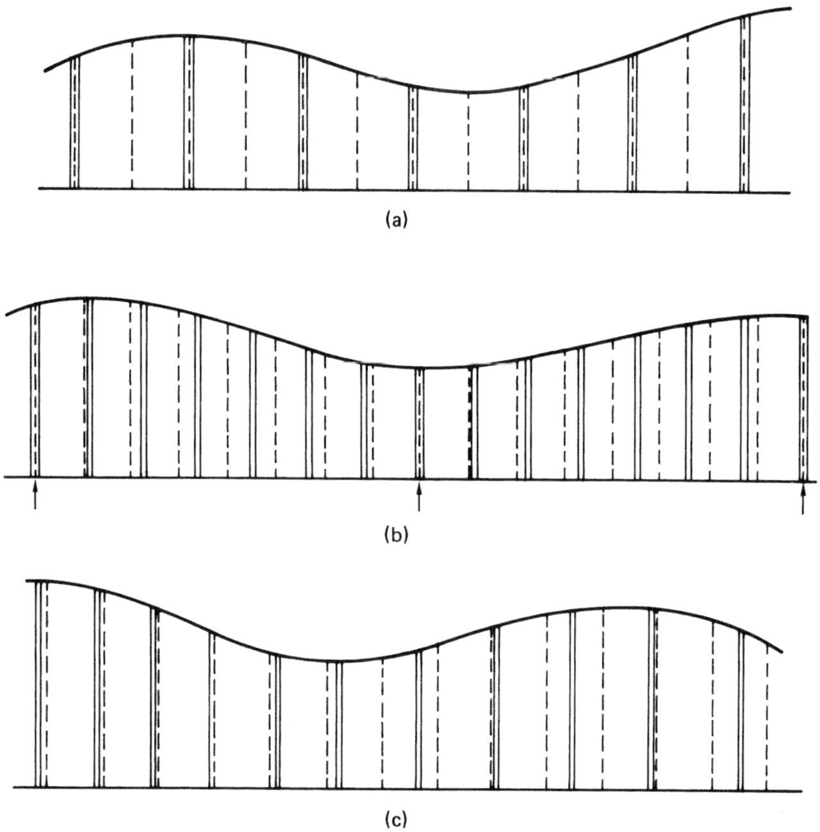

Figure 3.16 Categories of rate conversion. (a) Integer-ratio conversion, where the lower-rate samples are always coincident with those of the higher rate. There are a small number of phases needed. (b) Fractional-ratio conversion, where sample coincidence is periodic. A larger number of phases is required. Example here is conversion from 50.4 kHz to 44.1 kHz (8/7). (c) Variable-ratio conversion, where there is no fixed relationship, and a large number of phases are required.

There are three basic but related categories of rate conversion, as shown in Figure 3.16. The most straightforward (a) changes the rate by an integer ratio, up or down. The timing of the system is thus simplified because all samples (input and output) are present on edges of the higher-rate sampling clock. Such a system is generally adopted for oversampling convertors; the exact sampling rate immediately adjacent to the analog domain is not critical, and will be chosen to make the filters easier to implement.

Next in order of difficulty is the category shown at (b) where the rate is changed by the ratio of two small integers. Samples in the input periodically time-align with the output. Such devices can be used for converting between the various rates of ITU-601.

The most complex rate-conversion category is where there is no simple relationship between input and output sampling rates, and in fact they may vary. This situation shown at (c), is known as variable-ratio conversion. The temporal or spatial relationship of input and output samples is arbitrary. This problem will be met in effects machines which zoom or rotate images.

The technique of integer-ratio conversion is used in conjunction with oversampling convertors in digital video and audio and in motion estimation and compression systems where sub-sampled or reduced

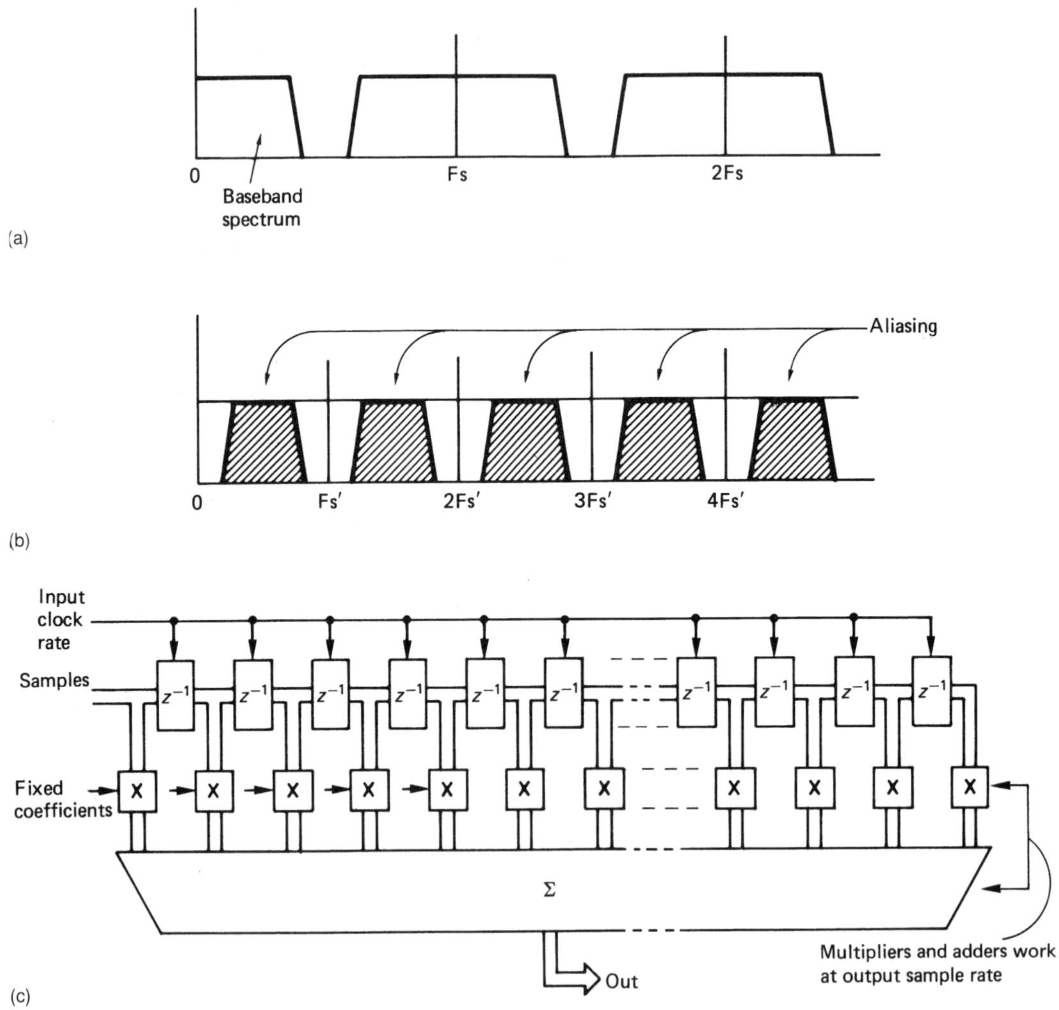

Figure 3.17 The spectrum of a typical digital sample stream at (a) will be subject to aliasing as in (b) if the baseband width is not reduced by an LPF. At (c) an FIR low-pass filter prevents aliasing. Samples are clocked transversely across the filter at the input rate, but the filter only computes at the output sample rate. Clearly this will only work if the two are related by an integer factor.

resolution versions of an input image are required. These applications will be detailed in Chapter 5.

Figure 3.17(a) shows the spectrum of a typical sampled system where the sampling rate is a little more than twice the analog bandwidth. Attempts to reduce the sampling rate by simply omitting samples, a process known as decimation, will result in aliasing, as shown in Figure 3.17(b). Intuitively it is obvious that omitting samples is the same as if the original sampling rate was lower. In order to prevent aliasing, it is necessary to incorporate low-pass filtering into the system where the cut-off frequency reflects the new, lower, sampling rate. An FIR type low-pass filter could be installed, as described earlier in this chapter, immediately prior to the stage where samples are omitted, but this would be wasteful, because for much of its time the FIR filter would be calculating sample values which are to be discarded. The more effective method is to combine the low-pass filter with the decimator so that the filter only calculates values to be retained in the output sample stream. Figure 3.17(c) shows how this is done. The filter makes one accumulation for every output sample, but that accumulation is the result of multiplying all relevant input samples in the filter window by an appropriate coefficient. The number of points in the filter is determined by the number of *input* samples in the period of the filter window, but the number of multiplications per second is obtained by multiplying that figure by the *output* rate. If the filter is not integrated with the decimator, the number of points has to be multiplied by the input rate. The larger the rate-reduction factor, the more advantageous the decimating filter ought to be, but this is not quite the case, as the greater the reduction in rate, the longer the filter window will need to be to accommodate the broader impulse response.

When the sampling rate is to be increased by an integer factor, additional samples must be created at even spacing between the existing ones. There is no need for the bandwidth of the input samples to be reduced since, if the original sampling rate was adequate, a higher one must also be adequate.

Figure 3.18 shows that the process of sampling-rate increase can be thought of in two stages. First, the correct rate is achieved by inserting samples of zero value at the correct instant, and then the additional samples are given meaningful values by passing the sample stream through a low-pass filter which cuts off at the Nyquist frequency of the original sampling rate. This filter is known as an interpolator, and one of its tasks is to prevent images of the lower input-sampling spectrum from appearing in the extended baseband of the higher-rate output spectrum.

All sampled systems have finite bandwidth and need a reconstruction filter to remove the frequencies above the baseband due to sampling.

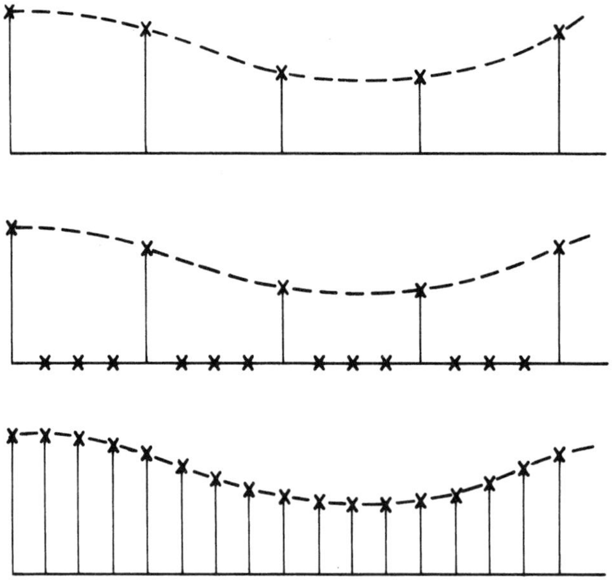

Figure 3.18 In integer-ratio sampling, rate increase can be obtained in two stages. First, zero-value samples are inserted to increase the rate, and then filtering is used to give the extra samples real values. The filter necessary will be an LPF with a response which cuts off at the Nyquist frequency of the input samples.

After reconstruction, one infinitely short digital sample ideally represents a $\sin x/x$ pulse whose central peak width is determined by the response of the reconstruction filter, and whose amplitude is proportional to the sample value. This implies that, in reality, one sample value has meaning over a considerable timespan, rather than just at the sample instant. This will be detailed in Chapter 4. Were this not true, it would be impossible to build an interpolator.

Performing the steps of rate increase separately is inefficient. The bandwidth of the information is unchanged when the sampling rate is increased; therefore the original input samples will pass through the filter unchanged, and it is superfluous to compute them. The combination of the two processes into an interpolating filter minimizes the amount of computation.

As the purpose of the system is purely to increase the sampling rate, the filter must be as transparent as possible, and this implies that a linear-phase configuration is mandatory, suggesting the use of an FIR structure. Figure 3.19 shows that the theoretical impulse response of such a filter is a $\sin x/x$ curve which has zero value at the position of adjacent input samples. In practice this impulse cannot be implemented because it is infinite. The impulse response used will be truncated and windowed as described earlier. To simplify this discussion, assume that a $\sin x/x$ impulse is to be used. There is a strong parallel with the operation of a

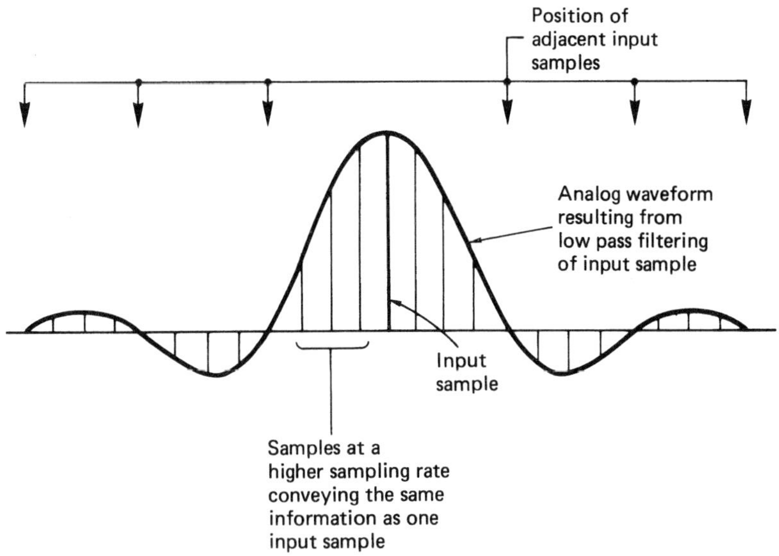

Figure 3.19 A single sample results in a sinx/x waveform after filtering in the analog domain. At a new, higher, sampling rate, the same waveform after filtering will be obtained if the numerous samples of differing size shown here are used. It follows that the values of these new samples can be calculated from the input samples in the digital domain in an FIR filter.

DAC where the analog voltage is returned to the time-continuous state by summing the analog impulses due to each sample. In a digital interpolating filter, this process is duplicated.[5]

If the sampling rate is to be doubled, new samples must be interpolated exactly halfway between existing samples. The necessary impulse response is shown in Figure 3.20; it can be sampled at the *output* sample period and quantized to form coefficients. If a single input sample is multiplied by each of these coefficients in turn, the impulse response of that sample at the new sampling rate will be obtained. Note that every other coefficient is zero, which confirms that no computation is necessary on the existing samples; they are just transferred to the output. The intermediate sample is computed by adding together the impulse responses of every input sample in the window. The figure shows how this mechanism operates. If the sampling rate is to be increased by a factor of four, three sample values must be interpolated between existing input samples. Figure 3.21 shows that it is only necessary to sample the impulse response at one-quarter the period of input samples to obtain three sets of coefficients which will be used in turn. In hardware-implemented filters, the input sample which is passed straight to the output is transferred by using a fourth filter phase where all coefficients are zero except the central one which is unity.

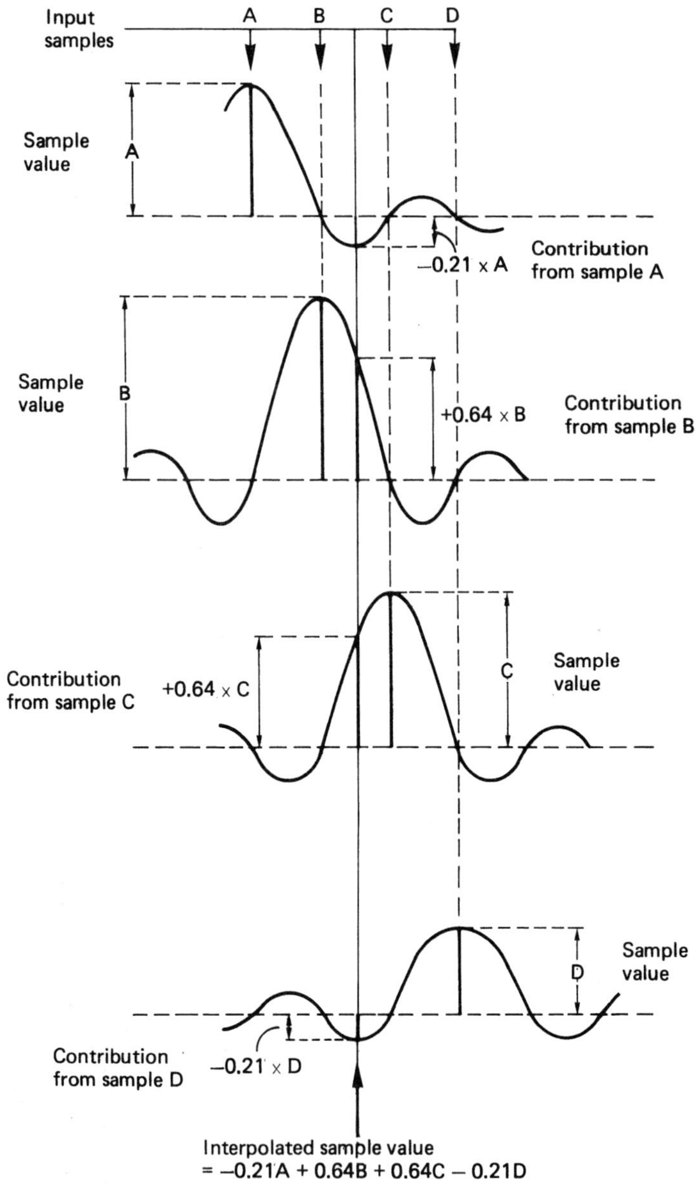

Figure 3.20 A two times oversampling interpolator. To compute an intermediate sample, the input samples are imagined to be $\sin x/x$ impulses, and the contributions from each at the point of interest can be calculated. In practice, rather more samples on either side need to be taken into account.

Fractional ratio conversion allows interchange between different images having different pixel array sizes. Fractional ratios also occur in the vertical axis of standards convertors. Figure 3.16 showed that when the two sampling rates have a simple fractional relationship m/n, there is a

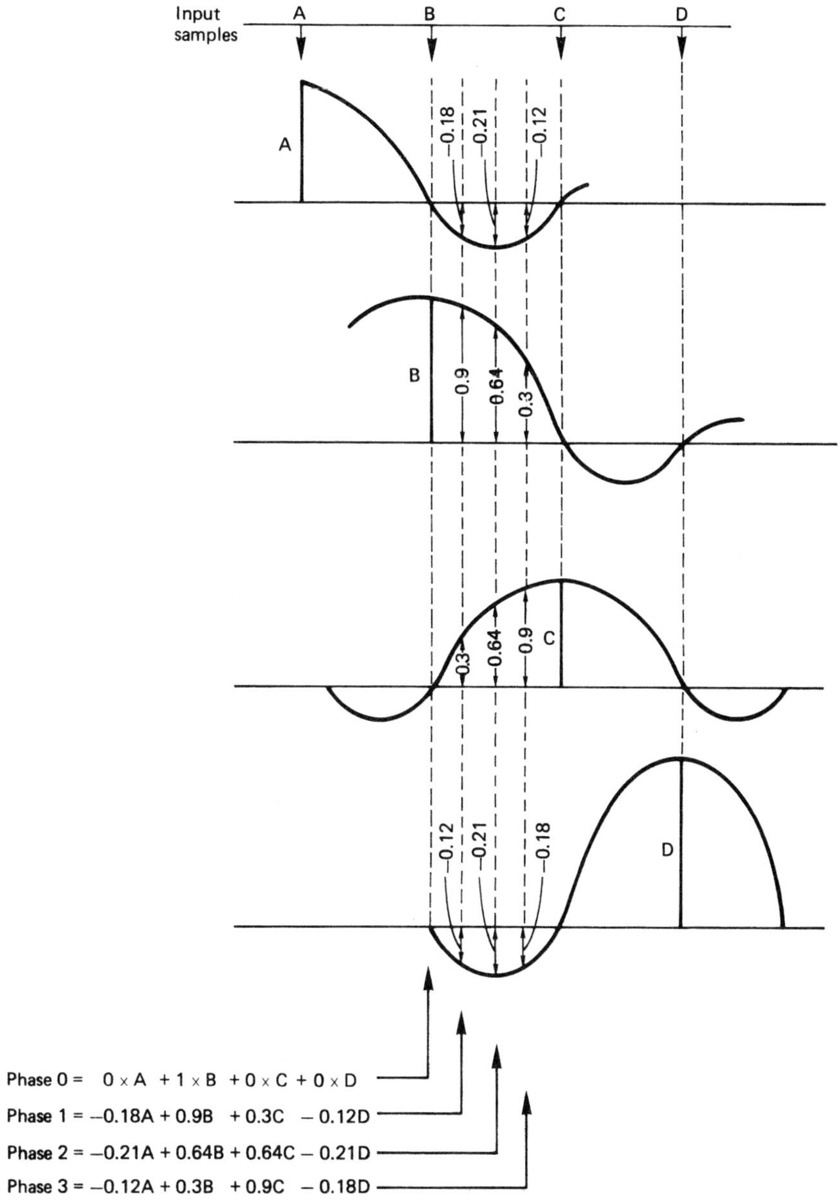

Figure 3.21 In 4× oversampling, for each set of input samples, four phases of coefficients are necessary, each of which produces one of the oversampled values.

periodicity in the relationship between samples in the two streams. It is possible to have a system clock running at the least-common multiple frequency which will divide by different integers to give each sampling rate.[6]

The existence of a common clock frequency means that a fractional-ratio convertor could be made by arranging two integer-ratio converters in

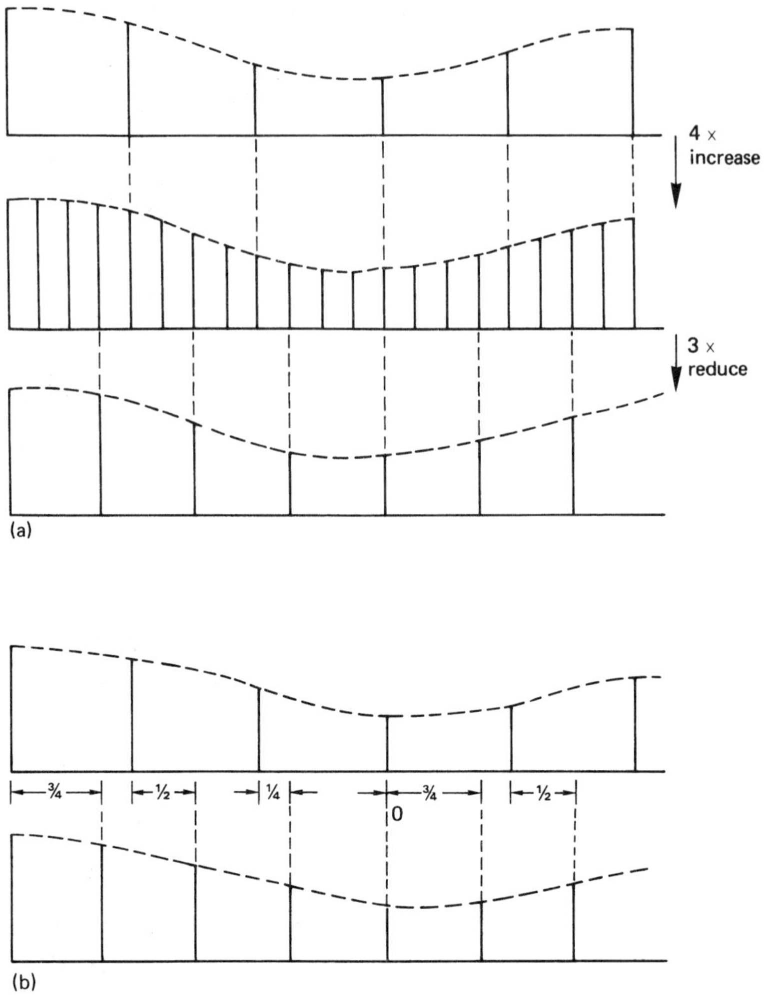

Figure 3.22 At (a), fractional-ratio conversion of 3/4 in this example is by increasing to 4× input prior to reducing by 3×. The inefficiency due to discarding previously computed values is clear. At (b), efficiency is raised since only needed values will be computed. Note how the interpolation phase changes for each output. Fixed coefficients can no longer be used.

series. This configuration is shown in Figure 3.22(a). The input-sampling rate is multiplied by m in an interpolator, and the result is divided by n in a decimator. Although this system would work, it would be grossly inefficient, because only one in n of the interpolator's outputs would be used. A decimator followed by an interpolator would also offer the correct sampling rate at the output, but the intermediate sampling rate would be so low that the system bandwidth would be quite unacceptable.

As has been seen, a more efficient structure results from combining the processes. The result is exactly the same structure as an integer-ratio interpolator, and requires an FIR filter. The impulse response of the filter is determined by the lower of the two sampling rates, and, as before, it prevents aliasing when the rate is being reduced, and prevents images when the rate is being increased. The interpolator has sufficient coefficient phases to interpolate m output samples for every input sample, but not all of these values are computed; only interpolations which coincide with an output sample are performed. It will be seen in Figure 3.22(b) that input samples shift across the transversal filter at the input sampling rate, but interpolations are only performed at the output sample rate. This is possible because a different filter phase will be used at each interpolation.

In the previous examples, the sample rate or spacing of the filter output had a constant relationship to the input, which meant that the two rates had to be phase-locked. This is an undesirable constraint in some applications, including image manipulators. In a variable-ratio interpolator, values will exist for the points at which input samples were made, but it is necessary to compute what the sample values would have been at absolutely any point between available samples. The general concept of the interpolator is the same as for the fractional-ratio convertor, except that an infinite number of filter phases is ideally necessary. Since a realizable filter will have a finite number of phases, it is necessary to study the degradation this causes. The desired continuous temporal or spatial axis of the interpolator is quantized by the phase spacing, and a sample value needed at a particular point will be replaced by a value for the nearest available filter phase. The number of phases in the filter therefore determines the accuracy of the interpolation. The effects of calculating a value for the wrong point are identical to those of sampling with clock jitter, in that an error occurs proportional to the slope of the signal. The result is program-modulated noise. The higher the noise specification, the greater the desired time accuracy and the greater the number of phases required. The number of phases is equal to the number of sets of coefficients available, and should not be confused with the number of points in the filter, which is equal to the number of coefficients in a set (and the number of multiplications needed to calculate one output value).

The sampling jitter accuracy necessary for eight-bit working is measured in picoseconds. This implies that something like 32 filter phases will be required for adequate performance in an eight-bit sampling-rate convertor.

3.7 Transforms and duality

The duality of transforms provides an interesting insight into what is happening in common processes. Fourier analysis holds that any periodic waveform can be reproduced by adding together an arbitrary number of

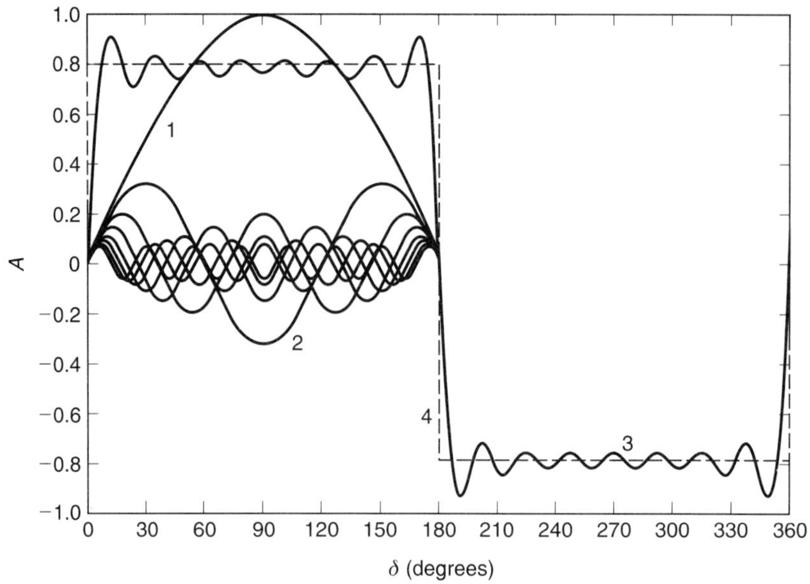

Figure 3.23 Fourier analysis of a square wave into fundamental and harmonics. *A*, amplitude; δ, phase of fundamental wave in degrees; 1, first harmonic (fundamental); 2, odd harmonics 3–15; 3, sum of harmonics 1–15; 4, ideal square wave.

harmonically related sinusoids of various amplitudes and phases. Figure 3.23 shows how a square wave can be built up of harmonics. The spectrum can be drawn by plotting the amplitude of the harmonics against frequency. It will be seen that this gives a spectrum which is a decaying wave. It passes through zero at all even multiples of the fundamental. The shape of the spectrum is a $\sin x/x$ curve. If a square wave has a $\sin x/x$ spectrum, it follows that a filter with a rectangular impulse response will have a $\sin x/x$ spectrum.

A low-pass filter has a rectangular spectrum, and this has a $\sin x/x$ impulse response. These characteristics are known as a transform pair. In transform pairs, if one domain has one shape of the pair, the other domain will have the other shape. Figure 3.24 shows a number of transform pairs.

At (a) a squarewave has a $\sin x/x$ spectrum and a $\sin x/x$ impulse has a square spectrum. In general the product of equivalent parameters on either side of a transform remains constant, so that if one increases, the other must fall. If (a) shows a filter with a wider bandwidth, having a narrow impulse response, then (b) shows a filter of narrower bandwidth which has a wide impulse response. This is duality in action. The limiting case of this behaviour is where one parameter becomes zero, the other goes to infinity. At (c) a time-domain pulse of infinitely short duration has a flat spectrum. Thus a flat waveform, i.e. DC, has only zero in its

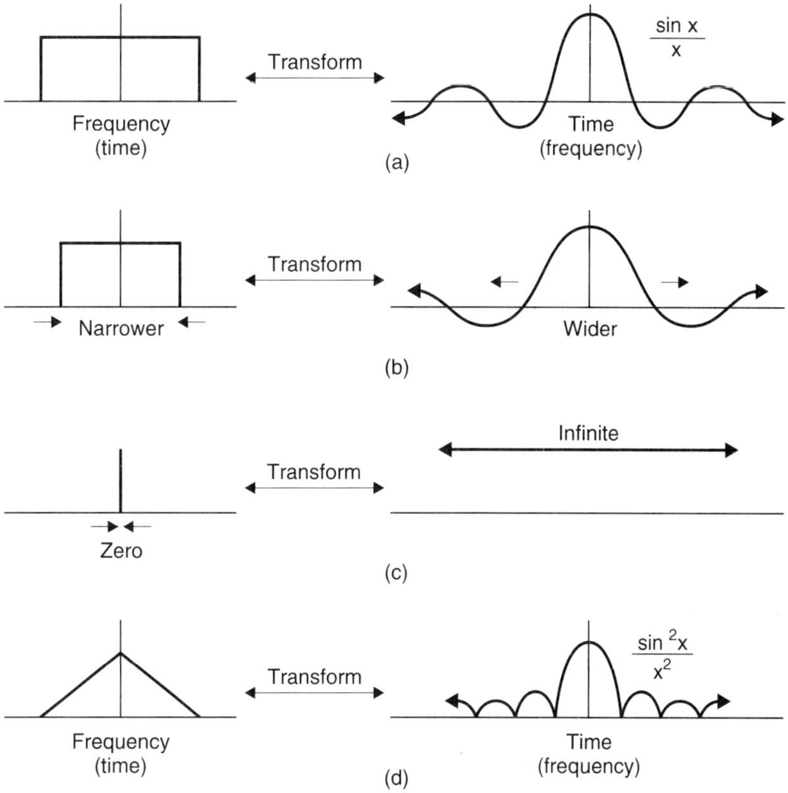

Figure 3.24 Transform pairs. At (a) the dual of a rectangle is a $\sin x/x$ function. If one is time domain, the other is frequency domain. At (b), narrowing one domain widens the other. The limiting case of this is (c). Transform of the $\sin x/x$ squared function is triangular.

spectrum. The impulse response of the optics of a laser disk (d) has a $\sin^2 x/x^2$ intensity function, and this is responsible for the triangular falling frequency response of the pickup. The lens is a rectangular aperture, but as there is no such thing as negative light, a $\sin x/x$ impulse response is impossible. The squaring process is consistent with a positive-only impulse response. Interestingly the transform of a Gaussian response in still Gaussian.

Duality also holds for sampled systems. A sampling process is periodic in the time domain. This results in a spectrum which is periodic in the frequency domain. If the time between the samples is reduced, the bandwidth of the system rises. Figure 3.25(a) shows that a continuous time signal has a continuous spectrum whereas at (b) the frequency transform of a sampled signal is also discrete. In other words sampled signals can only be analysed into a finite number of frequencies. The more accurate the frequency analysis has to be, the more samples are needed in the block. Making the block longer reduces the ability to locate a transient

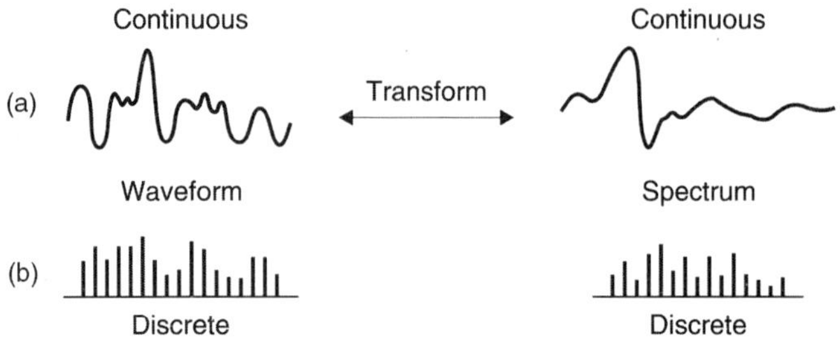

Figure 3.25 Continuous time signal (a) has continuous spectrum. Discrete time signal (b) has discrete spectrum.

in time. This is the Heisenberg inequality which is the limiting case of duality, because when infinite accuracy is achieved in one domain, there is no accuracy at all in the other.

3.8 The Fourier transform

Figure 3.23 showed that if the amplitude and phase of each frequency component is known, linearly adding the resultant components in an inverse transform results in the original waveform. In digital systems the waveform is expressed as a number of discrete samples. As a result the Fourier transform analyses the signal into an equal number of discrete frequencies. This is known as a discrete Fourier transform or DFT in which the number of frequency coefficients is equal to the number of input samples. The fast Fourier transform is no more than an efficient way of computing the DFT.[7] As was seen in the previous section, practical systems must use windowing to create short-term transforms.

It will be evident from Figure 3.26 that the knowledge of the phase of the frequency component is vital, as changing the phase of any component will seriously alter the reconstructed waveform. Thus the DFT must accurately analyse the phase of the signal components.

There are a number of ways of expressing phase. Figure 3.27 shows a point which is rotating about a fixed axis at constant speed. Looked at from the side, the point oscillates up and down at constant frequency. The waveform of that motion is a sine wave, and that is what we would see if the rotating point were to translate along its axis whilst we continued to look from the side.

One way of defining the phase of a waveform is to specify the angle through which the point has rotated at time zero ($T = 0$). If a second point is made to revolve at 90° to the first, it would produce a cosine wave when translated. It is possible to produce a waveform having arbitrary phase by adding together the sine and cosine waves in various

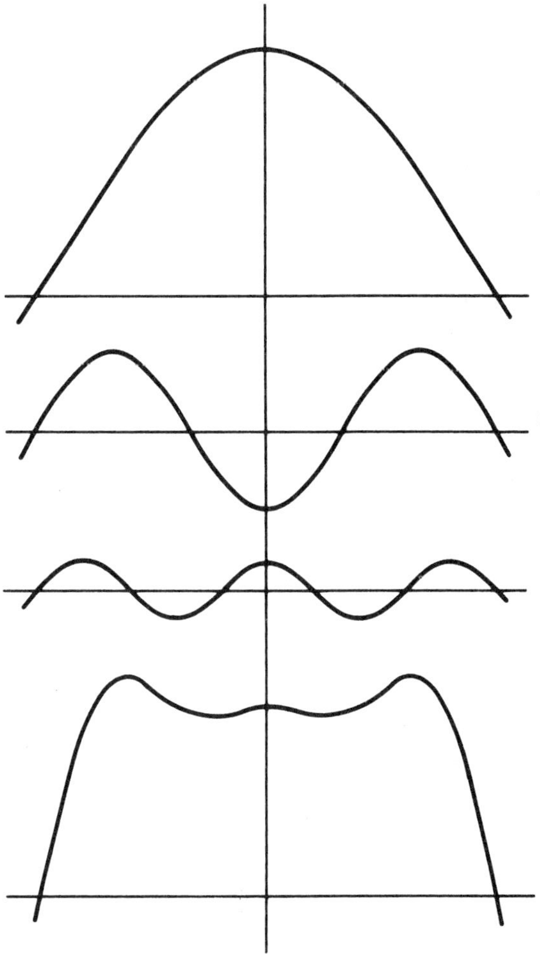

Figure 3.26 Fourier analysis allows the synthesis of any waveform by the addition of discrete frequencies of appropriate amplitude and phase.

proportions and polarities. For example, adding the sine and cosine waves in equal proportions results in a waveform lagging the sine wave by 45°.

Figure 3.27 shows that the proportions necessary are respectively the sine and the cosine of the phase angle. Thus the two methods of describing phase can be readily interchanged.

The discrete Fourier transform spectrum-analyses a string of samples by searching separately for each discrete target frequency. It does this by multiplying the input waveform by a sine wave, known as the basis function, having the target frequency and adding up or integrating the products. Figure 3.28(a) shows that multiplying by basis functions gives a non-zero integral when the input frequency is the same, whereas (b)

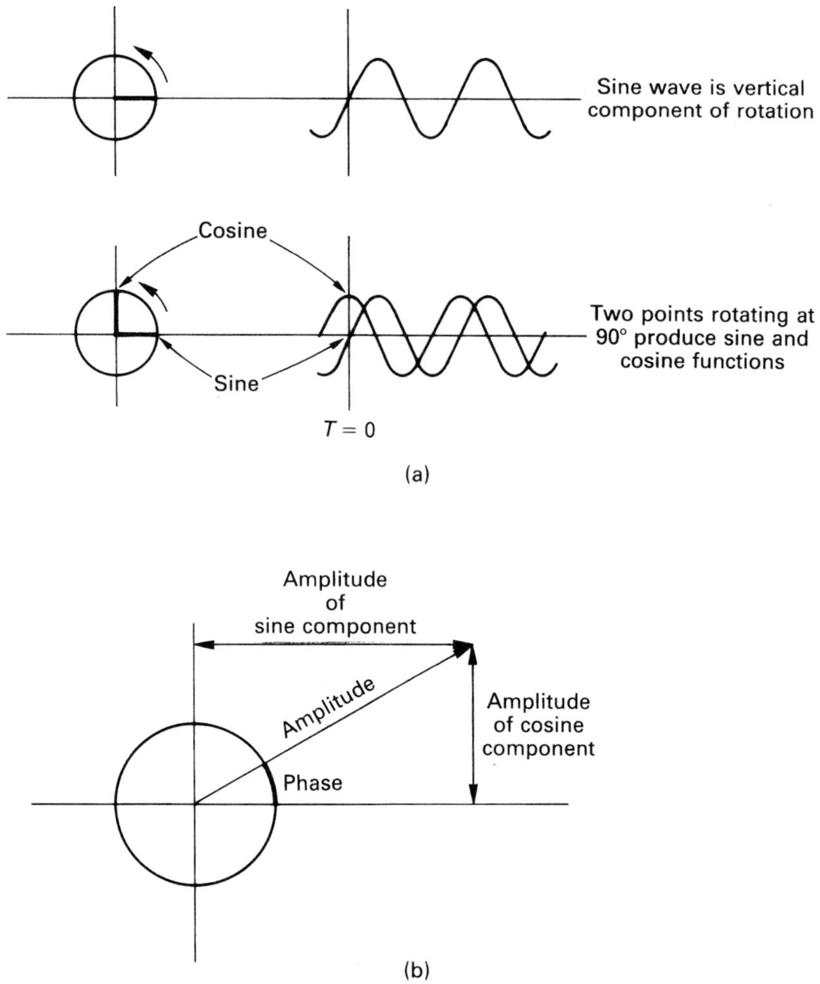

Figure 3.27 The origin of sine and cosine waves is to take a particular viewpoint of a rotation. Any phase can be synthesized by adding proportions of sine and cosine waves.

shows that with a different input frequency (in fact all other different frequencies) the integral is zero showing that no component of the target frequency exists. Thus from a real waveform containing many frequencies all frequencies except the target frequency are excluded. The magnitude of the integral is proportional to the amplitude of the target component.

Figure 3.28(c) shows that the target frequency will not be detected if it is phase shifted 90° as the product of quadrature waveforms is always zero. Thus the discrete Fourier transform must make a further search for the target frequency using a cosine basis function. It follows from the arguments above that the relative proportions of the sine and cosine integrals reveal the phase of the input component. Thus each discrete

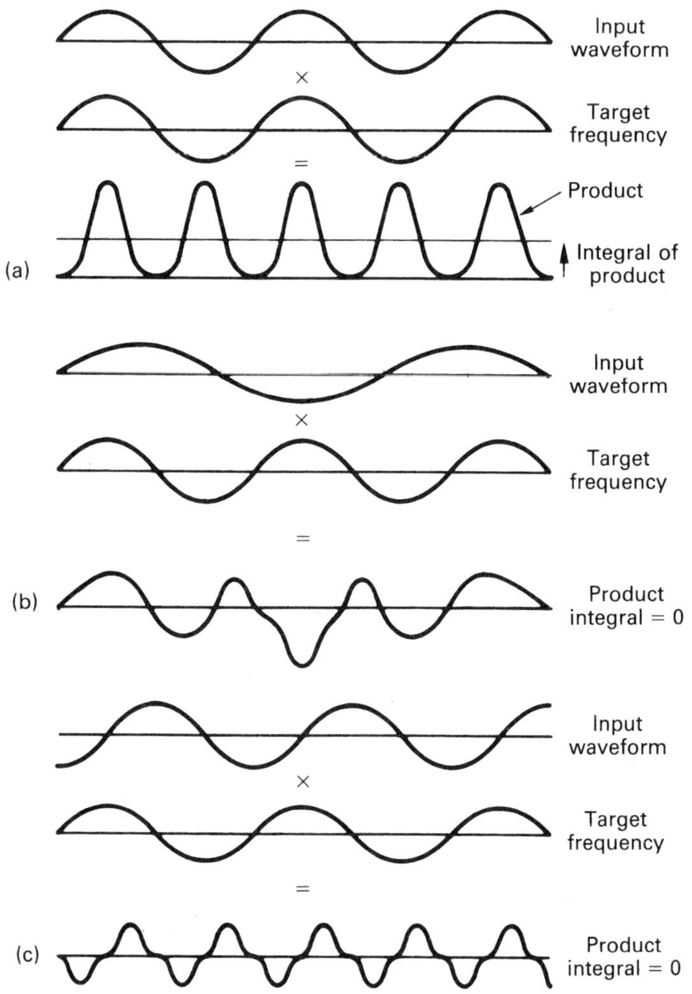

Figure 3.28 The input waveform is multiplied by the target frequency and the result is averaged or integrated. At (a) the target frequency is present and a large integral results. With another input frequency the integral is zero as at (b). The correct frequency will also result in a zero integral shown at (c) if it is at 90° to the phase of the search frequency. This is overcome by making two searches in quadrature.

frequency in the spectrum must be the result of a pair of quadrature searches.

Searching for one frequency at a time as above will result in a DFT, but only after considerable computation. However, a lot of the calculations are repeated many times over in different searches. The fast Fourier transform gives the same result with less computation by logically gathering together all the places where the same calculation is needed and making the calculation once.

The amount of computation can be reduced by performing the sine and cosine component searches together. Another saving is obtained by noting that every 180° the sine and cosine have the same magnitude but are simply inverted in sign. Instead of performing four multiplications on two samples 180° apart and adding the pairs of products it is more economical to subtract the sample values and multiply twice, once by a sine value and once by a cosine value.

The first coefficient is the arithmetic mean which is the sum of all the sample values in the block divided by the number of samples. Figure 3.29

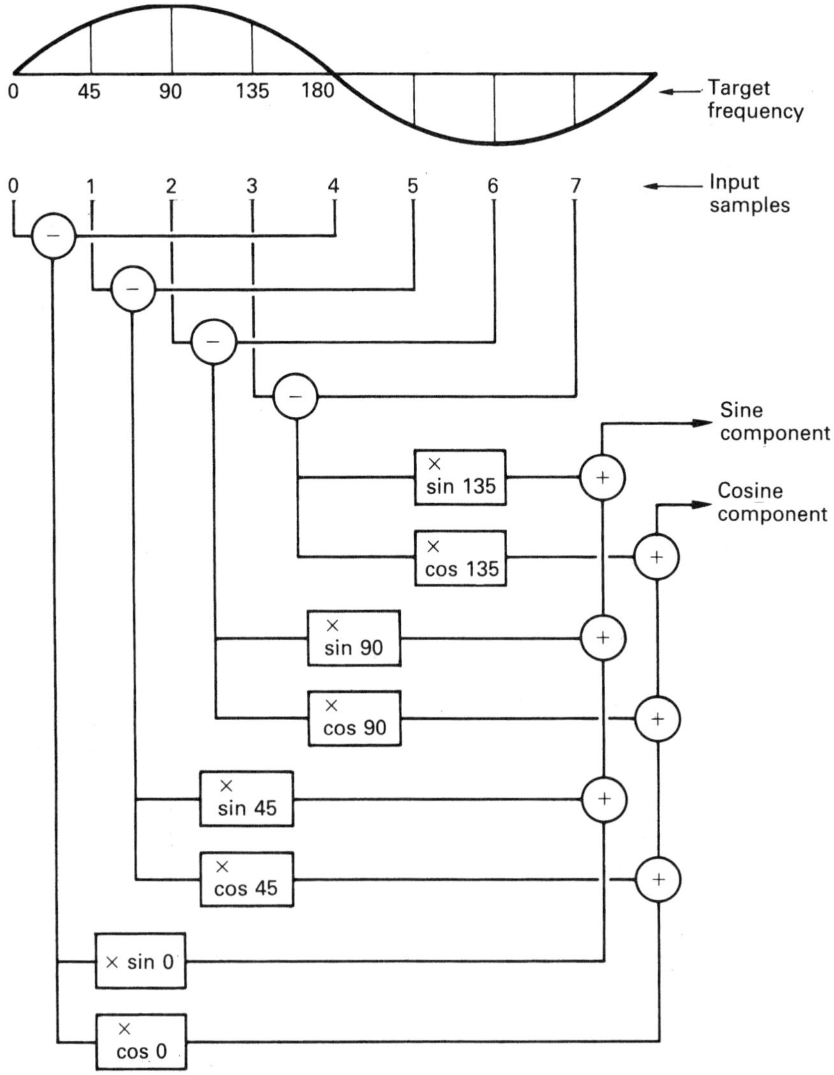

Figure 3.29 An example of a filtering search. Pairs of samples are subtracted and multiplied by sampled sine and cosine waves. The products are added to give the sine and cosine components of the search frequency.

shows how the search for the lowest frequency in a block is performed. Pairs of samples are subtracted as shown, and each difference is then multiplied by the sine and the cosine of the search frequency. The process shifts one sample period, and a new sample pair is subtracted and multiplied by new sine and cosine factors. This is repeated until all the sample pairs have been multiplied. The sine and cosine products are then added to give the value of the sine and cosine coefficients respectively.

It is possible to combine the calculation of the DC component which requires the sum of samples and the calculation of the fundamental which requires sample differences by combining stages shown in Figure 3.30(a) which take a pair of samples and add and subtract them. Such a stage is called a butterfly because of the shape of the schematic. Figure 3.30(b)

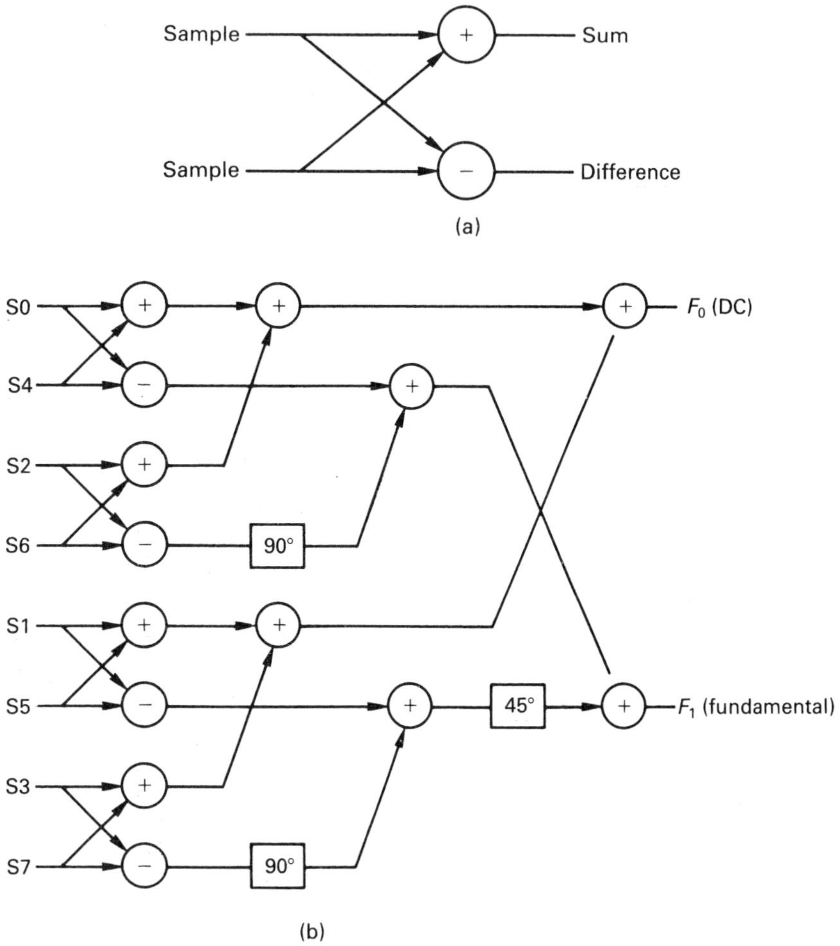

Figure 3.30 The basic element of an FFT is known as a butterfly as at (a) because of the shape of the signal paths in a sum and difference system. The use of butterflies to compute the first two coefficients is shown in (b).

shows how the first two components are calculated. The phase rotation boxes attribute the input to the sine or cosine component outputs according to the phase angle. As shown, the box labelled 90° attributes nothing to the sine output, but unity gain to the cosine output. The 45° box attributes the input equally to both components.

Figure 3.30(c) shows a numerical example. If a sinewave input is considered where zero degrees coincides with the first sample, this will produce a zero sine coefficient and non-zero cosine coefficient. Figure 3.30(d) shows the same input waveform shifted by 90°. Note how the coefficients change over.

Figure 3.30(e) shows how the next frequency coefficient is computed. Note that exactly the same first-stage butterfly outputs are used, reducing the computation needed.

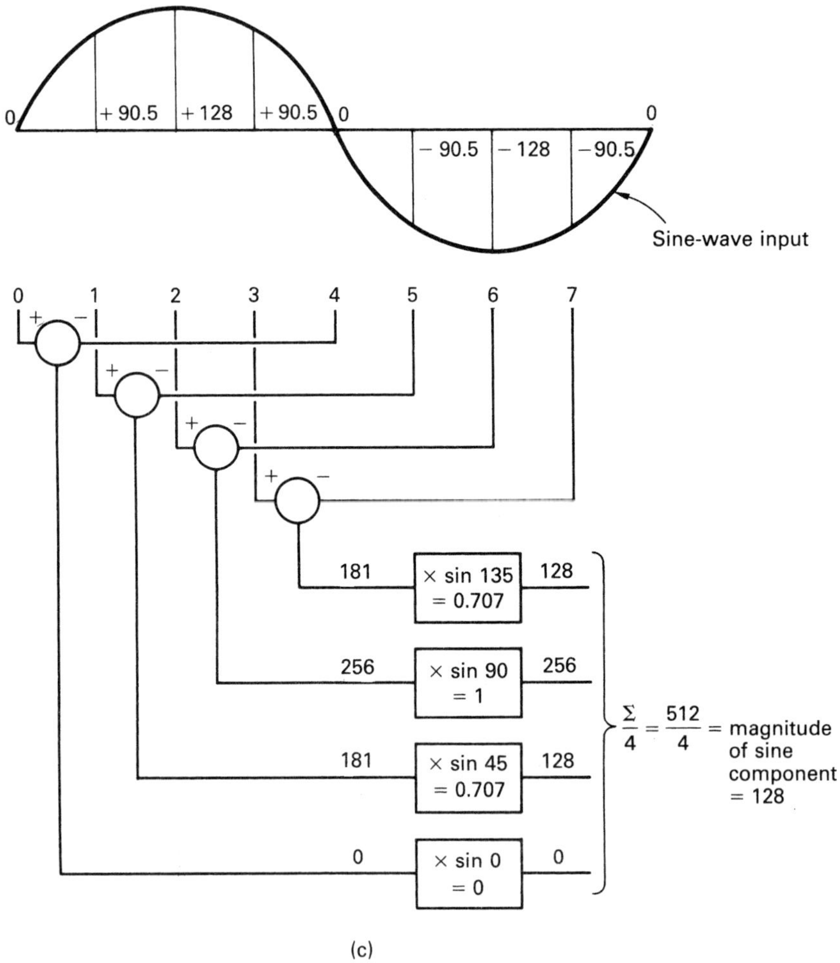

Figure 3.30(c) An actual calculation of a sine coefficient. This should be compared with the result shown in (d).

A similar process may be followed to obtain the sine and cosine coefficients of the remaining frequencies. The full FFT diagram for eight samples is shown in Figure 3.31(a). The spectrum this calculates is shown in (b). Note that only half of the coefficients are useful in a real band-limited system because the remaining coefficients represent frequencies above one half of the sampling rate.

In STFTs the overlapping input sample blocks must be multiplied by window functions. The principle is the same as for the application in FIR filters shown in section 3.5. Figure 3.32 shows that multiplying the search frequency by the window has exactly the same result except that this need be done only once and much computation is saved. Thus in the STFT the basis function is a windowed sine or cosine wave.

The FFT is used extensively in such applications as phase correlation, where the accuracy with which the phase of signal components can be

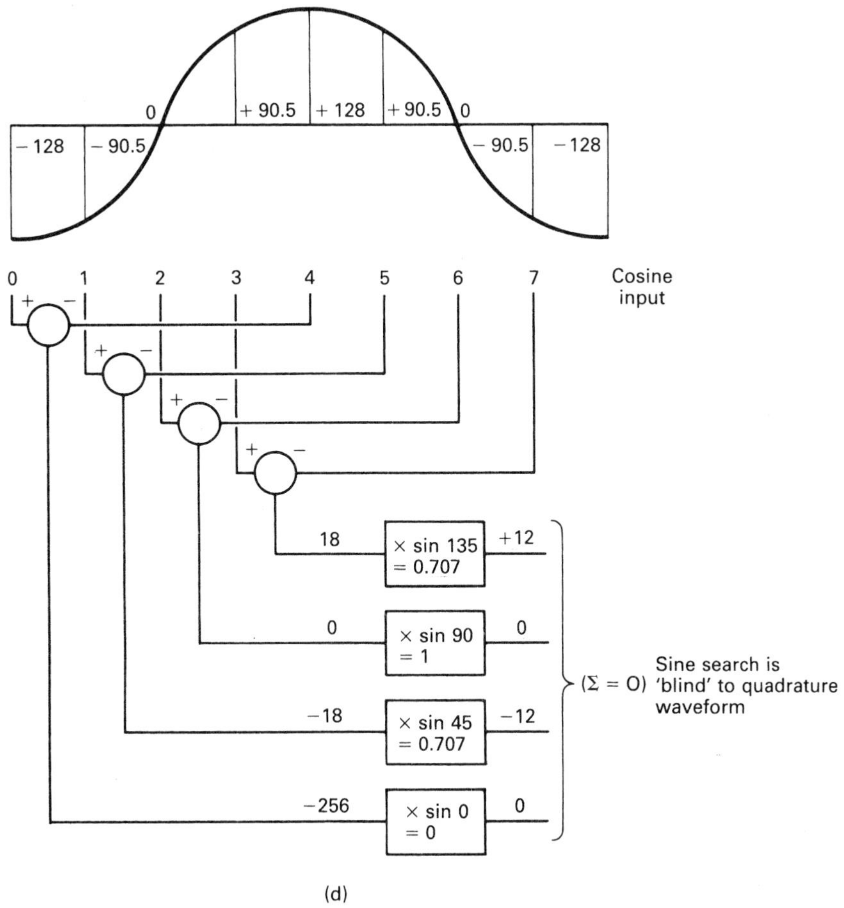

Figure 3.30(d) With a quadrature input the frequency is not seen.

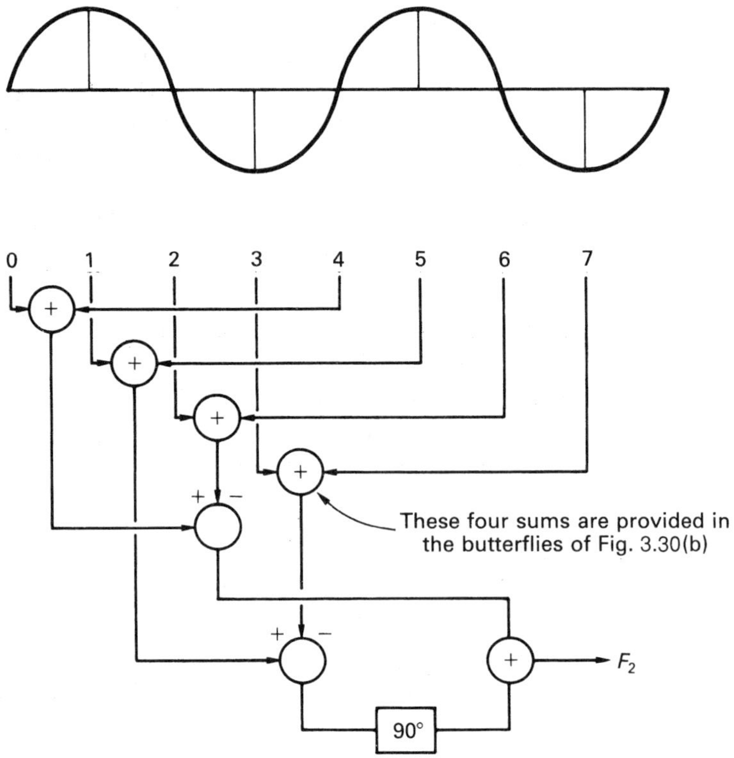

(e)

Figure 3.30(e) The butterflies used for the first coefficients form the basis of the computation of the next coefficient.

analysed is essential. It also forms the foundation of the discrete cosine transform.

3.9 The discrete cosine transform (DCT)

The DCT is a special case of a discrete Fourier transform in which the sine components of the coefficients have been eliminated leaving a single number. This is actually quite easy. Figure 3.33(a) shows a block of input samples to a transform process. By repeating the samples in a time-reversed order and performing a discrete Fourier transform on the double-length sample set a DCT is obtained. The effect of mirroring the input waveform is to turn it into an even function whose sine coefficients are all zero. The result can be understood by considering the effect of individually transforming the input block and the reversed block.

Figure 3.33(b) shows that the phase of all the components of one block are in the opposite sense to those in the other. This means that when the

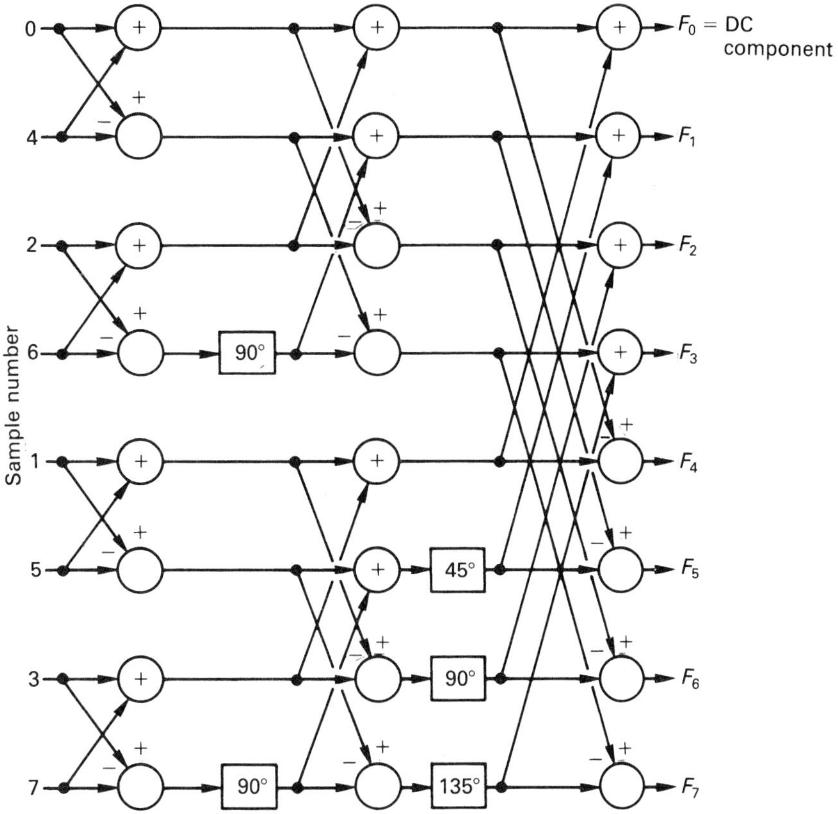

(a)

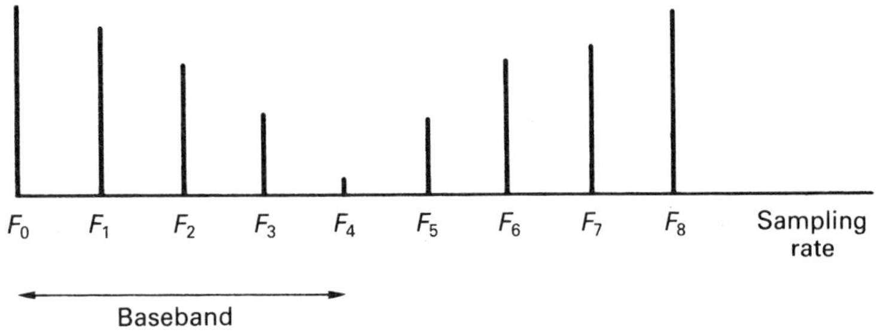

(b)

Figure 3.31 At (a) is the full butterfly diagram for an FFT. The spectrum this computes is shown at (b).

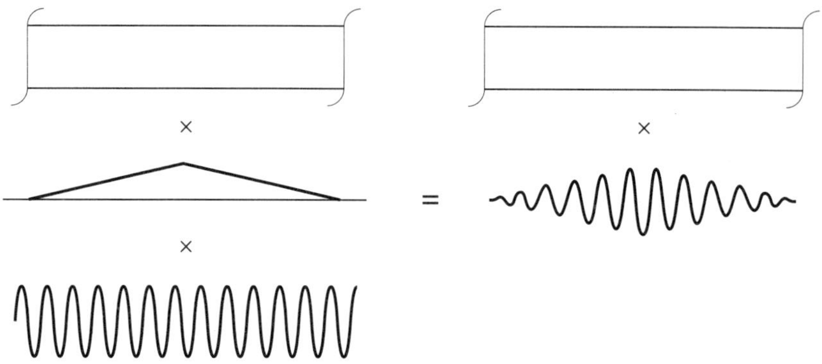

Figure 3.32 Multiplication of a windowed block by a sine wave basis function is the same as multiplying the raw data by a windowed basis function but requires less multiplication as the basis function is constant and can be precomputed.

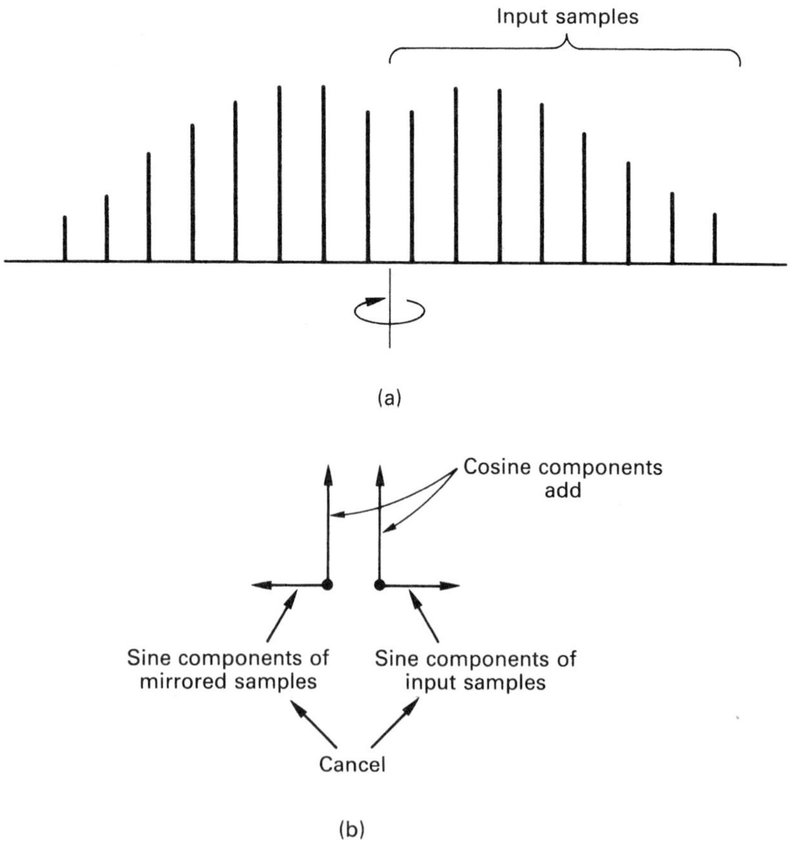

Figure 3.33 The DCT is obtained by mirroring the input block as shown at (a) prior to an FFT. The mirroring cancels out the sine components as at (b), leaving only cosine coefficients.

components are added to give the transform of the double length block all the sine components cancel out, leaving only the cosine coefficients, hence the name of the transform.[8] In practice the sine component calculation is eliminated. Another advantage is that doubling the block length by mirroring doubles the frequency resolution, so that twice as many useful coefficients are produced. In fact a DCT produces as many useful coefficients as input samples.

For image processing two-dimensional transforms are needed. In this case for every horizontal frequency, a search is made for all possible vertical frequencies. A two-dimensional DCT is shown in Figure 3.34. The DCT is separable in that the two-dimensional DCT can be obtained by computing in each dimension separately. Fast DCT algorithms are available.[9]

Figure 3.35 shows how a two-dimensional DCT is calculated by multiplying each pixel in the input block by terms which represent sampled cosine waves of various spatial frequencies. A given DCT coefficient is obtained when the result of multiplying every input pixel in the block is summed. Although most compression systems, including JPEG and MPEG, use square DCT blocks, this is not a necessity and

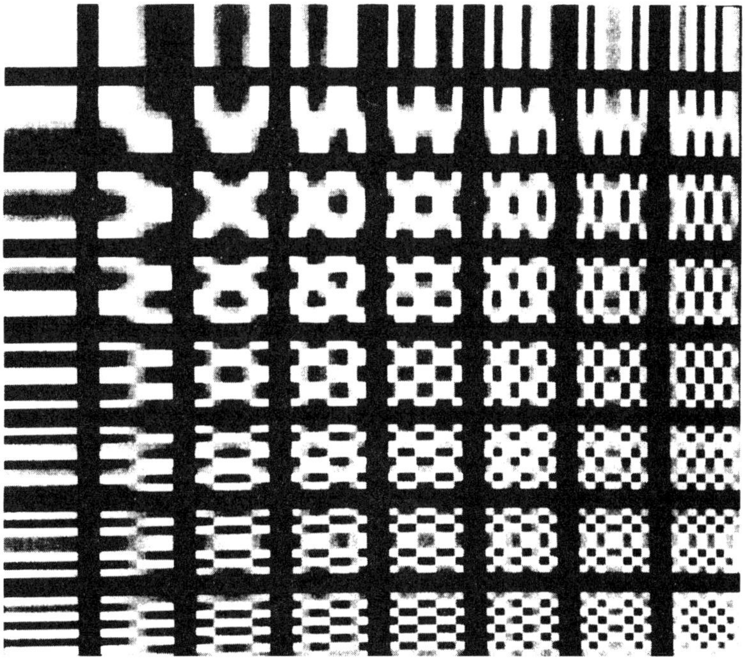

Figure 3.34 The discrete cosine transform breaks up an image area into discrete frequencies in two dimensions. The lowest frequency can be seen here at the top left corner. Horizontal frequency increases to the right and vertical frequency increases downwards.

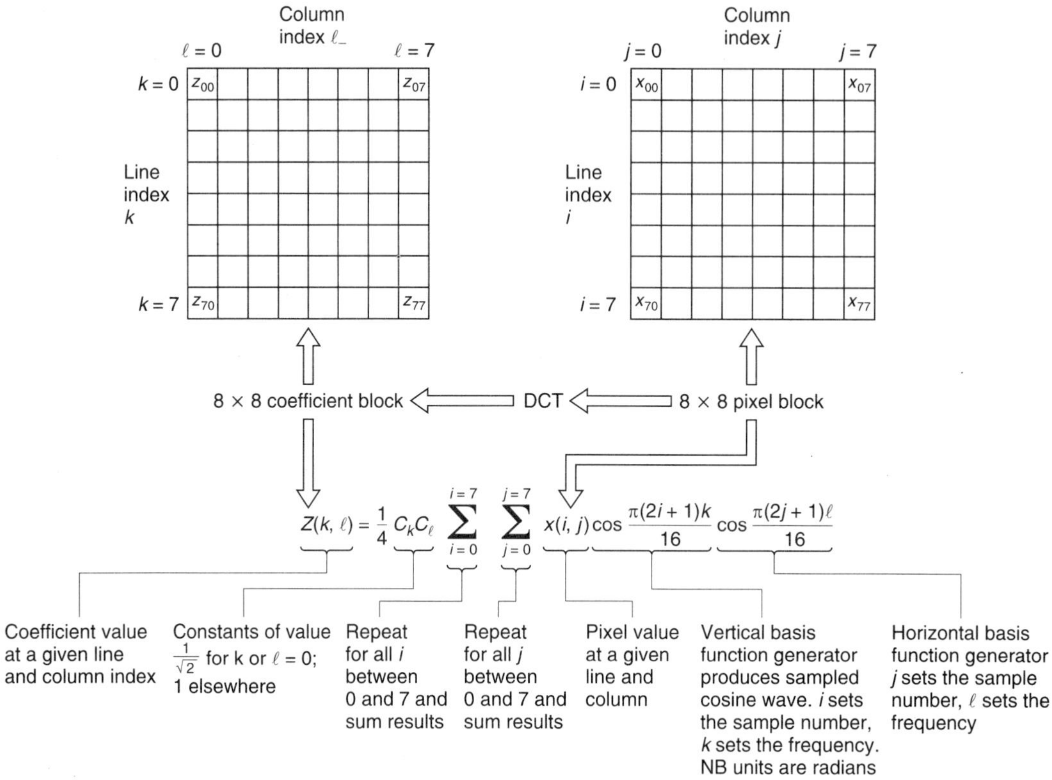

Figure 3.35 A two-dimensional DCT is calculated as shown here. Starting with an input pixel block one calculation is necessary to find a value for each coefficient. After 64 calculations using different basis functions the coefficient block is complete.

rectangular DCT blocks are possible and are used in, for example, the DV format.

The DCT is primarily used in MPEG-2 because it converts the input waveform into a form where redundancy can be easily detected and removed. More details of the DCT can be found in Chapter 9.

3.10 The wavelet transform

The wavelet transform was not discovered by any one individual, but has evolved via a number of similar ideas and was only given a strong mathematical foundation relatively recently.[10–13] The wavelet transform is similar to the Fourier transform in that it has basis functions of various frequencies which are multiplied by the input waveform to identify the frequencies it contains. However, the Fourier transform is based on periodic signals and endless basis functions and requires windowing. The wavelet transform is fundamentally windowed, as the basis functions

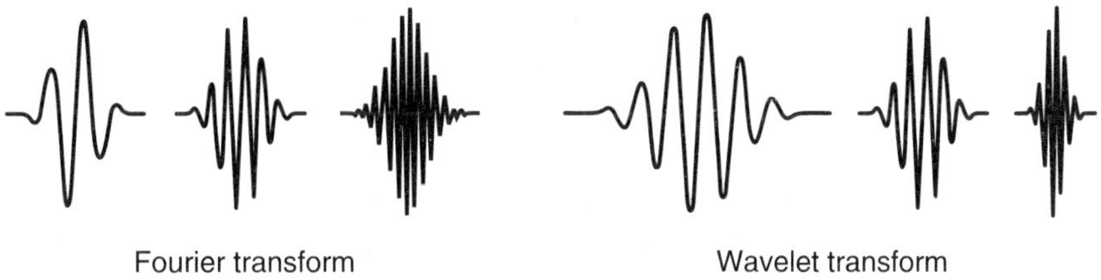

Figure 3.36 Unlike Fourier transforms, wavelet basis functions are scaled so that they contain the same number of cycles irrespective of frequency. As a result their frequency discrimination ability is a constant proportion of the centre frequency.

employed are not endless sine waves, but are finite on the time axis; hence the name. Wavelet transforms do not use a fixed window, but instead the window period is inversely proportional to the frequency being analysed. As a result a useful combination of time and frequency resolutions is obtained. High frequencies corresponding to transients in audio or edges in video are transformed with short basis functions and therefore are accurately located. Low frequencies are transformed with long basis functions which have good frequency resolution.

Figure 3.36 shows that that a set of wavelets or basis functions can be obtained simply by scaling (stretching or shrinking) a single wavelet on

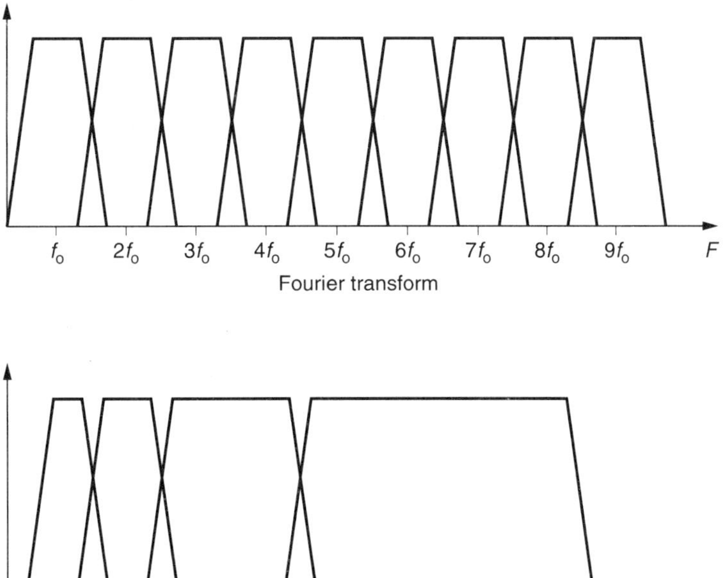

Figure 3.37 Wavelet transforms divide the frequency domain into octaves instead of the equal bands of the Fourier transform.

the time axis. Each wavelet contains the same number of cycles such that as the frequency reduces the wavelet gets longer. Thus the frequency discrimination of the wavelet transform is a constant fraction of the signal frequency. In a filter bank such a characteristic would be described as 'constant Q'. Figure 3.37 shows that the division of the frequency domain by a wavelet transform is logarithmic whereas in the Fourier transform the division is uniform. The logarithmic coverage is effectively dividing the frequency domain into octaves and as such parallels the frequency discrimination of human hearing.

References

1. Ray, S.F., *Applied Photographic Optics*, Oxford: Focal Press (1988) (Ch. 17)
2. van den Enden, A.W.M. and Verhoeckx, N.A.M., Digital signal processing: theoretical background. *Philips Tech. Rev.*, **42**, 110–144, (1985)
3. McClellan, J.H., Parks, T.W. and Rabiner, L.R., A computer program for designing optimum FIR linear-phase digital filters. *IEEE Trans. Audio and Electroacoustics*, **AU-21**, 506–526 (1973)
4. Dolph, C.L., A current distribution for broadside arrays which optimises the relationship between beam width and side-lobe level. *Proc. IRE*, **34**, 335–348 (1946)
5. Crochiere, R.E. and Rabiner, L.R., Interpolation and decimation of digital signals – a tutorial review. *Proc. IEEE*, **69**, 300–331 (1981)
6. Rabiner, L.R., Digital techniques for changing the sampling rate of a signal. In B. Blesser, B. Locanthi and T.G. Stockham Jr (eds), *Digital Audio*, pp.79–89, New York: Audio Engineering Society (1982)
7. Kraniauskas, P., *Transforms in Signals and Systems*, Chapter 6. Wokingham: Addison-Wesley (1992)
8. Ahmed, N., Natarajan, T. and Rao, K., Discrete Cosine Transform, *IEEE Trans. Computers*, **C-23**, 90–93 (1974)
9. De With, P.H.N., *Data compression techniques for digital video recording*, Ph.D thesis, Technical University of Delft (1992)
10. Goupillaud, P., Grossman, A. and Morlet, J., Cycle-Octave and related transforms in seismic signal analysis. *Geoexploration*, **23**, 85–102, Elsevier Science (1984/5)
11. Daubechies, I., The wavelet transform, time–frequency localisation and signal analysis. *IEEE Trans. Info. Theory*, **36**, No.5, 961–1005 (1990)
12. Rioul, O. and Vetterli, M., Wavelets and signal processing. *IEEE Signal Process. Mag.*, 14–38 (Oct. 1991)
13. Strang, G. and Nguyen, T., *Wavelets and Filter Banks*, Wellesly, MA: Wellesley–Cambridge Press (1996)

4

Sampling

4.1 Introduction

Sampling is a process of periodic measurement which can take place in space or time and in several dimensions at once. Figure 4.1(a) shows that in *temporal sampling* the frequency of the signal to be sampled and the sampling rate F_s are measured in Hertz (Hz), the standard unit of temporal frequency. In still images such as photographs there is no temporal change and Figure 4.1(b) shows that the sampling is *spatial*. The sampling rate is now a spatial frequency. The absolute unit of spatial frequency is cycles-per-metre, although for imaging purposes cycles-per-millimetre is more practical.

If the human viewer is considered, none of these units is useful because they don't take into account the viewing distance. The acuity of the eye is measured in cycles per degree. As Figure 4.1(c) shows, a large distant screen subtends the same angle as a small nearby screen. Figure 4.1(c) also shows that the nearby screen, possibly a computer monitor, needs to be able to display a higher spatial frequency than a distant cinema screen to give the same sharpness perceived at the eye. If the viewing distance is proportional to size, both screens could have the same number of pixels, leading to the use of a relative unit, shown in (d), which is cycles-per-picture-height (cph) in the vertical axis and cycles-per-picture-width (cpw) in the horizontal axis.

The computer screen has more cycles-per-millimetre than the cinema screen, but in this example has the same number of cycles-per-picture-height.

Spatial and temporal frequencies are related by the process of scanning as given by:

$$\text{Temporal frequency} = \text{Spatial frequency} \times \text{scanning velocity}$$

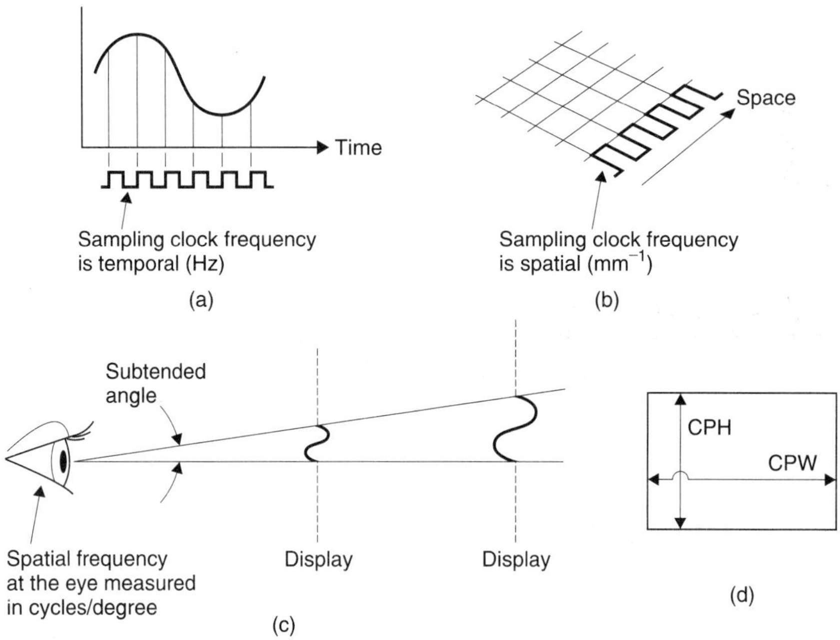

Figure 4.1 (a) Electrical waveforms are sampled temporally at a sampling rate measured in Hz. (b) Image information must be sampled spatially, but there is no single unit of spatial sampling frequency. (c) The acuity of the eye is measured as a subtended angle, and here two different displays of different resolutions give the same result at the eye because they are at a different distance. (d) Size-independent units such as cycles per picture height will also be found.

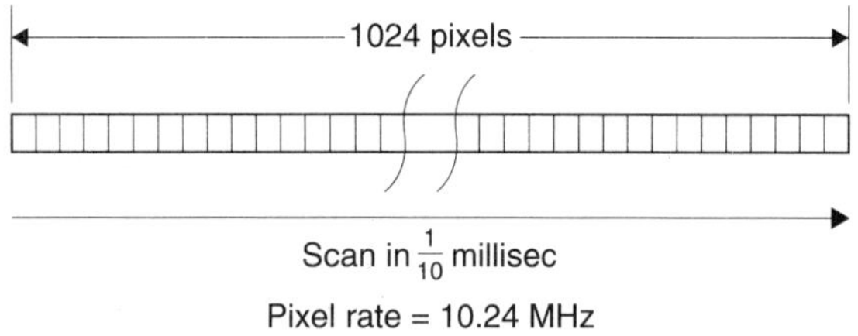

Figure 4.2 The connection between image resolution and pixel rate is the scanning speed. Scanning the above line in 1/10 ms produces a pixel rate of 10.24 MHz.

Figure 4.2 shows that if the 1024 pixels along one line of an SVGA monitor were scanned in one tenth of a millisecond, the sampling clock frequency would be 10.24 MHz.

Sampling theory does not require regular sample spacing, but it is the most efficient arrangement. As a practical matter if regular sampling is employed, the process of timebase correction can be used to eliminate any jitter due to recording or transmission.

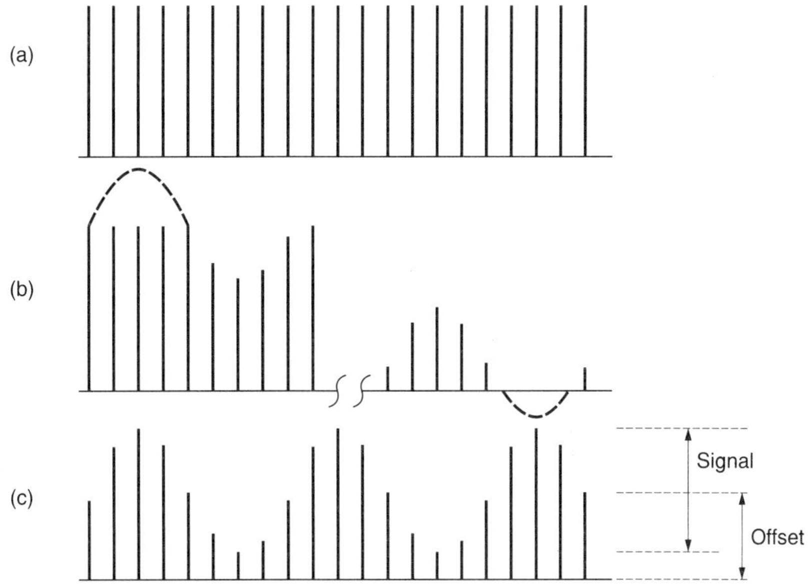

Figure 4.3 The sampling process requires a constant-amplitude pulse train as shown in (a). This is amplitude modulated by the waveform to be sampled. If the input waveform has excessive amplitude or incorrect level, the pulse train clips as shown in (b). For a bipolar waveform, the greatest signal level is possible when an offset of half the pulse amplitude is used to centre the waveform as shown in (c).

The sampling process originates with a pulse train which is shown in Figure 4.3(a) to be of constant amplitude and period. This pulse train can be temporal or spatial. The information to be sampled amplitude-modulates the pulse train in much the same way as the carrier is modulated in an AM radio transmitter. One must be careful to avoid overmodulating the pulse train as shown in (b) and this is achieved by suitably biasing the information waveform as at (c).

4.2 Sampling

In the same way that AM radio produces sidebands or identical images above and below the carrier, sampling also produces sidebands although the carrier is now a pulse train and has an infinite series of harmonics as shown in Figure 4.4(a). The sidebands repeat above and below each harmonic of the sampling rate as shown in (b). The consequence of this is that sampling does not alter the spectrum of the baseband signal at all. The spectrum is simply repeated. Consequently sampling need not lose any information.

The sampled signal can be returned to the continuous domain simply by passing it into a low-pass filter. This filter has a frequency response which prevents the images from passing, and only the baseband signal

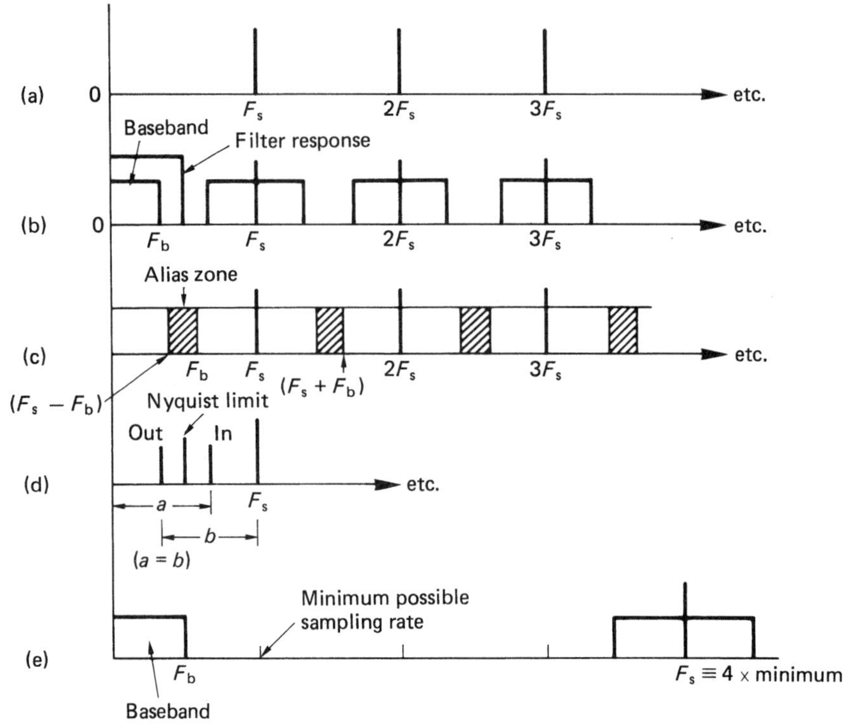

Figure 4.4 (a) Spectrum of sampling pulses. (b) Spectrum of samples. (c) Aliasing due to sideband overlap. (d) Beat-frequency production. (e) 4× oversampling.

emerges, completely unchanged. If considered in the frequency domain, this filter can be called an anti-image filter; if considered in the time domain it can be called a reconstruction filter. It can also be considered as a spatial filter if a sampled still image is being returned to a continuous image. Such a filter will be two-dimensional.

If an input is supplied having an excessive bandwidth for the sampling rate in use, the sidebands will overlap (Figure 4.4(c)) and the result is aliasing, where certain output frequencies are not the same as their input frequencies but instead become difference frequencies (d). It will be seen from Figure 4.4 that aliasing does not occur when the input bandwidth is equal to or less than half the sampling rate, and this derives the most fundamental rule of sampling, which is that the sampling rate must be at least twice the input bandwidth.

Nyquist[1] is generally credited with being the first to point out the need for sampling at twice the highest frequency in the signal in 1928, although the mathematical proofs were given independently by Shannon[2,3] and Kotelnikov. It subsequently transpired that Whittaker[4] beat them all to it, although his work was not widely known at the time. One half of the sampling frequency is often called the Nyquist frequency.

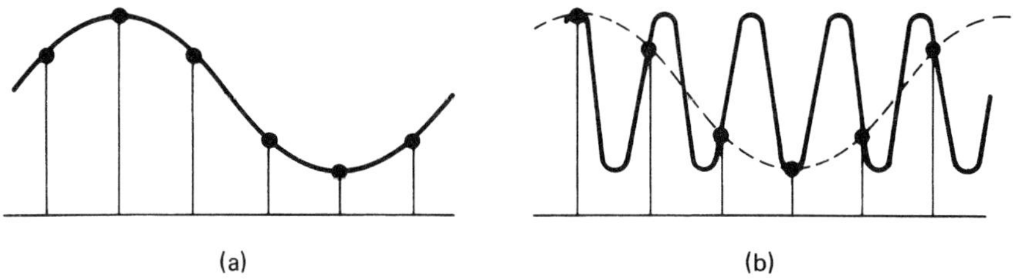

Figure 4.5 In (a), the sampling is adequate to reconstruct the original signal. In (b) the sampling rate is inadequate, and reconstruction produces the wrong waveform (detailed). Aliasing has taken place.

Whilst aliasing has been described above in the frequency domain, it can be described equally well in the time domain. In Figure 4.5(a) the sampling rate is obviously adequate to describe the waveform, but at (b) it is inadequate and aliasing has occurred. In some cases there is no control over the spectrum of input signals and in this case it becomes necessary to have a low-pass filter at the input to prevent aliasing. This anti-aliasing filter prevents frequencies of more than half the sampling rate from reaching the sampling stage.

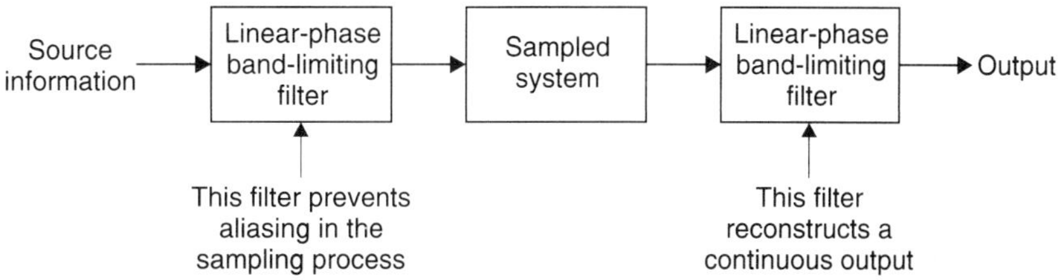

Figure 4.6 Sampling systems depend completely on the use of band-limiting filters before and after the sampling stage. Implementing these filters rigorously is non-trivial.

Figure 4.6 shows that all practical sampling systems consist of a pair of filters, the anti-aliasing filter before the sampling process and the reconstruction filter after it. It should be clear that the results obtained will be strongly affected by the quality of these filters which may be spatial or temporal according to the application.

4.3 Reconstruction

Perfect reconstruction was theoretically demonstrated by Shannon as shown in Figure 4.7. The input must be band limited by an ideal linear-phase low-pass filter with a rectangular frequency response and a bandwidth of one-half the sampling frequency. The samples must be

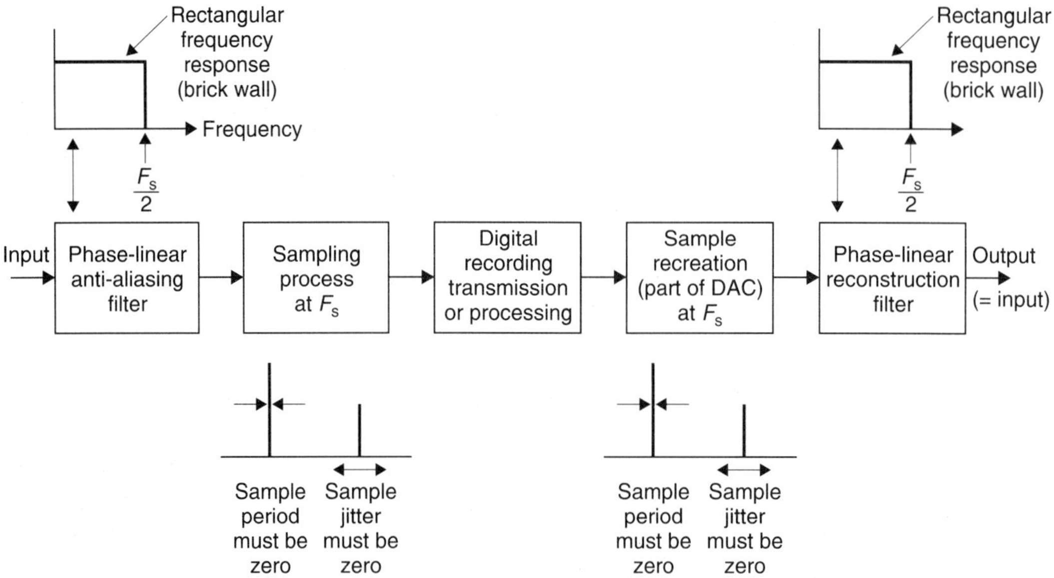

Figure 4.7 Shannon's concept of perfect reconstruction requires the hypothetical approach shown here. The anti-aliasing and reconstruction filters must have linear phase and rectangular frequency response. The sample period must be infinitely short and the sample clock must be perfectly regular. Then the output and input waveforms will be identical if the sampling frequency is twice the input bandwidth (or more).

taken at an instant with no averaging of the waveform. These instantaneous samples can then be passed through a second, identical filter which will perfectly reconstruct that part of the input waveform which was within the passband.

There are some practical difficulties in implementing Figure 4.7 exactly, but well-engineered systems can approach it and so it forms a useful performance target. It was shown in Chapter 3 that the impulse response of a linear-phase ideal low-pass filter is a $\sin x/x$ waveform, and this is repeated in Figure 4.8(a). Such a waveform passes through zero volts periodically. If the cut-off frequency of the filter is one-half of the sampling rate, the impulse passes through zero *at the sites of all other samples*. It can be seen from Figure 4.8(b) that at the output of such a filter, the voltage at the centre of a sample is due to that sample alone, since the value of *all* other samples is zero at that instant. In other words the continuous output waveform must pass through the tops of the input samples. In between the sample instants, the output of the filter is the sum of the contributions from many impulses (theoretically an infinite number), causing the waveform to pass smoothly from sample to sample.

It is a consequence of the band-limiting of the original anti-aliasing filter that the filtered analog waveform could only take one path between

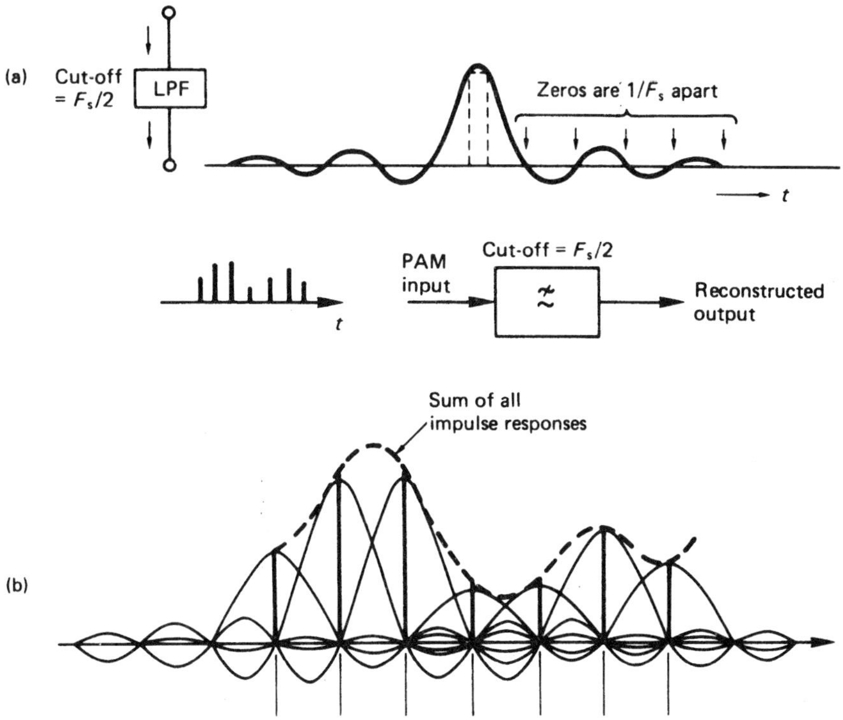

Figure 4.8 An ideal low-pass filter has an impulse response shown in (a). The impulse passes through zero at intervals equal to the sampling period. When convolved with a pulse train at the sampling rate, as shown in (b), the voltage at each sample instant is due to that sample alone as the impulses from all other samples pass through zero there.

the sample. As the reconstruction filter has the same frequency response, the reconstructed output waveform must be identical to the original band-limited waveform prior to sampling. A rigorous mathematical proof of reconstruction can be found in Porat[5] or Betts.[6]

Perfect reconstruction with a Nyquist sampling rate is a limiting condition which cannot be exceeded and can only be reached under ideal and impractical conditions. Thus in practice Nyquist rate sampling can only be approached. Zero-duration pulses are impossible and the ideal linear-phase filter with a vertical 'brick-wall' cut-off slope is impossible to implement. In the case of temporal sampling, as the slope tends to vertical, the delay caused by the filter goes to infinity. In the case of spatial sampling, sharp cut optical filters are impossible to build. Figure 4.9 shows that the spatial impulse response of an ideal lens is a symmetrical intensity function. Note that the function is positive only as the expression for intensity contains a squaring process. The negative excursions of the $\sin x/x$ curve can be handled in an analog or digital filter by negative voltages or numbers, but in optics there is no negative

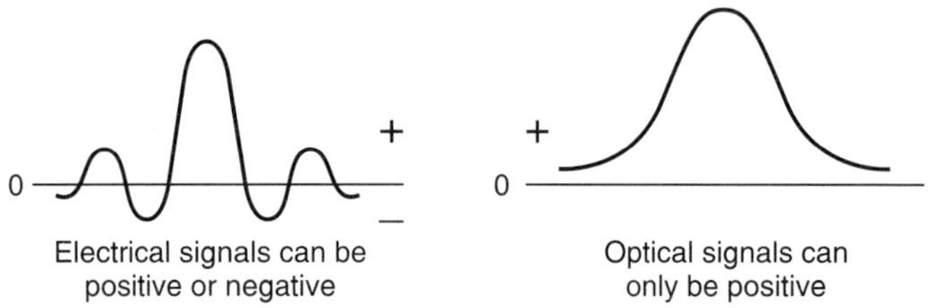

Figure 4.9 In optical systems the spatial impulse response cannot have negative excursions and so ideal filters in optics are more difficult to make.

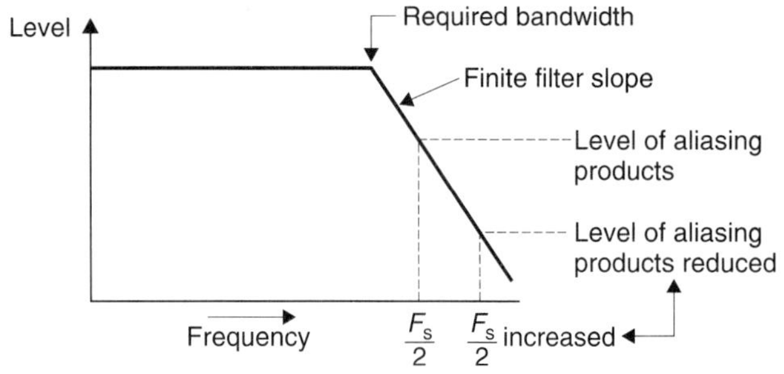

Figure 4.10 With finite slope filters, aliasing is always possible, but it can be set at an arbitrarily low level by raising the sampling rate.

light. The restriction to positive only impulse response limits the sharpness of optical filters.

In practice real filters with finite slopes can still be used as shown in Figure 4.10. The cut-off slope begins at the edge of the required pass band, and because the slope is not vertical, aliasing will always occur. However it can be seen from Figure 4.10 that the sampling rate can be raised to drive aliasing products to an arbitrarily low level. The perfect reconstruction process still works, but the system is a little less efficient in information terms because the sampling rate has to be raised. There is no absolute factor by which the sampling rate must be raised. A figure of 10 per cent is typical in temporal sampling, although it depends upon the filters which are available and the level of aliasing products that are acceptable.

There is another difficulty which is that the requirement for linear phase means the impulse response of the filter must be symmetrical. In the time domain, such filters cannot be *causal* because the output has to begin before the input occurs. A filter with a finite slope has a finite window and so a linear-phase characteristic can be obtained by incorporating a delay of one-half the window period so that the filter can be causal. This concept was described in Chapter 3.

4.4 Aperture effect

In practical sampling systems the sample impulse cannot be infinitely small in time or space. Figure 4.11 shows that real equipment may produce impulses whose possible shapes include rectangular and Gaussian. The result is an *aperture effect* where the frequency response of the sampling system is modified. The new response is the Fourier transform of the aperture function.

In the case where the pulses are rectangular, the proportion of the sample period occupied by the pulse is defined as the *aperture ratio* which is normally expressed as a percentage.

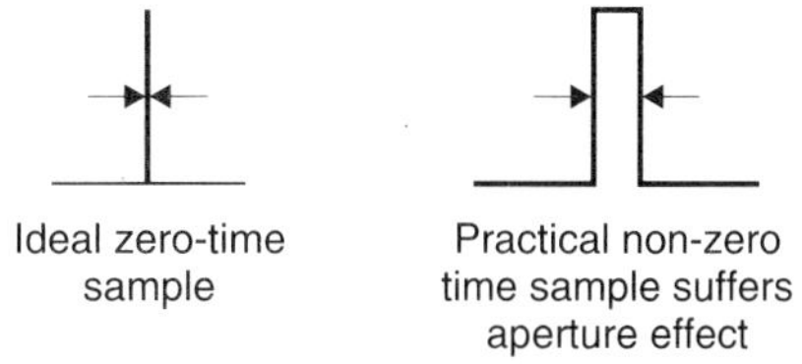

Figure 4.11 The ideal zero duration/size sample required by Figure 4.7 is not met in practice. Typical sample impulses look like this and have a filtering action called aperture effect.

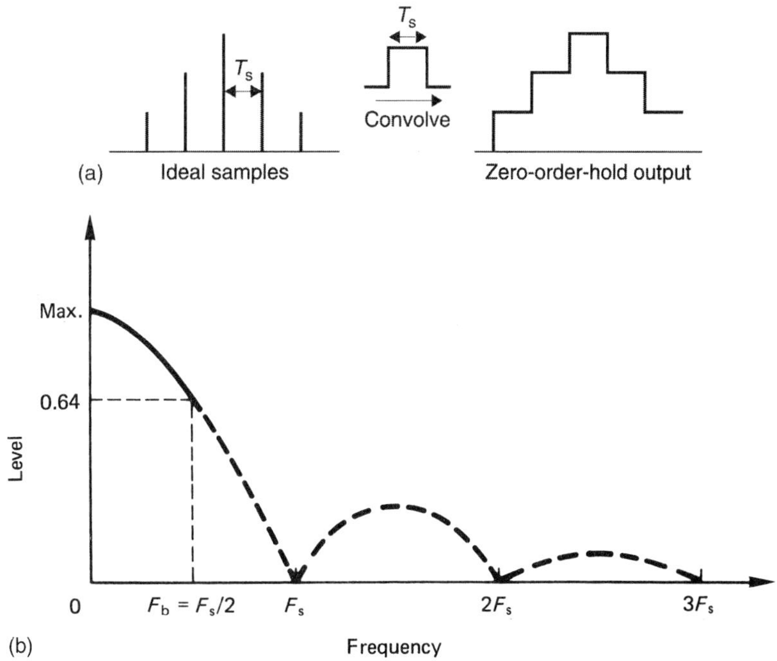

Figure 4.12 (a) In a zero-order-hold (ZOH) system, the samples are stretched to the sample period and the waveform looks like a staircase. (b) Frequency response with 100 per cent aperture nulls at multiples of sampling rate. Area of interest is up to half sampling rate.

The case where the pulses have been extended in width to become equal to the sample period is known as a zero-order-hold (ZOH) system and has a 100 per cent aperture ratio as shown in Figure 4.12(a). This produces a waveform which is more like a staircase than a pulse train.

To see how the use of ZOH compares with ideal Shannon reconstruction, it must be recalled that pulses of negligible width have a uniform spectrum and so the frequency response of the sampler and reconstructor is flat within the passband. In contrast, pulses of 100 per cent aperture ratio have a $\sin x/x$ spectrum which falls to a null at the sampling rate, and as a result is about 4 dB down at the Nyquist frequency as shown in Figure 4.12(b).

Figure 4.13(a) shows how ZOH is normally represented in texts with the pulses extending to the right of the sample. This representation is incorrect because it does not have linear phase as can be seen in (b). Figure 4.13(c) shows the correct representation where the pulses are

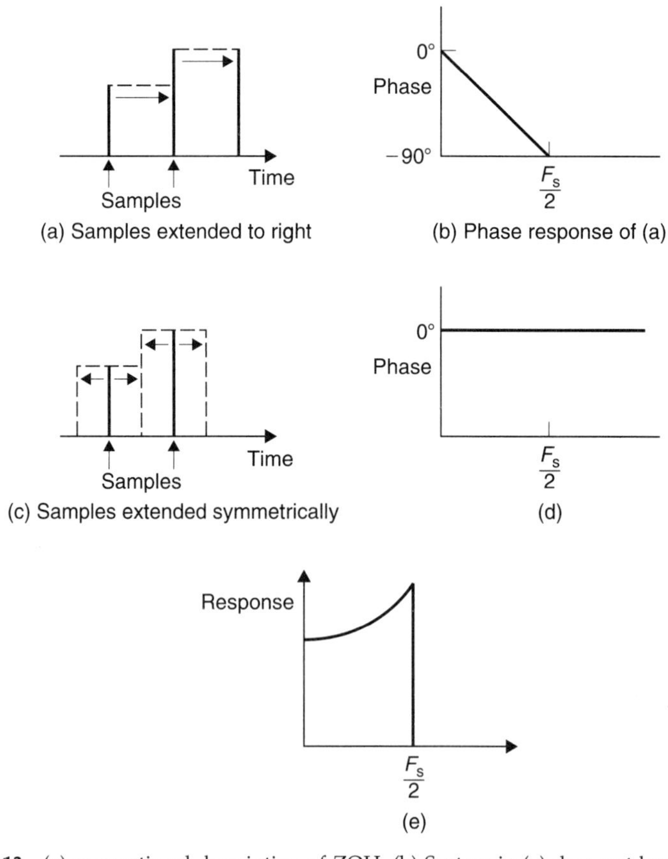

Figure 4.13 (a) conventional description of ZOH. (b) System in (a) does not have linear phase. (c) Linear phase ZOH system in which the samples are spread symmetrically. (d) Phase response of (c). (e) Flat response can be obtained using equalizer.

extended symmetrically about the sample to achieve linear phase (d). This is conceptually easy if the pulse generator is considered to cause a half-sample-period delay relative to the original waveform. If the pulse width is stable, the reduction of high frequencies is constant and predictable, and an appropriate filter response shown in (e) can render the overall response flat once more. Note that the equalization filter in (e) is conceptually a low-pass reconstruction filter in series with an inverse $\sin x/x$ response.

An alternative in the time domain is to use resampling which is shown in Figure 4.14. Resampling passes the zero-order-hold waveform through a further synchronous sampling stage which consists of an analog switch which closes briefly in the centre of each sample period. The output of the switch will be pulses which are narrower than the original. If, for example, the aperture ratio is reduced to 50 per cent of the sample period, the first frequency response null is now at twice the sampling rate, and the loss at the edge of the pass band is reduced. As the figure shows, the frequency response becomes flatter as the aperture ratio falls. The process should not be carried too far, as with very small aperture ratios there is

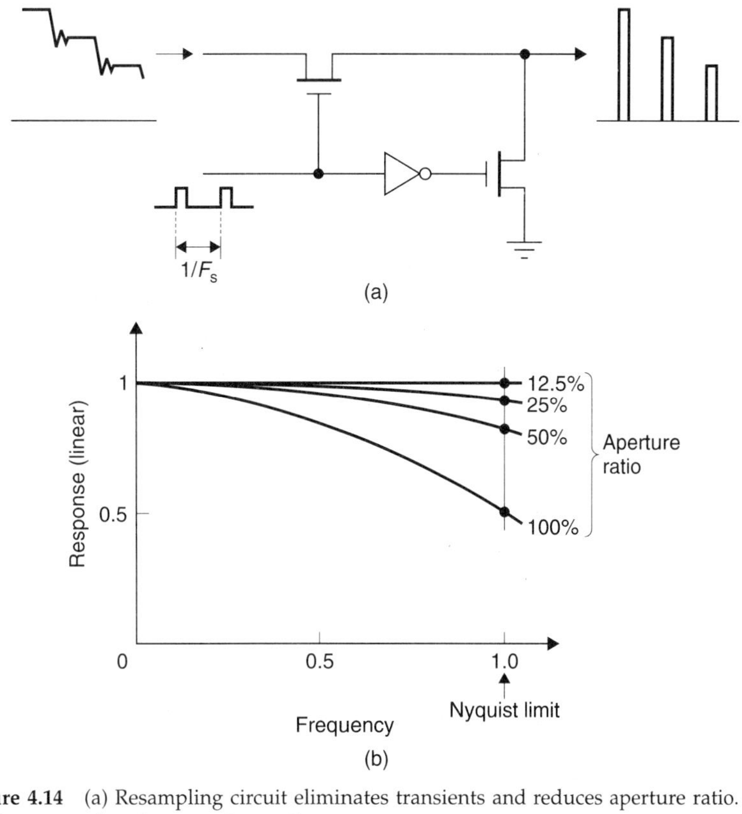

Figure 4.14 (a) Resampling circuit eliminates transients and reduces aperture ratio. (b) Response of various aperture ratios.

little energy in the pulses and noise can be a problem. A practical limit is around 12.5 per cent where the frequency response is virtually ideal.

It should be stressed that in real systems there will often be more than one aperture effect. The result is that the frequency responses of the various aperture effects multiply, which is the same as saying that their impulse responses convolve. Whatever fine words are used, the result is an increasing loss of high frequencies where a series of acceptable devices when cascaded produce an unacceptable result. This topic will be considered in Chapter 7 where high-resolution imaging systems are discussed.

In many systems, for reasons of economy or ignorance, reconstruction is simply not used and the system output is an unfiltered ZOH waveform. Figure 4.15 shows some examples of this kind of thing which are associated with the 'digital look'. It is important to appreciate that in well-engineered systems containing proper filters there is no such thing as the digital look.

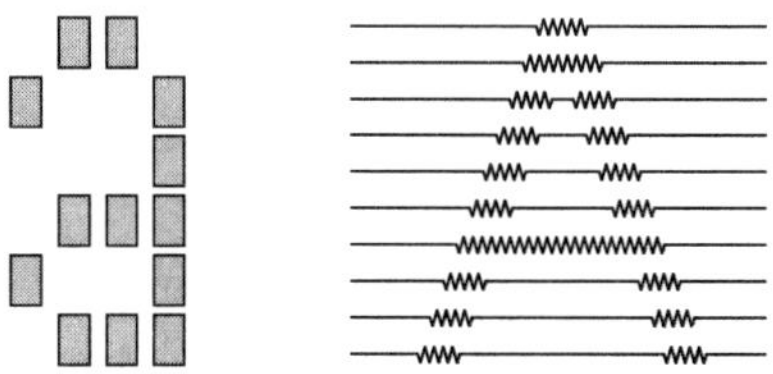

Figure 4.15 Some examples of sampled systems in which filtering is inadequate or absent.

It is always instructive to consider other industries to see how familiar technologies are used for different purposes. Figure 4.16(a) shows the lines of a racing yacht. In order to describe the three-dimensional hull shape to the builders, the designer puts the hull shape through a giant conceptual bread slicer and supplies a drawing of each slice. Essentially the hull has been spatially sampled. The designer would place the samples or stations close enough together to ensure that the surface detail was fully conveyed. This is the equivalent of using a high enough sampling rate.

Imagine the designer's reaction on being presented with an unfiltered ZOH hull shown in Figure 4.16(b) and being told that it was what he had asked for in the plans. This hull isn't going to win any races. Instead shipbuilders use reconstruction to interpolate the shape of the hull between the stations. In some cases this was done by bending a lead bar called a spline so that it made a fair transition between the frames. To this day computer algorithms which interpolate in this way are called splines. In shipbuilding the use of perfect reconstruction from samples preceded Whittaker, let alone Shannon.

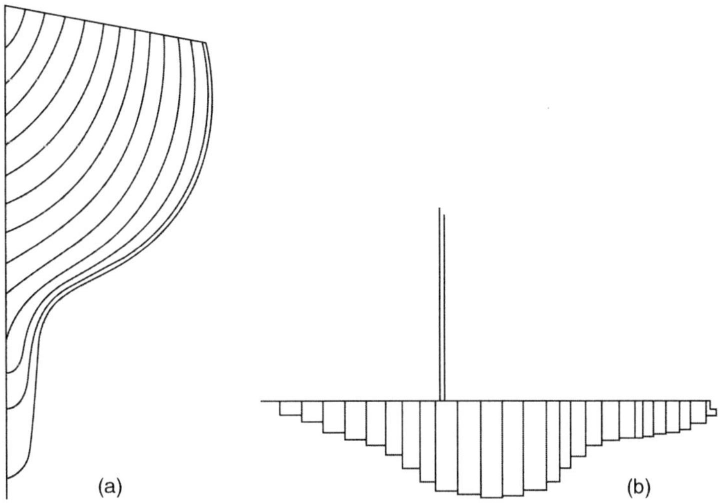

Figure 4.16 (a) A yacht hull can be described by samples called 'lines'. (b) A zero-order-hold yacht built from the lines of (a). An obvious mistake here, but one which is frequently made in convergent technologies.

Using unfiltered or ZOH output in audio or imaging systems is poor practice and won't win any races either. It is a pity that so many textbooks give the impression that this is how conversions should be performed.

4.5 Sampling clock jitter

The points at which samples are taken and re-created in time or space must be evenly spaced, otherwise unwanted signals can be added. In scanning systems, the scan must proceed with precisely uniform speed. Figure 4.17(a) shows the effect of noise on the vertical scan waveform of a CRT is spatial jitter of the vertical line positions. Figure 4.17(b) shows that another source of jitter is crosstalk or interference on the clock signal of a temporal sampling system, although a balanced clock line will be more immune to such crosstalk. The unwanted additional signal changes the time at which the sloping clock signal appears to cross the threshold voltage of the clock receiver.

Figure 4.18(a) shows the effect of sampling jitter on a sloping waveform. Samples are taken at the wrong times. When these samples have passed through a system, the timebase correction stage prior to the DAC will remove the jitter, and the result is shown at (b). The magnitude of the unwanted signal is proportional to the slope of the waveform and so the amount of jitter which can be tolerated falls at 6 dB per octave. As the resolution of the system is increased by the use of longer sample wordlength, tolerance to jitter is further reduced. The nature of the

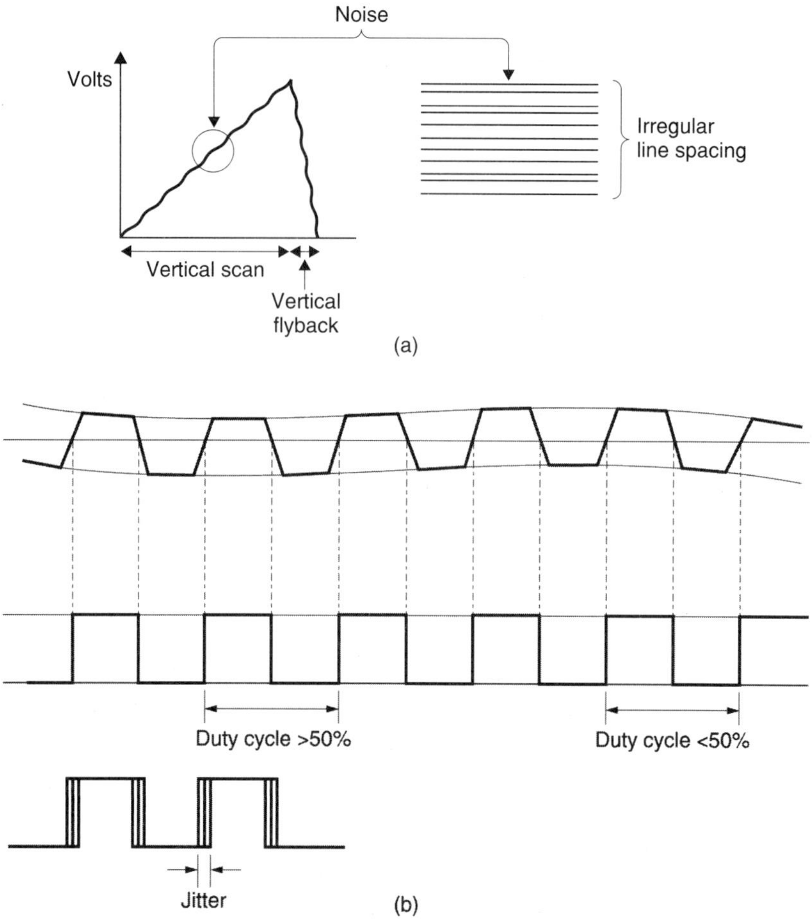

Figure 4.17 (a) Noise on the vertical scan waveform introduces jitter in the line position of a CRT. (b) Crosstalk in transmission can result in unwanted signals being added to the clock waveform. It can be seen here that a low-frequency interference signal affects the slicing of the clock and causes a periodic jitter.

unwanted signal depends on the spectrum of the jitter. If the jitter is random, the effect is noise-like and relatively benign unless the amplitude is excessive.

4.6 Quantizing

Quantizing is the process of expressing some infinitely variable quantity by discrete or stepped values and turns up in a remarkable number of everyday guises. Figure 4.19 shows that an inclined ramp enables infinitely variable height to be achieved, whereas a step-ladder allows only discrete heights to be had. A step-ladder quantizes height. When

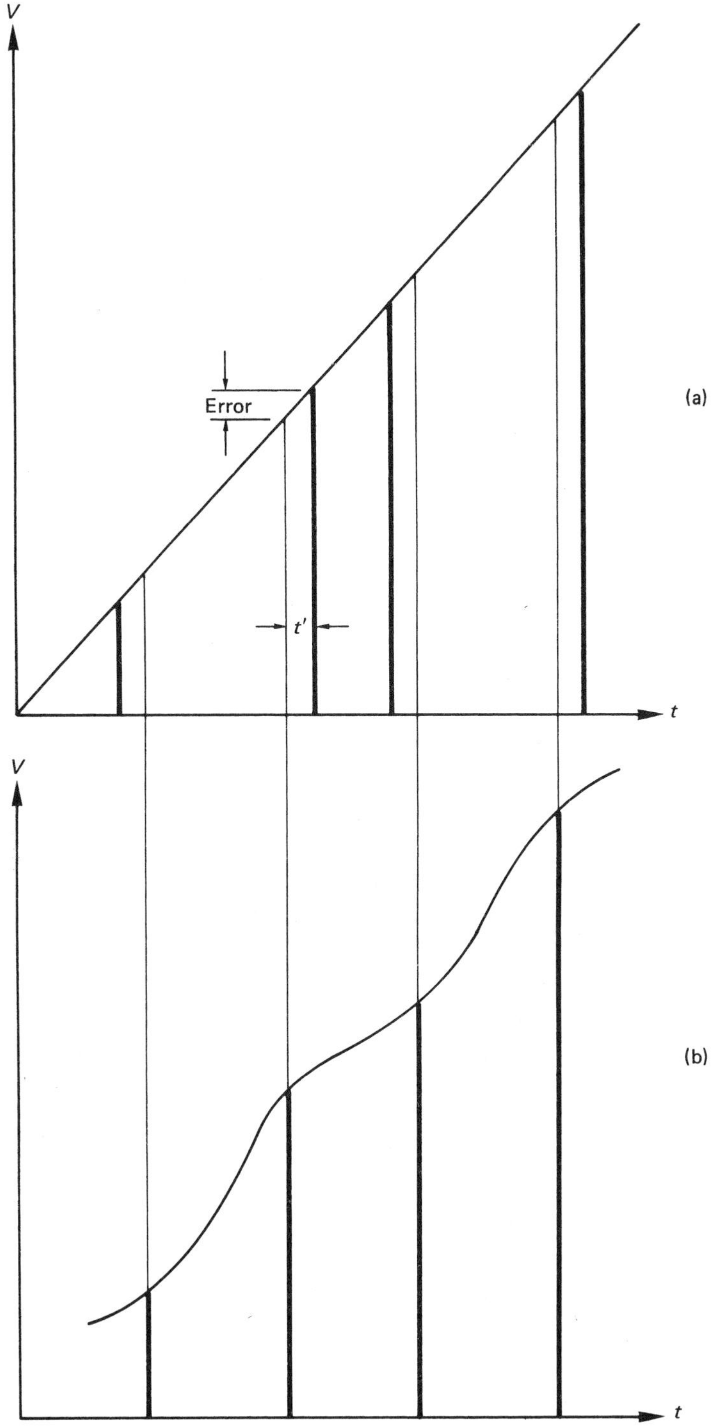

Figure 4.18 The effect of sampling timing jitter on noise. At (a) a sloping signal sampled with jitter has error proportional to the slope. When jitter is removed by reclocking, the result at (b) is noise.

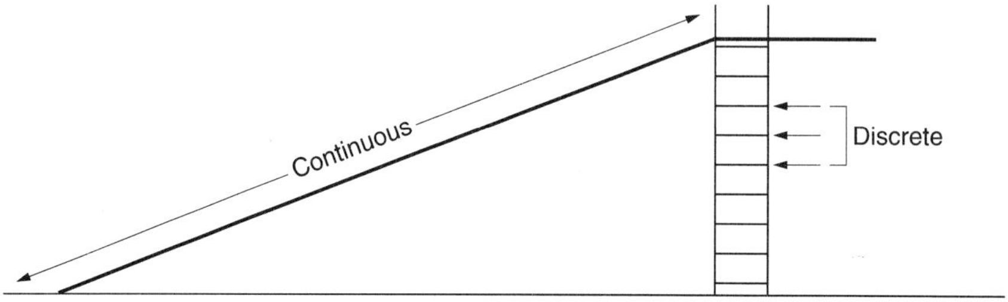

Figure 4.19 An analog parameter is continuous whereas a quantized parameter is restricted to certain values. Here the sloping side of a ramp can be used to obtain any height whereas a ladder only allows discrete heights.

accountants round off sums of money to the nearest pound or dollar they are quantizing. Time passes continuously, but the display on a digital clock changes suddenly every minute because the clock is quantizing time.

In audiovisual systems the values to be quantized are infinitely variable samples which can represent a voltage waveform, the brightness of a pixel and so on. Strict quantizing is a process which operates in a domain which is orthogonal to space or time and so it works in exactly the same way whether the samples have been taken spatially or temporally.

Figure 4.20(a) shows that the process of quantizing divides the voltage range up into quantizing intervals Q, also referred to as steps S. In applications such as telephony and video these may be of differing size, but for digital audio the quantizing intervals are made as identical as possible. If this is done, the binary numbers which result are truly proportional to the original analog voltage, and the digital equivalents of mixing and gain changing can be performed by adding and multiplying sample values. If the quantizing intervals are unequal this cannot be done accurately. When all quantizing intervals are the same, the term 'uniform quantizing' is used. The erroneous term 'linear quantizing' will also be found.

The term LSB (least significant bit) will also be found in place of quantizing interval in some treatments, but this is a poor term because quantizing works in the voltage domain. A bit is not a unit of voltage and can have only two values. In studying quantizing, voltages within a quantizing interval will be discussed, but there is no such thing as a fraction of a bit.

Whatever the exact voltage of the input signal, the quantizer will locate the quantizing interval in which it lies. In what may be considered a separate step, the quantizing interval is then allocated a code value which is typically some form of binary number. The information sent is the number of the quantizing interval in which the

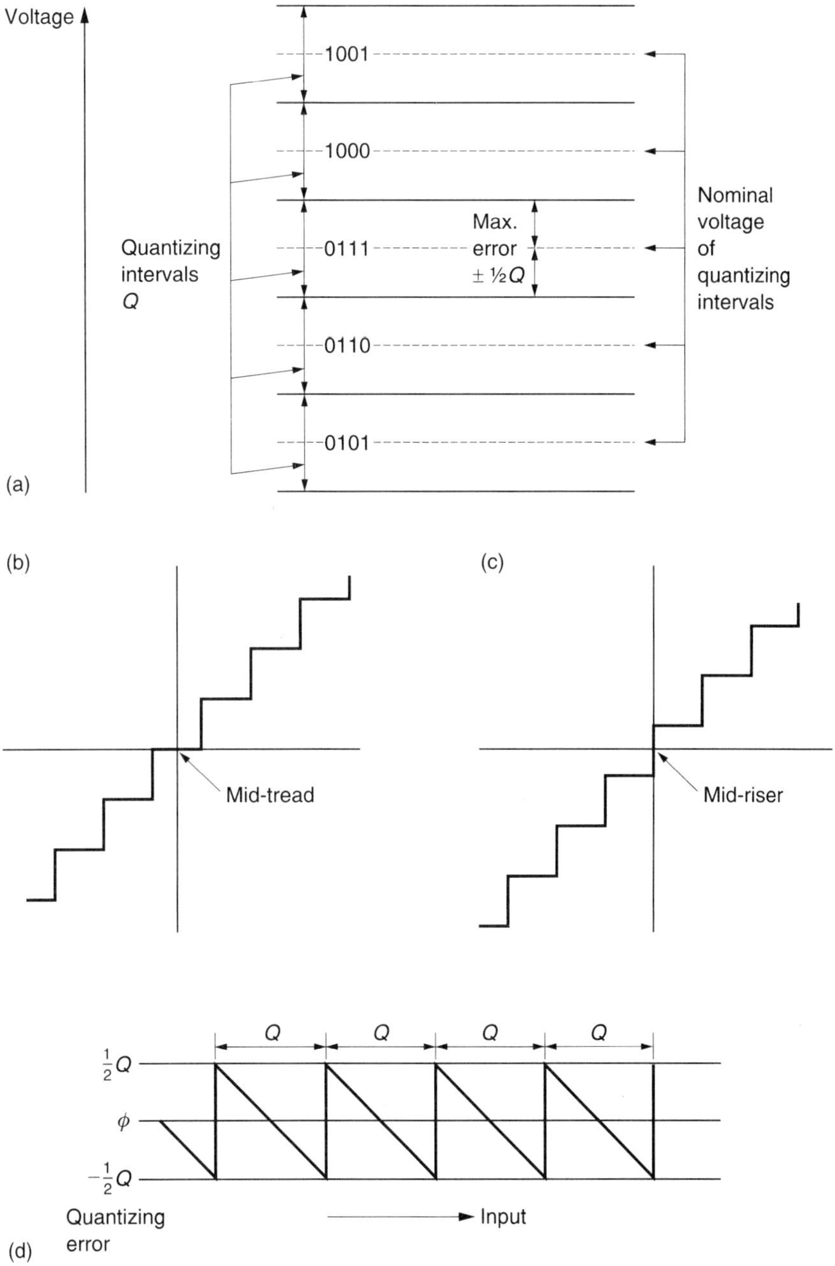

Figure 4.20 Quantizing assigns discrete numbers to variable voltages. All voltages within the same quantizing interval are assigned the same number which causes a DAC to produce the voltage at the centre of the intervals shown by the dashed lines in (a). This is the characteristic of the mid-tread quantizer shown in (b). An alternative system is the mid-riser system shown in (c). Here 0 V analog falls between two codes and there is no code for zero. Such quantizing cannot be used prior to signal processing because the number is no longer proportional to the voltage. Quantizing error cannot exceed $\pm 1/2Q$ as shown in (d).

input voltage lay. Whereabouts that voltage lay within the interval is not conveyed, and this mechanism puts a limit on the accuracy of the information which a real quantizer may approach but not exceed. When the number of the quantizing interval is converted back to the analog domain, it will result in a voltage at the centre of the quantizing interval as this minimizes the magnitude of the error between input and output. The number range is limited by the wordlength of the binary numbers used. In an eight-bit system, 256 different quantizing intervals exist, wheres in a sixteen-bit system there are 65 536. To be strictly correct, the quantizing intervals at the end of the range are infinite because all voltages outside the working range will be expressed as one or other of the limits.

4.7 Quantizing error

It is possible to draw a transfer function for such an ideal quantizer followed by an ideal DAC, and this is also shown in Figure 4.20. A transfer function is simply a graph of the output with respect to the input. In signal processing, when the term 'linearity' is used, this generally means the overall straightness of the transfer function. Linearity is a particular goal in audio, yet it will be seen that an ideal quantizer is anything but linear.

Figure 4.20(b) shows the transfer function is somewhat like a staircase, and blanking level is half-way up a quantizing interval, or on the centre of a tread. This is the so-called mid-tread quantizer which is universally used in video and audio. Figure 4.20(c) shows the alternative mid-riser transfer function which causes difficulty because it does not have a code value corresponding to black or silence and as a result the numerical code value is not proportional to the analog signal voltage.

Quantizing causes an error in the magnitude of the sample which is given by the difference between the actual staircase transfer function and the ideal straight line. This is shown in Figure 4.20(d) to be a sawtooth-like function which is periodic in Q. The amplitude cannot exceed $\pm \frac{1}{2} Q$ peak-to-peak unless the input is so large that clipping occurs.

When considering quantizing error it is important to avoid confusion with additional errors such as aperture effects. This treatment of quantizing error avoids that confusion by assuming Shannon point samples which have only magnitude in the domain they are measuring but no duration or size in the time or space domains. It is then correct to compare the quantized samples with the original samples to obtain what is effectively a sampled quantizing error waveform. To obtain the continuous quantizing error waveform the sample errors must be reconstructed. Any other approach gives misleading results.

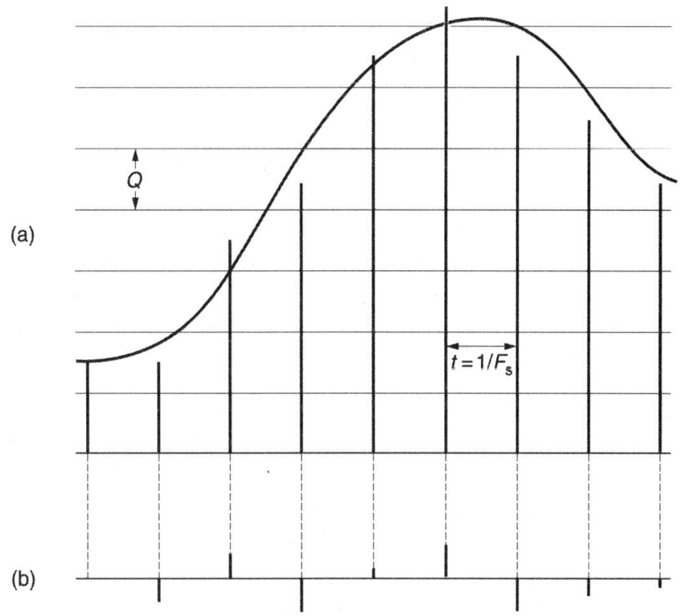

Figure 4.21 In (a) an arbitrary signal is represented to finite accuracy by PAM needles whose peaks are at the centre of the quantizing intervals. The errors caused can be thought of as an unwanted signal (b) added to the original.

This has been done in Figure 4.21. The curve is the input waveform and by definition the original samples lie on the curve. The horizontal lines in the drawing are the boundaries between the quantizing intervals, and by definition the quantized samples always reach the centre of a quantizing interval. The quantizing error is the difference in the two samples which is shown shaded. These quantizing errors are shown in (b) and can be thought of as samples of an unwanted signal which the quantizing process adds to the perfect original. The resulting continuous waveform due to this quantizing error is also shown in (b).

Quantizing error has some non-intuitive characteristics and it is dangerous to make assumptions about it. For example, Figure 4.22 shows

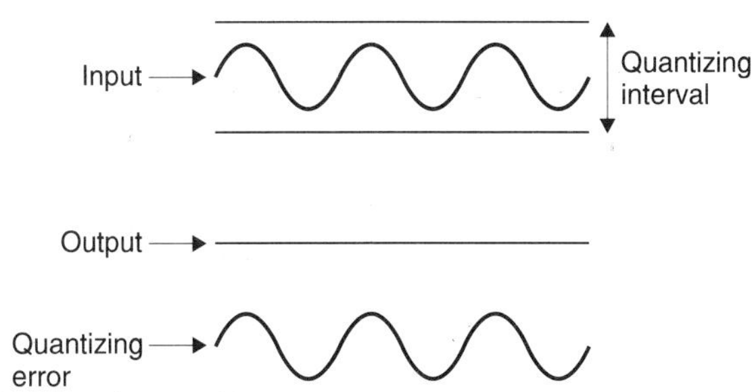

Figure 4.22 At low signal levels, the quantizing error and the input signal are identical. The output remains constant.

that if a very small amplitude input signal remains within one quantizing interval, the quantizing error *is* the signal and the quantized signal is unmodulated.

As the transfer function is non-linear, ideal quantizing can cause distortion. As a result practical equipment deliberately uses non-ideal quantizers to achieve linearity. The quantizing error of an ideal quantizer is a complex function, and it has been researched in great depth.[7–10] It is not intended to go into such depth here. The characteristics of an ideal quantizer will only be pursued far enough to convince the reader that such a device cannot be used in quality audiovisual applications.

As the magnitude of the quantizing error is limited, its effect can be minimized by making the signal larger. This will require more quantizing intervals and more bits to express them. The number of quantizing intervals multiplied by their size gives the quantizing range of the convertor. A signal outside the range will be clipped. Provided that clipping is avoided, the larger the signal, the less will be the effect of the quantizing error.

Where the input signal exercises the whole quantizing range and has a complex waveform (such as from a contrasty, detailed image or a complex piece of music), successive samples will have widely varying numerical values and the quantizing error on a given sample will be independent of that on others. In this case the size of the quantizing error will be distributed with equal probability between the limits. Figure 4.23(a) shows the resultant uniform probability density. In this case the unwanted signal added by quantizing is an additive broadband noise uncorrelated with the signal, and it is appropriate in this case to call it quantizing noise. This is not quite the same as thermal noise which has a Gaussian probability shown in Figure 4.23(b) (see section 1.7 for a treatment of statistics). The difference is of no consequence as in the large signal case the noise is masked by the signal. Under these conditions, a

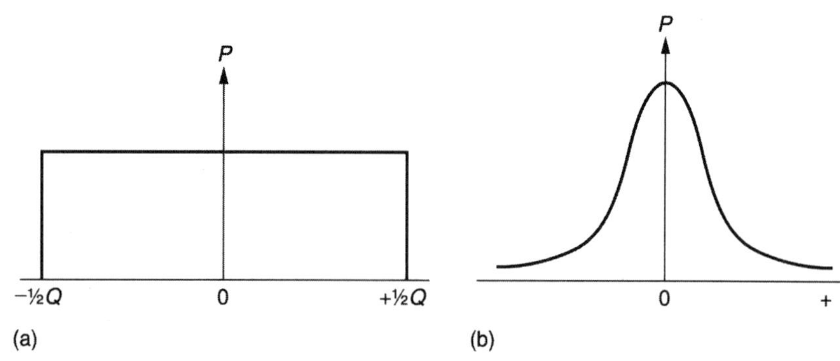

Figure 4.23 In (a) the amplitude of a quantizing error needle will be from $-1/2Q$ to $+1/2Q$ with equal probability. Note, however, that white noise in analog circuits generally has Gaussian amplitude distribution, shown in (b).

meaningful signal-to-noise ratio can be calculated as follows.

In a system using n-bit words. there will be 2^n quantizing intervals. The largest sinusoid which can fit without clipping will have this peak-to-peak amplitude. The peak amplitude will be half as great, i.e. $2^{n-1}Q$ and the rms amplitude will be this value divided by $\sqrt{2}$.

The quantizing error has an amplitude of $\frac{1}{2}Q$ peak which is the equivalent of $Q/\sqrt{12}$ rms. The signal-to-noise ratio for the large signal case is then given by:

$$20 \log_{10} \frac{\sqrt{12} \times 2^{n-1}}{\sqrt{2}} \text{ dB}$$

$$= 20 \log_{10} \left(\sqrt{6} \times 2^{n-1}\right) \text{ dB}$$

$$= 20 \log \left(2^n \times \frac{\sqrt{6}}{2}\right) \text{ dB}$$

$$= 20n \log 2 + 20 \log \frac{\sqrt{6}}{2} \text{ dB}$$

$$= 6.02n + 1.76 \text{ dB} \tag{4.1}$$

By way of example, an eight-bit system will offer very nearly 50 dB SNR.

Whilst the above result is true for a large complex input waveform, treatments which then assume that quantizing error is *always* noise give results which are at variance with reality. The expression above is only valid if the probability density of the quantizing error is uniform. Unfortunately at low depths of modulations in audio and with flat fields or simple pictures in image portrayal this is not the case as is already known from Figure 4.21.

At low modulation depth, quantizing error ceases to be random, and becomes a function of the input waveform and the quantizing structure as Figure 4.21 showed. Once an unwanted signal becomes a deterministic function of the wanted signal, it has to be classed as a distortion rather than a noise. Distortion can also be predicted from the non-linearity, or staircase nature, of the transfer function. With a large signal, there are so many steps involved that we must stand well back, and a staircase with enough steps appears to be a slope. With a small signal there are few steps and they can no longer be ignored.

Distortion precludes the use of an ideal quantizer for high-quality work. There is little point in studying the adverse effects further as they should be and can be eliminated completely in practical equipment by the use of dither. The importance of correctly dithering a quantizer cannot be emphasized enough, since failure to dither irrevocably distorts the converted signal: there can be no process which will subsequently remove that distortion. The signal-to-noise ratio derived above has no relevance to practical applications as it will be modified by the dither.

4.8 Introduction to dither

At high signal levels, quantizing error is effectively noise. As the depth of modulation falls, the quantizing error of an ideal quantizer becomes more strongly correlated with the signal and the result is distortion, visible as contouring. If the quantizing error can be decorrelated from the input in some way, the system can remain linear but noisy. Dither performs the job of decorrelation by making the action of the quantizer unpredictable and gives the system a noise floor like an analog system.[11,12]

In one approach, pseudo-random noise (see Chapter 2) with rectangular probability and a peak-to-peak amplitude of Q was added to the input signal prior to quantizing, but was subtracted after reconversion to analog. This is known as subtractive dither and was investigated by Schuchman[13] and much later by Sherwood.[14] Subtractive dither has the advantages that the dither amplitude is non-critical, the noise has full statistical independence from the signal[15] and has the same level as the quantizing error in the large signal undithered case.[16] Unfortunately, it suffers from practical drawbacks, since the original noise waveform must accompany the samples or must be synchronously re-created at the DAC. This is virtually impossible in a system where the signal may have been edited or where its level has been changed by processing, as the noise needs to remain synchronous and be processed in the same way. All practical digital video systems use non-subtractive dither where the dither signal is added prior to quantization and no attempt is made to remove it at the DAC.[17] The introduction of dither prior to a conventional quantizer inevitably causes a slight reduction in the signal-to-noise ratio attainable, but this reduction is a small price to pay for the elimination of non-linearities.

The ideal (noiseless) quantizer of Figure 4.21 has fixed quantizing intervals and must always produce the same quantizing error from the same signal. In Figure 4.24 it can be seen that an ideal quantizer can be dithered by linearly adding a controlled level of noise either to the input signal or to the reference voltage which is used to derive the quantizing intervals. There are several ways of considering how dither works, all of which are equally valid.

The addition of dither means that successive samples effectively find the quantizing intervals in different places on the voltage scale. The

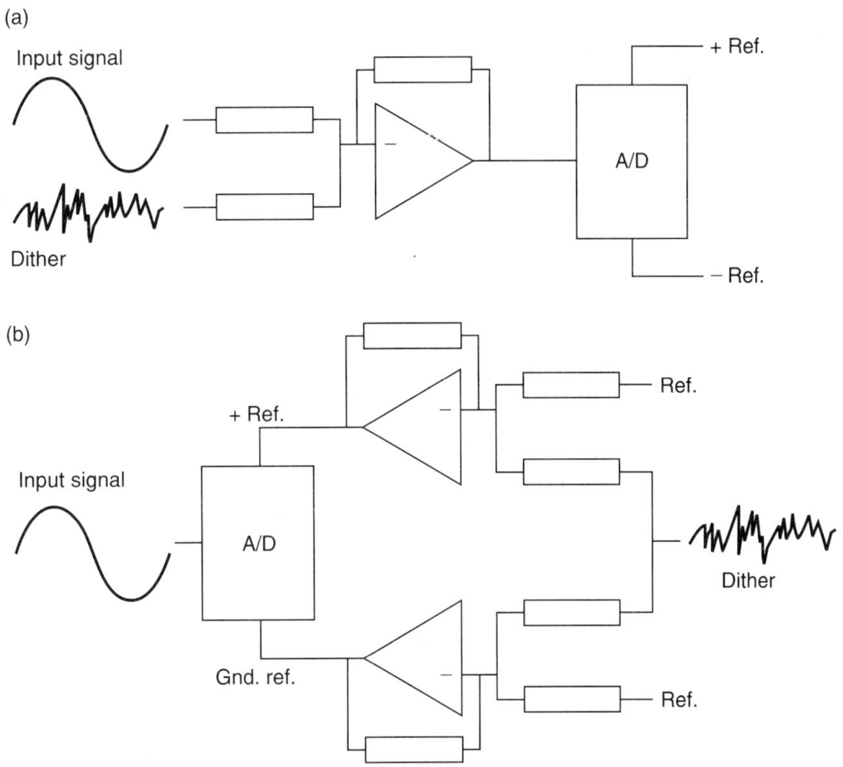

Figure 4.24 Dither can be applied to a quantizer in one of two ways. In (a) the dither is linearly added to the analog input signal, whereas in (b) it is added to the reference voltages of the quantizer.

quantizing error becomes a function of the dither, rather than a predictable function of the input signal. The quantizing error is not eliminated, but the subjectively unacceptable distortion is converted into a broadband noise which is more benign to the ear.

Some alternative ways of looking at dither are shown in Figure 4.25. Consider the situation where a low-level input signal is changing slowly within a quantizing interval. Without dither, the same numerical code is output for a number of samples and the variations within the interval are lost. Dither has the effect of forcing the quantizer to switch between two or more states. The higher the voltage of the input signal within a given interval, the more probable it becomes that the output code will take on the next higher value. The lower the input voltage within the interval, the more probable it is that the output code will take the next lower value. The dither has resulted in a form of duty cycle modulation, and the resolution of the system has been extended indefinitely instead of being limited by the size of the steps.

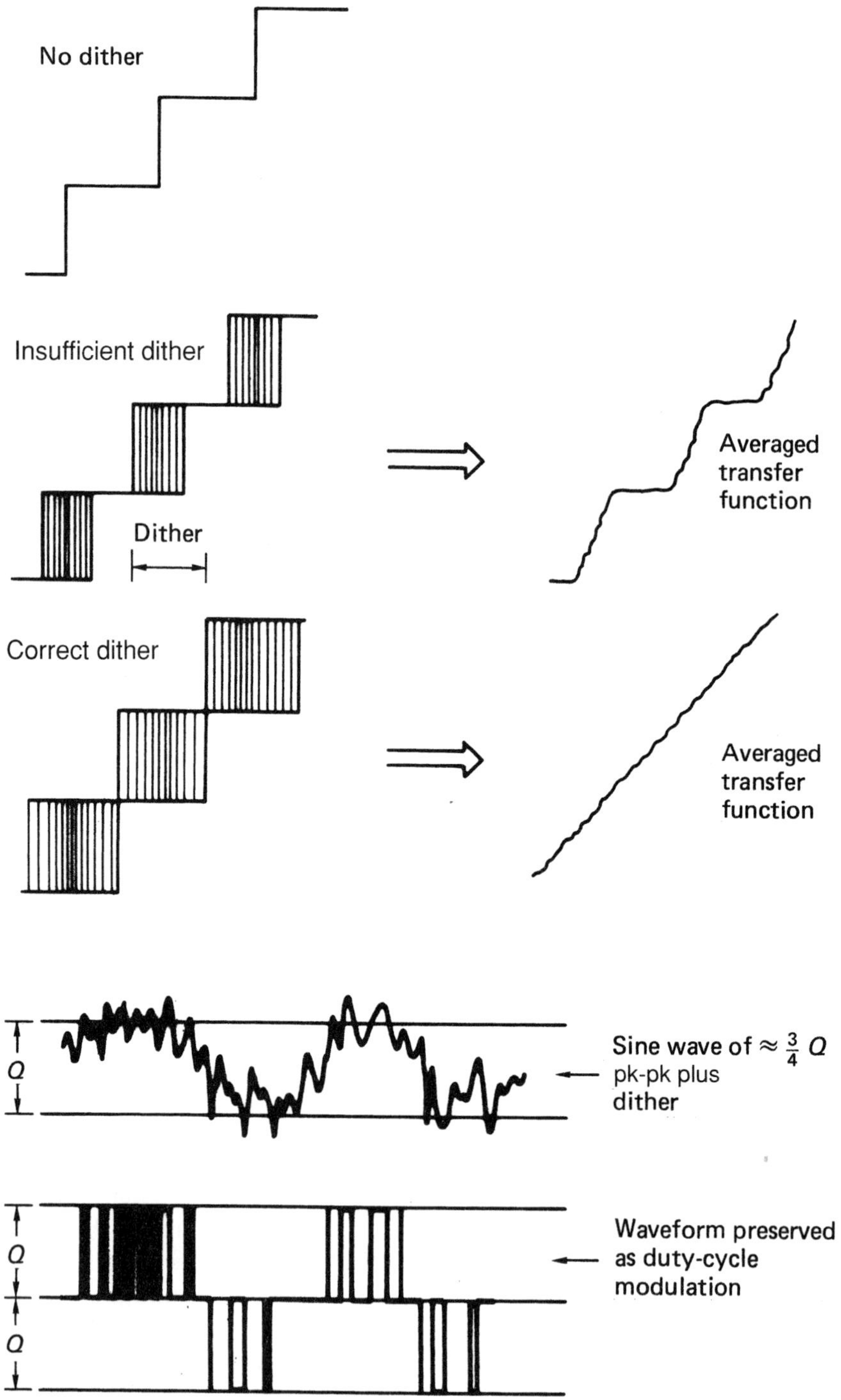

Figure 4.25 Wideband dither of the appropriate level linearizes the transfer function to produce noise instead of distortion. This can be confirmed by spectral analysis. In the voltage domain, dither causes frequent switching between codes and preserves resolution in the duty cycle of the switching.

Dither can also be understood by considering what it does to the transfer function of the quantizer. This is normally a perfect staircase, but in the presence of dither it is smeared horizontally until with a certain amplitude the average transfer function becomes straight.

4.9 Requantizing and digital dither

Recent ADC technology allows the wordlength of audio and video samples to be raised far above the capability of early devices. The situation then arises that an existing recorder or channel needs to be connected to the output of an ADC with greater wordlength. The words need to be shortened in some way.

In signal processing, when a sample value is attenuated, the extra low-order bits which come into existence below the radix point preserve the resolution of the signal and the dither in the least significant bit(s) which linearizes the system. The same word extension will occur in any process involving multiplication, such as digital filtering. It will subsequently be necessary to shorten the wordlength. Low-order bits must be removed to reduce the resolution whilst keeping the signal magnitude the same. Even if the original conversion was correctly dithered, the random element in the low-order bits will now be some way below the end of the intended word. If the word is simply truncated by discarding the unwanted low-order bits or rounded to the nearest integer the linearizing effect of the original dither will be lost.

Shortening the wordlength of a sample reduces the number of quantizing intervals available without changing the signal amplitude. As Figure 4.26 shows, the quantizing intervals become larger and the original signal is *requantized* with the new interval structure. This will introduce requantizing distortion having the same characteristics as quantizing distortion in an ADC. It then is obvious that when shortening the wordlength of a ten-bit convertor to eight bits, the two low-order bits must be removed in a way that displays the same overall quantizing structure as if the original convertor had been only of eight-bit wordlength. It will be seen from Figure 4.26 that truncation cannot be used because it does not meet the above requirement but results in signal-dependent offsets because it always rounds in the same direction. Proper numerical rounding is essential because it accurately simulates analog quantizing to the new interval size. Unfortunately the ten-bit convertor will have a dither amplitude appropriate to quantizing intervals one quarter the size of an eight-bit unit and the result will be highly non-linear.

In practice, in addition to rounding, there must be a mechanism whereby the requantizing error is converted to noise rather than

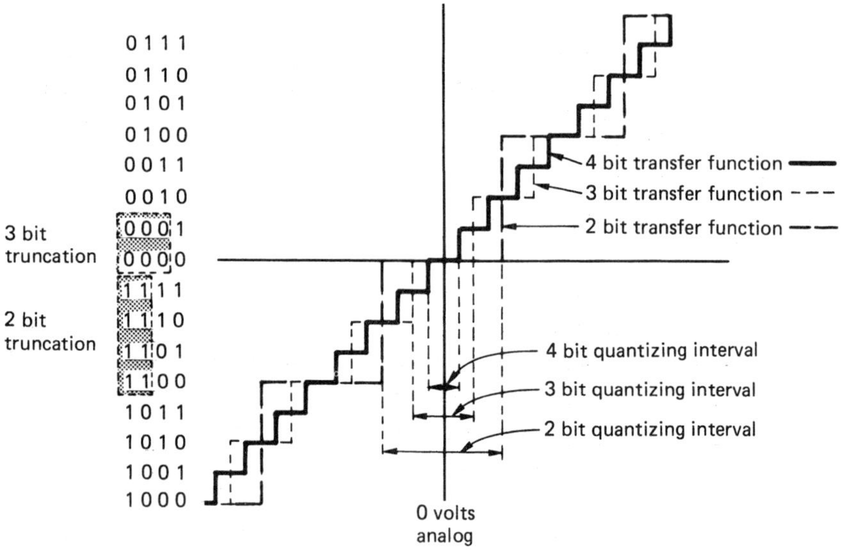

Figure 4.26 Shortening the wordlength of a sample reduces the number of codes which can describe the voltage of the waveform. This makes the quantizing steps bigger hence the term requantizing. It can be seen that simple truncation or omission of the bits does not give analogous behaviour. Rounding is necessary to give the same result as if the larger steps had been used in the original conversion.

distortion. One technique which meets this requirement is to use digital dithering[18] prior to rounding. This is directly equivalent to the analog dithering in an ADC.

Digital dither is a pseudo-random sequence of numbers. If it is required to simulate the analog dither signal of Figures 4.24 and 4.25, then it is obvious that the noise must be bipolar so that it can have an average voltage of zero. Two's complement coding can be used for the dither values.

Figure 4.27 shows a simple digital dithering system (i.e. one without noise shaping) for shortening sample wordlength. The output of a two's complement pseudo-random sequence generator (see Chapter 2) of appropriate wordlength is added to input samples prior to rounding. The most significant of the bits to be discarded is examined in order to determine whether the bits to be removed sum to more or less than half a quantizing interval. The dithered sample is either rounded down, i.e. the unwanted bits are simply discarded, or rounded up, i.e. the unwanted bits are discarded but one is added to the value of the new short word. The rounding process is no longer deterministic because of the added dither which provides a linearizing random component.

If this process is compared with that of Figure 4.24 it will be seen that the principles of analog and digital dither are identical; the processes simply take place in different domains using two's complement numbers

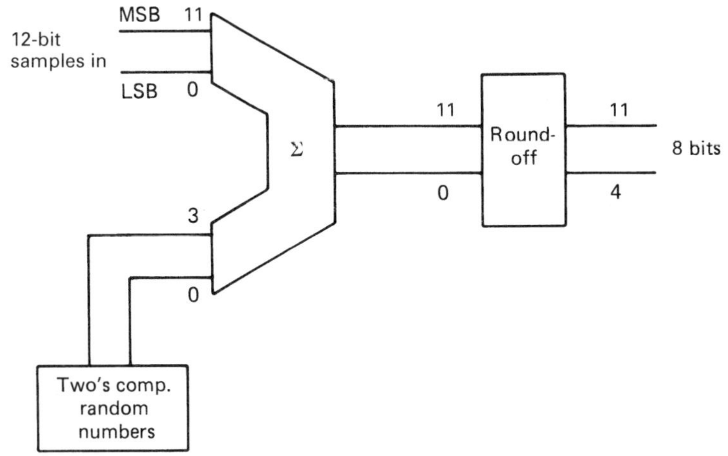

Figure 4.27 In a simple digital dithering system, two's complement values from a random number generator are added to low-order bits of the input. The dithered values are then rounded up or down according to the value of the bits to be removed. The dither linearizes the requantizing.

which are rounded or voltages which are quantized as appropriate. In fact quantization of an analog dithered waveform is identical to the hypothetical case of rounding after bipolar digital dither where the number of bits to be removed is infinite, and remains identical for practical purposes when as few as eight bits are to be removed. Analog dither may actually be generated from bipolar digital dither (which is no more than random numbers with certain properties) using a DAC.

4.10 Dither techniques

The intention here is to treat the processes of analog and digital dither as identical except where differences need to be noted. The characteristics of the noise used are rather important for optimal performance, although many sub-optimal but nevertheless effective systems are in use. The main parameters of interest are the peak-to-peak amplitude, the amplitude probability distribution function (pdf) and the spectral content.

The most comprehensive study of non-subtractive dither is due to Vanderkooy and Lipshitz[17–19] and the treatment here is based largely upon their work.

4.10.1 Rectangular pdf dither

Chapter 2 showed that the simplest form of dither (and therefore the easiest to generate) is a single sequence of random numbers which have uniform or rectangular probability. The amplitude of the dither is critical.

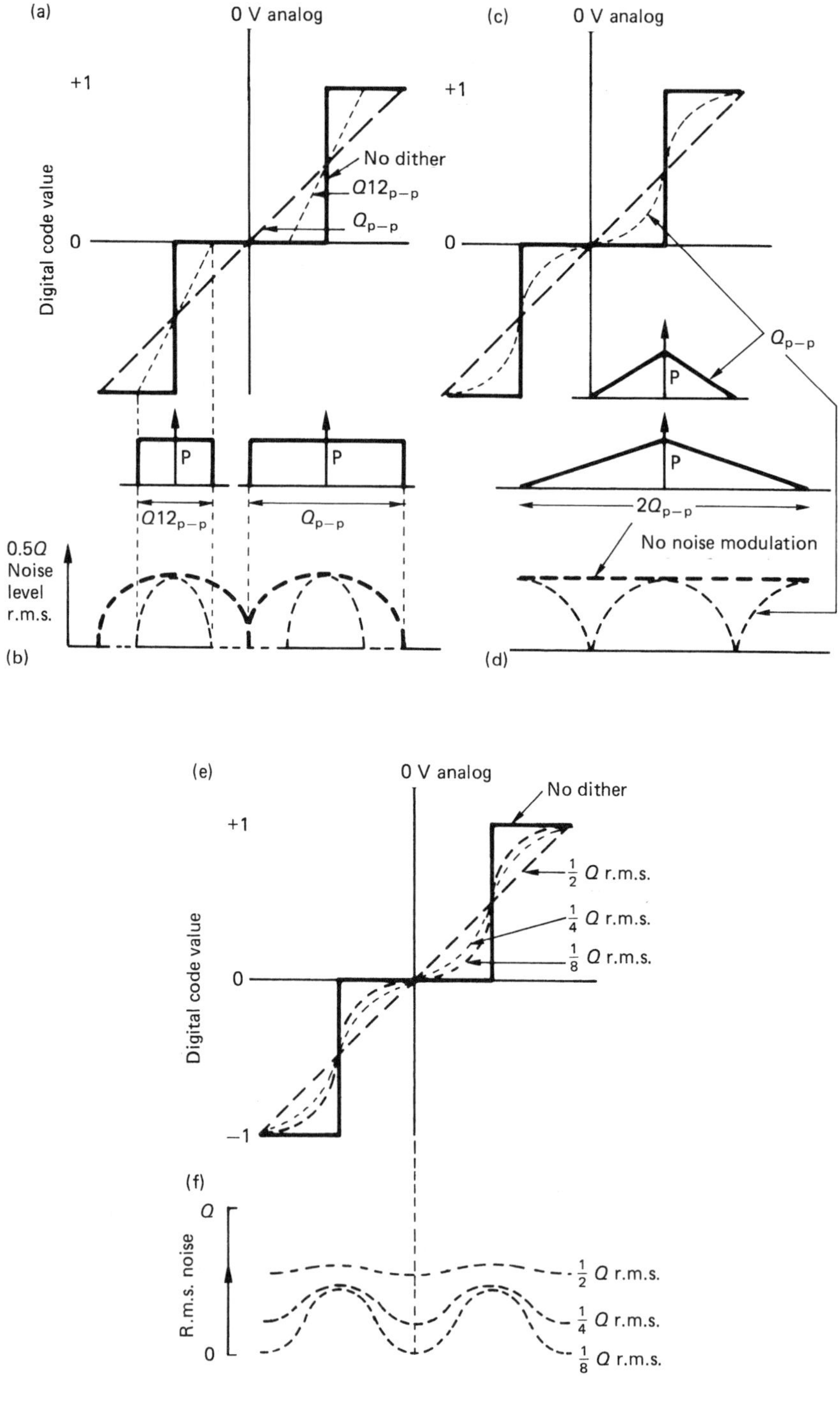

Figure 4.28 (a) Use of rectangular probability dither can linearize, but noise modulation (b) results. Triangular pdf dither (c) linearizes, and noise modulation is eliminated as at (d). Gaussian dither (e) can also be used, almost eliminating noise modulation at (f).

Figure 4.28(a) shows the time-averaged transfer function of one quantizing interval in the presence of various amplitudes of rectangular dither. The linearity is perfect at an amplitude of $1Q$ peak-to-peak and then deteriorates for larger or smaller amplitudes. The same will be true of all levels which are an integer multiple of Q. Thus there is no freedom in the choice of amplitude.

With the use of such dither, the quantizing noise is not constant. Figure 4.28(b) shows that when the analog input is exactly centred in a quantizing interval (such that there is no quantizing error) the dither has no effect and the output code is steady. There is no switching between codes and thus no noise. On the other hand when the analog input is exactly at a riser or boundary between intervals, there is the greatest switching between codes and the greatest noise is produced. Mathematically speaking, the first moment, or mean error is zero but the second moment, which in this case is equal to the variance, is not constant. From an engineering standpoint, the system is linear but suffers noise modulation: the noise floor rises and falls with the signal content and this is audible in the presence of low-frequency signals.

The dither adds an average noise amplitude of $Q/\sqrt{12}$ rms to the quantizing noise of the same level. In order to find the resultant noise level it is necessary to add the powers as the signals are uncorrelated. The total power is given by:

$$2 \times \frac{Q^2}{12} = \frac{Q^2}{6}$$

and the rms voltage is $Q/\sqrt{6}$. Another way of looking at the situation is to consider that the noise power doubles and so the rms noise voltage has increased by 3 dB in comparison with the undithered case. Thus for an n-bit wordlength, using the same derivation as expression (4.1) above, the signal-to-noise ratio for Q peak-to-peak rectangular dither will be given by:

$$6.02n - 1.24\,\text{dB} \tag{4.2}$$

Unlike the undithered case, this is a true signal-to-noise ratio and linearity is maintained at all signal levels. By way of example, for a ten-bit system nearly 59 dB signal-to-noise ratio is achieved. The 3 dB loss compared to the undithered case is a small price to pay for linearity.

4.10.2 Triangular pdf dither

The noise modulation due to the use of rectangular-probability dither is undesirable. It comes about because the process is too simple. The undithered quantizing error is signal dependent and the dither represents a single uniform-probability random process. This is only capable of decorrelating the quantizing error to the extent that its mean value is zero, rendering the system linear. The signal dependence is not eliminated, but is displaced to the next statistical moment. This is the variance and the result is noise modulation. If a further uniform-probability random process is introduced into the system, the signal dependence is displaced to the next moment and the second moment or variance becomes constant.

Adding together two statistically independent rectangular probability functions produces a triangular probability function. A signal having this characteristic can be used as the dither source.

Figure 4.28(c) shows the averaged transfer function for a number of dither amplitudes. Linearity is reached with a peak-to-peak amplitude of $2Q$ and at this level there is no noise modulation. The lack of noise modulation is another way of stating that the noise is constant. The triangular pdf of the dither matches the triangular shape of the quantizing error function.

The dither adds two noise signals with an amplitude of $Q/\sqrt{12}$ rms to the quantizing noise of the same level. In order to find the resultant noise level it is necessary to add the powers as the signals are uncorrelated. The total power is given by:

$$3 \times \frac{Q^2}{12} = \frac{Q^2}{4}$$

and the rms voltage is $Q/\sqrt{4}$. Another way of looking at the situation is to consider that the noise power is increased by 50 per cent in comparison to the rectangular dithered case and so the rms noise voltage has increased by 1.76 dB. Thus for an n-bit wordlength, using the same derivation as expressions (4.1) and (4.2) above, the signal-to-noise ratio for Q peak-to-peak rectangular dither will be given by:

$$6.02n - 3\,\text{dB} \tag{4.3}$$

Continuing the use of a ten-bit example, a signal-to-noise ratio of 57.2 dB is available which is 4.8 dB worse than the SNR of an undithered quantizer in the large signal case. It is a small price to pay for perfect linearity and an unchanging noise floor.

4.10.3 Gaussian pdf dither

Adding more uniform probability sources to the dither makes the overall probability function progressively more like the Gaussian distribution of analog noise. Figure 4.28(d) shows the averaged transfer function of a quantizer with various levels of Gaussian dither applied. Linearity is reached with $\frac{1}{2}Q$ rms and at this level noise modulation is negligible. The total noise power is given by:

$$\frac{Q^2}{4} + \frac{Q^2}{12} = \frac{3 \times Q^2}{12} + \frac{Q^2}{12}$$

$$= \frac{Q^2}{3}$$

and so the noise level will be $Q/\sqrt{3}$ rms. The noise level of an undithered quantizer in the large signal case is $Q/\sqrt{12}$ and so the noise is higher by a factor of:

$$\frac{Q}{\sqrt{3}} \times \frac{\sqrt{12}}{Q} = \frac{Q}{\sqrt{3}} \times \frac{2\sqrt{3}}{Q} = 2 = 6.02\,\text{dB}$$

Thus the signal-to-noise ratio is given by

$$6.02(n - 1) + 1.76\,\text{dB} \tag{4.4}$$

A ten-bit system with correct Gaussian dither has a signal-to-noise ratio of 56 dB.

This is inferior to the figure in expression (4.3) by 1.1 dB. In digital dither applications, triangular probability dither of 2Q peak-to-peak is optimum because it gives the best possible combination of nil distortion, freedom from noise modulation and signal-to-noise ratio. Using dither with more than two rectangular processes added is detrimental. Whilst this result is also true for analog dither, it is not practicable to apply it to a real ADC as all real analog signals contain thermal noise which is Gaussian. If triangular dither is used on a signal containing Gaussian noise, the results derived above are not obtained. ADCs should therefore use Gaussian dither of $Q/2$ rms and performance will be given by expression (4.4).

4.11 Basic digital-to-analog conversion

This direction of conversion will be discussed first, since ADCs often use embedded DACs in feedback loops.

The purpose of a digital-to-analog convertor is to take numerical values and reproduce the continuous electrical waveform that they represent. Figure 4.29 shows the major elements of a conventional conversion subsystem, i.e. one in which oversampling is not employed. The jitter in the clock needs to be removed with a VCO or VCXO. Sample values are buffered in a latch and fed to the convertor element which operates on

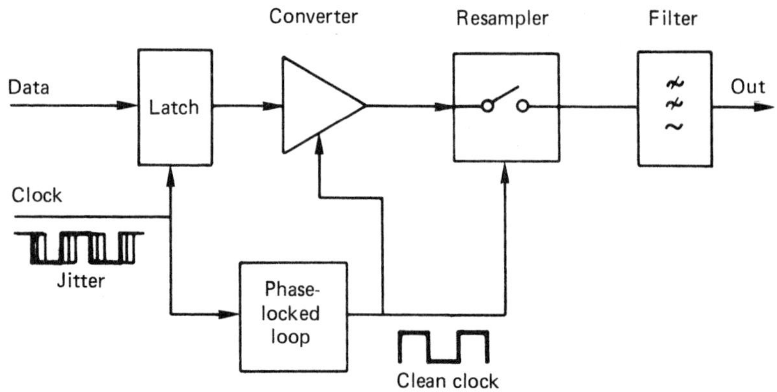

Figure 4.29 The components of a conventional convertor. A jitter-free clock drives the voltage conversion, whose output may be resampled prior to reconstruction.

each cycle of the clean clock. The output is then a voltage proportional to the number for at least a part of the sample period. A resampling stage may be found next, in order to remove switching transients, reduce the aperture ratio or allow the use of a convertor which takes a substantial part of the sample period to operate. The resampled waveform is then presented to a reconstruction filter which rejects frequencies above the audio band.

This section is primarily concerned with the implementation of the convertor element. The most common way of achieving this conversion is to control binary-weighted currents and sum them in a virtual earth. Figure 4.30 shows the classical *R*–2*R* DAC structure. This is relatively

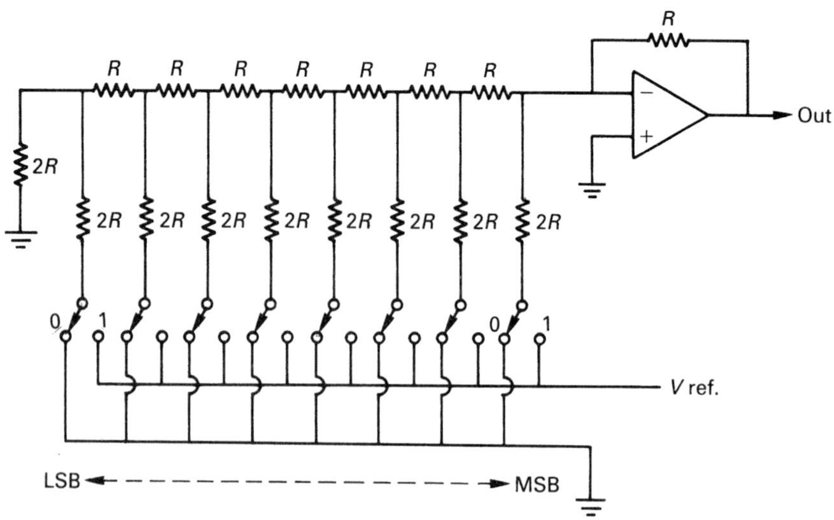

Figure 4.30 The classical *R*–2*R* DAC requires precise resistance values and 'perfect' switches.

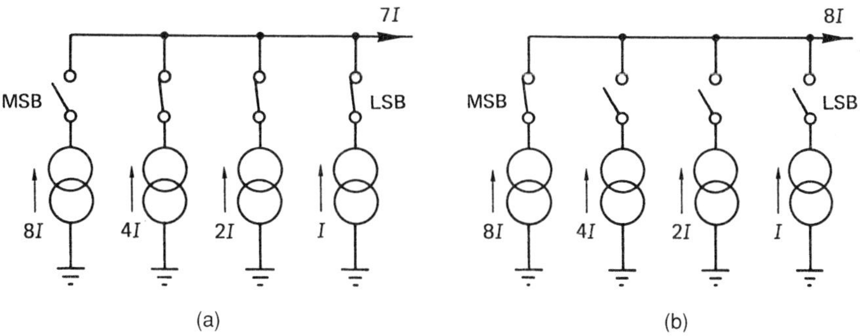

Figure 4.31 At (a) current flow with an input of 0111 is shown. At (b) current flow with input code one greater.

simple to construct, but the resistors have to be extremely accurate. To see why this is so, consider the example of Figure 4.31. At (a) the binary code is about to have a major overflow, and all the low-order currents are flowing. At (b), the binary input has increased by one, and only the most significant current flows. This current must equal the sum of all the others plus one. The accuracy must be such that the step size is within the required limits. In this eight-bit example, if the step size needs to be a rather casual 10 per cent accurate, the necessary accuracy is only one part in 2560, but for a ten-bit system it would become one part in 10 240. This degree of accuracy is difficult to achieve and maintain in the presence of ageing and temperature change.

4.12 Basic analog-to-digital conversion

The input to an ADC is a continuous-time, continuous-voltage waveform, and this is converted into a discrete-time, discrete-voltage format by a combination of sampling and quantizing. As these two processes are orthogonal they are totally independent and can be performed in either order. Figure 4.32(a) shows an analog sampler preceding a quantizer, whereas (b) shows an asynchronous quantizer preceding a digital sampler. Ideally, both will give the same results; in practice each has different advantages and suffers from different deficiencies. Both approaches will be found in real equipment.

The general principle of a quantizer is that different quantized voltages are compared with the unknown analog input until the closest quantized voltage is found. The code corresponding to this becomes the output. The comparisons can be made in turn with the minimal amount of hardware, or simultaneously with more hardware.

The flash convertor is probably the simplest technique available for PCM video conversion. The principle is shown in Figure 4.33. The

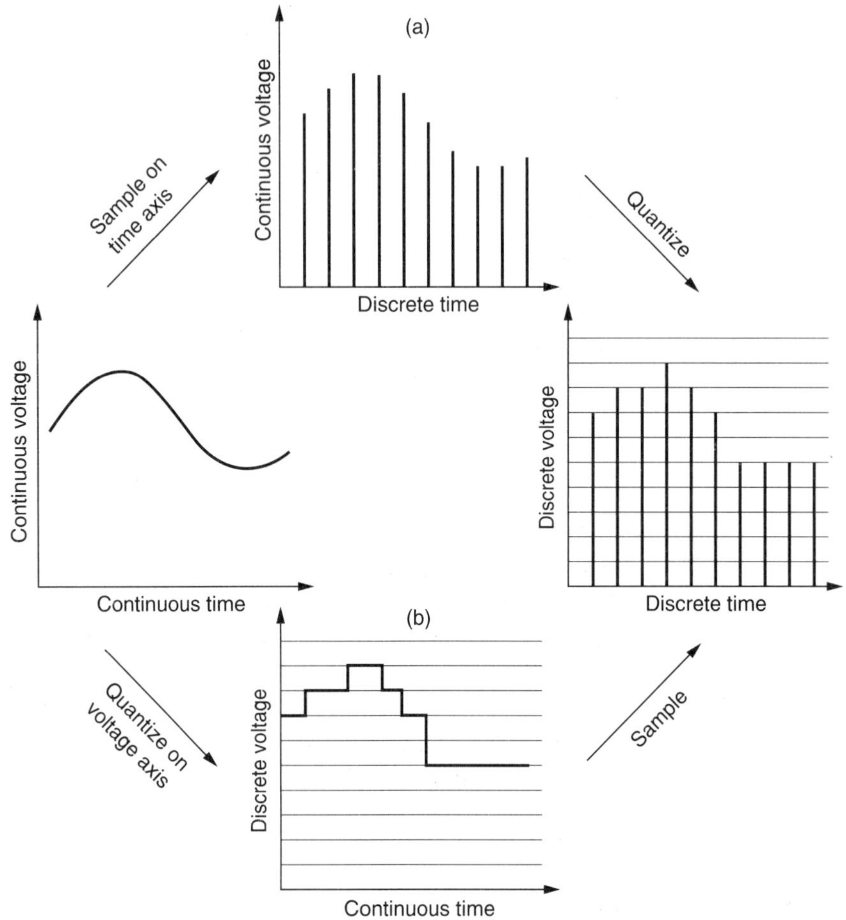

Figure 4.32 Since sampling and quantizing are orthogonal, the order in which they are performed is not important. In (a) sampling is performed first and the samples are quantized. This is common in audio convertors. In (b) the analog input is quantized into an asynchronous binary code. Sampling takes place when this code is latched on sampling clock edges. This approach is universal in video convertors.

threshold voltage of every quantizing interval is provided by a resistor chain which is fed by a reference voltage. This reference voltage can be varied to determine the sensitivity of the input. There is one voltage comparator connected to every reference voltage, and the other input of all the comparators is connected to the analog input. A comparator can be considered to be a one-bit ADC. The input voltage determines how many of the comparators will have a true output. As one comparator is necessary for each quantizing interval, then, for example, in an eight-bit system there will be 255 binary comparator outputs, and it is necessary to use a priority encoder to convert these to a binary code.

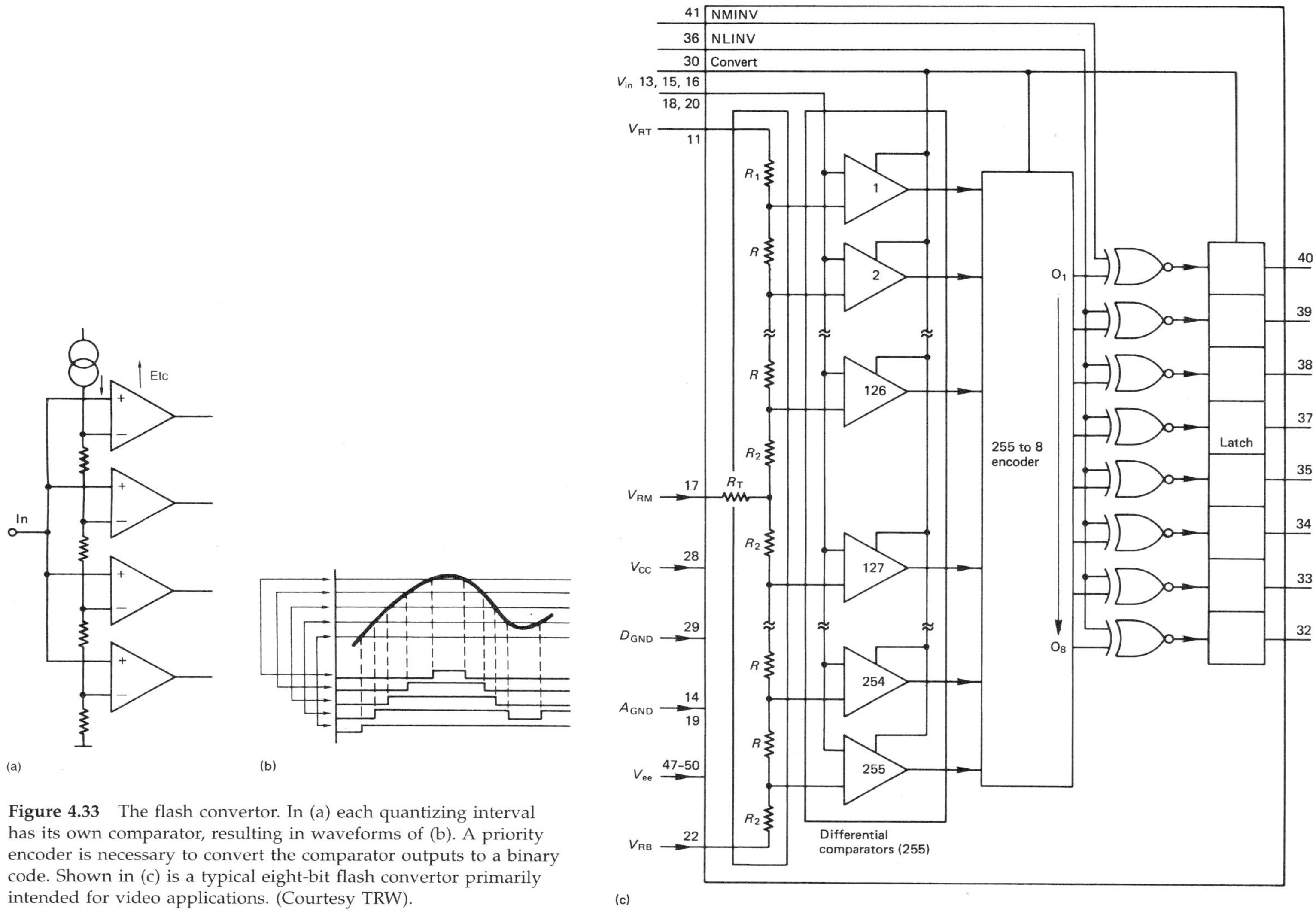

Figure 4.33 The flash convertor. In (a) each quantizing interval has its own comparator, resulting in waveforms of (b). A priority encoder is necessary to convert the comparator outputs to a binary code. Shown in (c) is a typical eight-bit flash convertor primarily intended for video applications. (Courtesy TRW).

Note that the quantizing stage is asynchronous; comparators change state as and when the variations in the input waveform result in a reference voltage being crossed. Sampling takes place when the comparator outputs are clocked into a subsequent latch. This is an example of quantizing before sampling as was illustrated in Figure 4.32. Although the device is simple in principle, it contains a lot of circuitry and can only be practicably implemented on a chip. The analog signal has to drive many inputs which results in a significant parallel capacitance, and a low-impedance driver is essential to avoid restricting the slewing rate of the input. The extreme speed of a flash convertor is a distinct advantage in oversampling. Because computation of all bits is performed simultaneously, no track/hold circuit is required, and droop is eliminated. Figure 4.33(c) shows a flash convertor chip. Note the resistor ladder and the comparators followed by the priority encoder. The MSB can be selectively inverted so that the device can be used either in offset binary or two's complement mode.

The flash convertor is ubiquitous in digital video because of the high speed necessary. For audio purposes, many more conversion techniques are available and these are considered in Chapter 5.

References

1. Nyquist, H., Certain topics in telegraph transmission theory. *AIEE Trans*, 617–644 (1928)
2. Shannon, C.E., A mathematical theory of communication. *Bell Syst. Tech. J.*, **27**, 379 (1948)
3. Jerri, A.J., The Shannon sampling theorem – its various extensions and applications: a tutorial review. *Proc. IEEE*, **65**, 1565–1596 (1977)
4. Whittaker, E.T., On the functions which are represented by the expansions of the interpolation theory. *Proc. R. Soc. Edinburgh*, 181–194 (1915)
5. Porat, B., *A Course in Digital Signal Processing*, New York: John Wiley (1996)
6. Betts, J.A., *Signal Processing Modulation and Noise*, Chapter 6, Sevenoaks: Hodder and Stoughton (1970)
7. Bennett, W. R., Spectra of quantized signals. *Bell System Tech. Journal*, **27**, 446–472 (1948)
8. Widrow, B., Statistical analysis of amplitude quantized sampled-data systems. *Trans. AIEE*, Part II, **79**, 555–568 (1961)
9. Lipshitz, S.P., Wannamaker, R.A. and Vanderkooy, J., Quantization and dither: a theoretical survey. *J. Audio Eng. Soc.*, **40**, 355–375 (1992)
10. Maher, R.C., On the nature of granulation noise in uniform quantization systems. *J. Audio Eng. Soc.*, **40**, 12–20 (1992)
11. Goodall, W. M., Television by pulse code modulation. *Bell System Tech. Journal*, **30**, 33–49 (1951)
12. Roberts, L. G., Picture coding using pseudo-random noise. *IRE Trans. Inform. Theory*, **IT-8**, 145–154 (1962)
13. Schuchman, L., Dither signals and their effect on quantizing noise. *Trans. Commun. Technol.*, **COM-12**, 162–165 (1964)
14. Sherwood, D.T., Some theorems on quantization and an example using dither. In *Conf. Rec., 19th Asilomar Conference on circuits, systems and computers*, Pacific Grove, CA (1985)

15. Lipshitz, S.P., Wannamaker, R.A. and Vanderkooy, J., Quantization and dither: a theoretical survey. *J. Audio Eng. Soc.*, **40**, 355–375 (1992)
16. Gerzon, M. and Craven, P.G., Optimal noise shaping and dither of digital signals. Presented at 87th Audio Eng. Soc. Conv., New York (1989), Preprint No. 2822 (J-1)
17. Vanderkooy, J. and Lipshitz, S.P., Resolution below the least significant bit in digital systems with dither. *J. Audio Eng. Soc.*, **32**, 106–113 (1984)
18. Vanderkooy, J. and Lipshitz, S.P., Digital dither. Presented at 81st Audio Eng. Soc. Conv., Los Angeles (1986), Preprint 2412 (C-8)
19. Vanderkooy, J. and Lipshitz, S.P., Digital dither. In *Audio in Digital Times*, New York: AES (1989)

5

Sound

5.1 Introduction

Sound is important in convergent systems both in its own right and as an accompaniment to some form of image. Traditionally the consumer could receive sound radio at a time decided by the broadcaster, or purchase prerecorded media. Digital technology allows a much greater variety of sound-delivery mechanisms. Sound radio is now broadcast digitally, with greater resistance to multipath reception than analog FM could offer, but still at a time decided by the broadcaster. Prerecorded media reached their pinnacle of sound quality with the Compact Disc, followed by the smaller but audibly inferior MiniDisc, but these are only digitized versions of earlier services.

However, network technology allows digital audio to be delivered to any desired quality and at any time. Figure 5.1 shows one service which is already established. The service provider maintains file servers which contain music in a compressed digital format (typically MPEG Layer III also known as MP3). The consumer can download these files to a PC over

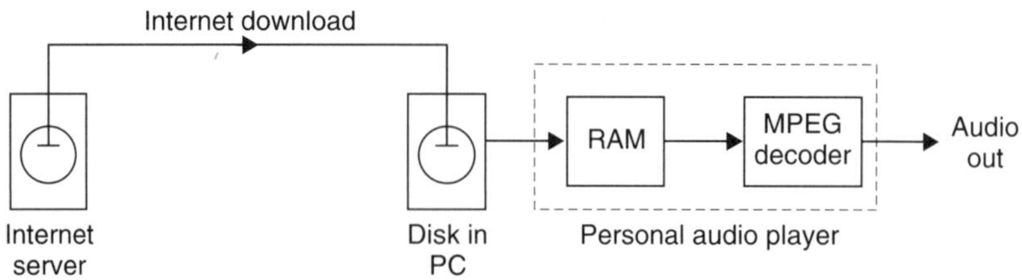

Figure 5.1 Using heavy compression, digital audio recordings can be transferred over the Internet to a PC and thence to a RAM-based player in non-real-time. The compression decoder in the player accesses the RAM to produce real-time audio.

the Internet, and can then transfer the files to a RAM-based portable player which contains an MPEG decoder. The sound quality is not outstanding, but the service has the advantage of immediacy and flexibility. The consumer can access audio files from anywhere and create a personalized album in a RAM player.

At greater cost, audio data can be exchanged between recording studios using mild or no compression, giving a faster alternative to the delivery of tapes. Clearly a range of sound qualities will be required according to the service, ranging from voice-grade message services to downloadable classical music. This chapter takes the approach that if it shows how to make the finest possible sound reproduction system, the reader can always take an economic decision to provide lower quality. Consequently the information provided here represents as far as possible the state of the art.

Digital multiplexing makes it easy to deliver surround sound and this adds greater involvement to certain moving-image material both in the home and in electronic cinemas. It has been shown beyond doubt that realistic sound causes the viewer to rate the subjective picture quality higher. This is true not only of electronic cinema but also for Internet video where the picture quality is frequently mediocre due to bit rate limitations.

The electronic cinema has the advantage over the home theatre that a greater sum can be invested in the sound equipment, although a small proportion of home theatre systems will also be highly specified. The flat display screen using plasma technology is often hailed as the ultimate TV set to hang on the wall, but a moment's thought will reveal that without flat loudspeaker technology of high quality, the flat screen is not a TV, but only a display. Most of today's flat screens contain loudspeakers which are truly appalling and inconsistent with the current high cost of such displays.

It should not be assumed that audio is used entirely for entertainment. Some audio applications, such as aircaft noise monitoring, submarine detection and battlefield simulators, result in specifications which are extremely high. Emergency evacuation instructions in public places come from audio systems which must continue to work in the presence of cable damage, combustion products, water and power loss.

By definition, the sound quality of an audio system can only be assessed by the human auditory system (HAS). Quality means different things to different people and can range from a realistic reproduction of classical music to the intelligible delivery of speech in a difficult acoustic. Many items of audio equipment can only be designed well with a good knowledge of the human hearing mechanism. The understanding of the HAS and how it relates to the criteria for accurate sound reproduction has increased enormously in recent years and these findings will be given here. From this knowledge it becomes obvious what will and will not work and it becomes clear how to proceed and to what degree of accuracy.

The traditional hi-fi enthusiast will not find much comfort here. There are no suggestions to use rare or exotic materials based on pseudoscience. The obvious and audible mistakes made in the design of much of today's hi-fi equipment are testimony to the fact that it comes from a heavily commoditized and somewhat disreputable industry where technical performance has hardly improved in twenty years. This chapter is not about hi-fi, it is about sound reproduction. All the criteria proposed here are backed with reputable research and all the technology described has been made and works as expected.

5.2 The deciBel

The first audio signals to be transmitted were on analog telephone lines. Where the wiring is long compared to the electrical wavelength (not to be confused with the acoustic wavelength) of the signal, a transmission line exists in which the distributed series inductance and the parallel capacitance interact to give the line a characteristic impedance. In telephones this turned out to be about 600 Ω. In transmission lines the best power delivery occurs when the source and the load impedance are the same; this is the process of matching.

It was often required to measure the power in a telephone system, and one milliWatt was chosen as a suitable unit. Thus the reference against which signals could be compared was the dissipation of one milliWatt in 600 Ω. Figure 5.2 shows that the dissipation of 1 mW in 600 Ω will be due to an applied voltage of 0.775 V rms. This voltage is the reference against which all audio levels are compared.

The deciBel is a logarithmic measuring system and has its origins in telephony[1] where the loss in a cable is a logarithmic function of the length. Human hearing also has a logarithmic response with respect to sound pressure level (SPL). In order to relate to the subjective response audio signal level measurements have also to be logarithmic and so the deciBel was adopted for audio.

Figure 5.3 shows the principle of the logarithm. To give an example, if it is clear that 10^2 is 100 and 10^3 is 1000, then there must be a power between 2 and 3 to which 10 can be raised to give any value between 100 and 1000. That power is the logarithm to base 10 of the value. e.g. $\log_{10} 300 = 2.5$ approx. Note that 10^0 is 1.

Logarithms were developed by mathematicians before the availability of calculators or computers to ease calculations such as multiplication, squaring, division and extracting roots. The advantage is that armed with

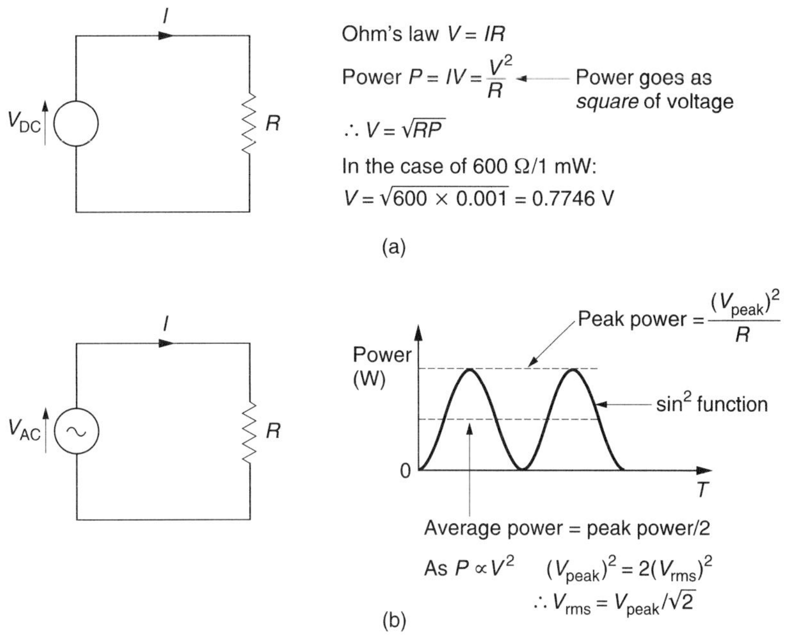

Figure 5.2 (a) Ohm's law: the power developed in a resistor is proportional to the square of the voltage. Consequently, 1 mW in 600 Ω requires 0.775 V. With a sinusoidal alternating input (b), the power is a sine square function which can be averaged over one cycle. A DC voltage which would deliver the same power has a value which is the square root of the mean of the square of the sinusoidal input.

a set of log tables, multiplication can be performed by adding, division by subtracting. Figure 5.3 shows some examples. It will be clear that squaring a number is performed by adding two identical logs and the same result will be obtained by multiplying the log by 2.

The slide rule is an early calculator which consists of two logarithmically engraved scales in which the length along the scale is proportional to the log of the engraved number. By sliding the moving scale, two lengths can easily be added or subtracted and as a result multiplication and division is readily obtained.

The logarithmic unit of measurement in telephones was called the Bel after Alexander Graham Bell, the inventor. Figure 5.4(a) shows that the Bel was defined as the log of the *power* ratio between the power to be measured and some reference power. Clearly the reference power must have a level of 0 Bels since $\log_{10} 1$ is 0.

The Bel was found to be an excessively large unit for many purposes and so it was divided into 10 deciBels, abbreviated to dB with a small d and a large B and pronounced 'deebee'. Consequently the number of dB is ten times the log of the power ratio. A device such as an amplifier can have a fixed power gain which is independent of signal level and this can

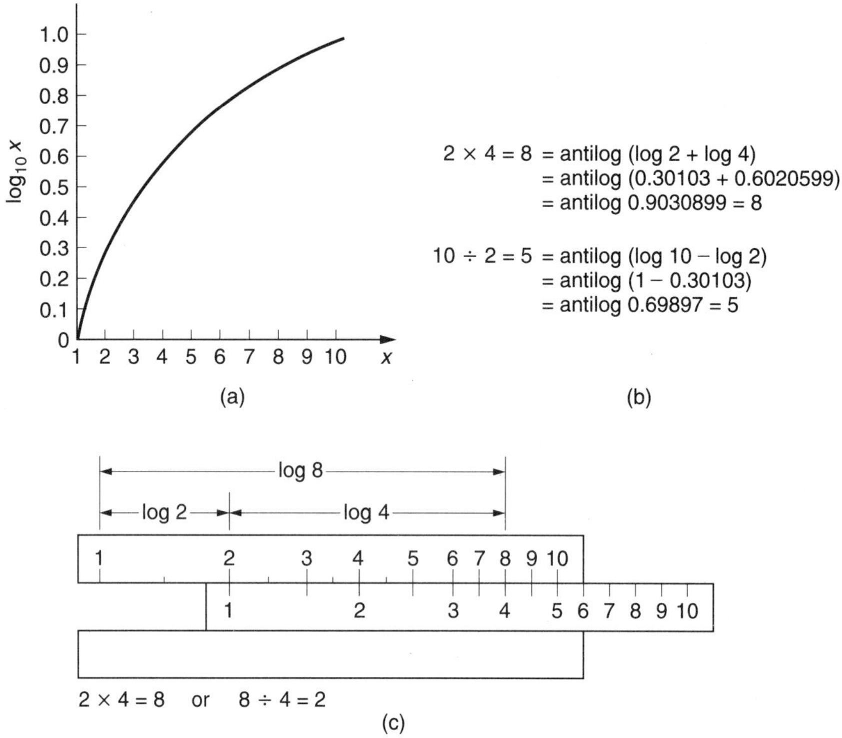

Figure 5.3 (a) The logarithm of a number is the power to which the base (in this case 10) must be raised to obtain the number. (b) Multiplication is obtained by adding logs, division by subtracting. (c) The slide rule has two logarithmic scales whose length can easily be added or subtracted.

be measured in dB. However, when measuring the power of a signal, it must be appreciated that the dB is a ratio and to quote the number of dBs without stating the reference is about as senseless as describing the height of a mountain as 2000 without specifying whether this is feet or metres. To show that the reference is one milliWatt into 600 Ω, the units will be dB(m). In radio engineering, the dB(W) will be found which is power relative to one Watt.

Although the dB(m) is defined as a power ratio, level measurements in audio are often done by measuring the signal voltage using 0.775 V as a reference in a circuit whose impedance is not necessarily 600 Ω. Figure 5.4(b) shows that as the power is proportional to the square of the voltage, the power ratio will be obtained by squaring the voltage ratio. As squaring in logs is performed by doubling, the squared term of the voltages can be replaced by multiplying the log by a factor of two. To give a result in deciBels, the log of the voltage ratio now has to be multiplied by 20.

Whilst 600 Ω matched-impedance working is essential for the long distances encountered with telephones, it is quite inappropriate for

$$1 \text{ Bel} = \log_{10} \frac{P_1}{P_2} \qquad 1 \text{ deciBel} = 1/10 \text{ Bel}$$

$$\text{Power ratio (dB)} = 10 \times \log_{10} \frac{P_1}{P_2}$$

(a)

As power α V^2, when using voltages:

$$\text{Power ratio (dB)} = 10 \log \frac{V_1^2}{V_2^2}$$

$$= 10 \times \log \frac{V_1}{V_2} \times 2$$

$$= 20 \log \frac{V_1}{V_2}$$

(b)

Figure 5.4 (a) The Bel is the log of the ratio between two powers, that to be measured and the reference. The Bel is too large so the deciBel is used in practice. (b) As the dB is defined as a power ratio, voltage ratios have to be squared. This is conveniently done by doubling the logs so the ratio is now multiplied by 20.

analog audio wiring in the studio or the home. The wavelength of audio in wires at 20 kHz is 15 km. Most studios are built on a smaller scale than this and clearly analog audio cables are *not* transmission lines and their characteristic impedance is swamped by the devices connected at each end. Consequently the reader is cautioned that anyone who attempts to sell exotic analog audio cables by stressing their transmission line characteristics is more of a salesman than a physicist.

In professional analog audio systems impedance matching is not only unnecessary it is also undesirable. Figure 5.5(a) shows that when impedance matching is required the output impedance of a signal source must be artificially raised so that a potential divider is formed with the load. The actual drive voltage must be twice that needed on the cable as the potential divider effect wastes 6 dB of signal level and requires unnecessarily high power supply rail voltages in equipment. A further problem is that cable capacitance can cause an undesirable HF roll-off in conjunction with the high source impedance.

In modern professional analog audio equipment, shown in Figure 5.5(b) the source has the lowest output impedance practicable. This means that any ambient interference is attempting to drive what amounts to a short circuit and can only develop very small voltages. Furthermore, shunt capacitance in the cable has very little effect. The destination has a somewhat higher impedance (generally a few kΩ) to avoid excessive

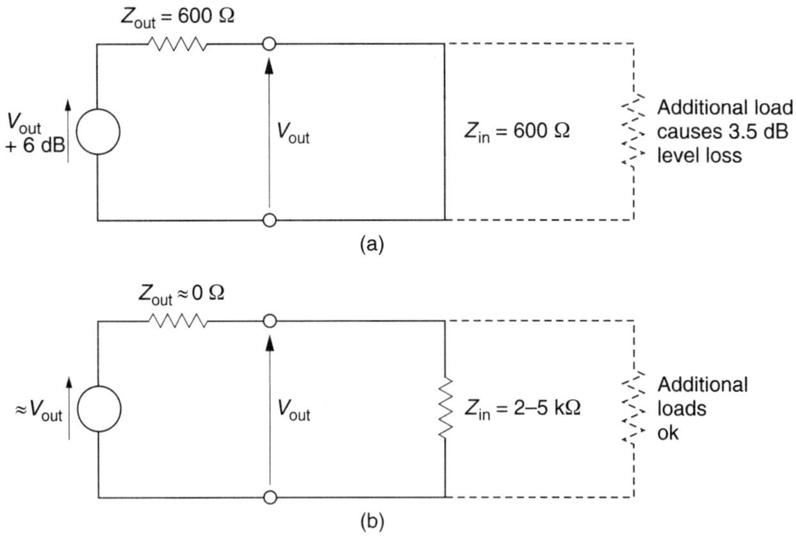

Figure 5.5 (a) Traditional impedance matched source wastes half the signal voltage in the potential divider due to the source impedance and the cable. (b) Modern practice is to use low-output impedance sources with high-impedance loads.

currents flowing and to allow several loads to be placed across one driver.

In the absence of a fixed impedance it is now meaningless to consider power. Consequently only signal voltages are measured. The reference remains at 0.775 V, but power and impedance are irrelevant. Voltages measured in this way are expressed in dB(u); the commonest unit of level in modern systems. Most installations boost the signals on interface cables by 4 dB. As the gain of receiving devices is reduced by 4 dB, the result is a useful noise advantage without risking distortion due to the drivers having to produce high voltages.

In order to make the difference between dB(m) and dB(u) clear, consider the lossless matching transformer shown in Figure 5.6. The

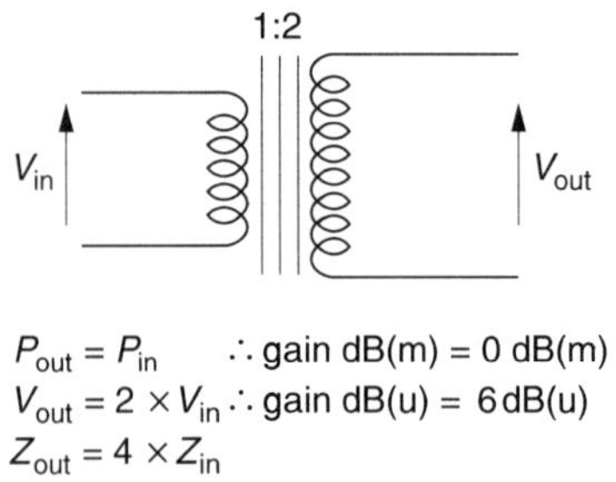

Figure 5.6 A lossless transformer has no power gain so the level in dB(m) on input and output is the same. However, there is a voltage gain when measurements are made in dB(u).

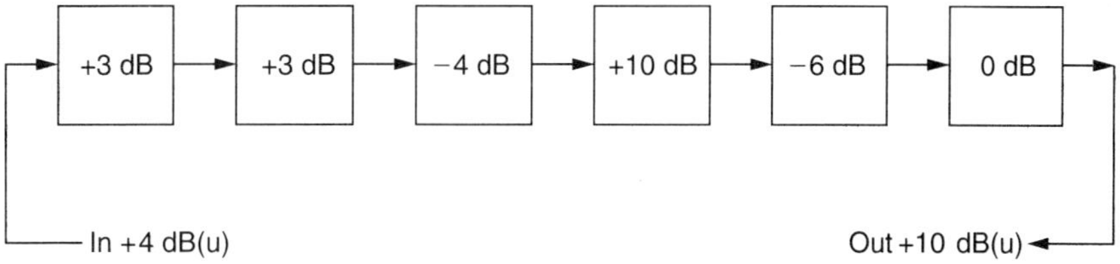

Figure 5.7 In complex systems each stage may have voltage gain measured in dB. By adding all of these gains together and adding to the input level in dB(u), the output level in dB(u) can be obtained.

turns ratio is 2:1 therefore the impedance matching ratio is 4:1. As there is no loss in the transformer, the power in is the same as the power out so that the transformer shows a gain of 0 dB(m). However, the turns ratio of 2:1 provides a voltage gain of 6 dB(u). The doubled output voltage will develop the same power into the quadrupled load impedance.

In a complex system signals may pass through a large number of processes, each of which may have a different gain. Figure 5.7 shows that if one stays in the linear domain and measures the input level in volts rms, the output level will be obtained by multiplying by the gains of all the stages involved. This is a complex calculation.

The difference between the signal level with and without the presence of a device in a chain is called the *insertion loss* measured in dB. However, if the input is measured in dB(u), the output level of the first stage can be obtained by adding the insertion loss in dB. The output level of the second stage can be obtained by further adding the loss of the second stage in dB and so on. The final result is obtained by adding together all of the insertion losses in dB and adding them to the input level in dB(u) to give the output level in dB(u). As the dB is a pure ratio it can multiply anything (by addition of logs) without changing the units. Thus dB(u) of level added to dB of gain are still dB(u).

In acoustic measurements, the sound pressure level (SPL) is measured in deciBels relative to a reference pressure of 2×10^{-5} Pascals (Pa) rms. In order to make the reference clear the units are dB(SPL). In measurements which are intended to convey an impression of subjective loudness, a weighting filter is used prior to the level measurement which reproduces the frequency response of human hearing which is most sensitive in the midrange. The most common standard frequency response is the so-called A-weighting filter, hence the term dB(A) used when a weighted level is being measured. At high or low frequencies, a lower reading will be obtained in dB(A) than in dB(SPL).

5.3 Audio level metering

There are two main reasons for having level meters in audio equipment: to line up or adjust the gain of equipment, and to assess the amplitude of the program material. Gain line-up is especially important in digital systems where an incorrect analog level can result in ADC clipping.

Line-up is often done using a 1 kHz sine wave generated at an agreed level such as 0 dB(u). If a receiving device does not display the same level, then its input sensitivity must be adjusted. Tape recorders and other devices which pass signals through are usually lined up so that their input and output levels are identical, i.e. their insertion loss is 0 dB. Line-up is important in large systems because it ensures that inadvertent level changes do not occur.

In measuring the level of a sine wave for the purposes of line-up, the dynamics of the meter are of no consequence, whereas on program material the dynamics matter a great deal. The simplest (and cheapest) level meter is essentially an AC voltmeter with a logarithmic response. As the ear is logarithmic, the deflection of the meter is roughly proportional to the perceived volume, hence the term Volume Unit (VU) meter.

In audio recording and broadcasting, the worst sin is to overmodulate the tape, the ADC or the transmitter by allowing a signal of excessive amplitude to pass. Real audio signals are rich in short transients which pass before the sluggish VU meter responds. Consequently the VU meter is also called the virtually useless meter in professional circles.

Broadcasters developed the peak program meter (PPM) which is also logarithmic, but which is designed to respond to peaks as quickly as the ear responds to distortion. Consequently the attack time of the PPM is carefully specified. If a peak is so short that the PPM fails to indicate its true level, the resulting overload will also be so brief that the HAS will not hear it. A further feature of the PPM is that the decay time of the meter is very slow, so that any peaks are visible for much longer and the meter is easier to read because the meter movement is less violent.

The original PPM as developed by the BBC was sparsely calibrated, but other users have adopted the same dynamics and added dB scales. Figure 5.8 shows some of the scales in use.

In broadcasting, the use of level metering and line-up procedures ensures that the level experienced by the viewer/listener does not change significantly from program to program. Consequently in a transmission suite, the goal would be to broadcast tapes at a level identical to that which was obtained during production. However, when making a recording prior to any production process, the goal would be to modulate the tape as fully as possible without clipping, as this would then give the best signal-to-noise ratio. The level would then be reduced if necessary in the production process.

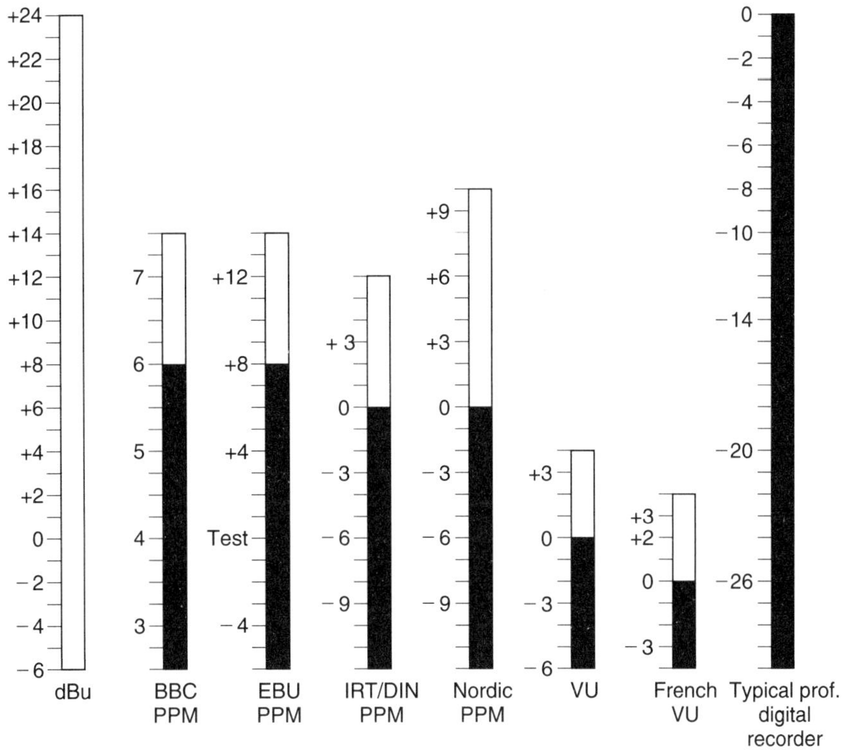

Figure 5.8 Some of the scales used in conjunction with the PPM dynamics. (After Francis Rumsey, with permission.)

Unlike analog recorders, digital systems do not have headroom, as there is no progressive onset of distortion until convertor clipping, the equivalent of saturation, occurs at 0 dBFs. Accordingly many digital recorders have level meters which read in dBFs. The scales are marked with 0 at the clipping level and all operating levels are below that. This causes no dificulty provided the user is aware of the consequences.

However, in the situation where a digital copy of an analog tape is to be made, it is very easy to set the input gain of the digital recorder so that line-up tone from the analog tape reads 0 dB. This lines up digital clipping with the analog operating level. When the tape is dubbed, all signals in the headroom suffer convertor clipping.

In order to prevent such problems, manufacturers and broadcasters have introduced artificial headroom on digital level meters, simply by calibrating the scale and changing the analog input sensitivity so that 0 dB analog is some way below clipping. Unfortunately there has been little agreement on how much artificial headroom should be provided, and machines which have it are seldom labelled with the amount. There is an argument which suggests that the amount of headroom should be a function of the sample wordlength, but this causes difficulties when transferring from one wordlength to another. In sixteen-bit working, 12 dB of headroom is a useful figure, but now that eighteen- and twenty-bit convertors are available, 18 dB may be more appropriate.

5.4 The ear

The human auditory system, the sense called hearing, is based on two obvious tranducers at the side of the head, and a number of less obvious mental processes which give us an impression of the world around us based on disturbances to the equilibrium of the air which we call sound. It is only possible briefly to introduce the subject here. The interested reader is referred to Moore[2] for an excellent treatment.

The HAS can tell us, without aid from any other senses, where a sound source is, how big it is, whether we are in an enclosed space and how big that is. If the sound source is musical, we can further establish information such as pitch and timbre, attack, sustain and decay. In order to do this, the auditory system must work in the time, frequency and space domains. A sound reproduction system which is inadequate in one of these domains will be unrealistic however well the other two are satisfied. Chapter 3 introduced the concept of uncertainty between the time and frequency domains and the ear cannot analyse both at once. The HAS circumvents this by changing its characteristics dynamically so that it can concentrate on one domain or the other.

The acuity of the HAS is astonishing. It can detect tiny amounts of distortion, and will accept an enormous dynamic range over a wide number of octaves. If the ear detects a different degree of impairment between two audio systems and an original or 'live' sound in properly conducted tests, we can say that one of them is superior. Thus quality is completely subjective and can only be checked by listening tests. However, any characteristic of a signal which can be heard can, in principle, also be measured by a suitable instrument although in general the availability of such instruments lags the requirement and the use of such instruments lags the availability. The subjective tests will tell us how sensitive the instrument should be. Then the objective readings from the instrument give an indication of how acceptable a signal is in respect of that characteristic.

Figure 5.9 shows that the structure of the ear is traditionally divided into the outer, middle and inner ears. The outer ear works at low impedance, the inner ear works at high impedance, and the middle ear is an impedance-matching device. The visible part of the outer ear is called the pinna which plays a subtle role in determining the direction of arrival of sound at high frequencies. It is too small to have any effect at low

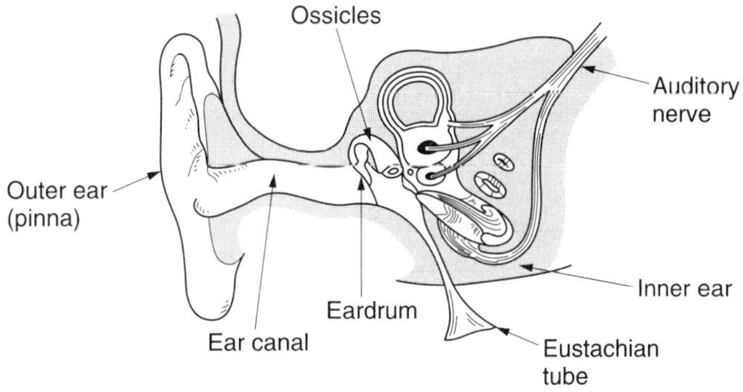

Figure 5.9 The structure of the human ear. See text for details.

frequencies. Incident sound enters the auditory canal or meatus. The pipe-like meatus causes a small resonance at around 4 kHz. Sound vibrates the eardrum or tympanic membrane which seals the outer ear from the middle ear. The inner ear or cochlea works by sound travelling though a fluid. Sound enters the cochlea via a membrane called the oval window. If airborne sound were to be incident on the oval window directly, the serious impedance mismatch would cause most of the sound to be reflected. The middle ear remedies that mismatch by providing a mechanical advantage.

The tympanic membrane is linked to the oval window by three bones known as ossicles which act as a lever system such that a large displacement of the tympanic membrane results in a smaller displacement of the oval window but with greater force. Figure 5.10 shows that the malleus applies a tension to the tympanic membrane rendering it conical in shape. The malleus and the incus are firmly joined together to form a lever. The incus acts upon the stapes through a spherical joint. As the area of the tympanic membrane is greater than that of the oval window, there is a further multiplication of the available force.

Consequently small pressures over the large area of the tympanic membrane are converted to high pressures over the small area of the oval

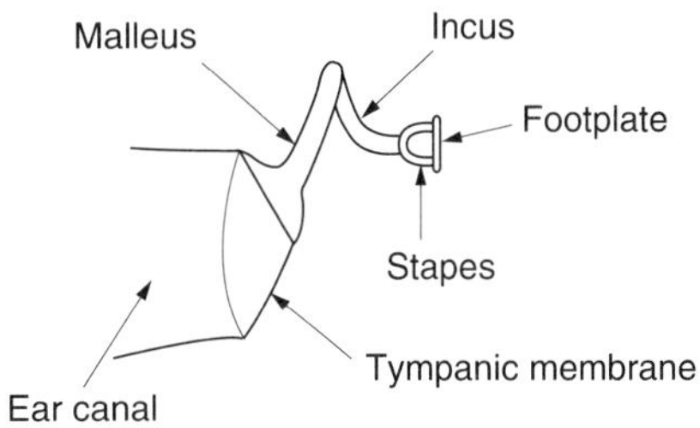

Figure 5.10 The malleus tensions the tympanic membrane into a conical shape. The ossicles provide an impedance-transforming lever system between the tympanic membrane and the oval.

window. The middle ear evolved to operate at natural sound levels and causes distortion at the high levels which can be generated with artificial amplification.

The middle ear is normally sealed, but ambient pressure changes will cause static pressure on the tympanic membrane which is painful. The pressure is relieved by the Eustachian tube which opens involuntarily while swallowing. Some of the discomfort of the common cold is due to these tubes becoming blocked. The Eustachian tubes open into the cavities of the head and must normally be closed to avoid one's own speech appearing deafeningly loud.

The ossicles are located by minute muscles which are normally relaxed. However, the middle ear reflex is an involuntary tightening of the *tensor tympani* and *stapedius* muscles which heavily damp the ability of the tympanic membrane and the stapes to transmit sound by about 12 dB at frequencies below 1 kHz. The main function of this reflex is to reduce the audibility of one's own speech. However, loud sounds will also trigger this reflex which takes some 60–120 ms to operate; too late to protect against transients such as gunfire.

The cochlea is the transducer proper, converting pressure variations in the fluid into nerve impulses. However, unlike a microphone, the nerve impulses are not an analog of the incoming waveform. Instead the cochlea has some analysis capability which is combined with a number of mental processes to make a complete analysis. As shown in Figure 5.11(a), the cochlea is a fluid-filled tapering spiral cavity within bony walls. The widest part, near the oval window, is called the *base* and the distant end is the *apex*. Figure 5.11(b) shows that the cochlea is divided lengthwise into three volumes by Reissner's membrane and the basilar membrane. The *scala vestibuli* and the *scala tympani* are connected by a small aperture at the apex of the cochlea known as the *helicotrema*. Vibrations from the stapes are transferred to the oval window and become fluid pressure variations which are relieved by the flexing of the round window.

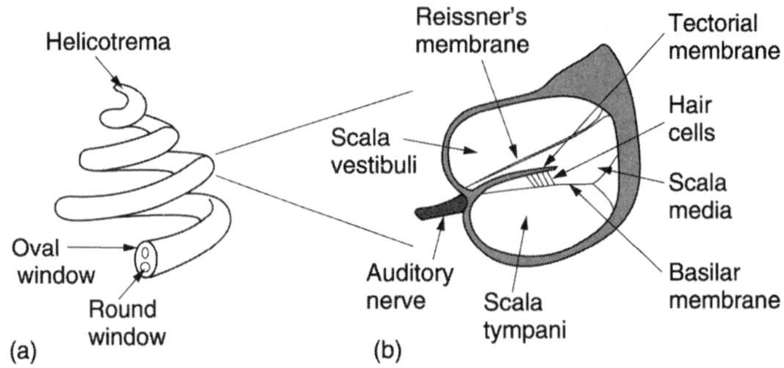

Figure 5.11 (a) The cochlea is a tapering spiral cavity. (b) The cross-section of the cavity is divided by Reissner's membrane and the basilar membrane.

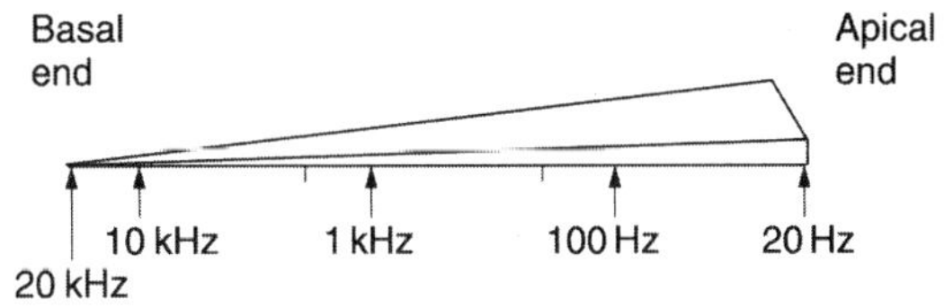

Figure 5.12 The basilar membrane tapers so its resonant frequency changes along its length.

Effectively the basilar membrane is in series with the fluid motion and is driven by it except at very low frequencies where the fluid flows through the helicotrema, decoupling the basilar membrane.

To assist in its frequency-domain operation, the basilar membrane is not uniform. Figure 5.12 shows that it tapers in width and varies in thickness in the opposite sense to the taper of the cochlea. The part of the basilar membrane which resonates as a result of an applied sound is a function of the frequency. High frequencies cause resonance near to the oval window, whereas low frequencies cause resonances further away. More precisely the distance from the apex where the maximum resonance occurs is a logarithmic function of the frequency. Consequently tones spaced apart in octave steps will excite evenly spaced resonances in the basilar membrane. The prediction of resonance at a particular location on the membrane is called *place theory*. Among other things, the basilar membrane is a mechanical frequency analyser. A knowledge of the way it operates is essential to an understanding of musical phenomena such as pitch discrimination, timbre, consonance and dissonance and to auditory phenomena such as critical bands, masking and the precedence effect.

The vibration of the basilar membrane is sensed by the organ of Corti which runs along the centre of the cochlea. The organ of Corti is active in that it contains elements which can generate vibration as well as sense it. These are connected in a regenerative fashion so that the *Q* factor, or frequency selectivity, of the ear is higher than it would otherwise be. The deflection of hair cells in the organ of Corti triggers nerve firings and these signals are conducted to the brain by the auditory nerve.

Nerve firings are not a perfect analog of the basilar membrane motion. A nerve firing appears to occur at a constant phase relationship to the basilar vibration; a phenomenon called phase locking, but firings do not necessarily occur on every cycle. At higher frequencies firings are intermittent, yet each is in the same phase relationship.

The resonant behaviour of the basilar membrane is not observed at the lowest audible frequencies below 50 Hz. The pattern of vibration does not appear to change with frequency and it is possible that the frequency is low enough to be measured directly from the rate of nerve firings.

5.5 Level and loudness

At its best, the HAS can detect a sound pressure variation of only 2×10^{-5} Pascals rms and so this figure is used as the reference against which sound pressure level (SPL) is measured. The sensation of loudness is a logarithmic function of SPL hence the use of the deciBel explained in section 5.2. The dynamic range of the HAS exceeds 130 dB, but at the extremes of this range, the ear is either straining to hear or is in pain.

The frequency response of the HAS is not at all uniform and it also changes with SPL. The subjective response to level is called loudness and is measured in *phons*. The phon scale and the SPL scale coincide at 1 kHz, but at other frequencies the phon scale deviates because it displays the actual SPLs judged by a human subject to be equally loud as a given level at 1 kHz. Figure 5.13 shows the so-called equal loudness contours which were originally measured by Fletcher and Munson and subsequently by Robinson and Dadson. Note the irregularities caused by resonances in the meatus at about 4 kHz and 13 kHz.

Usually, people's ears are at their most sensitive between about 2 kHz and 5 kHz, and although some people can detect 20 kHz at high level, there is much evidence to suggest that most listeners cannot tell if the upper frequency limit of sound is 20 kHz or 16 kHz.[3,4] For a long time it was thought that frequencies below about 40 Hz were unimportant, but it is now clear that reproduction of frequencies down to 20 Hz improves

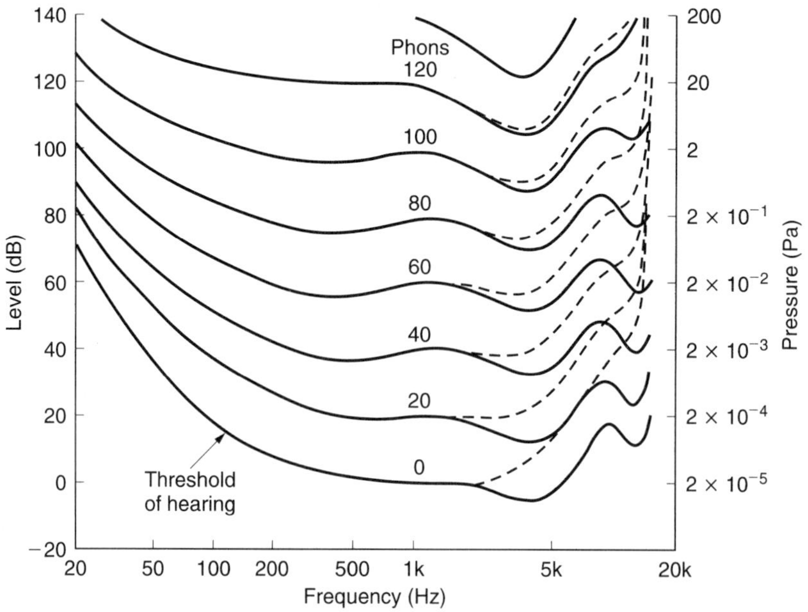

Figure 5.13 Contours of equal loudness showing that the frequency response of the ear is highly level dependent (solid line. age 20; dashed line, age 60).

reality and ambience.[5] The generally accepted frequency range for high-quality audio is 20–20 000 Hz, although for broadcasting an upper limit of 15 000 Hz is often applied.

The most dramatic effect of the curves of Figure 5.13 is that the bass content of reproduced sound is disproportionately reduced as the level is turned down. This would suggest that if a powerful yet high-quality reproduction system is available the correct tonal balance when playing a good recording can be obtained simply by setting the volume control to the correct level. This is indeed the case. A further consideration is that many musical instruments and the human voice change timbre with level and there is only one level which sounds correct for the timbre.

Oddly, there is as yet no standard linking the signal level in a transmission or recording system with the SPL at the microphone, although with the advent of digital microphones this useful information could easily be sent as metadata.

Loudness is a subjective reaction and is almost impossible to measure. In addition to the level-dependent frequency response problem, the listener uses the sound not for its own sake but to draw some conclusion about the source. For example, most people hearing a distant motorcycle will describe it as being loud. Clearly at the source, it *is* loud, but the listener has compensated for the distance. Paradoxically the same listener may then use a motor mower without hearing protection.

The best that can be done is to make some compensation for the level-dependent response using *weighting curves*. Ideally there should be many, but in practice the A, B and C weightings were chosen where the A curve is based on the 40-phon response. The measured level after such a filter is in units of dBA. The A curve is almost always used because it most nearly relates to the annoyance factor of distant noise sources. The use of A-weighting at higher levels is highly questionable.

5.6 Frequency discrimination

Figure 5.14 shows an uncoiled basilar membrane with the apex on the left so that the usual logarithmic frequency scale can be applied. The envelope of displacement of the basilar membrane is shown for a single frequency at (a). The vibration of the membrane in sympathy with a single frequency cannot be localized to an infinitely small area, and nearby areas are forced to vibrate at the same frequency with an amplitude that decreases with distance. Note that the envelope is asymmetrical because the membrane is tapering and due to frequency-dependent losses in the propagation of vibrational energy down the cochlea. If the frequency is changed, as in (b), the position of maximum displacement will also change. As the basilar membrane is continuous,

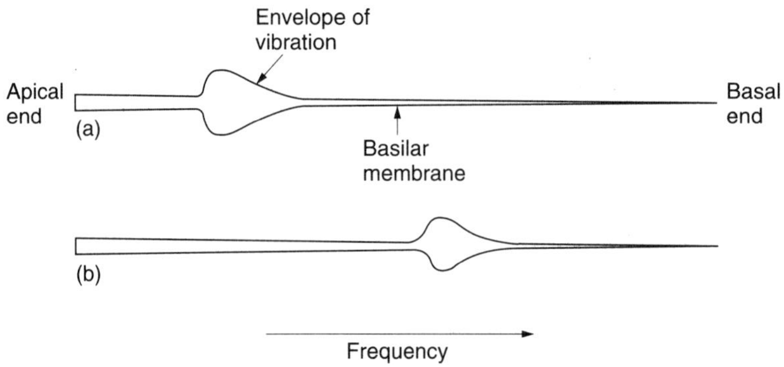

Figure 5.14 The basilar membrane symbolically uncoiled. (a) Single frequency causes the vibration envelope shown. (b) Changing the frequency moves the peak of the envelope.

the position of maximum displacement is infinitely variable, allowing extremely good pitch discrimination of about one twelfth of a semitone which is determined by the spacing of hair cells.

In the presence of a complex spectrum, the finite width of the vibration envelope means that the ear fails to register energy in some bands when there is more energy in a nearby band. Within those areas, other frequencies are mechanically excluded because their amplitude is insufficient to dominate the local vibration of the membrane. Thus the *Q* factor of the membrane is responsible for the degree of auditory masking, defined as the decreased audibility of one sound in the presence of another.

The term used in psychoacoustics to describe the finite width of the vibration envelope is *critical bandwidth*. Critical bands were first described by Fletcher.[6] The envelope of basilar vibration is a complicated function. It is clear from the mechanism that the area of the membrane involved will increase as the sound level rises. Figure 5.15 shows the bandwidth as a function of level.

As was shown in Chapter 3, the Heisenberg inequality teaches that the higher the frequency resolution of a transform, the worse the time accuracy. As the basilar membrane has finite frequency resolution measured in the width of a critical band, it follows that it must have finite time resolution. This also follows from the fact that the membrane is resonant, taking time to start and stop vibrating in response to a stimulus. There are many examples of this. Figure 5.16 shows the impulse response and Figure 5.17 the perceived loudness of a tone burst increases with duration up to about 200 ms due to the finite response time.

The HAS has evolved to offer intelligibility in reverberant environments which it does by averaging all received energy over a period of about 30 ms. Reflected sound which arrives within this time is integrated

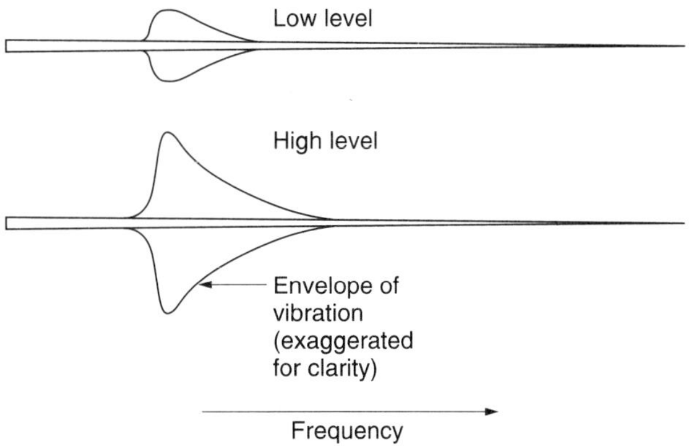

Figure 5.15 The critical bandwidth changes with SPL.

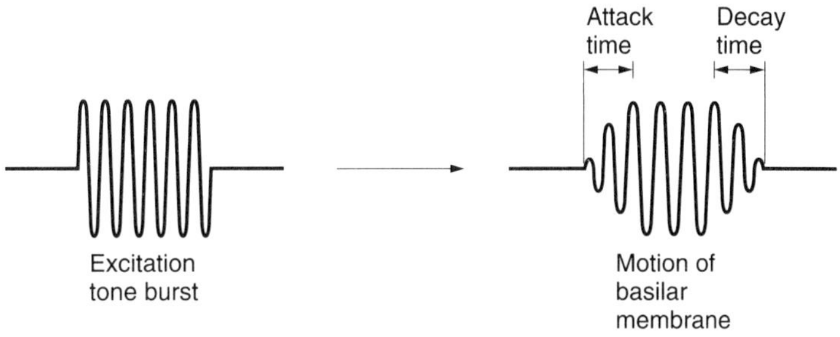

Figure 5.16 Impulse response of the ear showing slow attack and decay due to resonant behaviour.

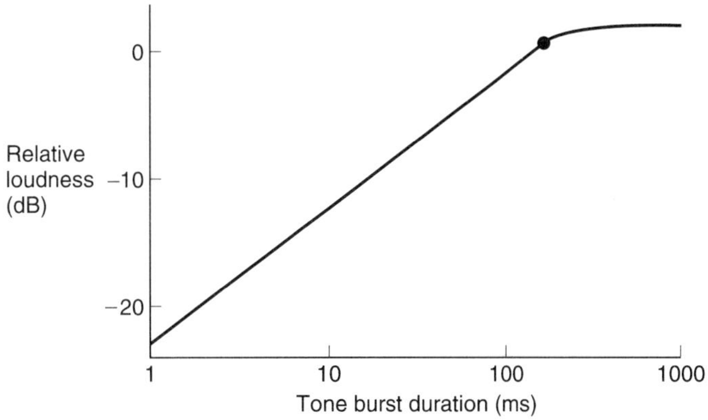

Figure 5.17 Perceived level of tone burst rises with duration as resonance builds up.

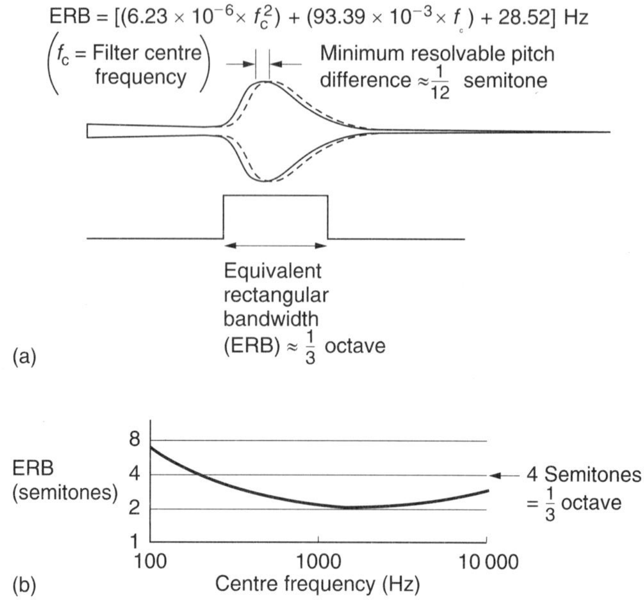

Figure 5.18 Effective rectangular bandwidth of critical band is much wider than the resolution of the pitch discrimination mechanism.

to produce a louder sensation, whereas reflected sound which arrives after that time can be temporally discriminated and is perceived as an echo. Microphones have no such ability which is why we often need to have acoustic treatment in areas where microphones are used.

A further example of the finite time discrimination of the HAS is the fact that short interruptions to a continuous tone are difficult to detect. Finite time resolution means that masking can take place even when the masking tone begins after and ceases before the masked sound. This is referred to as forward and backward masking.[7]

As the vibration envelope is such a complicated shape, Moore and Glasberg have proposed the concept of equivalent rectangular bandwidth to simplify matters. The ERB is the bandwidth of a rectangular filter which passes the same power as a critical band. Figure 5.18(a) shows the expression they have derived linking the ERB with frequency. This is plotted in (b) where it will be seen that one third of an octave is a good approximation. This is about thirty times broader than the pitch discrimination also shown in (b).

Figure 5.19 shows an electrical signal (a) in which two equal sine waves of nearly the same frequency have been linearly added together. Note that the envelope of the signal varies as the two waves move in and out of phase. Clearly the frequency transform calculated to infinite accuracy is that shown at (b). The two amplitudes are constant and there is no

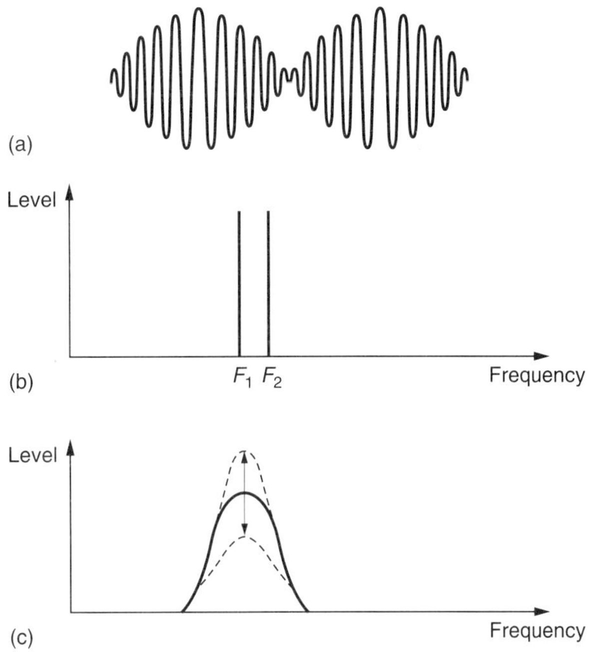

Figure 5.19 (a) Result of adding two sine waves of similar frequency. (b) Spectrum of (a) to infinite accuracy. (c) With finite accuracy only a single frequency is distinguished whose amplitude changes with the envelope of (a) giving rise to beats.

evidence of the envelope modulation. However, such a measurement requires an infinite time. When a shorter time is available, the frequency discrimination of the transform falls and the bands in which energy is detected become broader.

When the frequency discrimination is too wide to distinguish the two tones as in (c), the result is that they are registered as a single tone. The amplitude of the single tone will change from one measurement to the next because the envelope is being measured. The rate at which the envelope amplitude changes is called a *beat* frequency which is not actually present in the input signal. Beats are an artifact of finite frequency resolution transforms. The fact that the HVS produces beats from pairs of tones proves that it has finite resolution.

Measurement of when beats occur allows measurement of critical bandwidth. Figure 5.20 shows the results of human perception of a two-tone signal as the frequency **dF** difference changes. When **dF** is zero, described musically as *unison*, only a single note is heard. As **dF** increases, beats are heard, yet only a single note is perceived. The limited frequency resolution of the basilar membrane has *fused* the two tones together. As **dF** increases further, the sensation of beats ceases at 12–15 Hz and is replaced by a sensation of roughness or *dissonance*. The roughness is due to parts

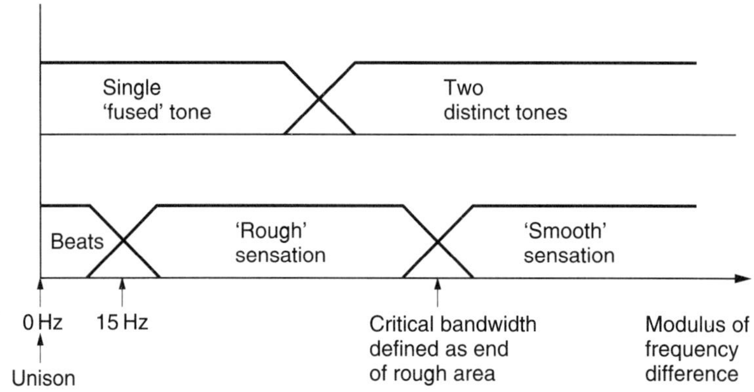

Figure 5.20 Perception of two-tone signal as frequency difference changes.

of the basilar membrane being unable to decide the frequency at which to vibrate. The regenerative effect may well become confused under such conditions. The roughness which persists until **dF** has reached the critical bandwidth beyond which two separate tones will be heard because there are now two discrete basilar resonances. In fact this is the definition of critical bandwidth.

5.7 Music and the ear

The characteristics of the HVS, especially critical bandwidth, are responsible for the way music has evolved. Beats are used extensively in music. When tuning a pair of instruments together, a small tuning error will result in beats when both play the same nominal note. In certain pipe organs, pairs of pipes are sounded together with a carefully adjusted pitch error which results in a pleasing tremolo effect.

With certain exceptions, music is intended to be pleasing and so dissonance is avoided. Two notes which sound together in a pleasing manner are described as harmonious or *consonant*. Two sine waves appear consonant if they separated by a critical bandwidth because the roughness of Figure 5.20 is avoided, but real musical instruments produce a series of harmonics in addition to the fundamental.

Figure 5.21 shows the spectrum of a harmonically rich instrument. The fundamental and the first few harmonics are separated by more than a critical band, but from the seventh harmonic more than one harmonic will be in one band and it is possible for dissonance to occur. Musical instruments have evolved to avoid the production of seventh and higher harmonics. Violins and pianos are played or designed to excite the strings at a node of the seventh harmonic to suppress this dissonance.

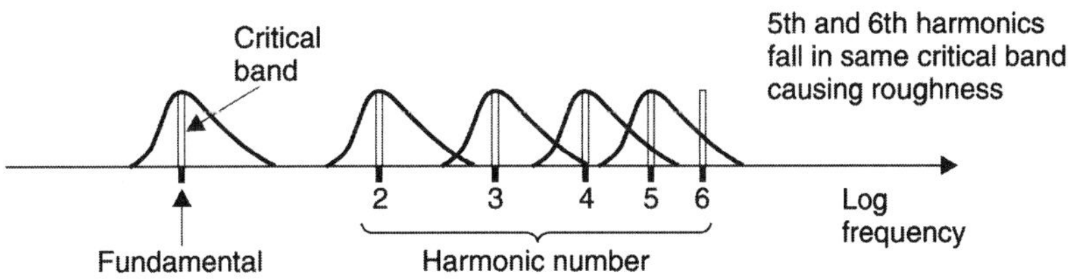

Figure 5.21 Spectrum of a real instrument with respect to critical bandwidth. High harmonics can fall in the same critical band and cause dissonance.

Harmonic distortion in audio equipment is easily detected even in minute quantities because the first few harmonics fall in non-overlapping critical bands. The sensitivity of the HAS to third harmonic distortion probably deserves more attention in audio equipment than the fidelity of the dynamic range or frequency response.

When two harmonically rich notes are sounded together, the harmonics will fall within the same critical band and cause dissonance unless the fundamentals have one of a limited number of simple relationships which makes the harmonics fuse. Clearly an octave relationship is perfect.

Figure 5.22 shows some examples. In (a) two notes with the ratio (interval) 3:2 are considered. The harmonics are either widely separated or fused and the combined result is highly consonant. The interval of 3:2

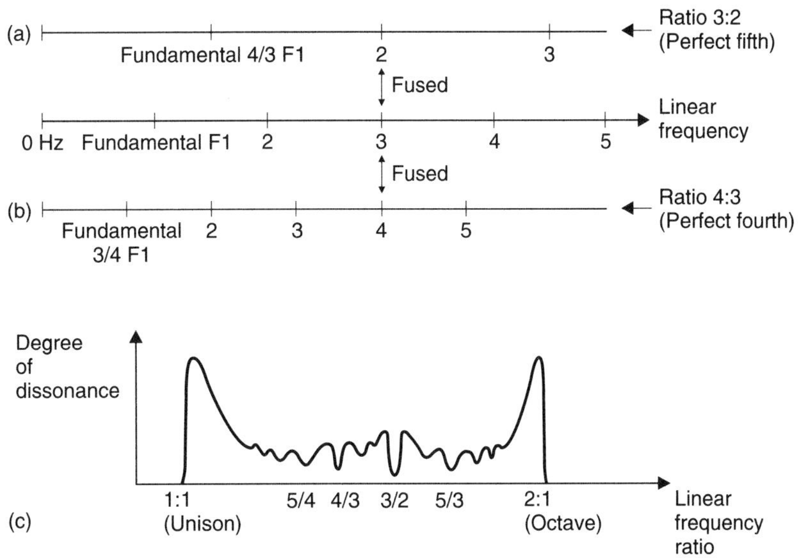

Figure 5.22 (a) Perfect fifth with a frequency ratio of 3:2 is consonant because harmonics are either in different critical bands or are fused. (b) Perfect fourth achieves the same result with 4:3 frequency ratio. (c) Degree of dissonance over range from 1:1 to 2:1.

is known to musicians as a perfect fifth. In (b) the ratio is 4:3. All harmonics are either at least a third of an octave apart or are fused. This relationship is known as a perfect fourth. The degree of dissonance over the range from 1:1 to 2:1 (unison to octave) was investigated by Helmholtz and is shown in Figure 5.22(c). Note that the dissonance rises at both ends where the fundamentals are within a critical bandwidth of one another. Dissonances in the centre of the scale are where some harmonics lie in a within a critical bandwidth of one another. Troughs in the curve indicate areas of consonance. Many of the troughs are not very deep, indicating that the consonance is not perfect. This is because of the effect shown in Figure 5.21 in which high harmonics get closer together with respect to critical bandwidth. When the fundamentals are closer together, the harmonics will become dissonant at a lower frequency, reducing the consonance. Figure 5.22(c) also shows the musical terms used to describe the consonant intervals.

It is clear from Figure 5.22(c) that the notes of the musical scale have empirically been established to allow the maximum consonance with pairs of notes and chords. Early instruments were tuned to the just diatonic scale in exactly this way. Unfortunately the just diatonic scale does not allow changes of key because the notes are not evenly spaced. A key change is where the frequency of every note in a piece of music is multiplied by a constant, often to bring the accompaniment within the range of a singer. In continuously tuned instruments such as the violin and the trombone this is easy, but with fretted or keyboard instruments such as a piano there is a problem.

The equal-tempered scale is a compromise between consonance and key changing. The octave is divided into twelve equal intervals called tempered semitones. On a keyboard, seven of the keys are white and produce notes very close to those of the just diatonic scale, and five of the keys are black. Music can be transposed in semitone steps by using the black keys. Figure 5.23 shows an example of transposition where a scale is played in several keys.

Frequency is an objective measure whereas *pitch* is the subjective near equivalent. Clearly frequency and level are independent, whereas pitch and level are not. Figure 5.24 shows the relationship between pitch and level. Place theory indicates that the hearing mechanism can sense a single frequency quite accurately as a function of the place or position of maximum basilar vibration. However, most periodic sounds and real musical instruments produce a series of harmonics in addition to the fundamental. When a harmonically rich sound is present the basilar membrane is excited at spaced locations. Figure 5.25(a) shows all harmonics, (b) shows even harmonics predominating and (c) shows odd harmonics predominating. It would appear that the HAS is accustomed to hearing harmonics in various amounts and the consequent regular

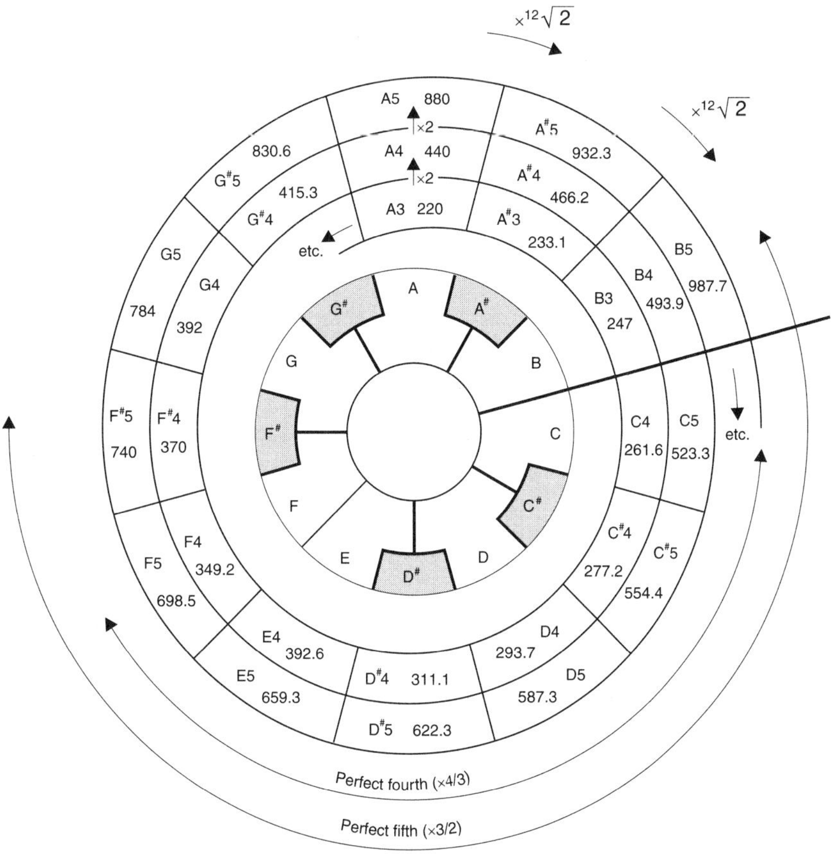

Figure 5.23 With a suitably tempered octave, scales can be played in different keys.

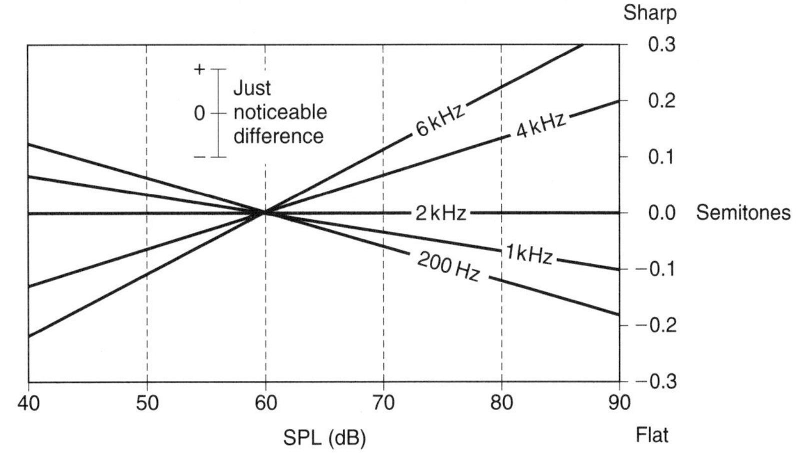

Figure 5.24 Pitch sensation is a function of level.

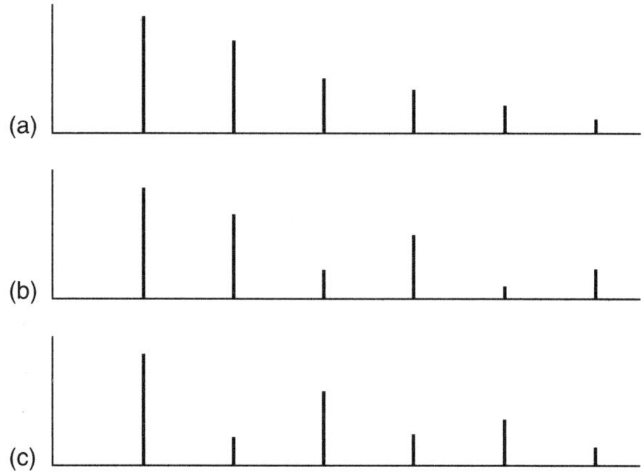

Figure 5.25 (a) Harmonic structure of rich sound. (b) Even harmonic predominance. (c) Odd harmonic predominance. Pitch perception appears independent of harmonic structure.

pattern of excitation. It is the overall pattern which contributes to the sensation of pitch even if individual partials vary enormously in relative level.

Experimental signals in which the fundamental has been removed leaving only the harmonics result in unchanged pitch perception. The pattern in the remaining harmonics is enough uniquely to establish the missing fundamental. Imagine the fundamental in (b) to be absent. Neither the second harmonic nor the third can be mistaken for the fundamental because if they were fundamentals a different pattern of harmonics would result. A similar argument can be put forward in the time domain, where the timing of phase-locked nerve firings responding to a harmonic will periodically coincide with the nerve firings of the fundamental. The ear is used to such time patterns and will use them in conjunction with the place patterns to determine the right pitch. At very low frequencies the place of maximum vibration does not move with frequency yet the pitch sensation is still present because the nerve firing frequency is used.

As the fundamental frequency rises it is difficult to obtain a full pattern of harmonics as most of them fall outside the range of hearing. The pitch discrimination ability is impaired and needs longer to operate. Figure 5.26 shows the number of cycles of excitation needed to discriminate pitch as a function of frequency. Clearly at around 5 kHz performance is failing because there are hardly any audible harmonics left. Phase locking also fails at about the same frequency. Musical instruments have evolved accordingly, with the highest notes of virtually all instruments found below 5 kHz.

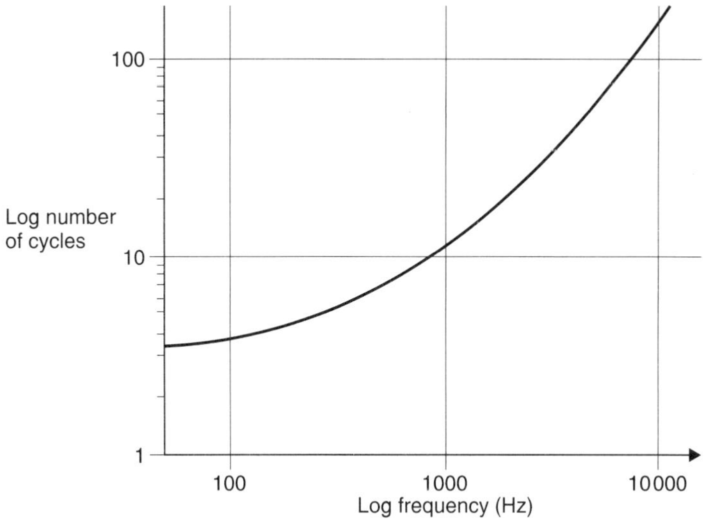

Figure 5.26 Pitch discrimination fails as frequency rises. The graph shows the number of cycles needed to distinguish pitch as a function of frequency.

5.8 The physics of sound

Sound is simply an airborne version of vibration which is why the two topics are inextricably linked. The air which carries sound is a mixture of gases, mostly nitrogen, some oxygen, a little carbon dioxide and so on. Gases are the highest energy state of matter, which is another way of saying that you have to heat ice to get water then heat it some more to get steam. The reason that a gas takes up so much more room than a liquid is that the molecules contain so much energy that they break free from their neighbours and rush around at high speed. As Figure 5.27(a) shows, the innumerable elastic collisions of these high-speed molecules produce pressure on the walls of any gas container. In fact the distance a molecule can go without a collision, the mean-free path, is quite short at

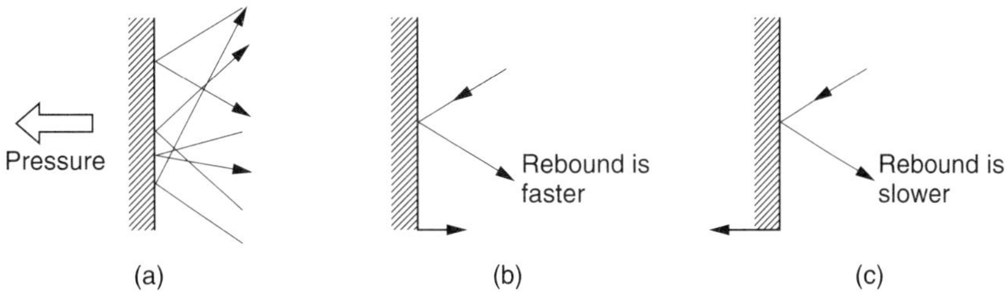

Figure 5.27 (a) The pressure exerted by a gas is due to countless elastic collisions between gas molecules and the walls of the container. (b) If the wall moves against the gas pressure, the rebound velocity increases. (c) Motion with the gas pressure reduces the particle velocity.

atmospheric pressure. Consequently gas molecules also collide with each other elastically, so that if left undisturbed, in a container at a constant temperature, every molecule would end up with essentially the same energy and the pressure throughout would be constant and uniform.

Sound disturbs this simple picture. Figure 5.27(b) shows that a solid object which moves *against* gas pressure increases the velocity of the rebounding molecules, whereas in Figure 5.27(c) one moving *with* gas pressure reduces that velocity. The average velocity and the displacement of all the molecules in a layer of air near to a moving body is the same as the velocity and displacement of the body. Movement of the body results in a local increase or decrease in pressure of some kind. Thus sound is both a pressure and a velocity disturbance. Integration of the velocity disturbance gives the displacement.

Despite the fact that a gas contains endlessly rushing colliding molecules, a small mass or *particle* of gas can have stable characteristics because the molecules leaving are replaced by new ones with identical statistics. As a result, acoustics seldom considers the molecular structure of air and the constant motion is neglected. Thus when particle velocity and displacement is considered in acoustics, this refers to the average values of a large number of molecules. The undisturbed container of gas referred to earlier will have a particle velocity and displacement of zero at all points.

When the volume of a fixed mass of gas is reduced, the pressure rises. The gas acts like a spring. However, a gas also has mass. Sound travels through air by an interaction between the mass and the springiness. Imagine pushing a mass via a spring. It would not move immediately because the spring would have to be compressed in order to transmit a force. If a second mass is connected to the first by another spring, it would start to move even later. Thus the speed of a disturbance in a mass/spring system depends on the mass and the stiffness.

After the disturbance had propagated the masses would return to their rest position. The mass/spring analogy is helpful for an early understanding, but is too simple to account for commonly encountered acoustic phenomena such as spherically expanding waves. It must be remembered that the mass and stiffness are distributed throughout the gas in the same way that inductance and capacitance are distributed in a transmission line. Sound travels through air without a net movement of the air.

Unlike solids, the elasticity of gas is a complicated process. If a fixed mass of gas is compressed, work has to be done on it. This will create heat in the gas. If the heat is allowed to escape and the compression does not change the temperature, the process is said to be *isothermal*. However, if the heat cannot escape the temperature will rise and give a disproportionate increase in pressure. This process is said to be *adiabatic* and the Diesel engine depends upon it. In most audio cases there is insufficient

$$\text{Velocity } V = \sqrt{\frac{\gamma R T}{M}}$$

γ = adiabatic constant (1.4 for air)
R = gas constant (8.31 J K^{-1} $mole^{-1}$)
T = absolute temp (K)
M = molecular weight (kg $mole^{-1}$)

Assume air is 21% O_2, 78% N_2, 1% Ar

$$\text{Molecular weight} = 21\% \times 16 \times 2 + 78\% \times 14 \times 2 + 1\% \times 18 \times 1$$
$$= 2.87 \times 10^{-2} \text{ kg mole}^{-1}$$

$$V = \sqrt{\frac{1.4 \times 8.31\ T}{2.87 \times 10^{-2}}} = 20.1\sqrt{T}$$

at 20°C $T = 293$ K $V = 20.1\sqrt{293} = 344$ m s^{-1}

Figure 5.28 Calculating the speed of sound from the elasticity of air.

time for much heat transfer and so air is considered to act adiabatically. Figure 5.28 shows how the speed of sound *c* in air can be derived by calculating its elasticity under adiabatic conditions.

If the volume allocated to a given mass of gas is reduced isothermally, the pressure and the density will rise by the same amount so that *c* does not change. If the temperature is raised at constant pressure, the density goes down and so the speed of sound goes up. Gases with lower density than air have a higher speed of sound. Divers who breathe a mixture of oxygen and helium to prevent 'the bends' must accept that the pitch of their voices rises remarkably. Digital pitch shifters can be used to facilitate communication.

The speed of sound is proportional to the square root of the absolute temperature. Temperature changes with respect to absolute zero (–273°C) also amount to around 1 per cent except in extremely inhospitable places. The speed of sound experienced by most of us is about 1000 feet per second or 344 metres per second. Temperature falls with altitude in the atmosphere and with it the speed of sound. The local speed of sound is defined as Mach 1. Consequently supersonic aircraft are fitted with Mach meters.

As air acts adiabatically, a propagating sound wave causes cyclic temperature changes. The speed of sound is a function of temperature, yet sound causes a temperature variation. One might expect some effects because of this. Fortunately, sounds which are below the threshold of pain have such a small pressure variation compared with atmospheric pressure that the effect is negligible and air can be assumed to be linear. However, on any occasion where the pressures are higher, this is not a valid assumption. In such cases the positive half-cycle significantly increases local temperature and the speed of sound, whereas the negative half-cycle reduces temperature and velocity. Figure 5.29 shows that this results in significant distortion of a sine wave, ultimately causing a *shock wave* which can travel faster than the speed of sound until the pressure has dissipated with distance. This effect is responsible for the sharp sound of a handclap.

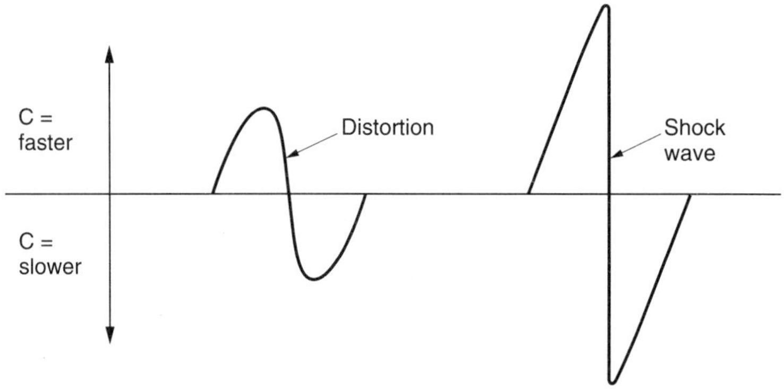

Figure 5.29 At high level, sound distorts itself by increasing the speed of propagation on positive half-cycles. The result is a shock wave.

This behaviour means that the speed of sound changes slightly with frequency. High frequencies travel slightly faster than low because there is less time for heat conduction to take place. Figure 5.30 shows that a complex sound source produces harmonics whose phase relationship with the fundamental advances with the distance the sound propagates. This allows one mechanism (there are others) by which the HAS can judge the distance from a known sound source. Clearly for realistic sound reproduction nothing in the audio chain must distort the phase relationship between frequencies. A system which accurately preserves such relationships is said to display linear phase.

Sound can be due to a one-off event known as percussion, or a periodic event such as the sinusoidal vibration of a tuning fork. The sound due to percussion is called transient whereas a periodic stimulus produces steady-state sound having a frequency f.

Because sound travels at a finite speed, the fixed observer at some distance from the source will experience the disturbance at some later time. In the case of a transient, the observer will detect a single replica of the original as it passes at the speed of sound. In the case of the tuning fork, a periodic sound, the pressure peaks and dips follow one another away from the source at the speed of sound. For a given rate of vibration

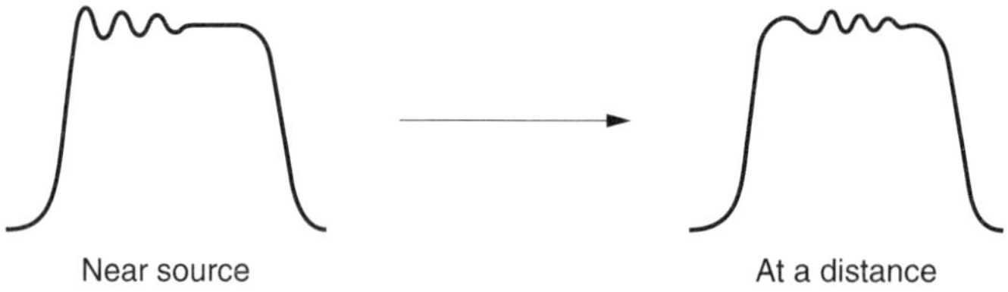

Figure 5.30 In a complex waveform, high frequencies travel slightly faster producing a relative phase change with distance.

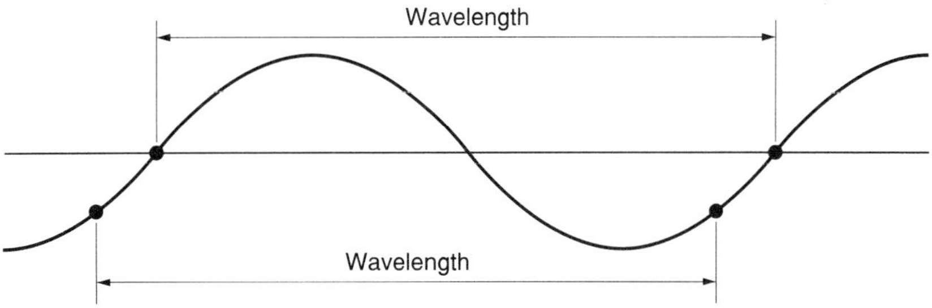

Figure 5.31 Wavelength is defined as the distance between two points at the same place on adjacent cycles. Wavelength is inversely proportional to frequency.

of the source, a given peak will have propagated a constant distance before the next peak occurs. This distance is called the wavelength, λ. Figure 5.31 shows that wavelength is defined as the distance between any two identical points on the whole cycle. If the source vibrates faster, successive peaks get closer together and the wavelength gets shorter. Wavelength is inversely proportional to the frequency. It is easy to remember that the wavelength of 1000 Hz is a foot (about 30 cm).

If there is relative motion between the source and the observer, the frequency of a periodic sound will be changed. Figure 5.32 shows a sound source moving towards the observer. At the end of a cycle, the source will be nearer the observer than at the beginning of the cycle. As a result the wavelength radiated in the direction of the observer will be shortened so that the pitch rises. The wavelength of sounds radiated away from the observer will be lengthened. The same effect will occur if the observer moves. This is the Doppler effect, which is most noticeable on passing motor vehicles whose engine notes appear to drop as they pass. Note that

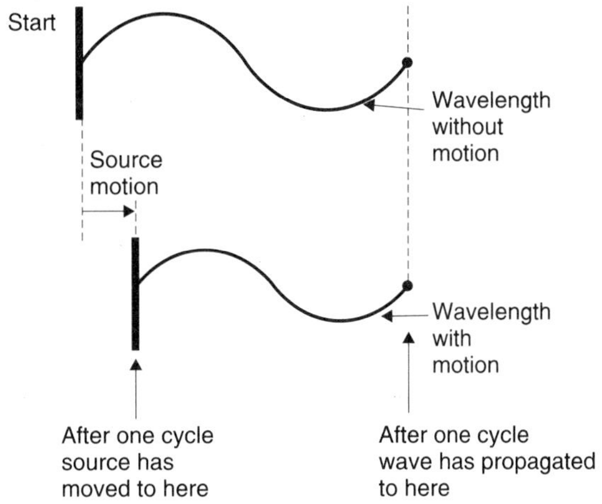

Figure 5.32 Periodic sounds are subject to Doppler shift if there is relative motion between the source and the observer.

the effect always occurs, but it is only noticeable on a periodic sound. Where the sound is aperiodic, such as broadband noise, the Doppler shift will not be heard.

Sound is a wave motion, and the way a wave interacts with any object depends upon the relative size of that object and the wavelength. The audible range of wavelengths is from around 17 millimetres to 17 metres so dramatic changes in the behaviour of sound over the frequency range should be expected.

Figure 5.33(a) shows that when the wavelength of sound is large compared to the size of a solid body, the sound will pass around it almost as if it were not there. When the object is large compared to the wavelength, then simple reflection takes place as in Figure 5.33(b). However, when the size of the object and the wavelength are comparable, the result can only be explained by diffraction theory.

The parameter which is used to describe this change of behaviour with wavelength is known as the wave number k and is defined as:

$$k = \frac{2\pi f}{c} = \frac{2\pi}{\lambda}$$

where f = frequency, c = the speed of sound and λ = wavelength. In practice the size of any object or distance a in metres is multiplied by k.

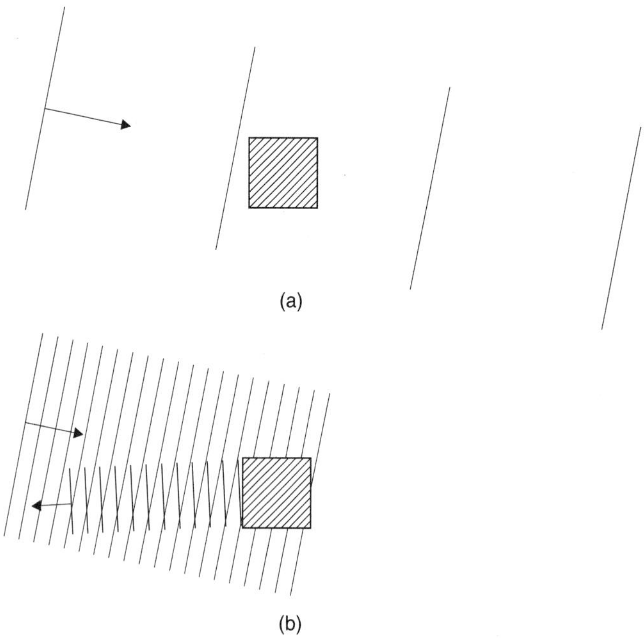

Figure 5.33 (a) Sound waves whose spacing is large compared to an obstacle simply pass round it. (b) When the relative size is reversed, an obstacle becomes a reflector.

A good rule of thumb is that below $ka = 1$, sound tends to pass around as in Figure 5.33(a) whereas above $ka = 1$, sound tends to reflect as in (b).

5.9 How sound is radiated

When sound propagates, there are changes in velocity **v**, displacement **x** and pressure **p**. Figure 5.34 shows that the velocity and the displacement are always in quadrature. This is obvious because velocity is the differential of the displacement. When the displacement reaches its maximum value and is on the point of reversing direction, the velocity is zero. When the displacement is zero the velocity is maximum.

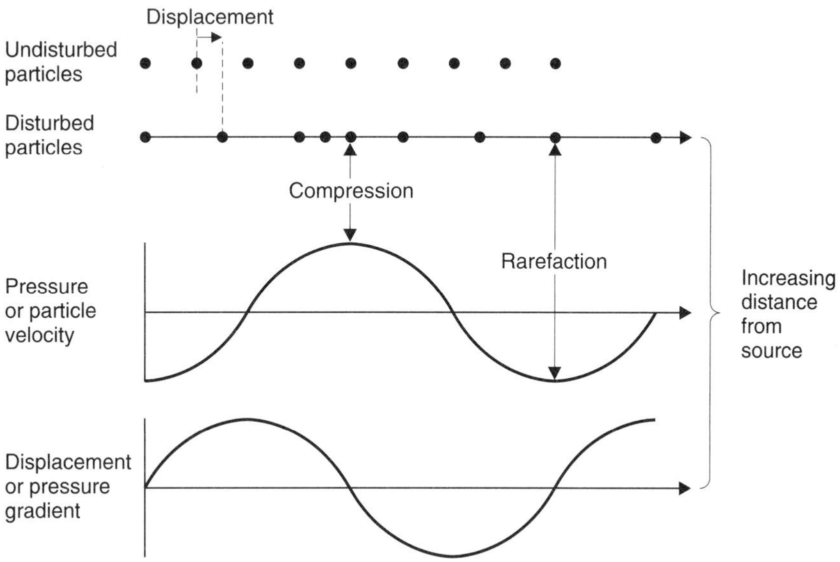

Figure 5.34 The pressure, velocity and displacement of particles as sound propagates.

The pressure and the velocity are linked by the *acoustic impedance z* which is given by *p/v*. Just like electrical impedances which can be reactive, the acoustic impedance is complex and varies with acoustic conditions. Consequently the phase relationship between velocity and pressure also varies. When any vibrating body is in contact with the air, a thin layer of air must have the same velocity as the surface of the body. The pressure which results from that velocity depends upon the acoustic impedance.

The wave number is useful to explain the way in which sound is radiated. Consider a hypothetical pulsating sphere as shown in Figure

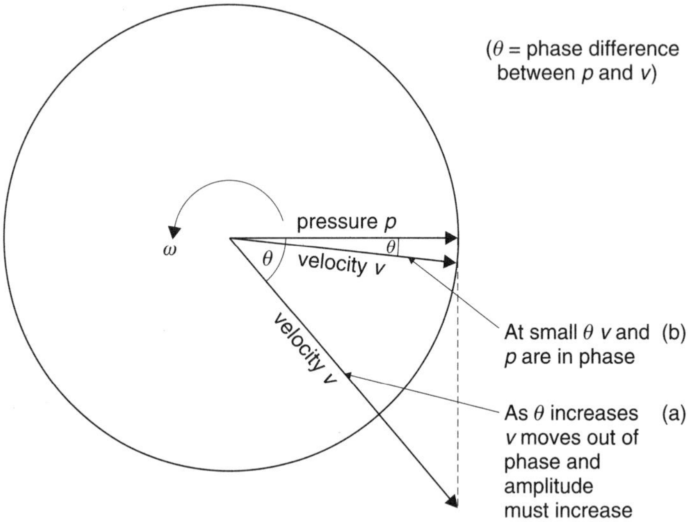

Figure 5.35 A pulsating sphere experiences an impedance which is a function of *ka*. With small *ka* pressure and velocity are in quadrature, but become coherent as *ka* rises.

5.35. The acoustic impedance changes with radius *a*. If the sphere pulsates very slowly, it will do work against air pressure as it expands and the air pressure will return the work as it contracts. There is negligible radiation because the impedance is reactive. Figure 5.35(a) shows that when *ka* is small there is a 90° phase shift between the pressure and the velocity. As the frequency or the radius rises, as in (b), the phase angle reduces from 90° and the pressure increases. When *ka* is large, the phase angle approaches zero and the pressure reaches its maximum value compared to the velocity. The impedance has become resistive.

When *ka* is very large, the spherical radiator is at a distance and the spherical waves will have become plane waves. Figure 5.34 showed the relationships between pressure, velocity and displacement for a plane wave. A small air mass may have kinetic energy due to its motion and kinetic energy due to its compression. The total energy is constant, but the distribution of energy between kinetic and potential varies throughout the wave. This relationship will not hold when *ka* is small. This can easily occur especially at low frequencies where the wavelengths can be several metres.

Microphones can transduce either the pressure or the velocity component of sound. When *ka* is large, the pressure and velocity waveforms in a spherical wave are identical. However it will be clear from Figure 5.35(a) and (b) that when *ka* is small the velocity exceeds the pressure component. This is the cause of the well-known proximity effect, also known as tip-up, which emphasizes low frequencies when velocity-sensing microphones are used close to a sound source. Figure 5.36 shows

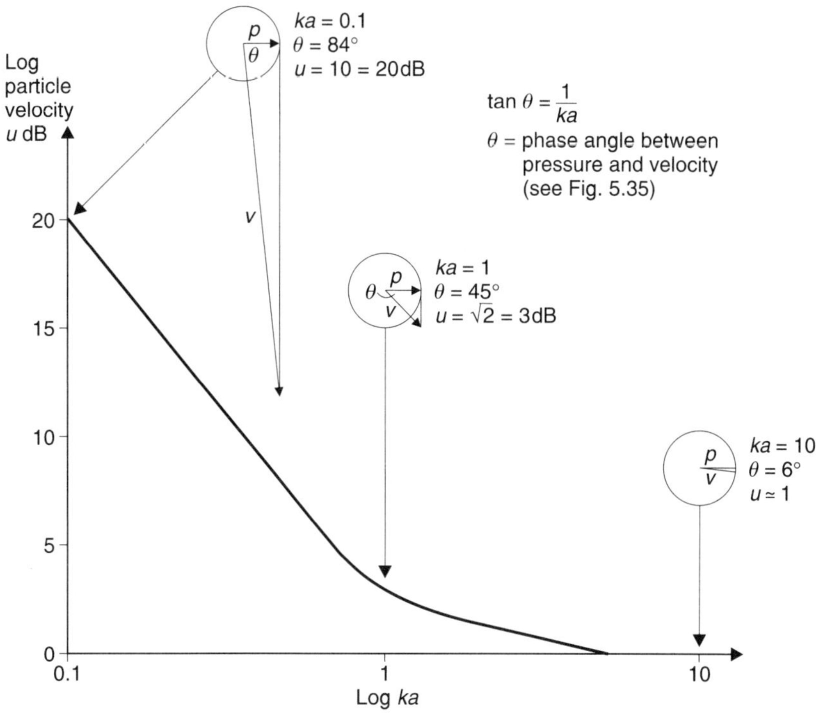

Figure 5.36 Proximity effect is due to raised velocity component of sound relative to pressure near to sound sources.

the response of a velocity microphone relative to that of a pressure microphone for different values of *ka*. Various combinations of distance and frequency are given for illustration. Practical microphones often incorporate some form of bass-cut filter to offset the effect.

The sensation of sound is proportional to the average velocity. However, the displacement is the integral of the velocity. Figure 5.37 shows that to obtain an identical velocity or slope the amplitude must increase as the inverse of the frequency. Consequently for a given SPL low-frequency sounds result in much larger air movement than high

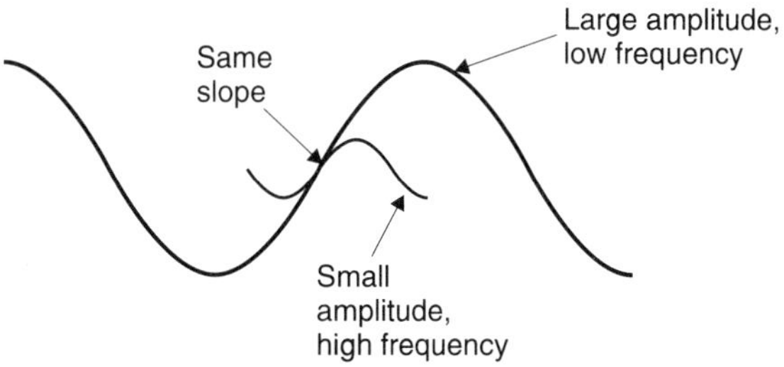

Figure 5.37 For a given velocity or slope, lower frequencies require greater amplitude.

frequency. The SPL is proportional to the *volume velocity* U of the source which is obtained by multiplying the vibrating area in m^2 by the velocity in m/s. As SPL is proportional to volume velocity, as frequency falls the volume or displacement must rise. This means that low-frequency sound can only be radiated effectively by large objects, hence all the bass instruments in the orchestra are much larger than their treble equivalents. This is also the reason why a loudspeaker cone is only seen to move at low frequencies.

The units of volume velocity are cubic metres per second and so sound is literally an alternating current. The pressure p is linked to the current by the impedance just as it is in electrical theory. There are direct analogies between acoustic and electrical parameters and equations which are helpful. One small difficulty is that whereas alternating electrical parameters are measured in rms units, acoustic units are not. Thus when certain acoustic parameters are multiplied together the product has to be divided by two. This happens automatically with rms units. Figure 5.38 shows the analogous equations.

Acoustic	**Electrical**
U = volume velocity (m^3/sec)	$\equiv I$ rms current (A)
p = pressure (Pa)	$\equiv V$ rms voltage (V)
Z = impedance $= \dfrac{P}{U}$	$\equiv \dfrac{V}{I} = Z$
P = power $= \dfrac{\lvert U\rvert^2 \times \text{Real}(Z)}{2}$ (W)	$\equiv I^2 \times$ Real Z(W)

↑
Note factor of 2 as U is not RMS

$\lvert U\rvert$ = amplitude of U Real (Z) = resistive part of impedance

Figure 5.38 Electrical units are rms whereas many acoustic units are not, hence the factor of two difference in otherwise analogous equations.

The intensity of a sound is the sound power passing through unit area. In the far field it is given by the product of the volume velocity and the pressure. In the near field the relative phase angle will have to be considered. Intensity is a vector quantity as it has direction which is considered to be perpendicular to the area in question. The total sound power is obtained by multiplying the intensity by the cross-sectional area through which it passes. Power is a scalar quantity because it can be radiated in all directions.

When a spherical sound wave is considered, there is negligible loss as it advances outwards. Consequently the sound power passing through the surface of an imaginary sphere surrounding the source is independent of the radius of that sphere. As the area of a sphere is proportional to the square of the radius, it will be clear that the intensity falls according to an inverse square law.

The inverse square law should be used with caution. There are a number of exceptions. As was seen in Figure 5.36, the proximity effect causes a deviation from the inverse square law for small *ka*. The area in which there is deviation from inverse square behaviour is called the *near field*.

In reverberant conditions a sound field is set up by reflections. As the distance from the source increases at some point the level no longer falls.

It is also important to remember that the inverse square law applies only to near-point sources. A line source radiates cylindrically and intensity is then inversely proportional to radius. Noise from a busy road approximates to a cylindrical source.

5.10 Acoustics

A proper understanding of the behaviour of sound requires familiarity with the principles of wave acoustics. Wave theory is used in many different disciplines including radar, sonar, optics, antenna and filter design and the principles remain the same. Consequently the designer of a loudspeaker may obtain inspiration from studying a radar antenna or a CD pickup.

Figure 5.39 shows that when two sounds of equal amplitude and frequency add together, the result is completely dependent on the relative phase of the two. At (a) when the phases are identical, the result is the arithmetic sum. At (b) where there is a 180° relationship, the result is complete cancellation. This is constructive and destructive interference. At any other phase and/or amplitude relationship, the result can only be obtained by vector addition as shown in (c).

The wave theory of propagation of sound is based on interference and suggests that a wavefront advances because an infinite number of point sources can be considered to emit spherical waves which will only add when they are all in the same phase. This can only occur in the plane of the wavefront. Figure 5.40(a) shows that at all other angles, interference between spherical waves is destructive. For any radiating body, such as a vibrating object, it is easy to see from Figure 5.40(b) that when *ka* is small, only weak spherical radiation is possible, whereas when *ka* is large, a directional plane wave can be propagated or beamed. Consequently high-frequency sound behaves far more directionally than low-frequency sound.

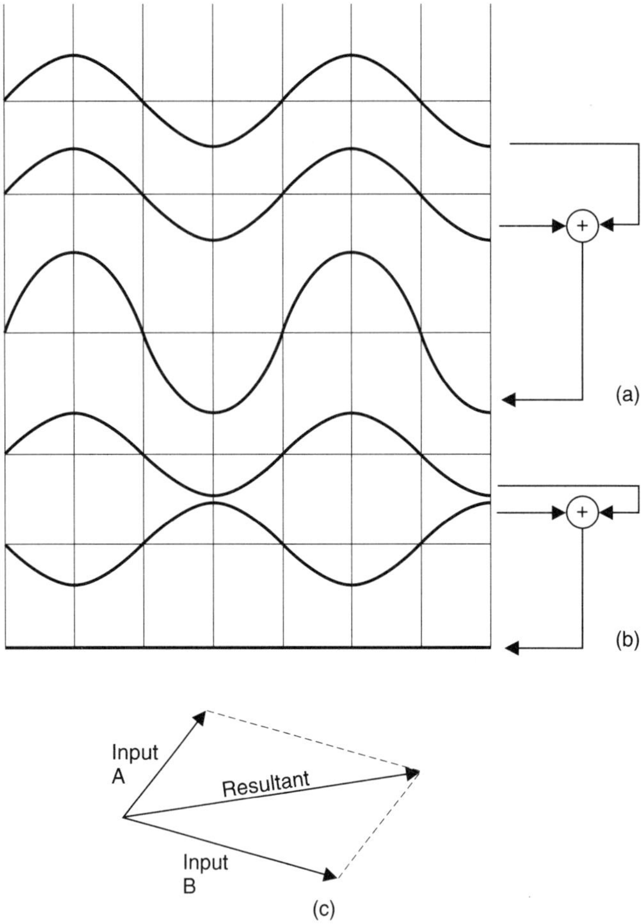

Figure 5.39 (a) Constructive interference between two in-phase signals. (b) Destructive interference between out-of-phase signals. (c) Vector addition is needed to find result of arbitrary phase relationship.

When a wavefront arrives at a solid body, it can be considered that the surface of the body acts as an infinite number of points which reradiate the incident sound in all directions. It will be seen that when *ka* is large and the surface is flat, constructive interference only occurs when the wavefront is *reflected* such that the angle of reflection is the same as the angle of incidence. When *ka* is small, the amount of reradiation from the body compared to the radiation in the wavefront is very small. Constructive interference takes place beyond the body as if it were absent, thus it is correct to say that the sound diffracts around the body.

Figure 5.41 shows two identical sound sources which are spaced apart by a distance of several wavelengths and which vibrate in-phase. At all points equidistant from the sources the radiation adds constructively. The

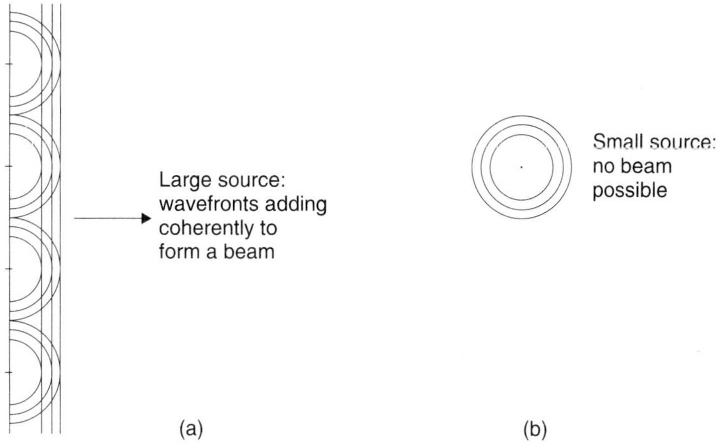

Figure 5.40 (a) Plane waves can be considered to propagate as an infinity of spherical waves which cancel out in all directions other than forward to form a beam. (b) Where the sound source is small no beam can be formed.

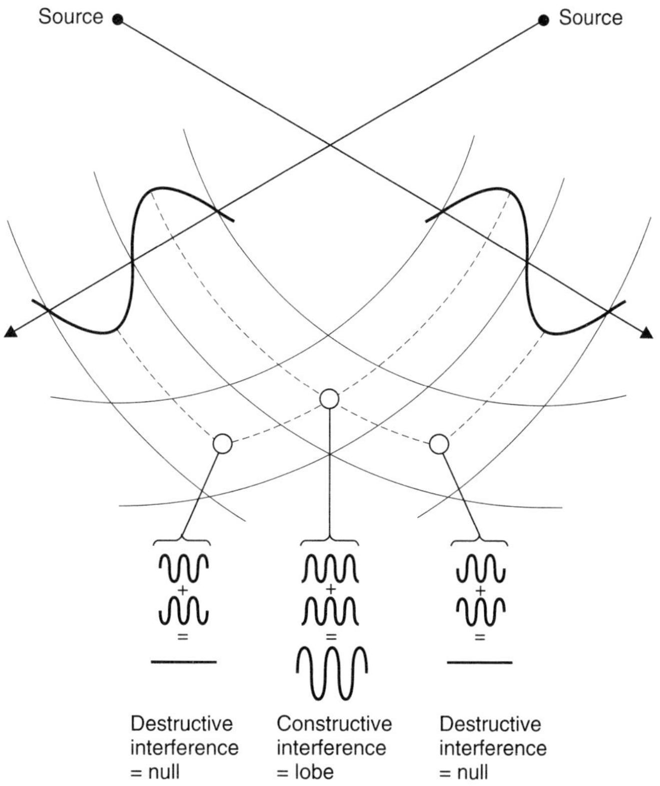

Figure 5.41 Constructive and destructive interference between two identical sources.

same is true where there are path length differences which are multiples of the wavelength. However, in certain directions the path length difference will result in relative phase reversal. Destructive interference means that sound cannot leave in those directions. The resultant diffraction pattern has a polar diagram which consists of repeating lobes with nulls between them.

This chapter has so far considered only the radiation of a pulsating sphere; a situation which is too simple to model many real-life sound radiators. The situation of Figure 5.41 can be extended to predict the results of vibrating bodies of arbitrary shape. Figure 5.42 shows a hypothetical rigid circular piston vibrating in an opening in a plane surface. This is apparently much more like a real loudspeaker. As it is rigid, all parts of it vibrate in the same phase. Following concepts advanced earlier, a rigid piston can be considered to be an infinite number of point sources. The result at an arbitrary point in space in front of the piston is obtained by integrating the waveform from every point source.

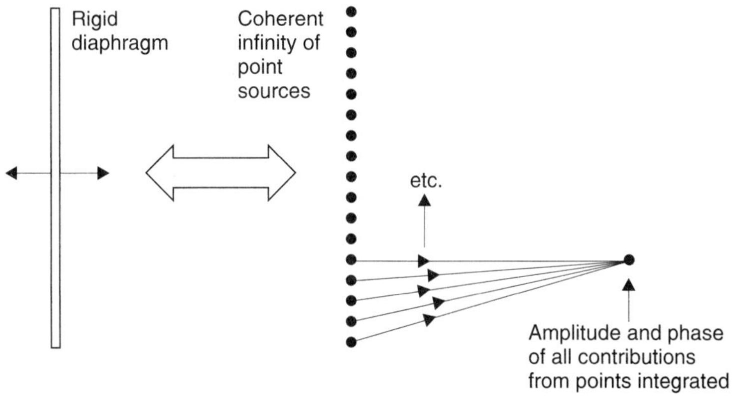

Figure 5.42 A rigid radiating surface can be considered as an infinity of coherent point sources. The result at a given location is obtained by integrating the radiation from each point.

A transducer can be affected dramatically by the presence of other objects, but the effect is highly frequency dependent. In Figure 5.43(a) a high frequency is radiated, and this simply reflects from the nearby object because the wavelength is short and the object is acoustically distant or in the *far field*. However, if the wavelength is made longer than the distance between the source and the object as in Figure 5.43(b), the object is acoustically close or in the *near field* and becomes part of the source. The effect is that the object reduces the solid angle into which radiation can take place as well as raising the acoustic impedance the transducer sees.

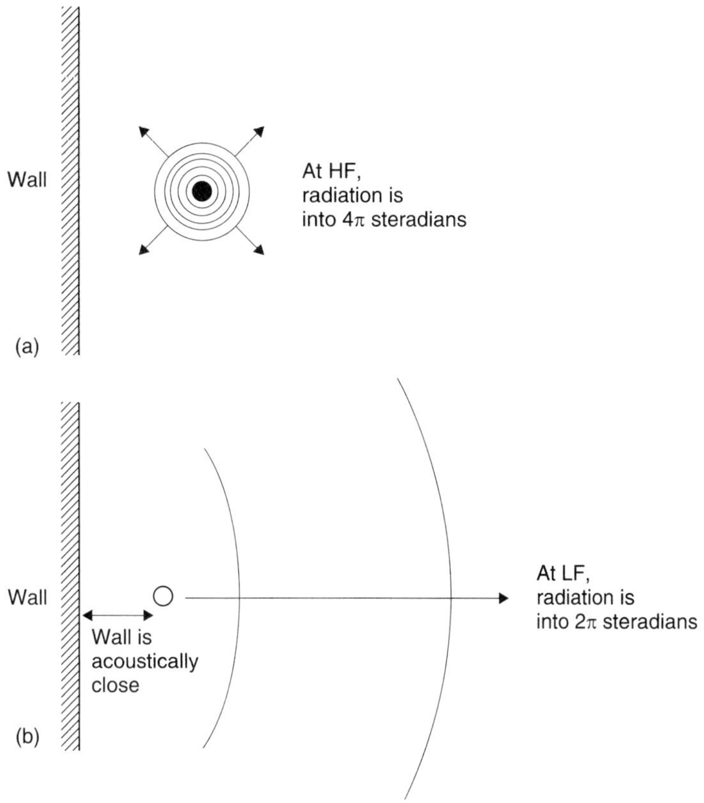

Figure 5.43 (a) At high frequencies an object is in the far field. (b) At low frequencies the same object is in the near field and increases velocity by constricting the radiation path.

The volume velocity of the source is confined into a smaller cross-sectional area and consequently the velocity must rise in inverse proportion to the solid angle.

In Figure 5.44 the effect of positioning a loudspeaker is shown. In free space (a) the speaker might show a reduction in low frequencies which disappears when it is placed on the floor (b). In this case placing the speaker too close to a wall, or even worse, in a corner, (c), will emphasize the low-frequency output. High-quality loudspeakers will have an adjustment to compensate for positioning. The technique can be useful in the case of small cheap loudspeakers whose LF response is generally inadequate. Some improvement can be had by corner mounting.

It will be evident that at low frequencies the long wavelengths make it impossible for two close-spaced radiators acoustically to get out of phase. Consequently when two radiators are working within one another's near field, they act like a single radiator. Each radiator will experience a doubled acoustic impedance because of the presence of the other. Thus

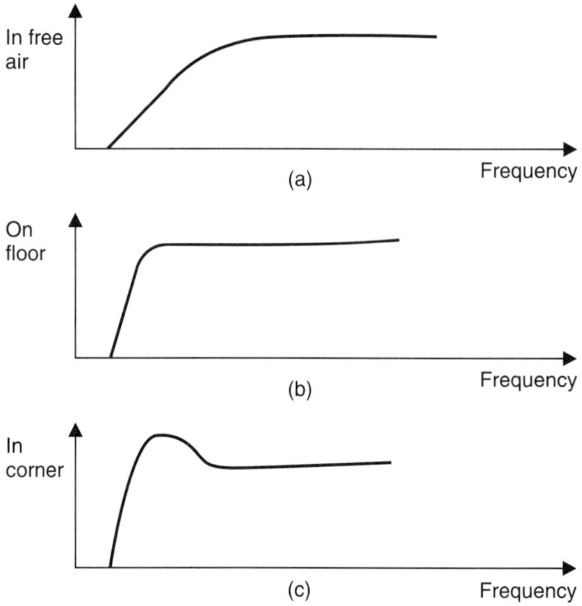

Figure 5.44 Loudspeaker positioning affects low-frequency response. (a) Speaker in free air appears bass deficient. (b) This effect disappears when floor mounted. (c) Bass is increased when mounted near a wall or corner.

the pressure for a given volume velocity will be doubled. As the intensity is proportional to the square of the pressure, it will be quadrupled.

The effect has to be taken into account when stereo loudspeakers are installed. At low frequencies the two speakers will be acoustically close and so will mutually raise their acoustic impedance causing a potential bass tip-up problem. When a pair of stereo speakers has been properly equalized, disconnecting one will result in the remaining speaker sounding bass light. In surround-sound systems there may be four or five speakers working in one another's near field at low frequencies, making considerable SPL possible and calling into question the need for a separate subwoofer.

In Figure 5.45 the effect of positioning a microphone very close to a source is shown. The microphone body reduces the area through which sound can escape in the near field and raises the acoustic impedance, emphasizing the low frequencies. This effect will be observed even with pressure microphones as it is different in nature to and adds to the proximity effect described earlier. This is most noticeable in public address systems where the gain is limited to avoid howl-round. The microphone must then be held close to obtain sufficient level and the plosive parts of speech are emphasized. The high signal levels generated often cause amplifier clipping, cutting intelligibility.

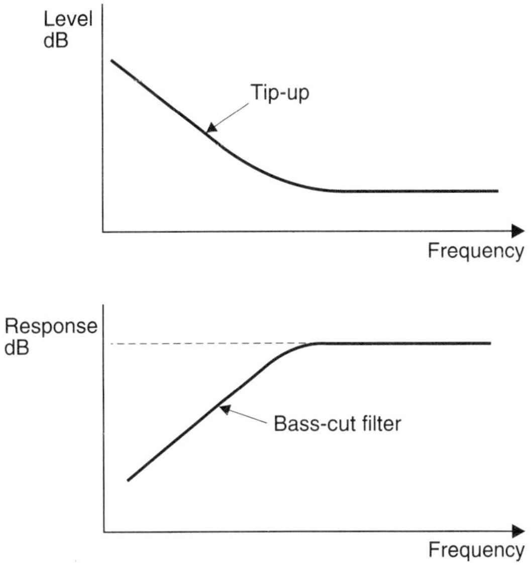

Figure 5.45 Bass tip-up due to close microphone positioning. A suitable filter will help intelligibility.

When inexperienced microphone users experience howl-round they often misguidedly cover the microphone with a hand in order to prevent the sound from the speakers reaching it. This is quite the reverse of the correct action as the presence of the hand raises the local impedance and actually makes the howl-round worse. The correct action is to move the microphone away from the body and (assuming a directional mic) to point it away from the loudspeakers. In general this will mean pointing the microphone at the audience.

In Figure 5.46 a supra-aural headphone (one which sits above the ear rather than surrounding it) in free space has a very poor LF response because it is a dipole source and at low frequency air simply moves from front to back in a short circuit. However, the presence of the listener's head obstructs the short circuit and the bass tip-up effect gives a beneficial extension of frequency response to the intended listener, whilst those not wearing the headphones only hear high frequencies. Many personal stereo players incorporate an LF boost to further equalize the losses. All practical headphones must be designed to take account of the presence of the user's head since headphones work primarily in the near field.

A dramatic example of bass tip-up is obtained by bringing the ear close to the edge of a cymbal shortly after it has been struck. The fundamental note which may only be a few tens of Hz can clearly be heard. As the cymbal is such a poor radiator at this frequency there is very little

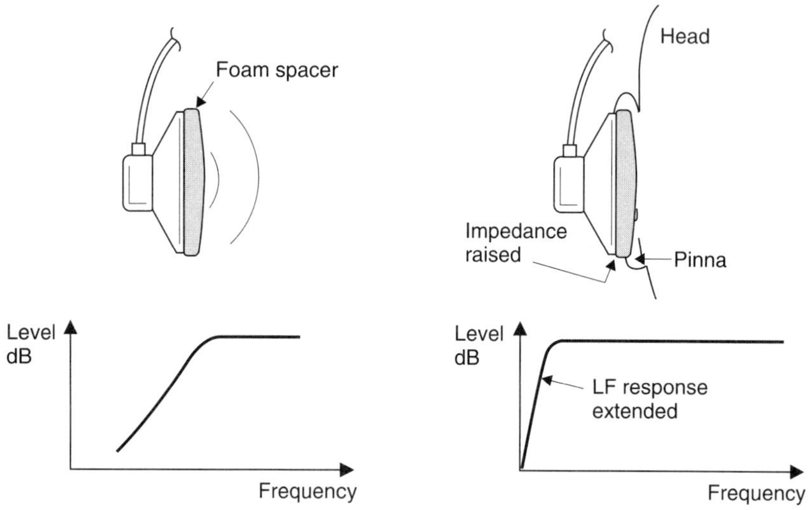

Figure 5.46 Supra-aural headphones rely on the bass tip-up in the near field to give a reasonable bass response.

damping of the fundamental which will continue for some time. At normal distances it is quite inaudible.

If sound enters a medium in which the speed is different, the wavelength will change causing the wavefront to leave the interface at a different angle. This is known as refraction. The ratio of velocity in air to velocity in the medium is known as the refractive index of that medium; it determines the relationship between the angles of the incident and refracted wavefronts. This doesn't happen much in real life, it requires a thin membrane with different gases each side to demonstrate the effect. However, as was shown above in connection with the Doppler effect, wind has the ability to change the wavelength of sound. Figure 5.47 shows that when there is a wind blowing, friction with the earth's surface

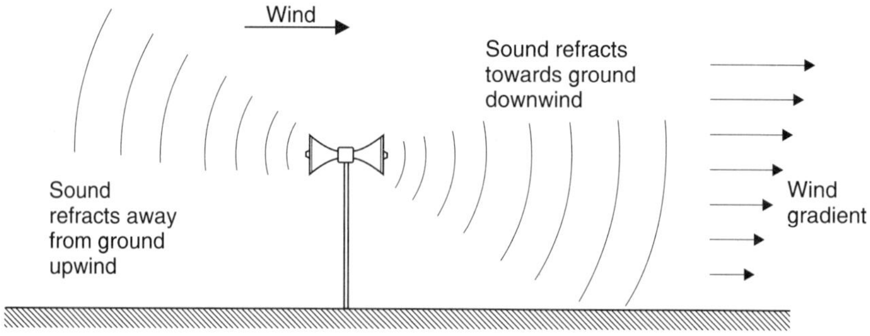

Figure 5.47 When there is a wind, the velocity gradient refracts sound downwards downwind of the source and upwards upwind of the source.

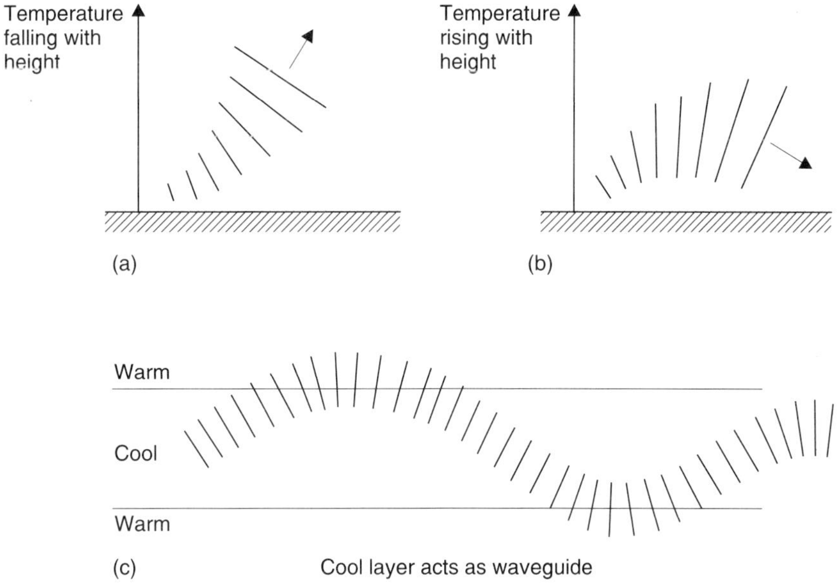

Figure 5.48 (a) Temperature fall with altitude refracts sound away from the earth. (b) Temperature inversion refracts sound back to earth. (c) Cool layer in the atmosphere can act as a waveguide.

causes a velocity gradient. Sound radiated upwind will have its wavelength shortened more away from the ground than near it, whereas the reverse occurs downwind.

Upwind it is difficult to hear a sound source because the radiation has been refracted upwards whereas downwind the radiation will be refracted towards the ground making the sound 'carry' better. Temperature gradients can have the same effect. As Figure 5.48(a) shows, the reduction in the speed of sound due to the normal fall in temperature with altitude acts to refract sound away from the earth. In the case of a temperature inversion (b) the opposite effect happens. Sometimes a layer of air forms in the atmosphere which is cooler than the air above and below it. Figure 5.48(c) shows that this acts as a waveguide because sound attempting to leave the layer is gently curved back in giving the acoustic equivalent of a mirage. In this way sound can travel hundreds of kilometres. Sometimes what appears to be thunder is heard on a clear sunny day. In fact it is the sound from a supersonic aircraft which may be a very long way away indeed.

When two sounds of equal frequency and amplitude are travelling in opposite directions, the result is a *standing wave* where constructive interference occurs at fixed points one wavelength apart with nulls between. This effect can often be found between parallel hard walls, where the space will contain a whole number of wavelengths. As Figure

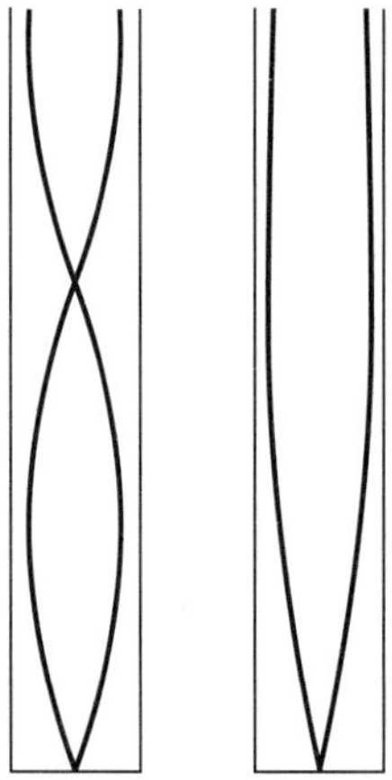

Figure 5.49 Standing waves in an organ pipe can exist at several different frequencies.

5.49 shows, a variety of different frequencies can excite standing waves at a given spacing. Wind instruments work on the principle of standing waves. The wind produces broadband noise, and the instrument resonates at the fundamental depending on the length of the pipe. The higher harmonics add to the richness or *timbre* of the sound produced.

In practice, many real materials do not reflect sound perfectly. As Figure 5.50 shows, some sound is reflected, some is transmitted and the remainder is absorbed. The proportions of each will generally vary with frequency. Only porous materials are capable of being effective sound absorbers. The air movement is slowed by viscous friction among the fibres. Such materials include wood, foam, cloth and carpet. Non-porous materials either reflect or transmit according to their mass. Thin, hard materials such as glass, reflect high frequencies but transmit low frequencies. Substantial mass is required to prevent transmission of low frequencies, there being no substitute for masonry.

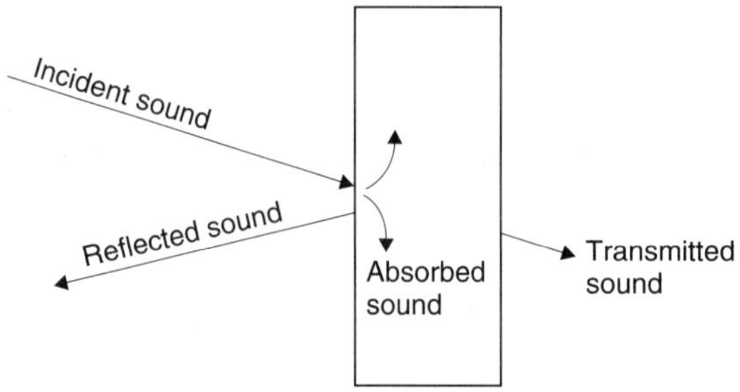

Figure 5.50 Incident sound is partially reflected, partially transmitted and partially absorbed. The proportions vary from one material to another and with frequency.

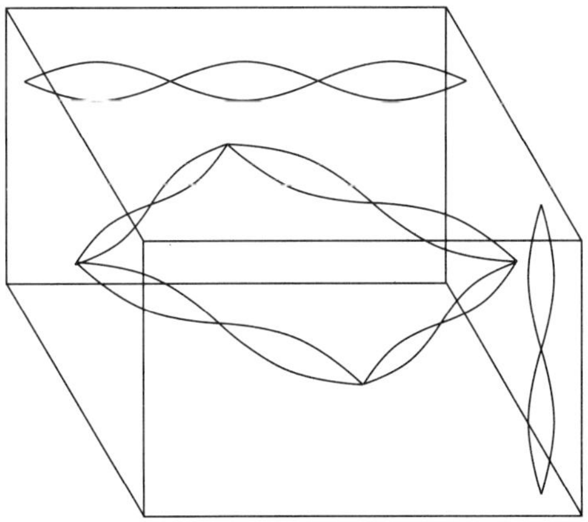

Figure 5.51 In a room, standing waves can be set up in three dimensions.

In real rooms with hard walls, standing waves can be set up in many dimensions, as Figure 5.51 shows. The frequencies at which the dominant standing waves occur are called eigentones. Any sound produced in such a room which coincides in frequency with an eigentone will be strongly emphasized as a resonance which might take some time to decay. Clearly a cube would be the worst possible shape for a studio as it would have a small number of very powerful resonances.

At the opposite extreme, an *anechoic chamber* is a room treated with efficent absorption on every surface. Figure 5.52 shows that long wedges of foam absorb sound by repeated reflection and absorption down to a

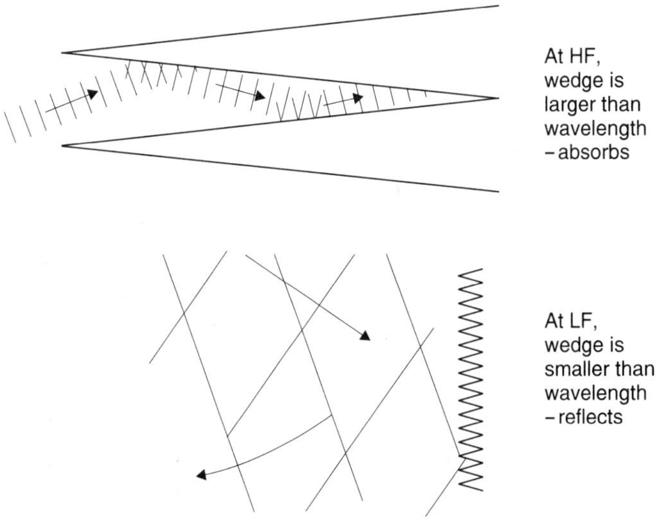

Figure 5.52 Anechoic wedges are effective until wavelength becomes too large to see them.

frequency determined by the length of the wedges (our friend *ka* again). Some people become distressed in anechoic rooms and musical instruments sound quiet, lifeless and boring. Sound of this kind is described as *dry.*

Reflected sound is needed in concert halls to amplify the instruments and add richness or *reverberation* to the sound. Since reflection cannot and should not be eliminated, practical studios, listening rooms and concert halls are designed so that resonances are made as numerous and close together as possible so that no single one appears dominant. Apart from choosing an irregular shape, this goal can be helped by the use of *diffusers* which are highly irregular reflectors. Figure 5.53 shows that if a two-plane

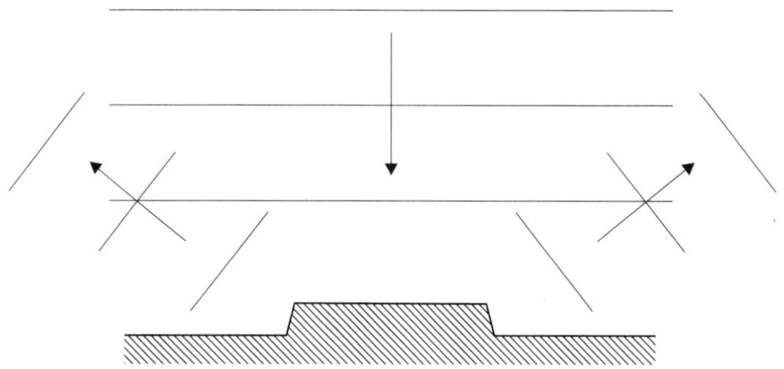

Figure 5.53 A diffuser prevents simple reflection of an incident wavefront by destructive interference. The diffracted sound must leave by another path.

stepped surface is made from a reflecting material, at some wavelengths there will be destructive interference between sound reflected from the upper surface and sound reflected from the lower. Consequently the sound cannot reflect back the way it came but must diffract off at any angle where constructive interference can occur. A diffuser made with steps of various dimensions will reflect sound in a complex manner. Diffusers are thus very good at preventing standing waves without the deadening effect that absorbing the sound would have.

In a hall having highly reflective walls, any sound will continue to reflect around for some time after the source has ceased. Clearly as more absorbent is introduced, this time will fall. The time taken for the sound to decay by 60 dB is known as the *reverberation time* of the room. The optimum reverberation time depends upon the kind of use to which the hall is put. Long reverberation times make orchestral music sound rich and full, but would result in intelligibility loss on speech. Consequently theatres and cinemas have short reverberation times, opera houses have medium times and concert halls have the longest. In some multi-purpose halls the reverberation can be modified by rotating wall panelling, although more recently this is done with electronic artificial reverberation using microphones, signal processors and loudspeakers.

Only porous materials make effective absorbers at high frequency, but these cannot be used in areas which are prone to dampness or where frequent cleaning is required. This is why indoor swimming pools are so noisy.

5.11 Directionality in hearing

An understanding of the mechanisms of direction sensing is important for the successful implementation of spatial illusions such as stereophonic and surround sound. The nerve impulses from the ears are processed in specific areas of the brain which appear to have evolved at different times to provide different types of information. The time-domain response works quickly, primarily aiding the direction-sensing mechanism, and is older in evolutionary terms. The frequency-domain response works more slowly, aiding the determination of pitch and timbre and developed later, presumably after speech evolved.

The earliest use of hearing was as a survival mechanism to augment vision. The most important aspect of the hearing mechanism was the ability to determine the location of the sound source. Figure 5.54 shows that the brain can examine several possible differences between the signals reaching the two ears. At (a) a phase shift will be apparent. At (b) the distant ear is shaded by the head resulting in a different frequency response compared to the nearer ear. At (c) a transient sound arrives later at the more distant ear. The inter-aural phase, delay and level mechanisms vary in their effectiveness depending on the nature of the sound to be located. At some point a fuzzy logic decision has to be made as to how the information from these different mechanisms will be weighted.

There will be considerable variation with frequency in the phase shift between the ears. At a low frequency such as 30 Hz, the wavelength is around 11.5 metres and so this mechanism must be quite weak at low frequencies. At high frequencies the ear spacing is many wavelengths producing a confusing and complex phase relationship. This suggests a frequency limit of around 1500 Hz which has been confirmed by experiment.

At low and middle frequencies sound will diffract round the head sufficiently well that there will be no significant difference between the level at the two ears. Only at high frequencies does sound become directional enough for the head to shade the distant ear causing what is called an inter-aural intensity difference (IID).

Phase differences are only useful at low frequencies and shading only works at high frequencies. Fortunately real-world sounds are timbral or

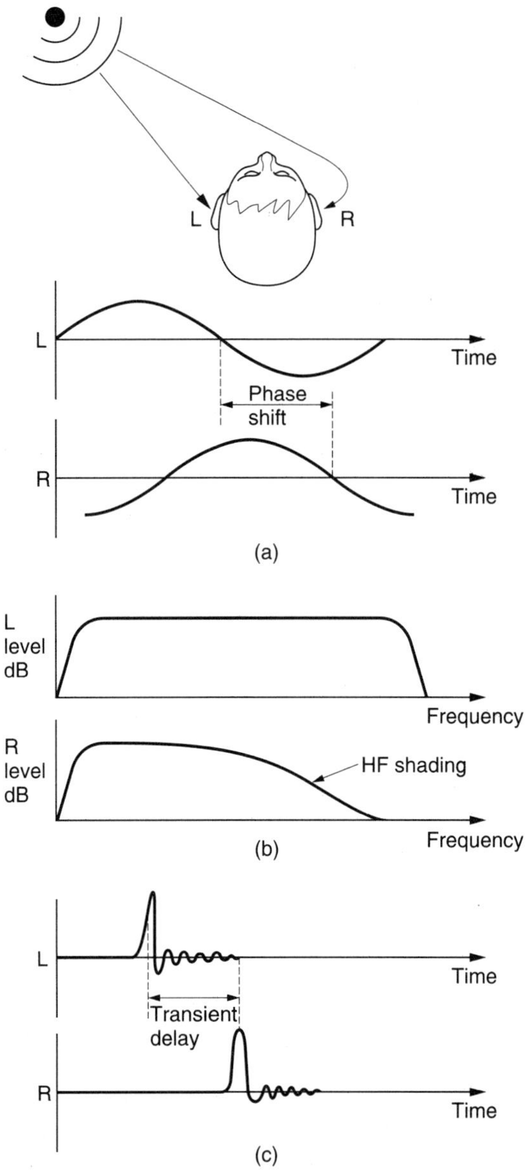

Figure 5.54 Having two spaced ears is cool. (a) Off-centre sounds result in phase difference. (b) Distant ear is shaded by head producing loss of high frequencies. (c) Distant ear detects transient later.

broadband and often contain transients. Timbral, broadband and transient sounds differ from tones in that they contain many different frequencies.

A transient has an unique aperiodic waveform which, as Figure 5.54(c) shows, suffers no ambiguity in the assessment of inter-aural delay (IAD) between two versions. Note that a 1° change in sound location causes an

IAD of around 10 microseconds. The smallest detectable IAD is a remarkable 6 microseconds. This should be the criterion for spatial reproduction accuracy.

A timbral waveform is periodic at the fundamental frequency but the presence of harmonics means that a greater number of nerve firings can be compared between the two ears. As the statistical deviation of nerve firings with respect to the incoming waveform is about 100 microseconds the only way in which an IAD of 6 microseconds can be resolved is if the timing of many nerve firings is correlated in some way in the brain.

Transient noises produce a one-off pressure step whose source is accurately and instinctively located. Figure 5.55 shows an idealized transient pressure waveform following an acoustic event. Only the initial transient pressure change is required for location. The time of arrival of the transient at the two ears will be different and will locate the source laterally within a processing delay of around a millisecond.

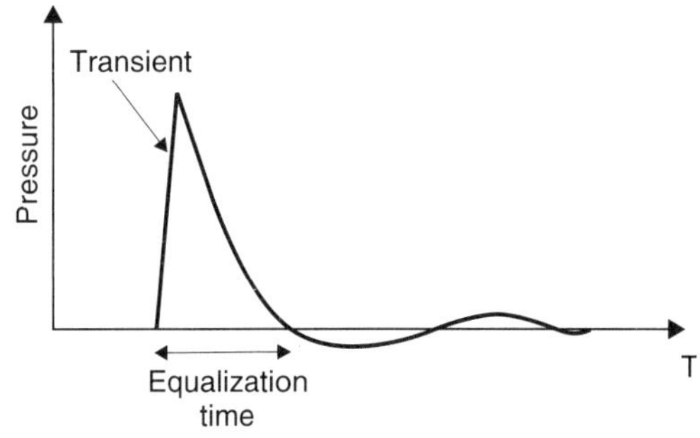

Figure 5.55 Following an acoustic event, a pressure step is created, but this cannot be sustained by the surrounding air and rapidly decays. The time of arrival difference of the transient at the two ears allows direction to be discerned and the time taken for the pressure to equalize allows the size of the source to be estimated.

Following the event which generated the transient, the air pressure equalizes. The time taken for this equalization varies and allows the listener to establish the likely size of the sound source. The larger the source, the longer the pressure-equalization time. Only after this does the frequency analysis mechanism tell anything about the pitch and timbre of the sound.

The above results suggest that anything in a sound reproduction system which impairs the reproduction of a transient pressure change will damage localization and the assessment of the pressure-equalization time. Clearly in an audio system which claims to offer any degree of precision, every component must be able to reproduce transients accurately and must have at least a minimum phase characteristic if it cannot be phase-linear. In this respect digital audio represents a distinct technical performance advantage although much of this is lost in poor transducer design, especially in loudspeakers.

It must be appreciated that the HAS can locate a number of different sound sources simultaneously. The HAS must constantly be comparing excitation patterns from the two ears with different delays. Strong correlation will be found where the delay corresponds to the interaural delay for a given source. This is apparent in the binaural threshold of hearing which is 3–6 dB better than monaural at around 4 kHz. This delay-varying mechanism will take time and it is to be expected that the HAS would then be slow to react to changes in source direction. This is indeed the case and experiments have shown that oscillating sources can only be tracked up to 2–3 Hz.[8] The ability to locate bursts of noise improves with burst duration up to about 700 milliseconds.

The perception we have of when a sound stops and starts is not very precise. This is just as well because we live in a reverberant world which is filled with sound reflections. If we could separately distinguish every different reflection in a reverberant room we would hear a confusing cacaphony. In practice we hear very well in reverberant surroundings, far better than microphones can, because of the transform nature of the ear and the way in which the brain processes nerve signals.

When two or more versions of a sound arrive at the ear, provided they fall within a time span of about 30 ms, they will not be treated as separate sounds, but will be fused into one sound. Only when the time separation reaches 50–60 ms do the delayed sounds appear as echoes from different directions. As we have evolved to function in reverberant surroundings, reflections do not impair our ability to locate the source of a sound. The fusion will be impaired if the spectra of the two sounds are too dissimilar.

A moment's thought will confirm that the *first* version of a transient sound to reach the ears must be the one which has travelled by the shortest path. Clearly this must be the direct sound rather than a reflection. Consequently the HAS has evolved to attribute source direction from the time of arrival difference at the two ears of the first version of a transient. Later versions which may arrive from elsewhere simply add to the perceived loudness but do not change the perceived location of the source.

This phenomenon is known as the precedence or Haas effect after the Dutch researcher who investigated it. Haas found that the precedence effect is so powerful that even when later-arriving sounds are artificially amplified (a situation which does not occur in nature) the location still appears to be that from which the first version arrives. Figure 5.56 shows how much extra level is needed to overcome the precedence effect as a function of arrival delay.

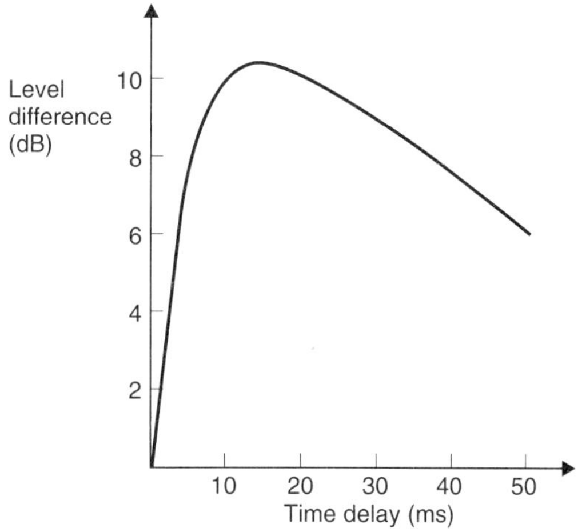

Figure 5.56 The precedence effect is powerful. This curve shows the extra level which is needed in a later sound to overcome the precedence effect.

Experiments have been conducted in which the delay and intensity clues are contradictory to investigate the way the weighting process works. The same sound is produced in two locations but with varying relative delay and shading-dependent level. The way in which the listener perceives an apparent sound direction reveals how the directional clues are weighted.

Within the maximum inter-aural delay of about 700 microseconds the precedence effect does not function and the perceived direction can be pulled away from that of the first-arriving source by an increase in level. Figure 5.57 shows that this area is known as the time–intensity trading region. Once the maximum inter-aural delay is exceeded, the HAS knows that the time difference must be due to reverberation and the trading ceases to change with level.

It is important to realize that in real life the HAS expects a familiar sound to have a familiar weighting of phase, time of arrival and shading clues. A high-quality sound reproduction system must do the same if a convincing spatial illusion is to be had. Consequently a stereo or surround system which attempts to rely on just one of these effects will not sound realistic. Worse still is a system which relies on one effect to be dominant but where another is contradictory.

In the presence of an array of simultaneous sound sources the HAS has an ability to concentrate on one of them based on its direction. The brain appears to be able to insert a controllable time delay in the nerve signals from one ear with respect to the other so that when sound arrives from a given direction the nerve signals from both ears are coherent. Sounds arriving from other directions are incoherent and are heard less well. This

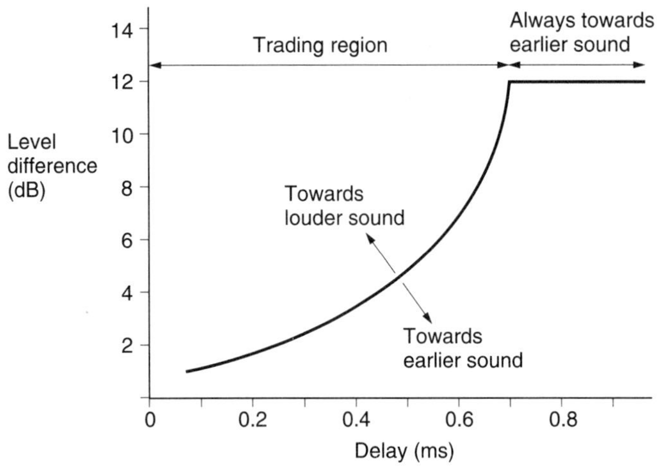

Figure 5.57 Time–intensity trading occurs within the inter-aural delay period.

is known as *attentional selectivity*[9] but is more usually referred to as the *cocktail party effect*.

Monophonic systems prevent the use of this effect completely because the first version of all sounds reaching the listener come from the same loudspeaker. Stereophonic systems allow the cocktail party effect to function in that the listener can concentrate on specific sound sources in a reproduced stereophonic image with the same facility as in the original sound.

One of the most compelling demonstrations of stereo is to make a stereophonic recording of a crowded function in a reverberant room. On replaying several times it will be possible to attentional selectivity to listen to a different conversation each time. Upon switching to mono it will be found that the result is completely unintelligible. A corollary of this experiment is that if this result is not obtained, there is a defect in the equipment or the hearing of the listener.

One of the most frustrating aspects of hearing impairment is that hearing loss in one ear destroys the ability to use the cocktail party effect. In quiet surroundings many people with hearing loss can follow what is said in normal tones. In a crowded room they are at a serious disadvantage because they cannot select a preferred sound source.

Laterally separated ears are ideal for determining the location of sound sources in the plane of the earth's surface, which is after all where most sound sources emanate. In comparison our ability to determine height in sound is very poor. As the ears are almost exactly half-way back on each side of the head it is quite possible for sound sources ahead or behind, above or below to produce almost the same relative delay, phase shift and shading resulting in an ambiguity. This leads to the concept of the *cone of confusion* where all sources on a cone with the listener at the vertex will result in the same IAD.

There are two main ways in which the ambiguity can be resolved. If a plausible source of sound can be seen, then the visual clue will dominate. Experience will also be used. People who look up when they hear birdsong may not be able to determine the height of the source at all, they may simply know, as we all do, that birds sing in trees.

A second way of resolving front/back ambiguity is to turn the head slightly. This is often done involuntarily and most people are not aware they are using the technique. In fact when people deliberately try harder to locate a sound they often keep their head quite still making the ambiguity worse. Section 5.14 will show why intensity stereo recordings are fundamentally incompatible with headphone reproduction. A further problem with headphones is that they turn with the wearer's head, disabling the ability to resolve direction by that means.

The convolutions of the pinna also have some effect at high frequencies where the wavelength of sound is sufficiently short. The pinna produces a comb-filtering spectral modification which is direction dependent. Figure 5.58 shows that different parts of the pinna cause reflections according to

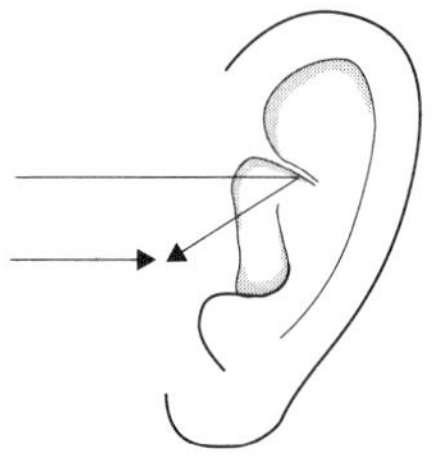

Figure 5.58 The pinna plays a part in determining direction at high frequencies where reflections cause recognizable notches in the spectrum which are a function of geometry.

the direction from which the sound has come. The different reflection mechanisms result in notches or cancellations at various frequencies. The hearing mechanism learns the position of these notches in order to make height judgements with suitable types of sound source.

Figure 5.59 shows that when standing, sounds from above reach the ear directly and via a ground reflection which has come via a longer path. (There is also a smaller effect due to reflection from the shoulders). At certain frequencies the extra path length will correspond to a 180° phase shift, causing cancellation at the ear. The result is a frequency response consisting of evenly spaced nulls which is called *comb filtering*. A moving object such as a plane flying over will suffer changing geometry which will cause the frequency of the nulls to fall towards the point where the overhead position is reached.

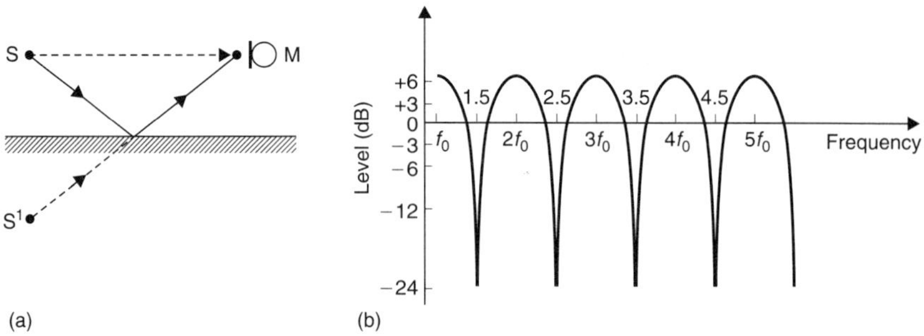

Figure 5.59 Comb-filtering effect produced by interference between a sound wave and a delayed version of itself. (a) Microphone M receives direct wave from source S and a delayed wave from image sound source S^1. (b) Frequency response shows alternating peaks and troughs resembling the teeth of a comb.

The direction-sensing ability has been examined by making binaural recordings using miniature microphones actually placed down the ear canals of a volunteer. When these are played back on headphones to the person whose ears were used for the recording, full localization of direction including front/rear and height discrimination is obtained. However, the differences between people's ears are such that the results of playing the recording to someone else are much worse. The same result is obtained if a dummy head is used.

Whilst binaural recordings give very realistic spatial effects, these effects are only obtained on headphones and consequently the technique is unsatisfactory for signals intended for loudspeaker reproduction and cannot be used in prerecorded music, radio or television.

When considering the localization ability of sound, it should be appreciated that vision can produce a very strong clue. If only one person can be seen speaking in a crowd, then any speech heard must be coming from that person. The same is true when watching films or television. This is a bonus because it means that the utmost precision is not required in the spatial accuracy of stereo or surround sound accompanying pictures. However, if the inaccuracy is too great fatigue may result and the viewer may have a displacement of localization for some time afterwards.[10]

5.12 Microphone principles

Digital techniques are popular in audio because they allow ease of processing, storage and transmission with great precision. In order to enter the digital domain it is essential to have transducers such as microphones and loudspeakers which can convert between real sound and an electrical equivalent. Figure 5.60(a) shows that even if the

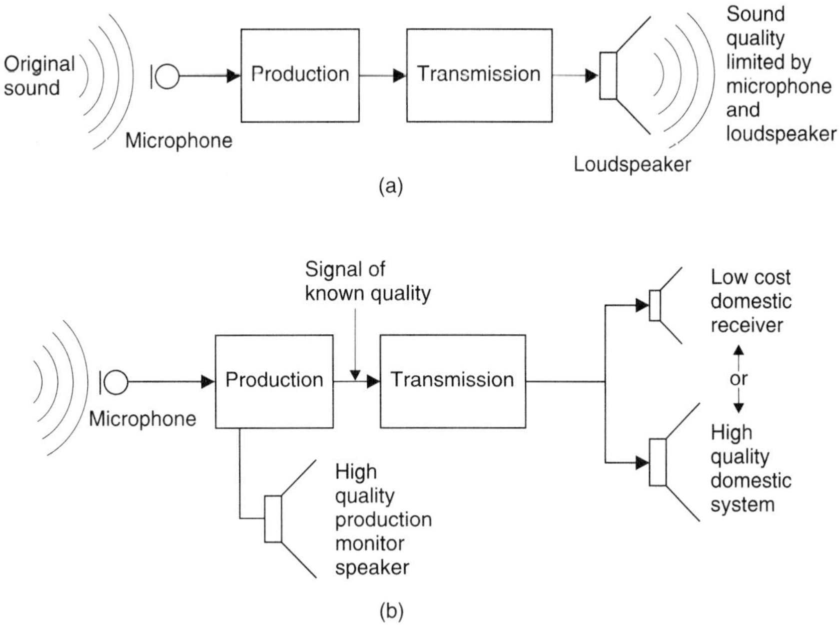

Figure 5.60 (a) The final sound quality of an audio system is limited by both microphones and loudspeakers. (b) Sound production must be performed using high-quality loudspeakers on the assumption that the transmitted quality should be limited only by the listener's equipment.

convertors and the digital system are ideal, the overall quality of a sound system is limited by the quality of both microphone and loudspeaker. In a broadcast sound system or when selling prerecorded material on media or over a network, the quality of the final loudspeaker is variable, dependent upon what the consumer can afford as shown in (b).

However, it must be assumed that at least a number of consumers will have high-quality systems. The quality of the sound should exceed or at least equal that of the consumer's equipment even after all the recording, production and distribution processes have been carried out. Consequently the microphone used in production must be of high quality. The microphone is a measuring device and its output consists of *information* rather than power. It is possible to conceive of an ideal microphone and the best practice approaches this quite closely. The loudspeakers used for monitoring the production process must also be of high quality so that any defect in the microphone or elsewhere can be identified. However, loudspeakers have to transduce power, not just information and this is harder.

The job of the microphone is to convert sound into an electrical signal. Sound consists of both pressure and velocity variations and microphones can use either or both in order to obtain various directional characteristics.[11] The polar or directional characteristics of a microphone are most

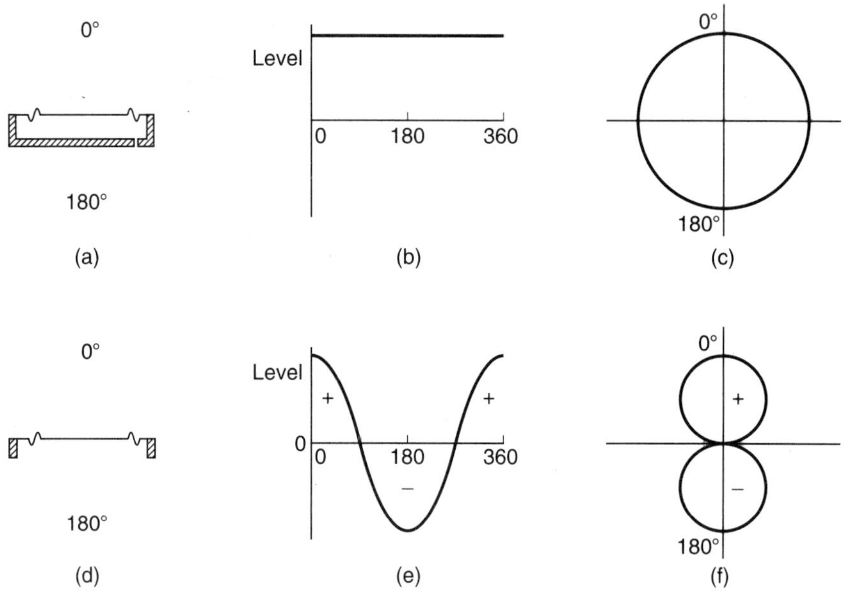

Figure 5.61 (a) Pressure microphone only allows sound to reach one side of the diaphragm. (b) Pressure microphone is omnidirectional for small *ka*. (c) Directional characteristic is more intuitive when displayed in polar form. (d) Velocity or pressure gradient microphone exposes both sides of diaphragm. (e) Output of velocity microphone is a sinusoidal function of direction. (f) In polar coordinates velocity microphone shows characteristic figure-of-eight shape for small *ka*.

important and are treated here before consideration of the operating principle. Polar characteristics assume even greater importance if the illusion of stereophony is to be made realistic.

Figure 5.61(a) shows a true pressure microphone which consists of a diaphragm stretched across an otherwise sealed chamber. In practice a small pinhole is provided to allow changes in atmospheric pressure to take place without causing damage. Some means is provided to sense the diaphragm motion and convert it into an electrical output signal. This can be done in several ways which will be considered below. The output of such a microphone for small values of *ka* is completely independent of direction as (b) shows.

Unlike the HAS, which is selective, microphones reproduce every sound which reaches them. Figure 5.62(a) shows the result of placing a microphone near to a hard wall. The microphone receives a combination of direct and reflected sound between which there is a path length difference. At frequencies where this amounts to a multiple of a wavelength, the reflection will reinforce the direct sound, but at intermediate frequencies cancellation will occur, giving a comb filtering effect. Clearly a conventional microphone should not be positioned near a reflecting object.

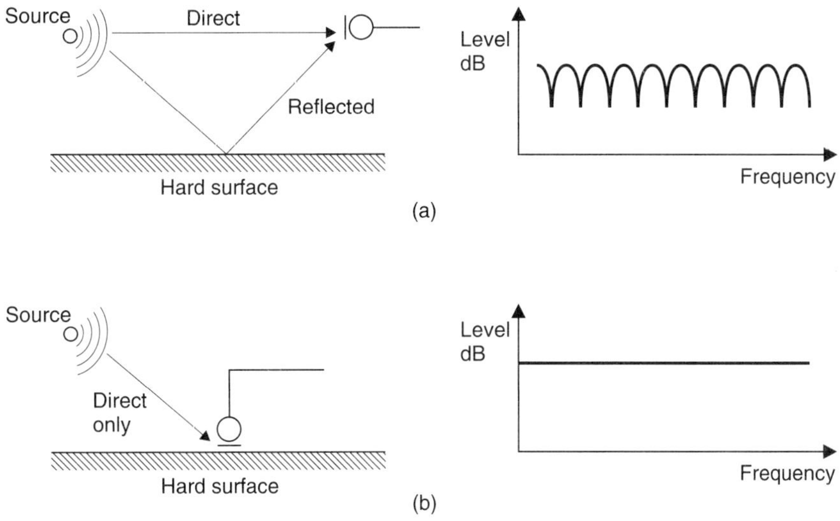

Figure 5.62 (a) Microphone placed several wavelengths from reflective object suffers comb filtering due to path-length difference. (b) Pressure zone microphone is designed to be placed at a boundary where there is no path-length difference.

The path length difference is zero at the wall itself. The pressure zone microphone (PZM) of Figure 5.62(b) is designed to be placed on flat surfaces where it will not suffer from reflections. A pressure capsule is placed facing and parallel to a flat surface at a distance which is small compared to the shortest wavelength of interest. The acoustic impedance rises at a boundary because only a half-space can be seen and the output of a PZM is beneficially doubled.

Figure 5.61(d) shows the *pressure gradient* microphone in which the diaphragm is suspended in free air from a symmetrical perimeter frame. The maximum excursion of the diaphragm will occur when it faces squarely across the incident sound. As (e) shows, the output will fall as the sound moves away from this axis, reaching a null at 90°. If the diaphragm were truly weightless then it would follow the variations in air velocity perfectly, hence the term *velocity microphone*. However as the diaphragm has finite mass then a pressure difference is required to make it move, hence the more accurate term pressure gradient microphone.

The pressure gradient microphone works by sampling the passing sound wave at two places separated by the front-to-back distance. Figure 5.63 shows that the pressure difference rises with frequency as the front-to-back distance becomes a greater part of the cycle. The force on the diaphragm rises at 6 dB/octave. Eventually the distance exceeds half the wavelength at the critical frequency where the pressure gradient effect falls rapidly. Fortunately the rear of the diaphragm will be starting to experience shading at this frequency so that the drive is only from the

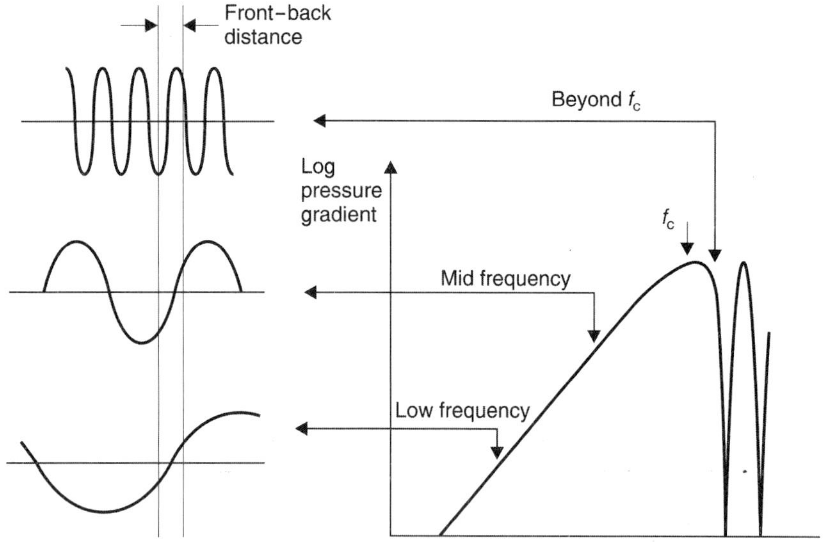

Figure 5.63 The pressure gradient microphone diaphragm experiences a pressure difference which rises with frequency up to the critical frequency, f_c.

front. This has the beneficial effect of transferring to pressure operation so that the loss of output is not as severe as the figure suggests. The pressure gradient signal is in phase with the particle displacement and is in quadrature with the particle velocity.

In practice the directional characteristics shown in Figure 5.61(b) and (e) are redrawn in *polar coordinates* such that the magnitude of the response of the microphone corresponds to the distance from the centre point at any angle. The pressure microphone (c) has a circular polar diagram as it is omnidirectional or *omni* for short. Omni microphones are good at picking up ambience and reverberation which makes them attractive for music and sound effects recordings in good locations. In acoustically poor locations they cannot be used because they are unable to discriminate between wanted and unwanted sound. Directional microphones are used instead.

The PG microphone has a polar diagram (f) which is the shape of a figure-of-eight. Note the null at 90° and that the polarity of the output reverses beyond 90° giving rise to the term *dipole*. The figure-of-eight microphone (sometimes just called 'an *eight*') responds in two directions giving a degree of ambience pickup, although the sound will be a little drier than that of an omni. A great advantage of the figure-of-eight microphone over the omni is that it can reject an unwanted sound. Rather than point the microphone at the wanted sound, a better result will be obtained by pointing the null or dip in the polar diagram at the source of the unwanted sound.

Unfortunately the pressure gradient microphone cannot distinguish between gradients due to sound and those due to gusts of wind. Consequently PG microphones are more sensitive to wind noise than omnis.

If an omni and an eight are mounted coincidentally, various useful results can be obtained by combining the outputs. Figure 5.64(a) shows that if the omni and eight signals are added equally, the result is a heart-shaped polar diagram called a *cardioid*. This response is obtained because at the back of the eight the output is antiphase and has to be subtracted from the output of the omni. With equal signals this results in a null at the rear and a doubling at the front. This useful polar response will naturally sound drier than an eight, but will have the advantage of rejecting more unwanted sound under poor conditions. In public address applications, use of a cardioid will help to prevent *feedback* or *howl-round* which occurs when the microphone picks up too much of the signal from the loudspeakers. Virtually all hand-held microphones have a cardioid response where the major lobe faces axially so that the microphone is

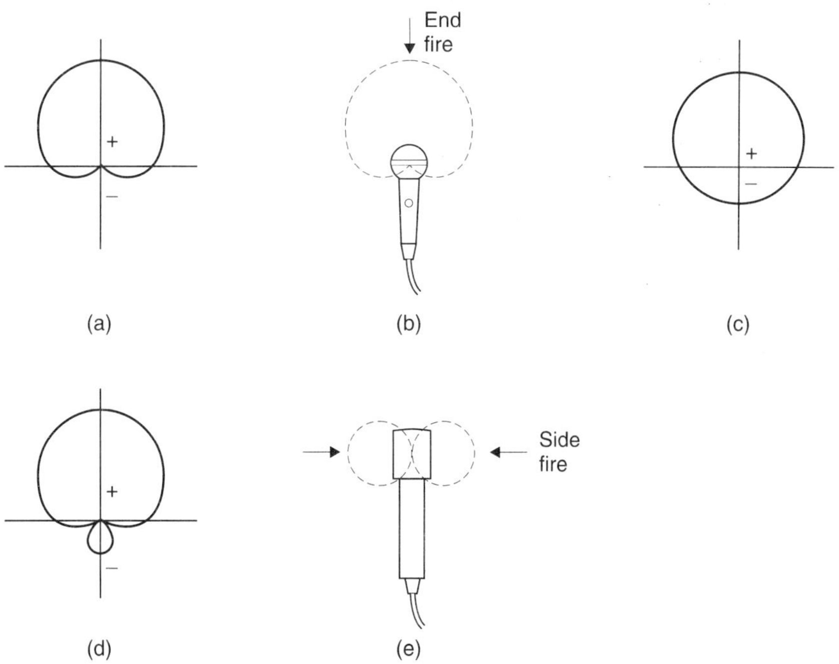

Figure 5.64 (a) Combining an omni response with that of an eight in equal amounts produces the useful cardioid directivity pattern. (b) Hand-held fixed cardioid response microphones are usually built in the end-fire configuration where the body is placed in the null. (c) Sub-cardioid obtained by having more omni in the mix gives better ambience pickup than cardioid. (d) Hyper-cardioid obtained by having more eight in the mix is more directional than cardioid but the presence of the rear lobe must be considered in practice. (e) Microphones with variable polar diagram are generally built in the side-fire configuration.

pointed *at* the sound source. This is known as an *end-fire* configuration shown in Figure 5.64(b).

Where a fixed cardioid-only response is required, this can be obtained using a single diaphragm where the chamber behind it is not sealed, but open to the air via an acoustic labyrinth. Figure 5.65(a) shows that the asymmetry of the labyrinth means that sound which is incident from the front reaches the rear of the diaphragm after a path difference allowing pressure gradient operation. Sound from the rear arrives at both sides of the diaphragm simultaneously, nulling the pressure gradient effect. Sound incident at 90° experiences half the path length difference, giving a reduced output in comparison with the on-axis case. The overall response has a cardioid polar diagram. This approach is almost universal in hand-held cardioid microphones.

In variable directivity microphones there are two such cardioid mechanisms facing in opposite directions as shown in Figure 5.65(b). The system was first devised by the Neumann Company.[12] The central baffle block contains a pattern of tiny holes, some of which are drilled right through and some of which are blind. The blind holes increase the volume behind the diaphragms, reducing the resonant frequency in pressure operation when the diaphragms move in anti-phase. The holes add damping because the viscosity of air is significant in such small cross-sections.

The through-drilled holes allow the two diaphragms to move in tandem so that pressure gradient operation is allowed along with further damping. Figure 5.65(c) shows that sound incident from one side acts on the *outside* of the diaphragm on that side directly, but passes *through* the other diaphragm and then through the cross-drilled holes to act on the

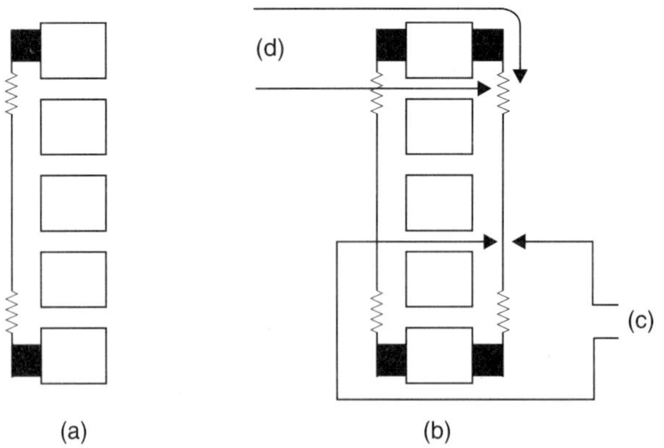

Figure 5.65 (a) Fixed cardioid response is obtained with a labyrinth delaying sound reaching the rear of the diaphragm. (b) Double cardioid capsule is the basis of the variable directivity microphone. (c) Sound arriving from the same side experiences a path-length difference to create a pressure gradient. (d) Sound arriving from the opposite side sees no path-length difference and fails to excite diaphragm.

inside of the first diaphragm. The path length difference creates the pressure gradient condition. Sound from the 'wrong' side (d) arrives at both sides of the far diaphragm without a path length difference.

The relative polarity and amplitude of signals from the two diaphragms can be varied by a control. By disabling one or other signal, a cardioid response can be obtained. Combining them equally results in an omni, whereas combining them with an inversion results in a figure-of-eight response. Unequal combination can obtain the sub-cardioid shown in Figure 5.64(c) or a hyper-cardioid shown in Figure 5.64(d).

Where a flexible polar response is required, the end-fire configuration cannot be used as the microphone body would then block the rearward access to the diaphragm. The *side-fire* configuration is shown in Figure 5.64(e) where the microphone is positioned *across* the approaching sound, usually in a vertical position. For picture applications where the microphone has to be out of shot such microphones are often slung from above pointing vertically downwards.

In most applications the polar diagrams noted above are adequate, but on occasions it proves to be quite impossible to approach the subject close enough and then a highly directional microphone is needed. Picking up ball sounds in sport is one application. Figure 5.66(a) shows that the *shotgun* microphone consists of a conventional microphone capsule which is mounted at one end of a slotted tube. Sound wavefronts approaching from an angle will be diffracted by the slots such that each slot becomes a reradiator launching sound down the inside of the tube. However, Figure 5.66(b) shows that the radiation from the slots travelling down the tube will not add coherently and will be largely cancelled. A wavefront approaching directly on axis as in (c) will pass directly down the outside and the inside of the tube as if the tube were not there and consequently will give a maximum output.

The directivity patterns shown here are only obtained where *ka* is small and are thus ideal. In practice at high frequencies *ka* will not be small and

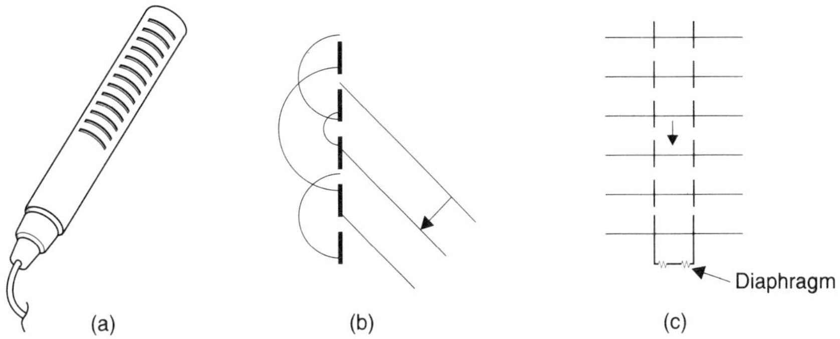

Figure 5.66 (a) Shotgun microphone has slotted tube. (b) Off-axis sound enters slots to produce multiple incoherent sources which cancel. (c) On-axis sound is unaware of tube.

the actual polar diagram will differ due to diffraction becoming significant.

Figure 5.67(a) shows the result of a high-frequency sound arriving off-axis at a large diaphragm. It will be clear that at different parts of the diaphragm the sound has a different phase and that in an extreme case cancellation will occur, reducing the output significantly.

When the sound is even further off-axis, shading will occur. Consequently at high frequency the polar diagram of a nominally omni microphone may look something like that shown in Figure 5.67(b). The HF polar diagram of an eight may resemble (c). Note the narrowing of the response such that proper reproduction of high frequencies is only achieved when the source is close to the axis.

The frequency response of a microphone should ideally be flat and this is often tested on-axis in anechoic conditions. However, in practical use the surroundings will often be reverberant and this will change the

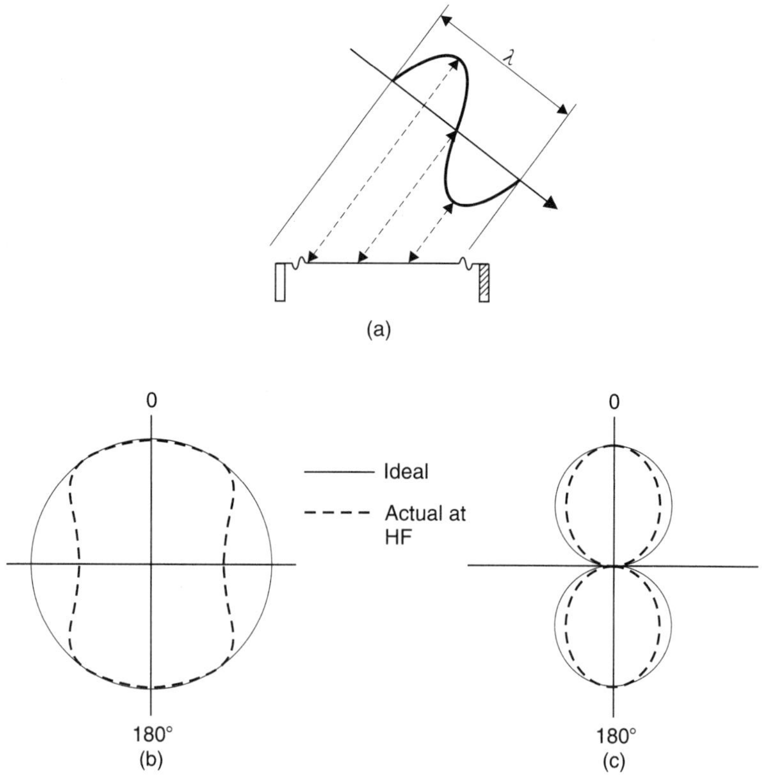

Figure 5.67 (a) Off-axis response is impaired when *ka* is not small because the wavefront reaches different parts of diaphragm at different times causing an aperture effect. (b) Polar diagram of practical omni microphone at high frequency shows narrowing of frontal response due to aperture effect and rear loss due to shading. (c) Practical eight microphone has narrowing response at high frequency.

response at high frequencies because the directivity is not independent of frequency. Consequently a microphone which is flat on-axis but which has a directivity pattern which narrows with frequency will sound dull in practical use. Conversely a microphone which has been equalized flat in reverberant surroundings may appear too bright to an on-axis source.

Pressure microphones being omnidirectional have the most difficulty in this respect because shading makes it almost impossible to maintain the omnidirectional response at high frequencies. Clearly an omni based on two opposing cardioids will be better at high frequencies than a single-pressure capsule. Another possibility is to mount the diaphragm horizontally and place a conical reflector above it.

It is possible to reduce *ka* by making the microphone diaphragm smaller but this results in smaller signals making low noise difficult to achieve. However, developments in low-noise circuitry will allow diaphragm size beneficially to be reduced.

In the case of the shotgun microphone, the tube will become acoustically small at low frequencies and will become ineffective causing the polar diagram to widen.

The electrical output from a microphone can suffer from distortion with very loud signals or from noise with very quiet signals. In passive microphones distortion will be due to the linear travel of the diaphragm being exceeded whereas in active microphones there is the additional possibility of the circuitry being unable to handle large-amplitude signals. Generally a maximum SPL will be quoted at which a microphone produces more than 0.5 per cent THD.

Noise will be due to thermal effects in the transducer itself and in the circuitry. Microphone noise is generally quoted as the SPL which would produce the same level as the noise. The figure is usually derived for the noise after A weighting (see section 5.5). The difference between the 0.5 per cent distortion SPL and the self-noise SPL is the dynamic range of the microphone: 110 dB is considered good but some units reach an exceptional 130 dB.

In addition to thermal noise, microphones may also pick up unwanted signals and hum fields from video monitors, lighting dimmers and radio transmissions. Considering the low signal levels involved, microphones have to be well designed to reject this kind of interference. The use of metal bodies and grilles is common to provide good RF screening.

The output voltage for a given SPL is called the sensitivity. The specification of sensitivity is subject to as much variation as the mounting screw thread. Some data sheets quote output voltage for 1 Pa, some for 0.1 Pa. Sometimes the output level is quoted in dBV, sometimes dBu (see section 5.2). The outcome is that in practice preamplifier manufacturers provide a phenomenal range of gain on microphone inputs and the user simply turns up the gain to get a reasonable level.

It should be noted that in reverberant conditions pressure and pressure gradient microphones can give widely differing results. For example, where standing waves are encountered, a pressure microphone positioned at a pressure node would give an increased output whereas a pressure gradient microphone in the same place would give a reduced output. The effect plays havoc with the polar diagram of a cardioid microphone.

The proximity effect should always be considered when placing microphones. As explained above, proximity effect causes an emphasis of low frequencies when a PG microphone is too close to a source. A true PG microphone such as an eight will suffer the most, whereas a cardioid will have 6 dB less proximity effect because half of the signal comes from an omni response.

5.13 Microphone mechanisms

There are two basic mechanisms upon which microphone operation is based: electrostatic and electrodynamic. The electrodynamic microphone operates on the principle that a conductor moving through a magnetic field will generate a voltage proportional to the rate of change of flux. As the magnetic flux is constant, then this results in an output proportional to the velocity of the conductor, i.e. it is a *constant velocity* transducer. The most common type has a moving coil driven by a diaphragm. In the ribbon microphone the diaphragm itself is the conductor.

The electrostatic microphone works on the variation in capacitance between a moving diaphragm and a fixed plate. As the capacitance varies directly with the spacing the electrostatic microphone is a *constant amplitude* transducer. There are two forms of electrostatic microphone: the condensor, or capacitor, microphone and the electret microphone.

The ribbon and electrostatic microphones have the advantage that there is extremely direct coupling between the sound waveform and the electrical output and so very high quality can be achieved. The moving-coil microphone is considered to be of lower quality but is cheaper and more robust.

Microphones can be made using other techniques but none can offer high quality and use is restricted to consumer or communications purposes or where something unbreakable is required.

Figure 5.68(a) shows that the vibrations of a diaphragm can alter the pressure on a quantity of carbon granules, altering their resistance to current flow. This construction was used for telephone mouthpieces for many years. Whilst adequate for speech, the noise level and distortion is high.

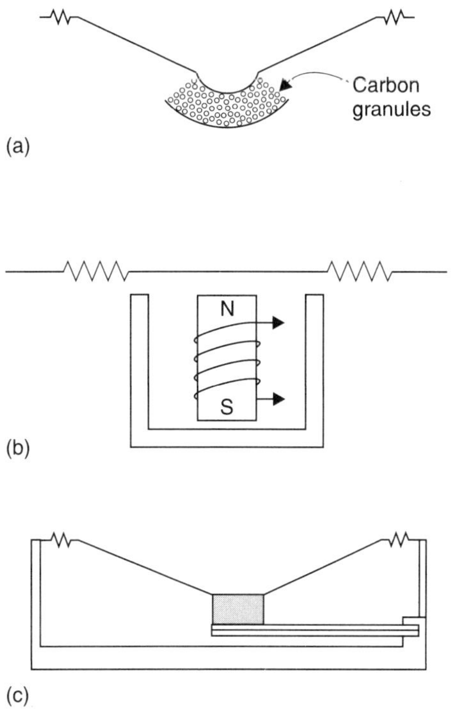

Figure 5.68 (a) Carbon microphone relies on variations of pressure affecting resistance of carbon granules. (b) Ferrous diaphragm of variable reluctance microphone changes flux as it moves. Coil responds to flux changes. (c) Piezo-electric microphone relies on voltage produced by bending a crystal.

Figure 5.68(b) shows the moving-iron or variable reluctance microphone in which a ferrous diaphragm vibrates adjacent to a permanent magnet. The variation of the air gap causes the flux of the magnet to vary and this induces a signal in a coil.

Figure 5.68(c) shows a piezo-electric or crystal microphone in which the diaphragm vibrations deform a bimorph crystal of Rochelle salt or barium titanate. This material produces a voltage when under strain. A high input impedance is required.

There are two basic implementations of the electrodynamic microphone; the ribbon and the moving coil. Figure 5.69(a) shows that in the ribbon microphone the diaphragm is a very light metallic foil which is suspended under light tension between the poles of a powerful magnet. The incident sound causes the diaphragm to move and the velocity of the motion results in an EMF being generated across the ends of the ribbon.

The most common form which the ribbon microphone takes is the figure-of-eight response although cardioid and pressure variants are possible using the techniques outlined above. The output voltage of the

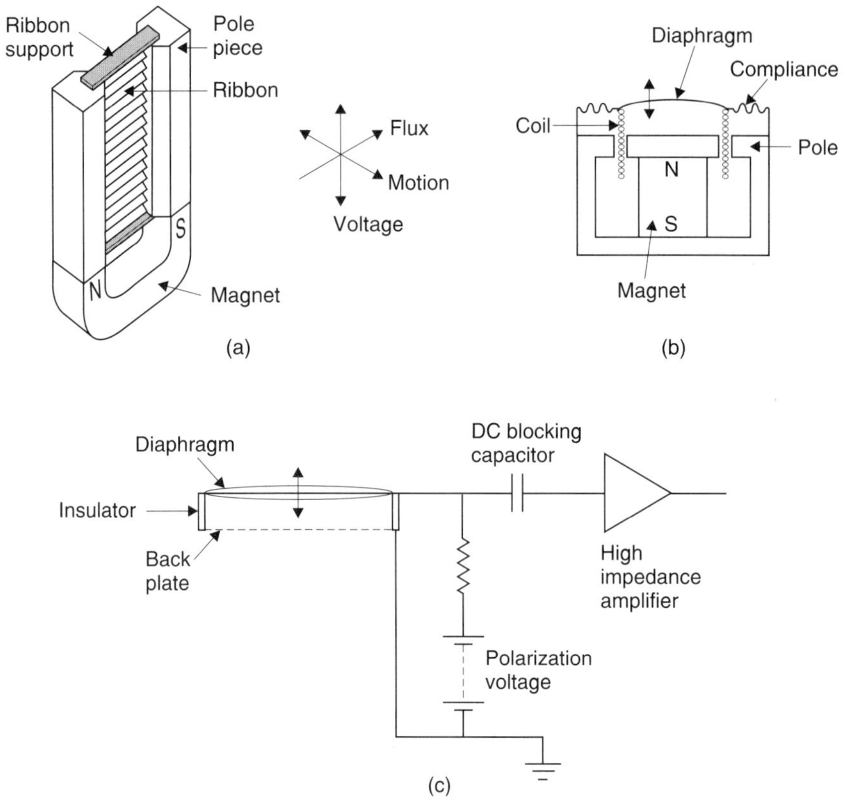

Figure 5.69 (a) Now obsolete ribbon microphone suspends conductive diaphragm in magnetic field. Low output impedance requires matching transformer. (b) The moving-coil microphone is robust but indirect coupling impairs quality. (c) Capacitor microphone has very tight coupling but requires high-impedance electronics and needs to be kept dry.

ribbon is very small but the source impedance of the ribbon is also very low and so it is possible to use a transformer to produce a higher output voltage at a more convenient impedance.

As the driving force on a pressure gradient transducer is proportional to frequency, the resonant frequency of the ribbon is set below the audio band at only a few Hz. Consequently the ribbon works in the mass-controlled region where for constant drive force the velocity falls at 6 dB/ octave. This balances the 6 dB/octave rise of the pressure gradient effect to produce a flat response. The very high compliance needed to set the resonance below the audio band means that the ribbon microphone is shock sensitive. If the body of the microphone is moved, the diaphragm will lag behind causing relative motion. Good mounting isolation is required.

The advantage of the ribbon microphone is that the motion of the ribbon is directly converted to an electrical signal. This is potentially very accurate. However, unless the transformer is of extremely high quality the inherent accuracy will be lost. A further problem is that to obtain reasonable sensitivity the diaphragm must be relatively large, giving a low cut-off frequency and leading to the directivity problems mentioned above. Traditionally the magnet was also large, leading to a heavy construction. A further problem is that the diaphragm is extremely delicate and a single exposure to wind might destroy it.

Although the ribbon microphone was at one time the best available it has been overshadowed by the capacitor microphone and is little used today. The ribbon principle deserves to be revisited with modern techniques. A smaller diaphragm and a physically smaller rare-earth magnet would push up the cut-off frequency by reducing the path length difference. The smaller output could be offset by incorporating an amplifier into an active design.

The most common version of the electrodynamic microphone is the moving-coil system shown in Figure 5.69(b). The diaphragm is connected to a cylindrical former upon which is wound a light coil of wire. The coil operates in the radial flux pattern of a cylindrical magnet. As the output is proportional to velocity, a moving-coil pressure microphone has to work in the resistance-controlled domain using a mid-band resonance which is heavily damped. The range is often extended by building in additional damped resonances. A moving-coil pressure gradient microphone would need to operate in mass-control.

As it is possible to wind many turns of wire on the coil, the output of such a microphone is relatively high. The structure is quite robust and can easily withstand wind and handling abuse. However, the indirect conversion, whereby the sound moves the diaphragm and the diaphragm moves the coil, gives impaired performance because the coil increases the moving mass and the mechanical coupling between the coil and diaphragm is never ideal. Consequently the moving-coil microphone, generally in a cardioid response form, finds common application in outdoor use, for speech or for public address, but is considered inadequate for accurate music work.

In the capacitor (or condensor) microphone the diaphragm is highly insulated from the body of the microphone and is fed with a high polarizing voltage via a large resistance. Figure 5.69(c) shows that a fixed metallic grid forms a capacitor in conjunction with the diaphragm. The diaphragm is connected to an amplifier having a very high impedance. The high impedances mean that there is essentially a constant charge condition. Consequently when incident sound moves the diaphragm and the capacitance between it and the grid varies, the result will be a change of diaphragm voltage which can be amplified to produce an output.

As the condenser mechanism has a constant amplitude characteristic, a pressure or omni condensor microphone needs to use *stiffness control* to obtain a flat response. The resonant frequency is placed above the audio band. In a PG condensor microphone *resistance control* has to be used where a well-damped mid-band resonant frequency is employed.

The condensor microphone requires active circuitry close to the capsule and this requires a source of DC power. This is often provided using the same wires as the audio output using the principle of *phantom powering*.

If the impedance seen by the condensor is not extremely high, charge can leak away when the diaphragm moves. This will result in poor output and phase shift at low frequencies. As the condensor microphone requires high impedances to work properly, it is at a disadvantage in damp conditions which means that in practice it has to be kept indoors in all but the most favourable weather. Some condensor microphones contain a heating element which is designed to drive out moisture. In older designs based on vacuum tubes, the heat from the tube filaments would serve the same purpose. If a capacitor microphone has become damp, it may fail completely or create a great deal of output noise until it has dried out.

In the electret microphone a material is employed which can produce a constant electric field without power. It is the electrostatic equivalent of a permanent magnet. An electret is a extremely good insulator which has been heated in an intense electric field. A conductor moving in such a field will produce a high-impedance output which will usually require to be locally amplified. The electret microphone can be made very light because no magnet is required. This is useful for hand-held and miniature designs.

In early designs the diaphragm itself was the polarized element, but this required an excessively heavy diaphragm. Later designs use a conductive diaphragm like that of a capacitor microphone and the polarized element is part of the backplate. These back-polarized designs usually offer a better frequency response. Whilst phantom power can be used, electret microphones are often powered by a small dry cell incorporated into the microphone body.

In variable directivity condensor microphones the double cardioid principle of Figure 5.65 is often used. However, the variable mixing of the two signals is achieved by changing the polarity and magnitude of the polarizing voltage on one diaphragm such that the diaphragm audio outputs can simply be added. Figure 5.70 shows that one diaphragm is permanently polarized with a positive voltage, whereas the other can be polarized with a range of voltages from positive, through zero, to negative.

When the polarizing voltages are the same, the microphone becomes omni, whereas if they are opposing it becomes an eight. Setting the variable voltage to zero allows the remaining diaphragm to function as a cardioid. A fixed set of patterns may be provided using a switch, or a

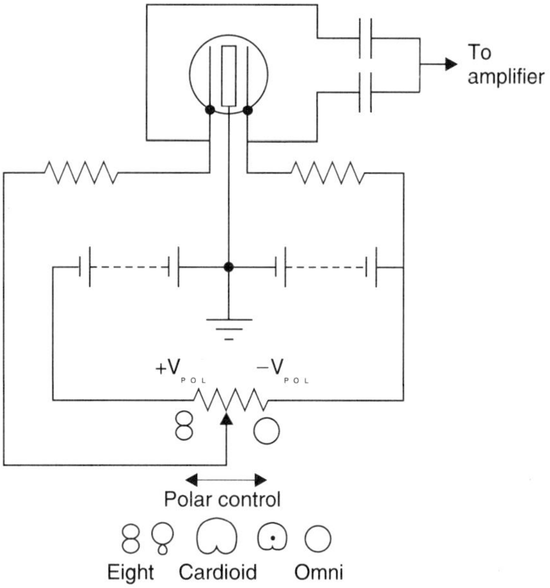

Figure 5.70 Variable directivity electrostatic microphone varies polarizing voltage and polarity on one diaphragm to change directivity.

continuously variable potentiometer may be supplied. Whilst this would appear to be more flexible it has the disadvantage of being less repeatable. It will be clear that this approach cannot be used with the electret microphone which usually has fixed directivity. The pressure zone microphone is an ideal application for the electret principle.

Where active microphones (those containing powered circuitry) are used, it is common to provide the power using the balanced audio cable in reverse. Figure 5.71 shows how phantom powering works. As the audio signal is transmitted differentially, the DC power can be fed to the microphone without interfering with the returning audio signal. The cable screen forms the return path for the DC power.

The use of female XLR connectors for audio inputs is because of phantom power. An audio input is a phantom power output and so requires the insulated contacts of the female connector. Many, but not all, passive microphones are wired such that their differential output is floating relative to the grounded case. These can be used with a cable carrying live phantom power. Provision is generally made to turn the phantom power off so that any type of passive or self-powered microphones can be used.

Variable-directivity microphones may have the directivity control on the microphone body, or they may be provided with a control box which can be some distance away. This can offer practical advantages when a microphone is slung out of reach.

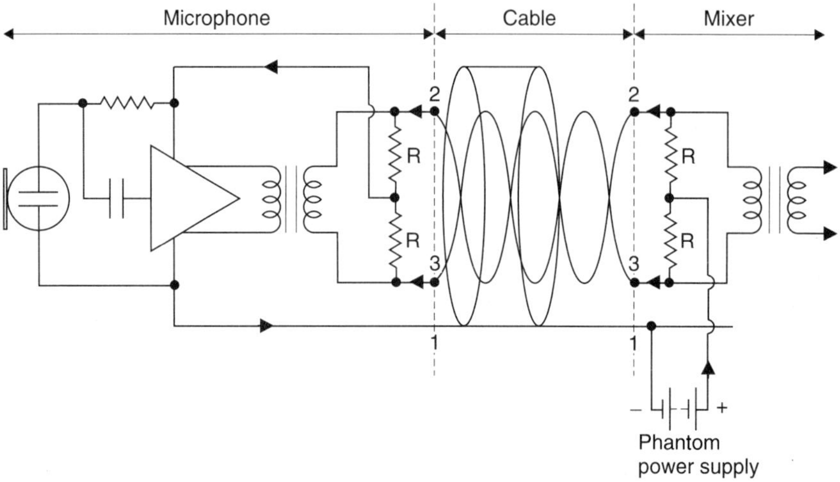

Figure 5.71 Phantom power system allows mixing console to power microphone down signal cable.

5.14 Stereo and surround sound

The most popular technique for giving an element of spatial realism in sound is *stereophony*, nowadays abbreviated to stereo, based on two simultaneous audio channels feeding two spaced loudspeakers as shown in Figure 5.72(a). The optimum listening arrangement for stereo is where the speakers and the listener are at different points of a triangle which is almost equilateral.

Delivering more than two channels with analog systems is difficult, but the Dolby Surround system managed to encode rear channel information into two signal channels which were stereo compatible. Further progress in surround sound was made as soon as digital delivery was feasible. In the digital domain any number of channels can be delivered without crosstalk using multiplexing. Figure 5.72(b) shows that in a typical surround installation, five speakers are used, namely Left, Centre, Right, Left rear and Right rear positioned as shown. It is usually beneficial if the rear speakers are mounted somewhat further apart than the front speakers. It is also possible to include a narrow-band signal which drives a monophonic subwoofer. This configuration is known as a 5.1 channel system.

Surround sound works on exactly the same principles as stereo and is no more than an extension of stereo. The principles of stereo will be described here first, before expanding into surround sound.

Stereophony works by creating differences of phase and time of arrival of sound *at the listener's ears*. It was shown above that these are the most powerful hearing mechanisms for determining direction. Figure 5.73(a)

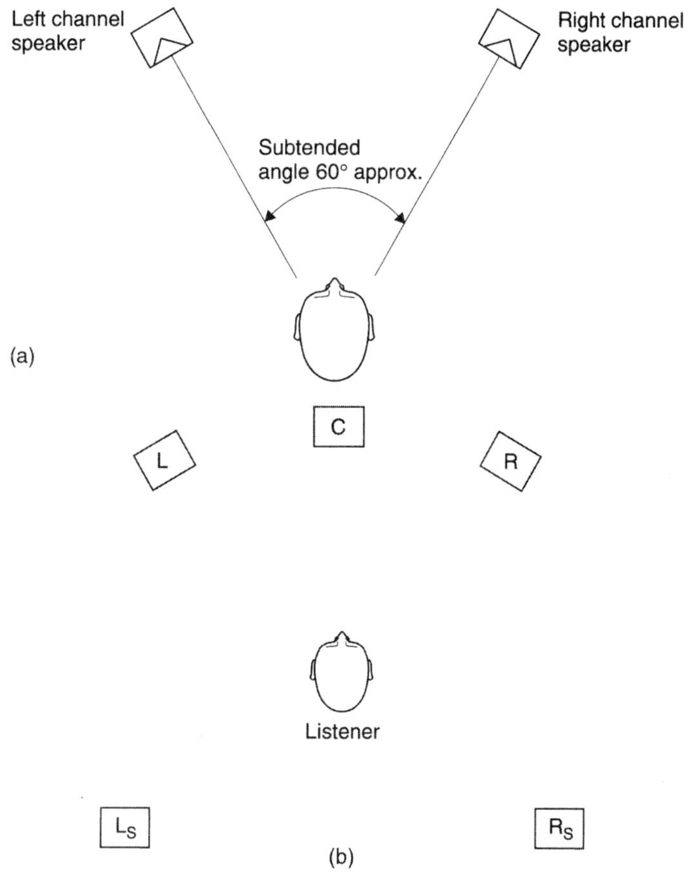

Figure 5.72 (a) Configuration user for stereo listening. (b) In surround sound, it is common practice to supplant the stereo pair of (a) with a centre speaker and a pair of rear speakers.

shows that this time of arrival difference is achieved by producing the same waveform at each speaker simultaneously, but with a difference in the relative level, rather than phase. Each ear picks up sound from both loudspeakers and sums the waveforms.

The sound picked up by the ear on the same side as the speaker is in advance of the same sound picked up by the opposite ear. When the level emitted by the left loudspeaker is greater than that emitted by the right, it will be seen from Figure 5.73(b) that the sum of the signals received at the left ear is a waveform which is phase advanced with respect to the sum of the waveforms received at the right ear. If the waveforms concerned are transient the result will be a time of arrival difference. These differences are interpreted as being due to a sound source left of centre.

The stereophonic illusion only works properly if the two loudspeakers are producing in-phase signals. In the case of an accidental phase

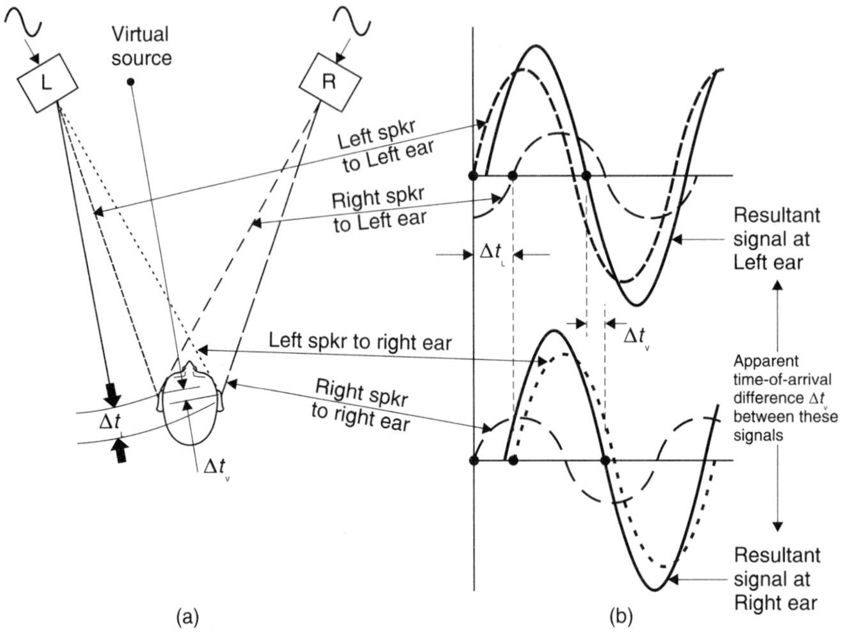

Figure 5.73 (a) Stereo illusion is obtained by producing the same waveform at both speakers, but with different amplitudes. (b) As both ears hear both speakers but at different times, relative level causes apparent time shift at the listener. Δt_L = inter-aural delay due to loudspeaker; Δt_V = inter-aural delay due to virtual source.

reversal, the spatial characteristic will be ill-defined and lack images. At low frequencies the two loudspeakers are in one another's near field and so antiphase connection results in bass cancellation. The same result will be obtained in a surround system if the phase of one or more channels differs from the rest.

As the apparent position of a sound source between the two speakers can be controlled solely by the relative level of the sound emitted by each one, stereo signals in this format are called *intensity stereo*. In intensity stereo it is possible to 'steer' a monophonic signal from a single microphone into a particular position in a stereo image using a form of differential gain control. Figure 5.74 shows that this device, known as a *panoramic potentiometer* or pan-pot for short, will produce equal outputs when the control is set to the centre. If the pan-pot is moved left or right, one output will increase and the other will reduce, moving or *panning* the stereo image to one side.

If the system is perfectly linear, more than one sound source can be panned into a stereo image, with each source heard in a different location. This is done using a stereo mixer, shown in Figure 5.75 in which monophonic inputs pass via pan-pots to a stereo mix bus. The majority of pop records are made in this way, usually with the help of a multi-

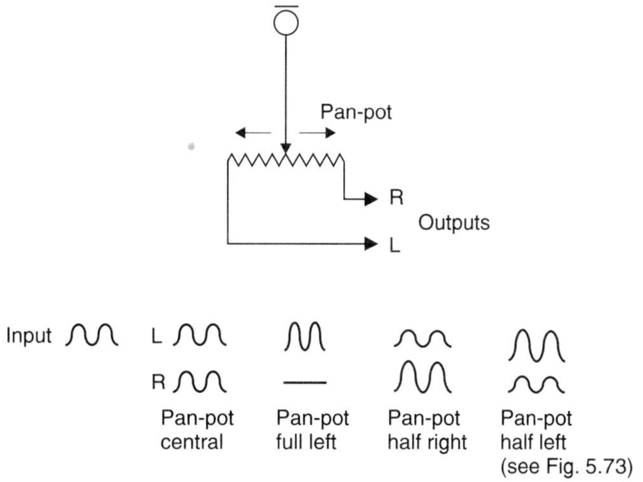

Figure 5.74 The panpot distributes a monophonic microphone signal into two stereo channels following the sound source to be positioned anywhere in the image.

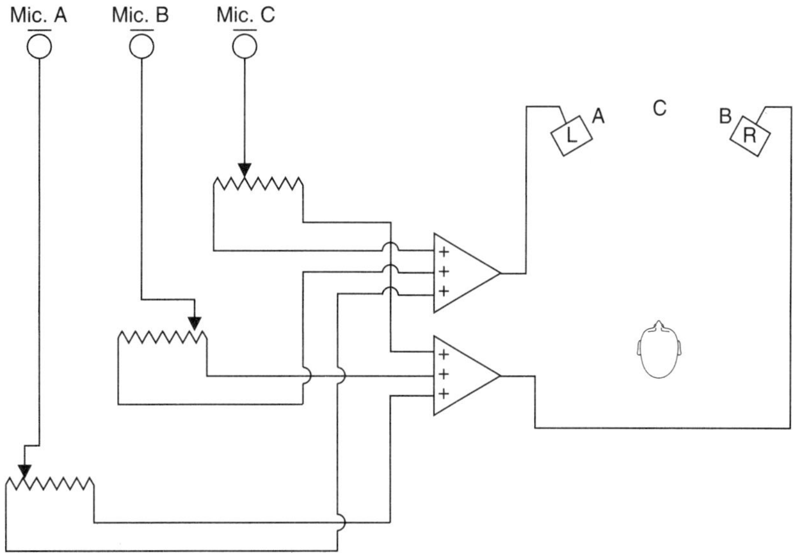

Figure 5.75 Multi-channel mixing technique pans multiple sound sources into one stereo image.

channel recorder with one track per microphone so that mixing and panning can be done at leisure. At one time these recorders were based on analog tape, but today the use of disk drives is becoming universal.

Figure 5.76(a) shows that Dolby Surround derives four channels, L, Centre, R and a surround channel which can be reproduced from two or more rear speakers. In fact a similar speaker arrangement to five-channel discrete can be used. Figure 5.76(b) shows a Dolby Surround encoder. The centre channel is attenuated 3 dB and added equally to L and R. The surround signal is attenuated 3 dB and band limited prior to being encoded with a modified Dolby-B process. The resultant signal is then phase shifted so that a 180° phase relationship is formed between the components which are added to the Lt and Rt signals.

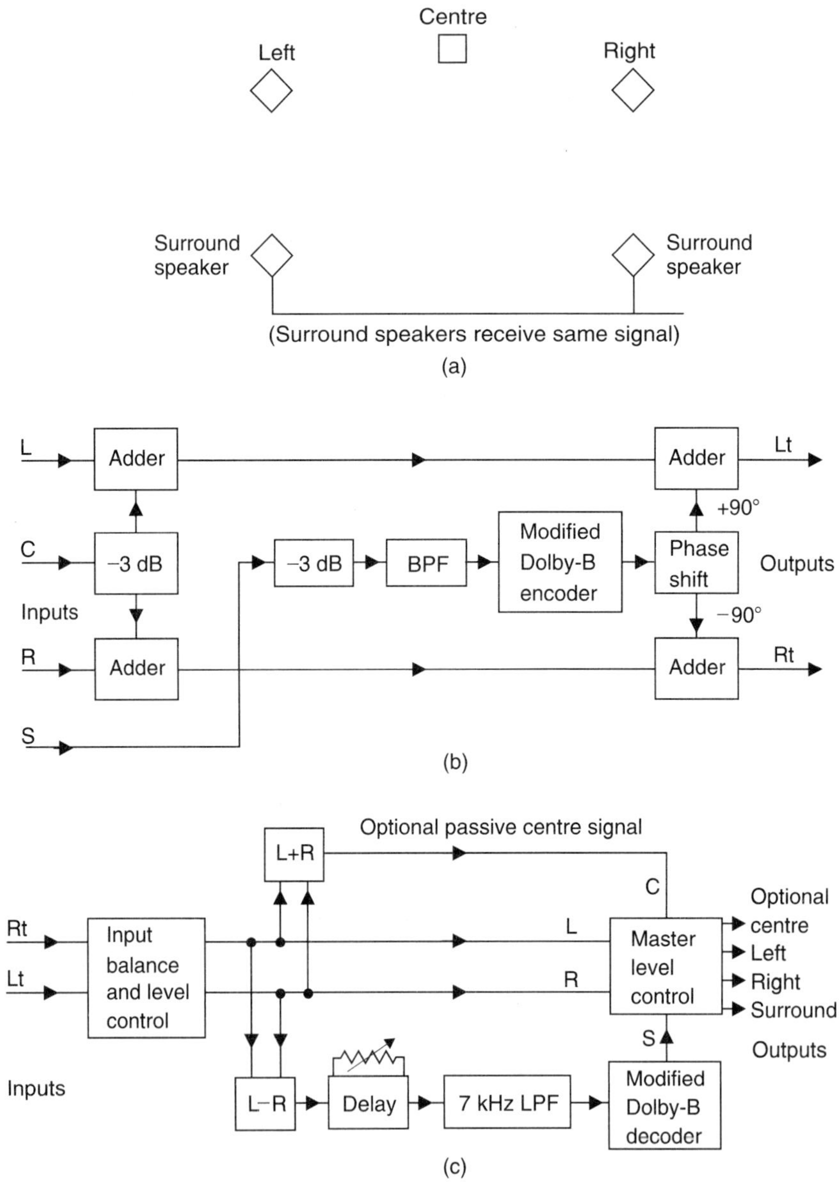

Figure 5.76 (a) Dolby surround sound speaker layout. (b) Dolby surround encoder; see text. (c) Simple passive decoder.

In a simple passive decoder (c) Lt and Rt are used to drive L and R speakers directly. In the absence of a C speaker, the L and R speakers will reproduce the C signal centrally. The added antiphase surround signal will fail to produce an image. If a C speaker is provided, adding Lt and Rt will produce a suitable signal to drive it, although this will result in narrowing of the frontal image. Subtracting Lt and Rt will result in sum of the surround signal and any difference between the original L, R signals. This is band limited then passed through the Dolby-B decoder to produce a surround output.

The Dolby-B-like processing is designed to reduce audibility of L minus R breakthrough on the S signal, particularly on sibilants. The degree of compression is less than that in true Dolby-B to prevent difficulties when Lt and Rt are used as direct speaker drive signals.

In the Pro-logic decoder, shown in Figure 5.76(d) the sum and difference stages are replaced with variable matrices which can act like a two-dimensional pan-pot or steering system. A simple decoder performs poorly when a single point source of sound is present in quiet surroundings whereas a steered decoder will reduce the crosstalk output from unwanted channels. The steering is done by analysing the input signals to identify dominant sound sources. Figure 5.76(d) shows that comparison of the Lt and Rt signals will extract left/right dominance, whereas comparison of sum and difference signals will extract front/rear dominance.

Given that a sound source can be panned between a pair of speakers in front of the listener, with a slight increase in complexity a sound source can be panned between Left, Centre and Right speakers. Figure 5.77 shows that this is done by treating Left and Centre as one stereo pair and Centre and Right as another. A virtual sound source can be positioned anywhere between the Left and Centre speakers by controlling the

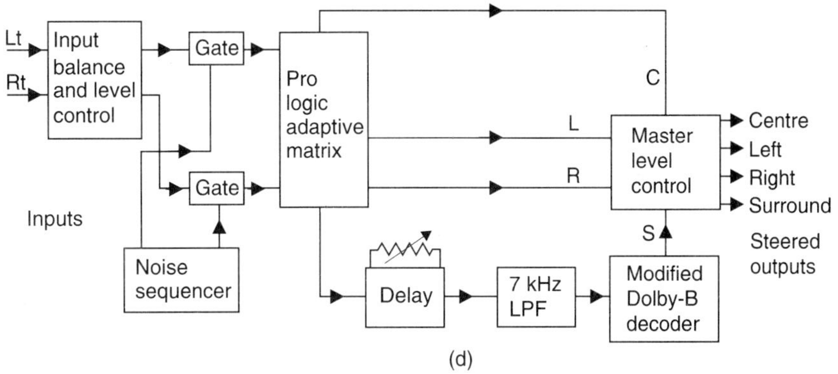

Figure 5.76 (d) Pro-logic decoder uses variable matrices driven by analysis of dominant sound source location.

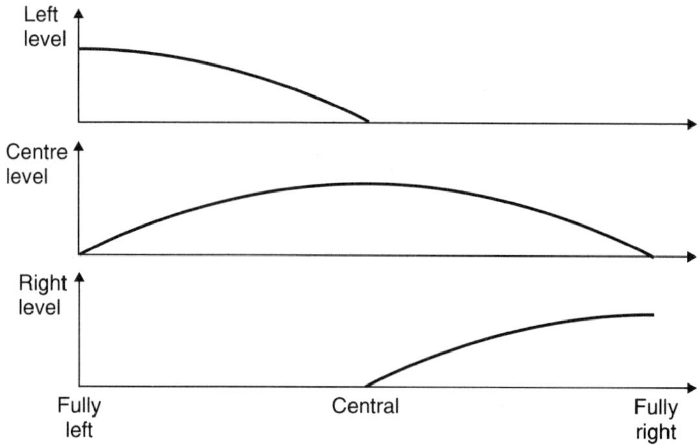

Figure 5.77 Panning between three speakers must be done by treating the system as two stereo pairs where the centre speaker is common to both pairs. Virtual sound sources between one pair should not result in any output from the remaining speaker.

relative level whilst the Right speaker remains silent. When the sound source is panned completely to the Centre speaker, further movement to the right is possible by feeding some signal to the Right speaker whilst the Left speaker remains silent.

The use of the Centre speaker comes from cinema practice and is intended to deliver central images more accurately for listeners positioned off-axis or to compensate for loudspeakers with poor imaging ability. With precision loudspeakers having good imaging, there is little difference between the performance of a Left, Centre, Right system and a simple Left, Right stereo system where the centre channel has been equally added to the Left and Right signals.

A front virtual image can be located anywhere between the Left and Right speakers, and by a similar argument a rear virtual image can be located anywhere between the Left rear and Right rear speakers. It will be clear that this is possible simply by considering the head to be turned through 180° in Figure 5.73.

Five-channel surround sound is something of a misnomer because there is no mechanism by which a virtual sound source can be made to appear to the side. Figure 5.78 shows that images can be positioned between the front speakers or between the rear speakers only. If an attempt is made to position a sound source to the side by feeding equal amounts of signal into, say, the Left and Left rear speakers, the result will be unsatisfactory to a listener facing forward. The sound source will appear at the front or the rear depending on the position of the listener and may jump between these locations. Some writers have reported that sound appears to come from above and to the side.

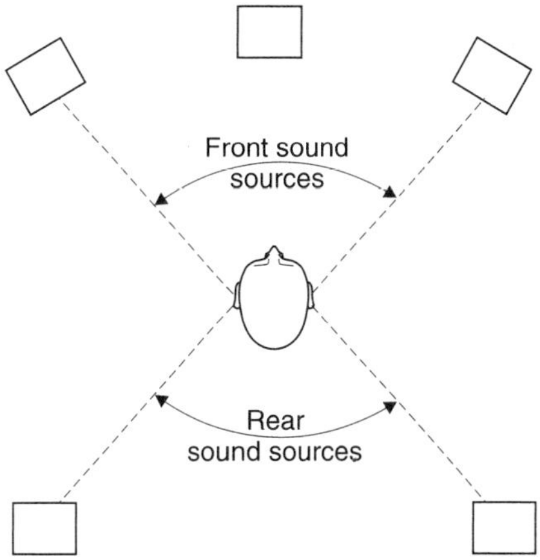

Figure 5.78 Five-channel suround sound is a misnomer because virtual sound sources can only be positioned in the locations shown. Sound from the side has to come from room reverberation or further loudspeakers.

With surround, stereo and mono equipment co-existing, it is necessary to consider compatibility so that, for example, acceptable results are obtained when listening to surround material on stereo equipment, or stereo material on mono equipment.

Well-recorded surround sound material can be converted to stereo quite easily. The redundancy of the centre channel in surround means that it the centre signal is added equally to the left and right signals, a good central image will still be obtained with good loudspeakers. Adding the rear channels to the appropriate front channels means that ambience and reverberation is still reproduced. It is possible for certain effects which rely on phase or time delay to succeed in surround but to produce artifacts in stereo. It is worth while monitoring in stereo at some point in a surround production to avoid such pitfalls.

There is a certain amount of compatibility between intensity stereo and mono systems. If the S gain of a stereo signal is set to zero, only the M signal will pass. This is the component of the stereo image due to sounds from straight ahead and is the signal used when monophonic audio has to be produced from stereo.

Sources positioned on the extreme edges of the sound stage will not appear as loud in mono as those in the centre and any antiphase ambience will cancel out, but in most cases the result is adequate. Clearly an accidental situation in which one channel is phase reversed is catastrophic in mono as the centre of the image will be cancelled out. Stereo signals from spaced microphones generally have poor mono compatibility because of comb filtering.

One characteristic of stereo is that the viewer is able to concentrate on a sound coming from a particular direction using the cocktail party effect.

Thus it will be possible to understand dialog which is quite low in level even in the presence of other sounds in a stereo mix. In mono the listener will not be able to use spatial discrimination and the result may be reduced intelligibility which is particularly difficult for those with hearing impairments.[13] Consequently it is good practice to monitor stereo material in mono to check for acceptable dialog.

A mono signal can also be reproduced on a stereo system by creating identical L and R signals, producing a central image only. Whilst there can be no real spatial information most people prefer mono on two speakers to mono on a single speaker.

5.15 Stereo and surround microphones

Pan-potted audio can never be as realistic as the results of using a stereo or surround microphone because the pan-pot causes all the sound to appear at one place in the stereo image. In the real world the direct sound should come from that location but reflections and reverberation should come from elsewhere. Artificial reverberation has to be used on pan-potted mixes.

The job of a stereo microphone is to produce two audio signals which have no phase or time differences but whose relative levels are a function of the direction from which sound arrives. The most spatially accurate technique involves the use of directional microphones which are coincidentally mounted but with their polar diagrams pointing in different directions. This configuration is known variously as a *crossed pair*, a *coincident pair* or a *Blumlein pair* after Alan Blumlein[14] who pioneered stereophony. Figure 5.79 shows a stereo microphone constructed by crossing a pair of figure-of-eight microphones at 90°.

The output from the two microphones will be equal for a sound source straight ahead, but as the source moves left, the output from the left-facing microphone will increase and the output from the right-facing microphone will reduce. When a sound source has moved 45° off-axis, it will be in the response null of one of the microphones and so only one loudspeaker will emit sound. Thus the fully left or fully right reproduction condition is reached at ±45°. The angle between nulls in L and R is called the acceptance angle which has some parallels with the field of view of a camera.

Sounds between 45° and 135° will be emitted out of phase and will not form an identifiable image. Important sound sources should not be placed in this region. Sounds between 135° and 225° are in-phase and are mapped onto the frontal stereo image. The all-round pickup of the crossed eight makes it particularly useful for classical music recording where it will capture the ambience of the hall.

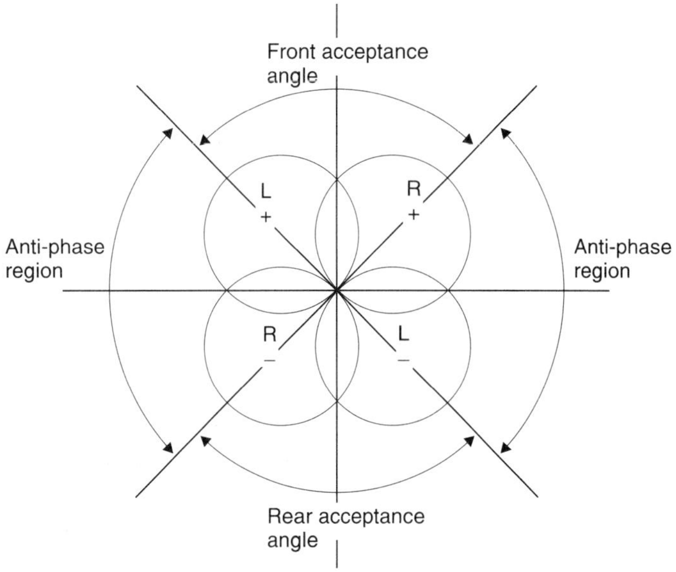

Figure 5.79 Crossed eight stereo microphone. Note acceptance angle between nulls.

Other polar diagrams can be used, for example the crossed cardioid, shown in Figure 5.80 is popular. There is no obvious correct angle at which cardioids should be crossed, and the actual angle will depend on the application. Commercially available stereo microphones are generally built on the side-fire principle with one capsule vertically above the other.

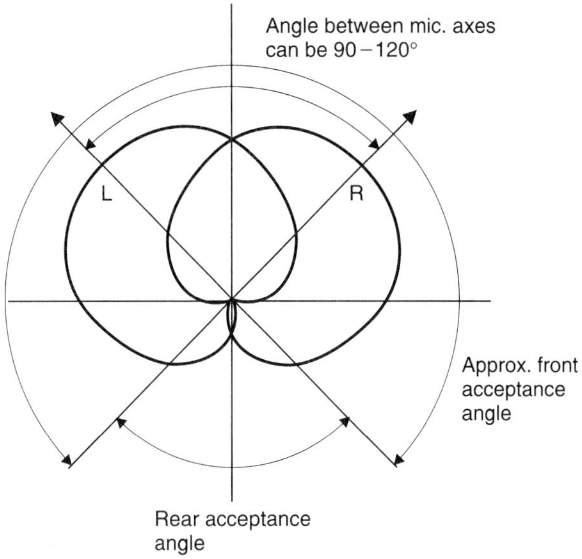

Figure 5.80 Crossed cardioid microphone.

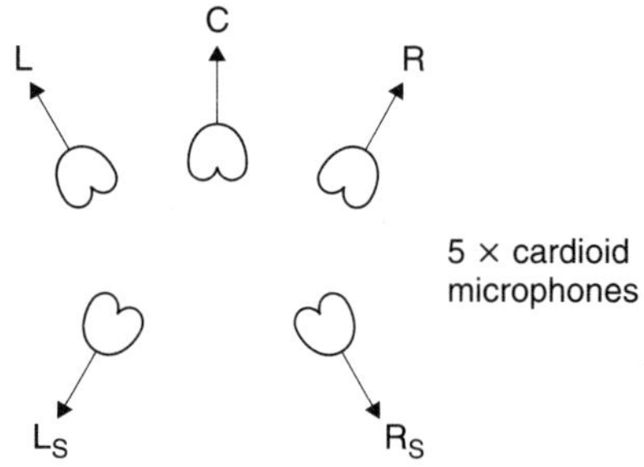

Figure 5.81 One form of surround-sound microphone uses one cardioid microphone per channel. This works but is inefficient and unnecessary.

The two capsules can be independently rotated to any desired angle. Usually the polar diagrams of the two capsules can be changed.

For surround sound, an array of microphones will be needed. Figure 5.81 shows that one approach is to use five cardioid microphones. The rear microphones can be conventional cardioids, but it is advantageous if the front microphones are given a hyper-cardioid bias to narrow their directivity pattern. The microphones should not be turned outwards too far otherwise sounds to the side may result in problematic equal outputs in the front and rear channels.

In the soundfield microphone, four capsules are fitted in a tetrahedron. By adding and subtracting proportions of these four signals in various ways it is possible to synthesize a stereo microphone having any acceptance angle and to point it in any direction relative to the body of the microphone. This can be done using the control box supplied with the microphone. Although complex, the soundfield microphone has the advantage that it can be electrically steered and so no physical access is needed after it is slung. If all four outputs are recorded, the steering process can be performed in post-production by connecting the control

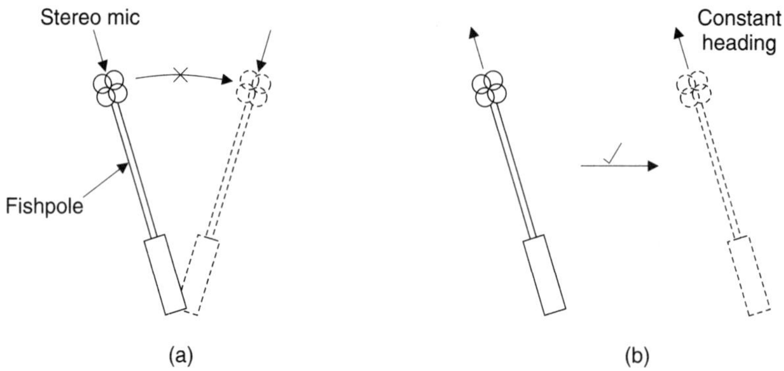

Figure 5.82 (a) Swinging a fishpole causes sound image to rotate. Tracking has to be used as in (b).

box to the recorder output. For surround sound purposes, additional matrices allow the same four signals to be used to synthesize further stereo microphones. If the directivities are carefully determined, Left, Centre and Right signals can be derived as well as the rear pair.

Clearly the use of stereo or surround sound will make it obvious if a microphone has been turned. In many applications the microphone is turned as a side effect of swinging a boom or fishpole, as in Figure 5.82(a). This is undesirable, and more precise handling techniques are necessary to keep the microphone heading constant as in (b).

5.16 M–S stereo

In audio production the apparent width of the stereo image may need to be adjusted, especially in television to obtain a good audio transition where there has been a change of shot or to match the sound stage to the picture. This can be done using *M–S stereo* and manipulating the difference between the two channels. Figure 5.83(a) shows that the two signals from the microphone, L and R, are passed through a *sum and difference* unit which produces two signals, M and S. The M or Mid signal is the sum of L and R whereas the S or Side signal is the difference

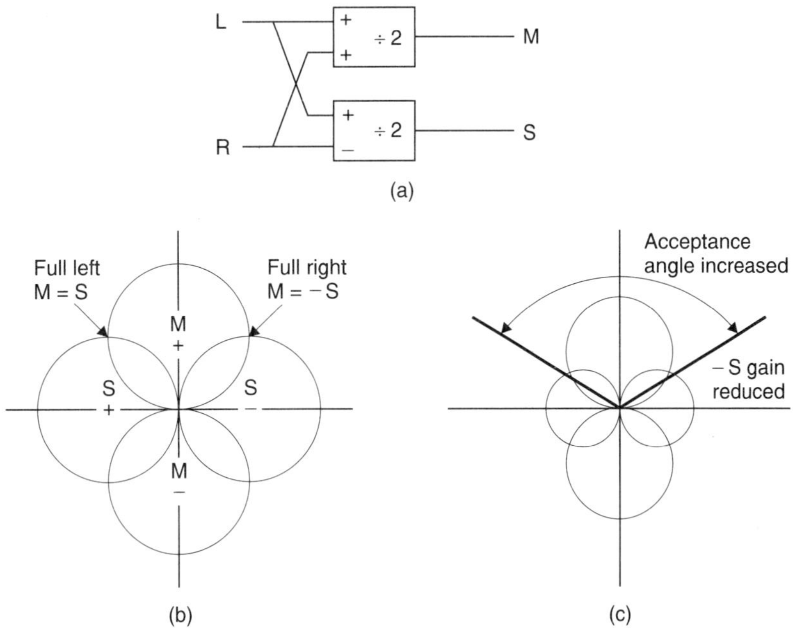

Figure 5.83 (a) M–S working adds and subtracts the L, R stereo signals to produce Mid and Side signals. In the case of a crossed eight, the M–S format is the equivalent of forward and sideways facing eights. (c) Changing the S gain alters the acceptance angle of the stereo microphone.

between L and R. The sums and differences are divided by two to keep the levels correct. These processes can be performed in the analog domain prior to conversion, or in the digital domain using the techniques shown in Chapter 2.

The result of this sum-difference process can be followed in Figure 5.83(b). A new polar diagram is drawn which represents the sum of L and R for all angles of approach. It will be seen that this results in a forward-facing eight, as if a monophonic microphone had been used, hence the term M or Mid. If the same process is performed using L–R, the result is a sideways-facing eight, hence the term S or Side. In L, R format the acceptance angle is between the nulls whereas in M–S format the acceptance angle is between the points where the M and S polar diagrams cross.

The S signal can now be subject to variable gain. Following this a second sum and difference unit is used to return to L, R format for monitoring. The S gain control effectively changes the size of the S polar diagram without affecting the M polar diagram. Figure 5.83(c) shows that reducing the S gain makes the acceptance angle wider whereas increasing the S gain makes it smaller. Clearly if the S gain control is set to unity, there will be no change to the signals.

Whilst M–S stereo can be obtained by using a conventional L, R microphone and a sum and difference network, it is clear from Figure 5.83(b) that M–S signals can be obtained directly using a suitable microphone. Figure 5.84 shows a number of M–S microphones in which the S capsule is always an eight. A variety of responses (other than omni) can be used for the M capsule.

The M–S microphone technique has a number of advantages. The narrowing polar diagram at high frequencies due to diffraction is less of a problem because the most prominent sound source will generally be in the centre of the stereo image and this is directly on the axis of the M

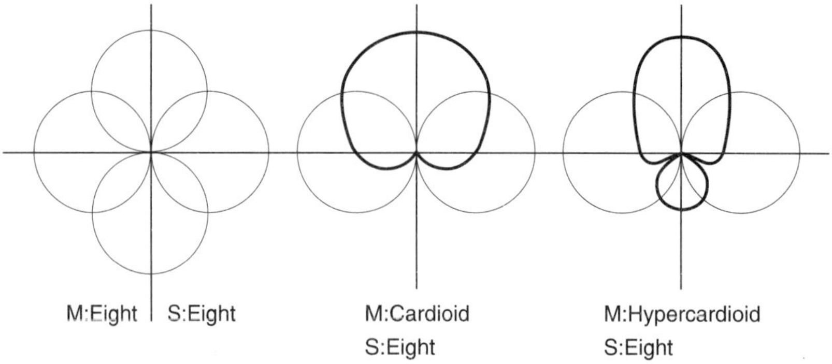

Figure 5.84 Various M–S microphone configurations. Note that the S microphone must always be an eight.

capsule. An image width control can easily be built into an M–S microphone. A favourite mono microphone can be turned into an M–S microphone simply by mounting a side-facing eight above it.

In surround sound, M–S techniques can be used directly for width control working on the rear speakers. In the case of the Left, Centre, Right speakers, increasing the level of the centre speaker whilst reducing those of the outer speakers will have the effect of reducing width.

5.17 Digitizing audio

As was introduced in Chapter 4, digitizing audio requires a number of processing stages. The analog signal from, for example, a microphone is subject to bandwidth limiting in an anti-aliasing filter, followed by sampling and quantizing to produce two's complement coded PCM data. The quality obtained will be affected by the all three of these stages and the necessary quality will be considered here.

Sampling theory is only the beginning of the process which must be followed to arrive at a suitable sampling rate. As was seen in section 4.3, the finite slope of realizable filters will compel designers to raise the sampling rate above the theoretical value. For consumer products, the lower the sampling rate, the better, since the cost of the medium is directly proportional to the sampling rate: thus sampling rates near to twice 20 kHz are to be expected.

Early digital audio recorders were built before modern high-density digital media were available. These were based on analog video recorders which were adapted to store audio samples by creating a signal called *pseudo-video* which could convey binary as black and white levels. The sampling rate of such a system is constrained to relate simply to the field rate and field structure of the television standard used, so that an integer number of samples can be stored on each usable TV line in the field. Such a recording can be made on a monochrome recorder, and these recordings are made in two standards, 525 lines at 60 Hz and 625 lines at 50 Hz. Thus it is possible to find a frequency which is a common multiple of the two and also suitable for use as a sampling rate.

The allowable sampling rates in a pseudo-video system can be deduced by multiplying the field rate by the number of active lines in a field (blanked lines cannot be used) and again by the number of samples in a line. By careful choice of parameters it is possible to use either 525/60 or 625/50 video with a sampling rate of 44.1 kHz.

In 60 Hz video, there are 35 blanked lines, leaving 490 lines per frame, or 245 lines per field for samples. If three samples are stored per line, the sampling rate becomes

$$60 \times 245 \times 3 = 44.1\,\text{kHz}$$

In 50 Hz video, there are 37 lines of blanking, leaving 588 active lines per frame, or 294 per field, so the same sampling rate is given by

$$50.00 \times 294 \times 3 = 44.1\,\text{kHz}$$

The sampling rate of 44.1 kHz came to be that of the Compact Disc. Even though CD has no video circuitry and today the production and mastering equipment is based on data technology, the standard sampling rate remains.

For landlines to FM stereo broadcast transmitters having a 15 kHz audio bandwidth, the sampling rate of 32 kHz is more than adequate, and has been in use for some time in the United Kingdom and Japan. This frequency is also in use in DVB audio and in DAB.

The professional sampling rate of 48 kHz was proposed as having a simple relationship to 32 kHz, being far enough above 40 kHz to allow for high-quality filters or variable-speed operation. Recently there have been proposals calling for dramatically increased audio sampling rates. These are misguided and will not be considered further here.

The signal-to-noise ratio obtained by a convertor cannot exceed a figure which is set by the output PCM wordlength. Chapter 4 showed how this is calculated as a function of the dither technique employed, although a useful rule of thumb is simply to multiply the wordlength by six to get an SNR in dB. For consumer purposes, sixteen bits is generally adequate for post-produced material. For professional purposes longer wordlengths are used to give some freedom in level setting and to allow sixteen-bit performance after generation loss in production steps.

5.18 Audio convertors

The DAC will be discussed first, since ADCs often use embedded DACs in feedback loops. The purpose of a digital-to-analog convertor is to take numerical values and reproduce the continuous waveform that they represent. The conversion techniques shown in Chapter 4 are simply not accurate enough for audio use where wordlengths of sixteen bits or more are required. Although PCM audio is universal because of the ease with which it can be recorded and processed numerically, there are several alternative related methods of converting an analog waveform to a bitstream. The output of these convertor types is not Nyquist rate PCM, but this can be obtained from them by appropriate digital signal processing. In advanced conversion systems it is possible to adopt an alternative convertor technique specifically to take advantage of a particular characteristic. The output is then digitally converted to Nyquist rate PCM in order to obtain the advantages of both.

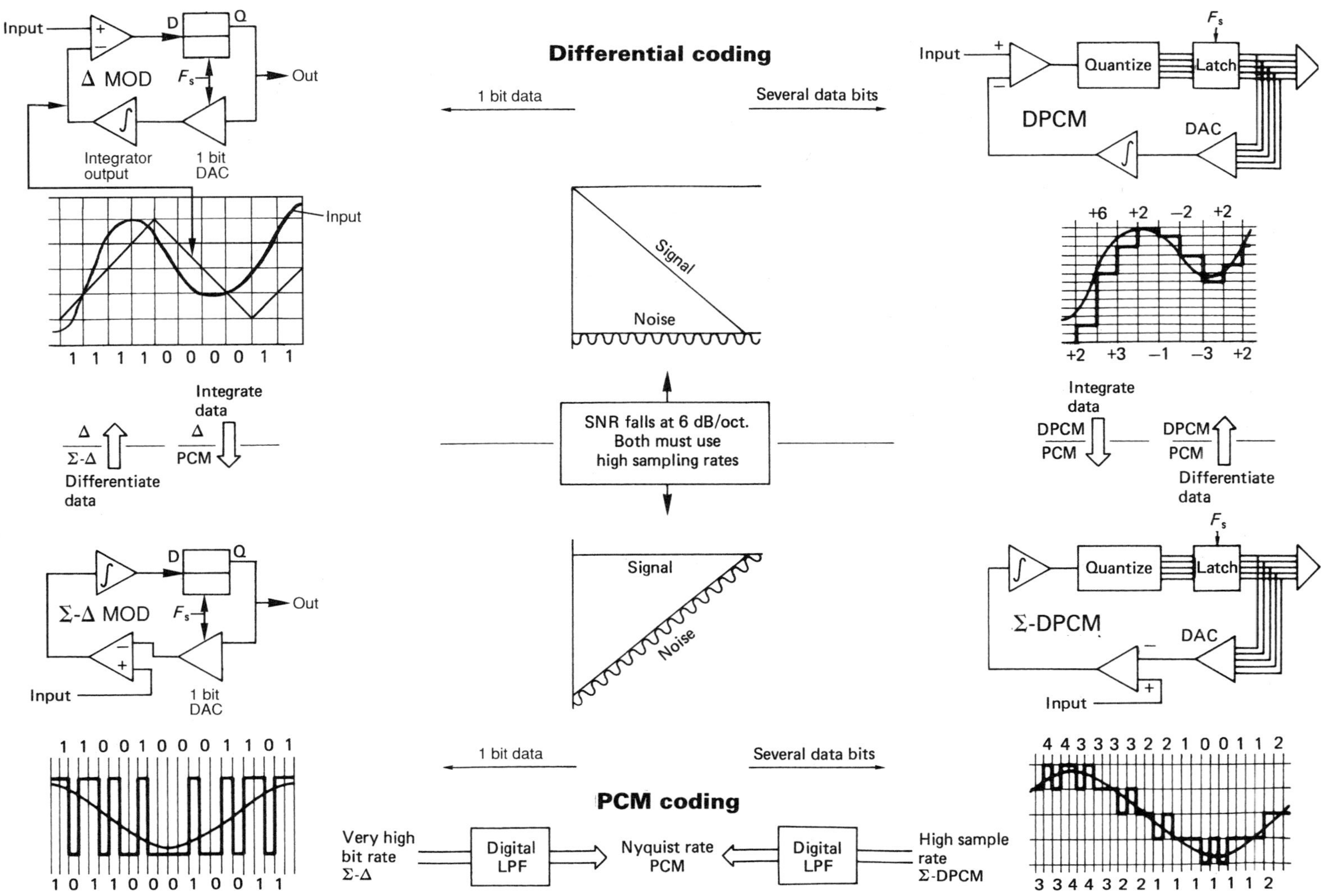

Figure 5.85 The four main alternatives to simple PCM conversion are compared here. Delta modulation is a one-bit case of differential PCM and conveys the slope of the signal. The digital output of both can be integrated to give PCM. Σ–Δ (sigma–delta) is a one-bit case of Σ-DPCM. The application of integrator before differentiator makes the output pure PCM, but tilts the noise floor; hence these can be referred to as 'noise-shaping' convertors.

Figure 5.85 introduces the alternative convertor structures. The top half of the diagram shows convertors which are differential. In differential coding the value of the output code represents the difference between the current sample voltage and that of the previous sample. The lower half of the diagram shows convertors which are PCM. In addition, the left side of the diagram shows single-bit convertors, whereas the right side shows multi-bit convertors.

In differential pulse code modulation (DPCM), shown at top right, the difference between the previous absolute sample value and the current one is quantized into a multi-bit binary code. It is possible to produce a DPCM signal from a PCM signal simply by subtracting successive samples; this is digital differentiation. Similarly, the reverse process is possible by using an accumulator or digital integrator (see Chapter 2) to compute sample values from the differences received. The problem with this approach is that it is very easy to lose the baseline of the signal if it commences at some arbitrary time. A digital high-pass filter can be used to prevent unwanted offsets.

Differential convertors do not have an absolute amplitude limit. Instead there is a limit to the maximum rate at which the input signal voltage can change. They are said to be slew rate limited, and thus the permissible signal amplitude falls at 6 dB per octave. As the quantizing steps are still uniform, the quantizing error amplitude has the same limits as PCM. As input frequency rises, ultimately the signal amplitude available will fall down to it.

If DPCM is taken to the extreme case where only a binary output signal is available then the process is described as delta modulation (top left in Figure 5.85). The meaning of the binary output signal is that the current analog input is above or below the accumulation of all previous bits. The characteristics of the system show the same trends as DPCM, except that there is severe limiting of the rate of change of the input signal. A DPCM decoder must accumulate all the difference bits to provide a PCM output for conversion to analog, but with a one-bit signal the function of the accumulator can be performed by an analog integrator.

If an integrator is placed in the input to a delta modulator, the integrator's amplitude response loss of 6 dB per octave parallels the convertor's amplitude limit of 6 dB per octave; thus the system amplitude limit becomes independent of frequency. This integration is responsible for the term sigma–delta modulation, since in mathematics sigma is used to denote summation. The input integrator can be combined with the integrator already present in a delta-modulator by a slight rearrangement of the components (bottom left in Figure 5.85). The transmitted signal is now the amplitude of the input, not the slope; thus the receiving integrator can be dispensed with, and all that is necessary to alter the DAC is an LPF to smooth the bits. The removal of the integration stage at the decoder now means that the quantizing error amplitude rises at 6 dB per octave, ultimately meeting the level of the wanted signal.

The principle of using an input integrator can also be applied to a true DPCM system and the result should perhaps be called sigma DPCM (bottom right in Figure 5.85). The dynamic range improvement over delta–sigma modulation is 6 dB for every extra bit in the code. Because the level of the quantizing error signal rises at 6 dB per octave in both delta–sigma modulation and sigma DPCM, these systems are sometimes referred to as 'noise-shaping' convertors, although the word 'noise' must be used with some caution. The output of a sigma DPCM system is again PCM, and a DAC will be needed to receive it, because it is a binary code.

As the differential group of systems suffer from a wanted signal that converges with the unwanted signal as frequency rises, they must all use very high sampling rates.[15] It is possible to convert from sigma DPCM to conventional PCM by reducing the sampling rate digitally. When the sampling rate is reduced in this way, the reduction of bandwidth excludes a disproportionate amount of noise because the noise shaping concentrated it at frequencies beyond the audio band. The use of noise shaping and oversampling is the key to the high resolution obtained in advanced convertors.

5.19 Oversampling in audio

Oversampling means using a sampling rate which is greater (generally substantially greater) than the Nyquist rate. Neither sampling theory nor quantizing theory *require* oversampling to be used to obtain a given signal quality, but Nyquist rate conversion places extremely high demands on component accuracy and analog filter performance when a convertor is implemented. Oversampling allows a given signal quality to be reached without requiring very close tolerance, and therefore expensive, components. Although it can be used alone, the advantages of oversampling are better realized when it is used in conjunction with noise shaping. Thus in practice the two processes are generally used together and the terms are often seen used in the loose sense as if they were synonymous. For a detailed and quantitative analysis of oversampling having exhaustive references the serious reader is referred to Hauser.[16]

In section 3.16, where dynamic element matching was described, it was seen that component accuracy was traded for accuracy in the time domain. Oversampling is another example of the same principle.

Figure 5.86 shows the main advantages of oversampling. At (a) it will be seen that the use of a sampling rate considerably above the Nyquist rate allows the anti-aliasing and reconstruction filters to be realized with

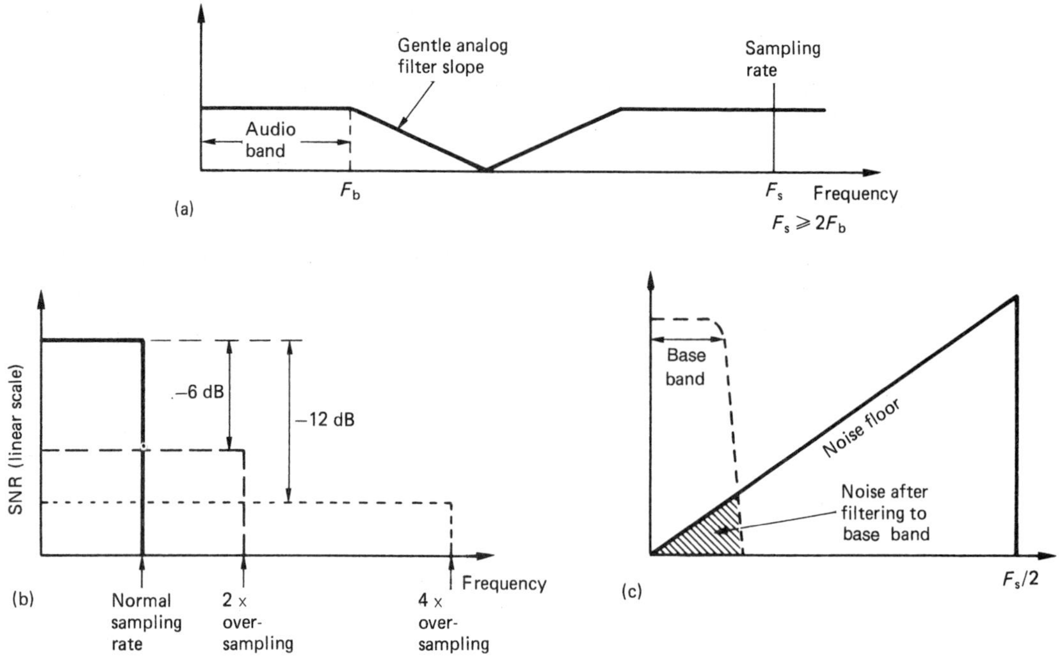

Figure 5.86 Oversampling has a number of advantages. In (a) it allows the slope of analog filters to be relaxed. In (b) it allows the resolution of convertors to be extended. In (c) *a noise-shaped* convertor allows a disproportionate improvement in resolution.

a much more gentle cut-off slope. There is then less likelihood of phase linearity and ripple problems in the audio passband.

Figure 5.86(b) shows that information in an analog signal is two-dimensional and can be depicted as an area which is the product of bandwidth and the linearly expressed signal-to-noise ratio. The figure also shows that the same amount of information can be conveyed down a channel with a SNR of half as much (6 dB less) if the bandwidth used is doubled, with 12 dB less SNR if bandwidth is quadrupled, and so on, provided that the modulation scheme used is perfect.

The information in an analog signal can be conveyed using some analog modulation scheme in any combination of bandwidth and SNR which yields the appropriate channel capacity. If bandwidth is replaced by sampling rate and SNR is replaced by a function of wordlength, the same must be true for a digital signal as it is no more than a numerical analog. Thus raising the sampling rate potentially allows the wordlength of each sample to be reduced without information loss.

Oversampling permits the use of a convertor element of shorter wordlength, making it possible to use a flash convertor. The flash convertor is capable of working at very high frequency and so large oversampling factors are easily realized. The flash convertor needs no track/hold system as it works instantaneously. If the sigma-DPCM convertor structure of Figure 5.85 is realized with a flash convertor element, it can be used with a high oversampling factor. Figure 5.86(c) shows that this class of convertor has a rising noise floor. If the highly oversampled output is fed to a digital low-pass filter which has the same frequency response as an analog anti-aliasing filter used for Nyquist rate sampling, the result is a disproportionate reduction in noise because the majority of the noise was outside the audio band. A high-resolution convertor can be obtained using this technology without requiring unattainable component tolerances.

Information theory predicts that if an audio signal is spread over a much wider bandwidth by, for example, the use of an FM broadcast transmitter, the SNR of the demodulated signal can be higher than that of the channel it passes through, and this is also the case in digital systems. The concept is illustrated in Figure 5.87. At (a) four-bit samples are

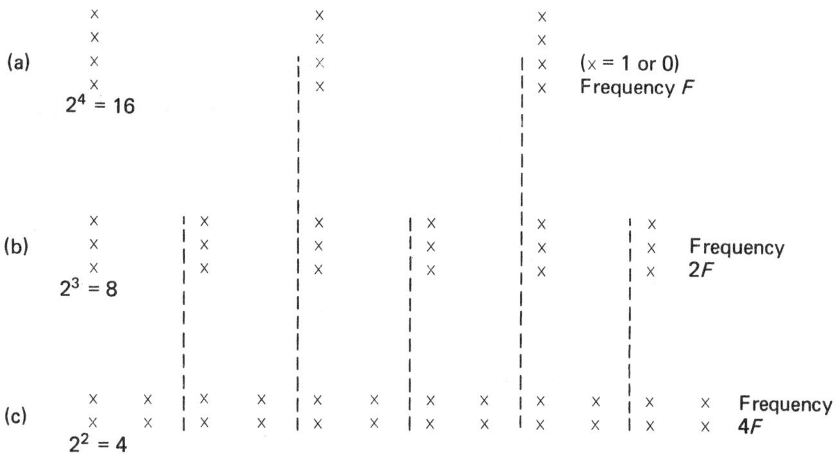

Figure 5.87 Information rate can be held constant when frequency doubles by removing one bit from each word. In all cases here it is $16F$. Note bit rate of (c) is double that of (a). Data storage in oversampled form is inefficient.

delivered at sampling rate F. As four bits have sixteen combinations, the information rate is $16F$. At (b) the same information rate is obtained with three-bit samples by raising the sampling rate to $2F$ and at (c) two-bit samples having four combinations require to be delivered at a rate of $4F$. Whilst the information rate has been maintained, it will be noticed that the bit-rate of (c) is twice that of (a). The reason for this is shown in Figure 5.88. A single binary digit can only have two states; thus it can only convey two pieces of information, perhaps 'yes' or 'no'. Two binary digits together can have four states, and can thus convey four pieces of information, perhaps 'spring summer autumn or winter', which is two

	0 = No 1 = Yes	00 = Spring 01 = Summer 10 = Autumn 11 = Winter	000 do 001 re 010 mi 011 fa 100 so 101 la 110 te 111 do	0000 0 0001 1 0010 2 0011 3 0100 4 0101 5 0110 6 0111 7 1000 8 1001 9 1010 A 1011 B 1100 C 1101 D 1110 E 1111 F	0000 ⋮ FFFF Digital audio sample values
No of bits	1	2	3	4	16
Information per word	2	4	8	16	65 536
Information per bit	2	2	≈3	4	4096

Figure 5.88 The amount of information per bit increases disproportionately as wordlength increases. It is always more efficient to use the longest words possible at the lowest word rate. It will be evident that sixteen bit PCM is 2048 times as efficient as delta modulation. Oversampled data are also inefficient for storage.

pieces of information per bit. Three binary digits grouped together can have eight combinations, and convey eight pieces of information, perhaps 'doh re mi fah so lah te or doh', which is nearly three pieces of information per digit. Clearly the further this principle is taken, the greater the benefit. In a sixteen-bit system, each bit is worth 4 K pieces of information. It is always more efficient, in information-capacity terms, to use the combinations of long binary words than to send single bits for every piece of information. The greatest efficiency is reached when the longest words are sent at the slowest rate which must be the Nyquist rate. This is one reason why PCM recording is more common than delta modulation, despite the simplicity of implementation of the latter type of convertor. PCM simply makes more efficient use of the capacity of the binary channel.

Oversampling is a method of overcoming practical implementation problems by replacing a single critical element or bottleneck by a number of elements whose overall performance is what counts. As Hauser[16] properly observed, oversampling tends to overlap the operations which are quite distinct in a conventional convertor. In earlier sections of this chapter, the vital subjects of filtering, sampling, quantizing and dither have been treated almost independently. Figure 5.89(a) shows that it is possible to construct an ADC of predictable performance by a taking a

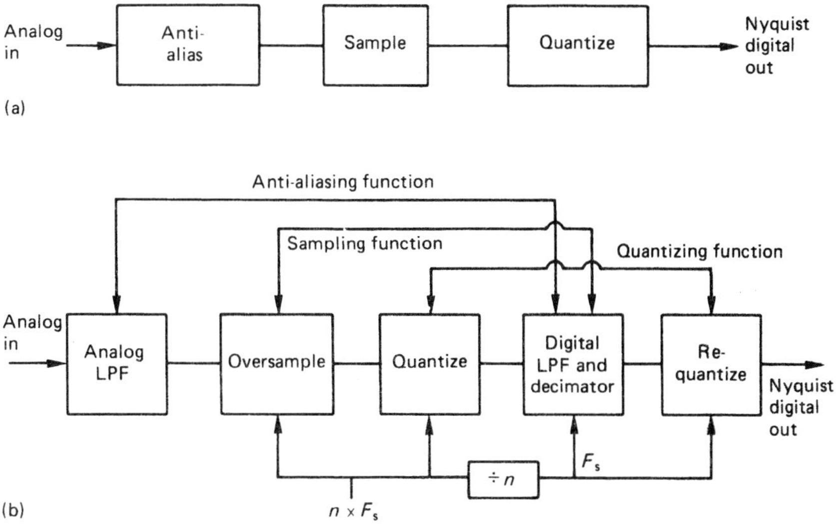

Figure 5.89 A conventional ADC performs each step in an identifiable location as in (a). With oversampling, many of the steps are distributed as shown in (b).

suitable anti-aliasing filter, a sampler, a dither source and a quantizer and assembling them like building bricks. The bricks are effectively in series and so the performance of each stage can only limit the overall performance. In contrast Figure 5.89(b) shows that with oversampling the overlap of operations allows different processes to augment one another allowing a synergy which is absent in the conventional approach.

If the oversampling factor is n, the analog input must be bandwidth limited to $n.F_s/2$ by the analog anti-aliasing filter. This unit need only have flat frequency response and phase linearity within the audio band. Analog dither of an amplitude compatible with the quantizing interval size is added prior to sampling at $n.F_s$ and quantizing.

Next, the anti-aliasing function is completed in the digital domain by a low-pass filter which cuts off at $F_s/2$. Using an appropriate architecture this filter can be absolutely phase-linear and implemented to arbitrary accuracy. Such filters are discussed in Chapter 4. The filter can be considered to be the demodulator of Figure 5.86 where the SNR improves as the bandwidth is reduced. The wordlength can be expected to increase. As Chapter 2 illustrated, the multiplications taking place within the filter extend the wordlength considerably more than the bandwidth reduction alone would indicate. The analog filter serves only to prevent aliasing into the audio band at the oversampling rate; the audio spectrum is determined with greater precision by the digital filter.

With the audio information spectrum now Nyquist limited, the sampling process is completed when the rate is reduced in the decimator. One sample in n is retained.

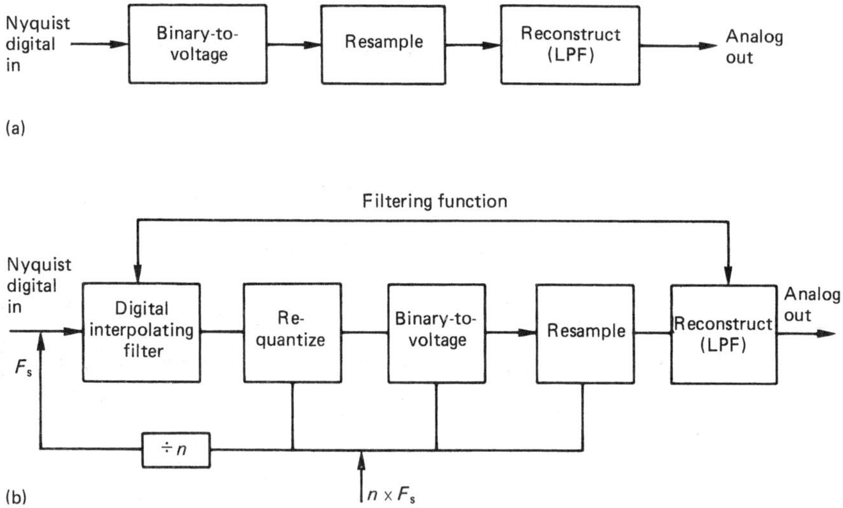

Figure 5.90 A conventional DAC in (a) is compared with the oversampling implementation in (b).

The excess wordlength extension due to the anti-aliasing filter arithmetic must then be removed. Digital dither is added, completing the dither process, and the quantizing process is completed by requantizing the dithered samples to the appropriate wordlength which will be greater than the wordlength of the first quantizer. Alternatively noise shaping may be employed.

Figure 5.90(a) shows the building-brick approach of a conventional DAC. The Nyquist rate samples are converted to analog voltages and then a steep-cut analog low-pass filter is needed to reject the sidebands of the sampled spectrum.

Figure 5.90(b) shows the oversampling approach. The sampling rate is raised in an interpolator which contains a low-pass filter that restricts the baseband spectrum to the audio bandwidth shown. A large frequency gap now exists between the baseband and the lower sideband. The multiplications in the interpolator extend the wordlength considerably and this must be reduced within the capacity of the DAC element by the addition of digital dither prior to requantizing. Again noise shaping may be used as an alternative.

If an oversampling convertor is considered which makes no attempt to shape the noise spectrum, it will be clear that if it contains a perfect quantizer, no amount of oversampling will increase the resolution of the system, since a perfect quantizer is blind to all changes of input within one quantizing interval, and looking more often is of no help. It was shown earlier that the use of dither would linearize a quantizer, so that input changes much smaller than the quantizing interval would be

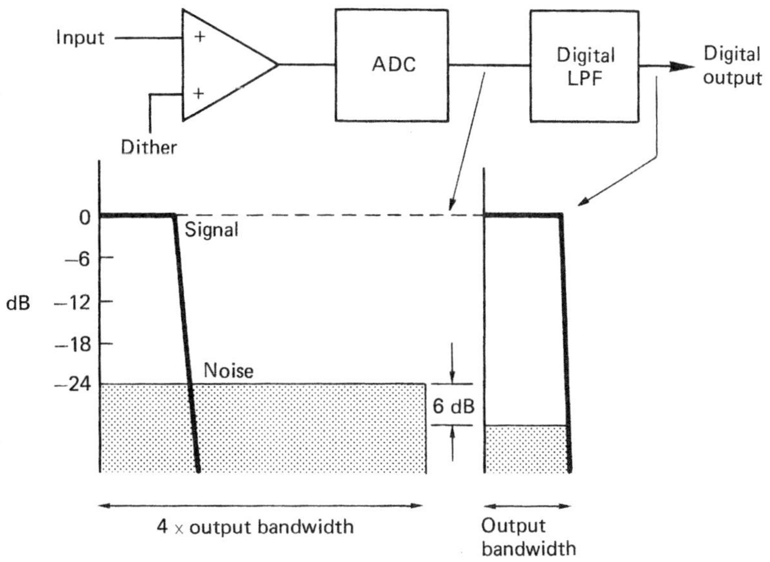

Figure 5.91 In this simple oversampled convertor, 4× oversampling is used. When the convertor output is low-pass filtered, the noise power is reduced to one-quarter, which in voltage terms is 6 dB. This is a suboptimal method and is not used.

reflected in the output and this remains true for this class of convertor.

Figure 5.91 shows an example of a white-noise-dithered quantizer, oversampled by a factor of four. Since dither is correctly employed, it is valid to speak of the unwanted signal as noise. The noise power extends over the whole baseband up to the Nyquist limit. If the basebandwidth is reduced by the oversampling factor of four back to the bandwidth of the original analog input, the noise bandwidth will also be reduced by a factor of four, and the noise power will be one-quarter of that produced at the quantizer. One-quarter noise power implies one-half the noise voltage, so the SNR of this example has been increased by 6 dB, the equivalent of one extra bit in the quantizer. Information theory predicts that an oversampling factor of four would allow an extension by two bits. This method is sub-optimal in that very large oversampling factors would be needed to obtain useful resolution extension, but it would still realize some advantages, particularly the elimination of the steep-cut analog filter.

The division of the noise by a larger factor is the only route left open, since all the other parameters are fixed by the signal bandwidth required. The reduction of noise power resulting from a reduction in bandwidth is only proportional if the noise is white, i.e. it has uniform power spectral density (PSD). If the noise from the quantizer is made spectrally non-uniform, the oversampling factor will no longer be the factor by which the noise power is reduced. The goal is to concentrate noise power at high frequencies, so that after low-pass filtering in the digital domain down to the audio input bandwidth, the noise power will be reduced by more than the oversampling factor.

5.20 Noise shaping

Noise shaping dates from the work of Cutler[17] in the 1950s. It is a feedback technique applicable to quantizers and requantizers in which the quantizing process of the current sample is modified in some way by the quantizing error of the previous sample.

When used with requantizing, noise shaping is an entirely digital process which is used, for example, following word extension due to the arithmetic in digital mixers or filters in order to return to the required wordlength. It will be found in this form in oversampling DACs. When used with quantizing, part of the noise-shaping circuitry will be analog. As the feedback loop is placed around an ADC it must contain a DAC. When used in convertors, noise shaping is primarily an implementation technology. It allows processes which are conveniently available in integrated circuits to be put to use in audio conversion. Once integrated circuits can be employed, complexity ceases to be a drawback and low-cost mass-production is possible.

It has been stressed throughout this chapter that a series of numerical values or samples is just another analog of an audio waveform. Chapter 2 showed that all analog processes such as mixing, attenuation or integration all have exact numerical parallels. It has been demonstrated that digitally dithered requantizing is no more than a digital simulation of analog quantizing. It should be no surprise that in this section noise shaping will be treated in the same way. Noise shaping can be performed by manipulating analog voltages or numbers representing them or both. If the reader is content to make a conceptual switch between the two, many obstacles to understanding fall, not just in this topic, but in digital audio in general.

The term 'noise shaping' is idiomatic and in some respects unsatisfactory because not all devices which are called noise shapers produce true noise. The caution which was given when treating quantizing error as noise is also relevant in this context. Whilst 'quantizing-error-spectrum shaping' is a bit of a mouthful, it is useful to keep in mind that noise shaping means just that in order to avoid some pitfalls. Some noise-shaper architectures do not produce a signal-decorrelated quantizing error and need to be dithered.

Figure 5.92(a) shows a requantizer using a simple form of noise shaping. The low-order bits which are lost in requantizing are the

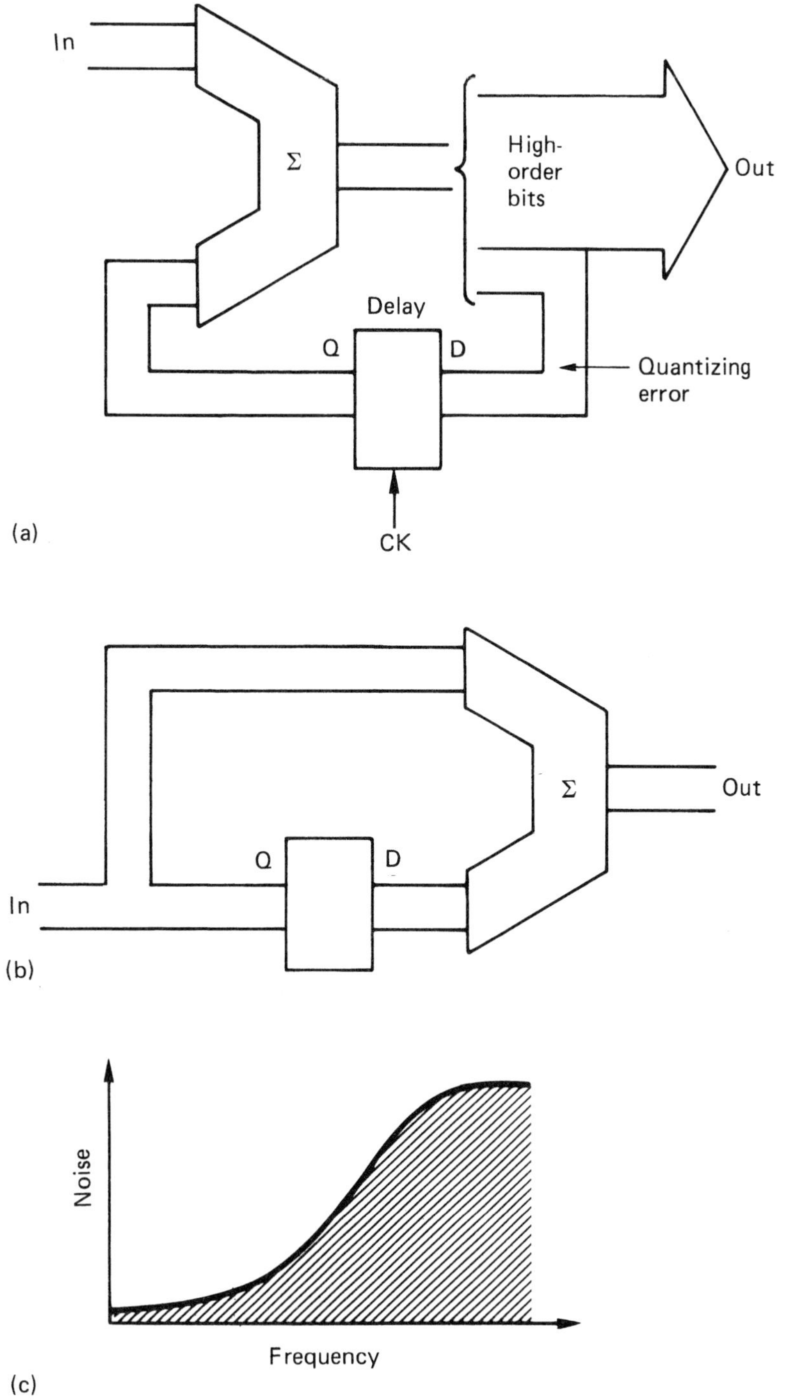

Figure 5.92 (a) A simple requantizer which feeds back the quantizing error to reduce the error of subsequent samples. The one-sample delay causes the quantizing error to see the equivalent circuit shown in (b) which results in a sinusoidal quantizing error spectrum shown in (c).

quantizing error. If the value of these bits is added to the next sample before it is requantized, the quantizing error will be reduced. The process is somewhat like the use of negative feedback in an operational amplifier except that it is not instantaneous, but encounters a one-sample delay. With a constant input, the mean or average quantizing error will be brought to zero over a number of samples, achieving one of the goals of additive dither. The more rapidly the input changes, the greater the effect of the delay and the less effective the error feedback will be. Figure 5.92(b) shows the equivalent circuit seen by the quantizing error, which is created at the requantizer and subtracted from itself one sample period later. As a result the quantizing error spectrum is not uniform, but has the shape of a raised sinewave shown at (c), hence the term 'noise shaping'. The noise is very small at DC and rises with frequency, peaking at the Nyquist frequency at a level determined by the size of the quantizing step. If used with oversampling, the noise peak can be moved outside the audio band.

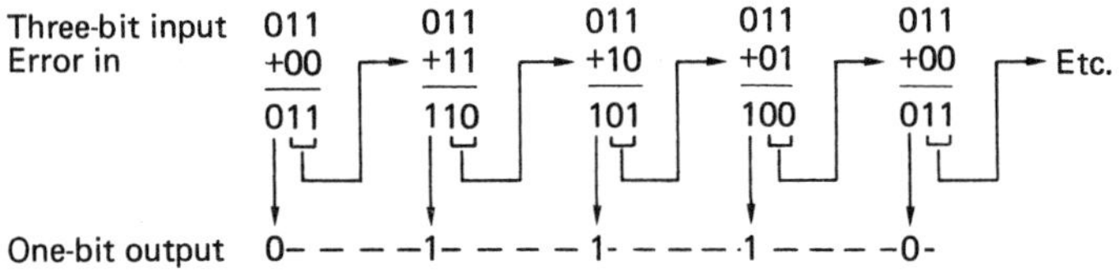

Figure 5.93 By adding the error caused by truncation to the next value, the resolution of the lost bits is maintained in the duty cycle of the output. Here, truncation of 011 by two bits would give continuous zeros, but the system repeats 0111, 0111, which, after filtering, will produce a level of three-quarters of a bit.

Figure 5.93 shows a simple example in which two low-order bits need to be removed from each sample. The accumulated error is controlled by using the bits which were neglected in the truncation, and adding them to the next sample. In this example, with a steady input, the roundoff mechanism will produce an output of 01110111 . . . If this is low-pass filtered, the three ones and one zero result in a level of three-quarters of a quantizing interval, which is precisely the level which would have been obtained by direct conversion of the full digital input. Thus the resolution is maintained even though two bits have been removed.

Noise shaping can also be used without oversampling. In this case the noise cannot be pushed outside the audio band. Instead the noise floor is shaped or weighted to complement the unequal spectral sensitivity of the ear to noise[18,19]. Unless we wish to violate Shannon's theory, this psychoacoustically optimal noise shaping can only reduce the noise power at certain frequencies by increasing it at others. Thus

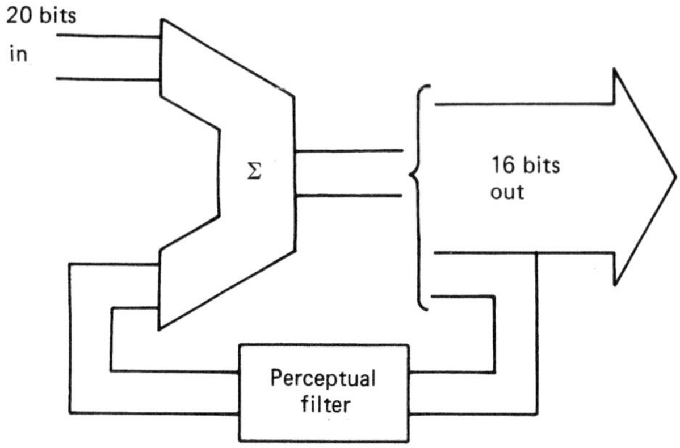

Figure 5.94 Perceptual filtering in a requantizer gives a subjectively improved SNR.

the average log psd over the audio band remains the same, although it may be raised slightly by noise induced by imperfect processing.

Figure 5.94 shows noise shaping applied to a digitally dithered requantizer. Such a device might be used when, for example, making a CD master from a twenty-bit recording format. The input to the dithered requantizer is subtracted from the output to give the error due to requantizing. This error is filtered (and inevitably delayed) before being subtracted from the system input. The filter is not designed to be the exact inverse of the perceptual weighting curve because this would cause extreme noise levels at the ends of the band. Instead the perceptual curve is levelled off[20] such that it cannot fall more than e.g. 40 dB below the peak.

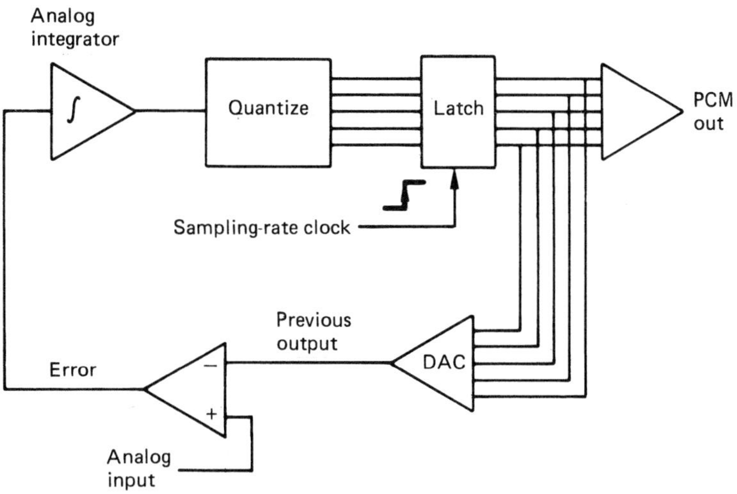

Figure 5.95 The sigma-DPCM convertor of Figure 5.85 is shown here in more detail.

Psychoacoustically optimal noise shaping can offer nearly three bits of increased dynamic range when compared with optimal spectrally flat dither. Enhanced Compact Discs recorded using these techniques are now available.

The sigma-DPCM convertor introduced above works well with noise shaping and is shown in more detail in Figure 5.95. The current digital sample from the quantizer is converted back to analog in the embedded DAC. The DAC output differs from the ADC input by the quantizing error. The DAC output is subtracted from the analog input to produce an error which is integrated to drive the quantizer in such a way that the error is reduced. With a constant input voltage the average error will be zero because the loop gain is infinite at DC. If the average error is zero, the mean or average of the DAC outputs must be equal to the analog input. The instantaneous output will deviate from the average in what is called an idling pattern. The presence of the integrator in the error feedback loop makes the loop gain fall with rising frequency. With the feedback falling at 6 dB per octave, the noise floor will rise at the same rate.

A greater improvement in dynamic range can be obtained if the integrator is supplanted to realize a higher-order filter.[21] The filter is in the feedback loop and so the noise will have the opposite response to the filter and will therefore rise more steeply to allow a greater SNR enhancement after decimation. Figure 5.96 shows the theoretical SNR enhancement possible for various loop filter orders and oversampling factors. A further advantage of high-order loop filters is that the quantizing noise can be decorrelated from the signal making dither

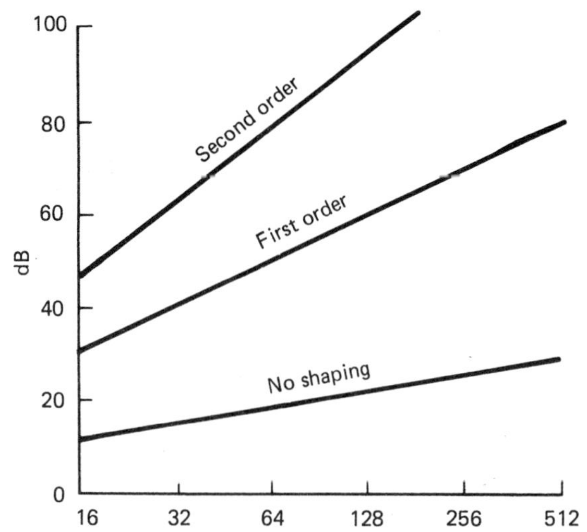

Figure 5.96 The enhancement of SNR possible with various filter orders and oversampling factors in noise-shaping convertors.

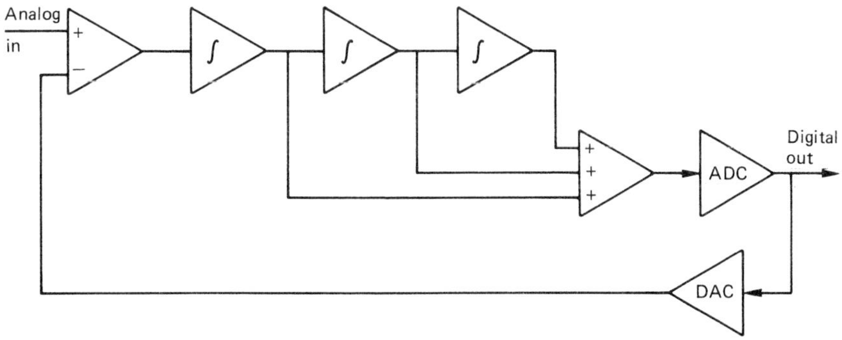

Figure 5.97 Stabilizing the loop filter in a noise-shaping convertor can be assisted by the incorporation of feedforward paths as shown here.

unnecessary. High-order loop filters were at one time thought to be impossible to stabilize, but this is no longer the case, although care is necessary. One technique which may be used is to include some feedforward paths as shown in Figure 5.97.

References

1. Martin, W.H., Decibel – the new name for the transmission unit. *Bell System Tech. J.* (Jan. 1929)
2. Moore, B.C.J., *An Introduction to the Psychology of Hearing*, London: Academic Press (1989)
3. Muraoka, T., Iwahara, M. and Yamada, Y., Examination of audio bandwidth requirements for optimum sound signal transmission. *J. Audio Eng. Soc.*, **29**, 2–9 (1982)
4. Muraoka, T., Yamada, Y. and Yamazaki, M., Sampling frequency considerations in digital audio. *J. Audio Eng. Soc.*, **26**, 252–256 (1978)
5. Fincham, L.R., The subjective importance of uniform group delay at low frequencies. Presented at the 74th Audio Engineering Society Convention, New York (1983), Preprint 2056 (H-1)
6. Fletcher, H., Auditory patterns. *Rev. Modern Physics*, **12**, 47–65 (1940)
7. Carterette, E.C. and Friedman, M.P., *Handbook of Perception*, 305–319, New York: Academic Press (1978)
8. Moore, B.C., *An Introduction to the Psychology of Hearing*, section 6.12, London: Academic Press (1989)
9. Cao, Y., Sridharan, S. and Moody, M., Co-talker separation using the cocktail party effect. *J. Audio Eng. Soc.*, **44**, No.12, 1084–1096 (1996)
10. Moore, B.C., *An Introduction to the Psychology of Hearing*, section 6.13, London: Academic Press (1989)
11. *AES Anthology: Microphones*, New York: Audio Engineering Society
12. Bauer, B.B., A century of microphones. *J. Audio Eng. Soc.*, **35**, 246–258 (1967)
13. Harvey, F.K. and Uecke, E.H., Compatibility problems in two channel stereophonic recordings. *J. Audio Eng. Soc.*, **10**, No 1, 8–12 (Jan. 1962)
14. Alexander, R.C., *The Life and Works of Alan Dower Blumlein*, Oxford: Focal Press (1999)
15. Adams, R.W., Companded predictive delta modulation: a low-cost technique for digital recording. *J. Audio Eng. Soc.*, **32**, 659–672 (1984)

16. Hauser, M.W., Principles of oversampling A/D conversion. *J. Audio Eng. Soc.*, **39**, 3–26 (1991)
17. Cutler, C.C., Transmission systems employing quantization. US Pat. No. 2.927,962 (1960)
18. Fielder, L.D., Human auditory capabilities and their consequences in digital audio convertor design. In *Audio in Digital Times*, New York: AES (1989)
19. Wannamaker, R.A., Psychoacoustically optimal noise shaping. *J. Audio Eng. Soc.*, **40**, 611–620 (1992)
20. Lipshitz, S.P., Wannamaker, R.A. and Vanderkooy, J., Minimally audible noise shaping. *J. Audio Eng. Soc.*, **39**, 836–852 (1991)
21. Adams, R.W., Design and implementation of an audio 18-bit A/D convertor using oversampling techniques. Presented at the 77th Audio Engineering Society Convention, Hamburg (1985), Preprint 2182

6

Light

6.1 Introduction

Light is a form of radiation and physical laws have been constructed to explain its behaviour. The general science of radiation is called *radiometry*. However, physical laws cannot explain the sense we call vision or the impression of colour. For applications of imaging technology such as television and cinema, light is what can be seen by a human being and this is the subject of *photometry*. In that context, any discussion must include the characteristics of the eye in all the relevant domains. Once the operation of the human visual system (HVS) is understood, it will be clear that, in order to obtain realism, imaging quality has to meet adequate criteria in a number of domains. These include at least contrast, noise level, colour accuracy, static and dynamic resolution, flicker and motion portrayal.

Once these topics are appreciated, it then becomes possible to analyse today's popular imaging technologies to see why they all look different and to suggest a way forward to a new level of realism which will be expected in applications such as simulators and electronic cinema.

Figure 6.1 shows some of the interactions between domains which complicate matters. Technically, contrast exists only in the brightness domain and is independent of resolution which exists in the image plane. In the HVS, the subjective parameter of sharpness is affected by both and so these cannot be treated separately. Sharpness is also affected by the accuracy of motion portrayal. It would appear that colour vision evolved later as an enhancement to monochrome vision. The resolution of the eye to colour changes is very poor.

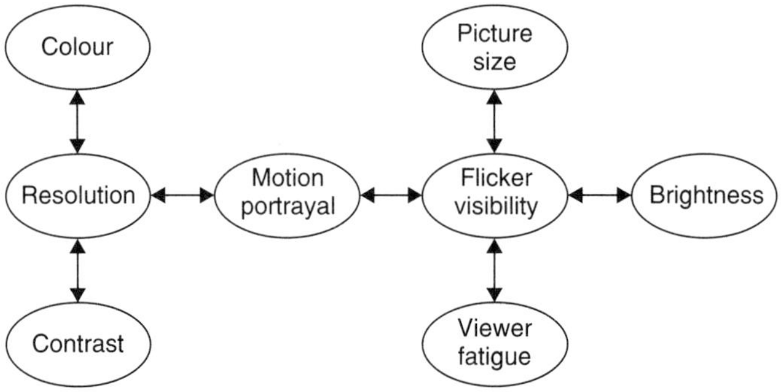

Figure 6.1 The various domains in which images can be analysed are not independent in the human visual system. Some of the interactions are shown here.

6.2 What is light?

Electromagnetic radiation exists over a fantastic range of frequencies, f, and corresponding wavelengths λ connected to the speed of light, c, by the equation:

$$c = f \times \lambda$$

The human visual system (HVS) has evolved to be sensitive to a certain range of frequencies which we call light. The frequencies are extremely high and it is the convention in optics to describe the wavelength instead. Figure 6.2 shows that the HVS responds to radiation in the range of 400 to 700 nanometres (nm = $m \times 10^{-9}$) according to a curve known as a *luminous efficiency function* having a value defined as unity at the peak which occurs at a wavelength of 555 nm under bright light conditions. Within that range different distributions of intensity with respect to wavelength exist, which are called *spectral power distributions* or SPDs. The

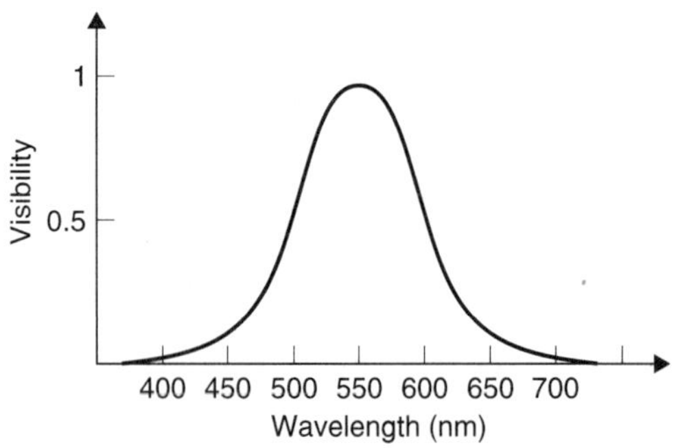

Figure 6.2 The luminous efficiency function shows the response of the HVS to light of different wavelengths.

variations in SPD give rise to the sensation that we call colour. A narrow-band light source with a wavelength of 400 nm appears violet and shorter wavelengths are called ultra-violet. Similarly light with a wavelength of 700 nm appears red and longer wavelengths are called infra-red. Although we cannot see infra-red radiation, we can feel it as the sensation of heat.

6.3 Sources of light

Light sources include a wide variety of heated bodies, from the glowing particles of carbon in candle flames to the sun. Radiation from a heated body covers a wide range of wavelengths. In physics, light and radiant heat are the same thing, differing only in wavelength, and it is vital to an understanding of colour to see how they relate. This was first explained by Max Planck who proposed the concept of a *black body*. Being perfectly non-reflective the only radiation which could come from it would be due to its temperature.

Figure 6.3 shows that the intensity and spectrum of radiation from a body are a function of the temperature. The peak of the distribution at each temperature is found on a straight line according to Wien's Law. Radiation from the sun contains ultra-violet radiation, but this is (or was) strongly scattered by the Earth's atmosphere and is accordingly weak. Incidentally this scattering of short wavelengths is why the sky appears blue. As temperature falls, the intensity of the radiation becomes too low to be useful. The wavelength range of human vision evolved to sense a reasonable dynamic range of black-body radiation between practical limits.

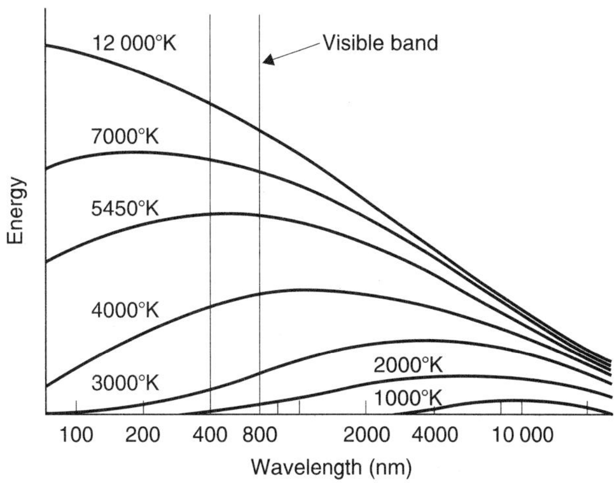

Figure 6.3 The radiated spectrum of a black body changes with temperature.

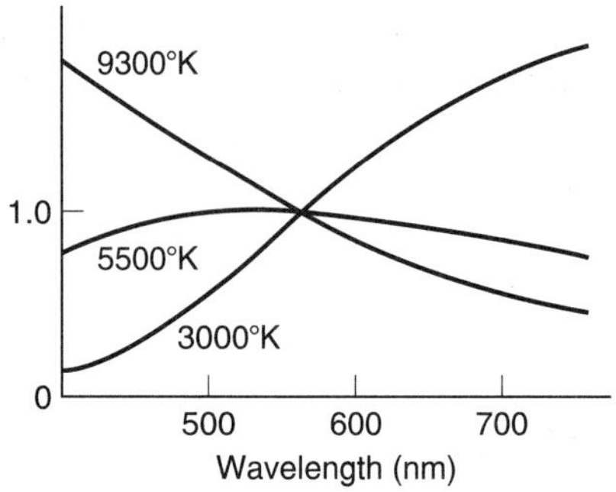

Figure 6.4 The spectra of Figure 6.3 normalized to the same intensity at mid-scale to show the red distribution at low temperatures changing to blue at very high temperatures.

The concept of *colour temperature* follows from Planck's work. Figure 6.4 shows a different version of Figure 6.3 in which the SPDs have been scaled so they all have the same level at one wavelength near the centre of the range of the HVS. A body at a temperature of around 3000° Kelvin (K) radiates an SPD centred in the infra-red, and the HVS perceives the only the left-hand end of the distribution as the colour red, hence the term 'red-hot'. As the temperature increases, at about 5000° K the peak of the SPD aligns with the peak of the sensitivity of the HVS and we see white, hence the term 'white hot'. Red hot and white hot are a layman's colour temperature terms. A temperature of 9000° K takes the peak of the SPD into the ultra-violet and we see the right-hand end of the distribution as blue. The term 'blue hot' is not found because such a temperature is not commonly reached on Earth.

It is possible to characterize a thermal *illuminant* or source of light simply by specifying the temperature in degrees K of a black body which appears to be the same colour to a human observer. Non-thermal illuminants such as discharge lamps may be given an equivalent colour temperature, but their SPD may be quite different from that of a heated body.

Although the radiation leaving the sun is relatively constant, the radiation arriving on Earth varies throughout the day. Figure 6.5(a) shows that at midday, the sun is high and the path through the atmosphere is short. The amount of scattering of the blue end of the spectum is minimal and the light has a blueish quality. However, at the end of the day, the sun is low and the path through the atmosphere is much longer as (b) shows. The extent of blue scattering is much greater and the remaining radiation reaching the observer becomes first orange as the sun gets low and finally red as it sets. Thus the colour temperature of sunlight is not constant. In addition to the factors mentioned, clouds will also change the colour temperature.

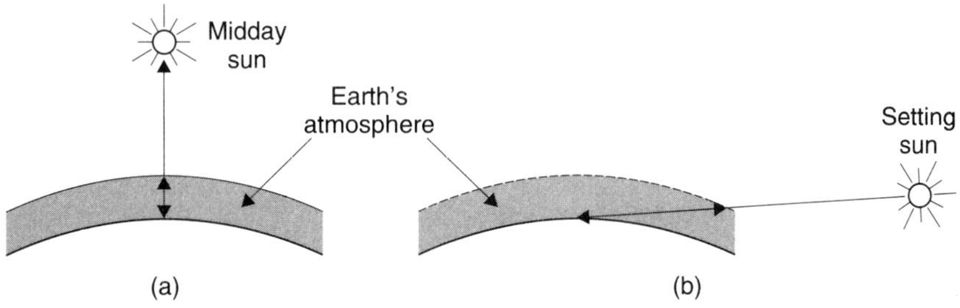

Figure 6.5 (a) at midday the path of sunlight through the atmosphere is short. (b) When the sun is low the path through the atmosphere is longer, making the effect of blue scattering more obvious.

Light can also be emitted by atoms in which electrons have been raised from their normal, stable, orbit to one of higher energy by some form of external stimulus other than heat which could be ultra-violet light or electrical.

Electrons which fall back to the valence band emit a quantum of energy as a photon whose frequency is proportional to the energy difference between the bands. The process is described by Planck's Law:

$$\text{Energy difference } E = H \times f$$

$$\text{where } H = \text{Planck's Constant}$$

$$= 6.6262 \times 10^{-34} \text{ Joules/Hertz}$$

The wavelength of the light emitted is a function of the characteristics of a particular atom, and a great variety exist. The SPD of light sources of this kind is very narrow, appearing as a *line* in the spectrum. Some materials are monochromatic, whereas some have two or more lines. Useful and efficient illuminants can be made using mixtures of materials to increase the number of lines, although the spectrum may be far from white in some cases. Such illuminants can be given an effective colour temperature, even though there is nothing in the light source at that temperature. The colour temperature is that at which a black body and the illuminant concerned give the same perceived result to the HVS. This type of light generation is the basis of mercury and sodium lights, fluorescent lights, dayglo paint, the aurora borealis, whiteners in washing powder, phosphors in CRT and plasma displays, lasers and LEDs. It should be noted that although these devices have colour temperatures as far as the HVS is concerned, their line spectrum structure may cause them to have unnatural effects on other colour-sensitive devices such as film and TV cameras.

6.4 Optical principles

Wave theory of light suggests that a wavefront advances because an infinite number of point sources can be considered to emit spherical waves which will only add when they are all in the same phase. This can only occur in the plane of the wavefront. Figure 6.6 shows that at all other angles, interference between spherical waves is destructive. Note the similarity with sound propagation described in Chapter 5.

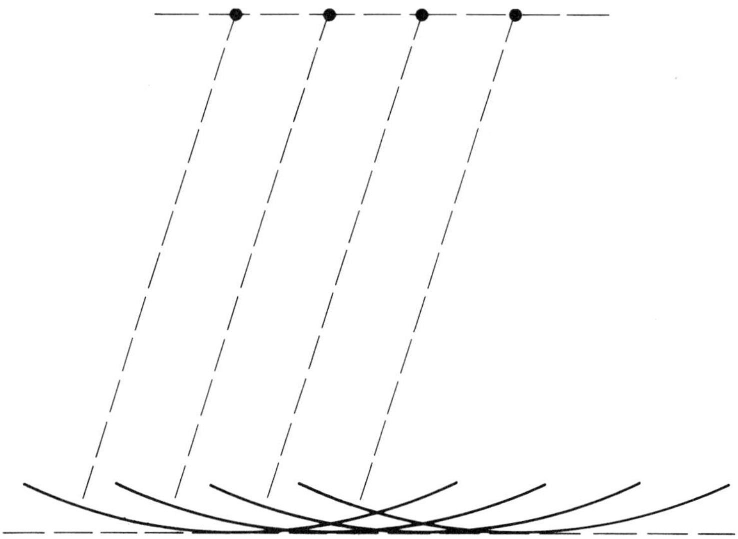

Figure 6.6 Plane-wave propagation considered as infinite numbers of spherical waves.

When such a wavefront arrives at an interface with a denser medium, such as the surface of a lens, the velocity of propagation is reduced; therefore the wavelength in the medium becomes shorter, causing the wavefront to leave the interface at a different angle (Figure 6.7). This is known as refraction. The ratio of velocity *in vacuo* to velocity in the medium is known as the refractive index of that medium; it determines the relationship between the angles of the incident and refracted wavefronts. Reflected light, however, leaves at the same angle to the normal as the incident light. If the speed of light in the medium varies with wavelength, dispersion takes place, where incident white light will be split into a rainbow-like spectrum leaving the interface at different angles. Glass used for chandeliers and cut glass is chosen to be highly dispersive, whereas glass for lenses in cameras and projectors will be chosen to have a refractive index which is as constant as possible with changing wavelength. The use of monochromatic light allows low-cost optics to be used as they only need to be corrected for a single

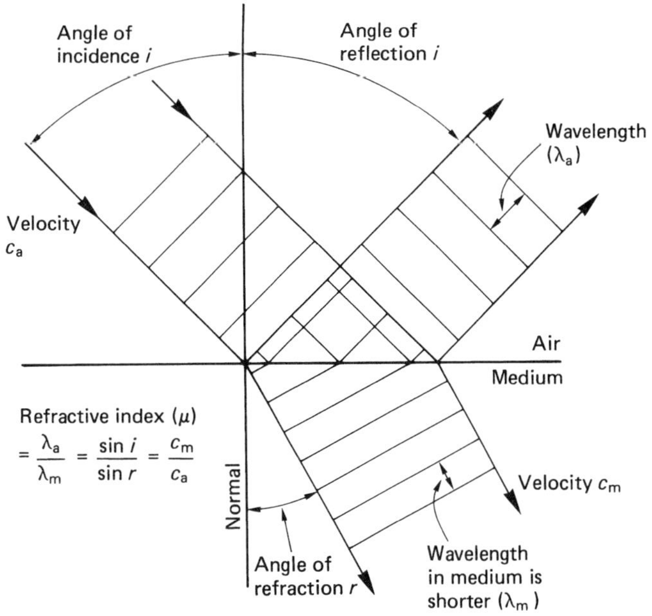

Figure 6.7 Reflection and refraction, showing the effect of the velocity of light in a medium.

wavelength. This is done in optical disk pickups and in colour projectors which use one optical system for each colour.

In natural light, the electric-field component will be in many planes. Light is said to be polarized when the electric field direction is constrained. The wave can be considered as made up from two orthogonal components. When these are in phase, the polarization is said to be linear. When there is a phase shift between the components, the polarization is said to be elliptical, with a special case at 90° called circular polarization. These types of polarization are contrasted in Figure 6.8.

In order to create polarized light, anisotropic materials are necessary. Polaroid material, invented by Edwin Land, is vinyl which is made anisotropic by stretching it while hot. This causes the long polymer molecules to line up along the axis of stretching. If the material is soaked in iodine, the molecules are rendered conductive, and short out any electric-field component along themselves. Electric fields at right angles are unaffected; thus the transmission plane is at right angles to the stretching axis.

Stretching plastics can also result in anisotropy of refractive index; this effect is known as birefringence. If a linearly polarized wavefront enters such a medium, the two orthogonal components propagate at different velocities, causing a relative phase difference proportional to the distance travelled. The plane of polarization of the light is rotated. Where the

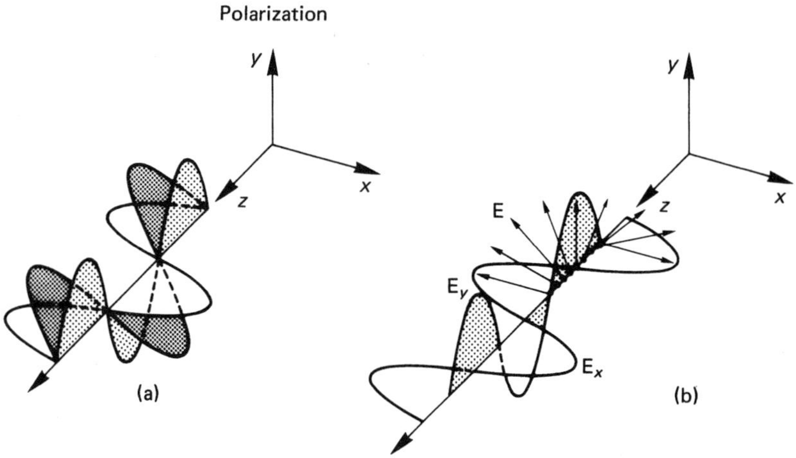

Figure 6.8 (a) Linear polarization: orthogonal components are in phase. (b) Circular polarization: orthogonal components are in phase quadrature.

thickness of the material is such that a 90° phase change is caused, the device is known as a quarter-wave plate. The action of such a device is shown in Figure 6.9. If the plane of polarization of the incident light is at 45° to the planes of greatest and least refractive index, the two orthogonal components of the light will be of equal magnitude, and this results in circular polarization. Similarly, circular-polarized light can be returned to the linear-polarized state by a further quarter-wave plate. Rotation of the

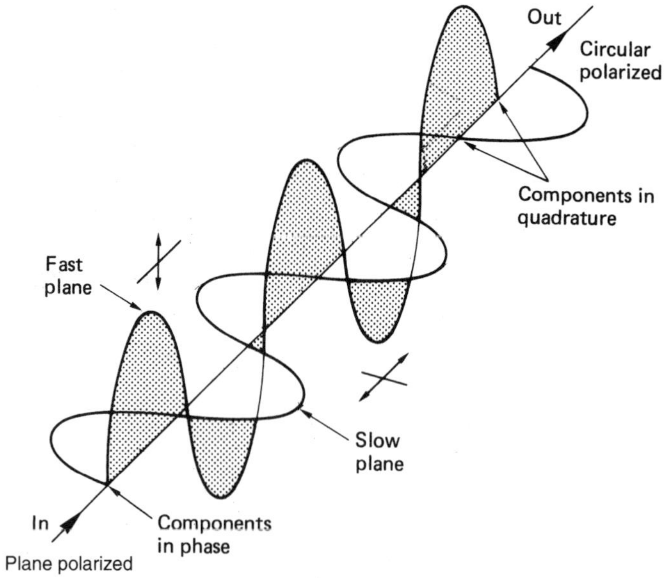

Figure 6.9 Different speed of light in different planes rotates the plane of polarization in a quarter-wave plate to give a circularly polarized output.

plane of polarization is a useful method of separating incident and reflected light in a laser disk pickup. Using a quarter-wave plate, the plane of polarization of light leaving the pickup will have been turned 45°, and on return it will be rotated a further 45°, so that it is now at right angles to the plane of polarization of light from the source. The two can easily be separated by a polarizing prism, which acts as a transparent block to light in one plane, but as a prism to light in the other plane, such that reflected light is directed towards the sensor.

6.5 Photometric units

Radiometric and photometric units are different because the latter are affected by the luminous efficiency function of the eye. Figure 6.10 shows the two sets of units for comparison. Figure 6.11 shows an imaginary point light source radiating equally in all directions. An imaginary sphere surrounds the source. The source itself has a power output, measured in *Watts*, and this power uniformly passes through the area of the sphere, so the power per unit area will follow an inverse square law. Power per unit area is known as intensity, with units of Watts per square metre. Given a surface radiating with a certain intensity, viewed at right angles to the surface the maximum *brightness* would be measured. Viewed from any other angle the brightness would fall off as a cosine function.

The above units are indifferent to wavelength and whether the HVS can see the radiation concerned. In photometry, the equivalent of power is *luminous flux*, whose unit is the *lumen*, the equivalent of intensity is

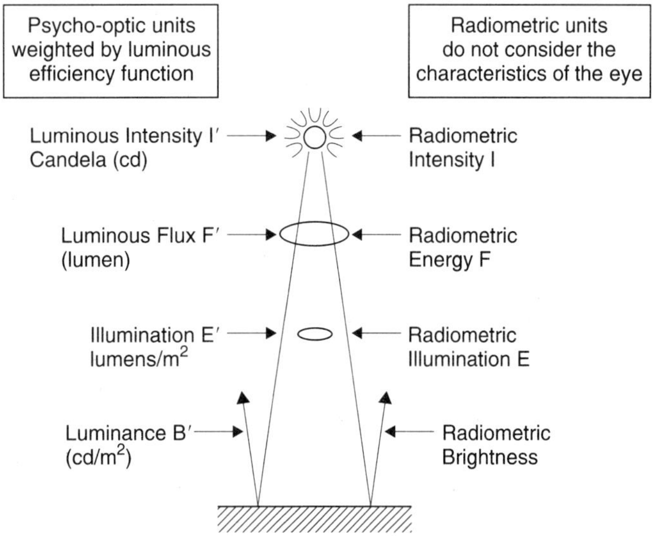

Figure 6.10 Radiometric and photometric units compared.

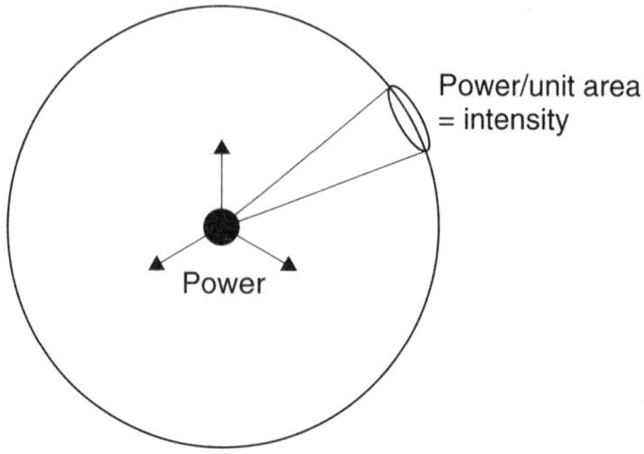

Figure 6.11 An imaginary point source radiating through a spherical area is helpful to visualize the units used to measure light.

luminous intensity measured in *candela* and the equivalent of brightness is *luminance* measured in *nits*.

It is difficult to maintain a standard of luminous flux so instead the candela is defined. The candela replaced the earlier unit of candle power and is defined in such a way as to make the two units approximately the same. One square centimetre of platinum at its freezing point of 2042° K radiates 60 cd.

The lumen is defined as the luminous flux radiated over a unit solid angle by a source whose intensity is one candela. The nit is defined as one candela per square metre. As an example, a CRT may reach 200–300 nit.

In an optical system, the power of the source is often concentrated in a certain direction and so for a fixed number of candela the brightness in that direction would rise. This is the optical equivalent of forward gain in an antenna.

The lumen is a weighted value based on the luminous efficiency function of the HVS. Thus the same numerical value in lumens will appear equally bright to the HVS whatever the colour. If three sources of light, red, green and blue each of one lumen are added, the total luminous flux will be three lumens but the result will not appear white.

It is worth while discussing this in some detail. Figure 6.12(a) shows three monochromatic light sources of variable intensity which are weighted by the luminous efficiency function of the HVS in order correctly to measure the luminous flux. In order to obtain one lumen from each source, the red and blue sources must be set to produce more luminous flux than the green source. This means that the spectral distribution of the source is no longer uniform and so it will not appear white. In contrast, Figure 6.12(b) shows three sources which have the same luminous flux. After weighting by the luminous efficiency function, each source produces a different number of lumens, but the eye perceives the effect as white. Essentially the eye has a non-uniform response, but in judging colour it appears to compensate for that so that a spectrum which

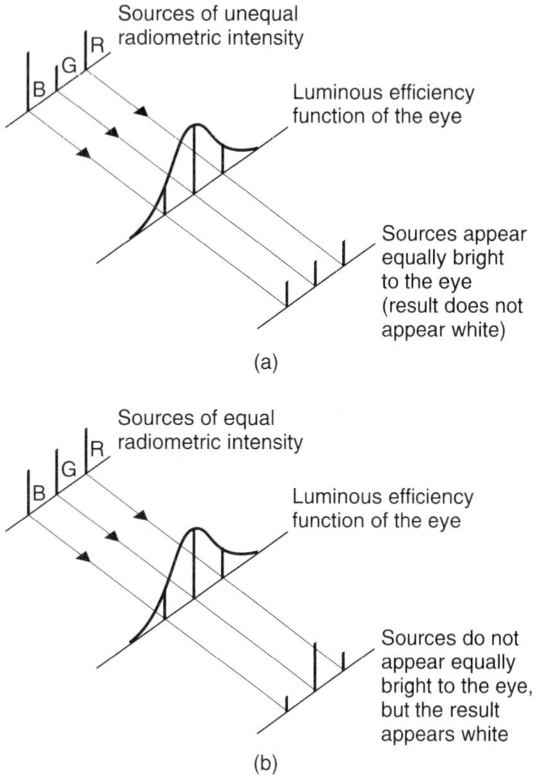

Figure 6.12 Three sources producing the same number of lumens are shown at (a) produce a different amount of luminous flux. Three sources having the same luminous flux (not the same number of lumens) appear white to the eye (b).

is physically white, i.e. having equal luminous flux at all visible wavelengths, also appears white to the eye.

As a consequence it is more convenient to have a set of units in which equal values result in white. These are known as *tristimulus units* and are obtained by weighting the value in lumens by a factor which depends on the response of the eye to each of the three wavelengths. The weighting factors add up to unity so that three tristimulus units, one of each colour, when added together produce one lumen. Tristimulus units will be considered further in section 6.14.

6.6 MTF, contrast and sharpness

All imaging devices, including the eye, have finite performance and the modulation transfer function (MTF) is a way of describing the ability of an imaging system to carry detail. The MTF is essentially an optical frequency response and is a function of depth of contrast with respect to spatial frequency. Prior to describing the MTF it is necessary to define some terms used in assessing image quality.

Spatial frequency is measured in cycles per millimetre (mm^{-1}). Contrast Index (CI) is shown in Figure 6.13(a). The luminance variation across an image has peaks and troughs and the relative size of these is used to calculate the contrast index as shown. A test image can be made having the same Contrast Index over a range of spatial frequencies as shown in Figure 6.13(b). If a non-ideal optical system is used to examine the test image, the output will have a Contrast Index which falls with rising spatial frequency.

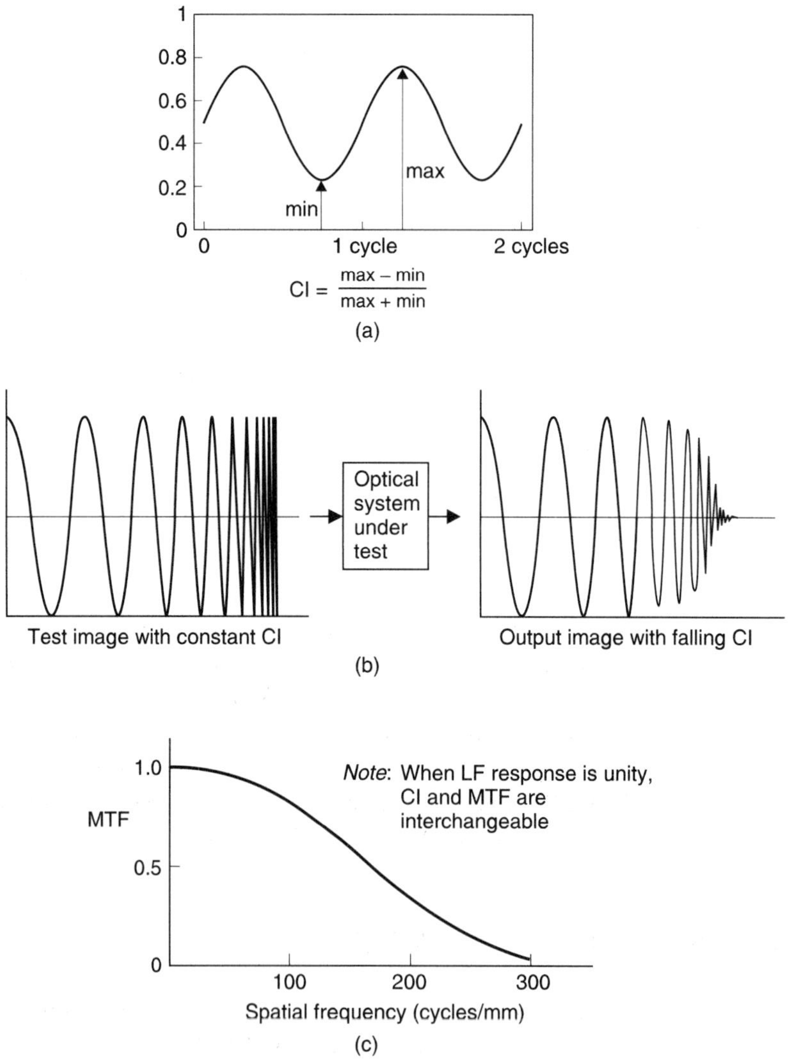

Figure 6.13 (a) The definition of contrast index (CI). (b) Frequency sweep test image having constant CI. (c) MTF is the ratio of output and input CIs.

The ratio of the output CI to the input CI is the MTF as shown in Figure 6.13(c). In the special case where the input CI is unity the output CI is identical to the output MTF. It is common to measure resolution by quoting the frequency at which the MTF has fallen to one half. This is known as the 50 per cent MTF frequency. The limiting resolution is defined as the point where the MTF has fallen to 10 per cent.

Whilst MTF resolution testing is objective, human vision is subjective and gives an impression we call sharpness. However, the assessment of sharpness is affected by contrast. Increasing the contrast of an image will result in an increased sensation of sharpness even though the MTF is unchanged. When CRTs having black areas between the phosphors were introduced, it was found that the improved contrast resulted in subjectively improved sharpness even though the MTF was unchanged. Similar results are obtained with CRTs having non-reflective coatings.

The perceived contrast of a display is also a function of the surroundings. Displays viewed in dark surroundings, such as cinema film and transparencies, appear to lack contrast whereas when the same technical contrast is displayed with light surroundings, the contrast appears correct. This is known as the *surround effect*. It can be overcome by artificially expanding the contrast prior to the display. This will be considered in section 6.9 where the subject of gamma is treated.

6.7 The human visual system

The HVS evolved as a survival tool. A species which could use vision to sense an impending threat, to locate food and a mate would have an obvious advantage. From an evolutionary standpoint, using the visual system to appreciate art or entertainment media is very recent. In a system having strong parallels to the hearing system described in Chapter 5, the HVS has two obvious transducers, namely the eyes, coupled to a series of less obvious but extremely sophisticated processes which take place in the brain. The result of these processes is what we call sight, a phenomenon which is difficult to describe.

At an average reading distance of 350 mm, the letters in this book subtend an angle to the eye of about a third of a degree. The lines from which the letters are formed are about one tenth of a millimetre across and subtend an angle of about one minute (one sixtieth of a degree). The field of view of the HVS is nearly a hemisphere. A short calculation will reveal how many pixels would be needed to convey that degree of resolution over such a wide field of view. The result is simply staggering. If we add colour and we also wish to update all those pixels to allow motion, it is possible to estimate what bandwidth would be needed.

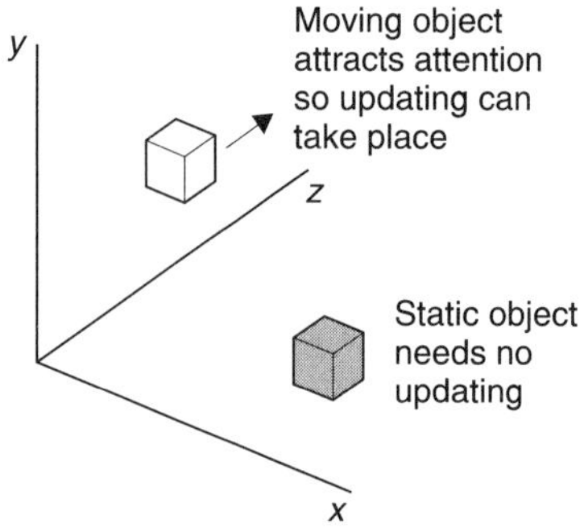

Figure 6.14 The human concept of reality can be likened to a three-dimensional store in the mind in which objects are placed as they are recognized. Moving objects attract the attention because they need to be updated in the model.

The result is so large that it is utterly inconceivable that the nerves from the eye to the brain could carry so much data, or that the brain could handle it. Clearly the HVS does not work in this way. Instead the HVS does what the species finds most useful. It helps create a model in the mind of the reality around it.

Figure 6.14 shows the concept. The model can be considered like a kind of three-dimensional frame store in which objects are stored as the HVS identifies them. Inanimate objects are so called because they don't move. They can be modelled once and left in the model until there is evidence to suggest that there has been a change. In contrast, animate objects need more attention, because they could be bringing benefit or detriment.

The HVS solves both of these requirements with the same mechanism. The eyes can swivel to scan the environment and their owner can move within it. This scanning process allows the model to be built using eyes with a relatively narrow field of view. Within this narrow field of view, the provision of high resolution and colour vision does not require absurd bandwidth, although it does require good lighting. Although the pixels are close together, the total number is fairly small.

Such narrow vision alone is not useful because events outside the field of vision do not alert the HVS to the need for an update of the model. Thus in addition there is a wider field of view which has relatively poor resolution and is colourblind, but which works at low light levels and responds primarily to small changes or movements.

Sitting at a laptop computer writing these words, I can only see a small part of the screen in detail. The rest of the study is known only from the model. On my right is a mahogany bracket clock, but in peripheral vision it appears as a grey lump. However, in my mind the wood and the brass are still the right colour. The ticking of the clock is coming from the same place in the model as the remembered object, reinforcing the illusion.

If I were to be replaced with a camera and a stereo microphone, and the two then turned to the right towards the clock, the visual image and the sound image would both move left. However, if I myself turn right this doesn't happen. The signals from the balance organs in the ear, the sound image model and the visual model produce data consistent with the fact that it was I that moved and the result is that the model doesn't move. Instead I have become another object in the model and am moving within it. The advantage of this detached approach is that my limbs are included in the model so that I can see an object and pick it up.

This interaction between the senses is very strong and disparities between the senses are a powerful clue that one is being shown an illusion. In advanced systems for use in electronic cinema or flight simulators, it is vital to maintain accurate tracking between the visual image, the sound image and the sense of balance. Disparities which are not obvious may often result in fatigue.

One consequence of seeing via a model is that we often see what we expect to see rather than what is before us. Optical illusions demonstrate this, and Maurits Escher turned it into an art form. The technique of camouflage destroys familiar shapes and confuses the modelling process. Animals and birds may freeze when predators approach because their lack of motion doesn't trigger peripheral vision.

6.8 The eye

The simple representation of Figure 6.15 shows that the eyeball is nearly spherical and is swivelled by muscles. The space between the cornea and the lens is filled with transparent fluid known as *aqueous humour*. The remainder of the eyeball is filled with a transparent jelly known as *vitreous humour*. Light enters the cornea, and the the amount of light admitted is controlled by the pupil in the iris. Light entering is involuntarIly focused on the retina by the lens in a process called *visual accommodation*. The lens is the only part of the eye which is not nourished by the bloodstream and its centre is technically dead. In a young person the lens is flexible and muscles distort it to perform the focusing action. In old age the lens loses some flexibility and causes *presbyopia* or limited accommodation. In some people the length of the eyeball is incorrect resulting in *myopia* (short-sightedness) or *hypermetropia* (long-sightedness). The cornea should have the same curvature in all meridia, and if this is not the case, *astigmatism* results.

The retina is responsible for light sensing and contains a number of layers. The surface of the retina is covered with arteries, veins and nerve fibres and light has to penetrate these in order to reach the sensitive layer. This contains two types of discrete receptors known as *rods* and *cones*

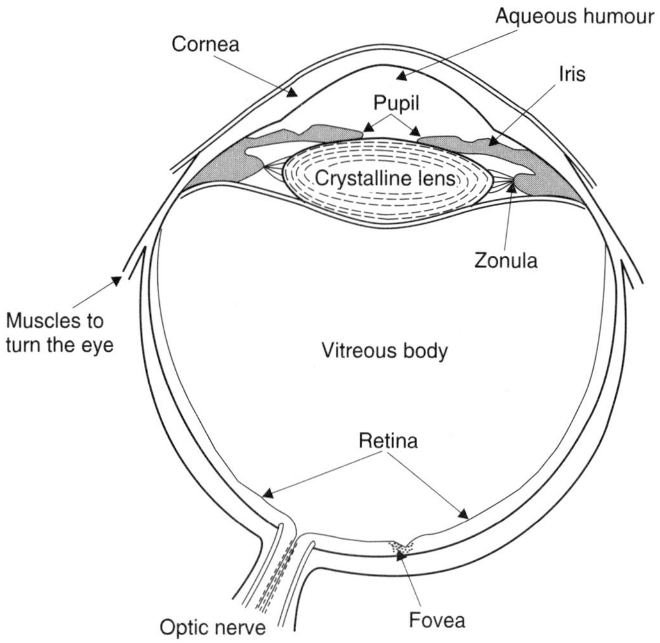

Figure 6.15 A simple representation of an eyeball; see text for details.

from their shape. The distribution and characteristics of these two receptors are quite different. Rods dominate the periphery of the retina whereas cones dominate a central area known as the *fovea* outside which their density drops off. Vision using the rods is monochromatic and has poor resolution but remains effective at very low light levels, whereas the cones provide high resolution and colour vision but require more light.

Figure 6.16 shows how the sensitivity of the retina slowly increases in response to entering darkness. The first part of the curve is the adaptation of cone or *photopic* vision. This is followed by the greater adaptation of the rods in *scotopic* vision. Figure 6.17 shows that the luminous efficiency function is different for scotopic vision, peaking at around 507 nm. This is known as the Purkinje effect. At such low light levels the fovea is essentially blind and small objects which can be seen in the peripheral rod vision disappear when stared at. A significant area of the retina, where the optic nerve connects, is completely blind. However we are not aware of a hole in our vision because we don't see the image on the retina literally. Instead we see the visual model which inserts information in the hole. The hole is in a different place in each eye which assists in this concealment process.

The cones in the fovea are densely packed and directly connected to the nervous system allowing the highest resolution. Resolution then falls off away from the fovea. As a result the eye must move to scan large areas of

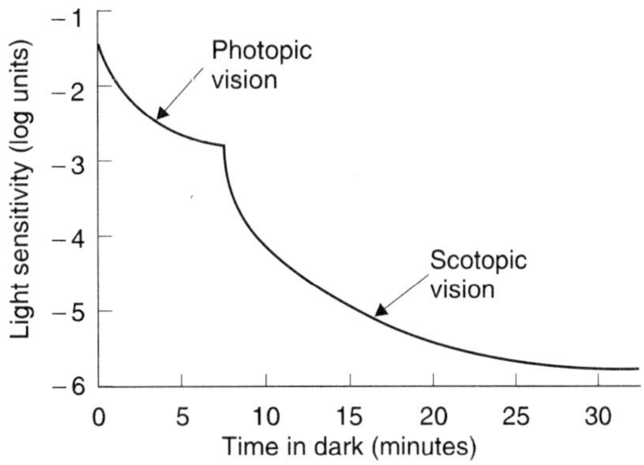

Figure 6.16 Retinal sensitivity changes after sudden darkness. The initial curve is due to adaptation of cones. At very low light levels cones are blind and monochrome rod vision takes over.

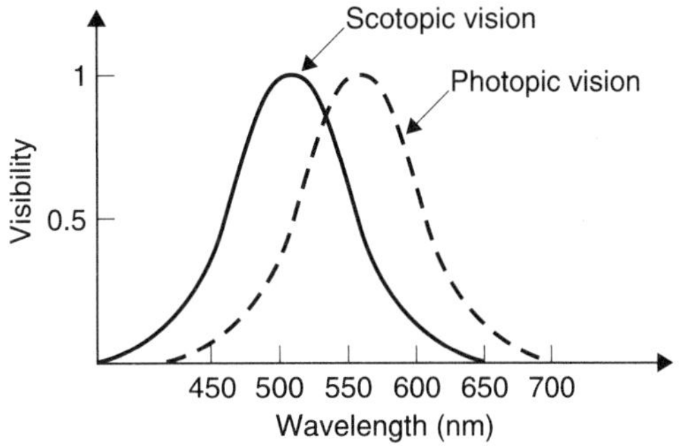

Figure 6.17 The luminous efficiency function is different for scotopic vision.

detail. The image perceived is not just a function of the retinal response, but is also affected by processing of the nerve signals. The overall acuity of the eye can be displayed as a graph of the response plotted against the degree of detail being viewed. Detail is generally measured in lines per millimetre or cycles per picture height, but this takes no account of the distance from the eye. A better unit for eye resolution is one based upon the subtended angle of detail as this will be independent of distance. Units of cycles per degree are then appropriate. Figure 6.18 shows the response of the eye to static detail. Note that the response to very low frequencies is also attenuated. An extension of this characteristic allows the vision system to ignore the fixed pattern of shadow on the retina due to the nerves and arteries.

The resolution of the eye is primarily a spatio-temporal compromise. The eye is a spatial sampling device; the spacing of the rods and cones on the retina represents a spatial sampling frequency and the finite area of the individual sensors results in an aperture effect. However, if these

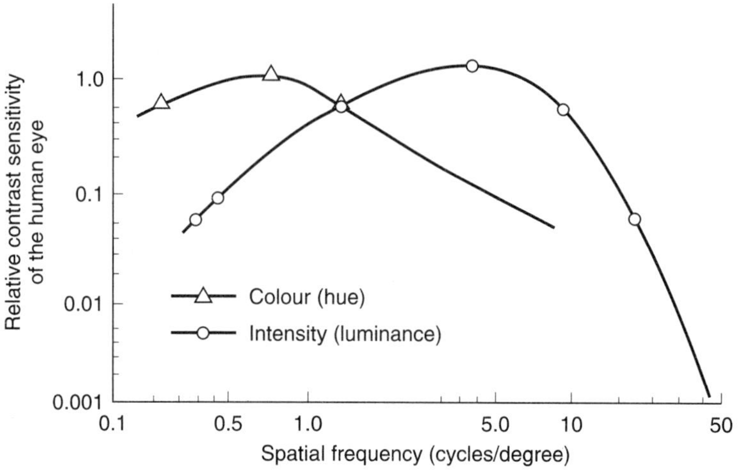

Figure 6.18 The response of the eye to static detail falls off at both low and high spatial frequencies.

parameters are measured and an MTF is estimated, it will be found that the measured acuity of the eye exceeds the value calculated.

This is possible because a form of oversampling is used. Figure 6.19 shows that the eye is in a continuous state of unconscious vibration called saccadic motion. This causes the sampling sites to exist in more than one location, effectively increasing the spatial sampling rate provided there is a temporal filter which is able to integrate the information from the various different positions of the retina.

This temporal filtering is partly responsible for *persistence of vision* and other effects. The HVS does not respond instantly to light, but requires between 0.15 and 0.3 second before the brain perceives an image, although that image could have been presented for an extremely short length of time. At low light levels the time taken to perceive an image increases. The position of moving objects is perceived with a lag which causes the geometry of stereoscopic depth perception to be in error, a phenomenon known as the Pulfrich effect.

Scotopic vision experiences a greater delay than photopic vision as more processes are required. Images are retained for about 0.1 second. Flashing lights are perceived to flicker until the *critical flicker frequency* is

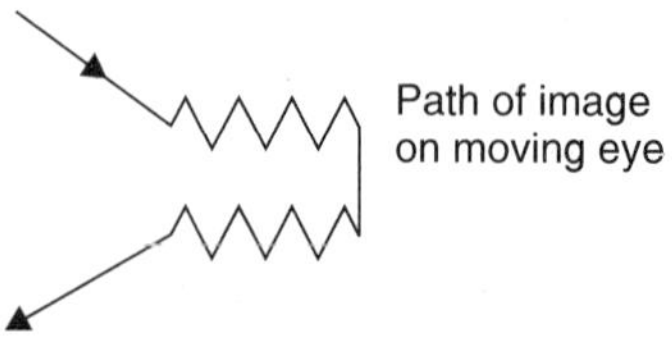

Figure 6.19 The eye is constantly moving and this causes the sampling sites on the retina to exist in more places, enhancing resolution.

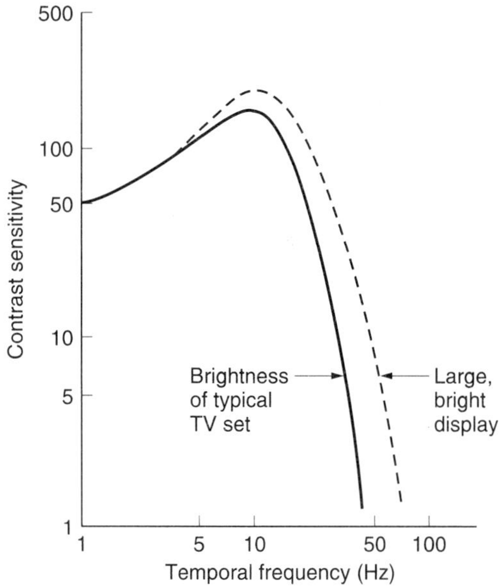

Figure 6.20 The critical flicker frequency is not constant but rises as brightness increases.

reached, when the light appears continuous for higher frequencies. Figure 6.20 shows how the CFF changes with brightness. The CFF in peripheral vision is higher than in foveal vision. This is consistent with using peripheral vision to detect movement.

The critical flicker frequency is also a function of the state of alertness of the individual. When people are tired or under stress, the rate at which the brain updates the model appears to slow down so that the CFF falls.[1]

The response of the eye is effectively two-dimensional as it is affected by spatial frequencies and temporal frequencies. Figure 6.21 shows the two-dimensional or spatio-temporal response of the eye. If the eye were static, a detailed object moving past it would give rise to temporal frequencies, as Figure 6.22(a) shows. The temporal frequency is given by the detail in the object, in lines per millimetre, multiplied by the speed. Clearly a highly detailed object can reach high temporal frequencies even at slow speeds, and Figure 6.21 shows that the eye cannot respond to high temporal frequencies; a fixed eye cannot resolve detail in moving objects. The solution is that in practice the eye moves to follow objects of interest. Figure 6.22(b) shows that when the eye is following an object the image becomes stationary on the retina and the temporal frequencies are brought to zero. The greatest resolution is then possible. Clearly whilst one object is being followed other objects moving differently will be blurred. This ability of the eye to follow motion has a great bearing on the

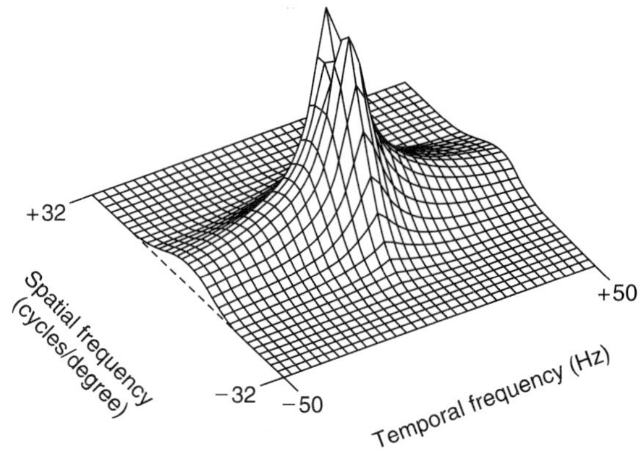

Figure 6.21 The response of the eye shown with respect to temporal and spatial frequencies. Note that even slow relative movement causes a serious loss of resolution. The eye tracks moving objects to prevent this loss.

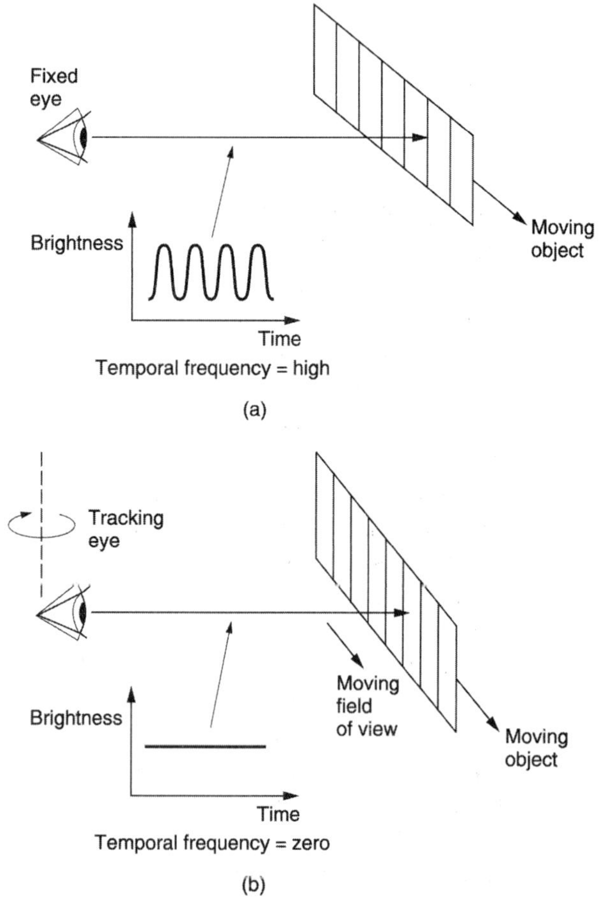

Figure 6.22 In (a) a detailed object moves past a fixed eye, causing temporal frequencies beyond the response of the eye. This is the cause of motion blur. In (b) the eye tracks the motion and the temporal frequency becomes zero. Motion blur cannot then occur.

way that discrete frames are perceived as a continuously moving picture and affects the design of motion-compensated equipment. This will be discussed further in section 6.10.

6.9 Gamma

Gamma is the power to which the voltage of a conventional analog video signal must be raised to produce a linear light representation of the original scene. At the bottom of it all, there are two reasons for gamma. One is the perennial search for economy and the other is a characteristic of the human visual system which allows the economy to be made. The truth is that gamma is a perceptive compression system. It allows a television picture of better perceived quality to pass through a signal path of given performance.

The true brightness of a television picture can be affected by electrical noise on the video signal. The best results will be obtained by considering how well the eye can perceive such noise. The contrast sensitivity of the eye is defined as the smallest brightness difference which is visible. In fact the contrast sensitivity is not constant, but increases proportionally to brightness. Thus whatever the brightness of an object, if that brightness changes by about 1 per cent it will be equally detectable.

If video signals were linear, at maximum brightness the signal would have to be a hundred times bigger than the noise. However, if the signal were half as bright, the noise level would also have to be halved, so the SNR would now have to be 6 dB better. If the signal were one tenth as bright, a noise level ten times lower would be needed. The characteristic of the eye means that noise is more visible in dark picture areas than in bright areas.

For economic reasons, video signals have to be made non-linear to render noise less visible. An inverse gamma function takes place on the linear light signal from the camera so that the video signal is non-linear for most of its journey. Figure 6.23 shows a typical inverse gamma function. As a true power function requires infinite gain near black, a linear segment is substituted. Where it is necessary to compensate for the surround effect (see section 6.6) the gamma and inverse gamma processes can be made slightly different so that an overall non-linearity results. This improves perceived contrast when viewing in dark surroundings.

The result of using gamma is that contrast variations in the original scene near black result in a larger signal amplitude than variations near white. The result is that noise picked up by the video signal has less effect on dark areas than on bright areas, countering the sensitivity of the eye. After a gamma function at the display, noise at near-black levels is compressed with respect to noise near-white levels. Thus a video

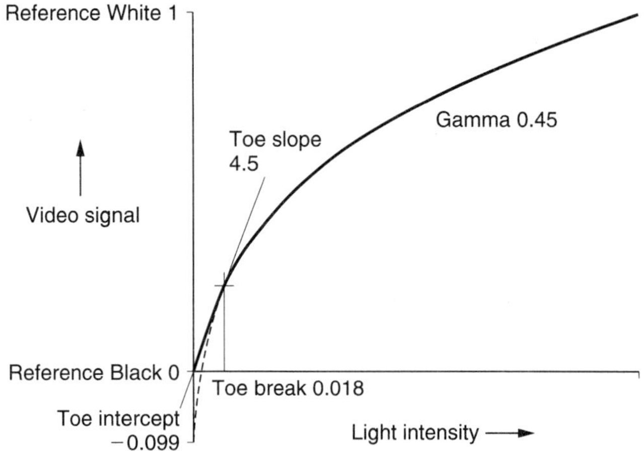

Figure 6.23 CCIR Rec. 709 inverse gamma function used at camera has a straight line approximation at the lower part of the curve to avoid boosting camera noise. Note that the output amplitude is greater for modulation near black.

transmission system using gamma has a lower perceived noise level than one without. Without gamma, vision signals would need around 30 dB better signal-to-noise ratio for the same perceived quality and digital video samples would need five or six extra bits.

There is a strong argument to retain gamma in the digital domain for analog compatibility. In the digital domain transmission noise is eliminated, but instead the conversion process introduces quantizing noise.

As all television signals, analog and digital, are subject to gamma correction, it is technically incorrect to refer to the *Y* signal as luminance, because this parameter is defined as linear in colorimetry. Charles Poynton[2] has suggested that the term *luma* should be used to describe the signal which results when luminance has been gamma corrected so that it is clear that a non-linear signal is being considered. That convention has been adopted throughout this book.

Figure 6.24 shows that digital luma can be considered in several equivalent ways. At (a) a linear analog luminance signal is passed through a gamma corrector to create luma and this is then quantized uniformly. At (b) the linear analog luminance signal is fed directly to a non-uniform quantizer. At (c) the linear analog luminance signal is uniformly quantized to produce digital luminance. This is converted to digital luma by a digital process having a non-linear transfer function.

Whilst the three techniques shown give the same result, (a) is the simplest, (b) requires a special ADC with gamma-spaced quantizing steps, and (c) requires a high-resolution ADC of perhaps fourteen to sixteen bits because it works in the linear luminance domain where noise

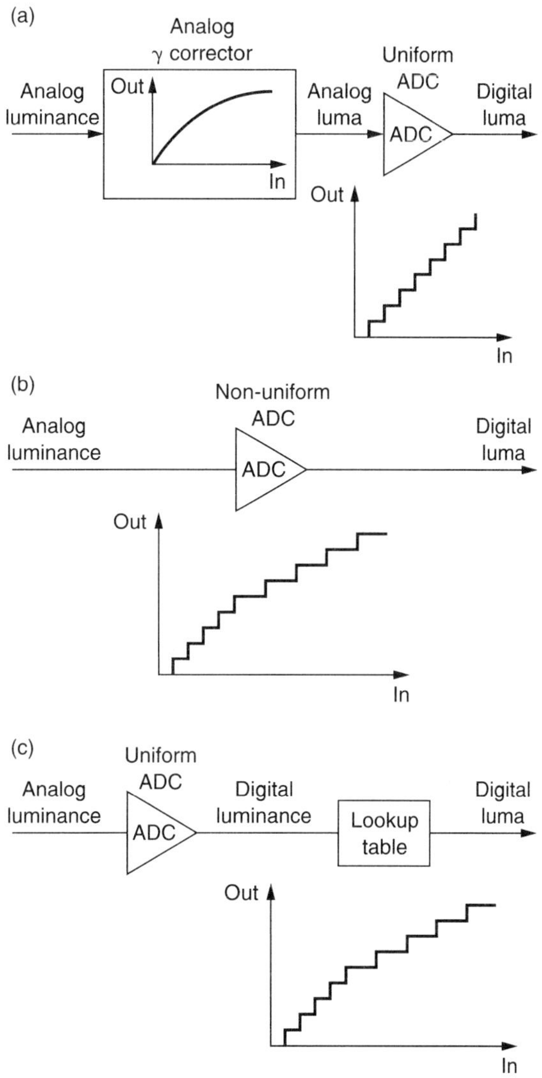

Figure 6.24 (a) Analog γ correction prior to ADC. (b) Non-uniform quantizer gives direct γ conversion. (c) Digital γ correction using look-up table

is highly visible. Technique (c) is used in digital processing cameras where long wordlength is common practice.

As digital luma with eight-bit resolution gives the same subjective performance as digital luminance with fourteen-bit resolution it will be clear why gamma can also be considered as a perceptive compression technique.

As gamma is derived from a characteristic of the eye, there is only one correct value, which is the one that gives an apparent sensitivity to noise which is independent of brightness. Too little gamma and we would see more noise in dark areas. Too much and we would see more noise in highlights. This is why it is regarded as a constant in television. All the more surprising that in computer graphics standards gamma varies considerably. As the use of computers in television spreads, this incompatibility can be a source of difficulty.

Clearly image data which are intended to be displayed on a television system must have the correct gamma characteristic or the grey scale will not be correctly reproduced. Image data from computer systems often have gamma characteristics which are incompatible with the standards adopted in video and a gamma conversion process will be required to obtain a correct display. This may take the form of a lookup table or an algorithm.

So what has gamma got to do with CRTs? The electrons emitted from the cathode have negative charge and so are attracted towards an anode which is supplied with a positive voltage. The voltage on the grid controls the current. The electron beam strikes the inside of the tube face which is coated with phosphor. The intensity of the light produced is effectively controlled by the intensity of the electron beam which is in turn controlled by the grid voltage. It is the relative voltage between the cathode and the grid which determines the beam current.

The relationship between the tube drive voltage and the phosphor brightness is not linear, but is an exponential function. The power is the same for all CRTs as it is a function of the physics of the electron gun and it has a value of around 2.8. It is a happy but pure coincidence that the gamma function of a CRT follows roughly the same curve as human contrast sensitivity.

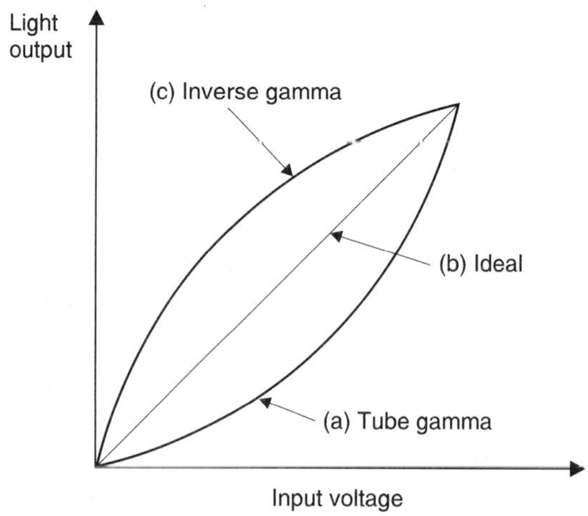

Figure 6.25 The non-linear characteristic of tube (a) contrasted with the ideal response (b). Non-linearity may be opposed by gamma correction with a response (c).

Consequently if video signals are pre-distorted at source by an inverse gamma, the gamma characteristic of the CRT will linearize the signal. Figure 6.25 shows the principle. CRT non-linearity is actually used to enhance the noise performance of a television system. If the CRT had no gamma characteristic, a gamma circuit would have been necessary ahead of it to linearize the gamma-corrected video signals. As all standard video signals are inverse gamma processed, it follows that if a non-CRT display such as a plasma or LCD device is to be used, some gamma conversion will be required at the display. In a plasma display, the amount of light emitted is controlled by the duration of the discharge and a voltage-to-pulse-length stage is needed in the drive electronics. It is straightforward to include a gamma effect in this conversion.

6.10 Motion portrayal and dynamic resolution

Althought the term 'motion pictures' is commonly used, it is inaccurate. Today's film, television and graphics systems do not present moving pictures at all. Instead they present a series of still pictures at a frequency known as the *frame rate*. The way that the human visual system interprets periodically updated still pictures to obtain an illusion of motion has only been put on a scientific basis relatively recently. Most of today's image-portrayal systems were designed empirically before this knowledge was available and it is hardly surprising that in the absence of a theory the results are often poor and myth abounds.

All high-quality non-stereoscopic image-portrayal systems should look the same to the viewer as the original scene when viewed through one eye. This must hold not only for the appearance of any objects but also for their motion. At the time of writing this cannot be said for film or television, which differ obviously from one another and from the original scene.

To suggest that re-creation of the original scene is the only acceptable goal is pedantic as this is probably not necessary. However, it can fairly be stated that the standards of realism of present-day systems are somewhat lacking and a degree of improvement is desirable, particularly in the portrayal of motion. That improvement is not especially difficult with modern technology as will be shown here.

As was shown in section 6.7, the eye uses involuntary tracking at all times. This means that the criterion for comparing moving image-portrayal systems has to be the apparent resolution perceived by the viewer in an object moving within the limits of accurate eye tracking. The traditional metric of static resolution in film and television has to be abandoned as unrepresentative of the viewing experience and replaced with a more appropriate metric known as *dynamic resolution*.

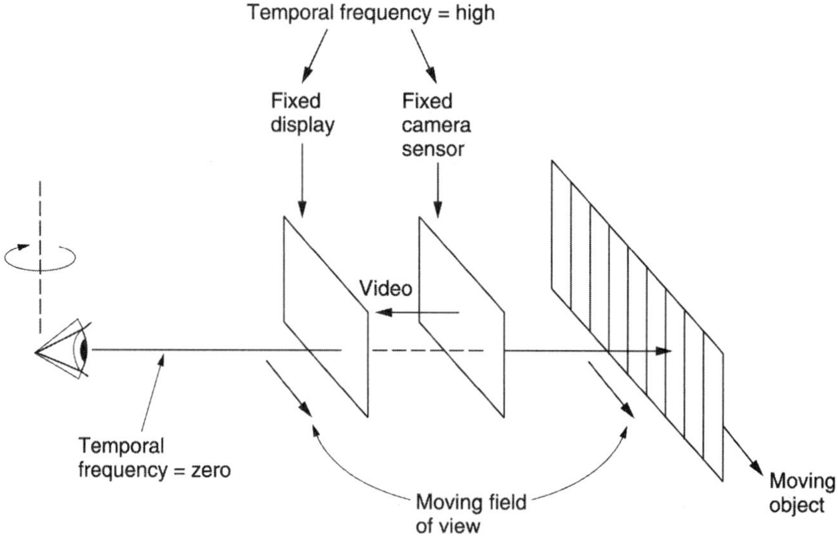

Figure 6.26 An object moves past a camera, and is tracked on a monitor by the eye. The high temporal frequencies cause allasing in the TV signal, but these are not perceived by the tracking eye as this reduces the temporal frequency to zero.

Figure 6.22(b) showed an eye tracking a real detailed moving object. The tracking process renders the object stationary with respect to the retina and so the eye can perceive detail. Figure 6.26 shows the eye tracking the same object, but this time on the screen of an image-portrayal system. The camera and display are fixed. This results in high temporal frequencies being present in the imaging system.

Consider an example of a moving object containing moderate detail of 80 cycles per picture width. If the object moves at a speed of one picture width per second, the temporal frequency due to the object modulation moving past a given pixel in the fixed camera is 80 Hz. In conventional systems, this temporal frequency is sampled at the frame rate, typically only 24, 25 or 30 Hz. According to conventional sampling theory, this is a recipe for aliasing, whereas film and television are known to work reasonably well. One may be forgiven for wondering what is going on and the explanation is based on the fact that eye tracking has a dramatic effect.

Figure 6.27 shows that when the moving eye tracks an object on the screen, the viewer is watching with respect to the optic flow axis, not the time axis, and these are not parallel when there is motion. The optic flow axis is defined as an imaginary axis in the spatio-temporal volume which joins the same points on objects in successive frames. Clearly when many objects move independently there will be one optic flow axis for each, although the HVS can only track one at a time.

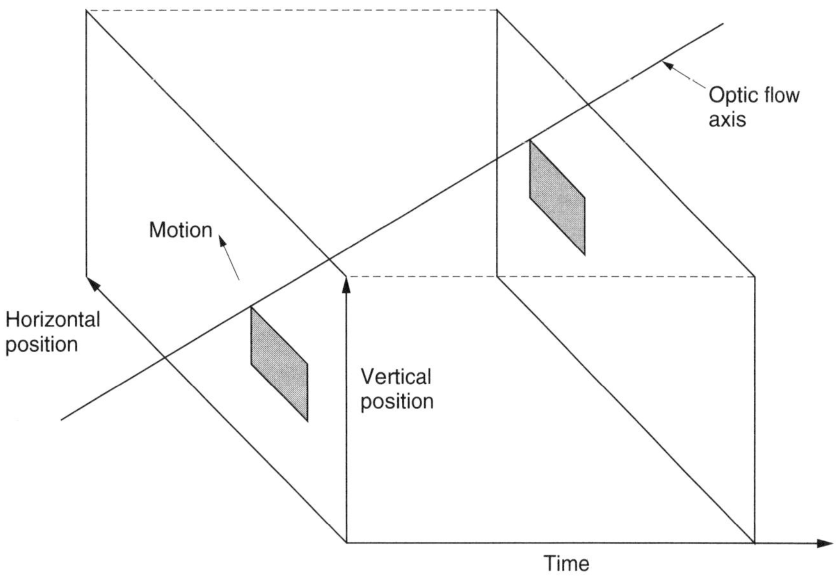

Figure 6.27 Objects travel in a three-dimensional space along the optic flow axis which is only parallel to the time axis if there is no movement.

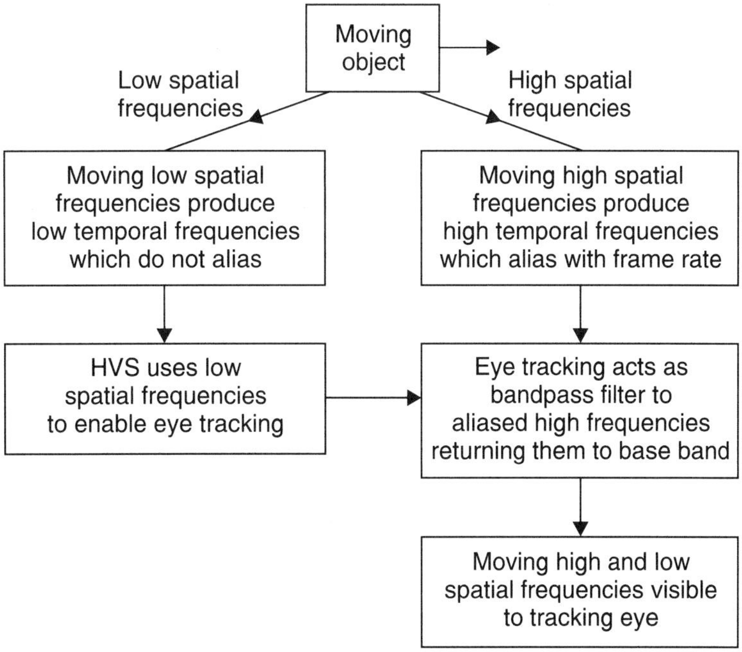

Figure 6.28 A real moving object contains a range of spatial frequencies. The low frequencies allow eye tracking to be performed, and once the eye is tracking correctly, the aliased high frequencies are heterodyned back to their correct baseband frequency so that detail can be seen in moving areas.

Figure 6.28(a) shows that real scenes contain many spatial frequencies rather than hypothetical sine waves. The bulk of an object is carried in low spatial frequencies and the temporal frequency due to motion is quite low and does not alias. This allows the eye to track a moving object. When the eye is tracking, it views the series of presented pictures along the optic flow axis. Figure 6.28(b) shows that this eye tracking arrests the temporal frequency due to moving detail, allowing the spatial detail to be seen. Note that aliasing occurs on the time axis, but this is not seen by the tracking eye. It is only eye tracking which allows the use of such low picture rates. However well low picture rates work on the tracked object, it is important to consider what happens on parts of the picture which are not being tracked.

It is a further consequence of Figure 6.28(a) that the observer perceives the direction of motion of an object before the object can be seen in detail. The detail can only be seen when the eye has achieved tracking.

When the eye is tracking, successive pictures appear in different places with respect to the retina. In other words if an object is moving down the screen and followed by the eye, the screen, and the background image portrayed on it, is actually moving up with respect to the retina.

6.11 Background strobing and frame rate

In real-life eye tracking, the motion of the background will be smooth, but in an image-portrayal system based on periodic presentation of frames, the background will be presented to the retina in a different position in each frame. The retina separately perceives each impression of the background leading to an effect called background strobing which is shown in Figure 6.29.

The criterion for the selection of a display frame rate in an imaging system is sufficient reduction of background strobing. It is a complete myth that the display rate simply needs to exceed the critical flicker frequency. Manufacturers of graphics displays which use frame rates well in excess of those used in film and television are doing so for a valid reason: it gives better results! Note that the display rate and the transmission rate need not be the same in an advanced system. The picture rate may artificially be increased prior to display.

6.12 Colour

There are many aspects of colour to consider in imaging systems. It is conventional to begin with colour science which explains what is happening both in physics and in the eye, as this will define the problem

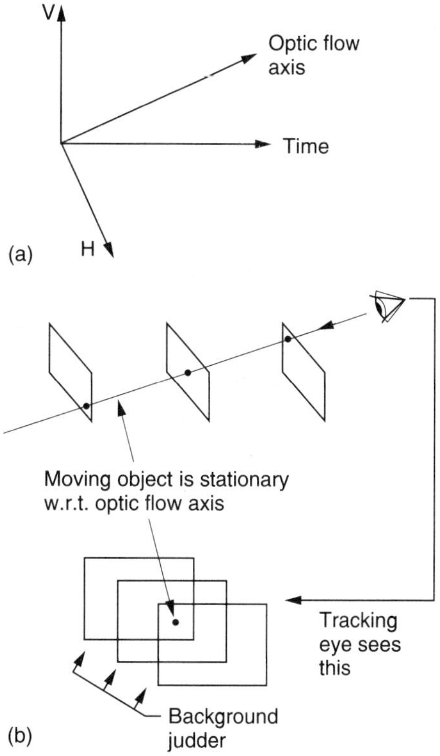

Figure 6.29 The optic flow axis (a) joins points on a moving object in successive pictures. (b) When a tracking eye follows a moving object on a screen, that screen will be seen in a different place at each picture. This is the origin of background strobing.

of colour portrayal. Ideally a sensor with at least the same colour acuity as the eye would be used to create colour data whose transmission is probably the easiest part of the system. An ideal display would be able to re-create the original colours.

Practicality and economics mean that ideal colour reproduction is seldom achieved in real systems, primarily because of difficulties in the display, but nevertheless good results can be obtained with a little care. The approach of this chapter will be to describe current practice, but without losing sight of the fact that improvements are possible. As convergence continues, it will increasingly become important for colour data to be transferable between previously separate disciplines. Computer data representing a coloured image may be used to drive a CRT display, a colour printer or a film recorder or to make plates for a press. In each case the same colours should be obtained as on the computer monitor. At the moment the disparity of technologies makes such transfers non-trivial.

6.13 Colour vision

When considering everyday objects at normal temperatures, the black-body radiation is negligible compared to the reflection of ambient light. Figure 6.30 shows that the colour perceived by the human observer is a function of the illuminant and the reflectivity of the object concerned.

The sensation of colour is entirely a fabrication of the human visual system and in the real world there is only a distribution of energy at different wavelengths. There is no fixed relationship between the two. The SPD of daylight varies throughout the day, and the SPD of many artificial light sources is different again. As a result the SPD reaching the eye in the reflection from some object is subject to a lot of variation. However, although this ought to cause things to change colour, this is not what we see. It would cause enormous practical difficulties if we saw 'true' colour. Imagine parking a white car at midday and being unable to locate it just before sunset because it has become red.

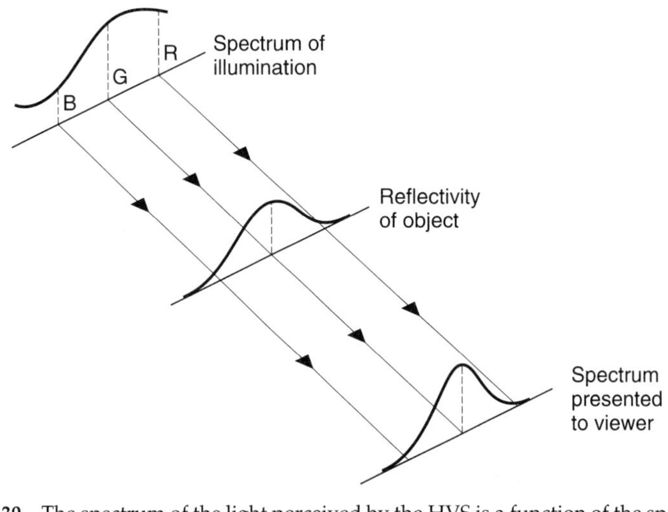

Figure 6.30 The spectrum of the light perceived by the HVS is a function of the spectrum of the illumination and the reflectivity of the object concerned. Thus it is incorrect to state that colour is a property of an object as this assumes a certain type of lighting.

Instead the HVS compensates so that we can recognize our property and our friends despite changes in natural or artificial illumination. In the absence of any reference, the eye automatically tries to colour balance an image so that familiar objects in it have familiar colours.

This characteristic of seeing the colour we expect means that the absolute accuracy of colour reproduction can be fairly poor. However, the differential accuracy of colour vision is astonishingly good. If during the filming of a movie or TV program, footage shot at midday is edited onto footage shot later on, the sudden jump of colour balance will be obvious to all. Film and TV cameras don't have the subconscious colour corrector of the HVS and steps have to be taken artificially to maintain the same colour balance. Another example of differential colour accuracy is the difficulty of matching paint on replacement car body panels.

The eye is able to distinguish between different SPDs because it has sensors in the retina called *cones* which respond in three different ways. Each type of cone has a different spectral response curve. The *rods* in the retina which operate at extremely low light levels only exist in one type and so there is no colour vision when the rods are in use. The full resolution of human vision is restricted to brightness variations. Our ability to resolve colour details is only about a quarter of that.

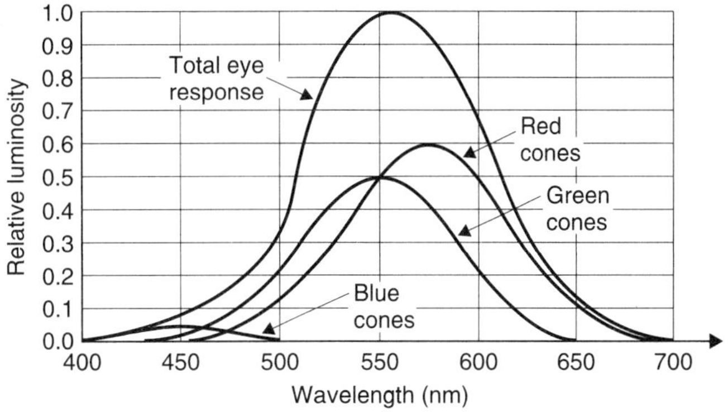

Figure 6.31 The approximate response of each type of cone in the retina.

Figure 6.31 shows an approximate response for each of the three types of cone. If light of a single wavelength is observed, the relative responses of the three sensors allows us to discern what we call the colour of the light. Note that at both ends of the visible spectrum there are areas in which only one receptor responds; all colours in those areas look the same. There is a great deal of variation in receptor response from one individual to the next and the standard curves used in colorimetry are not necessarily valid for an individual. In a surprising number of people the single receptor zones are extended and discrimination between, for example, red and orange is difficult.

The responses of Figure 6.31 are broad and this means that a considerable range of SPDs actually appear to have the same colour. The eye will perceive, for example, the same white sensation whether the light has flat SPD or whether it consists of three monochromatic components. Maxwell's triangle (Figure 6.32) was an early attempt to depict the operation of the eye graphically.

The HVS appears to average the SPD of the light it is analysing in two dimensions. The result of additively mixing any two colours will appear

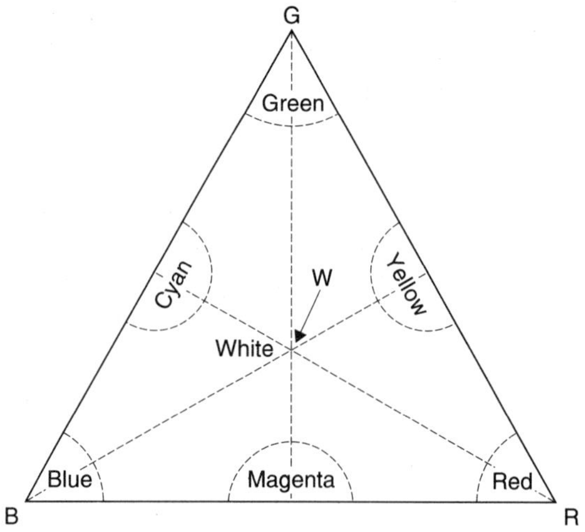

Figure 6.32 Maxwell's triangle was an early attempt at understanding colour vision.

on a straight line between them at a location which is a function of the relative intensity. Thus adding red and green will create yellow, and in turn yellow and blue will create white. It does not matter whether the yellow is spectral yellow or whether it is a mixture of red and green. These effects are summarized by Grassman's Law: sources of the same colour produce identical effects in a mixture regardless of their spectral composition.

As a result it is possible for somewhat different SPDs to be perceived as exactly the same colour. Such SPDs are known as *metamers*. Figure 6.33

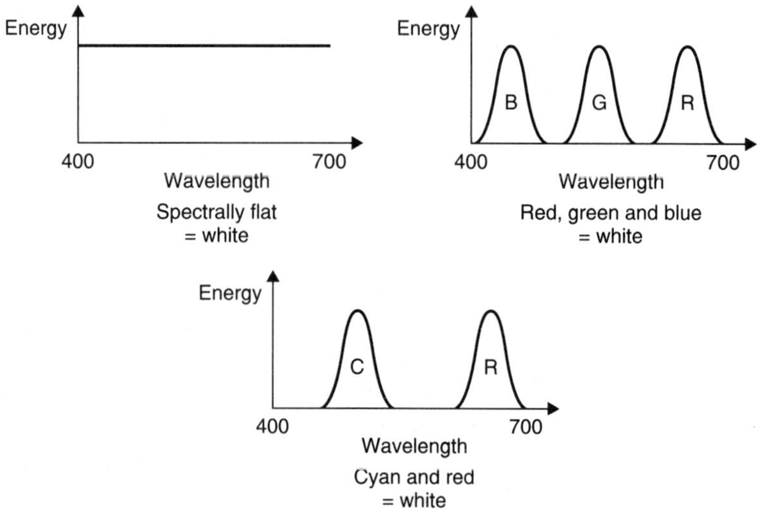

Figure 6.33 Metamers are spectral distributions which appear the same colour to the HVS.

shows some metamers. White light as perceived by the HVS can be spectrally uniform, a mixture of red and cyan or equal parts of red, green and blue, or an infinite number of such variations.

Metamerism is both good and bad. It is good because it allows colour-imaging equipment to be much simpler than otherwise. However, it is bad because it allows illuminants which are metamers of white but which are anything but spectrally uniform. An example is fluorescent light which appears white but makes coloured objects appear different because the narrow line spectra may not coincide with the reflectivity function of the object concerned. Try looking at mahogany in daylight and then under fluorescent light. This effect also plays havoc with colour film which is not expecting narrow spectra and will suffer strong colour casts, generally towards green which does nothing for flesh tones.

6.14 Colorimetry

The triple receptor or *trichromatic* characteristic of the eye is extremely fortunate as it means that it is possible to represent the full range of visible colours and brightness by only three signals. However, this is only true if the three signals are obtained in an appropriate way. It does *not* follow that it is possible to re-create the entire visible colour range with only three different light sources, and this distinction will be clarified here. Nevertheless with three sources a large range of colours is still possible. It is important to appreciate that some colours occur very rarely and the inability accurately to re-create them in systems designed for entertainment is not serious. However, for technical or security purposes it may be an issue.

There are two ways of creating colours, which amount to alternative ways of producing the same SPD. One can start with a wide spectrum such as white light and narrow it down by removing part of the spectrum with filters, or one can create weighted amounts of light at three discrete wavelengths which are added up. Cinema film operates on the former principle, known as *subtractive colour matching*, whereas colour CRTs operate on the latter, known as *additive colour matching*. Subtractive colour matching also occurs with paints and inks.

Colour is subjective and it is difficult to describe a colour accurately without an objective basis. The work on objective measurement of colour vision was carried out by the Commission Internationale d'Eclairage (CIE) in the 1920s.

The CIE chose three monochromatic primaries, 436 and 546 nm from mercury lamps and 700 nm from a neon lamp. Once the primaries have been selected, the proportions needed to reproduce a given colour can be found, and from these proportions it will be possible to specify the

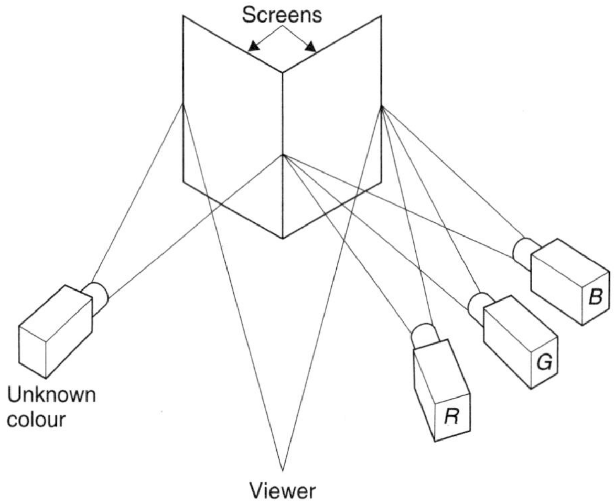

Figure 6.34 Simple colorimeter. Intensities of primaries on the right screen are adjusted to match the test colour on the left screen.

spectral characteristics of the three analysis filters needed to produce three signals representing the colours. These analysis filters are called *CIE colour matching functions*.

Figure 6.34 shows a colorimeter used for finding colour matching functions. It consists of two adjacent white screens. One screen is illuminated by three light sources, one of each of the primary colours selected for the system being designed. Initially, the second screen is illuminated with white light and the three sources are adjusted until the first screen displays the same white. This calibrates the sources. Light of a single wavelength is then projected on the second screen. The primaries are once more adjusted until both screens appear to have the same colour.

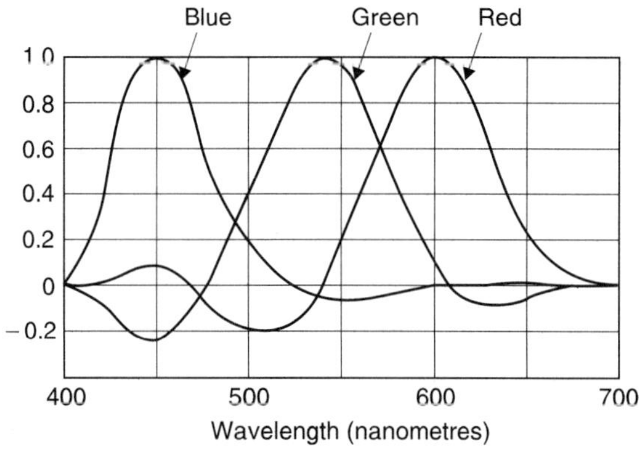

Figure 6.35 Colour mixture curves show how to mix primaries to obtain any spectral colour.

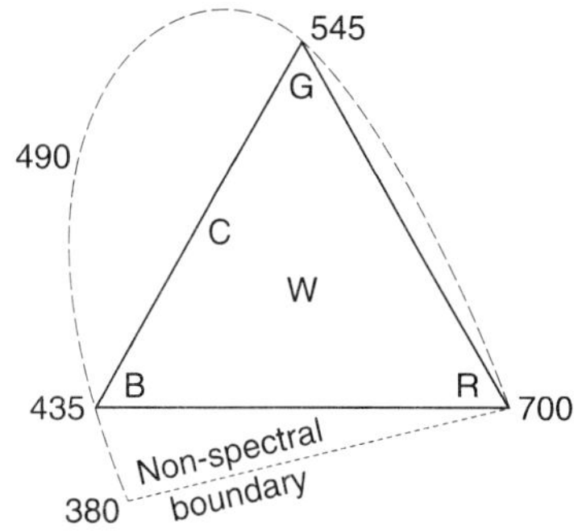

Figure 6.36 The problem with Maxwell's triangle is not that it is wrong, but incomplete in that there are colours which exist outside it.

The proportions of the primaries are noted. This process is repeated for the whole visible spectrum, resulting in *colour mixture curves* or *tristimulus values* shown in Figure 6.35.

In some cases it was found impossible to find a match. Figure 6.36 shows that the reason for the inability to match is that Maxwell's triangle in an incomplete description of colour vision. In fact the colours which can be perceived go outside the triangle, whereas the colour which can be created must reside within it. For example, if it is attempted to match pure cyan at a wavelength of 490 nm, this cannot be approached more closely than the limit set by the line between green and blue, which corresponds to the red source being turned off completely.

For analysis purposes a negative contribution can be simulated by shining some primary colour on the test screen until a match is obtained. The colour mixing curves dictate what the spectral response of the three sensors must be if distinct combinations of three signals are to be obtained for all visible colours.

6.15 The CIE chromaticity diagram

As there are three variables, they can only simultaneously be depicted in three dimensions. Figure 6.37 shows the *RGB* colour space which is basically a cube with black at the origin and white at the diagonally opposite corner. Figure 6.38 shows the colour mixture curves of Figure 6.35 plotted in *RGB* space. For each visible wavelength a vector exists whose direction is determined by the proportions of the three primaries. If the brightness is allowed to vary this will affect all three primaries and thus the length of the vector in the same proportion.

Depicting and visualizing the *RGB* colour space is not easy and it is also difficult to take objective measurements from it. The solution is to modify

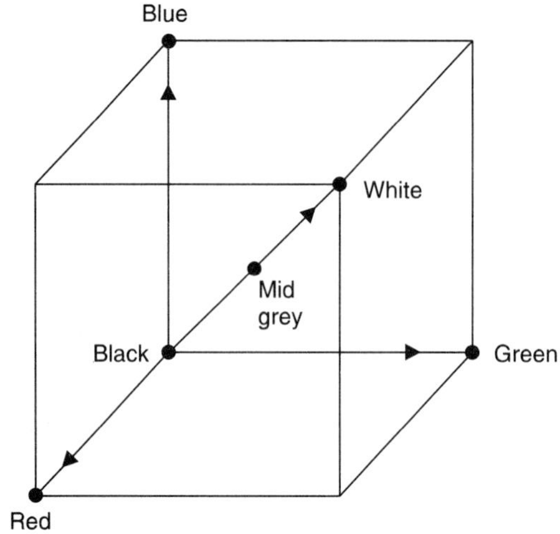

Figure 6.37 *RGB* colour space is three-dimensional and not easy to draw.

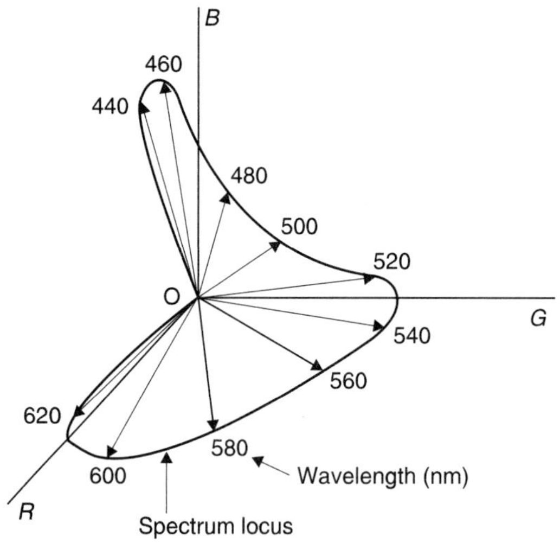

Figure 6.38 Colour mixture curves plotted in *RGB* space result in a vector whose locus moves with wavelength in three dimensions.

the diagram to allow it to be reproduced in two dimensions on flat paper. This is done by eliminating luminance (brightness) changes and depicting only the colour at constant brightness. Figure 6.39(a) shows how a constant luminance unit plane intersects the *RGB* space at unity on each axis. At any point on the plane the three components add up to one. A two-dimensional shape results when vectors representing all colours intersect the plane. Vectors may be extended if necessary to allow intersection. Figure 6.39(b) shows that the 500 nm vector has to be produced (extended) to meet the unit plane, whereas the 580 nm vector naturally intersects. Any colour can now uniquely be specified in two dimensions.

The points where the unit plane intersects the axes of *RGB* space form a triangle on the plot. The horseshoe-shaped locus of pure spectral colours goes outside this triangle because, as was seen above, the colour mixture curves require negative contributions for certain colours.

Negative values are a nuisance and can be eliminated by new coordinates called *X*, *Y* and *Z*. Figure 6.39(c) shows that in this representation the origin is in the same place for *XYZ* and *RGB*, but the *RGB* axes have been turned inwards just far enough that the spectrum locus does not extend beyond the *YZ*, *YX* or *ZX* planes. Thus at about 570 nm the spectrum locus touches $y = 1 - x$ and at about 500 nm it touches $Y = 1 - Z$ and so on.

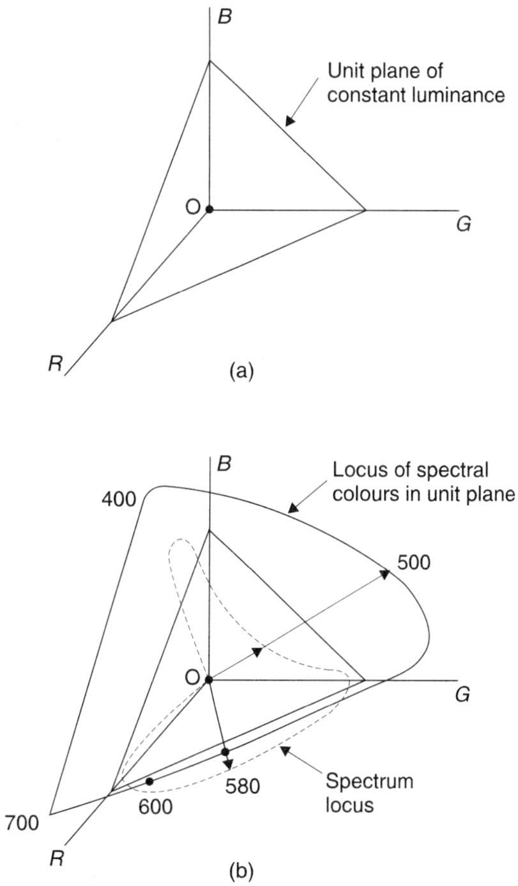

Figure 6.39 (a) A constant luminance plane intersects *RGB* space, allowing colours to be studied in two dimensions only. (b) The intersection of the unit plane by vectors joining the origin and the spectrum locus produces the locus of spectral colours which requires negative values of *R*, *G* and *B* to describe it.

The CIE standard *chromaticity diagram* shown in Figure 6.39(d) is obtained in this way by projecting the unity luminance plane onto the X, Y plane. As luminance has been eliminated by making $x + y + z = 1$, one of these parameters is redundant to describe the colour. By projecting onto the XY plane, the Z axis is the one which is made redundant. As a

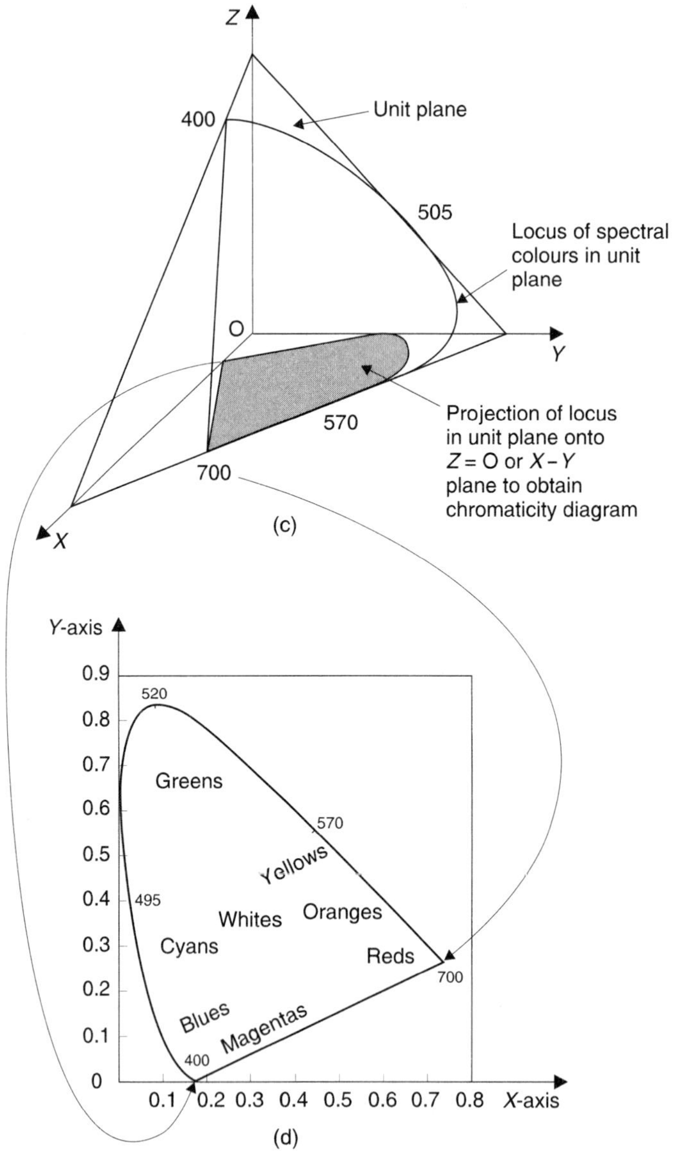

Figure 6.39 (*Continued*) In (c) a new coordinate system, X, Y, Z, is used so that only positive values are required. The spectrum locus now fits entirely in the triangular space where the unit plane intersects these axes. To obtain the CIE chromaticity diagram (d), the locus is projected onto the X–Y plane.

result only two *trichromatic coefficients*, x and y, are needed to convey all possible colours.

It is worth spending some time considering the CIE chromaticity diagram. The curved part of the locus is due to spectral or monochromatic colours over the visible range. The straight base is due to non-spectral colours obtained additively by mixing red and blue. Note that this base is not parallel to the X-axis because the R axis has been turned. It should be clear from Figure 6.40 that because there is a large cyan area outside the primary triangle, a corresponding quantity of 'negative red' is needed to match it. This results in a significant tilt of the R axis being needed to prevent negative values of r going below the ZX plane.

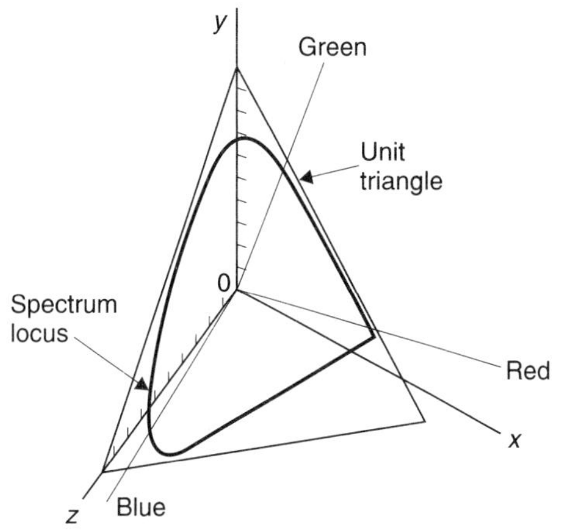

Figure 6.40 The RGB axes of Figure 6.37 are no longer orthogonal in CIE colour space. As shown here, the axes are turned inward sufficiently that no valid combination of R, G and B results in negative values of X,Y or Z.

Although the development of the CIE diagram has been traced starting from a stated set of primaries, it would not make any difference if the tests had been done with another set. For example, if a monochromatic source at 500 nm had been available, Figure 6.41 would apply. There would be a large set of yellows outside the primary triangle and this would have resulted in a large amount of 'negative blue' being needed to match. Thus the (different) RGB axes would still have to be turned in just enough to make them non-negative in XYZ space and this would have resulted in the same diagram.

Although colour is subjective, the independence of the CIE colour diagram from the primaries used to measure it makes it about as objective a tool as there is likely to be. Only colours within the the curve and its straight base exist. Combinations of x and y outside this area are invalid and meaningless. Valid combinations of x and y will be interpreted as the same colour by anyone who has access to the CIE document.

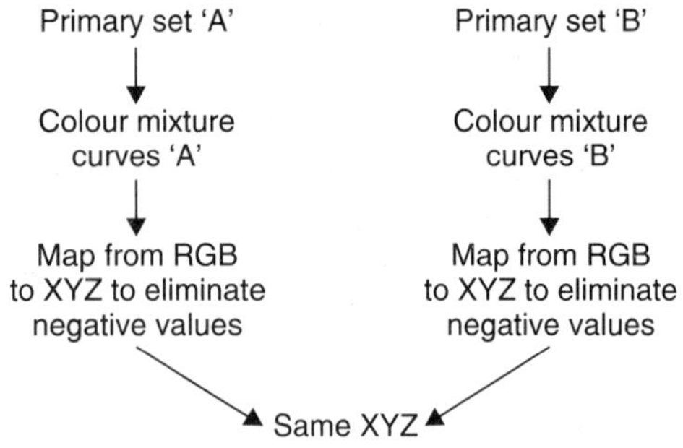

Figure 6.41 Starting with different primaries, the colour mixture curves would be different, but the *RGB* axes would need to be turned in *XYZ* space by a different amount so that the same diagram would result.

The projection chosen has the effect of bringing the red and blue primaries closer together than they are in the $x + y + z = 1$ plane. Thus the main drawback is that equal distances on the diagram do not correspond to equal subjective changes. The distance on the diagram between equal increments of wavelength are greater near the Y axis than elsewhere.

Whites appear in the centre of the chromaticity diagram corresponding to roughly equal amounts of primary colour ($x = y = z = 0.333\ldots$). More will be said about whites in due course. Two terms are used to describe colours: *hue* and *saturation*. Colours having the same hue lie on a straight line between the white point and the perimeter of the primary triangle.

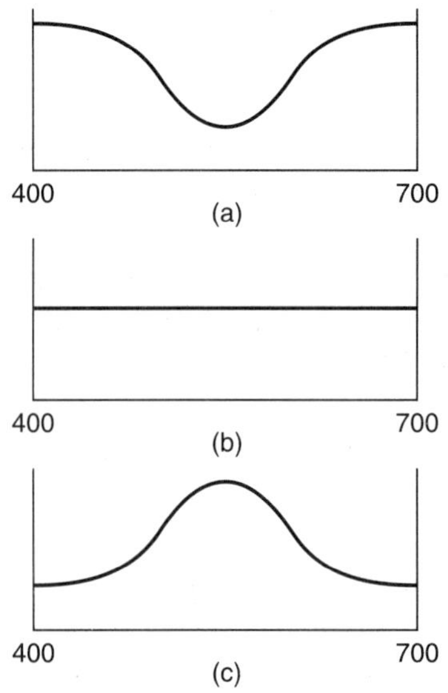

Figure 6.42 (a) The end-weighted spectrum perceived as purple. (b) The flat spectrum perceived as white. (c) The centre weighted spectrum perceived as green.

The saturation of the colour increases with distance from the white point. As an example, pink is a desaturated red. A saturated, or spectral, colour is monochromatic and has a single line spectrum. Desaturation results in an increasing level of energy at all other wavelengths

The peak photopic response of the eye at 550 nm is where the curve touches the line of $y = 1 - x$ at $y = 0.666\ldots, x = 0.333$. As white has the same x coordinate, the complementary colour to peak green must be where $x = 0.333\ldots$ crosses the non-spectral base line. It is useful to consider what happens on ascending this line from purple to green. Figure 6.42(a) shows that on the non-spectral line purple results from significant levels of red and blue but no green. This makes the spectrum end-weighted as shown. Figure 6.42(b) shows that white is due to equal amounts of primary, making the spectrum flat (literally white). Figure 6.42(c) shows that green is due to a centre-weighted spectrum.

6.16 Whites

Whites occupy the centre of the chromaticity diagram. As colour is subjective, there is no single white point. The closest to objectivity that is possible is CIE illuminant E which is defined as having uniform power through the visible spectrum. This corresponds to $x = y = z = 0.3333\ldots$ Figure 6.43 shows the location of various 'white' sources or *illuminants* on the chromaticity diagram. Illuminant A corresponds to the SPD of a

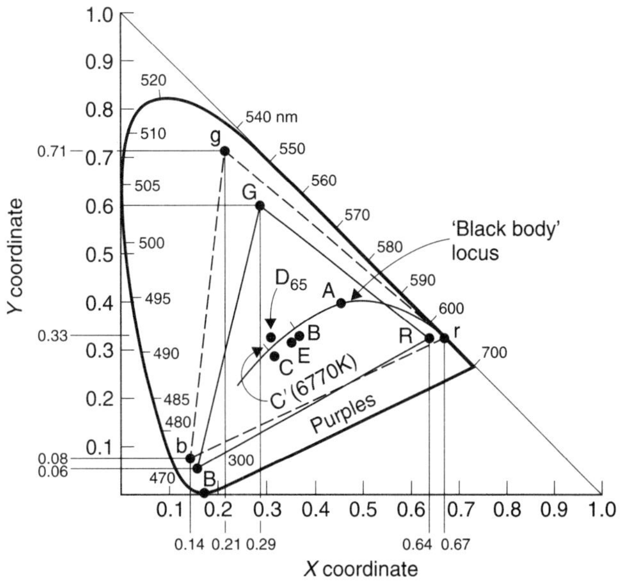

Figure 6.43 Position of various illuminants on the CIE diagram.

tungsten filament lamp having a colour temperature of 3200°K and appears somewhat yellow. Illuminant B corresponds to midday sunlight and illuminant C corresponds to typical daylight which is bluer because it consists of a mixture of sunlight and light scattered by the atmosphere. Illuminants B and C are effectively obsolete and have been replaced by the D series of illuminants which represent various types of daylight. D_{65} is the closest approximation to typical daylight. Colour systems which generate their own light, such as electronic displays, should use D_{65} white. In applications such as colour photographs and printing, the illumination under which the images will be viewed is out of the manufacturer's control. This could be daylight or artificial light and the D_{50} and D_{55} illuminants represent a compromise between natural and tungsten light.

Computer monitors are often used in high ambient lighting levels which requires a bright display. Many computer images are entirely synthetic and colour accuracy is of little consequence. As practical blue phosphors are more efficient than red and green phosphors, it is easy to increase the brightness of a display by incorporating more blue. This leads to a colour temperature of about 9300°K. This is fine for general-purpose computing but of no use at all for colour-imaging work. In this case the monitor will have to be recalibrated by turning down the blue drive signal.

6.17 Colour matching functions

The CIE chromaticity diagram eliminates brightness changes by considering only x and y. In a real sensing device, measuring x, y and z would allow brightness to be measured as well as the colour. Such a sensor must have three sensing elements, each having a different filtering effect or sensitivity with respect to wavelength. These filter specifications are known as colour matching functions which must be consistent with the derivation of the CIE diagram. In fact the way the CIE diagram is designed makes one of the colour matching functions, y, take the shape of the luminous efficiency function. Effectively y has the same spectral response as a monochrome camera would need in order to give the correct brightness for objects of any colour. The addition of x and z allow the hue and saturation of an object to be conveyed.

Figure 6.44 shows some examples of how the colour matching functions follow from the CIE diagram. It must be recalled that the valid region of the diagram is actually a projection of a plane given by $x + y + z = 1$. Thus for any spectral colour on the CIE diagram, the necessary values of x and y can be read off and the value of z can be calculated by a simple subtraction from 1. Plotting x, y and z against wavelength gives

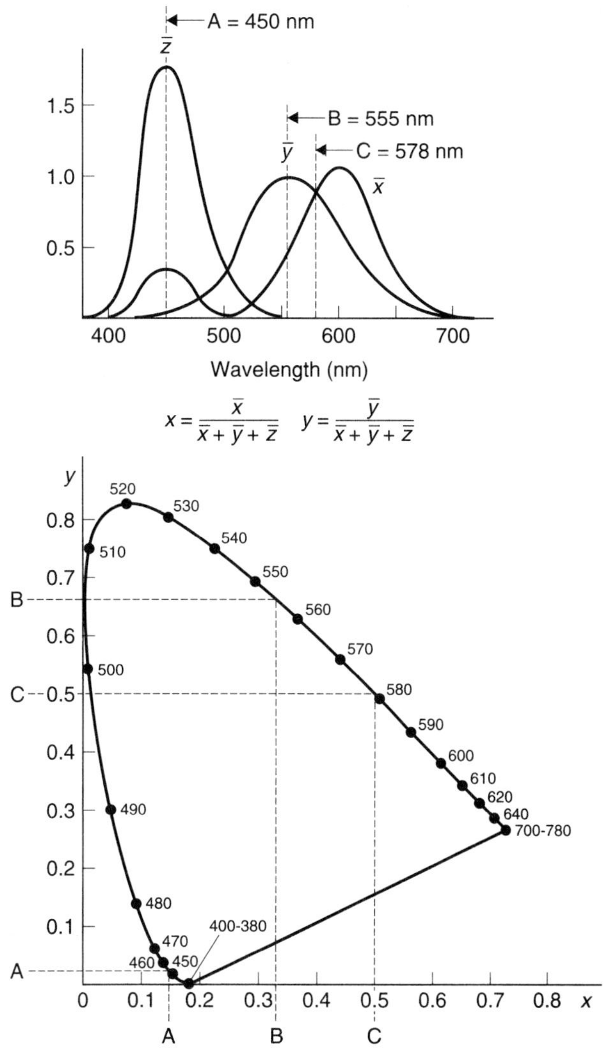

For point A at 450 nm, $\bar{z} = 1.75$ $\bar{x} = 0.35$ $\bar{y} = 0.05$

$$x = \frac{0.35}{0.35 + 0.05 + 1.75} = 0.16 \qquad y = \frac{0.05}{0.35 + 0.05 + 1.75} = 0.02$$

For point B at 555 nm, $\bar{z} = 0$ $\bar{x} = 0.5$ $\bar{y} = 1.0$

$$x = \frac{0.5}{0.5 + 1 + 0} = 0.33 \qquad y = \frac{1.0}{0.5 + 1 + 0} = 0.66$$

For point C at 578 nm, $\bar{z} = 0$ $\bar{x} = 0.87$ $\bar{y} = 0.87$

$$x = \frac{0.87}{0.87 + 0.87 + 0} = 0.5 \qquad y = \frac{0.87}{0.87 + 0.87 + 0} = 0.5$$

Figure 6.44 Deriving colour matching functions from the CIE diagram. For each x and y, the value of z can be calculated as $x + y + z = 1$.

the shape of the colour matching functions. These are then normalized so that at the peak of the y response the distribution coefficient has a value of unity.

Note that the three colour matching functions are positive only and so it is technically possible to make a three-sensor camera equipped with filters having these functions which can capture every nuance of colour that the HVS can perceive in the three output signals.

It does *not* follow that a display can be made having three light sources to which these signals are directly connected. The primaries necessary accurately to produce a display directly from xyz tristimuli cannot be implemented because they are outside the valid region of the colour diagram and do not exist.

6.18 Choice of primaries

In order to produce all possible colours, the CIE xyz tristimulus signal would have to control a display which was capable of generating a colour anywhere within the valid region of the chromaticity diagram. Strictly this would require tunable light sources which could produce monochromatic light at any visible wavelength. These are not commercially available and instead the most common solution is to provide only three primary colours loosely called red, green and blue, which are not necessarily monochromatic. Only colours within the triangle joining the primaries can be reproduced and clearly efforts should be made to obtain primaries which embrace as large an area as possible. Figure 6.45 shows how the colour range or gamut of television compares with paint and

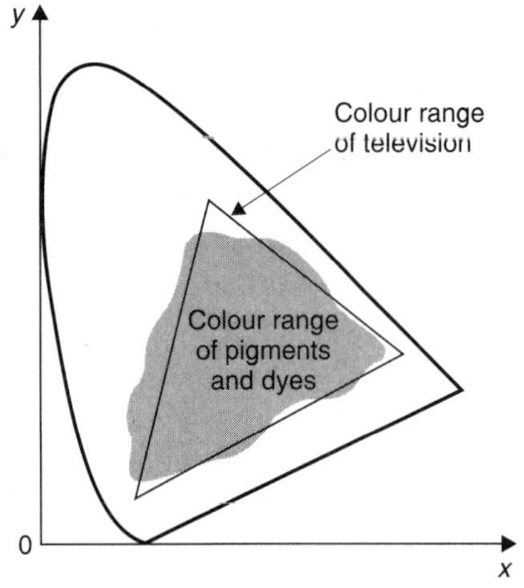

Figure 6.45 Comparison of the colour range of television and printing.

printing inks and illustrates that the comparison is favourable. Most everyday scenes fall within the colour gamut of television. Exceptions include saturated turquoise, spectrally pure iridescent colours formed by interference in duck's feathers or reflections in Compact Discs. For special purposes displays have been made having four primaries to give a wider colour range, but these are uncommon.

Figure 6.46 shows the primaries initially selected for NTSC. However, manufacturers looking for brighter displays substituted more efficient phosphors having a smaller colour range. This was later standardized as the SMPTE C phosphors using CIE D_{65} white. These were also adopted for PAL as ITU Rec. 709. In principle, the use of lasers as primaries is beneficial because they produce monochromatic light which, by definition, must be on the perimeter of the CIE diagram.

Once the primaries have been selected from those available, the next step is to determine how they can be driven. In principle, the CIE *xyz* tristimuli can be converted into primary drive signals using a suitable signal processor programmed with the necessary geometry. For any *xyz* triple, a given location on the chromaticity diagram would be addressed and this could be converted to the appropriate combinations of *RGB*. This

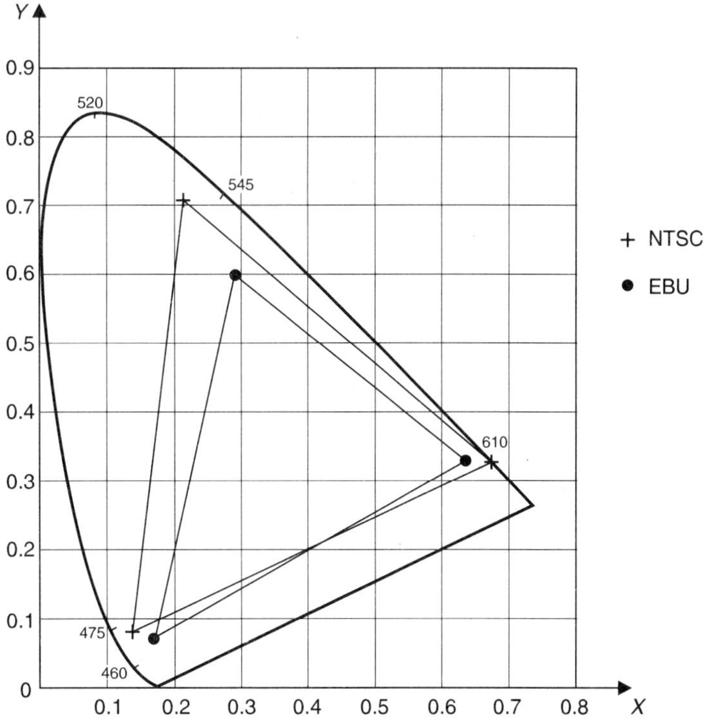

Figure 6.46 The primary colours for NTSC were initially as shown. These were later changed to more efficient phosphors which were also adopted for PAL. See text.

is only possible within the triangle formed by the primaries. Outside the triangle the mathematically correct result would be that one or more of the *RGB* signals would be negative, but as this is non-realizable, they would simply be clipped to zero.

It is possible to conceive of a display having more than three primaries which would offer a wider colour gamut. In this case the signal processor would convert the CIE *xyz* tristimuli into any convenient metamer of the true colour. In other words over a large part of the chromaticity diagram there will be more than one combination of four or more primaries which would give the same perceived result. As the primaries are approached, the possibility for metamerism falls.

The advantage of using the CIE *xyz* analysis functions is that the full colour gamut is inherent in the video signal and any recordings made of it. The visible gamut is limited only by the available display. If in the future displays with wider gamut become economic, existing video recordings would be displayed more realistically.

In traditional colour television systems this approach has not been taken. Television was perceived as an entertainment medium in which strict accuracy was not needed and the high cost of implementing CIE colour matching functions in cameras to produce accurate signals could not be justified if the accuracy could not be displayed. Thus for technical purposes conventional television cameras may be unsuitable.

Instead, traditional television cameras use colour matching functions which are easy to implement and compatible with the limited gamut of the standardized phosphors. Certain colours are not theoretically reproduceable, and those colours that are reproduced are often distorted to some extent. The approach used in television will be considered in Chapter 7.

References

1. Hosokawa, T., Mikami, K. and Saito, K., Basic study of the portable fatigue meter: effects of illumination, distance from eyes and age. *Ergonomics*, **40**, 887–894 (1997)
2. Poynton, C., *A Technical Introduction to Digital Video*, New York: John Wiley (1996)

7

Image portrayal

7.1 Introduction

This complex subject is difficult to approach because of the extensive interrelations between different areas. Figure 7.1 illustrates the number of dimensions involved. An image is two-dimensional and so there are the horizontal and vertical picture axes to consider. In film, the picture is continuous and sampling occurs only in the time axis. In analog television, the horizontal axis of the picture is continuous but the vertical axis is sampled into lines. In digital imaging the picture will be sampled in both axes to produce an array of pixels having a certain resolution. This chapter includes the theory necessary to link pixel counts to resolution.

In a monochrome image, each pixel describes a single quantity, namely the brightness. The range of this quantity determines the maximum contrast. At the bottom of the range there will be a noise floor. The relationship between the numerical value and the brightness may be linear or non-linear. In a coloured image each pixel becomes a vector, or multi-dimensional quantity which describes the hue and saturation in some way in addition to the brightness.

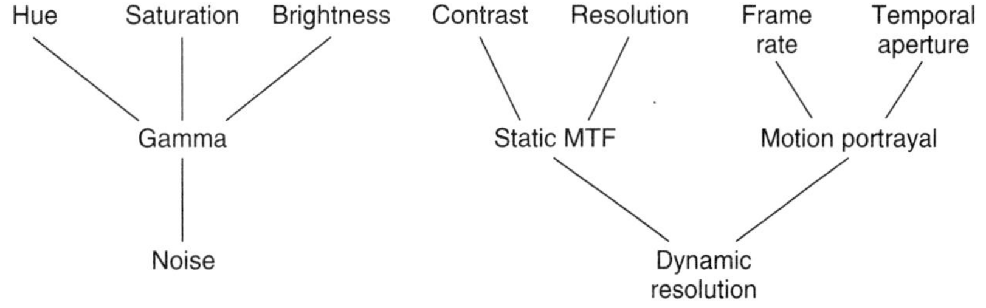

Figure 7.1 The dimensions involved in moving-image portrayal.

If motion is to be portrayed, the picture must be updated at the picture rate. Of course, the term 'moving pictures' is a misnomer; the pictures don't move at all, but instead attempt to create an illusion of movement in the mind of the viewer with varying degrees of success. A moving object simply adopts a different location in each picture. The object is not moving along the time axis, but along a fourth axis known as the optic flow axis. The optic flow axis is identified by motion-compensated standards convertors to eliminate judder and also by noise reducers and MPEG compressors because the greatest similarity from one picture to the next is along that axis. The success of these devices is testimony to the importance of the theory which will be considered in some depth here.

7.2 Film

Film is the oldest of the moving image-portrayal systems and standards were established well before any scientific understanding existed. Originally, 35 mm 'silent' film ran at a 18 frames per second, but on the introduction of 'talking pictures' it was found that the bandwidth of the linear optically modulated soundtrack was inadequate and the frame rate was raised to 24 Hz. Thus no psycho-optic criteria were used in determining the frame rate of film.

It is often stated that the resolution available from film cannot be matched by electronic imaging techniques, but this is only true if static resolution is considered and even then digital imaging is an advancing art. The very fine grain structure of the latest cinema film stock gives extremely high static resolution, but unfortunately the viewer cannot enjoy it.

It is impossible to project film at 24 Hz because the extreme flicker is too distressing. The conventional solution is shown in Figure 7.2. The projector has a pulldown mechanism which replaces one frame with the next while a rotating shutter cuts off the light. This shutter is fitted with two blades instead of one so that the light is admitted twice per frame.

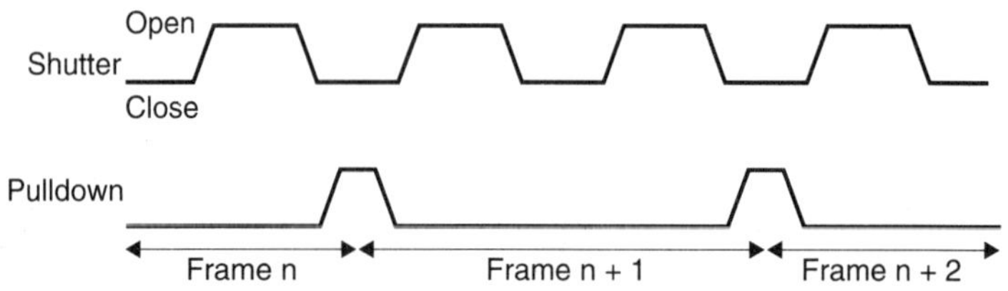

Figure 7.2 In conventional film projection, the shutter is opened twice for each film frame so that with a frame rate of 24 Hz, a flicker frequency of 48 Hz is seen.

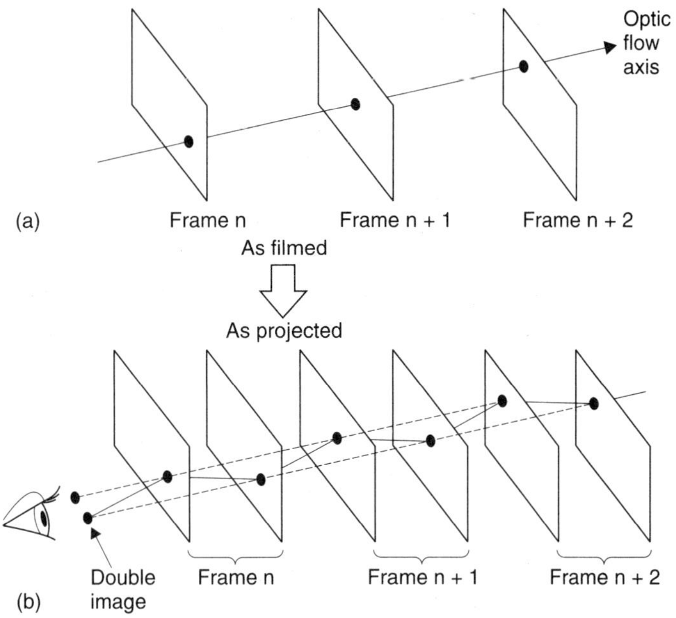

Figure 7.3 (a) The optic flow axis of the original scene is distorted by the double projection of each frame. (b) A tracking eye sees a double image in the presence of motion.

This raises the flicker frequency to 48 Hz, which is desirable, but a number of undesirable artifacts are also introduced.

Figure 7.3(a) shows that when an object moves, the frame repeat mechanism does not portray the motion properly. Instead of an accurate portrayal of the position of the object at 48 Hz, the position in each frame is simply repeated. The optic flow axis is not smooth, but is distorted. When the eye attempts to track a moving object, Figure 7.3(b) shows that the result will be a double image. The effect depends on the speed of motion.

At low speeds, the eye sees two images superimposed with a slight shift. This has the effect of cancelling out high-frequency detail in the direction of motion so the resolution is reduced. At higher speeds, two distinct images are seen.

A further effect of frame repeat is that although flicker rate is 48 Hz, the rate at which a new background location is presented is only 24 Hz. The result is that background strobing (see section 6.11) is extremely obvious.

The already limited dynamic resolution of film is further reduced by the phenomena of weave and hop. Weave is where the film moves laterally in the camera or projector and hop is where the film is not pulled down by exactly the same distance every frame. Film frames can also bow during projection so that they are not flat. This has the effect of a slight variation in magnification.

The larger film formats, such as 70 mm, primarily look better because the projector doesn't need such high magnification and the effect of weave and hop is reduced. It is also easier to get adequate light through the larger frames. Mike Todd, the developer of the Todd-AO 70 mm film standard, was aware of the dynamic problems of film and wanted to raise the frame rate to 30 Hz. To this day 70 mm projectors are still capable of running at 30 Hz, but Hollywood conservatism meant that the frame rate soon reverted to 24 Hz to make it easier to release films in both formats.

Although the reasons for these artifacts may not be understood, their existence certainly is. Cinematographers have to film in such a way that these artifacts are moderated. As film cannot portray rapid motion, cameras have to mounted very solidly and they must use fluid-damped pan and tilt bearings. Zooms must be very slow. Tracking shots are used where the camera travels at the same speed as the dominant action. The camera will often be mounted on a wheeled dolly for this purpose, and outdoors temporary rails will be laid to allow smooth tracking.

The serious level of background strobing is addressed by using a very large lens aperture to give a shallow depth of field. This requires the continuous attention of the focus puller, but puts the background out of focus, masking the effect of the 24 Hz strobing. Unfortunately in bright light the use of a large aperture results in a short exposure for each frame. This has the effect of making the background strobing more obvious because the short exposure reduces the amount of smear. A better result may be obtained by using a neutral density filter so that the large aperture can be retained with a longer exposure. The techniques needed to overcome the basic limitations of frame repeat have led to the 'film look'.

The gulf between static and dynamic resolution in film means that the actual resolution needed in electronic projections systems does not have to be very high to give a similar experience to the viewer.

The frames of early formats were not far from square in order to operate within the limited coverage of early lenses. To combat the competition from television, cinema adopted a wider screen format, but it went about it exactly the wrong way, using anamorphic lenses on camera and projector which squeezed the subject laterally onto the film and expanded it again during projection. Anamorphic optics place great demands on the film resolution in the horizontal axis, which is wasted in the vertical axis. The reason that the cinema industry got away with using anamorphic optics was partly because the dynamic resolution was so poor the loss was masked.

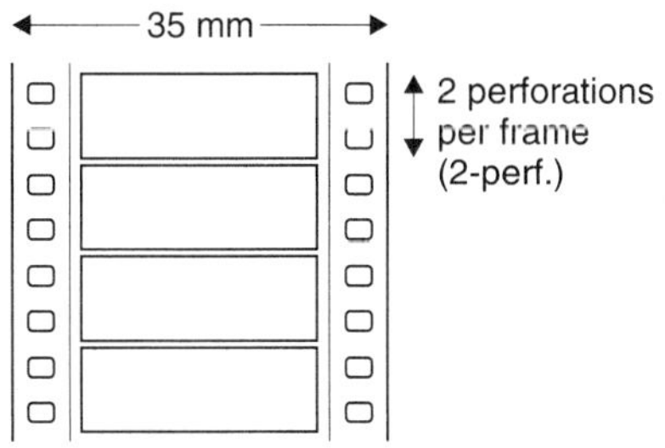

Figure 7.4 A film format suitable for convergent systems. The frame height is halved to create a wide frame without anamorphic optics and to allow a suitable frame rate without increasing the film speed.

Figure 7.4 shows a film format which is more appropriate to convergent systems. The conventional 35 mm four-perf. frame is effectively cut in half to produce a two-perf. format. This is an existing film format. Two-perf. has a number of advantages. It allows the frame rate to be doubled without increasing the film speed and it allows widescreen frames without the use of anamorphic optics. It might be thought that there would be a loss of static resolution due to the smaller frames, but this is not the case. To maintain resolution anamorphic film frames need to be bigger by the anamorphic ratio. For example, with 2:1 anamorphism, the film grain limits the horizontal resolution, whereas the vertical resolution is twice as good as it needs to be, meaning that half of the film area is wasted.

Two-perf. film running at 48, 50 or 60 Hz allows direct projection with a single blade shutter giving precise re-creation of motion and allowing the dynamic resolution to rise dramatically. The visibility of film grain is reduced because the grain in each frame is different and the higher frame rate allows the temporal filtering of the eye to operate. Such a format is also directly compatible with television standards.

Colour is obtained in film projection by subtractive filtering. White light from the projector's lamp passes through three different layers in the film in turn. Each layer is designed to attenuate a certain portion of the spectrum according to the density of the layer. If all the layers have maximum density, no light can pass. Variations in the relative density of the three layers allow different colours to be shown.

Colour accuracy in film is rather poor, but film manufacturers strive to make their product consistent so that the colour rendering stays the same for the entire movie. When film is transferred to the video or data domains, it is almost certain that the colour will appear distorted in some way and a process known as colour correction will be needed to give acceptable results.

7.3 Spatial sampling

Spatial sampling is a two-dimensional version of sampling, but Shannon's theory still applies. For the highest quality and realism, there must be no visible sampling artifacts. In legacy television sytems, there has always been a tradeoff between resolution and the level of artifacts such as aliasing and visible line structure. This was acceptable at the time these systems were designed over fifty years ago, but today it does not have to be accepted.

Figure 7.5 shows that to eliminate sampling artifacts requires a formal approach to Shannon perfect reconstruction as was introduced in Chapter 4. There must be a spatial anti-aliasing filter mechanism associated with the image sensor and a spatial reconstruction filter mechanism associated with the display. These filters and the sampling rate used must be specified at the same time to give the required resolution.

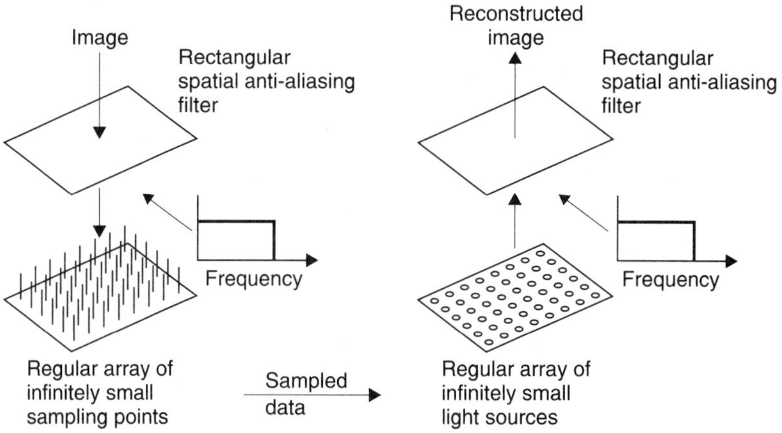

Figure 7.5 Ideal reconstruction of sampled images requires the approach shown here. This is impossible for several reasons discussed in the text.

It is desirable to prevent spatial aliasing, since the result is visually irritating. CCD sensors can alias in both horizontal and vertical dimensions, and so an anti-aliasing optical filter may be fitted between the lens and the sensor of a conventional camera. This takes the form of a plate which diffuses the image formed by the lens. Such a device can never have a sharp cut-off, and so there are effectively two choices. If aliasing is permitted, the theoretical information rate of the system can be approached. If aliasing is prevented, the information conveyed is below system capacity.

These considerations also apply at the television display. The display ought to filter out spatial frequencies above one half the spatial sampling rate. In a conventional CRT this means that a vertical optical filter should be fitted in front of the screen to render the raster invisible. Again the poor slope of a simply realizable filter would attenuate too much of the wanted spectrum, and so the technique is not used.

As the eye is axisymmetric, the resolution in the horizontal and vertical axes is the same and this would suggest that the vertical and horizontal sample spacing should also be the same. This is the origin of the term 'square pixels' shown in Figure 7.6(a) in which samples are taken in rows and columns on a grid. Transform duality suggests that the resulting two-dimensional spectrum will also have a grid structure. The corresponding spectrum is shown in (b). The baseband spectrum is in the centre of the diagram, and the repeating sampling sideband spectrum extends vertically and horizontally. The star-shaped spectrum is purely symbolic and results from viewing an image of a man-made object such as a building containing primarily horizontal and vertical elements. A pastoral scene would result in a more circular or elliptical spectrum. In order to return to the baseband image, the sidebands must be filtered out with a two-dimensional spatial filter. The shape of the two-dimensional frequency response shown in Figure 7.6(c) is known as a Brillouin zone.

Figure 7.6(d) shows an alternative sampling site matrix known as quincunx sampling because of the similarity to the pattern of five dots on a die. The resultant spectrum has the same characteristic pattern as shown in (e). Quincuncx sampling offers more possibilities for the shape of the Brillouin zones. Any shape which will tesselate can in principle be used. Figure 7.6(f) shows a diamond-shaped zone, whereas (g) shows cross-shaped zones. Clearly none of these two-dimensional frequency responses can be implemented in optical filters, but they can be implemented in the digital domain following optical sampling at higher rates.

Quincunx sampling attracted attention at one time because it has some interesting properties. Considering the horizontal azis, the highest horizontal frequency in the baseband is more than half of the horizontal sampling rate, as is the case for the vertical axis. We appear to be violating sampling theory, hence the term 'sub-Nyquist sampling' which will be found in connection with quincunx sampling. In fact there is no violation whatsoever, simply a compromise. The increase in horizontal and vertical resolution is achieved at the expense of reduced diagonal resolution.

Taking Nyquist spatial sampling one axis at a time doesn't convey the whole truth. It may be appropriate to have an additional criterion for two dimensions as follows: 'When sampling in two dimensions, the product of the vertical and horizontal sampling rates must be at least four times the product of the vertical and horizontal spatial bandwidths.'

Once this is appreciated, it becomes clear that sub-Nyquist sampling is an oxymoron. Quincunx sampling causes practical difficulties because it does not fit conveniently with data arrays in computing or with many types of sensor or display, although certain digital cameras for still images use quincunx sensors. With the development of compression techniques such as MPEG, the pressure to reduce sampling rates by arcane sampling methods disappeared.

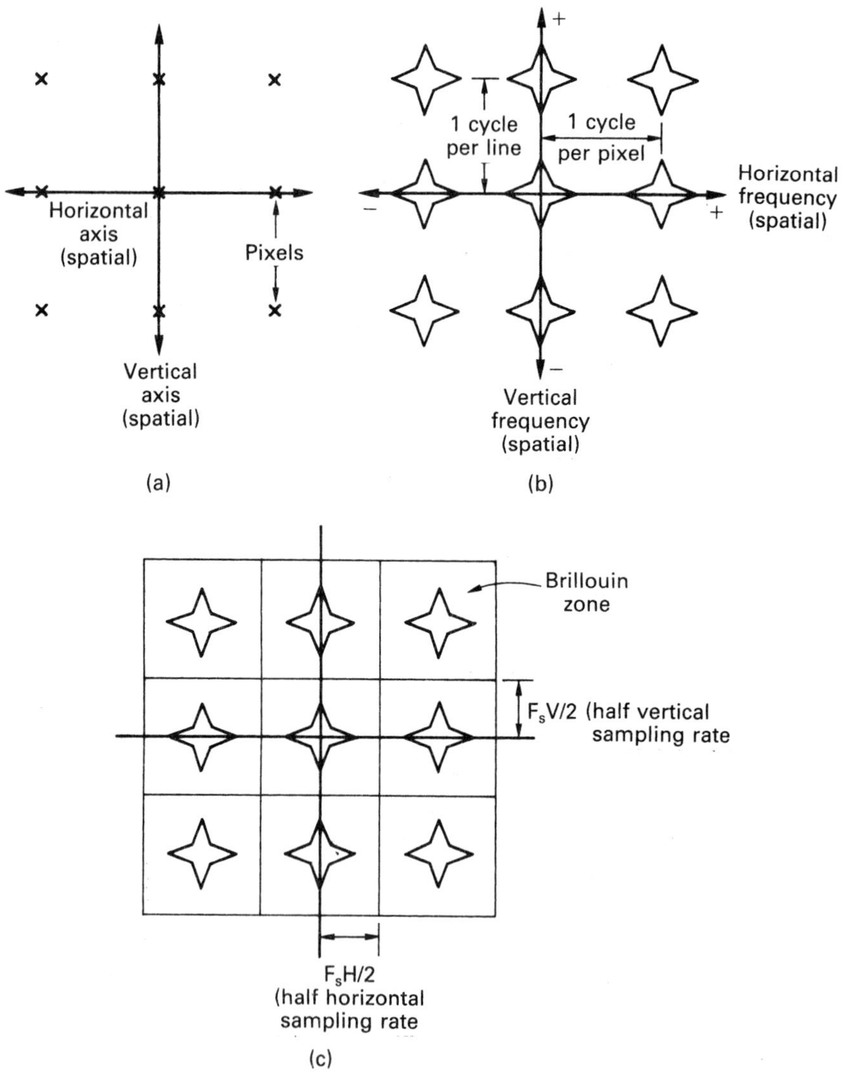

Figure 7.6 Image sampling spectra. The rectangular array of (a) has a spectrum shown at (b) having a rectangular repeating structure. Filtering to return to the baseband requires a two-dimensional filter whose response lies within the Brillouin zone shown at (c).

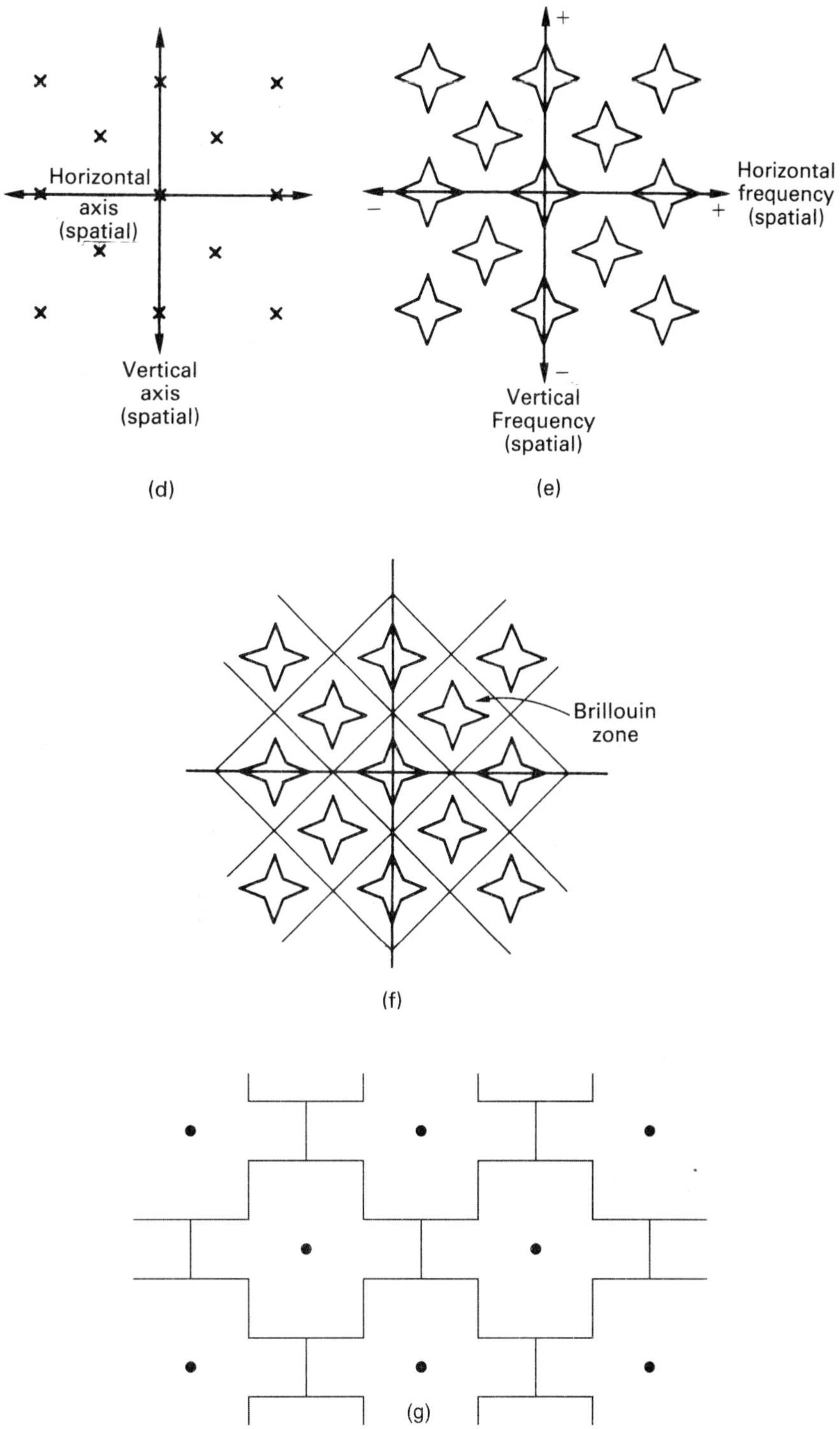

Figure 7.6 (*Continued*) Quincunx sampling is shown at (d) to have a similar spectral structure (e). An appropriate Brillouin zone is required as at (f). (g) An alternative Brillouin zone for quincunx sampling.

7.4 Spatial aperture effect

Figure 7.7(a) shows a test image consisting of alternating black and white bars. Considered as a spatial waveform, the modulation is a square wave which contains an indefinite series of odd harmonics in addition to the fundamental. This infinite bandwidth cannot be passed by any lens or sensor. Figure 7.7(b) shows that in practice the lens and sensor will both suffer from an aperture effect in addition to the effect of any deliberate anti-aliasing filter. These effects mean that conventional Nyquist rate sampling of images always gives relatively poor performance. The resolution achieved in practice is always significantly less than the pixel count would suggest.

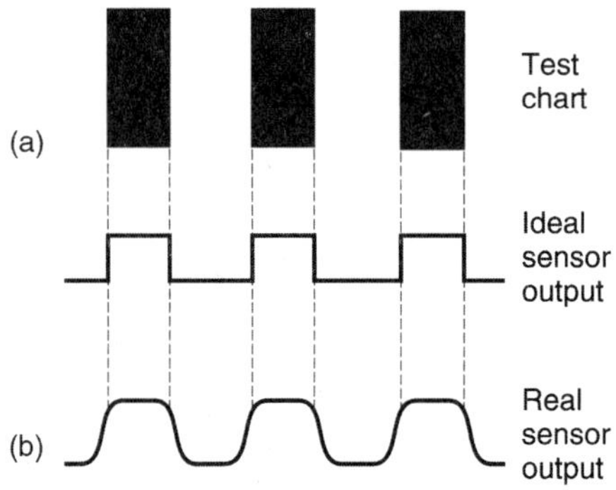

Figure 7.7 Ideal test image at (a) consists of alternating black and white bars. After the aperture effects of the lens and the sensor have been considered, there will be considerable softening of the edges corresponding to a loss of high spatial frequencies.

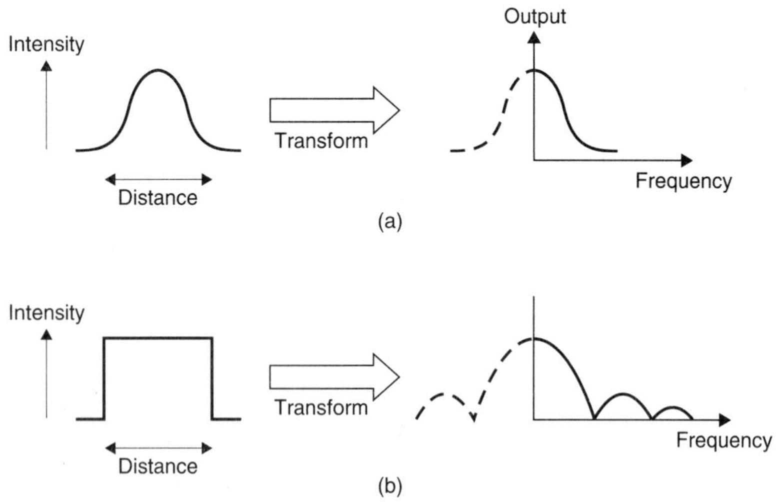

Figure 7.8 (a) CRT spot has a Gaussian intensity distribution and a Gaussian spatial frequency response. (b) CCD pixel has a rectangular aperture and a $\sin x/x$ spatial frequency response.

As the MTF of an aperture effect is given by the Fourier transform of the aperture function, analysis in the frequency domain must give a consistent result. The spatial frequency spectrum of the output can be obtained by multiplying the input spectrum by the frequency response of the lens and sensor.

Figure 7.8 shows some examples. At (a) the Fourier transform of a Gaussian impulse is seen also to be Gaussian. A cathode ray tube with a spot having a Gaussian intensity distribution will also have a Gaussian spatial frequency response. At (b) a CCD camera has discrete square sensors and a rectangular aperture function. Its frequency response will be the Fourier transform of a rectangle, which is a $\sin x/x$ function.

7.5 Spatial oversampling

Oversampling means using a sampling rate which is greater (generally substantially greater) than the Nyquist rate. As was seen in Chapter 4, sampling only works at the Nyquist rate if the samples are taken and reproduced as points with ideal filtering. In real imaging systems, samples are sensed and reproduced as finite areas and ideal optical filters are impossible. Oversampling allows these sensor issues substantially to be overcome.

Figure 7.9 shows how spatial oversampling can be used to increase the resolution of an imaging system. Assuming a 720 × 400 pixel system, Figure 7.9(a) shows that the aperture effect would result in an early roll-off of the MTF. Instead a 1440 × 800 pixel sensor is used, having a response shown at (b). This outputs four times as much data, but if these data are passed into a two-dimensional low-pass filter which decimates by a factor of two in each axis, the original bit rate will be obtained once more. This will be a digital filter which can have arbitrarily accurate peformance, including a flat passband and steep cut-off slope. The combination of the aperture effect of the 1440 × 800 pixel camera and the

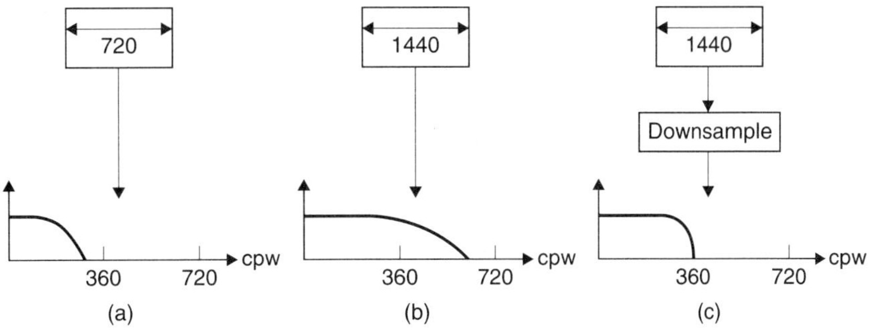

Figure 7.9 Spatial oversampling in a sensor. At (a) 720 × 400 pixel sensor and its spatial frequency response. (b) 1440 × 800 pixel sensor and response. (c) Output of sensor (b) after downsampling to 720 × 400 pixels.

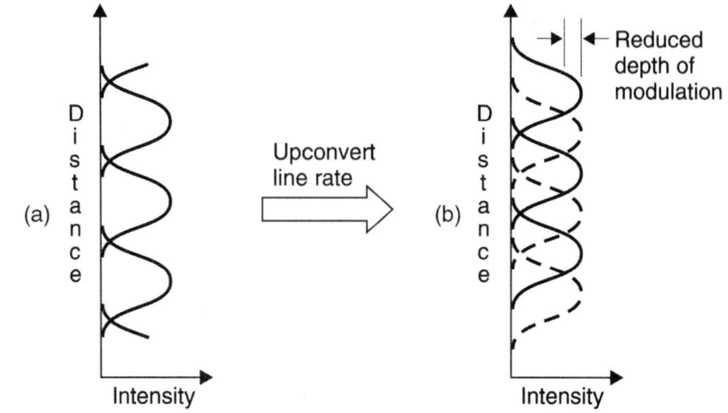

Figure 7.10 Spatial oversampling in a display. At (a) with conventional CRT display the line structure is visible and the spatial frequency response is impaired. At (b) an interpolator doubles the number of lines. The overlap of the intensity functions renders the raster less visible and improves the spatial frequency response.

LPF gives a spatial frequency response which is shown in (c). This is better than could be achieved with a 720 × 400 camera. The improvement in subjective quality is quite noticeable in practice.

In the case of display technology, oversampling can also be used, this time to render the raster or pixels invisible and to improve the aperture of the display. Once more a filter is required, but this now, for example, doubles the number of input pixels in each axis using interpolation. Again the filter can have arbitrarily high accuracy. The aperture effect of the display does not affect the passband of the input signal because of the use of oversampling, but it can instead be used to reduce the visibility of the line structure. Figure 7.10 shows that if the number of lines is doubled in an interpolator, the intensity function of the CRT spot is not halved in diameter, but is reduced by a smaller amount. The partial overlapping of the intensity functions reduces the depth of modulation at the new artificially small line spacing.

Figure 7.11 shows a system in which oversampling is used at both ends of the channel to obtain a higher resolution without increasing the channel data rate.

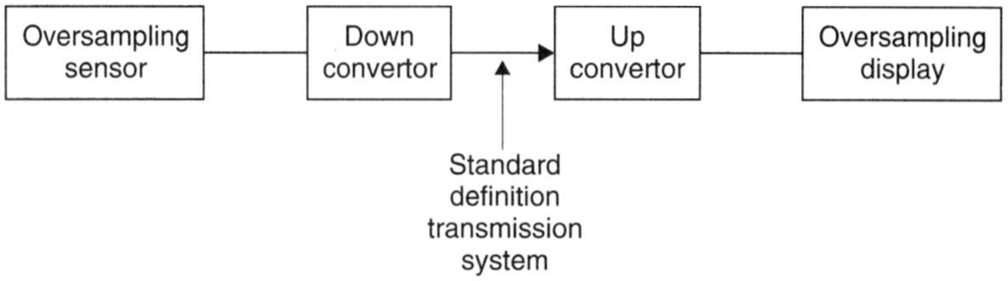

Figure 7.11 An oversampling television system in which both display and camera oversample so that an existing line standard can be used. Techniques such as this have effectively made high-definition television broadcasting unnecessary.

7.6 Temporal aperture effects

The conventional view of sampled moving images is that shown in Figure 7.12(a) in which there are three axes, vertical, horizontal and temporal. These orthogonal axes would suggest that what happens in, for example, the time axis does not affect the image plane. This is inadequate to explain the experience of the human viewer. It might be thought that the temporal sampling process could be returned to the continuous time domain by a temporal filter. In fact temporal filters destroy image quality in the presence of motion and should be avoided. The only acceptable temporal filter in a moving image-portrayal system is the persistence of vision of the eye. Although this is temporal with respect to the eye, the fact that the eye can track means that persistence of vision does not filter on the time axis of the display.

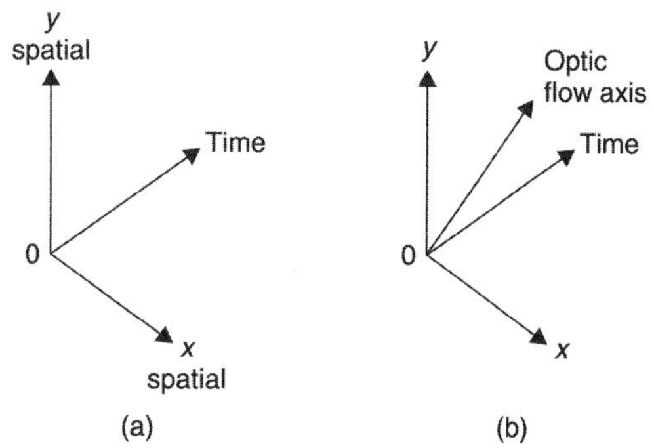

Figure 7.12 (a) The conventional view of image-portrayal systems is that everything can be explained in three axes, x, y and time. This is inadequate and (b) shows that the optic flow axis is necessary to explain how a tracking eye perceives motion portrayal.

Figure 7.12(b) shows that it is necessary to consider a fourth axis, namely the optic flow axis. The optic flow axis is not parallel to the time axis when there is motion. The HVS is watching along the optic flow axis and because it is not orthogonal to the image plane, it has a component in the image plane. Thus temporal filtering in the system *does not* have the same effect as persistence of vision.

The result is that events on the time axis can affect the image. Figure 7.13(a) shows that the ideal mechanism is for the image to be captured and displayed at a single vanishingly short point on the time axis, as the perfect reconstruction theory of sampling would suggest. In practice this is not possible, as finite light energy has to fall on all sensors and be created by all displays and this takes time. The result is a temporal aperture effect. Figure 7.13(b) shows that this reflects in the optic flow

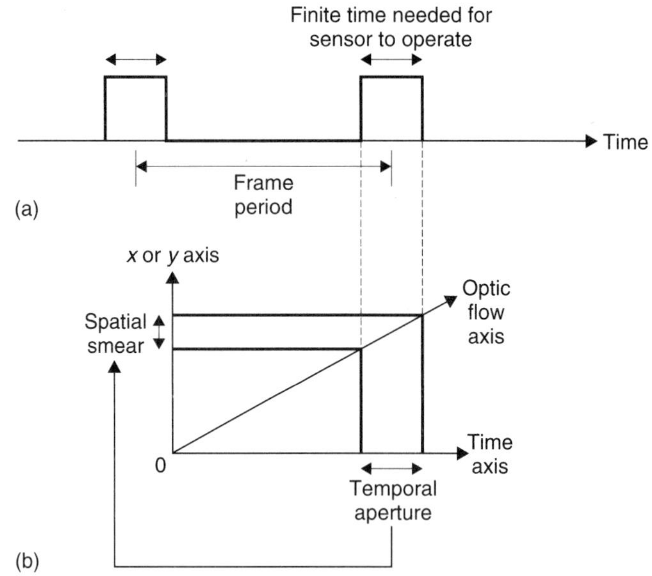

Figure 7.13 (a) Ideal sampling requires images to be sampled in an instant. This is impossible as all practical sensors require finite time to operate. This sampling time is a temporal aperture effect. As (b) shows, the temporal aperture reflects in the optic flow axis to cause image smear on the sensor.

axis to cause smear in the image plane which reduces resolution in moving objects.

The eye can resolve detail in moving objects by tracking and there is no fundamental reason why this should not be possible in a well-engineered image-portrayal system. These are, however, extremely rare. In most systems the level of motion-induced artifacts is so high that it is often better deliberately to induce smear to disguise what is happening. This is so common that it has led to the misguided belief that there will always be motion blur.

7.7 Analog video

It is difficult to convey two-dimensional images from one place to another directly, whereas electrical and radio signals are easily carried. The problem is to convert a two-dimensional image into a single voltage changing with time. The solution is to use the principle of scanning shown in Figure 7.14(a). The camera produces a *video signal* whose voltage is a function of the image brightness at a single point on the sensor. This voltage is converted back to the brightness of the same point on the display. The points on the sensor and display must be scanned synchronously if the picture is to be re-created properly. If this is done rapidly enough it is largely invisible to the eye. Figure 7.14(b) shows that the scanning is controlled by a triangular or *sawtooth* waveform in each dimension which causes a constant speed forward scan followed by a rapid return or *flyback*. As the horizontal scan is much more rapid than the vertical scan the image is broken up into lines which are not quite horizontal.

In the example of Figure 7.14(b), the horizontal scanning frequency or *line rate*, F_h, is an integer multiple of the vertical scanning frequency or *frame rate* and a *progressive scan* system results in which every frame is identical. Figure 7.14(c) shows an *interlaced scan* system in which there is an integer number of lines in *two* vertical scans or *fields*. The first field begins with a full line and ends on a half line and the second field begins with a half line and ends with a full line. The lines from the two fields interlace or mesh on the screen. Terrestrial analog broadcast systems such

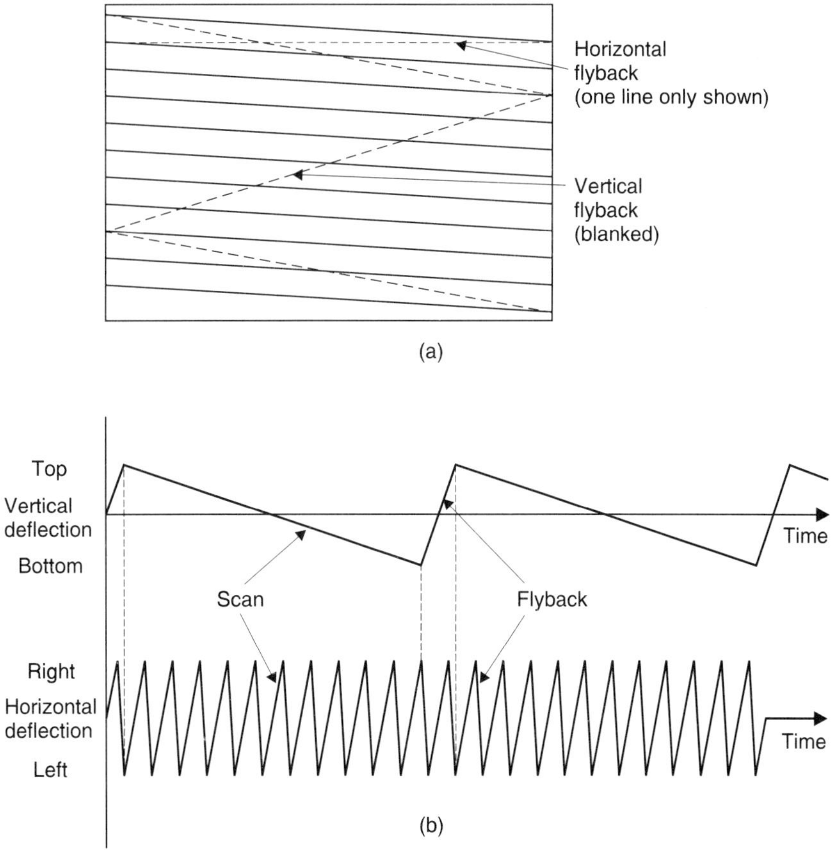

Figure 7.14 Scanning converts two-dimensional images into a signal which can be sent electrically. In (a) the scanning of camera and display must be identical. The scanning is controlled by horizontal and vertical sawtooth waveforms (b).

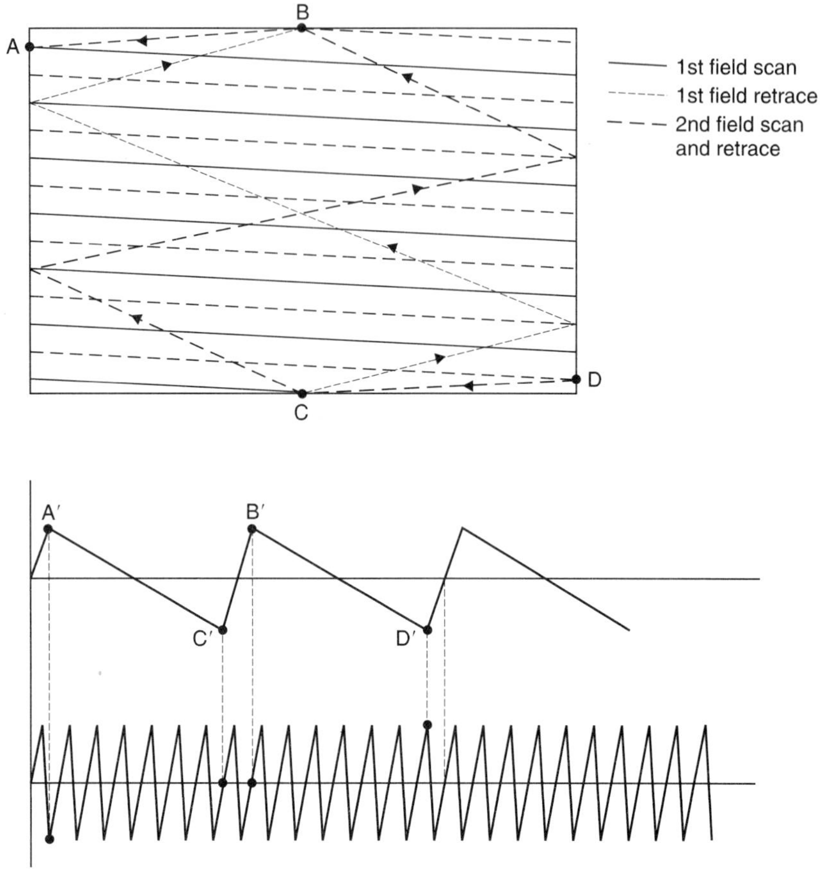

(c)

Figure 7.14 (*Continued*) Where two vertical scans are needed to complete a whole number of lines, the scan is interlaced as shown in (c). The frame is now split into two fields.

as PAL and NTSC use interlace. The additional complication of interlace has both merits and drawbacks which will be discussed in section 7.10.

7.8 Synchronizing

It is vital that the horizontal and vertical scanning at the camera is simultaneously replicated at the display. This is the job of the *synchronizing* or sync system which must send timing information to the display alongside the video signal. In very early television equipment this was achieved using two quite separate or *non-composite* signals. Figure 7.15(a) shows one of the first (US) television signal standards in which the video waveform had an amplitude of 1 volt peak to peak and the sync signal had an amplitude of 4 volts peak to peak. In practice, it was more convenient to combine both into a single electrical waveform then called *composite video* which carries the synchronizing information as well as the scanned brightness signal. The single signal is effectively shared by using some of the flyback period for synchronizing. The 4 volt sync signal was attenuated by a factor of ten and added to the video to produce a 1.4 volt peak to peak signal. This was the origin of the 10:4 video:sync relationship of US television practice. Later the amplitude was reduced to 1 volt peak to peak so that the signal had the same range as the original non-composite video. The 10:4 ratio was retained. As Figure 7.15(b) shows, this ratio results in some rather odd voltages and to simplify matters, a new unit called the *IRE* unit (after the Institute of Radio Engineers) was devised. Originally this was defined as 1 per cent of the video voltage swing, independent of the actual amplitude in use, but it came in practice to mean 1 per cent of 0.714 volt. In European systems shown in Figure 7.15(c) the messy numbers were avoided by using a 7:3 ratio and the waveforms are always measured in millivolts. Whilst such a signal was originally called composite video, today it would be referred to as monochrome video or *Ys*, meaning luma carrying syncs although in practice the s is often omitted.

Figure 7.15(d) shows how the two signals are separated. The voltage swing needed to go from black to peak white is less than the total swing available. In a standard analog video signal the maximum amplitude is 1 volt peak-to-peak. The upper part of the voltage range represents the variations in brightness of the image from black to white. Signals below that range are 'blacker than black' and cannot be seen on the display. These signals are used for synchronizing.

Figure 7.16(a) shows the line synchronizing system part-way through a field or frame. The part of the waveform which corresponds to the forward scan is called the *active line* and during the active line the voltage represents the brightness of the image. In between the active line periods are *horizontal blanking intervals* in which the signal voltage will be at or below black. Figure 7.16(b) shows that in some systems the active line voltage is superimposed on a *pedestal* or *black level set-up* voltage of 7.5 *IRE*. The purpose of this set-up is to ensure that the blanking interval signal is below black on simple displays so that it is guaranteed to be invisible on the screen. When set-up is used, black level and blanking level differ by the pedestal height. When set-up is not used, black level and blanking level are one and the same.

The blanking period immediately after the active line is known as the *front porch*, which is followed by the *leading edge of sync*. When the leading edge of sync passes through 50 per cent of its own amplitude, the horizontal retrace pulse is considered to have occurred. The flat part at the bottom of the horizontal sync pulse is known as *sync tip* and this is

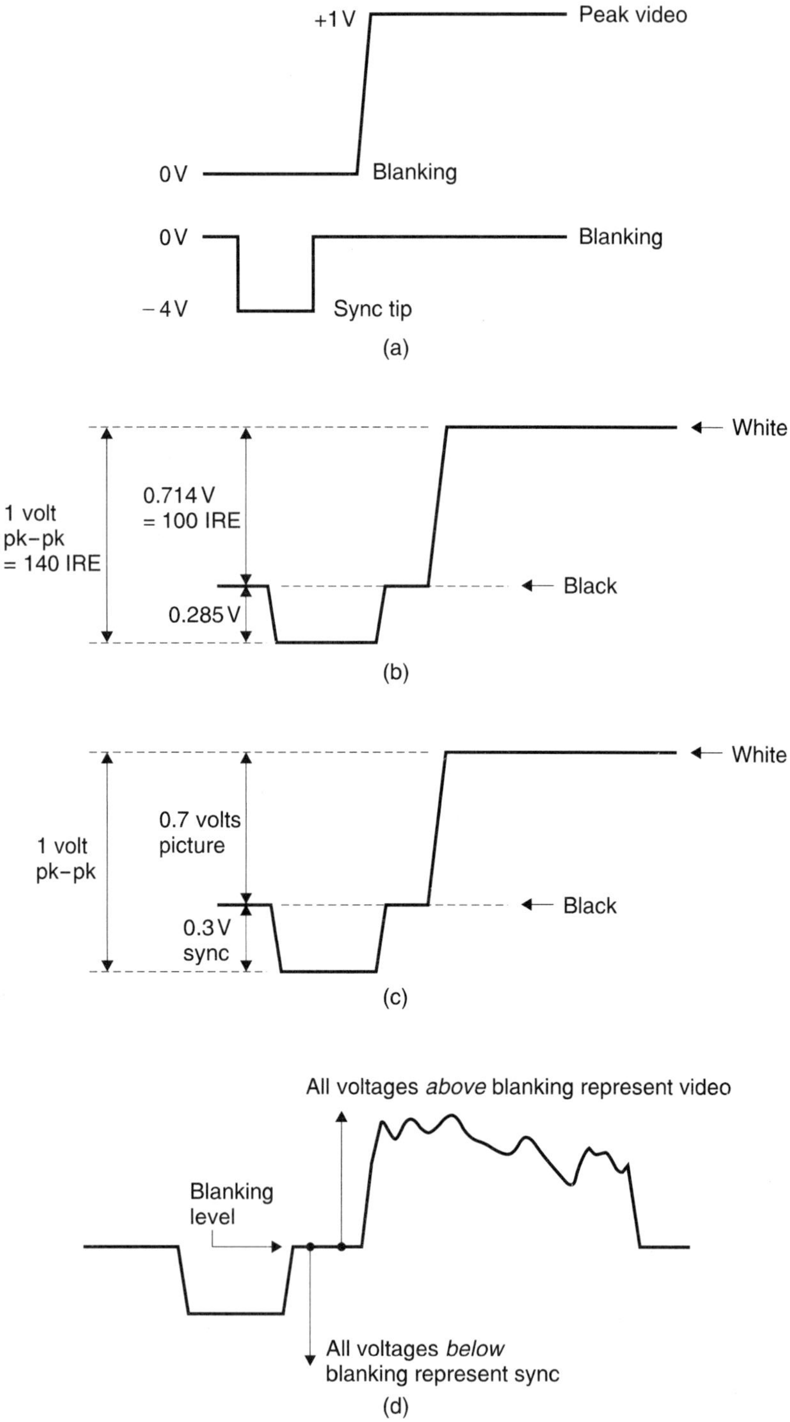

Figure 7.15 Early video used separate vision and sync signals shown in (a). The US one volt video waveform in (b) has 10:4 video/sync ratio. (c) European systems use 7:3 ratio to avoid odd voltages. (d) Sync separation relies on two voltage ranges in the signal.

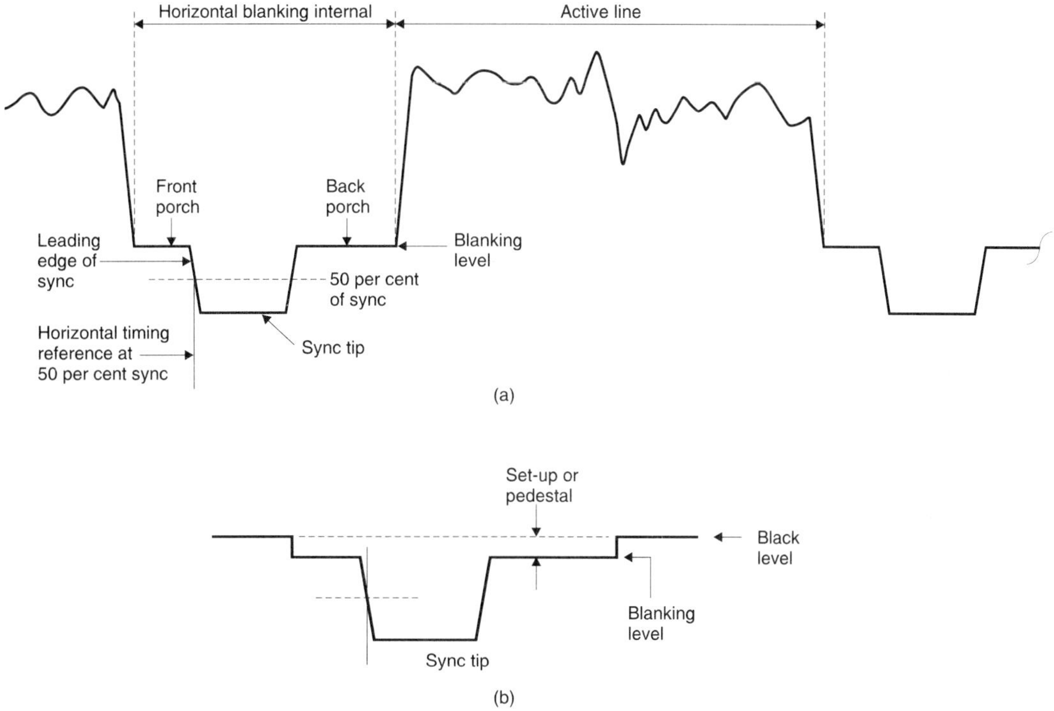

Figure 7.16 (a) Part of a video waveform with important features named. (b) Use of pedestal or set-up.

followed by the trailing edge of sync which returns the waveform to blanking level. The signal remains at blanking level during the *back porch* during which the display completes the horizontal flyback. The sync pulses have sloping edges because if they were square they would contain high frequencies which would go outside the allowable channel bandwidth on being broadcast.

The vertical synchronizing system is more complex because the vertical flyback period is much longer than the horizontal line period and horizontal synchronization must be maintained throughout it. The vertical synchronizing pulses are much longer than horizontal pulses so that they are readily distinguishable. Figure 7.17(a) shows a simple approach to vertical synchronizing. The signal remains predominantly at sync tip for several lines to indicate the vertical retrace, but returns to blanking level briefly immediately prior to the leading edges of the horizontal sync, which continues throughout. Figure 7.17(b) shows that the presence of interlace complicates matters, as in one vertical interval the vertical sync pulse coincides with a horizontal sync pulse whereas in the next the vertical sync pulse occurs half-way down a line. In practice the long vertical sync pulses were found to disturb the average signal voltage too much, and to reduce the effect extra *equalizing pulses* were put

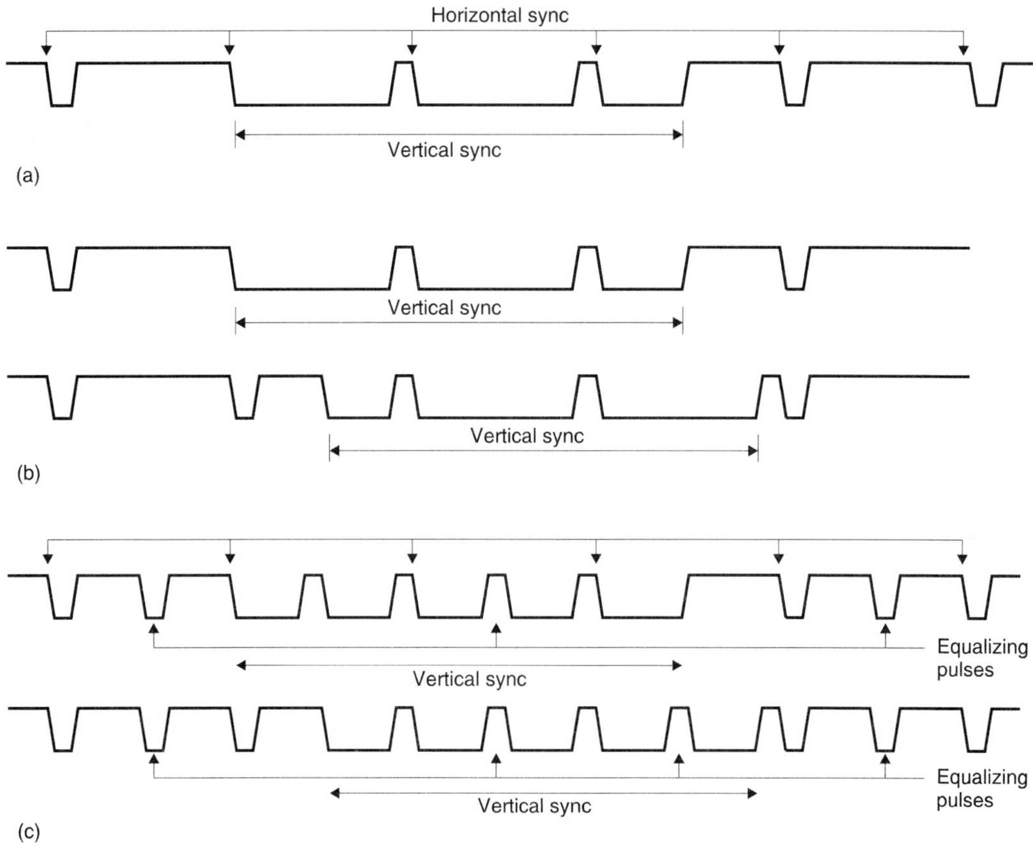

Figure 7.17 (a) A simple vertical pulse is longer than a horizontal pulse. (b) In an interlaced system there are two relationships between H and V. (c) The use of equalizing pulses to balance the DC component of the signal.

in, half-way between the horizontal sync pulses. The horizontal timebase system can ignore the equalizing pulses because it contains a flywheel circuit which only expects pulses roughly one line period apart. Figure 7.17(c) shows the final result of an interlaced system with equalizing pulses. The vertical blanking interval can be seen, with the vertical pulse itself towards the beginning.

Correct portrayal of a television image is only obtained when the synchronization system is working. Should the video signal be conveyed without the synchronizing information, a condition called sync loss occurs, causing the picture to break up.

7.9 Bandwidth and definition

As the conventional analog television picture is made up of lines, the line structure determines the *definition* or the fineness of detail which can be portrayed in the vertical axis. The limit is reached in theory when alternate lines show black and white. In a 625-line picture there are roughly 600 unblanked lines. If 300 of these are white and 300 are black then there will be 300 complete cycles of detail in one picture height. One unit of resolution,which is a unit of spatial frequency, is c/ph or cycles per picture height. In practical displays the contrast will have fallen to virtually nothing at this ideal limit and the resolution actually achieved is around 70 per cent of the ideal, or about 210 c/ph. The degree to which the ideal is met is known as the *Kell factor* of the display.

Definition in one axis is wasted unless it is matched in the other and so the horizontal axis should be able to offer the same performance. As the aspect ratio of conventional television is 4:3 then it should be possible to display 400 cycles in one picture width, reduced to about 300 cycles by the Kell factor. As part of the line period is lost due to flyback, 300 cycles per picture width becomes about 360 cycles per line period.

In 625-line television, the frame rate is 25 Hz and so the line rate F_h will be:

$$F_h = 625 \times 25 = 15\,625\,\text{Hz}$$

If 360 cycles of video waveform must be carried in each line period, then the bandwidth required will be given by:

$$15\,625 \times 360 = 5.625 \text{ MegaHertz}$$

In the 525-line system, there are roughly 500 unblanked lines allowing 250 c/ph theoretical definition, or 175 lines allowing for the Kell factor. Allowing for the aspect ratio, equal horizontal definition requires about 230 cycles per picture width. Allowing for horizontal blanking this requires about 280 cycles per line period.

In 525-line video, $F_h = 525 \times 30 = 15\,750\,\text{Hz}$ Thus the bandwidth required is:

$$15\,750 \times 280 = 4.4 \text{ MegaHertz}$$

If it is proposed to build a high-definition television system, one might start by doubling the number of lines and hence double the definition. Thus in a 1250-line format about 420 c/ph might be obtained. To achieve equal horizontal definition, bearing in mind the aspect ratio is now 16:9, then nearly 750 cycles per picture width will be needed. Allowing for horizontal blanking, then around 890 cycles per line period will be needed. The line frequency is now given by:

$$F_h = 1250 \times 25 = 31\,250\,\text{Hz}$$

and the bandwidth required is given by:

$$31\,250 \times 890 = 28 \text{ MegaHertz}$$

Note the dramatic increase in bandwidth. In general the bandwidth rises as the square of the resolution because there are more lines and more cycles needed in each line. It should be clear that, except for research purposes, high-definition television will never be broadcast as a conventional analog signal because the bandwidth required is simply uneconomic. If and when high-definition broadcasting becomes common, it will be compelled to use digital compression techniques to make it economic.

7.10 Interlace

Interlaced scanning is a crude compression technique which was developed empirically in the 1930s as a way of increasing the picture rate to reduce flicker without a matching increase in the video bandwidth. Instead of transmitting entire frames, the lines of the frame are sorted into odd lines and even lines. Odd lines are transmitted in one field, even lines in the next. A pair of fields is supposed to interlace to produce a frame, but it wil be seen that this frequently does not happen. Figure 7.18(a) shows that the vertical/temporal arrangement of lines in an interlaced system forms a quincunx pattern. Not surprisingly the vertical/temporal spectrum of an interlaced signal shows the same pattern.

Study of the vertical temporal spectrum allows many of the characteristics of interlace to be deduced. Like quincuncx spatial sampling, theoretically interlace has a triangular passband, as Figure 7.18(b) shows. The highest vertical resolution is obtained at the point shown, and this is only obtained with a temporal frequency of zero, i.e. when there is no motion. This is suggesting that interlaced systems have poor dynamic resolution.

Although the passband is triangular, a suitable reconstruction filter cannot be implemented in any known display. Figure 7.18(c) shows that in, for example, a CRT display, there is no temporal filter, only a vertical filter due to the aperture effect of the electron beam. As a result there are two problems. First, fine vertical detail will be displayed at the frame rate. The result is that although the field rate is above the CFF, a significant amount of frame rate energy is present to cause flicker. Second, in the presence of motion there will be vertical aliasing.

As was mentioned in Chapter 3, transform duality holds that any phenomenon can be described in both domains. Figure 7.18(d) shows that vertical detail such as an edge may only be present in one field of the pair and this results in frame rate flicker called 'interlace twitter'.

Figure 7.19(a) shows a dynamic resolution analysis of interlaced scanning. When there is no motion, the optic flow axis and the time axis are parallel and the apparent vertical sampling rate is the number of lines

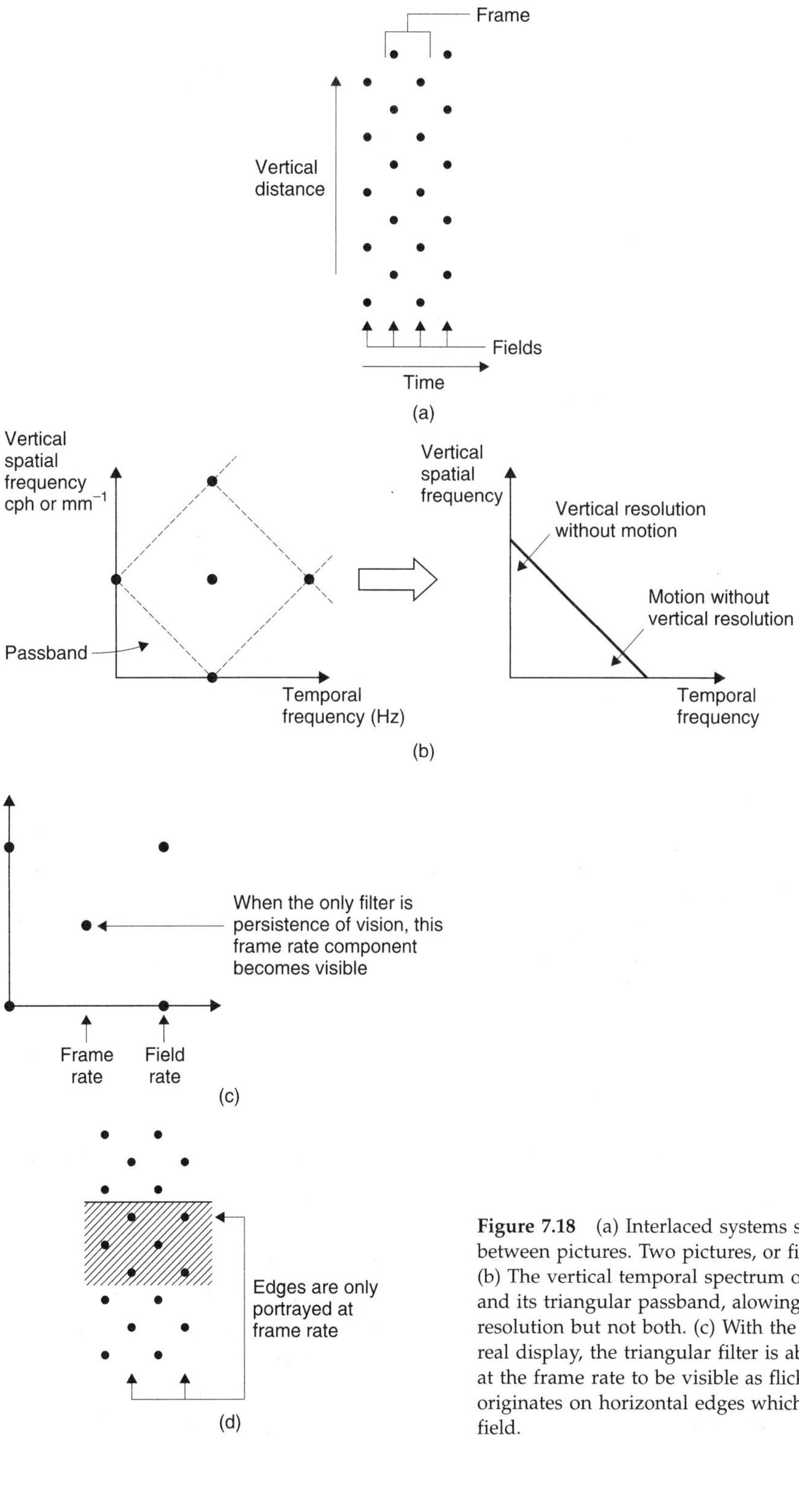

Figure 7.18 (a) Interlaced systems shift the lines in between pictures. Two pictures, or fields, make a frame. (b) The vertical temporal spectrum of an interlaced system and its triangular passband, allowing motion or vertical resolution but not both. (c) With the spectrum of (b) on a real display, the triangular filter is absent, allowing energy at the frame rate to be visible as flicker. (d) the flicker originates on horizontal edges which only appear in one field.

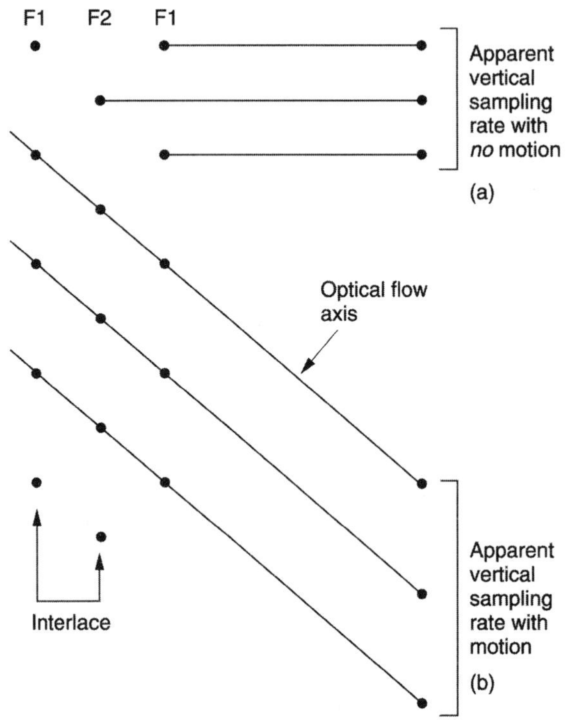

Figure 7.19 When an interlaced picture is stationary, viewing takes place along the time axis as shown in (a). When a vertical component of motion exists, viewing takes place along the optic flow axis. (b) The vertical sampling rate falls to one half its stationary value.

in a frame. However, when there is vertical motion, (b), the optic flow axis turns. In the case shown, the sampling structure due to interlace results in the vertical sampling rate falling to one half of its stationary value.

Consequently interlace does exactly what would be expected from a half-bandwidth filter. It halves the vertical resolution when any motion with a vertical component occurs. In a practical television system, there is no anti-aliasing filter in the vertical axis and so when the vertical sampling rate of an interlaced system is halved by motion, high spatial frequencies will alias or heterodyne causing annoying artifacts in the picture. This is easily demonstrated.

Figure 7.20(a) shows how a vertical spatial frequency well within the static resolution of the system aliases when motion occurs. In a progressive scan system this effect is absent and the dynamic resolution due to scanning can be the same as the static case.

Interlaced systems handle motion transverse to the scanning lines very poorly by aliasing, whereas motion parallel to the scanning lines results in a strange artifact. If the eye is tracking a horizontally moving object, the object itself will be portrayed quite well because the interlace mechanism will work. However, Figure 7.20(b) shows that the background strobing

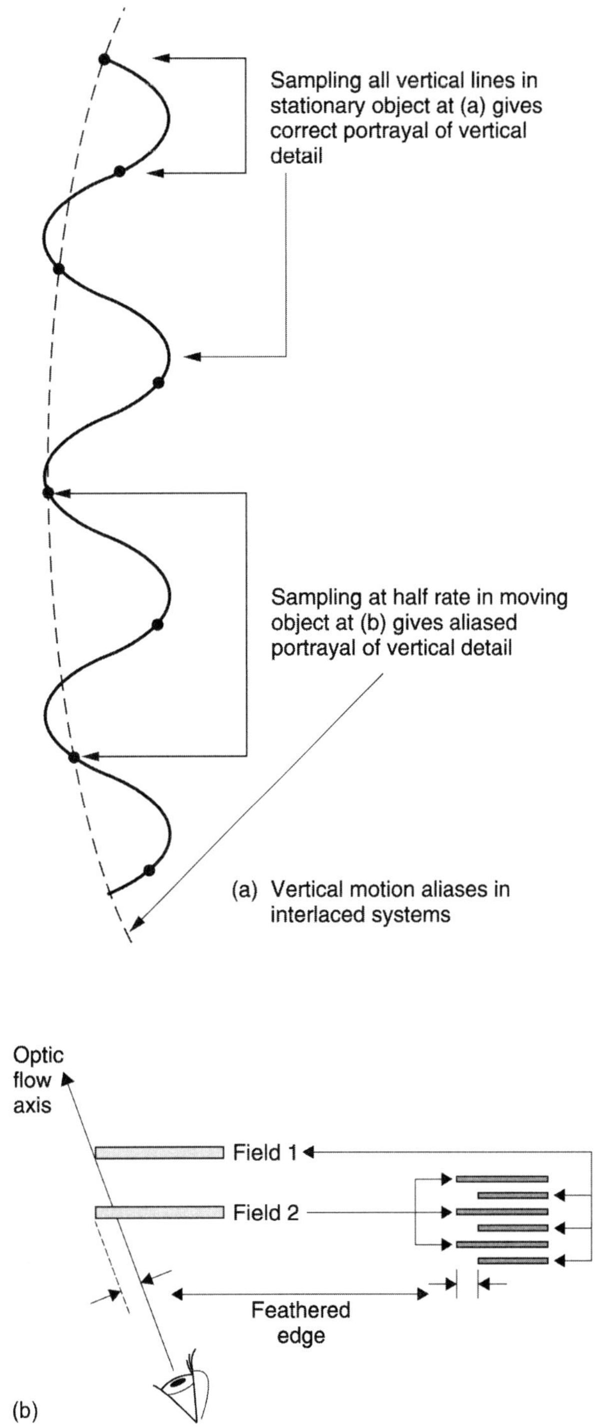

Figure 7.20 (a) The halving in sampling rate causes high spatial frequencies to alias. (b) To an eye following a horizontally moving object, vertical lines in the background will appear feathered because each field appears at a different place on the retina.

will appear *feathered* because only half of the lines are present in each version of the background. Vertical edges in the background appear as shown in the figure.

Feathering is less noticeable than vertical aliasing and for this reason interlaced television systems always have horizontal raster lines. In real life, horizontal motion is more common than vertical.

It is easy to calculate the vertical image motion velocity needed to obtain the half-bandwidth speed of interlace, because it amounts to one raster line per field. In 525/60 (NTSC) there are about 500 active lines, so motion as slow as one picture height in 8 seconds will halve the dynamic resolution. In 625/50 (PAL) there are about 600 lines, so the half-bandwidth speed falls to one picture height in 12 seconds. This is why NTSC, with fewer lines and lower bandwidth, doesn't look as soft as it should compared to PAL, because it has better dynamic resolution.

Figure 7.21 shows that the situation deteriorates rapidly if an attempt is made to use interlaced scanning in systems with a lot of lines. In 1250/50, the resolution is halved at a vertical speed of just one picture height in 24 seconds. In other words on real moving video a 1250/50 interlaced system has the same dynamic resolution as a 625/50 progressive system. By the same argument a 1080 I system has the same performance as a 480 P system.

Now that techniques such as digital compression and spatial over-sampling are available, the format used for display need not be the same as the transmission format. Thus it is difficult to justify the use of interlace in a transmission format. In fact interlace causes difficulties which are absent in progressive systems. Progressive systems are separable. Vertical filtering need not affect the time axis and vice versa. Interlaced systems are not separable, and two-dimensional filtering is mandatory. A vertical

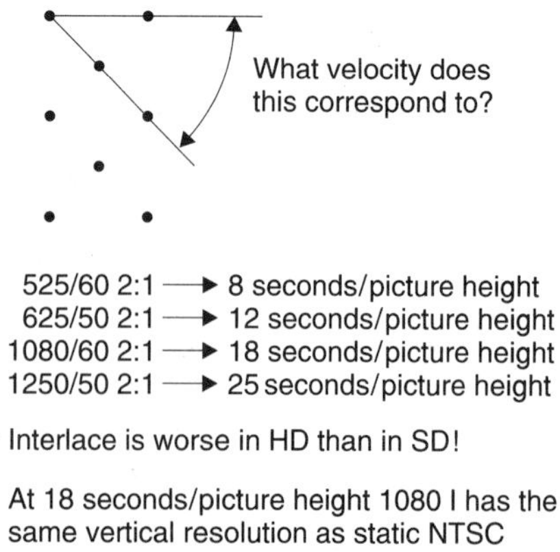

Figure 7.21 Interlace works best in systems with few lines, e.g. NTSC. Increasing the number of lines reduces performance if the frame rate is not also raised. Here are shown the vertical velocities at which various interlaces standards fail.

process requires motion compensation in an interlaced system whereas in a progressive system it does not. Interlace, however, makes motion estimation more difficult. When compression is used, compression systems should not be cascaded. As digital compression techniques based on transforms are now available, it makes no sense to use an interlaced, i.e. compressed, video signal as an input. Better results will be obtained if a progressive scan signal is used.

Computer-generated images and film are not interlaced, but consist of discrete frames spaced on a time axis. As digital technology is bringing computers and television closer the use of interlaced transmission is an embarrassing source of incompatibility. The future will bring image-delivery systems based on computer technology and oversampling cameras and displays which can operate at resolutions much closer to the theoretical limits. With the technology of the day, interlace had a purpose whereas it now impedes progress.

Interlace causes difficulty in any process which requires image manipulation. This includes DVEs, standards convertors and display convertors. All these devices give better results when working with progressively scanned data and if the source material is interlaced, a de-interlacing process will be necessary and will be considered in section 7.23.

7.11 Colour television

The precise approach to colour reproduction described in Chapter 6 is not adopted in colour television. Instead the approach is to find a set of primary CRT phosphors which give reasonable brightness and to engineer the rest of the system around them. Figure 7.22 shows the Rec. 709 primaries adopted in most TV systems along with the D_{65} white point. In order to determine the colour matching functions needed in the camera, the line from the white point through each primary is extended to the perimeter of the CIE diagram to find the centre wavelength of the filter at which its response will peak. Three filter responses are then specified. In practice the ideal responses are seldom provided. Figure 7.23(a) shows a more typical filter set from a colour TV camera.

The type of filters used have flat passbands which are not optimal. As can be seen from Figure 7.23(b) flat passbands make the three outputs from the camera identical for a range of wavelengths, whereas they should be unique for each wavelength. This loses subtlety from the reproduced colour.

A monochrome camera produces a single luma signal *Y* or *Ys* whereas a colour camera produces three signals, or *components*, *R*, *G* and *B* which are essentially monochrome video signals representing an image after filtering in each primary colour. In some systems sync is present on a

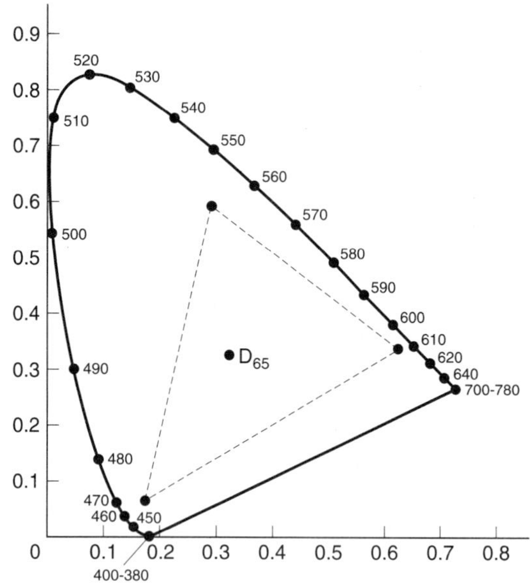

Figure 7.22 The primaries used in Rec. 709 television systems and the white point.

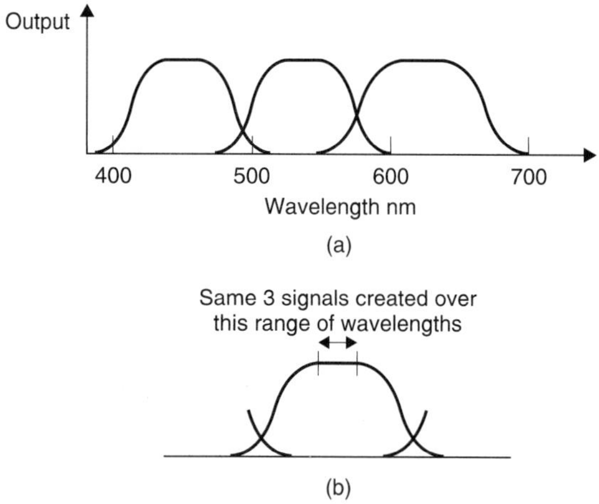

Figure 7.23 (a) Filter responses of a real camera are usually suboptimal. (b) Flat response curves result in the same combination of primaries for a range of colours.

separate signal (*RGBS*). Rarely is it present on all three components, whereas most commonly it is only present on the green component leading to the term *RGsB*. The use of the green component for sync has led to suggestions that the components should be called *GBR*. Like luma, *RGsB* signals may use 0.7 or 0.714 volt signals, with or without set-up.

RGB and *Y* signals are incompatible, yet when colour television was introduced it was a practical necessity that it should be possible to display colour signals on a monochrome display and vice versa.

Creating or *transcoding* a luma signal from R, Gs and B is relatively easy. Chapter 6 introduced the spectral response of the eye which has a peak in the green region. Green objects will produce a larger stimulus than red objects of the same brightness, with blue objects producing the least stimulus. A luma signal can be obtained by adding R, G and B together, not in equal amounts, but in a sum which is *weighted* by the relative response of the eye. Once the primaries of a television system have been defined, the weighting factors can be determined from the luminous efficiency curve of the HVS. For Rec. 709 primaries:

$$Y = 0.299R + 0.587G + 0.114B$$

Syncs may be regenerated, but will be identical to those on the Gs input and when added to Y result in Ys as required.

If Ys is derived in this way, a monochrome display will show nearly the same result as if a monochrome camera had been used in the first place. The results are not identical because of the non-linearities introduced by gamma correction as will be seen in section 7.12.

As colour pictures require three signals, it should be possible to send Ys and two other signals which a colour display could arithmetically convert back to R, G and B. There are two important factors which restrict the form that the other two signals may take. One is to achieve reverse compatibility. The other is the requirement to conserve bandwidth for economic reasons.

If the source is a monochrome camera, it can only produce Ys and the other two signals will be completely absent. A colour display should be able to operate on the Ys signal only and show a monochrome picture.

The above requirements are met by sending two *colour difference signals* along with Ys. There are three possible colour difference signals, $R–Y$, $B–Y$ and $G–Y$. As the green signal makes the greatest contribution to Y, then the amplitude of $G–Y$ would be the smallest and would be most susceptible to noise. Thus $R–Y$ and $B–Y$ are used in practice as Figure 7.24 shows.

R and B are readily obtained by adding Y to the two colour difference signals. G is obtained by rearranging the expression for Y above such that:

$$G = \frac{Y - 0.3R - 0.11B}{0.59}$$

If a colour CRT is being driven, it is possible to apply inverted luma to the cathodes and the $R–Y$ and $B–Y$ signals directly to two of the grids so that

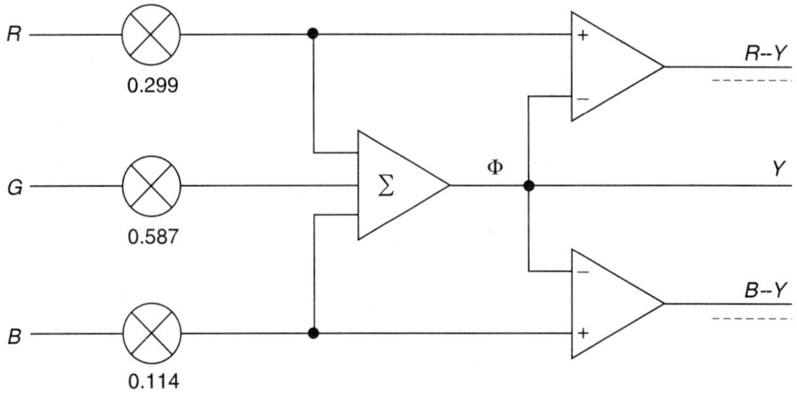

Figure 7.24 Colour components are converted to colour difference signals by the transcoding shown here.

the tube performs some of the matrixing. It is then only necessary to obtain $G–Y$ for the third grid, using the expression:

$$G–Y = -0.51(R–Y) - 0.186(B–Y)$$

If a monochrome source having only a *Ys* output is supplied to a colour display, $R–Y$ and $B–Y$ will be zero. It is reasonably obvious that if there are no colour difference signals the colour signals cannot be different from one another and $R = G = B$. As a result the colour display can produce only a neutral picture.

The use of colour difference signals is essential for compatibility in both directions between colour and monochrome, but it has a further advantage which follows from the way in which the HVS works. In order to produce the highest resolution in the fovea, the eye will use signals from all types of cone, regardless of colour. In order to determine colour the stimuli from three cones must be compared. There is evidence that the nervous system uses some form of colour difference processing to make this possible. As a result the full acuity of the human eye is available only in monochrome. Differences in colour cannot be resolved so well. A further factor is that the lens in the human eye is not achromatic and this means that the ends of the spectrum are not well focused. This is particularly noticeable on blue.

If the eye cannot resolve colour very well there is no point is expending valuable bandwidth sending high-resolution colour signals. Colour difference working allows the luma to be sent separately at full bandwidth. This determines the subjective sharpness of the picture. The colour difference signals can be sent with considerably reduced bandwidth, as little as one quarter that of luma, and the human eye is unable to tell.

In practice analog component signals are never received perfectly, but suffer from slight differences in relative gain. In the case of *RGB* a gain error in one signal will cause a colour cast on the received picture. A gain error in *Y* causes no colour cast and gain errors in *R–Y* or *B–Y* cause much smaller perceived colour casts. Thus colour difference working is also more robust than *RGB* working.

The overwhelming advantages obtained by using colour difference signals mean that in broadcast and production facilities *RGB* is seldom used. The outputs from the *RGB* sensors in the camera are converted directly to *Y*, *R–Y* and *B–Y* in the camera control unit and output in that form. Standards exist for both analog and digital colour difference signals to ensure compatibility between equipment from various manufacturers.

Whilst signals such as *Y*, *R*, *G* and *B* are *unipolar* or positive only, it should be stressed that colour difference signals are *bipolar* and may meaningfully take on levels below zero volts.

The wide use of colour difference signals has led to the development of test signals and equipment to display them. The most important of the test signals are the ubiquitous *colour bars*. Colour bars are used to set the gains and timing of signal components and to check that matrix operations are performed using the correct weighting factors. The origin of the colour bar test signal is shown in Figure 7.25. In *100 per*

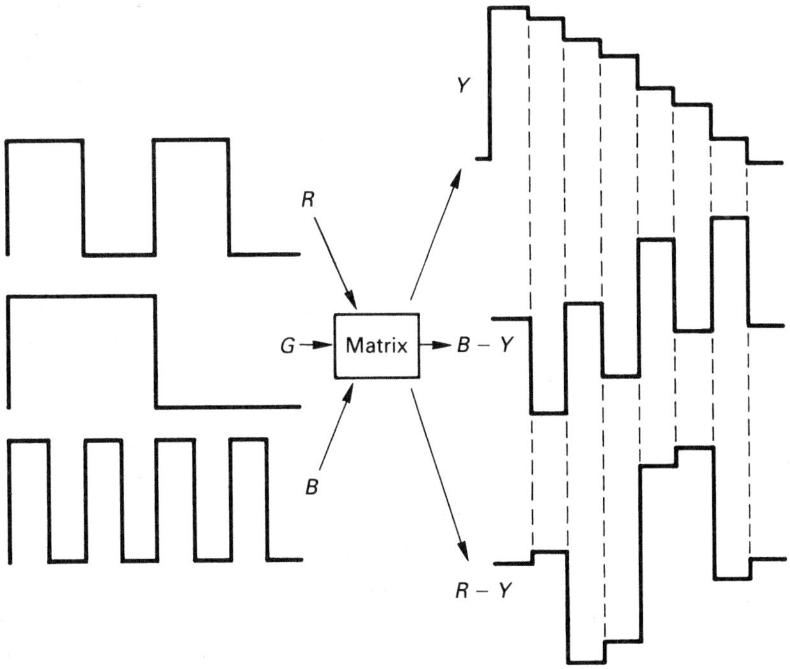

Figure 7.25 Origin of colour difference signals representing colours bars. Adding *R*, *G* and *B* according to the weighting factors produces an irregular luminance staircase.

cent amplitude bars, peak amplitude binary *RGB* signals are produced, having one, two and four cycles per screen width. When these are added together in a weighted sum, an eight-level luma staircase results because of the unequal weighting. The matrix also produces two colour difference signals, *R–Y* and *B–Y* as shown. Sometimes *75 per cent amplitude bars* are generated by suitably reducing the *RGB* signal amplitude. Note that in both cases the colours are fully saturated; it is only the brightness which is reduced to 75 per cent. Sometimes the white bar of a 75 per cent bar signal is raised to 100 per cent to make calibration easier. Such a signal is sometimes erroneously called a 100 per cent bar signal.

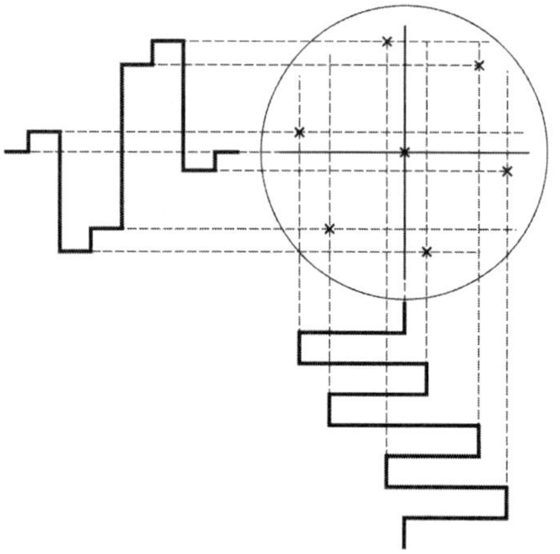

Figure 7.26 Colour difference signals can be shown two-dimensionally on a vectorscope.

Figure 7.26 shows that both colour difference signals can be displayed at once on a component vectorscope. The screen of a component vectorscope represents a constant luminance chromaticity diagram with white in the centre and saturation increasing outwards with radius. The *B–Y* signal causes horizontal deflection, and *R–Y* causes vertical deflection. It will be seen that this results in a display having six peripheral dots and two central dots. The central dots result from the white and black bars which are not colours and in which the colour difference signals are both zero.

R–Y and *B–Y* have voltage swings which are inconvenient because they are somewhat different from the gamut of *Y*. Figure 7.27(a) shows an SMPTE/EBU standard colour difference signal set in which the signals are called *Ys*, P_b and P_r. 0.3 volt syncs are on luma only and all three video signals have a 0.7 volt peak to peak swing with 100 per

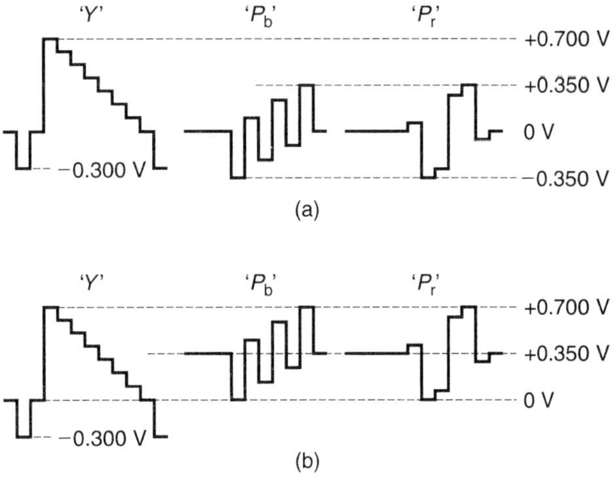

Figure 7.27 (a) 100 per cent colour bars represented by SMPTE/EBU standard colour difference signals. (b) Level comparison is easier in waveform monitors if the $B-Y$ and $R-Y$ signals are offset upwards.

cent bars. In order to obtain these voltage swings, the following gain corrections are made to the components:

$$P_r = 0.71327(R-Y) \text{ and } P_b = 0.56433(B-Y)$$

Within waveform monitors, the colour difference signals may be offset by 350 mV as in Figure 7.27(b) to match the luma range for display purposes.

7.12 Constant luminance

The use of matrix arithmetic in colour difference video systems only works perfectly if the signals represent linear light. In the presence of gamma this is not the case. As was seen in section 6.9, all video signals are subject to a non-linear gamma precompensation which is a power function. In traditional colour television, the non-linearity of the CRT is used to counteract the gamma precompensation used at the camera. As can be seen, this means that the conversions between *RGB* and colour difference formats must be made in the non-linear domain.

Figure 7.28(a) shows a colour difference system using gamma in which there is no bandwidth reduction of the colour difference signals. The effect of gamma is that some luminance is present in the colour difference signals and vice versa. As the encoding and decoding matrices are complementary, their use is transparent. However, in practice the bandwidth of the colour difference signals is reduced, as shown in Figure

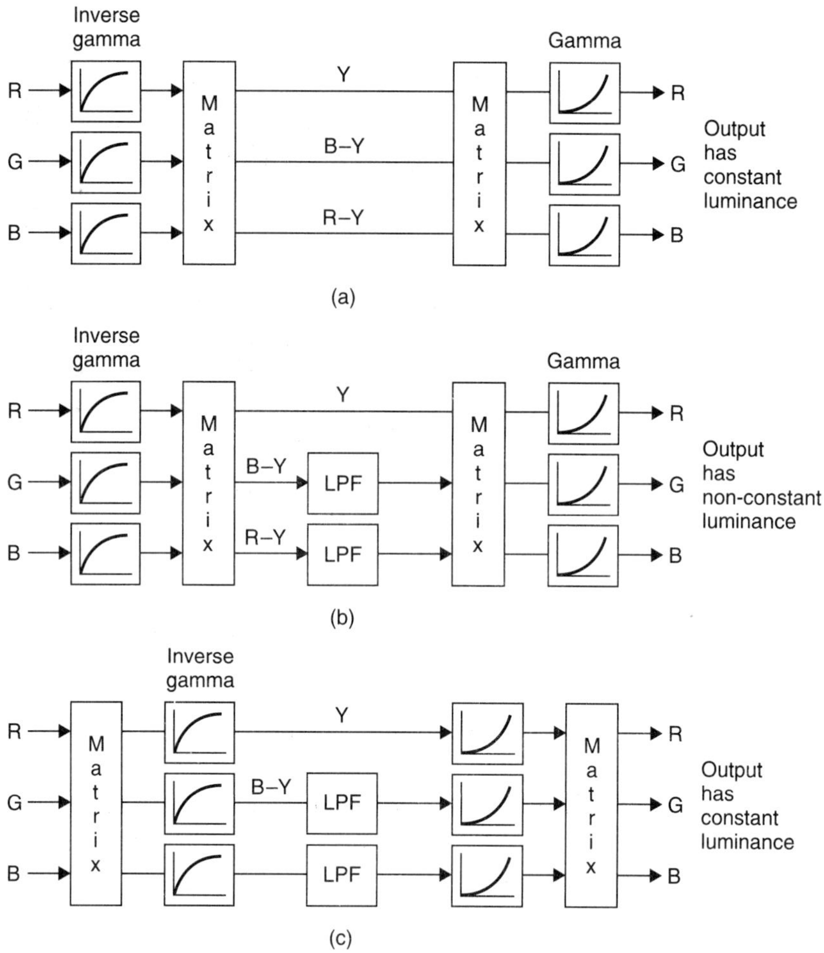

Figure 7.28 (a) Colour difference system with no bandwidth reduction is transparent because the matrices are fully reversible. (b) If the bandwidth of the colour difference signals is reduced, the use of gamma causes failure of constant luminance. (c) Constant luminance can be achieved if the matrices work in the linear light domain.

7.28(b), and this has the effect of removing that part of the luminance signal which was being carried in the colour difference signals.

The result is a phenomenon called *failure of constant luminance.* In the presence of large steps in the video signal at the boundaries of objects, the luminance level will be incorrect. If colour bars are observed after passing through such a system, the most obvious symptom is that at the green/ magenta transition in the centre of the screen there will be a dark line caused by a drop in the luminance level.

In systems designed to use the non-linearity of the CRT, the failure of constant luminance is accepted. However, when an alternative display technology is available, colour differences can correctly be calculated using the constant luminance system of Figure 7.28(c). As the matrix processes take place in the linear light domain, the problem is avoided. Whilst signals from a constant luminance encoder are incompatible with traditional television sets, there is no reason why they should not be used with proprietary systems such as in electronic cinema.

7.13 Analog colour television signals

Although analog video is obsolescent, analog equipment will continue in use for some time to come. Much archive material resides on analog formats. Convergent digital systems will be faced with accepting input from, or delivering output to, legacy analog systems and for this reason it is important to understand how they work at least well enough to avoid obvious pitfalls. The number of different approaches to colour television is large and confusing. Figure 7.29 shows how these relate. Note that in addition to variations in the colour modulation scheme, there will be differences in the number of scanning lines and in the frame rates used.

The starting point in in all cases is gamma preprocessed *RGB*, with Rec. 709 colorimetry. *RGB* can be digitized, but this is uncommon because of the high bit rate required. *RGB* can be matrixed to *Y*, *R–Y* and *B–Y*, but the colour difference signals will be scaled to produce Y, P_r P_b. The bandwidth of the colour difference signals is halved. Section 7.14 will show how this signal format can be digitized according to ITU Rec. 601 to produce a format widely used in television production equipment.

For analog broadcasting, colour difference signals can be converted to *composite video*. Figure 7.30 shows how a particular colour can be reached on a vectorscope display. In component signals, the dot is reached by travelling a given distance horizontally, followed by a given distance vertically. This is the way a map reference works; mathematicians call the components Cartesian coordinates. It is just as easy to reach the same dot by travelling a suitable distance at the appropriate heading or angle.

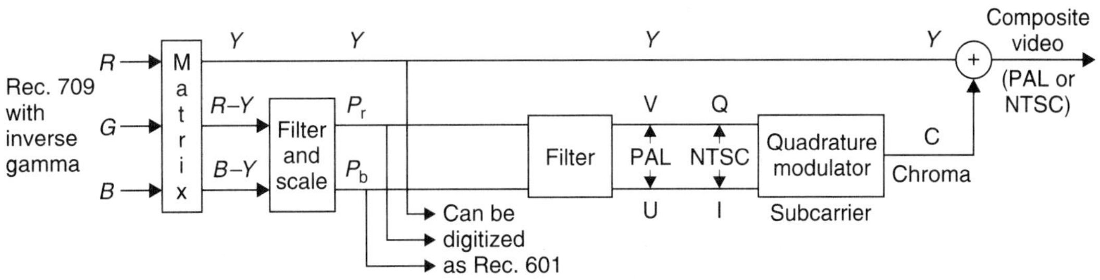

Figure 7.29 Traditional analog colour television signals and how they relate.

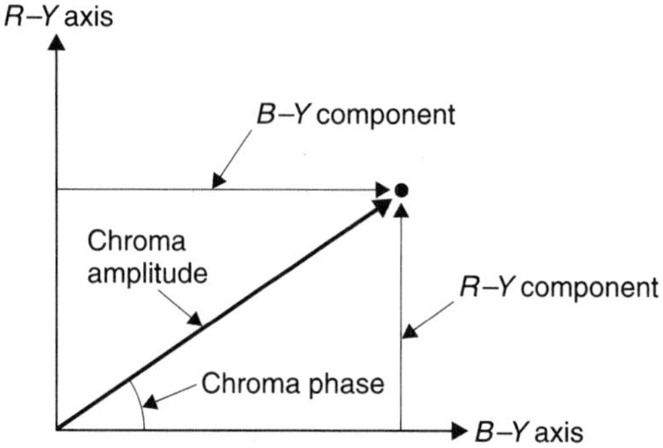

Figure 7.30 The equivalence of polar (radius and angle) and *XY* coordinates in locating a specific colour.

Mathematicians call this polar coordinates. Instead of two separate signals, we can convey distance and angle in the amplitude and phase of a single waveform. That is precisely how PAL and NTSC chroma work. The radius of the colour is given by the chroma amplitude which is proportional to the saturation, and the angle is the phase. The phase angle of the vector literally points to the appropriate hue in the chromaticity diagram.

Simultaneous modulation of amplitude and phase is performed by a quadrature modulator. Figure 7.31 shows how this works. A pair of amplitude modulators (analog multipliers) are supplied with the same carriers except that one has been phase shifted by 90°. The outputs of the two modulators are linearly added and the resultant signal will be found to be amplitude and phase modulated. The phase is a function of the relative proportions and polarities of the two inputs. The original subcarrier is suppressed in the output of the modulator. The picture

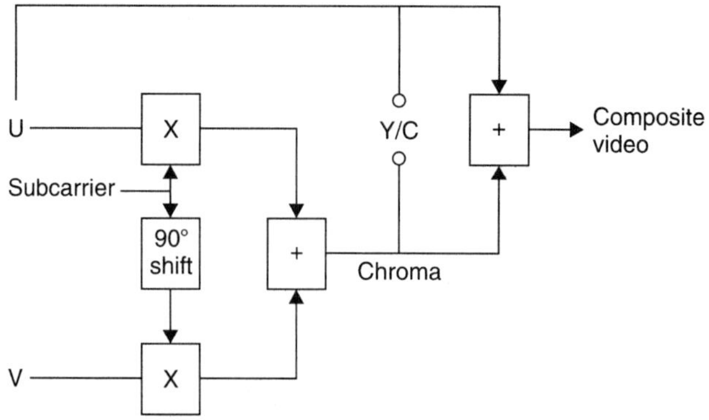

Figure 7.31 Quadrature modulator allows two signals to modulate one carrier in amplitude and phase to produce chroma. This may be kept separate in the *Y/C* system, or added to the luminance in composite systems.

frequencies in the baseband result in sidebands above and below the centre frequency after modulation. As a result it is incorrect to refer to the quadrature modulator output as subcarrier; the correct term is chroma. As the chroma signal carries the information from both colour difference signals, it is possible to carry a colour picture by sending two signals: luminance and chroma, abbreviated to *Y/C*. This is also shown in Figure 7.31. *Y/C* is used in S-VHS VCRs in which the chroma signal is kept separate from the luminance through the whole record and playback process in order to avoid cross effects. It is difficult to define a *Y/C* standard. As there are two signals involved, strictly speaking it is a component standard. A composite system linearly adds chroma to luminance for broadcasting. At the receiver the two signals must undergo *Y/C* separation before the chroma can be demodulated back to a pair of colour difference signals.

Demodulation is done using a pair of synchronous demodulators also driven in quadrature. These need reference carriers which are identical in phase to the original pair of carriers. As there is no subcarrier in the chroma signal it is necessary to send a reference subcarrier separately. This is the purpose of the burst which is sent during horizontal blanking. A heavily damped phase-locked loop synchronizes to the burst and continues to run for the rest of the line to provide a reference for the decoder.

One way of considering how quadrature modulation works is that when one of the carrier inputs reaches its peak, the other is passing through zero. At that time the signal voltage can only be a function of, say, the $B-Y$ input. Ninety degrees later the relationships exchange and the signal voltage can then only be a function of the $R-Y$ input. Demodulation is a question of sampling the signal every 90°. Odd samples reflect the state of one component; even samples reflect the state of the other. The demodulators have the effect of inverting alternate samples. A simple low-pass filter removes the harmonics of the subcarrier frequency to re-create the input waveform.

Composite video was originally designed as a monochrome-compatible system for broadcasting in which subcarrier-based colour-difference information was added to an existing line standard in such a way that existing sets could still display a monochrome picture. A further requirement was that the addition of colour should not increase the bandwidth of the TV channel. In that respect composite video has to be viewed as an early form of compression.

Whilst the details vary, all composite signals have in common the need to include a subcarrier-based *chroma* signal within the luminance band in such a way that it will be effectively invisible on an unmodified monochrome TV set. This is achieved in much the same way in all three systems. Figure 7.32 shows that if a chroma signal is linearly added to a

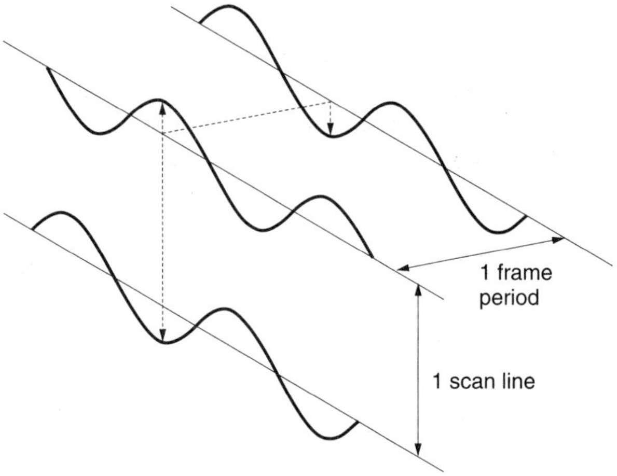

Figure 7.32 In composite video the subcarrier frequency is arranged so that inversions occur between adjacent lines and pictures to help reduce the visibility of the chroma.

luminance signal it has the effect of making it alternately too bright and too dark. If it is arranged that the chroma is inverted on the next picture line the effect is that areas which are too bright on one line are adjacent to areas which are too dark on the next. The eye will see the average brightness of the line pairs which is almost the original luminance. In the absence of gamma correction the cancellation would be perfect; in the presence of gamma it is imperfect but generally adequate.

Efforts are also made to ensure that the phase of the chroma also reverses from frame to frame so that the same point on the screen alternates in brightness on the time axis about the value determined by the luminance signal. Clearly the exact frequency of the subcarrier has to be carefully chosen with respect to line and frame rates. NTSC and PAL use quadrature modulation as shown above, so that two components can be sent simultaneously whereas SECAM frequency modulates the subcarrier and sends the components on alternate lines. The effect of composite modulation is to produce an extremely complex signal spectrum, especially in PAL.

Analog composite video is today obsolescent because it being replaced by digital transmissions employing compression schemes such as MPEG.

7.14 Digital colour signals

In principle any analog video signal can be digitized with a suitable sampling rate and wordlength. This is commonly done with colour difference signals. The luma signal, Y, retains the same name in the digital domain, whereas P_r is known as C_r and P_b is known as C_b.

Whilst signals such as *Y*, *R*, *G* and *B* are unipolar or positive only, colour difference signals are bipolar and may meaningfully take on negative values.

In colour difference working, the important requirement is for image manipulation in the digital domain. This is facilitated by a sampling rate which is a multiple of line rate because then there is a whole number of samples in a line and samples are always in the same position along the line and can form neat columns. A practical difficulty is that the line period of the 525 and 625 systems is slightly different. The problem was overcome by the use of a sampling clock which is an integer multiple of both line rates.

ITU-601 (formerly CCIR-601) recommends the use of certain sampling rates which are based on integer multiples of the carefully chosen fundamental frequency of 3.375 MHz. This frequency is normalized to 1 in the document.

In order to sample 625/50 luminance signals without quality loss, the lowest multiple possible is 4, which represents a sampling rate of 13.5 MHz. This frequency line-locks to give 858 samples per line period in 525/59.94 and 864 samples per line period in 625/50.

In the component analog domain, the colour difference signals used for production purposes typically have one half the bandwidth of the luminance signal. Thus a sampling rate multiple of 2 is used, resulting in 6.75 MHz. This sampling rate allows, respectively, 429 and 432 samples per line.

Component video sampled in this way has a 4:2:2 format. Whilst other combinations are possible, 4:2:2 is the format for which the majority of production equipment is constructed. Figure 7.33(a) shows the spatial arrangement given by 4:2:2 sampling. Luminance samples appear at half the spacing of colour difference samples, and every other luminance sample is co-sited with a pair of colour difference samples. Co-siting is important because it allows all attributes of one picture point to be conveyed with a three-sample vector quantity. Modification of the three samples allows such techniques as colour correction to be performed. This would be difficult without co-sited information. Co-siting is achieved by clocking the three ADCs simultaneously.

For lower bandwidths, particularly in prefiltering operations prior to compression, the sampling rate of the colour difference signal can be halved. 4:1:1 delivers colour bandwidth in excess of that required by analog composite video.

In 4:2:2 the colour difference signals are sampled horizontally at half the luminance sampling rate, yet the vertical colour difference sampling rates are the same as for luminance. Whilst this is not a problem in a production application, this disparity of sampling rates represents a data rate overhead which is undesirable in a compression environment. In this

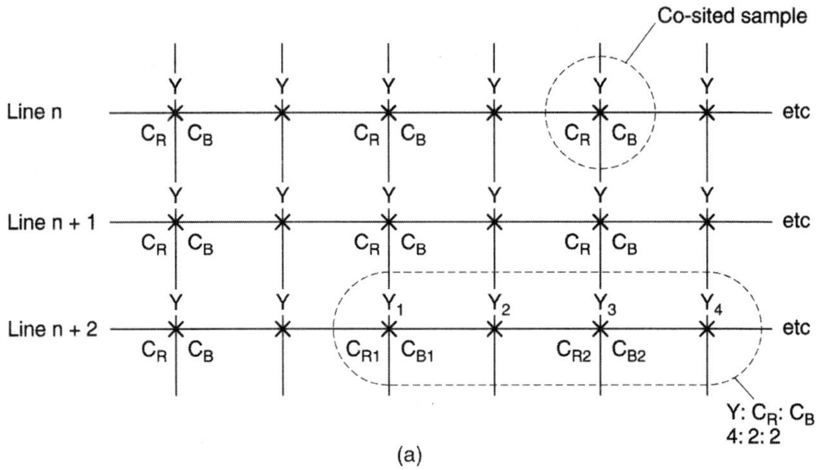

Figure 7.33(a) In CCIR-601 sampling mode 4:2:2, the line synchronous sampling rate of 13.5 MHz results in samples having the same position in successive lines, so that vertical columns are generated. The sampling rates of the colour difference signals C_R, C_B are one-half of that of luminance, i.e. 6.75 MHz, so that there are alternate *Y* only samples and co-sited samples which describe *Y*, C_R and C_B. In a run of four samples, there will be four *Y* samples, two C_R samples and two C_B samples, hence 4:2:2.

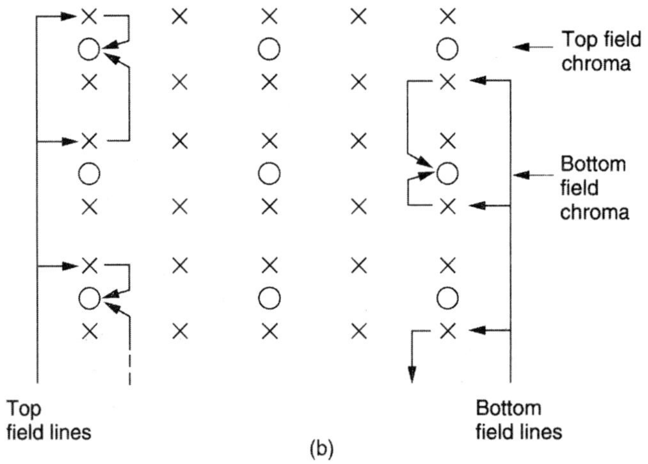

Figure 7.33(b) In 4:2:0 coding the colour difference pixels are downsampled vertically as well as horizontally. Note that the sample sites need to be vertically interpolated so that when two interlaced fields are combined the spacing is even.

case it is possible to halve the vertical sampling rate of the colour difference signals as well. Figure 7.33(b) shows that in MPEG-2 4:2:0 sampling, the colour difference signals are downsampled so that the same vertical and horizontal resolution is obtained.

The chroma samples in 4:2:0 are positioned half-way between luminance samples in the vertical axis so that they are evenly spaced when an interlaced source is used. To obtain a 4:2:2 output from 4:2:0 data a vertical interpolation process will be needed in addition to low-pass filtering.

The sampling rates of ITU-601 are based on commonality between 525- and 625-line systems. However, the consequence is that the pixel spacing is different in the horizontal and vertical axes. This is incompatible with computer graphics in which so-called 'square' pixels are used. This means that the horizontal and vertical spacing is the same, giving the same resolution in both axes. However, high-definition TV and computer graphics formats universally use 'square' pixels. Converting between square and non-square pixel data will require a rate-conversion process as described in section 3.6.

It is not necessary to digitize analog video syncs in component systems, since the sampling rate is derived from sync. The only useful video data are those sampled during the active line. All other parts of the video waveform can be re-created at a later time. It is only necessary to standardize the size and position of a digital active line. The position is specified as a given number of sampling clock periods from the leading edge of sync, and the length is simply a standard number of samples. The component digital active line is 720 luminance samples long. This is slightly longer than the analog active line and allows for some drift in the analog input. Ideally the first and last samples of the digital active line should be at blanking level.

Figure 7.34 shows that in 625-line systems[1] the control system waits for 132 sample periods before commencing sampling the line. Then 720 luminance samples and 360 of each type of colour difference sample are taken; 1440 samples in all. A further 12 sample periods will elapse before the next sync edge, making 132 + 720 + 12 = 864 sample periods. In 525-line systems[2] the analog active line is in a slightly different place and so the controller waits 122 sample periods before taking the same digital active line samples as before. There will then be 16 sample periods before the next sync edge, making 122 + 720 + 16 = 858 sample periods.

Figure 7.35 shows the luminance signal sampled at 13.5 MHz and two colour difference signals sampled at 6.75 MHz. Three separate signals with different clock rates are inconvenient and so multiplexing can be used. If the colour difference signals are multiplexed into one channel, then two 13.5 MHz channels will be required. If these channels are multiplexed into one, a 27 MHz clock will be required. The word order will be:

C_b, Y, C_r, Y, etc.

In order unambiguously to deserialize the samples, the first sample in the line is always C_b.

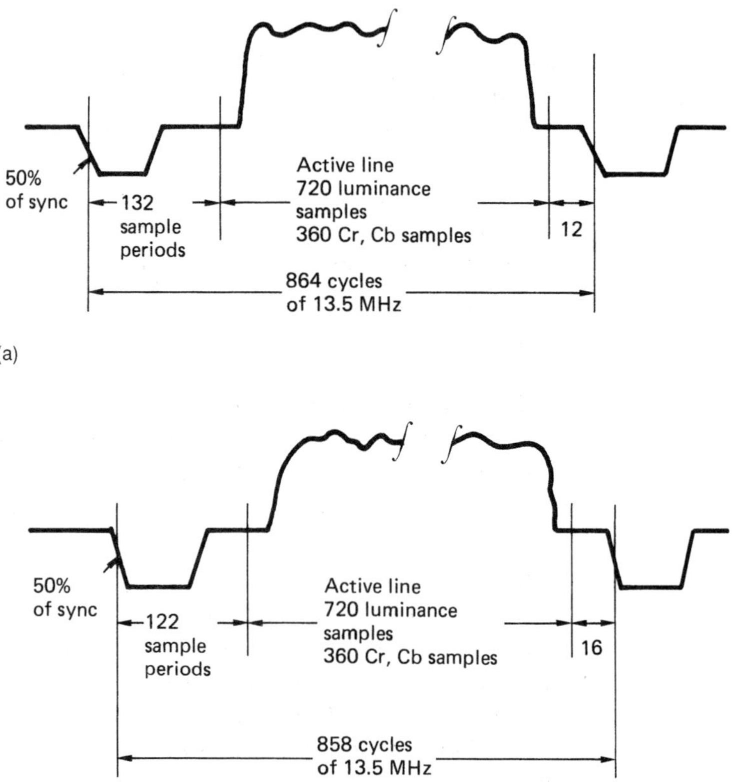

(a)

(b)

Figure 7.34 (a) In 625-line systems to CCIR-601, with 4:2:2 sampling, the sampling rate is exactly 864 times line rate, but only the active line is sampled, 132 sample periods after sync. (b) In 525 line systems to CCIR-601, with 4:2:2 sampling, the sampling rate is exactly 858 times line rate, but only the active line is sampled, 122 sample periods after sync. Note active line contains exactly the same quantity of data as for 50 Hz systems.

In addition to specifying the location of the samples, it is also necessary to standardize the relationship between the absolute analog voltage of the waveform and the digital code value used to express it so that all machines will interpret the numerical data in the same way. These relationships are in the voltage domain and are independent of the line standard used.

Both eight- and ten-bit resolution are allowed by the interface standards. Figure 7.36 shows how the luminance signal fits into the quantizing range of a eight-bit system. Black is at a level of 16_{10} and peak white is at 235_{10} so that there is some tolerance of imperfect analog signals. The sync pulse will clearly go outside the quantizing range, but this is of no consequence as conventional syncs are not transmitted. The visible voltage range fills the quantizing range and this gives the best possible resolution.

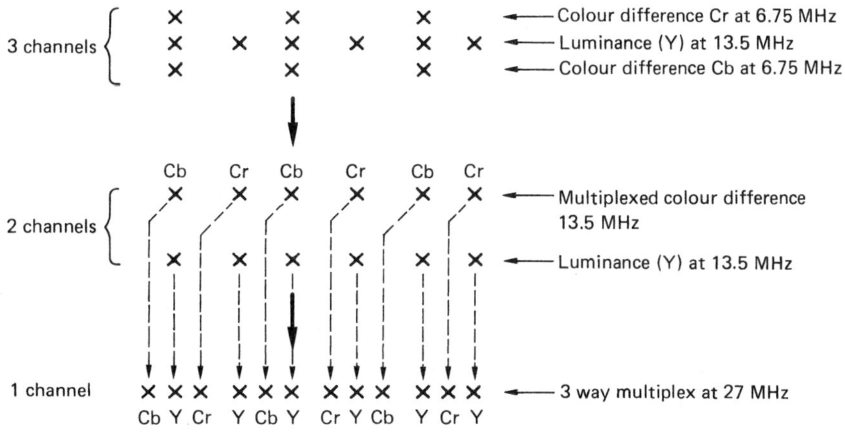

Figure 7.35 The colour difference sampling rate is one-half that of luminance, but there are *two* colour difference signals, C_r and C_b hence the colour difference data rate is equal to the luminance data rate, and a 27 MHz interleaved format is possible in a single channel.

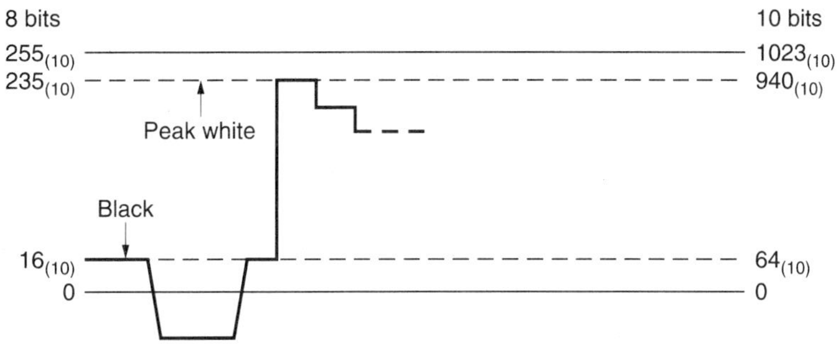

Figure 7.36 The standard luminance signal fits into eight or ten-bit quantizing structures as shown here.

The colour difference signals use offset binary, where 128_{10} is the equivalent of blanking voltage. The peak analog limits are reached at 16_{10} and 240_{10} respectively allowing once more some latitude for maladjusted analog inputs.

Note that the code values corresponding to all ones and all zeros, i.e. the two extreme ends of the quantizing range are not allowed to occur in the active line as they are reserved for synchronizing. Convertors must be followed by circuitry which catches these values and forces the LSB to a different value if out-of-range analog inputs are applied.

The peak-to-peak amplitude of Y is 220 quantizing intervals, whereas for the colour difference signals it is 225 intervals. There is thus a small gain difference between the signals. This will be cancelled out by the opposing gain difference at any future DAC, but must be borne in mind when digitally converting to other standards. Computer graphics standards often use the entire number scale with black at all zeros.

As conventional syncs are not sent, horizontal and vertical synchronizing is achieved by special bit patterns sent with each line. Immediately before the digital active line location is the *SAV* (start of active video) pattern, and immediately after is the *EAV* (end of active video) pattern. These unique patterns occur on every line and continue throughout the vertical interval.

Each sync pattern consists of four symbols. The first is all ones and the next two are all zeros. As these cannot occur in active video, their detection reliably indicates a sync pattern. The fourth symbol is a data byte which contains three data bits, *H*, *F* and *V*. These bits are protected by four redundancy bits which form a seven-bit Hamming codeword for the purpose of detecting and correcting errors. Figure 7.37 shows the structure of the sync pattern. The sync bits have the following meanings:

H is used to distinguish between *SAV*, where it is set to 0 and *EAV* where it is set to 1.

F defines the state of interlace and is 0 during the first field and 1 during the second field. *F* is only allowed to change at *EAV*. In interlaced systems, one field begins at the centre of a line, but there is no sync pattern at that location so the field bit changes at the end of the line in which the change took place.

V is 1 during vertical blanking and 0 during the active part of the field. It can only change at *EAV*.

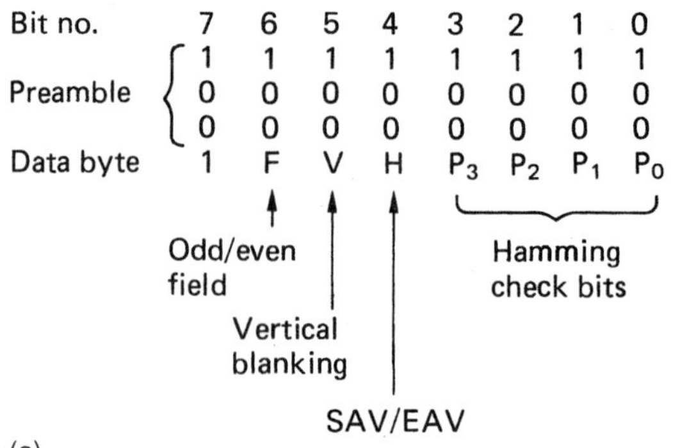

(a)

Figure 7.37(a) The 4-byte synchronizing pattern which precedes and follows every active line sample block has this structure.

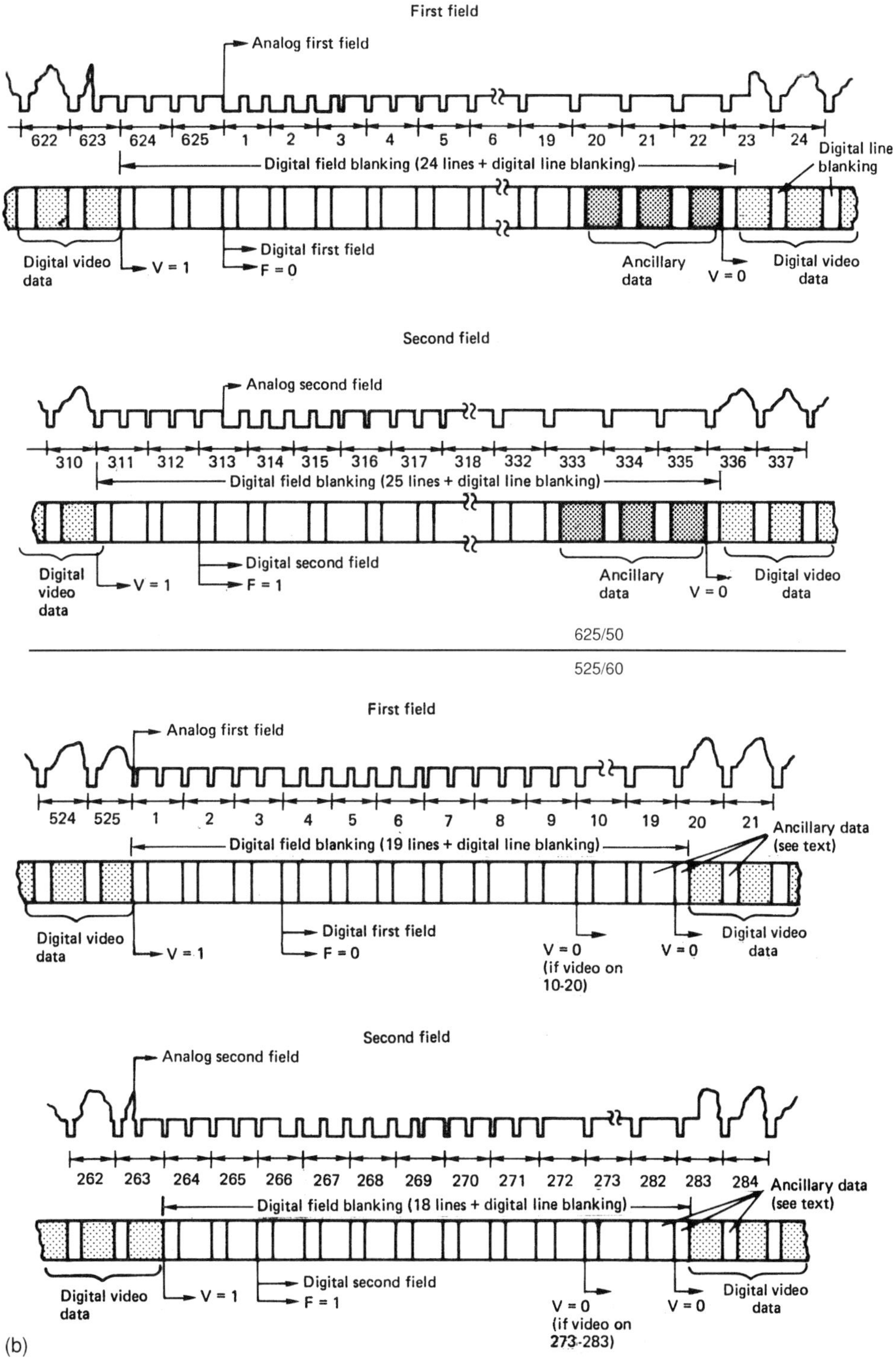

(b)

Figure 7.37(b) The relationships between analog video timing and the information in the digital timing reference signals for 625/50 (above) and 525/60 (below).

7.15 Digital colour space

Figure 7.38 shows the colour space available in eight-bit *RGB*. In computers, eight-bit *RGB* is common and claims are often seen that 16 million different colours are possible. This is nonsense.

A colour is a given combination of hue and saturation and is independent of brightness. Consequently all sets of *RGB* values having the same ratios produce the same colour. For example, $R = G = B$ always gives the same colour whatever the pixel value. Thus there are 256 brightnesses which have the same colour allowing a more believable 65 000 different colours.

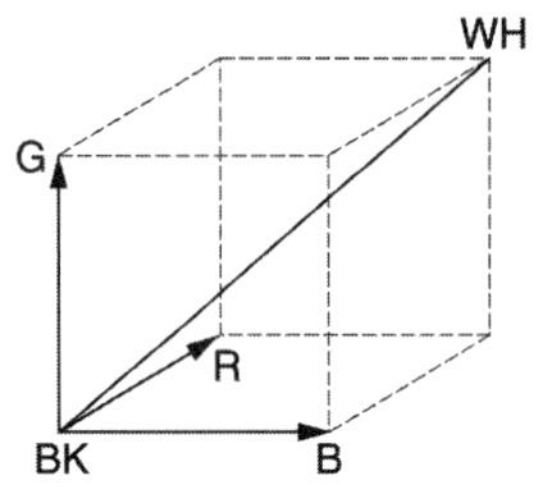

Figure 7.38 *RGB* space. If each component has eight-bit resolution, 16 million combinations are possible, but these are not all different colours as many will have the same hue and differ only in saturation.

Figure 7.39 shows the *RGB* cube mapped into eight-bit colour difference space so that it is no longer a cube. Now the grey axis goes straight up the middle because greys correspond to both C_r and C_b being zero. To visualize colour difference space, imagine looking down along the grey axis. This makes the black and white corners coincide in the centre. The remaining six corners of the legal colour difference space now correspond to the six boxes on a vectorscope. Although there are still 16 million combinations, many of these are now illegal. For example, as black or white are approached, the colour differences must fall to zero.

From an information theory standpoint, colour difference space is redundant. With some tedious geometry, it can be shown that less than a quarter of the codes are legal. The luminance resolution remains the same, but there is about half as much information in each colour axis. This due to the colour difference signals being bipolar. If the signal resolution has to be maintained, eight-bit *RGB* should be transformed to a longer wordlength in the colour difference domain, nine bits being adequate. At this stage the colour difference transform doesn't seem efficient because twenty-four-bit *RGB* converts to twenty-six-bit Y, C_r, C_b.

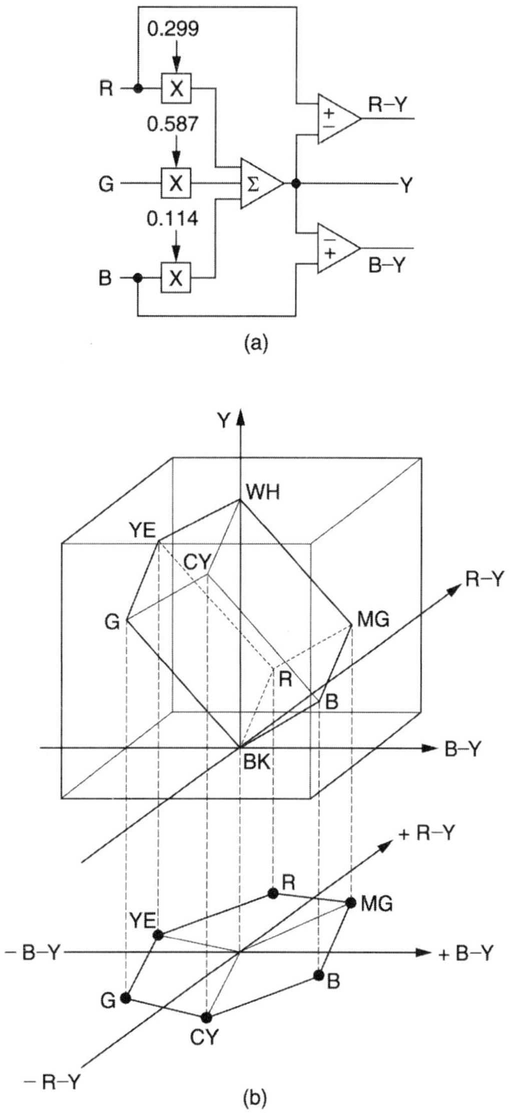

Figure 7.39 Colour difference space is entered from *RGB* via the matrix shown in (a). In colour difference space (b) the White–Black axis is vertical and colour space is an area orthogonal to that axis which moves up and down as brightness changes. Note that the conventional vectorscope display is the projection of the *RGB* cube onto the the colour plane.

In most cases the loss of colour resolution is invisible to the eye, and eight-bit resolution is retained. The results of the transform computation must be digitally dithered to avoid posterizing.

As was seen in section 6.7, the acuity of human vision is axisymmetric, making the so-called 'square pixel' the most efficient arrangement for luminance and colour difference signals alike. Figure 7.40 shows the

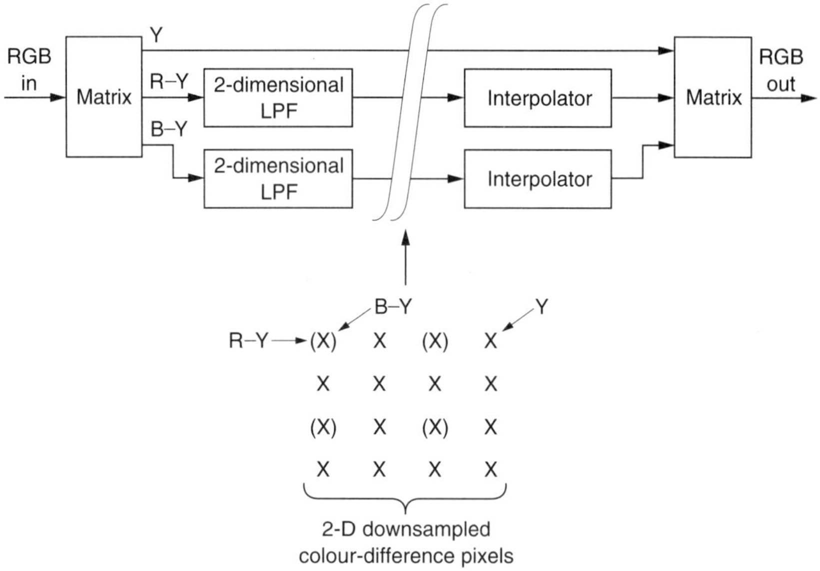

Figure 7.40 Ideal two-dimensionally downsampled colour-difference system. Colour resolution is half of luma resolution, but the eye cannot tell the difference.

ideal. The colour sampling is co-sited with the luminance sampling but the colour sample spacing is twice that of luminance. The colour difference signals after matrixing from *RGB* have to be low-pass filtered in two dimensions prior to downsampling in order to prevent aliasing of HF detail. At the display, the downsampled colour data have to be interpolated in two dimensions to produce colour information in every pixel. In an oversampling display the colour interpolation can be combined with the display upsampling stage.

Co-siting the colour and luminance pixels has the advantage that the transmitted colour values are displayed unchanged. Only the interpolated values need to be calculated. This minimizes generation loss in the filtering. Downsampling the colour by a factor of two in both axes means that the colour data are reduced to one quarter of the original amount. When viewed by the HVS this is essentially a lossless process.

7.16 Telecine

Telecine is a significant source of video signals as film continues to be an important medium. Film cameras and projectors both work by means of synchronized shutters and intermittently driven sprockets or claw mechanisms. When the shutter is closed, the film is mechanically advanced by one frame by driving the intermittent sprocket. When the film has come to rest at the next frame, the shutter opens again. This process is repeated at the frame rate of film, the most common of which is 24 Hz. In order to reduce flicker, the projector works in a slightly different way from the camera. For each film frame, the shutter opens two or three times, instead of once, multiplying the flicker frequency accordingly.

A conventional telecine machine outputs a standard broadcast video signal. Initially the output was analog, but later machines were developed which could output a standardized digital signal. The latest machines are essentially generic film scanners and output pixel data. These are known as datacines.

In telecine traditionally some liberties are taken because there was until recently no alternative. In 50 Hz telecine the film is driven at 25 fps, not 24, so that each frame results in two fields. In 60 Hz telecine the film runs at 24 fps, but odd frames result in two fields, even frames result in three fields; a process known as 3:2 pulldown. On average, there are two and a half fields per film frame giving a field rate of 60 Hz. The field repetition of telecine causes motion judder which is explained in section 7.21.

Essentially a telecine machine is a form of film projector which outputs a video signal instead of an image on a screen. Early telecine machines were no more than conventional projectors which shone light into a modified TV camera, but these soon gave way to more sophisticated devices. As television pictures are scanned vertically down the screen, it is possible to scan film using the linear motion of the film itself. In these machines there is no intermittent motion and the film is driven by a friction roller. This causes less wear to the film, and if the sprocket holes are damaged, there is less vertical instability in the picture position.

The first constant speed telecines used the 'flying spot' scanning principle. A CRT produces a small spot of white light which is focused on the film. The spot is driven back and forth across the tube by a sawtooth waveform and consequently scans the film transversely. The film modulates the intensity of the light passing through and sensors on the other side of the film produce a video output signal. It is easy to see how a constantly moving film can produce a progressively scanned video signal, but less easy to see how interlace or 3:2 pulldown can be achieved. A further problem is that on the film the bottom of one frame is only separated from the top of the next frame by a thin black bar. Scanning of the next frame would begin as soon as that of the previous frame had ended, leaving no time for the vertical interval required by the television display for vertical retrace.

In flying spot telecines, these problems were overcome by deflecting the spot along the axis of film motion in addition to the transverse scan. By deflecting the spot steadily against film motion for one frame and then jumping back for the next, the film frame would be scanned in less than real time, creating a vertical interval in the video output. By jumping the spot in the same direction as the film travel by one frame and making a further scan, two interlaced fields could be produced from one film frame.

The two-dimensional motion of the flying spot caused it to produce what is known as a 'patch' on the CRT. If the film is stopped, the shape of the patch can be changed to be the same as the shape of the frame in order to display a still picture in the video output. More complex patch generation allows a picture to be obtained with the film running at any linear speed. The patch slides along the CRT to follow a given frame, and then omits or repeats frames in order to produce a standard field rate in the video whatever the film frame rate. By controlling both the width and height of the patch independently, films of any frame size can be handled, and anamorphic formats can be linearized. Smaller parts of a film frame can be made to fill the TV screen by shrinking the patch, and the patch can be rotated for effect or to compensate for a film camera which was not level.

In order to obtain a 3:2 pulldown interlaced output, there must be five different patch positions on the CRT where one frame is scanned twice but the next is followed for three scans. There is a ten-field sequence before the geometry repeats, requiring ten different patches to be generated. This caused great difficulty in early flying spot telecines because any physical error in the relative positioning of the patches would cause the image on the TV screen to bounce vertically. The solution was to use digital field stores between the scanner and the video output. Each frame of the film could then be scanned into two fields, and the 3:2 pulldown effect is obtained by outputting from one of the field stores twice. Figure 7.41 shows the procedure which produces a correctly interlaced 60 Hz output.

Progress in field store technology made it possible to build a telecine in which the vertical motion of the patch was replaced by a process of electronic timebase correction. The line scanning mechanism is obtained

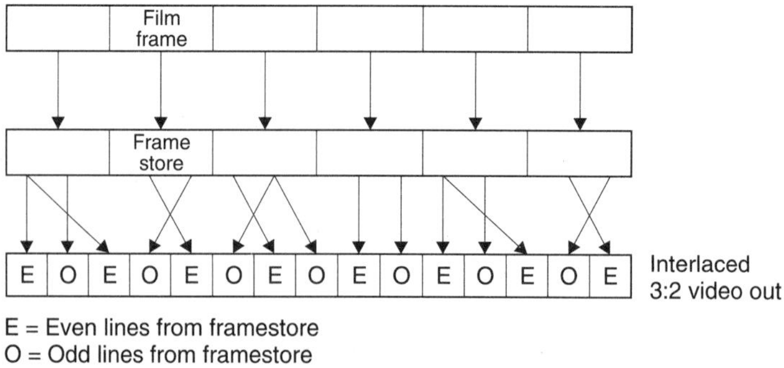

Figure 7.41 When a field store is available, 3:2 pulldown is obtained by repeating fields from the store, so the film scanning process is regular.

by projecting the steadily moving film onto a sensor consisting of a single line of CCD elements. The entire film frame is scanned progressively in one frame period and this information is stored. By reading alternate lines from the store, an interlaced output is possible. 3:2 pulldown is obtained in the same way. By reading the store faster than it is written, the film frame area can be fitted into the active picture area, leaving time for blanking. The linear sensor cannot move, so a still frame cannot be obtained. However, output is possible over a range of speeds using the frame store as a buffer.

Practical telecine machines need some form of colour correction. The colorimetry of film is subject to considerable variation and the spectral response of each emulsion layer is unlikely to be matched by the filter responses of the telecine optics. A basic colour corrector will have facilities to apply compensating DC offsets to the signals from the film as well as controlling the gamma of each component. A matrix calculation can compensate to some extent for television primaries which do not match the primary filtering used when the film was shot.

7.17 Conversion between television and computer formats

Computer terminals have evolved quite rapidly from devices which could display only a few lines of text in monochrome into high-resolution colour graphics displays which outperform conventional television.

The domains of computer graphics and television have in common only that images are represented. The degree of incompatibility is such that one could be forgiven for thinking that it was the outcome of a perverse competition. Nevertheless with sufficient care good results can be obtained. Figure 7.42 shows that the number of issues involved is quite large. If only one of these is not correctly addressed, the results will be disappointing. The number of processes also suggests that each must be

Colour primaries
Gamma
Digital gamut
Pixel aspect ratio
Interlace/progressive
Picture aspect ratio
Picture rate

Figure 7.42 The various issues involved in converting between broadcast video and computer graphics formats. The problem is non-trivial but failure to address any one of these aspects will result in impairment.

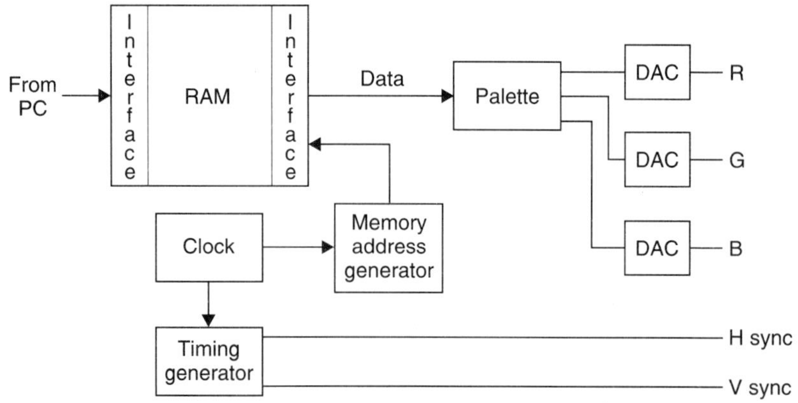

Figure 7.43 A typical computer graphics card. See text for details.

performed with adequate precision, otherwise there will be a tolerance build-up or generation loss problem.

Figure 7.43 shows a typical graphics card. The pixel values to be displayed are written into a frame store by the CPU and the display mechanism reads the frame store line by line to produce a raster scanned image. Pixel array sizes are described as $x \times y$ pixels and these have been subject to much greater variation than has been the case in television. Figure 7.44 shows some of the array sizes supported in graphics devices. As computer screens tend to be used in brighter ambient light than television screens, the displays have to be brighter and this makes flicker more visible. This can be overcome by running at a frame rate of 75 Hz.

320 × 200
320 × 350
360 × 400
640 × 200
720 × 400
720 × 350
640 × 350
640 × 400
640 × 480
640 × 473
800 × 600
1056 × 350
1056 × 480
1056 × 473
1118 × 350
1118 × 480
1118 × 473
1024 × 768

Figure 7.44 The array sizes which may be found in computer graphics.

Pin	
1	Red
2	Green
3	Blue
4	N/C
5	Ground
6	Red return
7	Green return
8	Blue return
9	Key pin
10	Sync return
11	Monitor ID (not used)
12	Ground if monochrome monitor
13	H sync
14	V sync
15	N/C

Figure 7.45 The standard IBM graphics connector and its associated signals.

A typical graphics card outputs analog *RGB* which can drive a CRT display. The analog outputs are provided by eight-bit DACs. Figure 7.45 shows the standard IBM graphics connector. In order to avoid storing twenty-four bits per pixel, some systems restrict the number of different colours which can be displayed at once.

Between the frame store and the DACs is a device called a palette or colour look-up table (CLUT). This can be preloaded with a range of colours which are appropriate for the image to be displayed. Whilst this is adequate for general-purpose computing, it is unsuitable for quality image portrayal.

Computer graphics takes a somewhat different view of gamma than does television. This may be due to the fact that early computer displays had no grey scale and simply produced binary video (black or white) in which linearity has no meaning. As computer graphics became more sophisticated, each pixel became a binary number and a grey scale was possible. The gamma of the CRT display was simply compensated by an inverse gamma look-up table (LUT) prior to the video DAC as shown in Figure 7.46(a). This approach means that the pixel data within the computer are in the linear light domain. This in itself is not a problem, but when linear light is represented by only eight-bit pixels, then contouring in dark areas is inevitable. Linear light needs to be expressed by around fourteen bits for adequate resolution as was seen in Chapter 6.

In order to improve the situation, certain manufacturers moved away from the linear light domain, but without going as far as conventional television practice. The solution was that the internal data would be subject to a partial inverse gamma, as shown in Figure 7.46(b), followed by a further partial inverse gamma stage in the LUT of the graphics card.

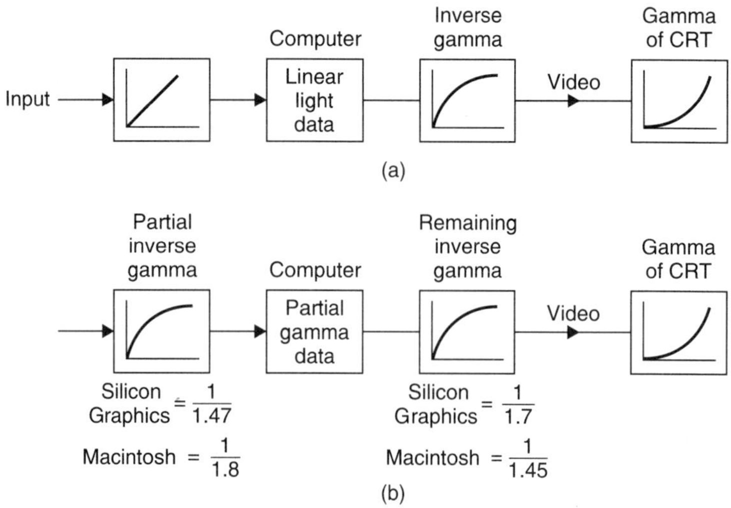

Figure 7.46 Computers and gamma: a dog's dinner. At (a) a simple system uses linear light-coding internals and an inverse gamma LUT prior to the CRT. With only eight-bit data this suffers excessive quantizing error. (b) Improved performance is obtained by having partial inverse gamma internal data in tandem with a further partial inverse gamma prior to the CRT. Unfortunately there are two conflicting incompatible standards.

The combined effect of the two inverse gammas was correctly to oppose the CRT gamma.

Unfortunately Silicon Graphics and Macintosh came up with systems in which the two gamma stages were completely incompatible even though the overall result in both cases is correct. Data from one format cannot be displayed on the other format (or as video) without gamma conversion. In the absence of gamma conversion the grey scale will be non-linear, crushing either dark areas or light areas depending on the direction of data transfer. Gamma conversion is relatively straightforward as a simple look-up table can be created with eight-bit data.

Whatever the direction of conversion, one of the formats involved is likely to be *RGB*. It is useful if this is made the internal format of the conversion. Figure 7.47 shows that if the input is colour difference based, conversion should be done early, whereas if the output is to be colour difference based, the conversion should be done late.

It is also worth considering the use of the linear light domain within the conversion process. This overcomes any quality loss due to failure of constant luminance and distortion due to interpolating gamma-based signals. Figure 7.48 shows the principle. The gamma of the input format is reversed at the input and the gamma of the output format is re-created after all other processing is complete. Gamma in television signals generally follows a single standard, whereas with a computer format it will be necessary to establish exactly what gamma was assumed.

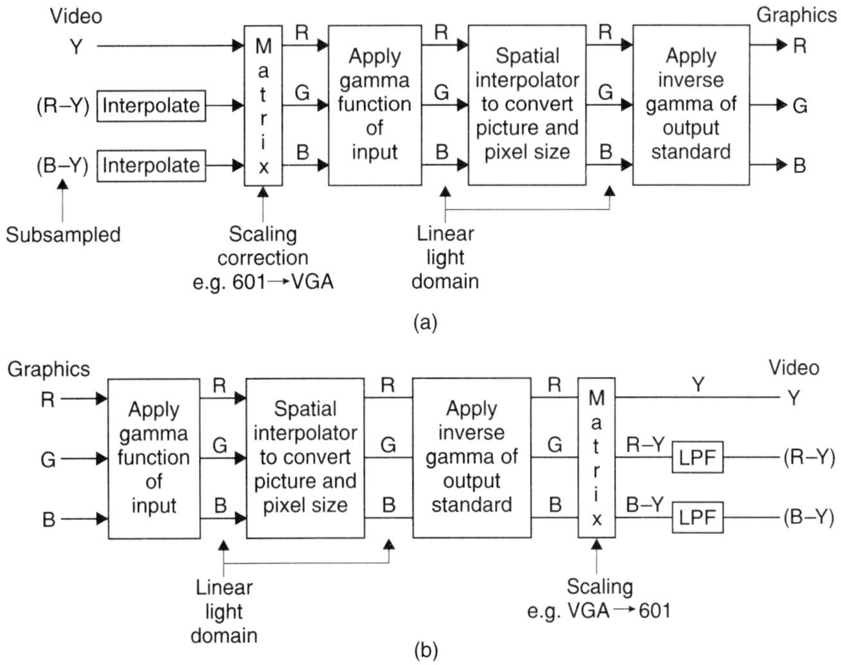

Figure 7.47 Possible strategies for video/computer conversion. (a) video to graphics *RGB*. (b) Graphics *RGB* to video.

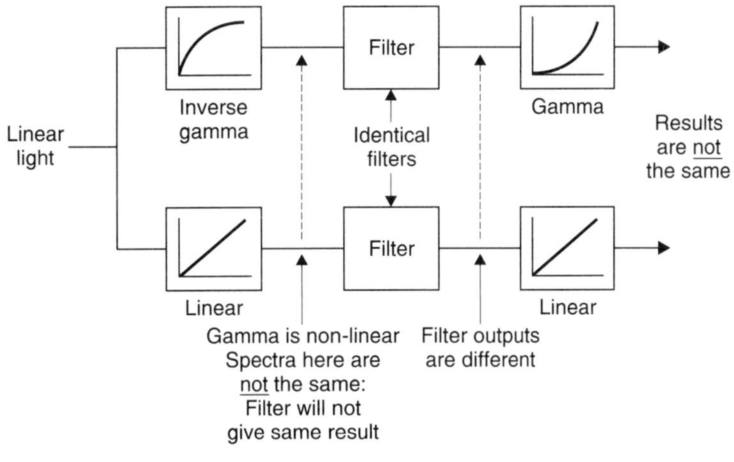

Figure 7.48 Gamma is a compression technique and for the finest results it should not be used in any image-manipulation process because the result will be distorted. Accurate work should be done in the linear light domain.

Computer formats tend to use the entire number scale from black to white, such that in eight-bit systems black is 00Hex and white is FF. However, television signals according to ITU 601 have some headroom above white and footroom below black. If gamma, headroom and footroom conversion is not properly performed, the result will be black crushing, white crushing, lack of contrast of a distorted grey scale.

Colorimetry may be a problem in conversion. Television signals generally abide by ITU 709 colorimetry, whereas computer graphic files could use almost any set of primaries. As was seen in Chapter 6, it is not unusual for computer screens to run at relatively high colour temperatures to give brighter pictures. If the primaries are known, then it is possible to convert between colour spaces using matrix arithmetic. Figure 7.49 shows that if two triangles are created on the chromaticity diagram, one for each set of primaries, then wherever the triangles overlap, ideal conversion is possible. In the case of colours where there is no overlap the best that can be done is to produce the correct hue by calculating the correct vector from the white point, even if the saturation is incorrect.

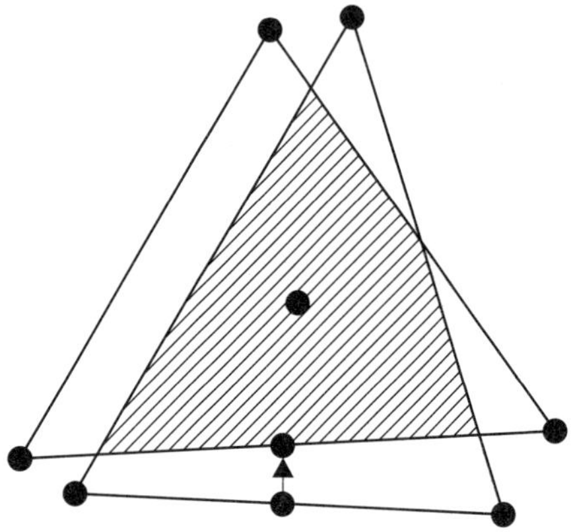

Figure 7.49 Conversion between colour spaces only works where the areas enclosed by the primary triangles overlap (shaded). Outside these areas the best that can be done is to keep the hue correct by accepting a saturation error.

Where the colorimetry is not known, accurate conversion is impossible. However, in practice acceptable results can be obtained by adjusting the primary gains to achieve an acceptable colour balance on a recognizable part of the image such as a white area or a flesh tone.

The image size or pixel count will be different and, with the exception of recent formats, the television signal will be interlaced and will not necessarily use square pixels. Spatial interpolation will be needed to move between pixel array sizes and pixel aspect ratios. The frame rate may also be different. The best results will be obtained using motion compensation. If both formats are progressively scanned, resizing and rate conversion are separable, but if interlace is involved the problem is not separable and resizing and rate conversion should be done simultaneously in a three-dimensional filter.

7.18 The importance of motion compensation

Section 2.16 introduced the concept of eye tracking and the optic flow axis. The optic flow axis is the locus of some point on a moving object which will be in a different place in successive pictures. Any device which computes with respect to the optic flow axis is said to be *motion compensated*. Until recently the amount of computation required in motion compensation was too expensive, but now this is no longer the case the technology has become very important in moving image-portrayal systems.

Figure 7.50(a) shows an example of a moving object which is in a different place in each of three pictures. The optic flow axis is shown. The object is not moving with respect to the optic flow axis and if this axis can be found some very useful results are obtained. The proces of finding the optic flow axis is called *motion estimation*. Motion estimation is literally a process which analyses successive pictures and determines how objects move from one to the next. It is an important enabling technology because of the way it parallels the action of the human eye.

Figure 7.50(b) shows that if the object does not change its appearance as it moves, it can be portrayed in two of the pictures by using data from one picture only, simply by shifting part of the picture to a new location. This can be done using vectors as shown. Instead of transmitting a lot of pixel data, a few vectors are sent instead. This is the basis of motion-compensated compression which is used extensively in MPEG as will be seen in Chapter 9.

Figure 7.50(c) shows that if a high-quality standards conversion is required between two different frame rates, the output frames can be synthesized by moving image data, not through time, but along the optic flow axis. This locates objects where they would have been if frames had been sensed at those times, and the result is a judder-free conversion. This process can be extended to drive image displays at a frame rate higher than the input rate so that flicker and background strobing are reduced. This technology is available in certain high-quality consumer television sets. This approach may also be used with 24 Hz film to eliminate judder in telecine machines.

Figure 7.50(d) shows that noise reduction relies on averaging two or more images so that the images add but the noise cancels. Conventional noise reducers fail in the presence of motion, but if the averaging process takes place along the optic flow axis, noise reduction can continue to operate.

The way in which eye tracking avoides aliasing is fundamental to the perceived quality of television pictures. Many processes need to manipulate moving images in the same way in order to avoid the obvious difficulty of processing with respect to a fixed frame of reference.

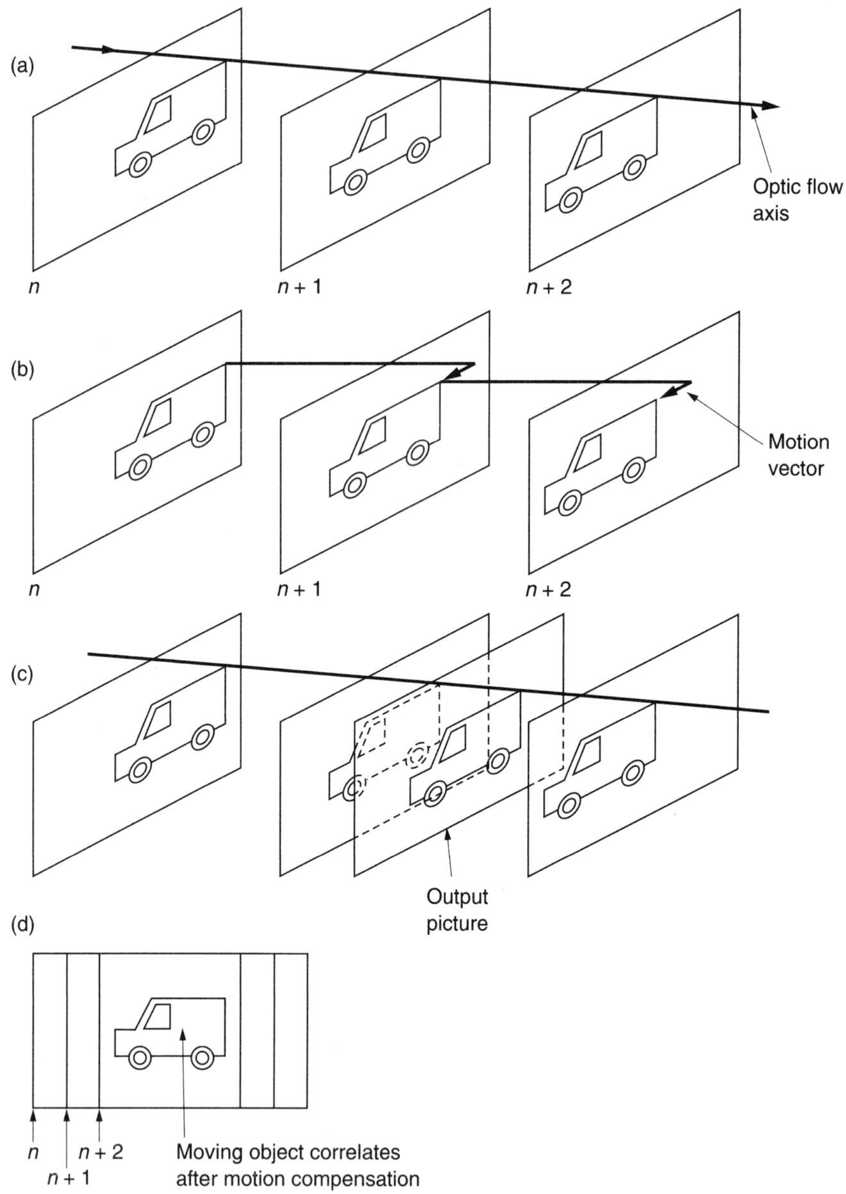

Figure 7.50 Motion compensation is an important technology. (a) The optic flow axis is found for a moving object. (b) The object in picture (n + 1) and (n + 2) can be re-created by shifting the object of picture n using motion vectors. MPEG uses this process for compression. (c) A standards convertor creates a picture on a new timebase by shifting object data along the optic flow axis. (d) With motion compensation a moving object can still correlate from one picture to the next so that noise reduction is possible.

Processes of this kind are referred to as *motion compensated* and rely on a quite separate process which has measured the motion.

Motion compensation is also important where interlaced video needs to be processed as it allows the best possible de-interlacing performance.

7.19 Motion-estimation techniques

There are three main methods of motion estimation which are to be found in various applications: block matching, gradient matching and phase correlation. Each have their own characteristics which are quite different.

Block matching is the simplest technique to follow. In a given picture, a block of pixels is selected and stored as a reference. If the selected block is part of a moving object, a similar block of pixels will exist in the next picture, but not in the same place. As Figure 7.51 shows, block matching simply moves the reference block around over the second picture looking for matching pixel values. When a match is found, the displacement needed to obtain it is used as a basis for a motion vector.

Whilst simple in concept, block matching requires an enormous amount of computation because every possible motion must be tested over the assumed range. Thus if the object is assumed to have moved over a 16-pixel range, then it will be necessary to test sixteen different horizontal displacements in each of sixteen vertical positions; in excess of 65 000 positions. At each position every pixel in the block must be compared with every pixel in the second picture. In typical video

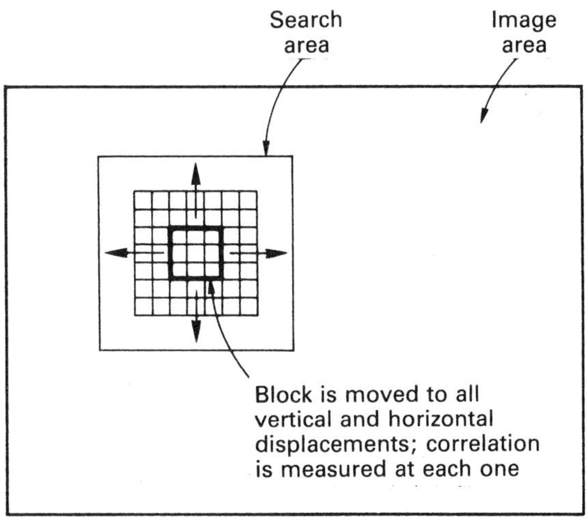

Figure 7.51 In block matching the search block has to be positioned at all possible relative motions within the search area and a correlation measured at each one.

displacements of twice the figure quoted here may be found, particularly in sporting events, and the computation then required becomes enormous. If the motion is required to subpixel accuracy, then before any matching can be attempted the picture will need to be interpolated.

7.20 Motion-compensated picture rate conversion

A conventional standards convertor is not transparent to motion portrayal, and the effect is judder and loss of resolution. Figure 7.52 shows what happens on the time axis in a conversion between 60 Hz and 50 Hz (in either direction). Fields in the two standards appear in different planes cutting through the spatio-temporal volume, and the job of the standards convertor is to interpolate along the time axis between input planes in one standard in order to estimate what an intermediate plane in the other standard would look like. With still images, this is easy, because planes can be slid up and down the time axis with no ill effect. If an object is moving, it will be in a different place in successive fields. Interpolating between several fields results in multiple images of the object. The position of the dominant image will not move smoothly, an effect which is perceived as judder. Motion compensation is designed to eliminate this undesirable judder.

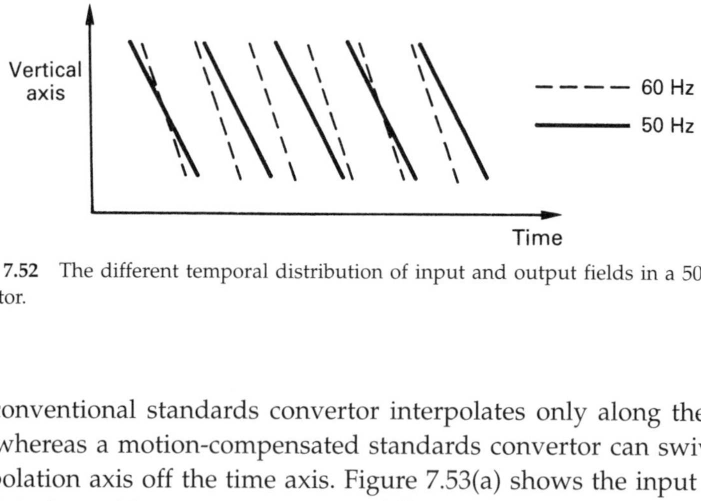

Figure 7.52 The different temporal distribution of input and output fields in a 50/60 Hz convertor.

A conventional standards convertor interpolates only along the time axis, whereas a motion-compensated standards convertor can swivel its interpolation axis off the time axis. Figure 7.53(a) shows the input fields in which three objects are moving in a different way. At (b) it will be seen that the interpolation axis is aligned with the optic flow axis of each moving object in turn.

Each object is no longer moving with respect to its own optic flow axis, and so on that axis it no longer generates temporal frequencies due to motion and temporal aliasing due to motion cannot occur.[3] Interpolation

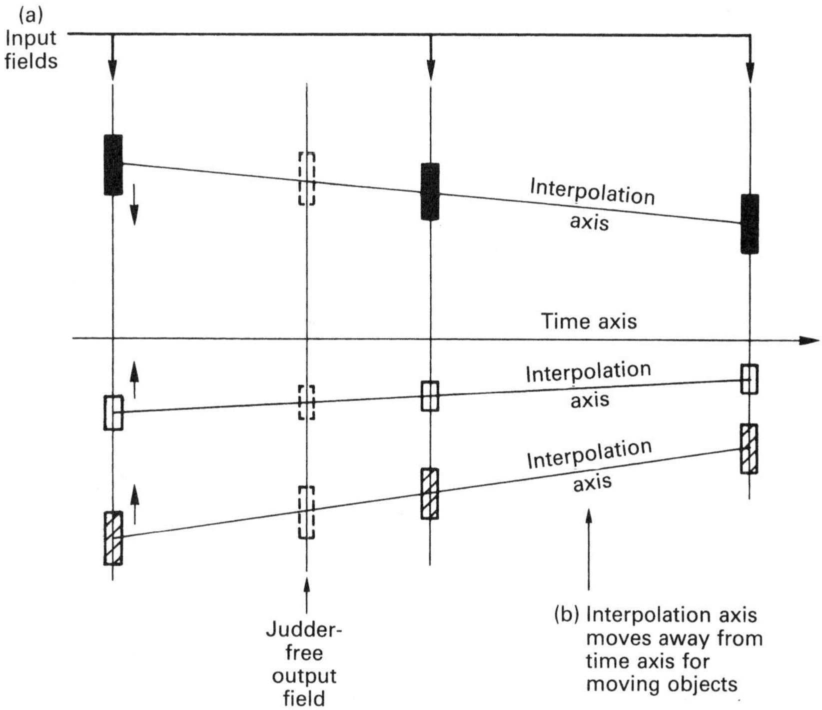

Figure 7.53 (a) Input fields with moving objects. (b) Moving the interpolation axes to make them parallel to the trajectory of each object.

along the optic flow axes will then result in a sequence of output fields in which motion is properly portrayed. The process requires a standards convertor which contains filters that are modified to allow the interpolation axis to move dynamically within each output field. The signals which move the interpolation axis are known as motion vectors. It is the job of the motion-estimation system to provide these motion vectors. The overall performance of the convertor is determined primarily by the accuracy of the motion vectors. An incorrect vector will result in unrelated pixels from several fields being superimposed and the result is unsatisfactory.

Figure 7.54 shows the sequence of events in a motion-compensated standards convertor. The motion estimator measures movements between successive fields. These motions must then be attributed to objects by creating boundaries around sets of pixels having the same motion. The result of this process is a set of motion vectors, hence the term 'vector assignation'. The motion vectors are then input to a modified four-field standards convertor in order to deflect the interfield interpolation axis.

The vectors from the motion estimator actually measure the distance moved by an object from one input field to another. What the standards

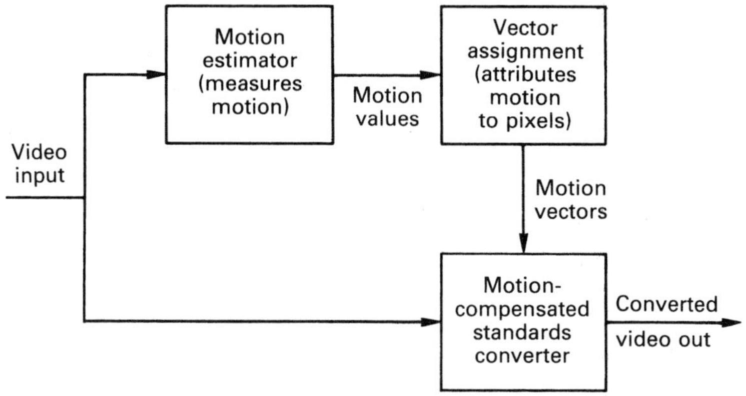

Figure 7.54 The essential stages of a motion-compensated standards convertor.

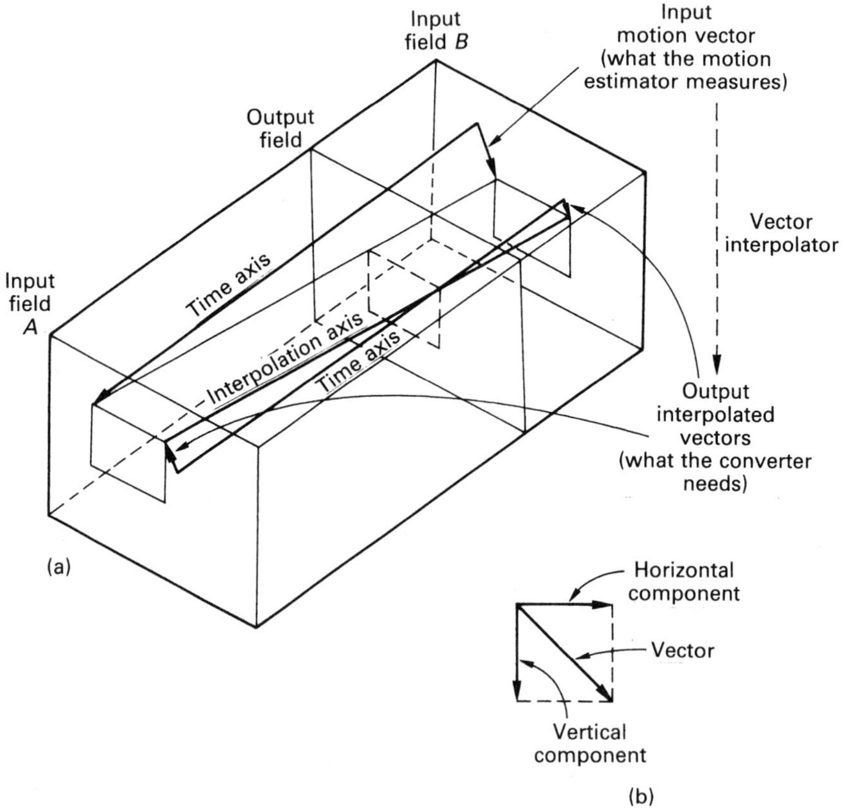

Figure 7.55 The motion vectors on the input field structure must be interpolated onto the output field structure as in (a). The field to be interpolated is positioned temporally between source fields and the motion vector between them is apportioned according to the location. Motion vectors are two-dimensional, and can be transmitted as vertical and horizontal components shown at (b) which control the spatial shifting of input fields.

convertor requires is the value of motion vectors at an output field. A vector interpolation stage is needed which computes where between the input fields A and B the current output field lies, and uses this to proportion the motion vector into two parts. Figure 7.55(a) shows that the first part is the motion between field A and the output field; the second is the motion between field B and the output field. Clearly the difference between these two vectors is the motion between input fields. These processed vectors are used to displace parts of the input fields so that the axis of interpolation lies along the optic flow axis. The moving object is stationary with respect to this axis so interpolation between fields along it will not result in any judder.

Whilst a conventional convertor only needs to interpolate vertically and temporally, a motion-compensated convertor also needs to interpolate horizontally to account for lateral movement in images. Figure 7.55(b) shows that the motion vector from the motion estimator is resolved into two components, vertical and horizontal. The spatial impulse response of the interpolator is shifted in two dimensions by these components. This shift may be different in each of the fields which contribute to the output field.

When an object in the picture moves, it will obscure its background. The vector interpolator in the standards convertor handles this automatically provided the motion estimation has produced correct vectors. Figure 7.56 shows an example of background handling. The moving

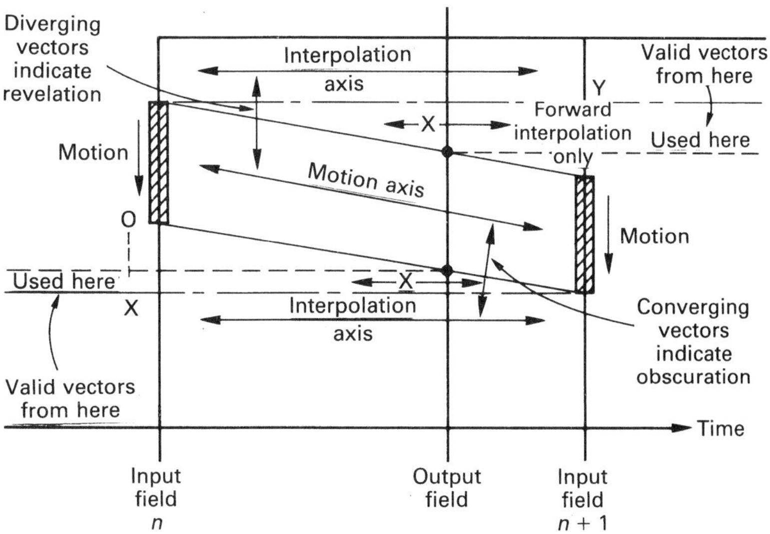

Figure 7.56 Background handling. When a vector for an output pixel near a moving object is not known, the vectors from adjacent background areas are assumed. Converging vectors imply obscuring is taking place which requires that interpolation can only use previous field data. Diverging vectors imply that the background is being revealed and interpolation can only use data from later fields.

object produces a finite vector associated with each pixel, whereas the stationary background produces zero vectors except in the area O – X where the background is being obscured. Vectors converge in the area where the background is being obscured, and diverge where it is being revealed. Image correlation is poor in these areas so no valid vector is assigned.

An output field is located between input fields, and vectors are projected through it to locate the intermediate position of moving objects. These are interpolated along an axis which is parallel to the optic flow axis. This results in address mapping which locates the moving object in the input field RAMs. However, the background is not moving and so the optic flow axis is parallel to the time axis. The pixel immediately below the leading edge of the moving object does not have a valid vector because it is in the area O – X where forward image correlation failed.

The solution is for that pixel to assume the motion vector of the background below point X, but only to interpolate in a backwards direction, taking pixel data from previous fields. In a similar way, the pixel immediately behind the trailing edge takes the motion vector for the background above point Y and interpolates only in a forward direction, taking pixel data from future fields. The result is that the moving object is portrayed in the correct place on its trajectory, and the background around it is filled in only from fields which contain useful data.

The technology of the motion-compensated standards convertor can be used in other applications. When video recordings are played back in slow motion, the result is that the same picture is displayed several times, followed by a jump to the next picture. Figure 7.57 shows that a moving object would remain in the same place on the screen during picture repeats, but jump to a new position as a new picture was played. The eye attempts to track the moving object, but, as Figure 7.57 also shows, the location of the moving object wanders with respect to the trajectory of the eye, and this is visible as judder.

Motion-compensated slow-motion systems are capable of synthesizing new images which lie between the original images from a slow-motion source. Figure 7.58 shows that two successive images in the original recording (using DVE terminology, these are source fields) are fed into the unit, which then measures the distance travelled by all moving objects between those images. Using interpolation, intermediate fields (target fields) are computed in which moving objects are positioned so that they lie on the eye trajectory. Using the principles described above, background information is removed as moving objects conceal it, and replaced as the rear of an object reveals it. Judder is thus removed and motion with a fluid quality is obtained.

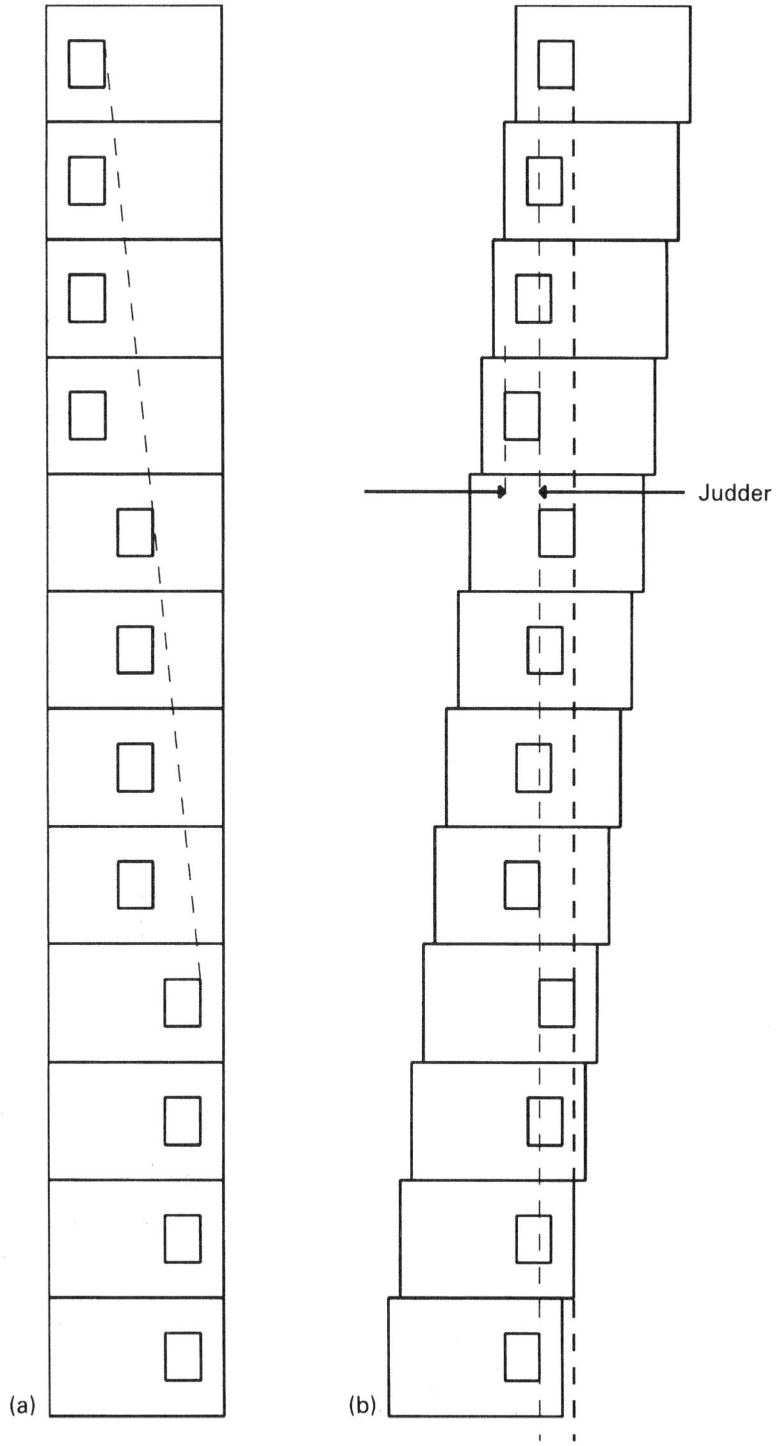

Figure 7.57 Conventional slow motion using field repeating with stationary eye shown at (a). With tracking eye at (b) the source of judder is seen.

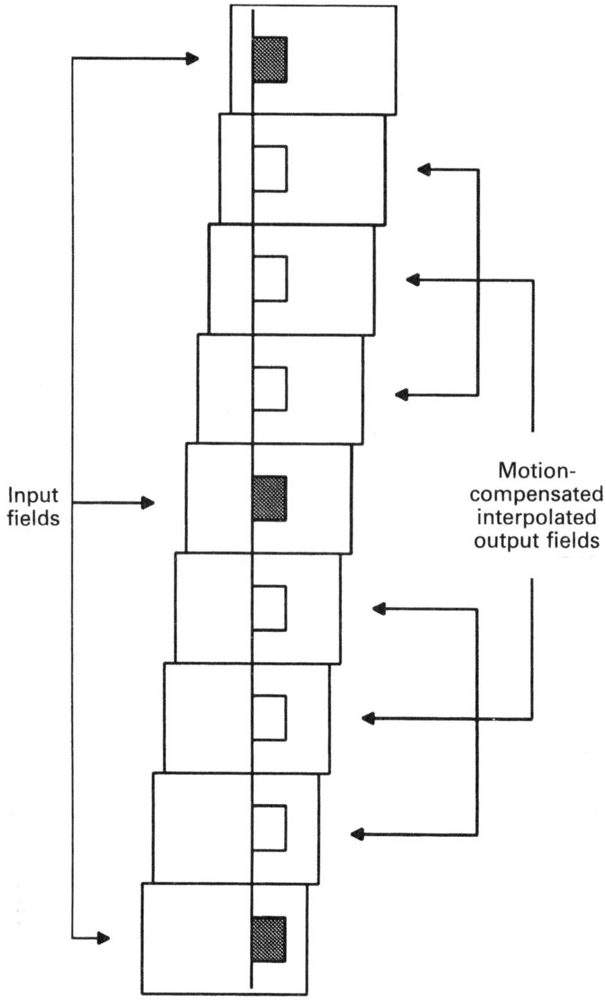

Figure 7.58 In motion-compensated slow motion, output fields are interpolated with moving objects displaying judder-free linear motion between input fields.

7.21 Motion-compensated telecine system

Figure 7.59(a) shows the time axis of film, where entire frames are simultaneously exposed, or sampled, at typically 24 Hz. The result is that the image is effectively at right angles to the time axis. During filming, some of the frame period is required to transport the film, and the shutter is closed whilst this takes place. The temporal aperture or exposure is thus somewhat shorter than the frame period.

When displayed in the cinema, each frame of a film is generally projected twice to produce a flicker frequency of 48 Hz. The result with a

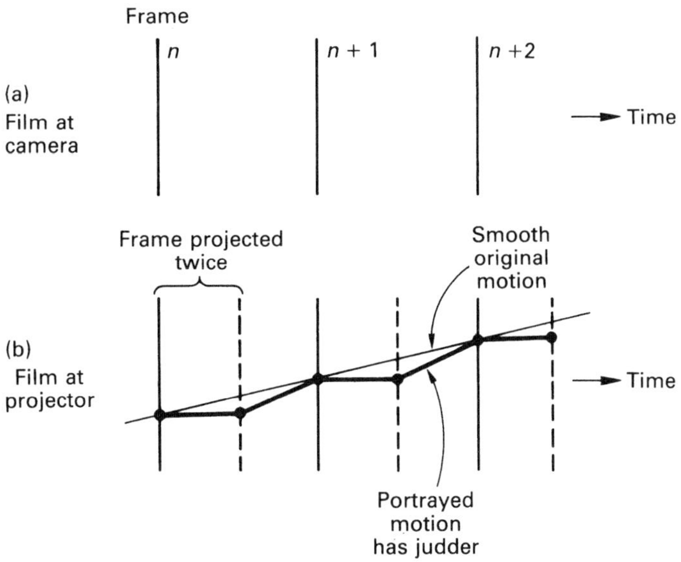

Figure 7.59 (a) The spatio-temporal characteristic of film. Note that each frame is repeated twice on projection. (b) The frame repeating results in motion judder as shown here.

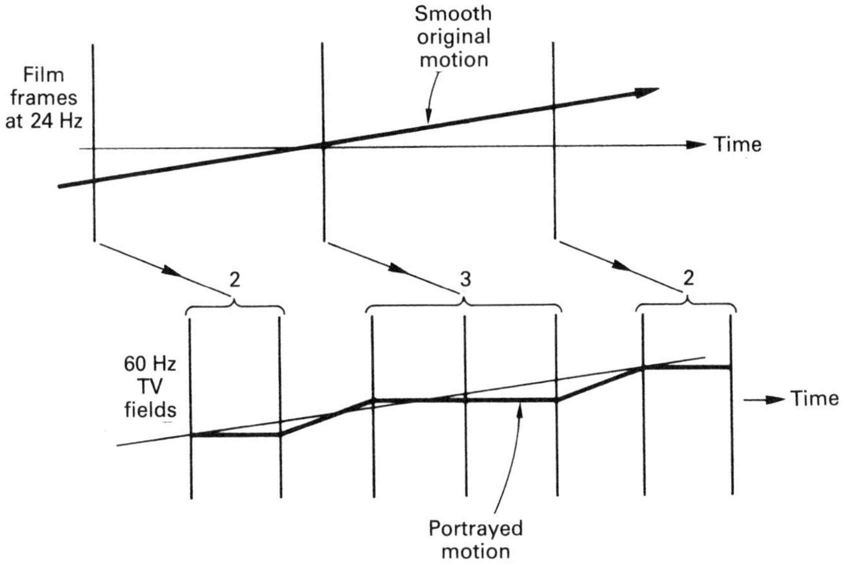

Figure 7.59 (c) Telecine machines must use 3:2 pulldown to produce 60 Hz field rate video.

moving object is that the motion is not properly portrayed and there is judder. Figure 7.59(b) shows the origin of the judder.

The same effect is evident if film is displayed on a CRT via a conventional telecine machine. In telecine the film is transported at 25 fps and each frame results in two fields in 50 Hz standards and this will result in judder as well. In 60 Hz telecine the film travels at 24 fps, but odd frames result in three fields, even frames result in two fields; the well-known 3/2 pulldown. Motion portrayal (or lack of it) in this case is shown in Figure 7.59(c).

In fact the telecine machine is a perfect application for motion compensation. As Figure 7.60 shows, each film frame is converted to a progressive scan image in a telecine machine, and then a motion-compensated standards conversion process is used to output whatever frame rate is required without judder, leading to much-improved subjective quality.

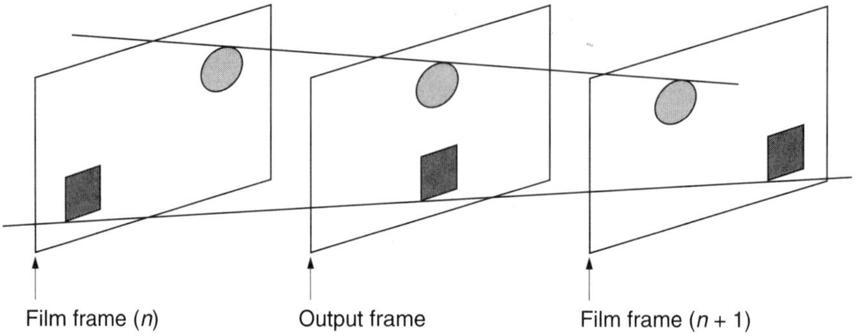

Figure 7.60 A film with a frame rate of 24 Hz cannot be displayed directly because of flicker. Using a motion-compensated standards conversion process extra frames can be synthesized in which moving objects are correctly positioned. Any television picture rate can then be obtained from film.

If the original film is not available, 50 and 60 Hz video recording can be used. In the case of 50 Hz, pairs of fields are combined to produce progressively scanned frames. In the case of 60 Hz, the third field in the 3/2 sequence is identified and discarded, prior to de-interlacing. Motion-compensated rate conversion then proceeds as before.

7.22 Camera shake compensation

As video cameras become smaller and lighter, it becomes increasingly difficult to move them smoothly and the result is camera shake. This is irritating to watch, as well as requiring a higher bit rate in compression systems. There are two solutions to the problem, one which is contained within the camera, and one which can be used at some later time on the video data.

Figure 7.61 shows that image-stabilizing cameras contain miniature gyroscopes which produce an electrical output proportional to their rate

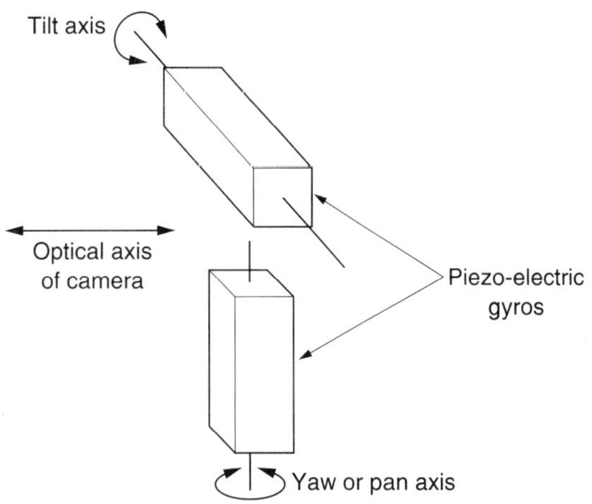

Figure 7.61 Image-stabilizing cameras sense shake using a pair of orthogonal gyros which sense movement of the optical axis.

of turn about a specified axis. A pair of these, mounted orthogonally, can produce vectors describing the camera shake. This can be used to oppose the shake by shifting the image. In one approach, the shifting is done optically. Figure 7.62 shows a pair of glass plates with the intervening space filled with transparent liquid. By tilting the plates a variable angle prism can be obtained and this is fitted in the optical system before the

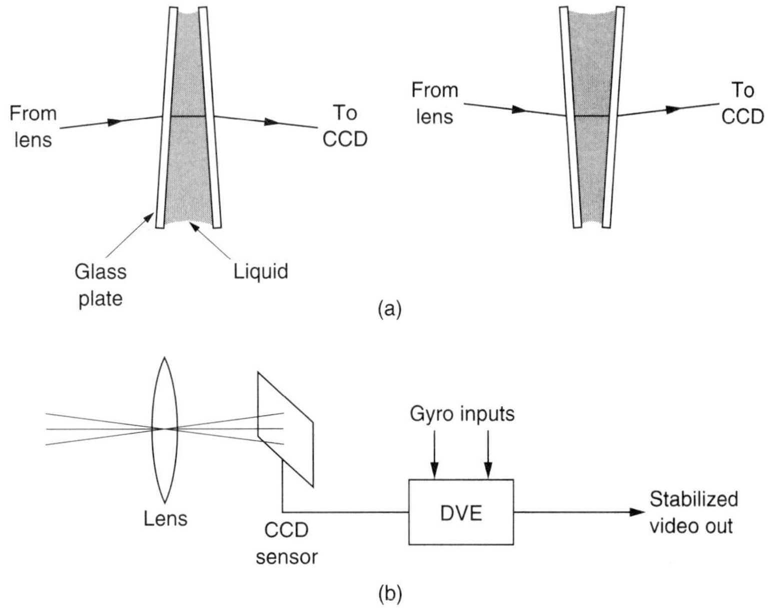

Figure 7.62 Image-stabilizing cameras. (a) The image is stabilized optically prior to the CCD sensors. (b) The CCD output contains image shake, but this is opposed by the action of a DVE configured to shift the image under control of the gyro inputs.

sensor. If the prism plates are suitably driven by servos from the gyroscopic sensors, the optical axis along which the camera is looking can remain constant despite shake. Shift is also possible by displacing some of the lens elements.

Alternatively, the camera can contain a DVE where the vectors from the gyroscopes cause the CCD camera output to be shifted horizontally or vertically so that the image remains stable. This approach is commonly used in consumer camcorders.

A great number of video recordings and films already exist in which there is camera shake. Film also suffers from weave in the telecine machine. In this case the above solutions are inappropriate and a suitable signal processor is required. Figure 7.63 shows that motion compensation can be used. If a motion estimator is arranged to find the motion between a series of pictures, camera shake will add a fixed component in each picture to the genuine object motions. This can be used to compute the optic flow axis of the camera, independently of the objects portrayed.

Operating over several pictures, the trend in camera movement can be separated from the shake by filtering, to produce a position error for each picture. Each picture is then shifted in a DVE in order to cancel the position error. The result is that the camera shake is gone and the camera movements appear smooth. In order to prevent the edges of the frame moving visibly, the DVE also performs a slight magnification so that the edge motion is always outside the output frame.

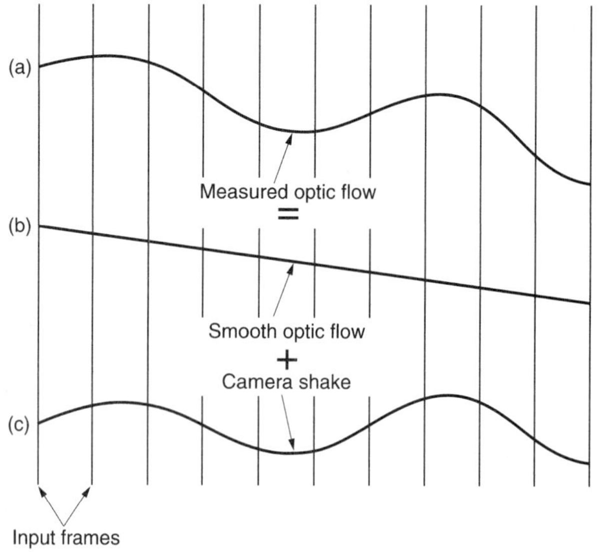

Figure 7.63 In digital image stabilizing the optic flow axis of objects in the input video is measured as in (a). This motion is smoothed to obtain a close approximation to the original motion (b). If this is subtracted from (a) the result is the camera shake motion (c) which is used to drive the image stabilizer.

7.23 Motion-compensated de-interlacing

The most efficient way of de-interlacing is to use motion compensation. Figure 7.64 shows that when an object moves in an interlaced system, the interlace breaks down with respect to the optic flow axis as was seen in section 2.17. If the motion is known, two or more fields can be shifted so that a moving object is in the same place in both. Pixels from both fields can then be used to describe the object with better resolution than would be possible from one field alone. It will be seen from Figure 7.65 that the combination of two fields in this way will result in pixels having a highly

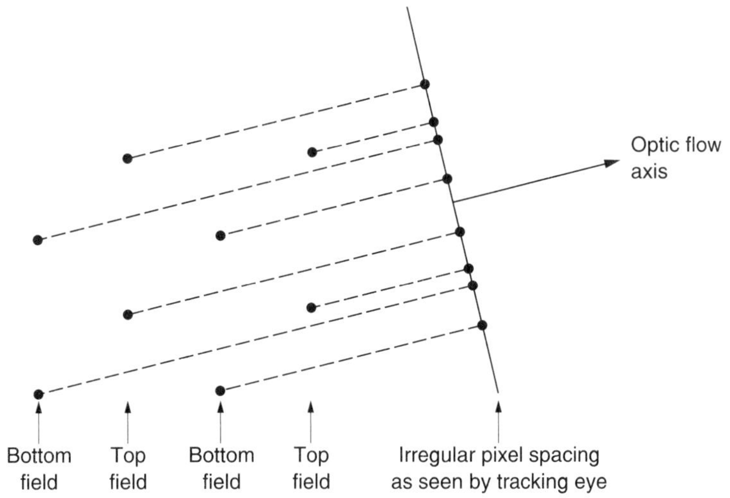

Figure 7.64 In the presence of vertical motion or motion having a vertical component, interlace breaks down and the pixel spacing with respect to the tracking eye becomes irregular.

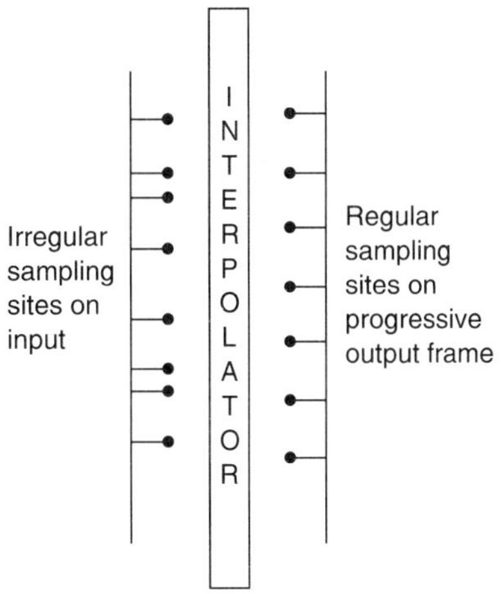

Figure 7.65 A de-interlacer needs an interpolator which can operate with input samples which are positioned arbitrarily rather than regularly.

irregular spacing and a special type of filter is needed to convert this back to a progressive frame with regular pixel spacing. At some critical vertical speeds there will be alignment between pixels in adjacent fields and no improvement is possible, but at other speeds the process will always give better results.

7.24 Aspect ratios

When television was in its infancy the production of cathode ray tubes (CRTs) was quite difficult because of the huge stress set up by the internal vacuum. Early tubes were circular as this shape resists pressure well. Early lenses had restricted coverage, and as the difficulty of obtaining coverage rises with distance from the optical axis, lens design is also eased by a circular picture. A square picture gives the largest area within a circle. Whatever the designers of television systems might have wanted for a picture aspect ratio, they had to compromise by choosing a rectangular shape which was close to the ideal square and this led to the 4:3 aspect ratio. Early film formats were also close to square for coverage reasons.

Now that lens and CRT design has advanced, these restrictions are no longer so severe. Newer types of display do not suffer the mechanical constraints of CRTs. As a result it is possible to have a wider picture without serious loss of quality and the aspect ratio of television will change to 16:9.

Figure 7.66 shows how a given picture is mapped onto an analog TV waveform. Neglecting the blanking interval which is needed for tube

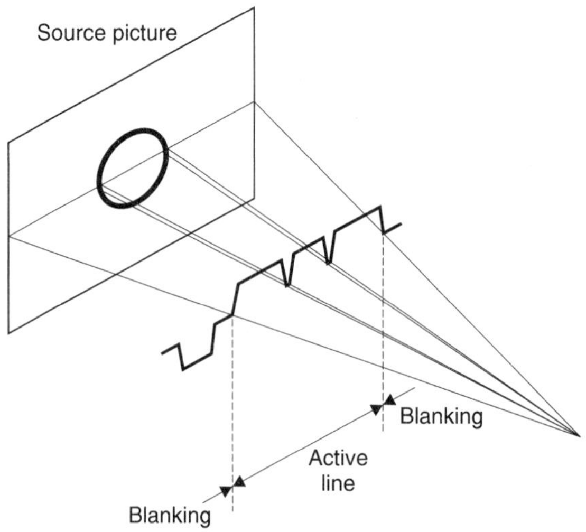

Figure 7.66 In all video standards, the source picture is mapped into a fixed percentage of the total line duration so that distance across the screen has a fixed proportional relationship to time along the line.

flyback, the distance across the picture is proportional to the time elapsed along the active line. The camera will break the picture into a standard number of lines, and again neglecting the vertical blanking interval, the distance down the picture will be proportional to the time through the frame in a non-interlaced system. If the format has a fixed number of lines per frame, the aspect ratio of the video format reflects in the ratio of the horizontal and vertical scan speeds. Neglecting blanking, the ratio of horizontal to vertical scan speed in an ideal 625-line system having a square picture would be 625 to 1. In a 4:3 system it would be more like 830 to 1. In a 16:9 system it would be about 1100 to 1. A viewpoint of this kind is useful because it is size independent. The picture can be any size as both axes then scale by the same amount.

Clearly if the display is to be compatible with the resultant video format, it must have the same aspect ratio so that the vertical and horizontal mapping retains the correct relationship. If this is done, objects portrayed on the display have the same shape as they had in the original picture. If it is not done correctly there will be distortion. Most test cards contain a circular component to test for this distortion as it is easy to see non-circularity. If a circular object in front of a camera apears circular on the display, their scanning is compatible because both have the same aspect ratio. This test, however, does NOT mean that both camera and display are meeting any standard. For example, both camera and display could be maladjusted to underscan by 10 per cent horizontally, yet the circularity test would still succeed. Thus the aspect ratio compatibility test should be made by checking the the display with an electronically generated precision circle prior to assessing the camera output. Any discrepancy would then be removed by adjusting the camera.

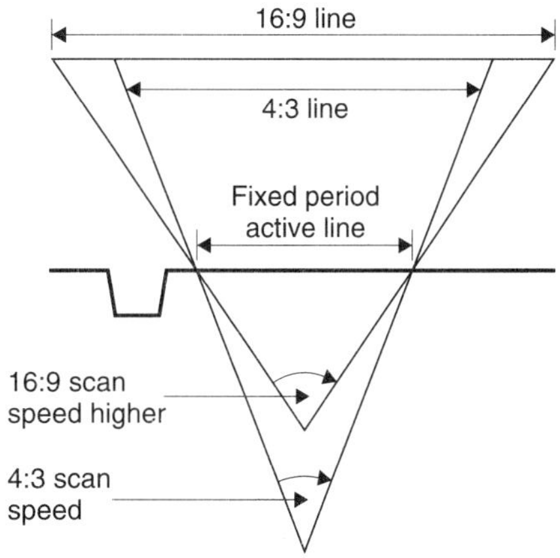

Figure 7.67 Using a higher scan speed, a longer source line can be mapped onto a standard active line. Note that for a given resolution, more bandwidth will be required because more cycles of detail will be scanned in a given time.

Figure 7.67 shows how a 16:9 picture is mapped onto a video signal. If the frame rate and the number of lines in the frame is kept the same, the wider picture is obtained by simply increasing the horizontal scan speed at the camera. This allows the longer line to be scanned within the existing active line period. A 16:9 CRT will display the resulting signal with correct circularity.

Any television camera can instantly be adapted to work in this way by fitting an anamorphic lens with a ratio of 1.333 . . .:1 which maps a 16:9 picture onto a 4:3 sensor. Clearly the viewfinder will need modification to reduce its vertical scan to 0.75 of its former deflection.

Redefinition of the scanning speed ratio at the camera has produced a different video standard which is now incompatible with 4:3 displays even though a waveform monitor confirms that it meets all the timing specifications. By stretching the horizontal scan the video has been rendered anamorphic. Figure 7.68(a) shows the result of displaying 16:9 video on a 4:3 monitor. The incompatible mapping causes circularity failure. Circular objects appear as vertical ellipses. Figure 7.68(b) shows the result of displaying 4:3 video on a 16:9 monitor. Circular objects appear as horizontal ellipses.

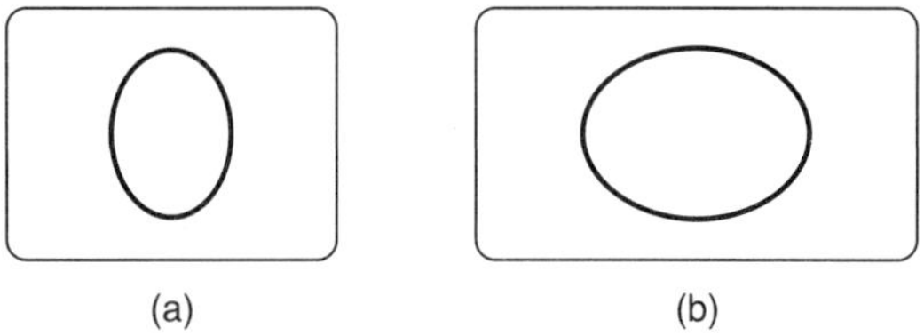

Figure 7.68 Displaying 16:9 video on a 4:3 monitor (a) results in a horizontal compression. The reverse case shown in (b) causes a horizontal stretch.

A form of standards convertor is needed which will allow interchange between the two formats. There are two basic applications of such convertors as can be seen in Figure 7.69. If 16:9 cameras and production equipment are used, an aspect ratio convertor is needed to view material on 4:3 monitors and to obtain a traditional broadcast output. Alternatively, conventional cameras can be used with a large safe area at top and bottom of the picture. 4:3 equipment is used for production and the aspect ratio convertor is then used to obtain a 16:9 picture output.

The criterion for conversion must be that circularity has to be maintained otherwise the pictures will appear distorted. Thus an aspect ratio convertor must change the aspect ratio of the picture frame, without changing the aspect ratio of portrayed objects.

If circularity is maintained, something else has to go. Figure 7.70(a) shows the result of passing 16:9 into a convertor for 4:3 display. If the

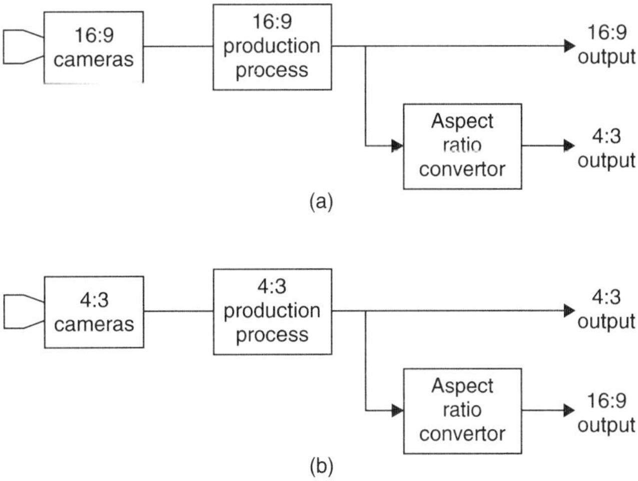

Figure 7.69 Two different approaches to dual-aspect ratio production which will be necessary during the change-over period.

screen must be filled, the convertor must perform a horizontal transform of 1.333 . . .:1 to maintain circularity. The result of doing this alone is that the edges of the input picture are lost as they will be pushed outside the active line length. This may be acceptable if a pan/scan control is available. Alternatively, if no part of the image can be lost, the convertor must perform a vertical transform of 0.75:1. This will result in the vertical blanking area of the 16:9 input entering the 4:3 screen area and the result will be black bars above and below the picture.

Figure 7.70(b) shows the reverse conversion process where 4:3 is being converted to 16:9. Again if 'full screen' mode is required, the convertor must perform a vertical transform of 1.333 . . .:1 to maintain circularity. This pushes the top and bottom of the input picture into 16:9 blanking. If

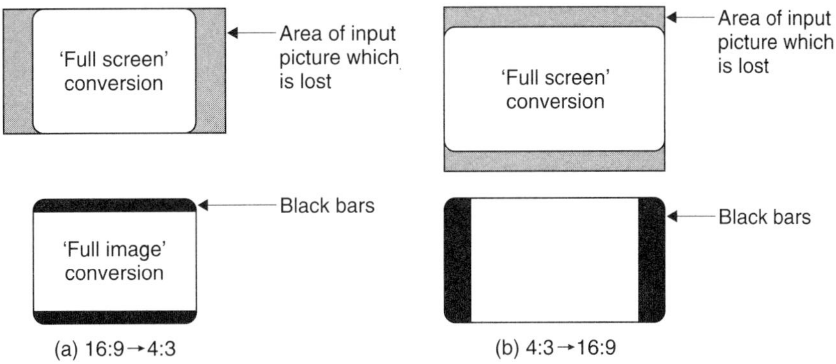

Figure 7.70 The extreme cases of 16:9 and 4:3 interchange are at the 'full image' and 'full screen' points.

the 4:3 material was shot with 16:9 safe areas this is no problem. However, if the input was intended for 4:3 it may have wanted detail near the top or bottom of the picture and a tilt (vertical pan) control may be provided to select the area which appears in the output. If no part of the image can be lost, i.e 'full image' mode is required, a horizontal transform of 0.75:1 is needed, and this must result in the horizontally blanked areas of the 4:3 input entering the 16:9 screen area.

The above steps represent the two extremes or full screen or no image loss. In practice there is a scale between those extremes in which the black bars can be made smaller in one axis by an image loss in the other axis. In practice, then, an aspect ratio convertor needs to perform vertical and horizontal transforms which may be magnification, translation or both. In order to maintain circularity, the ratio between the horizontal and vertical magnifications can only have three values, 1.333 . . .:1 for 16:9 to 4:3 conversion, 1:1 for bypass and 0.75:1 for 4:3 to 16:9 conversion. Thus having selected the mode, a single magnification control would vary the conversion between 'full screen' and 'full image' modes. When not in full image mode, pan and tilt controls allow the user to select the part of the input image which appears in the output.

References

1. EBU Doc. Tech. 3246
2. SMPTE 125M, Television – Bit Parallel Digital Interface – Component Video Signal 4:2:2
3. Lau, H. and Lyon, D., Motion compensated processing for enhanced slow motion and standards conversion. *IEE Conf. Publ. No. 358*, 62–66 (1992)

8

Presentation

The traditional television set with a CRT and a modest loudspeaker will continue for some time because it can be made at very low cost and is adequate for watching certain types of program. However, convergent technology allows the production and delivery of high-quality image and surround-sound data, leading to a requirement for presentation equipment which can do justice to it. The requirements of an electronic cinema will be for a large bright picture with adequate audio power, whereas in the home cinema there are additional constraints such as cost and physical size. High definition in the home will not succeed until the equipment can be made sufficiently compact. This is true not only for displays, but also for loudspeakers which traditionally have been large and unattractive. Surround sound requires the user to have five or more loudspeakers and with traditional technology this will be unwieldy if good quality is required, or give poor sound if size limits are imposed. The solution is to use active loudspeaker technology, as decribed below, to obtain sound of high quality from small enclosures.

8.1 Display principles

The large number of display technologies available all have rather different characteristics, both strengths and drawbacks, and to date no one technology is ideal. Figure 8.1 shows some of the ways in which displays can be categorized. The light may be generated by the display itself, or the display may modulate light from a separate source. This modulation mechanism may be infinitely variable, or analog, or it may be binary in which case some form of pulse width or duty cycle modulation becomes necessary. Displays may be parallel, where the whole image is

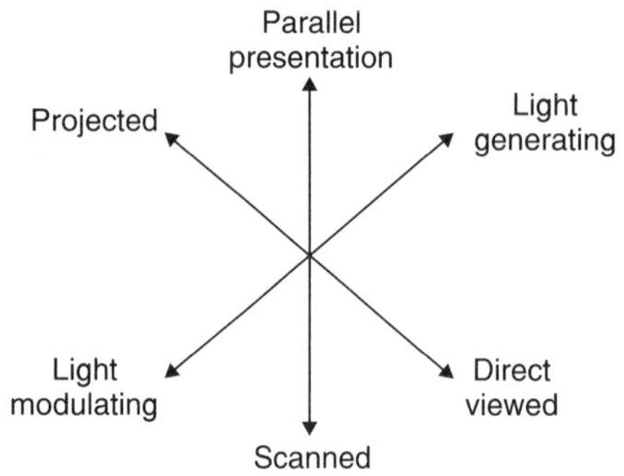

Figure 8.1 Categories of display technology. See text.

presented simultaneously, or scanned, where a single light spot travels at high speed to cover the whole picture area in one frame period. Some types of display are in the form of a projector, requiring a cinema-type screen, whereas other types are themselves the screen.

The applications of displays are almost unlimited and this is partly responsible for the wide range of technologies. In portable applications, weight and power consumption are overriding concerns whereas in critical monitoring areas colorimetry, level resolution, spatial and dynamic resolution are more important. In projection systems, high light output is a goal so that a large screen can be used.

8.2 The monochrome CRT

The cathode ray tube (CRT) is a relative of the vacuum tube and is shown in Figure 8.2. Inside a glass envelope a vacuum is formed initially by pumping and completed by igniting a material called a *getter* which burns any remaining oxygen to form a harmless solid. The pressure differential across the tube face results in considerable force. For example, the atmosphere exerts a force of about a ton on the face of a 20-inch diagonal tube. As glass is weak in tension the tube is strengthened with a steel band which is stretched around the perimeter of the screen. Figure 8.3 shows that the tube face is generally slightly domed outwards so that the thrust due to atmospheric pressure is converted to a radial out-thrust to which the steel band provides a reaction. The necessity to withstand atmospheric pressure over the screen area puts an upper limit on the size of CRTs. Large CRTs are necessarily heavy.

The cathode is coated with a barium compound and contains an insulated heating element which raises its temperature. This heating causes the coating to emit electrons. The electrons have negative charge and so are attracted towards an anode which is supplied with a positive

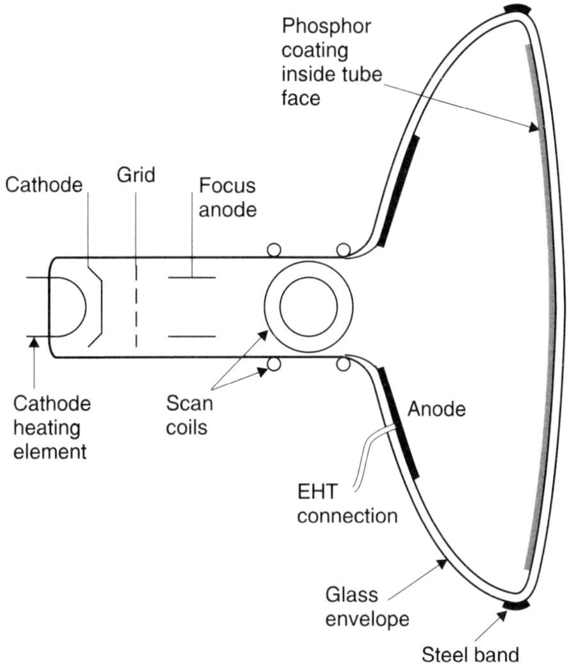

Figure 8.2 A simple CRT contains an electron gun and deflection mechanism for scanning. The cathode-to-grid voltage determines the beam current and hence brightness.

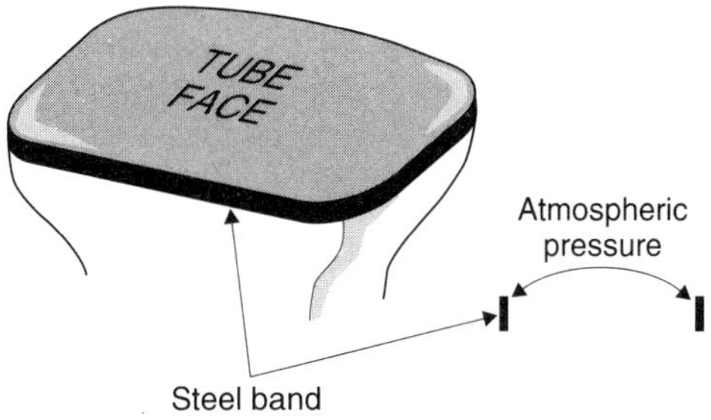

Figure 8.3 The thrust due to atmospheric pressure is resisted by doming or curving the tube face. This converts the pressure load into an out-thrust which can be resisted by a steel band stretched around the tube. Domed buildings are held up in much the same way. The large forces involved place practical limits on the size of CRT which can be made before it becomes too heavy to be useful.

voltage. Between the cathode and the anode is a wire mesh grid. If this grid is held at a suitable negative voltage with respect to the cathode it will repel electrons from the cathode and they will be prevented from reaching the anode. If the grid voltage is reduced the effect diminishes and some electrons can pass. The voltage on the grid controls the current.

The anode contains a hole through which the electrons emerge in a beam. They are further accelerated by more electrodes at successively higher voltages, the last of these being the EHT (extra high tension) electrode which runs at 15–25 kV. The electron beam strikes the inside of the tube face which is coated with material known as a phosphor. The impact of energetic electrons causes electrons in the phosphor to be driven to higher, unstable valence levels, and when they drop back, photons of a specific wavelength are released. By mixing a number of phosphor materials white light can be obtained.

The intensity of the light is effectively controlled by the intensity of the electron beam which is in turn controlled by the grid voltage. As it is the relative voltage between the cathode and the grid which determines the beam current, some tubes are driven by holding the grid at a constant voltage and varying the voltage on the cathode. The electron impact may also generate low-level X-rays and the face of the tube will be made from lead glass to absorb most of them.

The relationship between the tube drive voltage and the phosphor brightness is not linear, but an exponential function where the power is known as *gamma*. The power is the same for all CRTs as it is a function of the physics of the electron gun and it has a value of around 2.8. As was seen in section 6.8, the gamma function of a CRT follows roughly the same curve as human contrast sensitivity. Traditionally video signals are predistorted at source by an inverse gamma, such that the gamma characteristic of the CRT will linearize the signal.

Virtually all CRT-based displays are fitted with two controls conventionally and misleadingly marked *brightness* and *contrast*. Figure 8.4(a) shows what the 'brightness' control actually does. When correctly set, the lowest drive voltage, i.e. blanking level, results in the electron beam being just cut off so that the CRT displays black. If the 'brightness' is set too low, as in (b), the CRT cuts off prematurely and all inputs below a certain level are reproduced as black. The symptom is decribed as *black crushing*. If the control is set too high, as in (c), video blanking results in a substantial light output such that all displayed images are superimposed on a grey level.

It should be clear that there is only one correct setting for a brightness control because it is in fact a tube bias or black level control. In order correctly to set a black level control the grey stepped scale of a test card may be used. The black level control is advanced until the black part of the scale appears obviously grey, and then it is turned down until the the black part of the scale is just displayed as truly black, but not so far that the darkest grey step next to it becomes black as well. Once set in this way the CRT is correctly biased and further adjustment will only be needed if component values drift.

Special test signals exist in the television industry to assist with monitor alignment. One of these is known as PLUGE (Picture Line-Up GEnerator), pronounced 'plooj'. The PLUGE signal contains a black area

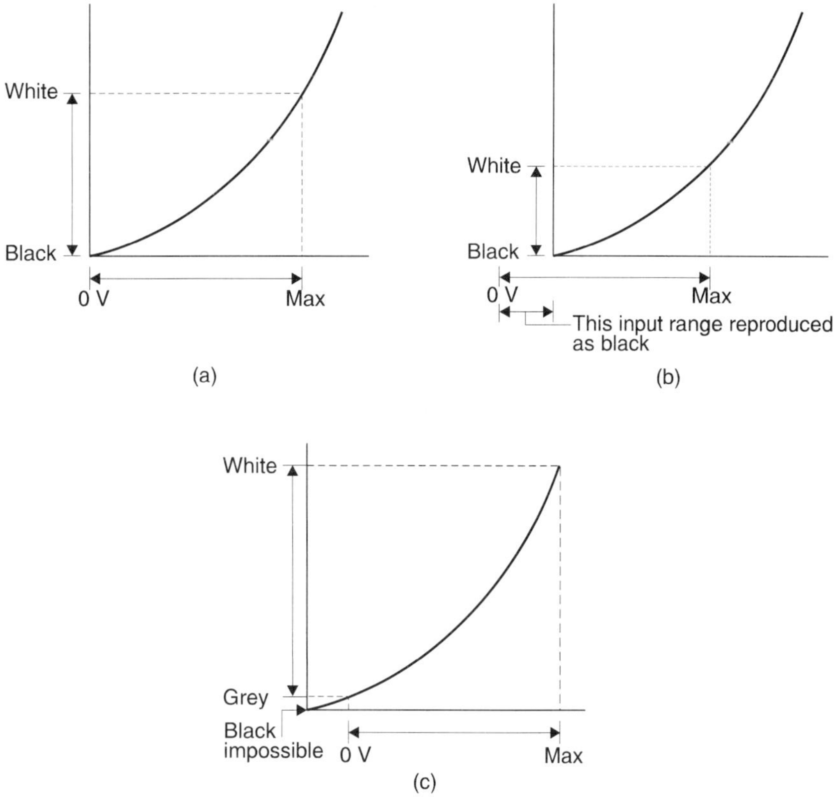

Figure 8.4 (a) Correctly set brightness control cuts off the electron beam at blanking level. (b) Control set too low causes black crushing. (c) Control set too high causes grey pedestal on picture, spoiling contrast. Brightness control is a misnomer as it has only one correct setting.

in which there are two 'black' bars which sit typically ±20 mV above and below black level. If the 'brightness' control is adjusted downwards from an initial excessively bright setting, it will be found that the two bars become indistinguishable from the black background, due to black crushing, at slightly different times. The correct setting is achieved when one bar has vanished but the other is still visible.

The 'below black' pulse in the PLUGE signal is technically illegal because it occurs during the active line and gamut-monitoring equipment may issue an alarm or error condition if asked to pass such a signal. This is normal.

The action of the 'contrast' control is shown in Figure 8.5. This has the effect of increasing the amplitude of white signals whilst leaving black level unchanged. Thus in order to increase the brightness of a correctly biased display, the contrast control should be advanced. If the contrast is excessive the electron beam becomes larger in diameter and the resolution of the display is reduced. In critical monitoring, a light meter

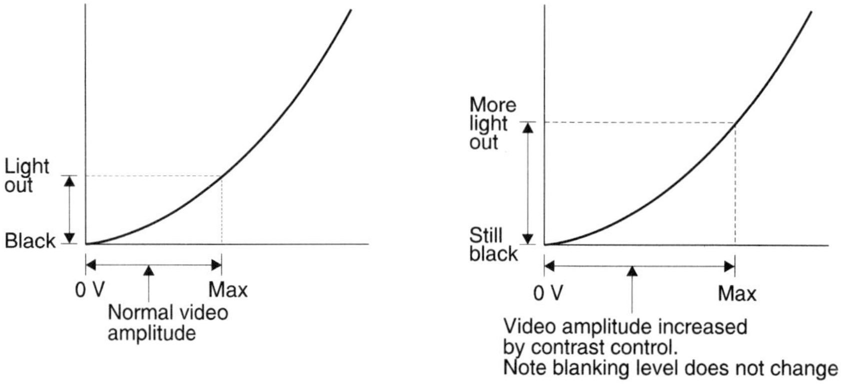

Figure 8.5 Action of contrast control. Paradoxically, the picture is made brighter by increasing contrast.

is used in conjunction with a peak-white input signal to allow a standard brightness to be achieved. The PLUGE signal contains a peak white area to assist with this.

In practice the contrast of a CRT is also affected quite badly by ambient lighting. With black input voltage cutting off the beam, the brightness of a CRT cannot fall below the brightness of reflected ambient light. Thus ambient light reduces contrast. For best results all display technologies should be viewed in subdued lighting where the best combination of contrast and resolution will be obtained. As all CRT tubes are reflective to some extent, it is important to ensure no bright objects are positioned where they could be seen reflected in the screen. Some CRTs are provided with non-reflective coatings which have a beneficial effect.

The electron beam is an electric current and this can be deflected electrostatically by voltages applied to plates at the neck of the tube, or magnetically by coils outside the tube. Electrostatic deflection is fine for the small tubes used in oscilloscopes, but the large deflection angles needed in TV tubes can only be obtained with magnetic deflection.

The horizontal deflection coils are generally driven by a transformer. During the flyback period the flux in the transformer changes rapidly and this can be used to generate the EHT supply by providing an additional winding on the transformer which feeds a high-voltage rectifier. There is some evidence to suggest that the X-rays or magnetic fields from CRTs may present a health hazard after prolonged exposure.

The rate at which the electron beam can retrace is limited by the inductance of the scan coils which limit the rate at which the deflection current can change. The active line has to be made considerably shorter than the line period so that sufficient retrace time is available. Losses in the transformer put a practical limit on the line scanning frequency which can be used, although better materials could overcome this.

Normally the horizontal and vertical retrace is invisible, but certain monitors have the facility to shift the scan phase with respect to incoming syncs by part of a line and part of a field. The result is that the blanking periods become visible for inspection on the screen in the form of a cross, hence the term *pulse cross monitor.*

8.3 The colour CRT

In order to display colour pictures, three simultaneous images must be generated, one for each primary colour. The colour CRT does this geometrically. Figure 8.6(a) shows that three electron beams pass down the tube from guns mounted in a triangular or delta array. Immediately before the tube face is mounted a perforated metal plate known as a shadow mask. The three beams approach holes in the shadow mask at a slightly different angle and so fall upon three different areas of phosphor

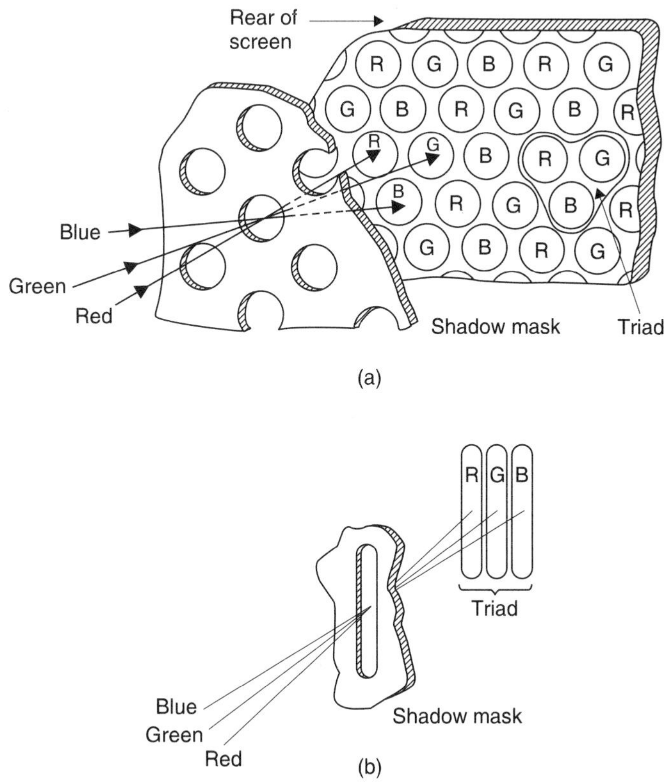

Figure 8.6 (a) Triads of phosphor dots are triangular and electron guns are arranged in a triangle. (b) Inline tube has strips of phosphor side by side.

which each produce a different primary colour. The sets of three phosphors are known as triads. Figure 8.6(b) shows an alternative arrangement in which the three electron guns are mounted in a straight line and the shadow mask is slotted and the triads are rectangular. This is known as a PIL (precision-in-line) tube). The triads can easily be seen upon close inspection of an operating CRT.

During the manufacturing process the shadow mask is fitted and the tube is assembled except for the electron guns. The inside of the tube is coated with photoresist and a light source is positioned at the point where the scan coils would deflect an electron beam such that the resist is exposed in all locations where one colour of phosphor should be deposited. The process is repeated for each phosphor.

In early tubes the space between the phosphor dots was grey. Later tubes replaced this with black in order to reduce reflection of ambient light and thereby increase contrast and apparent sharpness.

When the tube is completed, the scan coils have to be installed in exactly the right place otherwise the correct beam geometry will not result and beams may fall on part of the wrong phosphor in the triads. Adjusting the scan coils to ensure correct triad registration is called the *purity* adjustment. The shadow mask is heated by electron impact in service, and is not readily cooled because it is in a vacuum. Should the shadow mask overheat, it may distort due to thermal expansion and damage the purity. This effect limits the brightness of shadow mask CRTs. Purity can also be damaged by stray magnetic fields which may magnetize the shadow mask. Most monitors incorporate coils which degauss the shadow mask when the unit is first switched on. Many loudspeakers produce stray magnetic fields sufficiently strong to affect nearby CRTs and it is advisable to use loudspeakers which have been designed to contain their fields. Leakage field control will be discussed later in this chapter.

The three electron beams must also be arranged to scan over exactly the same area of the tube so that the three images correctly superimpose. Static shifts of the beams can be obtained by the *static convergence* controls which register the three beams in the tube centre. All three beams are deflected by the same horizontal and vertical scan coils, and the geometry is such that there will be registration errors between the beams which increase with the deflection. These errors are cancelled by providing subsidiary individual scan coils for two of the beams with correction waveforms. This is known as *dynamic convergence*. In order to adjust the convergence, a test pattern which produces a white cross-hatch is used. If the convergence is incorrect, rainbow-like lines can be seen instead of one white line. The inline tube has the advantage that the dynamic convergence waveforms are simpler to generate.

8.4 The projection CRT

A television projector may be made by using a similar optical system to a film projector in which the film in the gate is replaced by the face of a CRT. The cost of lenses means that the CRT has to be fairly small. This results in a high magnification factor between the CRT and the screen, requiring very high resolution on the CRT face. Obtaining enough light is a problem and normally driving a CRT at high beam currents will result in spreading of the spot which reduces resolution. Both of these problems are addressed at once by using three tubes; one for each colour. Each tube is essentially a monochrome tube in which the phosphor is selected to produce the appropriate primary colour. The approach needs no shadow mask and this improves efficiency and resolution.

Each tube generally has its own lens and these are usually mounted in a horizontal line so that the depth of the unit is minimized. This is an advantage when it is mounted from a ceiling. The geometry of three separate and displaced optical systems is such that the three primary images do not naturally superimpose or converge on the screen. Figure 8.7 shows that the lateral offset of the outer beams causes 'keystoning' in which the images are not rectangular. This is overcome by creating an inverse keystone raster on the CRT face by modifying the scan waveforms. In modern machines the convergence waveforms are generated by a microprocessor and the projector can converge itself automatically by generating test patterns through one lens whilst examining them through another.

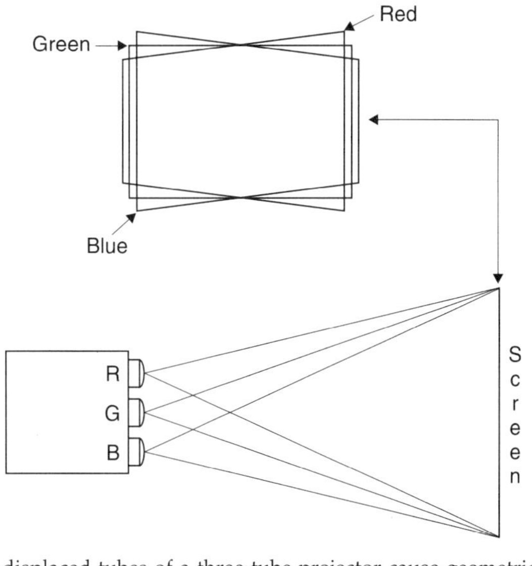

Figure 8.7 The displaced tubes of a three-tube projector cause geometric errors on the screen known as keystoning. The raster on each CRT has to be predistorted to make the three images converge.

8.5 Plasma displays

In the plasma display the source of light is an electrical discharge in a gas at low pressure. This generates ultra-violet light which excites phosphors in the same way that a fluorescent light operates. Each pixel consists of three such elements, one for each primary colour. Figure 8.8 shows that the pixels are controlled by arranging the discharge to take place between electrodes which are arranged in rows and columns.

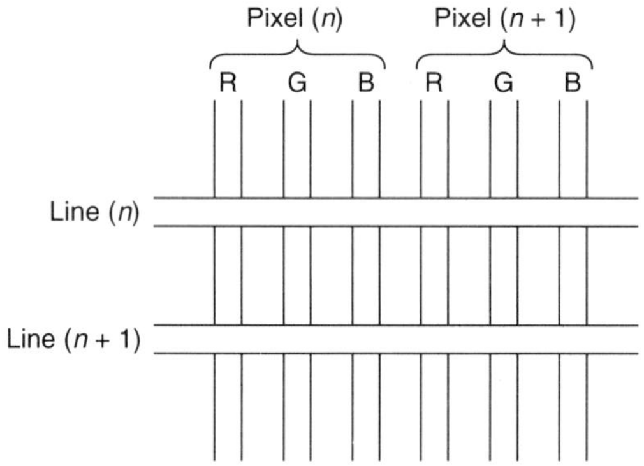

Figure 8.8 When a voltage is applied between a line or row electrode and a pixel electrode, a plasma discharge occurs. This excites a phosphor to produce visible light.

The advantage of the plasma display is that it can be made perfectly flat and it is very thin, even in large screen sizes. Plasma displays allow the practical size limit of CRTs to be exceeded.

The great difficulty with the plasma display is that the relationship between light output and drive voltage is highly non-linear. Below a certain voltage there is no discharge at all. Consequently the only way that the brightness can accurately be varied is to modulate the time for which the discharge takes place. The electrode signals are pulse width modulated.

Eight-bit digital video has 256 different brightnesses and it is difficult to obtain such a scale by pulse width modulation as the increments of pulse length would need to be generated by a clock of fantastic frequency. It is common practice to break the picture period up into many pulses, each of which is modulated in width. Despite this, plasma displays often show contouring or posterizing, indicating a lack of sufficient brightness levels. Multiple pulse drive also has some temporal effects which may be visible on moving material unless motion compensation is used. This will be considered further in section 8.8.

8.6 Scanning lasers

The laser is a useful source of light for colorimetric purposes because it is monochromatic. In theory three lasers of suitable wavelengths used as primaries could produce a range of colours which is unparalleled by any other technology.

The great difficulty with lasers is providing a scanning mechanism. This has traditionally been done with rotating multi-faceted mirrors, but a simple calculation will show that incredible rotational speeds are needed for high-definition images. The rotating parts have been mounted inside vacuum chambers to reduce air resistance and noise. As an alternative to scanning the whole image with a single beam, there have been attempts to divide the picture into strips, each of which has its own beam. This dramatically cuts the speed of the rotating parts, but it is very difficult to conceal the boundaries between the strips in the presence of motion and eye tracking. In order to do this properly a special motion-compensated signal processor will be required.

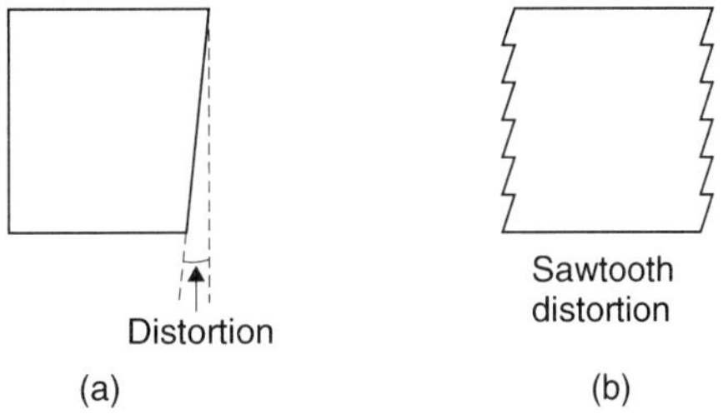

Figure 8.9 (a) Dynamic distortion of a moving vertical edge on a scanned display is minor and difficult to see. However, when the display is segmented so that it can be scanned by multiple beams (b), the dynamic distortion takes on an obvious sawtooth characteristic which requires non-trivial precompensation.

Figure 8.9 shows the problem. If a horizontally moving vertical line is displayed on a single beam scanned display, the dynamic distortion due to the use of a raster scan causes a small tilt of the vertical which is not noticeable. However, in a multi-beam system, the line takes on a sawtooth appearance which is very noticeable unless the image is predistorted in the opposite sense.

8.7 Micromirror projectors

In a micromirror projector, each pixel consists of a tiny mirror mounted on an equally tiny piezo-electric actuator which can tilt it when a control voltage is applied. Figure 8.10 shows that each mirror may be aligned so

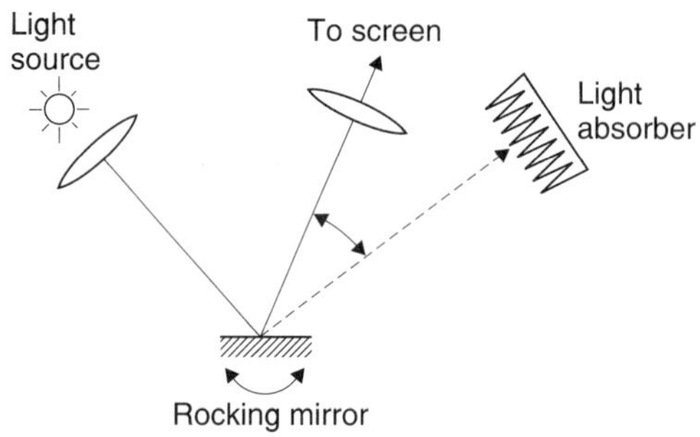

Figure 8.10 Micromirror projectors use arrays of minute mirrors which are individually actuated so that light from the source is reflected onto the screen or into an absorber.

that it reflects light from a source onto the screen or into a light absorber. The mechanism is binary: either light passes to the screen or it is absorbed. In order to obtain a grey scale, each mirror is driven by pulses of variable width. Fortunately the mirror elements are so small that they can move extremely rapidly. The same dynamic effect as in plasma displays can occur with long pulses, but the micromirror display has the advantage that it does not generate light, it only modulates light from another source. A powerful light source can be used to keep the pulses short, improving dynamic resolution. The colorimetry of the micromirror projector is entirely a function of the light sources used.

8.8 Temporal effects

Different display technologies suffer from different temporal effects and this is responsible for some of the visible differences between display types.

Figure 8.11(a) shows that in conventionally projected film, the temporal impulse is basically rectangular due to the continuously burning arc lamp and the mechanical shutter. Figure 8.11(b) shows that the significant temporal aperture causes a loss of dynamic resolution because the image is smeared with respect to the tracking eye. However, the smearing also reduces the impact of background judder.

Some film projectors have discharge lamps which flash when the film is stationary, so that no shutter is needed. The period of the discharge is very short, leading to better portrayal of moving objects but worse background judder because the background is strobed at a different location in each frame with respect to a tracking eye.

Figure 8.12 shows that the CRT phosphor continues to emit light in an exponentially decaying curve for some time after the electron beam has passed. This is known as *persistence*. It might be thought that long

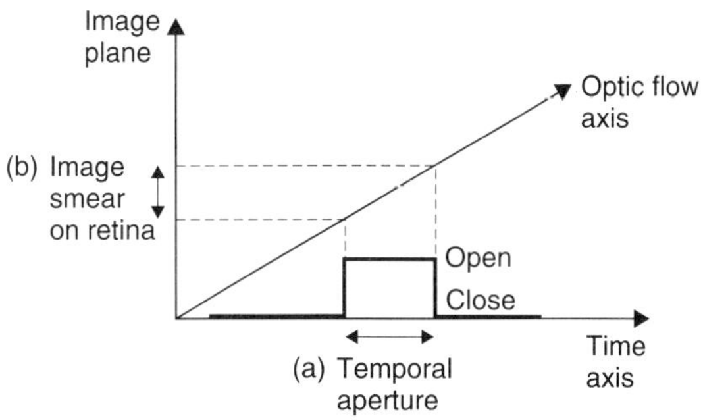

Figure 8.11 Film projector with a mechanical shutter has the temporal aperture shown in (a). This results in loss of dynamic resolution (b) as image is smeared across the field of view of the tracking eye.

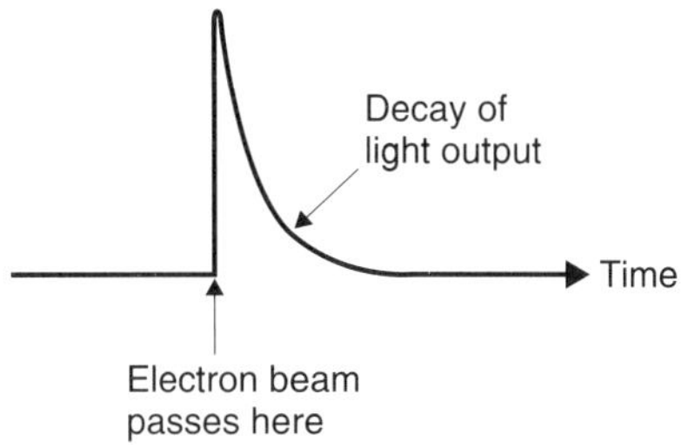

Figure 8.12 The temporal aperture of a CRT is an exponential decay. This short aperture gives good dynamic resolution which other display technologies struggle to match.

persistence could be used to reduce flicker but this is not the case. As the impulse response is so peaky, an extremely long persistence figure is needed to stretch the peak significantly. This would damage the dynamic resolution. CRTs for television normally have quite short persistence and their dynamic resolution is very good. Flicker is best reduced by raising the frame rate.

Figure 8.13 shows that if the eye is tracking a moving object on a plasma screen, viewing takes place on the optic flow axis. A dark area of the moving object will need only a short drive pulse, whereas a bright part will need a long pulse. The pulse length has a component along the optic flow axis giving rise to a dynamic effect in which moving lines appear wider the brighter they get. The solution is artificially to increase the display rate using a signal processor. This will need to be motion compensated. Instead of one long pulse, two shorter pulses will be used, reducing the dynamic effect. The perceived brightness is now a function of the sum of the two pulse widths and so a reduction in contouring is also possible.

The liquid crystal display has a very slow temporal response and the dynamic resolution is poor.

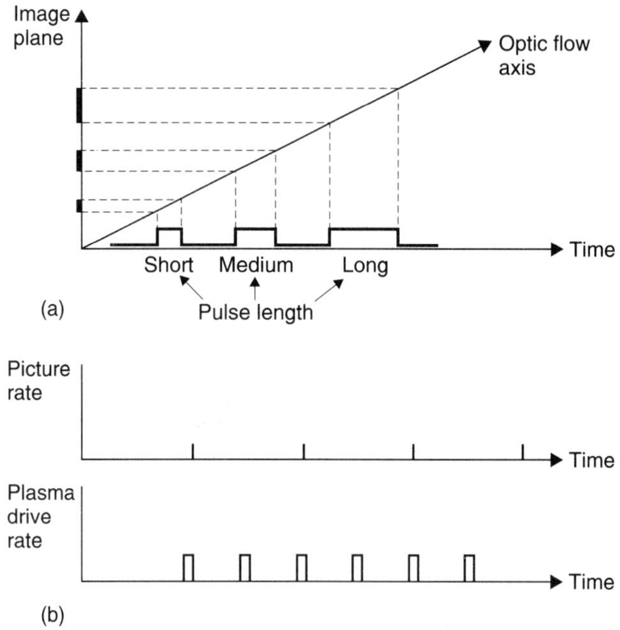

Figure 8.13 Plasma screens are pulse width modulated. This causes an unusual effect (a) whereby brighter areas are illuminated for longer, making them appear wider when moving. Practical screens need to use upconversion so that more and shorter drive pulses (b) can be used.

8.9 Display processors

As was seen in Chapter 7, it is advantageous to use spatial and/or temporal oversampling in displays. Spatial oversampling requires that the number of pixels on the screen in both axes shall be greater than the number of input pixels. This has the effect of putting the aperture effect of the display outside the image passband. The greater spatial frequency of the pixels in an oversampled display is more readily filtered out so that the viewer perceives a continuous image.

If interlace has a place in modern systems, it is in display technology. Figure 8.14 shows a progressive scan transmission system with a rectangular passband (a). For display purposes, the signal could be upconverted or oversampled by a factor of two in both dimensions to reduce flicker and render the raster invisible. Upconverting to a progressive scan format would require the display line rate to be quadrupled as (b) shows. The use of interlace in the display upconvertor shown at (c) allows the full input passband through but only requires the display line rate to be doubled. The benefits of oversampling are achieved without the display becoming very expensive. Temporal oversampling by a factor of two raises the frame rate of an interlaced system above the CFF so that interlace flicker is no longer visible.

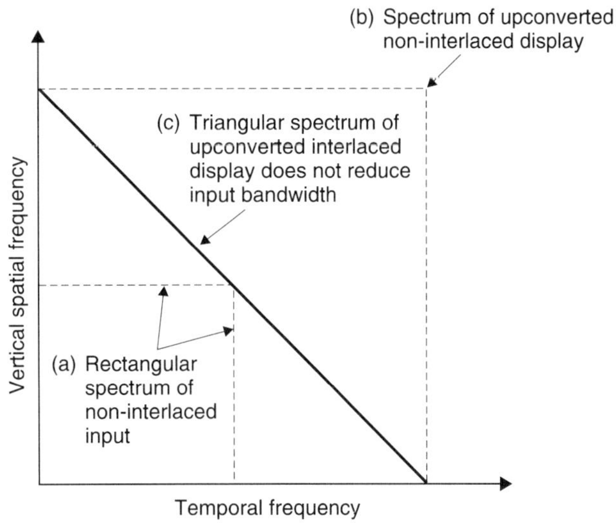

Figure 8.14 Interlace can be used in an oversampling display to reduce the line frequency of that display; see text for details.

8.10 Optical filtering

When a projection display is used there will be a lens of some kind to focus the image onto the screen. This allows an opportunity which is not available to direct displays to use the lens as a reconstruction filter to make the individual pixels or raster lines blend into a continuous image. This requires an understanding of Fourier optics.

Figure 8.15 shows that when a given spatial frequency is illuminated by light of a given wavelength, the information carrying the spatial frequency is carried in wavefronts which leave at an angle to the optical axis. As the spatial frequency increases, the wavefronts become more oblique, whereas a reduction in spatial frequency makes the wavefronts less oblique. The resolution limit of an optical system is reached when the

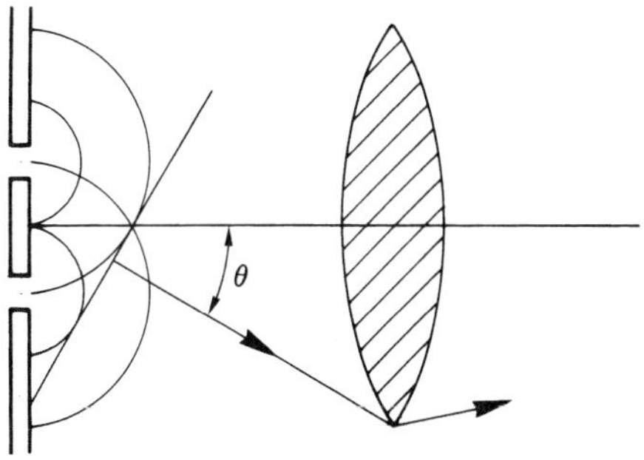

Figure 8.15 As detail in an image gets finer, the wavefronts describing it are angled further away from the normal.

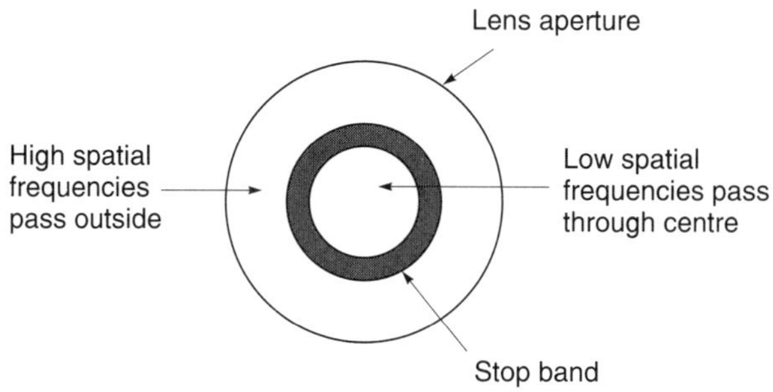

Figure 8.16 An optical bandstop filter using an annular stop to absorb certain spatial frequencies whilst allowing others to pass.

wavefronts are too oblique to enter the aperture of the lens. Effectively the lens is acting as a spatial spectrum analyser. The lowest frequencies pass through near the centre of the lens, but as spatial frequency rises an annular band of increasing radius admits the light through the lens.

This gives rise to the possibility of using the lens as a bandstop filter. Figure 8.16 shows that if an annular mask is made with suitable inner and outer dimensions and installed adjacent to the lens, it will attenuate certain spatial frequencies whilst allowing lower and higher frequencies to pass. If the frequency concerned is the spatial frequency of the pixels or scanning lines, that frequency will be much attenuated on the screen.

In three-lens projectors where each lens handles one of the primary colours, each image is monochromatic and the fixed wavelength makes the optical filter work very well.

8.11 Loudspeaker principles

An ideal loudspeaker should produce a particle velocity proportional to the input waveform and so must have a wide, flat frequency response with no resonances and minimum linear and non-linear distortion. This, however, is only part of the design problem.

In all practical loudspeakers some form of diaphragm has to be vibrated which then vibrates the air.[1] There are contradictory requirements. As can be seen in Figure 8.17, the SPL which the loudspeaker can generate is determined by the volume velocity. If the frequency is halved, the displacement must be doubled either by doubling the area of the diaphragm or by doubling the travel or some combination of both. Clearly a powerful loudspeaker which is able to reproduce the lowest audio frequencies must have a large diaphragm capable of considerable travel. As human hearing is relatively insensitive at LF a loudspeaker

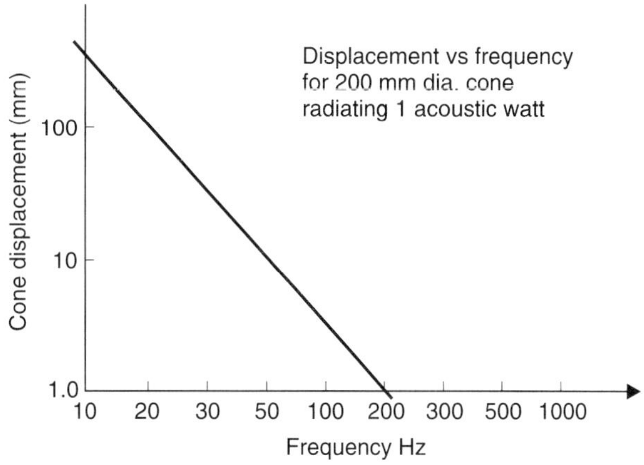

Figure 8.17 Volume velocity requirements dictate that low-frequency reproduction must involve large diaphragms or long travel.

which can only reproduce the lowest audible frequencies at low power is a waste of time.

Unfortunately any diaphragm which has sufficient area for low-frequency use will be too large at the highest audio frequencies resulting in *beaming* or high directivity which is undesirable. One solution is to use a number of drive units which each handle only part of the frequency range. Those producing low frequencies are called *woofers* and will have large diaphragms with considerable travel whereas those producing high frequencies are called *tweeters* and will have small diaphragms whose movement is seldom visible. In some systems mid-range units or *squawkers* are also used, having characteristics mid-way between the other types. A frequency-dividing system or *crossover network* is required to limit the frequency range of signals to each drive unit.

A good microphone produces an accurate version of sounds *approaching* it from many directions. Even if a loudspeaker reproduced the microphone waveform exactly, the resulting sound is *leaving* in many directions. Spatially a single loudspeaker is producing sound travelling in exactly the opposite direction to the original. Consequently reproduction of the original soundfield is simply not possible.

Figure 8.18 shows the problem. Sound approaching a microphone at (a) does so from a multiplicity of sources whereas sound leaving a single loudspeaker superimposes all these sources into one. Consequently a monophonic or single loudspeaker is doomed to condense every sound source and its reverberation to a single point. When listening in anechoic conditions (b) this is exactly what happens. Whilst the waveform might be reproduced with great precision, the spatial characteristics of such a sound are quite wrong.

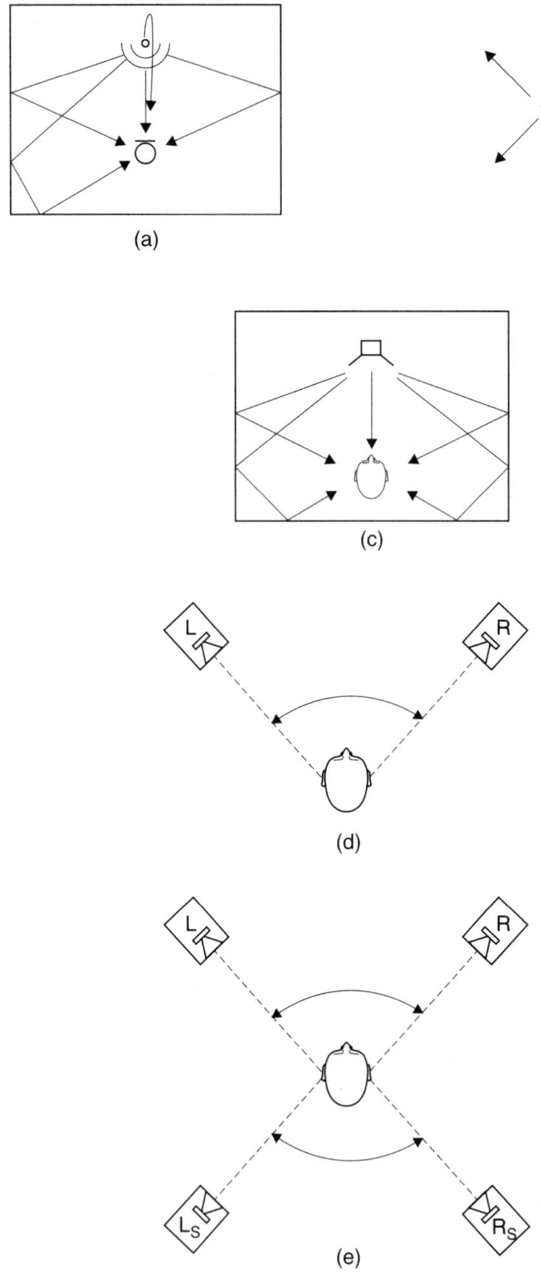

Figure 8.18 (a) Sound approaches microphone from many directions due to ambience and reverberation. (b) In anechoic conditions single loudspeaker produces exactly the opposite of (a). (c) Loudspeaker in reverberant conditions simulates situation of (a) at listener's ears. (d) Stereo systems can only re-create virtual sound sources over angle shown. (e) Surround-sound systems can create further virtual sources to the rear, but not to the side unless additional speakers are used.

However, when listening in a room having a degree of reverberation a better result is achieved irrespective of the reverberation content of the signal. The reverberation in the mono signal has only time delay and no spatial characteristics whatsoever whereas the reverberation in the listening room has true spatial characteristics. The human listener is accustomed to ambient sound approaching from all directions in real life and when this does not happen in a reproduction system the result is unsatisfactory.

Thus in all real listening environments a considerable amount of reverberant sound is required in addition to the direct sound from the loudspeakers. Figure 8.18(c) shows that the reverberation of the listening room results in sound approaching the listener from all sides giving a closer approximation to the situation in (a). Clearly better reverberation will be obtained when the loudspeaker is out in clear space in the room. So-called bookcase loudspeakers mounted on walls or shelves can never give good results.

Better spatial accuracy requires more channels and more loudspeakers. Whilst the ideal requires an infinite number of loudspeakers, it will be seen that, with care, as few as two speakers can give a convincing spatial illusion. The improvement in spatial performance using two speakers is enormous. Tests[2] have shown that most people prefer stereo with poor bandwidth and significant distortion to pristine mono. A further improvement can be obtained by using a further pair of speakers to the rear of the listener, with perhaps the addition of a centre speaker between the front ones.

Pairs of speakers can only give spatial accuracy for sound sources located between them. Figure 8.18(d) shows the angle over which stereo speakers deliver an accurate image. Figure 8.18(e) shows that in surround sound there is a further angle to the rear, suggesting that 4/5 channel surround sound is a misnomer as it is no more able to re-create sound sources at the side of the listener than is a stereo system. As a result, reverberation in the listening room must provide ambient sound from all remaining directions.

Clearly the resultant reverberant sound field can never be a replica of that at the microphone, but a plausible substitute is essential for realism and its absence results in an unsatisfactory result. Clearly the traditional use of heavily damped rooms for monitoring is suspect.

Given a room with reasonable reverberation characteristics, Figure 8.19 shows that the reverberant sound reaching the listener must have been radiated by the loudspeaker in a direction other than on its forward-facing axis. If realism is to be achieved, the polar diagram of the loudspeaker and its stability with frequency is extremely important. A common shortcoming with most drive units is that output becomes more directional with increasing frequency. Figure 8.20(a) shows that although

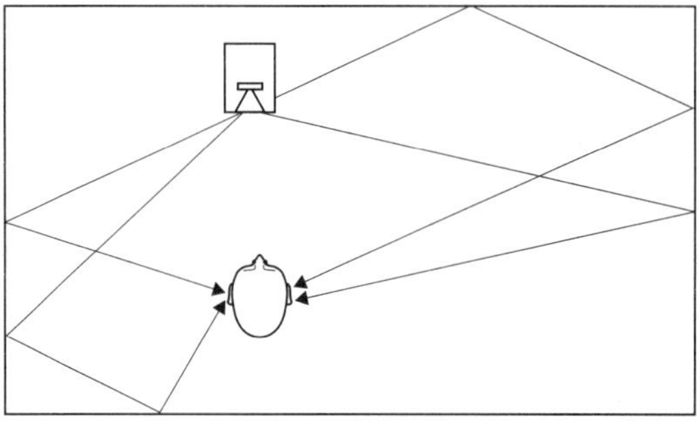

Figure 8.19 Most of the sound power reaching a listener in real conditions has been radiated at angles away from the central axis of the speaker. This means the off-axis speaker response is important.

the frequency response on-axis may be ruler flat giving a good quality direct sound, the frequency response off-axis may be quite badly impaired. In the case of a multiple-drive unit speaker, if the crossover frequencies are too high, each drive unit will have started beaming before it crosses over to the next which widens the directivity again. Figure 8.20(b) shows that the off-axis response is then highly irregular. As the off-axis output excites the essential reverberant field the tonal balance of the reverberation will not match that of the direct sound.[3] The skilled listener can determine the crossover frequency, which by definition ought not to be possible in a good loudspeaker.

The resultant conflict between on- and off-axis tonality may only be perceived subconsciously and cause *listening fatigue* where the initial

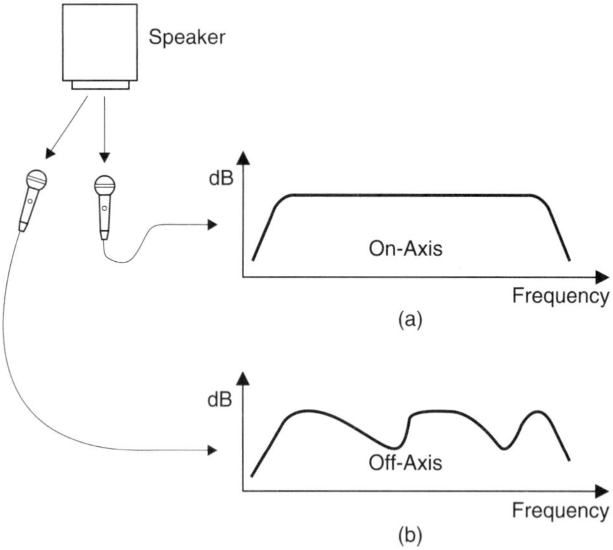

Figure 8.20 (a) Ideal on-axis response is achieved by many loudspeakers. (b) Off-axis response of most loudspeakers is irregular causing colouration of reverberant field.

impression of the loudspeaker is quite good but after a while one starts looking for excuses to stop listening. The hallmark of a good loudspeaker installation is that one can listen to it indefinitely and that of an excellent installation is where one does not want to stop.

Unfortunately such instances are rare. More often loudspeakers are used having such poor off-axis frequency response that the only remedy is to make the room highly absorbent so that the off-axis sound never reaches the listener. This has led to the well-established myth that reflections are bad and that extensive treatment to make a room dead is necessary for good monitoring. This approach has no psychoacoustic basis and has simply evolved as a practical way of using loudspeakers having poor directivity. The problem is compounded by the fact that an absorbent room requires more sound power to obtain a given SPL. Consequently heavily treated rooms require high-power loudspeakers which have high distortion and often further sacrifice polar response in order to achieve that high power.

A conventional box-shaped loudspeaker with drive units in the front will suffer extensive shading of the radiation to the rear and thus will create a coloured reverberant field. Clearly a much more effective way of exciting reverberation with an accurate tonal balance is for the loudspeaker to emit sound to the rear as well as to the front. Some surround-sound systems specify such speakers for the rear channels in order to give a better impression of ambience, but the approach is equally valid for the front speakers or for stereo speakers.

Loudspeakers have also been seen with additional drive units facing upwards in order to improve the balance between direct and reverberant sound. These techniques work well but obviously in a dead room are a waste of time as the additional radiation will never reach the listener. The fault is in the room, not the speaker.

8.12 Loudspeaker mechanisms

The two transduction mechanisms used in microphones are both reversible and so can also be applied to loudspeakers. The electrodynamic loudspeaker produces a force by passing current through a magnetic field whereas the electrostatic loudspeaker produces force due to the action of an electric field upon a charge.

The moving-coil loudspeaker[4] is by far the most common device. Figure 8.21 shows the structure of a typical low-cost unit containing an annular ferrite magnet. The magnet produces a radial field in which the coil operates. The coil drives the centre of the diaphragm which is supported by a *spider* allowing axial but not radial movement. The perimeter of the cone is supported by a flexible *surround*. The end of the

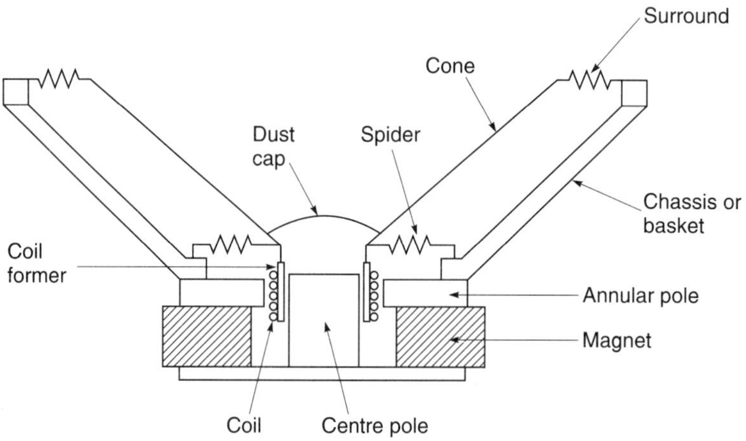

Figure 8.21 The components of a moving-coil loudspeaker.

coil is blanked off by a domed *dust cap* which is acoustically part of the cone. When the cone moves towards the magnet, air under the dust cap and the spider will be compressed and suitable vents must be provided to allow it to escape. If this is not done the air will force its way out at high speed causing turbulence and resulting in noise which is known as *chuffing*.

A major drawback of the moving-coil loudspeaker is that the drive force is concentrated in one place on the diaphragm whereas the air load is distributed over the surface. This can cause the diaphragm to *break up*, which is undesirable in a woofer which should act as a rigid piston. Figure 8.22 shows that a more even application of coil thrust can be obtained by using a large coil so that the distance from the point where the drive force is applied is reduced.

The coil in a loudspeaker has appreciable resistance and this results in heating. At high power, the heat can only be dissipated by a large temperature rise. This has the effect of raising the coil resistance, reducing the sensitivity of the speaker. The result is known as thermal compression.

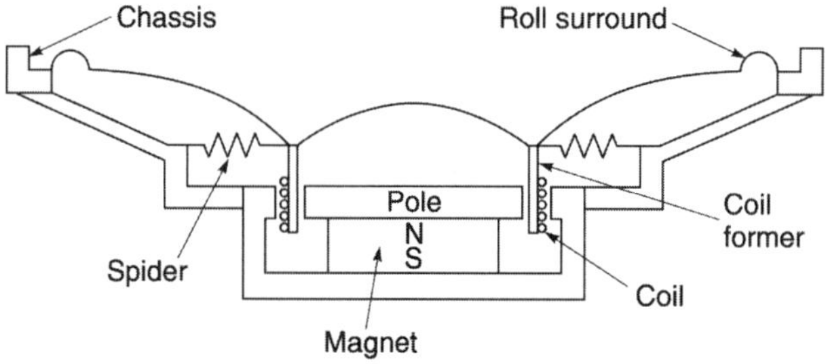

Figure 8.22 Woofer using large coil to distribute force more evenly.

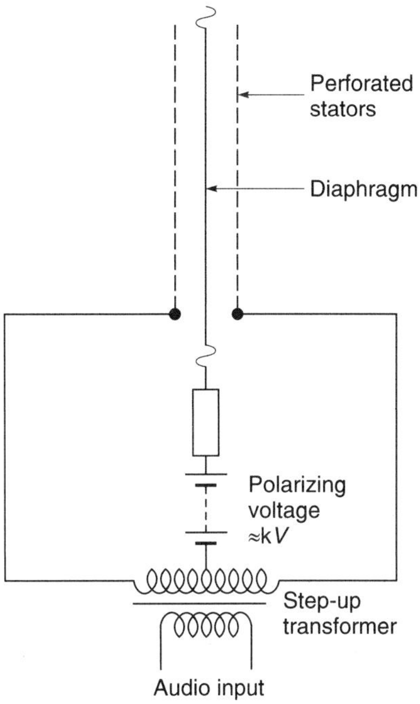

Figure 8.23 The electrostatic loudspeaker uses the force experienced by a charge in an electric field. The charge is obtained by polarizing the diaphragm.

As the density of air is so low, the mass of air a loudspeaker actually moves is a few per cent of the mass of the diaphragm. Consequently most of the drive power supplied to any kind of loudspeaker is wasted in accelerating the diaphragm back and forth and the efficiency is very poor. There is no prospect of this situation ever being resolved in electromagnetic speakers.

The electrostatic loudspeaker is shown in Figure 8.23. A slightly conductive diaphragm is connected to a high-voltage DC supply so that it becomes charged. The high resistivity of the diaphragm prevents the charge moving around so that at all audio frequencies it can be considered fixed. Any charge placed in an electric field will experience a force. The electric field is provided by electrodes either side of the diaphragm which are driven in antiphase, often by a centre-tapped transformer.

The advantage of the electrostatic loudspeaker is that the driving mechanism is fundamentally linear and the mechanical drive is applied uniformly all over the diaphragm. Consequently there is no reason why the diaphragm should break up. There is no heat-dissipation mechanism in the electrostatic speaker and thermal compression is completely absent. The electrostatic loudspeaker has the further advantage that it is also inherently a dipole, radiating as much sound to the rear as forward.

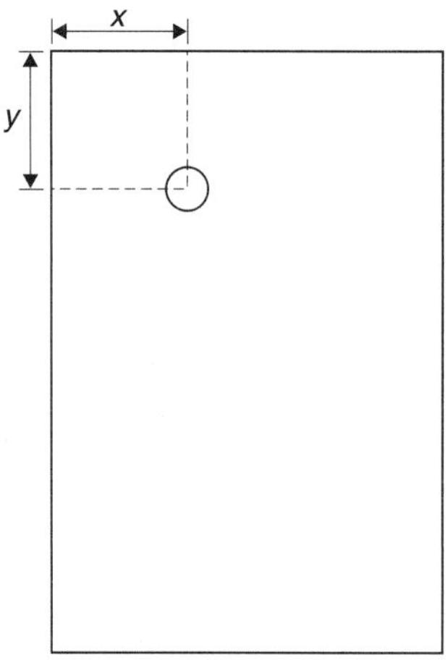

Figure 8.24 In distributed mode loudspeakers, the coil is critically positioned such that the panel resonances which occur are innumerable and uniform.

Recently a new type of loudspeaker has emerged which operates on bending waves in a flat panel.[5] Figure 8.24 shows that a moving-coil motor is used to excite the panel in a location which is carefully calculated. The panel will break up or resonate, but the correct choice of motor location will ensure that no mode dominates. Such distributed-mode loudspeakers (DML) can be very thin, and can also be made transparent so that displays can be seen through them. Radiation takes place from both sides of the panel. This is beneficial in exciting the reverberant field, but for wall mounting a suitable enclosure can absorb the rear radiation. The panel cannot be made to move as a piston and so performance at low frequencies is poor. A crossover to a conventional woofer will be needed if the full frequency range is required.

DML speakers have rather different characteristics from conventional speakers. Their large radiating area means that they do not act as point sources. Their acoustic near-field extends a considerable distance from the panel and in this area the inverse square law does not apply. The frequency response and directivity of correctly designed DML panels are chaotic. At a given listening location the direct sound will have a very irregular frequency response but with no dominant peaks. The reverberant sound will have another irregular frequency response. Masking in the ear results in an average frequency response being perceived and the result can be quite pleasing.

However, DML speakers also have some problems. The distributed-mode radiation destroys transient wavefronts and the spatial information they contain (see section 5.11). The lack of a point source means that stereophonic images are smeared. However, the chaotic behaviour and wide directivity makes DML speakers suitable for the rear speakers in surround-sound systems, especially those where radiation from both sides of the panel is allowed. The rear speakers primarily reproduce reverberation and ambience which is inherently chaotic.

The greatest strength of DML speakers is not in competition with conventional speakers. Instead DML should be seen as a technology which allows loudspeakers of reasonable quality to be incorporated into products or locations where the use of a conventional speaker would be impossible.

8.13 Directivity

One of the greatest challenges in a loudspeaker is to make the polar characteristics change smoothly with frequency in order to give an uncoloured reverberant field. Unfortunately crossing over between a number of drive units often does not achieve this. Figure 8.25 shows that

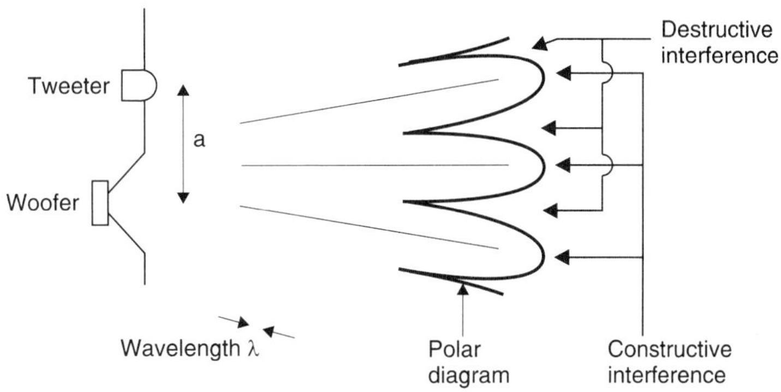

Figure 8.25 At the crossover frequency both drivers are operating and if *ka* is not small the polar diagram becomes highly irregular because of path-length differences.

at the crossover frequency both drive units separated by *a* are contributing equally to the radiation. If the wavelength is long compared to the dimensions the system acts as a single driver and the polar diagram will be undisturbed. However, with typical speaker components this will only be true below a few hundred Hz. If a crossover is attempted above that frequency a diffraction pattern will be created where the radiation will sum or cancel according to the path length differences between the two drivers. This results in an irregular polar diagram and some quite undesirable off-axis frequency responses.[6]

Clearly the traditional loudspeaker with many different drive units is flawed. Certain moving-coil and electrostatic transducers can approach the ideal with sufficient care. Figure 8.26(a) shows that if the flare angle

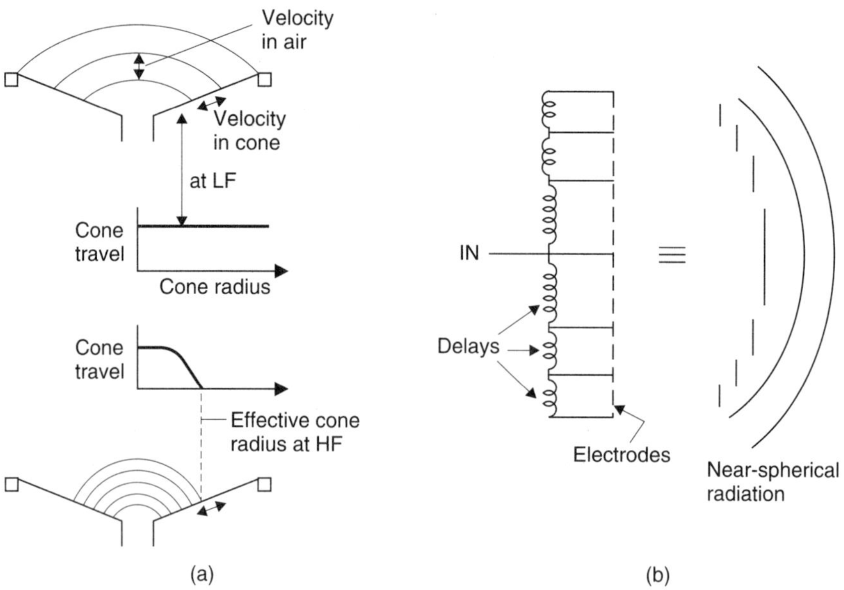

Figure 8.26 (a) A cone built as a lossy transmission line can reduce its diameter as a function of frequency, giving smooth directivity characteristics. (b) Using delay lines a flat electrostatic panel can be made to behave like a pulsating sphere.

of a cone-type moving-coil unit is correct for the material, the forward component of the speed of sound in the cone can be made slightly less than the speed of sound in the air, so that nearly spherical wavefronts can be launched. The cone is acting as a mechanical transmission line for vibrations which start at the coil former and work outwards. This should not be confused with cone break-up which is uncontrolled and detrimental. If frequency-dependent loss is introduced into the transmission line, the higher the frequency, the smaller is the area of the cone which radiates. Done correctly the result is a constant dispersion drive unit. There are vibrations travelling out across the cone surface and the cone surround must act as a matched terminator so that there can be no reflections.

The dome looks as if it ought to have a broad radiation pattern. Unfortunately this simplistic view is quite wrong.[1,7] The dome driver exhibits exactly the opposite of what is wanted. In practice domes can't be rigid because vibrations can travel right across the dome and bounce off the other side as shown in Figure 8.27(a). The palliative here is the soft dome which is made from a lossy material. However, with a lossy material, as frequency rises, the centre of the dome decouples and only the perimeter is fully driven, producing an annular radiator of maximum size as shown in Figure 8.27(b). Consequently the polar characteristics of domes are poor and the off-axis response is likely to be impaired. The

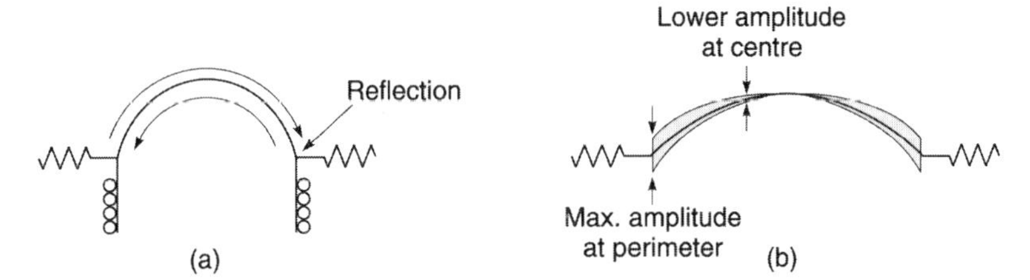

Figure 8.27 The problems of dome drivers. (a) Rigid dome cannot be terminated; vibrations travel across the dome and reflect. (b) Solution to reflections is the 'soft' dome which attenuates vibrations travelling from the coil.

only advantage of the dome driver is that a very large coil can be fitted which will allow high power dissipation. This allows high SPL to be generated in dead rooms where the poor directivity will be concealed.

The elegant directivity solution in an electrostatic speaker first proposed by Walker of Quad[8] is to make the mechanically flat diaphragm behave like a sphere by splitting the electrode structure into concentric rings fed by lossy delay lines as shown in Figure 8.26(b). This produces what is known as a *phased array*. The outward propagation of vibrations across the diaphragm again simulates quite closely a sector of a pulsating sphere. Matched termination at the perimeter is required to prevent reflections. There is no reason why such an approach should not work with a segmented ribbon speaker.

Using either of these techniques allows the construction of a single-drive unit which will work over the entire mid and treble range and display smooth directivity changes. A low-frequency crossover to a woofer completes the design. Such two-way speakers can display extremely good performance especially if implemented with active techniques.

Interestingly enough if strict polar response and distortion criteria are applied, the phased array electrostatic loudspeaker turns out to be capable of higher SPL than the moving-coil unit. This is because the phased array approach allows the electrostatic loudspeaker to have a very large area diaphragm without beaming taking place. Consequently at mid and high frequencies it can achieve very large volume velocities yet with very small displacements.

8.14 The moving-coil speaker

Unlike the electrostatic speaker, the moving-coil speaker is not fundamentally linear and a number of mechanisms are responsible for less than ideal behaviour. There are two basic criteria for linearity. First, the drive force of the coil should depend only on the current and not on the coil position. Second, the restoring force of the suspension should be exactly proportional to the displacement. Both of these effects are worse at low frequencies where the cone travel is greatest.

Rice and Kellog discovered around 1925 that the displacement of a moving-coil loudspeaker cone reaches a peak at the resonance, and falls at 6 dB per octave either side of that resonance as shown in Figure 8.28(a).

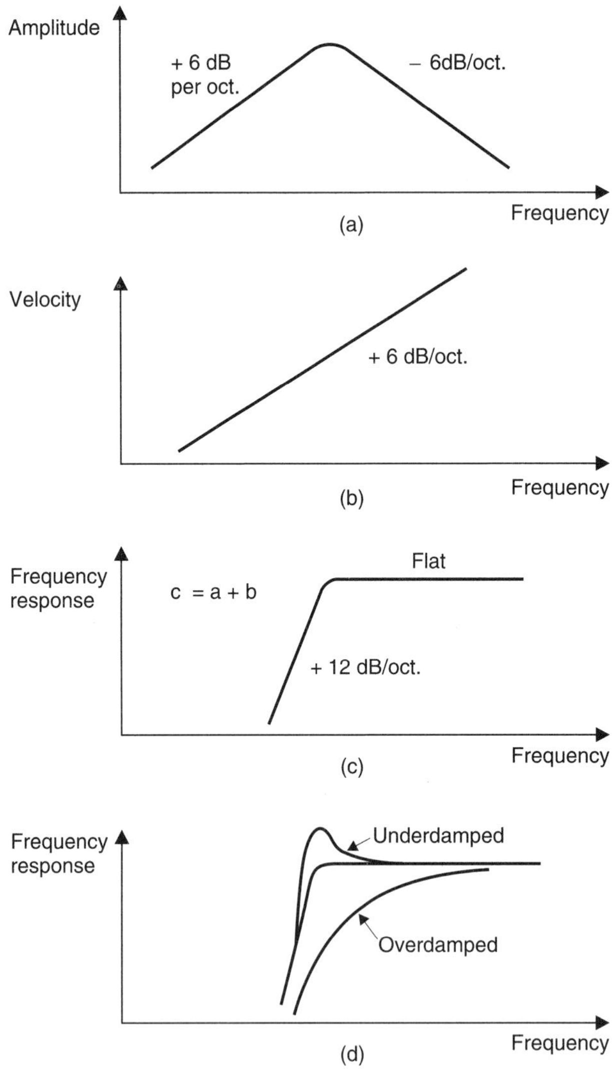

Figure 8.28 (a) The amplitude of a resonant system falls at 6 dB/octave away from the peak. (b) The velocity of the system in (a) is obtained by differentiating the displacement, resulting in a 6 dB/octave tilt. This gives a flat response region with a 12 dB/octave roll-off below resonance. (c) Moving coil motor acts as a transformer coupling resonant system to the coil resistance which acts as a damper. Motor design affects peakiness of resonance (d).

Radiation is proportional to cone *velocity* which is obtained by differentiating the displacement. Differentiation tilts the response by 6 dB/octave. Consequently as Figure 8.28(b) shows, the radiation is independent of frequency above resonance but falls at 12 dB/octave below.

Below resonance the motion is stiffness controlled. The displacement is proportional to coil current and velocity leads the current. Above resonance the system is mass controlled. The acceleration is proportional to coil current and velocity lags the current. Figure 8.29 shows the phase response through resonance. Note that at the resonant frequency the velocity is exactly in phase with the coil current. Because of this phase characteristic the polarity of a loudspeaker is a matter of opinion.

Manufacturers mark one terminal with a red spot or a + sign as an aid to wiring in the correct polarity. However, some use the convention that a positive DC voltage (e.g. from a battery) will cause forward motion of the cone, whereas others use the convention that the positive half-cycle of an AC voltage at a frequency above resonance will cause forward motion. It will be seen from Figure 8.29 that these two conventions are, of course, in phase opposition. The AC definition makes more sense as that is how the speaker is used. However, most manufacturers use the DC definition.

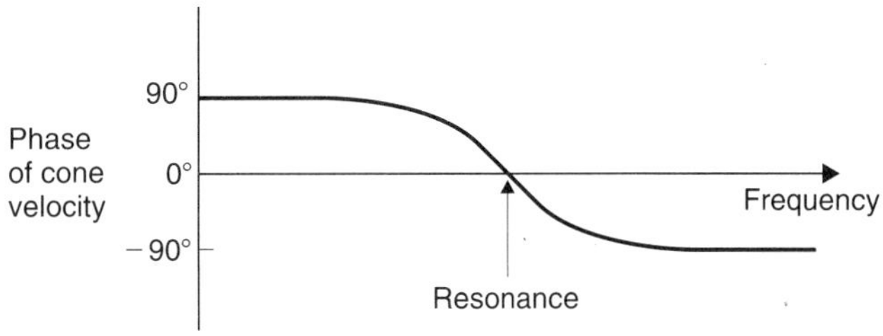

Figure 8.29 Phase response of loudspeaker passes through zero at resonance. The sharper the resonance the more rapid is the phase change.

The phase reversal of a moving-coil driver as it passes through resonance means that it is fundamentally incapable of reproducing the input waveform at frequencies near resonance. Clearly if it is intended to reproduce the input waveform accurately the fundamental resonance must be placed below the audio band at around 20 Hz or signal processing must be used to artificially lower the resonance.

Figure 8.30 shows that with an amplifier of low output resistance, the mechanical resonance is damped by the coil resistance. The moving-coil motor acts as a transformer coupling the resonant system to the damping resistance. Increasing the flux density or the length of coil in the gap increases the effective ratio of the transformer and makes the coil resistance appear lower, increasing the damping. The peakiness of the

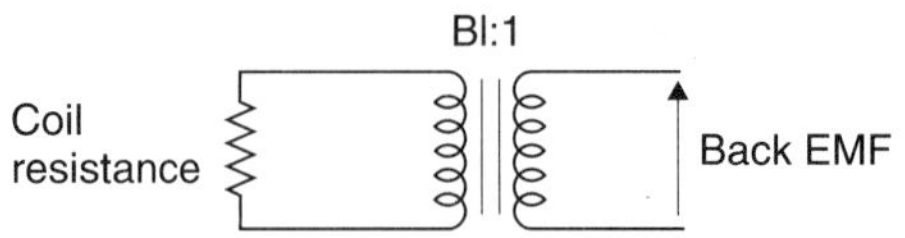

Figure 8.30 The Bl product of the motor coil determines the ratio of the coupling between the resonant system and the damping of the coil resistance.

resonance is adjusted in the design process by balancing the coil resistance, the strength of the magnet and the length of coil wire in the magnetic field. If the drive unit is not driven by a low-output impedance via low-resistance cables the resonance may be underdamped and a pronounced peak may occur.

The moving-coil speaker obtains a drive force due to the coil current reacting against the magnetic field. Figure 8.31 shows that the radial magnetic field is provided by a permanent magnet. If the moving coil motor is to be linear, the force produced must depend only on the current and not on the position. In the case of a tweeter, shown in Figure 8.31(a), the travel is usually so small that the coil can be made the same length as the flux gap as the leakage flux effectively extends the gap. In woofers the travel is significant and in order to obtain linearity the coil can be made shorter (b) or longer (c) than the flux gap. Clearly (c) is less efficient as power is wasted driving current through those parts of the coil which are

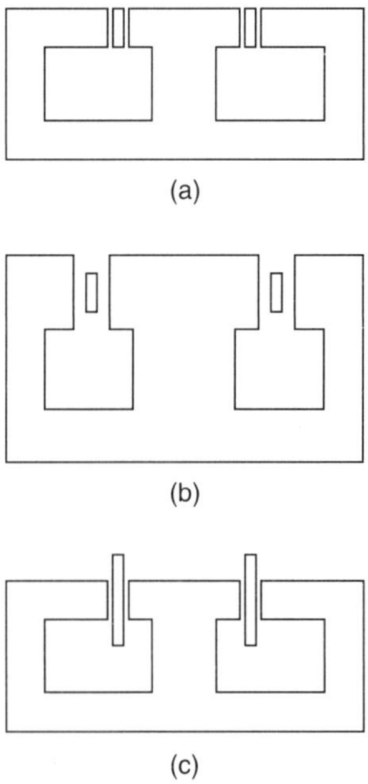

Figure 8.31 (a) Coil same length as gap. (b) Coil shorter than gap. (c) Coil longer than gap.

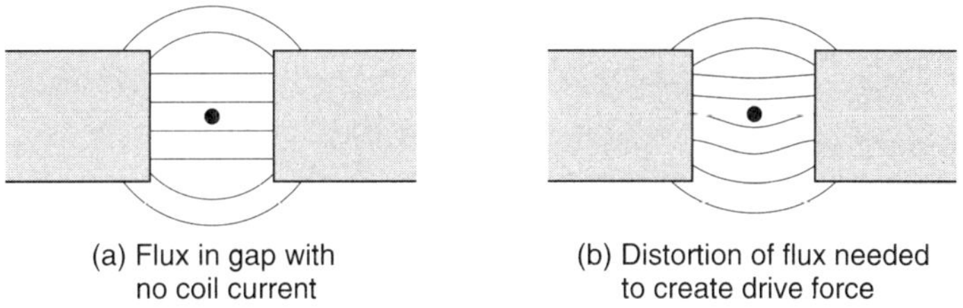

Figure 8.32 (a) Poor magnet design with asymmetrical flux. (b) Better design achieves flux symmetry.

not in the gap. However, (b) requires a massive magnet structure and is little used because of the weight and cost.

It is important that the flux distribution is symmetrical. Figure 8.32(a) shows a typical low-cost speaker with casual pole design. Figure 8.32(b) shows a better approach.

The volume of the air gap in which the coil operates is a critical factor. This is given by the gap width multiplied by the gap area. The wider the gap, the greater the magneto-motive force (mmf) needed to drive flux across the gap and the longer the magnet needs to be. The gap width will be set by the radial thickness of the coil plus operating clearances. The gap depth and the pole radius set the pole area and the greater the area over which a given flux density is required, the greater the total flux and the greater the cross sectional area of the magnet will need to be.

The low-cost ferrite magnet is a source of considerable problems in the television environment because it produces so much stray flux. This can cause colour purity errors and distortion of the picture on a CRT because it disturbs the magnetic deflection system. Whilst screening can be installed, a better solution for speakers to be used near CRTs is to employ

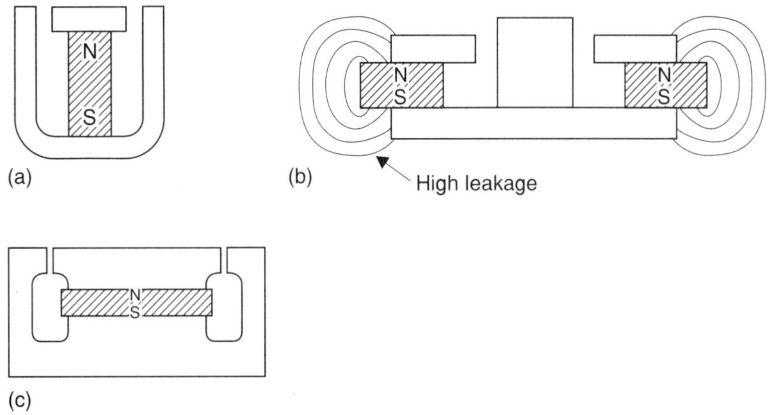

Figure 8.33 (a) Alnico requires columnar magnet. (b) Ferrite requires generous cross-sectional area and leaks badly. (c) Rare-earth magnet has very small volume and mass. Structures (a) and (c) have no external leakage.

a different magnetic circuit design as shown in Figure 8.33. Such a design completely contains its own flux because the magnet is inside the magnetic circuit. The magnet has to be smaller, but sufficient flux is easily available using rare-earth magnets. As Figure 8.33(c) shows, the rare-earth magnet has a very high energy product and only a small volume of material is required. This can easily be located inside the coil, leading to a very compact motor.

As there is no such thing as a magnetic insulator, a good deal of flux is lost to leakage where flux simply jumps from one pole to the next. Undercutting the pole pieces is of some help because it helps to keep as much air as possible in the shunt leakage path. However, the ferrite magnet fares poorly for leakage because its surface area is so large that the shunt reluctance is small. In ferrite designs often only a third of the magnet flux passes through the gap.

The rare-earth magnet can be so small that its shunt reluctance is significantly higher and there is much less leakage. Thus the magnet can be even smaller because the reduced leakage makes it more efficient. Whilst samarium–cobalt rare-earth magnets are expensive, the cost of neodymium–iron–boron magnets is falling and they are starting to become popular in loudspeakers because of their efficiency and low leakage. Rare-earth magnets may have ten times the energy of ferrite, but because the leakage is much reduced it is often possible to use a magnet only one twentieth the volume of a ferrite equivalent. The lower weight allowed by neodymium means that the entire drive unit weighs about one half as much as one having a ferrite magnet.

The coil must have good electrical conductivity and low mass. Most coils are copper, but aluminium has a better conductivity-to-weight ratio. Aluminium wire is available with a thin coating of copper to facilitate making connections. In most cases the coil is made by winding onto a cylindrical former which delivers the coil thrust to the neck of the cone.

The job of the cone is to couple the motion of the coil to a large volume of air. In a woofer the diaphragm is acoustically small and the cone should be rigid so that it acts as a piston. As excessive mass reduces efficiency, the best materials for woofer cones are those which offer the best ratio of modulus of elasticity to density. Other factors include the ability to resist high temperatures reached by the coil former where it joins the neck of the cone, and the inherent damping of the material which prevents resonances.

Early cones were made of paper but these are easily damaged and are susceptible to moisture absorption which changes the speaker characteristics as a function of humidity. The conical shape was adopted because it allows a great increase in stiffness over a flat sheet of material. Even greater stiffness is possible if the cone is flared as shown in Figure 8.34.

Figure 8.34 A flared 'cone' is even stiffer than a true cone.

Many different approaches have been tried for cone construction and in woofers at least, many of these have been successful. Figure 8.35 shows some possibilities for woofers. The sandwich construction uses two skins, typically of aluminium, with a low-density core, typically of expanded polystyrene. This is sometimes taken to the extreme case where the cone is solid, having a flat front. Aluminium cones can be turned into sandwich structures by anodizing. The hard oxide layer due to the anodizing step forms a rigid skin and the aluminium forms the core. Thermoplastics have been used for cones and have the advantage that they can be moulded at low cost, but are unsuitable for high-power applications. Recently composite materials have become economic and their high stiffness-to-density ratio which makes them attractive in aerospace is equally useful in loudspeakers.

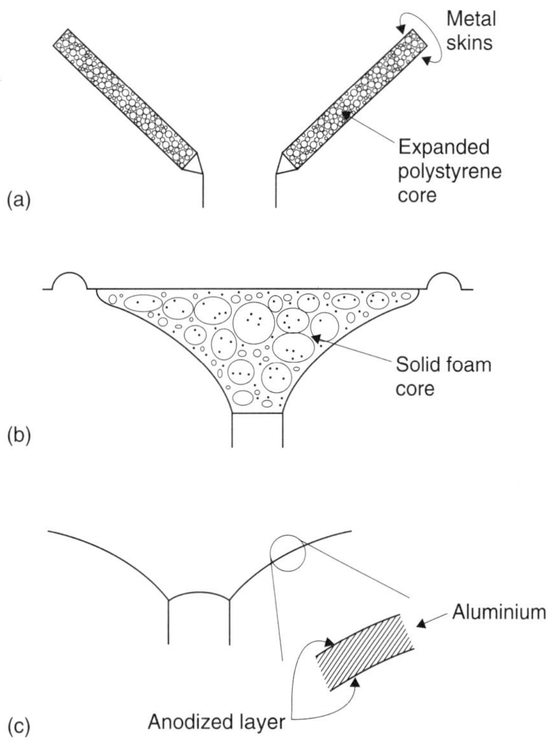

Figure 8.35 (a) Sandwich woofer cone. (b) Solid foam woofer diaphragm. (c) Anodized aluminium forms a sandwich.

In tweeters the cone design is more difficult because of the need to allow the cone to act as a transmission line without allowing uncontrolled break-up. This makes the stiffness and damping critical. In many cases one single material is unsuitable and the cone is made from a suitably stiff material which has an appropriate internal speed of sound and a separate damping layer may then be provided.

8.15 Low-frequency reproduction

An unenclosed diaphragm acts as a dipole and these become extremely inefficient at low frequencies because air simply moves from the front to the back, short-circuiting the radiation. In practice the radiation from the two sides of the diaphragm must be kept separate to create an efficient LF radiator. The concept of the *infinite baffle* is one in which the drive unit is mounted in an aperture in an endless plate. Such a device cannot be made and in practice the infinite baffle is folded round to make an *enclosure*. Sealed enclosures are often and erroneously called infinite baffles, but they do not have the same result. Unfortunately the enclosed air acts as a spring because inward movement of the diaphragm reduces the volume, raising the pressure.

The stiffness of this air spring acts in parallel with the stiffness of the diaphragm supports. The mass of the diaphragm and the total stiffness determines the frequency of *fundamental resonance* of the loudspeaker. To obtain reproduction of lowest frequencies, the resonance must be kept low and this implies a large box to reduce the stiffness of the air spring, and a high-compliance drive unit. When the air stiffness dominates the drive unit stiffness, the configuration is called *acoustic suspension*.

Acoustic suspension speakers were claimed to offer a more accurate compliance than the speaker's mechanical flexure, but this is not true.

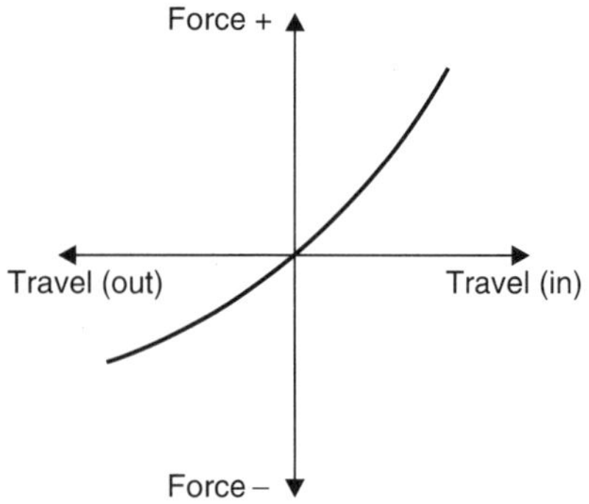

Figure 8.36 An air spring is non-linear producing more restoring force on compression than on rarefaction.

The air spring in a sealed box is fundamentally non-linear. This is easy to see by considering Figure 8.36. Here a diaphragm will displace a volume equal to the volume of the box. If the diaphragm moves inwards, the pressure becomes infinite. If the diaphragm moves outwards, the pressure is merely halved. It is simple to calculate the distortion given the diaphragm displacement and the box volume.

In early attempts to give satisfactory low-frequency performance from smaller boxes, a number of passive schemes have been tried. These include the reflex cabinet shown in Figure 8.37(a) which has a port containing an air mass. This is designed to resonate with the air spring at a frequency below that of the fundamental resonance of the driver so that as the driver response falls off the port output takes over. In some designs the air mass is replaced by a compliantly mounted diaphragm having no coil, known as an ABR or auxiliary bass radiator, (b).

Another alternative is the transmission line speaker shown in (c) in which the rear wave from the driver is passed down a long damped labyrinth which emerges at a port. The length is designed to introduce a 180° phase shift at the frequency where the port output is meant to augment the driver output. A true transmission line loudspeaker is quite large in order to make the labyrinth long enough. Some smaller models

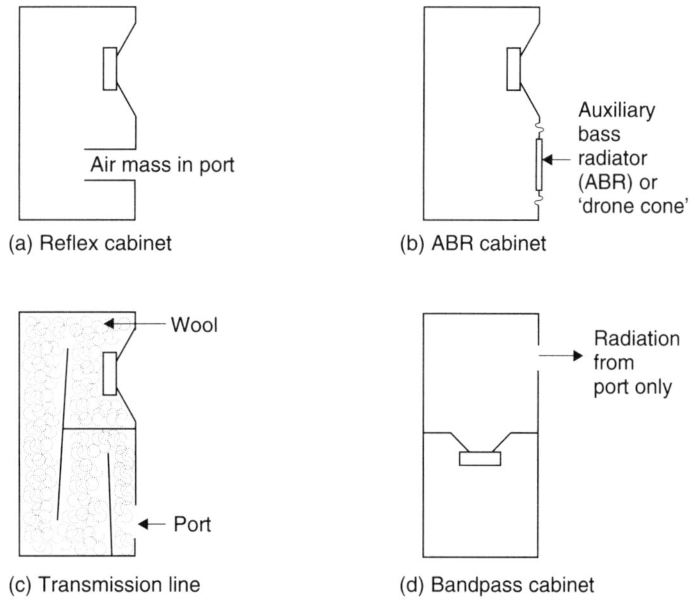

Figure 8.37 Various attempts to reproduce low frequencies. (a) Mass of air in reflex duct resonates with air spring in box. (b) Air mass replaced by undriven diaphragm or ABR. (c) Rear wave is phase shifted 180° in transmission line to augment front radiation. (d) Bandpass enclosure puts drive unit between two resonating chambers. None of these techniques can properly reproduce transients and active techniques have rendered them obsolete.

are available which claim to work on the transmission line principle but in fact the labyrinth is far too short and there is a chamber behind the drive unit which makes these heavily damped reflex cabinets.

More recently the *bandpass* enclosure (d) has become popular, probably because suitable computer programs are now available to assist the otherwise difficult design calculations. The bandpass enclosure has two chambers with the drive unit between them. All radiation is via the port.

The reflex, ABR, bandpass and transmission line principles have numerous drawbacks, the most serious of which are that the principle only works on continuous tone. Low-frequency transients suffer badly from linear distortion because the leading edge of the transients are removed and reproduced after the signal has finished to give the phenomenon of *hangover*. The low-frequency content of the sound lags behind the high frequencies in an unnatural way. In other words the input waveform is simply not reproduced by these tricks as is easily revealed by comparison with the original sound.

Different order filtering and different damping change the amount by which this lag takes place, but can never eliminate the problem, which is most noticeable on transient musical information such as percussion and on effects such as door slams. It is quite impossible to use such a low-frequency technique in conjunction with a linear phase electrostatic high-frequency unit or a constant directivity mid-top moving-coil unit because the quality mismatch is too obvious.

The only low-frequency structure which can approach the reproduction of the input waveform is the sealed box. In passive loudspeakers, in order to reproduce the lowest frequencies the box will need to be large to

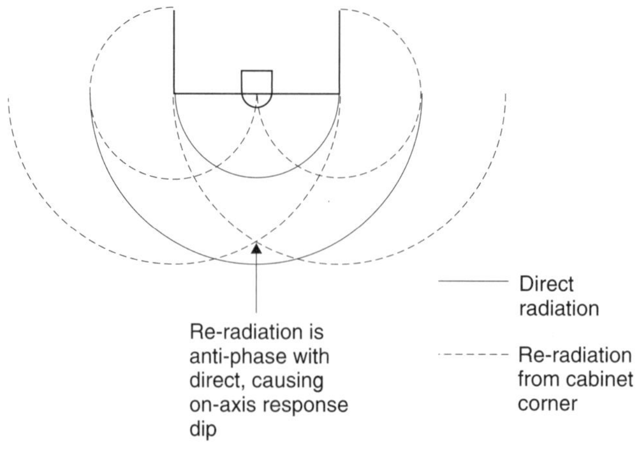

Figure 8.38 Attempting to radiate high frequency from a tweeter mounted in a large rectangular box produces frequency response irregularity due to diffraction from the box corners.

prevent the stiffness of the air spring raising the fundamental resonance. Unfortunately a large box forms a very poor place from which to radiate high frequencies. Figure 8.38 shows that when a high-frequency unit is fitted in a large box, diffraction results in reradiation at the corners.[9,10]

When the direct and reradiated sounds combine the result is constructive or destructive interference depending on the frequency. This causes ripples in the on-axis frequency response. The larger the box, the further down the spectrum these ripples go. The effect can be reduced by making the cabinet smaller and curved with no sharp corners.

8.16 Crossover networks

As the full-range drive unit is virtually impossible, practical loudspeakers need to employ several drive units, each optimized for a particular frequency range. A crossover network is needed so that signals of the right frequency are sent to the appropriate drive unit. Perhaps it is more accurate to say that the wrong frequencies are prevented from reaching drive units which cannot handle them.

Loudspeakers are highly traditional devices which continue to be built in the same way even though the restrictions which originally led to the approach have long since disappeared. At one time audio amplifiers were expensive and the multi-drive unit loudspeaker had to use a single amplifier to control cost. This meant that the crossover had to be performed at power level. Figure 8.39(a) shows a typical simple power level crossover. An inductor in series with the woofer reduces the input at high frequencies as its impedance rises whereas a capacitor in series with

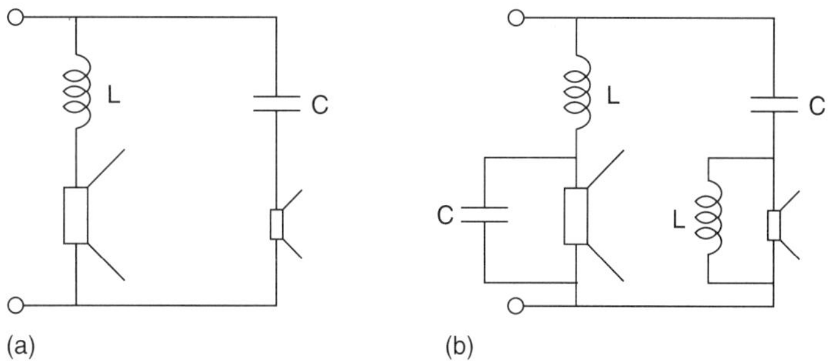

(a)

$$C_1 = \frac{1}{2\pi f_1 R_0}$$

$$L = \frac{R_0}{2\pi f_1}$$

(b)

$$C = \frac{1}{2\pi f_1 R_0 \sqrt{2}}$$

$$L = \frac{R_0 \sqrt{2}}{2\pi f_1}$$

Figure 8.39 (a) Simple 6 dB/octave crossover. (b) 12 dB/octave requires second-order filter.

the tweeter increases the input at high frequencies as its impedance falls. The crossover slope is only 6 dB per octave which means that the two drive units will still receive significant signal levels outside their operating bandwidth. A steeper crossover can be obtained by using a second-order filter (b) which achieves 12 dB/octave.

Unfortunately none of these simple approaches work properly. It is self-evident that the sum of the two crossover outputs ought to be the original signal. This is known as a *constant voltage* crossover.[11] However, passive crossover techniques simply cannot reach this goal and must be considered obsolete for high-quality applications.

Using analog computing techniques it is easy to create constant-voltage crossovers. A filter is used to prevent unwanted frequencies reaching a certain drive unit. If the output of that filter is subtracted from the input, as in Figure 8.40, the result is the frequencies which the drive unit can handle. By definition, the sum of the two signals is the original. With more complexity, such a crossover can be made symmetrical or asymmetrical and have slopes to suit the characteristics of the drive units. When properly engineered the crossover frequency simply cannot be determined by listening.

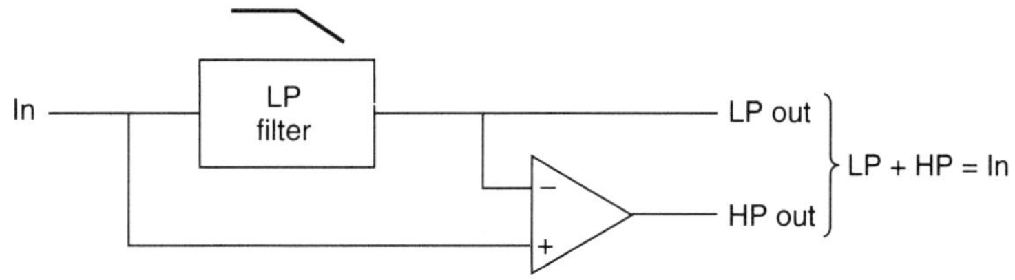

Figure 8.40 Active crossover with constant voltage characteristic gives precision that is impossible with passive crossovers.

8.17 Enclosures

The loudspeaker enclosure has to fulfil two functions. At low frequencies it must contain the back radiation from the woofer and at high frequencies its shape determines the diffraction characteristics which will affect the on-axis frequency response and the directivity.

At low frequencies an enclosure must be rigid so that internal pressures do not cause flexing. As the area of the enclosure walls is an order of magnitude greater than the woofer cone area, the slightest flexing can cause appreciable colouration of the sound. In other industries vessels to contain or resist pressure are invariably cylindrical or spherical. The aerosol can, the airliner and the submarine are good examples. The dogged adherence to the square box made from six flat panels illustrates that even today most loudspeakers are designed by tradition rather than physics.

At high frequencies the sharp corners on a square loudspeaker cause impedance changes and act as secondary radiators. This is also true of the woofer if this is exposed.[10] Many years ago Olsen[9] produced his definitive series of tests on speaker enclosure shapes, but this has been largely ignored.

Fortunately a small number of manufacturers are making loudspeakers in enclosures which rely on curvature for both stiffness and diffraction control. These are not necessarily expensive to make using moulding techniques, but the result is much less colouration of the sound and an opportunity for a more interesting visual appearance.

8.18 Active loudspeakers

With modern electronic techniques all passive schemes with their inevitable compromises and shortcomings must be considered obsolete. The traditional wideband power amplifier having low distortion and a flat frequency response which expects to see a loudspeaker with the same characteristics is both overly optimistic and an unnecessary restriction. What is required is a system whereby the radiated sound resembles the original line level signal. What goes on inside the box to achieve this is the designer's problem.

An active loudspeaker containing its own amplifiers can easily introduce equalization and signal processing which can artificially move the fundamental resonance down in frequency and achieve any desired damping factor. The crossover can be performed precisely and at low cost at line level instead of imprecisely at power level using large expensive components. Inverse distortion can be applied to compensate for drive unit deficiencies. The advantage of this approach is that the speaker can be made relatively phase-linear and will not suffer from hangover. The smaller cabinet also allows the radiation characteristics of the mid and high frequencies to be improved. The sensitivities of the drive units do not need to be matched so that there is more freedom in their design. In the absence of separate amplifier cabinets less space is needed overall and the dubious merits of exotic speaker cables become irrelevant.

Figure 8.41 shows the block diagram of a modern active loudspeaker. The line-level input passes to a crossover filter which routes low and high frequencies to each driver. Each drive unit has its own power amplifier. The low-frequency power amplifier is preceded by a compensation network which can electronically lower the resonance of the low-

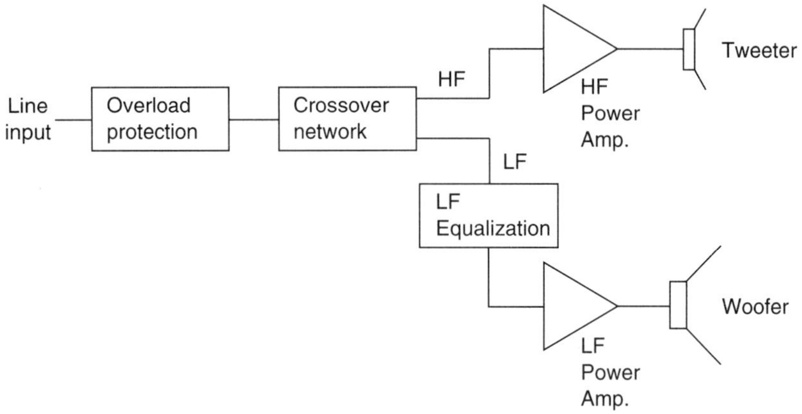

Figure 8.41 In an active loudspeaker the crossover function is performed at line level and separate amplifiers are used for each drive unit. The low-frequency response is controlled by equalization and electronic damping allowing accurate transient reproduction.

frequency driver and determine the damping factor. In some units the low-frequency diaphragm is fitted with a feedback transducer so that distortion can be further reduced.

Electronic compensation of the fundamental resonance of a woofer makes it possible to reduce the size of the enclosure dramatically. Techniques of this kind allow realistic reproduction of low frequencies from enclosures whose volume would have been considered impossible a few years ago. If the goal is to add loudspeakers to a plasma display, only a very small enclosure is available and passive loudspeakers simply cannot function adequately.

8.19 Loudspeaker criteria for stereo and surround sound

The accuracy required for spatial reproduction is much greater than for mono. Spatial reproduction includes conventional stereo with two speakers and the frontal image creation in a surround-sound system having a centre speaker in addition to the left and right speakers since the physics is the same in both cases. If there is any non-linearity in the system, different sound sources will intermodulate and produce phantom sound sources which appear to come from elsewhere in the image than either of the original sounds. As these phantom sources are spatially separate from the genuine sources, they are easier to detect.

Where non-ideal speakers are used, it is important that the two speakers are absolutely identical. If the frequency and phase responses are not identical, the location of the apparent sound source will move with frequency. Where a harmonically rich source is involved, it will appear to be wider than it really is. This is known as *smear*.

If the loudspeakers suffer from beaming at high frequency then a proper image will only be obtained at a small 'sweet spot' and all high frequencies will appear to emanate from the speakers, not from a central image. Small movements by the listener may cause quite large image changes. Irregular polar diagrams will also destroy stereo imaging. Such irregularities often occur near the crossover frequencies. Placing the drive units in a vertical line will prevent the horizontal polar diagram becoming too irregular. However, this idea is completely destroyed if such a speaker is placed on its side; a technique which is seen with depressing regularity. This may be because many loudspeakes are so mediocre that turning them on their side does not make them sound any worse.

Loudspeakers and amplifiers used for stereo or surround-sound production must have very low distortion and a precisely tracking frequency and phase response. Loudspeakers must have smoothly changing directivity characteristics. In practice a great deal of equipment fails to meet these criteria.

In many audio/visual applications the level of background noise is high and/or the room acoustic is deficient, making conventional monitoring difficult. In many cases there is little space left for loudspeakers once all the video equipment is installed. One solution is the *close-field* monitor which is designed and equalized so that the listener can approach very close to it. The term 'near-field' is often and erroneously used to describe close-field monitors. The essence of close-field monitoring is that direct sound reaches the listener so much earlier than the reverberant sound that the room acoustic becomes less important. In stereo close-field monitoring the loudspeakers are much closer together, even though the same angle is subtended to the listener.

References

1. Watkinson, J.R., Transducer drive mechanisms, in Borwick, J. (ed.), *Loudspeaker and Headphone Handbook*, 3rd edn, Ch.2: Oxford: Focal Press (2000)
2. Olson, H.F., Stereophonic sound reproduction in the home. *J. Audio Eng. Soc.*, **6**, No.2, 80–90 (1958)
3. Moir, J., Speaker directivity and sound quality. *Wireless World*, **85**, No. 1526 (Oct. 1979)
4. Rice, C.W. and Kellog, E.W., Notes on the development of a new type of hornless loudspeaker. *JAIEE*, **12**, 461–480 (1925)
5. Azima, H., Colloms, M. and Harris, N., Acoustic device. *EP 0 847 661 B1* (1999)
6. Shorter, D.E.L., A survey of performance criteria and design considerations for high-quality monitoring loudspeakers. *Proc. IEE*, **105**, Part B, No.24, 607–623 (Nov. 1958)

7. Kates, J.M., Radiation from a dome, in *AES Anthology: Loudspeakers*, Vol.1-Vol.25, New York: Audio Engineering Society (1978)
8. Walker, P.J., New developments in electrostatic loudspeakers. *J. Audio Eng. Soc.*, **28**, No.11, 795–799 (Nov.1980)
9. Olson, H.F., *Acoustical Engineering*, Philadelphia: Professional Audio Journals Inc. (1991)
10. Kates, J.M., Loudspeaker cabinet reflection effects. *J. Audio Eng. Soc.*, **27**, No. 5 (1979)

9

Compression

9.1 Introduction to compression

Compression, bit rate reduction and data reduction are all terms which mean basically the same thing in this context. In essence the same (or nearly the same) information is carried using a smaller quantity or rate of data. It should be pointed out that, in audio, *compression* traditionally means a process in which the dynamic range of the sound is reduced. Provided the context is clear, the two meanings can co-exist without a great deal of confusion.

There are several reasons why compression techniques are popular:

(a) Compression extends the playing time of storage devices such as file servers.

(b) Compression allows miniaturization. With less data to store, the same playing time is obtained with smaller hardware. This is the approach used in the DV video tape format, DVD and MiniDisc.

(c) Tolerances can be relaxed. With less data to record, storage density can be reduced making equipment which is more resistant to adverse environments and which requires less maintenance.

(d) In communication systems, compression allows a reduction in bandwidth, hence the use in digital television broadcasting. Where the communication is billed by the bit, compression will result in a reduction in cost. Compression may also make possible some process which would be impracticable without it, such as Internet video.

(e) If a given bandwidth is available to an uncompressed signal, compression allows faster than real-time transmission in the same bandwidth.

(f) If a given bandwidth is available, compression allows a better-quality signal in the same bandwidth.

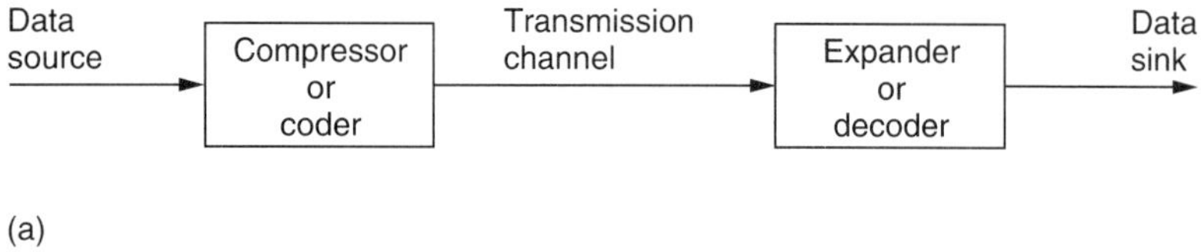

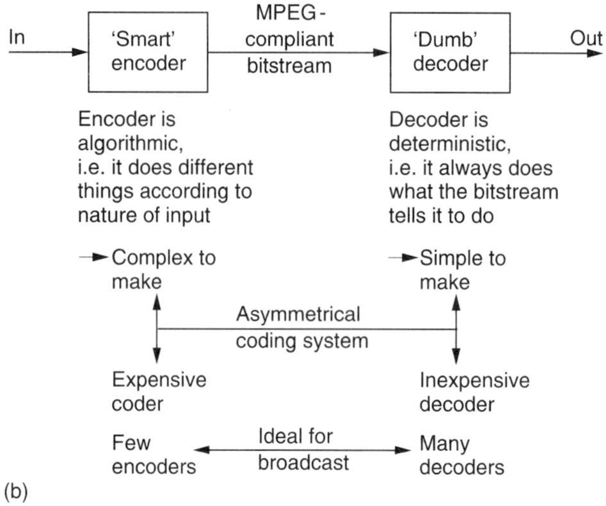

Figure 9.1 In (a) a compression system consists of compressor or coder, a transmission channel and a matching expander or decoder. The combination of coder and decoder is known as a codec. (b) MPEG is asymmetrical since the encoder is much more complex than the decoder.

Compression is summarized in Figure 9.1. It will be seen in (a) that the data rate is reduced at source by the *compressor.* The compressed data are then passed through a communication channel and returned to the original rate by the *expander.* The ratio between the source data rate and the channel data rate is called the *compression factor.* The term *coding gain* is also used. Sometimes a compressor and expander in series are referred to as a *compander.* The compressor may equally well be referred to as a *coder* and the expander a *decoder* in which case the tandem pair may be called a *codec.*

In audio and video compression, where the encoder is more complex than the decoder the system is said to be asymmetrical as in Figure 9.1(b). The encoder needs to be algorithmic or adaptive whereas the decoder is 'dumb' and carries out fixed actions. This is advantageous in applications such as broadcasting where the number of expensive complex encoders is small but the number of simple inexpensive decoders is large. In point-to-point applications or in recorders the advantage of asymmetrical coding is not so great.

Although there are many different coding techniques, all of them fall into one or other of these categories. In *lossless* coding, the data from the expander are identical bit-for-bit with the original source data. The so-called 'stacker' programs which increase the apparent capacity of disk drives in personal computers use lossless codecs. Clearly with computer programs the corruption of a single bit can be catastrophic. Lossless coding is generally restricted to compression factors of around 2:1.

It is important to appreciate that a lossless coder cannot guarantee a particular compression factor and the communications link or recorder used with it must be able to function with the variable output data rate. Source data which result in poor compression factors on a given codec are described as *difficult*. It should be pointed out that the difficulty is often a function of the codec. In other words data which one codec finds difficult may not be found difficult by another. Lossless codecs can be included in bit-error-rate testing schemes. It is also possible to cascade or *concatenate* lossless codecs without any special precautions.

In *lossy* coding, data from the expander are not identical bit-for-bit with the source data and as a result comparing the input with the output is bound to reveal differences. Lossy codecs are not suitable for computer data, but are used in audio and video as they allow greater compression factors than lossless codecs. Successful lossy codecs are those in which the errors are arranged so that a human viewer or listener finds them subjectively difficult to detect. Thus lossy codecs must be based on an understanding of psychoacoustic and psychovisual perception and are often called *perceptive* codes.

In perceptive coding, the greater the compression factor required, the more accurately must the human senses be modelled. Perceptive coders can be forced to operate at a fixed compression factor. This is convenient for practical transmission applications where a fixed data rate is easier to handle than a variable rate. The result of a fixed compression factor is that the subjective quality can vary with the 'difficulty' of the input material. Perceptive codecs should not be concatenated indiscriminately especially if they use different algorithms. As the reconstructed signal from a perceptive codec is not bit-for-bit accurate, clearly such a codec cannot be included in any bit error rate testing system as the coding differences would be indistinguishable from real errors.

Although the adoption of digital techniques to images is recent, compression itself is as old as television. Figure 9.2 shows some of the compression techniques used in traditional television systems.

One of the oldest techniques is interlace which has been used in analog television from the very beginning as a primitive way of reducing bandwidth. As was seen in Chapter 7, interlace is not without its problems, particularly in motion rendering. MPEG supports interlace simply because legacy interlaced signals exist and there is a requirement

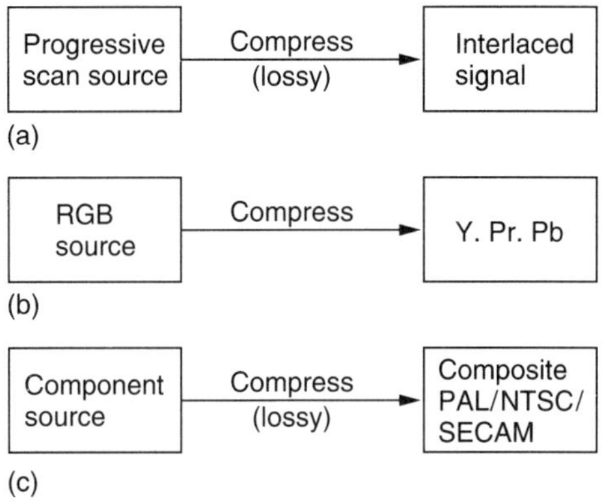

Figure 9.2 Compression is as old as television. (a) Interlace is a primitive way of halving the bandwidth. (b) Colour difference working invisibly reduces colour resolution. (c) Composite video transmits colour in the same bandwidth as monochrome.

to compress them. This should not be taken to mean that it is a good idea.

The generation of colour difference signals from *RGB* in video represents an application of perceptive coding. The human visual system (HVS) sees no change in quality although the bandwidth of the colour difference signals is reduced. This is because human perception of detail in colour changes is much less than in brightness changes. This approach is sensibly retained in MPEG.

Composite video systems such as PAL, NTSC and SECAM are all analog compression schemes which embed a subcarrier in the luminance signal so that colour pictures are available in the same bandwidth as monochrome. In comparison with a progressive scan *RGB* picture, interlaced composite video has a compression factor of 6:1.

In a sense MPEG can be considered to be a modern digital equivalent of analog composite video as it has most of the same attributes. For example, the eight-field sequence of a PAL subcarrier which makes editing diffficult has its equivalent in the GOP (group of pictures) of MPEG.[1]

In a PCM digital system the bit rate is the product of the sampling rate and the number of bits in each sample and this is generally constant. Nevertheless the *information* rate of a real signal varies. In all real signals, part of the signal is obvious from what has gone before or what may come later and a suitable receiver can predict that part so that only the true information actually has to be sent. If the characteristics of a predicting receiver are known, the transmitter can omit parts of the message in the knowledge that the receiver has the ability to re-create it. Thus all encoders must contain a model of the decoder.

One definition of information is that it is the unpredictable or surprising element of data. Newspapers are a good example of information because they only mention items which are surprising. Newspapers never carry items about individuals who have *not* been involved in an accident as this is the normal case. Consequently the phrase 'no news is good news' is remarkably true because if an information channel exists but nothing has been sent then it is most likely that nothing remarkable has happened.

The difference between the information rate and the overall bit rate is known as the redundancy. Compression systems are designed to eliminate as much of that redundancy as practicable or perhaps affordable. One way in which this can be done is to exploit statistical predictability in signals. The information content or *entropy* of a sample is a function of how different it is from the predicted value. Most signals have some degree of predictability. A sine wave is highly predictable, because all cycles look the same. According to Shannon's theory, any signal which is totally predictable carries no information. In the case of the sine wave this is clear because it represents a single frequency and so has no bandwidth.

At the opposite extreme a signal such as noise is completely unpredictable and as a result all codecs find noise *difficult*. There are two consequences of this characteristic. First, a codec which is designed using the statistics of real material should not be tested with random noise because it is not a representative test. Second, a codec which performs well with clean source material may perform badly with source material containing superimposed noise. Most practical compression units require some form of preprocessing before the compression stage proper and appropriate noise reduction should be incorporated into the preprocessing if noisy signals are anticipated. It will also be necessary to restrict the degree of compression applied to noisy signals.

All real signals fall part-way between the extremes of total predictability and total unpredictability or noisiness. If the bandwidth (set by the sampling rate) and the dynamic range (set by the wordlength) of the transmission system are used to delineate an area, this sets a limit on the information capacity of the system. Figure 9.3(a) shows that most real signals occupy only part of that area. The signal may not contain all frequencies, or it may not have full dynamics at certain frequencies.

Entropy can be thought of as a measure of the actual area occupied by the signal. This is the area that *must* be transmitted if there are to be no subjective differences or *artifacts* in the received signal. The remaining area is called the *redundancy* because it adds nothing to the information conveyed. Thus an ideal coder could be imagined which miraculously sorts out the entropy from the redundancy and sends only the former. An ideal decoder would then re-create the original impression of the information quite perfectly.

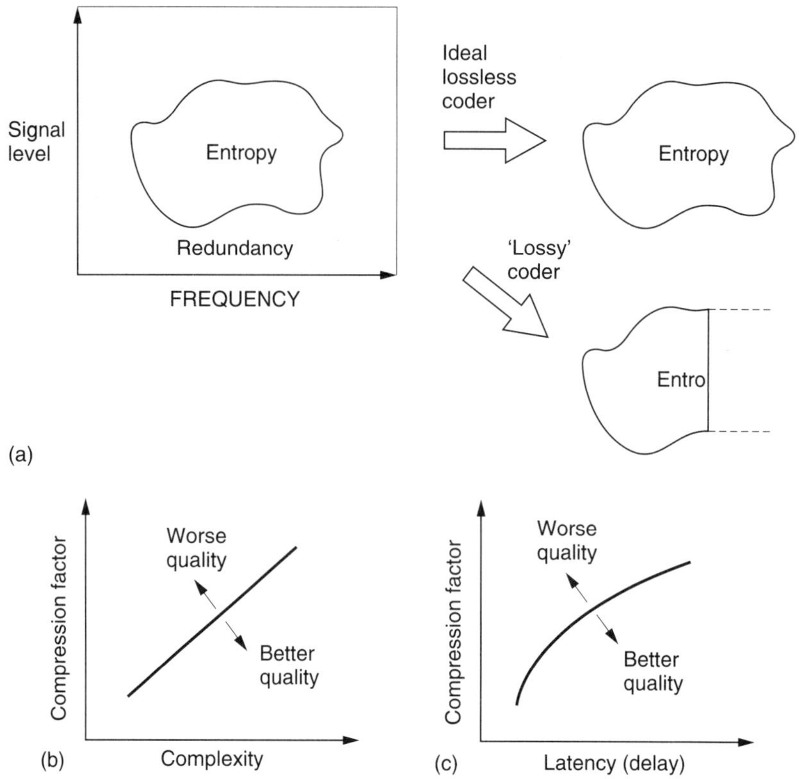

Figure 9.3 (a) A perfect coder removes only the redundancy from the input signal and results in subjectively lossless coding. If the remaining entropy is beyond the capacity of the channel some of it must be lost and the codec will then be lossy. An imperfect coder will also be lossy as it fails to keep all entropy. (b) As the compression factor rises, the complexity must also rise to maintain quality. (c) High compression factors also tend to increase latency or delay through the system.

As the ideal is approached, the coder complexity and the latency or delay both rise. Figure 9.3(b) shows how complexity increases with compression factor. This can be seen in the relative complexities of MPEG-1, 2 and 4. Figure 9.3(c) shows how increasing the codec latency can improve the compression factor. Obviously we would have to provide a channel which could accept whatever entropy the coder extracts in order to have transparent quality. As a result moderate coding gains which only remove redundancy need not cause artifacts and result in systems which are described as *subjectively lossless*.

If the channel capacity is not sufficient for that, then the coder will have to discard some of the entropy and with it useful information. Larger coding gains which remove some of the entropy must result in artifacts. It will also be seen from Figure 9.3 that an imperfect coder will fail to separate the redundancy and may discard entropy instead, resulting in artifacts at a suboptimal compression factor.

A single variable-rate transmission or recording channel is inconvenient and unpopular with channel providers because it is difficult to police. The requirement can be overcome by combining several compressed channels into one constant rate transmission in a way which flexibly allocates data rate between the channels. Provided the material is unrelated, the probability of all channels reaching peak entropy at once is very small and so those channels which are at one instant passing easy material will free up transmission capacity for those channels which are handling difficult material. This is the principle of statistical multiplexing.

Where the same type of source material is used consistently, e.g. English text, then it is possible to perform a statistical analysis on the frequency with which particular letters are utilized. Variable-length coding is used in which frequently used letters are allocated short codes and letters which occur infrequently are allocated long codes. This results in a lossless code. The well-known Morse code used for telegraphy is an example of this approach. The letter e is the most frequent in English and is sent with a single dot. An infrequent letter such as z is allocated a long complex pattern. It should be clear that codes of this kind which rely on a prior knowledge of the statistics of the signal are only effective with signals actually having those statistics. If Morse code is used with another language, the transmission becomes significantly less efficient because the statistics are quite different; the letter z, for example, is quite common in Czech.

The Huffman code[2] is one which is designed for use with a data source having known statistics and shares the same principles with the Morse code. The probability of the different code values to be transmitted is studied, and the most frequent codes are arranged to be transmitted with short wordlength symbols. As the probability of a code value falls, it will be allocated longer wordlength. The Huffman code is used in conjunction with a number of compression techniques and is shown in Figure 9.4.

The input or *source* codes are assembled in order of descending probability. The two lowest probabilities are distinguished by a single code bit and their probabilities are combined. The process of combining probabilities is continued until unity is reached and at each stage a bit is used to distinguish the path. The bit will be a zero for the most probable path and one for the least. The compressed output is obtained by reading the bits which describe which path to take going from right to left.

In the case of computer data, there is no control over the data statistics. Data to be recorded could be instructions, images, tables, text files and so on; each having their own code value distributions. In this case a coder relying on fixed source statistics will be completely inadequate. Instead a system is used which can learn the statistics as it goes along. The Lempel–Ziv–Welch (LZW) lossless codes are in this category. These codes build

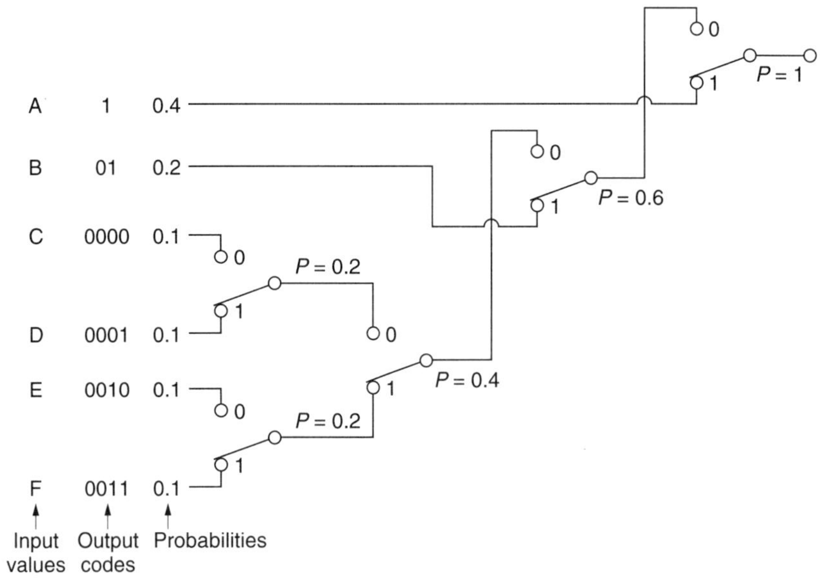

Figure 9.4 The Huffman code achieves compression by allocating short codes to frequent values. To aid deserializing the short codes are not prefixes of longer codes.

up a conversion table between frequent long source data strings and short transmitted data codes at both coder and decoder and initially their compression factor is below unity as the contents of the conversion tables are transmitted along with the data. However, once the tables are established, the coding gain more than compensates for the initial loss. In some applications, a continuous analysis of the frequency of code selection is made and if a data string in the table is no longer being used with sufficient frequency it can be deselected and a more common string substituted.

Lossless codes are less common for audio and video coding where perceptive codes are permissible. The perceptive codes often obtain a coding gain by shortening the wordlength of the data representing the signal waveform. This must increase the noise level and the trick is to ensure that the resultant noise is placed at frequencies where human senses are least able to perceive it. As a result although the received signal is measureably different from the source data, it can *appear* the same to the human listener or viewer at moderate compression factors. As these codes rely on the characteristics of human sight and hearing, they can only be fully tested subjectively.

The compression factor of such codes can be set at will by choosing the wordlength of the compressed data. Whilst mild compression will be undetectable, with greater compression factors, artifacts become noticeable. Figure 9.3 shows that this is inevitable from entropy considerations.

9.2 Compression standards

Standards are important in compression because without a suitable decoder, compressed data are meaningless. The MPEG standards are possibly the most well known, but they are certainly not the only standards. In video recording, the DV standard is also important. There are also a number of obsolescent standards which predated MPEG, and various proprietary schemes.

MPEG is actually an acronym for the Moving Pictures Experts Group which was formed by the ISO (International Standards Organization) to set standards for audio and video compression and transmission. The first compression standard for audio and video was MPEG-1.[3,4] MPEG-1 was initially designed to allow pictures and sound to be carried in the standard bit rate of a Compact Disc. Achieving such a low bit rate at the time required considerable spatial and temporal subsampling of standard definition television down to what is known as SIF (source intermediate format). Figure 9.5 shows that SIF discards every other field in the input

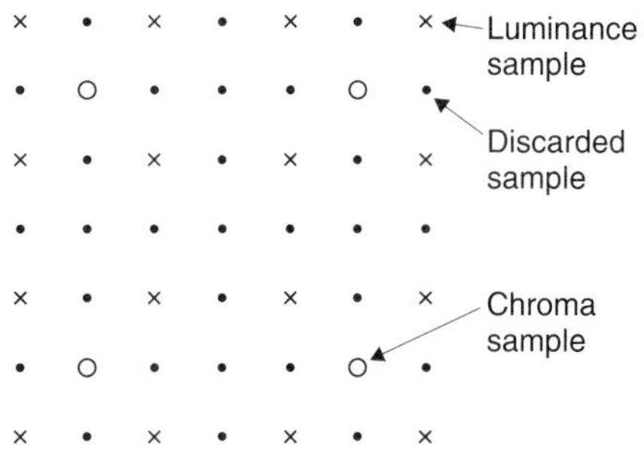

Figure 9.5 In MPEG-1, the input format is known as SIF (source intermediate format) and is created from interlaced video by discarding alternate fields and downsampling those that remain.

to halve the picture rate and eliminate interlace. Discarding alternate picture lines in this way halves vertical resolution and the horizontal resolution is also halved to match. Chroma data are further down-sampled. MPEG-1 was of limited quality and application and the subsequent MPEG-2 standard was considerably broader in scope and of wider appeal. For example, MPEG-2 supports interlace and a much wider range of picture sizes and bit rates. The MPEG-4 standard uses the tools of MPEG-2 but adds to them to allow even higher compression factors. MPEG standards are largely backward compatible such that an MPEG-2 decoder can understand MPEG-1 data and an MPEG-4 decoder can understand both MPEG-2 and MPEG-1 data.

The approach of the ISO to standardization in MPEG is novel because it is not the encoder which is standardized. Figure 9.6(a) shows that

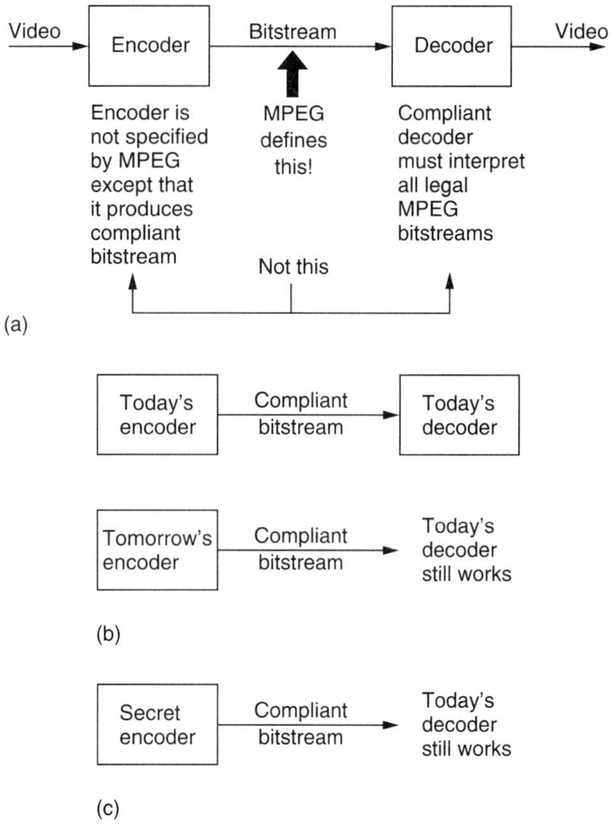

Figure 9.6 (a) MPEG defines the protocol of the bitstream between encoder and decoder. The decoder is defined by implication, the encoder is left very much to the designer. (b) This approach allows future encoders of better performance to remain compatible with existing decoders. (c) This approach also allows an encoder to produce a standard bitstream while its technical operation remains a commercial secret.

instead the way in which a decoder shall interpret the bitstream is defined. A decoder which can successfully interpret the bitstream is said to be *compliant*. Figure 9.6(b) shows that the advantage of standardizing the decoder is that over time encoding algorithms can improve yet compliant decoders will continue to function with them.

Manufacturers can supply encoders using algorithms which are proprietary and their details do not need to be published. A useful result is that there can be competition between different encoder designs which means that better designs will evolve. The user will have greater choice because different levels of cost and complexity can exist in a range of coders yet a compliant decoder will operate with them all.

MPEG is, however, much more than a compression scheme as it also standardizes the protocol and syntax under which it is possible to combine or multiplex audio data with video data to produce a digital equivalent of a television program. Many such programs can be combined in a single multiplex and MPEG defines the way in which such multiplexes can be created and transported. The definitions include the metadata which decoders require to demultiplex correctly and which users will need to locate programs of interest. As with all video systems there is a requirement for synchronizing or genlocking and this is particularly complex when a multiplex is assembled from many signals which are not necessarily synchronized to one another.

The applications of audio and video compression are limitless and the ISO has done well to provide standards which are appropriate to the wide range of possible compression products.

MPEG embraces video pictures from the tiny screen of a videophone to the high-definition images needed for electronic cinema. Audio coding stretches from speech-grade mono to multichannel surround sound.

Figure 9.7 shows the use of a codec with a recorder. The playing time of the medium is extended in proportion to the compression factor. In the case of tapes, the access time is improved because the length of tape needed for a given recording is reduced and so it can be rewound more quickly.

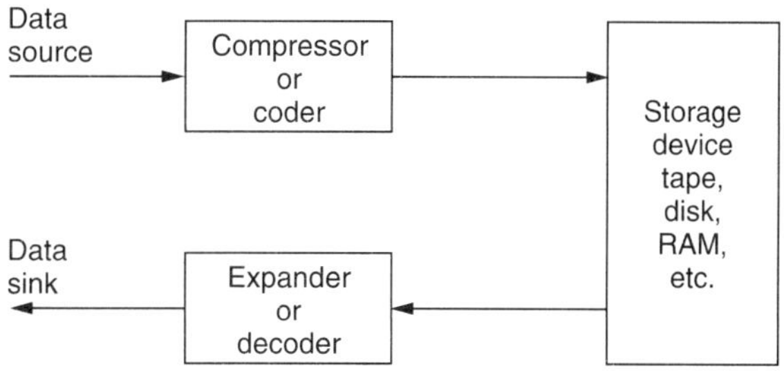

Figure 9.7 Compression can be used around a recording medium. The storage capacity may be increased or the access time reduced according to the application.

In the case of DVD (digital video disk, aka digital versatile disk) the challenge was to store an entire movie on one 12 cm disk. The storage density available with today's optical disk technology is such that recording of conventional uncompressed video would be out of the question.

In communications, the cost of data links is often roughly proportional to the data rate and so there is simple economic pressure to use a high compression factor. However, it should be borne in mind that implementing the codec also has a cost which rises with compression factor and so a degree of compromise will be inevitable. It should also be appreciated that the cost of communications is a moving target. The adoption of optical fibres has made bandwidth essentially limitless between major centres, leaving the bandwidth issue primarily in the so-called 'last mile' from such centres to the home. In the case of Video-On-Demand, technology such as ADSL (see Chapter 12) exists to convey data to the home on existing copper telephone lines, but the available bit rate is insufficient for entertainment-grade video without compression.

In workstations designed for the editing of audio and/or video, the source material is stored on hard disks for rapid access. Whilst top-grade systems may function without compression, many systems use compression to offset the high cost of disk storage. When a workstation is used for *off-line* editing, a high compression factor can be used and artifacts will be visible in the picture.

This is of no consequence as the picture is only seen by the editor who uses it to make an EDL (edit decision list) which is no more than a list of actions and the timecodes at which they occur. The original uncompressed material is then *conformed* to the EDL to obtain high-quality edited work. When *on-line* editing is being performed, the output of the workstation is the finished product and clearly a lower compression factor will have to be used.

Perhaps it is in broadcasting where the use of compression will have its greatest impact. There is only one electromagnetic spectrum and pressure from other services such as cellular telephones makes efficient use of bandwidth mandatory. Analog television broadcasting is an old technology and makes very inefficient use of bandwidth. Its replacement by a compressed digital transmission will be inevitable for the practical reason that the bandwidth is needed elsewhere.

Fortunately in broadcasting there is a mass market for decoders and these can be implemented as low-cost integrated circuits. Fewer encoders are needed and so it is less important if these are expensive. Whilst the cost of digital storage goes down year on year, the cost of electromagnetic spectrum goes up. Consequently in the future the pressure to use compression in recording will ease whereas the pressure to use it in radio communications will increase.

9.3 Profiles, levels and layers

MPEG-2 has too many applications to solve with a single standard and so it is subdivided into Profiles and Levels. Put simply a Profile describes a degree of complexity whereas a Level describes the picture size or resolution which goes with that Profile. Not all Levels are supported at all Profiles. Figure 9.8 shows the available combinations. In principle there are 24 of these, but not all have been defined. An MPEG decoder having a given Profile and Level must also be able to decode lower profiles and levels.

Levels \ Profiles	Simple	Main	4:2:2	SNR	Spatial	High
High		4:2:0 1920 × 1152 90 Mb/S				4:2:0 or 4:2:2 1920 × 1152 100 Mb/S
High 1440		4:2:0 1440 × 1152 60 Mb/S			4:2:0 1440 × 1152 60 Mb/S	4:2:0 or 4:2:2 1440 × 1152 80 Mb/S
Main	4:2:0 720 × 576 15 Mb/S NO B	4:2:0 720 × 576 15 Mb/S	4:2:2 720 × 608 50 Mb/S	4:2:0 720 × 576 15 Mb/S		4:2:0 or 4:2:2 720 × 576 20 Mb/S
Low		4:2:0 352 × 288 4 Mb/S		4:2:0 352 × 288 4 Mb/S		

Figure 9.8 Profiles and levels in MPEG-2. See text for details.

The simple profile does not support bidirectional coding and so only *I* and *P* pictures will be output. This reduces the coding and decoding delay and allows simpler hardware. The simple profile has only been defined at Main level (SP@ML).

The Main Profile is designed for a large proportion of uses. The low level uses a low-resolution input having only 352 pixels per line. The majority of broadcast applications will require the MP@ML (Main Profile at Main Level) subset of MPEG which supports SDTV (standard definition television).

The High-1440 level is a high-definition scheme which doubles the definition compared to main level. The high level not only doubles the resolution but maintains that resolution with 16:9 format by increasing the number of horizontal samples from 1440 to 1920.

In compression systems using spatial transforms and requantizing it is possible to produce scaleable signals. A scaleable process is one in which the input results in a main signal and a 'helper' signal. The main signal can be decoded alone to give a picture of a certain quality, but if the information from the helper signal is added some aspect of the quality can be improved.

Figure 9.9(a) shows that in a conventional MPEG coder, by heavily requantizing coefficients a picture with moderate signal-to-noise ratio results. If, however, that picture is locally decoded and subtracted pixel by pixel from the original, a 'quantizing noise' picture would result. This can be compressed and transmitted as the helper signal. A simple decoder decodes only the main 'noisy' bitstream, but a more complex decoder can decode both bitstreams and combine them to produce a low-noise picture. This is the principle of SNR scaleability.

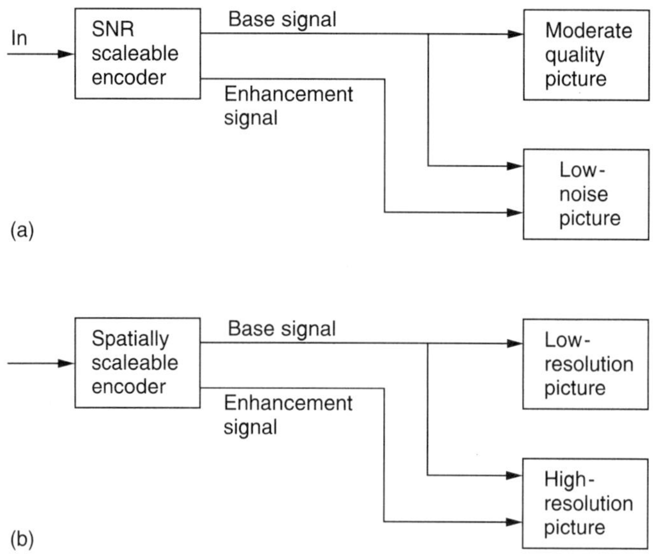

Figure 9.9 (a) An SNR scaleable encoder produces a 'noisy' signal and a noise cancelling signal. (b) A spatally scaleable encoder produces a low-resolution picture and a resolution-enhancing picture.

As an alternative, Figure 9.9(b) shows that by coding only the lower spatial frequencies in a HDTV picture a main bitstream can be made which an SDTV receiver can decode. If the lower-definition picture is locally decoded and subtracted from the original picture, a 'definition-enhancing' picture would result. This can be coded into a helper signal. A suitable decoder could combine the main and helper signals to re-create the HDTV picture. This is the principle of spatial scaleability.

The High profile supports both SNR and spatial scaleability as well as allowing the option of 4:2:2 sampling (see section 7.14).

The 4:2:2 profile has been developed for improved compatibility with existing digital television production equipment. This allows 4:2:2 working without requiring the additional complexity of using the high profile. For example, a HP@ML decoder must support SNR scaleability which is not a requirement for production.

In MPEG audio the different requirements are met using *layers*. Layer I is the least complex, but gives the lowest compression factor, Layer II is more complex, but maintains quality at lower bit rates, whereas Layer III is extremely complex and is optimized for very high compression factors. Subsequently MPEG-AAC (advanced audio coding) was developed which allows better audio quality through increased complexity. However, AAC is not compatible with the earlier systems.

9.4 Spatial and temporal redundancy in MPEG

Video signals exist in four dimensions: these are the attributes of the sample, the horizontal and vertical spatial axes and the time axis. Compression can be applied in any or all of those four dimensions. MPEG assumes eight-bit colour difference signal as the input, requiring rounding if the source is ten-bit. The sampling rate of the colour signals is less than that of the luminance. This is done by downsampling the colour samples horizontally and generally vertically as well. Essentially an MPEG system has three parallel simultaneous channels, one for luminance and two colour difference, which after coding are multiplexed into a single bitstream.

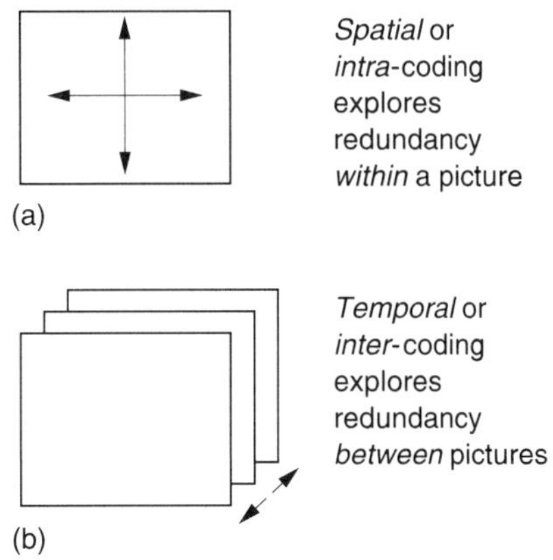

Figure 9.10 (a) Spatial or intra-coding works on individual images. (b) Temporal or inter-coding works on successive images.

Figure 9.10(a) shows that when individual pictures are compressed without reference to any other pictures, the time axis does not enter the process which is therefore described as *intra-coded* (intra = within) compression. The term *spatial coding* will also be found. It is an advantage of intra-coded video that there is no restriction to the editing which can be carried out on the picture sequence. As a result compressed VTRs intended for production use spatial coding. Cut editing may take place on the compressed data directly if necessary. As spatial coding treats each picture independently, it can employ certain techniques developed for the compression of still pictures. The ISO JPEG (Joint Photographic Experts Group) compression standards[5,6] are in this category. Where a succession of JPEG coded images are used for television, the term 'Motion JPEG' will be found.

Greater compression factors can be obtained by taking account of the redundancy from one picture to the next. This involves the time axis, as

Figure 9.10(b) shows, and the process is known as *inter-coded* (inter = between) or *temporal* compression.

Temporal coding allows a higher compression factor, but has the disadvantage that an individual picture may exist only in terms of the differences from a previous picture. Clearly editing must be undertaken with caution and arbitrary cuts simply cannot be performed on the MPEG bitstream. If a previous picture is removed by an edit, the difference data will then be insufficient to re-create the current picture.

Intra-coding works in three dimensions on the horizontal and vertical spatial axes and on the sample values. Analysis of typical television pictures reveals that whilst there is a high spatial frequency content due to detailed areas of the picture, there is a relatively small amount of energy at such frequencies. Often pictures contain sizeable areas in which the same or similar pixel values exist. This gives rise to low spatial frequencies. The average brightness of the picture results in a substantial zero frequency component. Simply omitting the high-frequency components is unacceptable as this causes an obvious softening of the picture.

A coding gain can be obtained by taking advantage of the fact that the amplitude of the spatial components falls with frequency. It is also possible to take advantage of the eye's reduced sensitivity to noise in high spatial frequencies. If the spatial frequency spectrum is divided into frequency bands the high-frequency bands can be described by fewer bits not only because their amplitudes are smaller but also because more noise can be tolerated. The wavelet transform and the discrete cosine transform used in MPEG allow two-dimensional pictures to be described in the frequency domain. These were discussed in Chapter 3.

Inter-coding takes further advantage of the similarities between successive pictures in real material. Instead of sending information for each picture separately, inter-coders will send the difference between the previous picture and the current picture in a form of differential coding. Figure 9.11 shows the principle. A picture store is required at the coder to allow comparison to be made between successive pictures and a similar store is required at the decoder to make the previous picture available. The difference data may be treated as a picture itself and subjected to some form of transform-based spatial compression.

The simple system of Figure 9.11(a) is of limited use as in the case of a transmission error, every subsequent picture would be affected. Channel switching in a television set would also be impossible. In practical systems a modification is required. One approach is the so-called 'leaky predictor' in which the next picture is predicted from a limited number of previous pictures rather than from an indefinite number. As a result errors cannot propagate indefinitely. The approach used in MPEG is that periodically some absolute picture data are transmitted in place of difference data.

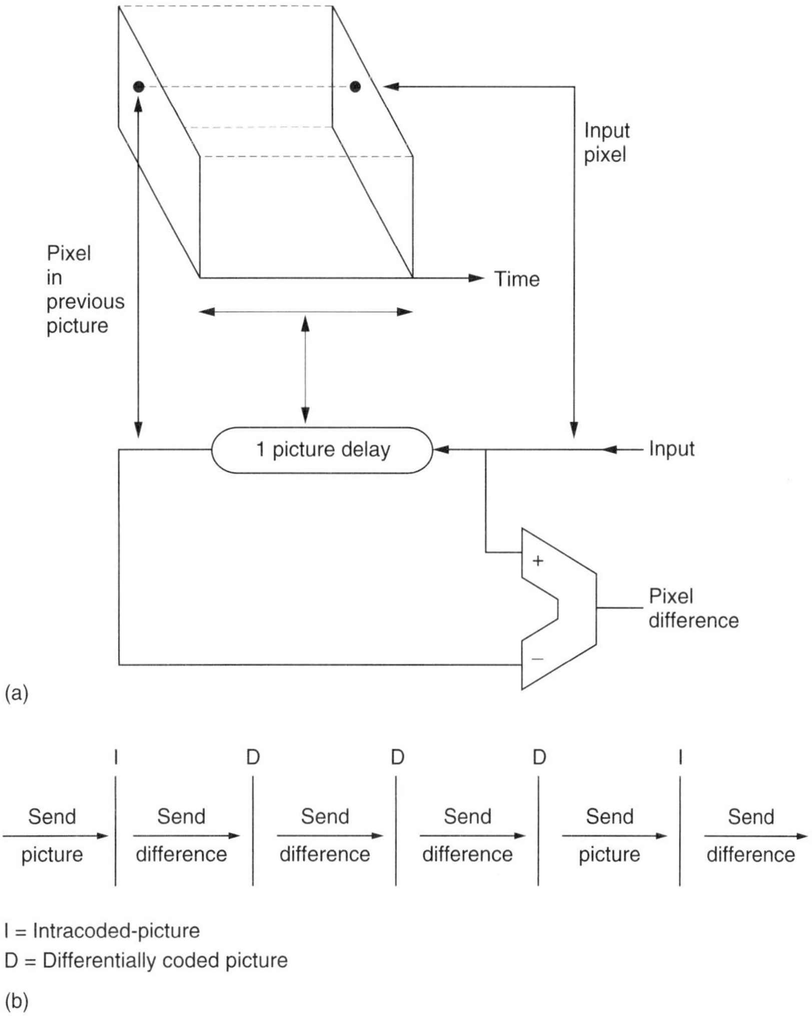

Figure 9.11 An inter-coded system (a) uses a delay to calculate the pixel differences between successive pictures. To prevent error propagation, intra-coded pictures (b) may be used periodically.

Figure 9.11(b) shows that absolute picture data, known as *I* or *intra pictures* are interleaved with pictures which are created using difference data, known as *P* or *predicted* pictures. The *I* pictures require a large amount of data, whereas the *P* pictures require less data. As a result the instantaneous data rate varies dramatically and buffering has to be used to allow a constant transmission rate. The leaky predictor needs less buffering as the compression factor does not change so much from picture to picture.

The *I* picture and all the *P* pictures prior to the next *I* picture are called a group of pictures (GOP). For a high compression factor, a large number of *P* pictures should be present between *I* pictures, making a long GOP. However, a long GOP delays recovery from a transmission error. The compressed bitstream can only be edited at *I* pictures as shown.

In the case of moving objects, although their appearance may not change greatly from picture to picture, the data representing them on a fixed sampling grid will change and so large differences will be generated between successive pictures. It is a great advantage if the effect of motion can be removed from difference data so that they reflect only the changes in appearance of a moving object since a much greater coding gain can then be obtained. This is the objective of motion compensation.

In real television program material objects move around before a fixed camera or the camera itself moves. Motion compensation is a process which effectively measures motion of objects from one picture to the next so that it can allow for that motion when looking for redundancy between pictures. Chapter 7 showed that moving pictures can be expressed in a three-dimensional space which results from the screen area moving along the time axis. In the case of still objects, the only motion is along the time axis. However, when an object moves, it does so along the *optic flow axis* which is not parallel to the time axis. The optic flow axis joins the same point on a moving object as it takes on various screen positions.

It will be clear that the data values representing a moving object change with respect to the time axis. However, looking along the optic flow axis the appearance of an object changes only if it deforms, moves into shadow or rotates. For simple translational motions the data representing an object are highly redundant with respect to the optic flow axis. Thus if the optic flow axis can be located, coding gain can be obtained in the presence of motion.

A motion-compensated coder works as follows. An *I* picture is sent, but is also locally stored so that it can be compared with the next input picture to find motion vectors for various areas of the picture. The *I* picture is then shifted according to these vectors to cancel inter-picture motion. The resultant *predicted* picture is compared with the actual picture to produce a *prediction error* also called a *residual*. The prediction error is transmitted with the motion vectors. At the receiver the original *I* picture is also held in a memory. It is shifted according to the transmitted motion vectors to create the predicted picture and then the prediction error is added to it to re-create the original. When a picture is encoded in this way MPEG calls it a *P* picture.

The concept of sending a prediction error is a useful approach because it allows both the motion estimation and compensation to be imperfect.

A good motion-compensation system will send just the right amount of vector data. With insufficient vector data, the prediction error will be large, but transmission of excess vector data will also cause the the bit rate to rise. There will be an optimum balance which minimizes the sum of the prediction error data and the vector data.

In MPEG-2 the balance is obtained by dividing the screen into areas called *macroblocks* which are 16 luminance pixels square. Each macroblock is steered by a vector. The location of the boundaries of a macroblock are fixed and so the vector does not move the macroblock. Instead the vector tells the decoder where to look in another frame to find pixel data to *fetch* to the macroblock. Figure 9.12(a) shows this concept. The shifting process is generally done by modifying the read address of a RAM using the vector. This can shift by one pixel steps. MPEG-2 vectors have half-pixel resolution so it is necessary to interpolate between pixels from RAM to obtain half-pixel shifted values.

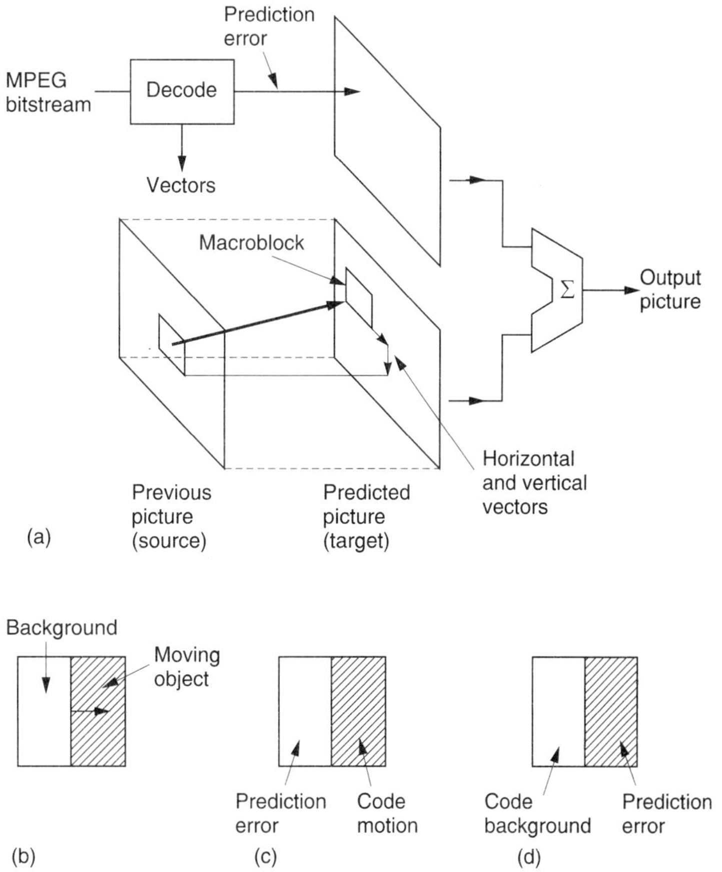

Figure 9.12 (a) In motion compensation, pixel data are brought to a fixed macroblock in the target picture from a variety of places in another picture. (b) Where only part of a macroblock is moving, motion compensation is non-ideal. The motion can be coded (c), causing a prediction error in the background, or the background can be coded (d) causing a prediction error in the moving object.

Real moving objects will not coincide with macroblocks and so the motion compensation will not be ideal but the prediction error makes up for any shortcomings. Figure 9.12(b) shows the case where the boundary of a moving object bisects a macroblock. If the system measures the moving part of the macroblock and sends a vector, the decoder will shift the entire block making the stationary part wrong. If no vector is sent, the moving part will be wrong. Both approaches are legal in MPEG-2 because the prediction error sorts out the incorrect values. An intelligent coder might try both approaches to see which required the least prediction error data.

The prediction error concept also allows the use of simple but inaccurate motion estimators in low-cost systems. The greater prediction error data are handled using a higher bit rate. On the other hand, if a precision motion estimator is available, a very high compression factor may be achieved because the prediction error data are minimized. MPEG-2 does not specify how motion is to be measured; it simply defines how a decoder will interpret the vectors. Encoder designers are free to use any motion-estimation system provided that the right vector protocol is created. Chapter 3 contrasted a number of motion-estimation techniques.

Figure 9.13(a) shows that a macroblock contains both luminance and colour difference data at different resolutions. Most of the MPEG-2 Profiles use a 4:2:0 structure which means that the colour is down-sampled by a factor of two in both axes. Thus in a 16 × 16 pixel block, there are only 8 × 8 colour difference sampling sites. MPEG-2 is based upon the 8 × 8 DCT (see section 3.9) and so the 16 × 16 block is the screen area which contains an 8 × 8 colour difference sampling block. Thus in

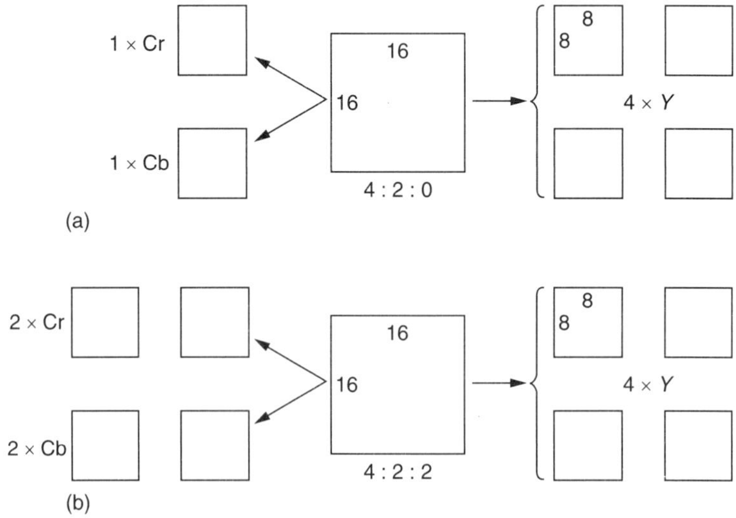

Figure 9.13 The structure of a macroblock. (A macroblock is the screen area steered by *one* vector.) (a) In 4:2:0, there are two chroma DCT blocks per macroblock whereas in 4:2:2 (b) there are four, 4:2:2 needs 33 per cent more data than 4:2:0.

4:2:0 in each macroblock there are four luminance DCT blocks, one $R - Y$ DCT block and one $B - Y$ DCT block, all steered by the same vector.

In the 4:2:2 Profile of MPEG-2, shown in Figure 9.13(b), the chroma is not downsampled vertically, and so there is twice as much chroma data in each macroblock which is otherwise substantially the same.

In MPEG-4 the motion-compensation process is taken further. The macroblock approach of MPEG-2 will always result in prediction errors because object boundaries seldom coincide with macroblock boundaries. MPEG-4 overcomes this limitation because its motion compensation is object based. Essentially in MPEG-4 it is possible to describe an arbitrarily shaped object which can then be steered with vectors.

9.5 *I* and *P* coding

Predictive (*P*) coding cannot be used indefinitely, as it is prone to error propagation. A further problem is that it becomes impossible to decode the transmission if reception begins part-way through. In real video signals, cuts or edits can be present across which there is little redundancy and which make motion estimators throw up their hands.

In the absence of redundancy over a cut, there is nothing to be done but to send the new picture information in absolute form. This is called *I* coding where *I* is an abbreviation of *intra* coding. As *I* coding needs no previous picture for decoding, then decoding can begin at *I* coded information.

MPEG is effectively a toolkit and there is no compulsion to use all the tools available. Thus an encoder may choose whether to use *I* or *P* coding, either once and for all or dynamically on a macroblock-by-macroblock basis.

For practical reasons, an entire frame may be encoded as *I* macroblocks periodically. This creates a place where the bitstream might be edited or where decoding could begin.

Figure 9.14 shows a typical application of the Simple Profile of MPEG-2. Periodically an *I* picture is created. Between *I* pictures are *P* pictures

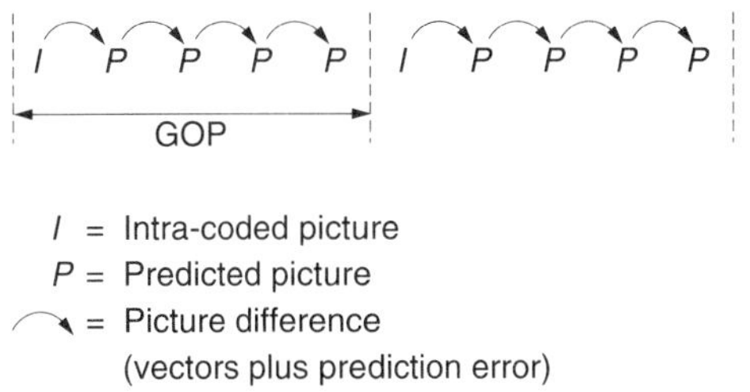

Figure 9.14 A Simple Profile MPEG-2 signal may contain periodic *I* pictures with a number of *P* pictures between.

which are based on the picture before. These *P* pictures predominantly contain macroblocks having vectors and prediction errors. However, it is perfectly legal for *P* pictures to contain *I* macroblocks. This might be useful where, for example, a camera pan introduces new material at the edge of the screen which cannot be created from an earlier picture.

Note that although what is sent is called a *P* picture, it is not a picture at all. It is a set of instructions to convert the previous picture into the current picture. If the previous picture is lost, decoding is impossible. An *I* picture together with all of the pictures before the next I picture form a *Group of Pictures* (GOP).

9.6 Bidirectional coding

Motion-compensated predictive coding is a useful compression technique, but it does have the drawback that it can only take data from a previous picture. Where moving objects reveal a background this is completely unknown in previous pictures and forward prediction fails. However, more of the background is visible in later pictures. Figure 9.15 shows the concept. In the centre of the diagram, a moving object has revealed some background. The previous picture can contribute nothing, whereas the next picture contains all that is required.

Bidirectional coding is shown in Figure 9.16. A bidirectional or *B* macroblock can be created using a combination of motion compensation

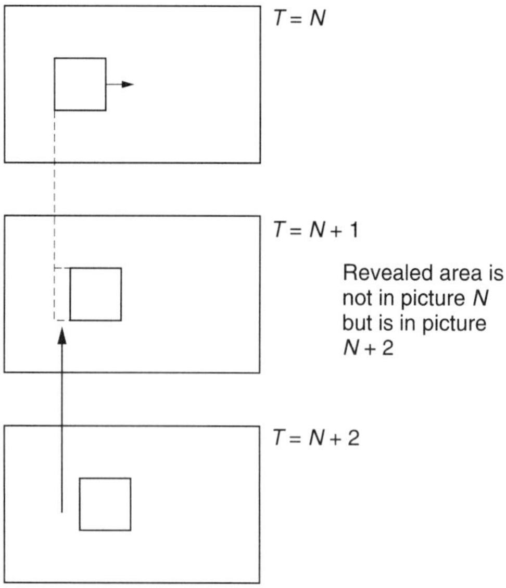

Figure 9.15 In bidirectional coding the revealed background can be efficiently coded by bringing data back from a future picture.

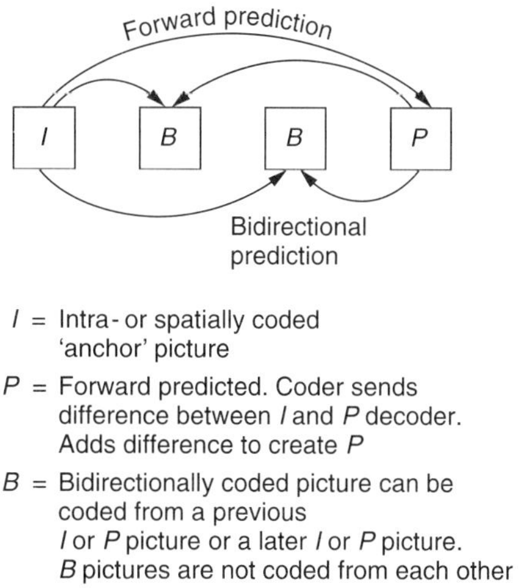

Figure 9.16 In bidirectional coding, a number of *B* pictures can be inserted between periodic forward predicted pictures. See text.

and the addition of a prediction error. This can be done by forward prediction from a previous picture or backward prediction from a subsequent picture. It is also possible to use an average of both forward and backward prediction. On noisy material this may result in some reduction in bit rate. The technique is also a useful way of portraying a dissolve.

The averaging process in MPEG-2 is a simple linear interpolation which works well when only one *B* picture exists between the reference pictures before and after. A larger number of *B* pictures would require weighted interpolation but MPEG-2 does not support this.

Typically two *B* pictures are inserted between *P* pictures or between *I* and *P* pictures. As can be seen, *B* pictures are never predicted from one another, only from *I* or *P* pictures. A typical GOP for broadcasting purposes might have the structure *IBBPBBPBBPBB*. Note that the last *B* pictures in the GOP require the *I* picture in the next GOP for decoding and so the GOPs are not truly independent. Independence can be obtained by creating a *closed GOP* which may contain *B* pictures but which ends with a *P* picture. It is also legal to have a *B* picture in which every macroblock is forward predicted, needing no future picture for decoding.

Bidirectional coding is very powerful. Figure 9.17 is a constant quality curve showing how the bit rate changes with the type of coding. On the left, only *I* or spatial coding is used, whereas on the right an *IBBP* structure is used. This means that there are two bidirectionally coded pictures in between a spatially coded picture (*I*) and a forward predicted picture (*P*). Note how for the same quality the system which only uses

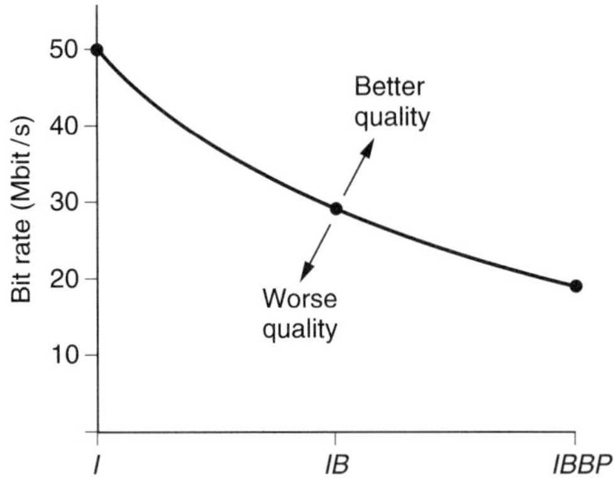

Figure 9.17 Bidirectional coding is very powerful as it allows the same quality with only 40 per cent of the bit rate of intra-coding. However, the encoding and decoding delays must increase. Coding over a longer time span is more efficient but editing is more difficult.

spatial coding needs two and a half times the bit rate that the bidirectionally coded system needs.

Clearly information in the future has yet to be transmitted and so is not normally available to the decoder. MPEG-2 gets around the problem by sending pictures in the wrong order. Picture reordering requires delay in the encoder and a delay in the decoder to put the order right again. Thus the overall codec delay must rise when bidirectional coding is used. This is quite consistent with Figure 9.3 which showed that as the compression factor rises the latency must also rise.

Figure 9.18 shows that although the original picture sequence is *IBBPBBPBBIBB* . . ., this is transmitted as *IPBBPBBIBB* . . . so that the future picture is already in the decoder before bidirectional decoding begins. Note that the *I* picture of the next GOP is actually sent before the last *B* pictures of the current GOP.

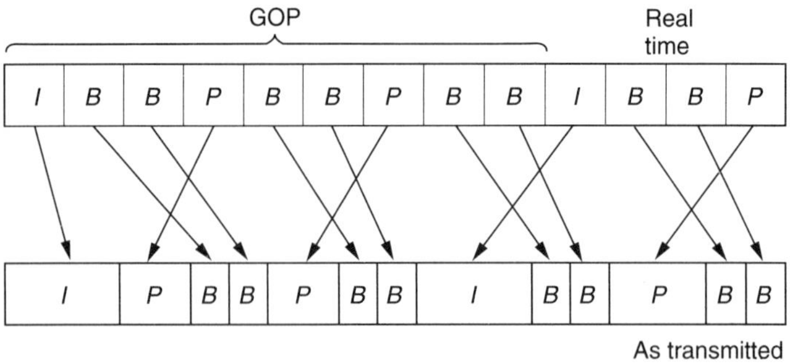

Figure 9.18 Comparison of pictures before and after compression showing sequence change and varying amount of data needed by each picture type. *I*, *P*, *B* pictures use unequal amounts of data.

Figure 9.18 also shows that the amount of data required by each picture is dramatically different. *I* pictures have only spatial redundancy and so need a lot of data to describe them. *P* pictures need fewer data because they are created by shifting the *I* picture with vectors and then adding a prediction error picture. *B* pictures need the least data of all because they can be created from *I* or *P*.

With pictures requiring a variable length of time to transmit, arriving in the wrong order, the decoder needs some help. This takes the form of picture-type flags and time stamps.

9.7 Coding applications

Figure 9.19 shows a variety of GOP structures. The simplest is the *III* .. sequence in which every picture is intra-coded. Pictures can be fully decoded without reference to any other pictures and so editing is straightforward. However, this approach requires about two and one half times the bit rate of a full bidirectional system. Bidirectional coding is most useful for final delivery of post-produced material either by broadcast or on prerecorded media as there is then no editing requirement. As a compromise the *IBIB* .. structure can be used which has some of the bit rate advantage of bidirectional coding but without too much latency. It is possible to edit an *IBIB* stream by performing some processing. If it is required to remove the video following a *B* picture, that *B* picture could not be decoded because it needs *I* pictures either side of it for bidirectional decoding. The solution is to decode the *B* picture first, and then re-encode it with forward prediction only from the previous *I* picture. The subsequent *I* picture can then be replaced by an edit process. Some quality loss is inevitable in this process but this is acceptable in applications such as ENG and industrial video.

I I I I I I ...	*I* only freely editable, needs high bit rate
I P P P P I P ...	Forward predicted only, needs less decoder memory, used in Simple Profile
I B B P B B P B ...	Forward and bidirectional, best compression factor, needs large decoder memory, hard to edit
I B I B I B ...	Lower bit rate than *I* only, editable with moderate processing

Figure 9.19 Various possible GOP structures used with MPEG. See text for details.

9.8 Spatial compression

Spatial compression in MPEG is used in *I* pictures on actual picture data and in *P* and *B* pictures on prediction error data. MPEG uses the discrete cosine transform described in section 3.7. The DCT works on blocks and in MPEG these are 8 × 8 pixels. Section 5.7 showed how the macroblocks of the motion-compensation structure are designed so they can be broken down into 8 × 8 DCT blocks. In a 4:2:0 macroblock there will be six DCT blocks whereas in a 4:2:2 macroblock there will be eight.

Figure 9.20 shows the table of basis functions or *wave table* for an 8 × 8 DCT. Adding these two-dimensional waveforms together in different proportions will give any original 8 × 8 pixel block. The coefficients of the DCT simply control the proportion of each wave which is added in the inverse transform. The top-left wave has no modulation at all because it conveys the DC component of the block. This coefficient will be a unipolar (positive only) value in the case of luminance and will typically be the largest value in the block as the spectrum of typical video signals is dominated by the DC component.

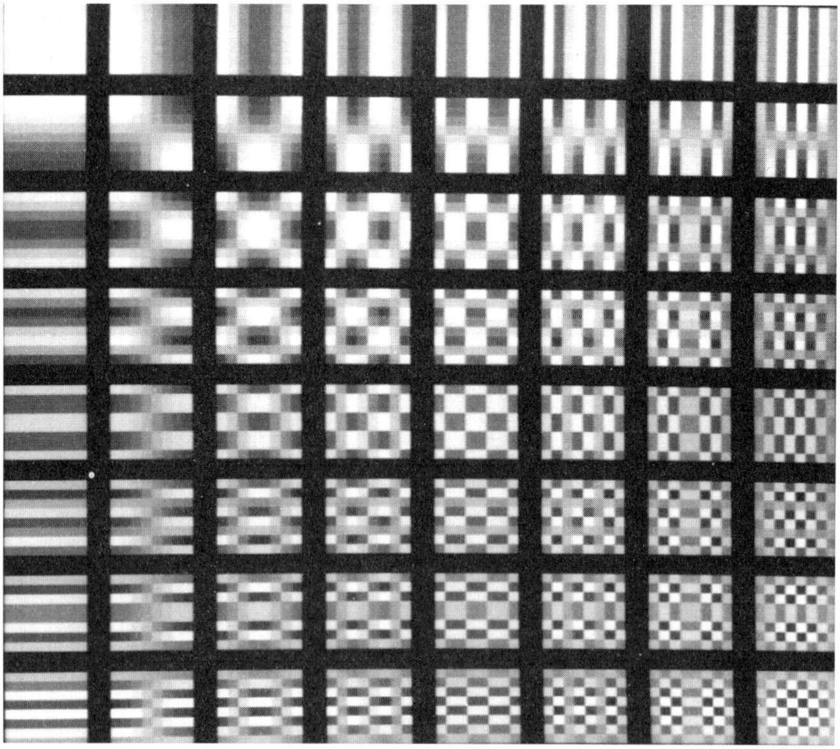

Figure 9.20 The discrete cosine transform breaks up an image area into discrete frequencies in two dimensions. The lowest frequency can be seen here at the top-left corner. Horizontal frequency increases to the right and vertical frequency increases downwards.

Increasing the DC coefficient adds a constant amount to every pixel. Moving to the right the coefficients represent increasing horizontal spatial frequencies and moving downwards the coefficients represent increasing vertical spatial frequencies. The bottom-right coefficient represents the highest diagonal frequencies in the block. All these coefficients are bipolar, where the polarity indicates whether the original spatial waveform at that frequency was inverted.

Figure 9.21 shows a one-dimensional example of an inverse transform. The DC coefficient produces a constant level throughout the pixel block. The remaining waves in the table are AC coefficients. A zero coefficient would result in no modulation, leaving the DC level unchanged. The wave next to the DC component represents the lowest frequency in the transform which is half a cycle per block. A positive coefficient would make the left side of the block brighter and the right side darker whereas a negative coefficient would do the opposite. The magnitude of the coefficient determines the amplitude of the wave which is added. Figure 9.21 also shows that the next wave has a frequency of one cycle per block. i.e. the block is made brighter at both sides and darker in the middle.

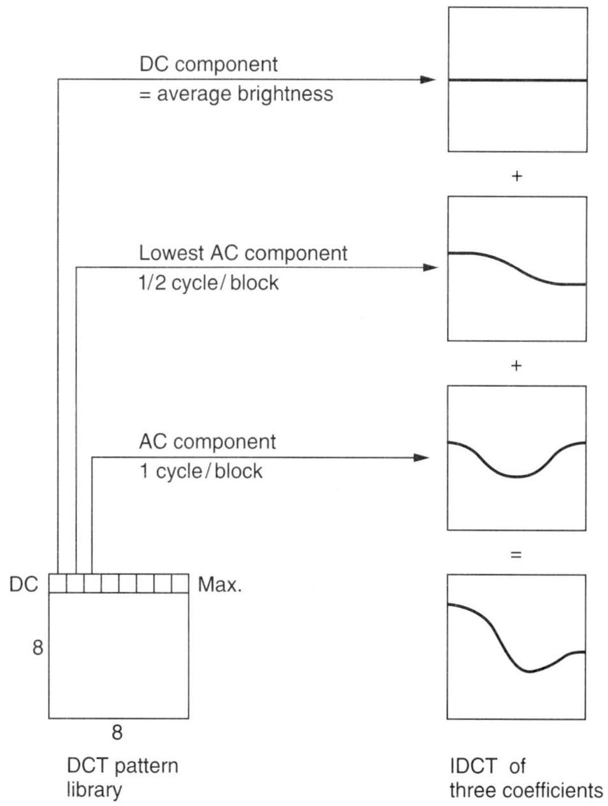

Figure 9.21 A one-dimensional inverse transform. See text for details.

Consequently an inverse DCT is no more than a process of mixing various pixel patterns from the wave table where the relative amplitudes and polarity of these patterns are controlled by the coefficients. The original transform is simply a mechanism which finds the coefficient amplitudes from the original pixel block.

The DCT itself achieves no compression at all. Sixty-four pixels are converted to sixty-four coefficients. However, in typical pictures, not all coefficients will have significant values; there will often be a few dominant coefficients. The coefficients representing the higher two-dimensional spatial frequencies will often be zero or of small value in large areas, due to blurring or simply plain undetailed areas before the camera.

Statistically, the further from the top-left corner of the wave table the coefficient is, the smaller will be its magnitude. Coding gain (the technical term for reduction in the number of bits needed) is achieved by transmitting the low-valued coefficients with shorter wordlengths. The zero-valued coefficients need not be transmitted at all. Thus it is not the DCT which compresses the data, it is the subsequent processing. The DCT simply expresses the data in a form which makes the subsequent processing easier.

Higher compression factors require the coefficient wordlength to be further reduced using requantizing. Coefficients are divided by some factor which increases the size of the quantizing step. The smaller number of steps which results permits coding with fewer bits, but of course with an increased quantizing error. The coefficients will be multiplied by a reciprocal factor in the decoder to return to the correct magnitude.

Inverse transforming a requantized coefficient means that the frequency it represents is reproduced in the output with the wrong amplitude. The difference between original and reconstructed amplitude is regarded as a noise added to the wanted data. Figure 9.22 shows that the visibility of such noise is far from uniform. The maximum sensitivity is found at DC and falls thereafter. As a result the top-left coefficient is often treated as a special case and left unchanged. It may warrant more error protection than other coefficients.

MPEG takes advantage of the falling sensitivity to noise. Prior to requantizing, each coefficient is divided by a different weighting constant as a function of its frequency. Figure 9.23 shows a typical weighting process. Naturally the decoder must have a corresponding inverse weighting. This weighting process has the effect of reducing the magnitude of high-frequency coefficients disproportionately. Clearly different weighting will be needed for colour difference data as colour is perceived differently.

P and *B* pictures are decoded by adding a prediction error image to a reference image. That reference image will contain weighted noise. One

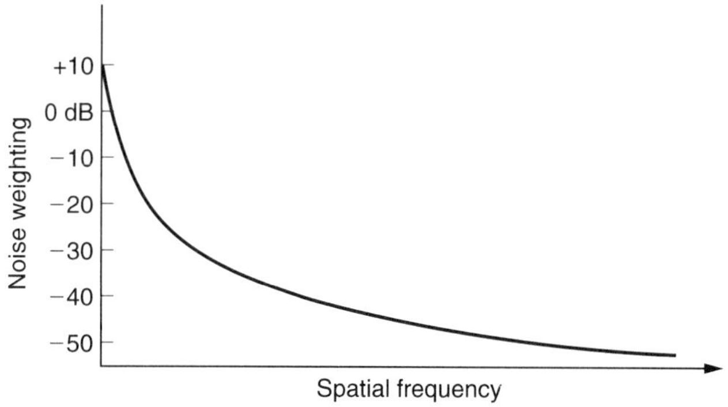

Figure 9.22 The sensitivity of the eye to noise is greatest at low frequencies and drops rapidly with increasing frequency. This can be used to mask quantizing noise caused by the compression process.

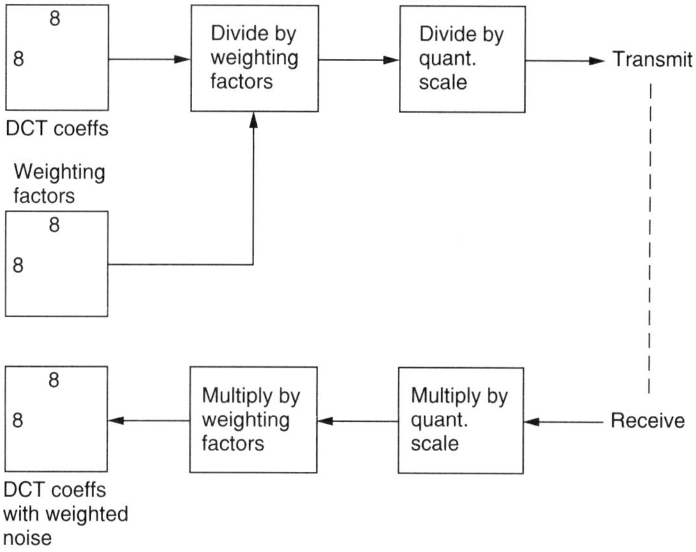

Figure 9.23 Weighting is used to make the noise caused by requantizing different at each frequency.

purpose of the prediction error is to cancel that noise to prevent tolerance build-up. If the prediction error were also to contain weighted noise this result would not be obtained. Consequently prediction error coefficients are flat weighted.

When forward prediction fails, such as in the case of new material introduced in a *P* picture by a pan, *P* coding would set the vectors to zero and encode the new data entirely as an unweighted prediction error. In this case it is better to encode that material as an *I* macroblock because then weighting can be used and this will require fewer bits.

Requantizing increases the step size of the coefficients, but the inverse weighting in the decoder results in step sizes which increase with frequency. The larger step size increases the quantizing noise at high frequencies where it is less visible. Effectively the noise floor is shaped to match the sensitivity of the eye. The quantizing table in use at the encoder can be transmitted to the decoder periodically in the bitstream.

9.9 Scanning and run-length/variable-length coding

Study of the signal statistics gained from extensive analysis of real material is used to measure the probability of a given coefficient having a given value. This probability turns out to be highly non-uniform, suggesting the possibility of a variable-length encoding for the coefficient values. On average, the higher the spatial frequency, the lower the value of a coefficient will be. This means that the value of a coefficient falls as a function of its radius from the DC coefficient.

Typical material often has many coefficients which are zero valued, especially after requantizing. The distribution of these also follows a pattern. The non-zero values tend to be found in the top-left corner of the DCT block, but as the radius increases, not only do the coefficient values fall, but it becomes increasingly likely that these small coefficients will be interspersed with zero-valued coefficients. As the radius increases further it is probable that a region where all coefficients are zero will be entered.

MPEG uses all these attributes of DCT coefficients when encoding a coefficient block. By sending the coefficients in an optimum order, by describing their values with Huffman coding and by using run-length encoding for the zero-valued coefficients it is possible to achieve a significant reduction in coefficient data which remains entirely lossless. Despite the complexity of this process, it does contibute to improved picture quality because for a given bit rate lossless coding of the coefficients must be better than requantizing, which is lossy. Of course, for lower bit rates both will be required.

It is an advantage to scan in a sequence where the largest coefficient values are scanned first. Then the next coefficient is more likely to be zero than the previous one. With progressively scanned material, a regular zig-zag scan begins in the top-left corner and ends in the bottom-right corner as shown in Figure 9.24. Zig-zag scanning means that significant values are more likely to be transmitted first, followed by the zero values. Instead of coding these zeros, an unique 'end of block' (EOB) symbol is transmitted instead.

As the zig-zag scan approaches the last finite coefficient it is increasingly likely that some zero value coefficients will be scanned.

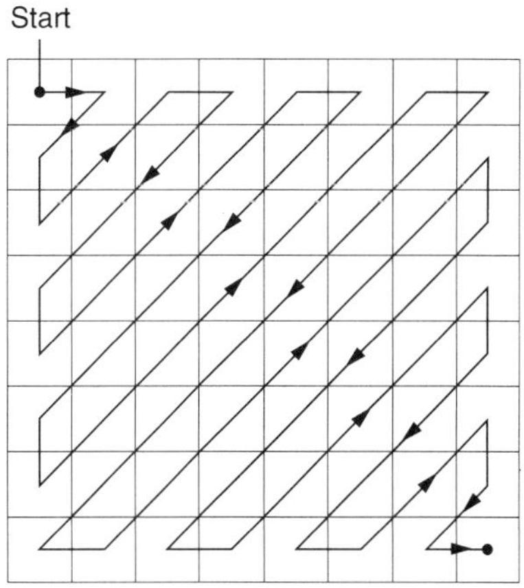

Figure 9.24 The zig-zag scan for a progressively scanned image.

Instead of transmitting the coefficients as zeros, the *zero-run-length*, i.e. the number of zero valued coefficients in the scan sequence is encoded into the next non-zero coefficient which is itself variable-length coded. This combination of run-length and variable-length coding is known as RLC/VLC in MPEG.

The DC coefficient is handled separately because it is differentially coded and this discussion relates to the AC coefficients. Three items need to be handled for each coefficient: the zero-run-length prior to this coefficient, the wordlength and the coefficient value itself. The wordlength needs to be known by the decoder so that it can correctly parse the bitstream. The wordlength of the coefficient is expressed directly as an integer called the *size*.

Figure 9.25(a) shows that a two-dimensional run/size table is created. One dimension expresses the zero-run-length; the other the size. A run length of zero is obtained when adjacent coefficients are non-zero, but a code of 0/0 has no meaningful run/size interpretation and so this bit pattern is used for the end-of-block (EOB) symbol.

In the case where the zero-run-length exceeds 14, a code of 15/0 is used signifying that there are fifteen zero-valued coefficients. This is then followed by another run/size parameter whose run-length value is added to the previous fifteen.

The run/size parameters contain redundancy because some combinations are more common than others. Figure 9.25(b) shows that each run/size value is converted to a variable-length Huffman codeword for transmission. As was shown in section 1.5, the Huffman codes are designed so that short codes are never a prefix of long codes so that the decoder can deduce the parsing by testing an increasing number of bits until a match with the look-up table is found. Having parsed and

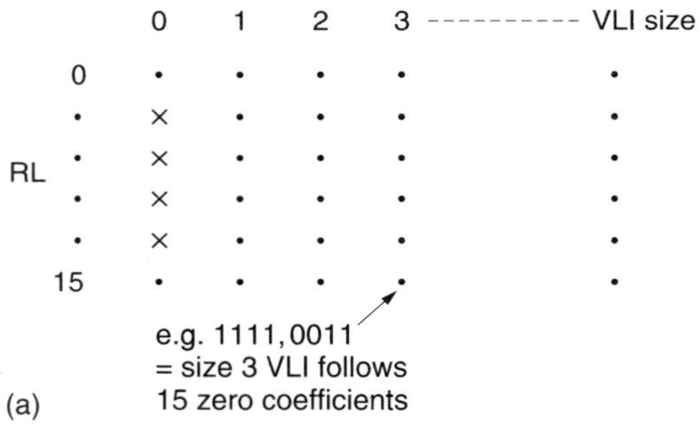

(a)

Run \ Size	0	1	2	3 → etc.
0	1010 (EOB)	00	01	100
1	–	1100	11011	
2	–	11100	11111001	
3	–	111010	111110111	
4	–	111011	1111111000	
5	–	1111010		
↓ etc.				

(b)

Coefficient to be transmitted	Coefficient code (↑ etc.)	Size parameter
15	1 1 1 1	4
14	1 1 1 0	
13	1 1 0 1	
12	1 1 0 0	
11	1 0 1 1	
10	1 0 1 0	
9	1 0 0 1	
8	1 0 0 0	
7	1 1 1	3
6	1 1 0	
5	1 0 1	
4	1 0 0	
3	1 1	2
2	1 0	
1	1	1
−1	0	
−2	0 1	2
−3	0 0	
−4	0 1 1	3
−5	0 1 0	
−6	0 0 1	
−7	0 0 0	
−8	0 1 1 1	4
−9	0 1 1 0	
−10	0 1 0 1	
−11	0 1 0 0	
−12	0 0 1 1	
−13	0 0 1 0	
−14	0 0 0 1	
−15	0 0 0 0	
	↓ etc.	

(c)

Figure 9.25 Run-length and variable-length coding simultaneously compresses runs of zero-valued coefficients and describes the wordlength of a non-zero coefficient.

decoded the Huffman run/size code, the decoder then knows what the coefficient wordlength will be and can correctly parse that.

The variable-length coefficient code has to describe a bipolar coefficient, i.e one which can be positive or negative. Figure 9.25(c) shows that for a particular size, the coding scale has a certain gap in it. For example, all values from –7 to +7 can be sent by a size 3 code, so a size 4 code only has to send the values of –15 to –8 and +8 to +15. The coefficient code is sent as a pure binary number whose value ranges from all zeros to all ones where the maximum value is a function of the size. The number range is divided into two, the lower half of the codes specifying negative values and the upper half specifying positive.

In the case of positive numbers, the transmitted binary value is the actual coefficient value, whereas in the case of negative numbers a constant must be subtracted which is a function of the size. In the case of a size 4 code, the constant is 15_{10}. Thus a size 4 parameter of 0111_2 (7_{10}) would be interpreted as 7 –15 = –8. A size of 5 has a constant of 31 so a transmitted coded of 01010_2 (10_2) would be interpreted as 10 –31 = –21.

This technique saves a bit because, for example, 63 values from –31 to +31 are coded with only five bits having only 32 combinations. This is possible because that extra bit is effectively encoded into the run/size parameter.

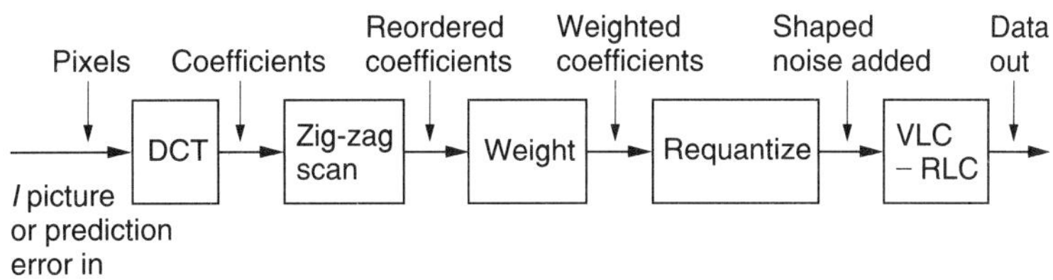

Figure 9.26 A complete spatial coding system which can compress an *I* picture or the prediction error in *P* and *B* pictures. See text for details.

Figure 9.26 shows the whole spatial coding subsystem. Macroblocks are subdivided into DCT blocks and the DCT is calculated. The resulting coefficients are multiplied by the weighting matrix and then requantized. The coefficients are then reordered by the zig-zag scan so that full advantage can be taken of run-length and variable-length coding. The last non-zero coefficient in the scan is followed by the EOB symbol.

In predictive coding, sometimes the motion-compensated prediction is nearly exact and so the prediction error will be almost zero. This can also happen on still parts of the scene. MPEG takes advantage of this by sending a code to tell the decoder there is no prediction error data for the macroblock concerned.

The success of temporal coding depends on the accuracy of the vectors. Trying to reduce the bit rate by reducing the accuracy of the vectors is false economy as this simply increases the prediction error. Consequently for a given GOP structure it is only in the the spatial coding that the overall bit rate is determined. The RLC/VLC coding is lossless and so its contribution to the compression cannot be varied. If the bit rate is too high, the only option is to increase the size of the coefficient-requantizing steps. This has the effect of shortening the wordlength of large coefficients, and rounding small coefficients to zero, so that the bit rate goes down. Clearly if taken too far the picture quality will also suffer because at some point the noise floor will become visible as some form of artifact.

9.10 A bidirectional coder

MPEG does not specify how an encoder is to be built or what coding decisions it should make. Instead it specifies the protocol of the bitstream at the output. As a result the MPEG-2 coder shown in Figure 9.27 is only an example.

Figure 9.27(a) shows the component parts of the coder. At the input is a chain of picture stores which can be bypassed for reordering purposes. This allows a picture to be encoded ahead of its normal timing when bidirectional coding is employed.

At the centre is a dual-motion estimator which can simultaneously measure motion between the input picture and earlier picture and a later picture. These reference pictures are held in frame stores. The vectors from the motion estimator are used locally to shift a picture in a frame store to form a predicted picture. This is subtracted from the input picture to produce a prediction error picture which is then spatially coded.

The bidirectional encoding process will now be described. A GOP begins with an *I* picture which is intra-coded. In Figure 9.27(b) the *I* picture emerges from the reordering delay. No prediction is possible on an *I* picture so the motion estimator is inactive. There is no predicted picture and so the prediction error subtractor is set simply to pass the input. The only processing which is active is the forward spatial coder which describes the picture with DCT coefficients. The output of the forward spatial coder is locally decoded and stored in the past picture frame store.

The reason for the spatial encode/decode is that the past picture frame store now contains exactly what the decoder frame store will contain, including the effects of any requantizing errors. When the same picture is used as a reference at both ends of a differential coding system, the errors will cancel out.

Having encoded the *I* picture, attention turns to the *P* picture. The input sequence is *IBBP*, but the transmitted sequence must be *IPBB*. Figure 9.27(c) shows that the reordering delay is bypassed to select the *P* picture. This passes to the motion estimator which compares it with the *I* picture and outputs a vector for each macroblock. The forward predictor uses these vectors to shift the *I* picture so that it more closely resembles the *P* picture. The predicted picture is then subtracted from the actual picture to produce a forward prediction error. This is then spatially coded. Thus the *P* picture is transmitted as a set of vectors and a prediction error image.

The *P* picture is locally decoded in the right-hand decoder. This takes the forward-predicted picture and adds the decoded prediction error to obtain exactly what the decoder will obtain.

Figure 9.27(d) shows that the encoder now contains an *I* picture in the left store and a *P* picture in the right store. The reordering delay is reselected so that the first *B* picture can be input. This passes to the motion estimator where it is compared with both the *I* and *P* pictures to produce forward and backward vectors. The forward vectors go to the forward predictor to make a *B* prediction from the *I* picture. The backward vectors go to the backward predictor to make a *B* prediction from the *P* picture. These predictions are simultaneously subtracted from the actual *B* picture to produce a forward prediction error and a backward prediction error. These are then spatially encoded. The encoder can then decide which direction of coding resulted in the best prediction; i.e. the smallest prediction error.

Not shown in the interests of clarity is a third signal path which creates a predicted *B* picture from the average of forward and backward predictions. This is subtracted from the input picture to produce a third prediction error. In some circumstances this prediction error may use fewer data than either forward or backward prediction alone.

As *B* pictures are never used to create other pictures, the decoder does not locally decode the *B* picture. After decoding and displaying the *B* picture the decoder will discard it. At the encoder the *I* and *P* pictures remain in their frame stores and the second *B* picture is input from the reordering delay.

Following the encoding of the second *B* picture, the encoder must reorder again to encode the second *P* picture in the GOP. This will be locally decoded and will replace the *I* picture in the left store. The stores and predictors switch designation because the left store is now a future *P* picture and the right store is now a past *P* picture. *B* pictures between them are encoded as before.

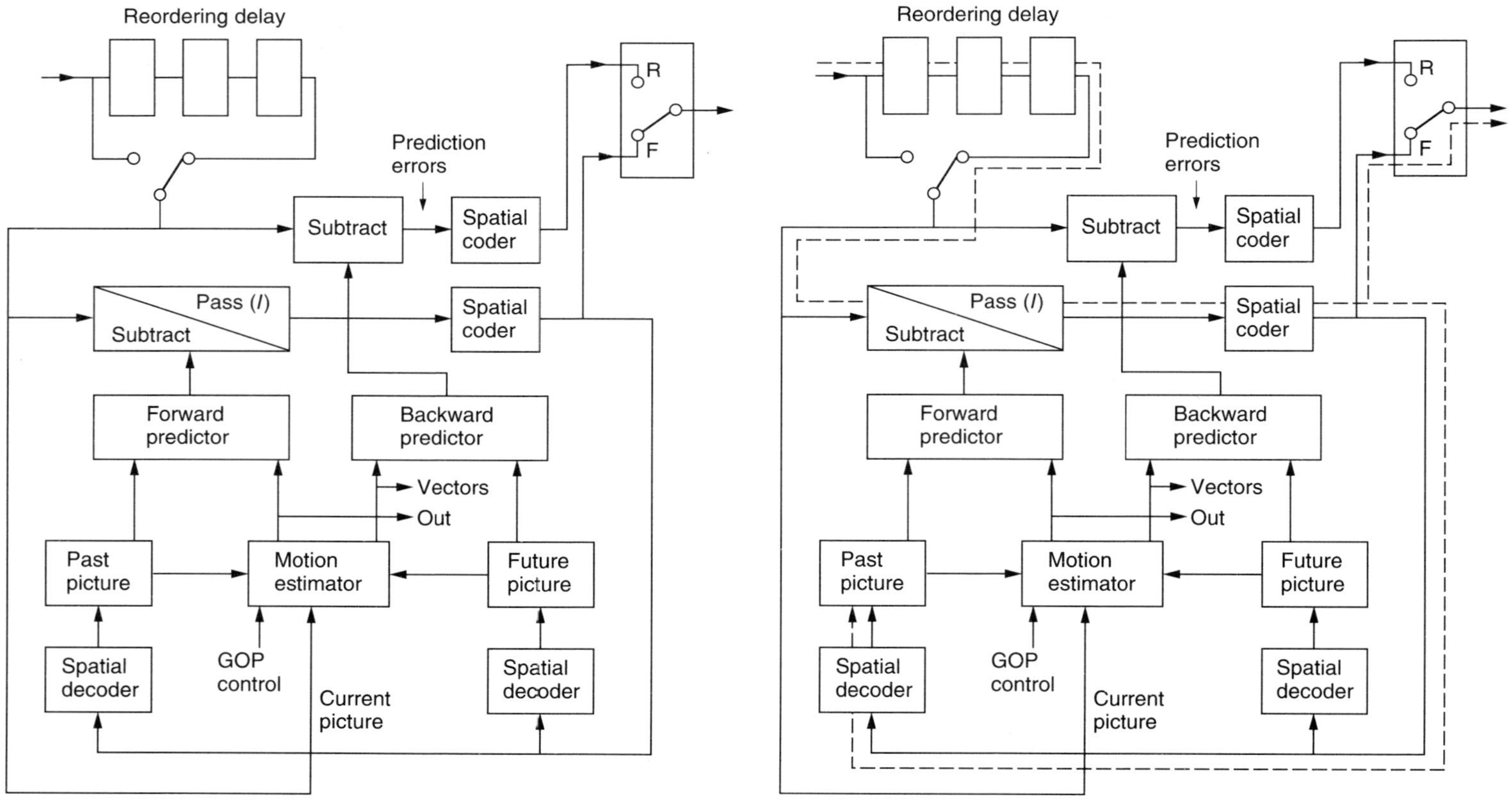

Reordering delay
Prediction errors
Subtract
Spatial coder
R
F
Pass (I)
Subtract
Spatial coder
Forward predictor
Backward predictor
Vectors
Out
Past picture
Motion estimator
Future picture
Spatial decoder
GOP control
Current picture
Spatial decoder

(a) (b)

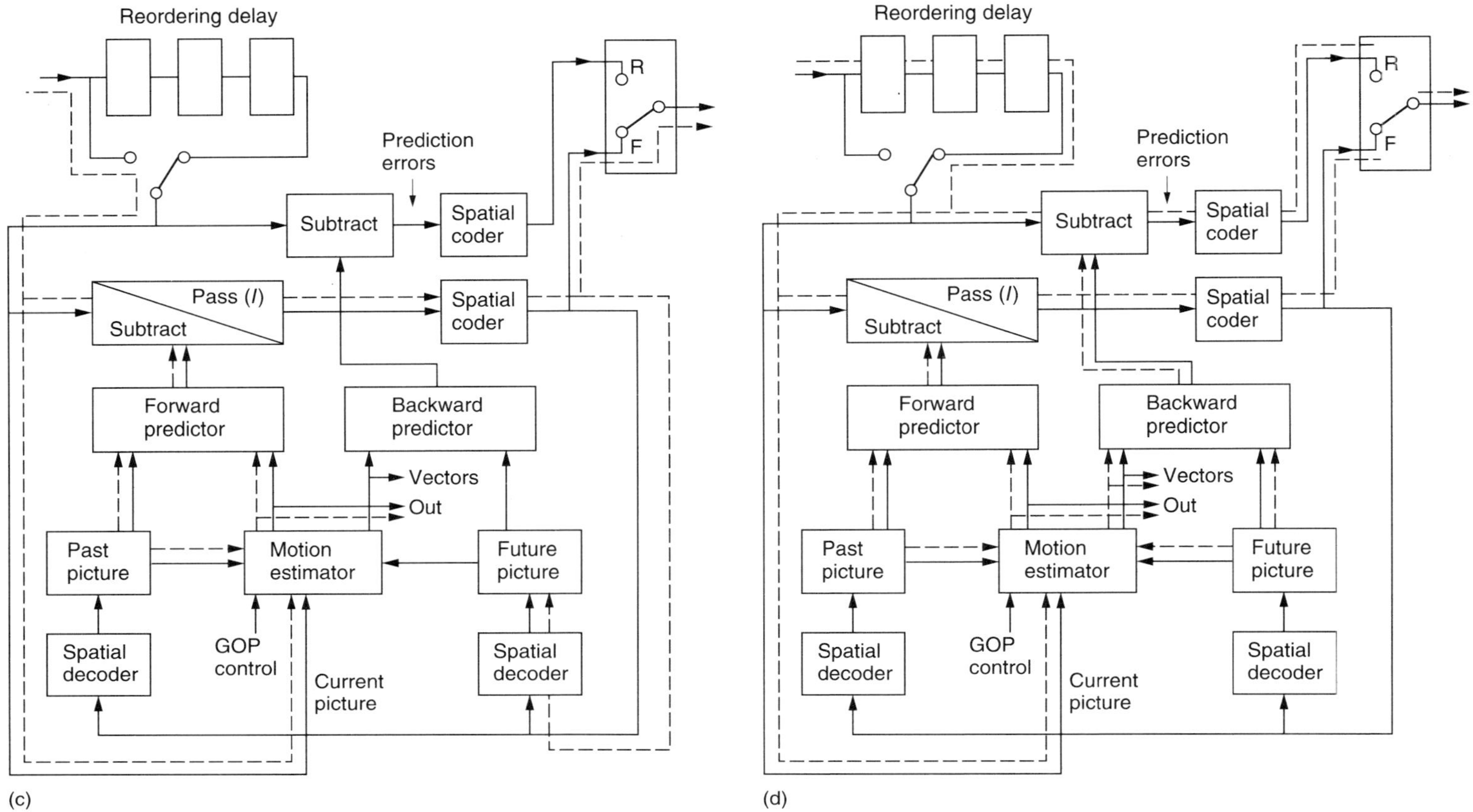

Figure 9.27 A bidirectional coder. (a) The essentional components. (b) Signal flow when coding an *I* picture. (c) Signal flow when coding a *P* picture. (d) Signal flow when bidirectional coding.

9.11 Slices

There is still some redundancy in the output of a bidirectional coder and MPEG is remarkably diligent in finding it. In *I* pictures, the DC coefficient describes the average brightness of an entire DCT block. In real video the DC component of adjacent blocks will be similar much of the time. A saving in bit rate can be obtained by differentially coding the DC coefficient.

In *P* and *B* pictures this is not done because these are prediction errors not actual images and the statistics are different. However, *P* and *B* pictures send vectors and instead the redundancy in these is explored. In a large moving object, many macroblocks will be moving at the same velocity and their vectors will be the same. Thus differential vector coding will be advantageous.

As has been seen above, differential coding cannot be used indiscriminately as it is prone to error propagation. Periodically absolute DC coefficients and vectors must be sent and the *slice* is the logical structure which supports this mechanism. In *I* pictures, the first DC coefficient in a slice is sent in absolute form, whereas the subsequent coefficients are sent differentially. In *P* or *B* pictures, the first vector in a slice is sent in absolute form, but the subsequent vectors are differential.

Slices are horizontal picture strips which are one macroblock (16 pixels) high and which proceed from left to right across the screen. The sides of the picture must coincide with the beginning or the end of a slice in MPEG-2, but otherwise the encoder is free to decide how big slices should be and where they begin.

In the case of a central dark building silhouetted against the bright sky, there would be two large changes in the DC coefficients, one at each edge of the building. It may be advantageous to the encoder to break the width of the picture into three slices, one each for the left and right areas of sky and one for the building. In the case of a large moving object, different slices may be used for the object and the background.

Each slice contains its own synchronizing pattern, so following a transmission error, correct decoding can resume at the next slice. Slice size can also be matched to the characteristics of the transmission channel. For example, in an error-free transmission system the use of a large number of slices in a packet simply wastes data capacity on surplus synchronizing patterns. However, in a non-ideal system it might be advantageous to have frequent resynchronizing.

9.12 Handling interlaced pictures

MPEG-1 handles interlaced inputs by discarding alternate fields to produce a non-interlaced signal. In MPEG-2, spatial coding, predictive

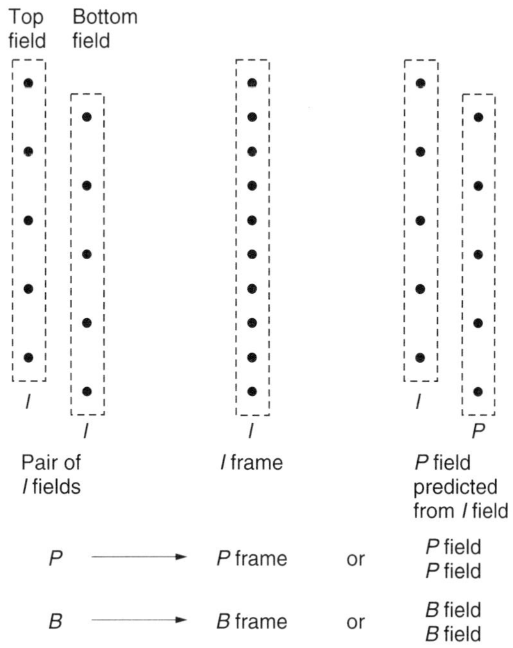

Figure 9.28 An interlaced frame consists of top and bottom fields. MPEG-2 can code a frame in the ways shown here.

coding and motion compensation can still be performed using interlaced source material at the cost of considerable complexity. Despite that complexity, coders cannot be expected to perform as well with interlaced material.

Figure 9.28 shows that in an incoming interlaced frame there are two fields each of which contain half of the lines in the frame. In MPEG-2 these are known as the *top field* and the *bottom field*. In video from a camera, these fields represent the state of the image at two different times. Where there is little image motion, this is unimportant and the fields can be combined obtaining more effective compression. However, in the presence of motion the fields become increasingly decorrelated because of the displacement of moving objects from one field to the next.

This characteristic determines that MPEG-2 must be able to handle fields independently or together. This dual approach permeates all aspects of MPEG-2 and affects the definition of pictures, macroblocks, DCT blocks and zig-zag scanning.

Figure 9.28 also shows how MPEG-2 designates interlaced fields. In picture types *I*, *P* and *B*, the two fields can be superimposed to make a *frame-picture* or the two fields can be coded independently as two *field-pictures*. As a third possibility, in *I* pictures only, the bottom field-picture can be predictively coded from the top field-picture to make an *IP* frame-picture.

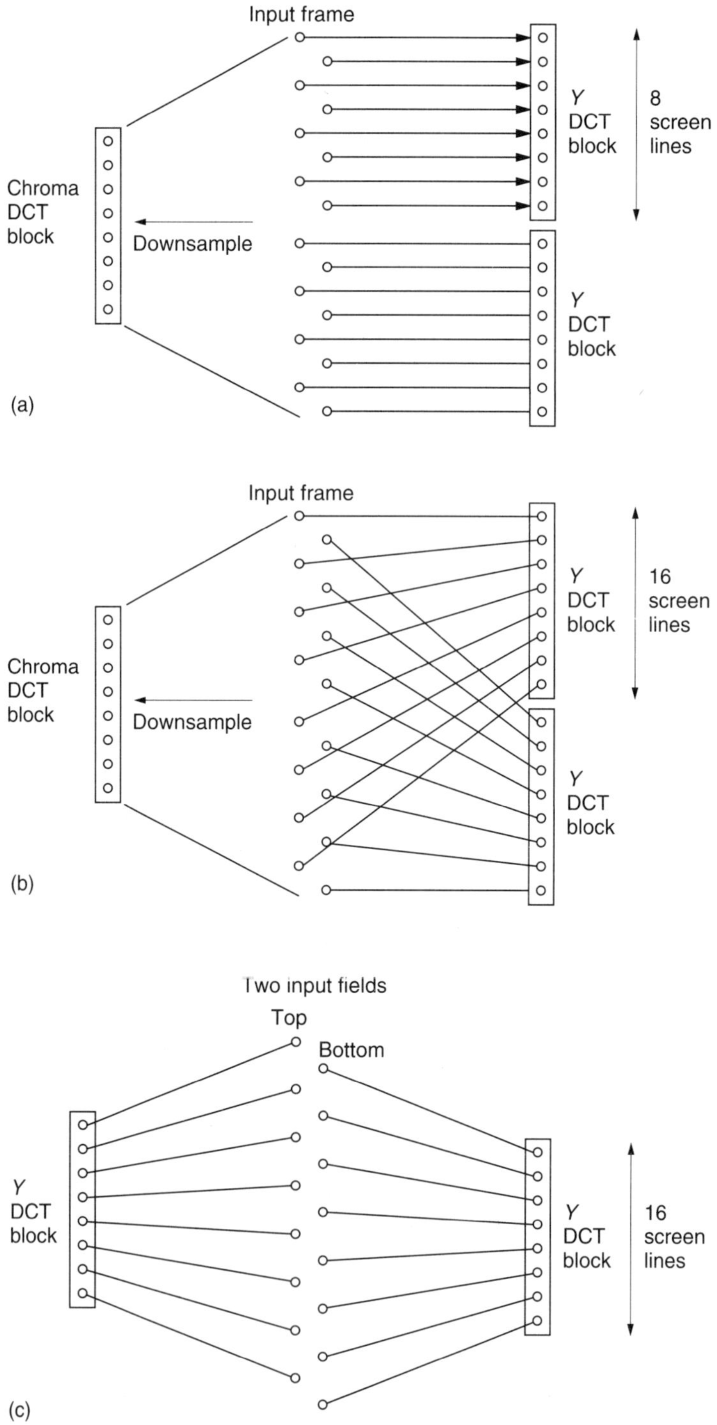

Figure 9.29 (a) In Frame-DCT, a picture is effectively de-interlaced. (b) In Field-DCT, each DCT block only contains lines from one field, but over twice the screen area. (c) The same DCT content results when field-pictures are assembled into blocks.

A frame-picture is one in which the macroblocks contain lines from both field types over a picture area 16 scan lines high. Each luminance macroblock contains the usual four DCT blocks but there are two ways in which these can be assembled. Figure 9.29(a) shows how a frame is divided into *frame DCT* blocks. This is identical to the progressive scan approach in that each DCT block contains eight contiguous picture lines. In 4:2:0, the colour difference signals have been downsampled by a factor of two and shifted as was shown in section 4.18. Figure 9.29(a) also shows how one 4:2:0 DCT block contains the chroma data from 16 lines in two fields.

Even small amounts of motion in any direction can destroy the correlation between odd and even lines and a frame DCT will result in an excessive number of coefficients. Figure 9.29(b) shows that instead the luminance component of a frame can also be divided into *field DCT* blocks. In this case one DCT block contains odd lines and the other contains even lines. In this mode the chroma still produces one DCT block from both fields as in Figure 9.29(a).

When an input frame is designated as two *field-pictures*, the macroblocks come from a screen area which is 32 lines high. Figure 9.29(c) shows that the DCT blocks contain the same data as if the input frame had been designated a *frame-picture* but with *field DCT*. Consequently it is only frame-pictures which have the option of field or frame DCT. These may be selected by the encoder on a macroblock-by-macroblock basis and, of course, the resultant bitstream must specify what has been done.

In a frame which contains a small moving area, it may be advantageous to encode as a frame-picture with frame DCT except in the moving area where field DCT is used. This approach may result in fewer bits than coding as two field-pictures.

In a field-picture and in a frame-picture using field DCT, a DCT block contains lines from one field type only and this must have come from a screen area sixteen scan lines high, whereas in progressive scan and frame DCT the area is only eight scan lines high. A given vertical spatial frequency in the image is sampled at points twice as far apart which is interpreted by the field DCT as a doubled spatial frequency, whereas there is no change in the horizontal spectrum.

Following the DCT calculation, the coefficient distribution will be different in field-pictures and field DCT frame-pictures. In these cases, the probability of coefficients is not a constant funtion of radius from the DC coefficient as it is in progressive scan, but is elliptical where the ellipse is twice as high as it is wide.

Using the standard 45° zig-zag scan with this different coefficient distribution would not have the required effect of putting all the significant coefficients at the beginning of the scan. To achieve this

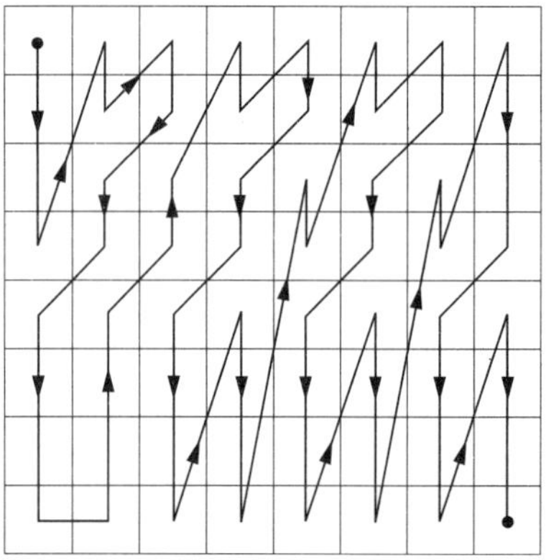

Figure 9.30 The zig-zag scan for an interlaced image has to favour vertical frequencies twice as much as horizontal.

requires a different zig-zag scan, which is shown in Figure 9.30. This scan, sometimes known as the Yeltsin walk, attempts to match the elliptical probability of interlaced coefficients with a scan slanted at 67.5° to the vertical. This is clearly suboptimal, and is one of the reasons why MPEG-2 does not work so well with interlaced video.

Motion estimation is more difficult in an interlaced system. Vertical detail can result in differences between fields and this reduces the quality of the match. Fields are vertically subsampled without filtering and so contain alias products. This aliasing will mean that the vertical waveform representing a moving object will not be the same in successive pictures and this will also reduce the quality of the match.

Even when the correct vector has been found, the match may be poor so the estimator fails to recognize it. If it is recognized, a poor match means that the quality of the prediction in *P* and *B* pictures will be poor and so a large prediction error or residual has to be transmitted. In an attempt to reduce the residual, MPEG-2 allows field-pictures to use motion-compensated prediction from either the adjacent field or from the same field type in another frame. In this case the encoder will use the better match. This technique can also be used in areas of frame-pictures which use field DCT.

The motion compensation of MPEG-2 has half-pixel resolution and this is inherently compatible with an interlace because an interpolator must be present to handle the half-pixel shifts. Figure 9.31(a) shows that in an interlaced system, each field contains half of the frame lines and so interpolating half-way between lines of one field type will actually create values lying on the sampling structure of the other field type. Thus it is equally possible for a predictive system to decode a given field type based on pixel data from the other field type or of the same type.

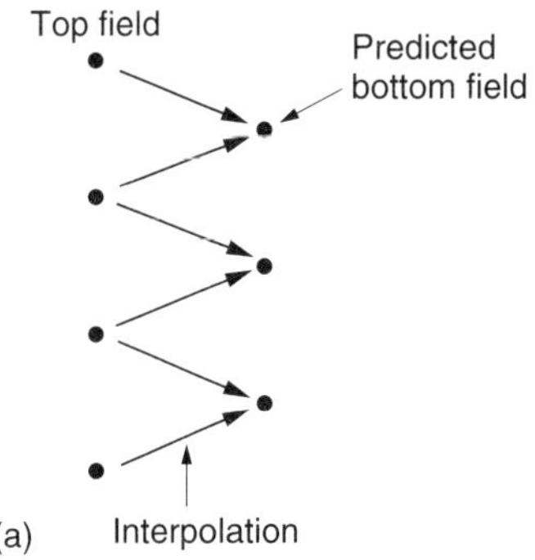

(a)

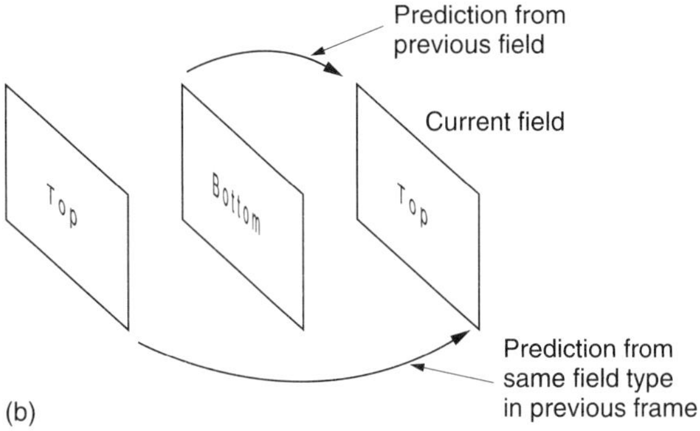

(b)

Figure 9.31 (a) Each field contains half of the frame lines and so interpolation is needed to create values lying on the sampling structure of the other field type, (b) Prediction can use data from the previous field or the one before that.

If when using predictive coding from the other field type the vertical motion vector contains a half-pixel component, then no interpolation is needed because the act of transferring pixels from one field to another results in such a shift.

Figure 9.31(b) shows that a macroblock in a given *P* field-picture can be encoded using a vector which shifts data from the previous field or from the field before that, irrespective of which frames these fields occupy. As noted above, field-picture macroblocks come from an area of screen 32 lines high and this means that the vector density is halved, resulting in larger prediction errors at the boundaries of moving objects.

As an option, field-pictures can restore the vector density by using 16 × 8 motion compensation where separate vectors are used for the top and bottom halves of the macroblock. Frame-pictures can also use 16 × 8 motion compensation in conjunction with field DCT. Whilst the 2 × 2 DCT block luminance structure of a macroblock can easily be divided vertically in two, in 4:2:0 the same screen area is represented by only one chroma macroblock of each component type. As it cannot be divided in half, this chroma is deemed to belong to the luminance DCT blocks of the upper field. In 4:2:2 no such difficulty arises.

MPEG-2 supports interlace simply because interlaced video exists in legacy systems and there is a requirement to compress it. However, where the opportunity arises to define a new system, interlace should be avoided. Legacy interlaced source material should be handled using a motion-compensated de-interlacer prior to compression in the progressive domain.

9.13 An MPEG-2 coder

Figure 9.32 shows a complete MPEG-2 coder. The bidirectional coder outputs coefficients and vectors, and the quantizing table in use. The vectors of *P* and *B* pictures and the DC coefficients of *I* pictures are differentially encoded in slices and the remaining coefficients are RLC/VLC coded. The multiplexer assembles all these data into a single bitstream called an elementary stream. The output of the encoder is a buffer which absorbs the variations in bit rate between different picture types. The buffer output has a constant bit rate determined by the demand clock. This comes from the transmission channel or storage device. If the bit rate is low, the buffer will tend to fill up, whereas if it is high the buffer will tend to empty. The buffer content is used to control the severity of the requantizing in the spatial coders. The more the buffer fills, the bigger the requantizing steps get.

The buffer in the decoder has a finite capacity and the encoder must model the decoder's buffer occupancy so that it neither overflows nor underflows. An overflow might occur if an *I* picture is transmitted when the buffer content is already high. The buffer occupancy of the decoder

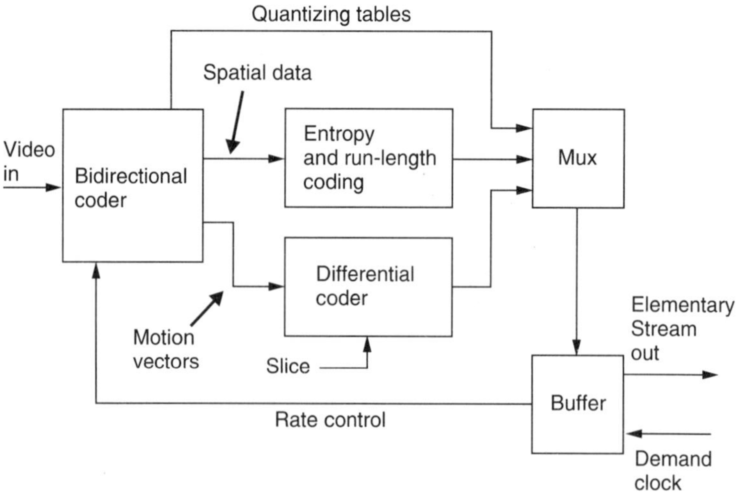

Figure 9.32 An MPEG 2 coder. See text for details.

depends somewhat on the memory access strategy of the decoder. Instead of defining a specific buffer size, MPEG-2 defines the size of a particular mathematical model of a hypothetical buffer. The decoder designer can use any strategy which implements the model, and the encoder can use any strategy which doesn't overflow or underflow the model. The elementary stream has a parameter called the video buffer verifier (VBV) which defines the minimum buffering assumptions of the encoder.

As was seen above, buffering is one way of ensuring constant quality when picture entropy varies. An intelligent coder may run down the buffer contents in anticipation of a difficult picture sequence so that a large amount of data can be sent.

MPEG does not define what a decoder should do if a buffer underflow or overflow occurs, but since both irrecoverably lose data it is obvious that there will be more or less of an interruption to the decoding. Even a small loss of data may cause loss of synchronization and in the case of long GOP the lost data may make the rest of the GOP undecodable. A decoder may chose to repeat the last properly decoded picture until it can begin to operate correctly again.

Buffer problems occur if the VBV model is violated. If this happens then more than one underflow or overflow can result from a single violation. Switching an MPEG bitstream can cause a violation because the two encoders concerned may have radically different buffer occupancy at the switch.

9.14 The elementary stream

Figure 9.33 shows the structure of the elementary stream from an MPEG-2 encoder. The structure begins with a set of coefficients representing a DCT block. Six or eight DCT blocks form the luminance and chroma content of one macroblock. In *P* and *B* pictures a macroblock will be associated with a vector for motion compensation. Macroblocks are associated into slices in which DC coefficients of *I* pictures and vectors in *P* and *B* pictures are differentially coded. An arbitrary number of slices forms a picture and this needs *I/P/B* flags describing the type of picture it is. The picture may also have a global vector which efficiently deals with pans.

Several pictures form a Group of Pictures (GOP) and the GOP begins with an *I* picture and may or may not include *P* and *B* pictures in a structure which may vary dynamically.

Several GOPs form a sequence which begins with a sequence header containing important data to help the decoder. It is possible to repeat the header within a sequence, and this helps lock-up in random access applications. The sequence header describes the MPEG-2 profile and

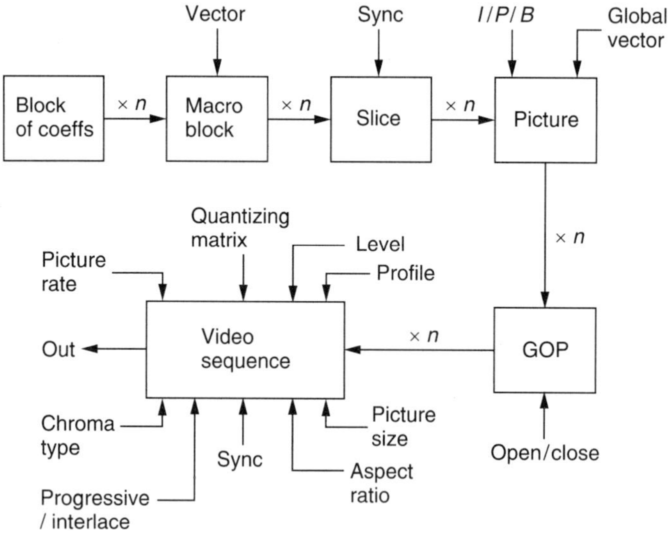

Figure 9.33 The structure of an elementary stream. MPEG defines the syntax precisely.

level, whether the video is progressive or interlaced, whether the chroma is 4:2:0 or 4:2:2, the size of the picture and the aspect ratio of the pixels. The quantizing matrix used in the spatial coder can also be sent. The sequence begins with a standardized bit pattern which is detected by a decoder to synchronize the deserialization.

9.15 An MPEG-2 decoder

The decoder is only defined by implication from the definitions of syntax and any decoder which can correctly interpret all combinations of syntax at a particular profile will be deemed compliant however it works.

The first problem a decoder has is that the input is an endless bitstream which contains a huge range of parameters many of which have variable length. Unique synchronizing patterns must be placed periodically throughout the bitstream so that the decoder can identify a known starting point. The pictures which can be sent under MPEG-2 are so flexible that the decoder must first find a sequence header so that it can establish the size of the picture, the frame rate, the colour coding used, etc.

The decoder must also be supplied with a 27 MHz system clock. In a DVD player, this would come from a crystal, but in a transmission system this would be provided by a numerically locked loop running from clock reference parameter in the bitstream (see Chapter 6). Until this loop has achieved lock the decoder cannot function properly.

Figure 9.34 shows a bidirectional decoder. The decoder can only begin decoding with an *I* picture and as this only uses intra-coding there will be

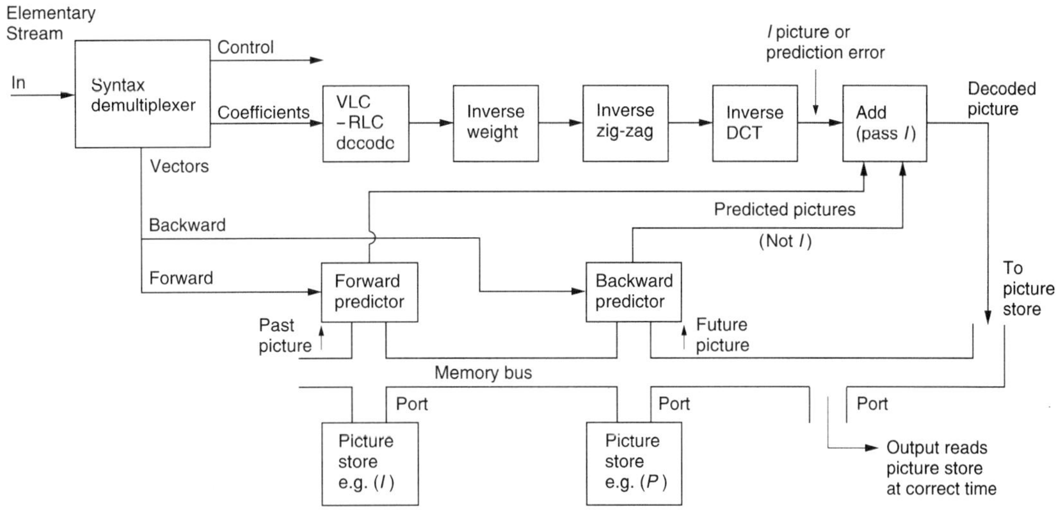

Figure 9.34 A bidirectional MPEG-2 decoder. See text for details.

no vectors. An *I* picture is transmitted as a series of slices. These slices begin with subsidiary synchronizing patterns. The first macroblock in the slice contains an absolute DC coefficient, but the remaining macroblocks code the DC coefficient differentially so the decoder must subtract the differential values from the previous value to obtain the absolute value.

The AC coefficients are sent as Huffman coded run/size parameters followed by coefficient value codes. The variable-length Huffman codes are decoded by using a look-up table and extending the number of bits considered until a match is obtained. This allows the zero-run-length and the coefficient size to be established. The right number of bits is taken from the bitstream corresponding to the coefficient code and this is decoded to the actual coefficient using the size parameter.

If the correct number of bits has been taken from the stream, the next bit must be the beginning of the next run/size code and so on until the EOB symbol is reached. The decoder uses the coefficient values and the zero-run-lengths to populate a DCT coefficient block following the appropriate zig-zag scanning sequence. Following EOB, the bitstream then continues with the next DCT block. Clearly this Huffman decoding will work perfectly or not at all. A single bit slippage in synchronism or a single corrupted data bit can cause a spectacular failure.

Once a complete DCT coefficient block has been received, the coefficients need to be inverse quantized and inverse weighted. Then an inverse DCT can be performed and this will result in an 8 × 8 pixel block. A series of DCT blocks will allow the luminance and colour information for an entire macroblock to be decoded and this can be placed in a framestore. Decoding continues in this way until the end of the slice when an absolute

DC coefficient will once again be sent. Once all the slices have been decoded, an entire picture will be resident in the framestore.

The amount of data needed to decode the picture is variable and the decoder just keeps going until the last macroblock is found. It will obtain data from the input buffer. In a constant bit rate transmission system, the decoder will remove more data to decode an *I* picture than has been received in one picture period, leaving the buffer emptier than it began. Subsequent *P* and *B* pictures need much fewer data and allow the buffer to fill again.

The picture will be output when the time stamp (see Chapter 6) sent with the picture matches the state of the decoder's time count.

Following the *I* picture may be another *I* picture or a *P* picture. Assuming a *P* picture, this will be predictively coded from the *I* picture. The *P* picture will be divided into slices as before. The first vector in a slice is absolute, but subsequent vectors are sent differentially. However, the DC coefficients are not differential.

Each macroblock may contain a forward vector. The decoder uses this to shift pixels from the *I* picture into the correct position for the predicted *P* picture. The vectors have half-pixel resolution and where a half-pixel shift is required, an interpolator will be used.

The DCT data are sent much as for an *I* picture. They will require inverse quantizing, but not inverse weighting because *P* and *B* coefficients are flat-weighted. When decoded this represents an error-cancelling picture which is added pixel-by-pixel to the motion-predicted picture. This results in the output picture.

If bidirectional coding is being used, the *P* picture may be stored until one or more *B* pictures have been decoded. The *B* pictures are sent essentially as a *P* picture might be, except that the vectors can be forward, backward or bidirectional. The decoder must take pixels from the *I* picture, the *P* picture, or both, and shift them according to the vectors to make a predicted picture. The DCT data decodes to produce an error-cancelling image as before.

In an interlaced system, the prediction mechanism may alternatively obtain pixel data from the previous field or the field before that. Vectors may relate to macroblocks or to 16×8 pixel areas. DCT blocks after decoding may represent frame lines or field lines. This adds up to a lot of different possibilities for a decoder handling an interlaced input.

9.16 Coding artifacts

This section describes the visible results of imperfect coding. Imperfect coding may be where the coding algorithm is suboptimal, where the coder latency is too short or where the compression factor in use is simply too great for the material.

In motion-compensated systems such as MPEG, the use of periodic intra-fields means that the coding noise varies from picture to picture and this may be visible as noise pumping. Noise pumping may also be visible where the amount of motion changes. If a pan is observed, as the pan speed increases the motion vectors may become less accurate and reduce the quality of the prediction processes. The prediction errors will get larger and will have to be more coarsely quantized. Thus the picture becomes noisier as the pan accelerates and the noise reduces as the pan slows down. The same result may be apparent at the edges of a picture during zooming. The problem is worse if the picture contains fine detail. Panning on grass or trees waving in the wind taxes most coders severely. Camera shake from a hand-held camera also increases the motion vector data and results in more noise as does film weave.

Input video noise or film grain degrades inter-coding as there is less redundancy between pictures and the difference data become larger, requiring coarse quantizing and adding to the existing noise.

Where a codec is really fighting the quantizing may become very coarse and as a result the video level at the edge of one DCT block may not match that of its neighbour. As a result the DCT block structure becomes visible as a mosaicing or tiling effect. Coarse quantizing also causes some coefficients to be rounded up and appear larger than they should be. High-frequency coefficients may be eliminated by heavy quantizing and this forces the DCT to act as a steep-cut low-pass filter. This causes fringeing or ringing around sharp edges and extra shadowy edges which were not in the original. This is most noticeable on text.

Excess compression may also result in colour bleed where fringeing has taken place in the chroma or where high-frequency chroma coefficients have been discarded. Graduated colour areas may reveal banding or posterizing as the colour range is restricted by requantizing. These artifacts are almost impossible to measure with conventional test gear.

Neither noise pumping nor blocking are visible on analog video recorders and so it is nonsense to liken the performance of a codec to the quality of a VCR. In fact noise pumping is extremely objectionable because, unlike steady noise, it attracts attention in peripheral vision and may result in viewing fatigue.

In addition to highly detailed pictures with complex motion, certain types of video signal are difficult for MPEG-2 to handle and will usually result in a higher level of artifacts than usual. Noise has already been mentioned as a source of problems. Timebase error from, for example, VCRs is undesirable because this puts succesive lines in different horizontal positions. A straight vertical line becomes jagged and this results in high spatial frequencies in the DCT process. Spurious coefficients are created which need to be coded.

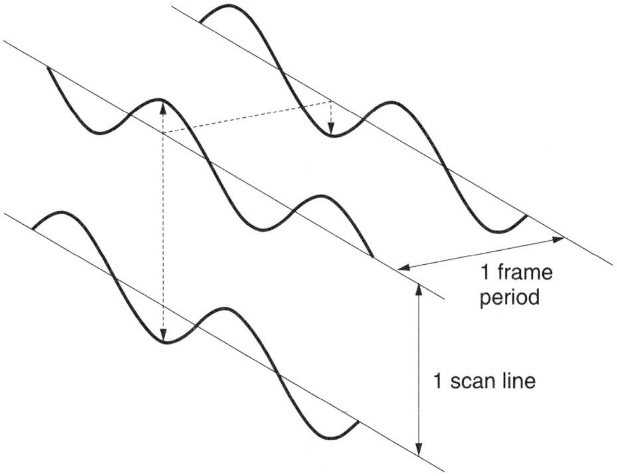

Figure 9.35 In composite video the subcarrier frequency is arranged so that inversions occur between adjacent lines and pictures to help reduce the visibility of the chroma.

Much archive video is in composite form and MPEG-2 can only handle this after it has been decoded to components. Unfortunately many general-purpose composite decoders have a high level of residual subcarrier in the outputs. This is normally not a problem because the subcarrier is designed to be invisible to the naked eye. Figure 9.35 shows that in PAL and NTSC the subcarrier frequency is selected so that a phase reversal is achieved between successive lines and frames.

Whilst this makes the subcarrier invisible to the eye, it is not invisible to an MPEG decoder. The subcarrier waveform is interpreted as a horizontal frequency, the vertical phase reversals are interpreted as a vertical spatial frequency and the picture-to-picture reversals increase the magnitude of the prediction errors. The subcarrier level may be low but it can be present over the whole screen and require an excess of coefficients to describe it.

Composite video should not in general be used as a source for MPEG-2 encoding, but where this is inevitable the standard of the decoder must be much higher than average, especially in the residual subcarrier specification. Some MPEG preprocessors support high-grade composite decoding options.

Judder from conventional linear standards convertors degrades the performance of MPEG-2. The optic flow axis is corrupted and linear filtering causes multiple images which confuse motion estimators and result in larger prediction errors. If standards conversion is necessary, the MPEG-2 system must be used to encode the signal in its original format and the standards convertor should be installed after the decoder. If a standards convertor has to be used before the encoder, then it must be a type which has effective motion compensation.

Film weave causes movement of one picture with respect to the next and this results in more vector activity and larger prediction errors. Movement of the centre of the film frame along the optical axis causes magnification changes which also result in excess prediction error data. Film grain has the same effect as noise: it is random and so cannot be compressed.

Perhaps because it is relatively uncommon, MPEG-2 cannot handle image rotation well because the motion-compensation system is designed only for translational motion. Where a rotating object is highly detailed, such as in certain fairground rides, the motion-compensation failure requires a significant amount of prediction error data and if a suitable bit rate is not available the level of artifacts will rise.

Flash guns used by still photographers are a serious hazard to MPEG-2 especially when long GOPs are used. At a press conference where a series of flashes may occur, the resultant video contains intermittent white frames which defeat prediction. A huge prediction error is required to turn the previous picture into a white picture, followed by another huge prediction error to return the white frame to the next picture. The output buffer fills and heavy requantizing is employed. After a few flashes the picture has generally gone to tiles.

9.17 Processing MPEG-2 and concatenation

Concatenation loss occurs when the losses introduced by one codec are compounded by a second codec. All practical compressers, MPEG-2 included, are lossy because what comes out of the decoder is not bit-identical to what went into the encoder. The bit differences are controlled so that they have minimum visibility to a human viewer.

MPEG-2 is a toolbox which allows a variety of manipulations to be performed in both the spatial and the temporal domain. There is a limit to the compression which can be used on a single frame, and if higher compression factors are needed, temporal coding will have to be used. The longer the run of pictures considered, the lower the bit rate needed, but the harder it becomes to edit.

The most editable form of MPEG-2 is to use *I* pictures only. As there is no temporal coding, pure cut edits can be made between pictures. The next best thing is to use a repeating *IB* structure which is locked to the odd/even field structure. Cut edits cannot be made as the *B* pictures are bidirectionally coded and need data from both adjacent *I* pictures for decoding. The *B* picture has to be decoded prior to the edit and re-encoded after the edit. This will cause a small concatenation loss.

Beyond the *IB* structure processing gets harder. If a long GOP is used for the best compression factor, an *IBBPBBP* . . . structure results. Editing this is very difficult because the pictures are sent out of order so that bidirectional decoding can be used. MPEG allows closed GOPs where the last *B* picture is coded wholly from the previous pictures and does not need the *I* picture in the next GOP. The bitstream can be switched at this point but only if the GOP structures in the two source video signals are synchronized (makes colour framing seem easy). Consequently in practice a long GOP bitstream will need to be decoded prior to any production step. Afterwards it will need to be re-encoded.

This is known as *naive* concatenation and an enormous pitfall awaits. Unless the GOP structure of the output is identical to and synchronized with the input the results will be disappointing. The worst case is where an *I* picture is encoded from a picture which was formerly a *B* picture. It is easy enough to lock the GOP structure of a coder to a single input, but if an edit is made between two inputs, the GOP timings could well be different.

As there are so many structures allowed in MPEG, there will be a need to convert between them. If this has to be done, it should only be in the direction which increases the GOP length and reduces the bit rate. Going the other way is inadvisable. The ideal way of converting from, say, the *IB* structure of a news system to the *IBBP* structure of an emission system is to use a recompressor. This is a kind of standards convertor which will give better results than a decode followed by an encode.

The DCT part of MPEG-2 itself is lossless. If all the coefficients are preserved intact an inverse transform yields the same pixel data. Unfortunately this does not yield enough compression for many applications. In practice the coefficients are made less accurate by removing bits, starting at the least significant end and working upwards. This process is weighted, or made progressively more aggressive as spatial frequency increases.

Small-value coefficients may be truncated to zero and large-value coefficients are most coarsely truncated at high spatial frequencies where the effect is least visible.

Figure 9.36(a) shows what happens in the ideal case where two *identical* coders are put in tandem and synchronized. The first coder quantizes the coefficients to finite accuracy and causes a loss on decoding. However, when the second coder performs the DCT calculation, the coefficients obtained will be identical to the quantized coefficients in the first coder and so if the second weighting and requantizing step is identical the same truncated coefficient data will result and there will be no further loss of quality.[7]

In practice this ideal situation is elusive. If the two DCTs become non-identical for any reason, the second requantizing step will introduce further error in the coefficients and the artifact level goes up. Figure 9.36(b) shows that non-identical concatenation can result from a large number of real-world effects.

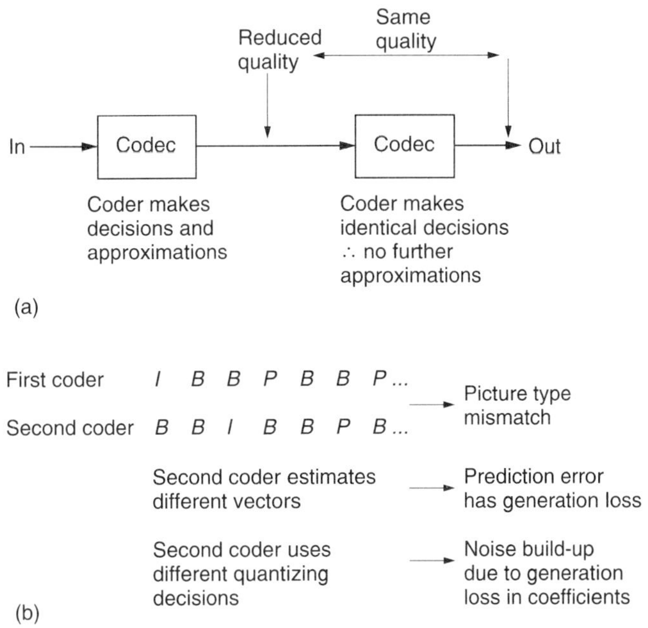

Figure 9.36 (a) Two identical coders in tandem which are synchronized make similar coding decisions and cause little loss. (b) There are various ways in which concatenated coders can produce non-ideal performance.

An intermediate processing step such as a fade will change the pixel values and thereby the coefficients. A DVE resize or shift will move pixels from one DCT block to another. Even if there is no processing step, this effect will also occur if the two codecs disagree on where the MPEG picture boundaries are within the picture. If the boundaries are correct there will still be concatenation loss if the two codecs use different weightings.

One problem with MPEG is that the compressor design is unspecified. Whilst this has advantages, it does mean that the chances of finding identical coders is minute because each manufacturer will have his own views on the best compression algorithm. In a large system it may be worth obtaining the coders from a single supplier.

It is now increasingly accepted that concatenation of compression techniques is potentially damaging, and results are worse if the codecs are different. Clearly feeding a digital coder such as MPEG-2 with a signal which has been subject to analog compression comes into the category of worse. Using interlaced video as a source for MPEG coding is suboptimal and using decoded composite video is even worse.

One way of avoiding concatenation is to stay in the compressed data domain. If the goal is just to move pictures from one place to another, decoding to traditional video so an existing router can be used is not ideal, although substantially better than going through the analog domain.

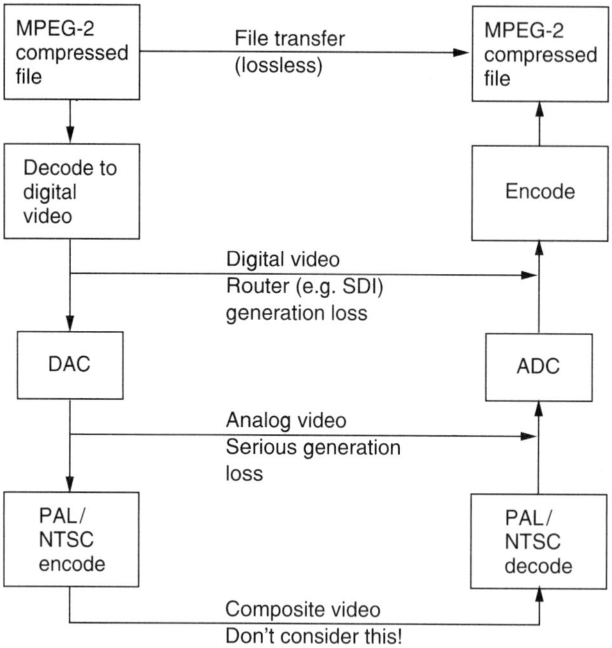

Figure 9.37 Compressed picture transport mechanisms contrasted.

Figure 9.37 shows some possibilities for picture transport. Clearly if the pictures exist as a compressed file on a server, a file transfer is the right way to do it as there is no possibility of loss because there has been no concatenation. File transfer is also quite indifferent to the picture format. It doesn't care whether the pictures are interlaced or not, whether the colour is 4:2:0 or 4:2:2.

Decoding to SDI (serial digital interface) standard is sometimes done so that existing serial digital routing can be used. This is concatenation and has to be done carefully. The compressed video can only use interlace with non-square pixels and the colour coding has to be 4:2:2 because SDI only allows that. If a compressed file has 4:2:0 the chroma has to be interpolated up to 4:2:2 for SDI transfer and then subsampled back to 4:2:0 at the second coder and this will cause generation loss. An SDI transfer also can only be performed in real time, thus negating one of the advantages of compression. In short, traditional SDI is not really at home with compression.

As 4:2:0 progressive scan gains popularity and video production moves steadily towards non-format-specific hardware using computers and data networks, use of the serial digital interface will eventually decline. In the short term, if an existing SDI router has to be used, one solution is to produce a bitstream which is sufficiently similar to SDI that a router will pass it. Systems such as SDDI and ASI (see Chapter 12) work in this way. In short, the signal level, frequency and impedance is pure SDI, but the data protocol is different so that a bit-accurate file transfer can be performed. This has two advantages. First, the compressed data format can be anything appropriate and non-interlaced and/or 4:2:0 can be handled in any picture size, aspect ratio or frame rate. Second, a faster than real-time transfer can be used depending on the compression factor of the file.

An improved way of reducing concatenation loss has emerged from the ATLANTIC research project.[8] Figure 9.38 shows that the second encoder in a concatenated scheme does not make its own decisions from the incoming video, but is instead steered by information from the first bitstream. As the second encoder has less intelligence, it is known as a *dim* encoder.

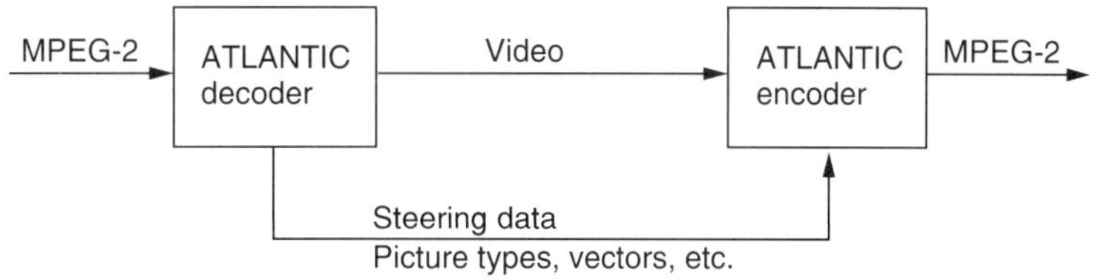

Figure 9.38 In an ATLANTIC system, the second encoder is steered by information from the decoder.

The information bus carries all the structure of the original MPEG-2 bitstream which would be lost in a conventional decoder. The ATLANTIC decoder does more than decode the pictures. It also places on the information bus all parameters needed to make the dim encoder re-enact what the initial MPEG-2 encode did as closely as possible.

The GOP structure is passed on so that pictures are re-encoded as the same type. Positions of macroblock boundaries become identical so that DCT blocks contain the same pixels and motion vectors relate to the same screen data. The weighting and quantizing tables are passed so that coefficient truncation is identical. Motion vectors from the original bitsream are passed on so that the dim encoder does not need to perform motion estimation. In this way predicted pictures will be identical to the original prediction and the prediction error data will be the same.

One application of this approach is in recompression, where an MPEG-2 bitstream has to have its bit rate reduced. This has to be done by heavier requantizing of coefficients, but if as many other parameters as possible can be kept the same, such as motion vectors, the degradation will be minimized. In a simple recompressor just requantizing the coefficients means that the predictive coding will be impaired. In a proper encode, the quantizing error due to coding, say, an *I* picture is removed from the *P* picture by the prediction process. The prediction error of P is obtained by subtracting the decoded I picture rather than the original I picture.

In simple recompression this does not happen and there may be a tolerance build-up known as drift.[9] A more sophisticated recompressor will need to repeat the prediction process using the decoded output pictures as the prediction reference.

MPEG-2 bitstreams will often be decoded for the purpose of switching. Local insertion of commercial breaks into a centrally originated bitstream is one obvious requirement. If the decoded video signal is switched, the information bus must also be switched. At the switch point identical re-encoding becomes impossible because prior pictures required for predictive coding will have disappeared. At this point the dim encoder has to become bright again because it has to create an MPEG-2 bitstream without assistance.

It is possible to encode the information bus into a form which allows it to be invisibly carried in the serial digital interface. Where a production process such as a vision mixer or DVE performs no manipulation, i.e. becomes bit transparent, the subsequent encoder can extract the information bus and operate in 'dim' mode. Where a manipulation is performed, the information bus signal will be corrupted and the encoder has to work in 'bright' mode. The encoded information signal is known as a 'mole'[10] because it burrows through the processing equipment!

There will be a generation loss at the switch point because the re-encode will be making different decisions in bright mode. This may be difficult to detect because the human visual system is slow to react to a vision cut and defects in the first few pictures after a cut are masked.

In addition to the video computation required to perform a cut, the process has to consider the buffer occupancy of the decoder. A downstream decoder has finite buffer memory, and individual encoders model the decoder buffer occupancy to ensure that it neither overflows nor underflows. At any instant the decoder buffer can be nearly full or nearly empty without a problem provided there is a subsequent correction. An encoder which is approaching a complex I picture may run down the buffer so it can send a lot of data to describe that picture. Figure 9.39(a) shows that if a decoder with a nearly full buffer is suddenly switched to an encoder which has been running down its buffer occupancy, the decoder buffer will overflow when the second encoder sends a lot of data.

An MPEG-2 switcher will need to monitor the buffer occupancy of its own output to avoid overflow of downstream decoders. Where this is a possibility the second encoder will have to recompress to reduce the output bit rate temporarily. In practice there will be a recovery period where the buffer occupancy of the newly selected signal is matched to that of the previous signal. This is shown in Figure 9.39(b).

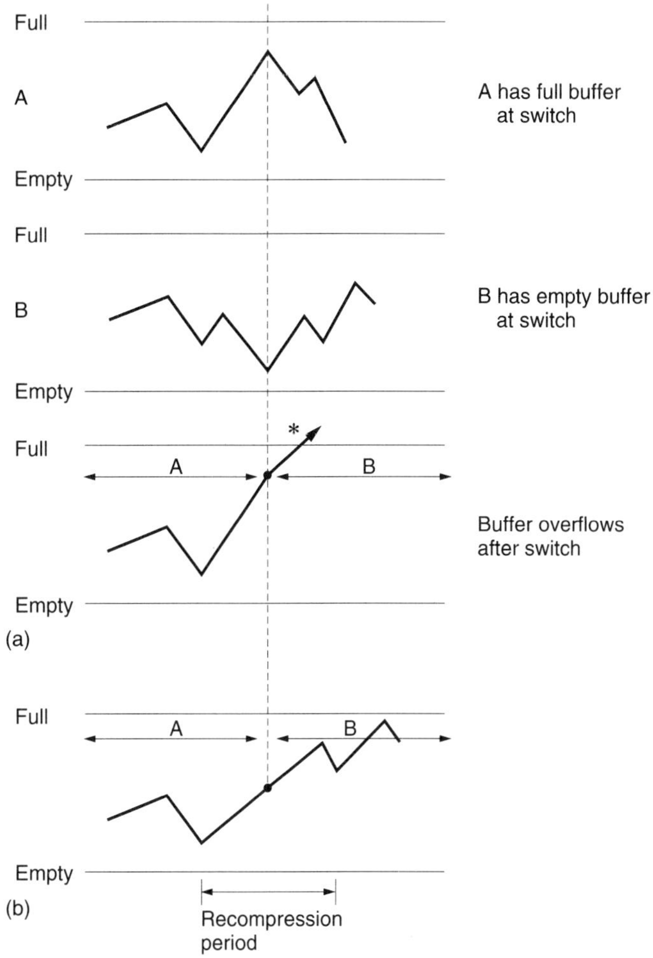

Figure 9.39 (a) A bitstream switch at a different level of buffer occupancy can cause a decoder overflow. (b) Recompression after a switch to return to correct buffer occupancy.

9.18 Audio compression

Perceptive coding relies on the principle of auditory masking, which was considered in Chapter 5. Masking causes the ear/brain combination to be less sensitive to sound at one frequency in the presence of another at a nearby frequency. If a first tone is present in the input, then it will mask signals of lower level at nearby frequencies. The quantizing of the first tone and of further tones at those frequencies can be made coarser. Fewer bits are needed and a coding gain results. The increased quantizing distortion is allowable if it is masked by the presence of the first tone.

The functioning of the ear is noticeably level dependent and perceptive coders take this into account. However, all signal processing takes

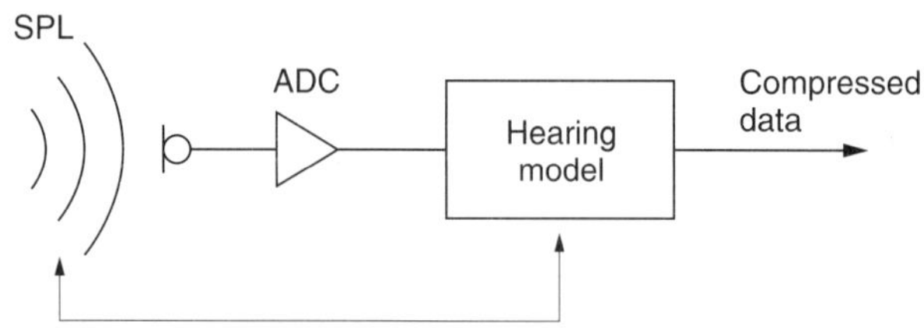

Figure 9.40 Audio coders must be level calibrated so that the psychoacoustic decisions in the coder are based on correct sound pressure levels.

place in the electrical or digital domain with respect to electrical or numerical levels whereas the hearing mechanism operates with respect to true sound pressure level. Figure 9.40 shows that in an ideal system the overall gain of the microphones and ADCs is such that the PCM codes have a relationship with sound pressure which is the same as that assumed by the model in the codec. Equally the overall gain of the DAC and loudspeaker system should be such that the sound pressure levels which the codec assumes are those actually heard. Clearly the gain control of the microphone and the volume control of the reproduction system must be calibrated if the hearing model is to function properly. If, for example, the microphone gain was too low and this was compensated by advancing the loudspeaker gain, the overall gain would be the same but the codec would be fooled into thinking that the sound pressure level was less than it really was and the masking model would not then be appropriate.

The above should come as no surprise as analog audio codecs such as the various Dolby systems have required and implemented line-up procedures and suitable tones. However obvious the need to calibrate coders may be, the degree to which this is recognized in the industry is almost negligible to date and this can only result in suboptimal performance.

9.19 Sound quality measurement

As has been seen, one way in which coding gain is obtained is to requantize sample values to reduce the wordlength. Since the resultant requantizing error is a distortion mechanism it results in energy moving from one frequency to another. The masking model is essential to estimate how audible the effect of this will be. The greater the degree of compression required, the more precise the model must be. If the masking model is inaccurate, then equipment based upon it may produce audible artifacts under some circumstances. Artifacts may also result if the model is not properly implemented. As a result, development of audio compression units requires careful listening tests with a wide range of source material[11,12] and precision loudspeakers. The presence of artifacts at a given compression factor indicates only that performance is below expectations; it does not distinguish between the implementation and the model. If the implementation is verified, then a more detailed model must be sought. Naturally comparative listening tests are only valid if all the codecs have been level calibrated and if the loudspeakers cause less loss of information than any of the codecs, a requirement which is frequently overlooked.

Properly conducted listening tests are expensive and time consuming, and alternative methods have been developed which can be used objectively to evaluate the performance of different techniques. The noise to masking ratio (NMR) is one such measurement.[13] Figure 9.41 shows how NMR is measured. Input audio signals are fed simultaneously to a data-reduction coder and decoder in tandem and to a compensating delay whose length must be adjusted to match the codec delay. At the output of the delay, the coding error is obtained by subtracting the codec output from the original. The original signal is spectrum-analysed into critical bands in order to derive the masking threshold of the input audio, and this is compared with the critical band spectrum of the error. The NMR in each critical band is the ratio between the masking threshold and the quantizing error due to the codec. An average NMR for all bands can be computed. A positive NMR in any band indicates that artifacts are potentially audible. Plotting the average NMR against time is a powerful technique, as with an ideal codec the NMR should be stable with different types of program material. If this is not the case the codec could perform quite differently as a function of the source material. NMR excursions can

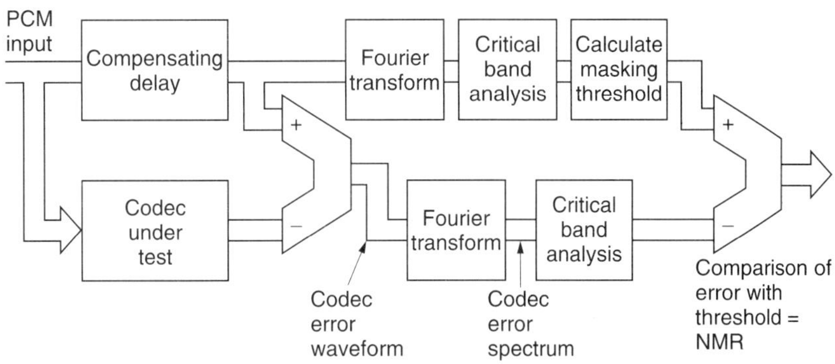

Figure 9.41 The noise-to-masking ratio is derived as shown here.

be correlated with the waveform of the audio input to analyse how the extra noise was caused and to redesign the codec to eliminate it.

Practical systems should have a finite NMR in order to give a degree of protection against difficult signals which have not been anticipated and against the use of post-codec equalization or several tandem codecs which could change the masking threshold. There is a strong argument that devices used for audio production should have a greater NMR than consumer or program delivery devices.

9.20 Audio compression tools

There are many different techniques available for audio compression, each having advantages and disadvantages. Real compressors will combine several techniques or tools in various ways to achieve different combinations of cost and complexity. Here it is intended to examine the tools separately before seeing how they are used in actual compression systems.

The simplest coding tool is companding which is a digital parallel of the noise reducers used in analog tape recording. Figure 9.42(a) shows that in companding the input signal level is monitored. Whenever the input level falls below maximum, it is amplified at the coder. The gain

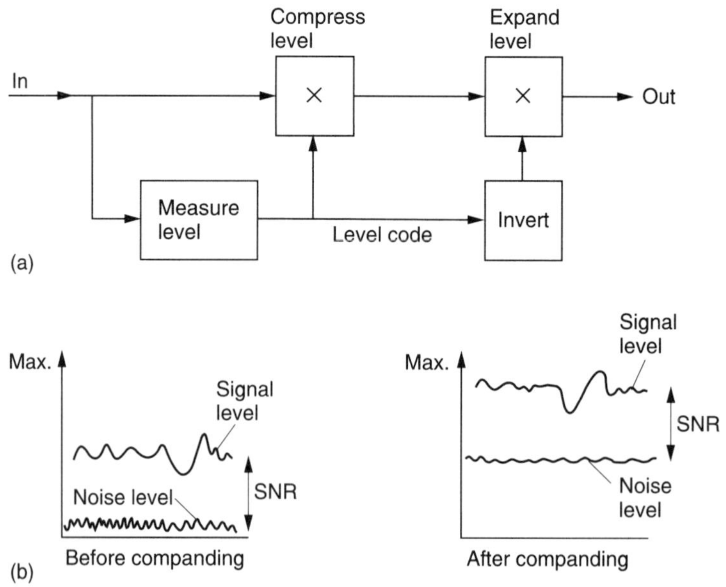

Figure 9.42 Digital companding. In (a) the encoder amplifies the input to maximum level and the decoder attenuates by the same amount. (b) In a companded system, the signal is kept as far as possible above the noise caused by shortening the sample wordlength.

which was applied at the coder is added to the data stream so that the decoder can apply an equal attenuation. The advantage of companding is that the signal is kept as far away from the noise floor as possible. In analog noise reduction this is used to maximize the SNR of a tape recorder, whereas in digital compression it is used to keep the signal level as far as possible above the distortion introduced by various coding steps.

One common way of obtaining coding gain is to shorten the wordlength of samples so that fewer bits need to be transmitted. Figure 9.42(b) shows that when this is done, the distortion will rise by 6 dB for every bit removed. This is because removing a bit halves the number of quantizing intervals which then must be twice as large, doubling the error amplitude.

Clearly if this step follows the compander of (a), the audibility of the distortion will be minimized. As an alternative to shortening the wordlength, the uniform quantized PCM signal can be converted to a non-uniform format. In non-uniform coding, shown at (c), the size of the quantizing step rises with the magnitude of the sample so that the distortion level is greater when higher levels exist.

Companding is a relative of floating-point coding shown in Figure 9.43 where the sample value is expressed as a mantissa and a binary exponent which determines how the mantissa needs to be shifted to have its correct absolute value on a PCM scale. The exponent is the equivalent of the gain setting or scale factor of a compander.

Clearly in floating point the signal-to-noise ratio is defined by the number of bits in the mantissa, and as shown in Figure 9.44, this will vary as a sawtooth function of signal level, as the best value, obtained when the mantissa is near overflow, is replaced by the worst value when the mantissa overflows and the exponent is incremented. Floating-point notation is used within DSP chips as it eases the computational problems involved in handling long wordlengths. For example, when multiplying floating-point numbers, only the mantissae need to be multiplied. The exponents are simply added.

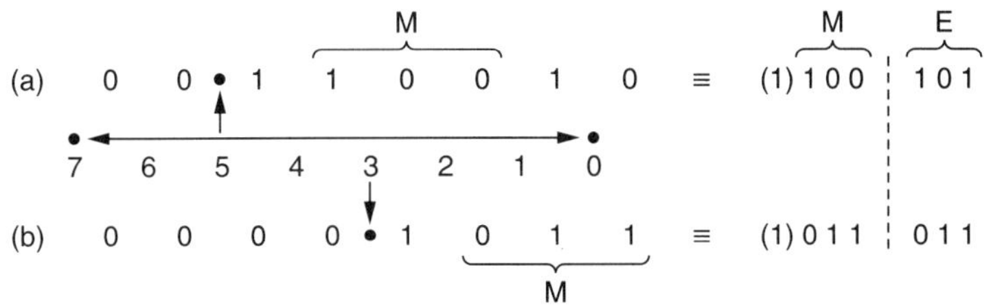

Figure 9.43 In this example of floating-point notation, the radix point can have eight positions determined by the exponent E. The point is placed to the left of the first '1', and the next 4 bits to the right form the mantissa M. As the MSB of the mantissa is always 1, it need not always be stored.

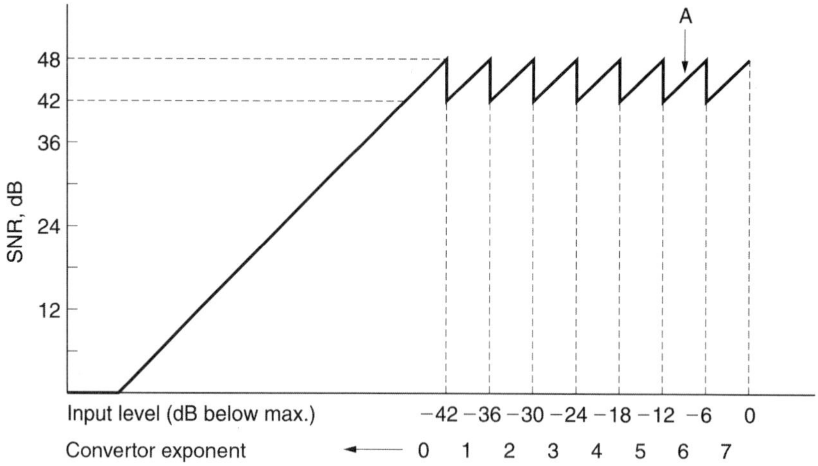

Figure 9.44 In this example of an eight-bit mantissa, three-bit exponent system, the maximum SNR is 6 dB × 8 = 48 dB with maximum input of 0 dB. As input level falls by 6 dB, the convertor noise remains the same, so SNR falls to 42 dB. Further reduction in signal level causes the convertor to shift range (point A in the diagram) by increasing the input analog gain by 6 dB. The SNR is restored, and the exponent changes from 7 to 6 in order to cause the same gain change at the receiver. The noise modulation would be audible in this simple system. A longer mantissa word is needed in practice.

A floating-point system requires one exponent to be carried with each mantissa and this is wasteful because in real audio material the level does not change so rapidly and there is redundancy in the exponents. A better alternative is floating-point block coding, also known as near-instantaneous companding, where the magnitude of the largest sample in a block is used to determine the value of an exponent which is valid for the whole block. Sending one exponent per block requires a lower data rate in than true floating point.[14]

In block coding the requantizing in the coder raises the quantizing error, but it does so over the entire duration of the block. Figure 9.45 shows that if a transient occurs towards the end of a block, the decoder will reproduce the waveform correctly, but the quantizing noise will start at the beginning of the block and may result in a burst of distortion products (also called pre-noise or pre-echo) which is audible before the transient. Temporal masking may be used to make this inaudible. With a 1 ms block, the artifacts are too brief to be heard.

Another solution is to use a variable time window according to the transient content of the audio waveform. When musical transients occur, short blocks are necessary and the coding gain will be low.[15] At other times the blocks become longer allowing a greater coding gain.

Whilst the above systems used alone do allow coding gain, the compression factor has to be limited because little benefit is obtained from masking. This is because the techniques above produce distortion

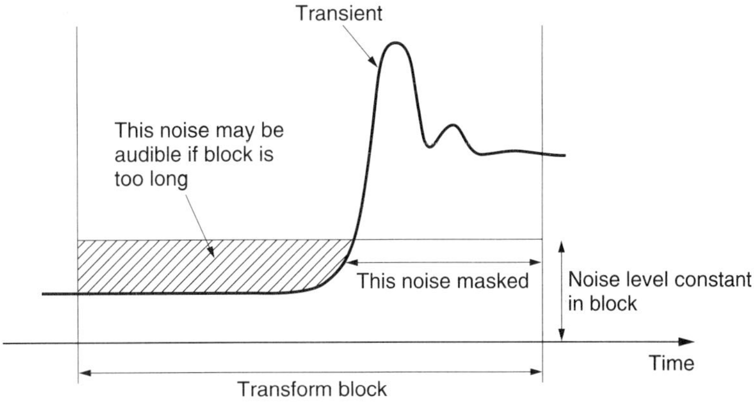

Figure 9.45 If a transient occurs towards the end of a transform block, the quantizing noise will still be present at the beginning of the block and may result in a pre-echo where the noise is audible before the transient.

which may be found anywhere over the entire audio band. If the audio input spectrum is narrow, this noise will not be masked.

Sub-band coding[16] splits the audio spectrum up into many different frequency bands. Once this has been done, each band can be individually processed. In real audio signals many bands will contain lower-level signals than the loudest one. Individual companding of each band will be more effective than broadband companding. Sub-band coding also allows the level of distortion products to be raised selectively so that distortion is only created at frequencies where spectral masking will be effective.

It should be noted that the result of reducing the wordlength of samples in a sub-band coder is often referred to as noise. Strictly, noise is an unwanted signal which is decorrelated from the wanted signal. This is not generally what happens in audio compression. Although the original audio conversion would have been correctly dithered, the linearizing random element in the low-order bits will be some way below the end of the shortened word. If the word is simply rounded to the nearest integer the linearizing effect of the original dither will be lost and the result will be quantizing distortion. As the distortion takes place in a bandlimited system the harmonics generated will alias back within the band. Where the requantizing process takes place in a sub-band, the distortion products will be confined to that sub-band as shown in Figure 9.46. Such distortion is anharmonic.

Following any perceptive coding steps, the resulting data may be further subject to lossless binary compression tools such as prediction, Huffman coding or a combination of both.

Audio is usually considered to be a time-domain waveform as this is what emerges from a microphone. As has been seen in Chapter 3, spectral analysis allows any periodic waveform to be represented by a set of

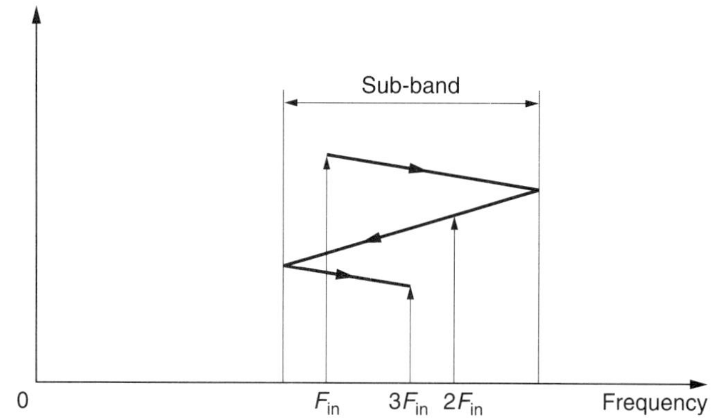

Figure 9.46 Requantizing a band-limited signal causes harmonics which will always alias back within the band.

harmonically related components of suitable amplitude and phase. In theory it is perfectly possible to decompose a periodic input waveform into its constituent frequencies and phases, and to record or transmit the transform. The transform can then be inverted and the original waveform will be precisely recreated.

Although one can think of exceptions, the transform of a typical audio waveform changes relatively slowly much of the time. The slow speech of an organ pipe or a violin string, or the slow decay of most musical sounds allow the rate at which the transform is sampled to be reduced, and a coding gain results. At some frequencies the level will be below maximum and a shorter wordlength can be used to describe the coefficient. Further coding gain will be achieved if the coefficients describing frequencies which will experience masking are quantized more coarsely.

In practice there are some difficulties; real sounds are not periodic, but contain transients which transformation cannot accurately locate in time. The solution to this difficulty is to cut the waveform into short segments and then to transform each individually. The delay is reduced, as is the computational task, but there is a possibility of artifacts arising because of the truncation of the waveform into rectangular time windows. A solution is to use window functions, and to overlap the segments as shown in Figure 9.47. Thus every input sample appears in just two transforms, but with variable weighting depending upon its position along the time axis.

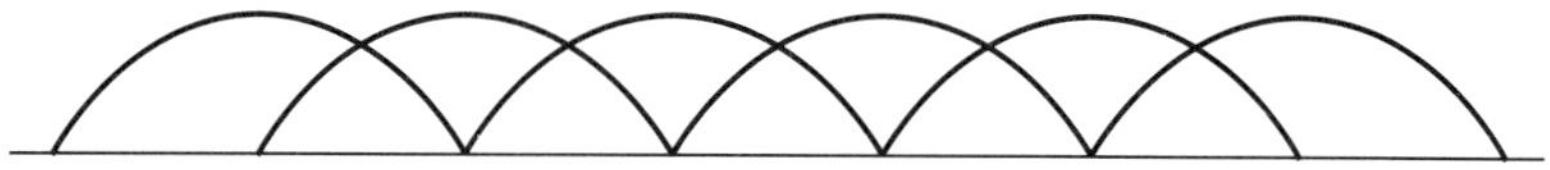

Figure 9.47 Transform coding can only be practically performed on short blocks. These are overlapped using window functions in order to handle continuous waveforms.

The DFT (discrete frequency transform) does not produce a continuous spectrum, but instead produces coefficients at discrete frequencies. The frequency resolution (i.e. the number of different frequency coefficients) is equal to the number of samples in the window. If overlapped windows are used, twice as many coefficients are produced as are theoretically necessary. In addition the DFT requires intensive computation, owing to the requirement to use complex arithmetic to render the phase of the components as well as the amplitude. An alternative is to use discrete cosine transforms (DCT) or the modified discrete cosine transform (MDCT) which has the ability to eliminate the overhead of coefficients due to overlapping the windows and return to the critically sampled domain.[17] Critical sampling is a term which means that the number of coefficients does not exceed the number which would be obtained with non-overlapping windows.

9.21 Sub-band coding

Sub-band coding takes advantage of the fact that real sounds do not have uniform spectral energy. The wordlength of PCM audio is based on the dynamic range required and this is generally constant with frequency although any pre-emphasis will affect the situation. When a signal with an uneven spectrum is conveyed by PCM, the whole dynamic range is occupied only by the loudest spectral component, and all the other components are coded with excessive headroom. In its simplest form, sub-band coding works by splitting the audio signal into a number of frequency bands and companding each band according to its own level. Bands in which there is little energy result in small amplitudes which can be transmitted with short wordlength. Thus each band results in variable-length samples, but the sum of all the sample wordlengths is less than that of PCM and so a coding gain can be obtained. Sub-band coding is not restricted to the digital domain; the analog Dolby noise-reduction systems use it extensively.

The number of sub-bands to be used depends upon what other compression tools are to be combined with the sub-band coding. If it is intended to optimize compression based on auditory masking, the sub-bands should preferably be narrower than the critical bands of the ear, and therefore a large number will be required. This requirement is frequently not met: ISO/MPEG Layers I and II use only 32 sub-bands. Figure 9.48 shows the critical condition where the masking tone is at the top edge of the sub-band. It will be seen that the narrower the sub-band, the higher the requantizing 'noise' that can be masked. The use of an excessive number of sub-bands will, however, raise complexity and the coding delay, as well as risking pre-ringing on transients which may exceed the temporal masking.

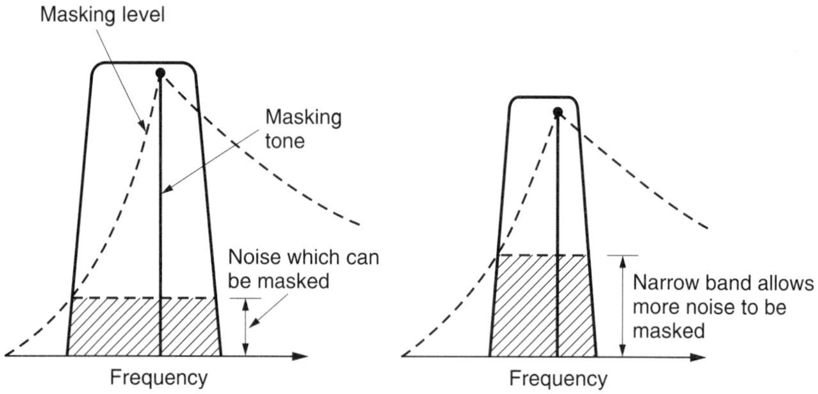

Figure 9.48 In sub-band coding the worst case occurs when the masking tone is at the top edge of the sub-band. The narrower the band, the higher the noise level which can be masked.

The bandsplitting process is complex and requires a lot of computation. One bandsplitting method which is useful is quadrature mirror filtering.[18] The QMF is is a kind of twin FIR filter which converts a PCM sample stream into two sample streams of half the input sampling rate, so that the output data rate equals the input data rate. The frequencies in the lower half of the audio spectrum are carried in one sample stream, and the frequencies in the upper half of the spectrum are carried in the other. Whilst the lower-frequency output is a PCM band-limited representation of the input waveform, the upper frequency output isn't. A moment's thought will reveal that it could not be so because the sampling rate is not high enough. In fact the upper half of the input spectrum has been heterodyned down to the same frequency band as the lower half by the clever use of aliasing. The waveform is unrecognizable, but when heterodyned back to its correct place in the spectrum in an inverse step, the correct waveform will result once more.

Sampling theory states that the sampling rate needed must be at least twice the bandwidth in the signal to be sampled. If the signal is band limited, the sampling rate need only be more than twice the signal

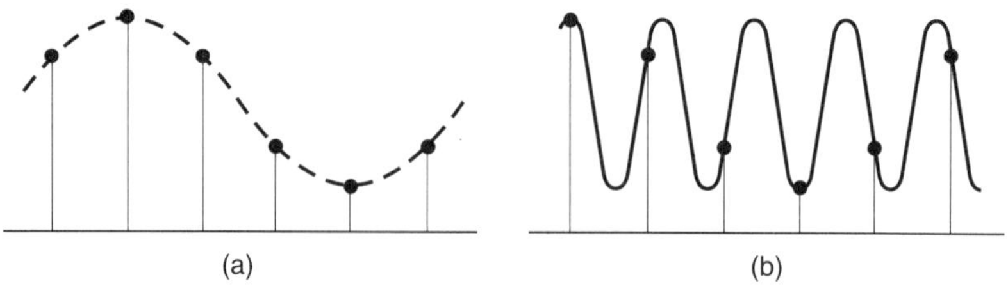

Figure 9.49 The sample stream shown would ordinarily represent the waveform shown in (a), but if it is known that the original signal could exist only between two frequencies then the waveform in (b) must be the correct one. A suitable bandpass reconstruction filter, or synthesis filter, will produce the waveform in (b).

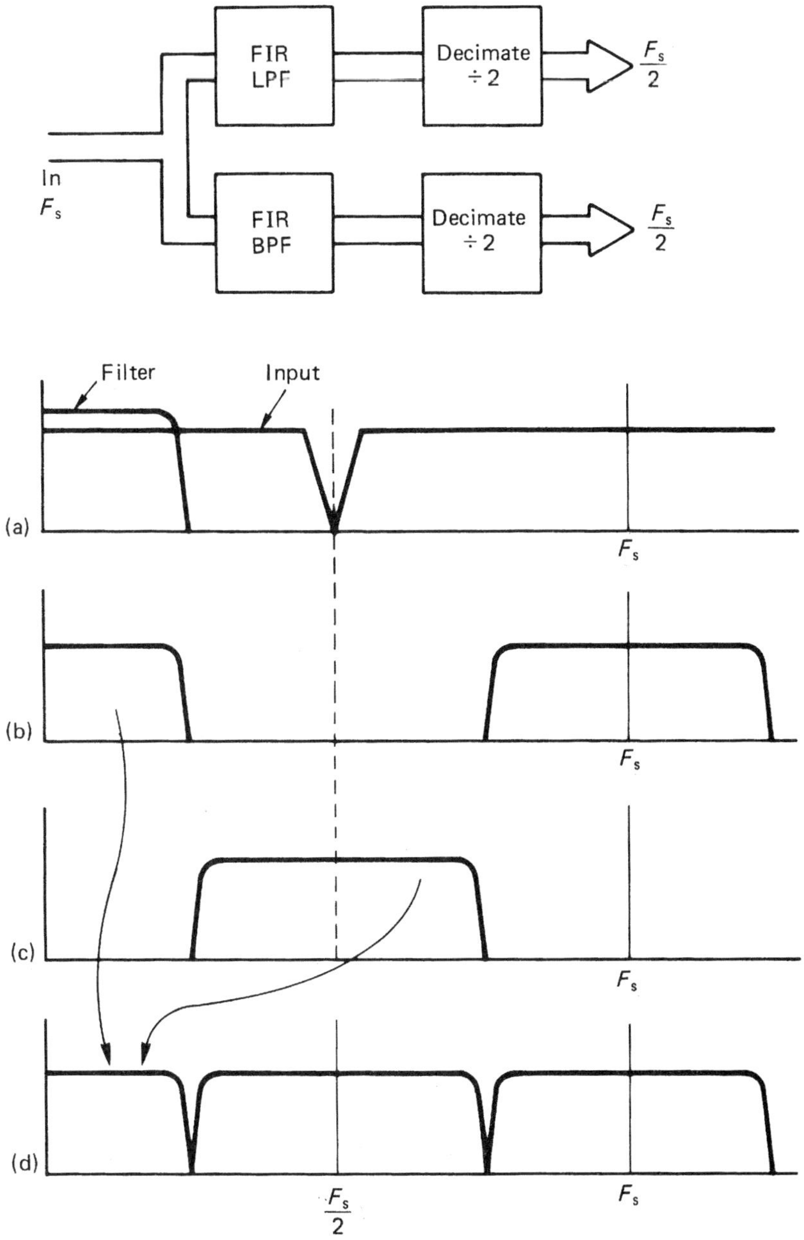

Figure 9.50 The quadrature mirror filter. At (a) the input spectrum has an audio baseband extending up to half the sampling rate. The input is passed through an FIR low-pass filter which cuts off at one-quarter of the sampling rate to give the spectrum shown at (b). The input also passes in parallel through a second FIR filter whose impulse response has been multiplied by a cosinusoidal waveform in order to amplitude-modulate it. The resultant impulse gives the filter a mirror image frequency response shown at (c). The spectra of both (b) and (c) show that both are oversampled by a factor of two because they are half empty. As a result both can be decimated by a factor of two, resulting at (d) in two identical Nyquist-sampled frequency bands of half the original width.

bandwidth not the signal *frequency*. Downsampled signals of this kind can be reconstructed by a reconstruction or *synthesis* filter having a bandpass response rather than a low-pass response. As only signals within the passband can be output, it is clear from Figure 9.49 that the waveform which will result is the original as the intermediate aliased waveform lies outside the passband.

Figure 9.50 shows the operation of a simple QMF. At (a) the input spectrum of the PCM audio is shown, having an audio baseband extending up to half the sampling rate and the usual lower sideband extending down from there up to the sampling frequency. The input is passed through a FIR low-pass filter which cuts off at one quarter of the sampling rate to give the spectrum shown at (b). The input also passes in parallel through a second FIR filter which is physically identical, but the coefficients are different. The impulse response of the FIR LPF is multiplied by a cosinusoidal waveform which amplitude modulates it. The resultant impulse gives the filter a frequency response shown at (c). This is a mirror image of the LPF response. If certain criteria are met, the overall frequency response of the two filters is flat. The spectra of both (b) and (c) show that both are oversampled by a factor of 2 because they are half-empty. As a result both can be decimated by a factor of two, which is the equivalent of dropping every other sample. In the case of the lower half of the spectrum, nothing remarkable happens. In the case of the upper half of the spectrum, it has been resampled at half the original frequency as shown at (d). The result is that the upper half of the audio spectrum aliases or heterodynes to the lower half.

An inverse QMF will recombine the bands into the original broadband signal. It is a feature of a QMF/inverse QMF pair that any energy near the band edge which appears in both bands due to inadequate selectivity in the filtering reappears at the correct frequency in the inverse filtering process provided that there is uniform quantizing in all the sub-bands. In practical coders, this criterion is not met, but any residual artifacts are sufficiently small to be masked.

The audio band can be split into as many bands as required by cascading QMFs in a tree. However, each stage can only divide the input spectrum in half. In some coders certain sub-bands will have passed through one splitting stage more than others and will be half their bandwidth.[19] A delay is required in the wider sub-band data for time alignment.

A simple quadrature mirror is computationally intensive because sample values are calculated which are later decimated or discarded, and an alternative is to use polyphase pseudo-QMF filters[20] or wave filters[21] in which the filtering and decimation process is combined. Only wanted sample values are computed. A polyphase QMF operates in a manner not unlike the polyphase operation of a FIR filter used for interpolation in

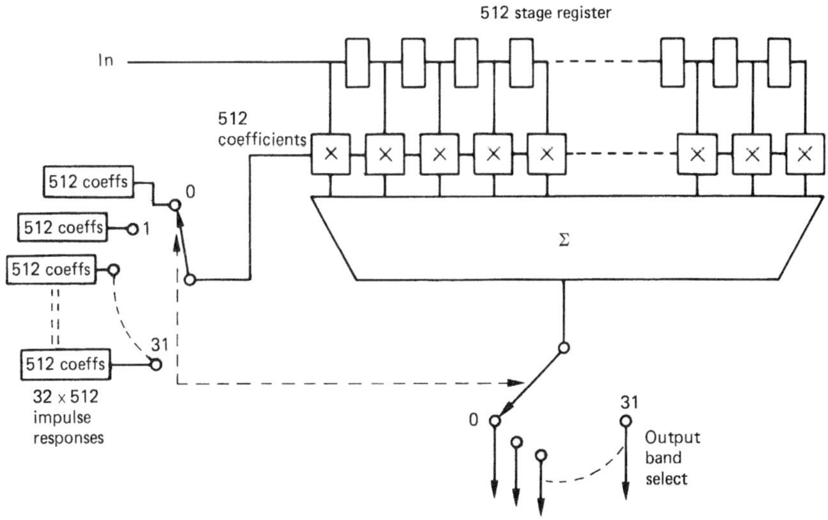

Figure 9.51 In polyphase QMF the same input samples are subject to computation using coefficient sets in many different time-multiplexed phases. The decimation is combined with the filtering so only wanted values are computed.

sampling rate conversion (see section 3.6). In a polyphase filter a set of samples is shifted into position in the transversal register and then these are multiplied by different sets of coefficients and accumulated in each of several phases to give the value of a number of different samples between input samples. In a polyphase QMF, the same approach is used.

Figure 9.51 shows an example of a 32-band polyphase QMF having a 512-sample window. With 32 sub-bands, each band will be decimated to $^1/_{32}$ of the input sampling rate. Thus only one sample in 32 will be retained after the combined filter/decimate operation. The polyphase QMF only computes the value of the sample which is to be retained in each sub-band. The filter works in 32 different phases with the same samples in the transversal register. In the first phase, the coefficients will describe the impulse response of a low-pass filter, the so-called prototype filter, and the result of 512 multiplications will be accumulated to give a single sample in the first band. In the second phase the coefficients will be obtained by multiplying the impulse response of the prototype filter by a cosinusoid at the centre frequency of the second band. Once more 512 multiply accumulates will be required to obtain a single sample in the second band. This is repeated for each of the 32 bands, and in each case a different centre frequency is obtained by multiplying the prototype impulse by a different modulating frequency. Following 32 such computations, 32 output samples, one in each band, will have been computed. The transversal register then shifts 32 samples and the process repeats.

The principle of the polyphase QMF is not so different from the techniques used to compute a frequency transform and effectively blurs the distinction between sub-band coding and transform coding.

The QMF technique is restricted to bands of equal width. It might be thought that this is a drawback because the critical bands of the ear are non-uniform. In fact this is only a problem when very high compression factors are required. In all cases it is the masking model of hearing which must have correct critical bands. This model can then be used to determine how much masking and therefore coding gain is possible within the actual sub-bands used. Uniform width sub-bands will not be able to obtain as much masking as bands which are matched to critical bands, but for many applications the additional coding gain is not worth the added filter complexity.

9.22 Compression formats

There are numerous formats intended for audio compression and these can be divided into international standards and proprietary designs.

The ISO (International Standards Organization) and the IEC (International Electrotechnical Commission) recognized that compression would have an important part to play and in 1988 established the ISO/IEC/MPEG (Moving Picture Experts Group) to compare and assess various coding schemes in order to arrive at an international standard for compressing video. The terms of reference were extended the same year to include audio and the MPEG/Audio group was formed.

MPEG audio coding is used for DAB (digital audio broadcasting) and for the audio content of digital television broadcasts to the DVB standard.

In the USA, it has been decided to use an alternative compression technique for the audio content of ATSC (Advanced Television Systems Committee) digital television broadcasts. This is the AC-3[22] system developed by Dolby Laboratories. The MPEG transport stream structure has also been standardized to allow it to carry AC-3 coded audio. The digital video disk can also carry AC-3 or MPEG audio coding.

Other popular proprietary codes include apt-X which is a mild compression factor/short delay codec and ATRAC which is the codec used in MiniDisc.

9.23 MPEG Audio compression

The subject of audio compression was well advanced when the MPEG/Audio group was formed. As a result it was not necessary for the group to produce *ab initio* codecs because existing work was considered suitable. As part of the Eureka 147 project, a system known as MUSICAM[23] (Masking pattern adapted Universal Sub-band Integrated Coding And Multiplexing) was developed jointly by CCETT in France, IRT in Germany and Philips in the Netherlands. MUSICAM was designed to be suitable for DAB (digital audio broadcasting).

As a parallel development, the ASPEC[24] (Adaptive Spectral Perceptual Entropy Coding) system was developed from a number of earlier systems as a joint proposal by AT&T Bell Labs, Thomson, the Fraunhofer Society and CNET. ASPEC was designed for use at high compression factors to allow audio transmission on ISDN.

These two systems were both fully implemented by July 1990 when comprehensive subjective testing took place at the Swedish Broadcasting Corporation.[11,25,26] As a result of these tests, the MPEG/Audio group combined the attributes of both ASPEC and MUSICAM into a standard[27,28] having three levels of complexity and performance.

These three different levels, which are known as *layers*, are needed because of the number of possible applications. Audio coders can be operated at various compression factors with different quality expectations. Stereophonic classical music requires different quality criteria from monophonic speech. The complexity of the coder will be reduced with a smaller compression factor. For moderate compression, a simple codec will be more cost effective. On the other hand, as the compression factor is increased, it will be necessary to employ a more complex coder to maintain quality.

MPEG Layer I is a simplified version of MUSICAM which is appropriate for the mild compression applications at low cost. Layer II is identical to MUSICAM and is used for DAB and for the audio content of DVB digital television broadcasts. Layer III is a combination of the best features of ASPEC and MUSICAM and is mainly applicable to telecommunications where high compression factors are required.

At each layer, MPEG Audio coding allows input sampling rates of 32, 44.1 and 48 kHz and supports output bit rates of 32, 48, 56, 64, 96, 112, 128, 192, 256 and 384 kbits/s. The transmission can be mono, dual channel (e.g. bilingual), or stereo. Another possibility is the use of joint stereo mode in which the audio becomes mono above a certain frequency. This allows a lower bit rate with the obvious penalty of reduced stereo fidelity.

The layers of MPEG Audio coding (I, II and III) should not be confused with the MPEG-1 and MPEG-2 television coding standards. MPEG-1 and MPEG-2 flexibly define a range of systems for video and audio coding, whereas the layers define types of audio coding.

The earlier MPEG-1 standard compresses audio and video into about 1.5 Mbits/s. The audio coding of MPEG-1 may be used on its own to

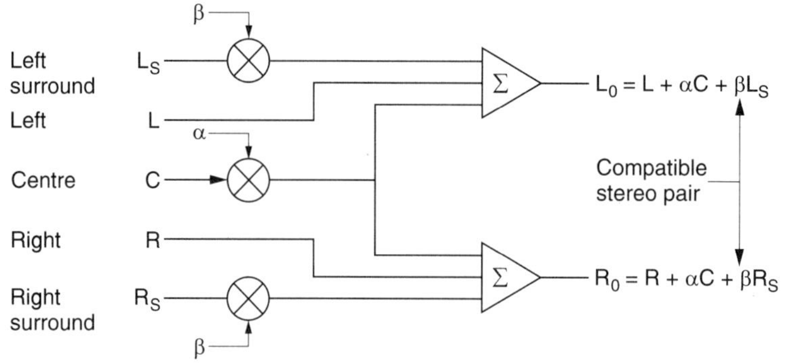

Figure 9.52 To allow compatibility with two-channel systems, a stereo signal pair is derived from the five surround signals in this manner.

encode one or two channels at bit rates up to 448 kbits/s. MPEG-2 allows the number of channels to increase to five: Left, Right, Centre, Left surround, Right surround and Subwoofer. In order to retain reverse compatibility with MPEG-1, the MPEG-2 coding converts the five-channel input to a compatible two-channel signal, L_0, R_0, by matrixing[29] as shown in Figure 9.52. The data from these two channels are encoded in a standard MPEG-1 audio frame, and this is followed in MPEG-2 by an ancillary data frame which an MPEG-1 decoder will ignore. The ancillary frame contains data for another three audio channels. Figure 9.53 shows that there are eight modes in which these three channels can be obtained. The encoder will select the mode which gives the least data rate for the prevailing distribution of energy in the input channels. An MPEG-2 decoder will extract those three channels in addition to the MPEG-1 frame and then recover all five original channels by an inverse matrix which is steered by mode select bits in the bitstream.

L	R	C
L	R_S	C
L_S	R	C
L_S	R_S	C
L	R	L_S
L	R	R_S
L_S	R	R_S
L	R_S	L_S

Figure 9.53 In addition to sending the stereo compatible pair, one of the above combinations of signals can be sent. In all cases a suitable inverse matrix can recover the original five channels.

The requirement for MPEG-2 Audio to be backward compatible with MPEG-1 audio coding was essential for some markets, but did compromise the performance because certain useful coding tools could not be used. Consequently the MPEG Audio group evolved a multi-channel standard which was not backward compatible because it incorporated additional coding tools in order to achieve higher performance. This came to be known as MPEG-2 AAC (advanced audio coding).

9.24 MPEG Layer I

Figure 9.54 shows a block diagram of a Layer I coder which is a simplified version of that used in the MUSICAM system. A polyphase filter divides the audio spectrum into 32 equal sub-bands. The output of the filter bank is critically sampled. In other words the output data rate is no higher than the input rate because each band has been heterodyned to a frequency range from zero upwards.

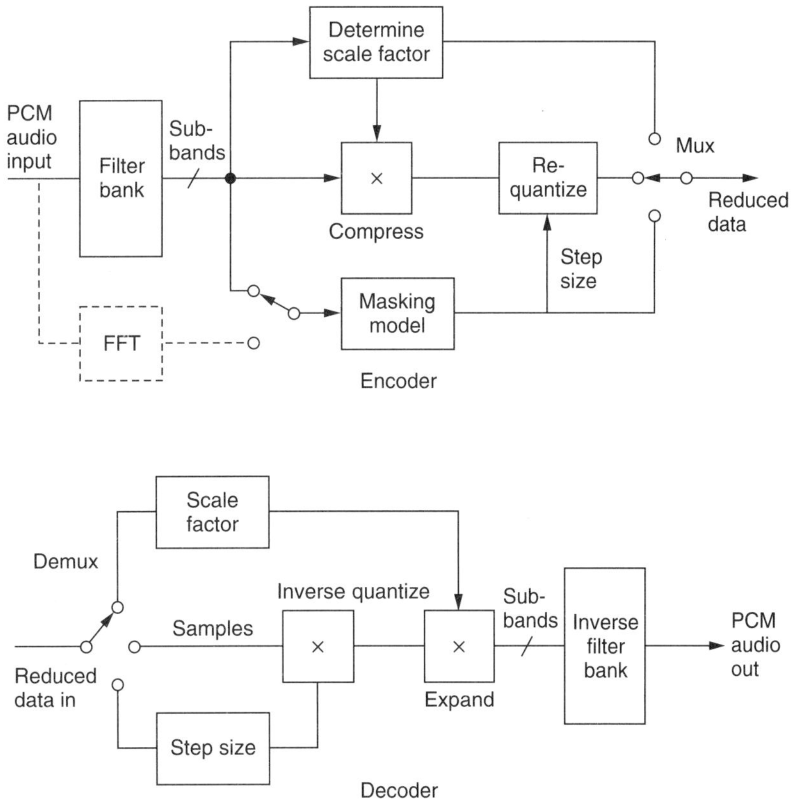

Figure 9.54 A simple sub-band coder. The bit allocation may come from analysis of the sub-band energy, or, for greater reduction, from a spectral analysis in a side chain.

Sub-band compression takes advantage of the fact that real sounds do not have uniform spectral energy. The wordlength of PCM audio is based on the dynamic range required and this is generally constant with frequency although any pre-emphasis will affect the situation. When a signal with an uneven spectrum is conveyed by PCM, the whole dynamic range is occupied only by the loudest spectral component, and all the other components are coded with excessive headroom. In its simplest form, sub-band coding works by splitting the audio signal into a number of frequency bands and companding each band according to its own level. Bands in which there is little energy result in small amplitudes which can be transmitted with short wordlength. Thus each band results in variable-length samples, but the sum of all the sample wordlengths is less than that of the PCM input and so a degree of coding gain can be obtained.

A Layer I compliant encoder, i.e. one whose output can be understood by a standard decoder, can be made which does no more than this. Provided the syntax of the bitstream is correct, the decoder is not concerned with how the coding decisions were made. However, higher compression factors require the distortion level to be increased and this should only be done if it is known that the distortion products will be masked. Ideally the sub-bands should be narrower than the critical bands of the ear. Figure 9.48 showed the critical condition where the masking tone is at the top edge of the sub-band. The use of an excessive number of sub-bands will, however, raise complexity and the coding delay. The use of 32 equal sub-bands in MPEG Layers I and II is a compromise. Efficient polyphase bandsplitting filters can only operate with equal-width sub-bands and the result, in an octave-based hearing model, is that sub-bands are too wide at low frequencies and too narrow at high frequencies.

To offset the lack of accuracy in the sub-band filter a parallel fast Fourier transform is used to drive the masking model. The standard suggests masking models, but compliant bitstreams can result from other models. In Layer I a 512-point FFT is used. The output of the FFT is used to determine the masking threshold which is the sum of all masking sources. Masking sources include at least the threshold of hearing which may locally be raised by the frequency content of the input audio. The degree to which the threshold is raised depends on whether the input audio is sinusoidal or atonal (broadband, or noise-like).

In the case of a sine wave, the magnitude and phase of the FFT at each frequency will be similar from one window to the next, whereas if the sound is atonal the magnitude and phase information will be chaotic.

The masking threshold is a effectively a graph of just noticeable noise as a function of frequency. Figure 9.55(a) shows an example. The masking threshold is calculated by convolving the FFT spectrum with the cochlea

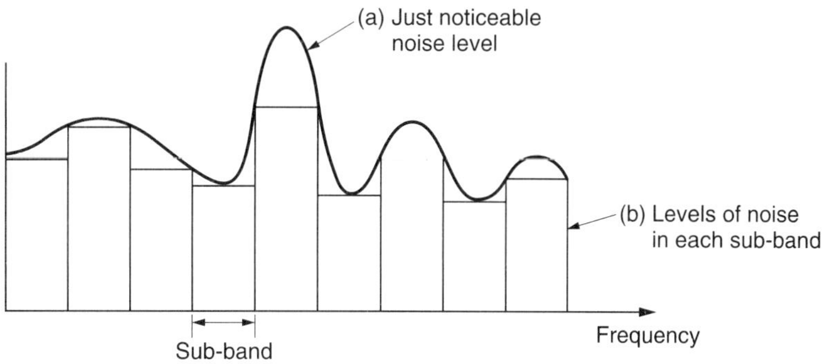

Figure 9.55 A continuous curve (a) of the just-noticeable noise level is calculated by the masking model. The levels of noise in each sub-band (b) must be set so as not to exceed the level of the curve.

spreading function (see section 5.6) with corrections for tonality. The level of the masking threshold cannot fall below the absolute masking threshold which is the threshold of hearing.

The masking threshold is then superimposed on the actual frequencies of each sub-band so that the allowable level of distortion in each can be established. This is shown in Figure 9.55(b).

Constant size input blocks are used, containing 384 samples. At 48 kHz, 384 samples corresponds to a period of 8 ms. After the sub-band filter each band contains 12 samples per block. The block size is too long to avoid the pre-masking phenomenon of Figure 9.45. Consequently the masking model must ensure that heavy requantizing is not used in a block which contains a large transient following a period of quiet. This can be done by comparing parameters of the current block with those of the previous block as a significant difference will indicate transient activity.

The samples in each sub-band block or *bin* are companded according to the peak value in the bin. A six-bit scale factor is used for each sub-band which applies to all 12 samples. The gain step is 2 dB and so with a six-bit code over 120 dB of dynamic range is available.

A fixed output bit rate is employed, and as there is no buffering the size of the coded output block will be fixed. The wordlengths in each bin will have to be such that the sum of the bits from all the sub-bands equals the size of the coded block. Thus some sub-bands can have long wordlength coding if others have short wordlength coding. The process of determining the requantization step size, and hence the wordlength in each sub-band, is known as bit allocation. In Layer I all sub-bands are treated in the same way and fourteen different requantization classes are used. Each one has an odd number of quantizing intervals so that all codes are referenced to a precise zero level.

Where masking takes place, the signal is quantized more coarsely until the distortion level is raised to just below the masking level. The coarse quantization requires shorter wordlengths and allows a coding gain. The bit allocation may be iterative as adjustments are made to obtain an equal NMR across all sub-bands. If the allowable data rate is adequate, a positive NMR will result and the decoded quality will be optimal. However, at lower bit rates and in the absence of buffering a temporary increase in bit rate is not possible. The coding distortion cannot be masked and the best the encoder can do is to make the (negative) NMR equal across the spectrum so that artifacts are not emphasized unduly in any one sub-band. It is possible that in some sub-bands there will be no data at all, either because such frequencies were absent in the program material or because the encoder has discarded them to meet a low bit rate.

The samples of differing wordlength in each bin are then assembled into the output coded block. Unlike a PCM block, which contains samples of fixed wordlength, a coded block contains many different wordlengths which may vary from one sub-band to the next. In order to deserialize the block into samples of various wordlength and demultiplex the samples into the appropriate frequency bins, the decoder has to be told what bit allocations were used when it was packed, and some synchronizing means is needed to allow the beginning of the block to be identified.

The compression factor is determined by the bit-allocation system. It is trivial to change the output block size parameter to obtain a different compression factor. If a larger block is specified, the bit allocator simply iterates until the new block size is filled. Similarly the decoder need only deserialize the larger block correctly into coded samples and then the expansion process is identical except for the fact that expanded words contain less noise. Thus codecs with varying degrees of compression are available which can perform different bandwidth/performance tasks with the same hardware.

Figure 9.56(a) shows the format of the Layer I elementary stream. The frame begins with a sync pattern to reset the phase of deserialization, and a header which describes the sampling rate and any use of pre-emphasis. Following this is a block of 32 four-bit allocation codes. These specify the wordlength used in each sub-band and allow the decoder to deserialize the sub-band sample block. This is followed by a block of 32 six-bit scale factor indices, which specify the gain given to each band during companding. The last block contains 32 sets of 12 samples. These samples vary in wordlength from one block to the next, and can be from 0 to fifteen bits long. The deserializer has to use the 32 allocation information codes to work out how to deserialize the sample block into individual samples of variable length.

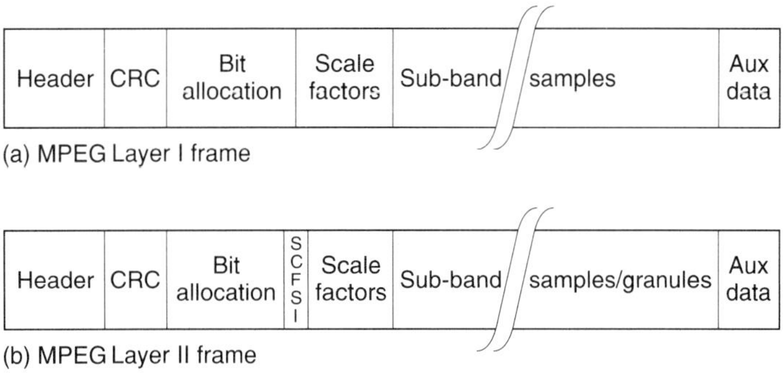

Figure 9.56 (a) The MPEG Layer I data frame has a simple structure. (b) in the Layer II frame, the compression of the scale factors requires the additional SCFSI code described in the text.

The Layer I MPEG decoder is shown in Figure 9.57. The elementary stream is deserialized using the sync pattern and the variable length samples are assembled using the allocation codes. The variable length samples are returned to fifteen-bit wordlength by adding zeros. The scale factor indices are then used to determine multiplication factors used to return the waveform in each sub-band to its original amplitude. The 32 sub-band signals are then merged into one spectrum by the synthesis filter. This is a set of bandpass filters which heterodynes every sub-band to the correct place in the audio spectrum and then adds them to produce the audio output.

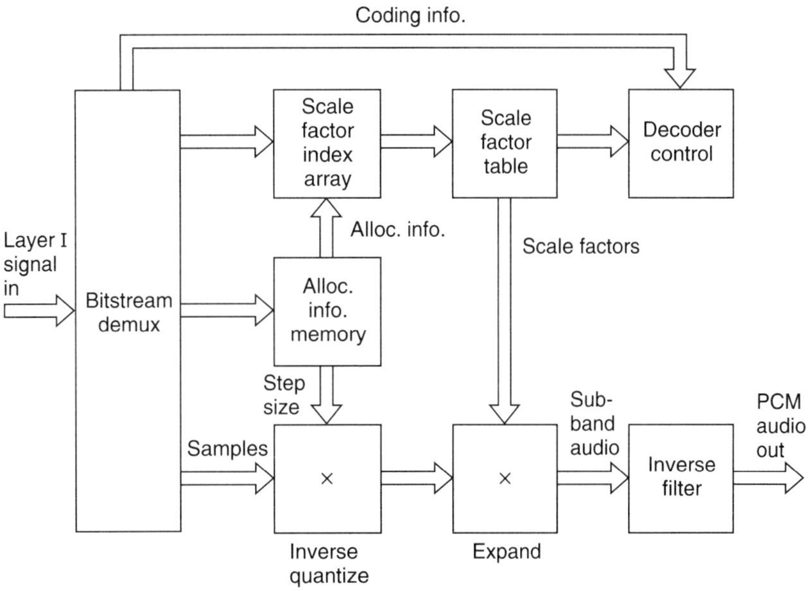

Figure 9.57 The Layer I decoder. See text for details.

9.25 MPEG Layer II

MPEG Layer II audio coding is identical to MUSICAM. The same 32-band filterbank and the same block companding scheme as Layer I is used. In order to give the masking model better spectral resolution, the side chain FFT has 1024 points. The FFT drives the masking model which may be the same as is suggested for Layer I. The block length is increased to 1152 samples. This is three times the block length of Layer I, corresponding to 24 ms at 48 kHz.

Figure 9.56(b) shows the Layer II elementary stream structure. Following the sync pattern the bit-allocation data are sent. The requantizing process of Layer II is more complex than in Layer I. The sub-bands are categorized into three frequency ranges, low, medium and high, and the requantizing in each range is different. Low-frequency samples can be quantized into fifteen different wordlengths, mid-frequencies into seven different wordlengths and high frequencies into only three different wordlengths. Accordingly the bit-allocation data uses words of four, three and two bits depending on the sub-band concerned. This reduces the amount of allocation data to be sent. In each case one extra combination exists in the allocation code. This is used to indicate that no data are being sent for that sub-band.

The 1152 sample block of Layer II is divided into three blocks of 384 samples so that the same companding structure as Layer I can be used. The 2 dB step size in the scale factors is retained. However, not all the scale factors are transmitted, because they contain a degree of redundancy. In real program material, the difference between scale factors in successive blocks in the same band exceeds 2 dB less than 10 per cent of the time. Layer II coders analyse the set of three successive scale factors in each sub-band. On a stationary program, these will be the same and only one scale factor out of three is sent. As the transient content increases in a given sub-band, two or three scale factors will be sent. A two-bit code known as SCFSI (scale factor select information) must be sent to allow the decoder to determine which of the three possible scale factors have been sent for each sub-band. This technique effectively halves the scale factor bit rate.

As for Layer I, the requantizing process always uses an odd number of steps to allow a true centre zero step. In long wordlength codes this is not a problem, but when three, five or nine quantizing intervals are used, binary is inefficient because some combinations are not used. For example, five intervals need a three-bit code having eight combinations leaving three unused.

The solution is that when three, five or nine-level coding is used in a sub-band, sets of three samples are encoded into a *granule*. Figure 9.58 shows how granules work. Continuing the example of five quantizing

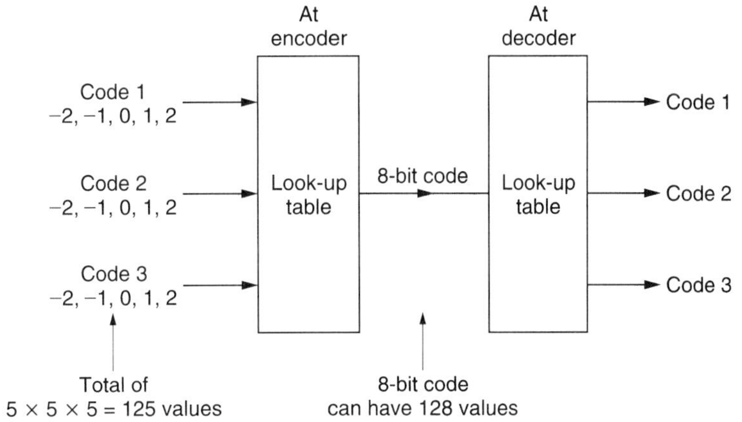

Figure 9.58 Codes having ranges smaller than a power of two are inefficient. Here three codes with a range of five values which would ordinarily need 3 × 3 bits can be carried in a single eight-bit word.

intervals, each sample could have five different values, therefore all combinations of three samples could have 125 different values. As 128 values can be sent with a seven-bit code, it will be seen that this is more efficient than coding the samples separately as three five-level codes would need nine bits. The three requantized samples are used to address a look-up table which outputs the granule code. The decoder can establish that granule coding has been used by examining the bit-allocation data.

The requantized samples/granules in each sub-band, bit-allocation data, scale factors and scale factor select codes are multiplexed into the output bit stream.

The Layer II decoder is shown in Figure 9.59. This is not much more complex than the Layer I decoder. The demultiplexing will separate the sample data from the side information. The bit-allocation data will

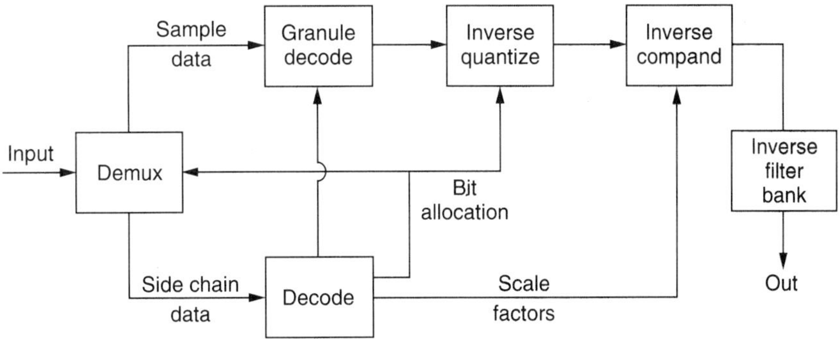

Figure 9.59 A Layer II decoder is slightly more complex than the Layer I decoder because of the need to decode granules and scale factors.

specify the wordlength or granule size used so that the sample block can be deserialized and the granules decoded. The scale factor select information will be used to decode the compressed scale factors to produce one scale factor per block of 384 samples. Inverse quantizing and inverse sub-band filtering takes place as for Layer I.

9.26 MPEG Layer III

Layer III is the most complex layer, and is only really necessary when the most severe data rate constraints must be met. It is also known as MP3 in its application of music delivery over the Internet. It is a transform code based on the ASPEC system with certain modifications to give a degree of commonality with Layer II. The original ASPEC coder used a direct MDCT on the input samples. In Layer III this was modified to use a hybrid transform incorporating the existing polyphase 32-band QMF of Layers I and II and retaining the block size of 1152 samples. In Layer 3, the 32 sub-bands from the QMF are further processed by a critically sampled MDCT.

The windows overlap by two to one. Two window sizes are used to reduce pre-echo on transients. The long window works with 36 sub-band samples corresponding to 24 ms, at 48 kHz and resolves eighteen different frequencies, making 576 frequencies altogether. Coding products are spread over this period which is acceptable in stationary material but not in the vicinity of transients. In this case the window length is reduced to 8 ms. Twelve sub-band samples are resolved into six different frequencies making a total of 192 frequencies. This is the Heisenberg inequality: by increasing the time resolution by a factor of three, the frequency resolution has fallen by the same factor.

Figure 9.60 shows the available window types. In addition to the long and short symmetrical windows there is a pair of transition windows, know as start and stop windows which allow a smooth transition between the two window sizes. In order to use critical sampling, MDCTs must resolve into a set of frequencies which is a multiple of four. Switching between 576 and 192 frequencies allows this criterion to be met. Note that an 8 ms window is still too long to eliminate pre-echo. Pre-echo is eliminated using buffering. The use of a short window minimizes the size of the buffer needed.

Layer III provides a suggested (but not compulsory) pychoacoustic model which is more complex than that suggested for Layers I and II, primarily because of the need for window switching. Pre-echo is associated with the entropy in the audio rising above the average value and this can be used to switch the window size. The perceptive model is used to take advantage of the high-frequency resolution available from

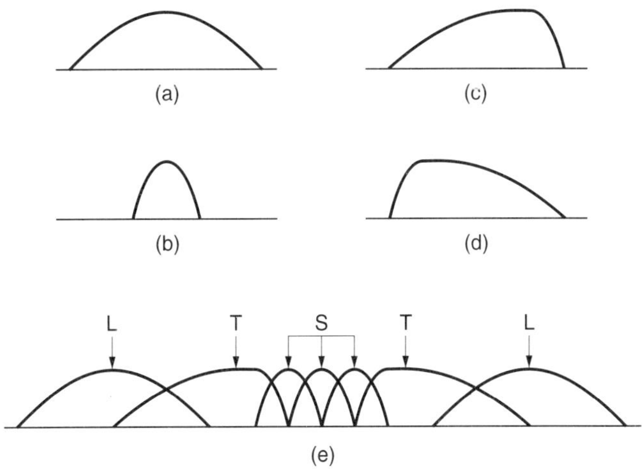

Figure 9.60 The window functions of Layer III coding. At (a) is the normal long window, whereas (b) shows the short window used to handle transients. Switching between window sizes requires transition windows (c) and (d). An example of switching using transition windows is shown in (e).

the DCT which allows the noise floor to be shaped much more accurately than with the 32 sub-bands of Layers I and II. Although the MDCT has high frequency resolution, it does not carry the phase of the waveform in an identifiable form and so is not useful for discriminating between tonal and atonal inputs. As a result a side FFT which gives conventional amplitude and phase data is still required to drive the masking model.

Non-uniform quantizing is used, in which the quantizing step size becomes larger as the magnitude of the coefficient increases. The quantized coefficients are then subject to Huffman coding. This is a technique where the most common code values are allocated the shortest wordlength. Layer III also has a certain amount of buffer memory so that pre-echo can be avoided during entropy peaks despite a constant output bit rate.

Figure 9.61 shows a Layer III encoder. The output from the sub-band filter is 32 continuous band-limited sample streams. These are subject to 32 parallel MDCTs. The window size can be switched individually in each sub-band as required by the characteristics of the input audio. The parallel FFT drives the masking model which decides on window sizes as well as producing the masking threshold for the coefficient quantizer. The distortion control loop iterates until the available output data capacity is reached with the most uniform NMR.

The available output capacity can vary owing to the presence of the buffer. Figure 9.62 shows that the buffer occupancy is fed back to the quantizer. During stationary program material, the buffer contents are deliberately run down by slight coarsening of the quantizing. The buffer

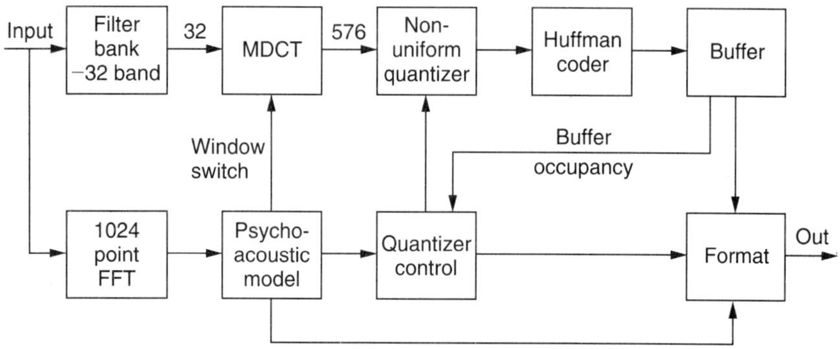

Figure 9.61 The Layer III coder. Note the connection between the buffer and the quantizer which allows different frames to contain different amounts of data.

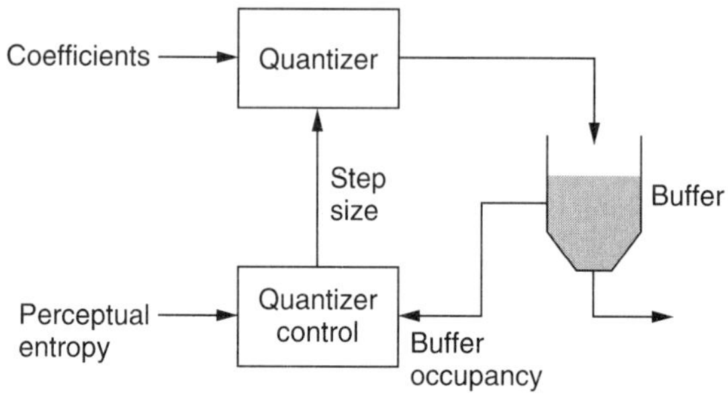

Figure 9.62 The variable rate coding of Layer III. An approaching transient via the perceptual entropy signal causes the coder to quantize more heavily in order to empty the buffer. When the transient arrives, the quantizing can be made more accurate and the increased data can be accepted by the buffer.

empties because the output rate is fixed but the input rate has been reduced. When a transient arrives, the large coefficients which result can be handled by filling the buffer, avoiding raising the output bit rate whilst also avoiding the pre-echo which would result if the coefficients were heavily quantized.

In order to maintain synchronism between encoder and decoder in the presence of buffering, headers and side information are sent synchronously at frame rate. However, the position of boundaries between the main data blocks which carry the coefficients can vary with respect to the position of the headers in order to allow a variable frame size. Figure 9.63 shows that the frame begins with an unique sync pattern which is followed by the side information. The side information contains a parameter called *main data begin* which specifies where the main data for the present frame began in the transmission. This parameter allows the decoder to find the coefficient block in the decoder buffer. As the frame headers are at fixed locations, the main data blocks may be interrupted by the headers.

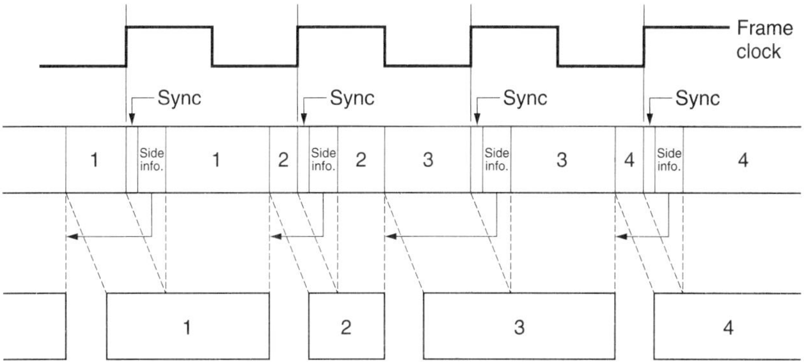

Figure 9.63 In Layer III, the logical frame rate is constant and is transmitted by equally spaced sync patterns. The data blocks do not need to coincide with sync. A pointer after each sync pattern specifies where the data block starts. In this example block 2 is smaller whereas 1 and 3 have enlarged.

9.27 MPEG-2 AAC

The MPEG standards system subsequently developed an enhanced system known as advanced audio coding (AAC).[30,31] This was intended to be a standard which delivered the highest possible performance using newly developed tools that could not be used in any standard which was backward compatible. AAC also forms the core of the audio coding of MPEG-4.

AAC supports up to 48 audio channels with default support of monophonic, stereo and 5.1 channel (3/2) audio. The AAC concept is based on a number of coding tools known as *modules* which can be combined in different ways to produce bitstreams at three different profiles.

The main profile requires the most complex encoder which makes use of all the coding tools. The low-complexity (LC) profile omits certain tools and restricts the power of others to reduce processing and memory requirements. The remaining tools in LC profile coding are identical to those in main profile such that a main profile decoder can decode LC profile bitstreams.

The scaleable sampling rate (SSR) profile splits the input audio into four equal frequency bands each of which results in a self-contained bitstream. A simple decoder can decode only one, two or three of these bitstreams to produce a reduced bandwidth output. Not all the AAC tools are available to SSR profile.

The increased complexity of AAC allows the introduction of lossless coding tools. These allow a lower bit rate for the same or improved quality at a given bit rate where the reliance on lossy coding is reduced. There is greater attention given to the interplay between time-domain and frequency-domain precision in the human hearing system.

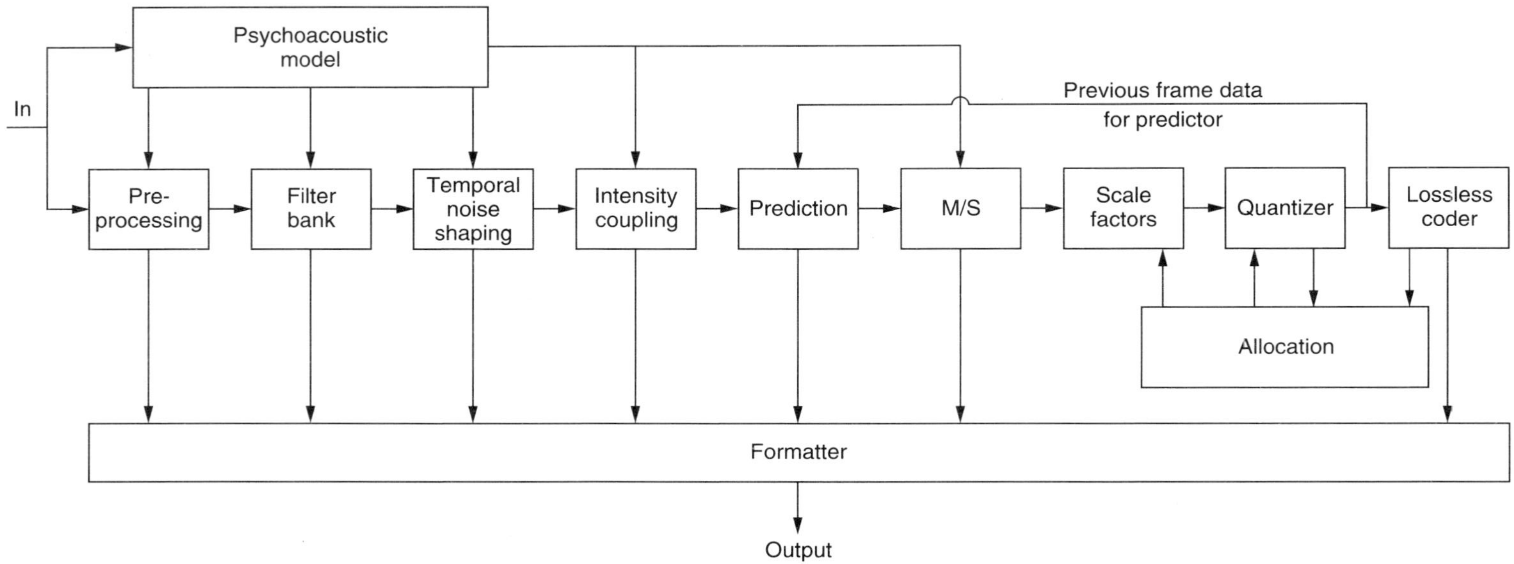

Figure 9.64 The AAC encoder. Signal flow is from left to right whereas side-chain data flow is vertical.

Figure 9.64 shows a block diagram of an AAC main profile encoder. The audio signal path is straight through the centre. The formatter assembles any side-chain data along with the coded audio data to produce a compliant bitstream. The input signal passes to the filter bank and the perceptual model in parallel.

The filter bank consists of a 50 per cent overlapped critically sampled MDCT which can be switched between block lengths of 2048 and 256 samples. At 48 kHz the filter allows resolutions of 23 Hz and 21 ms or 187 Hz and 2.6 ms. As AAC is a multichannel coding system, block length switching cannot be done indiscriminately as this would result in loss of block phase between channels. Consequently if short blocks are selected, the coder will remain in short block mode for integer multiples of eight blocks. This is illustrated in Figure 9.65 which also shows the use of transition windows between the block sizes as was done in Layer III.

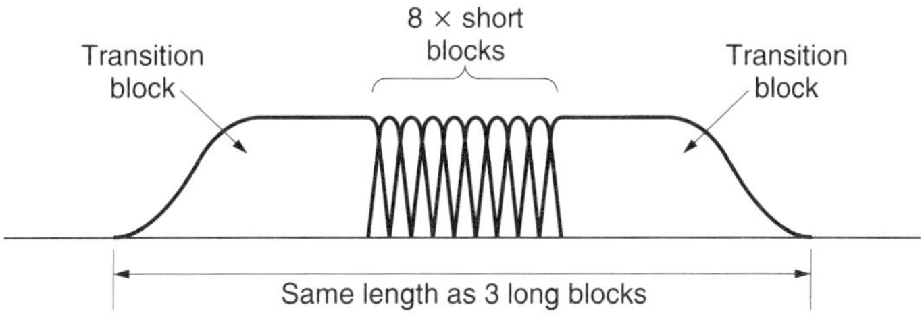

Figure 9.65 In AAC short blocks must be used in multiples of 8 so that the long block phase is undisturbed. This keeps block synchronism in multichannel systems.

The shape of the window function interferes with the frequency selectivity of the MDCT. In AAC it is possible to select either a sine window or a Kaiser–Bessel derived (KBD) window as a function of the input audio spectrum. As was seen in Chapter 3, filter windows allow different compromises between bandwidth and rate of roll-off. The KBD window rolls off later but is steeper and thus gives better rejection of frequencies more than about 200 Hz apart, whereas the sine window rolls off earlier but less steeply and so gives better rejection of frequencies less than 70 Hz.

Following the filter bank is the intra-block predictive coding module. When enabled this module finds redundancy between the coefficients within one transform block. In Chapter 3 the concept of transform duality was introduced, in which a certain characteristic in the frequency domain would be accompanied by a dual characteristic in the time domain and vice versa. Figure 9.66 shows that in the time domain, predictive coding works well on stationary signals but fails on transients. The dual of this characteristic is that in the frequency domain, predictive coding works well on transients but fails on stationary signals.

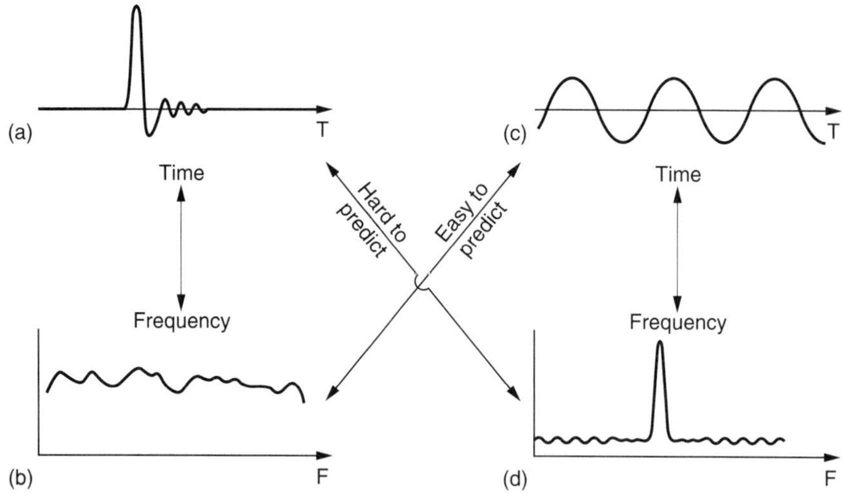

Figure 9.66 Transform duality suggests that predictability will also have a dual characteristic. A time predictor will not anticipate the transient in (a), whereas the broad spectrum of signal (a), shown in (b), will be easy for a predictor advancing down the frequency axis. In contrast, the stationary signal (c) is easy for a time predictor, whereas in the spectrum of (c) shown at (d) the spectral spike will not be predicted.

Equally, a predictive coder working in the time domain produces an error spectrum which is related to the input spectrum. The dual of this characteristic is that a predictive coder working in the frequency domain produces a prediction eror which is related to the input time domain signal.

This explains the use of the term *temporal noise shaping* (TNS) used in the AAC documents.[32] When used during transients, the TNS module produces distortion which is time-aligned with the input such that pre-echo is avoided. The use of TNS also allows the coder to use longer blocks more of the time. This module is responsible for a significant amount of the increased performance of AAC.

Figure 9.67 shows that the coefficients in the transform block are serialized by a commutator. This can run from the lowest frequency to the highest or in reverse. The prediction method is a conventional forward predictor structure in which the result of filtering a number of earlier coefficients (20 in main profile) is used to predict the current one. The prediction is subtracted from the actual value to produce a prediction error or residual which is transmitted. At the decoder, an identical predictor produces the same prediction from earlier coefficient values and the error in this is cancelled by adding the residual.

Following the intra-block prediction, an optional module known as the intensity/coupling stage is found. This is used for very low bit rates where spatial information in stereo and surround formats is discarded to keep down the level of distortion. Effectively over at least part of the

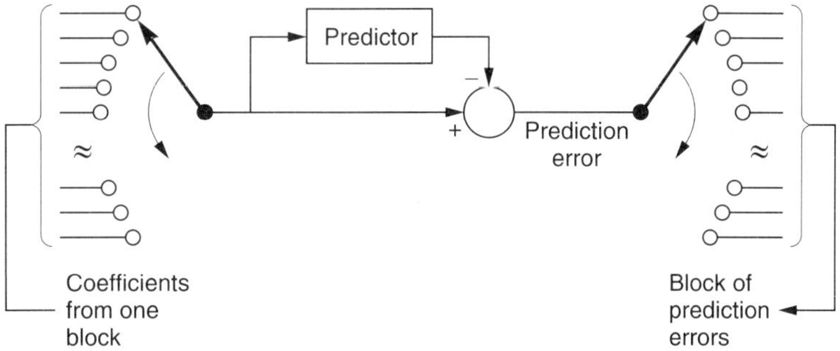

Figure 9.67 Predicting along the frequency axis is performed by running along the coefficients in a block and attempting to predict the value of the current coefficient from the values of some earlier ones. The prediction error is transmitted.

spectrum a mono signal is transmitted along with amplitude codes which allow the signal to be panned in the spatial domain at the decoder.

The next stage is the inter-block prediction module. Whereas the intra-block predictor is most useful on transients, the inter-block predictor module explores the redundancy between successive blocks on stationary signals.[33] This prediction only operates on coefficients below 16 kHz. For each DCT coefficient in a given block, the predictor uses the quantized coefficients from the same locations in two previous blocks to estimate the present value. As before, the prediction is subtracted to produce a residual which is transmitted. Note that the use of quantized coefficients to drive the predictor is necessary because this is what the decoder will have to do.

The predictor is adaptive and calculates its own coefficients from the signal history. The decoder uses the same algorithm so that the two predictors always track. The predictors run all the time whether prediction is enabled or not in order to keep the prediction coefficients adapted to the signal.

Audio coefficients are associated into sets known as *scale factor bands* for later companding. Within each scale factor band inter-block prediction can be turned on or off depending on whether a coding gain results.

Protracted use of prediction makes the decoder prone to bit errors and drift and removes decoding entry points from the bitstream. Consequently the prediction process is reset cyclically. The predictors are assembled into groups of 30 and after a certain number of a frames a different group is reset until all have been reset. Predictor reset codes are transmitted in the side data. Reset will also occur if short frames are selected.

In stereo and 3/2 surround formats there is less redundancy because the signals also carry spatial information. The effecting of masking may be up to 20 dB less when distortion products are at a different location in the stereo image from the masking sounds. As a result stereo signals require much higher bit rate than two mono channels, particularly on transient material which is rich in spatial clues.

In some cases a better result can be obtained by converting the signal to a mid-side (M/S) or sum/difference format before quantizing. In surround sound the M/S coding can be applied to the front L/R pair and the rear L/R pair of signals.

The M/S format can be selected on a block-by-block basis for each scale factor band.

Next comes the lossy stage of the coder where distortion is selectively introduced as a function of frequency as determined by the masking threshold. This is done by a combination of amplification and requantizing. As mentioned, coefficients (or residuals) are grouped into scale factor bands. As Figure 9.68 shows, the number of coefficients varies in order to

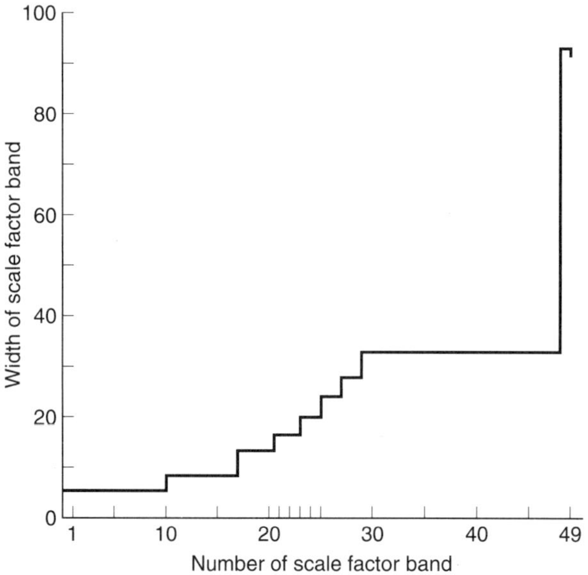

Figure 9.68 In AAC the fine-resolution coefficients are grouped together to form scale factor bands. The size of these varies to loosely mimic the width of critical bands.

divide the coefficients into approximate critical bands. Within each scale factor band, all coefficients will be multiplied by the same scale factor prior to requantizing. Coefficients which have been multiplied by a large scale factor will suffer less distortion by the requantizer whereas those which have been multiplied by a small scale factor will have more distortion. Using scale factors, the psychoacoustic model can shape the distortion as a function of frequency so that it remains masked. The scale factors allow gain control in 1.5 dB steps over a dynamic range equivalent to twenty-four-bit PCM and are transmitted as part of the side data so that the decoder can re-create the correct magnitudes.

The scale factors are differentially coded with respect to the first one in the block and the differences are then Huffman coded.

The requantizer uses non-uniform steps which give better coding gain and has a range of ±8191. The global step size (which applies to all scale factor bands) can be adjusted in 1.5 dB steps. Following requantizing the coefficients are Huffman coded.

There are many ways in which the coder can be controlled and any that results in a compliant bitstream is acceptable although the highest performance may not be reached. The requantizing and scale factor stages will need to be controlled in order to make best use of the available bit rate and the buffering. This is non-trivial because of the use of Huffman coding after the requantizer makes it impossible to predict the exact amount of data which will result from a given step size. This means that the process must iterate.

Whatever bit rate is selected, a good encoder will produce consistent quality by selecting window sizes, intra- or inter-frame prediction and using the buffer to handle entropy peaks. This suggests a connection between buffer occupancy and the control system. The psychoacoustic model will analyse the incoming audio entropy and during periods of average entropy it will empty the buffer by slightly raising the quantizer step size so that the bit rate entering the buffer falls. By running the buffer down, the coder can temporarily support a higher bit rate to handle transients or difficult material.

Simply stated, the scale factor process is controlled so that the distortion spectrum has the same shape as the masking threshold and the quantizing step size is controlled to make the level of the distortion spectrum as low as possible within the allowed bit rate. If the bit rate allowed is high enough, the distortion products will be masked.

9.28 Dolby AC-3

Dolby AC-3[22] is in fact a family of transform coders based on time-domain aliasing cancellation (TDAC) which allow various compromises between coding delay and bit rate to be used. In the modified discrete cosine transform (MDCT), windows with 50 per cent overlap are used. Thus twice as many coefficients as necessary are produced. These are sub-sampled by a factor of two to give a critically sampled transform, which results in potential aliasing in the frequency domain. However, by making a slight change to the transform, the alias products in the second half of a given window are equal in size but of opposite polarity to the alias products in the first half of the next window, and so will be cancelled on reconstruction. This is the principle of TDAC.

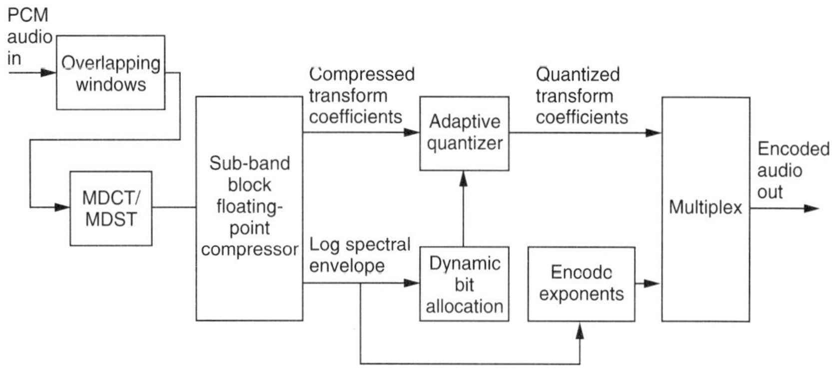

Figure 9.69 Block diagram of the Dolby AC-3 coder. See text for details.

Figure 9.69 shows the generic block diagram of the AC-3 coder. Input audio is divided into 50 per cent overlapped blocks of 512 samples. These are subject to a TDAC transform which uses alternate modified sine and cosine transforms. The transforms produce 512 coefficients per block, but these are redundant and after the redundancy has been removed there are 256 coefficients per block.

The input waveform is constantly analysed for the presence of transients and if these are present the block length will be halved to prevent pre-noise. This halves the frequency resolution but doubles the temporal resolution.

The coefficients have high frequency resolution and are selectively combined in sub-bands which approximate the critical bands. Coefficients in each sub-band are normalized and expressed in floating-point block notation with common exponents. The exponents in fact represent the logarithmic spectral envelope of the signal and can be used to drive the perceptive model which operates the bit allocation. The mantissae of the transform coefficients are then requantized according to the bit allocation.

The output bitstream consists of the requantized coefficients and the log spectral envelope in the shape of the exponents. There is a great deal of redundancy in the exponents. In any block, only the first exponent, corresponding to the lowest frequency, is transmitted absolutely. Remaining coefficients are transmitted differentially. Where the input has a smooth spectrum the exponents in several bands will be the same and the differences will then be zero. In this case exponents can be grouped using flags.

Further use is made of temporal redundancy. An AC-3 sync frame contains six blocks. The first block of the frame contains absolute exponent data, but where stationary audio is encountered, successive blocks in the frame can use the same exponents.

The receiver uses the log spectral envelope to deserialize the mantissae of the coefficients into the correct wordlengths. The highly redundant exponents are decoded starting with the lowest frequency coefficient in the first block of the frame and adding differences to create the remainder. The exponents are then used to return the coefficients to fixed-point notation. Inverse transforms are then computed, followed by a weighted overlapping of the windows to obtain PCM data.

References

1. MPEG Video Standard: ISO/IEC 13818–2: Information technology – generic coding of moving pictures and associated audio information: Video (1996) (aka ITU-T Rec. H-262 (1996))
2. Huffman, D.A., A method for the construction of minimum redundancy codes. *Proc. IRE*, **40**, 1098–1101 (1952)
3. Le Gall, D., MPEG: a video compression standard for multimedia applications. *Communications of the ACM*, **34**, No.4, 46–58 (1991)
4. ISO/IEC JTC1/SC29/WG11 MPEG, International standard ISO 11172 'Coding of moving pictures and associated audio for digital storage media up to 1.5 Mbits/s' (1992)
5. ISO Joint Photographic Experts Group standard JPEG-8-R8
6. Wallace, G.K., Overview of the JPEG (ISO/CCITT) still image compression standard. ISO/JTC1/SC2/WG8 N932 (1989)
7. Stone, J. and Wilkinson, J., Concatenation of video compression systems. Presented at 137th SMPTE Tech. Conf. New Orleans (1995)
8. Wells, N.D., The ATLANTIC project: Models for programme production and distribution. *Proc. Euro. Conf. Multimedia Applications Services and Techniques (ECMAST)*, 243–253 (1996)
9. Werner, O., Drift analysis and drift reduction for multiresolution hybrid video coding. *Image Communication*, **8**, 387–409 (1996)
10. Knee, M.J. and Wells, N.D., Seamless concatenation – a 21st century dream. Presented at Int. Television. Symp. Montreux (1997)
11. Grewin, C. and Ryden, T., Subjective assessments on low bit-rate audio codecs. *Proc. 10th. Int. Audio Eng. Soc. Conf.*, 91–102, New York: Audio Engineering Society (1991)
12. Gilchrist, N.H.C., Digital sound: the selection of critical programme material and preparation of the recordings for CCIR tests on low bit rate codecs. *BBC Res. Dept. Rep.*, RD 1993/1
13. Colomes, C. and Faucon, G., A perceptual objective measurement system (POM) for the quality assessment of perceptual codecs. Presented at 96th Audio Eng. Soc. Conv. Amsterdam (1994), Preprint No. 3801 (P4.2)
14. Caine, C.R., English, A.R. and O'Clarey, J.W.H. NICAM-3: near-instantaneous companded digital transmission for high-quality sound programmes. *J. IERE*, **50**, 519–530 (1980)
15. Davidson, G.A. and Bosi, M., AC-2: High quality audio coding for broadcast and storage. *Proc. 46th Ann. Broadcast Eng. Conf.*, Las Vegas, 98–105 (1992)
16. Crochiere, R.E., Sub-band coding. *Bell System Tech. J.*, **60**, 1633–1653 (1981)
17. Princen, J.P., Johnson, A. and Bradley, A.B., Sub-band/transform coding using filter bank designs based on time domain aliasing cancellation. *Proc. ICASSP*, 2161–2164 (1987)
18. Jayant, N.S. and Noll, P., *Digital Coding of Waveforms: Principles and applications to speech and video*, Englewood Cliffs, NJ: Prentice Hall (1984)
19. Theile, G., Stoll, G. and Link, M., Low bit rate coding of high quality audio signals: an introduction to the MASCAM system. *EBU Tech. Review*, No. 230, 158–181 (1988)

20. Chu, P.L., Quadrature mirror filter design for an arbitrary number of equal bandwidth channels. *IEEE Trans. ASSP*, **ASSP-33**, 203–218 (1985)
21. Fettweis, A., Wave digital filters: Theory and practice. *Proc. IEEE*, **74**, 270–327 (1986)
22. Davis, M.F., The AC-3 multichannel coder. Presented at 95th AES Conv., Preprint 2774
23. Wiese, D., MUSICAM: flexible bitrate reduction standard for high quality audio. Presented at Digital Audio Broadcasting Conference, London (March 1992)
24. Brandenburg, K., ASPEC coding. *Proc. 10th. Audio Eng. Soc. Int. Conf.* 81–90, New York: Audio Engineering Society (1991)
25. ISO/IEC JTC1/SC2/WG11 N0030: MPEG/AUDIO test report, Stockholm (1990)
26. ISO/IEC JTC1/SC2/WG11 MPEG 91/010: The SR report on: The MPEG/AUDIO subjective listening test. Stockholm (1991)
27. ISO/IEC JTC1/SC29/WG11 MPEG, International standard ISO 11172–3 'Coding of moving pictures and associated audio for digital storage media up to 1.5 Mbits/s, Part 3: Audio' (1992)
28. Brandenburg, K. and Stoll, G., ISO-MPEG-1 Audio: A generic standard for coding of high quality audio. *JAES*, **42**, 780–792 (1994)
29. Bonicel, P. *et al.*, A real time ISO/MPEG2 multichannel decoder. Presented at 96th Audio Eng. Soc. Conv. (1994), Preprint No. 3798 (P3.7)4.30
30. ISO/IEC 13818–7, Information Technology – Generic coding of moving pictures and associated audio, Part 7: Advanced audio coding (1997)
31. Bosi, M. *et al*, ISO/IEC MPEG-2 Advanced Audio Coding. *JAES*, **45**, 789–814 (1997)
32. Herre, J. and Johnston, J.D., Enhancing the performance of perceptual audio coders by using temporal noise shaping (TNS). Presented at 101st AES Conv., Preprint 4384 (1996)
33. Fuchs, H., Improving MPEG audio coding by backward adaptive linear stereo prediction. Presented at 99th AES Conv., Preprint 4086 (1995)

10

Digital coding principles

Recording and communication are quite different tasks, but they have a great deal in common. Digital transmission consists of converting data into a waveform suitable for the path along which it is to be sent. Digital recording is basically the process of recording a digital transmission waveform on a suitable medium. In this chapter the fundamentals of digital recording and transmission are introduced along with descriptions of the coding and error-correction techniques used in practical applications.

10.1 Introduction

Data can be recorded on many different media and conveyed using many forms of transmission. The generic term for the path down which the information is sent is the *channel*. In a transmission application, the channel may be a point-to-point cable, a network stage or a radio link. In a recording application the channel will include the record head, the medium and the replay head.

In digital circuitry there is a great deal of noise immunity because the signal has only two states, which are widely separated compared with the amplitude of noise. In both digital recording and transmission this is not always the case. In magnetic recording, noise immunity is a function of track width and reduction of the working signal-to-noise ratio of a digital track allows the same information to be carried in a smaller area of the medium, improving economy of operation. In broadcasting, the noise immunity is a function of the transmitter power and reduction of working SNR allows lower power to be used with consequent economy. These reductions also increase the random error rate, but, as was seen in

Chapter 1, an error-correction system may already be necessary in a practical system and it is simply made to work harder.

In real channels, the signal may *originate* with discrete states which change at discrete times, but the channel will treat it as an analog waveform and so it will not be *received* in the same form. Various frequency-dependent loss mechanisms will reduce the amplitude of the signal. Noise will be picked up as a result of stray electric fields or magnetic induction and in radio receivers the circuitry will contribute some noise. As a result the received voltage will have an infinitely varying state along with a degree of uncertainty due to the noise. Different frequencies can propagate at different speeds in the channel; this is the phenomenon of group delay. An alternative way of considering group delay is that there will be frequency-dependent phase shifts in the signal and these will result in uncertainty in the timing of pulses.

In digital circuitry, the signals are generally accompanied by a separate clock signal which reclocks the data to remove jitter as was shown in Chapter 1. In contrast, it is generally not feasible to provide a separate clock in recording and transmission applications. In the transmission case, a separate clock line would not only raise cost, but is impractical because at high frequency it is virtually impossible to ensure that the clock cable propagates signals at the same speed as the data cable except over short distances. In the recording case, provision of a separate clock track is impractical at high density because mechanical tolerances cause phase errors between the tracks. The result is the same; timing differences between parallel channels which are known as skew.

The solution is to use a self-clocking waveform and the generation of this is a further essential function of the coding process. Clearly if data bits are simply clocked serially from a shift register in so-called direct recording or transmission this characteristic will not be obtained. If all the data bits are the same, for example all zeros, there is no clock when they are serialized.

It is not the channel which is digital; instead the term describes the way in which the received signals are *interpreted*. When the receiver makes discrete decisions from the input waveform it attempts to reject the uncertainties in voltage and time. The technique of channel coding is one where transmitted waveforms are restricted to those which still allow the receiver to make discrete decisions despite the degradations caused by the analog nature of the channel.

10.2 Types of transmission channel

Transmission can be by electrical conductors, radio or optical fibre. Although these appear to be completely different, they are in fact just different examples of electromagnetic energy travelling from one place to another. If the energy is made time-variant, information can be carried.

Electromagnetic energy propagates in a manner which is a function of frequency, and our partial understanding requires it to be considered as electrons, waves or photons so that we can predict its behaviour in given circumstances.

At DC and at the low frequencies used for power distribution, electromagnetic energy is called electricity and needs to be transported completely inside conductors. It has to have a complete circuit to flow in, and the resistance to current flow is determined by the cross-sectional area of the conductor. The insulation around the conductor and the spacing between the conductors has no effect on the ability of the conductor to pass current. At DC an inductor appears to be a short circuit, and a capacitor appears to be an open circuit.

As frequency rises, resistance is exchanged for impedance. Inductors display increasing impedance with frequency, capacitors show falling impedance. Electromagnetic energy increasingly tends to leave the conductor. The first symptom is the skin effect: the current flows only in the outside layer of the conductor effectively causing the resistance to rise.

As the energy is starting to leave the conductors, the characteristics of the space between them become important. This determines the impedance. A change of impedance causes reflections in the energy flow and some of it heads back towards the source. Constant-impedance cables with fixed conductor spacing are necessary, and these must be suitably terminated to prevent reflections. The most important characteristic of the insulation is its thickness as this determines the spacing between the conductors.

As frequency rises still further, the energy travels less in the conductors and more in the insulation between them, and their composition becomes important and they begin to be called dielectrics. A poor dielectric like PVC absorbs high-frequency energy and attenuates the signal. So-called low-loss dielectrics such as PTFE are used, and one way of achieving low loss is to incorporate as much air into the dielectric as possible by making it in the form of a foam or extruding it with voids.

High-frequency signals can also be propagated without a medium, and are called radio. As frequency rises further the electromagnetic energy is termed light which can also travel without a medium, but can be also be guided through a suitable medium. Figure 10.1(a) shows an early type of optical fibre in which total internal reflection is used to guide the light. It will be seen that the length of the optical path is a function of the angle at which the light is launched. Thus at the end of a long fibre sharp transitions would be smeared by this effect. Later optical fibres are made with a radially varying refractive index such that light diverging from the

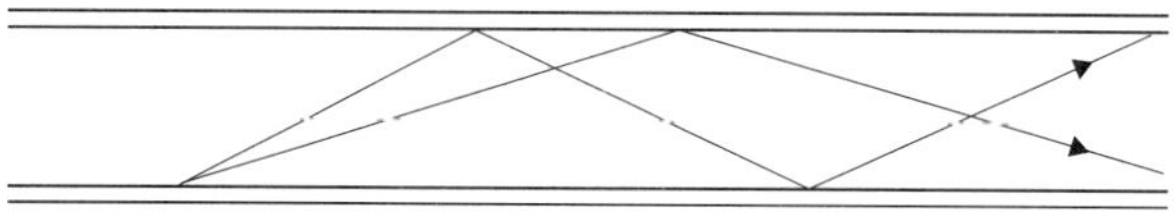
(a)

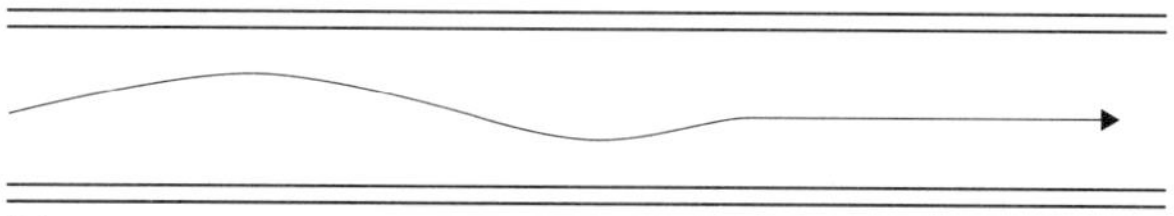
(b)

Figure 10.1 (a) Early optical fibres operated on internal reflection, and signals could take a variety of paths along the fibre, hence multi-mode. (b) Later fibres used graduated refractive index which meant that light was guided to the centre of the fibre and only one mode was possible.

axis is automatically refracted back into the fibre. Figure 10.1(b) shows that in single-mode fibre light can travel only down one path and so the smearing of transitions is avoided.

10.3 Transmission lines

Frequency-dependent behaviour is the most important factor in deciding how best to harness electromagnetic energy flow for information transmission. It is obvious that the higher the frequency, the greater the possible information rate, but in general, losses increase with frequency, and flat frequency response is elusive. The best that can be managed is that over a narrow band of frequencies, the response can be made reasonably constant with the help of equalization. Unfortunately raw data when serialized have an unconstrained spectrum. Runs of identical bits can produce frequencies much lower than the bit rate would suggest. One of the essential steps in a transmission system is to modify the spectrum of the data into something more suitable.

At moderate bit rates, say a few megabits per second, and with moderate cable lengths, say a few metres, the dominant effect will be the capacitance of the cable due to the geometry of the space between the conductors and the dielectric between. The capacitance behaves under these conditions as if it were a single capacitor connected across the signal. The effect of the series source resistance and the parallel capacitance is that signal edges or transitions are turned into exponential curves as the capacitance is effectively being charged and discharged through the source impedance.

As cable length increases, the capacitance can no longer be lumped as if it were a single unit; it has to be regarded as being distributed along the

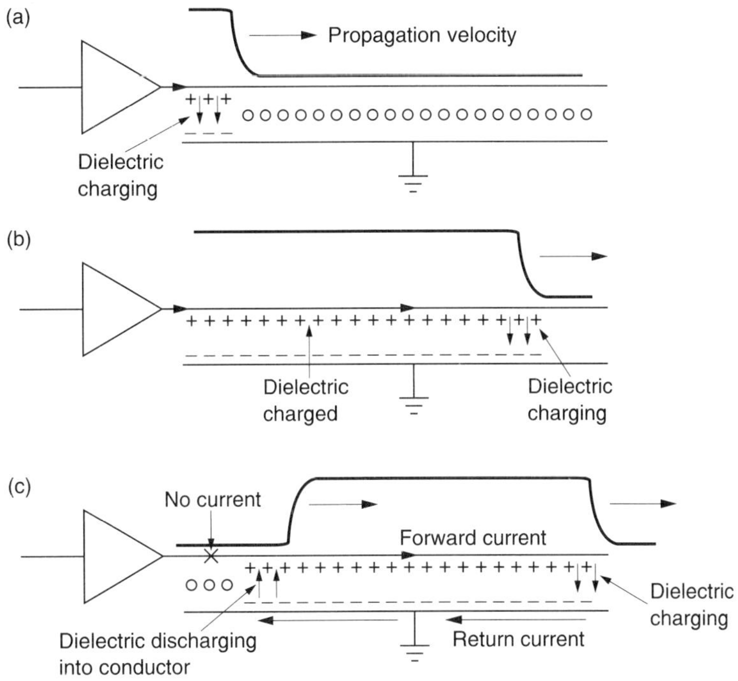

Figure 10.2 A transmission line conveys energy packets which appear with respect to the dielectric. In (a) the driver launches a pulse which charges the dielectric at the beginning of the line. As it propagates the dielectric is charged further along as in (b). When the driver ends the pulse, the charged dielectric discharges into the line. A current loop is formed where the current in the return loop flows in the opposite direction, to the current in the 'hot' wire.

cable. With rising frequency, the cable inductance also becomes significant, and it too is distributed.

The cable is now a transmission line and pulses travel down it as current loops which roll along as shown in Figure 10.2. If the pulse is positive, as it is launched along the line, it will charge the dielectric locally as at (a). As the pulse moves along, it will continue to charge the local dielectric as at (b). When the driver finishes the pulse, the trailing edge of the pulse follows the leading edge along the line. The voltage of the dielectric charged by the leading edge of the pulse is now higher than the voltage on the line, and so the dielectric discharges into the line as at (c). The current flows forward as it is in fact the same current which is flowing into the dielectric at the leading edge. There is thus a loop of current rolling down the line flowing forward in the 'hot' wire and backwards in the return.

The constant to-ing and fro-ing of charge in the dielectric results in dielectric loss of signal energy. Dielectric loss increases with frequency and so a long transmission line acts as a filter. Thus the term 'low-loss' cable refers primarily to the kind of dielectric used.

Transmission lines which transport energy in this way have a characteristic impedance caused by the interplay of the inductance along the conductors with the parallel capacitance. One consequence of that transmission mode is that correct termination or matching is required between the line and both the driver and the receiver. When a line is correctly matched, the rolling energy rolls straight out of the line into the load and the maximum energy is available. If the impedance presented by the load is incorrect, there will be reflections from the mismatch. An open circuit will reflect all the energy back in the same polarity as the original, whereas a short circuit will reflect all the energy back in the opposite

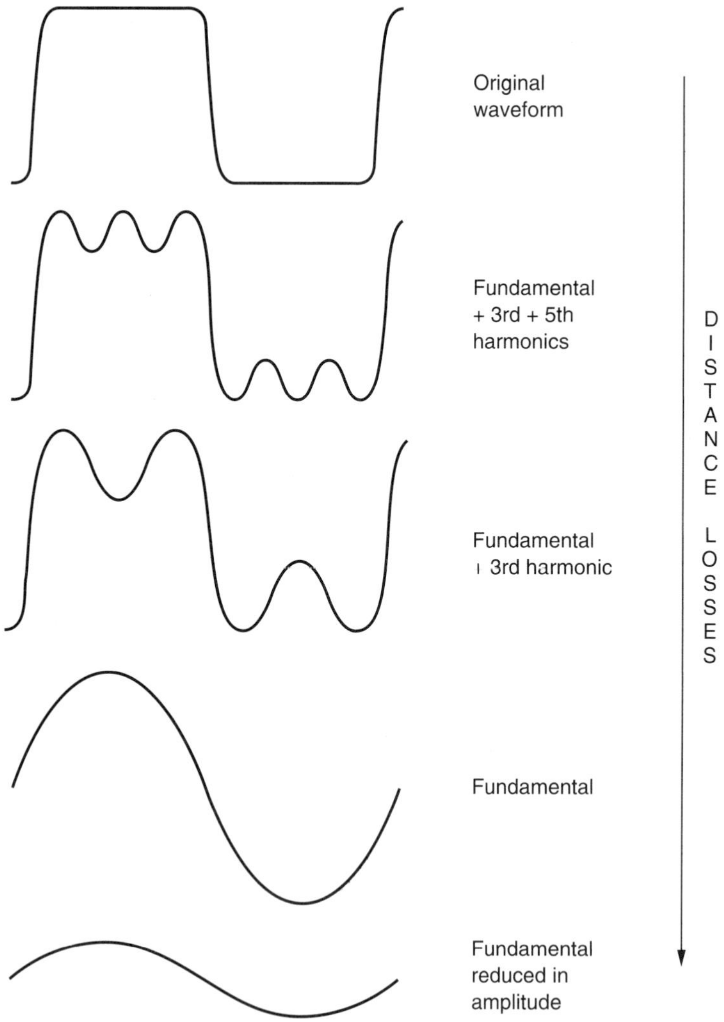

Figure 10.3 A signal may be square at the transmitter, but losses increase with frequency, and as the signal propagates, more of the harmonics are lost until only the fundamental remains. The amplitude of the fundamental then falls with further distance.

polarity. Thus impedances above or below the correct value will have a tendency towards reflections whose magnitude depends upon the degree of mismatch and whose polarity depends upon whether the load is too high or too low. In practice it is the need to avoid reflections which is the most important reason to terminate correctly.

A perfectly square pulse contains an indefinite series of harmonics, but the higher ones suffer progressively more loss. A square pulse at the driver becomes less and less square with distance as Figure 10.3 shows. The harmonics are progressively lost until in the extreme case all that is left is the fundamental. A transmitted square wave is received as a sine wave. Fortunately data can still be recovered from the fundamental signal component.

Once all the harmonics have been lost, further losses cause the amplitude of the fundamental to fall. The effect worsens with distance and it is necessary to ensure that data recovery is still possible from a signal of unpredictable level.

10.4 Types of recording medium

Digital media do not need to have linear transfer functions, nor do they need to be noise-free or continuous. All they need to do is to allow the player to be able to distinguish the presence or absence of replay events, such as the generation of pulses, with reasonable (rather than perfect) reliability. In a magnetic medium, the event will be a flux change from one direction of magnetization to another. In an optical medium, the event must cause the pickup to perceive a change in the intensity of the light falling on the sensor. This may be obtained through selective absorption of light by dyes, or by phase contrast (see Chapter 11). In magneto-optical disks the recording itself is magnetic, but it is made and read using light.

10.5 Magnetic recording

Magnetic recording relies on the hysteresis of certain magnetic materials. After an applied magnetic field is removed, the material remains magnetized in the same direction. By definition the process is non-linear.

Figure 10.4 shows the construction of a typical digital record head. A magnetic circuit carries a coil through which the record current passes and generates flux. A non-magnetic gap forces the flux to leave the magnetic circuit of the head and penetrate the medium. The current through the head must be set to suit the coercivity of the tape, and is

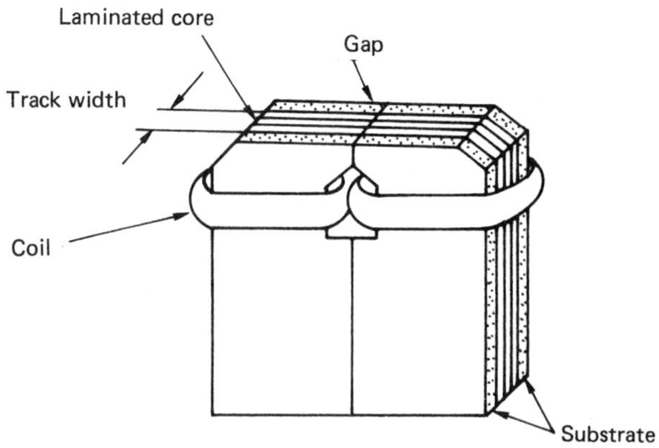

Figure 10.4 A digital record head is similar in principle to an analog head but uses much narrower tracks.

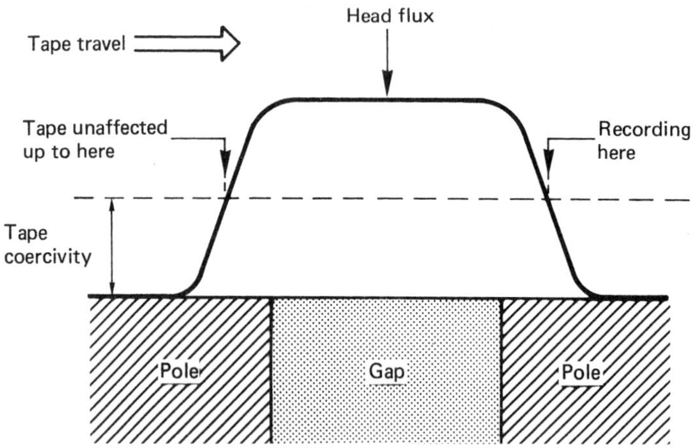

Figure 10.5 The recording is actually made near the trailing pole of the head where the head flux falls below the coercivity of the tape.

arranged to almost saturate the track. The amplitude of the current is constant, and recording is performed by reversing the direction of the current with respect to time. As the track passes the head, this is converted to the reversal of the magnetic field left on the tape with respect to distance. The magnetic recording is therefore bipolar. Figure 10.5 shows that the recording is actually made just after the trailing pole of the record head where the flux strength from the gap is falling. As in analog recorders, the width of the gap is generally made quite large to ensure that the full thickness of the magnetic coating is recorded, although this cannot be done if the same head is intended to replay.

Figure 10.6 shows what happens when a conventional inductive head, i.e. one having a normal winding, is used to replay the bipolar track made by reversing the record current. The head output is proportional to the

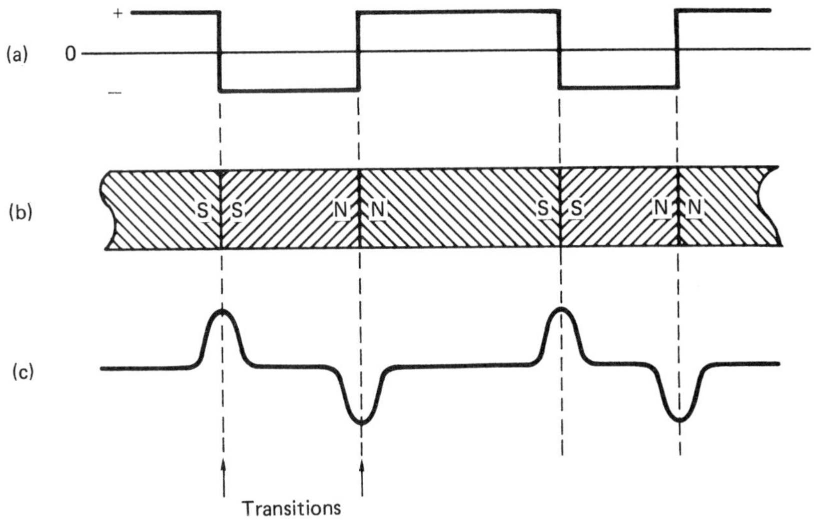

Figure 10.6 Basic digital recording. At (a) the write current in the head is reversed from time to time, leaving a binary magnetization pattern shown at (b). When replayed, the waveform at (c) results because an output is only produced when flux in the head changes. Changes are referred to as transitions.

rate of change of flux and so only occurs at flux reversals. In other words, the replay head differentiates the flux on the track. The polarity of the resultant pulses alternates as the flux changes and changes back. A circuit is necessary which locates the peaks of the pulses and outputs a signal corresponding to the original record current waveform. There are two ways in which this can be done.

The amplitude of the replay signal is of no consequence and often an AGC system is used to keep the replay signal constant in amplitude. What matters is the time at which the write current, and hence the flux stored on the medium, reverses. This can be determined by locating the peaks of the replay impulses, which can conveniently be done by differentiating the signal and looking for zero crossings. Figure 10.7 shows that this results in noise between the peaks. This problem is overcome by the gated peak detector, where only zero crossings from a pulse which exceeds the threshold will be counted. The AGC system allows the thresholds to be fixed. As an alternative, the record waveform can also be restored by integration, which opposes the differentiation of the head as in Figure 10.8.[1]

The head shown in Figure 10.4 has a frequency response shown in Figure 10.9. At DC there is no change of flux and no output. As a result inductive heads are at a disadvantage at very low speeds. The output rises with frequency until the rise is halted by the onset of thickness loss. As the frequency rises, the recorded wavelength falls and flux from the shorter magnetic patterns cannot be picked up so far away. At some

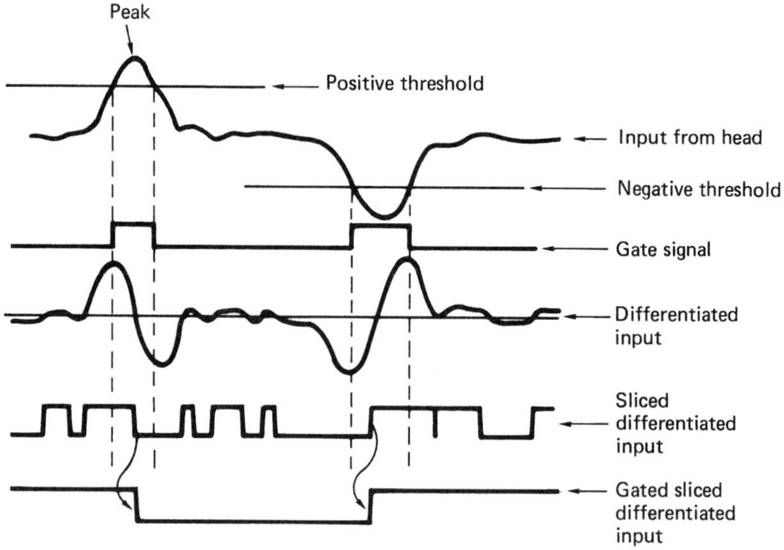

Figure 10.7 Gated peak detection rejects noise by disabling the differentiated output between transitions.

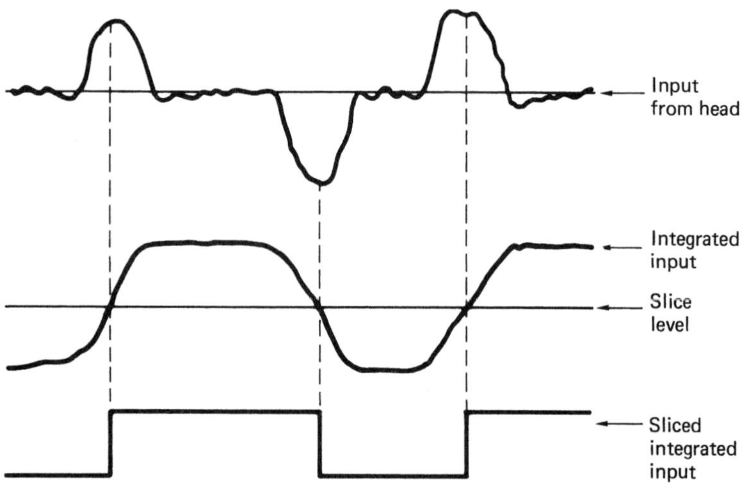

Figure 10.8 Integration method for re-creating write-current waveform.

point, the wavelength becomes so short that flux from the back of the tape coating cannot reach the head and a decreasing thickness of tape contributes to the replay signal.[2] In digital recorders using short wavelengths to obtain high density, there is no point in using thick coatings. As wavelength further reduces, the familiar gap loss occurs, where the head gap is too big to resolve detail on the track. The construction of the head results in the same action as that of a two-point

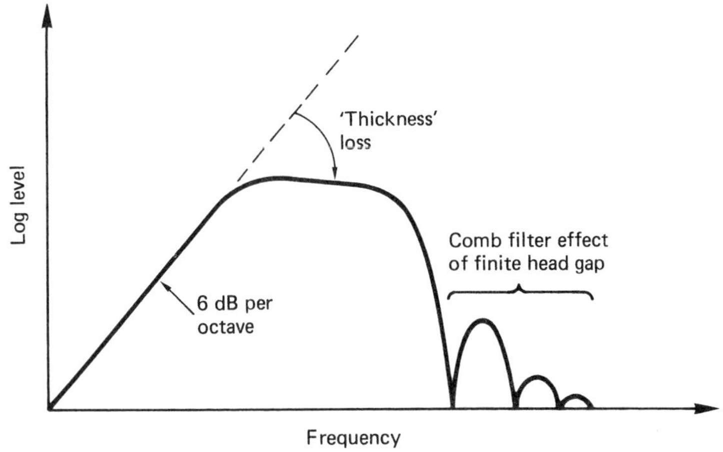

Figure 10.9 The major mechanisms defining magnetic channel bandwidth.

transversal filter, as the two poles of the head see the tape with a small delay interposed due to the finite gap. As expected, the head response is like a comb filter with the well-known nulls where flux cancellation takes place across the gap. Clearly the smaller the gap, the shorter the wavelength of the first null. This contradicts the requirement of the record head to have a large gap. In quality analog audio recorders, it is the norm to have different record and replay heads for this reason, and the same will be true in digital machines which have separate record and playback heads. Clearly where the same pair of heads are used for record and play, the head gap size will be determined by the playback requirement.

As can be seen, the frequency response is far from ideal, and steps must be taken to ensure that recorded data waveforms do not contain frequencies which suffer excessive losses.

A more recent development is the magneto-resistive (M-R) head. This is a head which measures the flux on the tape rather than using it to generate a signal directly. Flux measurement works down to DC and so offers advantages at low tape speeds. Unfortunately flux-measuring heads are not polarity conscious but sense the modulus of the flux and if used directly they respond to positive and negative flux equally, as shown in Figure 10.10. This is overcome by using a small extra winding in the head carrying a constant current. This creates a steady bias field which adds to the flux from the tape. The flux seen by the head is now unipolar and changes between two levels and a more useful output waveform results.

Recorders which have low head-to-medium speed use M-R heads, whereas recorders with high bit rates, such as DVTRs tend to use inductive heads.

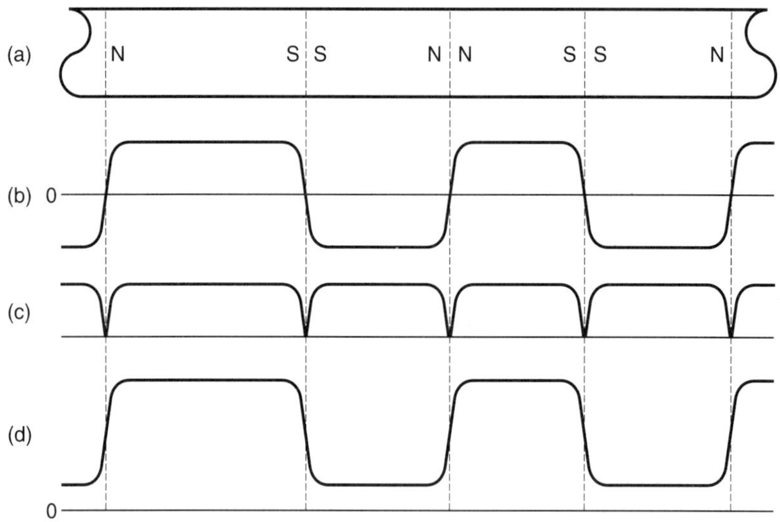

Figure 10.10 The sensing element in a magneto-resistive head is not sensitive to the polarity of the flux, only the magnitude. At (a) the track magnetization is shown and this causes a bidirectional flux variation in the head as at (b), resulting in the magnitude output at (c). However, if the flux in the head due to the track is biased by an additional field. It can be made unipolar as at (d) and the correct waveform is obtained.

Heads designed for use with tape work in actual contact with the magnetic coating. The tape is tensioned to pull it against the head. There will be a wear mechanism and a need for periodic cleaning. In the hard disk, the rotational speed is high in order to reduce access time, and the drive must be capable of staying on line for extended periods. In this case the heads do not contact the disk surface, but are supported on a

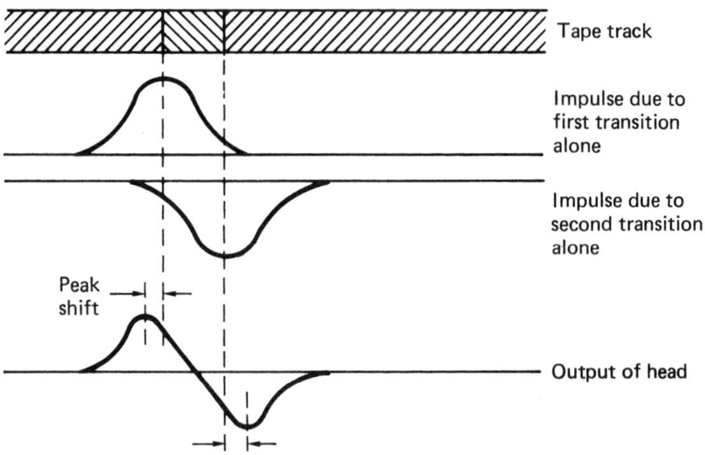

Figure 10.11 Readout pulses from two closely recorded transitions are summed in the head and the effect is that the peaks of the waveform are moved outwards. This is known as peak-shift distortion and equalization is necessary to reduce the effect.

boundary layer of air. The presence of the air film causes spacing loss, which restricts the wavelengths at which the head can replay. This is the penalty of rapid access.

Digital media must operate at high density for economic reasons. This implies that shortest possible wavelengths will be used. Figure 10.11 shows that when two flux changes, or transitions, are recorded close together, they affect each other on replay. The amplitude of the composite signal is reduced, and the position of the peaks is pushed outwards. This is known as inter-symbol interference, or peak-shift distortion and it occurs in all magnetic media.

The effect is primarily due to high-frequency loss and it can be reduced by equalization on replay, as is done in most tapes, or by precompensation on record as is done in hard disks.

10.6 Azimuth recording and rotary heads

Figure 10.12(a) shows that in azimuth recording, the transitions are laid down at an angle to the track by using a head which is tilted. Machines using azimuth recording must always have an even number of heads, so that adjacent tracks can be recorded with opposite azimuth angle. The two track types are usually referred to as A and B. Figure 10.12(b) shows the effect of playing a track with the wrong type of head. The playback process suffers from an enormous azimuth error. The effect of azimuth error can be understood by imagining the tape track to be made from many identical parallel strips. In the presence of azimuth error, the strips at one edge of the track are played back with a phase shift relative to

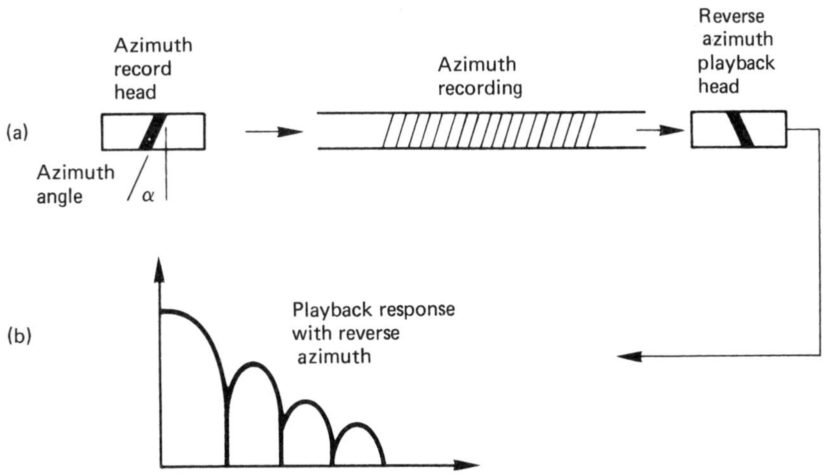

Figure 10.12 In azimuth recording (a), the head gap is tilted. If the track is played with the same head, playback is normal, but the response of the reverse azimuth head is attenuated (b).

strips at the other side. At some wavelengths, the phase shift will be 180° and there will be no output; at other wavelengths, especially long wavelengths, some output will reappear. The effect is rather like that of a comb filter, and serves to attenuate crosstalk due to adjacent tracks so that no guard bands are required. Since no tape is wasted between the tracks, more efficient use is made of the tape. The term 'guard-band-less' recording is often used instead of, or in addition to, the term 'azimuth recording'. The failure of the azimuth effect at long wavelengths is a characteristic of azimuth recording, and it is necessary to ensure that the spectrum of the signal to be recorded has a small low-frequency content. The signal will need to pass through a rotary transformer to reach the heads, and cannot therefore contain a DC component.

In some rotary head recorders there is no separate erase process, and erasure is achieved by overwriting with a new waveform. Overwriting is only successful when there are no long wavelengths in the earlier recording, since these penetrate deeper into the tape, and the short wavelengths in a new recording will not be able to erase them. In this case the ratio between the shortest and longest wavelengths recorded on tape should be limited.

Restricting the spectrum of the code to allow erasure by overwrite also eases the design of the rotary transformer.

10.7 Optical and magneto-optical disks

Optical recorders have the advantage that light can be focused at a distance whereas magnetism cannot. This means that there need be no physical contact between the pickup and the medium and no wear mechanism.

In the same way that the recorded wavelength of a magnetic recording is limited by the gap in the replay head, the density of optical recording is limited by the size of light spot which can be focused on the medium. This is controlled by the wavelength of the light used and by the aperture of the lens. When the light spot is as small as these limits allow, it is said to be diffraction limited.

The frequency response of an optical disk is shown in Figure 10.13. The response is best at DC and falls steadily to the optical cut-off frequency. Although the optics work down to DC, this cannot be used for the data recording. DC and low frequencies in the data would interfere with the focus and tracking servos and, as will be seen, difficulties arise when attempting to demodulate a unipolar signal. In practice the signal from the pickup is split by a filter. Low frequencies go to the servos, and higher frequencies go to the data circuitry. As a result the optical disk channel has the same inability to handle DC as does a magnetic recorder, and the same techniques are needed to overcome it.

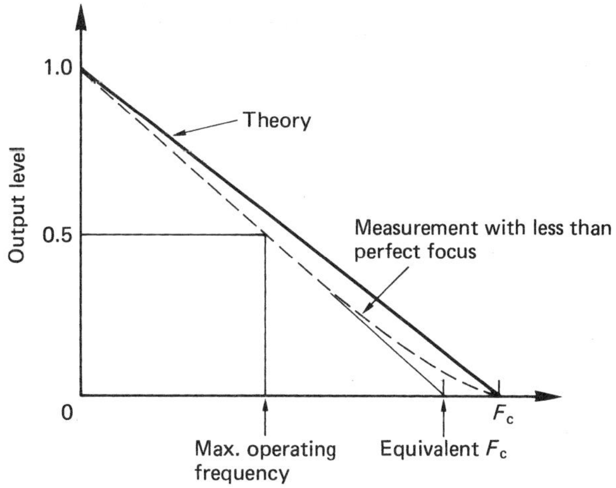

Figure 10.13 Frequency response of laser pickup. Maximum operating frequency is about half of cut-off frequency F_c.

When a magnetic material is heated above its Curie temperature, it becomes demagnetized, and on cooling will assume the magnetization of an applied field which would be too weak to influence it normally. This is the principle of magneto-optical recording. The heat is supplied by a finely focused laser, the field is supplied by a coil which is much larger.

Figure 10.14 shows that the medium is initially magnetized in one direction only. In order to record, the coil is energized with a current in

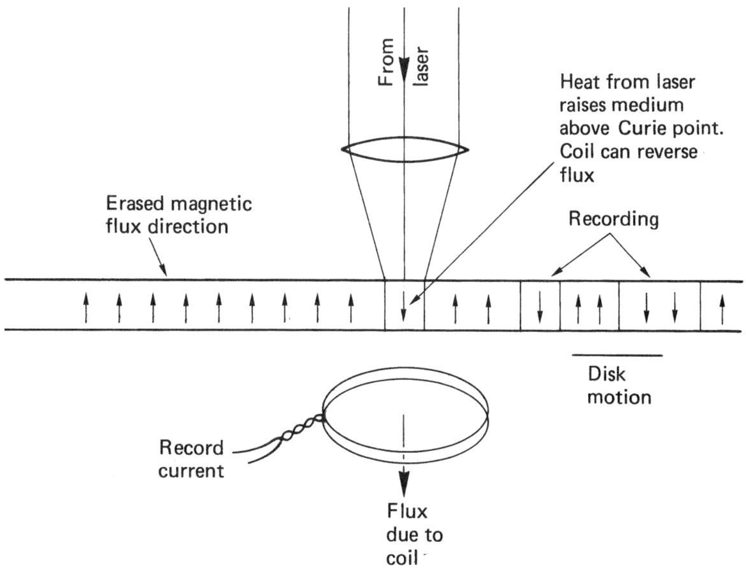

Figure 10.14 The thermomagneto-optical disk uses the heat from a laser to allow magnetic field to record on the disk.

the opposite direction. This is too weak to influence the medium in its normal state, but when it is heated by the recording laser beam the heated area will take on the magnetism from the coil when it cools. Thus a magnetic recording with very small dimensions can be made even though the magnetic circuit involved is quite large in comparison.

Readout is obtained using the Kerr effect or the Faraday effect, which are phenomena whereby the plane of polarization of light can be rotated by a magnetic field. The angle of rotation is very small and needs a sensitive pickup. The pickup contains a polarizing filter before the sensor. Changes in polarization change the ability of the light to get through the polarizing filter and result in an intensity change which once more produces a unipolar output.

The magneto-optic recording can be erased by reversing the current in the coil and operating the laser continuously as it passes along the track. A new recording can then be made on the erased track.

A disadvantage of magneto-optical recording is that all materials having a Curie point low enough to be useful are highly corrodible by air and need to be kept under an effectively sealed protective layer.

The magneto-optical channel has the same frequency response as that shown in Figure 3.24.

10.8 Equalization and data separation

The characteristics of most channels are that signal loss occurs which increases with frequency. This has the effect of slowing down rise times and thereby sloping off edges. If a signal with sloping edges is sliced, the time at which the waveform crosses the slicing level will be changed, and this causes jitter. Figure 10.15 shows that slicing a sloping waveform in the presence of baseline wander causes more jitter.

On a long cable, high-frequency rolloff can cause sufficient jitter to move a transition into an adjacent bit period. This is called inter-symbol interference and the effect becomes worse in signals which have greater asymmetry, i.e. short pulses alternating with long ones. The effect can be reduced by the application of equalization, which is typically a high-frequency boost, and by choosing a channel code which has restricted asymmetry.

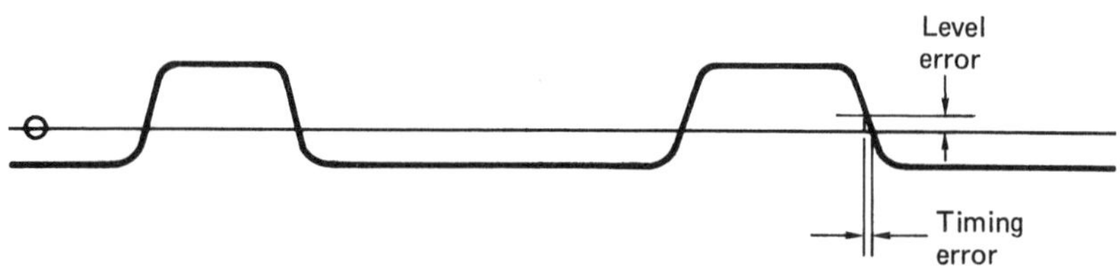

Figure 10.15 A DC offset can cause timing errors.

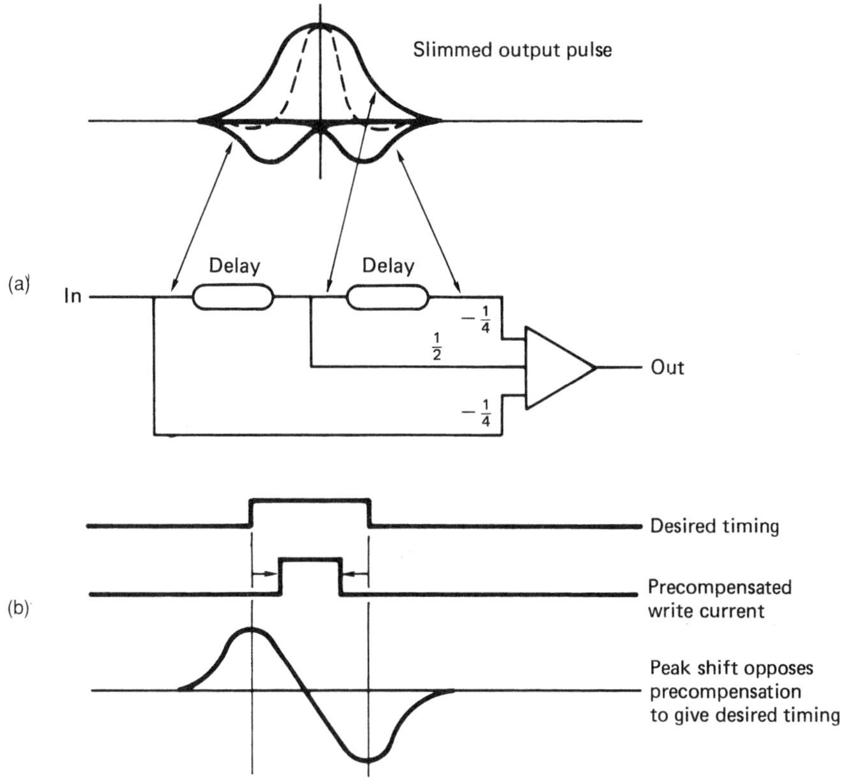

Figure 10.16 Peak-shift distortion is due to the finite width of replay pulses. The effect can be reduced by the pulse slimmer shown in (a) which is basically a transversal filter. The use of a linear operational amplifier emphasizes the analog nature of channels. Instead of replay pulse slimming, transitions can be written with a displacement equal and opposite to the anticipated peak shift as shown in (b).

Compensation for peak shift distortion in recording requires equalization of the channel,[3] and this can be done by a network after the replay head, termed an equalizer or pulse sharpener,[4] as in Figure 10.16(a). This technique uses transversal filtering to oppose the inherent transversal effect of the head. As an alternative, pre-compensation in the record stage can be used as shown in (b). Transitions are written in such a way that the anticipated peak shift will move the readout peaks to the desired timing.

The important step of information recovery at the receiver or replay circuit is known as data separation. The data separator is rather like an analog-to-digital convertor because the two processes of sampling and quantizing are both present. In the time domain, the sampling clock is derived from the clock content of the channel waveform. In the voltage domain, the process of *slicing* converts the analog waveform from the channel back into a binary representation. The slicer is thus a form of quantizer which has only one-bit resolution. The slicing process makes a discrete decision about the voltage of the incoming signal in order to reject noise. The sampler makes discrete decisions along the time axis in order to reject jitter. These two processes will be described in detail.

10.9 Slicing and jitter rejection

The slicer is implemented with a comparator which has analog inputs but a binary output. In a cable receiver, the input waveform can be sliced directly. In an inductive magnetic replay system, the replay waveform is differentiated and must first pass through a peak detector (Figure 10.7) or an integrator (Figure 10.8). The signal voltage is compared with the midway voltage, known as the threshold, baseline or slicing level by the comparator. If the signal voltage is above the threshold, the comparator outputs a high level, if below, a low level results.

Figure 10.17 shows some waveforms associated with a slicer. At (a) the transmitted waveform has an uneven duty cycle. The DC component, or average level, of the signal is received with high amplitude, but the pulse amplitude falls as the pulse gets shorter. Eventually the waveform cannot be sliced. At (b) the opposite duty cycle is shown. The signal level drifts to the opposite polarity and once more slicing is impossible. The phenomenon is called baseline wander and will be observed with any signal whose average voltage is not the same as the slicing level. At (c) it will be seen that if the transmitted waveform has a relatively constant average voltage, slicing remains possible up to high frequencies even in the presence of serious amplitude loss, because the received waveform remains symmetrical about the baseline.

It is clearly not possible simply to serialize data in a shift register for so-called direct transmission, because successful slicing can only be obtained if the number of ones is equal to the number of zeros; there is little chance of this happening consistently with real data. Instead, a modulation code or channel code is necessary. This converts the data into a waveform which is DC-free or nearly so for the purpose of transmission.

The slicing threshold level is naturally zero in a bipolar system such as magnetic inductive replay or a cable. When the amplitude falls it does so symmetrically and slicing continues. The same is not true of M-R heads and optical pickups, which both respond to intensity and therefore produce a unipolar output. If the replay signal is sliced directly, the threshold cannot be zero, but must be some level approximately half the amplitude of the signal as shown in Figure 10.18(a). Unfortunately when the signal level falls it falls toward zero and not towards the slicing level. The threshold will no longer be appropriate for the signal as can be seen at (b). This can be overcome by using a DC-free coded waveform. If a

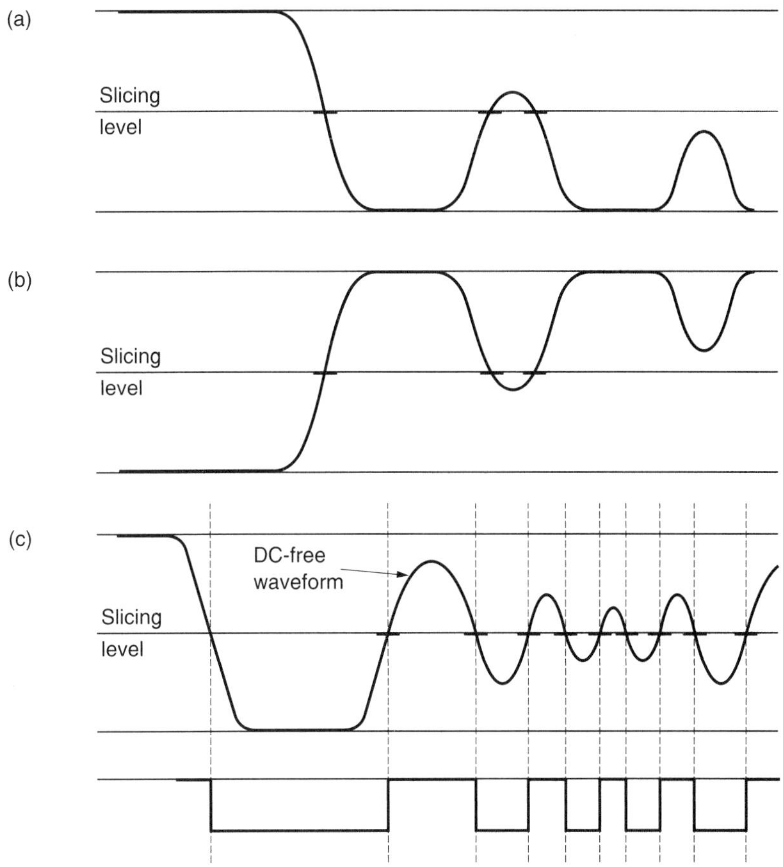

Figure 10.17 Slicing a signal which has suffered losses works well if the duty cycle is even. If the duty cycle is uneven, as at (a), timing errors will become worse until slicing fails. With the opposite duty cycle, the slicing falls in the opposite direction as at (b). If, however, the signal is DC free, correct slicing can continue even in the presence of serious losses, as (c) shows.

series capacitor is connected to the unipolar signal from an optical pickup, the waveform is rendered bipolar because the capacitor blocks any DC component in the signal. The DC-free channel waveform passes through unaltered. If an amplitude loss is suffered, (c) shows that the resultant bipolar signal now reduces in amplitude about the slicing level and slicing can continue.

The binary waveform at the output of the slicer will be a replica of the transmitted waveform, except for the addition of jitter or time uncertainty in the position of the edges due to noise, baseline wander, inter-symbol interference and imperfect equalization.

Binary circuits reject noise by using discrete voltage levels which are spaced further apart than the uncertainty due to noise. In a similar manner, digital coding combats time uncertainty by making the time axis

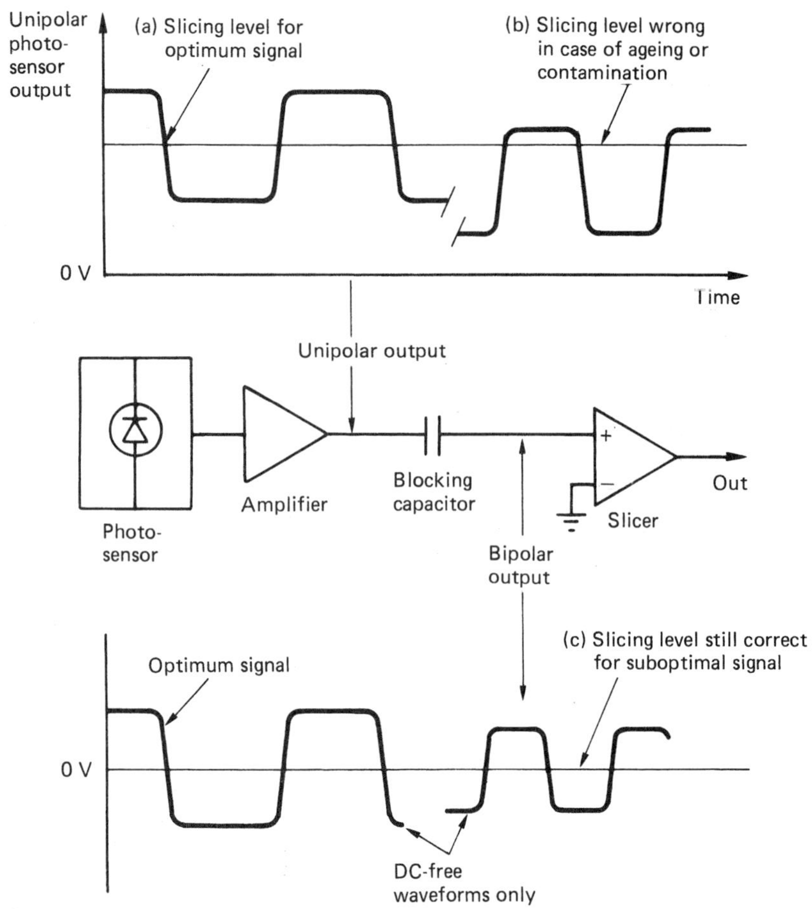

Figure 10.18 (a) Slicing a unipolar signal requires a non-zero threshold. (b) If the signal amplitude changes, the threshold will then be incorrect. (c) If a DC-free code is used, a unipolar waveform can be converted to a bipolar waveform using a series capacitor. A zero threshold can be used and slicing continues with amplitude variations.

discrete using events, known as transitions, spaced apart at integer multiples of some basic time period, called a detent, which is larger than the typical time uncertainty. Figure 10.19 shows how this jitter-rejection mechanism works. All that matters is to identify the detent in which the transition occurred. Exactly where it occurred within the detent is of no consequence.

As ideal transitions occur at multiples of a basic period, an oscilloscope, which is repeatedly triggered on a channel-coded signal carrying random data, will show an eye pattern if connected to the output of the equalizer. Study of the eye pattern reveals how well the coding used suits the channel. In the case of transmission, with a short cable, the losses will be small, and the eye opening will be virtually square except for some edge sloping due to cable capacitance. As cable length increases, the harmonics

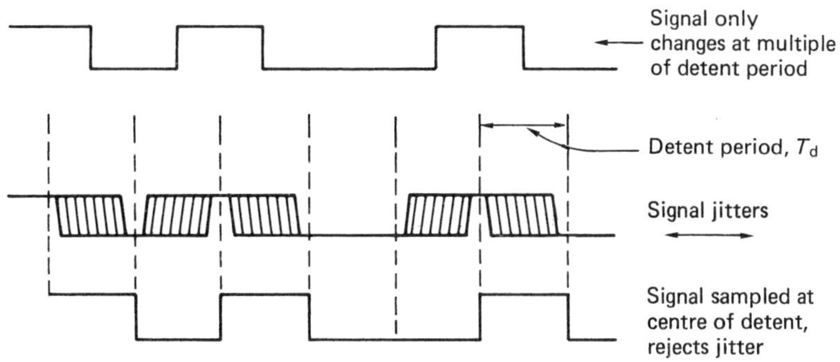

Figure 10.19 A certain amount of jitter can be rejected by changing the signal at multiples of the basic detent period T_d.

are lost and the remaining fundamental gives the eyes a diamond shape. The same eye pattern will be obtained with a recording channel where it is uneconomic to provide bandwidth much beyond the fundamental.

Noise closes the eyes in a vertical direction, and jitter closes the eyes in a horizontal direction, as in Figure 10.20. If the eyes remain sensibly open, data separation will be possible. Clearly more jitter can be tolerated if there is less noise, and vice versa. If the equalizer is adjustable, the optimum setting will be where the greatest eye opening is obtained.

In the centre of the eyes, the receiver must make binary decisions at the channel bit rate about the state of the signal, high or low, using the slicer output. As stated, the receiver is sampling the output of the slicer, and it needs to have a sampling clock in order to do that. In order to give the best rejection of noise and jitter, the clock edges which operate the sampler must be in the centre of the eyes.

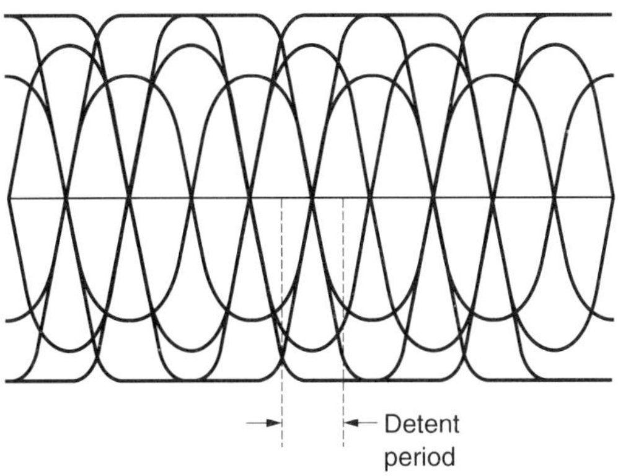

Figure 10.20 A transmitted waveform will appear like this on an oscilloscope as successive parts of the waveform are superimposed on the tube. When the waveform is rounded off by losses, diamond-shaped eyes are left in the centre, spaced apart by the detent period.

As has been stated, a separate clock is not practicable in recording or transmission. A fixed-frequency clock at the receiver is of no use as even if it was sufficiently stable, it would not know what phase to run at.

The only way in which the sampling clock can be obtained is to use a phase-locked loop to regenerate it from the clock content of the self-clocking channel-coded waveform. In phase-locked loops, the voltage-controlled oscillator is driven by a phase error measured between the output and some reference, such that the output eventually has the same frequency as the reference. If a divider is placed between the VCO and the phase comparator, as in section 2.9, the VCO frequency can be made to be a multiple of the reference. This also has the effect of making the loop more heavily damped. If a channel-coded waveform is used as a reference to a PLL, the loop will be able to make a phase comparison whenever a transition arrives and will run at the channel bit rate. When there are several detents between transitions, the loop will *flywheel* at the last known frequency and phase until it can rephase at a subsequent transition. Thus a continuous clock is re-created from the clock content of the channel waveform. In a recorder, if the speed of the medium should change, the PLL will change frequency to follow. Once the loop is locked, clock edges will be phased with the average phase of the jittering edges of the input waveform. If, for example, rising edges of the clock are phased to input transitions, then falling edges will be in the centre of the eyes. If these edges are used to clock the sampling process, the maximum jitter and noise can be rejected. The output of the slicer when sampled by the PLL edge at the centre of an eye is the value of a channel bit. Figure 10.21 shows the complete clocking system of a channel code from encoder to data separator.

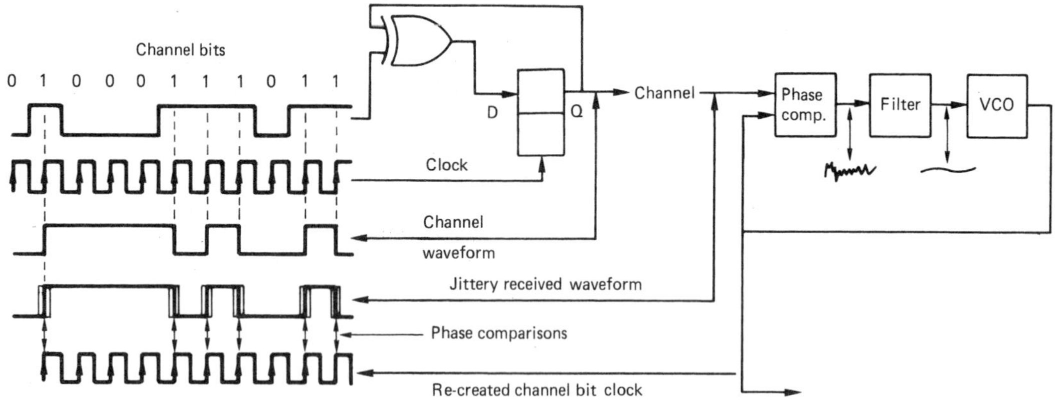

Figure 10.21 The clocking system when channel coding is used. The encoder clock runs at the channel bit rate, and any transitions in the channel must coincide with encoder clock edges. The reason for doing this is that, at the data separator, the PLL can lock to the edges of the channel signal, which represent an intermittent clock, and turn it into a continuous clock. The jitter in the edges of the channel signal causes noise in the phase error of the PLL, but the damping acts as a filter and the PLL runs at the average phase of the channel bits, rejecting the jitter.

Clearly data cannot be separated if the PLL is not locked, but it cannot be locked until it has seen transitions for a reasonable period. In recorders, which have discontinuous recorded blocks to allow editing, the solution is to precede each data block with a pattern of transitions whose sole purpose is to provide a timing reference for synchronizing the phase-locked loop. This pattern is known as a preamble. In interfaces, the transmission can be continuous and there is no difficulty remaining in lock indefinitely. There will simply be a short delay on first applying the signal before the receiver locks to it.

One potential problem area which is frequently overlooked is to ensure that the VCO in the receiving PLL is correctly centred. If it is not, it will be running with a static phase error and will not sample the received waveform at the centre of the eyes. The sampled bits will be more prone to noise and jitter errors. VCO centring can simply be checked by displaying the control voltage. This should not change significantly when the input is momentarily interrupted.

10.10 Channel coding

It is not practicable simply to serialize raw data in a shift register for the purpose of recording or for transmission except over relatively short distances. Practical systems require the use of a modulation scheme, known as a channel code, which expresses the data as waveforms which are self-clocking in order to reject jitter, separate the received bits and to avoid skew on separate clock lines. The coded waveforms should further be DC-free or nearly so to enable slicing in the presence of losses and have a narrower spectrum than the raw data both for economy and to make equalization easier.

Jitter causes uncertainty about the time at which a particular event occurred. The frequency response of the channel then places an overall limit on the spacing of events in the channel. Particular emphasis must be placed on the interplay of bandwidth, jitter and noise, which will be shown here to be the key to the design of a successful channel code.

Figure 10.22 shows that a channel coder is necessary prior to the record stage, and that a decoder, known as a data separator, is necessary after the replay stage. The output of the channel coder is generally a logic level signal which contains a 'high' state when a transition is to be generated. The waveform generator produces the transitions in a signal whose level and impedance is suitable for driving the medium or channel. The signal may be bipolar or unipolar as appropriate.

Some codes eliminate DC entirely, which is advantageous for cable transmission, optical media and rotary head recording. Some codes can reduce the channel bandwidth needed by lowering the upper spectral

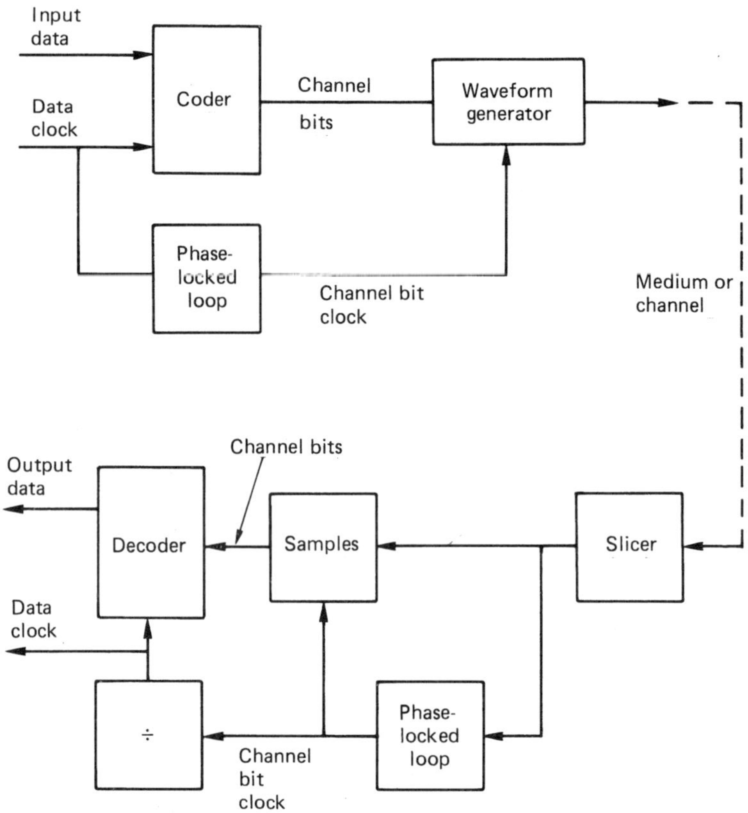

Figure 10.22 The major components of a channel coding system. See text for details.

limit. This permits higher linear density, usually at the expense of jitter rejection. Other codes narrow the spectrum by raising the lower limit. A code with a narrow spectrum has a number of advantages. The reduction in asymmetry will reduce peak shift and data separators can lock more readily because the range of frequencies in the code is smaller. In theory the narrower the spectrum, the less noise will be suffered, but this is only achieved if filtering is employed. Filters can easily cause phase errors which will nullify any gain.

A convenient definition of a channel code (for there are certainly others) is: 'A method of modulating real data such that they can be reliably received despite the shortcomings of a real channel, while making maximum economic use of the channel capacity.'

The basic time periods of a channel-coded waveform are called positions or detents, in which the transmitted voltage will be reversed or stay the same. The symbol used for the units of channel time is T_d.

One of the fundamental parameters of a channel code is the density ratio (DR). One definition of density ratio is that it is the worst-case ratio of the number of data bits recorded to the number of transitions in the channel. It can also be thought of as the ratio between the Nyquist rate of the data (one-half the bit rate) and the frequency response required in the channel. The storage density of data recorders has steadily increased due to improvements in medium and transducer technology, but modern storage densities are also a function of improvements in channel coding.

As jitter is such an important issue in digital recording and transmission, a parameter has been introduced to quantify the ability of a channel code to reject time instability. This parameter, the jitter margin, also known as the window margin or phase margin (T_w), is defined as the permitted range of time over which a transition can still be received correctly, divided by the data bit-cell period (T).

Since equalization is often difficult in practice, a code which has a large jitter margin will sometimes be used because it resists the effects of inter-symbol interference well. Such a code may achieve a better performance in practice than a code with a higher density ratio but poor jitter performance.

A more realistic comparison of code performance will be obtained by taking into account both density ratio and jitter margin. This is the purpose of the figure of merit (FoM), which is defined as DR $\times T_w$.

10.11 Simple codes

In the Non-Return to Zero (NRZ) code shown in Figure 10.23(a), the record current does not cease between bits, but flows at all times in one direction or the other dependent on the state of the bit to be recorded. This results in a replay pulse only when the data bits change from state to another. As a result if one pulse was missed, the subsequent bits would be inverted. This was avoided by adapting the coding such that the record current would change state or invert whenever a data one occurred, leading to the term Non-Return to Zero Invert or NRZI shown in Figure 10.23(b). In NRZI a replay pulse occurs whenever there is a data one. Clearly neither NRZ or NRZI are self-clocking, but require a separate clock track. Skew between

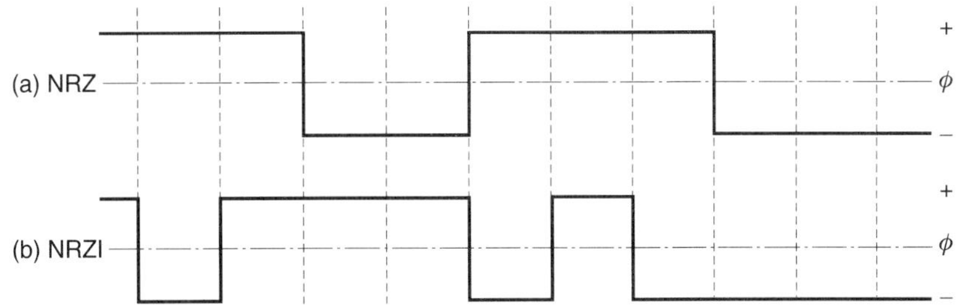

Figure 10.23 In the NRZ code (a) a missing replay pulse inverts every following bit. This was overcome in the NRZI code (b) which reverses write current on a data one.

tracks can only be avoided by working at low density and so the system cannot be used directly for digital video. However, virtually all the codes used for magnetic recording are based on the principle of the reversing the record current to produce a transition.

The FM code, also known as Manchester code or bi-phase mark code, shown in Figure 10.24(a) was the first practical self-clocking binary code and it is suitable for both transmission and recording. It is DC-free and very easy to encode and decode. It is the code specified for the AES/EBU digital audio interconnect standard. In the field of recording it remains in use today only where density is not of prime importance, for example in SMPTE/EBU timecode for professional audio and video recorders.

In FM there is always a transition at the bit-cell boundary which acts as a clock. For a data one, there is an additional transition at the bit-cell centre. Figure 10.24(a) shows that each data bit can be represented by two channel bits. For a data zero, they will be 10, and for a data one they will be 11. Since the first bit is always one, it conveys no information, and is responsible for the density ratio of only one-half. Since there can be two transitions for each data bit, the jitter margin can only be half a bit, and the resulting FoM is only 0.25. The high clock content of FM does, however, mean that data recovery is possible over a wide range of speeds; hence the use for timecode. The lowest frequency in FM is due to a stream of zeros and is equal to half the bit rate. The highest frequency is due to

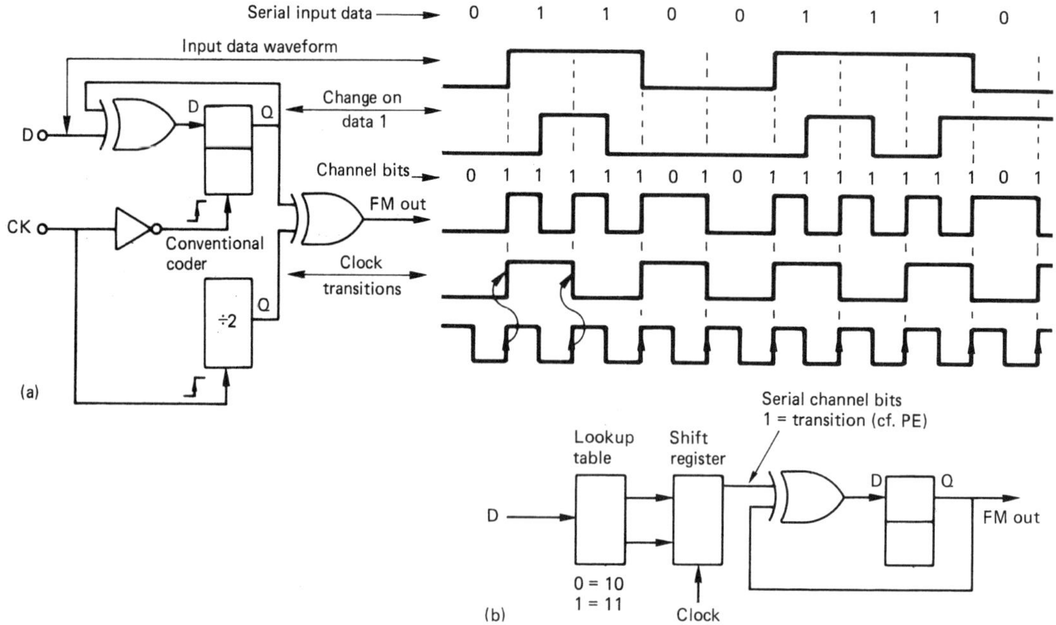

Figure 10.24 In (a) are the FM waveform from a conventional coder and the channel bits which may be used to describe transitions in it. A coder based on a look-up table is shown at (b).

a stream of ones, and is equal to the bit rate. Thus the fundamentals of FM are within a band of one octave. Effective equalization is generally possible over such a band. FM is not polarity conscious and can be inverted without changing the data.

Figure 10.24(b) shows how an FM coder works. Data words are loaded into the input shift register which is clocked at the data bit rate. Each data bit is converted to two channel bits in the codebook or look-up table. These channel bits are loaded into the output register. The output register is clocked twice as fast as the input register because there are twice as many channel bits as data bits. The ratio of the two clocks is called the code rate, in this case it is a rate one-half code. Ones in the serial channel bit output represent transitions whereas zeros represent no change. The channel bits are fed to the waveform generator which is a one-bit delay, clocked at the channel bit rate, and an exclusive-OR gate. This changes state when a channel bit one is input. The result is a coded FM waveform where there is always a transition at the beginning of the data bit period, and a second optional transition whose presence indicates a one.

In modified frequency modulation (MFM), also known as Miller code,[5] the highly redundant clock content of FM was reduced by the use of a phase-locked loop in the receiver which could flywheel over missing clock transitions. This technique is implicit in all the more advanced codes. Figure 10.25(a) shows that the bit-cell centre transition on a data one was retained, but the bit-cell boundary transition is now only required between successive zeros. There are still two channel bits for every data bit, but adjacent channel bits will never be one, doubling the minimum time between transitions, and giving a DR of 1. Clearly the

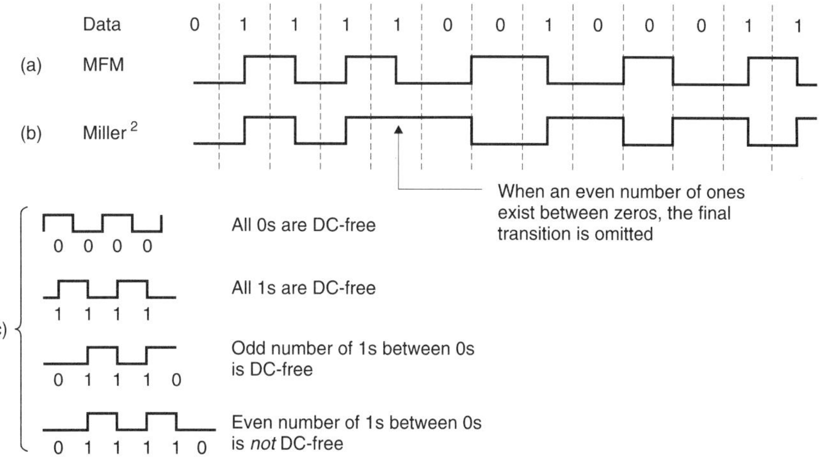

Figure 10.25 MFM or Miller code is generated as shown here. The minimum transition spacing is twice that of FM or PE. MFM is not always DC-free as shown in (c). This can be overcome by the modification of (b) which results in the Miller[2] code.

coding of the current bit is now influenced by the preceding bit. The maximum number of prior bits which affect the current bit is known as the constraint length L_c, measured in data-bit periods. For MFM $L_c = T$. Another way of considering the constraint length is that it assesses the number of data bits which may be corrupted if the receiver misplaces one transition. If L_c is long, all errors will be burst errors.

MFM doubled the density ratio compared to FM and PE without changing the jitter performance; thus the FoM also doubles, becoming 0.5. It was adopted for many rigid disks at the time of its development, and remains in use on double-density floppy disks. It is not, however, DC-free. Figure 10.25(b) shows how MFM can have DC content under certain conditions.

The Miller^2 code is derived from MFM, and Figure 10.25(c) shows that the DC content is eliminated by a slight increase in complexity.[6,7] Wherever an even number of ones occurs between zeros, the transition at the last one is omitted. This creates two additional, longer run lengths and increases the T_{max} of the code. The decoder can detect these longer run lengths in order to re-insert the suppressed ones. The FoM of Miller^2 is 0.5 as for MFM.

10.12 Group codes

Further improvements in coding rely on converting patterns of real data to patterns of channel bits with more desirable characteristics using a conversion table known as a codebook. If a data symbol of m bits is considered, it can have 2^m different combinations. As it is intended to discard undesirable patterns to improve the code, it follows that the number of channel bits n must be greater than m. The number of patterns which can be discarded is:

$$2^n - 2^m$$

One name for the principle is group code recording (GCR), and an important parameter is the code rate, defined as:

$$R = \frac{m}{n}$$

It will be evident that the jitter margin T_w is numerically equal to the code rate, and so a code rate near to unity is desirable. The choice of patterns which are used in the codebook will be those that give the desired balance between clock content, bandwidth and DC content.

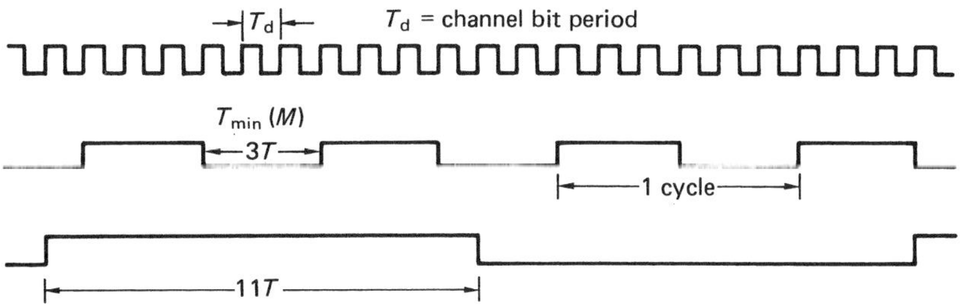

Figure 10.26 A channel code can control its spectrum by placing limits on T_{min} (*M*) and T_{max} which define upper and lower frequencies. The ratio of T_{max}/T_{min} determines the asymmetry of waveform and predicts DC content and peak shift.

Figure 10.26 shows that the upper spectral limit can be made to be some fraction of the channel bit rate according to the minimum distance between ones in the channel bits. This is known as T_{min}, also referred to as the minimum transition parameter *M* and in both cases is measured in data bits *T*. It can be obtained by multiplying the number of channel detent periods between transitions by the code rate. Unfortunately, codes are measured by the number of consecutive zeros in the channel bits, given the symbol *d*, which is always one less than the number of detent periods. In fact T_{min} is numerically equal to the density ratio.

$$T_{min} = M = \mathrm{DR} = \frac{(d + 1) \times m}{n}$$

It will be evident that choosing a low code rate could increase the density ratio, but it will impair the jitter margin. The figure of merit is:

$$\mathrm{FoM} = \mathrm{DR} \times T_w = \frac{(d + 1) \times m^2}{n^2}$$

since $T_w = m/n$

Figure 10.26 also shows that the lower spectral limit is influenced by the maximum distance between transitions T_{max}. This is also obtained by multiplying the maximum number of detent periods between transitions by the code rate. Again, codes are measured by the maximum number of zeros between channel ones, *k*, and so:

$$T_{max} = \frac{(k + 1) \times m}{n}$$

and the maximum/minimum ratio *P* is:

$$P = \frac{(k + 1)}{(d + 1)}$$

The length of time between channel transitions is known as the *run length*. Another name for this class is the run-length-limited (RLL) codes.[8] Since m data bits are considered as one symbol, the constraint length L_c will be increased in RLL codes to at least m. It is, however, possible for a code to have run-length limits without it being a group code.

In practice, the junction of two adjacent channel symbols may violate run-length limits, and it may be necessary to create a further codebook of symbol size $2n$ which converts violating code pairs to acceptable patterns. This is known as merging and follows the golden rule that the substitute $2n$ symbol must finish with a pattern which eliminates the possibility of a subsequent violation. These patterns must also differ from all other symbols.

Substitution may also be used to different degrees in the same nominal code in order to allow a choice of maximum run length, e.g. 3PM. The maximum number of symbols involved in a substitution is denoted by r. There are many RLL codes and the parameters d,k,m,n, and r are a way of comparing them.

Group codes are used extensively in recording and transmission. DVTRs and magnetic disks use group codes optimized for jitter rejection whereas optical disks use group codes optimized for density ratio.

10.13 Randomizing and encryption

Randomizing is not a channel code, but a technique which can be used in conjunction with almost any channel code. It is widely used in digital audio and video broadcasting and in a number of recording and transmission formats. The randomizing system is arranged outside the channel coder. Figure 10.27 shows that, at the encoder, a pseudo-random sequence is added modulo-2 to the serial data. This process makes the signal spectrum in the channel more uniform, drastically reduces T_{max} and reduces DC content. At the receiver the transitions are converted back to a serial bitstream to which the same pseudo-random sequence is

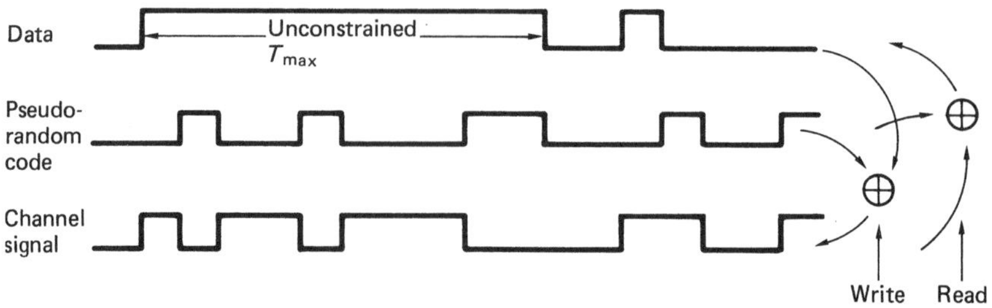

Figure 10.27 Modulo-2 addition with a pseudo-random code removes unconstrained runs in real data. Identical process must be provided on replay.

again added modulo-2. As a result the random signal cancels itself out to leave only the serial data, provided that the two pseudo-random sequences are synchronized to bit accuracy.

Many channel codes, especially group codes, display pattern sensitivity because some waveforms are more sensitive to peak shift distortion than others. Pattern sensitivity is only a problem if a sustained series of sensitive symbols needs to be recorded. Randomizing ensures that this cannot happen because it breaks up any regularity or repetition in the data. The data randomizing is performed by using the exclusive-OR function of the data and a pseudo-random sequence as the input to the channel coder. On replay the same sequence is generated, synchronized to bit accuracy, and the exclusive-OR of the replay bitstream and the sequence is the original data.

The generation of randomizing polynomials was described in section 2.8. Clearly the sync pattern cannot be randomized, since this causes a Catch-22 situation where it is not possible to synchronize the sequence for replay until the sync pattern is read, but it is not possible to read the sync pattern until the sequence is synchronized!

In recorders, the randomizing is block based, since this matches the block structure on the medium. Where there is no obvious block structure, convolutional, or endless randomizing can be used. In convolutional randomizing, the signal sent down the channel is the serial data waveform which has been convolved with the impulse response of a digital filter. On reception the signal is deconvolved to restore the original data.

Convolutional randomizing is used in the serial digital interface (SDI) which carries the production digital video. Figure 10.28(a) shows that the filter is an infinite impulse response (IIR) filter which has recursive paths from the output back to the input. As it is a one-bit filter its output cannot decay, and once excited, it runs indefinitely. The filter is followed by a transition generator which consists of a one-bit delay and an exclusive-OR gate. An input 1 results in an output transition on the next clock edge. An input 0 results in no transition.

A result of the infinite impulse response of the filter is that frequent transitions are generated in the channel which result in sufficient clock content for the phase-locked loop in the receiver.

Transitions are converted back to 1s by a differentiator in the receiver. This consists of a one-bit delay with an exclusive-OR gate comparing the input and the output. When a transition passes through the delay, the input and the output will be different and the gate outputs a 1 which enters the deconvolution circuit.

Figure 10.28(b) shows that in the deconvolution circuit a data bit is simply the exclusive-OR of a number of channel bits at a fixed spacing. The deconvolution is implemented with a shift register having the

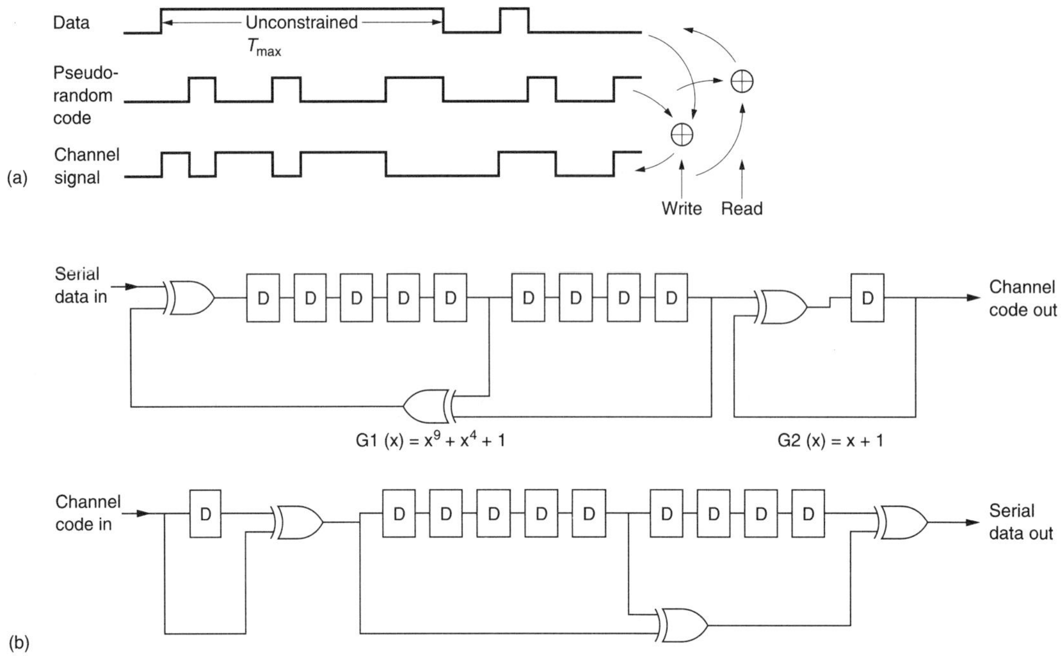

Figure 10.28 (a) Convolutional randomizing encoder transmits exclusive-OR of three bits at a fixed spacing in the data. One bit delay, far right, produces channel transitions from data ones. Decoder, (b), has opposing one-bit delay to return from transitions to data levels, followed by an opposing shift register which exactly reverses the coding process.

exclusive-OR gates connected in a reverse pattern to that in the encoder. The same effect as block randomizing is obtained, in that long runs are broken up and the DC content is reduced, but it has the advantage over block randomizing that no synchronizing is required to remove the randomizing, although it will still be necessary for deserialization. Clearly the system will take a few clock periods to produce valid data after commencement of transmission, but this is no problem on a permanent wired connection where the transmission is continuous.

In a randomized transmission, if the receiver is not able to re-create the pseudo-random sequence, the data cannot be decoded. This can be used as the basis for encryption in which only authorized users can decode transmitted data. In an encryption system, the goal is security whereas in a channel-coding system the goal is simplicity. Channel coders use pseudo-random sequences because these are economical to create using feedback shift registers. However, there are a limited number of pseudo-random sequences and it would be too easy to try them all until the correct one was found. Encryption systems use the same processes, but the key sequence which is added to the data at the encoder is truly random. This makes it much harder for unauthorized parties to access the data. Only a receiver in possession of the correct sequence can decode the channel signal. If the sequence is made long enough, the probability of stumbling across the sequence by trial and error can be made sufficiently small. Security systems of this kind can be compromised if the delivery of the key to the authorized user is intercepted.

10.14 Partial response

It has been stated that a magnetic head acts as a transversal filter, because it has two poles which scan the medium at different times. In addition the output is differentiated, so that the head may be thought of as a $(1 - D)$ impulse response system, where D is the delay which is a function of the tape speed and gap size. It is this delay which results in inter-symbol interference. Conventional equalizers attempt to oppose this effect, and succeed in raising the noise level in the process of making the frequency response linear. Figure 10.29 shows that the frequency response necessary

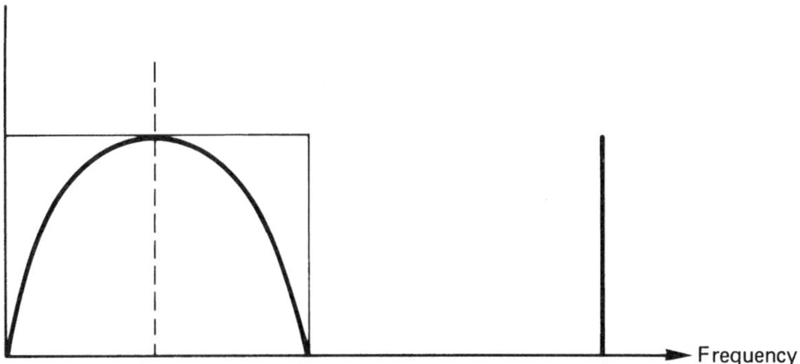

Figure 10.29 Class IV response has spectral nulls at DC and the Nyquist rate, giving a noise advantage, since magnetic replay signal is weak at both frequencies in a high-density channel.

to pass data with insignificant peak shift is a bandwidth of half the bit rate, which is the Nyquist rate. In Class IV partial response, the frequency response of the system is made to have nulls at DC and at the bit rate. Such a frequency response is particularly advantageous for rotary head recorders as it is DC-free and the low-frequency content is minimal, hence the use in Digital Betacam. The required response is is achieved by an overall impulse response of $(1 - D^2)$ where D is now the bit period. There are a number of ways in which this can be done.

If the head gap is made equal to one bit, the $(1 - D)$ head response may be converted to the desired response by the use of a $(1 + D)$ filter, as in

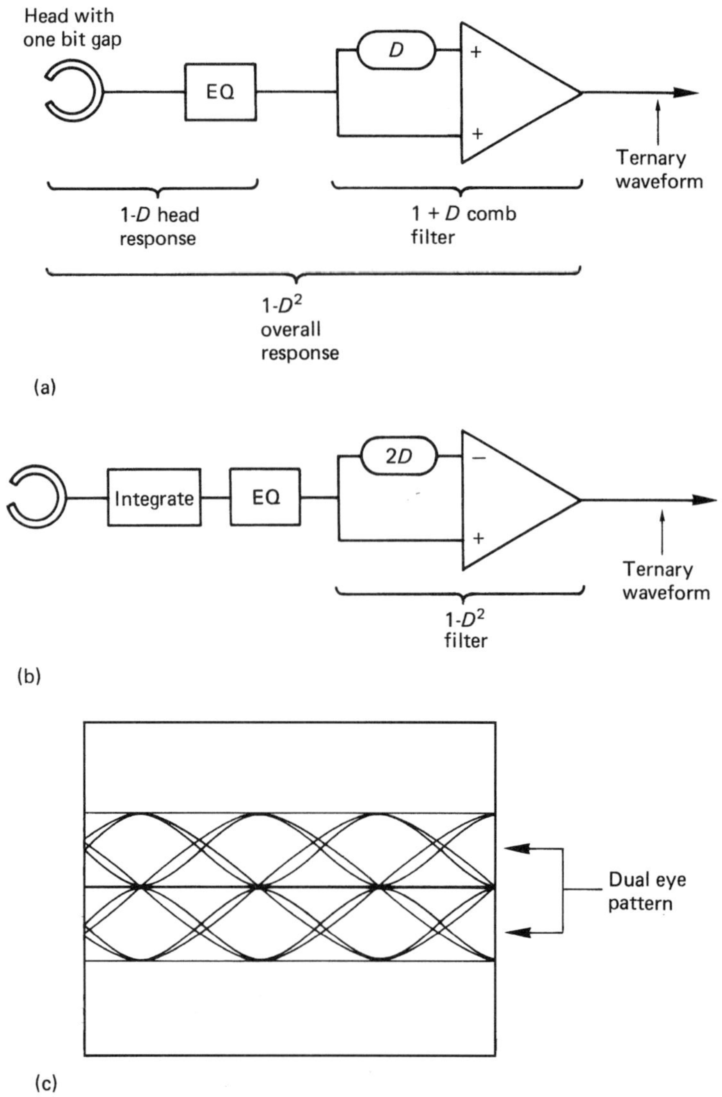

Figure 10.30 (a), (b) Two ways of obtaining partial response. (c) Characteristic eye pattern of ternary signal.

Figure 10.30(a).[9] Alternatively, a head of unspecified gapwidth may be connected to an integrator, and equalized flat to reproduce the record current waveform before being fed to a $(1 - D^2)$ filter as in Figure 10.30(b).[10]

The result of both of these techniques is a ternary signal. The eye pattern has two sets of eyes as in Figure 10.30(c).[11] When slicing such a signal, a smaller amount of noise will cause an error than in the binary case.

The treatment of the signal thus far represents an equalization technique, and not a channel code. However, to take full advantage of Class IV partial response, suitable precoding is necessary prior to recording, which does then constitute a channel-coding technique. This precoding is shown in Figure 10.31(a). Data are added modulo-2 to themselves with a two-bit delay. The effect of this precoding is that the outer levels of the ternary signals, which represent data ones, alternate in polarity on all odd bits and on all even bits. This is because the precoder

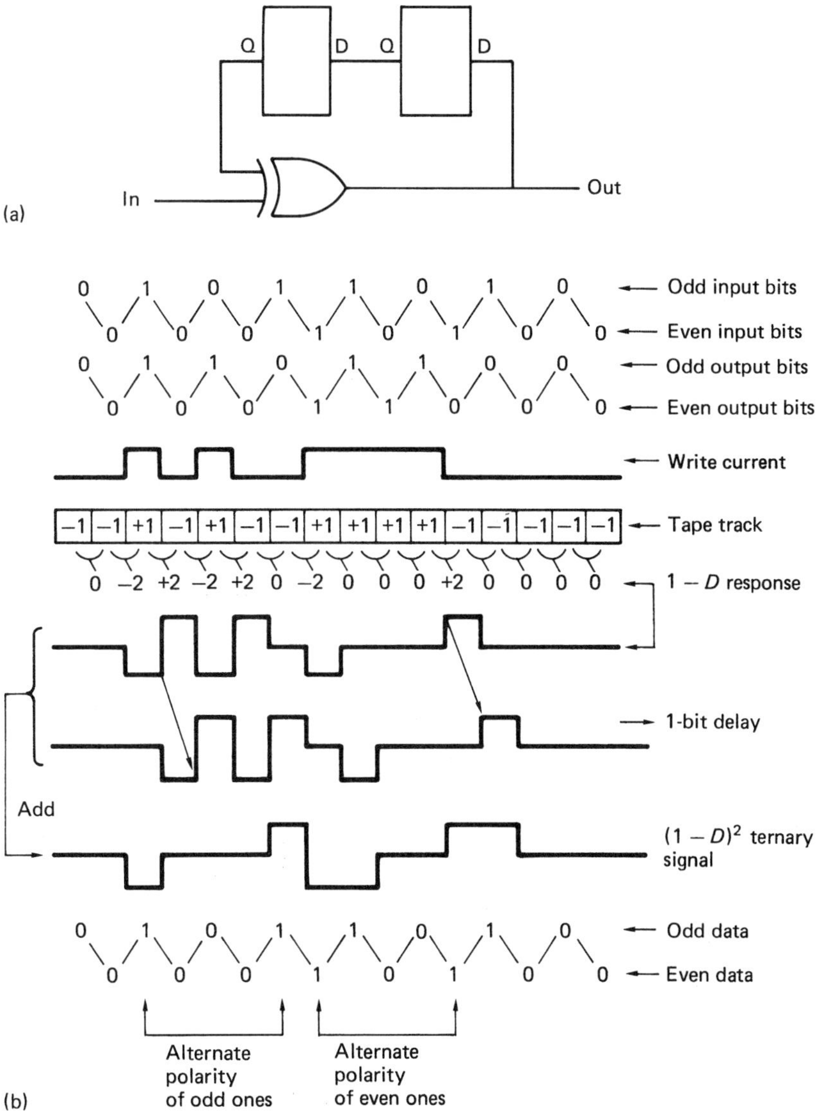

Figure 10.31 Class IV precoding at (a) causes redundancy in replay signal as derived in (b).

acts like two interleaved one-bit delay circuits, as in Figure 10.31(b). As this alternation of polarity is a form of redundancy, it can be used to recover the 3 dB SNR loss encountered in slicing a ternary eye pattern.

Viterbi decoding[12] can be used for this purpose. In Viterbi decoding, each channel bit is not sliced individually; the slicing decision is made in the context of adjacent decisions. Figure 10.32 shows a replay waveform

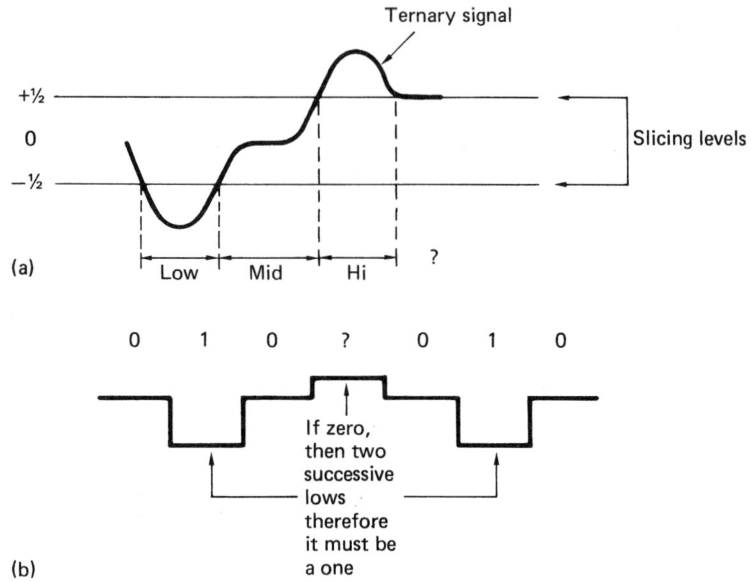

Figure 10.32 (a) A ternary signal suffers a noise penalty because there are two slicing levels. (b) The redundancy is used to determine the bit value in the presence of noise. Here the pulse height has been reduced to make it ambiguous 1/0, but only 1 is valid as zero violates the redundancy rules.

which is so noisy that, at the decision point, the signal voltage crosses the centre of the eye, and the slicer alone cannot tell whether the correct decision is an inner or an outer level. In this case, the decoder essentially allows both decisions to stand, in order to see what happens. A symbol representing indecision is output. It will be seen from the figure that as subsequent bits are received, one of these decisions will result in an absurd situation, which indicates that the other decision was the right one. The decoder can then locate the undecided symbol and set it to the correct value.

Viterbi decoding requires more information about the signal voltage than a simple binary slicer can discern. Figure 10.33 shows that the replay waveform is sampled and quantized so that it can be processed in digital logic. The sampling rate is obtained from the embedded clock content of the replay waveform. The digital Viterbi processing logic must be able to

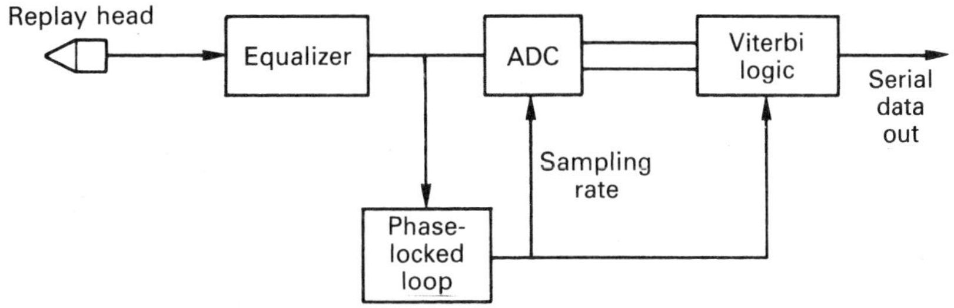

Figure 10.33 A Viterbi decoder is implemented in the digital domain by sampling the replay waveform with a clock locked to the embedded clock of the channel code.

operate at high speed to handle serial signals from a DVTR head. Its application in Digital Betacam is eased somewhat by the adoption of compression which reduces the data rate at the heads by a factor of two.

Clearly a ternary signal having a dual eye pattern is more sensitive than a binary signal, and it is important to keep the maximum run length T_{max} small in order to have accurate AGC. The use of pseudo-random coding along with partial response equalization and precoding is a logical combination.[13]

There is then considerable overlap between the channel code and the error-correction system. Viterbi decoding is primarily applicable to channels with random errors due to Gaussian statistics, and they cannot cope with burst errors. In a head-noise-limited system, however, the use of a Viterbi detector could increase the power of an separate burst error-correction system by relieving it of the need to correct random errors due to noise. The error-correction system could then concentrate on correcting burst errors unimpaired.

10.15 Synchronizing

Once the PLL in the data separator has locked to the clock content of the transmission, a serial channel bitstream and a channel bit clock will emerge from the sampler. In a group code, it is essential to know where a group of channel bits begins in order to assemble groups for decoding to data bit groups. In a randomizing system it is equally vital to know at what point in the serial data stream the words or samples commence. In serial transmission and in recording, channel bit groups or randomized data words are sent one after the other, one bit at a time, with no spaces in between, so that although the designer knows that a data block contains, say, 128 bytes, the receiver simply finds 1024 bits in a row. If the exact position of the first bit is not known, then it is not possible to put all the bits in the right places in the right bytes; a process known as deserializing. The effect of sync slippage is devastating, because a one-bit disparity between the bit count and the bitstream will corrupt every symbol in the block.

The synchronization of the data separator and the synchronization to the block format are two distinct problems, which are often solved by the same sync pattern. Deserializing requires a shift register which is fed with serial data and read out once per word. The sync detector is simply a set of logic gates which are arranged to recognize a specific pattern in the register. The sync pattern is either identical for every block or has a restricted number of versions and it will be recognized by the replay circuitry and used to reset the bit count through the block. Then by counting channel bits and dividing by the group size, groups can be deserialized and decoded to data groups. In a randomized system, the pseudo-random sequence generator is also reset. Then by counting derandomized bits from the sync pattern and dividing by the wordlength enables the replay circuitry to deserialize the data words.

Even if a specific code were excluded from the recorded data so it could be used for synchronizing, this cannot ensure that the same pattern cannot be falsely created at the junction between two allowable data words. Figure 10.34 shows how false synchronizing can occur due to concatenation. It is thus not practical to use a bit pattern which is a data code value in a simple synchronizing recognizer. The problem is overcome in some synchronous systems by using the fact that sync patterns occur exactly once per block and therefore contain redundancy. If the pattern is seen by the recognizer at block rate, a genuine sync condition exists. Sync patterns seen at other times must be false. Such systems take a few milliseconds before sync is achieved, but once achieved it should not be lost unless the transmission is interrupted.

In run-length-limited codes false syncs are not a problem. The sync pattern is no longer a data bit pattern but is a specific waveform. If the sync waveform contains run lengths which violate the normal coding limits, there is no way that these run lengths can occur in encoded data,

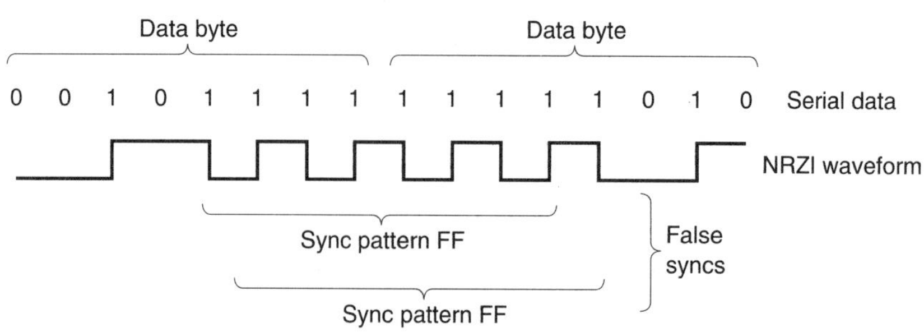

Figure 10.34 Concatenation of two words can result in the accidental generation of a word which is reserved for synchronizing.

nor any possibility that they will be interpreted as data. They can, however, be readily detected by the replay circuitry.

In a group code there are many more combinations of channel bits than there are combinations of data bits. Thus after all data bit patterns have been allocated group patterns, there are still many unused group patterns which cannot occur in the data. With care, group patterns can be found which cannot occur due to the concatenation of any pair of groups representing data. These are then unique and can be used for synchronizing.

10.16 Basic error correction

There are many different types of recording and transmission channel and consequently there will be many different mechanisms which may result in errors. Bit errors in video cause 'sparkles' in the picture whose effect depends upon the significance of the affected bit. Errors in compressed data are more serious as they may cause the decoder to lose sync.

In magnetic recording, data can be corrupted by mechanical problems such as media dropout and poor tracking or head contact, or Gaussian thermal noise in replay circuits and heads. In optical recording, contamination of the medium interrupts the light beam. When group codes are used, a single defect in a group changes the group symbol and may cause errors up to the size of the group. Single-bit errors are therefore less common in group-coded channels. Inside equipment, data are conveyed on short wires and the noise environment is under the designer's control. With suitable design techniques, errors can be made effectively negligible whereas in communication systems, there is considerably less control of the electromagnetic environment.

Irrespective of the cause, all these mechanisms cause one of two effects. There are large isolated corruptions, called error bursts, where numerous bits are corrupted all together in an area which is otherwise error-free, and there are random errors affecting single bits or symbols. Whatever the mechanism, the result will be that the received data will not be exactly the same as those sent. In binary the discrete bits will be each either right or wrong. If a binary digit is known to be wrong, it is only necessary to invert its state and then it must be right. Thus error correction itself is trivial; the hard part is working out *which* bits need correcting.

There are a number of terms which have idiomatic meanings in error correction. The raw BER (bit error rate) is the error rate of the medium, whereas the residual or uncorrected BER is the rate at which the error-correction system fails to detect or miscorrects errors. In practical digital systems, the residual BER is negligibly small. If the error correction is turned off, the two figures become the same.

Error correction works by adding some bits to the data which are calculated from the data. This creates an entity called a codeword which spans a greater length of time than one bit alone. The statistics of noise means that whilst one bit may be lost in a codeword, the loss of the rest of the codeword because of noise is highly improbable. As will be described later in this chapter, codewords are designed to be able to correct totally a finite number of corrupted bits. The greater the timespan over which the coding is performed, or, on a recording medium, the greater area over which the coding is performed, the greater will be the reliability achieved, although this does mean that an encoding delay will be experienced on recording, and a similar or greater decoding delay on reproduction.

Shannon [14] disclosed that a message can be sent to any desired degree of accuracy provided that it is spread over a sufficient timespan. Engineers have to compromise, because an infinite coding delay in the recovery of an error-free signal is not acceptable. Digital interfaces such as SDI (see Chapter 12) do not employ error correction because the build-up of coding delays in large production systems is unacceptable.

If error correction is necessary as a practical matter, it is then only a small step to put it to maximum use. All error correction depends on adding bits to the original message, and this, of course, increases the number of bits to be recorded, although it does not increase the information recorded. It might be imagined that error correction is going to reduce storage capacity, because space has to be found for all the extra bits. Nothing could be further from the truth. Once an error-correction system is used, the signal-to-noise ratio of the channel can be reduced, because the raised BER of the channel will be overcome by the error-correction system. Reduction of the SNR by 3 dB in a magnetic track can be achieved by halving the track width, provided that the system is not dominated by head or preamplifier noise. This doubles the recording density, making the storage of the additional bits needed for error correction a trivial matter. By a similar argument, the power of a digital transmitter can be reduced if error correction is used. In short, error correction is not a nuisance to be tolerated; it is a vital tool needed to maximize the efficiency of storage devices and transmission. Convergent systems would not be economically viable without it.

Figure 10.35 shows the broad subdivisions of error handling. The first stage might be called error avoidance and includes such measures as creating bad block files on hard disks or using verified media. Properly terminating network cabling is also in this category. Placing the audio blocks near to the centre of the tape in DVTRs is a further example. The data pass through the channel, which causes whatever corruptions it feels like. On receipt of the data the occurrence of errors is first detected, and this process must be extremely reliable, as it does not matter how effective the correction or how good the concealment algorithm if it is not known that

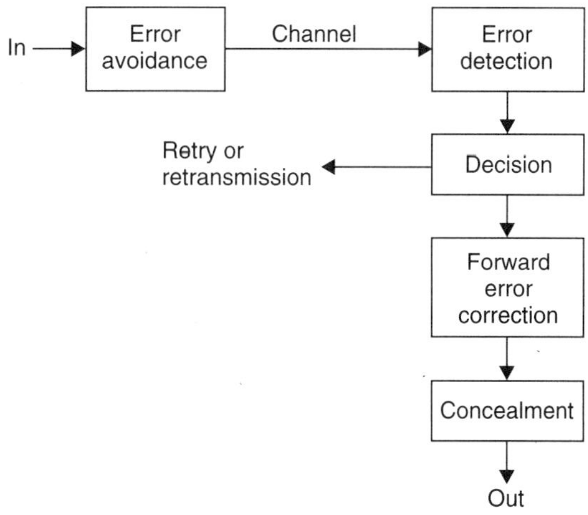

Figure 10.35 Error-handling strategies can be divided into avoiding errors, detecting errors and deciding what to do about them. Some possibilities are shown here. Of all these the detection is the most critical, as nothing can be done if the error is not detected.

they are necessary! The detection of an error then results in a course of action being decided.

In the case of a file transfer, real-time operation is not required. If a disk drive detects a read error a retry is easy as the disk is turning at several thousand rpm and will quickly re-present the data. An error due to a dust particle may not occur on the next revolution. A packet in error in a network will result in a retransmission. Many magnetic tape systems have *read after write*. During recording, offtape data are immediately checked for errors. If an error is detected, the tape may abort the recording, reverse to the beginning of the current block and erase it. The data from that block may then be recorded further down the tape. This is the recording equivalent of a retransmission in a communications system.

In many cases of digital video or audio replay a retry or retransmission is not possible because the data are required in real time. In this case the solution is to encode the message using a system which is sufficiently powerful to correct the errors in real time. These are called forward error-correcting schemes (FEC). The term 'forward' implies that the transmitter does not need to take any action in the case of an error; the receiver will perform the correction.

10.17 Concealment by interpolation

There are some practical differences between data recording for video and the computer data recording application. Although video or audio recorders seldom have time for retries, they have the advantage that there is a certain amount of redundancy in the information conveyed. Thus if an error cannot be corrected, then it can be concealed. If a sample is lost, it is possible to obtain an approximation to it by interpolating between samples in the vicinity of the missing one. Clearly concealment of any kind cannot be used with computer instructions or compressed data, although concealment can be applied after compressed signals have been decoded.

If there is too much corruption for concealment, the only course in video is to repeat the previous field or frame in a freeze as it is unlikely that the corrupt picture is watchable. In audio the equivalent is muting.

In general, if use is to be made of concealment on replay, the data must generally be reordered or shuffled prior to recording. To take a simple example, odd-numbered samples are recorded in a different area of the medium from even-numbered samples. On playback, if a gross error occurs on the medium, depending on its position, the result will be either corrupted odd samples or corrupted even samples, but it is most unlikely that both will be lost. Interpolation is then possible if the power of the correction system is exceeded. In practice the shuffle employed in digital video recorders is two-dimensional and rather more complex. Further details can be found in Chapter 11. The concealment technique described here is only suitable for PCM recording. If compression has been employed, different concealment techniques will be needed.

It should be stressed that corrected data are indistinguishable from the original and thus there can be no visible or audible artifacts. In contrast, concealment is only an approximation to the original information and could be detectable. In practical equipment, concealment occurs infrequently unless there is a defect requiring attention, and its presence is difficult to see.

10.18 Parity

The error-detection and error-correction processes are closely related and will be dealt with together here. The actual correction of an error is simplified tremendously by the adoption of binary. As there are only two symbols, 0 and 1, it is enough to know that a symbol is wrong, and the

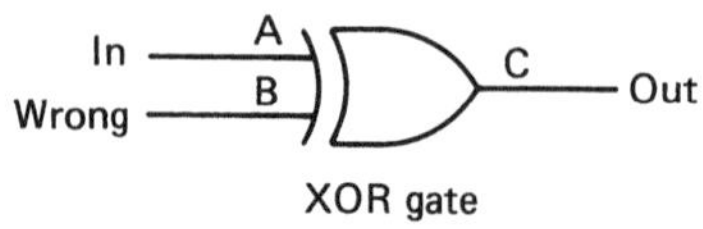

Truth table of XOR gate

A	B	C
0	0	0
0	1	1
1	0	1
1	1	0

$$A \oplus B = C$$

Figure 10.36 Once the position of the error is identified, the correction process in binary is easy.

correct value is obvious. Figure 10.36 shows a minimal circuit required for correction once the bit in error has been identified. The XOR (exclusive-OR) gate shows up extensively in error correction and the figure also shows the truth table. One way of remembering the characteristics of this useful device is that there will be an output when the inputs are different. Inspection of the truth table will show that there is an even number of ones in each row (zero is an even number) and so the device could also be called an even parity gate. The XOR gate is also an adder in modulo-2.

Parity is a fundamental concept in error detection. In Figure 10.37, the example is given of a four-bit data word which is to be protected. If an extra bit is added to the word which is calculated in such a way that the total number of ones in the five-bit word is even, this property can be tested on receipt. The generation of the parity bit can be performed by a number of the ubiquitous XOR gates configured into what is known as a

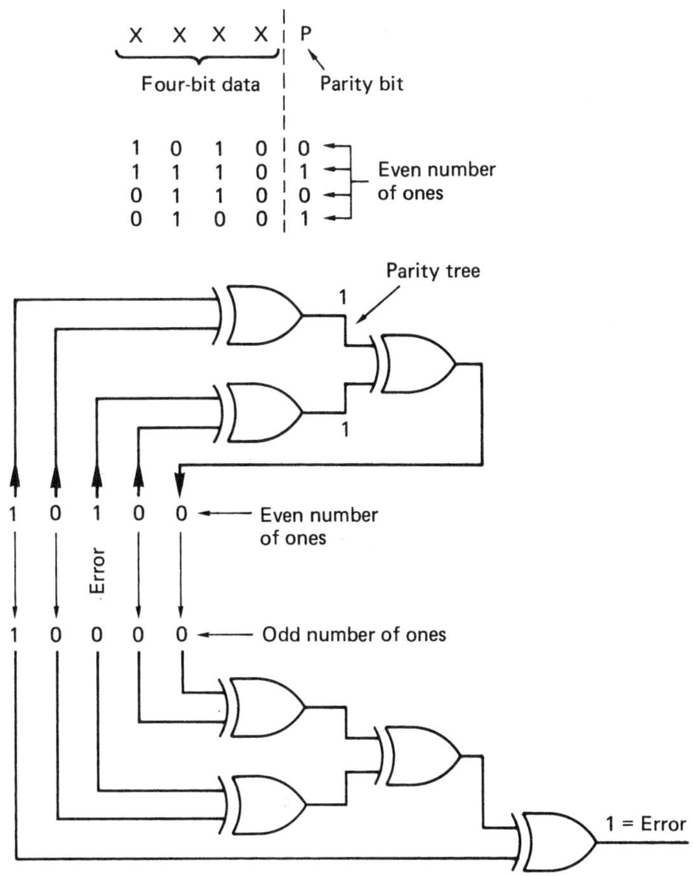

Figure 10.37 Parity checking adds up the number of ones in a word using, in this example, parity trees. One error bit and odd numbers of errors are detected. Even numbers of errors cannot be detected.

parity tree. In the figure, if a bit is corrupted, the received message will be seen no longer to have an even number of ones. If two bits are corrupted, the failure will be undetected. This example can be used to introduce much of the terminology of error correction. The extra bit added to the message carries no information of its own, since it is calculated from the other bits. It is therefore called a *redundant* bit.

The addition of the redundant bit gives the message a special property, i.e. the number of ones is even. A message having some special property *irrespective of the actual data content* is called a *codeword*. All error correction relies on adding redundancy to real data to form codewords for transmission. If any corruption occurs, the intention is that the received message will not have the special property; in other words if the received message is not a codeword there has definitely been an error. The receiver can check for the special property without any prior knowledge of the data content. Thus the same check can be made on all received data. If the received message is a codeword, there probably has not been an error. The word 'probably' must be used because the figure shows that two bits in error will cause the received message to be a codeword, which cannot be discerned from an error-free message.

If it is known that generally the only failure mechanism in the channel in question is loss of a single bit, it is *assumed* that receipt of a codeword means that there has been no error. If there is a probability of two error bits, that becomes very nearly the probability of failing to detect an error, since all odd numbers of errors will be detected, and a four-bit error is much less likely. It is paramount in all error-correction systems that the protection used should be appropriate for the probability of errors to be encountered. An inadequate error-correction system is actually worse

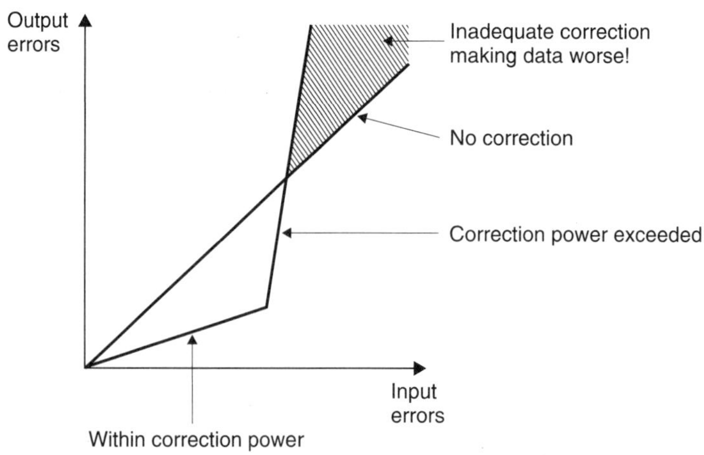

Figure 10.38 An error-correction system can only reduce errors at normal error rates at the expense of increasing errors at higher rates. It is most important to keep a system working to the left of the knee in the graph.

than not having any correction. Error correction works by trading probabilities. Error-free performance with a certain error rate is achieved at the expense of performance at higher error rates. Figure 10.38 shows the effect of an error-correction system on the residual BER for a given raw BER. It will be seen that there is a characteristic knee in the graph. If the expected raw BER has been misjudged, the consequences can be disastrous. Another result demonstrated by the example is that we can only guarantee to detect the same number of bits in error as there are redundant bits.

10.19 Block and convolutional codes

Figure 10.39(a) shows a strategy known as a crossword code, or product code. The data are formed into a two-dimensional array, in which each location can be a single bit or a multi-bit symbol. Parity is then generated on both rows and columns. If a single bit or symbol fails, one row parity check and one column parity check will fail, and the failure can be located at the intersection of the two failing checks. Although two symbols in error confuse this simple scheme, using more complex coding in a two-dimensional structure is very powerful, and further examples will be given throughout this chapter.

The example of Figure 10.39(a) assembles the data to be coded into a block of finite size and then each codeword is calculated by taking a different set of symbols. This should be contrasted with the operation of the circuit of (b). Here the data are not in a block, but form an endless stream. A shift register allows four symbols to be available simultaneously to the encoder. The action of the encoder depends upon the delays. When symbol 3 emerges from the first delay, it will be added (modulo-2) to symbol 6. When this sum emerges from the second delay, it will be added to symbol 9 and so on. The codeword produced is shown in Figure 10.39(c) where it will be seen to be bent such that it has a vertical section and a diagonal section. Four symbols later the next codeword will be created one column further over in the data.

This is a convolutional code because the coder always takes parity on the same pattern of symbols which is convolved with the data stream on an endless basis. Figure 10.39(c) also shows that if an error occurs, it can be located because it will cause parity errors in two codewords. The error will be on the diagonal part of one codeword and on the vertical part of the other so that it can be located uniquely at the intersection and corrected by parity.

Comparison with the block code of Figure 10.39(a) will show that the convolutional code needs less redundancy for the same single symbol location and correction performance as only a single redundant symbol is

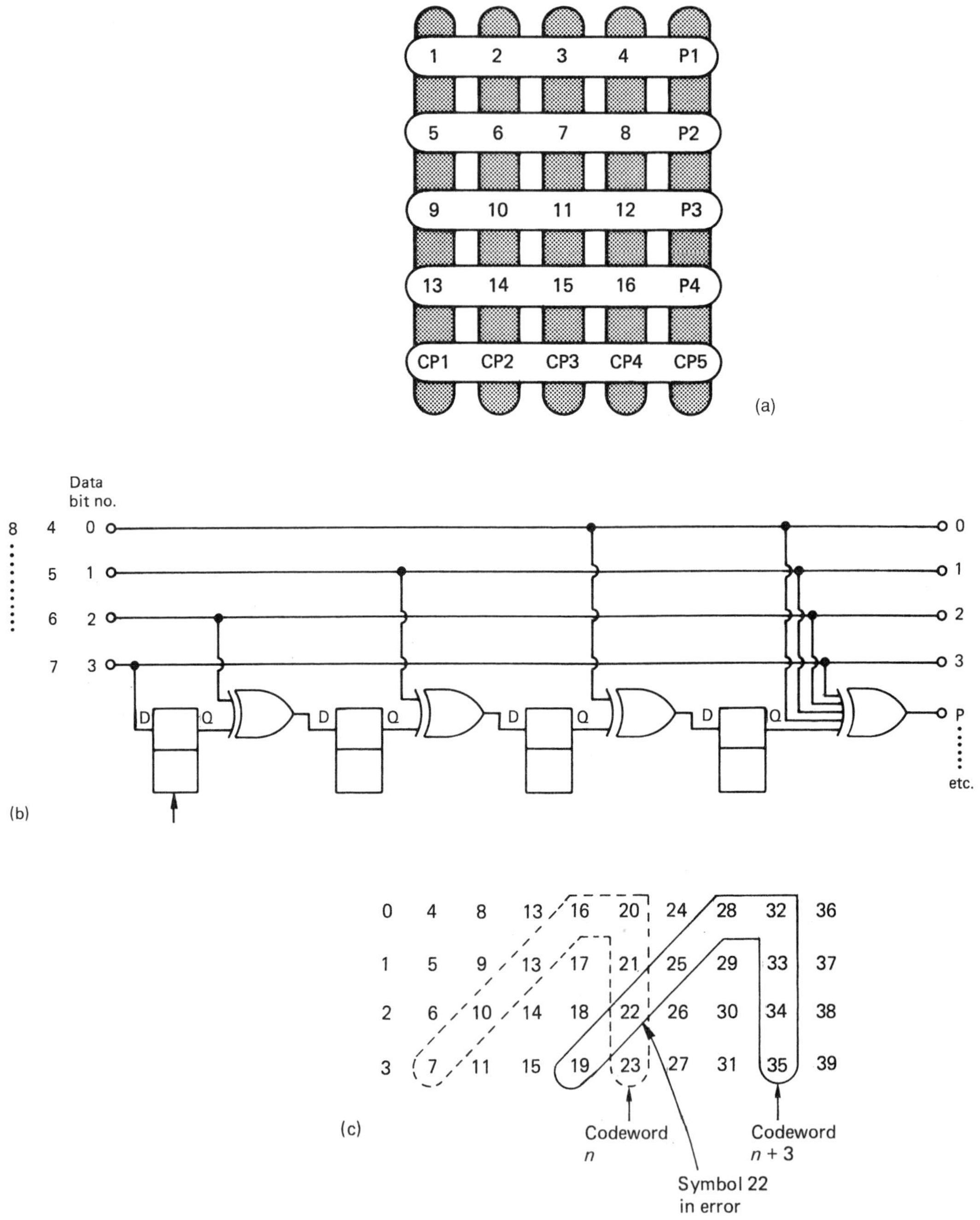

Figure 10.39 A block code is shown in (a). Each location in the block can be a bit or a word. Horizontal parity checks are made by adding P1, P2, etc., and cross-parity or vertical checks are made by adding CP1, CP2, etc. Any symbol in error will be at the intersection of the two failing codewords. In (b) a convolutional coder is shown. Symbols entering are subject to different delays which result in the codewords in (c) being calculated. These have a vertical part and a diagonal part. A symbol in error will be at the intersection of the diagonal part of one code and the vertical part of another.

required for every four data symbols. Convolutional codes are computed on an endless basis which makes them inconvenient in recording applications where editing is anticipated. Here the block code is more appropriate as it allows edit gaps to be created between codes. In the case of uncorrectable errors, the convolutional principle causes the syndromes to be affected for some time afterwards and the results in miscorrections of symbols which were not actually in error. This is called error propagation and is a characteristic of convolutional codes. Recording media tend to produce somewhat variant error statistics because media defects and mechanical problems cause errors which do not fit the classical additive noise channel. Convolutional codes can easily be taken beyond their correcting power if used with real recording media.

In transmission and broadcasting, the error statistics are more stable and the editing requirement is absent. As a result convolutional codes tend to be used in digital broadcasting as will be seen in Chapter 12.

10.20 Cyclic codes

In digital recording applications, the data are stored serially on a track, and it is desirable to use relatively large data blocks to reduce the amount of the medium devoted to preambles, addressing and synchronizing. The principle of codewords having a special characteristic will still be employed, but they will be generated and checked algorithmically by equations. The syndrome will then be converted to the bit(s) in error by solving equations.

Where data can be accessed serially, simple circuitry can be used because the same gate will be used for many XOR operations. The circuit of Figure 10.40 is a kind of shift register, but with a particular feedback arrangement which leads it to be known as a twisted-ring counter. If seven message bits A–G are applied serially to this circuit, and each one of them is clocked, the outcome can be followed in the diagram. As bit A is presented and the system is clocked, bit A will enter the left-hand latch. When bits B and C are presented, A moves across to the right. Both XOR gates will have A on the upper input from the right-hand latch, the left one has D on the lower input and the right one has B on the lower input. When clocked, the left latch will thus be loaded with the XOR of A and D, and the right one with the XOR of A and B. The remainder of the sequence can be followed, bearing in mind that when the same term appears on both inputs of an XOR gate, it goes out, as the exclusive-OR of something with itself is nothing. At the end of the process, the latches contain three different expressions. Essentially, the circuit makes three parity checks through the message, leaving the result of each in the three stages of the register. In the figure, these expressions have been used to

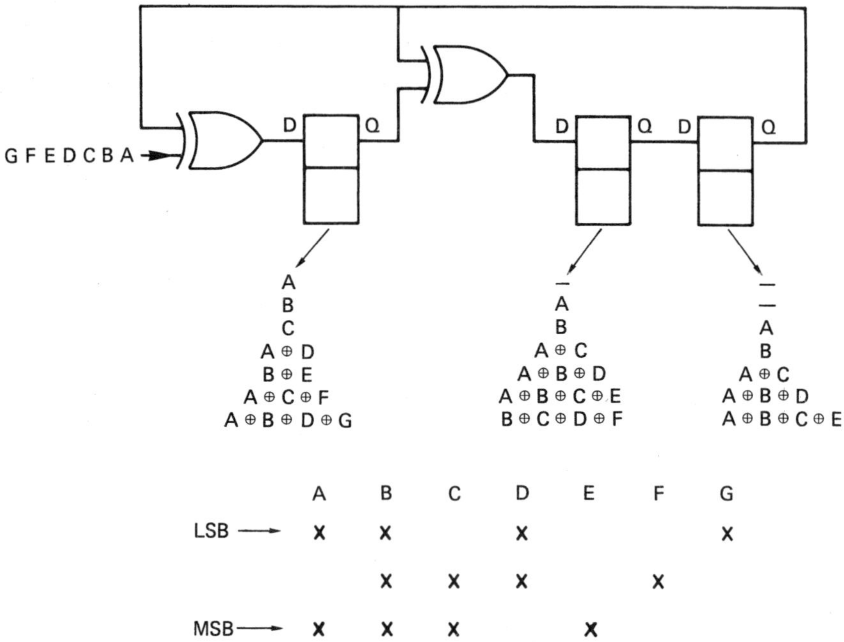

Figure 10.40 When seven successive bits A–G are clocked into this circuit, the contents of the three latches are shown for each clock. The final result is a parity-check matrix.

draw up a check matrix. The significance of these steps can now be explained.

The bits A B C and D are four data bits, and the bits E F and G are redundancy. When the redundancy is calculated, bit E is chosen so that there are an even number of ones in bits A B C and E; bit F is chosen such that the same applies to bits B C D and F, and similarly for bit G. Thus the four data bits and the three check bits form a seven-bit codeword. If there is no error in the codeword, when it is fed into the circuit shown, the result of each of the three parity checks will be zero and every stage of the shift register will be cleared. As the register has eight possible states, and one of them is the error-free condition, then there are seven remaining states, hence the seven-bit codeword. If a bit in the codeword is corrupted, there will be a non-zero result. For example, if bit D fails, the check on bits A B D and G will fail, and a one will appear in the left-hand latch. The check on bits B C D F will also fail, and the centre latch will set. The check on bits A B C E will not fail, because D is not involved in it, making the right-hand bit zero. There will be a syndrome of 110 in the register, and this will be seen from the check matrix to correspond to an error in bit D. Whichever bit fails, there will be a different three-bit syndrome which uniquely identifies the failed bit. As there are only three latches, there can be eight different syndromes. One of these is zero, which is the error-free condition, and so there are seven remaining error syndromes. The length of the codeword cannot exceed seven bits, or there would not be enough syndromes to correct all the bits. This can also be made to tie in with the generation of the check matrix. If fourteen bits, A to N, were fed into the circuit shown, the result would be that the check matrix repeated twice, and if a syndrome of 101 were to result, it could not be determined whether bit D or bit K failed. Because the check repeats every seven bits, the code is said to be a cyclic redundancy check (CRC) code.

It has been seen that the circuit shown makes a matrix check on a received word to determine if there has been an error, but the same circuit can also be used to generate the check bits. To visualize how this is done, examine what happens if only the data bits A B C and D are known, and the check bits E F and G are set to zero. If this message, ABCD000, is fed into the circuit, the left-hand latch will afterwards contain the XOR of A B C and zero, which is, of course what E should be. The centre latch will contain the XOR of B C D and zero, which is what F should be and so on. This process is not quite ideal, however, because it is necessary to wait for three clock periods after entering the data before the check bits are available. Where the data are simultaneously being recorded and fed into the encoder, the delay would prevent the check bits being easily added to the end of the data stream. This problem can be overcome by slightly modifying the encoder circuit as shown in Figure 10.41. By moving the position of the input to the right, the operation of the circuit is advanced so that the check bits are ready after only four clocks. The process can be followed in the diagram for the four data bits A B C and D. On the first clock, bit A enters the left two latches, whereas on the second clock, bit B will appear on the upper input of the left XOR gate, with bit A on the lower input, causing the centre latch to load the XOR of A and B and so on.

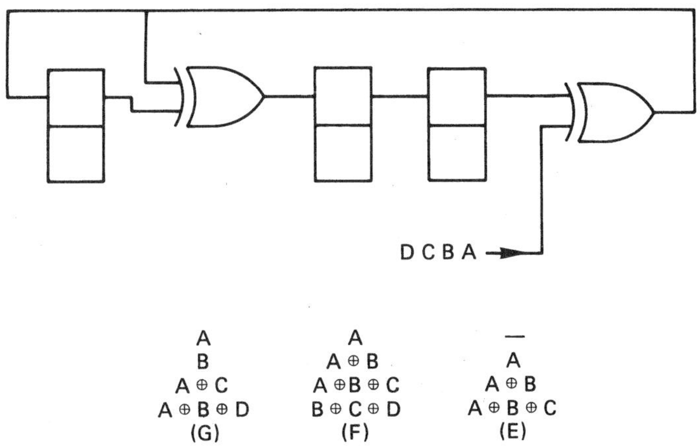

Figure 10.41 By moving the insertion point three places to the right, the calculation of the check bits is completed in only four clock periods and they can follow the data immediately. This is equivalent to premultiplying the data by x^3.

The way in which the cyclic codes work has been described in engineering terms, but it can be described mathematically if analysis is contemplated.

Just as the position of a decimal digit in a number determines the power of ten (whether that digit means one, ten or a hundred), the position of a binary digit determines the power of two (whether it means one, two or four). It is possible to rewrite a binary number so that it is expressed as a list of powers of two. For example, the binary number 1101 means 8 + 4 + 1, and can be written:

$$2^3 + 2^2 + 2^0$$

In fact, much of the theory of error correction applies to symbols in number bases other than 2, so that the number can also be written more generally as

$$x^3 + x^2 + 1 \ (2^0 = 1)$$

which also looks much more impressive. This expression, containing as it does various powers, is of course a polynomial, and the circuit of Figure 10.40 which has been seen to construct a parity-check matrix on a codeword can also be described as calculating the remainder due to dividing the input by a polynomial using modulo-2 arithmetic. In modulo-2 there are no borrows or carries, and addition and subtraction are replaced by the XOR function, which makes hardware implementation very easy. In Figure 10.42 it will be seen that the circuit of Figure 10.43 actually divides the codeword by a polynomial which is

$$x^3 + x + 1 \text{ or } 1011$$

This can be deduced from the fact that the right-hand bit is fed into two lower-order stages of the register at once. Once all the bits of the message have been clocked in, the circuit contains the remainder. In mathematical terms, the special property of a codeword is that it is a polynomial which yields a remainder of zero when divided by the generating polynomial. The receiver will make this division, and the result should be zero in the error-free case. Thus the codeword itself disappears from the division. If an error has occurred it is considered that this is due to an error polynomial which has been added to the codeword polynomial. If a codeword divided by the check polynomial is zero, a non-zero syndrome must represent the error polynomial divided by the check polynomial. Thus if the syndrome is multiplied by the check polynomial, the latter will be cancelled out and the result will be the error polynomial. If this is added modulo-2 to the received word, it will cancel out the error and leave the corrected data.

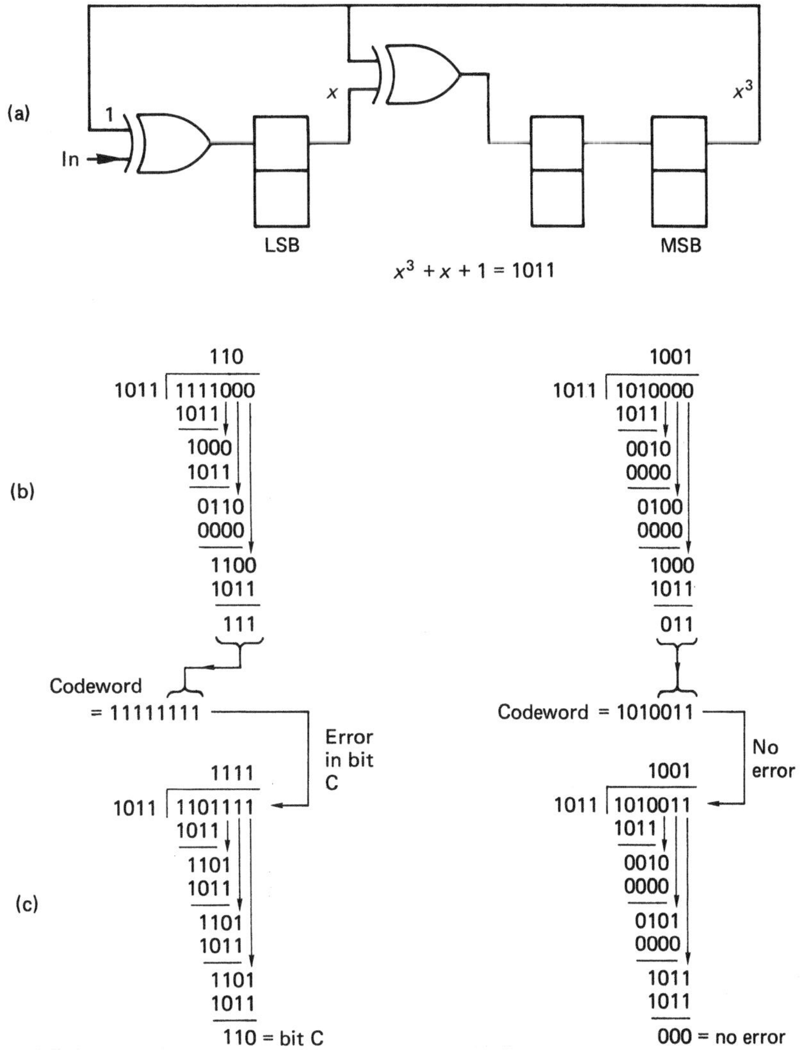

Figure 10.42 Circuit of Figure 10.40 divides by $x^3 + x + 1$ to find remainder. At (b) this is used to calculate check bits. At (c) right, zero syndrome, no error.

Some examples of modulo-2 division are given in Figure 10.42 which can be compared with the parallel computation of parity checks according to the matrix of Figure 10.40.

The process of generating the codeword from the original data can also be described mathematically. If a codeword has to give zero remainder when divided, it follows that the data can be converted to a codeword by adding the remainder when the data are divided. Generally speaking the remainder would have to be subtracted, but in modulo-2 there is no distinction. This process is also illustrated in Figure 10.42. The four data bits have three zeros placed on the right-hand end, to make the wordlength

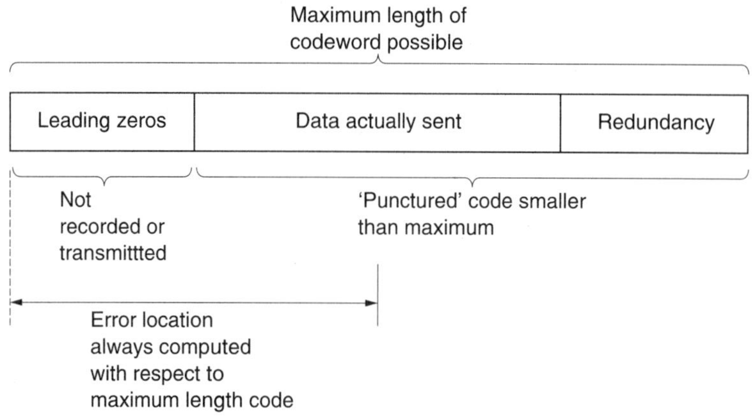

Figure 10.43 Codewords are often shortened, or punctured, which means that only the end of the codeword is actually transmitted. The only precaution to be taken when puncturing codes is that the computed position of an error will be from the beginning of the codeword, not from the beginning of the message.

equal to that of a codeword, and this word is then divided by the polynomial to calculate the remainder. The remainder is added to the zero-extended data to form a codeword. The modified circuit of Figure 10.41 can be described as premultiplying the data by x^3 before dividing.

CRC codes are of primary importance for detecting errors, and several have been standardized for use in digital communications. The most common of these are:

$$x^{16} + x^{15} + x^2 + 1 \text{ (CRC-16)}$$

$$x^{16} + x^{12} + x^5 + 1 \text{ (CRC-CCITT)}$$

The sixteen-bit cyclic codes have codewords of length $2^{16} - 1$ or 65 535 bits long. This may be too long for the application. Another problem with very long codes is that with a given raw BER, the longer the code, the more errors will occur in it. There may be enough errors to exceed the power of the code. The solution in both cases is to shorten or *puncture* the code. Figure 10.43 shows that in a punctured code, only the end of the codeword is used, and the data and redundancy are preceded by a string of zeros. It is not necessary to record these zeros, and, of course, errors cannot occur in them. Implementing a punctured code is easy. If a CRC generator starts with the register cleared and is fed with serial zeros, it will not change its state. Thus it is not necessary to provide the zeros, encoding can begin with the first data bit. In the same way, the leading zeros need not be provided during playback. The only precaution needed is that if a syndrome calculates the location of an error, this will be from the beginning of the codeword not from the beginning of the data. Where codes are used for detection only, this is of no consequence.

10.21 Introduction to the Reed–Solomon codes

The Reed–Solomon codes (Irving Reed and Gustave Solomon) are inherently burst correcting[15] because they work on multi-bit symbols rather than individual bits. The R–S codes are also extremely flexible in use. One code may be used both to detect and correct errors and the number of bursts which are correctable can be chosen at the design stage by the amount of redundancy. A further advantage of the R–S codes is that they can be used in conjunction with a separate error-detection mechanism in which case they perform only the correction by erasure. R–S codes operate at the theoretical limit of correcting efficiency. In other words, no more efficient code can be found.

In the simple CRC system described in section 4.18, the effect of the error is detected by ensuring that the codeword can be divided by a polynomial. The CRC codeword was created by adding a redundant symbol to the data. In the Reed–Solomon codes, several errors can be isolated by ensuring that the codeword will divide by a number of polynomials. Clearly if the codeword must divide by, say, two polynomials, it must have two redundant symbols. This is the minimum case of an R–S code. On receiving an R–S coded message there will be two syndromes following the division. In the error-free case, these will both be zero. If both are not zero, there is an error.

It has been stated that the effect of an error is to add an error polynomial to the message polynomial. The number of terms in the error polynomial is the same as the number of errors in the codeword. The codeword divides to zero and the syndromes are a function of the error only. There are two syndromes and two equations. By solving these simultaneous equations it is possible to obtain two unknowns. One of these is the position of the error, known as the *locator* and the other is the error bit pattern, known as the *corrector*. As the locator is the same size as the code symbol, the length of the codeword is determined by the size of the symbol. A symbol size of eight bits is commonly used because it fits in conveniently with both sixteen-bit audio samples and byte-oriented computers. An eight-bit syndrome results in a locator of the same wordlength. Eight bits have 2^8 combinations, but one of these is the error-free condition, and so the locator can specify one of only 255 symbols. As each symbol contains eight bits, the codeword will be $255 \times 8 = 2040$ bits long.

As further examples, five-bit symbols could be used to form a codeword 31 symbols long, and three-bit symbols would form a codeword seven symbols long. This latter size is small enough to permit some worked examples, and will be used further here. Figure 10.44 shows that in the seven-symbol codeword, five symbols of three bits each, A–E, are the data, and P and Q are the two redundant symbols. This simple

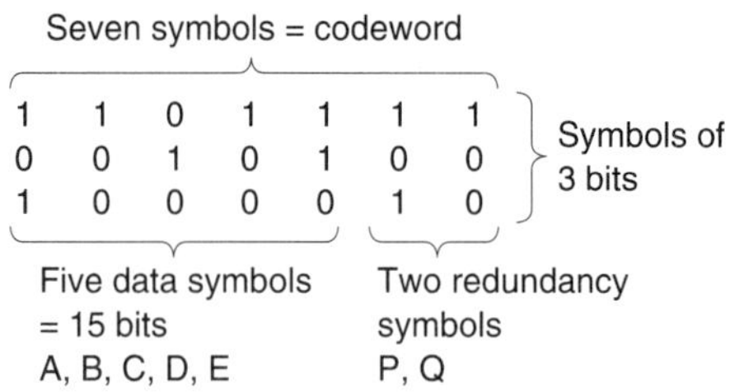

Figure 10.44 A Reed–Solomon codeword. As the symbols are of three bits, there can only be eight possible syndrome values. One of these is all zeros, the error-free case, and so it is only possible to point to seven errors; hence the codeword length of seven symbols. Two of these are redundant, leaving five data symbols.

example will locate and correct a single symbol in error. It does not matter, however, how many bits in the symbol are in error.

The two check symbols are solutions to the following equations:

$$\mathrm{A} \oplus \mathrm{B} \oplus \mathrm{C} \oplus \mathrm{D} \oplus \mathrm{E} \oplus \mathrm{P} \oplus \mathrm{Q} = 0 \ (\oplus = \text{XOR symbol})$$

$$a^7\,\mathrm{A} \oplus a^6\,\mathrm{B} \oplus a^5\,\mathrm{C} \oplus a^4\,\mathrm{D} \oplus a^3\,\mathrm{E} \oplus a^2\,\mathrm{P} \oplus a\mathrm{Q} = 0$$

where a is a constant. The original data A–E followed by the redundancy P and Q pass through the channel.

The receiver makes two checks on the message to see if it is a codeword. This is done by calculating syndromes using the following expressions, where the (′) implies the received symbol which is not necessarily correct:

$$\mathrm{S}_0 = \mathrm{A}' \oplus \mathrm{B}' \oplus \mathrm{C}' \oplus \mathrm{D}' \oplus \mathrm{E}' \oplus \mathrm{P}' \oplus \mathrm{Q}'$$

(This is in fact a simple parity check.)

$$\mathrm{S}_1 = a^7\,\mathrm{A}' \oplus a^6\,\mathrm{B}' \oplus a^5\,\mathrm{C}' \oplus a^4\,\mathrm{D}' \oplus a^3\mathrm{E}' \oplus a^2\,\mathrm{P}' \oplus a\mathrm{Q}'$$

If two syndromes of all zeros are not obtained, there has been an error. The information carried in the syndromes will be used to correct the error. For the purpose of illustration, let it be considered that D′ has been corrupted before moving to the general case. D′ can be considered to be the result of adding an error of value E to the original value D such that $\mathrm{D}' = \mathrm{D} \oplus E$.

$$\text{As } \mathrm{A} \oplus \mathrm{B} \oplus \mathrm{C} \oplus \mathrm{D} \oplus \mathrm{E} \oplus \mathrm{P} \oplus \mathrm{Q} = 0$$

$$\text{then } \mathrm{A} \oplus \mathrm{B} \oplus \mathrm{C} \oplus (\mathrm{D} \oplus E) \oplus \mathrm{E} \oplus \mathrm{P} \oplus \mathrm{Q} = E = \mathrm{S}_0$$

$$\text{As } \mathrm{D}' = \mathrm{D} \oplus E$$

$$\text{then } \mathrm{D} = \mathrm{D}' \oplus E = \mathrm{D}' \oplus \mathrm{S}_0$$

Thus the value of the corrector is known immediately because it is the same as the parity syndrome S_0. The corrected data symbol is obtained simply by adding S_0 to the incorrect symbol.

At this stage, however, the corrupted symbol has not yet been identified, but this is equally straightforward.

$$\text{As } a^7 \text{ A} \oplus a^6 \text{ B} \oplus a^5 \text{ C} \oplus a^4 \text{ D} \oplus a^3 \text{ E} \oplus a^2 \text{ P} \oplus a\text{Q} = 0$$

Then:

$$a^7 \text{ A} \oplus a^6 \text{ B} \oplus a^5 \text{ C} \oplus a^4 (\text{D} \oplus E) \oplus a^3 \text{ E} \oplus a^2 \text{ P} \oplus a\text{Q} = a^4 E = \text{S}_1$$

Thus the syndrome S_1 is the error bit pattern E, but it has been raised to a power of a which is a function of the position of the error symbol in the block. If the position of the error is in symbol k, then k is the locator value and:

$$\text{S}_0 \times a^{\text{k}} = \text{S}_1$$

Hence:

$$a^{\text{k}} = \frac{\text{S}_1}{\text{S}_0}$$

The value of k can be found by multiplying S_0 by various powers of a until the product is the same as S_1. Then the power of a necessary is equal to k. The use of the descending powers of a in the codeword calculation is now clear because the error is then multiplied by a different power of a dependent upon its position, known as the locator, because it gives the position of the error. The process of finding the error position by experiment is known as a Chien search.

Whilst the expressions above show that the values of P and Q are such that the two syndrome expressions sum to zero, it is not yet clear how P and Q are calculated from the data. Expressions for P and Q can be found by solving the two R–S equations simultaneously. This has been done in Appendix 10.1. The following expressions must be used to calculate P and Q from the data in order to satisfy the codeword equations. These are:

$$\text{P} = a^6 \text{ A} \oplus a\text{B} \oplus a^2\text{C} \oplus a^5 \text{ D} \oplus a^3\text{E}$$

$$\text{Q} = a^2 \text{ A} \oplus a^3\text{B} \oplus a^6 \text{ C} \oplus a^4 \text{ D} \oplus a\text{E}$$

In both the calculation of the redundancy shown here and the calculation of the corrector and the locator it is necessary to perform numerous multiplications and raising to powers. This appears to present a formidable calculation problem at both the encoder and the decoder.

This would be the case if the calculations involved were conventionally executed. However, the calculations can be simplified by using logarithms. Instead of multiplying two numbers, their logarithms are added. In order to find the cube of a number, its logarithm is added three times. Division is performed by subtracting the logarithms. Thus all the manipulations necessary can be achieved with addition or subtraction, which is straightforward in logic circuits.

The success of this approach depends upon simple implementation of log tables. As was seen in section 4.20, raising a constant, a, known as the *primitive element* to successively higher powers in modulo-2 gives rise to a Galois field. Each element of the field represents a different power n of a. It is a fundamental of the R–S codes that all the symbols used for data, redundancy and syndromes are considered to be elements of a Galois field. The number of bits in the symbol determines the size of the Galois field, and hence the number of symbols in the codeword.

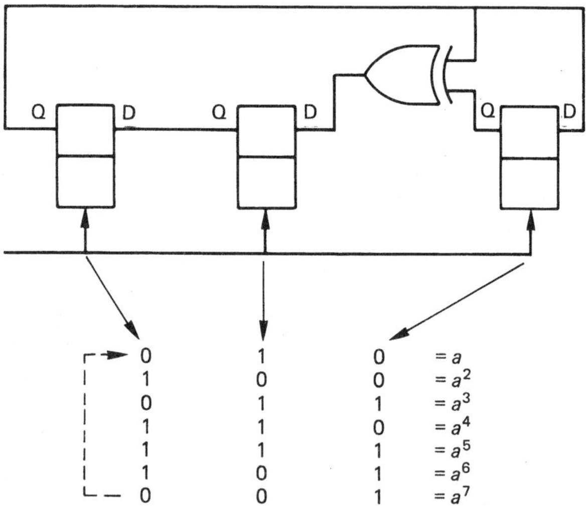

Figure 10.45 The bit patterns of a Galois field expressed as powers of the primitive element a. This diagram can be used as a form of log table in order to multiply binary numbers. Instead of an actual multiplication, the appropriate powers of a are simply added.

In Figure 10.45, the binary values of the elements are shown alongside the power of a they represent. In the R–S codes, symbols are no longer considered simply as binary numbers, but also as equivalent powers of a. In Reed–Solomon coding and decoding, each symbol will be multiplied by some power of a. Thus if the symbol is also known as a power of a it is only necessary to add the two powers. For example, if it is necessary to multiply the data symbol 100 by a^3, the calculation proceeds as follows, referring to Figure 10.45.

$$100 = a^2 \text{ so } 100 \times a^3 = a^{(2+3)} = a^5 = 111$$

Note that the results of a Galois multiplication are quite different from binary multiplication. Because all products must be elements of the field, sums of powers which exceed seven wrap around by having seven subtracted. For example:

$$a^5 \times a^6 = a^{11} = a^4 = 110$$

Figure 10.46 shows some examples of circuits which will perform this kind of multiplication. Note that they require a minimum amount of logic.

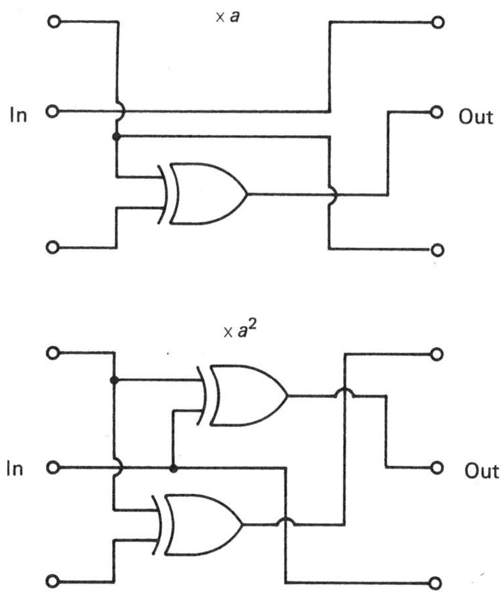

Figure 10.46 Some examples of GF multiplier circuits.

Figure 10.47 shows an example of the Reed–Solomon encoding process. The Galois field shown in Figure 10.45 has been used, having the primitive element $a = 010$. At the beginning of the calculation of P, the symbol A is multiplied by a^6. This is done by converting A to a power of a. According to Figure 10.48, $101 = a^6$ and so the product will be $a^{(6+6)} = a^{12} = a^5 = 111$. In the same way, B is multiplied by a, and so on, and the products are added modulo-2. A similar process is used to calculate Q.

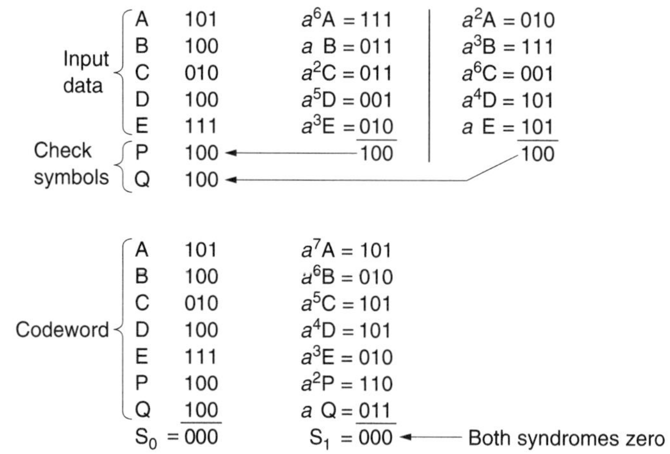

Figure 10.47 Five data symbols A–E are used as terms in the generator polynomials derived in Appendix 10.1 to calculate two redundant symbols P and Q. An example is shown at the top. Below is the result of using the codeword symbols A–Q as terms in the checking polynomials. As there is no error, both syndromes are zero.

Figure 10.48 shows a circuit which can calculate P or Q. The symbols A–E are presented in succession, and the circuit is clocked for each one. On the first clock, a^6A is stored in the left-hand latch. If B is now provided at the input, the second GF multiplier produces a B and this is added to the output of the first latch and when clocked will be stored in the second latch which now contains a^6A + aB. The process continues in this fashion

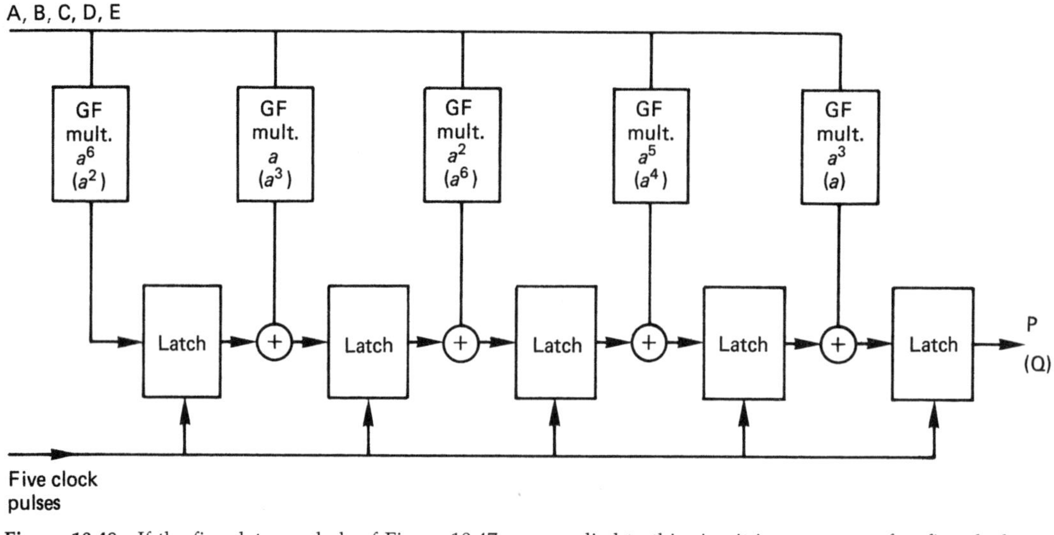

Figure 10.48 If the five data symbols of Figure 10.47 are supplied to this circuit in sequence, after five clocks, one of the check symbols will appear at the output. Terms without brackets will calculate P, bracketed terms calculate Q.

7	A	101	a^7A = 101
6	B	100	a^6B = 010
5	C	010	a^5C = 101
4	D′	101	a^4D′ = 011
3	E	111	a^3E = 010
2	P	100	a^2P = 110
1	Q	100	a Q = 011
	S_0 =	001	S_1 = 110

$$\frac{S_1}{S_0} = \frac{a^4}{1} = a^4$$

$k = 4$ (points to a^4D′ = 011)

D′ + S_0 = 101 + 001
D = 100

7	A	101	a^7A = 101
6	B	100	a^6B = 010
5	C′	110	a^5C = 100
4	D	100	a^4D = 101
3	E	111	a^3E = 010
2	P	100	a^2P = 110
1	Q	100	a Q = 011
	S_0 =	100	S_1 = 001

$$\frac{S_1}{S_0} = \frac{1}{a^2} = \frac{1}{a^2} \times \frac{a^5}{a^5} = a^5$$

$k = 5$ (points to a^5C = 100)

C′ + S_0 = 110 + 100
C = 010

7	A′	111	a^7A = 111
6	B	100	a^6B = 010
5	C	010	a^5C = 101
4	D	100	a^4D = 101
3	E	111	a^3E = 010
2	P	100	a^2P = 110
1	Q	100	a Q = 011
	S_0 =	010	S_1 = 010

$$\frac{S_1}{S_0} = \frac{a}{a} = 001 = a^7$$

$k = 7$ (points to a^7A = 111)

A′ + S_0 = 111 + 010
A = 101

Figure 10.49 Three examples of error location and correction. The number of bits in error in a symbol is irrelevant; if all three were wrong, S_0 would be 111, but correction is still possible.

until the complete expression for P is available in the right-hand latch. The intermediate contents of the right-hand latch are ignored.

The entire codeword now exists, and can be recorded or transmitted. Figure 10.47 also demonstrates that the codeword satisfies the checking equations. The modulo-2 sum of the seven symbols, S_0, is 000 because each column has an even number of ones. The calculation of S_1 requires multiplication by descending powers of a. The modulo-2 sum of the products is again zero. These calculations confirm that the redundancy calculation was properly carried out.

Figure 10.49 gives three examples of error correction based on this codeword. The erroneous symbol is marked with a dash. As there has been an error, the syndromes S_0 and S_1 will not be zero.

Figure 10.50 shows circuits suitable for parallel calculation of the two syndromes at the receiver. The S_0 circuit is a simple parity checker which accumulates the modulo-2 sum of all symbols fed to it. The S_1 circuit is more subtle, because it contains a Galois field (GF) multiplier in a feedback loop, such that early symbols fed in are raised to higher powers than later symbols because they have been recirculated through the GF multiplier more often. It is possible to compare the operation of these circuits with the example of Figure 10.49 and with subsequent examples to confirm that the same results are obtained.

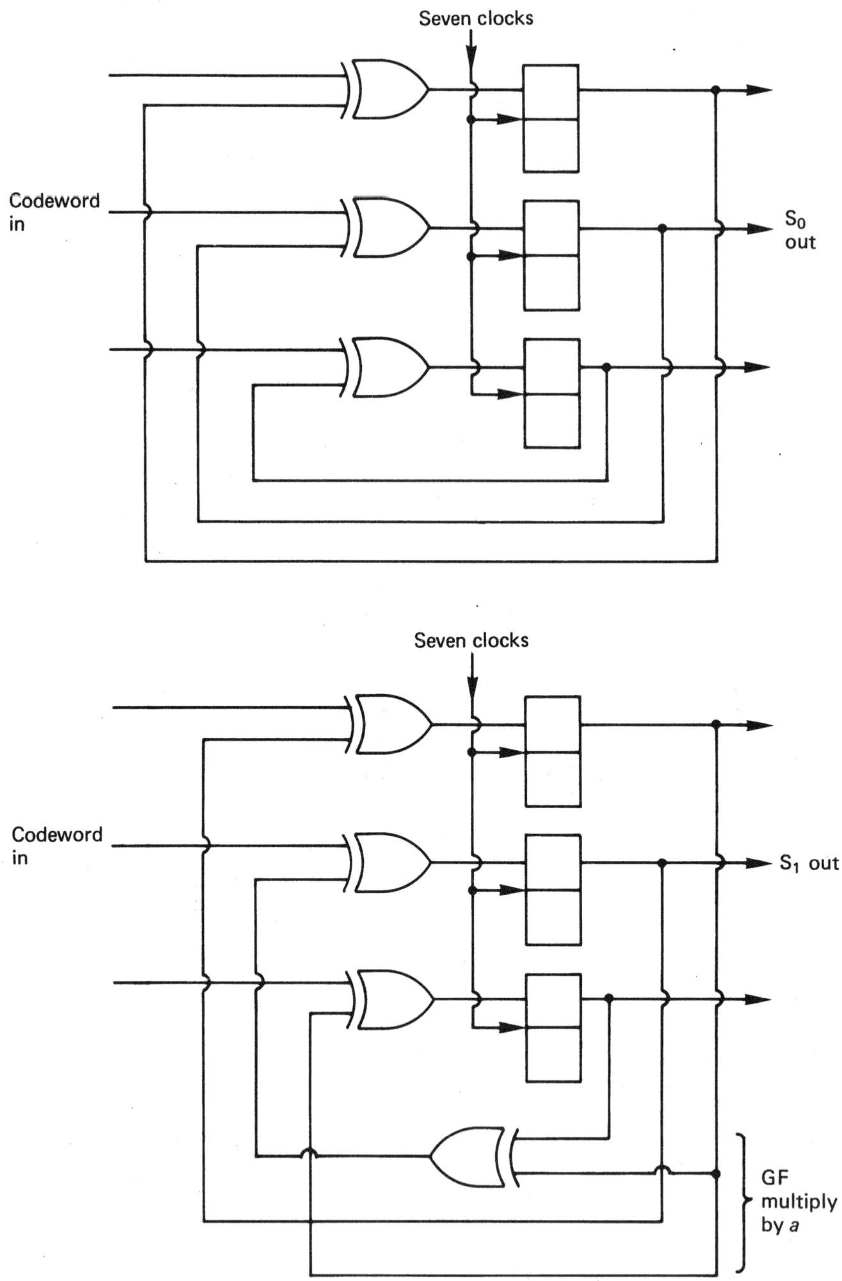

Figure 10.50 Circuits for parallel calculation of syndromes S_0, S_1, S_0 is a simple parity check. S_1 has a GF multiplication by a in the feedback, so that A is multiplied by a^7, B is multiplied by a^6, etc., and all are summed to give S_1.

10.22 Correction by erasure

In the examples of Figure 10.49, two redundant symbols P and Q have been used to locate and correct one error symbol. If the positions of errors are known by some separate mechanism (see product codes, section 10.24) the locator need not be calculated. The simultaneous equations may instead be solved for two correctors. In this case the number of symbols which can be corrected is equal to the number of redundant

A	101	a^7A =	101
B	100	a^6B =	010
$(C \oplus E_C)$	001	$a^5\ (C \oplus E_C)$	111
$(D \oplus E_D)$	010	$a^4\ (D \oplus E_D)$	111
E	111	a^3E =	010
P	100	a^2P =	110
Q	100	a Q =	011
S_1 =	101	S_1 =	000

$$S_0 = E_C \oplus E_D \qquad S_1 = a^5 E_C \oplus a^4 E_D$$

$$S_1 = a^5 E_C \oplus a^4 (S_0 \oplus E_C)$$

$$= a^5 E_C \oplus a^4 S_0 \oplus a^4 E_C$$

$$\therefore E_C = \frac{S_1 \oplus a^4 S_0}{a^5 \oplus a^4} = \frac{000 \oplus 011}{001} = 011$$

$$C = (C \oplus E_C) \oplus E_C = 001 \oplus 011 = \underline{010}$$

$$S_1 = a^5 (S_0 \ominus E_D) \oplus a^4 E_D$$

$$= a^5 S_0 \oplus a^5 E_D \oplus a^4 E_D$$

$$\therefore E_D = \frac{S_1 \oplus a^5 S_0}{a^5 \oplus a^4} = \frac{000 \oplus 110}{001} = 110$$

$$D = (D \oplus E_D) + E_D = 010 \oplus 110 = \underline{100}$$

(a)

A	101	a^7A	=	101	
B	100	a^6B	=	010	$S_0 = C \oplus D$
C	$\underline{000}$	a^5C	=	$\underline{000}$	$S_1 = a^5C \oplus a^4D$
D	$\underline{000}$	a^4D	=	$\underline{000}$	
E	111	a^3E	=	010	
P	100	a^2P	=	110	
Q	100	a Q	=	011	
S_0	= 100	S_1	=	000	

$$S_1 = a^5 S_0 \oplus a^5 D \oplus a^4 D = a^5 S_0 \oplus D$$

$$\therefore D = S_1 \oplus a^5 S_0 = 000 \oplus 100 = \underline{100}$$

$$S_1 = a^5 C \oplus a^4 C \oplus a^4 S_0 = C \oplus a^4 S_0$$

$$\therefore C = S_1 \oplus a^4 S_0 = 000 \oplus 010 = \underline{010}$$

(b)

Figure 10.51 If the location of errors is known, then the syndromes are a known function of the two errors as shown in (a). It is, however, much simpler to set the incorrect symbols to zero, i.e. to *erase* them as in (b). Then the syndromes are a function of the wanted symbols and correction is easier.

symbols. In Figure 10.51(a) two errors have taken place, and it is known that they are in symbols C and D. Since S_0 is a simple parity check, it will reflect the modulo-2 sum of the two errors. Hence

$$S_0 = EC \oplus ED$$

The two errors will have been multiplied by different powers in S_1, such that:

$$S_1 = a^5\ EC \oplus a^4\ ED$$

These two equations can be solved, as shown in the figure, to find *EC* and *ED*, and the correct value of the symbols will be obtained by adding these correctors to the erroneous values. It is, however, easier to set the values of the symbols in error to zero. In this way the nature of the error is rendered irrelevant and it does not enter the calculation. This setting of symbols to zero gives rise to the term erasure. In this case,

$$S_0 = C \oplus D$$

$$S_1 = a^5C + a^4D$$

Erasing the symbols in error makes the errors equal to the correct symbol values and these are found more simply as shown in Figure 10.51(b).

Practical systems will be designed to correct more symbols in error than in the simple examples given here. If it is proposed to correct by erasure an arbitrary number of symbols in error given by t, the codeword must be divisible by t different polynomials. Alternatively if the errors must be located and corrected, $2t$ polynomials will be needed. These will be of the form $(x + a^n)$ where n takes all values up to t or $2t$. a is the primitive element discussed in Chapter 2.

Where four symbols are to be corrected by erasure, or two symbols are to be located and corrected, four redundant symbols are necessary, and the codeword polynomial must then be divisible by

$$(x + a^0)\ (x + a^1)\ (x + a^2)\ (x + a^3)$$

Upon receipt of the message, four syndromes must be calculated, and the four correctors or the two error patterns and their positions are determined by solving four simultaneous equations. This generally requires an iterative procedure, and a number of algorithms have been developed for the purpose.[16–18] Modern DVTR formats use eight-bit R–S codes and erasure extensively. The primitive polynomial commonly used with GF(256) is

$$x^8 + x^4 + x^3 + x^2 + 1$$

The codeword will be 255 bytes long but will often be shortened by puncturing. The larger Galois fields require less redundancy, but the computational problem increases. LSI chips have been developed specifically for R–S decoding in many high-volume formats.

10.23 Interleaving

The concept of bit interleaving was introduced in connection with a single-bit correcting code to allow it to correct small bursts. With burst-correcting codes such as Reed–Solomon, bit interleave is unnecessary. In most channels, particularly high-density recording channels used for digital video or audio, the burst size may be many bytes rather than bits, and to rely on a code alone to correct such errors would require a lot of redundancy. The solution in this case is to employ symbol interleaving, as shown in Figure 10.52. Several codewords are encoded from input data,

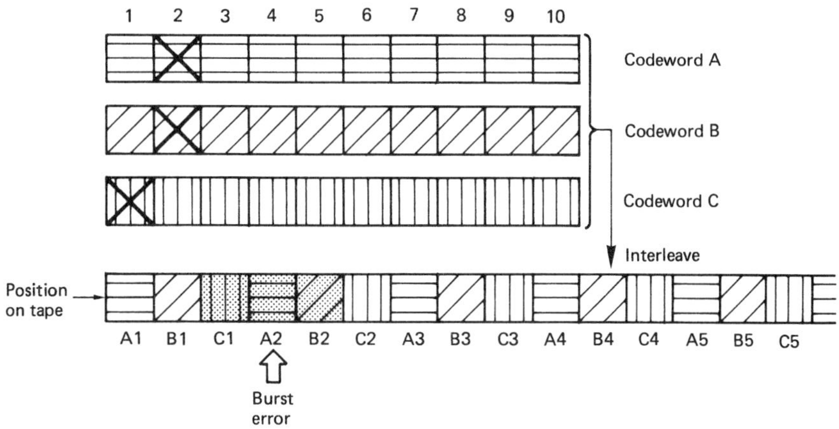

Figure 10.52 The interleave controls the size of burst errors in individual codewords.

but these are not recorded in the order they were input, but are physically reordered in the channel, so that a real burst error is split into smaller bursts in several codewords. The size of the burst seen by each codeword is now determined primarily by the parameters of the interleave, and Figure 10.53 shows that the probability of occurrence of bursts with respect to the burst length in a given codeword is modified. The number of bits in the interleave word can be made equal to the burst-correcting ability of the code in the knowledge that it will be exceeded only very infrequently.

There are a number of different ways in which interleaving can be performed. Figure 10.54 shows that in block interleaving, words are

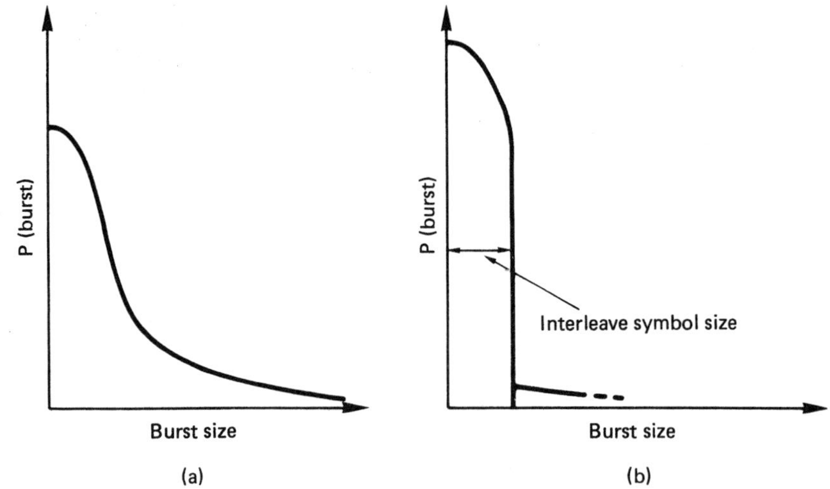

Figure 10.53 (a) The distribution of burst sizes might look like this. (b) Following interleave, the burst size within a codeword is controlled to that of the interleave symbol size, except for gross errors which have low probability.

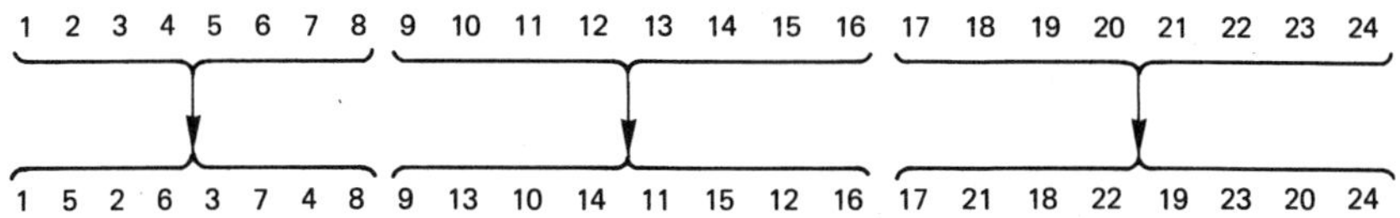

Figure 10.54 In block interleaving, data are scrambled within blocks which are themselves in the correct order.

reordered within blocks which are themselves in the correct order. This approach is attractive for rotary-head recorders, because the scanning process naturally divides the tape up into blocks. The block interleave is achieved by writing samples into a memory in sequential address locations from a counter, and reading the memory with non-sequential addresses from a sequencer. The effect is to convert a one-dimensional sequence of samples into a two-dimensional structure having rows and columns.

The alternative to block interleaving is convolutional interleaving where the interleave process is endless. In Figure 10.55 symbols are assembled into short blocks and then delayed by an amount proportional to the position in the block. It will be seen from the figure that the delays have the effect of shearing the symbols so that columns on the left side of the diagram become diagonals on the right. When the columns on the right are read, the convolutional interleave will be obtained. Convolutional interleave works well in transmission applications such as DVB where there is no natural track break. Convolutional interleave has the advantage of requiring less memory to implement than a block code. This

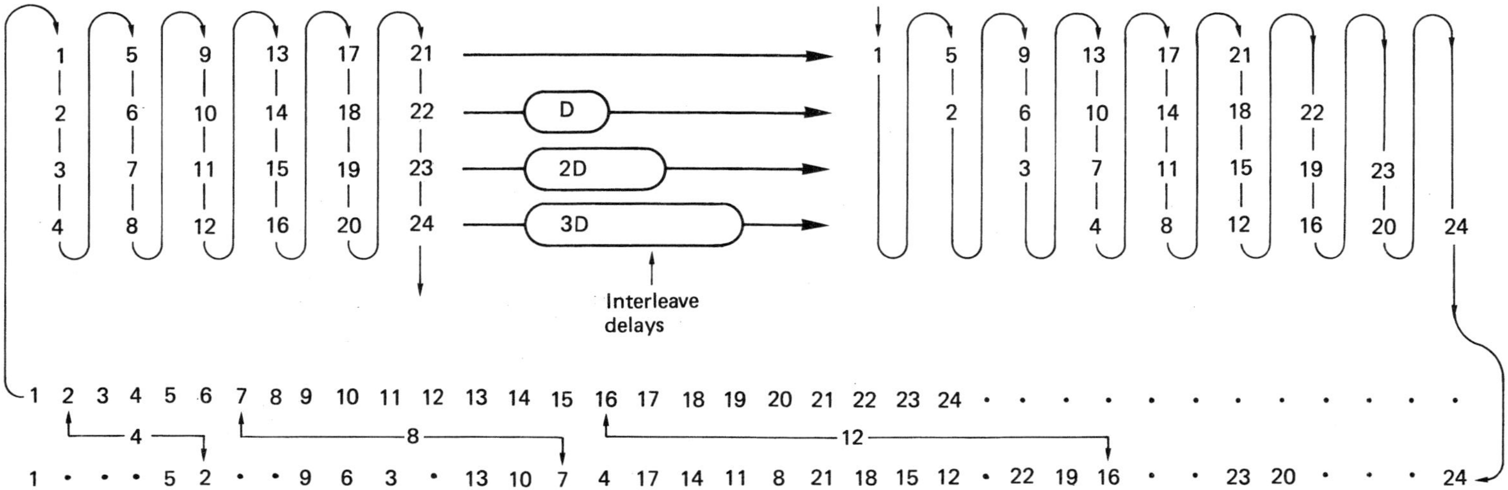

Figure 10.55 In convolutional interleaving, samples are formed into a rectangular array, which is sheared by subjecting each row to a different delay. The sheared array is read in vertical columns to provide the interleaved output. In this example, samples will be found at 4, 8 and 12 places away from their original order.

is because a block code requires the entire block to be written into the memory before it can be read, whereas a convolutional code requires only enough memory to cause the required delays.

10.24 Product codes

In the presence of burst errors alone, the system of interleaving works very well, but it is known that in most practical channels there are also uncorrelated errors of a few bits due to noise. Figure 10.56 shows an

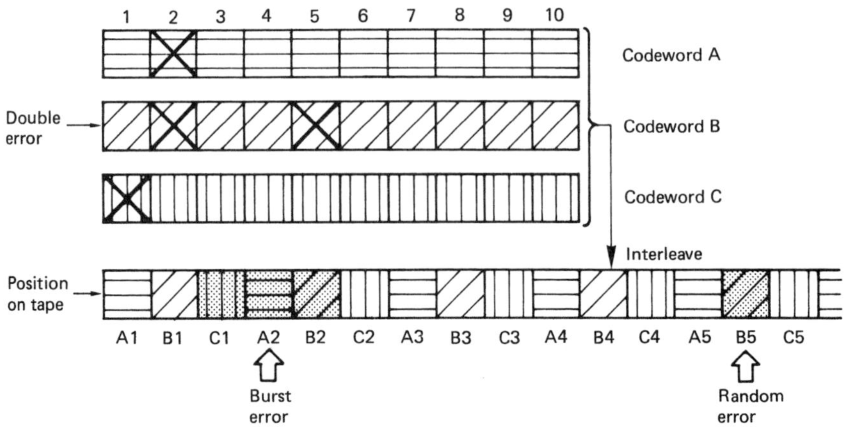

Figure 10.56 The interleave system falls down when a random error occurs adjacent to a burst.

interleaving system where a dropout-induced burst error has occurred which is at the maximum correctable size. All three codewords involved are working at their limit of one symbol. A random error due to noise in the vicinity of a burst error will cause the correction power of the code to be exceeded. Thus a random error of a single bit causes a further entire symbol to fail. This is a weakness of an interleave solely designed to handle dropout-induced bursts. Practical high-density equipment must address the problem of noise-induced or random errors and burst errors occurring at the same time. This is done by forming codewords both before and after the interleave process. In block interleaving, this results in a *product code,* whereas in the case of convolutional interleave the result is called *cross-interleaving.*

Figure 10.57 shows that in a product code the redundancy calculated first and checked last is called the outer code, and the redundancy calculated second and checked first is called the inner code. The inner code is formed along tracks on the medium. Random errors due to

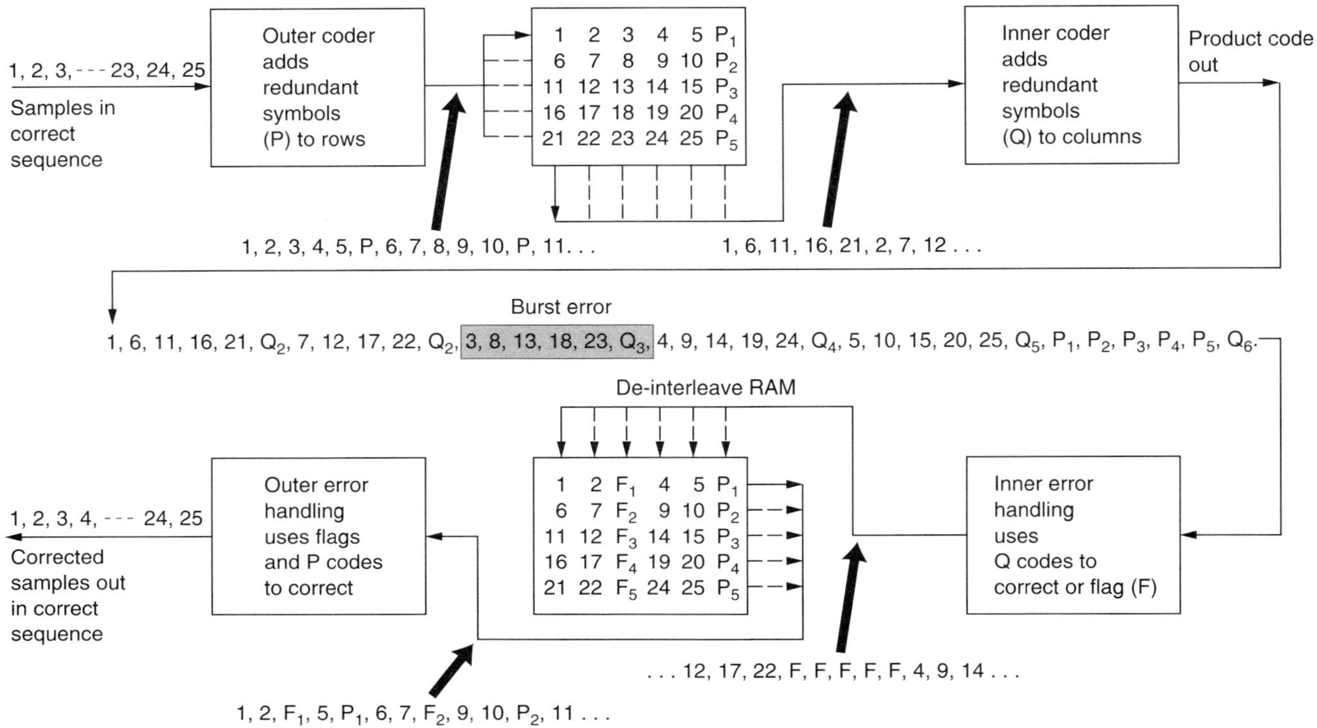

Figure 10.57 In addition to the redundancy P on rows, inner redundancy Q is also generated on columns. On replay, the Q code checker will pass on flags F if it finds an error too large to handle itself. The flags pass through the de-interleave process and are used by the outer error correction to identify which symbol in the row needs correcting with P redundancy. The concept of crossing two codes in in this way is called a product code.

noise are corrected by the inner code and do not impair the burst-correcting power of the outer code. Burst errors are declared uncorrectable by the inner code which flags the bad samples on the way into the de-interleave memory. The outer code reads the error flags in order to correct the flagged symbols by erasure. The error flags are also known as erasure flags. As it does not have to compute the error locations, the outer code needs half as much redundancy for the same correction power. Thus the inner code redundancy does not raise the code overhead. The combination of codewords with interleaving in several dimensions yields an error-protection strategy which is truly synergistic, in that the end result is more powerful than the sum of the parts. Needless to say, the technique is used extensively in modern storage formats.

Appendix 10.1 Calculation of Reed–Solomon generator polynomials

For a Reed–Solomon codeword over GF(2^3), there will be seven three-bit symbols. For location and correction of one symbol, there must be two redundant symbols P and Q, leaving A-E for data.

The following expressions must be true, where a is the primitive element of $x^3 \oplus x \oplus 1$ and $\oplus$ is XOR throughout:

$$\mathrm{A} \oplus \mathrm{B} \oplus \mathrm{C} \oplus \mathrm{D} \oplus \mathrm{E} \oplus \mathrm{P} \oplus \mathrm{Q} = 0 \qquad (1)$$

$$a^7\mathrm{A} \oplus a^6\mathrm{B} \oplus a^5\mathrm{C} \oplus a^4\mathrm{D} \oplus a^3\mathrm{E} \oplus a^2\mathrm{P} \oplus a\mathrm{Q} = 0 \qquad (2)$$

Dividing equation (2) by a:

$$a^6\mathrm{A} \oplus a^5\mathrm{B} \oplus a^4\mathrm{C} \oplus a^3\mathrm{D} \oplus a^2\mathrm{E} \oplus a\mathrm{P} \oplus \mathrm{Q} = 0$$

$$= \mathrm{A} \oplus \mathrm{B} \oplus \mathrm{C} \oplus \mathrm{D} \oplus \mathrm{E} \oplus \mathrm{P} \oplus \mathrm{Q}$$

Cancelling Q, and collecting terms:

$$(a^6 \oplus 1)\mathrm{A} \oplus (a^5 \oplus 1)\mathrm{B} \oplus (a^4 \oplus 1)\mathrm{C} \oplus (a^3 \oplus 1)\mathrm{D} \oplus (a^2 \oplus 1)\mathrm{E}$$

$$= (a + 1)\mathrm{P}$$

Using section 2.8 to calculate $(a^n + 1)$, e.g. $a^6 + 1 = 101 + 001 = 100 = a^2$:

$$a^2\mathrm{A} \oplus a^4\mathrm{B} \oplus a^5\mathrm{C} \oplus a\mathrm{D} \oplus a^6\mathrm{E} = a^3\mathrm{P}$$

$$a^6\mathrm{A} \oplus a\mathrm{B} \oplus a^2\mathrm{C} \oplus a^5\mathrm{D} \oplus a^3\mathrm{E} = \mathrm{P}$$

Multiply equation (1) by a^2 and equating to equation (2):

$$a^2\text{A} \oplus a^2\text{B} \oplus a^2\text{C} \oplus a^2\text{D} \oplus a^2\text{E} \oplus a^2\text{P} \oplus a^2\text{Q} = 0$$

$$= a^7\text{A} \oplus a^6\text{B} \oplus a^5\text{C} \oplus a^4\text{D} \oplus a^3\text{E} \oplus a^2\text{P} \oplus a\text{Q}$$

Cancelling terms a^2P and collecting terms (remember $a^2 \oplus a^2 = 0$):

$$(a^7 \oplus a^2)\text{A} \oplus (a^6 \oplus a^2)\text{B} \oplus (a^5 \oplus a^2)\text{C} \oplus (a^4 \oplus a^2)\text{D} \oplus$$

$$(a^3 \oplus a^2)\text{E} = (a^2 \oplus a)\text{Q}$$

Adding powers according to section 2.8, e.g.

$$a^7 \oplus a^2 = 001 \oplus 100 = 101 = a^6:$$

$$a^6\text{A} \oplus \text{B} \oplus a^3\text{C} \oplus a\text{D} \oplus a^5\text{E} = a^4\text{Q}$$

$$a^2\text{A} \oplus a^3\text{B} \oplus a^6\text{C} \oplus a^4\text{D} \oplus a\text{E} = \text{Q}$$

References

1. Deeley, E.M., Integrating and differentiating channels in digital tape recording. *Radio Electron. Eng.*, **56**, 169–173 (1986)
2. Mee, C.D., *The Physics of Magnetic Recording*, Amsterdam and New York: Elsevier–North Holland Publishing (1978)
3. Jacoby, G.V., Signal equalization in digital magnetic recording. *IEEE Trans. Magn.*, **MAG-11**, 302–305 (1975)
4. Schneider, R.C., An improved pulse-slimming method for magnetic recording. *IEEE Trans. Magn.*, **MAG-11**, 1240–1241 (1975)
5. Miller, A., US Patent. No.3 108 261
6. Mallinson, J.C. and Miller, J.W., Optimum codes for digital magnetic recording. *Radio and Electron. Eng.*, **47**, 172–176 (1977)
7. Miller, J.W., DC-free encoding for data transmission system. US Patent 4 027 335 (1977)
8. Tang, D.T., Run-length-limited codes. IEEE International Symposium on Information Theory (1969)
9. Yokoyama, K., Digital video tape recorder. *NHK Technical Monograph*, No.31 (March 1982)
10. Coleman, C.H. *et al.*, High data rate magnetic recording in a single channel. *J. IERE*, **55**, 229–236 (1985)
11. Kobayashi, H., Application of partial response channel coding to magnetic recording systems. *IBM J. Res. Dev.*, **14**, 368–375 (1970)
12. Forney, G.D., Jr, The Viterbi algorithm, *Proc. IEEE*, **61**, 268–278 (1973)
13. Wood, R.W. and Petersen, D.A., Viterbi detection of Class IV partial response on a magnetic recording channel. *IEEE Trans. Commun.*, **34**, 454–461 (1968)
14. Shannon, C.E., A mathematical theory of communication. *Bell System Tech. J.*, **27**, 379 (1948)
15. Reed, I.S. and Solomon, G., Polynomial codes over certain finite fields. *J. Soc. Indust. Appl. Math.*, **8**, 300–304 (1960)

16. Berlekamp, E.R., *Algebraic Coding Theory,* New York: McGraw-Hill (1967). Reprint edition: Laguna Hills, CA: Aegean Park Press (1983)
17. Sugiyama, Y. *et al.*, An erasures and errors decoding algorithm for Goppa codes. *IEEE Trans. Inf. Theory,* **IT-22** (1976)
18. Peterson, W.W. and Weldon, E.J., *Error Correcting Codes*, 2nd edn, Cambridge, MA: MIT Press (1972)

11

Storage devices

11.1 Introduction

Digital technology depends heavily on reliable storage devices. A number of storage technologies co-exist because there is as yet no one ideal solution. Given the use of error correction to allow arbitrary reliability, the main ways of comparing storage devices are cost per bit and access time. These attributes are usually incompatible. The hard disk drive has evolved to provide rapid access whereas the rotary head tape has evolved to provide low-cost bulk storage. Technology will continue to advance, and as a result recording densities of all media will continue to increase, along with improvements in transfer rate. The relative merits of different media will stay the same; disks will always be faster than tape, tape will always be cheaper. Clearly it makes sense to combine these in some way.

In a network-based system it is useful to have tape and disk drives which can transfer faster than real time in order to speed up the process. The density of tape recording has a great bearing on the cost per bit. One limiting factor is the track width. In current DVTR formats, the track width is much greater than theoretically necessary because of the difficulty of mechanically tracking with the heads. This is compounded by the current insistence on editing to picture accuracy on the tape itself. This is a convention inherited from analog VTRs, and it is unnecessary in digital machines. Digital VTRs employ read–modify–write, and this makes the edit precision in the data independent of the block size on tape. Future DVTRs may only be able to edit once per second, by employing edit gaps. This allows the tracks to be much narrower and the recording density can rise. Picture accurate editing requires the block to read intact, edited elsewhere, and written back whole. The obvious way to do this is on a disk. Thus a future for hybrid storage systems is to integrate the DVTR with the disk system and give it a format that it could not use as a standalone unit. This brings the DVTR very close in functionality to the streaming tape recorder which has evolved in the computer industry.

11.2 Disk storage

Disk drives came into being as random-access file-storage devices for digital computers. The explosion in personal computers has fuelled demand for low-cost high-density disk drives and the rapid access offered is increasingly finding applications in digital video. After lengthy development, optical disks are also emerging in digital video applications.

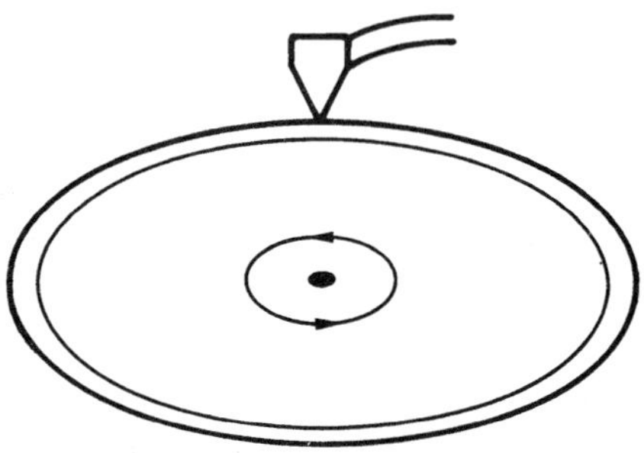

Figure 11.1 The rotating store concept. Data on the rotating circular track are repeatedly presented to the head.

Figure 11.1 shows that, in a disk drive, the data are recorded on a circular track. In hard-disk drives, the disk rotates at several thousand rev/min so that the head-to-disk speed is of the order of 100 miles per hour. At this speed no contact can be tolerated, and the head flies on a boundary layer of air turning with the disk at a height measured in microinches. The longest time it is necessary to wait to access a given data block is a few milliseconds. To increase the storage capacity of the drive without a proportional increase in cost, many concentric tracks are recorded on the disk surface, and the head is mounted on a positioner which can rapidly bring the head to any desired track. Such a machine is termed a moving-head disk drive. An increase in capacity could be obtained by assembling many disks on a common spindle to make a disk pack. The small size of magnetic heads allows the disks to placed close together. If the positioner is designed so that it can remove the heads away from the disk completely, it can be exchanged. The exchangeable-pack moving-head disk drive became the standard for mainframe and minicomputers for a long time.

Later came the so-called Winchester technology disks, where the disk and positioner formed a compact sealed unit which allowed increased storage capacity but precluded exchange of the disk pack alone.

Disk drive development has been phenomenally rapid. The first flying head disks were about 3 feet across. Subsequently disk sizes of 14, 8, $5\frac{1}{4}$, $3\frac{1}{2}$ and $1\frac{7}{8}$ inches were developed. Despite the reduction in size, the storage capacity is not compromised because the recording density has increased and continues to increase. In fact there is an advantage in making a drive smaller because the moving parts are then lighter and travel a shorter distance, improving access time.

There are numerous types of optical disk, which have different characteristics. The basic principles of optical disk readout were introduced in section 10.7. Optical disks fall into three broad groups which can usefully be compared:

1 The Compact Disc, its data derivative CD-ROM and the later DVD are examples of a read-only laser disk, which is designed for mass duplication by stamping. They cannot be recorded.
2 Some laser disks can be recorded, but once recorded they cannot be edited or erased because some permanent mechanical or chemical change has been made. These are usually referred to as write-once-read-many (WORM) disks.
3 Erasable optical disks have essentially the same characteristic as magnetic disks, in that new and different recordings can be made in the same track indefinitely, but there is usually a separate erase cycle needed before a new recording can be made since overwrite is not always possible.

Figure 11.2 introduces the essential subsystems of a disk drive which will be discussed here. Magnetic drives and optical drives are similar in that both have a spindle drive mechanism to revolve the disk, and a

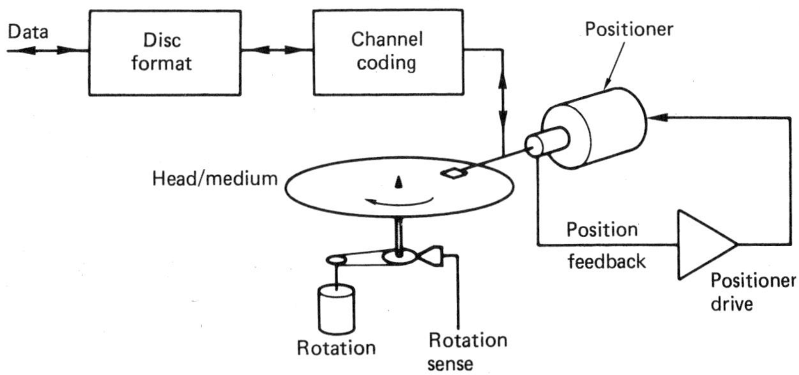

Figure 11.2 The main subsystems of a typical disk drive.

positioner to give radial access across the disk surface. In the optical drive, the positioner has to carry a collection of lasers, lenses, prisms, gratings and so on, and will be rather larger than a magnetic head. The heavier pickup cannot be accelerated as fast as a magnetic-drive positioner, and access time is slower. A large number of pickups on one positioner makes matters worse. For this reason and because of the larger spacing needed between the disks, multi-platter optical disks are uncommon. Instead 'juke box' mechanisms have been developed to allow a large library of optical disks to be mechanically accessed by one or more drives. Access time is sometimes reduced by having more than one positioner per disk; a technique adopted rarely in magnetic drives. A penalty of the very small track pitch possible in laser disks, which gives the enormous storage capacity, is that very accurate track following is needed, and it takes some time to lock onto a track. For this reason tracks on laser disks are usually made as a continuous spiral, rather than the concentric rings of magnetic disks. In this way, a continuous data transfer involves no more than track following once the beginning of the file is located.

Rigid disks are made from aluminium alloy. Magnetic-oxide types use an aluminium oxide substrate, or undercoat, giving a flat surface to which the oxide binder can adhere. Later metallic disks having higher coercivity are electroplated with the magnetic medium. In both cases the surface finish must be extremely good owing to the very small flying height of the head. As the head-to-disk speed and recording density are functions of track radius, the data are confined to the outer areas of the disks to minimize the change in these parameters. As a result, the centre of the pack is often an empty well. In fixed (i.e. non-interchangeable) disks the drive motor is often installed in the centre well.

The information layer of optical disks may be made of a variety of substances, depending on the working principle. This layer is invariably protected beneath a thick transparent layer of glass or polycarbonate.

Exchangeable optical and magnetic disks are usually fitted in protective cartridges. These have various shutters which retract on insertion in the drive to allow access by the drive spindle and heads. Removable packs usually seat on a taper to ensure concentricity and are held to the spindle by a permanent magnet. A lever mechanism may be incorporated into the cartridge to assist their removal.

11.3 Magnetic disks

In all technologies there are specialist terms, and those relating to magnetic disks will be explained here. Figure 11.3 shows a typical multiplatter magnetic disk pack in conceptual form. Given a particular

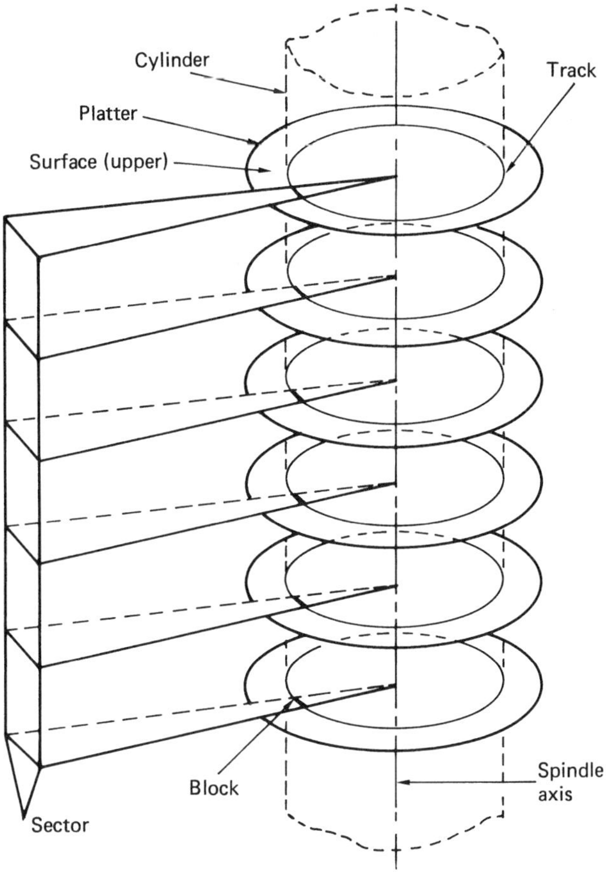

Figure 11.3 Disk terminology. Surface: one side of a platter. Track: path described on a surface by a fixed head. Cylinder: imaginary shape intersecting all surfaces at tracks of the same radius. Sector: angular subdivision of pack. Block: that part of a track within one sector. Each block has a unique cylinder, head and sector address.

set of coordinates (cylinder, head, sector), known as a disk physical address, one unique data block is defined. A common block capacity is 512 bytes. The subdivision into sectors is sometimes omitted for special applications. A disk drive can be randomly accessed, because any block address can follow any other, but unlike a RAM, at each address a large block of data is stored, rather than a single word.

Magnetic disk drives permanently sacrifice storage density in order to offer rapid access. The use of a flying head with a deliberate air gap between it and the medium is necessary because of the high medium speed, but this causes a severe separation loss which restricts the linear density available. The air gap must be accurately maintained, and consequently the head is of low mass and is mounted flexibly.

The aerohydrodynamic part of the head is known as the slipper; it is designed to provide lift from the boundary layer which changes rapidly with changes in flying height. It is not initially obvious that the difficulty with disk heads is not making them fly, but making them fly close enough to the disk surface. The boundary layer travelling at the disk surface has the same speed as the disk, but as height increases, it slows down due to drag from the surrounding air. As the lift is a function of relative air speed, the closer the slipper comes to the disk, the greater the lift will be. The slipper is therefore mounted at the end of a rigid cantilever sprung towards the medium. The force with which the head is pressed towards the disk by the spring is equal to the lift at the designed flying height. Because of the spring, the head may rise and fall over small warps in the disk. It would be virtually impossible to manufacture disks flat enough to dispense with this feature. As the slipper negotiates a warp it will pitch and roll in addition to rising and falling, but it must be prevented from yawing, as this would cause an azimuth error. Downthrust is applied to the aerodynamic centre by a spherical thrust button, and the required degrees of freedom are supplied by a thin flexible gimbal. The slipper has to bleed away surplus air in order to approach close enough to the disk, and holes or grooves are usually provided for this purpose in the same way that pinch rollers on some tape decks have grooves to prevent tape slip.

In exchangeable-pack drives, there will be a ramp on the side of the cantilever which engages a fixed block when the heads are retracted in order to lift them away from the disk surface.

Figure 11.4 shows how disk heads are made. The magnetic circuit of disk heads was originally assembled from discrete magnetic elements. As the gap and flying height became smaller to increase linear recording density, the slipper was made from ferrite, and became part of the magnetic circuit. This was completed by a small C-shaped ferrite piece which carried the coil. Ferrite heads were restricted in the coercivity of disk they could write without saturating. In thin-film heads, the magnetic circuit and coil are both formed by deposition on a substrate which becomes the rear of the slipper.

In a moving-head device it is not practicable to position separate erase, record and playback heads accurately. Erase is by overwriting, and reading and writing are carried out by the same head. The presence of the air film causes severe separation loss, and peak shift distortion is a major problem. The flying height of the head varies with the radius of the disk track, and it is difficult to provide accurate equalization of the replay channel because of this. The write current is often controlled as a function of track radius so that the changing reluctance of the air gap does not change the resulting record flux. Automatic gain control (AGC) is used on replay to compensate for changes in signal amplitude from the head.

Equalization may be used on recording in the form of precompensation, which moves recorded transitions in such a way as to oppose the effects of peak shift in addition to any replay equalization used.

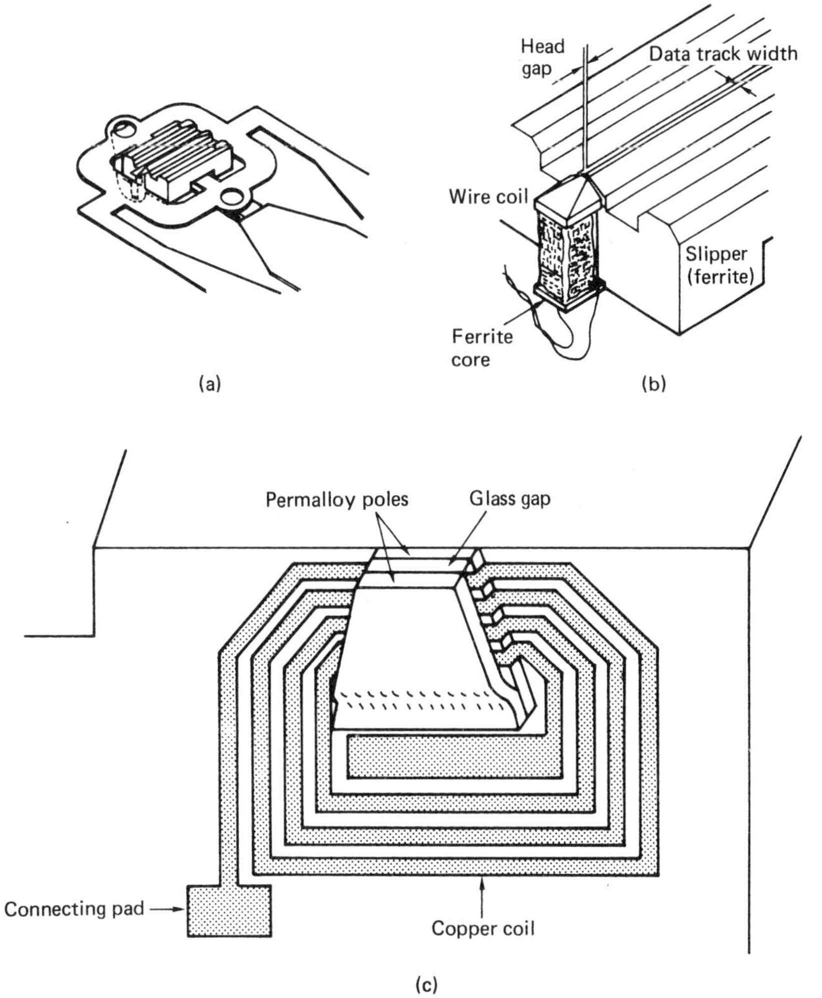

Figure 11.4 (a) Winchester head construction showing large air bleed grooves. (b) Close-up of slipper showing magnetic circuit on trailing edge. (c) Thin film head is fabricated on the end of the slipper using microcircuit technology.

Early disks used FM coding, which was easy to decode, but had a poor density ratio. The invention of MFM revolutionized hard disks, and further progress led to run-length-limited codes such as 2/3 and 2/7 which had a high density ratio without sacrificing the large jitter window necessary to reject peak shift distortion. Partial response is also suited to disks.

Typical drives have several heads, but with the exception of special-purpose parallel-transfer machines, only one head will be active at any one time, which means that the read and write circuitry can be shared between the heads. The read channel usually incorporates AGC, which will be overridden by the control logic between data blocks in order to search for address marks, which are short unmodulated areas of track. As a block preamble is entered, the AGC will be enabled to allow a rapid gain adjustment.

11.4 Accessing the blocks

The servo system required to move the heads rapidly between tracks, and yet hold them in place accurately for data transfer, is a fascinating and complex piece of engineering. In exchangeable pack drives, the disk positioner moves on a straight axis which passes through the spindle. Motive power is generally by moving-coil drive, because of the small moving mass which this technique permits.

When a drive is track-following, it is said to be detented, in fine mode or in linear mode depending on the manufacturer. When a drive is seeking from one track to another, it can be described as being in coarse mode or velocity mode. These are the two major operating modes of the servo.

Moving-coil actuators do not naturally detent and require power to stay on-track. The servo system needs positional feedback of some kind. The purpose of the feedback will be one or more of the following:

1 To count the number of cylinders crossed during a seek
2 To generate a signal proportional to carriage velocity
3 To generate a position error proportional to the distance from the centre of the desired track

Magnetic and optical drives obtain these feedback signals in different ways. Many positioners incorporate a tacho which may be a magnetic moving-coil type or its complementary equivalent the moving-magnet type. Both generate a voltage proportional to velocity, and can give no positional information.

A seek is a process where the positioner moves from one cylinder to another. The speed with which a seek can be completed is a major factor in determining the access time of the drive. The main parameter controlling the carriage during a seek is the cylinder difference, which is obtained by subtracting the current cylinder address from the desired cylinder address. The cylinder difference will be a signed binary number representing the number of cylinders to be crossed to reach the target, direction being indicated by the sign. The cylinder difference is loaded into a counter which is decremented each time a cylinder is crossed. The counter drives a DAC which generates an analog voltage proportional to the cylinder difference. As Figure 11.5 shows, this voltage, known as the scheduled velocity, is compared with the output

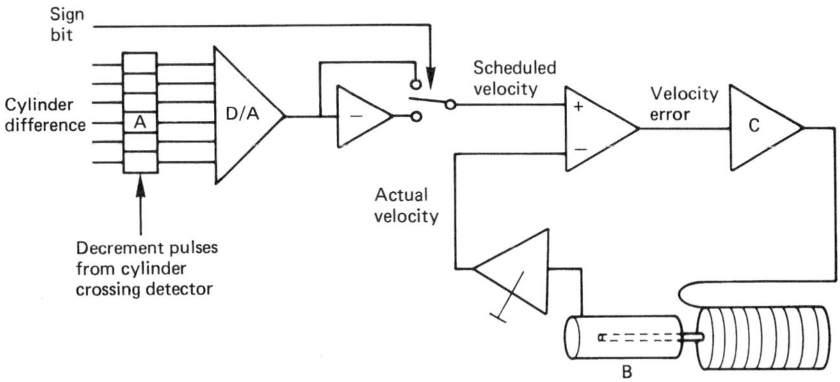

Figure 11.5 Control of carriage velocity by cylinder difference. The cylinder difference is loaded into the difference counter A. A digital-to-analog convertor generates an analog voltage from the cylinder difference, known as the scheduled velocity. This is compared with the actual velocity from the transducer B in order to generate the velocity error which drives the servo amplifier C.

of the carriage-velocity tacho. Any difference between the two results in a velocity error which drives the carriage to cancel the error. As the carriage approaches the target cylinder, the cylinder difference becomes smaller, with the result that the run-in to the target is critically damped to eliminate overshoot.

Figure 11.6(a) shows graphs of scheduled velocity, actual velocity and motor current with respect to cylinder difference during a seek. In the first half of the seek, the actual velocity is less than the scheduled velocity, causing a large velocity error which saturates the amplifier and provides maximum carriage acceleration. In the second half of the graphs, the scheduled velocity is falling below the actual velocity, generating a negative velocity error which drives a reverse current through the motor to slow the carriage down. The scheduled deceleration slope can clearly not be steeper than the saturated acceleration slope. Areas A and B on the graph will be about equal, as the kinetic energy put into the carriage has to be taken out. The current through the motor is continuous, and would result in a heating problem, so to counter this, the DAC is made non-linear so that above a certain cylinder difference no increase in scheduled velocity will occur. This results in the graph of Figure 11.6(b). The actual velocity graph is called a velocity profile. It consists of three regions: acceleration, where the system is saturated; a constant velocity plateau, where the only power needed is to overcome friction; and the scheduled run-in to the desired cylinder. Dissipation is only significant in the first and last regions.

The track-following accuracy of a drive positioner will be impaired if there is bearing runout, and so the spindle bearings are made to a high degree of precision.

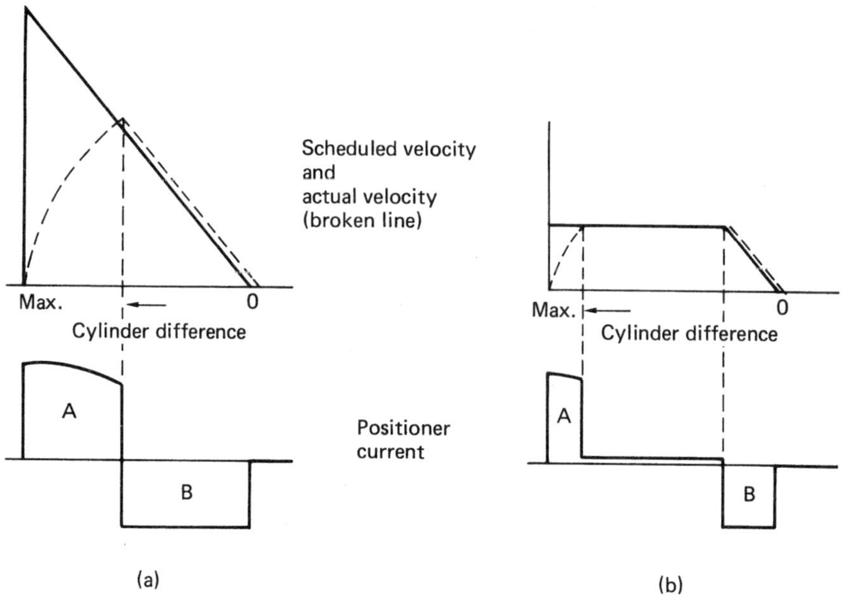

Figure 11.6 In the simple arrangement at (a) the dissipation in the positioner is continuous, causing a heating problem. The effect of limiting the scheduled velocity above a certain cylinder difference is apparent in (b) where heavy positioner current only flows during acceleration and deceleration. During the plateau of the velocity profile, only enough current to overcome friction is necessary. The curvature of the acceleration slope is due to the back EMF of the positioner motor.

In order to control reading and writing, the drive control circuitry needs to know which cylinder the heads are on, and which sector is currently under the head. Sector information used to be obtained from a sensor which detects holes or slots cut in the hub of the disk. Modern drives will obtain this information from the disk surface as will be seen. The result is that a sector counter in the control logic remains in step with the physical rotation of the disk. The desired sector address is loaded into a register, which is compared with the sector counter. When the two match, the desired sector has been found. This process is referred to as a search, and usually takes place after a seek. Having found the correct physical place on the disk, the next step is to read the header associated with the data block to confirm that the disk address contained there is the same as the desired address.

11.5 Servo-surface disks

One of the major problems to be overcome in the development of high-density disk drives was that of keeping the heads on-track despite changes of temperature. The very narrow tracks used in digital recording have similar dimensions to the amount a disk will expand as it warms up. The cantilevers and the drive base all expand and contract, conspiring with thermal drift in the cylinder transducer to limit track pitch. The breakthrough in disk density came with the introduction of the servo-surface drive. The position error in a servo-surface drive is derived from a head reading the disk itself. This virtually eliminates thermal effects on head positioning and allows great increases in storage density.

In a multiplatter drive, one surface of the pack holds servo information which is read by the servo head. In a ten-platter pack this means that 5 per cent of the medium area is lost, but this is unimportant since the increase in density allowed is enormous. Using one side of a single-platter cartridge for servo information would be unacceptable as it represents 50 per cent of the medium area, so in this case the servo information can be interleaved with sectors on the data surfaces. This is known as an embedded-servo technique. These two approaches are contrasted in Figure 11.7.

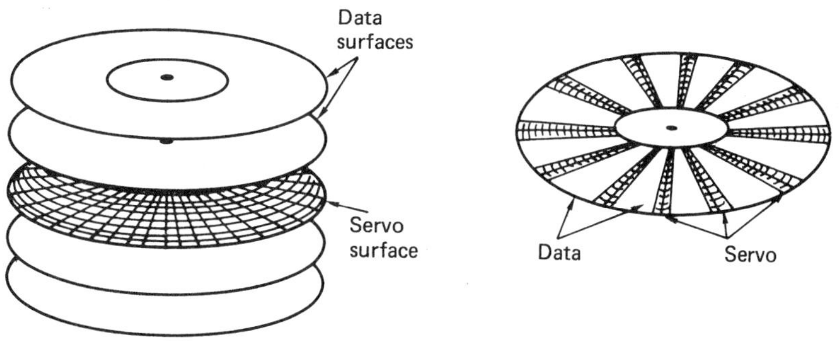

Figure 11.7 In a multiplatter disk pack, one surface is dedicated to servo information. In a single platter, the servo information is embedded in the data on the same surfaces.

The servo surface is written at the time of disk pack manufacture, and the disk drive can only read it. Writing the servo surface has nothing to do with disk formatting, which affects the data storage areas only. As there are exactly the same number of pulses on every track on the servo surface, it is possible to describe the rotational position of the disk simply by counting them. All that is needed is an unique pattern of missing pulses once per revolution to act as an index point, and the sector transducer can also be eliminated.

The advantage of deriving the sector count from the servo surface is that the number of sectors on the disk can be varied. Any number of sectors can be accommodated by feeding the pulse signal through a programmable divider, so the same disk and drive can be used in numerous different applications.

11.6 Winchester technology

In order to offer extremely high capacity per spindle, which reduces the cost per bit, a disk drive must have very narrow tracks placed close together, and must use very short recorded wavelengths, which implies that the flying height of the heads must be small. The so-called Winchester technology is one approach to high storage density. The technology was developed by IBM, and the name came about because the model number of the development drive was the same as that of the famous rifle.

Reduction in flying height magnifies the problem of providing a contaminant-free environment. A conventional disk is well protected whilst inside the drive, but outside the drive the effects of contamination become intolerable.

In exchangeable-pack drives, there is a real limit to the track pitch that can be achieved because of the difficulty or cost of engineering head-alignment mechanisms to make the necessary minute adjustments to give interchange compatibility.

The essence of Winchester technology is that each disk pack has its own set of read/write and servo heads, with an integral positioner. The whole is protected by a dust-free enclosure, and the unit is referred to as a head disk assembly, or HDA.

As the HDA contains its own heads, compatibility problems do not exist, and no head alignment is necessary or provided for. It is thus possible to reduce track pitch considerably compared with exchangeable pack drives. The sealed environment ensures complete cleanliness which permits a reduction in flying height without loss of reliability, and hence leads to an increased linear density. If the rotational speed is maintained, this can also result in an increase in data transfer rate. The HDA is completely sealed, but some have a small filtered port to equalize pressure.

An exchangeable-pack drive must retract the heads to facilitate pack removal. With Winchester technology this is not necessary. An area of the disk surface is reserved as a landing strip for the heads. The disk surface is lubricated, and the heads are designed to withstand landing and take-off without damage. Winchester heads have very large air-bleed grooves to allow low flying height with a much smaller downthrust from the cantilever, and so they exert less force on the disk surface during contact. When the term 'parking' is used in the context of Winchester technology, it refers to the positioning of the heads over the landing area.

Disk rotation must be started and stopped quickly to minimize the length of time the heads slide over the medium. This is conveniently achieved with a servo-controlled brushless motor which has dynamic braking ability. A major advantage of contact start/stop is that more than one head can be used on each surface if retraction is not needed. This leads to two gains: first, the travel of the positioner is reduced in proportion to the number of heads per surface, reducing access time; and, second, more data can be transferred at a given detented carriage position before a seek to the next cylinder becomes necessary. This increases the speed of long transfers. Figure 11.8 illustrates the relationships of the heads in such a system.

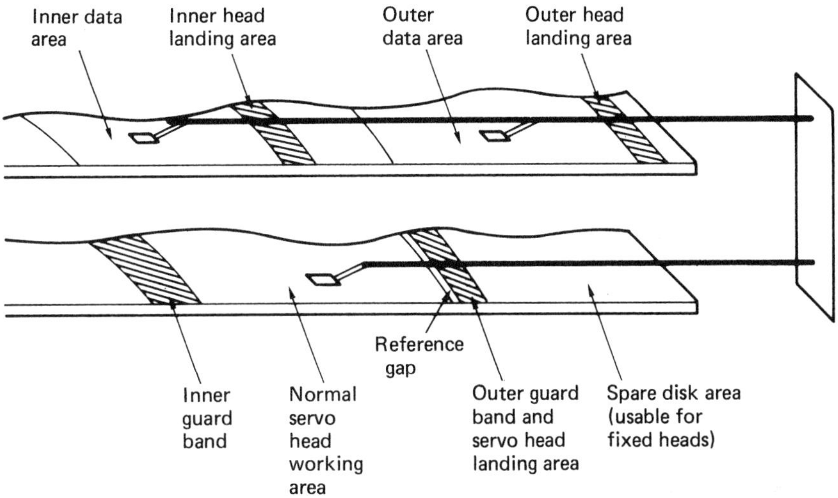

Figure 11.8 When more than one head is used per surface, the positioner still only requires one servo head. This is often arranged to be equidistant from the read/write heads for thermal stability.

Figure 11.9 shows that rotary positioners are feasible in Winchester drives; they cannot be used in exchangeable-pack drives because of interchange problems. There are some advantages to a rotary positioner. It can be placed in the corner of a compact HDA allowing smaller overall size. The manufacturing cost will be less than a linear positioner because fewer bearings and precision bars are needed. Significantly, a rotary positioner can be made faster since its inertia is smaller. With a linear positioner all parts move at the same speed. In a rotary positioner, only the heads move at full speed, as the parts closer to the shaft must move more slowly. The principle of many rotary positioners is exactly that of a moving-coil ammeter, where current is converted directly into torque.

One characteristic of rotary positioners is that there is a component of windage on the heads which tends to pull the positioner in towards the spindle. Windage can be overcome in rotary positioners by feeding the current cylinder address to a ROM which sends a code to a DAC. This produces an offset voltage which is fed to the positioner driver to generate a torque which balances the windage whatever the position of the heads.

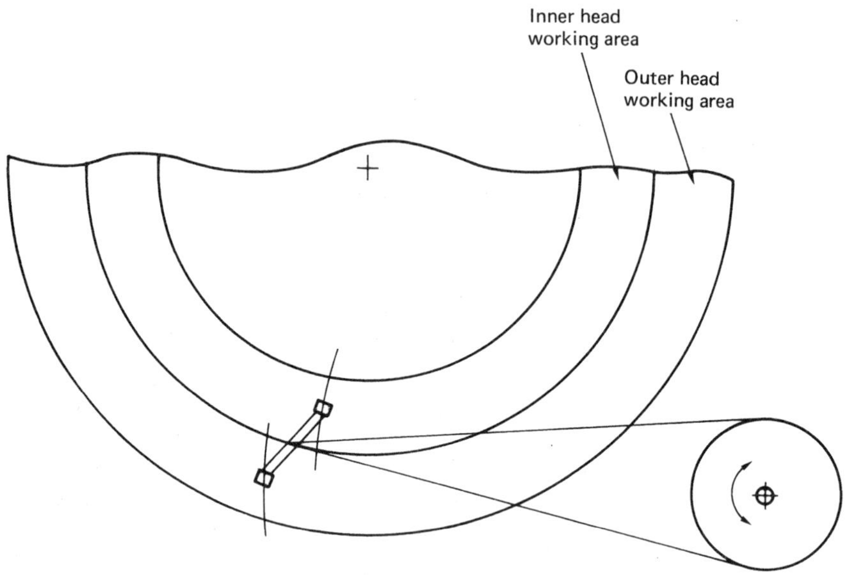

Figure 11.9 A rotary positioner with two heads per surface. The tolerances involved in the spacing between the heads and the axis of rotation mean that each arm records data in an unique position. Those data can only be read back by the same heads, which rules out the use of a rotary positioner in exchangeable-pack drives. In a head disk assembly the problem of compatibility does not arise.

When extremely small track spacing is contemplated, it cannot be assumed that all the heads will track the servo head due to temperature gradients. In this case the embedded-servo approach must be used, where each head has its own alignment patterns. The servo surface is often retained in such drives to allow coarse positioning, velocity feedback and index and write-clock generation, in addition to locating the guard bands for landing the heads.

Winchester drives have been made with massive capacity, but the problem of backup is then magnified, and the general trend has been for the physical size of the drive to come down as the storage density increases in order to improve access time and to facilitate the construction of storage arrays (see section 11.9). Very small Winchester disk drives are now available which plug into standard integrated circuit sockets. These are competing with RAM for memory applications where non-volatility is important.

11.7 The disk controller

A disk controller is a unit which is interposed between the drives and the rest of the system. It consists of two main parts; that which issues control signals to and obtains status from the drives, and that which handles the data to be stored and retrieved. Both parts are synchronized by the control sequencer. The essentials of a disk controller are determined by the characteristics of drives and the functions needed, and so they do not vary greatly. It is desirable for economic reasons to use a commercially available disk controller intended for computers. Such controllers are adequate for still store applications, but cannot support the data rate required for real-time moving video unless data reduction is employed. Disk drives are generally built to interface to a standard controller interface, such as the SCSI bus. The disk controller will then be a unit which interfaces the drive bus to the host computer system.

The execution of a function by a disk subsystem requires a complex series of steps, and decisions must be made between the steps to decide what the next will be. There is a parallel with computation, where the function is the equivalent of an instruction, and the sequencer steps needed are the equivalent of the microinstructions needed to execute the instruction. The major failing in this analogy is that the sequence in a disk drive must be accurately synchronized to the rotation of the disk.

Most disk controllers use direct memory access, which means that they have the ability to transfer disk data in and out of the associated memory without the assistance of the processor. In order to cause a file transfer, the disk controller must be told the physical disk address (cylinder, sector, track), the physical memory address where the file begins, the size of the file and the direction of transfer (read or write). The controller will then position the disk heads, address the memory, and transfer the samples. One disk transfer may consist of many contiguous disk blocks, and the controller will automatically increment the disk-address registers as each block is completed. As the disk turns, the sector address increases until the end of the track is reached. The track or head address will then be incremented and the sector address reset so that transfer continues at the beginning of the next track. This process continues until all the heads have been used in turn. In this case both the head address and sector address will be reset, and the cylinder address will be incremented, which causes a seek. A seek which takes place because of a data transfer is called an implied seek, because it is not necessary formally to instruct the system to perform it. As disk drives are block-structured devices, and the error correction is codeword-based, the controller will always complete a block even if the size of the file is less than a whole number of blocks. This is done by packing the last block with zeros.

The status system allows the controller to find out about the operation of the drive, both as a feedback mechanism for the control process and to handle any errors. Upon completion of a function, it is the status system which interrupts the control processor to tell it that another function can be undertaken.

In a system where there are several drives connected to the controller via a common bus, it is possible for non data-transfer functions such as seeks to take place in some drives simultaneously with a data transfer in another.

Before a data transfer can take place, the selected drive must physically access the desired block, and confirm this by reading the block header. Following a seek to the required cylinder, the positioner will confirm that the heads are on-track and settled. The desired head will be selected, and then a search for the correct sector begins. This is done by comparing the desired sector with the current sector register, which is typically incremented by dividing down servo-surface pulses. When the two counts are equal, the head is about to enter the desired block. Figure 11.10

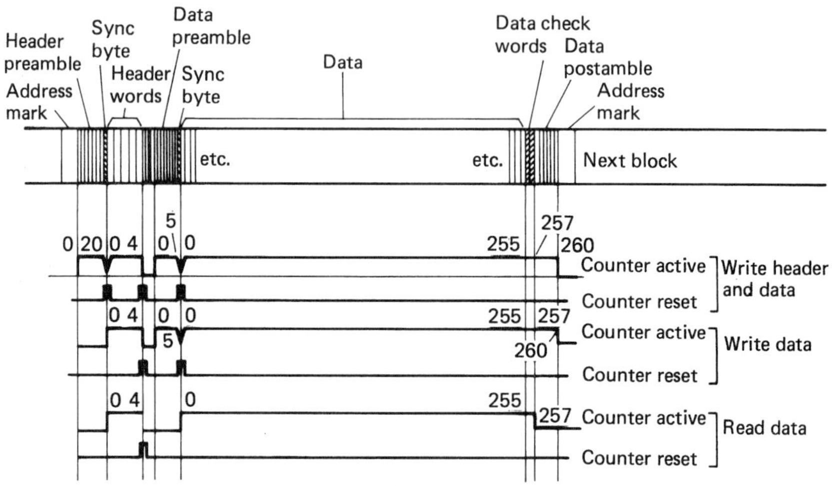

Figure 11.10 The format of a typical disk block related to the count process which is used to establish where in the block the head is at any time. During a read the count is derived from the actual data read, but during a write, the count is derived from the write clock.

shows the structure of a typical magnetic disk track. In between blocks are placed address marks, which are areas without transitions which the read circuits can detect. Following detection of the address mark, the sequencer is roughly synchronized to begin handling the block. As the block is entered, the data separator locks to the preamble, and in due course the sync pattern will be found. This sets to zero a counter which divides the data-bit rate by eight, allowing the serial recording to be correctly assembled into bytes, and also allowing the sequencer to count the position of the head through the block in order to perform all the necessary steps at the right time.

The first header word is usually the cylinder address, and this is compared with the contents of the desired cylinder register. The second

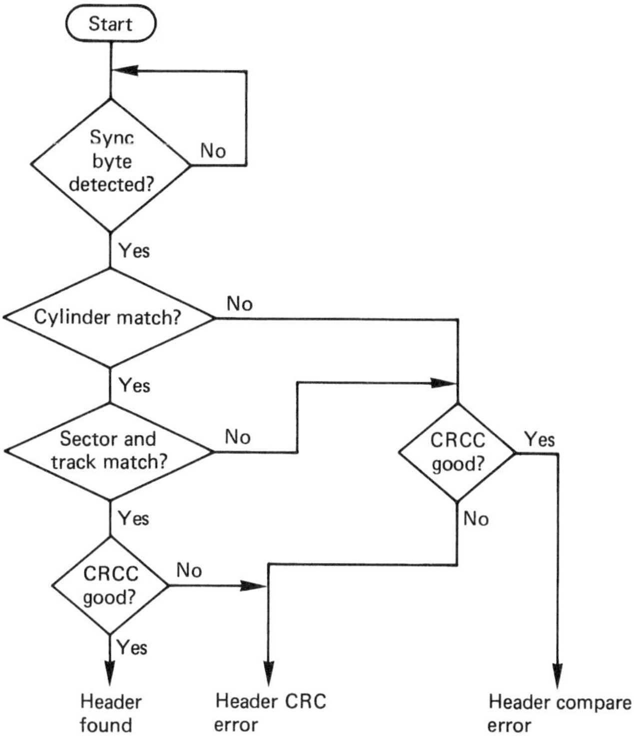

Figure 11.11 The vital process of position confirmation is carried out in accordance with the above flowchart. The appropriate words from the header are compared in turn with the contents of the disk-address registers in the subsystem. Only if the correct header has been found and read properly will the data transfer take place.

header word will contain the sector and track address of the block, and these will also be compared with the desired addresses. There may also be bad-block flags and/or defect-skipping information. At the end of the header is a CRCC which will be used to ensure that the header was read correctly. Figure 11.11 shows a flowchart of the position verification, after which a data transfer can proceed. The header reading is completely automatic. The only time it is necessary formally to command a header to be read is when checking that a disk has been formatted correctly.

During the read of a data block, the sequencer is employed again. The sync pattern at the beginning of the data is detected as before, following which the actual data arrive. These bits are converted to byte or sample parallel, and sent to the memory by DMA. When the sequencer has counted the last data-byte off the track, the redundancy for the error-correction system will be following.

During a write function, the header-check function will also take place as it is perhaps even more important not to write in the wrong place on a disk. Once the header has been checked and found to be correct, the write process for the associated data block can begin. The preambles, sync pattern, data block, redundancy and postamble have all to be written contiguously. This is taken care of by the sequencer, which is obtaining timing information from the servo surface to lock the block structure to the angular position of the disk. This should be contrasted with the read function, where the timing comes directly from the data.

When video samples are fed into a disk-based system, from a digital interface or from an A/D converter, they will be placed in a buffer memory, from which the disk controller will read them by DMA. The continuous-input sample stream will be split up into disk blocks for disk storage.

The disk transfers must by definition be intermittent, because there are headers between contiguous sectors. Once all the sectors on a particular cylinder have been used, it will be necessary to seek to the next cylinder, which will cause a further interruption to the data transfer. If a bad block is encountered, the sequence will be interrupted until it has passed. The instantaneous data rate of a parallel transfer drive is made higher than the continuous video data rate, so that there is time for the positioner to move whilst the video output is supplied from the FIFO memory. In replay, the drive controller attempts to keep the FIFO as full as possible by issuing a read command as soon as one block space appears in the FIFO. This allows the maximum time for a seek to take place before reading must resume. Figure 11.12 shows the action of the FIFO. Whilst recording, the drive controller attempts to keep the FIFO as empty as possible by issuing write commands as soon as a block of data is present. In this way the amount of time available to seek is maximized in the presence of a continuous video sample input.

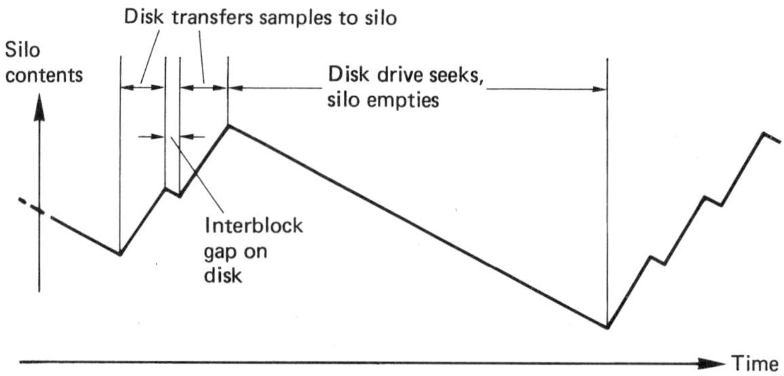

Figure 11.12 During a video replay sequence, silo is constantly emptied to provide samples, and is refilled in blocks by the drive.

11.8 Defect handling

The protection of data recorded on disks differs considerably from the approach used on other media in digital video. This has much to do with the intolerance of data processors to errors when compared with video data. In particular, it is not possible to interpolate to conceal errors in a computer program or a data file.

In the same way that magnetic tape is subject to dropouts, magnetic disks suffer from surface defects whose effect is to corrupt data. The shorter wavelengths employed as disk densities increase are affected more by a given size of defect. Attempting to make a perfect disk is subject to a law of diminishing returns, and eventually a state is reached where it becomes more cost-effective to invest in a defect-handling system.

In the construction of bad-block files, a brand new disk is tested by the operating system. Known patterns are written everywhere on the disk, and these are read back and verified. Following this the system gives the disk a volume name, and creates on it a directory structure which keeps records of the position and size of every file subsequently written. The physical disk address of every block which fails to verify is allocated to a file which has an entry in the disk directory. In this way, when genuine data files come to be written, the bad blocks appear to the system to be in use storing a fictitious file, and no attempt will be made to write there. Some disks have dedicated tracks where defect information can be written during manufacture or by subsequent verification programs, and these permit a speedy construction of the system bad-block file.

11.9 RAID arrays

Whilst the MTBF of a disk drive is very high, it is a simple matter of statistics that when a large number of drives is assembled in a system the time between failures becomes shorter. Disk drives are sealed units and the disks cannot be removed if there is an electronic failure. Even if this were possible the system cannot usually afford down time whilst such a data recovery takes place.

Consequently any system in which the data are valuable must take steps to ensure data integrity. This is commonly done using RAID (redundant array of inexpensive disks) technolgy. Figure 11.13 shows that in a RAID array data blocks are spread across a number of drives.

An-error correcting check symbol (typically Reed–Solomon) is stored on a redundant drive. The error correction is powerful enough to fully correct any error in the block due to a single failed drive. In RAID arrays the drives are designed to be hot-plugged (replaced without removing

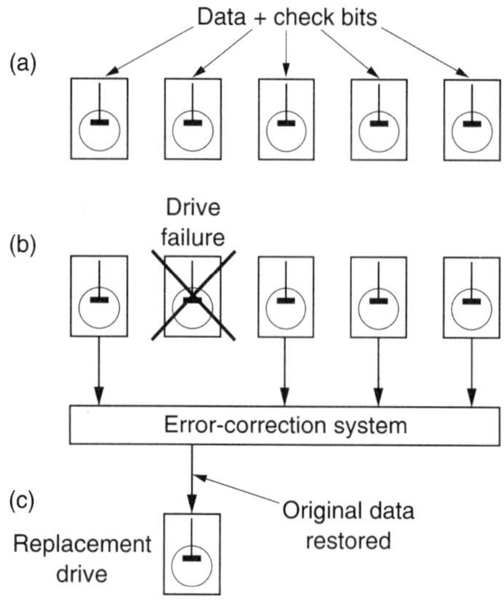

Figure 11.13 In RAID technology, data and redundancy are spread over a number of drives (a). In the case of a drive failure (b) the error-correction system can correct for the loss and continue operation. When the drive is replaced (c) the data can be rewritten so that the system can then survive a further failure.

power) so if a drive fails it is simply physically replaced with a new one. The error-correction system will rewrite the drive with the data which were lost with the failed unit.

When a large number of disk drives are arrayed together, it is necessary and desirable to spread files across all the drives in a RAID array. Whilst this ensures data integrity, it also means that the data transfer rate is multiplied by the number of drives sharing the data. This means that the data transfer rate can be extremely high and new approaches are necessary to move the data in and out of the disk system.

11.10 Disk servers

The disk controller will automatically divide files up into blocks of the appropriate size for recording. If any partial blocks are left over, these will be zero stuffed. Consequently disk stores are not constrained to files of a particular size. Unlike a DVTR which always stores the same amount of data per field, a disk system can store a different amount of data for each field if needs be.

This means that disks are not standards dependent. A disk system can mix 4:4:4, 4:2:2 and 4:2:0 files and it doesn't care whether the video is interlaced or not or compressed or not. It can mix 525- and 625-line files and it can mix 4:3 and 16:9 aspect ratios. This an advantage in news systems where compression is used. If a given compression scheme is used at the time of recording e.g. DVCPRO, the video can remain in the compressed data domain when it is loaded onto the disk system for editing. This avoids concatenation of codecs which is generally bad news in compressed systems.

One of the happy consequences of the move to disk drives in production is that the actual picture format used need no longer be fixed. With computer graphics and broadcast video visibly merging, interlace may well be doomed. In the near future it will be possible to use non-interlaced HD cameras, and downconvert to a non-interlaced intermediate resolution production format.

As production units such as mixers, character generators, paint systems and DVEs become increasingly software driven, such a format is much easier to adopt than in the days of analog where the functionality was frozen into the circuitry. Following production the intermediate format can be converted to any present or future emission standard.

11.11 Optical disk principles

In order to record MO disks or replay any optical disk, a source of monochromatic light is required. The light source must have low noise otherwise the variations in intensity due to the noise of the source will mask the variations due to reading the disk. The requirement for a low-noise monochromatic light source is economically met using a semiconductor laser.

In the LED, the light produced is incoherent or noisy. In the laser, the ends of the semiconductor are optically flat mirrors, which produce an optically resonant cavity. One photon can bounce to and fro, exciting others in synchronism, to produce coherent light. This is known as Light Amplification by Stimulated Emission of Radiation, mercifully abbreviated to LASER, and can result in a runaway condition, where all available energy is used up in one flash. In injection lasers, an equilibrium is reached between energy input and light output, allowing continuous operation with a clean output. The equilibrium is delicate, and such devices are usually fed from a current source. To avoid runaway when temperature change disturbs the equilibrium, a photosensor is often fed back to the current source. Such lasers have a finite life, and become steadily less efficient. The feedback will maintain output, and it is possible to anticipate the failure of the laser by monitoring the drive voltage needed to give the correct output.

Many rerecordable or eraseable optical disks rely on magneto-optics as considered in section 10.7. The storage medium is magnetic, but the writing mechanism is the heat produced by light from a laser; hence the term 'thermomagneto-optics'. The advantage of this writing mechanism is that there is no physical contact between the writing head and the medium. The distance can be several millimetres, some of which is taken up with a protective layer to prevent corrosion. Originally, this layer was glass, but engineering plastics have now taken over.

The laser beam will supply a relatively high power for writing, since it is supplying heat energy. For reading, the laser power is reduced, such that it cannot heat the medium past the Curie temperature, and it is left on continuously.

Whatever the type of disk being read, it must be illuminated by the laser beam. Some of the light reflected back from the disk re-enters the aperture of objective lens. The pickup must be capable of separating the reflected light from the incident light. When playing prerecorded disks such as CDs or DVDs, the phase contrast readout process results in a variation of intensity of the light returning to the pickup. When playing MO disks, the intensity does not change, but the magnetic recording on the disk rotates the plane of polarization one way or the other depending on the direction of the vertical magnetization. Figure 11.14(a) shows that a polarizing prism is required to linearly polarize the light from the laser on its way to the disk. Light returning from the disk has had its plane of polarization rotated by approximately ±1°. This is an extremely small rotation. Figure 11.14(b) shows that the returning rotated light can be considered to be composed of two orthogonal components. R_x is the component which is in the same plane as the illumination and is called the ordinary component and R_y is the component due to the Kerr effect rotation and is known as the magneto-optic component. A polarizing beam splitter mounted squarely would reflect the magneto-optic component R_y very well because it is at right angles to the transmission plane of the prism, but the ordinary component would pass straight on in the direction of the laser. By rotating the prism slightly a small amount of the ordinary component is also reflected. Figure 11.14(c) shows that when combined with the magneto-optic component, the angle of rotation has increased. Detecting this rotation requires a further polarizing prism or analyser as shown. The prism is twisted such that the transmission plane is at 45° to the planes of R_x and R_y. Thus with an unmagnetized disk, half of the light is transmitted by the prism and half is reflected. If the magnetic field of the disk turns the plane of polarization towards the transmission plane of the prism, more light is transmitted and less is reflected. Conversely if the plane of polarization is rotated away from the transmission plane, less light is transmitted and more is reflected. If two sensors are used, one for transmitted light and one for reflected light, the difference between the two sensor outputs will be a waveform representing the angle of polarization and thus the recording on the disk. This differential analyser eliminates common-mode noise in the reflected beam.

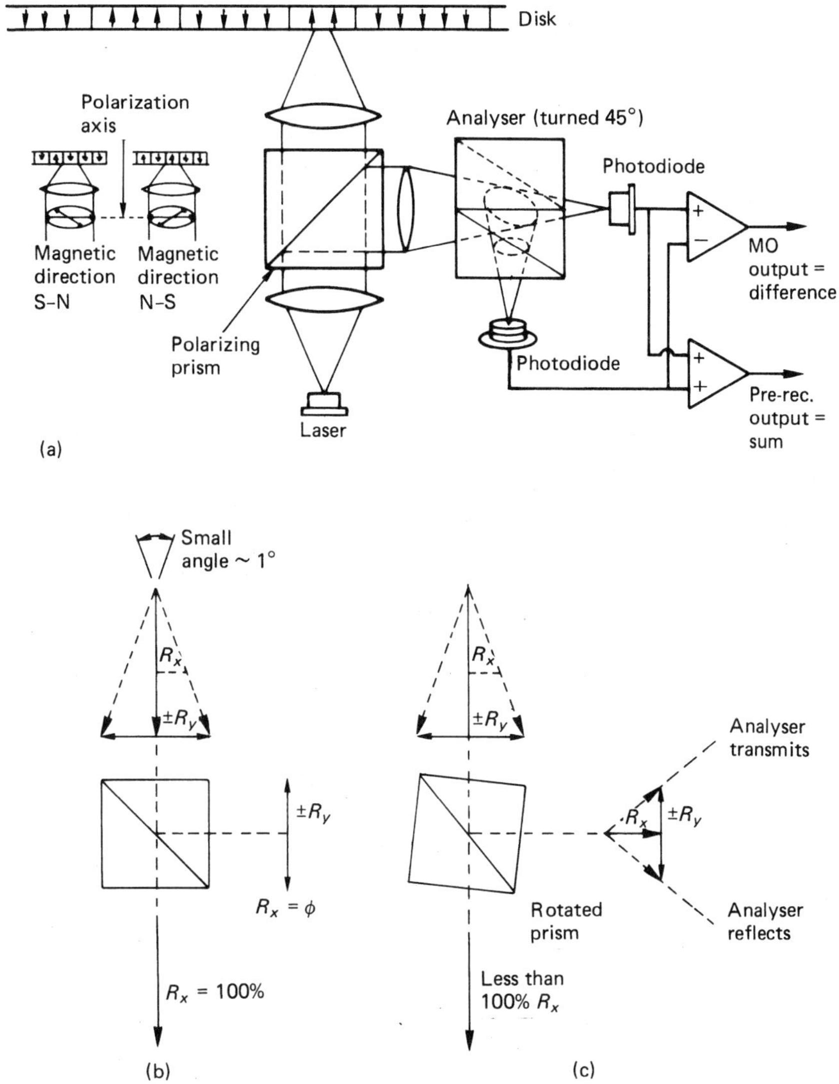

Figure 11.14 A pickup suitable for the replay of magneto-optic disks must respond to very small rotations of the plane of polarization.

High-density recording implies short wavelengths. Using a laser focused on the disk from a distance allows short wavelength recordings to be played back without physical contact, whereas conventional magnetic recording requires intimate contact and implies a wear mechanism, the need for periodic cleaning, and susceptibility to contamination.

The information layer is read through the thickness of the disk; this approach causes the readout beam to enter and leave the disk surface through the largest possible area. Despite the minute spot size of about 1 micrometre diameter, light enters and leaves through a 1 mm diameter circle. As a result, surface debris has to be three orders of magnitude larger than the readout spot before the beam is obscured. This approach has the further advantage in MO drives that the magnetic head, on the opposite side to the laser pickup, is then closer to the magnetic layer in the disk.

11.12 Focus and tracking systems

The frequency response of the laser pickup and the amount of crosstalk are both a function of the spot size and care must be taken to keep the beam focused on the information layer. If the spot on the disk becomes too large, it will be unable to discern the smaller features of the track, and can also be affected by the adjacent track. Disk warp and thickness irregularities will cause focal-plane movement beyond the depth of focus of the optical system, and a focus servo system will be needed. The depth of field is related to the numerical aperture, which is defined, and the accuracy of the servo must be sufficient to keep the focal plane within that depth, which is typically ±1 μm.

The track pitch of a typical optical disk is of the order of a micrometre, and this is much smaller than the accuracy to which the player chuck or the disk centre hole can be made; on a typical player, runout will swing several tracks past a fixed pickup. The non-contact readout means that there is no inherent mechanical guidance of the pickup and a suitable servo system must be provided.

The focus servo moves a lens along the optical axis in order to keep the spot in focus. Since dynamic focus-changes are largely due to warps, the focus system must have a frequency response in excess of the rotational speed. A moving-coil actuator is often used owing to the small moving mass which this permits. Figure 11.15 shows that a cylindrical magnet assembly almost identical to that of a loudspeaker can be used, coaxial with the light beam. Alternatively a moving magnet design can be used. A rare-earth magnet allows a sufficiently strong magnetic field without excessive weight.

A focus-error system is necessary to drive the lens. There are a number of ways in which this can be derived, the most common of which will be described here.

In Figure 11.16 a cylindrical lens is installed between the beam splitter and the photosensor. The effect of this lens is that the beam has no focal point on the sensor. In one plane, the cylindrical lens appears parallel-sided, and has negligible effect on the focal length of the main system, whereas in the other plane, the lens shortens the focal length. The image will be an ellipse whose aspect ratio changes as a function of the state of

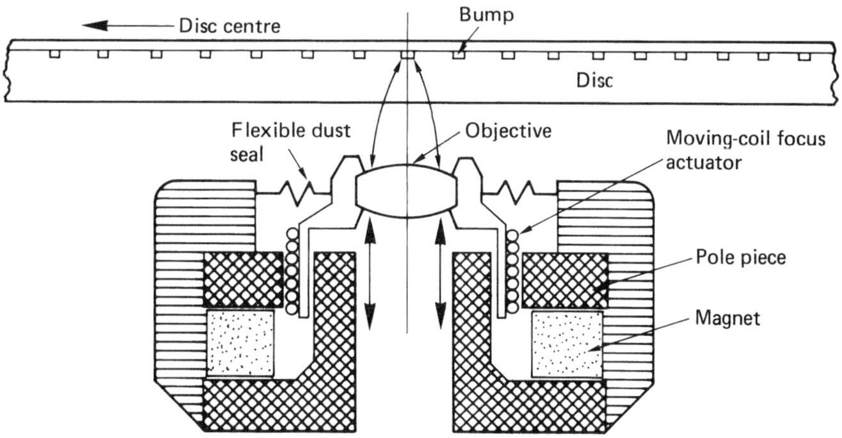

Figure 11.15 Moving-coil-focus servo can be coaxial with the light beam as shown.

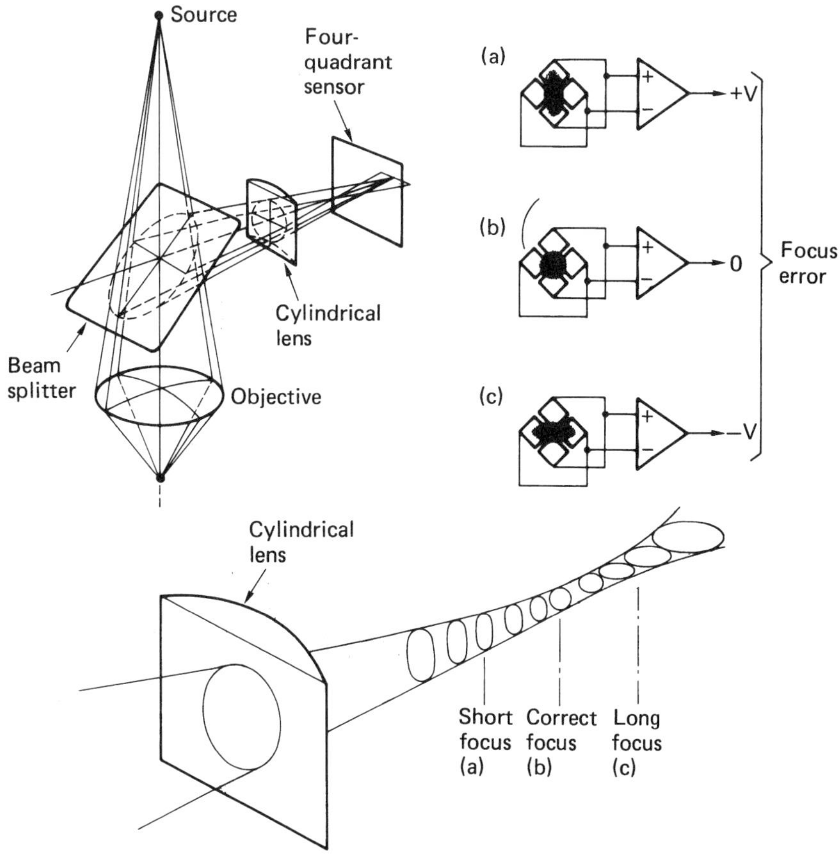

Figure 11.16 The cylindrical lens focus method produces an elliptical spot on the sensor whose aspect ratio is detected by a four-quadrant sensor to produce a focus error.

focus. Between the two foci, the image will be circular. The aspect ratio of the ellipse, and hence the focus error, can be found by dividing the sensor into quadrants. When these are connected as shown, the focus-error signal is generated. The data readout signal is the sum of the quadrant outputs.

Figure 11.17 shows the knife edge-method of determining focus. A split sensor is also required. At (a) the focal point is coincident with the knife edge, so it has little effect on the beam. At (b) the focal point is to the right

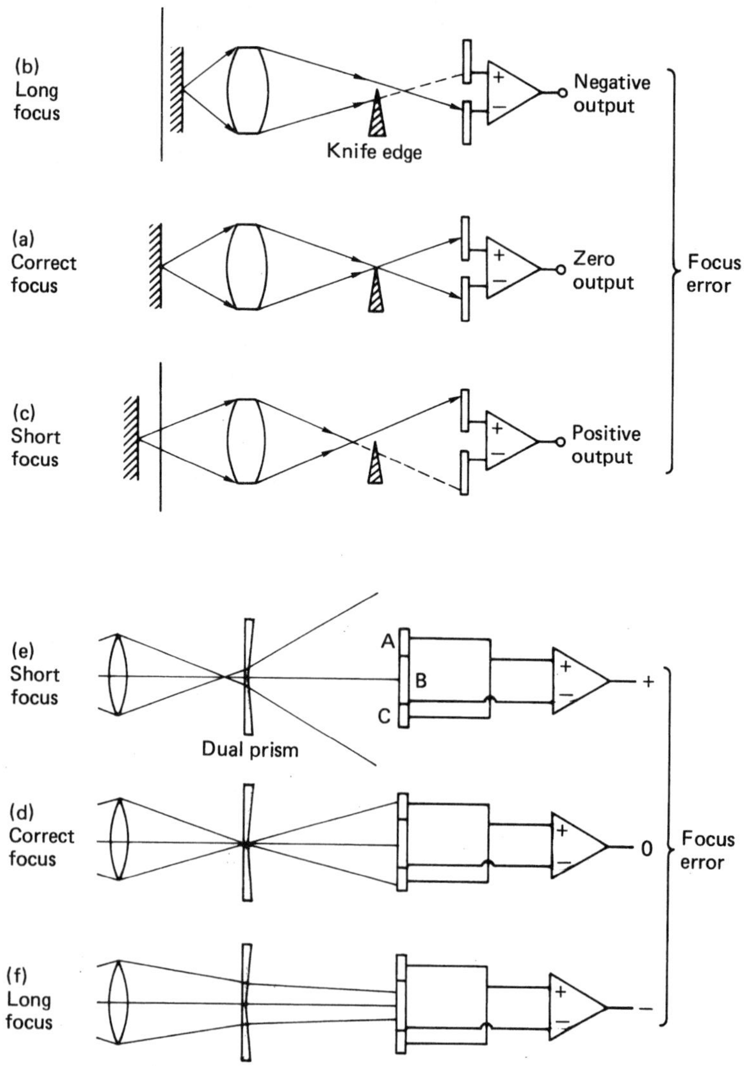

Figure 11.17 (a)–(c) Knife-edge focus-method requires only two sensors, but is critically dependent on knife-edge position. (d)–(f) Twin-prism method requires three sensors (A, B, C), where focus error is (A + C) – B. Prism alignment reduces sensitivity without causing focus error.

of the knife edge, and rising rays are interrupted, reducing the output of the upper sensor. At (c) the focal point is to the left of the knife edge, and descending rays are interrupted, reducing the output of the lower sensor. The focus error is derived by comparing the outputs of the two halves of the sensor. A drawback of the knife-edge system is that the lateral position of the knife edge is critical, and adjustment is necessary. To overcome this problem, the knife edge can be replaced by a pair of prisms, as shown in Figure 11.17(d)–(f). Mechanical tolerances then only affect the sensitivity, without causing a focus offset.

The cylindrical lens method is compared with the knife-edge/prism method in Figure 11.18, which shows that the cylindrical lens method has a much smaller capture range. A focus-search mechanism will be required, which moves the focus servo over its entire travel, looking for a zero crossing. At this time the feedback loop will be completed, and the sensor will remain on the linear part of its characteristic. The spiral track of CD and MiniDisc starts at the inside and works outwards. This was deliberately arranged because there is less vertical runout near the hub, and initial focusing will be easier.

In addition to the track runout mentioned above, there are further mechanisms which cause tracking error. A warped disk will not present its surface at 90° to the beam, but will constantly change the angle of incidence during two whole cycles per revolution. Owing to the change of refractive index at the disk surface, the tilt will change the apparent position of the track to the pickup, and Figure 11.19 shows that this makes

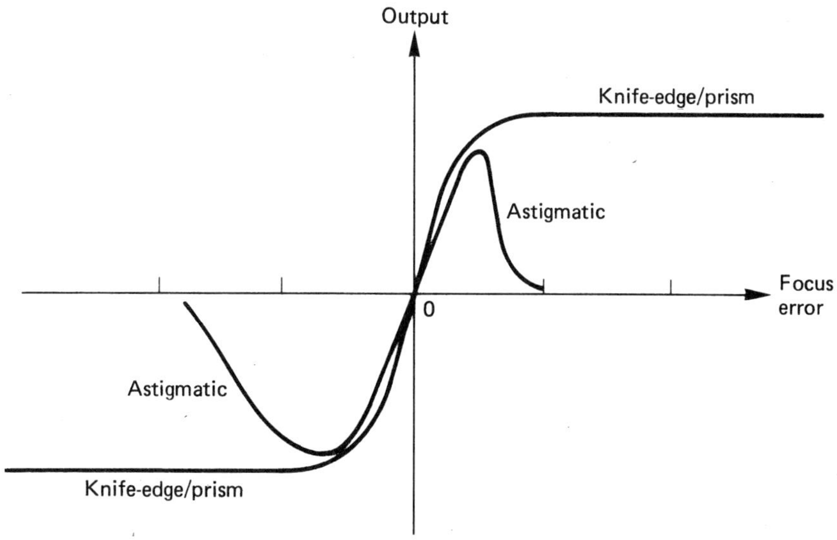

Figure 11.18 Comparison of capture range of knife-edge/prism method and astigmatic (cylindrical lens) system. Knife edge may have range of 1 mm, whereas astigmatic may only have a range of 40 micrometres, requiring a focus-search mechanism.

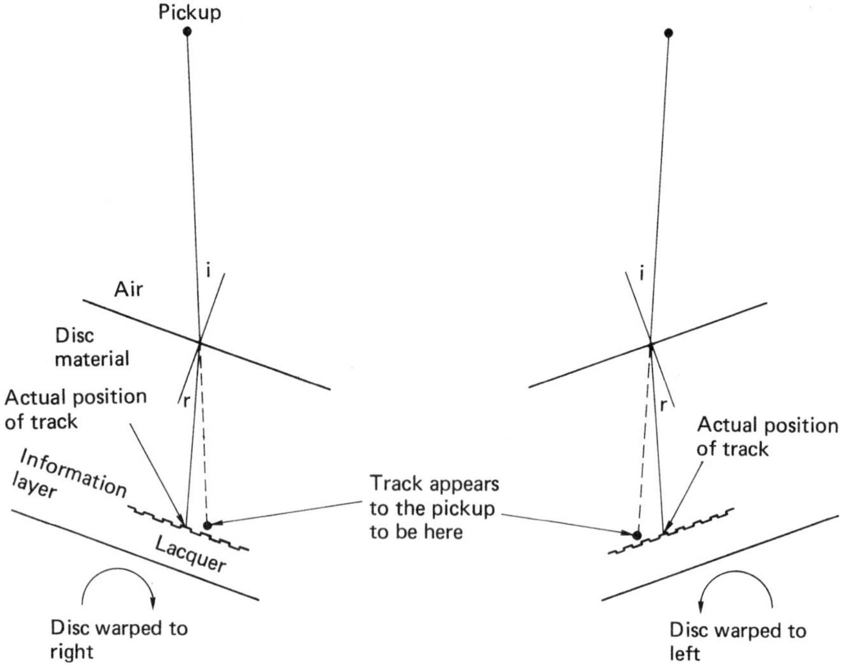

Figure 11.19 Owing to refraction, the angle of incidence (*i*) is greater than the angle of refraction (*r*). Disk warp causes the apparent position of the track (dotted line) to move, requiring the tracking servo to correct.

it appear wavy. Warp also results in coma of the readout spot. The disk format specifies a maximum warp amplitude to keep these effects under control. Finally, vibrations induced in the player from outside, particularly in portable and automotive players, will tend to disturb tracking. A track-following servo is necessary to keep the spot centralized on the track in the presence of these difficulties. There are several ways in which a tracking error can be derived.

In the three-spot method, two additional light beams are focused on the disk track, one offset to each side of the track centre-line. Figure 11.20 shows that, as one side spot moves away from the track into the mirror area, there is less destructive interference and more reflection. This causes the average amplitude of the side spots to change differentially with tracking error. The laser head contains a diffraction grating which produces the side spots, and two extra photosensors onto which the reflections of the side spots will fall. The side spots feed a differential amplifier, which has a low-pass filter to reject the channel-code information and retain the average brightness difference. Some players use a delay line in one of the side-spot signals whose period is equal to the time taken for the disk to travel between the side spots. This helps the differential amplifier to cancel the channel code.

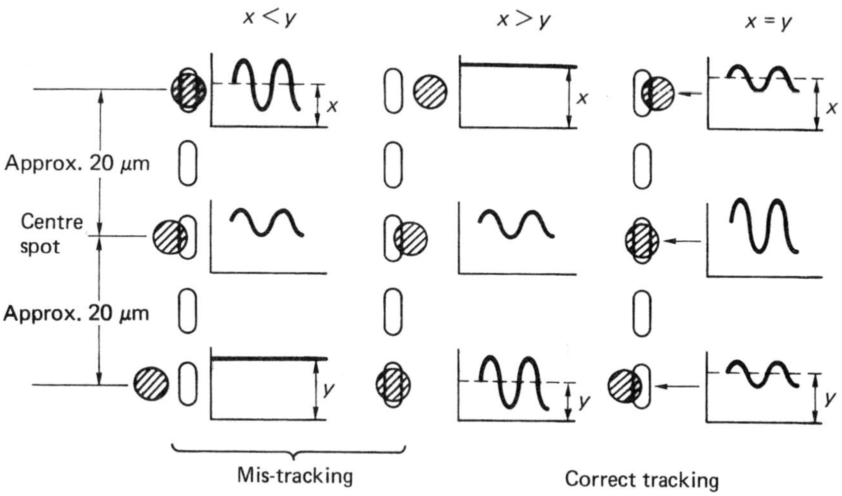

Figure 11.20 Three-spot method of producing tracking error compares average level of side-spot signals. Side spots are produced by a diffraction grating and require their own sensors.

The side spots are generated as follows. When a wavefront reaches an aperture which is small compared to the wavelength, the aperture acts as a point source, and the process of diffraction can be observed as a spherical wavefront leaving the aperture as in Figure 11.21. Where the wavefront passes through a regular structure, known as a diffraction grating, light on the far side will form new wavefronts wherever radiation is in phase, and Figure 11.22 shows that these will be at an angle to the normal depending on the spacing of the structure and the wavelength of the light. A diffraction grating illuminated by white light will produce a dispersed spectrum at each side of the normal. To obtain a fixed angle of diffraction, monochromatic light is necessary.

The alternative approach to tracking-error detection is to analyse the diffraction pattern of the reflected beam. The effect of an off-centre spot is

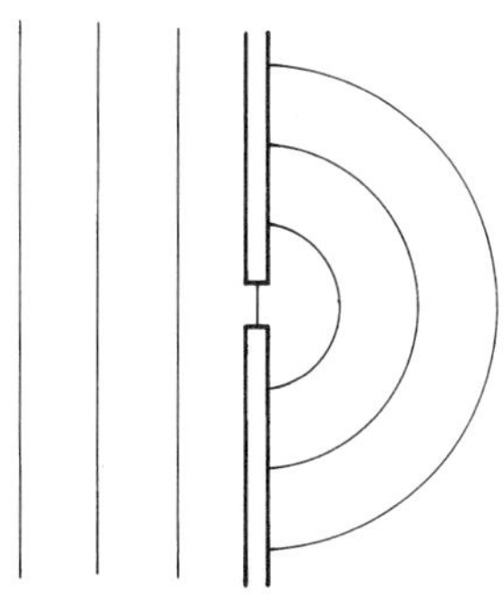

Figure 11.21 Diffraction as a plane wave reaches a small aperture.

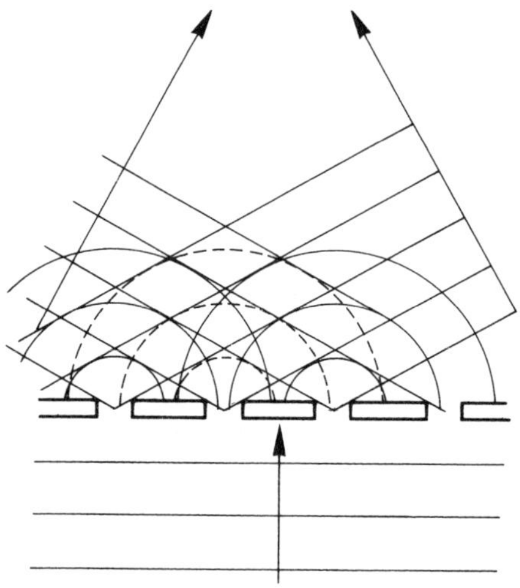

Figure 11.22 In a diffraction grating, constructive interference can take place at more than one angle for a single wavelength.

to rotate the radial diffraction pattern about an axis along the track. Figure 11.23 shows that, if a split sensor is used, one half will see greater modulation than the other when off-track. Such a system may be prone to develop an offset due either to drift or to contamination of the optics, although the capture range is large. A further tracking mechanism is often added to obviate the need for periodic adjustment. Figure 11.24 shows that in this dither-based system, a sinusoidal drive is fed to the tracking servo, causing a radial oscillation of spot position of about ±50 nm. This results in modulation of the envelope of the readout signal, which can be synchronously detected to obtain the sense of the error. The dither can be produced by vibrating a mirror in the light path, which enables a high frequency to be used, or by oscillating the whole pickup at a lower frequency.

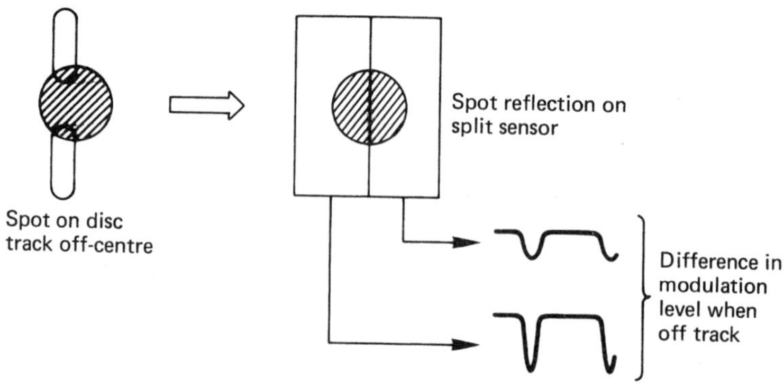

Figure 11.23 Split-sensor method of producing tracking error focuses image of spot onto sensor. One side of spot will have more modulation when off track.

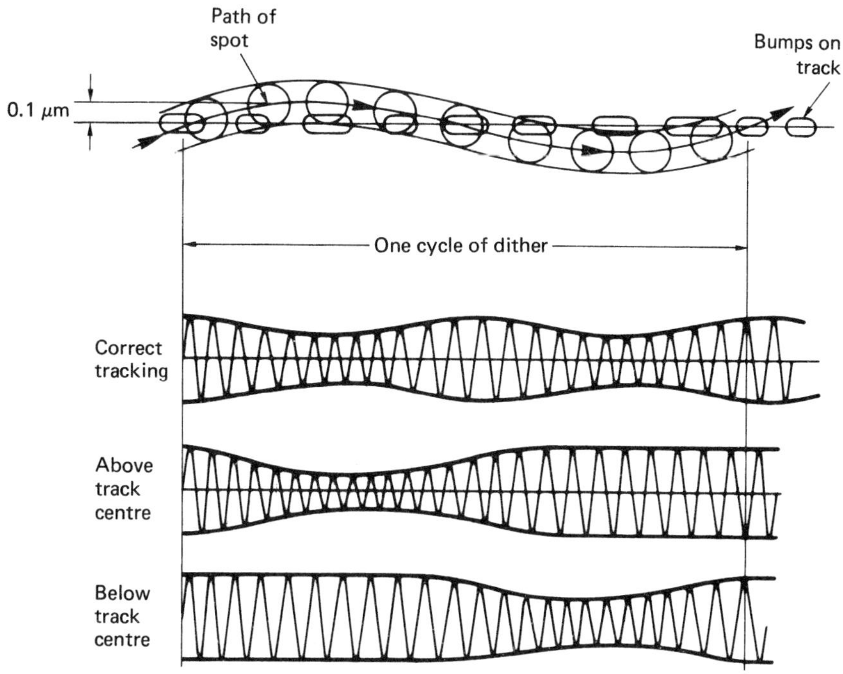

Figure 11.24 Dither applied to readout spot modulates the readout envelope. A tracking error can be derived.

In prerecorded disks there is obviously a track to follow, but in recordable disks provision has to be made for track following during the first recording of a blank disk. This is typically done by pressing the tracks in the form of continuous grooves. The grooves may be produced with a lateral wobble so that the wobble frequency can be used to measure the speed of the track during recording.

11.13 Structure of a DVD player

Figure 11.25 shows the block diagram of a typical DVD player, and illustrates the essential components. The most natural division within the block diagram is into the control/servo system and the data path. The control system provides the interface between the user and the servo mechanisms, and performs the logical interlocking required for safety and the correct sequence of operation.

The servo systems include any power-operated loading drawer and chucking mechanism, the spindle-drive servo, and the focus and tracking servos already described.

Power loading is usually implemented on players where the disk is placed in a drawer. Once the drawer has been pulled into the machine,

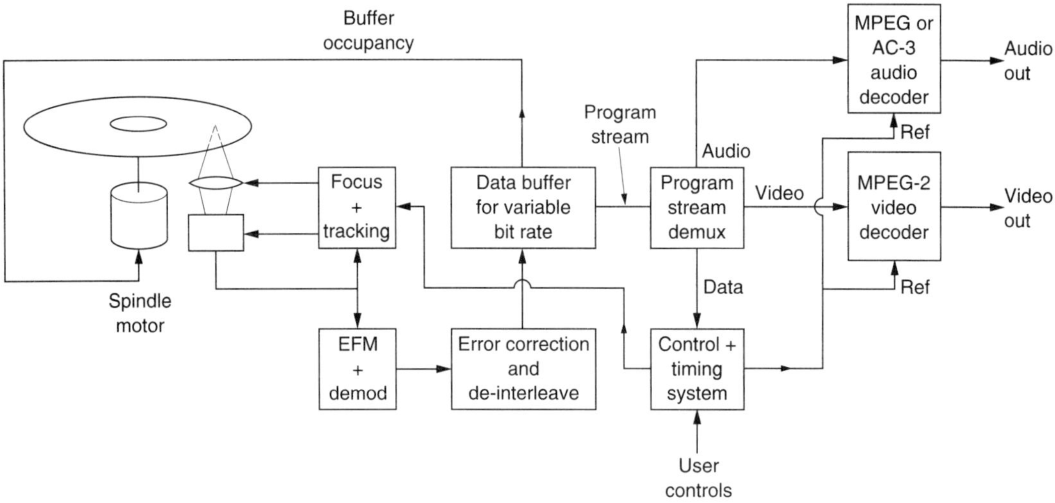

Figure 11.25 A DVD player's essential parts. See text for details.

the disk is lowered onto the drive spindle, and clamped at the centre, a process known as chucking. In the simpler top-loading machines, the disk is placed on the spindle by hand, and the clamp is attached to the lid so that it operates as the lid is closed.

The lid or drawer mechanisms have a safety switch which prevents the laser operating if the machine is open. This is to ensure that there can be no conceivable hazard to the user. In actuality there is very little hazard in a DVD pickup. This is because the beam is focused a few millimetres away from the objective lens, and beyond the focal point the beam diverges and the intensity falls rapidly. It is almost impossible to position the eye at the focal point when the pickup is mounted in the player, but it would be foolhardy to attempt to disprove this.

The data path consists of the data separator, the de-interleaving and error-correction process followed by a RAM buffer which supplies the MPEG decoder.

The data separator converts the EFMplus readout waveform into data. Following data separation the error-correction and de-interleave processes take place.

Because of the interleave system, there are two opportunities for correction, first, using the inner code prior to de-interleaving, and second, using the outer code after de-interleaving. In Chapter 9 it was shown that interleaving is designed to spread the effects of burst errors among many different codewords, so that the errors in each are reduced. However, the process can be impaired if a small random error, due perhaps to an imperfection in manufacture, occurs close to a burst error caused by surface contamination. The function of the inner redundancy is to correct single-symbol errors, so that the power of interleaving to handle bursts is undiminished, and to generate error flags for the outer system when a gross error is encountered.

The EFMplus coding is a group code which means that a small defect which changes one channel pattern into another could have corrupted up to eight data bits. In the worst case, if the small defect is on the boundary between two channel patterns, two successive bytes could be corrupted. However, the final odd/even interleave on encoding ensures that the two bytes damaged will be in different inner codewords; thus a random error can never corrupt two bytes in one inner codeword, and random errors are therefore always correctable.

The de-interleave process is achieved by writing sequentially into a memory and reading out using a sequencer. The outer decoder will then correct any burst errors in the data. As MPEG data are very sensitive to error the error-correction performance has to be extremely good.

Following the de-interleave and outer error-correction process an MPEG program stream (see Chapter 9) emerges. Some of the program stream data will be video, some will be audio and this will be routed to the appropriate decoder. It is a fundamental concept of DVD that the bit rate of this program stream is not fixed, but can vary with the difficulty of the program material in order to maintain consistent image quality. The bit rate is changed by changing the speed of the disk. However, there is a complication because the disk uses constant linear velocity rather than constant angular velocity. It is not possible to obtain a particular bit rate with a fixed spindle speed.

The solution is to use a RAM buffer between the transport and the MPEG decoders. The RAM is addressed by counters which are arranged to overflow, giving the memory a ring structure as described in Chapter 1. Writing into the memory is done using clocks derived from the disk whose frequency rises and falls with runout, whereas reading is done by the decoder which, for each picture, will take as much data as are required from the buffer.

The buffer will only function properly if the two addresses are kept apart. This implies that the amount of data read from the disk over the long term must equal the amount of data used by the MPEG decoders. This is done by analysing the address relationship of the buffer. If the disk is turning too fast, the write address will move towards the read address; if the disk is turning too slowly, the write address moves away from the read address. Subtraction of the two addresses produces an error signal which can be fed to the spindle motor.

The speed of the motor is unimportant. The important factor is that the data rate needed by the decoder is correct, and the system will drive the spindle at whatever speed is necessary so that the buffer neither underflows nor overflows.

The MPEG decoder will convert the compressed elementary streams into PCM video and audio and place the pictures and audio blocks into RAM. These will be read out of RAM whenever the time stamps recorded with each picture or audio block match the state of a time stamp counter. If bidirectional coding is used, the RAM readout sequence will convert the recorded picture sequence back to the real-time sequence. The time stamp counter is derived from a crystal oscillator in the player which is divided down to provide the 90 kHz time stamp clock.

As a result the frame rate at which the disk was mastered will be replicated as the pictures are read from RAM. Once a picture buffer is read out, this will trigger the decoder to decode another picture. It will read data from the buffer until this has been completed and thus indirectly influence the disk speed.

Owing to the use of constant linear velocity, the disk speed will be wrong if the pickup is suddenly made to jump to a different radius using manual search controls. This may force the data separator out of lock, or cause a buffer overflow and the decoder may freeze briefly until this has been remedied.

The control system of a CD player is inevitably microprocessor-based, and as such does not differ greatly in hardware terms from any other microprocessor-controlled device. Operator controls will simply interface to processor input ports and the various servo systems will be enabled or

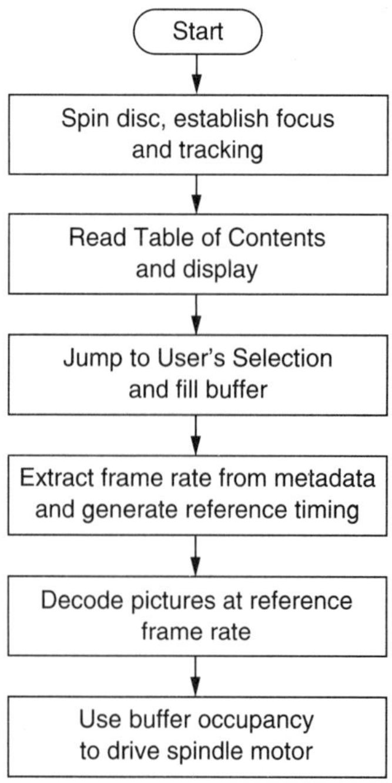

Figure 11.26 Simple processes required for a DVD player to operate.

overridden by output ports. Software, or more correctly firmware, connects the two. The necessary controls are Play and Eject, with the addition in most players of at least Pause and some buttons which allow rapid skipping through the program material.

Although machines vary in detail, the flowchart of Figure 11.26 shows the logic flow of a simple player, from start being pressed to pictures and sound emerging. At the beginning, the emphasis is on bringing the various servos into operation. Towards the end, the disc subcode is read in order to locate the beginning of the first section of the program material.

When track-following, the tracking-error feedback loop is closed, but for track crossing, in order to locate a piece of music, the loop is opened, and a microprocessor signal forces the laser head to move. The tracking error becomes an approximate sinusoid as tracks are crossed. The cycles of tracking error can be counted as feedback to determine when the correct number of tracks have been crossed. The 'mirror' signal obtained when the readout spot is half a track away from target is used to brake pickup motion and re-enable the track-following feedback.

11.14 Digital video tape

Whilst numerous experimental machines were built previously, the first production DVTR, launched in 1987, used the D-1 format which recorded colour difference data according to CCIR-601 on $\frac{3}{4}$-inch tape. Whilst it represented a tremendous achievement, the D-1 format was too early to take advantage of high-coercivity tapes and its recording density was quite low, leading to large cassettes and high running costs. The majority of broadcasters then used composite signals, and a component recorder could not easily be used in such an environment. Where component applications existed, the D-1 format could not compete economically with Betacam SP and M-II analog formats. As a result D-1 found application only in high-end post-production suites.

The D-2 format came next, but this was a composite digital format, handling conventional PAL and NTSC signals in digital form, and derived from a format developed by Ampex for a robotic cart. machine. The choice of composite recording was intended to allow broadcasters directly to replace analog recorders with a digital machine. D-2 retained the cassette shell of D-1 but employed higher-coercivity tape and azimuth recording (see Chapter 10) to improve recording density and playing time. Early D-2 machines had no flying erase heads, and difficulties arose with audio edits. D-2 was also hampered by the imminent arrival of the D-3 format.

D-3 was designed by NHK, and put into production by Panasonic. This had twice the recording density of D-2; three times that of D-1. This permitted the use of $\frac{1}{2}$-inch tape, making a digital camcorder a possibility. D-3 used the same sampling structure as D-2 for its composite recordings. Coming later, D-3 had learned from earlier formats and had a more powerful error-correction strategy than earlier formats, particularly in audio recording.

By this time the economics of VLSI chips had made made data reduction in VTRs viable, and the first application was the Ampex DCT format which used approximately 2:1 data reduction so that component video could be recorded on an updated version of the $\frac{3}{4}$-inch cassettes and transports designed for D-2.

When Sony were developing the Digital Betacam format, compatibility with the existing analog Betacam format was a priority. Digital Betacam uses the same cassette shells as the analog format, and certain models of the digital recorder can play existing analog tapes. Sony also adopted data reduction, but this was in order to allow the construction of a digital component VTR which offered sufficient playing time within the existing cassette dimensions.

The D-5 component format is backward compatible with D-3. The same cassettes are used and D-5 machines can play D-3 tapes. However, in standard definition, compression is not used; the tape speed is doubled in the component format in order to increase the bit rate. With mild compression D-5 recorders can handle high-definition video.

During the development of the DVTR, hard disk storage was developing rapidly and as costs fell, the advantages of disk-based video storage began to erode the DVTR market. In this environment the most successful tape-based solution recently has been the DV format and its production relative DVCPRO. DV has used compression to allow a highly miniaturized mechanism which is ideal for portable use and which outperforms disk-based technology in that application.

In the future recording technology will continue to advance and further formats are inevitable as manufacturers perceive an advantage over their competition. This does not mean that the user need slavishly change to every new format, as the cost of format change is high. Astute users retain their current format for long enough to allow a number of new formats to be introduced. They will then make a quantum leap to a format which is much better than the present one, missing out those between and minimizing the changeover costs.

11.15 The rotary head tape transport

The high bit rate of digital video could be accommodated by a conventional tape deck having many parallel tracks, but each would need its own read/write electronics and the cost would be high. However, the main problem with such an approach is that the data rate is proportional to the tape speed. The provision of stunt modes such as still frame or picture in shuttle are difficult or impossible. The rotary head recorder has the advantage that the spinning heads create a high head-to-tape speed offering a high bit rate recording with a small number of heads and without high tape speed. The head-to-tape speed is dominated by the rotational speed, and the linear tape speed can vary enormously without changing the frequencies produced by the head by very much. Whilst mechanically complex, the rotary head transport has been raised to a high degree of refinement and offers the highest recording density and thus lowest cost per bit of all digital recorders. Figure 11.27 shows that the tape

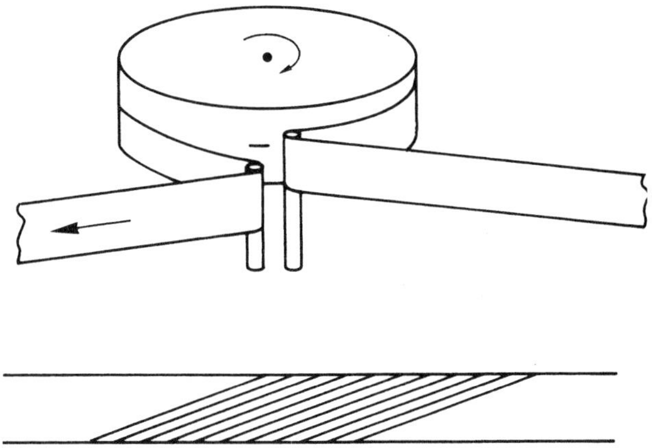

Figure 11.27 Rotary-head recorder. A helical scan records long diagonal tracks.

is led around a rotating drum in a helix such that the entrance and exit heights are different. As a result the rotating heads cross the tape at an angle and record a series of slanting tracks. The rotating heads turn at a speed which is locked to the video field rate so that a whole number of tracks results in each input field. Time compression can be used so that the switch from one track to the next falls within a gap between data blocks. Clearly the slant tracks can only be played back properly if linear tape motion is controlled in some way. This is the job of the linear control track which carries a pulse corresponding to every slant track. The control track is played back in order to control the capstan. The breaking up of fields into several tracks is called segmentation and it is used to keep the tracks reasonably short. The segments are invisibly reassembled in memory on replay to restore the original fields.

Figure 11.28 shows the important components of a rotary head helical scan tape transport. There are four servo systems which must correctly interact to obtain all modes of operation: two reel servos, the drum servo

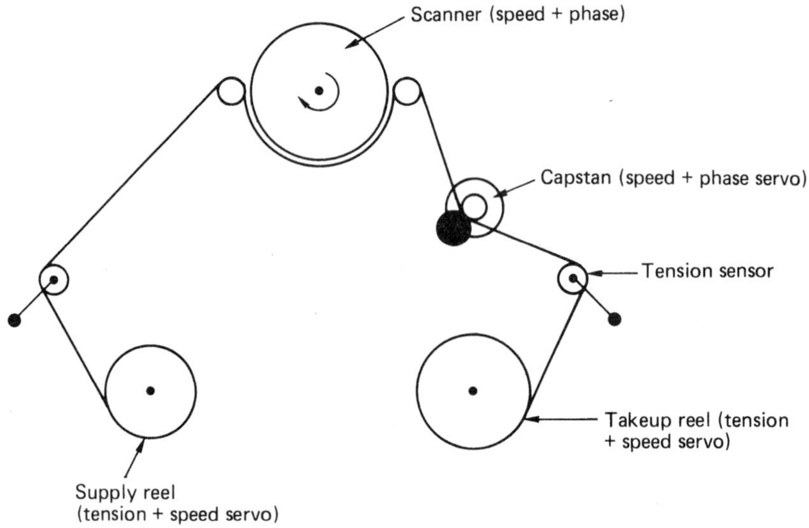

Figure 11.28 The four servos essential for proper operation of a helical-scan DVTR. Cassette-based units will also require loading and threading servos, and for variable speed a track-following servo will be necessary.

and the capstan servo. The capstan and reel servos together move and tension the tape, and the drum servo moves the heads. For variable-speed operation a further servo system will be necessary to deflect the heads.

There are two approaches to capstan drive, those which use a pinch roller and those which do not. In a pinch roller drive, the tape is held against the capstan by pressure from a resilient roller which is normally pulled towards the capstan by a solenoid. The capstan only drives the tape over a narrow speed range, generally the range in which broadcastable pictures are required. Outside this range, the pinch roller retracts, the tape will be driven by reel motors alone, and the reel motors will need to change their operating mode; one becomes a velocity servo whilst the other remains a tension servo.

In a pinch-roller-less transport, the tape is wrapped some way around a relatively large capstan, to give a good area of contact. The tape is always in contact with the capstan, irrespective of operating mode, and so the reel servos never need to change mode. A large capstan has to be used to give sufficient contact area, and to permit high shuttle speed without excessive motor rpm. This means that at play speed it will be turning slowly, and must be accurately controlled and free from cogging. A multi-pole ironless rotor pancake type brush motor is often used, or a sinusoidal drive brushless motor.

The simplest operating mode to consider is the first recording on a blank tape. In this mode, the capstan will rotate at constant speed, and drive the tape at the linear speed specified for the format. The drum must rotate at a precisely determined speed, so that the correct number of tracks per unit distance will be laid down on the tape. Since in a segmented recording each track will be a constant fraction of a television field, the drum speed must ultimately be determined by the incoming video signal to be recorded. The phase of the drum rotation with respect to input video timing depends upon the time delay necessary to shuffle and interleave the video samples. This time will vary from a minimum of about one segment to more than a field depending on the format.

In order to obtain accurate tracking on replay, a phase comparison will be made between offtape control track pulses and pulses generated by the rotation of the drum. If the phase error between these is used to modify the capstan drive, the error can be eliminated, since the capstan drives the tape which produces the control track segment pulses. Eliminating this timing error results in the rotating heads following the tape tracks properly. Artificially delaying or advancing the reference pulses from the drum will result in a tracking adjustment. Alternatively, the capstan phase can be controlled by analysing tracking signals embedded in the slant tracks. This approach is more accurate and allows a finer track pitch leading to higher recording density. The fixed head is also eliminated.

11.16 Digital video cassettes

The main advantages of a cassette are that the medium is better protected from contamination whilst out of the transport, and that an unskilled operator or a mechanical elevator can load the tape. The digital cassette contains two fully flanged reels side by side. The centre of each hub is fitted with a thrust pad and when the cassette is not in the drive a spring acts on this pad and presses the lower flange of each reel firmly against the body of the cassette to exclude dust. When the cassette is in the machine the relative heights of the reel turntables and the cassette supports are such that the reels seat on the turntables before the cassette comes to rest. This opens a clearance space between the reel flanges and the cassette body by compressing the springs.

The use of a cassette means that it is not as easy to provide a range of sizes as it is with open reels. Simply putting smaller reels in a cassette with the same hub spacing does not produce a significantly smaller cassette. The only solution is to specify different hub spacings for different sizes of cassette. This gives the best volumetric efficiency for storage, but it does mean that the transport must be able to reposition the reel drive motors if it is to play more than one size of cassette.

Cassettes typically have hinged doors to protect the tape when not in a transport, and a reel-locking mechanism to prevent the tape forming a slack loop in storage. There is also typically a write protect tab. Most

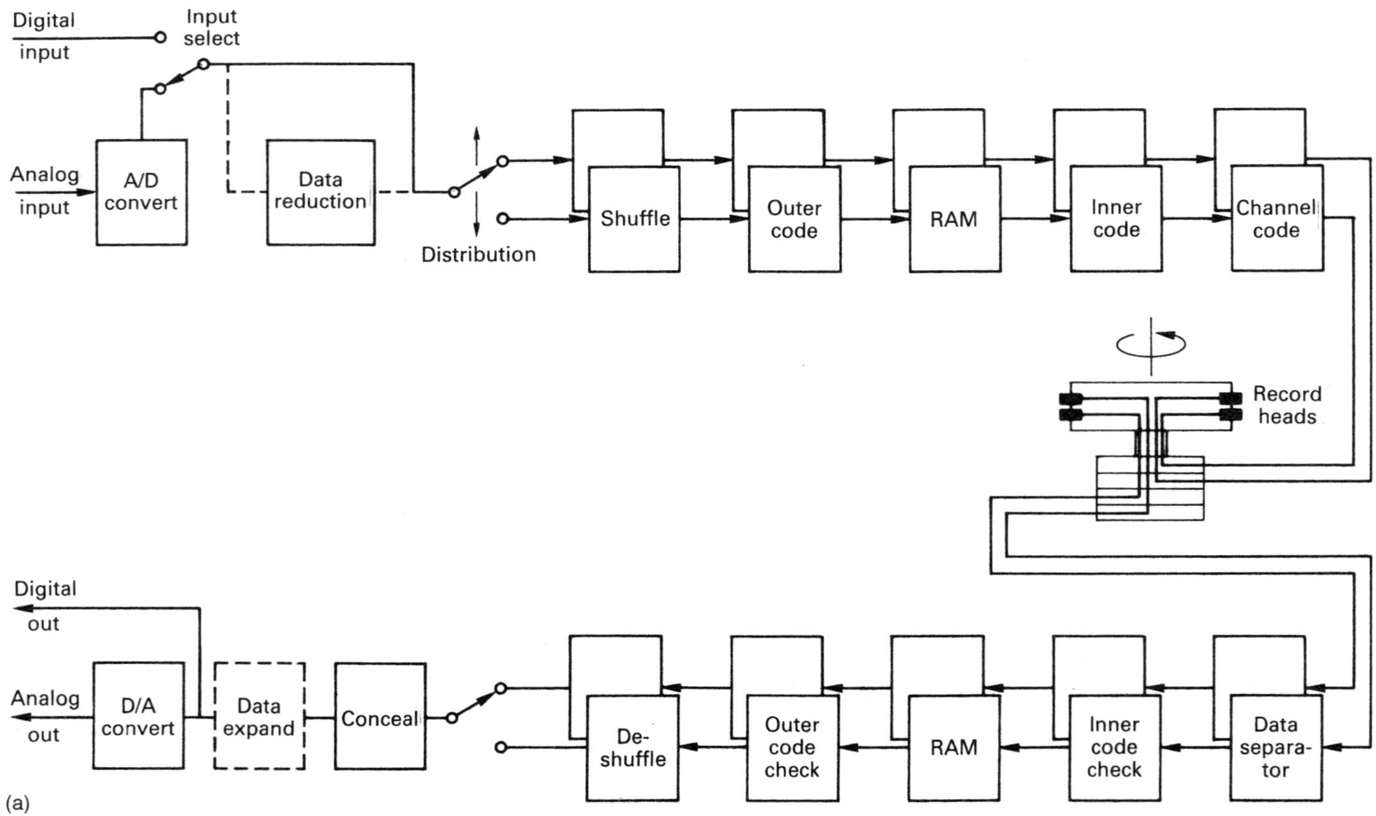
Digital
input
Input
select
Analog
input
A/D
convert
Data
reduction
Distribution
Shuffle
Outer
code
RAM
Inner
code
Channel
code
Record
heads
Digital
out
Analog
out
D/A
convert
Data
expand
Conceal
De-
shuffle
Outer
code
check
RAM
Inner
code
check
Data
separa-
tor

(a)

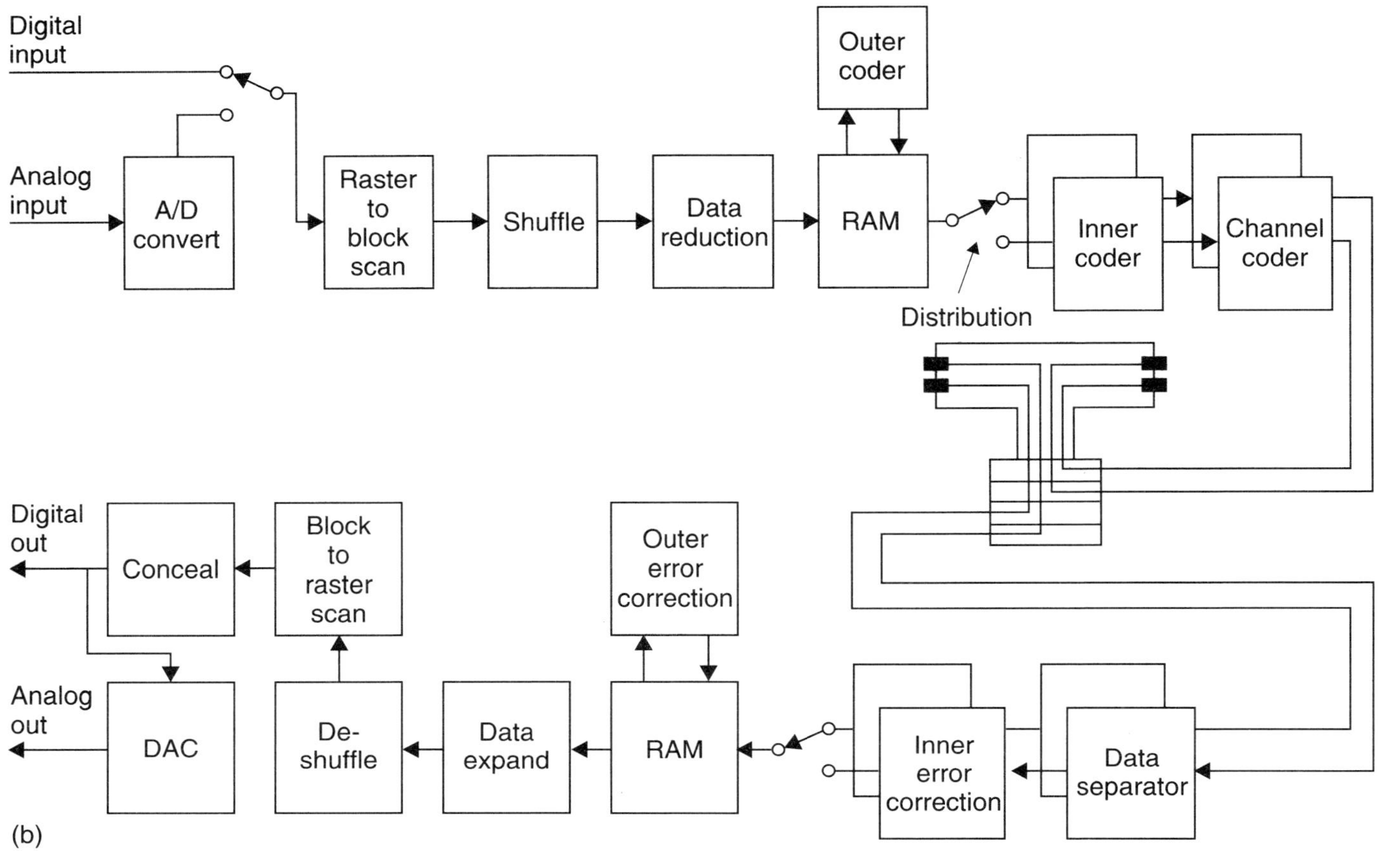

Figure 11.29 (a) Block diagram of full bit rate DVTR showing processes introduced in this chapter. In (b) a DVTR using data reduction is shown.

cassettes have provision for a barcode for use in automated handling systems. Some contain the equivalent of a smart card which carries metadata describing the recording. This can be read quickly without lacing the tape and independently of how far the tape has been wound.

11.17 DVTR block diagram

Figure 11.29(a) shows a representative block diagram of a PCM (i.e. uncompressed) DVTR. Following the convertors will be the distribution of odd and even samples and a shuffle process for concealment purposes. An interleaved product code will be formed prior to the channel coding stage which produces the recorded waveform. On replay the data separator decodes the channel code and the inner and outer codes perform correction as in section 10.24. Following the de-shuffle the data channels are recombined and any necessary concealment will take place. Figure 11.29(b) shows the block diagram of a DVTR using compression. Data from the convertors are rearranged from the normal raster scan to the DCT blocks upon which the compression system works. A common size is eight pixels horizontally by four or eight vertically. The blocks are then shuffled spatially. This has two functions; first, it aids concealment purposes and second, it makes the entropy of the picture more uniform. The shuffled blocks are passed through the compression process. The output of this is distributed and then assembled into product codes and channel coded as for a conventional recorder. On replay data separation and error correction takes place as before, but there is now a matching decoder which outputs DCT blocks. These are then de-shuffled prior to the error-concealment stage. As concealment is more difficult with pixel blocks, data from another field may be employed for concealment as well as data within the field.

The various DVTR formats largely employ the same processing stages, but there are considerable differences in the order in which these are applied. Distribution is shown in Figure 11.30(a). This is a process of sharing the input bit rate over two or more signal paths so that the bit rate recorded in each is reduced. The data are subsequently recombined on playback. Each signal path requires its own tape track and head. The parallel tracks which result form a *segment*.

Segmentation is shown in Figure 11.30(b). This is the process of sharing the data resulting from one video field over several segments. The replay system must have some means to ensure that associated segments are reassembled into the original field. This is generally a function of the control track.

Figure 11.30(c) shows a product code. Data to be recorded are protected by two error-correcting codeword systems at right angles; the inner code

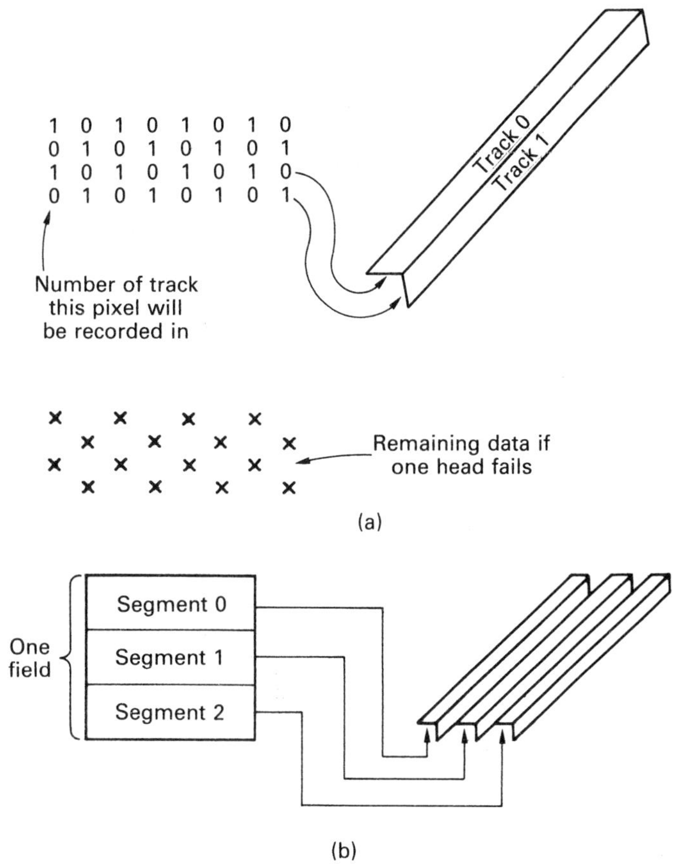

Figure 11.30 The fundamental stages of DVTR processing. At (a), distribution spreads data over more than one track to make concealment easier and to reduce the data rate per head. At (b) segmentation breaks video fields into manageable track lengths.

and the outer code (see Chapter 10). When it is working within its capacity the error-correction system returns corrupt data to their original value and its operation is undetectable.

If errors are too great for the correction system, concealment will be employed. Concealment is the *estimation* of missing data values from surviving data nearby. Nearby means data on vertical, horizontal or time axes as shown in Figure 11.30(d). Concealment relies upon distribution, as all tracks of a segment are unlikely to be simultaneously lost, and upon the *shuffle* shown in Figure 11.30(e). Shuffling reorders the pixels prior to recording and is reversed on replay. The result is that uncorrectable errors due to dropouts are not concentrated, but are spread out by the de-shuffle, making concealment easier. A different approach is required where compression is used because the data recorded are not pixels representing a point, but coefficients representing a DCT blocks and it is these which must be shuffled.

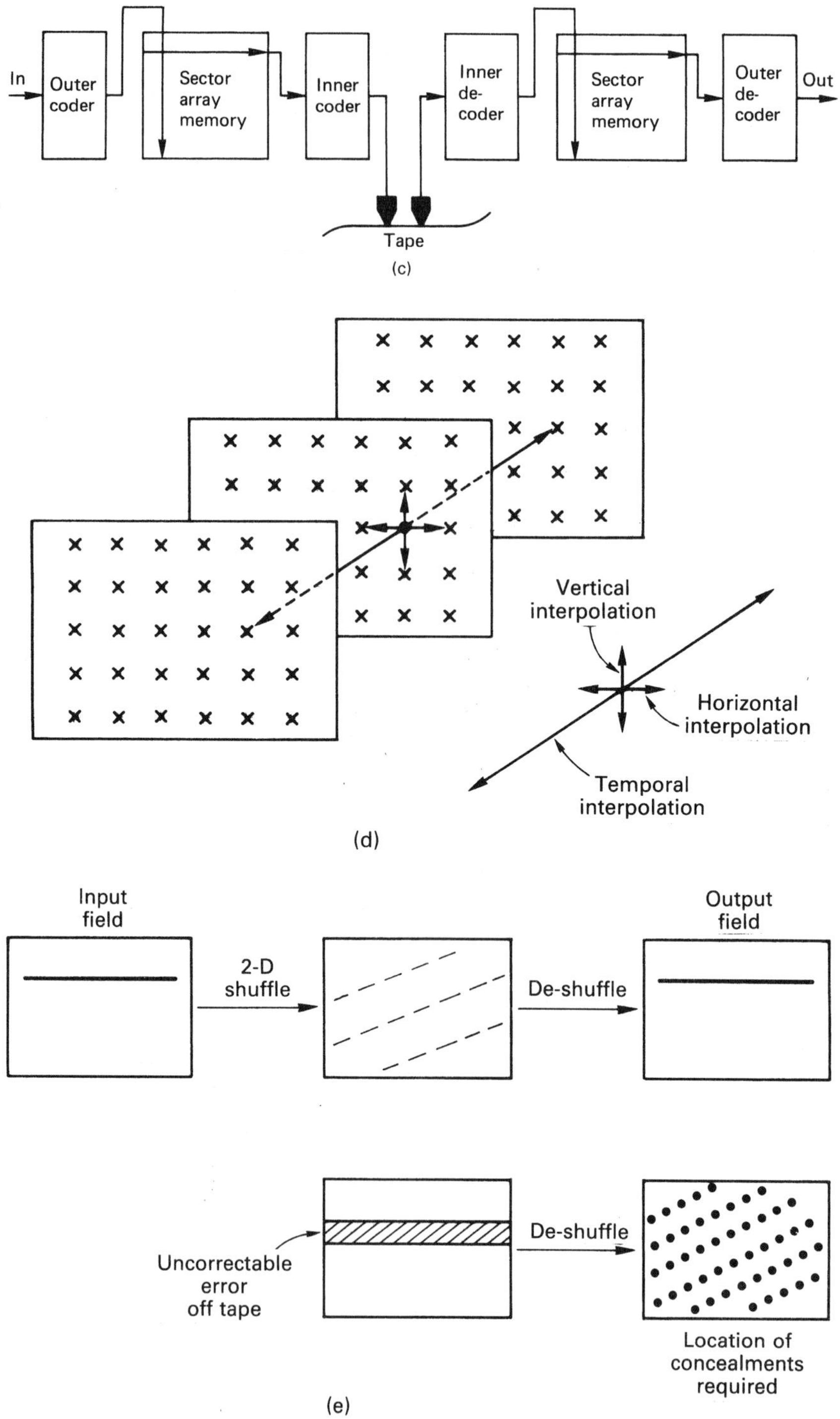

Figure 11.30 (*Continued*) Product codes (c) correct mixture of random and burst errors. Correction failure requires concealment which may be in three dimensions as shown in (d). Irregular shuffle (e) makes concealments less visible.

There are two approaches to error correction in segmented recordings. In D-1 and D-2 the approach shown in Figure 11.31(a) is used. Here, following distribution the input field is segmented first, then each segment becomes an independent shuffled product code. This requires less RAM to implement, but it means that from an error correction standpoint each tape track is self-contained and must deal alone with any errors encountered.

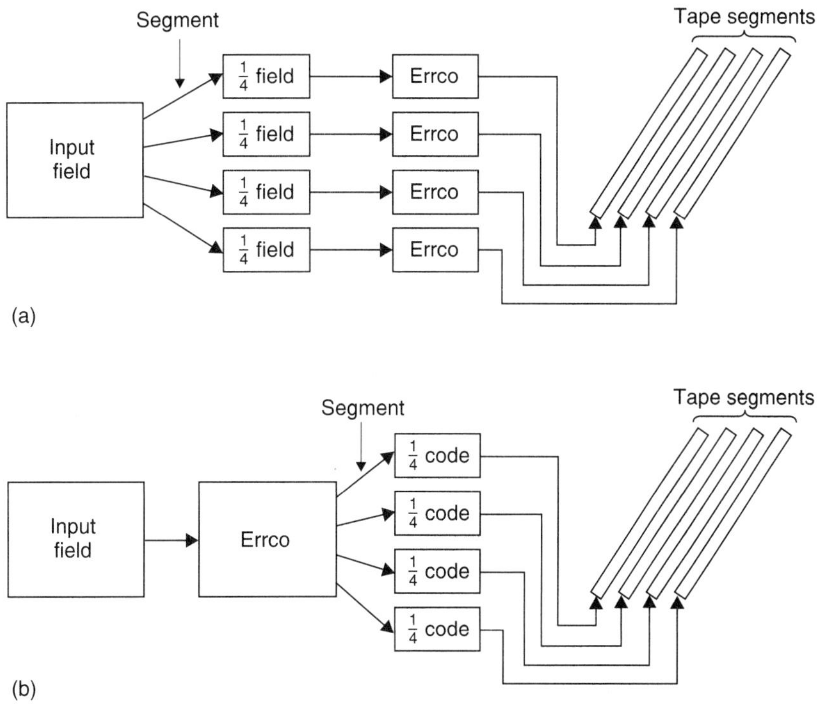

Figure 11.31 Early formats would segment data before producing product codes as in (a). Later formats perform product coding first, and then segment for recording as in (b). This gives more robust performance.

Later formats, beginning with D-3, use the approach shown in Figure 11.31(b). Here following distribution the entire field is used to produce one large shuffled product code in each channel. The product code is then segmented for recording on tape. Although more RAM is required to assemble the large product code, the result is that outer codewords on tape spread across several tracks and redundancy in one track can compensate for errors in another. The result is that size of a single burst error which can be fully corrected is increased. As RAM is now cheaper than when the first formats were designed, this approach is becoming more common.

11.18 Picture in shuttle

A rotary head recorder cannot follow the tape tracks properly when the tape is shuttled. Instead the heads cross the tracks at an angle and intermittently pick up short data blocks. Each of these blocks is an inner error-correcting codeword and this can be checked to see if the block was properly recovered. If this is the case, the data can be used to update a frame store which displays the shuttle picture. Clearly the shuttle picture is a mosaic of parts of many fields. In addition to helping the concealment of errors, the shuffle process is beneficial to obtaining picture-in-shuttle. Owing to shuffle, a block recovered from the tape contains data from many places in the picture, and this gives a better result than if many pixels were available from one place in the picture. The twinkling effect seen in shuttle is due to the updating of individual pixels following de-shuffle.

When compression is used, the picture is processed in blocks, and these will be visible as mosaicing in the shuttle picture as the frame store is updated by the blocks.

11.19 DV and DVCPRO

This component format uses quarter-inch wide metal evaporated (ME) tape which is only 7 micrometres thick in conjunction with compression to allow realistic playing times in miniaturized equipment. The format has jointly been developed by all the leading VCR manufacturers. Whilst DV was originally intended as a consumer format it was clear that such a format is ideal for professional applications such as news gathering and simple production because of the low cost and small size. This led to the development of the DVCPRO format.

In addition to component video there are also two channels of sixteen-bit uniformly quantized digital audio at 32, 44.1 or 48 kHz, with an option of four audio channels using twelve-bit non-uniform quantizing at 32 kHz.

Figure 11.32 shows that two cassette sizes are supported. The standard size cassette offers $4\frac{1}{2}$ hours of recording time and yet is only a little larger than an audio Compact Cassette. The small cassette is even smaller than a DAT cassette yet plays for one hour. Machines designed to play both tape sizes will be equipped with moving-reel motors. Both cassettes are equipped with fixed identification tabs and a moveable write-protect tab. These tabs are sensed by switches in the transport.

DV has adopted many of the features first seen in small formats such as the DAT digital audio recorder and the 8 mm analog video tape format. Of these the most significant is the elimination of the control track

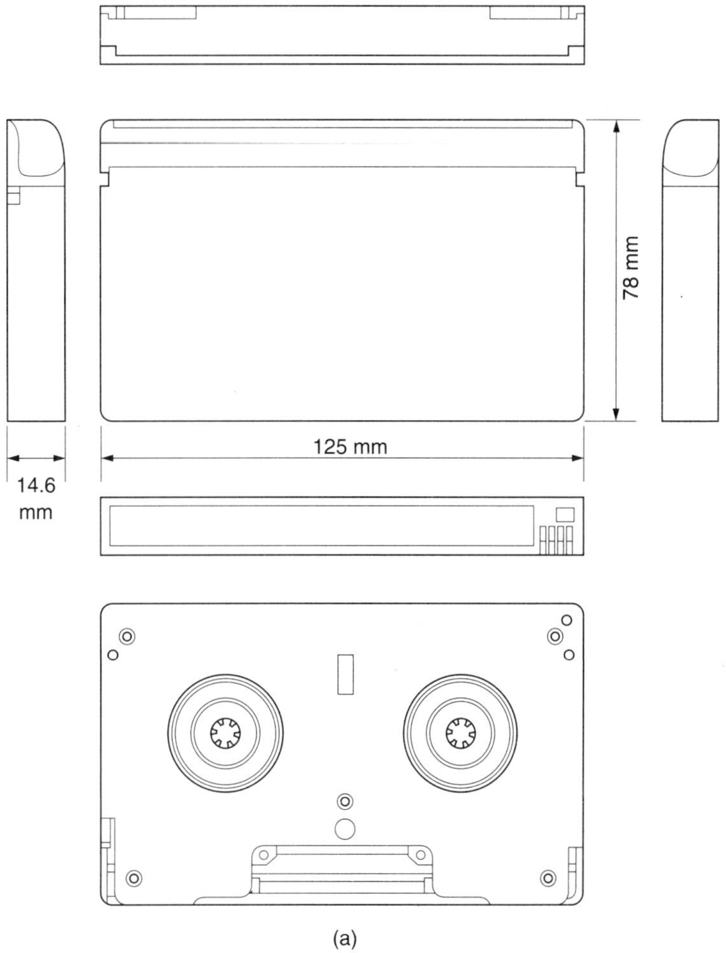

Figure 11.32 The cassettes developed for the 1/4-inch DVC format. At (a) the standard cassette which holds 4.5 hours of program material.

permitted by recording tracking signals in the slant tracks themselves. The adoption of metal evaporated tape and embedded tracking allows extremely high recording density. Tracks recorded with slant azimuth are only 10 μm wide and the minimum wavelength is only 0.49 μm resulting in a superficial density of over 0.4 Megabits per square millimetre.

Segmentation is used in DVC in such a way that as much commonality as possible exists between 50 and 60 Hz versions. The transport runs at 300 tape tracks per second; Figure 11.33 shows that 50 Hz frames contain 12 tracks and 60 Hz frames contain 10 tracks.

The tracking mechanism relies upon buried tones in the slant tracks. From a tracking standpoint there are three types of track shown in Figure 11.34; F_0, F_1 and F_2. F_1 contains a low-frequency pilot and F_2 a high-frequency pilot. F_0 contains no pilot tone, but the recorded data spectrum

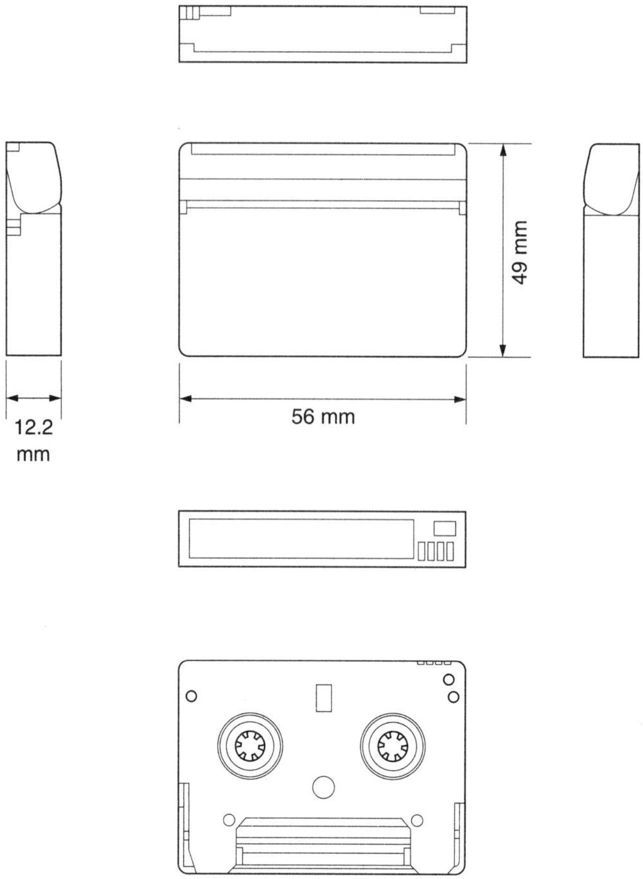

Figure 11.32 (*Continued*) The small cassette, shown at (b) is intended for miniature equipment and plays for 1 hour.

contains notches at the frequencies of the two tones. Figure 11.34 also shows that every other track will contain F_0 following a four-track sequence.

The embedded tracking tones are recorded throughout the track by inserting a low frequency into the channel-coded data. Every 24 data bits an extra bit is added whose value has no data meaning but whose polarity affects the average voltage of the waveform. By controlling the average voltage with this bit, low frequencies can be introduced into the channel-coded spectrum to act as tracking tones. The tracking tones have sufficiently long wavelength that they are not affected by head azimuth and can be picked up by the 'wrong' head. When a head is following an F_0 type track, one edge of the head will detect F_1 and the other edge will detect F_2. If the head is centralized on the track, the amplitudes of the two tones will be identical. Any tracking error will result in the relative

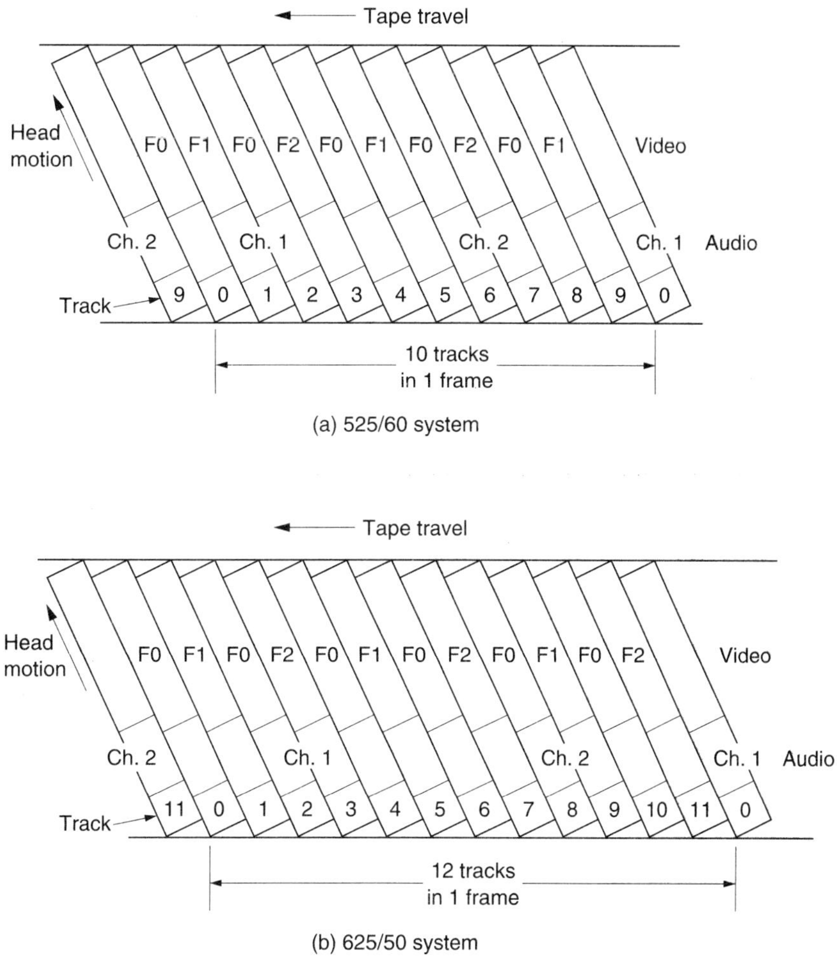

Figure 11.33 In order to use a common transport for 50 and 60 Hz standards the segmentation shown here is used. The segment rate is constant but 10 or 12 segments can be used in a frame.

amplitudes of the F_1 F_2 tones changing. This can be used to modify the capstan phase in order to correct the tracking error. As azimuth recording is used requiring a minimum of two heads, one head of the pair will always be able to play a type F_0 track.

In simple machines only one set of heads will be fitted and these will record or play as required. In more advanced machines, separate record and replay heads will be fitted. In this case the replay head will read the tracking tones during normal replay, but in editing modes, the record head would read the tracking tones during the pre-roll in order to align itself with the existing track structure.

Figure 11.35 shows the track dimensions. The tracks are approximately 33 mm long and lie at approximately 9° to the tape edge. A transport with

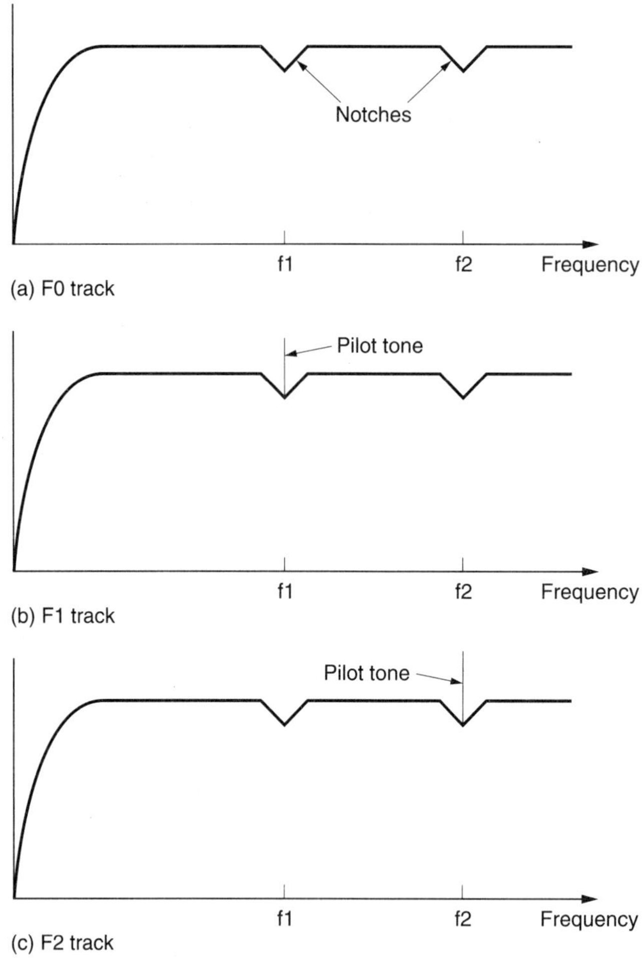

Figure 11.34 The tracks are of three types shown here. The F_0 track (a) contains spectral notches at two selected frequencies. The other two track types (b), (c) place a pilot tone in one or other of the notches.

a 180° wrap would need a drum of only 21 mm diameter. For camcorder applications with the small cassette this would allow a transport no larger than an audio 'Walkman'. With the larger cassette it would be advantageous to use time compression to allow a larger drum with partial wrap to be used. This would simplify threading and make room for additional heads in the drum for editing functions.

The audio, video and subcode data are recorded in three separate sectors with edit gaps between so that they can be independently edited in insert mode. In the case where all three data areas are being recorded in insert mode, there must be some mechanism to keep the new tracks synchronous with those which are being overwritten. In a conventional VTR this would be the job of the control track.

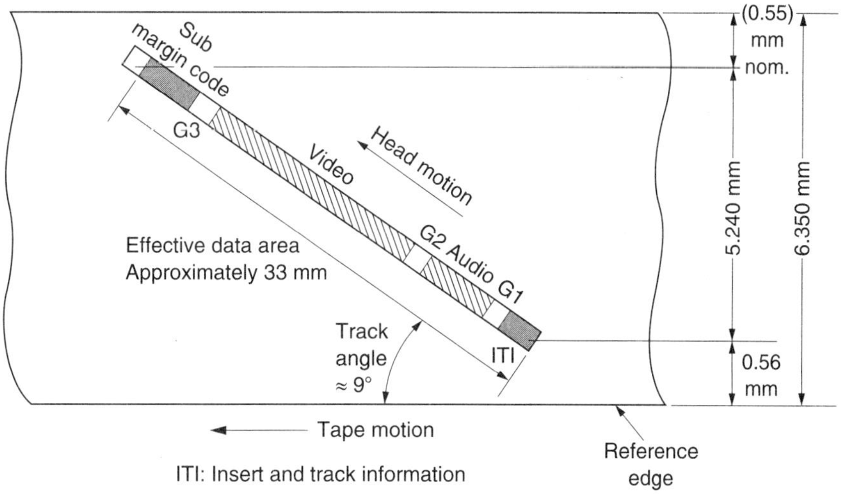

Figure 11.35 The dimensions of the DVC track. Audio, video and subcode can independently be edited. Insert and Track Information block aligns heads during insert.

In DV there is no control track and the job of tracking during insert is undertaken by part of each slant track. Figure 11.35 shows that the track begins with the insert and track information (ITI) block. During an insert edit the ITI block in each track is always read by the record head. This identifies the position of the track in the segmentation sequence and in the tracking tone sequence and allows the head to identify its physical position both along and across the track prior to an insert edit. The remainder of the track can then be recorded as required.

As there are no linear tracks, the subcode is designed to be read in shuttle for access control purposes. It will contain timecodes and flags.

Figure 11.36 shows a block diagram of the DV signal system. The input video is eight-bit component digital according to CCIR-601, but compression of about 5:1 is used. The colour difference signals are subsampled prior to compression. In 60 Hz machines, 4:1:1 sampling isused, allowing a colour difference bandwidth in excess of that possible with NTSC. In 50 Hz machines, 4:2:0 sampling is used. The colour difference sampling rate is still 6.75 MHz, but the two colour difference signals are sent on sequential lines instead of simultaneously. The result is that the vertical colour difference resolution matches the horizontal resolution.

A 16:9 aspect ratio can be supported in standard definition by increasing the horizontal pixel spacing as is done in Digital Betacam. High-definition signals can be supported using a higher compression factor.

As in other DVTRs, the error-correction strategy relies upon a combination of shuffle and product codes. Frames are assembled in RAM, and partitioned into blocks of 8 × 8 pixels. In the luminance channel, four

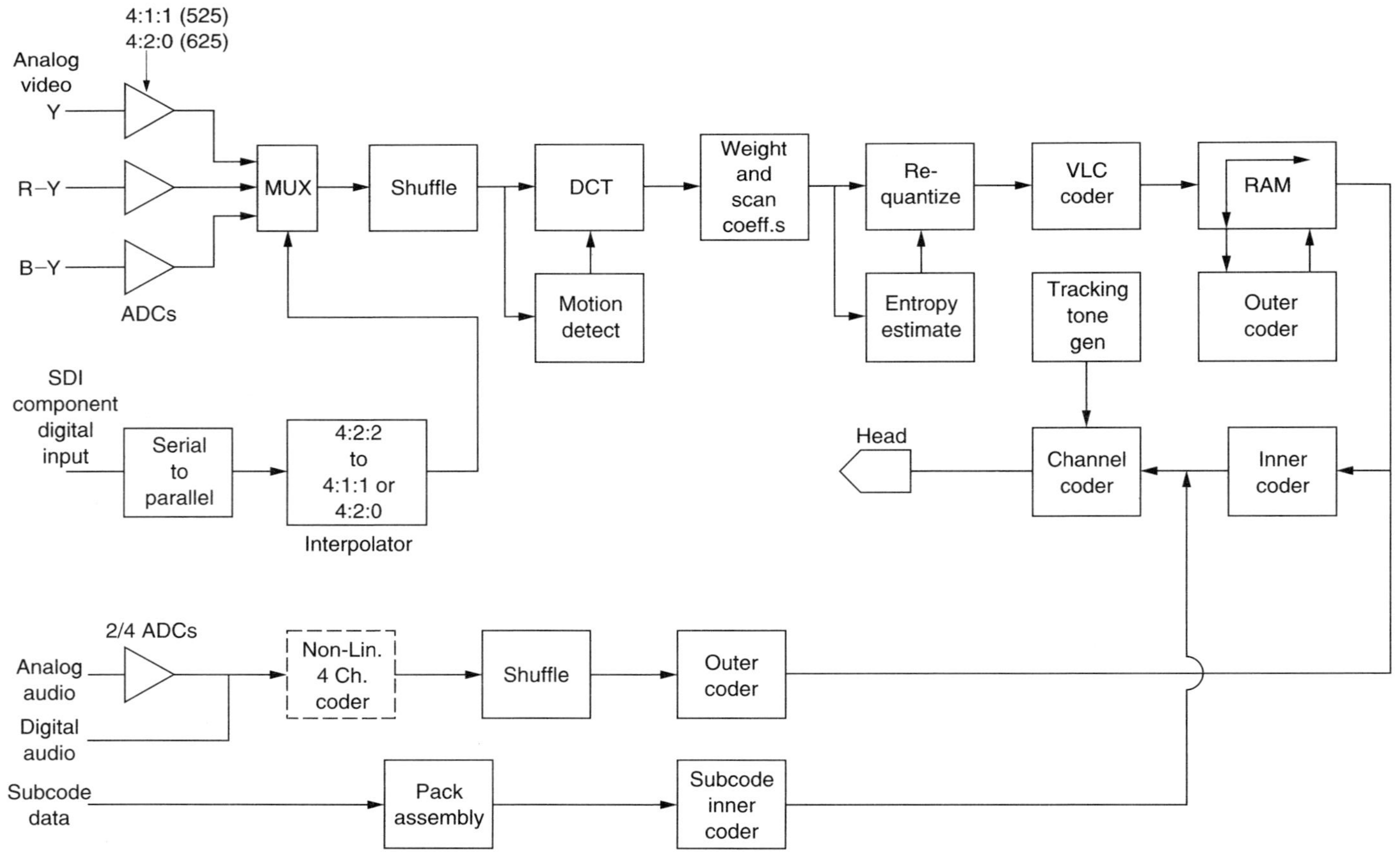

Figure 11.36 Block diagram of DVC signal system. This is similar to larger formats except that a high compression factor allows use of a single channel with no distribution.

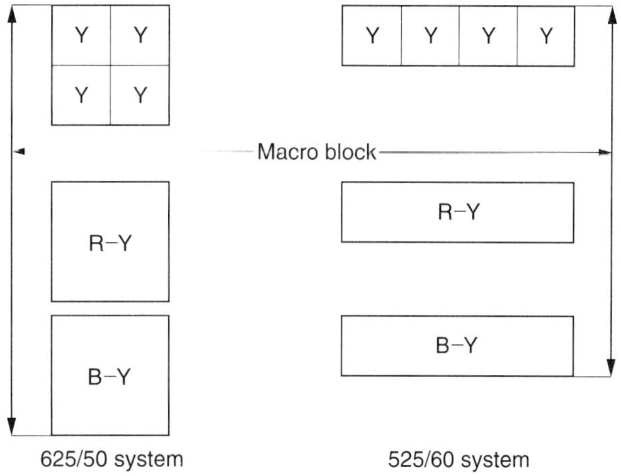

Figure 11.37 In DVC a macroblock contains information from a fixed screen area. As the colour resolution is reduced, there are twice as many luminance pixels.

of these blocks cover the same screen area as one block in each colour difference signal as Figure 11.37 shows. The four luminance blocks and the two colour difference blocks are together known as a macroblock. The shuffle is based upon reordering of macroblocks. Following the shuffle compression takes place. The compression system is DCT based and uses techniques described in Chapter 9. Compression acts within frame boundaries so as to permit frame accurate editing.

Intra-frame compression uses 8 × 8 pixel DCT blocks and allows a higher compression factor because advantage can be taken of redundancy between the two fields when there is no motion. If motion is detected, then moving areas of the two fields will be independently coded in 8 × 4 pixel blocks to prevent motion blur. Following the motion compensation the DCT coefficients are weighted, zig-zag scanned and requantized prior to variable-length coding. As in other compressed VTR formats the requantizing is adaptive so that the same amount of data is output irrespective of the input picture content. The entropy block occupies one sync block and contains data compressed from five macroblocks.

The DV product codes are shown in Figure 11.38. The video product block is shown at (a). This block is common to both 525- and 625-line formats. Ten such blocks record one 525-line frame whereas 12 blocks are required for a 625-line frame.

The audio channels are shuffled over a frame period and assembled into the product codes shown in Figure 11.38(b). Video and audio sync blocks are identical except for the ID numbering. The subcode structure is different. Figure 11.38(c) shows the structure of the subcode block. The subcode is not a product block because these can only be used for error correction when the entire block is recovered. The subcode is intended to

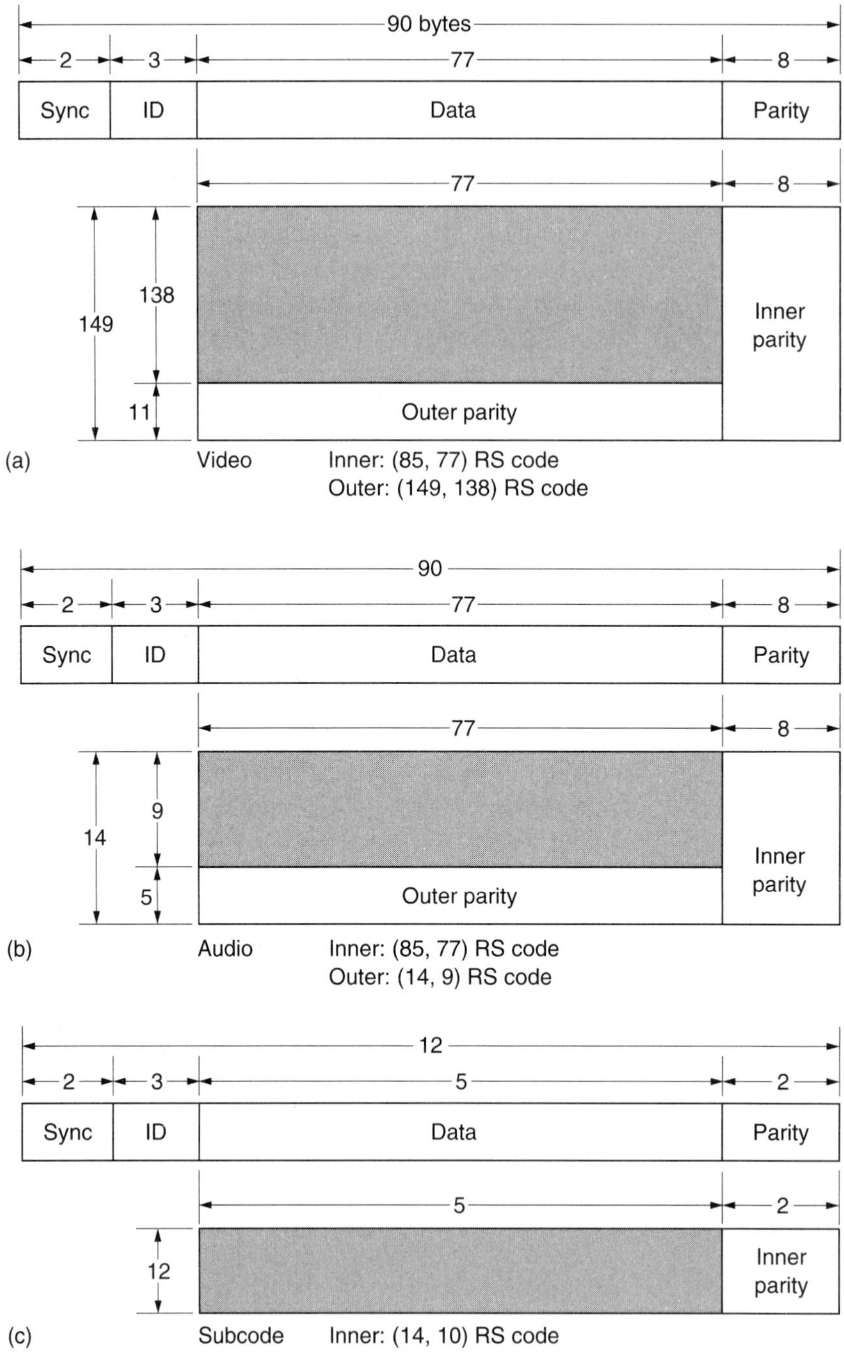

Figure 11.38 The product codes used in DVC. Video and audio codes at (a) and (b) differ only in size and use the same inner code structure. Subcode at (c) is designed to be read in shuttle and uses short sync blocks to improve chances of recovery.

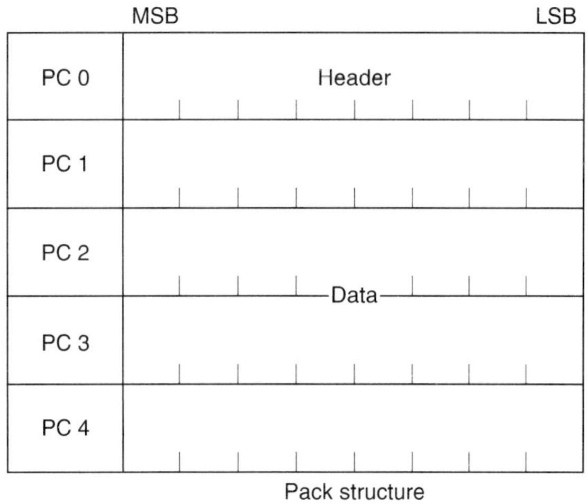

Figure 11.39 Structure of a pack.

be read in shuttle where only parts of the track are recovered. Accordingly only inner codes are used and these are much shorter than the video/audio codes, containing only 5 data bytes, known as a pack. The structure of a pack is shown In Figure 11.39. The subcode block in each track can accommodate 12 packs. Packs are repeated throughout the frame so that they have a high probability of recovery in shuttle. The pack header identifies the type of pack, leaving four bytes for pack data, e.g. timecode.

Following the assembly of product codes, the data are then channel coded for recording on tape. A scrambled NRZI channel code is used which is similar to the system used in D-1 except that the tracking tones are also inserted by the modulation process.

In the DVCPRO format the extremely high recording density and long playing time of the consumer DVC was not a requirement. Instead ruggedness and reliable editing were needed. In developing DVCPRO, Panasonic chose to revert to metal particle tape as used in most other DVTRs. This requires wider tracks, and this was achieved by increasing the tape linear speed. The wider tracks also reduce the mechanical precision needed for interchange and editing. However, the DVCPRO transport can still play regular DVC tapes.

The DVCPRO format has proved to be extremely popular and a number of hard disk-based editors are now designed to import native DVCPRO data to cut down on generation loss. With a suitable tape drive this can be done at 4 × normal speed. The SDTI interface (see Chapter 12) can also carry native DVC data. As DVCPRO has developed, later format variants increase the bit rate of the transport so that the compression factor can be reduced or high-definition pictures can be recorded.

12

Communication systems

12.1 Introduction

The approach taken here must necessarily be broad and must include in principle any system which can deliver data over distance. There appears to be an unwritten rule that anything to do with communications has to be described entirely using acronyms; a rule which this chapter intends to break in the interests of clarity. Figure 12.1 shows some of the ways in

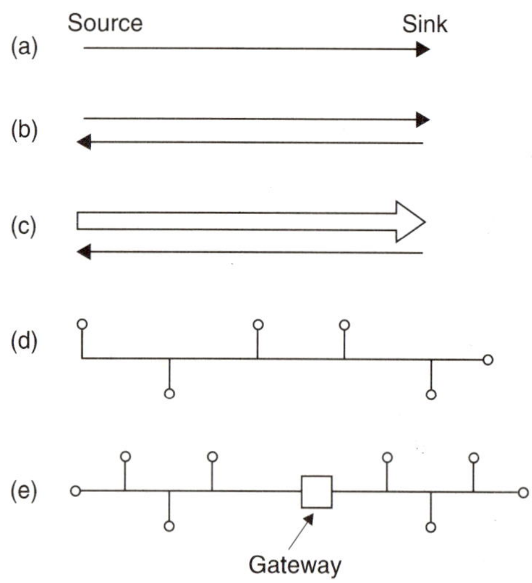

Figure 12.1 Some ways of classifying communications systems. At (a) the unidirectional point-to-point connection used in many digital audio and video interconnects. (b) Symmetrical bidirectional point-to-point system. (c) Asymmetrical point-to-point system. (d) A network must have some switching or addressing ability in addition to delivering data. (e) Networks can be connected by gateways.

which the subject can be classified. The simplest is a unidirectional point-to-point signal path shown at (a). This is common in digital production equipment and includes the AES/EBU digital audio interface and the serial digital interface (SDI) for digital video. Bidirectional point-to-point signals include the RS-232 and RS-422 duplex systems. Bidirectional signal paths may be symmetrical, i.e. have the same capacity in both directions (b), or asymmetrical, having more capacity in one direction than the other (c). In this case the low capacity direction may be known as a *back channel*.

Back channels are useful in a number of applications. Video-on-demand and interactive video are both systems in which the inputs from the viewer are relatively small, but result in extensive data delivery to the viewer. Archives and databases have similar characteristics.

When more than two devices can be interconnected in such a way that any one can communicate at will with any other, the result is a network as in Figure 12.1(d). The traditional telephone system is a network, and although the original infrastructure assumed analog speech transmission, subsequent developments in modems have allowed data transmission.

The computer industry has developed its own network technology, a long-serving example being Ethernet. Computer networks can work over various distances, giving rise to LANs (local area networks), MANs (metropolitan area networks) and WANs (wide area networks). Such networks can be connected together to form *internetworks* or internets for short, including *the* Internet. A private network, linking all employees of a given company, for example, may be referred to as an intranet.

Figure 12.1(e) shows that networks are connected together by *gateways*. In this example a private network (typically a local area network within an office block) is interfaced to an *access network* (typically a metropolitan area network with a radius of the order of a few kilometres) which in turn connects to the *transport network*. The access networks and the transport network together form a public network.

The different requirements of networks of different sizes have led to different protocols being developed. Where a gateway exists between two such networks, the gateway will often be required to perform protocol conversion. Such a device may be referred to as *network termination* equipment. Protocol conversion represents unnecessary cost and delay and recent protocols such as ATM are sufficiently flexible that they can be adopted in any type of network to avoid conversion.

Networks also exist which are optimized for storage devices. These range from the standard buses linking hard drives with their controllers to SANs (storage area networks) in which distributed storage devices behave as one large store.

Communication must also include broadcasting, which initially was analog, but has also adopted digital techniques so that transmitters

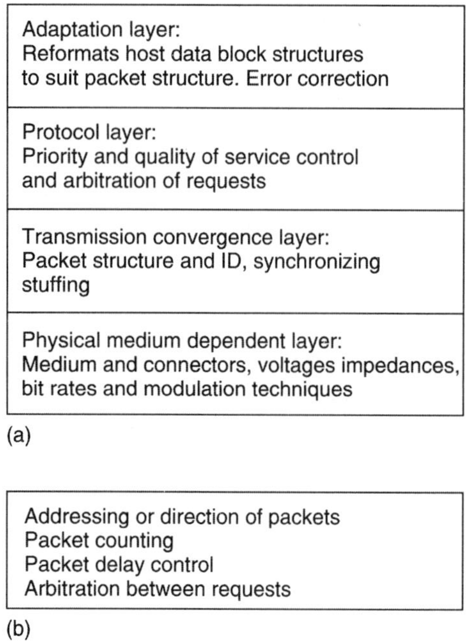

Figure 12.2 (a) Layers are important in communications because they have a degree of independence such that one can be replaced by another leaving the remainder undisturbed. (b) The functions of a network protocol. See text.

effectively radiate data. Traditional analog broadcasting was uni-directional, but with the advent of digital techniques, various means for providing a back channel have been developed.

To have an understanding of communications it is important to appreciate the concept of layers shown in Figure 12.2(a). The lowest layer is the *physical medium dependent* layer. In the case of a cabled interface, this layer would specify the dimensions of the plugs and sockets so that a connection could be made, and the use of a particular type of conductor such as co-axial, STP (screened twisted pair) or UTP (unscreened twisted pair). The impedance of the cable may also be specified. The medium may also be optical fibre which will need standardization of the terminations and the wavelength(s) in use.

Once a connection is made, the physical medium dependent layer standardizes the voltage of the transmitted signal and the frequency at which the voltage changes (the channel bit rate). This may be fixed at a single value, chosen from a set of fixed values, or, rarely, variable. Practical interfaces need some form of channel coding (see Chapter 10) in order to embed a bit clock in the data transmission.

The physical medium dependent layer allows binary transmission, but this needs to be structured or formatted. The *transmission convergence* layer takes the binary signalling of the physical medium dependent layer and builds a packet or cell structure. This consists at least of some form of synchronization system so that the start and end of serialized messages can be recognized and an addressing or labelling scheme so that packets can reliably be routed and recognized. Real cables and optical fibres run at fixed bit rates and a further function of the transmission convergence layer is the insertion of null or stuffing packets where insufficient user data exist.

In broadcasting, the physical medium dependent layer may be one which contains some form of radio signal and a modulation scheme. The modulation scheme will be a function of the kind of service. For example, a satellite modulation scheme would be quite different from one used in a terrestrial service.

In all real networks requests for transmission will arise randomly. Network resources need to be applied to these requests in a structured way to prevent chaos, data loss or lack of throughput. This raises the requirement for a protocol layer. TCP (transmission control protocol) and ATM (asynchronous transfer mode) are protocols. A protocol is an agreed set of actions in given circumstances. In a point-to-point interface the protocol is trivial, but in a network it is complex. Figure 12.2(b) shows some of the functions of a network protocol. There must be an addressing mechanism so that the sender can direct the data to the desired location, and a mechanism by which the receiving device confirms that all the data have been correctly received. In more advanced systems the protocol may allow variations in *quality of service* whereby the user can select (and pay for) various criteria such as packet delay and delay variation and the packet error rate. This allows the system to deliver isochronous (near-real-time) MPEG data alongside asynchronous (non-time-critical) data such as e-mail by appropriately prioritizing packets.

The protocol layer arbitrates between demands on the network and delivers packets at the required quality of service. The user data will not necessarily have been packeted, or if it was the packet size may be different from those used in the network. This situation arises, for example, when MPEG transport packets are to be sent via ATM. The solution is to use an *adaptation layer.*

Adaptation layers reformat the original data into the packet structure needed by the network at the sending device, and reverse the process at the destination device. Practical networks must have error checking/correction. Figure 12.3 shows some of the possibilities. In short interfaces, no errors are expected and a simple parity check or checksum with an error indication is adequate. In bidirectional applications a checksum failure would result in a retransmission request or cause the receiver to fail to acknowledge the transmission so that the sender would try again. In real-time systems, there may not be time for a retransmission, and an FEC (forward error correction) system will be needed in which enough

1 No correction or checking
2 Detection only
3 Error detection and retransmit request
4 Error detection and FEC to handle random errors
5 FEC and interleaving to handle packet loss
6 Automatic rerouting following channel failure

Figure 12.3 Different approaches to error checking used in various communications systems.

redundancy is included with every data block to permit on-the-fly correction at the receiver. The sensitivity to error is a function of the type of data, and so it is a further function of the adaptation layer to take steps such as interleaving and the addition of FEC codes.

12.2 Production-related interfaces

As audio and video production equipment made the transition from analog to digital technology, computers and networks were still another world and the potential of the digital domain was largely neglected because the digital interfaces which were developed simply copied analog practice but transmitted binary numbers instead of the original signal waveform. These interfaces are simple and have no addressing or handshaking ability. Creating a network requires switching devices called routers which are controlled independently of the signals themselves. Although obsolescent, there are substantial amounts of equipment in service adhering to these standards which will remain in use for some time.

The AES/EBU (Audio Engineering Society/European Broadcast Union) interface was developed to provide a short distance point-to-point connection for PCM digital audio and subsequently evolved to handle compressed audio data.

The serial digital interface (SDI) was developed to allow up to ten-bit samples of standard definition interlaced component or composite digital video to be communicated serially.[1] 16:9 format component signals with 18 MHz sampling rate can also be handled. As if to emphasize the gulf which then existed between television and computing, the SDI as first standardized had no error detection ability at all. This was remedied by a later option known as EDH (error detection and handling). The interface allows ancillary data including transparent conveyance of embedded AES/EBU digital audio channels during video blanking periods.

SDI is highly specific to two broadcast television formats and does not support progressive scan or compression. Pictures of arbitrary size or frame rate are not supported. Subsequently the electrical and channel coding layer of SDI was used to create SDTI (serial data transport interface) which is used for transmitting, among other things, elementary streams from video compressors. ASI (asynchronous serial interface) uses only the electrical interface of SDI but with a different channel code and protocol and is used for transmitting MPEG transport streams through SDI-based equipment.

12.3 SDI

The serial digital interface was designed to allow easy conversion to and from traditional analog component video for production purposes. Only 525/59.94/2:1 and 625/50/2:1 formats are supported with 4:2:2 sampling. The sampling structure of SDI was detailed in section 7.14 and only the transmission technique will be considered here.

Chapter 10 introduced the concepts of DC components and uncontrolled clock content in serial data for recording and the same issues are important in interfacing, leading to a coding requirement. SDI uses convolutional randomizing, as shown in Figure 10.28, in which the signal sent down the channel is the serial data waveform which has been convolved with the impulse response of a digital filter. On reception the signal is deconvolved to restore the original data.

The components necessary for an SDI link are shown in Figure 12.4. Parallel component or composite data having a wordlength of up to ten bits form the input. These are fed to a ten-bit shift register which is clocked at ten times the input rate, which will be 270 MHz or $40 \times F_{sc}$. If there are only eight bits in the input words, the missing bits are forced to zero for transmission except for the all-ones condition which will be forced to ten ones. The serial data from the shift register are then passed through the scrambler, in which a given bit is converted to the exclusive-OR of itself and two bits which are five and nine clocks ahead. This is followed by another stage, which converts channel ones into transitions. The resulting signal is fed to a line driver which converts the logic level into an alternating waveform of 800 millivolts peak-to-peak. The driver output impedance is carefully matched so that the signal can be fed down 75 Ohm co-axial cable using BNC connectors.

The scrambling process at the encoder spreads the signal spectrum and makes that spectrum reasonably constant and independent of the picture content. It is possible to assess the degree of equalization necessary by comparing the energy in a low-frequency band with that in higher frequencies. The greater the disparity, the more equalization is needed. Thus fully automatic cable equalization is easily achieved. The receiver must generate a bit clock at 270 MHz or $40 \times F_{sc}$ from the input signal, and this clock drives the input sampler and slicer which converts the cable waveform back to serial binary. The local bit clock also drives a

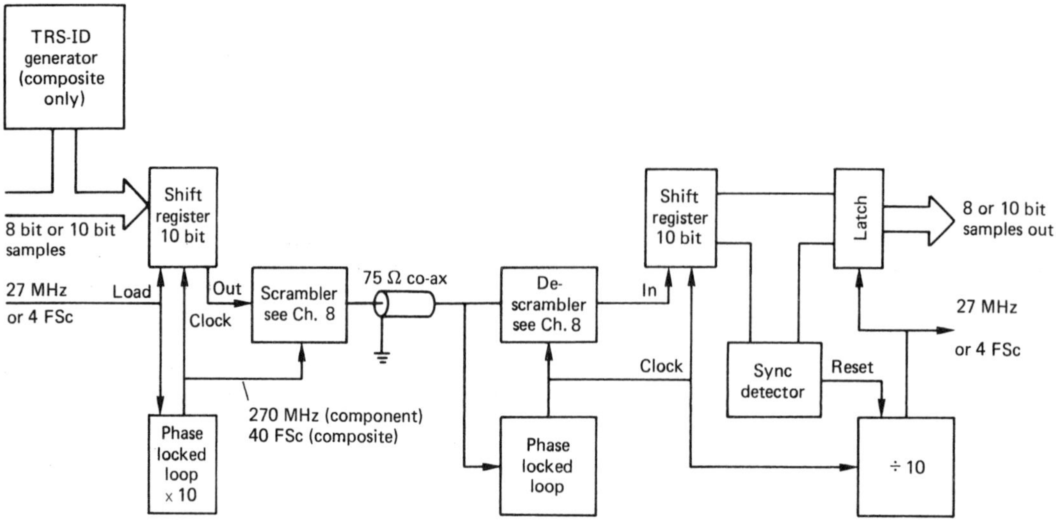

Figure 12.4 Major components of a serial scrambled link. Input samples are converted to serial form in a shift register clocked at ten times the sample rate. The serial data are then scrambled for transmission. On reception, a phase-locked loop recreates the bit rate clock and drives the de-scrambler and serial-to-parallel conversion. On detection of the sync pattern, the divide-by-ten counter is rephased to load parallel samples correctly into the latch. For composite working the bit rate will be 40 times subcarrier, and a sync pattern generator (top left) is needed to inject TRS-ID into the composite data stream.

circuit which simply reverses the scrambling at the transmitter. The first stage returns transitions to ones, and the second stage is a mirror image of the encoder which reverses the exclusive-OR calculation to output the original data. Since transmission is serial, it is necessary to obtain word synchronization, so that correct deserialization can take place.

In the component parallel input, the *SAV* and *EAV* sync patterns are present and the all-ones and all-zeros bit patterns these contain can be detected in the thirty-bit shift register and used to reset the deserializer.

On detection of the synchronizing symbols, a divide-by-ten circuit is reset, and the output of this will clock words out of the shift register at the correct times. This output will also become the output word clock.

It is a characteristic of all randomizing techniques that certain data patterns will interact badly with the randomizing algorithm to produce a channel waveform which is low in clock content. These so-called pathological data patterns[2] are extremely rare in real program material, but can be specially generated for testing purposes.

12.4 SDTI

SDI is closely specified and is only suitable for transmitting 2:1 interlaced 4:2:2 digital video in 525/60 or 625/50 systems. Since the development of

SDI, it has become possible economically to compress digital video and the SDI standard cannot handle this. SDTI (serial data transport interface) is designed to overcome that problem by converting SDI into an interface which can carry a variety of data types whilst retaining compatibility with existing SDI router infrastructures.

SDTI[3] sources produce a signal which is electrically identical to an SDI signal and which has the same timing structure. However, the digital active line of SDI becomes a data packet or *item* in SDTI. Figure 12.5 shows how SDTI fits into the existing SDI timing. Between EAV and SAV (horizontal blanking in SDI) an ancillary data block is incorporated. The structure of this meets the SDI standard, and the data within describe the contents of the following digital active line.

The data capacity of SDTI is about 200 Mbits/s because some of the 270 Mbits/s is lost due to the retention of the SDI timing structure. Each digital active line finishes with a CRCC (cyclic redundancy check character) to check for correct transmission.

SDTI raises a number of opportunities, including the transmission of compressed data at faster than real time. If a video signal is compressed at 4:1, then one quarter as much data would result. If sent in real time the bandwidth required would be one quarter of that needed by uncompressed video. However, if the same bandwidth is available, the compressed data could be sent in 1/4 of the usual time. This is particularly advantageous for data transfer between compressed camcor-

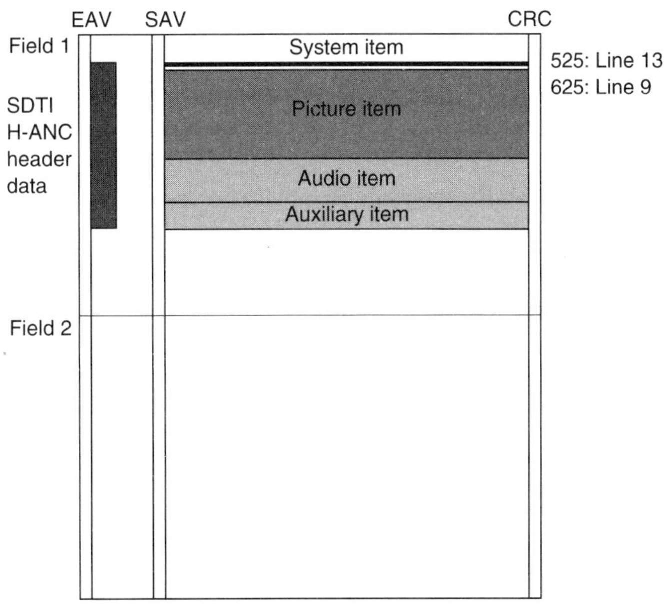

Figure 12.5 SDTI is a variation of SDI which allows transmission of generic data. This can include compressed video and non-real-time transfer.

ders and non-linear editing workstations. Alternatively, four different 50 Mbits/s signals could be conveyed simultaneously.

Thus an SDTI transmitter takes the form of a multiplexer which assembles packets for transmission from input buffers. The transmitted data can be encoded according to MPEG, MotionJPEG, Digital Betacam or DVC formats and all that is necessary is that compatible devices exist at each end of the interface. In this case the data are transferred with bit accuracy and so there is no generation loss associated with the transfer. If the source and destination are different, i.e. having different formats or, in MPEG, different group structures, then a conversion process with attendant generation loss would be needed.

12.5 ASI

The asynchronous serial interface is designed to allow MPEG transport streams to be transmitted over standard SDI cabling and routers. ASI offers higher performance than SDTI because it does not adhere to the SDI timing structure. Transport stream data do not have the same statistics as PCM video and so the scrambling technique of SDI cannot be used. Instead ASI uses an 8/10 group code (see section 10.12) to eliminate DC components and ensure adequate clock content).

SDI equipment is designed to run at a closely defined bit rate of 270 Mbits/s and has phase-locked loops in receiving and repeating devices which are intended to remove jitter. These will lose lock if the channel bit rate changes. Transport streams are fundamentally variable in bit rate and to retain compatibility with SDI routing equipment ASI uses stuffing bits to keep the transmitted bit rate constant.

The use of an 8/10 code means that although the channel bit rate is 270 Mbits/s, the data bit rate is only 80 per cent of that, i.e 216 Mbits/s. A small amount of this is lost to overheads.

12.6 AES/EBU

The AES/EBU digital audio interface, originally published in 1985, was proposed to embrace all the functions of existing formats in one standard. The goal was to ensure interconnection of professional digital audio equipment irrespective of origin. The EBU ratified the AES proposal with the proviso that the optional transformer coupling was made mandatory and led to the term AES/EBU interface, also called EBU/AES by some Europeans and standardized as IEC 958.

The interface has to be self-clocking and self-synchronizing, i.e. the single signal must carry enough information to allow the boundaries between individual bits, words and blocks to be detected reliably. To fulfil these requirements, the FM channel code is used (see Chapter 10) which is DC-free, strongly self-clocking and capable of working with a changing sampling rate. Synchronization of deserialization is achieved by violating the usual encoding rules.

The use of FM means that the channel frequency is the same as the bit rate when sending data ones. Tests showed that in typical analog audio-cabling installations, sufficient bandwidth was available to convey two digital audio channels in one twisted pair. The standard driver and receiver chips for RS-422A[4] data communication (or the equivalent CCITT-V.11) are employed for professional use, but work by the BBC[5] suggested that equalization and transformer coupling were desirable for longer cable runs, particularly if several twisted pairs occupy a common shield. Successful transmission up to 350 m has been achieved with these techniques.[6] Figure 12.6 shows the standard configuration. The output impedance of the drivers will be about 110 Ohms, and the impedance of the cable and receiver should be similar at the frequencies of interest. The driver was specified in AES-3–1985 to produce between 3 and 10 V peak-to-peak into such an impedance but this was changed to between 2 and 7 V in AES-3–1992 to better reflect the characteristics of actual RS-422 driver chips.

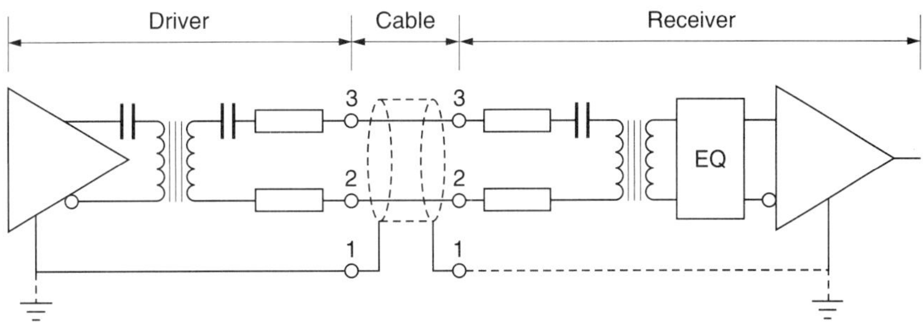

Figure 12.6 Recommended electrical circuit for use with the standard two-channel interface.

In Figure 12.7, the specification of the receiver is shown in terms of the minimum eye pattern (see section 10.9) which can be detected without error. It will be noted that the voltage of 200 mV specifies the height of the eye opening at a width of half a channel bit period. The actual signal amplitude will need to be larger than this, and even larger if the signal contains noise. Figure 12.8 shows the recommended equalization characteristic which can be applied to signals received over long lines.

The purpose of the standard is to allow the use of existing analog cabling, and as an adequate connector in the shape of the XLR is already

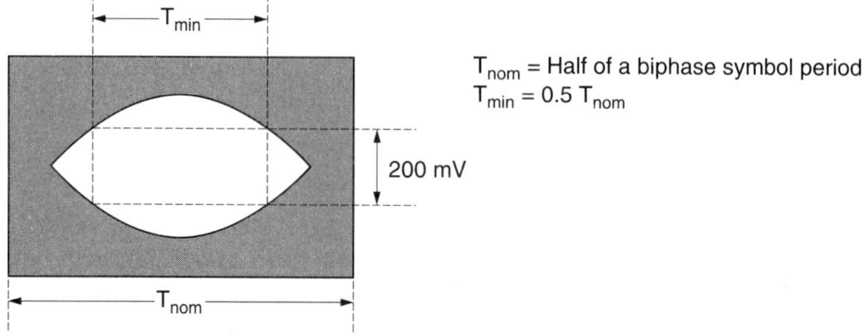

Figure 12.7 The minimum eye pattern acceptable for correct decoding of standard two-channel data.

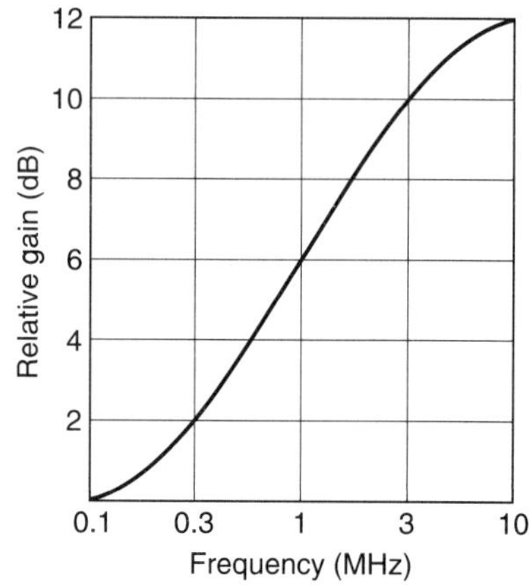

Figure 12.8 EQ characteristic recommended by the AES to improve reception in the case of long lines.

in wide service, the connector made to IEC 268 Part 12 has been adopted for digital audio use. Effectively, existing analog audio cables having XLR connectors can be used without alteration for digital connections.

There is a separate standard[7] for a professional interface using coaxial cable for distances of around 1000 m. This is simply the AES/EBU protocol but with a 75 Ohm coaxial cable carrying a one-volt signal so that it can be handled by analog video distribution amplifiers. Impedance converting transformers allow balanced 110 Ohm to unbalanced 75 Ohm matching.

In Figure 12.9 the basic structure of the professional and consumer formats can be seen. One subframe consists of 32 bit-cells, of which four will be used by a synchronizing pattern. Subframes from the two audio channels, A and B, alternate on a time-division basis, with the least significant bit sent first. Up to twenty-four-bit sample wordlength can be used, which should cater for all conceivable future developments, but

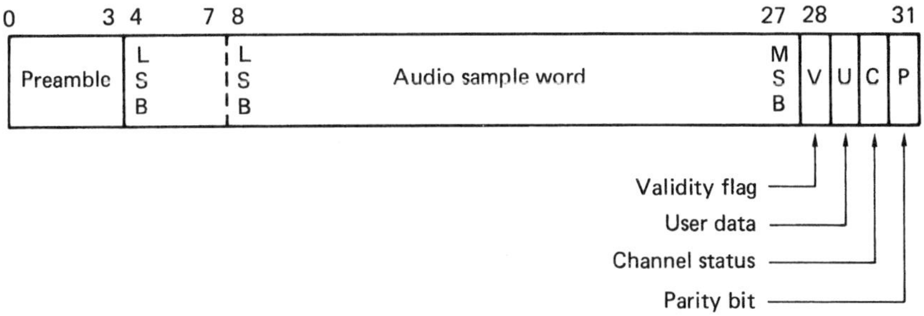

Figure 12.9 The basic subframe structure of the AES/EBU format. Sample can be twenty bits with four auxiliary bits, or twenty-four bits. LSB is transmitted first.

normally twenty-bit maximum length samples will be available with four auxiliary data bits, which can be used for a voice-grade channel in a professional application.

The format specifies that audio data must be in two's complement coding. If different wordlengths are used, the MSBs must always be in the same bit position otherwise the polarity will be misinterpreted. Thus the MSB has to be in bit 27 irrespective of wordlength. Shorter words are leading-zero filled up to the twenty-bit capacity. The channel status data included from AES-3–1992 signalling of the actual audio wordlength used so that receiving devices could adjust the digital dithering level needed to shorten a received word which is too long or pack samples onto a storage device more efficiently.

Four status bits accompany each subframe. The validity flag will be reset if the associated sample is reliable. Whilst there have been many aspirations regarding what the V bit could be used for, in practice a single bit cannot specify much, and if combined with other V bits to make a word, the time resolution is lost. AES-3–1992 described the V bit as indicating that the information in the associated subframe is 'suitable for conversion to an analog signal'. Thus it might be reset if the interface was being used for non-PCM audio data such as the output of an audio compressor.

The parity bit produces even parity over the subframe, such that the total number of ones in the subframe is even. This allows for simple detection of an odd number of bits in error, but its main purpose is that it makes successive sync patterns have the same polarity, which can be used to improve the probability of detection of sync. The user and channel-status bits are discussed later.

Two of the subframes described above make one frame, which repeats at the sampling rate in use. The first subframe will contain the sample from channel A, or from the left channel in stereo working. The second subframe will contain the sample from channel B, or the right channel in

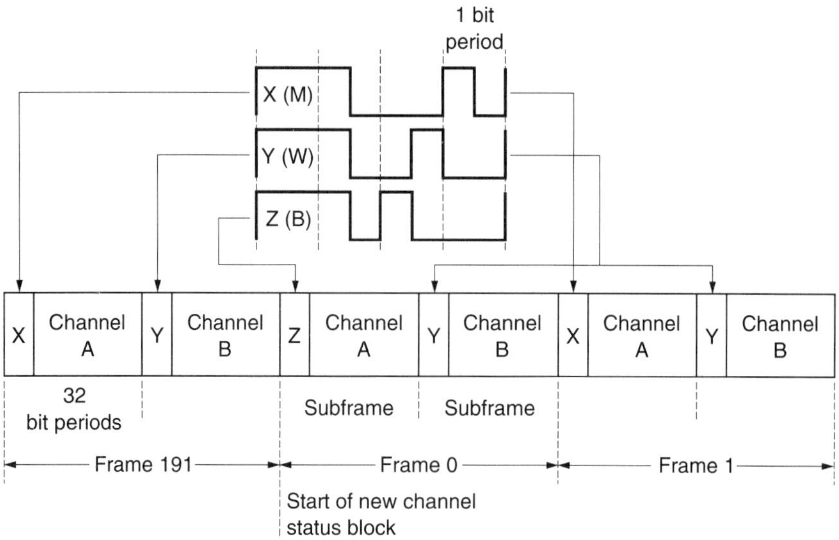

Figure 12.10 Three different preambles (X, Y and Z) are used to synchronize a receiver at the start of subframes.

stereo. At 48 kHz, the bit rate will be 3.072 MHz, but as the sampling rate can vary, the clock rate will vary in proportion.

In order to separate the audio channels on receipt the synchronizing patterns for the two subframes are different as Figure 12.10 shows. These sync patterns begin with a run length of 1.5 bits which violates the FM channel coding rules and so cannot occur due to any data combination. The type of sync pattern is denoted by the position of the second transition which can be 0.5, 1.0 or 1.5 bits away from the first. The third transition is designed to make the sync patterns DC-free.

The channel status and user bits in each subframe form serial data streams with one bit of each per audio channel per frame. The channel status bits are given a block structure and synchronized every 192 frames, which at 48 kHz gives a block rate of 250 Hz, corresponding to a period of 4 ms. In order to synchronize the channel-status blocks, the channel A sync pattern is replaced for one frame only by a third sync pattern which is also shown in Figure 12.10. The AES standard refers to these as X,Y and Z whereas IEC 958 calls them M,W and B. As stated, there is a parity bit in each subframe, which means that the binary level at the end of a subframe will always be the same as at the beginning. Since the sync patterns have the same characteristic, the effect is that sync patterns always have the same polarity and the receiver can use that information to reject noise. The polarity of transmission is not specified, and indeed an accidental inversion in a twisted pair is of no consequence, since it is only the transition that is of importance, not the direction.

In both the professional and consumer formats, the sequence of channel-status bits over 192 subframes builds up a 24-byte channel-status block. However, the contents of the channel status data is completely different between the two applications. The professional channel status structure is shown in Figure 12.11. Byte 0 determines the use of emphasis and the sampling rate. Byte 1 determines the channel usage mode, i.e. whether the data transmitted are a stereo pair, two unrelated mono signals or a single mono signal, and details the user bit handling and byte 2 determines wordlength. Byte 3 is applicable only to multichannel applications. Byte 4 indicates the suitability of the signal as a sampling rate reference. There are two slots of four bytes each which are used for alphanumeric source and destination codes. These can be used for routing. The bytes contain seven-bit ASCII characters (printable characters only) sent LSB first with the eighth bit set to zero acording to AES-3–1992. The destination code can be used to operate an automatic router,

Byte	
0	Basic control data
1	Mode and user bit management
2	Audio wordlength
3	Vectored target from byte 1 (reserved for multichannel applications)
4	AES11 sync ref. identification (bits 0–1), otherwise reserved
5	Reserved
6–9	Source identification (4 bytes of 7 bit ASCII, no parity)
10–13	Destination identification (4 bytes of 7 bit ASCII, no parity)
14–17	Local sample address code (32 bit binary)
18–21	Time-of-day sample address code (32 bit binary)
22	Channel status reliability flags
23	CRCC

Figure 12.11 Overall format of the professional channel-status block.

and the source code will allow the origin of the audio and other remarks to be displayed at the destination.

Bytes 14–17 convey a thirty-two-bit sample address which increments every channel status frame. It effectively numbers the samples in a relative manner from an arbitrary starting point. Bytes 18–21 convey a similar number, but this is a time-of-day count, which starts from zero at midnight. As many digital audio devices do not have real-time clocks built in, this cannot be relied upon. AES-3–92 specified that the time-of-day bytes should convey the real time at which a recording was made, making it rather like timecode. There are enough combinations in thirty-two bits to allow a sample count over 24 hours at 48 kHz. The sample count has the advantage that it is universal and independent of local supply frequency. In theory if the sampling rate is known, conventional Hours, minutes, seconds, frames timecode can be calculated from the sample count, but in practice it is a lengthy computation and users have proposed alternative formats in which the data from EBU or SMPTE timecode are transmitted directly in these bytes. Some of these proposals are in service as *de facto* standards.

The penultimate byte contains four flags which indicate that certain sections of the channel-status information are unreliable. This allows the transmission of an incomplete channel-status block where the entire structure is not needed or where the information is not available. The final byte in the message is a CRCC which converts the entire channel-status block into a codeword (see Chapter 10). The channel status message takes 4 ms at 48 kHz and in this time a router could have switched to another signal source. This would damage the transmission, but will also result in a CRCC failure so the corrupt block is not used.

12.7 Telephone-based systems

In his career as an inventor Alexander Graham Bell built man-lifting kites, aircraft and hydrofoils and developed the tetrahedral space frame. He was also involved in teaching the deaf to speak. Bell's wife Mabel had lost all hearing at the age of five from scarlet fever and it was through his work that they met. Bell argued that if a machine could be built which would display speech in some way, a deaf person would be able to modify his or her speech to obtain the same display as the teacher. A microphone was a fundamental part of the system, and having developed one, Bell went on to create the telephone, allowing speech to travel down telegraph wires.

The success of the telephone has led to vast number of subscribers being connected with copper wires and this is a valuable network infrastructure. As technology has developed, the telephone has become

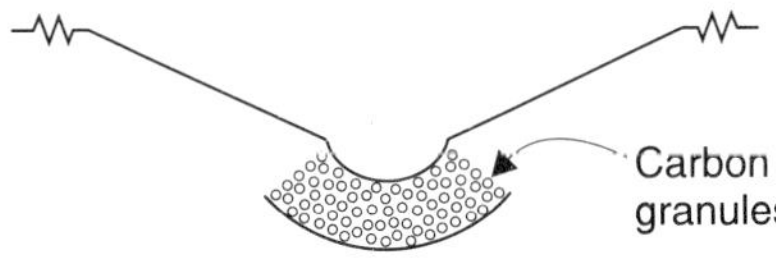

Figure 12.12 Carbon microphone relies on variations of pressure affecting resistance of carbon granules.

part of a global telecommunications industry. Simple economics suggests that in many cases improving the existing telephone cabling with modern modulation schemes is a good way of providing new communications services.

The original telephone microphone worked as shown in Figure 12.12. The sound vibrates the diaphragm which changes the compression (hence the resistance) of carbon granules. Such a microphone needs a power source, and this is provided by a 48 V battery at the exchange which forms part of a current loop that joins the two subscribers and includes the microphone and the earpiece. The modulated current produces a sound at the earpiece.

In practice some deliberate crosstalk is introduced into the system so that each subscriber hears some of their own voice in the earpiece. This is called sidetone and it is psychoacoustically necessary to allow the user to judge how loud to speak by providing a feedback mechanism. Without sidetone people tend to shout into the mouthpiece because it seems to be inert.

The length of wire in the loop is subject to enormous variation, and with it the loop resistance and losses. A high loop resistance will reduce the loop current and lower the signal. A voltage-dependent resistor in the phone compensates for the line length to try to keep the loop current steady.

As the goal of the telephone is to deliver the spoken information, its performance is measured in terms of intelligibility. The bandwidth is from about 300 Hz to 3 kHz and there is significant waveform distortion and noise. This, however, does not prevent speech being understood.

The long wires used in telephony are transmission lines with an impedance of about 600 Ohm at audio frequencies. The line loss is a logarithmic function of distance which led to the development of the deciBel to quantify the phenomenon.

Dialling and ringing is achieved down the same wires as are used by the conversation. When a telephone is hung up, a switch operates that open-circuits the current loop so that the exchange battery is no longer supplying power. The same hook switch connects the ringer to the lines via a capacitor which blocks the DC power. The telephone is made to ring by an AC signal generated at the exchange. The ringing frequency varies

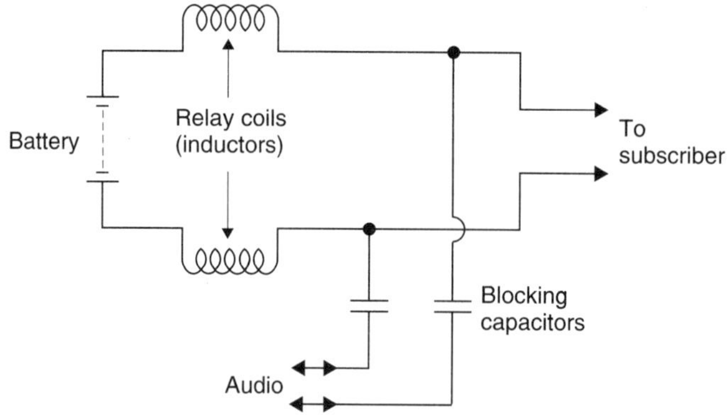

Figure 12.13 The traditional telephone system shares the same wires between signalling and speech using inductors which pass DC and capacitors which pass AC.

from country to country, but 20 Hz is common. This can pass through the DC-blocking capacitor. Figure 12.13 shows that at the exchange, the battery is fitted with inductors which block the ringing current.

The ringer in the telephone forms a tuned circuit which resonates at the ringing frequency. This raises efficiency which is important where long lines are used. In the original telephone the ringer would be a solenoid-operated bell, but in recent equipment there is an electronic synthesizer and loudspeaker driven by the AC ringing power. Connecting too many telephones to a line may mean that after the ring power is divided there is insuffcient to make each one ring reliably. Individual telephones vary in the ring power needed and so have what is called a ring equivalent number or REN which allows the engineer to calculate whether a particular combination of units will work.

Figure 12.13 also shows that the ring-blocking inductors may be the windings of relays which are in series with the current loop. When a telephone handset is lifted to make a call, the hook switch completes the current loop and the relays at the exchange will pull in to notify the exchange that a call is about to be made. When the handset is lifted to answer a call, the hook switch also stops the ringer.

For economic reasons, there are fewer paths through the telephone system than there are subscribers. This is because telephones were not used continuously until teenagers discovered them. Before a call can be made, the exchange has to find a free path and assign it to the calling telephone. Traditionally this was done electromechanically. A path which was already in use would be carrying loop current. When the exchange sensed that a handset was off-hook, a rotary switch would advance and sample all the paths until it found one without loop current where it would stop. This was signalled to the calling telephone by sending a dial tone.

In an early self-dialling telephone, on receipt of the dial tone the caller used a rotary dial to input the number. This was a simple mechanical pulse generator which broke the current loop at each pulse. The exchange relay would drop out each time the loop broke so that the relay contacts replicated the action of the rotary dial contacts. The exchange would use the pulses to operate uniselectors. Uniselectors were ten-way rotary switches which could be advanced one position at a time by a solenoid and a ratchet. Connecting the pulses from a rotary dial to a uniselector would cause the latter to move to the contact corresponding to the digit dialled.

The development of electronics revolutionized telephone exchanges. Whilst the loop current, AC ringing and hook switch sensing remained for compatibility, the electromechanical exchange gave way to electronic exchanges where the dial pulses were interpreted by digital counters which then drove crosspoint switches to route the call. The communication remained analog.

The next advance permitted by electronic exchanges was touch-tone dialling, also called DTMF. Touch-tone dialling is based on seven discrete frequencies shown in Figure 12.14. The telephone contains tone generators and tuned filters in the exchange can detect each frequency individually. The numbers 0 through 9 and two non-numerical symbols, asterisk and hash, can be transmitted using twelve unique tone pairs. A tone pair can reliably be detected in about 100 ms and this makes dialling much faster than the pulse system.

Tone	1	2	3	4	5	6	7	8
Frequency Hz	697	770	852	941	1209	1336	1477	1633

Key	0	1	2	3	4	5	6	7	8	9	*	#
Tone pair	4,6	1,5	1,6	1,7	2,5	2,6	2,7	3,5	3,6	3,7	4,5	4,7

Figure 12.14 DTMF dialling works on tone pairs.

The frequencies chosen for DTMF are logarithmically spaced so that the filters can have constant bandwidth and response time, but they do not correspond to the conventional musical scale. In addition to dialling speed, because the DTMF tones are within the telephone audio bandwidth, they can also be used for signalling during a call.

The first electronic exchanges simply used digital logic to perform the routing function. The next step was to use a fully digital system where the copper wires from each subscriber terminate in an interface or *line card* containing ADCs and DACs. The sampling rate of 8 kHz retains the traditional analog bandwidth, and eight-bit quantizing is used. This is not linear, but uses logarithmically sized quantizing steps so that the quantizing error is greater on larger signals. The result is a 64 kbit/s data rate in each direction.

Packets of data can be time-division multiplexed into high bit-rate data buses which can carry many calls simultaneously. The routing function becomes simply one of watching the bus until the right packet comes along for the selected destination. 64 kbit/s data switching came to be known as IDN (integrated digital network). As a data bus doesn't care whether it carries 64 kbit/s of speech or 64 kbit/s of something else, communications systems based on IDN tend to be based on multiples of that rate.

Such a system is called ISDN (integrated services digital network) which is basically a use of the telephone system that allows dial-up data transfer between subscribers in much the same way as a conventional phone call is made.

As it is based on IDN, ISDN works on units of 64 kbit/s, known as 'B channels', so that the communications channel carries the ISDN data just as easily as a voice call. However, for many applications, this bit rate isn't enough and ISDN joins together more than one B channel to raise the bit rate. In the lowest cost option, known as Basic Rate ISDN, two B channels are available, allowing 128 kbit/s communication.

Physically, the ISDN connection between the subscriber and the exchange consists of two twisted pairs; one for transmit and one for receive. The existing telephone wiring cannot be used. The signalling data, known as the D channel and running at 16 kbit/s, is multiplexed into the bitstream. A Basic Rate ISDN link has two B channels and one D channel multiplexed into the twisted pair. The B channels can be used for separate calls or ganged together.

Each twisted pair carries 2×64 plus 1×16 kbit/s of data, plus synchronizing patterns which allow the B and D information to be deserialized and separated. This results in a total rate of 192 kbit/s. The network echoes the D bits sent by the terminal. This is used to prove the connection exists in both directions and to detect if more than one terminal has tried to get on the lines at the same time.

Figure 12.15 shows what the signalling waveform of ISDN looks like. A three-level channel code called AMI (alternate mark inversion) is used. The outer two levels (positive or negative voltage) both represent data 0

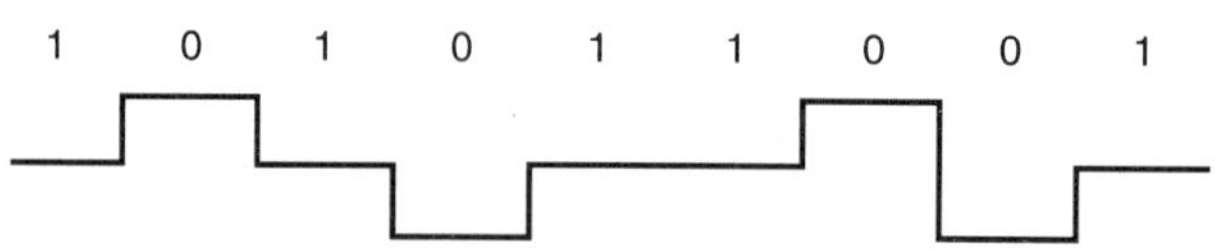

Figure 12.15 ISDN uses a modulation scheme known as AMI to deliver data over telephone-type twisted pairs.

whereas the centre level (zero volts) represents a data 1. Successive zeros must use alternating polarity. Whatever the data bit pattern, AMI coding means that the transmitted waveform is always DC-free because ones cause no offset and any zero is always balanced by the next zero which has opposite polarity.

For wider bandwidth, the Primary Rate ISDN system allows, in many parts of the world, up to 30 B channels in a system called E1, whereas in North America a system called T1 is used which offers 23 or 24 B channels. Naturally the more bit rate that is used, the more the call costs.

For compatibility with IDN, E1 and T1 still use individual 64-kilobit channels and the provision of wider bandwidth depends upon units called inverse multiplexers (I-MUXes) which distribute the source data over several B channels. The set of B channels used in an ISDN call do not necessarily all pass down the same route. Depending on how busy lines are, some B channels may pass down a physically different path between subscribers. The data arrive unchanged, but the time axis will be disrupted because the different paths may introduce different delays.

Figure 12.16 shows that the multiplexer at the receiving end has to combine the data from a number of B channels and apply suitable delays to each so that the final result is the original bitstream. The I-MUX has to put special time-variant codes in each B-channel signal so that the multiplexer can time-align them.

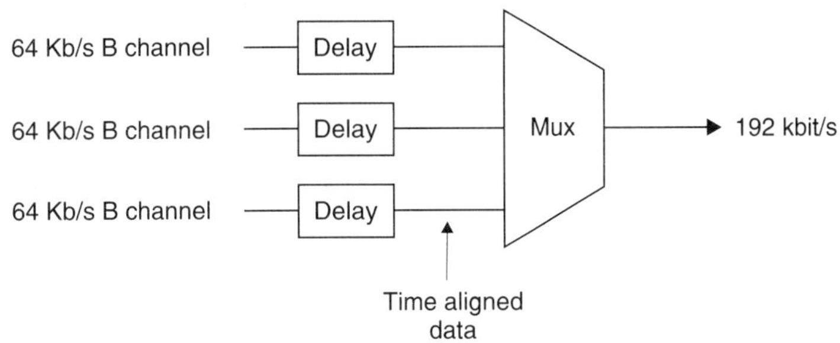

Figure 12.16 ISDN works on combining channels of fixed bit rate to approximate the bit rate needed for the application.

An alternative is where a telco has made full use of the synchronizing means within the networks. Where suitable control systems are implemented, once a single B channel call has been conected, the remaining B channels are logically attached so that they must follow the same routing, avoiding differential delays.

With the subsequent development of broadband networks (B-ISDN) the original ISDN is now known as N-ISDN where the N stands for narrow-band. B-ISDN is the ultimate convergent network able to carry any type of data and uses the well-known ATM (asynchronous transfer mode) protocol. Broadband and ATM are considered in a later section.

One of the difficulties of the AMI coding used in N-ISDN are that the data rate is limited and new cabling to the exchange is needed. ADSL (asymmetric digital subscriber line) is an advanced coding scheme which obtains high bit rate delivery and a back channel down existing subscriber telephone wiring.

ADSL works on frequency-division multiplexing using 4 kHz wide channels and 249 of these provide the delivery or downstream channel and 25 provide the back channel. Figure 12.17(a) shows that the existing bandwidth used by the traditional analog telephone is retained. The back channel occupies the lowest-frequency channels, with the downstream channels above. Figure 12.17(b) shows that at each end of the existing telephone wiring a device called a *splitter* is needed. This is basically a high-pass/low-pass filter which directs audio-frequency signals to the telephones and high-frequency signals to the modems.

Telephone wiring was never designed to support high-frequency signalling and is non-ideal. There will be reflections due to impedance mismatches which will cause an irregular frequency response in addition to high-frequency losses and noise which will all vary with cable length. ADSL can operate under these circumstances because it constantly monitors the conditions in each channel. If a given channel has adequate signal level and low noise, the full bit rate can be used, but in another

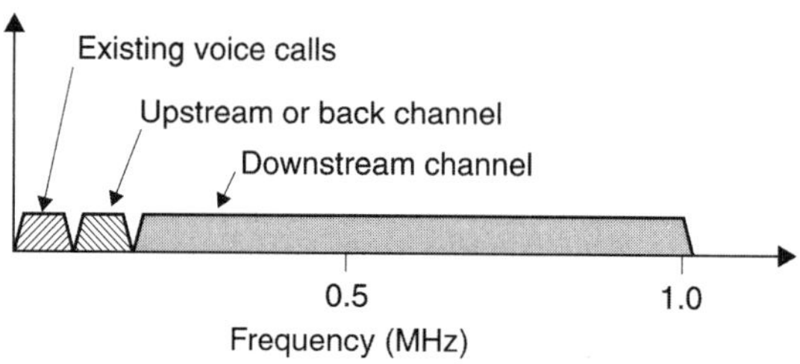

(a)

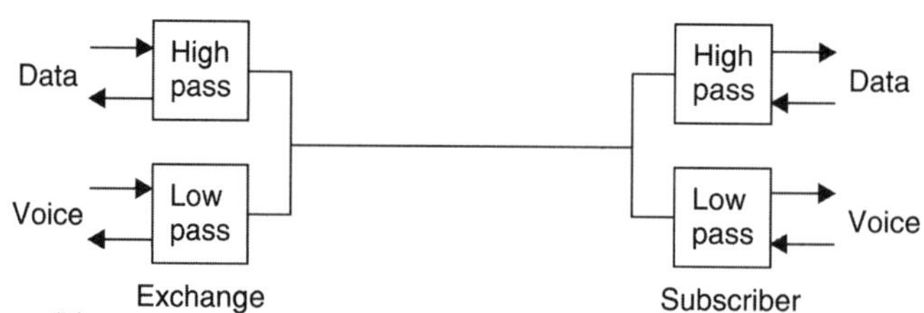

(b)

Figure 12.17 (a) ADSL allows the existing analog telephone to be retained, but adds delivery and back channels at higher frequencies. (b) A splitter is needed at each end of the subscriber's line.

channel there may be attenuation and the bit rate will have to be reduced. By independently coding the channels, the optimum data throughput for a given cable is obtained.

Each channel is modulated using DMT (discrete multitone technique) in which combinations of discrete frequencies are used. Within one channel symbol, there are 15 combinations of tones and so the coding achieves 15 bits/s/Hz. With a symbol rate of 4 kHz, each channel can deliver 60 kbits/s, making 14.9 Mbit/s for the downstream channel and 1.5 Mbit/s for the back channel. It should be stressed that these figures are theoretical maxima which are not reached in real cables. Practical ADSL systems deliver multiples of the ISDN channel rate up to about 6 Mbits/s, enough to deliver MPEG-2 coded video.

Over shorter distances, VDSL can reach up to 50 Mbits/s. Where ADSL and VDSL are being referred to as a common technology, the term xDSL will be found.

12.8 Digital television broadcasting

Digital television broadcasting relies on the combination of a number of fundamental technologies. These are: MPEG-2 compression to reduce the bit rate, multiplexing to combine picture and sound data into a common bitstream, digital modulation schemes to reduce the RF bandwidth needed by a given bit rate and error correction to reduce the error statistics of the channel down to a value acceptable to MPEG data.

MPEG compressed video is highly sensitive to bit errors, primarily because they confuse the recognition of variable-length codes so that the decoder loses synchronization. However, MPEG is a compression and multiplexing standard and does not specify how error correction should be performed. Consequently a transmission standard must define a system which has to correct essentially all errors such that the delivery mechanism is transparent.

Essentially a transmission standard specifies all the additional steps needed to deliver an MPEG transport stream from one place to another. This transport stream will consist of a number of elementary streams of video and audio, where the audio may be coded according to MPEG audio standard or AC-3. In a system working within its capabilities, the picture and sound quality will be determined only by the performance of the compression system and not by the RF transmission channel. This is the fundamental difference between analog and digital broadcasting. In analog television broadcasting, the picture quality may be limited by composite video encoding artifacts as well as transmission artifacts such as noise and ghosting. In digital television broadcasting the picture quality is determined instead by the compression artifacts and interlace artifacts if interlace has been retained.

If the received error rate increases for any reason, once the correcting power is used up, the system will degrade rapidly as uncorrected errors enter the MPEG decoder. In practice decoders will be programmed to recognize the condition and blank or mute to avoid outputting garbage. As a result digital receivers tend either to work well or not at all.

It is important to realize that the signal strength in a digital system does not translate directly to picture quality. A poor signal will increase the number of bit errors. Provided that this is within the capability of the error-correction system, there is no visible loss of quality. In contrast, a very powerful signal may be unusable because of similarly powerful reflections due to multipath propagation.

Whilst in one sense an MPEG transport stream is only data, it differs from generic data in that it must be presented to the viewer at a particular rate. Generic data are usually asynchronous, whereas baseband video and audio are synchronous. However, after compression and multiplexing audio and video are no longer precisely synchronous and so the term *isochronous* is used. This means a signal which was at one time synchronous and will be displayed synchronously, but which uses buffering at transmitter and receiver to accommodate moderate timing errors in the transmission.

Clearly another mechanism is needed so that the time axis of the original signal can be re-created on reception. The time stamp and program clock reference system of MPEG does this.

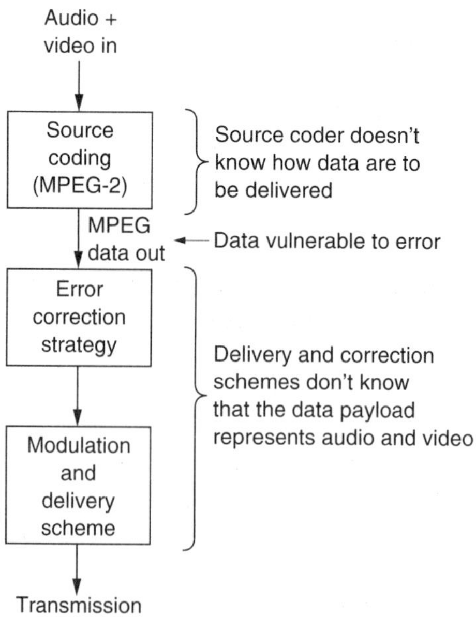

Figure 12.18 Source coder doesn't know delivery mechanism and delivery doesn't need to know what the data mean.

Figure 12.18 shows that the concepts involved in digital television broadcasting exist at various levels which have an independence not found in analog technology. In a given configuration a transmitter can radiate a given payload data bit rate. This represents the useful bit rate and does not include the necessary overheads needed by error correction, multiplexing or synchronizing. It is fundamental that the transmission system does not care what this payload bit rate is used for. The entire capacity may be used up by one high-definition channel, or a large number of heavily compressed channels may be carried. The details of this data usage are the domain of the *transport stream*. The multiplexing of transport streams is defined by the MPEG standards, but these do not define any error-correction or transmission technique.

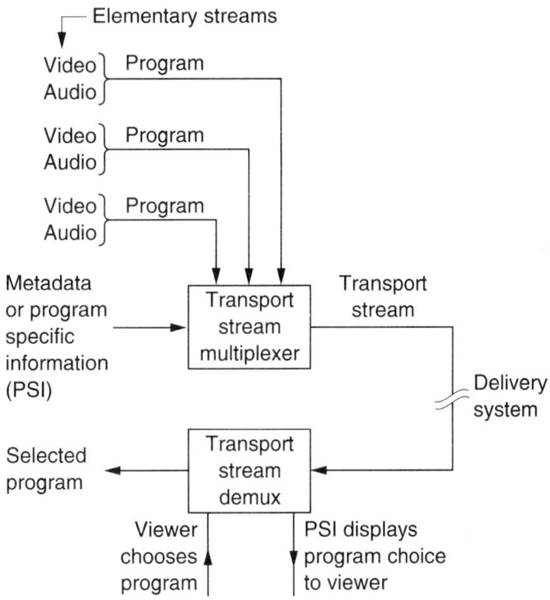

Figure 12.19 Program Specific Information helps the demultiplexer to select the required program.

At the lowest level in Figure 12.19 the source coding scheme, in this case MPEG compression, results in one or more elementary streams, each of which carries a video or audio channel. Elementary streams are multiplexed into a transport stream. The viewer then selects the desired elementary stream from the transport stream. Metadata in the transport stream ensure that when a video elementary stream is chosen, the appropriate audio elementary stream will automatically be selected.

12.9 MPEG packets and time stamps

The video elementary stream is an endless bitstream representing pictures which take a variable length of time to transmit. Bidirectional coding means that pictures are not necessarily in the correct order. Storage and transmission systems prefer discrete blocks of data and so elementary streams are packetized to form a PES (packetized elementary stream). Audio elementary streams are also packetized. A packet is shown in Figure 12.20. It begins with a header containing an unique packet start code and a code which identifies the type of data stream. Optionally the packet header also may contain one or more *time stamps* which are used for synchronizing the video decoder to real time and for obtaining lip-sync.

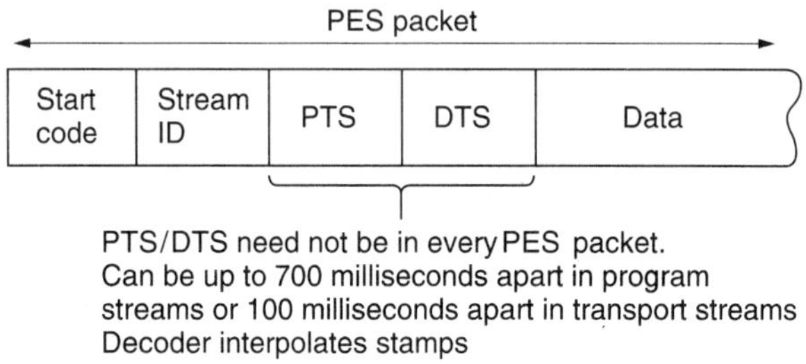

Figure 12.20 A PES packet structure is used to break up the continuous elementary stream.

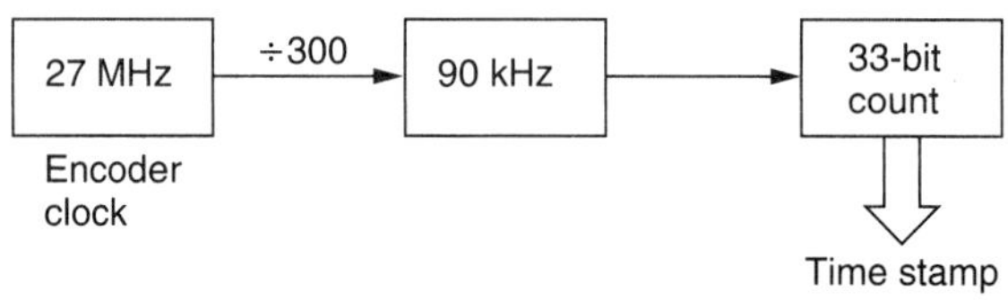

Figure 12.21 Time stamps are the result of sampling a counter driven by the encoder clock.

Figure 12.21 shows that a time stamp is a sample of the state of a counter which is driven by a 90 kHz clock. This is obtained by dividing down the master 27 MHz clock of MPEG-2. This 27 MHz clock must be locked to the video frame rate and the audio sampling rate of the program concerned. There are two types of time stamp: PTS and DTS. These are abbreviations for presentation time stamp and decode time stamp. A presentation time stamp determines when the associated picture should be displayed on the screen, whereas a decode time stamp determines when it should be decoded. In bidirectional coding these times can be quite different.

Audio packets only have presentation time stamps. Clearly if lip-sync is to be obtained, the audio sampling rate of a given program must have been locked to the same master 27 MHz clock as the video and the time stamps must have come from the same counter driven by that clock.

In practice the time between input pictures is constant and so there is a certain amount of redundancy in the time stamps. Consequently PTS/DTS need not appear in every PES packet. Time stamps can be up to 100 ms apart in transport streams. As each picture type (*I*, *P* or *B*) is flagged in the bitstream, the decoder can infer the PTS/DTS for every picture from the ones actually transmitted.

The MPEG-2 transport stream is intended to be a multiplex of many TV programs with their associated sound and data channels, although a single program transport stream (SPTS) is possible. The transport stream is based upon packets of constant size so that multiplexing, adding error-correction codes and interleaving in a higher layer is eased. Figure 12.22 shows that these are always 188 bytes long.

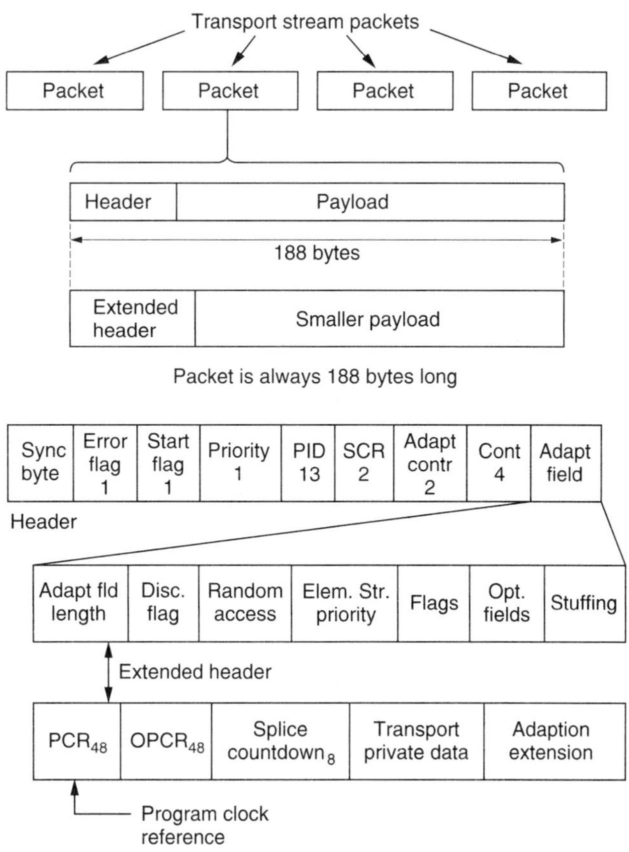

Figure 12.22 Transport stream packets are always 188 bytes long to facilitate multiplexing and error correction.

Transport stream packets always begin with a header. The remainder of the packet carries data known as the payload. For efficiency, the normal header is relatively small, but for special purposes the header may be extended. In this case the payload gets smaller so that the overall size of the packet is unchanged. Transport stream packets should not be confused with PES packets which are larger and which vary in size. PES packets are broken up to form the payload of the transport stream packets.

The header begins with a sync byte which is an unique pattern detected by a demultiplexer. A transport stream may contain many different elementary streams and these are identified by giving each an unique thirteen-bit Packet Identification Code or PID which is included in the header. A multiplexer seeking a particular elementary stream simply checks the PID of every packet and accepts only those which match.

In a multiplex there may be many packets from other programs in between packets of a given PID. To help the demultiplexer, the packet header contains a continuity count. This is a four-bit value which increments at each new packet having a given PID.

This approach allows statistical multiplexing as it does matter how many or how few packets have a given PID; the demux will still find them. Statistical multiplexing has the problem that it is virtually impossible to make the sum of the input bit rates constant. Instead the multiplexer aims to make the average data bit rate slightly less than the maximum and the overall bit rate is kept constant by adding 'stuffing' or null packets. These packets have no meaning, but simply keep the bit rate constant. Null packets always have a PID of 8191 (all ones) and the demultiplexer discards them.

12.10 Program clock reference

A transport stream is a multiplex of several TV programs and these may have originated from widely different locations. It is impractical to expect all the programs in a transport stream to be genlocked and so the stream is designed from the outset to allow unlocked programs. A decoder running from a transport stream has to genlock to the encoder and the transport stream has to have a mechanism to allow this to be done independently for each program. The synchronizing mechanism is called Program Clock Reference (PCR).

Figure 12.23 shows how the PCR system works. The goal is to re-create at the decoder a 27 MHz clock which is synchronous with that at the encoder. The encoder clock drives a forty-eight-bit counter which continuously counts up to the maximum value before overflowing and beginning again.

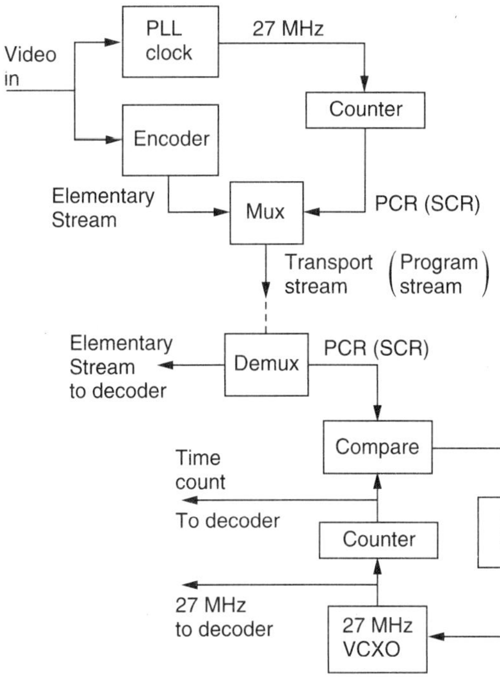

Figure 12.23 Program or System Clock Reference codes regenerate a clock at the decoder. See text for details.

A transport stream multiplexer will periodically sample the counter and place the state of the count in an extended packet header as a PCR (see Figure 12.22). The demultiplexer selects only the PIDs of the required program, and it will extract the PCRs from the packets in which they were inserted.

The PCR codes are used to control a numerically locked loop (NLL) described in section 2.9. The NLL contains a 27 MHz VCXO (voltage-controlled crystal oscillator) a variable-frequency oscillator based on a crystal which has a relatively small frequency range.

The VCXO drives a forty-eight-bit counter in the same way as in the encoder. The state of the counter is compared with the contents of the PCR and the difference is used to modify the VCXO frequency. When the loop reaches lock, the decoder counter would arrive at the same value as is contained in the PCR and no change in the VCXO would then occur. In practice the transport stream packets will suffer from transmission jitter and this will create phase noise in the loop. This is removed by the loop filter so that the VCXO effectively averages a large number of phase errors.

A heavily damped loop will reject jitter well, but will take a long time to lock. Lockup time can be reduced when switching to a new program if the decoder counter is jammed to the value of the first PCR received in the new program. The loop filter may also have its time constants shortened during lockup.

Once a synchronous 27 MHz clock is available at the decoder, this can be divided down to provide the 90 kHz clock which drives the time stamp mechanism.

The entire timebase stability of the decoder is no better than the stability of the clock derived from PCR. MPEG-2 sets standards for the maximum amount of jitter which can be present in PCRs in a real transport stream.

Clearly if the 27 MHz clock in the receiver is locked to one encoder it can only receive elementary streams encoded with that clock. If it is attempted to decode, for example, an audio stream generated from a different clock, the result will be periodic buffer overflows or underflows in the decoder. Thus MPEG defines a program in a manner which relates to timing. A program is a set of elementary streams which have been encoded with the same master clock.

12.11 Program Specific Information (PSI)

In a real transport stream, each elementary stream has a different PID, but the demultiplexer has to be told what these PIDs are and what audio belongs with what video before it can operate. This is the function of PSI which is a form of metadata. Figure 12.24 shows the structure of PSI.

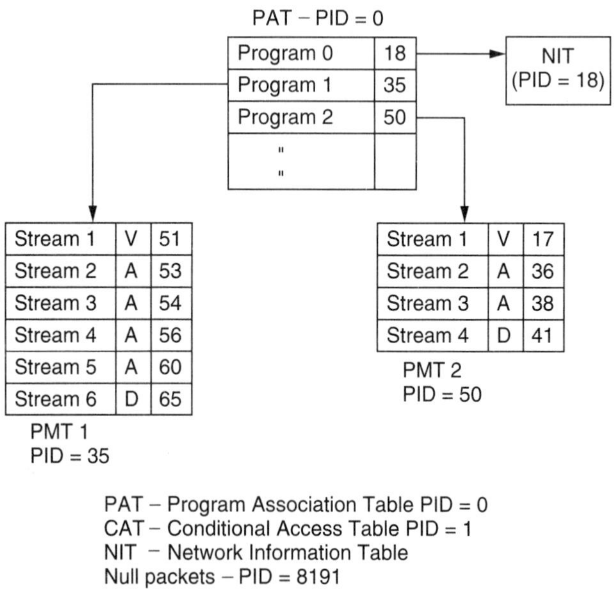

Figure 12.24 MPEG-2 Program Specific Information (PSI) is used to tell a demultiplexer what the transport stream contains.

When a decoder powers up, it knows nothing about the incoming transport stream except that it must search for all packets with a PID of zero. PID zero is reserved for the Program Association Table (PAT). The PAT is transmitted at regular intervals and contains a list of all the programs in this transport stream. Each program is further described by its own Program Map Table (PMT) and the PIDs of of the PMTs are contained in the PAT.

Figure 12.24 also shows that the PMTs fully describe each program. The PID of the video elementary stream is defined, along with the PID(s) of the associated audio and data streams. Consequently when the viewer selects a particular program, the demultiplexer looks up the program number in the PAT, finds the right PMT and reads the audio, video and data PIDs. It then selects elementary streams having these PIDs from the transport stream and routes them to the decoders.

Program 0 of the PAT contains the PID of the Network Information Table (NIT). This contains information about what other transport streams are available. For example in the case of a satellite broadcast, the NIT would detail the orbital position, the polarization, carrier frequency and modulation scheme. Using the NIT a set-top box could automatically switch between transport streams.

Apart from 0 and 8191, a PID of 1 is also reserved for the Conditional Access Table (CAT). This is part of the access control mechanism needed to support pay per view or subscription viewing.

12.12 Transport stream multiplexing

A transport stream multiplexer is a complex device because of the number of functions it must perform. A fixed multiplexer will be considered first. In a fixed multiplexer, the bit rate of each of the programs must be specified so that the sum does not exceed the payload bit rate of the transport stream. The payload bit rate is the overall bit rate less the packet headers and PSI rate.

In practice the programs will not be synchronous to one another, but the transport stream must produce a constant packet rate given by the bit rate divided by 188 bytes, the packet length. Figure 12.25 shows how this is handled. Each elementary stream entering the multiplexer passes through a buffer which is divided into payload-sized areas. Note that periodically the payload area is made smaller because of the requirement to insert PCR.

MPEG-2 decoders also have a quantity of buffer memory. The challenge to the multiplexer is to take packets from each program in such a way that neither its own buffers nor the buffers in any decoder either overflow or underflow. This requirement is met by sending packets from

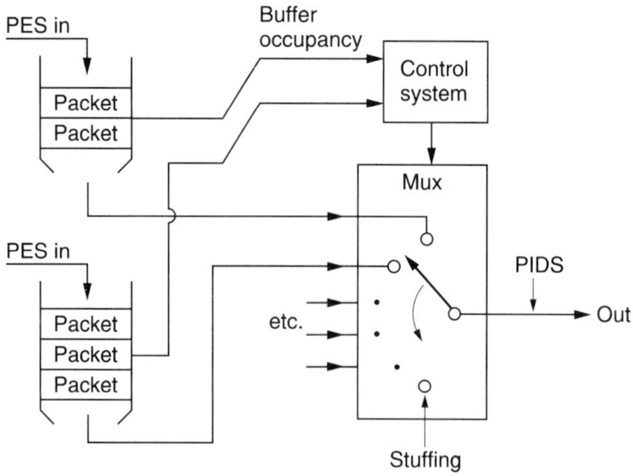

Figure 12.25 A transport stream multiplexer can handle several programs which are asynchronous to one another and to the transport stream clock. See text for details.

all programs as evenly as possible rather than bunching together a lot of packets from one program. When the bit rates of the programs are different, the only way this can be handled is to use the buffer contents indicators. The fuller a buffer is, the more likely it should be that a packet will be read from it. This a buffer content arbitrator can decide which program should have a packet allocated next.

If the sum of the input bit rates is correct, the buffers should all slowly empty because the overall input bit rate has to be less than the payload bit rate. This allows for the insertion of Program Specific Information. Whilst PATs and PMTs are being transmitted, the program buffers will fill up again. The multiplexer can also fill the buffers by sending more PCRs as this reduces the payload of each packet. In the event that the multiplexer has sent enough of everything but still can't fill a packet then it will send a null packet with a PID of 8191. Decoders will discard null packets and as they convey no useful data, the multiplexer buffers will all fill whilst null packets are being transmitted.

The use of null packets means that the bit rates of the elementary streams do not need to be synchronous with one another or with the transport stream bit rate. As each elementary stream can have its own PCR, it is not necessary for the different programs in a transport stream to be genlocked to one another; in fact they don't even need to have the same frame rate.

This approach allows the transport stream bit rate to be accurately defined and independent of the timing of the data carried. This is important because the transport stream bit rate determines the spectrum of the transmitter and this must not vary.

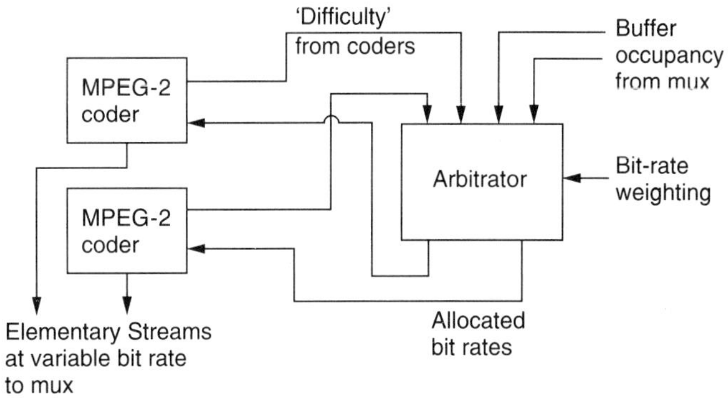

Figure 12.26 A statistical multiplexer contains an arbitrator which allocates bit rate to each program as a function of program difficulty.

In a statistical multiplexer or STATMUX, the bit rate allocated to each program can vary dynamically. Figure 12.26 shows that there must be tight connection between the STATMUX and the associated compressors. Each compressor has a buffer memory which is emptied by a demand clock from the STATMUX. In a normal, fixed bit rate, coder the buffer content feeds back and controls the requantizer. In statmuxing this process is less severe and only takes place if the buffer is very close to full, because the degree of coding difficulty is also fed to the STATMUX.

The STATMUX contains an arbitrator which allocates more packets to the program with the greatest coding difficulty. Thus if a particular program encounters difficult material it will produce large prediction errors and begin to fill its output buffer. As the STATMUX has allocated more packets to that program, more data will be read out of that buffer, preventing overflow. Of course this is only possible if the other programs in the transport stream are handling typical video.

In the event that several programs encounter difficult material at once, clearly the buffer contents will rise and the requantizing mechanism will have to operate.

12.13 Remultiplexing

In real life a program creator may produce a transport stream which carries all its programs simultaneously. A service provider may take in several such streams and create its own transport stream by selecting different programs from different sources. In an MPEG-2 environment this requires a remultiplexer, also known as a transmultiplexer. Figure 12.27 shows what a remultiplexer does.

Remultiplexing is easier when all the incoming programs have the same bit rate. If a suitable combination of programs is selected it is

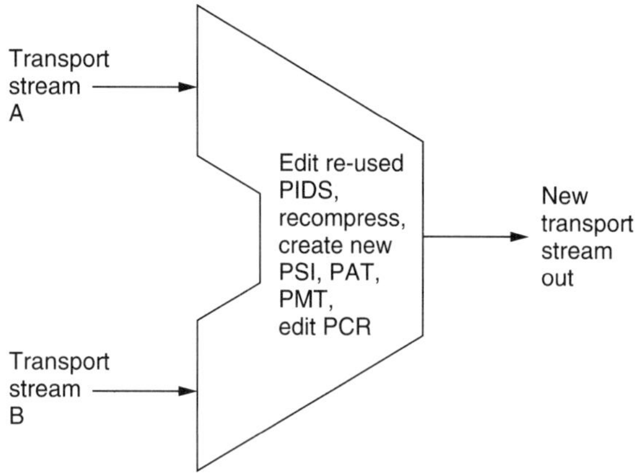

Figure 12.27 A remultiplexer creates a new transport stream from selected programs in other transport streams.

obvious that the output transport stream will always have sufficient bit rate. Where statistical multiplexing has been used, there is a possibility that the sum of the bit rates of the selected programs will exceed the bit rate of the output transport stream. To avoid this, the remultiplexer will have to employ recompression.

Recompression requires a partial decode of the bitstream to identify the DCT coefficients. These will then be requantized to reduce the bit rate until it is low enough to fit the output transport stream.

Remultiplexers have to edit the Program Specific Information (PSI) such that the Program Association Table (PAT) and the Program Map Tables (PMT) correctly reflect the new transport stream content. It may also be necessary to change the packet identification codes (PIDs) since the incoming transport streams could inadvertently have used the same values.

When Program Clock Reference (PCR) data are included in an extended packet header, they represent a real-time clock count and if the associated packet is moved in time the PCR value will be wrong. Remultiplexers have to re-create a new multiplex from a number of other multiplexes and it is inevitable that this process will result in packets being placed in different locations in the output transport stream than they had in the input. In this case the remultiplexer must edit the PCR values so that they reflect the value the clock counter would have had at the location at which the packet now resides.

12.14 Broadcast modulation techniques

A key difference between analog and digital transmission is that the transmitter output is switched between a number of discrete states rather

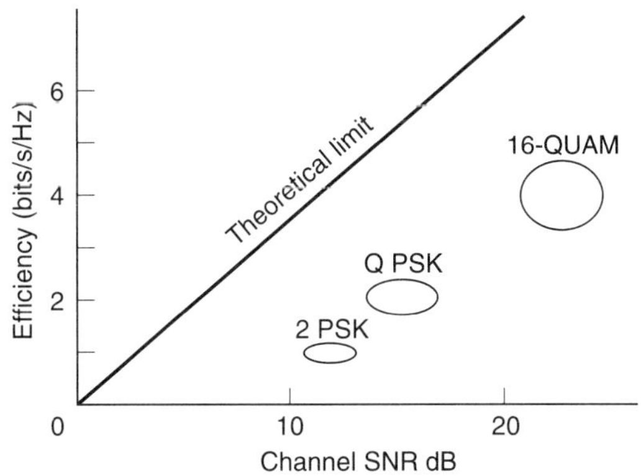

Figure 12.28 Where a better SNR exists, more data can be sent down a given bandwidth channel.

than continuously varying. The process is called channel coding, which is the digital equivalent of modulation. A good code minimizes the channel bandwidth needed for a given bit rate. This quality of the code is measured in bits/s/Hz and is the equivalent of the density ratio in recording. Figure 12.28 shows, not surprisingly, that the less bandwidth required, the better the signal-to-noise ratio has to be. The figure shows the theoretical limit as well as the performance of a number of codes which offer different balances of bandwidth/noise performance.

Where the SNR is poor, as in satellite broadcasting, the amplitude of the signal will be unstable, and phase modulation is used. Figure 12.29 shows that phase-shift keying (PSK) can use two or more phases. When four phases in quadrature are used, the result is Quadrature Phase Shift Keying or QPSK. Each period of the transmitted waveform can have one of four phases and therefore conveys the value of two data bits. 8-PSK uses eight phases and can carry three bits per symbol where the SNR is adequate. PSK is generally encoded in such a way that a knowledge of absolute phase is not needed at the receiver. Instead of encoding the

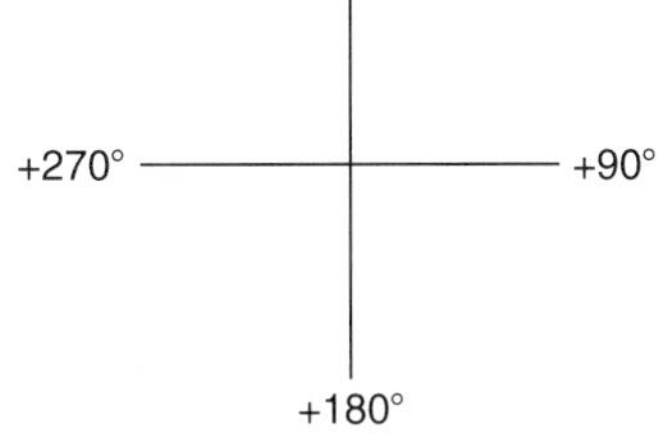

Data	Phase shift
0 0	0°
0 1	90°
1 0	270°
1 1	180°

Figure 12.29 Differential quadrature phase shift keying (DQPSK).

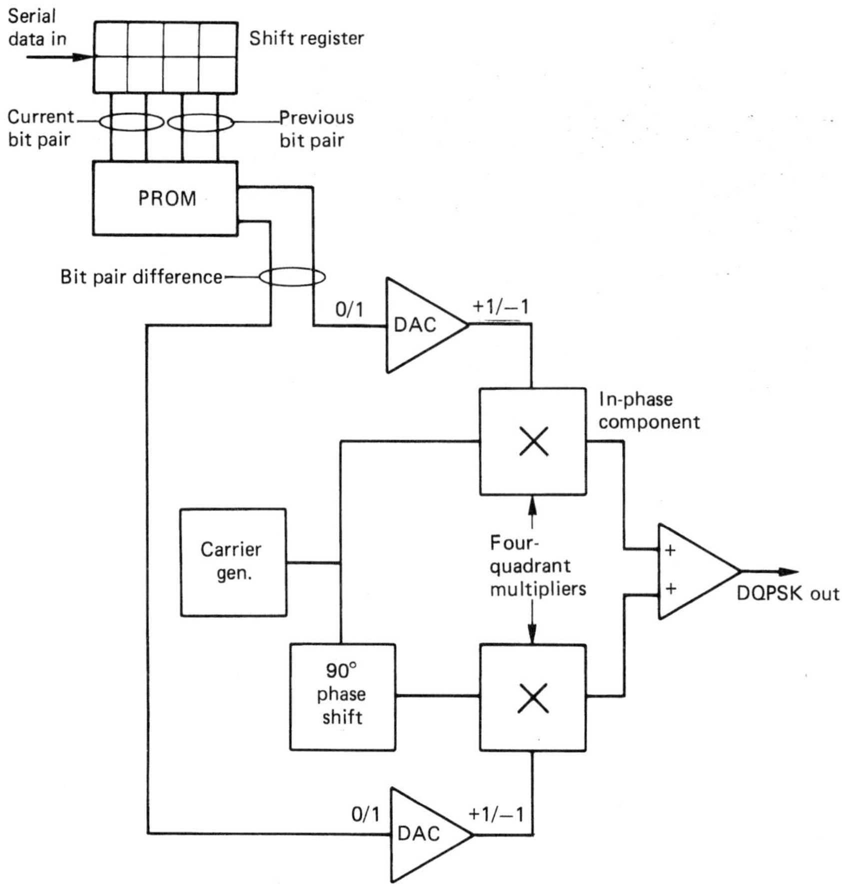

Figure 12.30 A QPSK coder conveys two bits for each modulation period. See text for details.

signal phase directly, the data determine the magnitude of the phase shift between symbols. A QPSK coder is shown in Figure 12.30.

In terrestrial transmission more power is available than, for example, from a satellite and so a stronger signal can be delivered to the receiver. Where a better SNR exists, an increase in data rate can be had using multi-level signalling or *m*-ary coding instead of binary. Figure 12.31 shows that the ATSC system uses an eight-level signal (8-VSB) allowing three bits to be sent per symbol. Four of the levels exist with normal carrier phase and four exist with inverted phase so that a phase-sensitive rectifier is needed in the receiver. Clearly the data separator must have a three-bit ADC which can resolve the eight signal levels. The gain and offset of the signal must be precisely set so that the quantizing levels register precisely with the centres of the eyes. The transmitted signal contains sync pulses which are encoded using specified code levels so that the data separator can set its gain and offset.

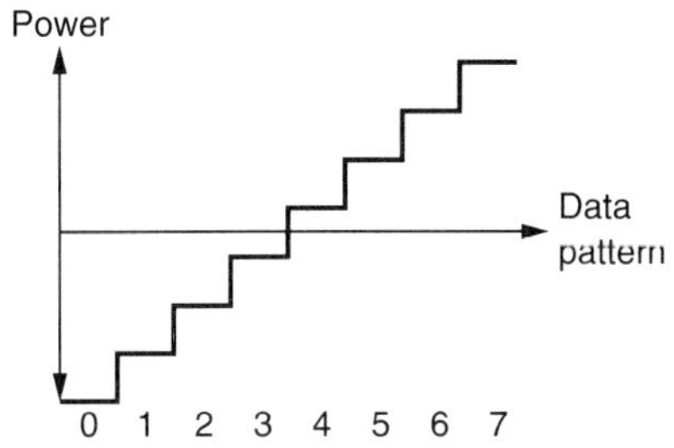

Figure 12.31 In 8VSB the transmitter operates in eight different states enabling three bits to be sent per symbol.

Multi-level signalling systems have the characteristic that the bits in the symbol have different error probability. Figure 12.32 shows that a small noise level will corrupt the low-order bit, whereas twice as much noise will be needed to corrupt the middle bit and four times as much will be needed to corrupt the high-order bit. In ATSC the solution is that the lower two bits are encoded together in an inner error-correcting scheme so that they represent only one bit with similar reliability to the top bit. As a result the 8-VSB system actually delivers two data bits per symbol even though eight-level signalling is used.

The modulation of the carrier results in a double-sideband spectrum, but following analog TV practice most of the lower sideband is filtered off leaving a vestigial sideband only, hence the term 8-VSB. A small DC offset is injected into the modulator signal so that the four in-phase levels are slightly higher than the four out-of-phase levels. This has the effect of creating a small pilot at the carrier frequency to help receiver locking.

Multi-level signalling can be combined with PSK to obtain multi-level Quadrature Amplitude Modulation (QUAM). Figure 12.33 shows the example of 64-QUAM. Incoming six-bit data words are split into two three-bit words and each is used to amplitude modulate a pair of

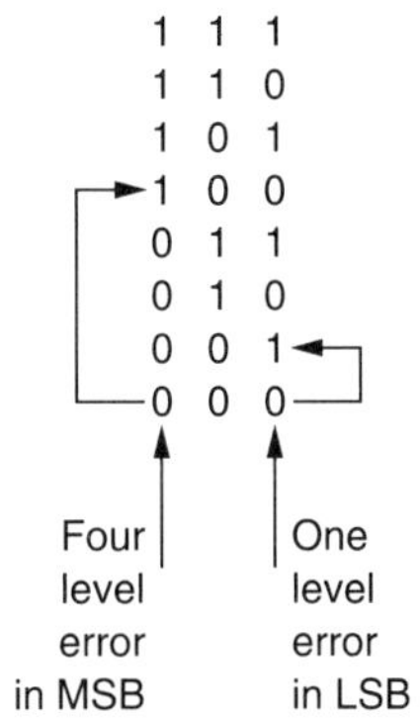

Figure 12.32 In multi-level signalling the error probability is not the same for each bit.

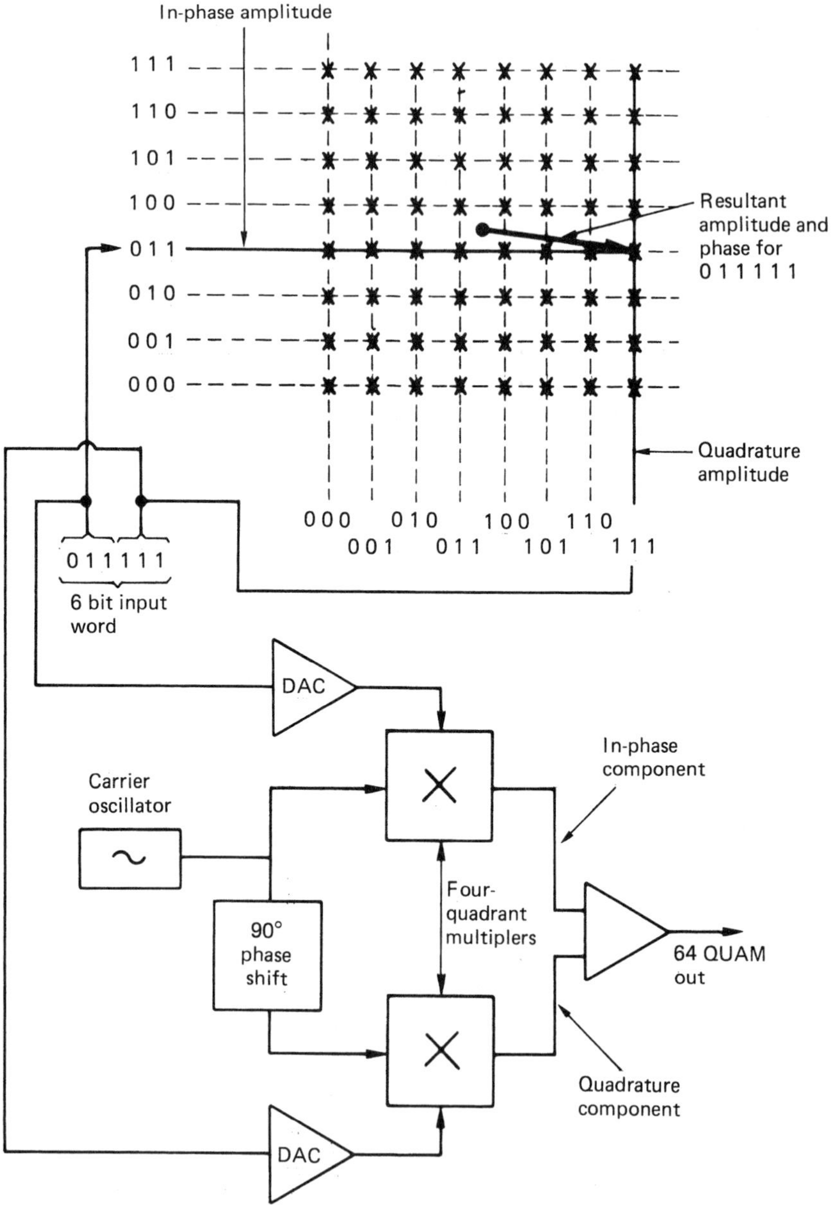

Figure 12.33 In 64-QUAM, two carriers are generated with a quadrature relationship. These are independently amplitude modulated to eight discrete levels in four quadrant multipliers. Adding the signals produces a QUAM signal having 64 unique combinations of amplitude and phase. Decoding requires the waveform to be sampled in quadrature like a colour TV subcarrier.

sinusoidal carriers which are generated in quadrature. The modulators are four-quadrant devices such that 2^3 amplitudes are available, four which are in phase with the carrier and four in antiphase. The two AM carriers are linearly added and the result is a signal which has 2^6 or 64 combinations of amplitude and phase. There is a great deal of similarity between QUAM and the colour subcarrier used in analog television in which the two colour difference signals are encoded into one amplitude and phase modulated waveform. On reception, the waveform is sampled twice per cycle in phase with the two original carriers and the result is a pair of eight-level signals. 16-QUAM is also possible, delivering only four bits per symbol but requiring a lower SNR.

The data bit patterns to be transmitted can have any combinations whatsoever, and if nothing were done, the transmitted spectrum would be non-uniform. This is undesirable because peaks cause interference with other services, whereas energy troughs allow external interference in. The randomizing technique of section 10.13 is used to overcome the problem. The process is known as energy dispersal. The signal energy is spread uniformly throughout the allowable channel bandwidth so that it has less energy at a given frequency.

A pseudo-random sequence generator is used to generate the randomizing sequence. Figure 12.34 shows the randomizer used in DVB. This sixteen-bit device has a maximum sequence length of 65 535 bits, and is preset to a standard value at the beginning of each set of eight transport

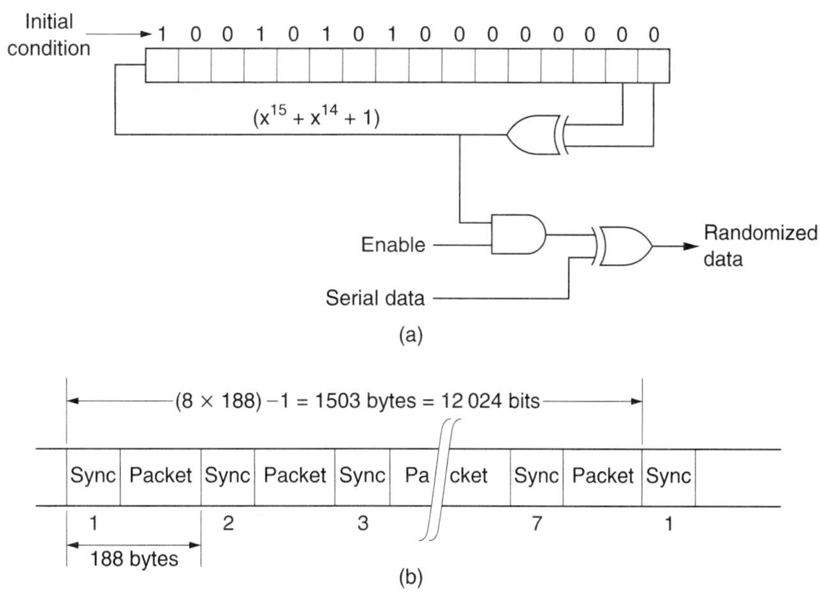

Figure 12.34 The randomizer of DVB is pre-set to the initial condition once every eight transport stream packets. The maximum length of the sequence is 65 535 bits, but only the first 12 024 bits are used before resetting again (b).

stream packets. The serialized data are XORed with the LSB of the Galois field, which randomizes the output which then goes to the modulator. The spectrum of the transmission is now determined by the spectrum of the prs.

On reception, the de-randomizer must contain the identical ring counter which must also be set to the starting condition to bit accuracy. Its output is then added to the data stream from the demodulator. The randomizing will effectively then have been added twice to the data in modulo-2, and as a result is cancelled out leaving the original serial data.

12.15 OFDM

The way that radio signals interact with obstacles is a function of the relative magnitude of the wavelength and the size of the object. AM sound radio transmissions with a wavelength of several hundred metres can easily diffract around large objects. The shorter the wavelength of a transmission, the larger objects in the environment appear to it and these objects can then become reflectors. Reflecting objects produce a delayed signal at the receiver in addition to the direct signal. In analog television transmissions this causes the familiar ghosting. In digital transmissions, the symbol rate may be so high that the reflected signal may be one or more symbols behind the direct signal, causing inter-symbol interference. As the reflection may be continuous, the result may be that almost every symbol is corrupted. No error-correction system can handle this. Raising the transmitter power is no help at all as it simply raises the power of the reflection in proportion.

The only solution is to change the characteristics of the RF channel in some way to either prevent the multipath reception or to prevent it being a problem. The RF channel includes the modulator, transmitter, antennae, receiver and demodulator.

As with analogue UHF TV transmissions, a directional antenna is useful with digital transmission as it can reject reflections. However, directional antennae tend to be large and they require a skilled permanent installation. Mobile use on a vehicle or vessel is simply impractical.

Another possibility is to incorporate a ghost canceller into the receiver. The transmitter periodically sends a standardized known waveform called a training sequence. The receiver knows what this waveform looks like and compares it with the received signal. In theory it is possible for the receiver to compute the delay and relative level of a reflection and so insert an opposing one. In practice if the reflection is strong it may prevent the receiver finding the training sequence.

The most elegant approach is to use a system in which multipath reception conditions cause only a small increase in error rate which the

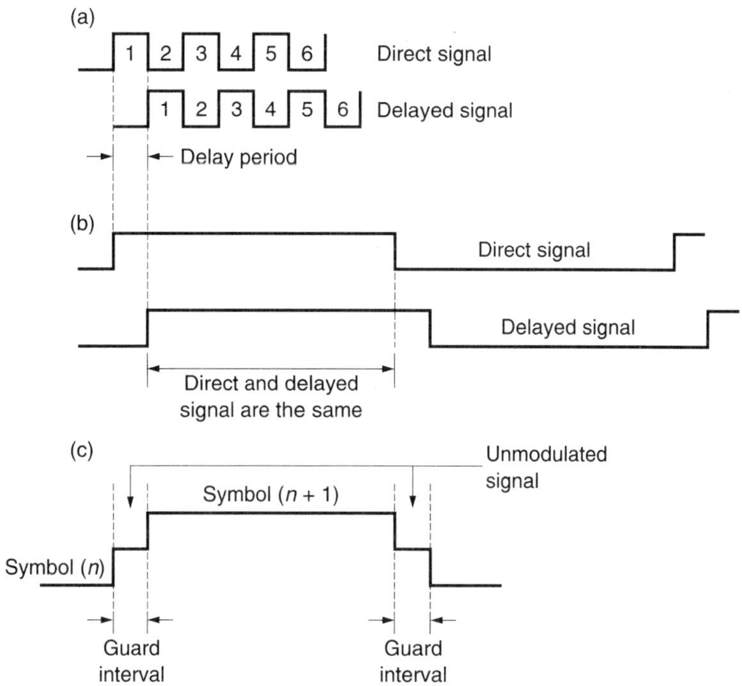

Figure 12.35 (a) High bit rate transmissions are prone to corruption due to reflections. (b) If the bit rate is reduced the effect of reflections is eliminated, in fact reflected energy can be used. (c) Guard intervals may be inserted between symbols.

error-correction system can manage. This approach is used in DVB. Figure 12.35(a) shows that when using one carrier with a high bit rate, reflections can easily be delayed by one or more bit periods, causing interference between the bits. Figure 12.35(b) shows that instead, OFDM sends many carriers each having a low bit rate. When a low bit rate is used, the energy in the reflection will arrive during the same bit period as the direct signal. Not only is the system immune to multipath reflections, but the energy in the reflections can actually be used. This characteristic can be enhanced by using guard intervals shown in (c). These reduce multipath bit overlap even more.

Note that OFDM is not a modulation scheme, and each of the carriers used in a OFDM system still needs to be modulated using any of the digital coding schemes described above. What OFDM does is to provide an efficient way of packing many carriers close together without mutual interference.

A serial data waveform basically contains a train of rectangular pulses. The transform of a rectangle is the function $\sin x/x$ and so the baseband pulse train has a $\sin x/x$ spectrum. When this waveform is used to modulate a carrier the result is a symmetrical $\sin x/x$ spectrum centred on

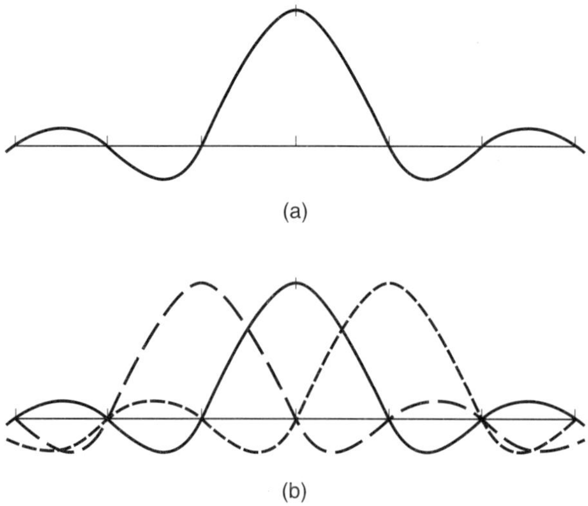

Figure 12.36 In OFDM the carrier spacing is critical, but when correct the carriers become independent and most efficient use is made of the spectrum. (a) Spectrum of bitstream has regular nulls. (b) Peak of one carrier occurs at null of another.

the carrier frequency. Figure 12.36(a) shows that nulls in the spectrum appear spaced at multiples of the bit rate away from the carrier.

Further carriers can be placed at spacings such that each is centred at the nulls of the others as is shown in (b). The distance between the carriers is equal to 90° or one quadrant of sin$x$. Owing to the quadrant spacing, these carriers are mutually orthogonal, hence the term orthogonal frequency division. A large number of such carriers (in practice several thousand) will be interleaved to produce an overall spectrum which is almost rectangular and which fills the available transmission channel.

When guard intervals are used, the carrier returns to an unmodulated state between bits for a period which is greater than the period of the reflections. Then the reflections from one transmitted bit decay during the guard interval before the next bit is transmitted. The use of guard intervals reduces the bit rate of the carrier because for some of the time it is radiating carrier not data. A typical reduction is to around 80 per cent of the capacity without guard intervals.

This capacity reduction does, however, improve the error statistics dramatically, such that much less redundancy is required in the error-correction system. Thus the effective transmission rate is improved. The use of guard intervals also moves more energy from the sidebands back to the carrier. The frequency spectrum of a set of carriers is no longer perfectly flat but contains a small peak at the centre of each carrier.

The ability to work in the presence of multipath cancellation is one of the great strengths of OFDM. In DVB, more than 2000 carriers are used in single transmitter systems. Provided there is exact synchronism, several transmitters can radiate exactly the same signal so that a single-frequency network can be created throughout a whole country. SFNs require a variation on OFDM which uses over 8000 carriers.

With OFDM, directional antennae are not needed and, given sufficient field strength, mobile reception is perfectly feasible. Of course, directional antennae may still be used to boost the received signal outside normal service areas or to enable the use of low-powered transmitters.

An OFDM receiver must perform fast Fourier transforms (FFTs) on the whole band at the symbol rate of one of the carriers. The amplitude and/or phase of the carrier at a given frequency effectively reflects the state of the transmitted symbol at that time slot and so the FFT partially demodulates as well.

In order to assist with tuning in, the OFDM spectrum contains pilot signals. These are individual carriers which are transmitted with slightly more power than the remainder. The pilot carriers are spaced apart through the whole channel at agreed frequencies which form part of the transmission standard.

Practical reception conditions, including multipath reception, will cause a significant variation in the received spectrum and some equalization will be needed. Figure 12.37 shows what the possible

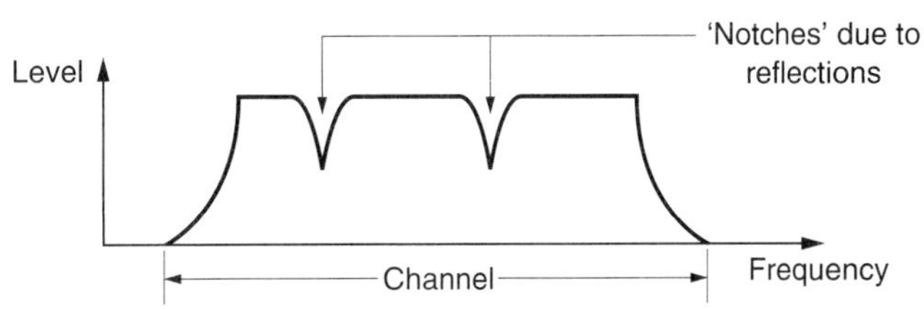

Figure 12.37 Multipath reception can place notches in the channel spectrum. This will require equalization at the receiver.

spectrum looks like in the presence of a powerful reflection. The signal has almost been cancelled at certain frequencies. However, the FFT performed in the receiver is effectively a spectral analysis of the signal and so the receiver computes for free the received spectrum. As in a flat spectrum the peak magnitude of all the coefficients would be the same (apart from the pilots), equalization is easily performed by multiplying the coefficients by suitable constants until this characteristic is obtained.

Although the use of transform-based receivers appears complex, when it is considered that such an approach simultaneously allows effective equalization the complexity is not significantly higher than that of a conventional receiver which needs a separate spectral analysis system just for equalization purposes.

The only drawback of OFDM is that the transmitter must be highly linear to prevent intermodulation between the carriers. This is readily achieved in terrestrial transmitters by derating the transmitter so that it runs at a lower power than it would in analog service. This is not practicable in satellite transmitters which are optimized for efficiency, so OFDM is not really suitable for satellite use.

12.16 Error correction in digital television broadcasting

As in recording, broadcast data suffer from both random and burst errors and the error-correction strategies of digital television broadcasting have to reflect that. Figure 12.38 shows a typical system in which inner and

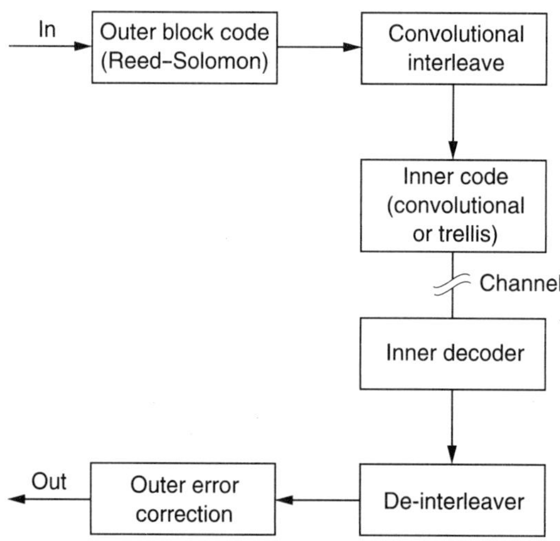

Figure 12.38 Error-correcting strategy of digital television broadcasting systems.

outer codes are employed. The Reed-Solomon codes are universally used for burst-correcting outer codes, along with an interleave which will be convolutional rather than the block-based interleave used in recording media. The inner codes will not be R–S, as more suitable codes exist for the statistical conditions prevalent in broadcasting. DVB uses a parity-based variable-rate system in which the amount of redundancy can be adjusted according to reception conditions. ATSC uses a fixed-rate parity-based system along with trellis coding to overcome co-channel interference from analog NTSC transmitters.

12.17 DVB

The DVB system is subdivided into systems optimized for satellite, cable and terrestrial delivery. This section concentrates on the terrestrial delivery system. Figure 12.39 shows a block diagram of a DVB-T transmitter.

Incoming transport stream packets of 188 bytes each are first subject to R–S outer coding. This adds 16 bytes of redundancy to each packet, resulting in 204 bytes. Outer coding is followed by interleaving. The

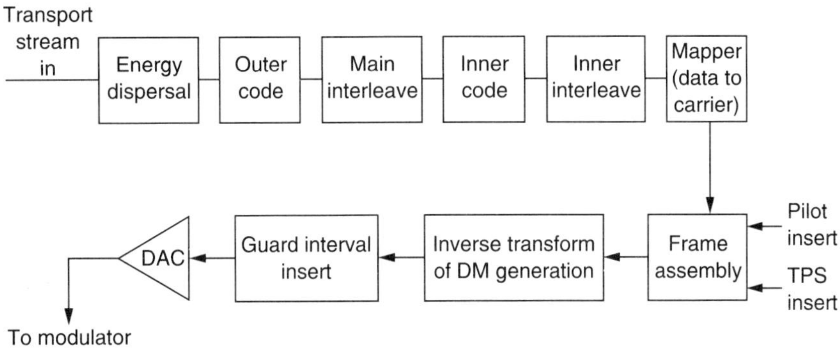

Figure 12.39 DVB-T transmitter block diagram. See text for details.

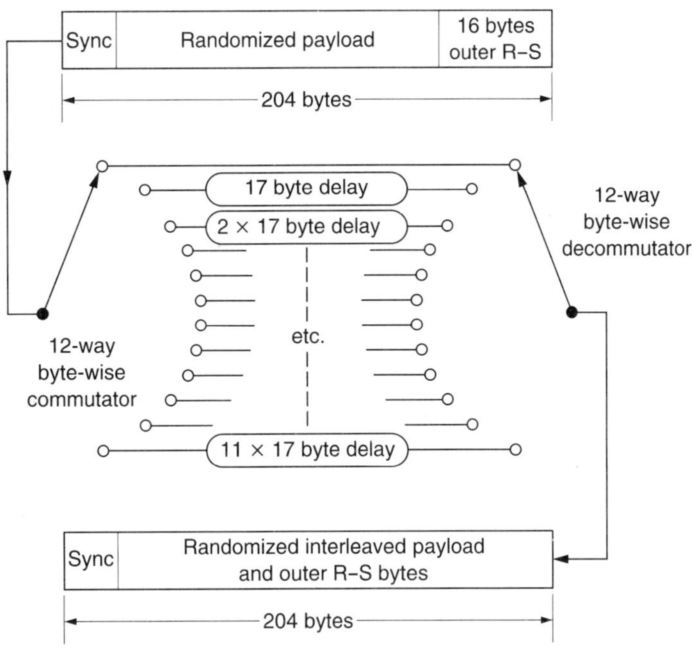

Figure 12.40 The interleaver of DVB uses 12 incrementing delay channels to reorder the data. The sync byte passes through the undelayed channel and so is still at the head of the packet after interleave. However, the packet now contains non-adjacent bytes from 12 different packets.

interleave mechanism is shown in Figure 12.40. Outer code blocks are commutated on a byte basis into twelve parallel channels. Each channel contains a different amount of delay, typically achieved by a ring-buffer RAM. The delays are integer multiples of 17 bytes, designed to skew the data by one outer block ($12 \times 17 = 204$). Following the delays, a commutator reassembles interleaved outer blocks. These have 204 bytes as before, but the effect of the interleave is that adjacent bytes in the input are 17 bytes apart in the output. Each output block contains data from twelve input blocks making the data resistant to burst errors.

Following the interleave, the energy-dispersal process takes place. The pseudo-random sequence runs over eight outer blocks and is synchronized by inverting the transport stream packet sync symbol in every eighth block. The packet sync symbols are not randomized.

The inner coding process of DVB is shown in Figure 12.41. Input data are serialized and pass down a shift register. Exclusive-OR gates produce convolutional parity symbols *X* and *Y*, such that the output bit rate is twice the input bit rate. Under the worst reception conditions, this 100 per cent redundancy offers the most powerful correction with the penalty that a low data rate is delivered. However, Figure 12.41 also shows that

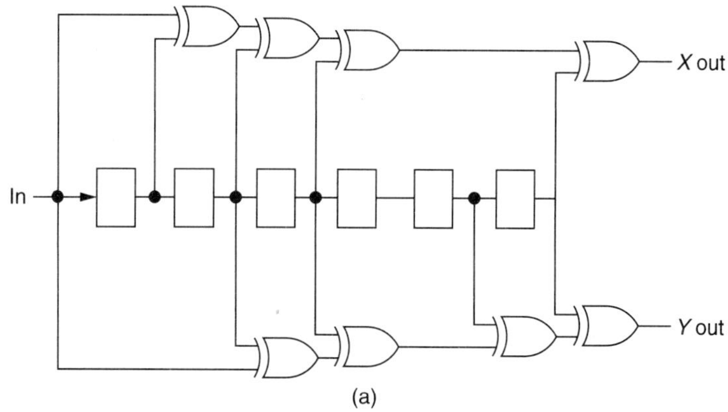

(a)

Rate	Transmitted sequence
1/2	X_1 Y_1
2/3	X_1 Y_1 Y_2
3/4	X_1 Y_1 Y_2 X_3
5/6	X_1 Y_1 Y_2 X_3 Y_4 X_6
7/8	X_1 Y_1 Y_2 Y_3 Y_4 X_5 X_6 X_7

(b)

Figure 12.41 (a) The mother inner coder of DVB produces 100 per cent redundancy, but this can be punctured by subsampling the *X* and *Y* data to give five different code rates as (b) shows.

a variety of inner redundancy factors can be used from 1/2 down to 1/8 of the transmitted bit rate. The *X*, *Y* data from the inner coder are subsampled, such that the coding is punctured.

The DVB standard allows the use of QPSK, 16-QUAM or 64-QUAM coding in an OFDM system. There are five possible inner code rates, and four different guard intervals which can be used with each modulation scheme. Thus for each modulation scheme there are 20 possible transport stream bit rates in the standard DVB channel, each of which requires a different receiver SNR. The broadcaster can select any suitable balance between transport stream bit rate and coverage area. For a given transmitter location and power, reception over a larger area may require a channel code with a smaller number of bits/s/Hz and this reduces the bit rate which can be delivered in a standard channel. Alternatively, a higher amount of inner redundancy means that the proportion of the transmitted bit rate which is data goes down. Thus for wider coverage the broadcaster will have to send fewer programs in the multiplex or use higher compression factors.

12.18 The DVB receiver

Figure 12.42 shows a block diagram of a DVB receiver. The off-air RF signal is fed to a mixer driven by the local oscillator. The IF output of the mixer is bandpass filtered and supplied to the ADC which outputs a digital IF signal for the FFT stage. The FFT is analysed initially to find the higher-level pilot signals. If these are not in the correct channels the local

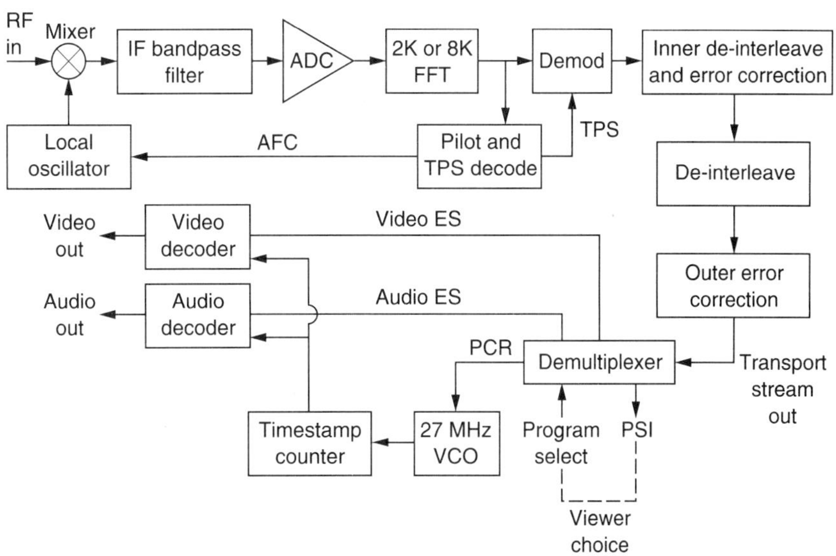

Figure 12.42 DVB receiver block diagram. See text for details.

oscillator frequency is incorrect and it will be changed until the pilots emerge from the FFT in the right channels. The data in the pilots will be decoded in order to tell the receiver how many carriers, what inner redundancy rate, guard band rate and modulation scheme are in use in the remaining carriers. The FFT magnitude information is also a measure of the equalization required.

The FFT outputs are demodulated into 2K or 8K bitstreams and these are multiplexed to produce a serial signal. This is subject to inner error correction which corrects random errors. The data are then de-interleaved to break up burst errors and then the outer R–S error correction operates. The output of the R–S correction will then be derandomized to become an MPEG transport stream once more. The derandomizing is synchronized by the transmission of inverted sync patterns.

The receiver must select a PID of 0 and wait until a Program Association Table (PAT) is transmitted. This will describe the available programs by listing the PIDs of the Program Map Tables (PMT). By looking for these packets the receiver can determine what PIDs to select to receive any video and audio elementary streams.

When an elementary stream is selected, some of the packets will have extended headers containing program clock reference (PCR). These codes are used to synchronize the 27 MHz clock in the receiver to the one in the MPEG encoder of the desired program. The 27 MHz clock is divided down to drive the time stamp counter so that audio and video emerge from the decoder at the correct rate and with lip sync.

It should be appreciated that time stamps are relative, not absolute. The time stamp count advances by a fixed amount each picture, but the exact count is meaningless. Thus the decoder can establish the frame rate of the video only from time stamps, but not the precise timing. In practice the receiver has finite buffering memory between the demultiplexer and the MPEG decoder. If the displayed video timing is too late, the buffer will tend to overflow whereas if the displayed video timing is too early the decoding may not be completed. The receiver can advance or retard the time stamp counter during lock-up so that it places the output timing mid-way between these extremes.

12.19 ATSC

The ATSC system is an alternative way of delivering a transport stream, but it is considerably less sophisticated than DVB, and supports only one transport stream bit rate of 19.28 Mbits/s. If any change in the service area is needed, this will require a change in transmitter power.

Figure 12.43 shows a block diagram of an ATSC transmitter. Incoming transport stream packets are randomized, except for the sync pattern, for energy dispersal. Figure 12.44 shows the randomizer.

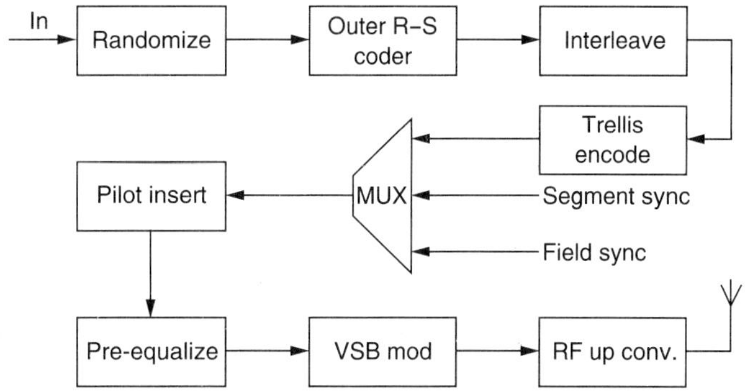

Figure 12.43 Block diagram of ATSC transmitter. See text for details.

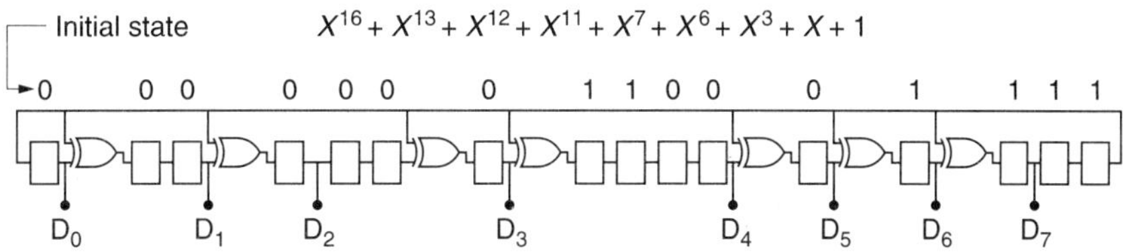

Figure 12.44 The randomizer of ATSC. The twisted ring counter is preset to the initial state shown each data field. It is then clocked once per byte and the eight outputs D_0–D_7 are X-ORed with the data byte.

The outer correction code includes the whole packet except for the sync byte. Thus there are 187 bytes of data in each codeword and 20 bytes of R–S redundancy are added to make a 207-byte codeword. After outer coding, a convolutional interleaver shown in Figure 12.45 is used. This reorders data over a time span of about 4 ms. Interleave simply exchanges content between packets, but without changing the packet structure.

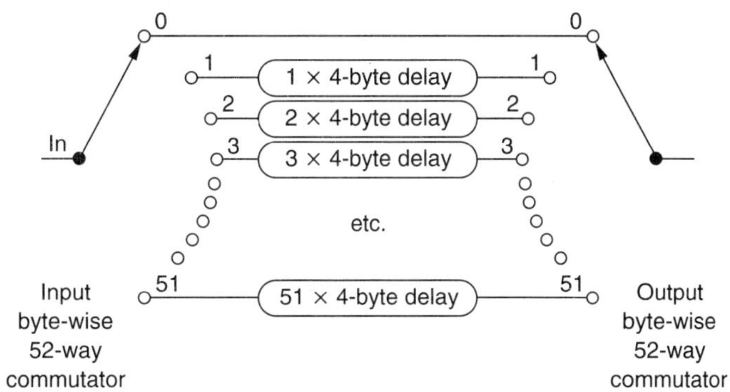

Figure 12.45 The ATSC convolutional interleaver spreads adjacent bytes over a period of about 4 ms.

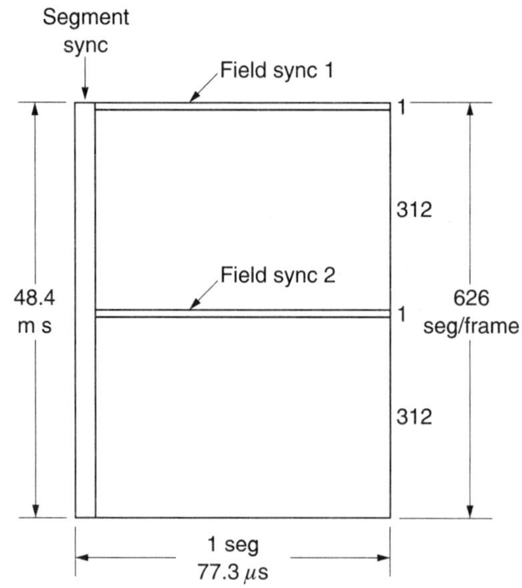

Figure 12.46 The ATSC data frame is transmitted one segment at a time. Segment sync denotes the beginning of each segment and the segments are counted from the field sync signals.

Figure 12.46 shows that the result of outer coding and interleave is a data frame which is divided into two fields of 313 segments each. The frame is tranmitted by scanning it horizontallly a segment at a time. There is some similarity with a traditional analog video signal here, because there is a sync pulse at the beginning of each segment and a field sync which occupies two segments of the frame. *Data segment sync* repeats every 77.3 ms, a segment rate of 12 933 Hz, whereas a frame has a period of 48.4 ms. The field sync segments contain a training sequnce to drive the adaptive equalizer in the receiver.

The data content of the frame is subject to trellis coding which converts each pair of data bits into three channel bits inside an inner interleave. The trellis coder is shown in Figure 12.47 and the interleave in Figure 12.48. Figure 12.47 also shows how the three channel bits map to the eight signal levels in the 8-VSB modulator.

Figure 12.49 shows the data segment after eight-level coding. The sync pattern of the transport stream packet, which was not included in the error-correction code, has been replaced by a segment sync waveform. This acts as a timing reference to allow deserializing of the segment, but as the two levels of the sync pulse are standardized, it also acts as an amplitude reference for the eight-level slicer in the receiver.

The eight-level signal is subject to a DC offset so that some transmitter energy appears at the carrier frequency to act as a pilot. Each eight-level symbol carries two data bits and so there are 832 symbols in each

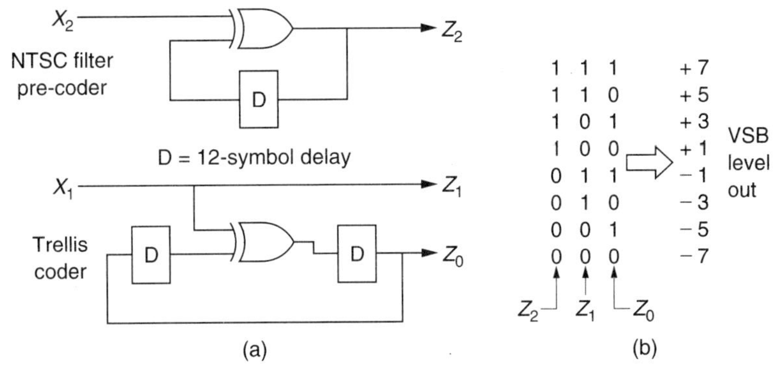

Figure 12.47 (a) The precoder and trellis coder of ATSC converts two data bits X_1, X_2 to three output bits Z_0, Z_1, Z_2. (b) The Z_0, Z_1, Z_2 output bits map to the eight-level code as shown.

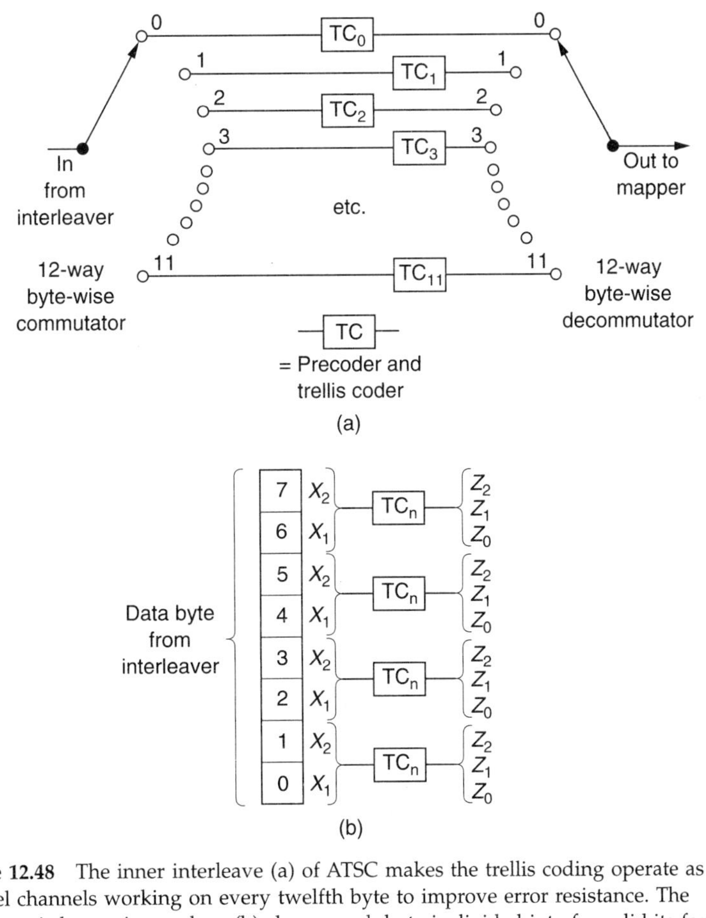

Figure 12.48 The inner interleave (a) of ATSC makes the trellis coding operate as twelve parallel channels working on every twelfth byte to improve error resistance. The interleave is byte-wise, and, as (b) shows, each byte is divided into four di-bits for coding into the tri-bits Z_0, Z_1, Z_2.

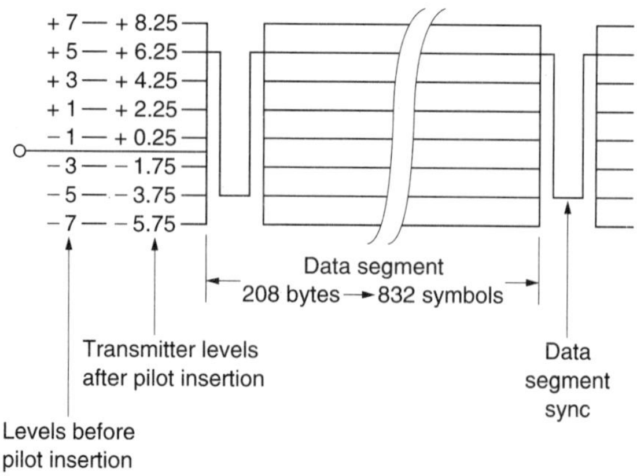

Figure 12.49 ATSC data segment. Note the sync pattern which acts as a timing and amplitude reference. The eight levels are shifted up by 1.25 to create a DC component resulting in a pilot at the carrier frequency.

segment. As the segment rate is 12 933 Hz, the symbol rate is 10.76 MHz and so this will require 5.38 MHz of bandwidth in a single sideband,

Figure 12.50 shows the transmitter spectrum. The lower sideband is vestigial and an overall channel width of 6 MHz results.

Figure 12.51 shows an ATSC receiver. The first stages of the receiver are designed to lock to the pilot in the transmitted signal. This then allows the eight-level signal to be sampled at the right times. This process will allow location of the segment sync and then the field sync signals. Once the receiver is synchronized, the symbols in each segment can be decoded. The inner or trellis coder corrects for random errors, then following de-interleave the R–S coder corrects burst errors, After derandomizing, standard transport stream sync patterns are added to the output data.

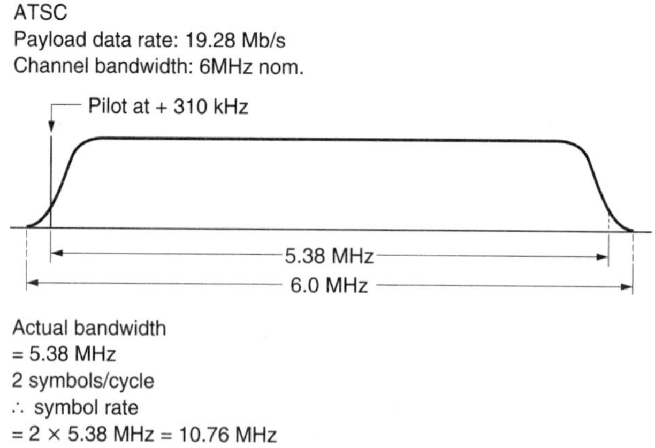

Figure 12.50 The spectrum of ATSC and its associated bit and symbol rates. Note pilot at carrier frequency created by DC offset in multi-level coder.

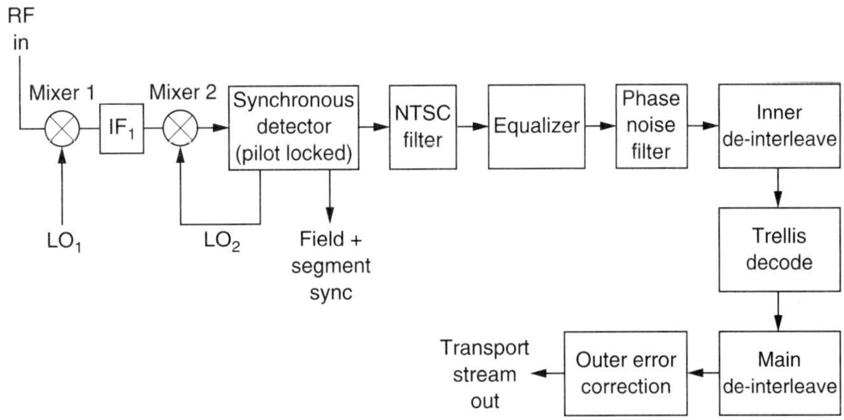

Figure 12.51 An ATSC receiver. Double conversion can be used so that the second conversion stage can be arranged to lock to the transmitted pilot.

In practice ATSC transmissions will experience co-channel interference from NTSC transmitters and the ATSC scheme allows the use of an NTSC rejection filter. Figure 12.52 shows that most of the energy of NTSC is at the carrier, subcarrier and sound carrier frequencies. A comb filter with a suitable delay can produce nulls or notches at these frequencies. However, the delay-and-add process in the comb filter also causes another effect. When two eight-level signals are added together, the result is a sixteen-level signal. This will be corrupted by noise of half the level that would corrupt an eight-level signal. However, the sixteen-level signal contains redundancy because it corresponds to the combinations of four bits whereas only two bits are being transmitted. This allows a form of error correction to be used.

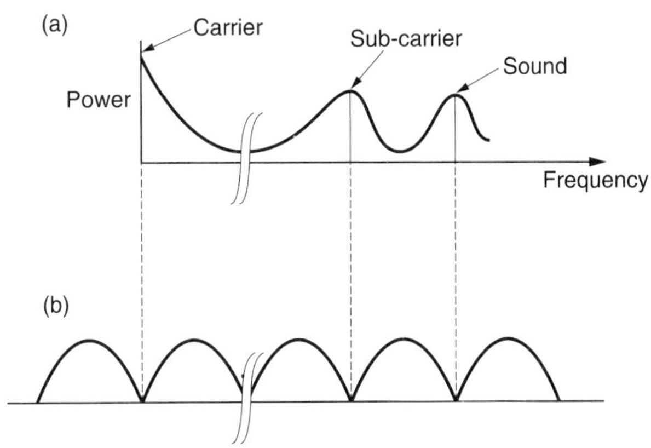

Figure 12.52 Spectrum of typical analog transmitter showing (a) maximum power at carrier, subcarrier and audio carrier. A comb filter (b) with a suitable delay can notch out NTSC interference. The precoding of ATSC is designed to work with the necessary receiver delay.

The ATSC inner precoder results in a known relationship existing between symbols independent of the data. The time delays in the inner interleave are designed to be compatible with the delay in the NTSC rejection comb filter. This limits the number of paths the received waveform can take through a time/voltage graph called a trellis. Where a signal is in error it takes a path sufficiently near to the correct one that the correct one can be implied.

ATSC uses a training sequence sent once every data field, but is otherwise helpless against multipath reception as tests have shown. In urban areas, ATSC must have a correctly oriented directional antenna to reject reflections. Unfortunately the American viewer has been brought up to believe that television reception is possible with a pair of 'rabbit's ears' on top of the TV set and ATSC will not work like this. Mobile reception is not practicable. As a result the majority of the world's broadcasters appear to be favouring an OFDM-based system.

12.20 Networks

A network is basically a communication resource which is shared for economic reasons. Like any shared resource, decisions have to be made somewhere and somehow about how the resource is to be used. In the absence of such decisions the resultant chaos will be such that the resource might as well not exist.

In communications networks the resource is the ability to convey data from any node or port to any other. On a particular cable, clearly only one transaction of this kind can take place at any one instant even though in practice many nodes will simultaneously be wanting to transmit data. Arbitration is needed to determine which node is allowed to transmit.

There are a number of different arbitration protocols and these have evolved to support the needs of different types of network. In small networks, such as LANs, a single point failure which halts the entire network may be acceptable, whereas in a public transport network owned by a telecommunications company, the network will be redundant so that if a particular link fails data may be sent via an alternative route. A link which has reached its maximum capacity may also be supplanted by transmission over alternative routes.

In physically small networks, arbitration may be carried out in a single location. This is fast and efficient, but if the arbitrator fails it leaves the system completely crippled. The processor buses in computers work in this way. In centrally arbitrated systems the arbitrator needs to know the structure of the system and the status of all the nodes. Following a configuration change, due perhaps to the installation of new equipment, the arbitrator needs to be told what the new configuration is, or have a mechanism which allows it to explore the network and learn the configuration. Central arbitration is only suitable for small networks which change their configuration infrequently.

In other networks the arbitration is distributed so that some decision-making ability exists in every node. This is less efficient but is does allow at least some of the network to continue operating after a component failure. Distributed arbitration also means that each node is self-sufficient and so no changes need to be made if the network is reconfigured by adding or deleting a node. This is the only possible approach in wide area networks where the structure may be very complex and change dynamically in the event of failures or overload.

Ethernet uses distributed arbitration. FireWire is capable of using both types of arbitration. A small amount of decision-making ability is built into every node so that distributed arbitration is possible. However, if one of the nodes happens to be a computer, it can run a centralized arbitration algorithm.

The physical structure of a network is subject to some variation as Figure 12.53 shows. In radial networks (a), each port has a unique cable connection to a device called a *hub*. The hub must have one connection for every port and this limits the number of ports. However, a cable failure will result in the loss of only one port. In a ring system (b) the nodes are connected like a daisy chain with each node acting as a feedthrough. In this case the arbitration requirement must be distributed. With some

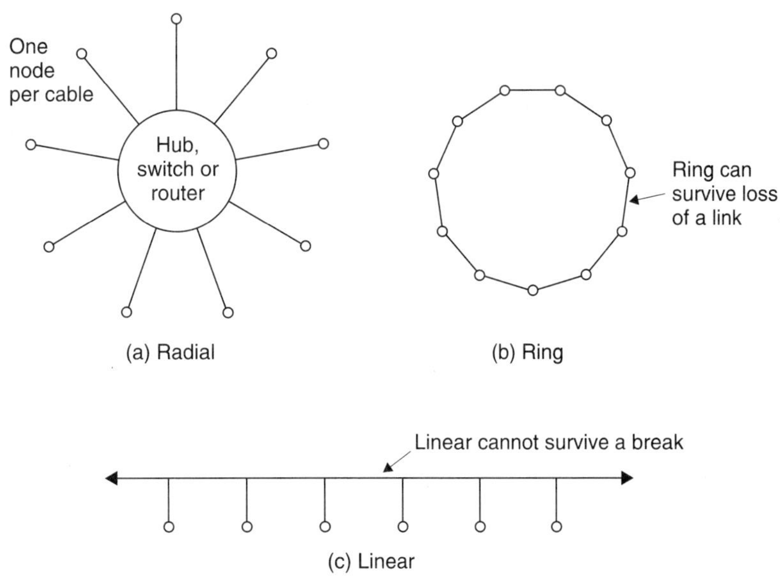

Figure 12.53 Network configurations. At (a) the radial system uses one cable to each node. (b) Ring system uses less cable than radial. (c) Linear system is simple but has no redundancy.

protocols, a single cable break doesn't stop the network operating. Depending on the protocol, simultaneous transactions may be possible provided they don't require the same cable. For example, in a storage network a disk drive may be outputting data to an editor while another drive is backing up data to a tape streamer. For the lowest cost, all nodes are physically connected in parallel to the same cable. Figure 12.53(c) shows that a cable break would divide the network into two halves, but it is possible that the impedance mismatch at the break could stop both halves working.

12.21 Network arbitration

One of the concepts involved in arbitration is priority which is fundamental to providing an appropriate quality of service. If two processes both want to use a network, the one with the highest priority would normally go first. Attributing priority must be done carefully because some of the results are non-intuitive. For example, it may be beneficial to give a high priority to a humble device which has a low data rate for the simple reason that if it is given use of the network it won't need it for long. In a television environment transactions concerned with on-air processes would have priority over file transfers concerning production and editing.

When a device gains access to the network to perform a transaction, generally no other transaction can take place until it has finished. Consequently it is important to limit the amount of time that a given port can stay on the bus. In this way when the time limit expires, a further arbitration must take place. The result is that the network resource rotates between transactions rather than one transfer hogging the resource and shutting out everyone else.

It follows from the presence of a time (or data quantity) limit that ports must have the means to break large files up into frames or cells and re-assemble them on reception. This process is sometimes called *adaptation*. If the data to be sent originally exist at a fixed bit rate, some buffering will be needed so that the data can be time-compressed into the available frames. Each frame must be contiguously numbered and the system must transmit a file size or word count so that the receiving node knows when it has received every frame in the file.

The error-detection system interacts with this process because if any frame is in error on reception, the receiving node can ask for a retransmission of the frame. This is more efficient than retransmitting the whole file. Figure 12.54 shows the flow chart for a receiving node.

Breaking files into frames helps to keep down the delay experienced by each process using the network. Figure 12.55 shows that each frame may

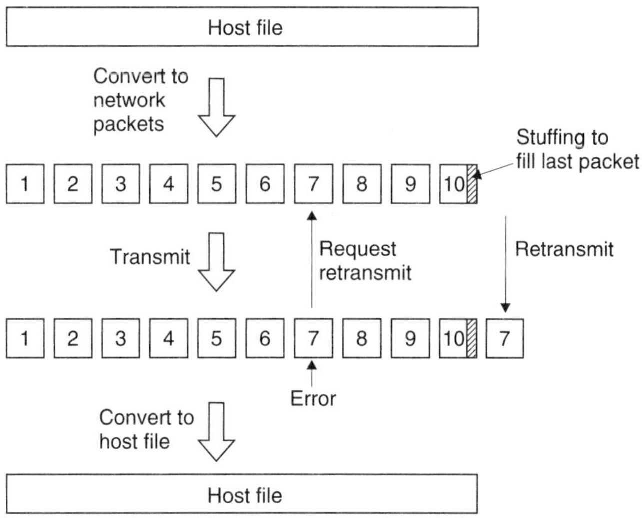

Figure 12.54 Receiving a file which has been divided into packets allows for the retransmission of just the packet in error.

be stored ready for transmission in a silo memory. It is possible to make the priority a function of the number of frames in the silo, as this is a direct measure of how long a process has been kept waiting. Isochronous systems must do this in order to meet maximum delay specifications. In Figure 12.55 once frame transmission has completed, the arbitrator will determine which process sends a frame next by examining the depth of all the frame buffers. MPEG transport stream multiplexers and networks delivering MPEG data must work in this way because the transfer is isochronous and the amount of buffering in a decoder is limited for economic reasons.

A central arbitrator is relatively simple to implement because when all decisions are taken centrally there can be no timing difficulty (assuming a well-engineered system). In a distributed system, there is an extra difficulty due to the finite time taken for signals to travel down the data paths between nodes.

Figure 12.56 shows the structure of Ethernet which uses a protocol called CSMA/CD (carrier sense multiple access with collision detect) developed by DEC and Xerox. This is a distributed arbitration network where each node follows some simple rules. The first of these is not to transmit if an existing bus signal is detected. The second is not to transmit more than a certain quantity of data before releasing the bus. Devices wanting to use the bus will see bus signals and so will wait until the present bus transaction finishes. This must happen at some point because of the frame size limit. When the frame is completed, signalling on the bus should cease. The first device to sense the bus becoming free and to

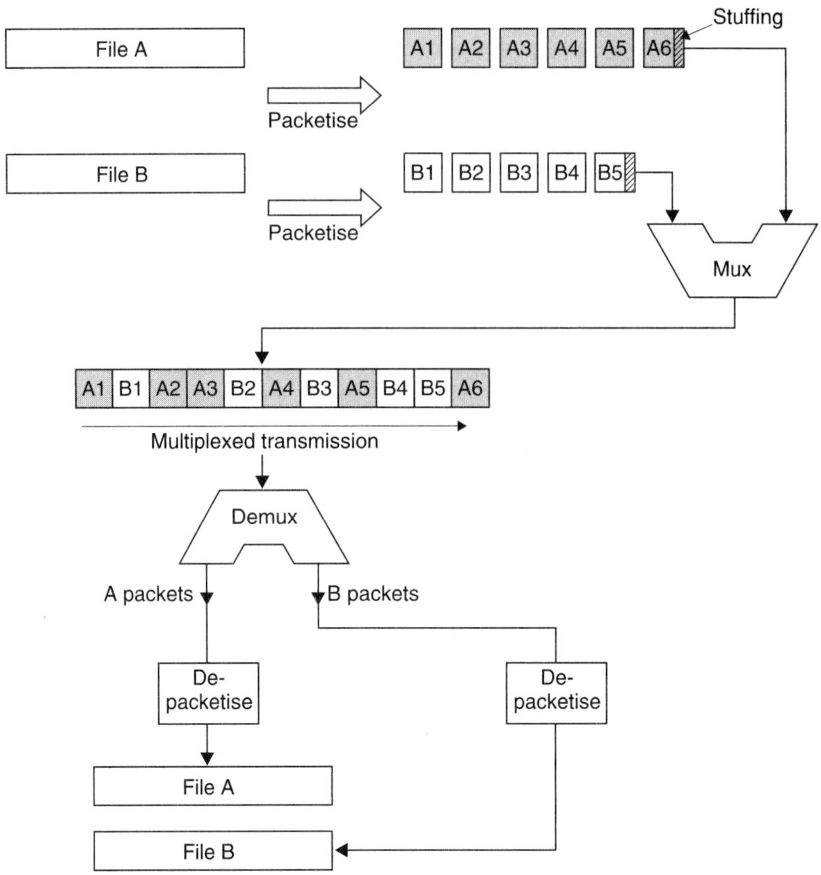

Figure 12.55 Files are broken into frames or packets for multiplexing with packets from other users. Short packets minimize the time between the arrival of successive packets. The priority of the multiplexing must favour isochronous data over asynchronous data.

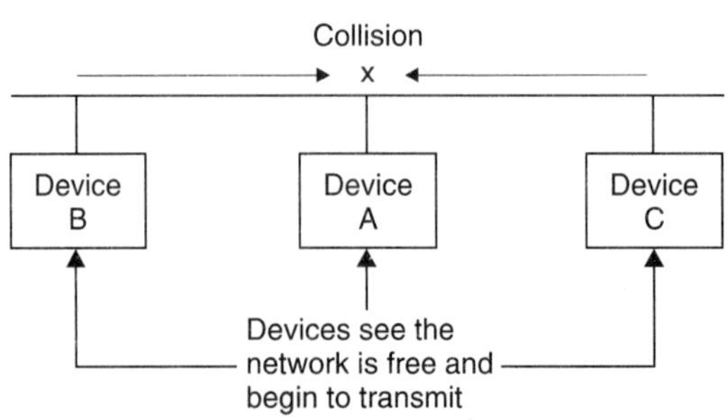

Figure 12.56 In Ethernet collisions can occur because of the finite speed of the signals. A 'back-off' algorithm handles collisions, but they do reduce the network throughput.

assert its own signal will prevent any other nodes transmitting according to the first rule. Where numerous devices are present it is possible to give them a priority structure by providing a delay between sensing the bus coming free and beginning a transaction. High-priority devices will have a short delay so they get in first. Lower-priority devices will only be able to start a transaction if the high-priority devices don't need to transfer.

It might be thought that these rules would be enough and everything would be fine. Unfortunately the finite signal speed means that there is a flaw in the system. Figure 12.56 shows why. Device A is transmitting and devices B and C both want to transmit and have equal priority. At the end of A's transaction, devices B and C see the bus become free at the same instant and start a transaction. With two devices driving the bus, the resultant waveform is meaningless. This is known as a collision and all nodes must have means to recover from it. First, each node will read the bus signal at all times. When a node drives the bus, it will also read back the bus signal and compare it with what was sent. Clearly if the two are the same all is well, but if there is a difference, this must be because a collision has occurred and two devices are trying to determine the bus voltage at once.

If a collision is detected, both colliding devices will sense the disparity between the transmitted and readback signals, and both will release the bus to terminate the collision. However, there is no point is adhering to the simple protocol to reconnect because this will simply result in another collision. Instead each device has a built-in delay which must expire before another attempt is made to transmit. This delay is not fixed, but is controlled by a random number generator and so changes from transaction to transaction.

The probability of two node devices arriving at the same delay is infinitesimally small. Consequently if a collision does occur, both devices will drop the bus, and they will start their back-off timers. When the first timer expires, that device will transmit and the other will see the transmission and remain silent. In this way the collision is not only handled, but is prevented from happening again.

The performance of Ethernet is usually specified in terms of the bit rate at which the cabling runs. However, this rate is academic because it is not available all the time. In a real network bit rate is lost by the need to send headers and error-correction codes and by the loss of time due to interframe spaces and collision handling. As the demand goes up, the number of collisions increases and throughput goes down. Collision-based arbitrators do not handle congestion well.

An alternative method of arbitration developed by IBM is shown in Figure 12.57. This is known as a *token ring* system. All the nodes have an input and an output and are connected in a ring which must be complete for the system to work. Data circulate in one direction only. If data are not

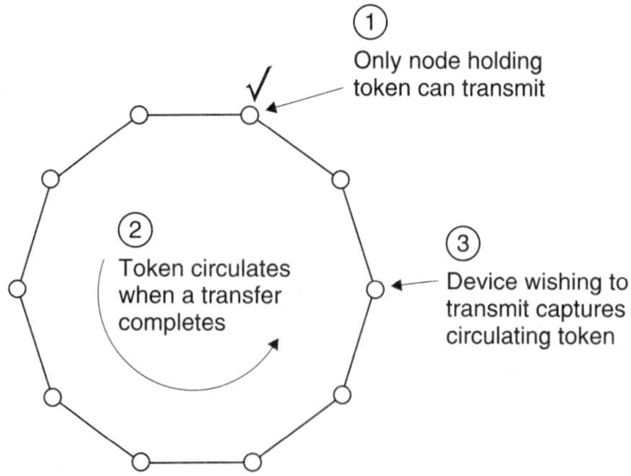

Figure 12.57 In a token ring system only the node in possession of the token can transmit so collisions are impossible. In very large rings the token circulation time causes loss of throughput.

addressed to a node which receives them, the data will be passed on. When the data arrive at the addressed node, that node will capture the data as well as passing them on with an acknowledge added. Thus the data packet travels right around the ring back to the sending node. When the sending node receives the acknowledge, it will transmit a token packet. This token packet passes to the next node, which will pass it on if it does not wish to transmit. If no device wishes to transmit, the token will circulate endlessly. However, if a device has data to send, it simply waits until the token arrives again and captures it. This node can now transmit data in the knowledge that there cannot be a collision because no other node has the token.

In simple token ring systems, the transmitting node transmits idle characters after the data packet has been sent in order to maintain synchronization. The idle character transmission will continue until the acknowledge arrives. In the case of long packets the acknowledge will arrive before the packet has all been sent and no idle characters are necessary. However, with short packets idle characters will be generated. These idle characters use up ring bandwidth.

Later token ring systems use *early token release* (ETR). After the packet has been transmitted, the sending node sends a token straight away. Another node wishing to transmit can do so as soon as the current packet has passed.

It might be thought that the nodes on the ring would transmit in their physical order, but this is not the case because a priority system exists. Each node can have a different priority if necessary. If a high-priority node wishes to transmit, as a packet from elsewhere passes through that node, the node will set *reservation bits* with its own priority level. When the sending node finishes and transmits a token, it will copy that priority level into the token. In this way nodes with a lower priority level will pass the token on instead of capturing it. The token will ultimately arrive at the high-priority node.

The token ring system has the advantage that it does not waste throughput with collisions and so the full capacity is always available. However, if the ring is broken the entire network fails.

In Ethernet the performance is degraded by the number of transactions, not the number of nodes, whereas in token ring the performance is degraded by the number of nodes.

12.22 FireWire

FireWire[8] is actually an Apple Computers Inc. trade name for the interface which is formally known as IEEE 1394–1995. It was originally intended as a digital audio network, but grew out of recognition. FireWire is more than just an interface as it can be used to form networks and if used with a computer effectively extends the computer's data bus. Figure 12.58 shows that devices are simply connected together as any combination of daisy-chain or star network.

Any pair of devices can communicate in either direction, and arbitration ensures that only one device transmits at once. Intermediate devices simply pass on transmissions. This can continue even if the intermediate device is powered down as the FireWire carries power to keep repeater functions active.

Communications are divided into *cycles* which have a period of 125 μs. During a cycle, there are 64 time slots. During each time slot, any one node can communicate with any other, but in the next slot, a different pair

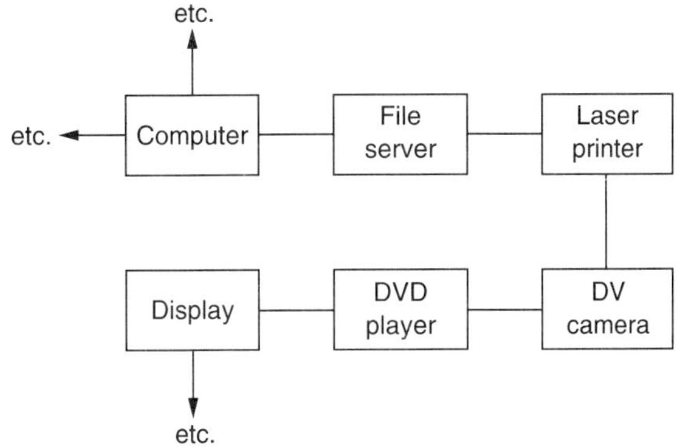

Figure 12.58 FireWire supports radial (star) or daisy-chain connection. Two-port devices pass on signals destined for a more distant device – they can do this even when powered down.

of nodes may communicate. Thus FireWire is best described as a time-division multiplexed (TDM) system. There will be a new arbitration between the nodes for each cycle.

FireWire is eminently suitable for video/computer convergent applications because it can simultaneously support asynchronous transfers of non-real-time computer data and isochronous transfers of real-time audio/video data. It can do this because the arbitration process allocates a fixed proportion of slots for isochronous data (about 80 per cent) and these have a higher priority in the arbitration than the asynchronous data. The higher the data rate a given node needs, the more time slots it will be allocated. Thus a given bit rate can be guaranteed throughout a transaction; a prerequisite of real-time A/V data transfer.

It is the sophistication of the arbitration system which makes FireWire remarkable. Some of the arbitration is in hardware at each node, but some is in software which only needs to be at one node. The full functionality requires a computer somewhere in the system which runs the isochronous bus management arbitration. Without this only asynchronous transfers are possible. It is possible to add or remove devices whilst the system is working. When a device is added the system will recognize it through a periodic learning process. Essentially every node on the system transmits in turn so that the structure becomes clear.

The electrical interface of FireWire is shown in Figure 12.59. It consists of two twisted pairs for signalling and a pair of power conductors. The twisted pairs carry differential signals of about 220 mV swinging around a common mode voltage of about 1.9 V with an impedance of 112 Ω. Figure 12.60 shows how the data are transmitted. The host data are simply serialized and used to modulate twisted pair A. The other twisted pair (B) carries a signal called a *strobe*, which is the exclusive-OR of the data and the clock. Thus whenever a run of identical bits results in no transitions in the data, the strobe signal will carry transitions. At the

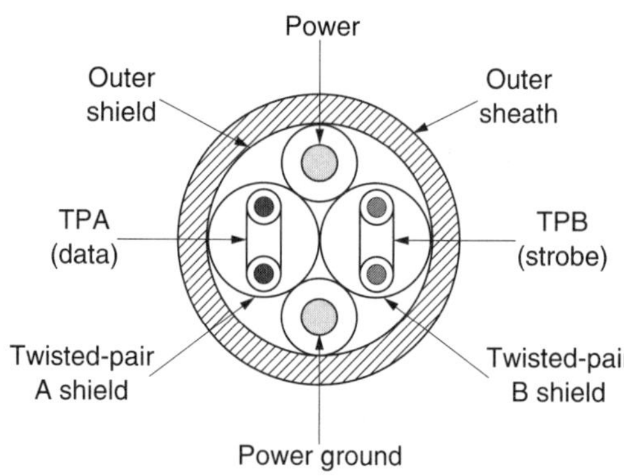

Figure 12.59 FireWire uses twin twisted pairs and a power pair.

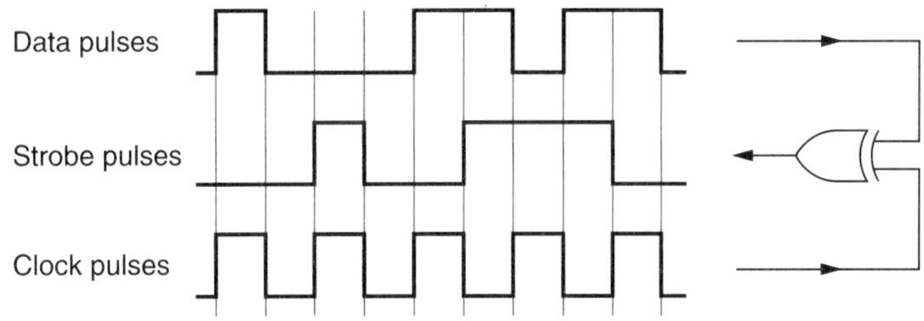

Figure 12.60 The strobe signal is the X-OR of the data and the bit clock. The data and strobe signals together form a self-clocking system.

receiver another exclusive-OR gate adds data and strobe to re-create the clock.

This signalling technique is subject to skew between the two twisted pairs and this limits cable lengths to about 10 metres between nodes. Thus FireWire is not a long-distance interface technique, instead it is very useful for interconnecting a large number of devices in close proximity. Using a copper interconnect, FireWire can run at 100, 200 or 400 Mbits/s, depending on the specific hardware. It is proposed to create an optical fibre version which would run at gigabit speeds.

12.23 Broadband networks and ATM

Broadband ISDN (B-ISDN) is the successor to N-ISDN and in addition to offering more bandwidth, gives practical solutions to the delivery of any conceivable type of data. The flexibility with which ATM operates means that intermittent or one-off data transactions which only require asynchronous delivery can take place alongside isochronous MPEG video delivery. This is known as *application independence* whereby the sophistication of isochronous delivery does not raise the cost of asynchronous data. In this way, generic data, video, speech and combinations of the above can co-exist.

ATM is multiplexed, but it is not time-division multiplexed. TDM is inefficient because if a transaction does not fill its allotted bandwidth, the capacity is wasted. ATM does not offer fixed blocks of bandwidth, but allows infinitely variable bandwidth to each transaction. This is done by converting all host data into small fixed-size cells at the adaptation layer. The greater the bandwidth needed by a transaction, the more cells per second are allocated to that transaction. This approach is superior to the fixed bandwidth approach, because if the bit rate of a particular transaction falls, the cells released can be used for other transactions so that the full bandwidth is always available.

As all cells are identical in size, a multiplexer can assemble cells from many transactions in an arbitrary order. The exact order is determined by

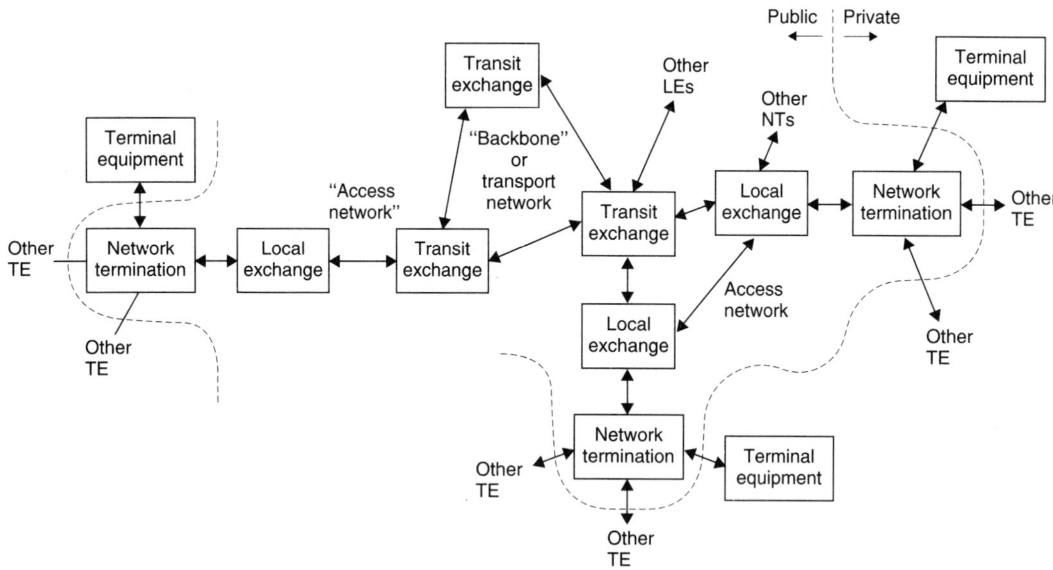

Figure 12.61 Structure and terminology of a broadband network. See text.

the quality of service required, where the time positioning of isochronous data would be determined first, with asynchronous data filling the gaps.

Figure 12.61 shows how a broadband system might be implemented. The transport network would typically be optical fibre based, using SONET (synchronous optical network) or SDH (synchronous digital hierarchy). These standards differ in minor respects. Figure 12.62 shows the bit rates available in each. Lower bit rates will be used in the access networks which will use different technology such as xDSL.

SONET and SDH assemble ATM cells into a structure known as a *container* in the interests of efficiency. Containers are passed intact between exchanges in the transport network. The cells in a container need not belong to the same transaction, they simply need to be going the same way for at least one transport network leg.

The cell-routing mechanism of ATM is unusual and deserves explanation. In conventional networks, a packet must carry the complete destination address so that at every exchange it can be routed closer to its destination. The exact route by which the packet travels cannot be

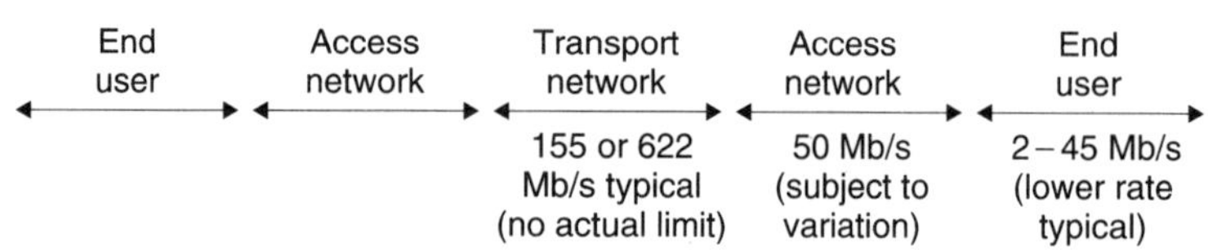

Figure 12.62 Bit rates available in SONET and SDH.

anticipated and successive packets in the same transaction may take different routes. This is known as a *connectionless* protocol.

In contrast, ATM is a *connection oriented* protocol. Before data can be transferred, the network must set up an end-to-end route. Once this is done, the ATM cells do not need to carry a complete destination address. Instead they only need to carry enough addressing so that an exchange or switch can distinguish between all the expected transactions.

The end-to-end route is known as a *virtual channel* which consists of a series of *virtual links* between switches. The term 'virtual channel' is used because the system acts like a dedicated channel even though physically it is not. When the transaction is completed the route can be dismantled so that the bandwidth is freed for other users. In some cases, such as delivery of a TV station's output to a transmitter, or as a replacement for analog cable TV the route can be set up continuously to form what is known as a *permanent virtual channel.*

The addressing in the cells ensures that all cells with the same address take the same path, but owing to the multiplexed nature of ATM, at other times and with other cells a completely different routing scheme may exist. Thus the routing structure for a particular transaction always passes cells by the same route, but the next cell may belong to another transaction and will have a different address causing it to be routed in another way.

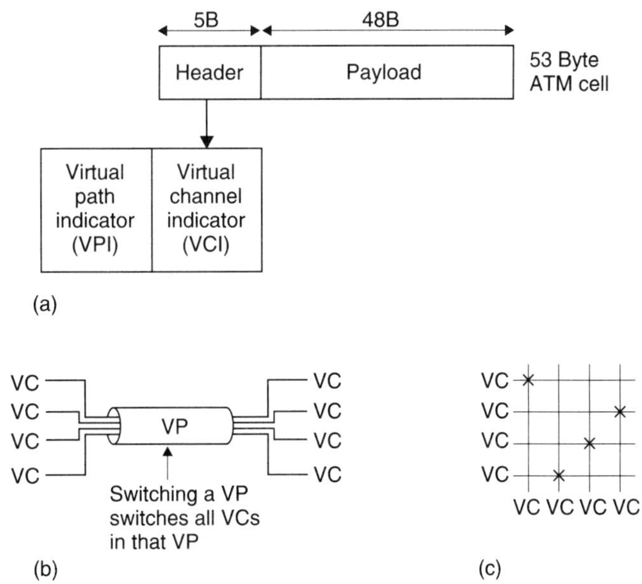

Figure 12.63 The ATM cell (a) carries routing information in the header. ATM paths carrying a group of channels can be switched in a virtual path switch (b). Individual channel switching requires a virtual channel switch which is more complex and causes more delay.

The addressing structure is hierarchical. Figure 12.63(a) shows the ATM cell and its header. The cell address is divided into two fields, the virtual channel identifier and the virtual path identifier. Virtual paths are logical groups of virtual channels which happen to be going the same way. An example would be the output of a video-on-demand server travelling to the first switch. The virtual path concept is useful because all cells in the same virtual path can share the same container in a transport network. A virtual path switch shown in Figure 12.63(b) can operate at the container level whereas a virtual channel switch (c) would need to dismantle and reassemble containers.

When a route is set up, at each switch a table is created. When a cell is received at a switch the VPI and/or VCI code is looked up in the table and used for two purposes. First, the configuration of the switch is obtained, so that this switch will correctly route the cell, second, the VPI and/or VCI codes may be updated so that they correctly control the next switch. This process repeats until the cell arrives at its destination.

In order to set up a path, the initiating device will initially send cells containing an ATM destination address, the bandwidth and quality of service required. The first switch will reply with a message containing the VPI/VCI codes which are to be used for this channel. The message from the initiator will propagate to the destination, creating look-up tables in each switch. At each switch the logic will add the requested bandwidth to the existing bandwidth in use to check that the requested quality of service can be met. If this succeeds for the whole channel, the destination will reply with a connect message which propagates back to the initiating device as confirmation that the channel has been set up. The connect message contains an unique call reference value which identifies this transaction. This is necessary because an initiator such a file server may be initiating many channels and the connect messages will not necessarily return in the same order as the set-up messages were sent.

The last switch will confirm receipt of the connect message to the destination and the initiating device will confirm receipt of the connect message to the first switch.

12.24 ATM AALs

ATM works by dividing all real data messages into cells of 48 bytes each. At the receiving end, the original message must be re-created. This can take many forms. Figure 12.64 shows some possibilities. The message may be a generic data file having no implied timing structure or a serial bitstream with a fixed clock frequency, known as UDT (unstructured data transfer). It may be a burst of data bytes from a TDM system.

The application layer in ATM has two sub-layers shown in Figure 12.65. The first is the segmentation and reassembly (SAR) sublayer which must

Generic data file having no timebase
Constant bit rate serial data stream
Audio/video data requiring a timebase
Compressed A/V data with fixed bit rate
Compressed A/V data with variable bit rate

Figure 12.64 Types of data which may need adapting to ATM.

ATM Application Layer	Convergence sublayer	Recovers timing of original data
	Segmentation and reassembly	Divides data into cells for transport Reassembles original data format

Figure 12.65 ATM adaption layer has two sublayers, segmentation and convergence.

divide the message into cells and rebuild it to get the binary data right. The second is the convergence sublayer (CS) which recovers the timing structure of the original message. It is this feature which makes ATM so appropriate for delivery of audio/visual material. Conventional networks such as the Internet don't have this ability.

In order to deliver a particular quality of service, the adaptation layer and the ATM layer work together. Effectively the adaptation layer will place constraints on the ATM layer, such as cell delay, and the ATM layer will meet those constraints without needing to know why. Provided the constraints are met, the adaptation layer can rebuild the message. The variety of message types and timing constraints leads to the adaptation layer having a variety of forms.

The adaptation layers which are most relevant to MPEG applications are AAL-1 and AAL-5. AAL-1 is suitable for transmitting MPEG-2 multi-program transport streams at constant bit rate and is standardized for this purpose in ETS 300814 for DVB application. AAL-1 has an integral forward error correction (FEC) scheme. AAL-5 is optimized for single-program transport streams (SPTS) at a variable bit rate and has no FEC.

AAL-1 takes as an input the 188-byte transport stream packets which are created by a standard MPEG-2 multiplexer. The transport stream bit rate must be constant but it does not matter if statistical multiplexing has been used within the transport stream.

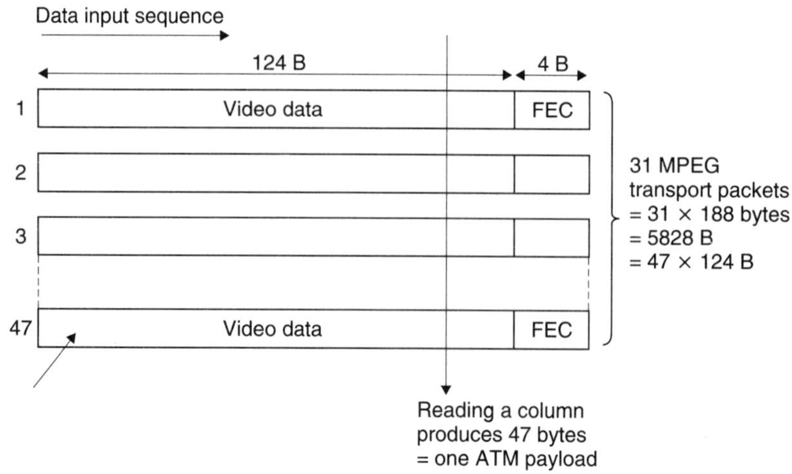

Figure 12.66 The interleave structure used in AAL-1.

The Reed–Solomon FEC of AAL-1 uses a codeword of size 128 so that the codewords consist of 124 bytes of data and 4 bytes of redundancy, making 128 bytes in all. Thirty-one 188-byte TS packets are restructured into this format. The 256-byte codewords are then subject to a block interleave. Figure 12.66 shows that 47 such codewords are assembled in rows in RAM and then columns are read out.

These columns are 47 bytes long and, with the addition of an AAL header byte make up a 48-byte ATM packet payload. In this way the interleave block is transmitted in 128 ATM cells.

The result of the FEC and interleave is that the loss of up to four cells in 128 can be corrected, or a random error of up to two bytes can be corrected in each cell. This FEC system allows most errors in the ATM layer to be corrected so that no retransmissions are needed. This is important for isochronous operation.

The AAL header has a number of functions. One of these is to identify the first ATM cell in the interleave block of 128 cells. Another function is to run a modulo-8 cell counter to detect missing or out-of-sequence ATM cells. If a cell simply fails to arrive, the sequence jump can be detected and used to flag the FEC system so that it can correct the missing cell by erasure (see section 10.22). In a manner similar to the use of program clock reference (PCR) in MPEG, AAL-1 embeds a timing code in ATM cell headers. This is called the synchronous residual time stamp (SRTS) and in conjunction with the ATM network clock allows the receiving AAL device to reconstruct the original data bit rate. This is important because in MPEG applications it prevents the PCR jitter specification being exceeded.

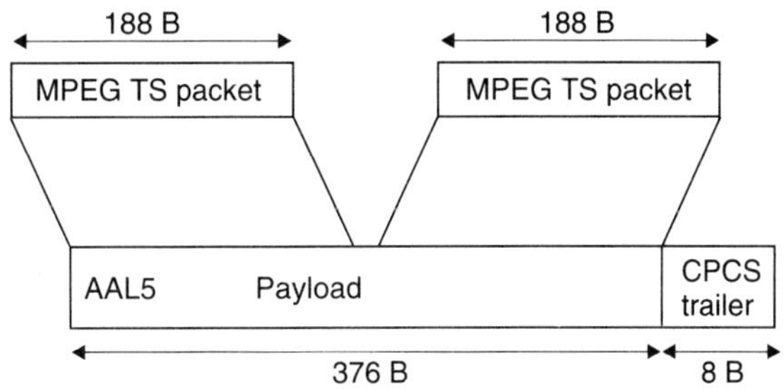

Figure 12.67 The AAL-5 adaptation layer can pack MPEG transport packets in this way.

In AAL-5 there is no error correction and the adaptation layer simply reformats MPEG TB blocks into ATM cells. Figure 12.67 shows one way in which this can be done. Two TS blocks of 188 bytes are associated with an 8-byte trailer known as CPCS (common part convergence sublayer). The presence of the trailer makes a total of 384 bytes which can be carried in eight ATM cells. AAL-5 does not offer constant delay and external buffering will be required, controlled by reading the MPEG PCRs in order to reconstruct the original time axis.

References

1. SMPTE 259M–10-bit 4:2:2 Component and 4FSc NTSC Composite Digital Signals – Serial Digital Interface
2. Eguchi, T., Pathological check codes for serial digital interface systems. Presented at SMPTE Conference, Los Angeles, October 1991
3. SMPTE 305M – Serial Data Transport Interface
4. EIA RS-422A. Electronic Industries Association, 2001 Eye Street NW, Washington, DC 20006, USA
5. Smart, D.L., Transmission performance of digital audio serial interface on audio tie lines. *BBC Designs Dept Technical Memorandum*, 3.296/84
6. European Broadcasting Union, Specification of the digital audio interface. *EBU Doc. Tech.*, 3250
7. Rorden, B. and Graham, M., A proposal for integrating digital audio distribution into TV production. *J. SMPTE* 606–608 (September, 1992)
8. Wicklegren, I.J., The facts about FireWire. *IEEE Spectrum*, 19–25 (1997)

Index

Focal Press

www.focalpress.com

Join Focal Press on-line

As a member you will enjoy the following benefits:

- an email bulletin with **information on new books**
- a regular **Focal Press Newsletter**:
    - featuring a selection of new titles
    - keeps you informed of **special offers, discounts and freebies**
    - alerts you to **Focal Press news and events** such as author signings and seminars
- complete access to **free content** and reference material on the focalpress site, such as the focalXtra articles and commentary from our authors
- a **Sneak Preview** of selected titles (sample chapters) *before* they publish
- a chance to have your say on our **discussion boards** and **review books** for other Focal readers

Focal Club Members are invited to give us feedback on our products and services. Email: worldmarketing@focalpress.com – we want to hear your views!

Membership is FREE. To join, visit our website and register. If you require any further information regarding the on-line club please contact:

Emma Hales, Marketing Manager
Email: emma.hales@repp.co.uk
Tel: +44 (0) 1865 314556
Fax: +44 (0)1865 315472
Address: Focal Press, Linacre House,
Jordan Hill, Oxford, UK, OX2 8DP

Catalogue

For information on all Focal Press titles, our full catalogue is available online at www.focalpress.com and all titles can be purchased here via secure online ordering, or contact us for a free printed version:

USA
Email: christine.degon@bhusa.com

Europe and rest of world
Email: jo.coleman@repp.co.uk
Tel: +44 (0)1865 314220

Potential authors

If you have an idea for a book, please get in touch:

USA
Lilly Roberts, Editorial Assistant
Email: lilly.roberts@bhusa.com
Tel: +1 781 904 2639
Fax: +1 781 904 2640

Europe and rest of world
Christina Donaldson, Editorial Assistant
Email: christina.donaldson@repp.co.uk
Tel: +44 (0)1865 314027
Fax: +44 (0)1865 314572